FINLAND
Helsinki
St. Petersburg
Stockholm
Tallinn
ESTONIA
Baltic
Sea
Nizhniy Novgorod
Volga
Riga
LATVIA
Moscow
RUSSIA
LITHUANIA
Vilnius
(RUSSIA)
Minsk
BELARUS
Ural
KAZAKHSTAN
Vistula
Warsaw
POLAND
Kiev
Kharkov
UKRAINE
Dnieper
CARPATHIAN
MTS.
SLOVAKIA
Budapest
MOLDOVA
Kishinev
HUNGARY
Caspian
Sea
ROMANIA
Crimea
CAUCASUS MTS.
Belgrade
Bucharest
GEORGIA
T'bilisi
Baku
AZERBAIJAN
Black Sea
SERBIA
Danube
ARMENIA
Yerevan
BULGARIA
(YUGOSLAVIA)
Sofia
AZERBAIJAN
Skopje
MACEDONIA
Tiranë
Ankara
ALBANIA
TURKEY
IRAN
Aegean
Sea
GREECE
Sea
Athens
Tigris
Euphrates
SYRIA
Baghdad
IRAQ
CYPRUS
LEBANON
Beirut
Damascus
Crete
Mediterranean
Sea
KUWAIT
Kuwait
Amman
Jerusalem
ISRAEL
JORDAN
Cairo
SAUDI ARABIA
EGYPT
Nile

A History of WESTERN SOCIETY

Sixth Edition

John P. McKay
University of Illinois at Urbana-Champaign

Bennett D. Hill
Georgetown University

John Buckler
University of Illinois at Urbana-Champaign

HOUGHTON MIFFLIN COMPANY
Boston New York

Sponsoring Editor: Andrea Shaw
Development Editor: Dale Anderson
Assistant Editor: Lisa Rothrauff
Senior Project Editor: Christina M. Horn
Editorial Assistant: Leah Y. Mehl
Production/Design Coordinator: Jennifer Meyer Dare
Manufacturing Manager: Florence Cadran
Senior Marketing Manager: Sandra McGuire

Credits **Pages 12 and 19:** Excerpts from *The Sumerians: Their History, Culture and Character,* by S. N. Kramer. Copyright © 1963 by University of Chicago Press. Reprinted with permission. **Page 880:** Parody by Henry Labouchère, quoted in *The Social History of the Machine Gun,* by John Ellis. Copyright © 1975 by John Ellis. Reprinted by permission of Pantheon Books, a division of Random House, Inc.

Cover Image: *Girl with a Red Hat,* by Jan Vermeer, ca 1666. National Gallery of Art, Washington, D.C./Superstock.
Cover Designer: Diana Coe
Photo Researcher: Linda Sykes

Printed in the U.S.A.
Library of Congress Catalog Card Number: 98-72226
ISBN: 0-395-90431-5
1 2 3 4 5 6 7 8 9-VH-02 01 00 99 98

About the Authors

John P. McKay Born in St. Louis, Missouri, John P. McKay received his B.A. from Wesleyan University (1961), his M.A. from the Fletcher School of Law and Diplomacy (1962), and his Ph.D. from the University of California, Berkeley (1968). He began teaching history at the University of Illinois in 1966 and became a professor there in 1976. John won the Herbert Baxter Adams Prize for his book *Pioneers for Profit: Foreign Entrepreneurship and Russian Industrialization, 1885–1913* (1970). He has also written *Tramways and Trolleys: The Rise of Urban Mass Transport in Europe* (1976) and has translated Jules Michelet's *The People* (1973). His research has been supported by fellowships from the Ford Foundation, the Guggenheim Foundation, the National Endowment for the Humanities, and IREX. He has written well over a hundred articles, book chapters, and reviews, which have appeared in numerous publications, including *The American Historical Review, Business History Review, The Journal of Economic History,* and *Slavic Review.* Recently, he contributed extensively to C. Stewart and P. Fritzsche, eds., *Imagining the Twentieth Century* (1997).

Bennett D. Hill A native of Philadelphia, Bennett D. Hill earned an A.B. from Princeton (1956) and advanced degrees from Harvard (A.M., 1958) and Princeton (Ph.D., 1963). He taught history at the University of Illinois at Urbana, where he was department chairman from 1978 to 1981. He has published *English Cistercian Monasteries and Their Patrons in the Twelfth Century* (1968), *Church and State in the Middle Ages* (1970), and articles in *Analecta Cisterciensia, The New Catholic Encyclopaedia, The American Benedictine Review,* and *The Dictionary of the Middle Ages.* His reviews have appeared in *The American Historical Review, Speculum, The Historian,* the *Journal of World History,* and *Library Journal.* He has been a Fellow of the American Council of Learned Societies and served on the editorial board of *The American Benedictine Review,* on committees of the National Endowment for the Humanities, and as Vice President of the American Catholic Historical Association (1995–1996). A Benedictine monk of St. Anselm's Abbey in Washington, D.C., he is also a Visiting Professor at Georgetown University.

John Buckler Born in Louisville, Kentucky, John Buckler received his B.A. (summa cum laude) from the University of Louisville in 1967. Harvard University awarded him the Ph.D. in 1973. From 1984 to 1986 he was an Alexander von Humboldt Fellow at the Institut für Alte Geschichte, University of Munich. He has lectured at the Fondation Hardt at the University of Geneva and at the University of Freiburg. He has also participated in numerous international conferences. He is currently a professor of Greek history at the University of Illinois. In 1980 Harvard University Press published his *Theban Hegemony, 371–362* B.C. He has also published *Philip II and the Sacred War* (Leiden 1989) and co-edited *BOIOTIKA: Vorträge vom 5. Internationalen Böotien-Kolloquium* (Munich 1989). He has contributed articles to *The American Historical Association's Guide to Historical Literature* (Oxford 1995), *The Oxford Classical Dictionary* (Oxford 1996), and *Encyclopedia of Greece and the Hellenic Tradition* (London 1999). His other articles have appeared in journals both here and abroad, including the *American Journal of Ancient History, Classical Philology, Rheinisches Museum für Philologie, Klio, Classical Quarterly, Wiener Studien,* and many others.

Contents in Brief

Contents

Chapter 6

Chapter 7

Chapter 8

Chapter 9

✣ Chapter 16

✣ Chapter 17

Chapter 21

Chapter 22

Chapter 23

Maps

Preface

A History of Western Society grew out of the authors' desire to infuse new life into the study of Western civilization. We knew full well that historians were using imaginative questions and innovative research to open up vast new areas of historical interest and knowledge. We also recognized that these advances had dramatically affected the subject of European economic, intellectual, and, especially, social history, while new research and fresh interpretations were also revitalizing the study of the traditional mainstream of political, diplomatic, and religious development. Despite history's vitality as a discipline, however, it seemed to us that both the broad public and the intelligentsia were generally losing interest in the past.

It was our conviction, based on considerable experience introducing large numbers of students to the broad sweep of Western civilization, that a book reflecting current trends could excite readers and inspire a renewed interest in history and our Western heritage. Our strategy was twofold. First, we made social history a core element of our work. We not only incorporated recent research by social historians but also sought to recreate the life of ordinary people in appealing human terms. At the same time we were determined to give great economic, political, cultural, and intellectual developments the attention they unquestionably deserve. We wanted to give individual readers and instructors a balanced, integrated perspective so that they could pursue—on their own or in the classroom—those themes and questions that they found particularly exciting and significant. In an effort to realize fully the potential of our fresh yet balanced approach, we made many changes, large and small, in the editions that followed.

Changes in the New Edition

In preparing the sixth edition we have worked hard to keep our book up-to-date and to strengthen our distinctive yet balanced approach. Five main lines of revision guided our many changes.

New "Individuals in Society" Feature

First, in each chapter of the sixth edition we have added a short study of a fascinating man or woman or group of people, which is carefully integrated into the main discussion in the text. This new "Individuals in Society" feature grows out of our long-standing focus on people's lives and the varieties of historical experience, and we believe that readers will empathize with these flesh-and-blood human beings as they themselves seek to define their own identities today. The spotlighting of individuals, both famous and obscure, carries forward the greater attention to cultural and intellectual developments that we used to invigorate our social history in the fifth edition, and it reflects changing interests within the historical profession as well as the development of "micro history."

The range of men and women we consider is great. Several are famous historical actors, such as the Roman orator Cicero (Chapter 5), the mystical Saint Teresa of Ávila (Chapter 14), the charismatic Russian rebel Stenka Razin (Chapter 17), the ruthless British imperialist Cecil Rhodes (Chapter 26), and the creator of communist Yugoslavia, Marshal Tito (Chapter 30). Other individuals illuminate aspects of their times but are not well-known: a solid Roman soldier (Chapter 6); a serf who gained freedom and success (Chapter 10); a Jewish businesswoman and mother of thirteen (Chapter 16); a talented midwife in colonial America (Chapter 20); and a pioneering professional woman in nineteenth-century Berlin (Chapter 24). Collective biographies of the Jews of medieval Speyer (Chapter 9) and the Protestant villagers resisting Nazi evil in Le Chambon in southern France (Chapter 29) probe the dimensions of collective identity and social action. Creative artists and intellectuals include the Greek playwright Menander (Chapter 4), the Italian Renaissance painter Gentile Bellini (Chapter 13), the Jewish philosopher Moses Mendelssohn (Chapter 18), the influential romantic writer Germaine de Staël (Chapter 23), and the left-wing socialist theorist Rosa Luxemburg (Chapter 27).

Expanded Ethnic and Geographic Scope

Second, in this edition we have added significantly more discussion of groups and regions that are frequently shortchanged in the general histories of Europe and Western civilization. This expanded scope is, we feel, an important improvement. It reflects the renewed awareness within the profession of Europe's enormous historical diversity, as well as the efforts of contemporary Europeans to understand the ambivalent and contested meanings of their national, regional, ethnic, and pan-European identities. Examples of this enlarged scope include early Greek influence in the western Mediterranean (Chapter 3) and subsequent developments there (Chapter 4); greatly expanded treatment of Europe's borderlands—Iberia, Ireland, Scotland, eastern Europe, and the Baltic area—in the Middle Ages (Chapters 9, 11, 12); developments in absolutist Sweden and southern Russia (Chapter 17); Spanish urban life (Chapter 24); and completely new and detailed discussion of twentieth-century eastern Europe (Chapters 27, 30, and 31). A broader treatment of Jewish history has been integrated into the text throughout this edition, just as the history of women and gender was integrated in the fifth edition. Examples include anti-Semitism during the Spanish Inquisition (Chapter 13) and in tsarist Russia (Chapter 27); Jewish Enlightenment thought in Germany (Chapter 18); and the unfolding of the Holocaust during the Second World War (Chapter 29).

Organizational Changes

Third, our expanded ethnic and geographic scope is one of several organizational improvements. Chapters 30 and 31 have been completely rewritten in order to present and interpret the historic changes that have transformed Europe and the world in the last fifteen years. Thus Chapter 30 treats the entire cold war era to the mid-1980s, while Chapter 31 analyzes the decline and collapse of communism, the re-emergence and reconstruction of eastern Europe, German unification and its consequences, ethnic conflicts and civil war in the Balkans, economic and cultural changes, immigration and globalization, the European Union, and the future in the new millennium. Chapter 6 has also been extensively reorganized to include a section on Late Antiquity. Chapters 9, 11, and 12 have been recast to highlight the interactions between English, German, and Spanish colonizers and the peoples they encountered and sometimes conquered. Discussions of politics after 1815 in Chapter 23 and of the public health revolution in Chapter 24 have been sharpened and tightened up.

Incorporation of Recent Scholarship

Fourth, as in all previous revisions we have made a conscientious effort to keep our book up-to-date with new and significant scholarship. Because the authors are committed to a balanced approach that reflects the true value of history, we have continued to incorporate important new findings on political, economic, cultural, and intellectual developments in this edition. Revisions of this nature include Chaldean Babylonia and the Kassites (Chapter 2), the Greek polis (Chapter 3), the Etruscans and the pre-Etruscans (Chapter 5), the Byzantine Empire (Chapter 7), the Merovingian and Carolingian kingdoms (Chapter 8), consumerism in Renaissance Italy (Chapter 13), absolutism in Western Europe (Chapter 16), the Enlightenment in Germany (Chapter 18), women in health care, business, and the liberal professions (Chapters 20, 22, and 24), the social aspects of Italian unification and the consequences of the Franco-Prussian War (Chapter 23), the action of left-wing socialists in Germany (Chapter 27), the causes of the Great Depression and the policies of the New Deal in the United States (Chapter 28), factors influencing Nazi voters in 1932 and Soviet collectivization (Chapter 29), and the collapse of communism (Chapter 31). In short, recent research keeps the broad sweep of our history fresh.

Revised Full-Color Art and Map Programs

Finally, the illustrative component of our work has been carefully revised. We have added many new illustrations to our extensive art program, which includes nearly two hundred color reproductions, letting great art and important events come alive. As in earlier editions, all illustrations have been carefully selected to complement the text, and all carry informative captions based on thorough research that enhance their value. Artwork remains an integral part of our book; the past can speak in pictures as well as in words. The use of full color serves to clarify the maps and graphs and to enrich the textual material. The maps and map captions have been updated to correlate directly to the text, and new maps have been added in Chapters 9 and 31.

DISTINCTIVE FEATURES

In addition to the new "Individuals in Society" study, distinctive features from earlier editions guide the reader in the process of historical understanding. Many of these features also show how historians sift through and evaluate evidence. Our goal is to suggest how historians actually work and think. We want the reader to think critically and to realize that history is neither a list of cut-and-dried facts nor a senseless jumble of conflicting opinions. To help students and instructors realize this goal, we have significantly expanded the discussion of "what is history" in Chapter 1 of this edition.

Revised Primary-Source Feature

In the fifth edition we added a two-page excerpt from a primary source at the end of each chapter. This important feature, entitled "Listening to the Past," extends and illuminates a major historical issue considered in the chapter, and it has been well received by instructors and students. In the new edition we have reviewed our selections and made judicious substitutions. For example, in Chapter 3 Thucydides describes the great plague of Athens and in Chapter 4 Tacitus depicts the meeting of Greek and Egyptian culture. The writings of Godric of Finchdale (Chapter 10) and Christine de Pisan (Chapter 12) shed new light on the Middle Ages, while Calvin outlines his plan for Geneva in Chapter 14. A former African slave details his captivity and sale in Chapter 19, while a Japanese patriot urges military reforms to counter European imperialism in Chapter 26. A soldier and a Viennese woman recount their experiences in the First World War in Chapter 27, and the Solidarity activist Adam Michnik defends nonviolent resistance to communism from prison in Chapter 31.

Each primary source opens with a problem-setting introduction and closes with "Questions for Analysis" that invite students to evaluate the evidence as historians would. Drawn from a range of writings addressing a variety of social, cultural, political, and intellectual issues, these sources promote active involvement and critical interpretation. Selected for their interest and importance and carefully fitted into their historical context, these sources do indeed allow the student to "listen to the past" and to observe how history has been shaped by individual men and women, some of them great aristocrats, others ordinary folk.

Problems of Historical Interpretation

The addition of more problems of historical interpretation in the fifth edition was well received, so we have increased their number again in this edition. We believe that the problematic element helps our readers develop the critical-thinking skills that are among the most precious benefits of studying history. New examples of this more open-ended, interpretive approach include the debate over the transition from Antiquity to the early Middle Ages (Chapter 6), the question of European racism in the Middle Ages (Chapter 12), the issue of gender in the Italian cities of the Renaissance (Chapter 13), the renewed debate on personal and collective responsibilities for the Holocaust (Chapter 29), the dynamics of the great purges in the Soviet Union (Chapter 29), the process of reconstruction in eastern Europe and the debate over globalization (Chapter 31).

Improved Chapter Features

Other distinctive features from earlier editions have been reviewed and improved in the sixth edition. To help guide the reader toward historical understanding, we pose specific historical questions at the beginning of each chapter. These questions are then answered in the course of each chapter, and each chapter concludes with a concise summary of its findings. All of the questions and summaries have been re-examined and frequently revised in order to maximize the usefulness of this popular feature.

In addition to posing chapter-opening questions and presenting more problems in historical interpretation, we have quoted extensively from a wide variety of primary sources in the narrative, demonstrating in our use of these quotations how historians evaluate evidence. Thus primary sources are examined as an integral part of the narrative as well as presented in extended form in the "Listening to the Past" chapter feature. We believe that such an extensive program of both integrated and separate primary source excerpts will help readers learn to interpret and think critically.

Each chapter concludes with carefully selected suggestions for further reading. These suggestions are briefly described to help readers know where to turn to continue thinking and learning about the Western world. Also chapter bibliographies have been thoroughly revised and updated to keep them current with the vast amount of new work being done in many fields.

Revised Timelines

The timelines appearing in earlier editions have been revised in this edition. Once again we provide a unified timeline in an appendix at the end of the book. Comprehensive and easy to locate, this useful timeline allows students to compare simultaneous political, economic, social, cultural, intellectual, and scientific developments over the centuries.

Flexible Format

Western civilization courses differ widely in chronological structure from one campus to another. To accommodate the various divisions of historical time into intervals that fit a two-quarter, three-quarter, or two-semester period, *A History of Western Society* is being published in four versions, three of which embrace the complete work:

- One-volume hardcover edition: A HISTORY OF WESTERN SOCIETY
- Two-volume paperback: A HISTORY OF WESTERN SOCIETY, *Volume I: From Antiquity to the Enlightenment* (Chapters 1–17); *Volume II: From Absolutism to the Present* (Chapters 16–31)
- Three-volume paperback: A HISTORY OF WESTERN SOCIETY, *Volume A: From Antiquity to 1500* (Chapters 1–13); *Volume B: From the Renaissance to 1815* (Chapters 12–21); *Volume C: From the Revolutionary Era to the Present* (Chapters 21–31)
- A HISTORY OF WESTERN SOCIETY, *Since 1300* (Chapters 12–31), for courses on Europe since the Renaissance

Note that overlapping chapters in both the two- and the three-volume sets permit still wider flexibility in matching the appropriate volume with the opening and closing dates of a course term.

ANCILLARIES

Learning and teaching ancillaries, listed below, also contribute to the usefulness of the text.

- *Study Guide*
- *Online Study Guide*
- *Instructor's Resource Manual*
- *Test Items*
- *Computerized Test Items*
- *GeoQuest™: an interactive map CD-ROM*
- *Bibliobase™: custom coursepacks in Western civilization*
- *Power Presentation Manager*
- *Map Transparencies*

The excellent *Study Guide* has been thoroughly revised by Professor James Schmiechen of Central Michigan University. Professor Schmiechen has been a tower of strength ever since he critiqued our initial prospectus, and he has continued to give us many valuable suggestions as well as his warmly appreciated support. His *Study Guide* contains learning objectives, chapter summaries, chapter outlines, review questions, extensive multiple-choice exercises, self-check lists of important concepts and events, and a variety of study aids and suggestions. The sixth edition also retains the study-review exercises on the interpretation of visual sources and major political ideas as well as suggested issues for discussion and essay, chronology reviews, and sections on studying effectively. These sections take the student through reading and studying activities such as underlining, summarizing, identifying main points, classifying information according to sequence, and making historical comparisons. To enable both students and instructors to use the *Study Guide* with the greatest possible flexibility, the guide is available in two volumes, with considerable overlapping of chapters. Instructors and students who use only Volumes A and B of the text have all the pertinent study materials in a single volume, *Study Guide, Volume I* (Chapters 1–21); likewise, those who use only Volumes B and C of the text also have all the necessary materials in one volume, *Study Guide, Volume II* (Chapters 12–31). An *Online Study Guide* is also available for students. Accessible through Houghton Mifflin's @history website (www.hmco.com/college/), it functions as a tutorial, providing rejoinders to all multiple-choice questions that explain why the student's response is or is not correct.

The *Instructor's Resource Manual,* prepared by Professor John Marshall Carter, contains instructional objectives, annotated chapter outlines, suggestions for lectures and discussion, paper and class activity topics, primary-source exercises, map activities, and lists of audio-visual resources. The accompanying *Test Items,* by Professor Charles Crouch of Georgia Southern University, offer identification, multiple-choice, map, and essay questions for a total of approximately two thousand test items. These test items are available to adopters in a Windows version that includes editing capability.

An exciting addition to our map program is a CD-ROM of thirty interactive maps—GeoQuest™, available for both instructors and students.

We are also proud to announce the creation of our on-line primary-source collection, Bibliobase™. This resource will allow instructors to select from over six hundred documents to create their own customized reader for courses in Western civilization. Visit our web site at **www.bibliobase.com** for more information.

To add an exciting multimedia component to lectures, we have created Power Presentation Manager (PPM), a software tool that enables teachers to prepare visual aids for lectures electronically. Using both textual and visual materials, instructors can customize their lectures by incorporating their own material into the PPM and combining it with the electronic resources available. Please contact your Houghton Mifflin Company representative for more information about this innovative and exciting multimedia program.

Finally, a set of full-color Map Transparencies of all the maps in the text is available on adoption.

Acknowledgments

It is a pleasure to thank the many instructors who read and critiqued the manuscript through its development:

Christopher Bellitto
St. Joseph's Seminary

William D. Burgess
East Tennessee State University

Carolyn A. Conley
University of Alabama at Birmingham

Charles Crouch
Georgia Southern University

Robert L. Dise, Jr.
University of Northern Iowa

Greg Eghigian
University of Texas, Arlington

Linda Frey
University of Montana

Mary T. Furgol
Montgomery College

Amy G. Gordon
Denison University

Daniel Gordon
University of Massachusetts, Amherst

Piotr Gorecki
University of Cracow

Jeffrey Herf
Ohio University

David Hudson
California State University, Fresno

Charles Ingrao
Purdue University

David Kammerance
Florence Darlington Technical College

Jonathan Katz
Oregon State University

James K. Kieswetter
Eastern Washington University

Cynthia Kosso
Northern Arizona University

James Lehning
University of Utah

Alex Lichtenstein
Florida International University

Sean Farrell Moran
Oakland University

Ross L. Pattison
Dutchess Community College

Kathleen Paul
University of South Florida

Linda J. Piper
University of Georgia

Norman G. Raiford
Greenville Technical College

Kenneth Schellhage
Northern Michigan University

David S. Sefton
Eastern Kentucky University

Michael Slaven
California University of Pennsylvania

Kay Slocum
Kent State University

Roger P. Snow
University of Great Falls

William Stiebing
University of New Orleans

Bruce M. Taylor
University of Dayton

Thomas Turley
Santa Clara University

Richard D. Weigel
Western Kentucky University

James M. Woods
Georgia Southern University

It is also a pleasure to thank our many editors at Houghton Mifflin for their efforts over many years. To Christina Horn, who guided production in the ever-more intensive email age, and to Dale Anderson, our development editor, we express our special appreciation. And we thank Carole Frohlich for her contributions in photo research and selection.

Many of our colleagues at the University of Illinois and at Georgetown University continued to provide information and stimulation, often without even knowing it. We thank them for it. Bennett Hill wishes to express his appreciation to Ramón de la Fuente for his assistance in the preparation of this sixth edition. John Buckler wishes to thank Professor Nicholas Yalouris, former General Inspector of Antiquities, for his kind permission to publish the newly discovered mosaic from Elis, Greece, in Chapter 3. John McKay happily acknowledges the fine research assistance provided by Camille Monahan and thanks her for it. He also expresses his deep appreciation to Jo Ann McKay for her sharp-eyed editorial support and unfailing encouragement.

Each of us has benefited from the criticism of his coauthors, although each of us assumes responsibility for what he has written. John Buckler has written the first six chapters; Bennett Hill has continued the narrative through Chapter 16; and John McKay has written Chapters 17 through 31. Finally, we continue to welcome the many comments and suggestions that have come from our readers, for they have helped us greatly in this ongoing endeavor.

J. P. M. B. D. H. J. B.

A History of WESTERN SOCIETY

CHAPTER 1

Near Eastern Origins

Mummy mask of Prince Yuya, the father-in-law of Amenhotep III. *(Egyptian Museum, Cairo/E.T. Archive)*

The culture of the modern Western world has its origins in the ancient Near East, a region that includes the lands bordering the Mediterranean's eastern shore, the Arabian peninsula, parts of northeast Africa, and perhaps above all Mesopotamia, the area of modern Iraq. In these areas many human beings abandoned their life of roaming and hunting to settle in stable agricultural communities. From these communities grew cities and civilizations, societies that invented concepts and techniques that have become integral parts of contemporary life. Fundamental to the development of Western culture was the invention of writing by the Sumerians of Mesopotamia, which allowed knowledge of the past to be preserved and facilitated the spread and accumulation of learning, lore, literature, and science. Mathematics, astronomy, and architecture were also innovations of the ancient Near Eastern civilizations. So, too, were the first law codes, as well as religious concepts that still permeate daily life.

But how do we know and understand these things? Before embarking on the study of history, it is necessary to ask, "What is it?" Only then can the peoples and events of tens of thousands of years be placed into a coherent whole. Once the nature of history is understood, further questions can be asked and reasonably answered. Specifically for this chapter,

- How did nomadic hunters become urban dwellers?
- How did Western culture originate in Mesopotamia, and what caused Mesopotamian culture to become predominant throughout most of the ancient Near East?
- How did the Egyptians contribute to this vast story?
- What did the arrival of the Hittites on the frontiers of Mesopotamia and Egypt mean to the more advanced cultures of their new neighbors?

These are the questions we will explore in this chapter.

 What Is History and Why?

History is the effort to reconstruct the past to discover what people thought, what they did, and how their beliefs and actions continue to influence human life. In order to appreciate the past fully, we must put it into perspective so that we can understand the factors that have helped to shape us as individuals, the society in which we live, and the nature of other peoples' societies. Why else should we study civilizations as separated from ours through time, distance, and culture as classical Greece, medieval Germany, and modern Russia? Although many of the people involved in these epochs are long dead, what they did has touched everyone alive today.

To answer the questions above, historians examine primary sources, the firsthand accounts of people who lived through the events, people in the best position to know what happened. Historians normally use a variety of evidence in their search for an accurate understanding of the past. Most important are documents written by people who recorded their experiences and analyzed the significance of them. They investigated what happened, who was responsible for it, why it happened, and what it meant. Another written historical source is the chronicle. Writers of chronicles noted events in their chronological order (therefore the name) and sometimes added a brief explanation of the events.

Historians also rely on other, nonliterary evidence. In nearly all periods of early history, people inscribed laws, treaties with other states, and honors to individuals in stone. Governments still engrave similar documents in bronze. Even today, one cannot visit a Civil War battlefield without encountering a plaque giving information about what happened there. In the medieval period scribes produced thousands of documents giving detailed accounts of agricultural life on manors—how they were run, what the local customs were, and how society actually functioned. These scribes, many of them Christian monks, also left a record of religious and political affairs.

With the modern period has come an explosion of information. In addition to the traditional sources of historical knowledge, we have official statistics covering virtually everything from the annual number of deaths in automobile accidents to the daily results of the stock market. Public and private archives preserve a wealth of material that is useful in understanding governments, corporations, and private people. All these materials are the raw resources of historians.

In the face of the evidence, historians must determine what is accurate and what is false or biased. They do so by taking the earliest information first. They compare various versions of particular events or large trends with one another. Some people who have left us with evidence of the past were more intelligent or better informed than others. Therefore, their testimony is preferred and indeed strengthened by other writers who independently reported the same things. When two or more dependable sources record the same thing in the same way, historians conclude that they present an accurate account of events.

Once historians have determined which sources are reliable, they use this information to conclude that they have established a fact or that they are in a position to understand the significance of the information. Understanding the past does not necessarily come easily, which is one of the joys and frustrations of history. Unlike the more exact physical sciences, history cannot reproduce experiments under controlled conditions, because no two historical events are precisely alike. People cannot be put into test tubes, and they are not as predictable as atoms or hydrocarbons. That is hardly surprising, for history is about people, the most complex organisms on this planet.

To complicate matters, for many epochs of history only the broad outlines are known, so interpretation is especially difficult. For example, historians know that the Hittite Empire collapsed at the height of its power, but interpretations of the causes of the catastrophe are still speculative. On the other end of the spectrum, some developments are so vast and complex that historians must master mountains of data before they can even begin to interpret them properly. Events as diverse as the end of the western Roman Empire, the origins of the Industrial Revolution, and the causes of the French Revolution are very complicated because so many people brought so many different forces to bear for so many reasons. In such cases, there is never one simple explanation that will satisfy everyone, which testifies to the complexity of life in developed societies.

Still another matter complicates an accurate understanding of the past. The attempt to understand history is uniquely human. Interpretations of the past sometimes change because people's points of view change in the course of life. The values and attitudes of one generation may not be shared by another. Despite such differences in interpretation, the efforts of historians to examine and understand the past can give them a perspective that is valuable to the present. It is through this process of analysis and interpretation of evidence that historians come to understand not only the past but its relation to life today.

Social history, an important subject of this book, is itself an example of the historian's reappraisal of the meaning of the past. For centuries people took the basic facts, details, and activities of life for granted. Obviously, people lived in certain types of houses, ate certain foods that they either raised or bought, and reared families. These matters seemed so ordinary that few serious historians gave them much thought. Yet within this generation a growing number of scholars have demonstrated that studies of the ways in which people have lived over the years deserve as much attention as the reigns of monarchs, the careers of great political figures, and the outcomes of big battles.

The topics of history and human societies lead to the question, "What is civilization?" *Civilization* is a word easier to describe than to define. It comes from the Latin adjective *civilis,* which refers to a citizen. Citizens willingly and mutually bind themselves in political, economic, and social organizations in which individuals merge themselves, their energies, and their interests in a larger community.

Civilization, however, goes far beyond politics. It also includes an advanced stage of social development, which entails enlightenment and education. Civilized society is refined, possessing the notion of law to govern the conduct of its members. It includes a code of manners and social conduct that creates an atmosphere of harmony and peace within the community. It creates art and generates science and philosophy to explain the larger world. It creates theology so that people can go beyond superstition in their pursuit of religion.

In the course of time, civilization has come to embrace not only a people's system of social and political organization but also their particular shared way of thinking and believing, their art, and other facets of their culture—the complex whole that sets one people apart from other peoples who have different shared values and practices. One way to understand this idea is to observe the origins and development of the chief Western civilizations, analyzing similarities and differences among them. The term *Western* in this context means the ideas, customs, and institutions that developed primarily in Europe, the Americas, and their colonies throughout the world. These ideas, customs, and institutions set Western civilization apart from other civilizations, such as the African and Asian, that developed their unique way of life as a result of different demands, challenges, and opportunities, both human and geographical. Yet even the term *Western* has its irony. Some of the roots of this civilization lie in western Asia and northern Africa. Mesopotamia, and to a lesser extent Egypt, created concepts that are basic to Western thought and conduct. They were not the deciding features, but they helped to shape European cultures. The term *Western* in this context means the ideas, customs, and institutions that set Western civilization apart from others. Yet no civilization stands alone. Each influences its neighbors, all the while preserving the essentials that make it distinctive.

At the fundamental level, the similarities of Western civilization are greater than the differences. Almost all people in Europe and the Americas share some values, even though they may live far apart, speak different languages, and have different religions and political and social systems. These values are the bonds that hold a civilization together. By studying these shared cultural values, which stretch through time and across distance, we can see how the various events of the past have left their impression on the present and even how the present may influence the future.

 THE FIRST HUMAN BEINGS

On December 27, 1831, young Charles Darwin stepped aboard the H.M.S. *Beagle* to begin a voyage to South America and the Pacific Ocean. In the course of that five-year voyage, he became convinced that species of animals and human beings had evolved from lower forms. At first Darwin was reluctant to publicize his theories because they ran counter to the biblical account of creation, which claimed that God had made Adam in one day. Finally, however, in 1859 he published *On the Origin of Species*. In 1871 he followed it with *The Descent of Man,* in which he argued that human beings and apes are descended from a common ancestor. Even before Darwin had proclaimed his theories, evidence to support them had come to light. In 1856 the fossilized bones of an early form of man were discovered in the Neander Valley of Germany. Called Neanderthal man after the place of his discovery, he was physically more primitive than modern man (*Homo sapiens,* or thinking man), but he was clearly a human being and not an ape. He offered proof of Darwin's theory that *Homo sapiens* had evolved from less-developed forms.

The theories of Darwin, supported by the evidence of fossilized remains, ushered in a new scientific era in which scientists and scholars have re-examined the very nature of human beings and their history. Men and women of the twentieth century have made many discoveries and solved some old problems, but they also have raised many new ones. Although the fossil remains of primitive unicellular organisms can be dated back roughly two and a half billion years, the fossil record is far from complete. Thus the whole story of evolution cannot yet be known.

Ever since Darwin published his theories of evolution, scholars have tried to find the "missing link" to the one fossil that would establish the point from which human beings and apes went their own evolutionary ways. However, recent finds have caused them to question the very concept of the missing link and its implications. Fossil remains in China suggest that evolution was more complicated than paleoanthropologists—scientists who study early human beings—previously thought and even that human beings may not have originated in Africa. It is not simply that paleoanthropologists, like historians, must interpret their data; they must rethink everything that they have discovered in the light of their latest findings. That point was reinforced in Spain in June 1997. Spanish archaeologists discovered fossil remains of an early hominoid, which revealed characteristics between modern human beings and Neanderthals. This find demonstrates that these early peoples roamed southern Europe as early as 800,000 years ago.

Many contemporary paleoanthropologists now suggest that the search for a missing link is a blind alley. Given the small numbers of these primates and the extent of the globe, there is an almost infinitesimal chance of finding a skeleton that can be considered the missing link between other primates and human beings. Instead, they stress the need to study all of these fossil remains to open new vistas for the understanding of evolution. That conclusion should not be surprising. In 1969, Loren Eiseley, a noted American anthropologist, offered the wisest and humblest observation: "The human interminglings of hundreds of thousands of years of prehistory are not to be clarified by a single generation of archeologists."[1]

Despite the enormous uncertainty surrounding human development, a reasonably clear picture can be drawn of two important early periods: the Paleolithic or Old Stone Age, and the Neolithic or New Stone Age. The immensely long Paleolithic Age, which lasted from about 400,000 to 7000 B.C., takes its scholarly name from the crude stone tools the earliest hunters chipped from flint and obsidian, a black volcanic rock. During the much shorter Neolithic Age, which lasted from about 7000 to 3000 B.C., human beings began using new types of stone tools and, more important, pursuing agriculture.

Paleolithic Cave Painting All Paleolithic peoples relied primarily on hunting for their survival. This scene, painted on the wall of a cave in southern France, depicts the animals that this group normally hunted. Paleolithic peoples may have hoped that by drawing these animals they gained a magical power over them. *(D. Mazonowicz, New York City)*

The Paleolithic Age

Paleolithic peoples hunted a huge variety of animals, ranging from elephants in Spain to deer in China. The hunters were thoroughly familiar with the habits and migratory patterns of the animals on which they relied. But success in the hunt also depended on the quality and effectiveness of the hunters' social organization. Paleolithic hunters were organized—they hunted in groups. They used their knowledge of the animal world and their power of thinking to plan how to down their prey. Paleolithic peoples also nourished themselves by gathering nuts, berries, and seeds. Just as they knew the habits of animals, so they had vast knowledge of the plant kingdom. Some Paleolithic peoples even knew how to plant wild seeds to supplement their food supply. Thus they relied on every part of the environment for survival.

The basic social unit of Paleolithic societies was probably the family, but family bonds were no doubt stronger and more extensive than those of families in modern, urban, and industrialized societies. It is likely that the bonds of kinship were strong not just within the nuclear family of father, mother, and children but throughout the extended family of uncles, aunts, cousins, nephews, and nieces. People in nomadic societies typically depend on the extended family for cooperative work and mutual protection. The ties of kinship probably also extended beyond the family to the tribe. A tribe was a group of families led by a patriarch, a dominant male who governed the group. Tribe members considered themselves descendants of a common ancestor. Most tribes probably consisted of thirty to fifty people.

As in the hunt, so too in other aspects of life—group members had to cooperate to survive. The adult males normally hunted abroad and between hunts made stone weapons. The women's realm was primarily the camp, but they too ranged through the neighborhood gathering nuts, grains, and fruits to supplement the group's diet. The women's primary responsibility was the bearing of children, who were essential to the continuation of the group. Women also had to care for the children, especially the infants. Part of women's work was tending the fire, which served for warmth, cooking, and protection against wild animals.

Some of the most striking accomplishments of Paleolithic peoples were intellectual. They used reason to govern their actions. Thought and language permitted the lore and experience of the old to be passed on to the young. An invisible world also opened up to *Homo sapiens*. The Neanderthals developed the custom of burying their dead and leaving offerings with the body, perhaps in the belief that somehow life continued after death.

Paleolithic peoples produced the first art. They decorated cave walls with lifelike paintings of animals and scenes of the hunt. Located deep in the caves, some of these paintings still survive, such as those at Altamira in Spain and Lascaux in France. Paleolithic peoples also began to fashion clay models of pregnant women and of animals. By portraying the animals as realistically as possible, the artist-hunters may have hoped to gain power over them. The statuettes of pregnant women seem to express a wish for fertile women to have babies and thus ensure the group's survival. The wall paintings and clay statuettes of Paleolithic peoples represent the earliest yearnings of human beings to control their environment.

The Neolithic Age

Hunting is at best a precarious way of life, even when the diet is supplemented with seeds and fruits. Paleolithic tribes either moved with the herds and adapted themselves to new circumstances or perished. Several long ice ages—periods when huge glaciers covered vast parts of Europe—subjected the small bands of Paleolithic hunters to extreme hardship.

Not long after the last ice age, around 7000 B.C., some hunters and gatherers began to rely chiefly on agriculture for their sustenance. Others continued the old pastoral and nomadic ways. Indeed, agriculture itself evolved over the course of time, and Neolithic peoples had long known how to grow crops. The real transformation of human life occurred when huge numbers of people began to rely primarily and permanently on the grain they grew and the animals they domesticated. Agriculture made possible a more stable and secure life. Neolithic peoples flourished, fashioning an energetic, creative era. They were responsible for many fundamental inventions and innovations that the modern world takes for granted. First, obviously, is systematic agriculture—that is, the reliance of Neolithic peoples on agriculture as their primary, not merely subsidiary, source of food. Thus they developed the primary economic activity of the entire ancient world and the basis of all modern life. With the settled routine of Neolithic farmers came the evolution of towns and eventually cities. Neolithic farmers usually raised more food than they could consume, and their surpluses permitted larger, healthier populations. Population growth in turn created an even greater reliance on settled farming, as only systematic agriculture could sustain the increased numbers of people. Since surpluses of food could also be bartered for other commodities, the Neolithic era witnessed the beginnings of large-scale exchange of goods. In time the increasing complexity of Neolithic societies led to the development of writing, prompted by the need to keep records and later by the urge to chronicle experiences, learning, and beliefs.

The transition to settled life also had a profound impact on the family. The shared needs and pressures that encourage extended-family ties are less prominent in settled than in nomadic societies. Bonds to the extended family weakened. In towns and cities, the nuclear family was more dependent on its immediate neighbors than on kinfolk.

However, the nomadic way of life and the family relationships it nurtured continued to flourish alongside settled agriculture. Dramatic evidence of this fact came to light on September 19, 1991, when a hiker in the Tyrolean Alps in Italy discovered the frozen body of a Neolithic herdsman. The corpse is the oldest found intact, and its preservation results from the man having been covered for some 5,300 years by glacial ice. Although the discoverers unfortunately did irreparable damage to the site, enough remains to give a unique impression of European nomadic life and a surprising glimpse of its sophistication. The "Iceman," as he is now called, was found equipped with the implements of everyday life. Among them are advanced bows and arrows that prove a remarkable knowledge of ballistics. A number of tools, some of bone, wood, and even copper, show that European people were making the transition from the Neolithic Age to the time when they relied primarily on metals for their tools. Dental evidence suggests that the Iceman's diet consisted of milled grain. These findings strongly suggest that the Iceman was a hunter and gatherer, but also that he and his society depended on milled grain as a vital part of their diet. The Iceman proves that nomadic and pastoral life could and did coincide peacefully with the emerging agricultural settlements. Often farmers and nomads bartered with one another, each group trading its surpluses for those of the other. Although nomadic peoples continued to exist throughout the Neolithic period and into modern times, the future belonged to the Neolithic farmers and their descendants. While the development of systematic agriculture may not have been revolutionary, the changes that it ushered in certainly were.

Until recently, scholars thought that agriculture originated in the ancient Near East and gradually spread elsewhere. Contemporary work, however, points to a more complex pattern of development. For unknown reasons people all over the world seem to have begun domesticating plants and animals. In the Near East the process took place at roughly the same time, between 8000 and 3500 B.C., at four main points of origin. The inhabitants of sites as far apart as Tepe Yahya in modern Iran, Jarmo in Iraq, Jericho in Palestine, and Hacilar in modern Turkey (Map 1.1) raised wheat, barley, peas, and lentils. They also kept herds of sheep, pigs, and possibly goats.

Once people began to rely on farming for their livelihood, they settled in permanent villages and built houses. The location of the village was crucial. Early farmers chose places where the water supply was constant and adequate for their crops and flocks. At first, villages were small, consisting of a few households. By about 7000 B.C., however, as the population expanded and prospered, villages usually developed into walled towns. Walls offered protection and permitted a more secure, stable way of life than that of the nomad. They also prove that towns grew in size, population, and wealth, for these fortifications were so large that they could have been raised only by a large labor force. They indicate, moreover, that towns were developing social and political organization. The fortifications, the work of the whole community, would have been impossible without central planning.

These fortifications also prove that Neolithic peoples made strides in warfare. The budding towns needed protection, and attackers needed a more systematic approach in their assaults. The obvious solution to both problems was the creation of organized armies. Paintings from Spain depict small armies armed with bows and protected by rudimentary armor of cloth or skins. These pictures also portray warriors deployed in both column and line formations—simple military tactics. In

Return of the Iceman This scene captures the discovery of a Neolithic herdsman who was trapped in the ice about 5,300 years ago. The discovery was made by chance in September 1991. In an ancient accident, he was sealed in ice with all of his tools, thus providing modern scholars with a unique view of the past. The discovery is so important that scientists have not yet done an autopsy on the corpse. *(Paul Hanny/Liaison)*

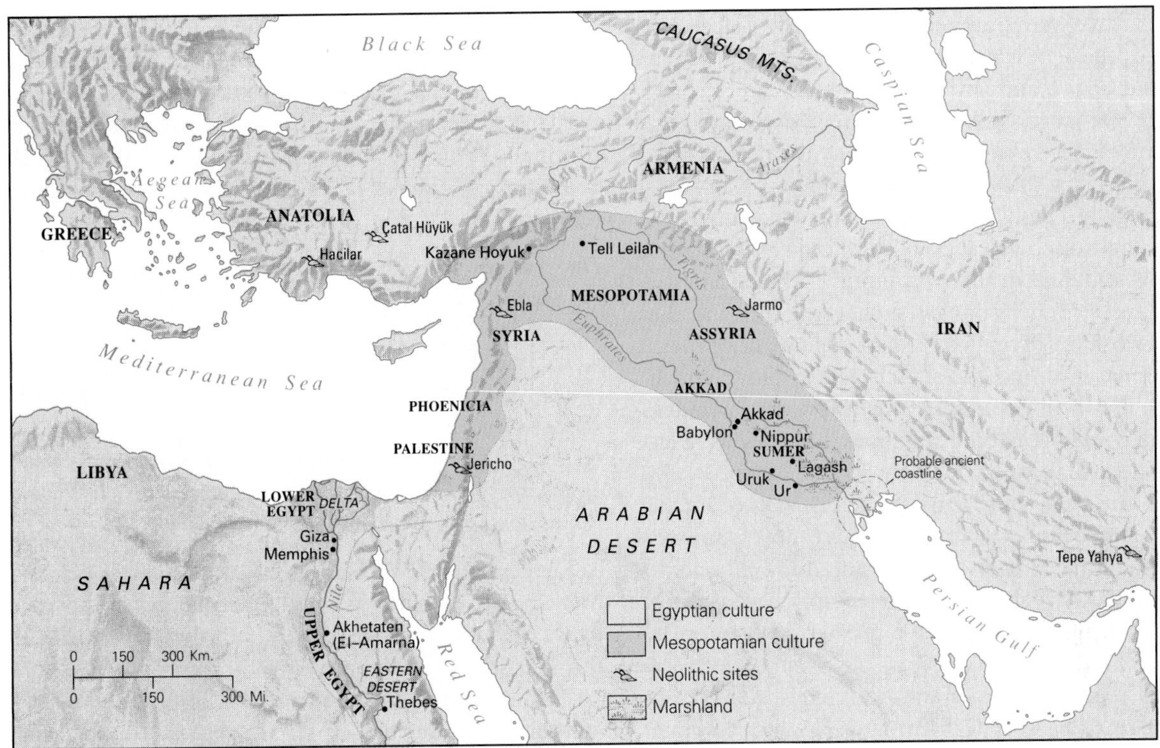

MAP 1.1 Spread of Cultures in the Ancient Near East This map illustrates the spread of the Mesopotamian and Egyptian cultures through a semicircular stretch of land often called the Fertile Crescent. From this area knowledge and use of agriculture spread throughout the western part of Asia Minor.

the eastern Mediterranean, warriors used the sling extensively in addition to the bow and arrow. A large graveyard discovered near the Nile River in ancient Nubia (modern Egypt) testifies to the ferocity of Neolithic warfare. At least 40 percent of the skeletons studied had multiple wounds, and it is likely that the rest of those found likewise died of wounds. Finds elsewhere in the Mediterranean basin also provide evidence that the graveyard in Nubia presents a picture of organized warfare typical of the Neolithic period.

More important than fortifications and organized armies was the prosperity that led to a dramatic increase in population. No census figures exist for this period, but the number and size of the towns prove that Neolithic society was expanding. Early farmers found that agriculture provided a larger and much more dependable food supply than hunting and gathering. No longer did the long winter months mean the threat of starvation. Farmers learned to store the surplus for the winter. Because the farming community was better fed than ever before, it was also more resistant to diseases that kill people suffering from malnutrition. Thus Neolithic farmers were healthier and lived longer than their predecessors.

Agricultural surplus also made possible the division of labor. It freed some members of the community from the necessity of raising food. Artisans and craftsmen devoted their attention to making the new stone tools farming demanded—hoes and sickles for field work and mortars and pestles for grinding the grain. Other artisans began to shape clay into pottery vessels, which were used to store grain, wine, and oil and to serve as kitchen utensils. Still others wove baskets and cloth. People who could specialize in particular crafts produced more and better goods than any single farmer could.

Until recently it was impossible to say much about these goods. But in April 1985, archaeologists announced the discovery near the Dead Sea in modern Israel of a unique deposit of Neolithic artifacts. Found buried in a cave were fragments of the earliest cloth yet discovered, the oldest painted mask, remains of woven baskets and boxes, and jewelry. The textiles are surprisingly elaborate, some woven in eleven intricate designs. These artifacts give eloquent testimony to the sophistication and artistry of Neolithic craftworkers.

Prosperity and stable conditions nurtured other innovations and discoveries. Neolithic farmers improved their tools and agricultural techniques. They domesticated bigger, stronger animals, such as the bull and the horse, to work for them. To harness the power of these animals, they invented tools such as the plow, which came into use by 3000 B.C. The first plows had wooden shares and could break only light soils, but they were far more efficient than stone hoes. By 3000 B.C., the wheel had been invented, and farmers devised ways of hitching bulls and horses to wagons. These developments enabled Neolithic farmers to raise more food more efficiently and easily than ever before, simply because animals and machines were doing a greater proportion of the work.

In arid regions such as Mesopotamia and Egypt, farmers learned to irrigate their land and later to drain it to prevent the buildup of salt in the soil. By diverting water from rivers, they were able to open new land to cultivation. River waters flooding the fields deposited layers of rich mud, which increased the fertility of the soil. Thus the rivers, together with the manure of domesticated animals, kept replenishing the land. The results included a further increase in population and wealth. Irrigation, especially on a large scale, demanded group effort. The entire community had to plan which land to irrigate and how to lay out the canals. Then everyone had to help dig the canals. The demands of irrigation underscored the need for strong central authority within the community. Successful irrigation projects in turn strengthened such central authority by proving it effective and beneficial. Thus corporate spirit and governments to which individuals were subordinate—the makings of urban life—began to evolve.

Mesopotamian Civilization

Mesopotamia is the Greek name for the land between the Euphrates and Tigris Rivers. Both rivers have their headwaters in the mountains of Armenia in modern Turkey. Both are fed by numerous tributaries, and the entire river system drains a vast mountainous region. Overland routes in Mesopotamia usually follow the Euphrates because the banks of the Tigris are frequently steep and difficult. North of the ancient city of Babylon the land levels out into a barren expanse. The desert continues south of Babylon, and in 1857 the English geologist and traveler W. K. Loftus depicted it in grim terms:

There is no life for miles around. No river glides in grandeur at the base of its [the ancient city of Uruk] mounds; no green date groves flourish near its ruins. The jackal and the hyena appear to shun the dull aspect of its tombs. The king of birds never hovers over the deserted waste. A blade of grass or an insect finds no existence there. The shrivelled lichen alone, clinging to the weathered surface of the broken brick, seems to glory in its universal dominion upon those barren walls.[2]

Farther south the desert gives way to a 6,000-square-mile region of marshes, lagoons, mud flats, and reed banks. At last, in the extreme south the Euphrates and the Tigris unite and empty into the Persian Gulf.

This forbidding area became the home of many folk and the land of the first cities. The region around Akkad (or Agade, probably located somewhere near modern Baghdad) was occupied by bands of Semitic nomads, people linked by the fact that their languages all belonged to the group of languages known as Semitic, a group that includes Hebrew and Arabic. These Semites in time assimilated Sumerian culture and were instrumental in spreading it to other neighboring areas. The Sumerians established themselves in the south and were perhaps migrants from the east. Their origins are still uncertain, and they were not the only people to inhabit Mesopotamia. By 3000 B.C., however, they had established a number of cities in the southernmost part of Mesopotamia, which became known as Sumer. The Sumerians soon changed the face of the land and made Mesopotamia the "cradle of civilization" (see Map 1.1).

The Role of Environment

From the outset geography had a profound effect on the evolution of Mesopotamian civilization. In this region agriculture is possible only with irrigation and good drainage. Consequently, the Sumerians and later the Akkadians built their cities along the Tigris and Euphrates and the branches of these rivers. Some major cities, such as Ur and Uruk, took root on tributaries of the Euphrates, while others, notably Lagash, were built

SIGNIFICANT EVENTS IN MESOPOTAMIAN HISTORY

Period	Events
ca 3000 B.C.	Sumerians become prevalent in southern Mesopotamia
ca 2600 B.C.	Mesopotamian culture spreads to northern Mesopotamia
ca 2331 B.C.	Sargon captures Sumer and creates the new kingdom of Akkad
ca 1792 B.C.	Hammurabi wins control of Mesopotamia; Babylon becomes the new capital of Mesopotamia
ca 1595 B.C.	Hittites and Kassites destroy Hammurabi's dynasty

on branches of the Tigris. The rivers supplied fish, a major element of the city dwellers' diet. The rivers also provided reeds and clay for building materials. Since this entire area lacks stone, mud brick became the primary building block of Mesopotamian architecture.

Although the rivers sustained life, they also destroyed it by frequent floods that ravaged entire cities. Moreover, they restrained political development by making Sumer a geographical maze. Among the rivers, streams, and irrigation canals stretched open desert or swamp where nomadic tribes roamed. Communication among the isolated cities was difficult and at times dangerous. Thus each Sumerian city became a state, independent of the others and protective of its independence. Any city that tried to unify the country was resisted by the other cities. The political history of Sumer is one of almost constant warfare. Although Sumer was eventually unified, unification came late and was always tenuous.

The Invention of Writing and the First Schools

The origins of writing probably go back to the ninth millennium B.C., when Near Eastern peoples used clay tokens as counters for record keeping. By the fourth millennium people had realized that drawing pictures of the tokens on clay was simpler than making tokens. This breakthrough in turn suggested that more information could be conveyed by adding pictures of still other objects. The result was a complex system of pictographs, in which each sign pictured an object. These pictographs were the forerunners of a Sumerian form of writing known as *cuneiform,* from the Latin term for "wedge-shaped," used to describe the strokes of the stylus.

How did this pictographic system work, and how did it evolve into cuneiform writing? At first, if a scribe wanted to indicate a star, he simply drew a picture of it (line A of Figure 1.1) on a wet clay tablet, which became rock-hard when baked. Anyone looking at the picture would know what it meant and would think of the word for star. This complicated and laborious system had serious limitations. It could not represent abstract ideas or combinations of ideas. For instance, how could it depict a slave woman?

The solution appeared when the scribe discovered that signs could be combined to express meaning. To refer to a slave woman the scribe used the sign for woman (line B) and the sign for mountain (line C)—literally, "mountain woman" (line D). Because the Sumerians regularly obtained their slave women from the mountains, this combination of signs was easily understandable.

The next step was to simplify the system. Instead of drawing pictures, the scribe made conventionalized signs that were generally understood to represent ideas. Thus the signs became *ideograms:* they symbolized ideas. The sign for star could also be used to indicate heaven, sky, or even god.

The real breakthrough came when the scribe learned to use signs to represent sounds. For instance, the scribe drew two parallel wavy lines to indicate the word

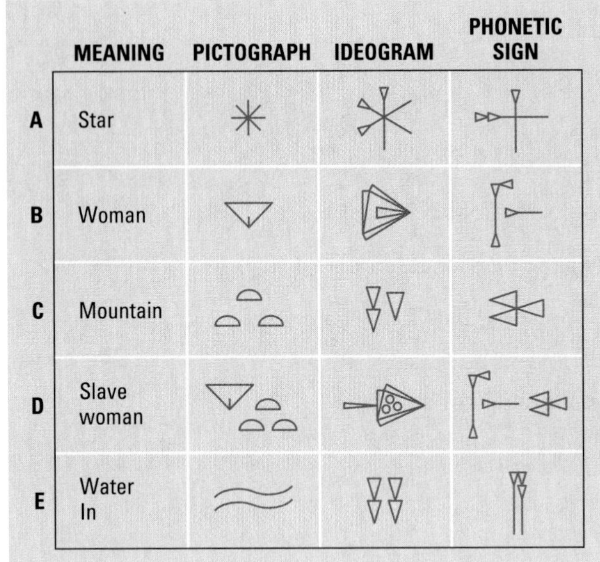

MEANING
PICTOGRAPH
IDEOGRAM
PHONETIC SIGN
A
Star
B
Woman
C
Mountain
D
Slave woman
E
Water
In

FIGURE 1.1 Sumerian Writing *(Excerpted from S. N. Kramer,* The Sumerians: Their History, Culture and Character, *University of Chicago Press, Chicago, 1963, pp. 302–306)*

a or "water" (line E). Besides water, the word *a* in Sumerian also meant "in." The word *in* expresses a relationship that is very difficult to represent pictorially. Instead of trying to invent a sign to mean "in," some clever scribe used the sign for water because the two words sounded alike. This phonetic use of signs made possible the combining of signs to convey abstract ideas.

The Sumerian system of writing was so complicated that only professional scribes mastered it, and even they had to study it for many years. By 2500 B.C. scribal schools flourished throughout Sumer. Most students came from wealthy families and were male. Each school had a master, teachers, and monitors. Discipline was strict, and students were caned for sloppy work and misbehavior. One graduate of a scribal school had few fond memories of the joy of learning:

My headmaster read my tablet, said:
"There is something missing," caned me.
. . . .
The fellow in charge of silence said:
"Why did you talk without permission," caned me.
The fellow in charge of the assembly said:
"Why did you stand at ease without permission," caned me.[3]

The Sumerian system of schooling set the educational standards for Mesopotamian culture, and the Akkadians and, later, the Babylonians adopted its practices and techniques. Mesopotamian education always had a practical side because of the economic and administrative importance of scribes. Most scribes took administrative positions in the temple or palace, where they kept records of business transactions, accounts, and inventories. But scribal schools did not limit their curriculum to business affairs. They were also centers of culture and scholarship. Topics of study included mathematics, botany, and linguistics. Advanced students copied and studied the classics of Sumerian literature. Talented students and learned scribes wrote compositions of their own. As a result, many literary, mathematical, and religious texts survive today, giving a full picture of Mesopotamian intellectual and spiritual life.

Mesopotamian Thought and Religion

The Mesopotamians made significant and sophisticated advances in mathematics using a numerical system based on units of sixty, ten, and six. They developed the concept of place value—that the value of a number depends on where it stands in relation to other numbers. Mesopotamian mathematical texts are of two kinds: tables and problems. Scribes compiled tables of squares and square roots, cubes and cube roots, and reciprocals. They wrote texts of problems, which dealt not only with equations and pure mathematics but also with concrete problems, such as how to plan irrigation ditches. The Mesopotamians did not consider mathematics a purely theoretical science. The building of cities, palaces, temples, and canals demanded practical knowledge of geometry and trigonometry.

Mesopotamian medicine was a combination of magic, prescriptions, and surgery. Mesopotamians believed that demons and evil spirits caused sickness and that magic spells could drive them out. Or, they believed, the physician could force the demon out by giving the patient a foul-tasting prescription. As medical knowledge grew, some prescriptions were found to work and thus were true medicines. Surgeons practiced a dangerous occupation, and the penalties for failure were severe. One section of Hammurabi's law code (see page 17) decreed: "If a physician performed a major operation on a seignior with a bronze lancet and has caused the seignior's death, or he opened up the eye-socket of a seignior and has destroyed the seignior's eye, they shall cut off his hand."[4] No wonder that one medical text warned physicians to have nothing to do with a dying person.

Im-dugud The god Im-dugud is represented here as a lion-headed eagle flanked by two stags. Im-dugud was a benevolent god, whose spreading wings fill the sky with clouds. He thus brings the rain that sustains the crops. *(Courtesy of the Trustees of the British Museum)*

Mesopotamian thought had a profound impact in theology and religion. The Sumerians originated many beliefs, and their successors added to them. The Mesopotamians believed that many gods run the world, but they did not consider all gods and goddesses equal. Some deities had very important jobs, taking care of music, law, sex, and victory, while others had lesser tasks, overseeing leatherworking and basketweaving. The god in charge of metalworking was hardly the equal of the god of wisdom.

Mesopotamian gods lived their lives much as human beings lived theirs. The gods were anthropomorphic, or human in form. Unlike men and women, they were powerful and immortal and could make themselves invisible. Otherwise, Mesopotamian gods and goddesses were very human: they celebrated with food and drink, and they raised families. They enjoyed their own "Garden of Eden," a green and fertile place. They could be irritable, vindictive, and irresponsible.

The Mesopotamians considered natural catastrophes the work of the gods. At times the Sumerians described their chief god, Enlil, as "the raging flood which has no rival." The gods, they believed, even used nature to punish the Mesopotamians. According to the myth of the Deluge, which gave rise to the biblical story of Noah, the god Enki warned Ziusudra, the Sumerian Noah:

A flood will sweep over the cult-centers;
To destroy the seed of mankind . . .
Is the decision, the word of the assembly of the gods.[5]

The Mesopotamians did not worship their deities because the gods were benevolent. Human beings were too insignificant to pass judgment on the conduct of the gods, and the gods were too superior to honor human morals. Rather, the Mesopotamians worshiped the gods because they were mighty. Likewise, it was not the place of men and women to understand the gods. The Sumerian equivalent to the biblical Job once complained to his god:

The man of deceit has conspired against me,
And you, my god, do not thwart him,
You carry off my understanding.[6]

The motives of the gods were not always clear. In times of affliction one could only pray and offer sacrifices to appease them.

The Mesopotamians had many myths to account for the creation of the universe. According to one Sumerian myth (echoed in Genesis, the first book of the Bible), only the primeval sea existed at first. The sea produced heaven and earth, which were united. Heaven and earth gave birth to Enlil, who separated them and made possible the creation of the other gods. Babylonian beliefs were similar. In the beginning was the primeval sea, the goddess Tiamat, who gave birth to the gods. When Tiamat tried to destroy the gods, Marduk, the chief god of the Babylonians, proceeded to kill her and divide her body and thus created the sky and earth. These myths are the earliest known attempts to answer the question, "How did it all begin?" The Mesopotamians obviously thought about these matters, as about the gods, in human terms. They never organized their beliefs into a philosophy, but their myths offered understandable explanations of natural phenomena. The myths were emotionally satisfying, and that was their greatest appeal.

In addition to myths, the Sumerians produced the first epic poem, the *Epic of Gilgamesh,* which evolved as a reworking of at least five earlier myths. An epic poem is a narration of the achievements, labors, and sometimes the failures of heroes that embodies a people's or a nation's conception of its own past. Historians can use epic poems to learn about various aspects of a society, and to that extent epics can be used as historical sources. The Sumerian epic recounts the wanderings of Gilgamesh—the semihistorical king of Uruk—and his companion Enkidu, their fatal meeting with the goddess Ishtar, after which Enkidu dies, and Gilgamesh's subsequent search for eternal life. During his search Gilgamesh learns that life after death is so dreary that he returns to Uruk, where he becomes a good king and ends his life happily. The *Epic of Gilgamesh* is not only an excellent piece of literature but also an intellectual triumph. It shows the Sumerians grappling with such enduring questions as life and death, humankind and deity, and immortality. Despite its great antiquity, it addresses questions of importance to people today. (See the feature "Listening to the Past: A Quest for Immortality" on pages 34–35.)

Sumerian Society

Their harsh environment fostered a grim, even pessimistic, spirit among the Mesopotamians. The Sumerians sought to please and calm the gods, especially the patron deity of the city. Encouraged and directed by the traditional priesthood, which was dedicated to understanding the ways of the gods, the people erected shrines in the center of each city and then built their houses around them. The best way to honor the gods was to make the shrine as grand and as impressive as possible, for gods who had a splendid temple might think twice about sending floods to destroy the city.

Sumerian society was a complex arrangement of freedom and dependence, and its members were divided into four categories: nobles, free clients of the nobility, commoners, and slaves. The nobility consisted of the king and his family, the chief priests, and high palace officials. Generally, the king rose to power as a war leader, elected by the citizenry, who established a regular army, trained it, and led it into battle. The might of the king and the frequency of warfare quickly made him the supreme figure in the city, and kingship soon became hereditary. The symbol of royal status was the palace, which rivaled the temple in grandeur.

The king and the lesser nobility held extensive tracts of land that were, like the estates of the temple, worked by slaves and clients. Clients were free men and women who were dependent on the nobility. In return for their labor, the clients received small plots of land to work for themselves. Although this arrangement assured the clients of a livelihood, the land they worked remained the possession of the nobility or the temple. Thus not only did the nobility control most—and probably the best—land, they also commanded the obedience of a huge segment of society. They were the dominant force in Mesopotamian society.

Commoners were free citizens. They were independent of the nobility; however, they could not rival the nobility in social status and political power. Commoners belonged to large patriarchal families who owned land in their own right. Commoners could sell their land, if the family approved, but even the king could not legally take their land without their approval. Commoners had a voice in the political affairs of the city and full protection under the law.

Until comparatively recent times, slavery has been a fact of life throughout the history of Western society. Some Sumerian slaves were foreigners and prisoners of war. Some were criminals who had lost their freedom as punishment for their crimes. Still others served as slaves to repay debts. These were more fortunate than the others, because the law required that they be freed after three years. But all slaves were subject to whatever treatment their owners might mete out. They could be beaten and even branded. Yet they were not considered dumb beasts. Slaves engaged in trade and made profits. Indeed, many slaves were able to buy their freedom.

Aerial View of Ur This photograph gives a good idea of the size and complexity of Ur, one of the most powerful cities in Mesopotamia. In the lower right-hand corner stands the massive ziggurat of Umammu. *(Georg Gerster/Comstock)*

They could borrow money and received at least some legal protection.

THE SPREAD OF MESOPOTAMIAN CULTURE

The Sumerians established the basic social, economic, and intellectual patterns of Mesopotamia, but the Semites played a large part in spreading Sumerian culture far beyond the boundaries of Mesopotamia. The interaction of the Sumerians and Semites, in fact, gives one of the very first glimpses of a phenomenon that can still be seen today. History provides abundant evidence of peoples of different origins coming together, usually on the borders of an established culture. The result was usually cultural change, outweighing any hostility, for each side learned from the other. The outcome in these instances was the evolution of a new culture that consisted of two or more old parts. Although the older culture almost invariably looked on the newcomers as inferior, the new just as invariably contributed something valuable to the old. So it was in 2331 B.C. The Semitic chieftain Sargon conquered Sumer and created a new empire. The symbol of his triumph was a new capital, the city of Akkad. Sargon, the first "world conqueror," led his armies to the Mediterranean Sea. Although his empire lasted only a few generations, it spread Mesopotamian culture throughout the Fertile Crescent, the belt of rich farmland that extends from Mesopotamia in the east up through Syria in the north and down to Egypt in the west (see Map 1.1).

Sargon's impact and the extent of Mesopotamian influence even at this early period have been dramatically revealed at Ebla in modern Syria. In 1964 archaeologists there unearthed a once-flourishing Semitic civilization that had assimilated political, intellectual, and artistic aspects of Mesopotamian culture. In 1975 the excavators uncovered thousands of clay tablets that proved that the people of Ebla had learned the art of writing from the Mesopotamians. Eblaite artists borrowed heavily from Mesopotamian art but developed their own style, which in turn influenced Mesopotamian artists. The Eblaites transmitted the heritage of Mesopotamia to other Semitic centers in Syria.

Further evidence of these developments came to light in November 1993, when American and Turkish archaeologists reported evidence of Sumerian influences far removed from Mesopotamia. At Tell Leilan in northern Syria and at Kazam Hoyuk in southern Turkey, researchers found proof of large urban centers that shared Sumerian culture as early as ca 2600 B.C. Finds included evidence of widespread literacy, a functioning bureaucracy, and links with Ebla and Mesopotamia. These discoveries also point to another conclusion. These frontier cities came under Sumerian influence not by conquest but because they found Mesopotamian culture attractive and useful. In this process, a universal culture developed in the ancient Near East, a culture basically Mesopotamian but fertilized by the traditions, genius, and ways of many other peoples.

The question to answer is why Mesopotamian culture had such an immediate and wide appeal. In the first place it was successful and enjoyed the prestige of its success. Newcomers wanted to find a respectable place in this old and venerated culture. It also provided an easy means of communication among people on a broad scale. The Eblaites could efficiently deal with the Mesopotamians and others who embraced this culture in ways that all could understand. Culture ignores borders. Despite local variations, so much common ground existed that similar political and economic institutions, exchange of ideas and religious beliefs, methods of writing, and a shared etiquette served as links among all who embraced Mesopotamian culture.

The Triumph of Babylon

Although the empire of Sargon was extensive, it was short-lived. The Akkadians, too, failed to solve the problems posed by Mesopotamia's geography and population pattern. Most scholars have attributed the fall of the Akkadian empire to internal problems and external invasions. Yet dramatic discoveries announced in August 1993 suggest strongly that climate also played a role in the demise of Akkadian power. Archaeologists have found evidence of a long, harsh drought, perhaps lasting as long as three hundred years, that struck the northern regions of the empire. The areas most severely affected were in modern Iraq, Syria, and parts of southern Turkey. Abandonment of the northern cities led to a stream of refugees to the south, overtaxing the economic resources of the cities there and straining their social and political structures. Cuneiform tablets had earlier mentioned this migration. The turmoil that resulted from this large influx of peoples may have contributed to the fighting that consumed the Akkadian empire.

It was left to the Babylonians to unite Mesopotamia politically and culturally. The Babylonians were Amorites, a Semitic people who had migrated from Arabia and settled on the site of Babylon along the middle Euphrates, where that river runs close to the Tigris. Babylon enjoyed an excellent geographical position and was ideally suited to be the capital of Mesopotamia. It dominated trade on the Tigris and Euphrates Rivers: all commerce to and from Sumer and Akkad had to pass by its walls. It also looked beyond Mesopotamia. Babylonian merchants followed the Tigris north to Assyria and Anatolia. The Euphrates led merchants to Syria, Palestine, and the Mediterranean. The city grew great because of its commercial importance and soundly based power.

Babylon was also fortunate to have a farseeing and able king, Hammurabi (r. 1792–1750 B.C.). Hammurabi set out to do three things: make Babylon secure, unify Mesopotamia, and win for the Babylonians a place in Mesopotamian civilization. The first two he accomplished by conquering Assyria in the north and

Sumer and Akkad in the south. Then he turned to his third goal.

Politically, Hammurabi joined in his kingship the Semitic concept of the tribal chieftain and the Sumerian idea of urban kingship. Culturally, he encouraged the spread of myths that explained how Marduk, the god of Babylon, had been elected king of the gods by the other Mesopotamian deities. Hammurabi's success in making Marduk the god of all Mesopotamians made Babylon the religious center of Mesopotamia. Through Hammurabi's genius the Babylonians made their own contribution to Mesopotamian culture—a culture vibrant enough to maintain its identity while assimilating new influences. Hammurabi's conquests and the activity of Babylonian merchants spread this enriched culture north to Anatolia and west to Syria and Palestine.

Life Under Hammurabi

One of Hammurabi's most memorable accomplishments was the proclamation of a law code that offers a wealth of information about daily life in Mesopotamia. Hammurabi's was not the first law code in Mesopotamia; indeed, the earliest goes back to about 2100 B.C. Like earlier lawgivers, Hammurabi proclaimed that he issued his laws on divine authority "to establish law and justice in the language of the land, thereby promoting the welfare of the people." Hammurabi's code inflicted such penalties as mutilation, whipping, and burning. Despite its severity, a spirit of justice and a sense of responsibility pervade the code. Hammurabi genuinely felt that his duty was to govern the Mesopotamians as righteously as possible. He tried to regulate the relations of his people so that they could live together in harmony.

The practical impact of Hammurabi's code is much debated. There is much disagreement about whether it recorded laws already established, promulgated new laws, or simply proclaimed what was just and proper. It is also unknown whether Hammurabi's proclamation, like others before it, was legally binding on the courts. At the very least, Hammurabi pronounced to the world what principles of justice he encouraged, while giving everyone visible evidence of his intentions as ruler of Babylonia.

The Code of Hammurabi has two striking characteristics. First, the law differed according to the social status of the offender. Aristocrats were not punished as harshly as commoners, nor commoners as harshly as slaves. Second, the code demanded that the punishment fit the crime. It called for "an eye for an eye, and a tooth for a tooth," at least among equals. However, an aristocrat who destroyed the eye of a commoner or slave could pay a fine instead of losing his own eye. Otherwise, as long as criminal and victim shared the same social status, the victim could demand exact vengeance.

Law Code of Hammurabi Hammurabi ordered his code to be inscribed on a stone pillar and set up in public. At the top of the pillar Hammurabi is depicted receiving the scepter of authority from the god Shamash. *(Hirmer Verlag München)*

Hammurabi's code began with legal procedure. There were no public prosecutors or district attorneys, so individuals brought their own complaints before the court. Each side had to produce written documents or witnesses to support its case. In cases of murder, the accuser had to prove the defendant guilty; any accuser who failed to do so was put to death. This strict law was designed to prevent people from lodging groundless charges. The Mesopotamians were very worried about witchcraft and sorcery. Anyone accused of witchcraft, even if the charges were not proved, underwent an ordeal by water. The gods themselves would decide the case. The defendant was thrown into the Euphrates, which was considered the instrument of the gods. A defendant who sank was guilty; a defendant who floated was innocent. Another procedural regulation covered the conduct of judges. Once a judge had rendered a verdict, he could not change it. Any judge who did so was fined heavily and deposed. In short, the code tried to guarantee a fair trial and a just verdict.

Consumer protection is not a modern idea; it goes back to Hammurabi's day. Merchants and businessmen had to guarantee the quality of their goods and services. A boat builder who did sloppy work had to repair the boat at his own expense. A boatman who lost the owner's boat or sank someone else's boat replaced it and its cargo. House builders guaranteed their work with their lives. Careless work could result in the collapse of a house and the death of its inhabitants. If that happened, the builder was put to death. A merchant who tried to increase the interest rate on a loan forfeited the entire amount. Hammurabi's laws tried to ensure that consumers got what they paid for and paid a just price.

Because farming was essential to Mesopotamian life, Hammurabi's code dealt extensively with agriculture. Tenant farming was widespread, and tenants rented land on a yearly basis. Instead of money they paid a portion of their crops as rent. Unless the land was carefully cultivated, it quickly reverted to wasteland. Therefore, tenants faced severe penalties for neglecting the land or not working it at all. Since irrigation was essential to grow crops, tenants had to keep the canals and ditches in good repair. Otherwise the land would be subject to floods and farmers would face crippling losses. Anyone whose neglect of the canals resulted in damaged crops had to bear all the expense of the lost crops. Those tenants who could not pay the costs were forced into slavery.

Hammurabi gave careful attention to marriage and the family. As elsewhere in the Near East, marriage had aspects of a business agreement. The prospective groom and the father of the future bride arranged everything. The man offered the father a bridal gift, usually money. If the man and his bridal gift were acceptable, the father provided his daughter with a dowry. After marriage the dowry belonged to the woman (although the husband normally administered it) and was a means of protecting her rights and status. Once the two men agreed on financial matters, they drew up a contract; no marriage was considered legal without one. Either party could break off the marriage, but not without paying a stiff penalty. Fathers often contracted marriages while their children were still young. The girl either continued to live in her father's house until she reached maturity or went to live in the house of her father-in-law. During this time she was legally considered a wife. Once she and her husband came of age, they set up their own house.

The wife was expected to be rigorously faithful. The penalty for adultery was death. According to Hammurabi's code: "If the wife of a man has been caught while lying with another man, they shall bind them and throw them into the water."[7] The husband had the power to spare his wife by obtaining a pardon for her from the king. He could, however, accuse his wife of adultery even if he had not caught her in the act. In such a case she could try to clear herself before the city council that investigated the charge. If she was found innocent, she could take her dowry and leave her husband. If a woman decided to take the direct approach and kill her husband, she was impaled.

The husband had virtually absolute power over his household. He could even sell his wife and children into slavery to pay debts. Sons did not lightly oppose their fathers, and any son who struck his father could have his hand cut off. A father was free to adopt children and include them in his will. Artisans sometimes adopted children to teach them the family trade. Although the father's power was great, he could not disinherit a son without just cause. Cases of disinheritance became matters for the city to decide, and the code ordered the courts to forgive a son for his first offense. Only if a son wronged his father a second time could he be disinherited.

Law codes, preoccupied as they are with the problems of society, provide a bleak view of things. Other Mesopotamian documents give a happier glimpse of life. Although Hammurabi's code dealt with marriage in a hard-fisted fashion, a Mesopotamian poem tells of two people meeting secretly in the city. Their parting is delightfully romantic:

PERIODS OF EGYPTIAN HISTORY

Period	Dates	Significant Events
Archaic	3100–2660 B.C.	Unification of Egypt
Old Kingdom	2660–2180 B.C.	Construction of the pyramids
First Intermediate	2180–2080 B.C.	Political chaos
Middle Kingdom	2080–1640 B.C.	Recovery and political stability
Second Intermediate	1640–1570 B.C.	Hyksos "invasion"
New Kingdom	1570–1075 B.C.	Creation of an Egyptian empire Akhenaten's religious policy

The king's surroundings had to be worthy of a god. Only a magnificent palace was suitable for his home; in fact, the very word *pharaoh* means "great house." Only later, in the Eighteenth Dynasty (see page 25), did it come to mean "king." The king's tomb also had to reflect his might and exalted status. To this day the great pyramids at Giza near Cairo bear silent but magnificent testimony to the god-kings of Egypt.

The Pharaoh's People

Because the common folk stood at the bottom of the social and economic scale, they were always at the mercy of grasping officials. The arrival of the tax collector was never a happy occasion. One Egyptian scribe described the worst that could happen:

And now the scribe lands on the river-bank and is about to register the harvest-tax. The janitors carry staves and the Nubians rods of palm, and they say, Hand over the corn, though there is none. The cultivator is beaten all over, he is bound and thrown into a well, soused and dipped head downwards. His wife has been bound in his presence and his children are in fetters.[11]

That was an extreme situation. Nonetheless, taxes might amount to 20 percent of the harvest, and tax collection could be brutal.

Egyptian society seems to have been a curious mixture of freedom and constraint. Slavery did not become widespread until the New Kingdom. There was neither a caste system nor a color bar, and humble people could rise to the highest positions if they possessed talent. On the other hand, most ordinary folk were probably little more than serfs who could not easily leave the land of their own free will. Peasants were also subject to forced labor, including work on the pyramids and canals. Young men were drafted into the pharaoh's army, which served both as a fighting force and as a labor corps.

The vision of thousands of people straining to build the pyramids and countless artists adorning the pharaoh's tomb brings to the modern mind a distasteful picture of oriental despotism. Indeed, the Egyptian view of life and society is alien to those raised on the Western concepts of individual freedom and human rights. To ancient Egyptians the pharaoh embodied justice and order—harmony among human beings, nature, and the divine. If the pharaoh was weak or allowed anyone to challenge his unique position, he opened the way to chaos. Twice in Egyptian history the pharaoh failed to maintain rigid centralization. During those two eras, known as the First and Second Intermediate Periods, Egypt was exposed to civil war and invasion. Yet the monarchy survived, and in each period a strong pharaoh arose to crush the rebels or expel the invaders and restore order.

The Hyksos in Egypt (1640–1570 B.C.)

While Egyptian civilization flourished behind its bulwark of sand and sea, momentous changes were taking place in the ancient Near East, changes that would leave their mark even on rich, insular Egypt. These changes

Pyramids of Giza Giza was the burial place of the pharaohs of the Old Kingdom and of their aristocracy, whose smaller rectangular tombs surround the two foremost pyramids. The small pyramid seen behind the third pyramid probably belonged to a pharaoh's wife. *(Courtesy, Museum of Fine Arts, Boston)*

involved enormous and remarkable movements, especially of peoples who spoke Semitic tongues.

The original home of the Semites was perhaps the Arabian peninsula. Some tribes moved into northern Mesopotamia, others into Syria and Palestine, and still others into Egypt. Shortly after 1800 B.C. people whom the Egyptians called Hyksos, which means "Rulers of the Uplands," began to settle in the Nile Delta. Many scholars have sought the origins of the Hyksos. The evidence available indicates that they entered Egypt from the areas of modern Israel and Lebanon. Yet that is only a partial explanation. The movements of the Hyksos were in fact part of a larger pattern of migration of peoples during this period. The history of Mesopotamia records many such wanderings of people in search of better homes for themselves. Such nomads normally settled in and accommodated themselves with the native cultures. The process was mutual, for each group had something to give and to learn from the other.

So it was in Egypt, but Egyptian tradition, as later recorded by the priest Manetho in the third century B.C., depicted the coming of the Hyksos as a brutal invasion:

> *In the reign of Toutimaios—I do not know why—the wind of god blew against us. Unexpectedly from the regions of the east men of obscure race, looking forward confidently to victory, invaded our land, and without a battle easily seized it all by sheer force. Having subdued those in authority in the land, they then barbarously burned our cities and razed to the ground the temples of the gods. They fell upon all the natives in an entirely hateful fashion, slaughtering them and leading both their children and wives into slavery. At last they made one of their people king, whose name was Salitis. This man resided at Memphis, leaving in Upper and Lower Egypt tax collectors and garrisons in strategic places.*[12]

The Hyksos created a capital city at Avaris, located at an as yet undiscovered site somewhere in the northeastern Nile Delta, but they probably exerted direct rule no farther south.

Although the Egyptians portrayed the Hyksos as a conquering horde, they were probably no more than nomads looking for good land. Their entry into the delta was probably gradual and generally peaceful. The Hyksos "invasion" was one of the fertilizing periods of Egyptian history; it introduced new ideas and techniques into Egyptian life.

The Hyksos brought with them the method of making bronze and casting it into tools and weapons that became standard in Egypt. They thereby brought Egypt fully into the Bronze Age culture of the Mediterranean world, a culture in which the production and use of bronze implements became basic to society. Bronze tools made farming more efficient than ever before because they were sharper and more durable than the copper tools they replaced. The Hyksos' use of bronze armor and weapons as well as horse-drawn chariots and the composite bow, made of laminated wood and horn and far more powerful than the simple wooden bow, revolutionized Egyptian warfare. However much the Egyptians learned from the Hyksos, Egyptian culture eventually absorbed the newcomers. The Hyksos came to worship Egyptian gods and modeled their monarchy on the pharaonic system.

The New Kingdom: Revival and Empire (1570–1200 B.C.)

Politically, Egypt was only in eclipse. The Egyptian sun shone again when a remarkable line of kings, the pharaohs of the Eighteenth Dynasty, arose to challenge the Hyksos. These pharaohs pushed the Hyksos out of the delta, subdued Nubia in the south, and conquered Palestine and parts of Syria in the northeast. They fought inconclusively with the Hurrians, who had migrated into the upper Euphrates from the north and created there the new Hurrian kingdom of Mitanni. In this way, Egyptian warrior-pharaohs inaugurated the New Kingdom—a period in Egyptian history characterized by enormous wealth and conscious imperialism. During this period, probably for the first time, widespread slavery became a feature of Egyptian life. The pharaoh's armies returned home leading hordes of slaves, who constituted a new labor force for imperial building projects. (See the feature "Individuals in Society: The Life and Times of Ah-mose the Egyptian.")

The kings of the Eighteenth Dynasty created the first Egyptian empire. They ruled Palestine and Syria through their officers and incorporated into the kingdom of Egypt the neighboring region of Nubia. Egyptian religion and customs flourished in Nubia, making a huge impact on African culture there and in neigh-

Hippopotamus Hunt This wall painting depicts the success of two men in a small boat who have killed a hippopotamus, seen in the lower right-hand corner. Behind the hippopotamus swims a crocodile hoping for a snack. *(Egyptian Museum SMPK, Berlin/Bildarchiv Preussischer Kulturbesitz)*

boring areas. The warrior-kings celebrated their success with monuments on a scale unparalleled since the pharaohs of the Old Kingdom had built the pyramids. Even today the colossal granite statues of these pharaohs and the rich tomb objects of Tutankhamen ("King Tut") testify to the might and splendor of the New Kingdom.

One of the most extraordinary of this unusual line of kings was Akhenaten (r. 1367–1350 B.C.), a pharaoh more concerned with religion than with conquest. Nefertiti, his wife and queen, encouraged his religious bent. The precise nature of Akhenaten's religious beliefs remains debatable. The problem began during his own lifetime. His religion was often unpopular among the people and the traditional priesthood, and its practice declined in the later years of his reign. After his death, it was condemned and denounced; consequently, not much is known about it. Most historians, however, agree that Akhenaten and Nefertiti were monotheists; that is, they believed that the sun-god Aton, whom they worshiped, was universal, the only god. They considered all other Egyptian gods and goddesses frauds and disregarded their worship. Yet their belief suffered from an obvious flaw. The pharaoh himself was considered the son of god, and monotheism obviously cannot have two gods. What Akhenaten meant by monotheism is that only Aton among the traditional Egyptian deities was god.

Akhenaten and Aton This relief shows the pharaoh and his family giving offerings to Aton, who is represented as the sun. It also demonstrates a new realism in Egyptian art. *(Egyptian Museum, Cairo)*

To genuine religious sentiments were added the motives of the traditional priesthood. Although many priests were scandalized by Akhenaten's brand of monotheism, many others were concerned more about their own welfare. By deposing the old gods Akhenaten destroyed the priests' livelihood and their reason for existence. On grounds of pure self-interest, the established priesthood opposed Akhenaten. Opposition in turn drove the pharaoh to intolerance and persecution. With a vengeance he tried to root out the old gods and their rituals.

Akhenaten's monotheism, imposed from above, failed to find a place among the people. The prime reason for Akhenaten's failure is that his god had no connection with the past of the Egyptian people, who trusted the old gods and felt comfortable praying to them. Average Egyptians were no doubt distressed and disheartened when their familiar gods were outlawed, for those gods were the heavenly powers that had made Egypt powerful and unique. The fanaticism and persecution that accompanied the new monotheism were in complete defiance of the Egyptian tradition of tolerant polytheism, or worship of several gods. Thus, when Akhenaten died, his religion died with him.

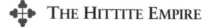

The Hittite Empire

At about the time the Hyksos entered the Nile Delta, the Hittites, who had long been settled in Anatolia (modern Turkey), became a major power in that region cultures that they found. Soon they fell under the powerful spell of the more advanced Mesopotamian culture. The Hittites adopted the cuneiform script for their own language. Hittite kings published law codes, just as Hammurabi had done. Royal correspondence followed Mesopotamian forms. The Hittites delighted in Mesopotamian myths, legends, epics, and art. To the credit of the Hittites, they used these Mesopotamian borrowings to create something of their own.

The Era of Hittite Greatness (ca 1475–ca 1200 B.C.)

The Hittites, like the Egyptians of the New Kingdom, eventually produced an energetic and capable line of kings who restored order and rebuilt Hittite power. They did so by controlling the aristocracy, securing central Anatolia, and regaining Syria. A technological aspect of their success was the introduction of iron to war and agriculture, in the form of weapons and tools. Around 1300 B.C. the Hittites stopped the Egyptian army of Rameses II at the Battle of Kadesh in Syria. Having fought each other to a standstill, the Hittites and Egyptians first made peace, then an alliance. Alliance was followed by friendship, and friendship by active cooperation. The two greatest powers of the early Near East tried to make war between them impossible.

They next included the Babylonians in their diplomacy. All three empires developed an official etiquette in which they treated one another as "brothers." They made alliances for offensive and defensive protection, and swore to uphold one another's authority. These contacts facilitated the exchange of ideas throughout the Near East. Furthermore, the Hittites passed much knowledge and lore from the Near East to the newly arrived Greeks in Europe (see chapter 3). The details of Hittite contact with the Greeks are unknown, but enough literary themes and physical objects exist to prove the connection.

THE FALL OF EMPIRES AND THE SURVIVAL OF CULTURES (CA 1200 B.C.)

The height of Hittite and Egyptian power came to a tumultuous end, but the achievements of these peoples lasted long after their governments had been overthrown or diminished in power. New political alignments appeared, but to some degree they all adopted and adapted the examples of their predecessors. They likewise embraced the cultures of those whom they had replaced on the political map.

Political Chaos

Like the Hittite kings, Rameses II (ca 1290–1224 B.C.) used the peace after the Battle of Kadesh to promote the prosperity of his own kingdom. Free from the expense and waste of warfare, he concentrated the income from the natural wealth and the foreign trade of Egypt on internal affairs. In the age-old tradition of the pharaohs, he began new building projects that brought both employment to his subjects and grandeur to Egypt. From Nubia to the delta of the Nile he bedecked his kingdom with grand new monuments. Once again, Egypt was wealthy and secure within its natural boundaries. In many ways, he was the last great pharaoh of Egypt.

This stable and generally peaceful situation endured until the late thirteenth century B.C., when both the Hittite and the Egyptian empires were destroyed by invaders. The most famous of these marauders, called the "Sea Peoples" by the Egyptians, remain one of the puzzles of ancient history. Despite much new work, modern archaeology is still unable to identify the Sea Peoples satisfactorily. The reason for this uncertainty is that the Sea Peoples were a collection of peoples who went their own, individual ways after their attacks on the Hittites and Egyptians. It is known, however, that their incursions were part of a larger movement of peoples. Although there is serious doubt about whether the Sea Peoples alone overthrew the Hittites, they did deal both the Hittites and the Egyptians a hard blow, making the Hittites vulnerable to overland invasion from the north and driving the Egyptians back to the Nile Delta. The Hittites fell under the external blows, but the Egyptians, shaken and battered, retreated to the delta and held on.

Cultural Endurance and Dissemination

The Egyptians and Mesopotamians established basic social, economic, and cultural patterns in the ancient Near East. Moreover, they spread them far beyond their homelands. Egypt exerted vast influence in Palestine and Syria, while Mesopotamia was influential in southern Anatolia (modern Turkey). Yet it is a mistake to think that these older civilizations moved into a cultural vacuum.

In Palestine and southern Syria the Egyptians found Semitic peoples living in small walled towns. Municipal life was quite advanced, with towns that included urban centers and small outlying hamlets. Although these societies were primarily based on agriculture, there is ample evidence of international trade. In short, both Palestine and Syria possessed an extensive political, social, and religious organization even before the arrival of the Egyptians. Contact had begun as early as the Bronze Age, when the Egyptians had moved along the eastern Mediterranean coast. The contact immediately led to trade. The Egyptians exploited the turquoise and copper trade in the area, and exported local pottery and other goods. Sometimes the Egyptians traded peacefully, but at other times they resorted to military invasion.

Farther north the Egyptians made maritime contact with the Phoenicians, most clearly seen from the excavations at Byblos. The two peoples exchanged not only goods but also technological knowledge. The Egyptians learned many shipbuilding techniques, their own boats being better designed for the Nile than the open sea. The Phoenicians in turn adopted aspects of Egyptian technology. Yet the cultural exchange between the two peoples was by far more important. The Phoenicians honored some Egyptian gods and adopted Egyptian artistic motifs. They learned the Egyptian script and became acquainted with some Egyptian myths. At the same time some deities of Byblos made their appearance in Egypt. Despite armed conflict, trade, not warfare, generally characterized relations in the area.

The situation in northern Syria was similar to that in southern Syria and Palestine. Cities were common, normally ruled by royal families. The families usually shared power and dealt jointly with foreign affairs. They often left the internal administration of the cities to local elders. The cities were primarily mercantile centers but also rich in agricultural produce, timber, and metal deposits. The need for record keeping soon led to the development of writing. These northern Semites adopted Sumerian writing in order to understand their neighbors to the east, but they also adapted it to write their own northern Semitic language. Their texts provide a wealth of information about the life of northern Syria. In the process, northern Syrians gained a solid knowledge of Mesopotamian literature, mathematics, and culture. Both local and Sumerian deities were honored. Despite Mesopotamian influence, northern Syria maintained its native traditions. The cultural exchange was a mixture of adoption, adaptation, contrast, and finally balance, as the two cultures came to understand each other.

Southern Anatolia presented a somewhat similar picture. Human settlement there consisted of trading colonies and small agricultural communities. Thousands of cuneiform tablets testify to commercial and cultural exchanges with Mesopotamia. In Anatolia kingship and temple were closely allied, but the government was not a theocracy (rule by a priestly order). A city assembly worked together with the king, and provincial cities were administered by a prince. The political and social organization was one of a firmly established native culture that gladly received foreign ideas while keeping its own identity.

A pattern emerged in Palestine, Syria, and Anatolia. In these areas native cultures established themselves during the prehistoric period. Upon coming into contact with the Egyptian and Mesopotamian civilizations, they adopted many aspects of these cultures, adapting them to their own traditional customs. Yet they also contributed to the advance of Egyptian and Mesopotamian cultures by introducing new technologies and religious ideas. The result was the emergence of a huge group of communities stretching from Egypt in the south to Anatolia in the north and from the Levant in the west to Mesopotamia in the east. Each enjoyed its own individual character, while at the same time sharing many common features with its neighbors.

Summary

For thousands of years Paleolithic peoples roamed this planet seeking game. Although many groups of Paleolithic peoples relied partly on agriculture, they lived a largely nomadic life. Only in the Neolithic Age—with the invention of new stone tools, a reliance on sustained agriculture, and the domestication of animals—did people begin to live in permanent locations. These villages evolved into towns, where people began to create new social bonds and political organizations. The result was economic prosperity.

The earliest area where these developments led to genuine urban societies is Mesopotamia. Here the Sumerians and then other Mesopotamians developed writing, which enabled their culture to be passed on to others. The wealth of the Mesopotamians made it possible for them to devote time to history, astronomy, urban planning, medicine, and other arts and sciences. Mesopotamian culture was so rich and advanced that neighboring peoples eagerly adopted it, thereby spreading it through much of the Near East.

Nor were the Mesopotamians alone in advancing the civilization of the day. In Egypt another strong culture developed, one that made an impact in Africa, the Near East, and, later, in Greece. The Egyptians too enjoyed such prosperity that they developed writing of their own, mathematical skills, and religious beliefs that influenced the lives of their neighbors. Into this world came the Hittites, an Indo-European people who were culturally less advanced than the Mesopotamians and Egyptians. The Hittites learned from their neighbors and rivals, but they also introduced their own sophisticated political system for administering their empire, a system that in some ways influenced both their contemporaries and later peoples.

NOTES

1. L. Eiseley, *The Unexpected Universe* (New York: Harcourt Brace Jovanovich, 1969), p. 102.
2. W. K. Loftus, *Travels and Researches in Chaldaea and Susiana* (New York: R. Carter & Brothers, 1857), p. 163.
3. Quoted in S. N. Kramer, *The Sumerians* (Chicago: University of Chicago Press, 1963), p. 238. John Buckler is the translator of all uncited quotations from a foreign language in Chapters 1–6.
4. J. B. Pritchard, ed., *Ancient Near Eastern Texts,* 3d ed. (Princeton, N.J.: Princeton University Press, 1969), p. 175. Hereafter called ANET.
5. Ibid., p. 44.
6. Ibid., p. 590.
7. Ibid., p. 171.
8. Kramer, p. 251.
9. ANET, p. 372.
10. Herodotus, *The Histories* 2.14.
11. Quoted in A. H. Gardiner, "Ramesside Texts Relating to the Taxation and Transport of Corn," *Journal of Egyptian Archaeology* 27 (1941): 19–20.
12. Manetho, *History of Egypt,* frag. 42.75–77.

SUGGESTED READING

Some very illuminating general studies of Near Eastern developments have recently reached print. A broad-ranging work, A. Kuhrt, *The Ancient Near East,* 2 vols. (1995), covers the region from the earliest time to Alexander's conquest, as does C. Snell, *Life in the Ancient Near East, 3100–332* B.C.E., which also covers social history. H. J. Nissen, *Archaic Bookkeeping* (1993), discusses both the development of early writing and its use in the administration of the ancient economy. Most welcome is the publication of D. Schmandt-Besserat's two-volume work on the origins of writing: *Before Writing,* vol. 1 (1992), which explores the development of cuneiform writing, and vol. 2 (1992), which provides actual evidence on the topic.

D. T. Potts, *Mesopotamian Civilization* (1996), presents a view of the Mesopotamians from their material remains but is not purely architectural. G. Stein and M. S. Rothman, *Chiefdoms and Early States in the Near East* (1994), provides a clear view of the political evolution of the region. An ambitious work is M. Hudson and B. Levine, *Privatization in the Ancient Near East and the Classical World* (1996), which treats the concept of private property. A very ambitious and thoughtful book, G. Algaze, *The Uruk World System* (1993), examines how the early Mesopotamians expanded their civilization. G. Pettinato, *Ebla* (1991), gives a thorough description of the site and its importance.

D. P. Silverman, *Ancient Egypt* (1997), provides the latest general account of the region, although N. Grimal, *A History of Ancient Egypt* (1992), is still good. S. Donadoni, ed., *The Egyptians* (1997), treats various aspects of Egyptian history and life. D. Meeks and C. Favard-Meeks, *Daily Life of the Egyptian Gods* (1996), with a learned and original point of view, discusses how the Egyptian gods are sometimes treated in literature as an ethnic group not so very different from human beings. A. R. David, *Pyramid Builders of Ancient Egypt,* 2d ed. (1996), studies the lives of the people who actually labored to build the pyramids for their pharaohs. A. Blackman, *Gods, Priests and Men* (1993), is a series of studies in the religion of pharaonic Egypt. G. Robbins, *Women in Ancient Egypt* (1993), which is richly illustrated, adds visual information to the literary sources. W. L. Moran, *The Amarna Letters* (1992), is a translation of the Egyptian documents so important to the understanding of the events of the New Kingdom.

Perhaps owing to the endemic political unrest, little new work has come from other parts of the Middle East. Somewhat dated but still solid is O. R. Gurney, *The Hittites,* 2d ed. (1954), a fine introduction by an eminent scholar. Good also is J. G. MacQueen, *The Hittites and Their Contemporaries in Asia Minor,* 2d ed. (1986). J. P. Mallory, *In Search of the Indo-Europeans* (1989), uses language, archaeology, and myth to study the Indo-Europeans. The 1960s were prolific years for archaeology in Turkey. A brief survey by one of the masters of the field is J. Mellaart, *The Archaeology of Modern Turkey* (1978), which also tests a great number of widely held historical interpretations. The Sea Peoples have been studied by T. and M. Dothan, *People of the Sea* (1992), who concentrate their work on the Philistines.

A truly excellent study of ancient religions, from Sumer to the late Roman Empire, is M. Eliade, ed., *Religions of Antiquity* (1989), which treats concisely but amply all of the religions mentioned in Chapters 1–6.

LISTENING TO THE PAST

A Quest for Immortality

The human desire to escape the grip of death, to achieve immortality, is one of the oldest wishes of all peoples. The Sumerian Epic of Gilgamesh *is the earliest recorded treatment of this topic. The oldest elements of the epic go back at least to the third millennium* B.C. *According to tradition, Gilgamesh was a king of Uruk whom the Sumerians, Babylonians, and Assyrians considered a hero-king and a god. In the story Gilgamesh and his friend Enkidu set out to attain immortality and join the ranks of the gods. They attempt to do so by performing wondrous feats against fearsome agents of the gods, who are determined to thwart them.*

During their quest Enkidu dies. Gilgamesh, more determined than ever to become immortal, begins seeking anyone who might tell him how to do so. His journey involves the effort not only to escape from death but also to reach an understanding of the meaning of life.

The passage begins with Enkidu speaking of a dream that foretells his own death.

Listen, my friend [Gilgamesh], this is the dream I dreamed last night. The heavens roared, and earth rumbled back an answer; between them I stood before an awful being, the sombre-faced man-bird; he had directed on me his purpose. His was a vampire face, his foot was a lion's foot, his hand was an eagle's talon. He fell on me and his claws were in my hair, he held me fast and I smothered; then he transformed me so that my arms became wings covered with feathers. He turned his stare towards me, and he led me away to the palace of Irkalla, the Queen of Darkness [the goddess of the underworld; in other words, an agent of death], to the house from which none who enters ever returns, down the road from which there is no coming back.

At this point Enkidu dies, whereupon Gilgamesh sets off on his quest for the secret of immortality. During his travels he meets with Siduri, the wise and good-natured goddess of wine, who gives him the following advice.

Gilgamesh, where are you hurrying to? You will never find that life for which you are looking. When the gods created man they allotted to him death, but life they retained in their own keeping. As for you, Gilgamesh, fill your belly with good things; day and night, night and day, dance and be merry, feast and rejoice. Let your clothes be fresh, bathe yourself in water, cherish the little child that holds your hand, and make your wife happy in your embrace; for this too is the lot of man.

Ignoring Siduri's advice, Gilgamesh continues his journey, until he finds Utnapishtim. Meeting Utnapishtim is especially important because, like Gilgamesh, he was once a mortal, but the gods so favored him that they put him in an eternal paradise. Gilgamesh puts to Utnapishtim the question that is the reason for his quest.

Oh, father Utnapishtim, you who have entered the assembly of the gods, I wish to question you concerning the living and the dead, how shall I find the life for which I am searching?

Utnapishtim said, "There is no permanence. Do we build a house to stand forever, do we seal a contract to hold for all time? Do brothers divide an inheritance to keep forever, does the flood-time of rivers endure? . . . What is there between the master and the servant when both have fulfilled their doom? When the Anunnaki [the gods of the underworld], the judges, come together, and Mammetun [the goddess of fate] the mother of destinies, together they decree the fates of men. Life and death they allot but the day of death they do not disclose.

Then Gilgamesh said to Utnapishtim the Faraway, "I look at you now, Utnapishtim, and your appearance is no different from mine; there is nothing strange in your features. I thought I should find you like a hero prepared for battle, but you lie here taking your ease on your back. Tell me truly, how was it that you came to enter the company of the gods and to possess everlasting life?" Utnapishtim said to Gilgamesh, "I shall reveal to you a mystery, I shall tell you a secret of the gods."

Utnapishtim then tells Gilgamesh of a time when the great god Enlil had become angered with the Sumerians and encouraged the other gods to wipe out humanity. The god Ea, however, warned Utnapishtim about the gods' decision to send a great flood to destroy the Sumerians. He commanded Utnapishtim to build a boat big enough to hold his family, various artisans, and all animals in order to survive the flood that was to come. Although Enlil was infuriated by the Sumerians' survival, Ea rebuked him. Then Enlil relented and blessed Utnapishtim with eternal paradise. After telling the story, Utnapishtim foretells Gilgamesh's fate.

Utnapishtim said, ". . . The destiny was fulfilled which the father of the gods, Enlil of the mountain, had decreed for Gilgamesh: In nether-earth the darkness will show him a light: of mankind, all that are known, none will leave a monument for generations to compare with his. The heroes, the wise men, like the new moon have their waxing and waning. Men will say, Who has ever ruled with might and power like his? As in the dark month, the month of shadows, so without him there is no light. O Gilgamesh, this was the meaning of your dream [of immortality]. You were given the kingship, such was your destiny, everlasting life was not your destiny. Because of this do not be sad at heart, do not be grieved or oppressed; he [Enlil] has given you power to bind and to loose, to be the darkness and the light of mankind. He has given unexampled supremacy over the people, victory in battle from which no fugitive returns, in forays and assaults from which there is no going back. But do not abuse this power, deal justly with your servants in the palace, deal justly before the face of the Sun."

Gilgamesh, from decorative panel of a lyre unearthed at Ur. *(The University Museum, University of Pennsylvania, neg. T4-108)*

Questions for Analysis

1. What does the *Epic of Gilgamesh* reveal about Sumerian attitudes toward the gods and human beings?
2. At the end of his quest, did Gilgamesh achieve immortality? If so, what was the nature of that immortality?
3. What does the epic tell us about Sumerian views of the nature of human life? Where do human beings fit into the cosmic world?

Source: THE EPIC OF GILGAMESH, translated by N. K. Sanders. Penguin Classics 1960, Second revised edition, 1972, pp. 91–119.

CHAPTER

2 Small Kingdoms and Mighty Empires in the Near East

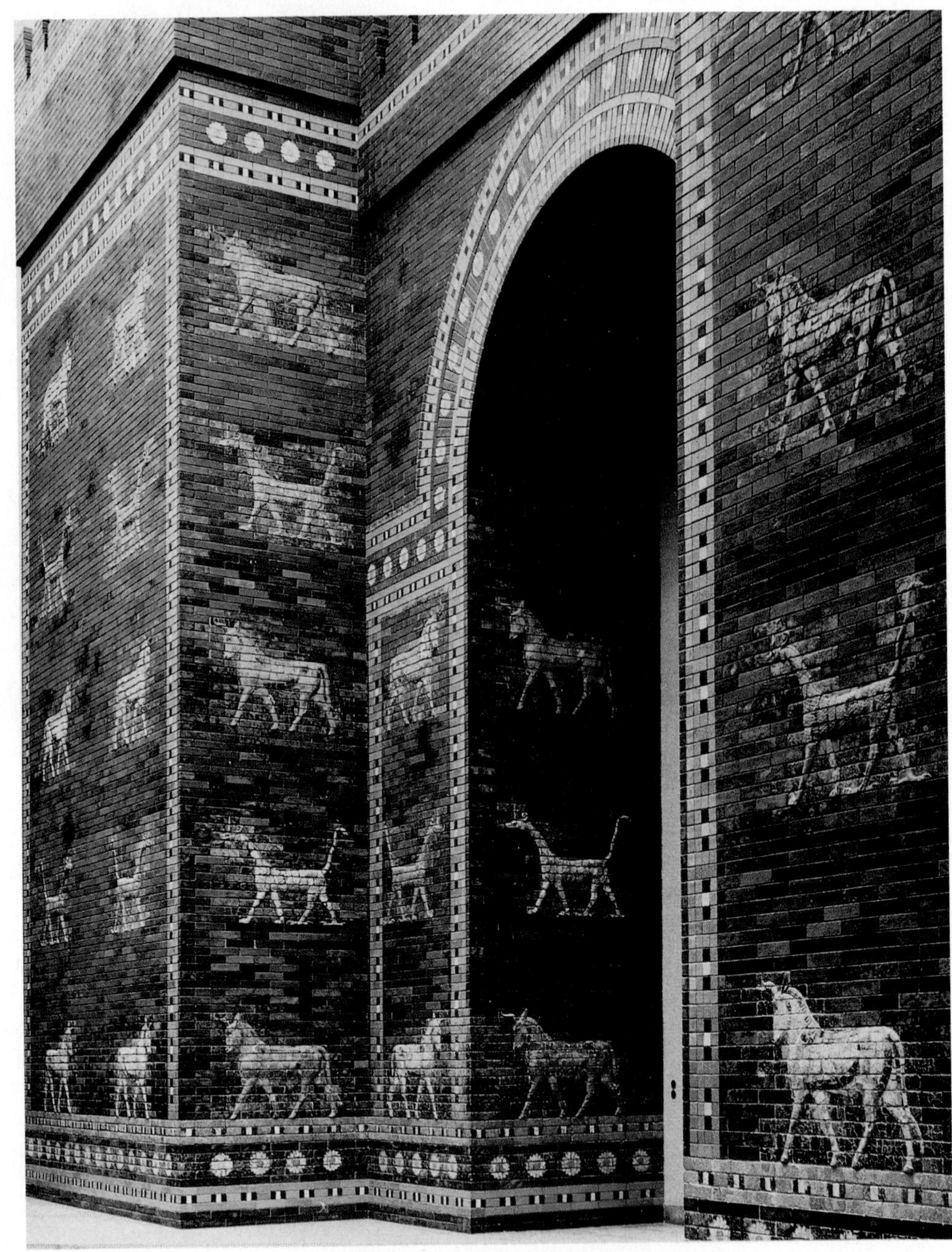

Reconstruction of the "Ishtar Gate," Babylon, early sixth century B.C. Located in the Berlin Museum. *(Staatliche Museen zu Berlin/Bildarchiv Preussicher Kulturbesitz)*

The migratory invasions that brought down the Hittites and stunned the Egyptians in the late thirteenth century B.C. ushered in an era of confusion and weakness. Although much was lost in the chaos, the old cultures of the ancient Near East survived to nurture new societies. In the absence of powerful empires, the Phoenicians, Syrians, Hebrews, and many other peoples carved out small independent kingdoms, until the Near East was a patchwork of them. During this period Hebrew culture and religion evolved under the influence of urbanism, kings, and prophets.

In the ninth century B.C. this jumble of small states gave way to an empire that for the first time embraced the entire Near East. Yet the very ferocity of the Assyrian Empire led to its downfall only two hundred years later. In 550 B.C. the Persians and Medes, who had migrated into Iran, created a "world empire" stretching from Anatolia in the west to the Indus Valley in the east. For over two hundred years the Persians gave the ancient Near East peace and stability.

- How did Egypt, its political greatness behind it, pass on its cultural heritage to its African neighbors?
- How did the Hebrew state evolve, and what was daily life like in Hebrew society?
- What forces helped to shape Hebrew religious thought, still powerfully influential in today's world?
- What enabled the Assyrians to overrun their neighbors, and how did their cruelty finally cause their undoing?
- Last, how did Iranian nomads create the Persian Empire?

This chapter will look at these questions.

Recovery and Diffusion

If the fall of empires was a time of massive political disruption, it also ushered in a period of cultural diffusion, an expansion of what had already blossomed in the broad region. Even though empires fell, many small kingdoms survived, along with a largely shared culture. These small states and local societies had learned much from the great powers, but they nonetheless retained their own lore and native traditions, which they passed on to their neighbors, thus diffusing a Near Eastern culture that was slowly becoming common in nature. The best-known examples can be found along the coast of the eastern Mediterranean, where various peoples—some of them newcomers—created homes and petty kingdoms in Syria, Phoenicia, and Palestine. After the Sea Peoples raided Egypt, a branch of them, known in the Bible as Philistines, settled along the coast of Palestine (Map 2.1). Establishing themselves in five cities somewhat inland from the sea, the Philistines set about farming and raising flocks.

Egypt, a Shattered Kingdom

The invasions of the Sea Peoples brought the great days of Egyptian power to an end. The long wars against invaders weakened and impoverished Egypt, causing political upheaval and economic chaos. One scribe left behind a somber portrait of Egypt stunned and leaderless:

> *The land of Egypt was abandoned and every man was a law to himself. During many years there was no leader who could speak for others. Central government lapsed, small officials and headmen took over the whole land. Any man, great or small, might kill his neighbor. In the distress and vacuum that followed . . . men banded together to plunder one another. They treated the gods no better than men, and cut off the temple revenues.*[1]

No longer able to dream of foreign conquests, Egypt looked to its own security from foreign invasion. Egyptians suffered a four-hundred-year period of political fragmentation, a new dark age known to Egyptian specialists as the Third Intermediate Period (eleventh–seventh centuries B.C.). (See the feature "Individuals in Society: Wen-Amon.")

The decline of Egypt was especially sharp in foreign affairs. Whereas the pharaohs of the Eighteenth Dynasty had held sway as far abroad as Syria, their weak successors found it unsafe to venture far from home. In the wake of the Sea Peoples, numerous small kingdoms sprang up in the Near East, each fiercely protective of its own independence. To them Egypt was a memory, and foreign princes often greeted Egyptian officials with suspicion or downright contempt. In the days of Egypt's greatness, petty kings would never have dared to treat Egyptian officials in such a humiliating fashion.

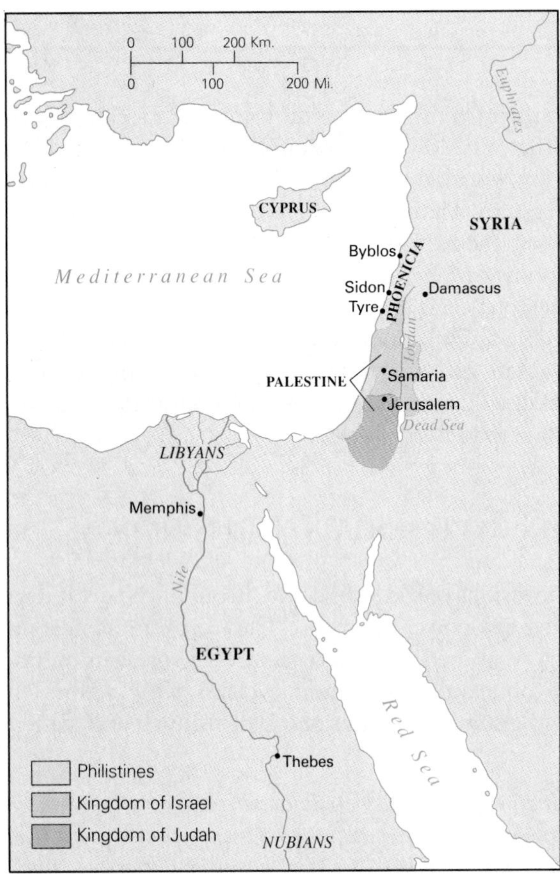

MAP 2.1 Small Kingdoms of the Near East This map illustrates the political fragmentation of the Near East after the great wave of invasions that occurred during the thirteenth century B.C.

Disrupted at home and powerless abroad, Egypt fell prey to invasion by its African neighbors. Libyans from North Africa filtered into the Nile Delta, where they established independent dynasties. Indeed, from 950 to 730 B.C. northern Egypt was ruled by Libyan pharaohs. The Libyans built cities, and for the first time a sturdy urban life grew up in the delta. Although the coming of the Libyans changed the face of the delta, the Libyans genuinely admired Egyptian culture and eagerly adopted Egypt's religion and way of life.

In southern Egypt, meanwhile, the pharaoh's decline opened the way to the energetic Nubians, who extended their authority northward throughout the Nile Valley. Nubian influence in these years was pervasive but not destructive. Since the imperial days of the Eighteenth Dynasty (see pages 25–26), the Nubians, too, had adopted many features of Egyptian culture. Now Nubian kings and aristocrats embraced Egyptian culture wholesale. The thought of destroying the heritage of the pharaohs would have struck them as stupid and barbaric. Thus the Nubians and the Libyans repeated an old Near Eastern phenomenon: new peoples conquered old centers of political and military power but were assimilated into the older culture.

The reunification of Egypt occurred late and unexpectedly. With Egypt distracted and disorganized by foreign invasions, an independent African state, the kingdom of Kush, grew up in the region of modern Sudan with its capital at Nepata. Like the Libyans, the Kushites worshiped Egyptian gods and used Egyptian hieroglyphs. In the eighth century B.C. their king, Piankhy, swept through the entire Nile Valley from Nepata in the south to the delta in the north. United once again, Egypt enjoyed a brief period of peace during which Egyptians continued to assimilate their conquerors. In the kingdom of Kush, Egyptian methods of administration and bookkeeping, arts and crafts, and economic practices became common, especially among the aristocracy. Nonetheless, reunification of the realm did not lead to a new Egyptian empire.

Yet Egypt's legacy to its African neighbors remained vibrant and rich. By trading and exploring southward along the coast of the Red Sea, the Egyptians introduced their goods and ideas as far south as the land of Punt, probably a region on the Somali coast. As early as the New Kingdom, Egyptian pharaohs had exchanged gifts with the monarchs of Punt, and contact between the two areas persisted. Egypt was the primary civilizing force in Nubia, which became another version of the pharaoh's realm, complete with royal pyramids and Egyptian deities. Egyptian religion penetrated as far south as Ethiopia.

One of the sturdy peoples who rose to prominence were the Phoenicians, a Semitic-speaking people who had long inhabited several cities along the coast of modern Lebanon. They had lived under the shadow of the Hittites and Egyptians, but in this period the Phoenicians enjoyed full independence. Unlike the Philistine newcomers, who turned from seafaring to farming, the Phoenicians took to the sea and became outstanding merchants and explorers. In trading ventures they sailed as far west as modern Tunisia, where in 813 B.C. they founded the city of Carthage, which would one day struggle with Rome for domination of the western Mediterranean. Phoenician culture was urban, based on the prosperous commercial centers of Tyre, Sidon, and Byblos. The Phoenicians' overwhelm-

Individuals in Society

Wen-Amon

Surprising as it may sound, the life of a bureaucrat is not always easy. Wen-Amon, an official of the temple of Amon-Re at Karnak in Egypt, learned that on an authorized mission to Phoenicia. He left his own narrative of his travels, which date to sometime in the eleventh century B.C. Egypt, the shattered kingdom, could no longer exert the authority that it had enjoyed under the pharaohs of the New Kingdom. Despite this political disruption, Egyptian officials continued to expect the traditional respect of the people whom they called "Asiatics." These Asiatics, however, had begun to doubt the power of Egypt and expressed their independence by openly opposing its authority.

Wen-Amon personally experienced this changed atmosphere when he was sent to Byblos in Phoenicia to obtain lumber for Amon-Re's ceremonial barge. Wen-Amon's detailed account of his experiences comes in the form of an official report to the chief priest of the temple.

Entrusted with ample funds in silver to pay for the lumber, Wen-Amon set out on his voyage. He docked at Dor, in modern Israel, which was independent of the pharaoh, but the local prince received him graciously. While his ship was at anchor, one of Wen-Amon's own sailors vanished with the silver. Wen-Amon immediately reported the robbery to the prince and demanded that he investigate the theft. Wen-Amon pointed out that the silver belonged to Amon-Re and the great men of Egypt. The prince flatly told Wen-Amon that he did not care whether Wen-Amon and the others were important men. He pointed out that an Egyptian, one of Wen-Amon's own men, had stolen the silver. It was not the prince's problem. No earlier Asian prince would have dared speak to a high Egyptian official in such terms.

Although rebuffed, Wen-Amon found a ship from Byblos and robbed it of an equivalent amount of silver. When he left Dor and entered the harbor of Byblos, the prince there, who had learned of the theft, ordered him to leave. For twenty-nine days there was an impasse. Each day that Wen-Amon remained, the prince told him to get out, but respect both for the great days of Egypt and for Amon-Re kept the prince from laying hands on Wen-Amon. Finally, the prince sent for Wen-Amon and asked for his papers. A heated argument ensued, with the prince shouting, "I am not your servant. I am not the servant of he who sent you either." Then he asked Wen-Amon what silly voyage he was making. By this time the Egyptian was greatly annoyed, and he reminded the prince of the greatness of Amon-Re. He flatly stated that unless the prince honored the great god, he and his land would have neither health nor prosperity. When the two calmed down, the prince agreed to send the timber to Egypt.

Pillars of the great temple of Amon at Karnak, New Kingdom. *(Marc Bernheim/Woodfin Camp & Associates)*

After the timber was loaded aboard his ship, Wen-Amon saw eleven enemy ships entering the harbor. They anchored, and those in charge reported to the prince of Byblos that they had come for the Egyptians. He refused to hand them over, saying that he would never arrest a messenger of Amon-Re. He agreed, however, to send Wen-Amon away first and allow the enemy ships to pursue the Egyptians. Stormy seas blew the Egyptian ship into Hittite territory. When Wen-Amon landed there, Queen Heteb granted him protection and asylum.

The papyrus breaks off at this point, but it is obvious that Wen-Amon weathered his various storms to return safely to Egypt. The document illustrates the presumption of power by Wen-Amon and his bluster at the lack of respect shown him. It also shows how Egypt's neighbors no longer feared Egyptian power. Finally, it illustrates the impact of Egyptian culture and religion on the peoples living along the coast of the Levant. Although Egyptian political power was in eclipse, its cultural legacy endured.

Questions for Analysis

1. What do Wen-Amon's experiences tell us about political conditions in the eastern Mediterranean?
2. Since Wen-Amon could no longer depend upon the majesty of Egypt for respect, how did he fulfill his duty?

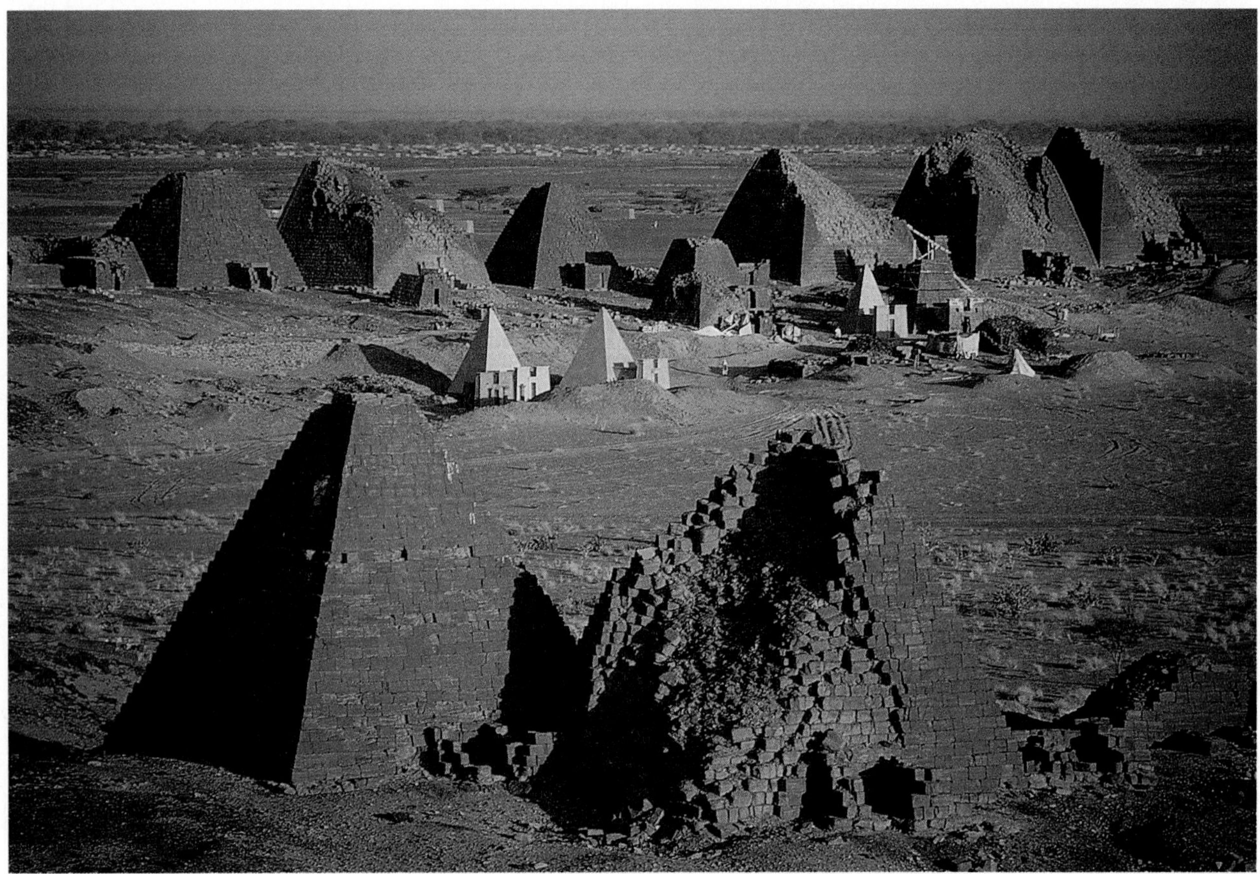

Nubian Pyramids The Nubians adopted many aspects of Egyptian culture and customs. The pyramids shown here are not as magnificent as their Egyptian predecessors, but they serve the same purpose of honoring the dead king. Their core was constructed of bricks, which were then covered with stone blocks. At the doors of the pyramids stood monumental gates to the interiors of the tombs. *(Michael Yamashita)*

ing cultural achievement was the development of an alphabet (Figure 2.1): they, unlike other literate peoples, used one letter to designate one sound, a system that vastly simplified writing and reading. The Greeks modified this alphabet and then used it to write their own language.

Typical of the new climate of freedom that the fall of empires provided for individual cities was Ugarit in modern Syria. Ugarit and later Tyre and Sidon became international ports and trading centers in the Near East. They were so commercially important that other powers left them independent, simply because they were economically indispensable. Ugarit was situated on the coast along many major trade routes. The city had contacts with Mesopotamia in the east, southern Syria and Palestine in the south, and Egypt even farther south. Through Egypt the Ugarites obtained myrrh, a gum resin used in perfumes, medicines, and incense, from southern Arabia. They obtained ebony from central Africa through well-established Egyptian routes. Their indirect reach extended as far east as Afghanistan, from which they acquired tin and lapis lazuli, a bright blue gem much in favor throughout the Near East. Ugarit also traded with Cyprus and Crete to the west. It exported purple wool, various metals, and luxury goods.

Ugarit stands as an excellent example of an affluent, cosmopolitan small state that thrived during this tumultuous period. Not militarily or politically powerful, the harbor city of Ugarit preserved and enhanced a cultural pattern that endured for a millennium and has left an indelible stamp on the nature of the modern Western world.

ROMAN	HIEROGLYPHIC	REPRESENTS	UGARITIC	PHOENICIAN	GREEK
G	[illegible]	Throw stick	T	[illegible]	Γ
E	[illegible]	Man with raised arms	[illegible]	[illegible]	E
K	[illegible]	Basket with handle	[illegible]	[illegible]	K
M	[illegible]	Water	[illegible]	[illegible]	M
N	[illegible]	Snake	[illegible]	[illegible]	N
O	[illegible]	Eye	[illegible]	O	O
P	[illegible]	Mouth	[illegible]	?	Π
R	[illegible]	Head	[illegible]	9	P
S	[illegible]	Pool with lotus flowers	[illegible]	W	Σ
B	[illegible]	House	[illegible]	9	B
A	[illegible]	Ox-head	[illegible]	K	A

FIGURE 2.1 Origins of the Alphabet List of Roman, Hieroglyphic, Ugaritic, Phoenician, and Greek sign forms. *(Source: A. B. Knapp,* The History and Culture of Ancient Western Asia and Egypt, *Dorsey Press, Chicago, 1988, p. 191. Reprinted by permission of Wadsworth Publishing Company.)*

THE CHILDREN OF ISRAEL

The fall of the Hittite Empire and Egypt's collapse created a vacuum of power in the western Near East that allowed for the rise of numerous small states. South of Phoenicia arose a small kingdom, the land of the ancient Jews or Hebrews. It is difficult to say precisely who the Hebrews were and what brought them to this area, because virtually the only source for much of their history is the Bible, which is essentially a religious document. Even though it contains much historical material, it also contains many Hebrew myths and legends. Moreover, it was compiled at different times, with the earliest parts dating to between about 950 and 800 B.C.

Earlier Mesopotamian and Egyptian sources refer to people called the Hapiru, which seems to mean homeless, independent nomads. According to Hebrew tradition, the followers of Abraham migrated from Mesopotamia, but Egyptian documents record Hapiru already in Syria and Palestine in the second millennium B.C. The Hebrews were probably a part of them. Together with other seminomadic peoples, they probably migrated into the Nile Delta seeking good land. According to the Bible the Egyptians enslaved them. One group, however, under the leadership of Moses, perhaps a semimythical figure, left Egypt in what the Hebrews remembered as the Exodus. From Egypt they wandered in the Sinai Peninsula, until they settled in Palestine in the thirteenth century B.C. Their arrival was by no means peaceful. In a series of vicious wars and savage slaughters, they slowly won a place.

In Palestine the Hebrews encountered the Philistines; the Amorites, relatives of Hammurabi's Babylonians; and the Semitic-speaking Canaanites. Despite the numerous wars, contact between the Hebrews and their new neighbors was not always hostile. The Hebrews freely mingled with the Canaanites, and some went so far as to worship Baal, an ancient Semitic fertility god represented as a golden calf. Archaeological research supports the biblical account of these developments. In

Standing Sphinx The sphinx was both a decorative and protective figure in ancient art and society. This ivory is a splendid illustration of the sphinx itself—part human, part bird, and part lion. This sphinx also displays the richness of Phoenician art at this period. *(Iraq Museum, Baghdad)*

1990 an expedition sponsored by Harvard University discovered a statue of a golden calf in its excavations of Ashkelon in modern Israel. Despite the anger expressed in the Bible over Hebrew worship of Baal, there is nothing surprising about the phenomenon. Once again, newcomers adapted themselves to the culture of an older, well-established people.

The greatest danger to the Hebrews came from the Philistines, whose superior technology and military organization at first made them invincible. In Saul (ca 1000 B.C.), a farmer of the tribe of Benjamin, the Hebrews found a champion and a spirited leader. In the biblical account, Saul carried the war to the Philistines, often without success. Yet in the meantime he established a monarchy over the twelve Hebrew tribes. Thus, under the peril of the Philistines, the Hebrews evolved from scattered, independent units into a centralized political organization in which the king directed the energies of the people. From this period derives the name *Israelites* for these erstwhile nomads.

Saul's work was carried on by David of Bethlehem, who in his youth had followed Saul into battle against the Philistines. Through courage and cunning, David pushed back the Philistines and waged war against his other neighbors. To give his kingdom a capital, he captured the city of Jerusalem, which he enlarged, fortified, and made the religious and political center of his realm. David's military successes won the Hebrews unprecedented security, and his forty-year reign was a period of vitality and political consolidation. His work in consolidating the monarchy and enlarging the kingdom paved the way for his son Solomon.

Solomon (ca 965–925 B.C.) applied his energies to creating a nation out of a collection of tribes ruled by a king. He divided the kingdom, for purposes of effective administration, into twelve territorial districts cutting across the old tribal borders. To Solomon the twelve tribes of Israel were far less important than the Hebrew nation. To bring his kingdom up to the level of its more sophisticated neighbors, he set about a building program to make Israel a respectable Near Eastern state. Work was begun on a magnificent temple in Jerusalem, on cities, palaces, fortresses, and roads. Solomon worked to bring Israel into the commercial mainstream of the world around it and kept up good relations with Phoenician cities to the north. To finance all of the construction and other activities that he initiated, Solomon imposed taxes far greater than any levied before, much to the displeasure of his subjects.

Solomon dedicated the temple in grand style and made it the home of the Ark of the Covenant, the cherished chest that contained the holiest of Hebrew religious articles. The temple in Jerusalem was intended to be the religious heart of the kingdom and the symbol of Hebrew unity. It also became the stronghold of the priesthood, for a legion of priests was needed to conduct religious sacrifices, ceremonies, and prayers. Yet Solomon's efforts were hampered by strife. In the eyes of some people, he was too ready to unite other religions with the worship of the Hebrew god Yahweh, and the financial demands of his building program drained the resources of his people. His use of forced labor for building projects further fanned popular resentment. However, Solomon turned a rude kingdom into a state with broad commercial horizons and greater knowledge of the outside world. At his death, the Hebrews broke into two political halves (see Map 2.1). The northern part of the kingdom of David and Solomon became Israel, with its capital at Samaria. The southern half was Judah, and Jerusalem remained its center. With political division went a religious rift: Israel, the northern kingdom, established rival sanctuaries for gods other than Yahweh. The Hebrew nation was divided, but at least it was divided into two far more sophisticated political units than before the time of Solomon. Nonetheless, war soon broke out between them, as recorded in the Bible. Unexpected and independent evidence of this warfare came to light in August 1993, when an Israeli archaeologist found an inscription that refers to the "House of David," the royal line of Israel. The stone celebrates an Israelite victory from the early ninth century B.C. This discovery is the first mention of King David's royal family outside the Bible and helps to confirm the biblical account of the fighting between the two kingdoms.

Eventually, the northern kingdom of Israel was wiped out by the Assyrians, but the southern kingdom of Judah survived numerous calamities until the Babylonians crushed it in 587 B.C. The survivors were sent into exile in Babylonia, a period commonly known as the "Babylonian Captivity." From 587 to 538 B.C., men

Megiddo This aerial view of the substantial fortress of Megiddo, in modern Israel, was a stronghold on the frontiers of Syria and Egypt. Standing atop a small plateau, it was heavily fortified and commanded a fertile plain. It also stood astride the major road between Egypt and the north, making it strategically valuable. It was the scene of a major battle in which the Egyptians routed a Canaanite army. *(Rolf Michael Kneller)*

Nomadic Semitic Tribe This Egyptian fresco captures the essentials of nomadic life. These Semites have captured a gazelle and an ibex. The four men behind the leaders are portrayed with their weapons, a bow and spears, which were used for both hunting and defense. Bringing up the rear is a domesticated burro. *(Erich Lessing /Art Resource, NY)*

known as the prophets kept Yahweh's religion alive in the midst of far older Babylonian religious practices. They predicted that Yahweh would permit the Israelites to return to their homeland if they only remained true to him. In 538 B.C. the Persians, under their king Cyrus the Great, permitted some forty thousand exiles to return to Jerusalem. During and especially after the Babylonian Captivity, the exiles redefined their beliefs and practices, and thus established what they believed was the law of Yahweh. Those who lived by these precepts can be called *Jews.*

The Evolution of Jewish Religion

Hand in hand with their political evolution from fierce nomads to urban dwellers, the Hebrews were evolving spiritual ideas that still permeate Western society. Their chief literary product, the Hebrew Bible, has fundamentally influenced both Christianity and Islam and still exerts a compelling force on the modern world.

Fundamental to an understanding of Jewish religion is the concept of the Covenant, a formal agreement between Yahweh and the Hebrew people. According to the Bible, the god Yahweh, the Christian "Jehovah," appeared to Moses on Mount Sinai. There Yahweh made a covenant with the Hebrews that was in fact a contract: if the Hebrews worshiped Yahweh as their only god, he would consider them his chosen people and protect them from their enemies. The Hebrews believed that Yahweh had led them out of bondage in Egypt and had helped them to conquer their new land, the Promised Land. In return, the Hebrews worshiped Yahweh and Yahweh alone. They also obeyed Yahweh's Ten Commandments, an ethical code of conduct revealed to them by Moses.

Yahweh was unique because he was a lone god. Unlike the gods of Mesopotamia and Egypt, Yahweh was not the son of another god, nor did he have a divine wife or family. Initially anthropomorphic, Yahweh gradually lost human form and became totally spiritual. Although Yahweh could assume human form, he was not to be depicted in any form. Thus the Hebrews considered graven images—statues and other physical representations—idolatrous.

At first Yahweh was probably viewed as no more than the god of the Hebrews, who sometimes faced competition from Baal and other gods in Palestine. Enlil, Marduk, Amon-Re, and the others sufficed for foreigners. In time, however, the Hebrews came to regard Yahweh as the only god. This was the beginning of true monotheism.

Unlike Akhenaten's monotheism, Hebrew monotheism was not an unpopular religion. It became the religion of a whole people, deeply felt and cherished. Some might fall away from Yahweh's worship, and various holy men had to exhort the Hebrews to honor the Covenant, but on the whole the people clung to Yahweh. Yet the Hebrews did not consider it their duty to spread the belief in the one god. The Hebrews rarely proselytized, as later Christians did. As the chosen people, their chief duty was to maintain the worship of Yahweh as he demanded. That worship was embodied in the Ten Commandments, which forbade the Hebrews to steal, murder, lie, or commit adultery. The Covenant was a constant force in Hebrew life (see the feature "Listening to the Past: The Covenant Between Yahweh and the Hebrews" on pages 60–61), and the Old Testament records one occasion when the entire nation formally reaffirmed it:

And the king [of the Jews] stood by a pillar, and made a covenant before the lord, to walk after the lord, and to keep his commandments and his testimonies and his statutes with all their heart and all their soul, to perform the words of this covenant that were written in this book [Deuteronomy]. And all the people stood to the covenant.[2]

From the Ten Commandments evolved Hebrew law, a code of law and custom originating with Moses and built on by priests and prophets. The earliest part of this code, the Torah or Mosaic law, was often as harsh as Hammurabi's code, which had a powerful impact on it. Later tradition, largely the work of prophets who lived from the eleventh to the fifth centuries B.C., was more humanitarian. The work of the prophet Jeremiah (ca 626 B.C.) exemplifies this gentler spirit. According to Jeremiah, Yahweh demanded righteousness from his people and protection for the weak and helpless.

Jeremiah's emphasis is on mercy and justice, on avoiding wrongdoing to others because it is displeasing to Yahweh. These precepts replaced the old law's demand for "an eye for an eye." Jeremiah's message is thus representative of a subtle and positive shift in Hebrew thinking. Jeremiah proclaimed that the god of anger was also the god of forgiveness: "Return, thou backsliding Israel, saith the lord; and I will not cause mine anger to fall upon you; for I am merciful, saith the lord, and I will not keep anger forever."[3] Although Yahweh would punish wrongdoing, he would not destroy those who repented. One generation might be punished for its misdeeds, but Yahweh's mercy was a promise of hope for future generations.

The uniqueness of this phenomenon can be seen by comparing the essence of Hebrew monotheism with the religious outlook of the Mesopotamians. Whereas the Mesopotamians considered their gods capricious, the Hebrews knew what Yahweh expected. The Hebrews believed that their god would protect them and make them prosper if they obeyed his commandments. The Mesopotamians thought human beings insignificant compared to the gods, so insignificant that the gods might even be indifferent to them. The Hebrews, too, considered themselves puny in comparison to Yahweh. Yet they were Yahweh's chosen people, whom he had promised never to abandon. Finally, though the

The Golden Calf According to the Hebrew Bible, Moses descended from Mt. Sinai, where he had received the Ten Commandments, to find the Hebrews worshiping a golden calf, which was against Yahweh's laws. In July 1990 an American archaeological team found this model of a gilded calf inside a pot. The figurine, which dates to about 1550 B.C., is strong evidence for the existence of the cult represented by the calf in Palestine. *(Courtesy of the Leon Levy Expedition to Ashkelon. Photo: Carl Andrews)*

Mesopotamians believed that the gods generally preferred good to evil, their religion did not demand ethical conduct. The Hebrews could please their god only by living up to high moral standards as well as worshiping him.

Daily Life in Israel

Historians generally know far more about the daily life of the aristocracy and the wealthy in ancient societies than about the conditions of the common people. Jewish society is an exception simply because the Bible, which lays down laws for all Jews, has much to say about peasants and princes alike. Comparisons with the social conditions of Israel's ancient neighbors and modern anthropological work among Palestinian Arabs shed additional light on biblical practices. Thus the life of the common people in ancient Israel is better known than, for instance, the lives of ordinary Romans or ancient Chinese.

The nomadic Hebrews first entered modern Palestine as tribes, numerous families who thought of themselves as all related to one another. At first, good farmland, pastureland, and water spots were held in common by the tribe. Common use of land was—and still is—characteristic of nomadic peoples. Typically each family or group of families in the tribe drew lots every year to determine who worked which fields. But as formerly nomadic peoples turned increasingly to settled agriculture, communal use of land gave way to family ownership. In this respect the experience of the ancient Hebrews seems typical of that of many early peoples. Slowly the shift from nomad to farmer affected far more than just how people fed themselves. Family relationships reflected evolving circumstances. With the transition to settled agriculture, the tribe gradually became less important than the extended family. With the advent of village life and finally full-blown urban life, the extended family in turn gave way to the nuclear family.

For women, however, the evolution of Jewish society led to less freedom of action, especially in religious life. At first women served as priestesses in festivals and religious cults. Some were considered prophetesses of Yahweh, although they never conducted his official rituals. In the course of time, however, the worship of Yahweh became more male-oriented and male-dominated. Increasingly, he also became the god of holiness, and to worship him people must be pure in mind and body. Women were seen as ritually impure because of menstruation and childbirth. Because of these "impurities," women now played a much reduced role in religion. Even when they did participate in religious rites, they were segregated from the men. For the most part, women were largely confined to the home and the care of the family.

Marriage was one of the most important and joyous events in Hebrew family life. The typical marriage in ancient Israel was monogamous, and a virtuous wife was revered and honored.

The newly married couple was expected to begin a family at once. Children, according to the Book of Psalms, "are an heritage of the lord: and the fruit of the womb is his reward."[4] The desire for children to perpetuate the family was so strong that if a man died before he could sire a son, his brother was legally obliged to marry the widow. The son born of the brother was thereafter considered the offspring and heir of the dead man. If the brother refused, the widow had her revenge by denouncing him to the elders and publicly spitting in his face.

As in most other societies, in ancient Israel the early education of children was in the mother's hands. She taught her children right from wrong and gave them their first instruction in the moral values of society. As boys grew older, they received more education from their fathers. Fathers instructed their sons in religion and the history of their people. Many children were taught to read and write, and the head of each family was probably able to write. Fathers also taught sons the family craft or trade. Boys soon learned that inattention could be painful, for Jewish custom advised fathers to be strict: "He that spareth his rod hateth his son: but he that loveth him chasteneth him betimes."[5]

The land was precious to the family, not simply because it provided a living, but also because it was a link to the past. Ironically, the success of the first Hebrew kings endangered the future of many family farms. With peace, more settled conditions, and increasing prosperity, some Jews began to amass larger holdings by buying out poor and struggling farmers. Far from discouraging this development, the kings created their own huge estates. In many cases slaves, both Jewish and foreign, worked these large farms and estates shoulder to shoulder with paid free men. In still later times, rich landowners rented plots of land to poor, free families; the landowners provided the renters with seed and livestock and normally took half the yield as rent. Although many Bible prophets denounced the destruction of the family farm, the trend continued toward large estates that were worked by slaves and hired free men.

The development of urban life among the Jews created new economic opportunities, especially in crafts and trades. People specialized in certain occupations, such as milling flour, baking bread, making pottery, weaving, and carpentry. All these crafts were family trades. Sons worked with their father, daughters with their mother. If the business prospered, the family might be assisted by a few paid workers or slaves. The practitioners of a craft usually lived in a particular section of town, a custom still prevalent in the Middle East today.

Commerce and trade developed later than crafts. In the time of Solomon foreign trade was the king's domain. Aided by the Phoenicians, Solomon built a fleet to trade with Red Sea ports. Solomon also participated in the overland caravan trade. Otherwise trade with neighboring countries was handled by foreigners, usually Phoenicians. Jews dealt mainly in local trade, and in most instances craftsmen and farmers sold directly to their customers. Many of Israel's wise men disapproved of commerce and considered it unseemly and immoral to profit from the work of others.

These social and economic developments also left their mark on daily life by prompting the compilation of two significant works, the Torah and the Talmud. The Torah is basically the Mosaic law, or the first five books of the Bible. The Talmud is a later work, begun during the Babylonian Captivity and completed by the end of the sixth century B.C. The Talmud records civil and ceremonial law and Jewish legend. The dietary rules of the Jews provide an excellent example of both the relationship between the Torah and the Talmud and their effect on ordinary life and culture. According to the Torah, people were not to eat meat that they found in the field. This very sensible prohibition protected them from eating dangerous food. Yet if meat from the countryside could not be eaten, some rules were needed for meat in the city. The solution found in the Talmud was a set of regulations for the proper way to conduct ritual slaughter. Some of these rules were very burdensome. The ritual defined the knife to be used in the slaughter and the way in which it was to be used. Accompanying these precise acts were prayers to be given when the animal's throat was cut. So too with the Torah's prohibition against cooking a kid in its mother's milk. This interpretation of Mosaic law went to such lengths that milk and meat could not be eaten at the same table, and different bowls must be used to serve them. Even different towels must be used to cleanse them. What had begun as simple and sensible dietary rules had become a complicated ritual, but one that many Orthodox Jews follow today.

ASSYRIA, THE MILITARY MONARCHY

Small kingdoms like those of the Phoenicians and the Hebrews could exist only in the absence of a major power. The beginning of the ninth century B.C. saw the rise of such a power: the Assyrians of northern Mesopotamia, whose chief capital was at Nineveh on the Tigris River. The Assyrians were a Semitic-speaking people heavily influenced, like so many other peoples of the Near East, by the Mesopotamian culture of Babylon to the south. They were also one of the most warlike peoples in history, largely because throughout their history they were threatened by neighboring folk. Living in an open, exposed land, the Assyrians experienced frequent and devastating attacks by the wild, war-loving tribes to their north and east and by the Babylonians to the south. The constant threat to survival experienced by the Assyrians promoted political cohesion and military might. Yet they were also a mercantile people who had long pursued commerce with both the Babylonians in the south and other peoples in the north.

The Power of Assyria

For over two hundred years the Assyrians labored to dominate the Near East. In 859 B.C. the new Assyrian king, Shalmaneser, unleashed the first of a long series of attacks on the peoples of Syria and Palestine. Year after relentless year, Assyrian armies hammered at the peoples of the west. These ominous events inaugurated two turbulent centuries marked by Assyrian military campaigns, constant efforts by Syria and the two Jewish kingdoms to maintain or recover their independence, and eventual Assyrian conquest of Babylonia and northern Egypt. In addition, periodic political instability occurred in Assyria itself, which prompted stirrings of freedom throughout the Near East.

Under the Assyrian kings Tiglath-pileser III (774–727 B.C.) and Sargon II (r. 721–705 B.C.), both mighty warriors, the Near East trembled as never before under the blows of Assyrian armies. The Assyrians stepped up their attacks on Anatolia, Syria, and Palestine. The kingdom of Israel and many other states fell; others, like the

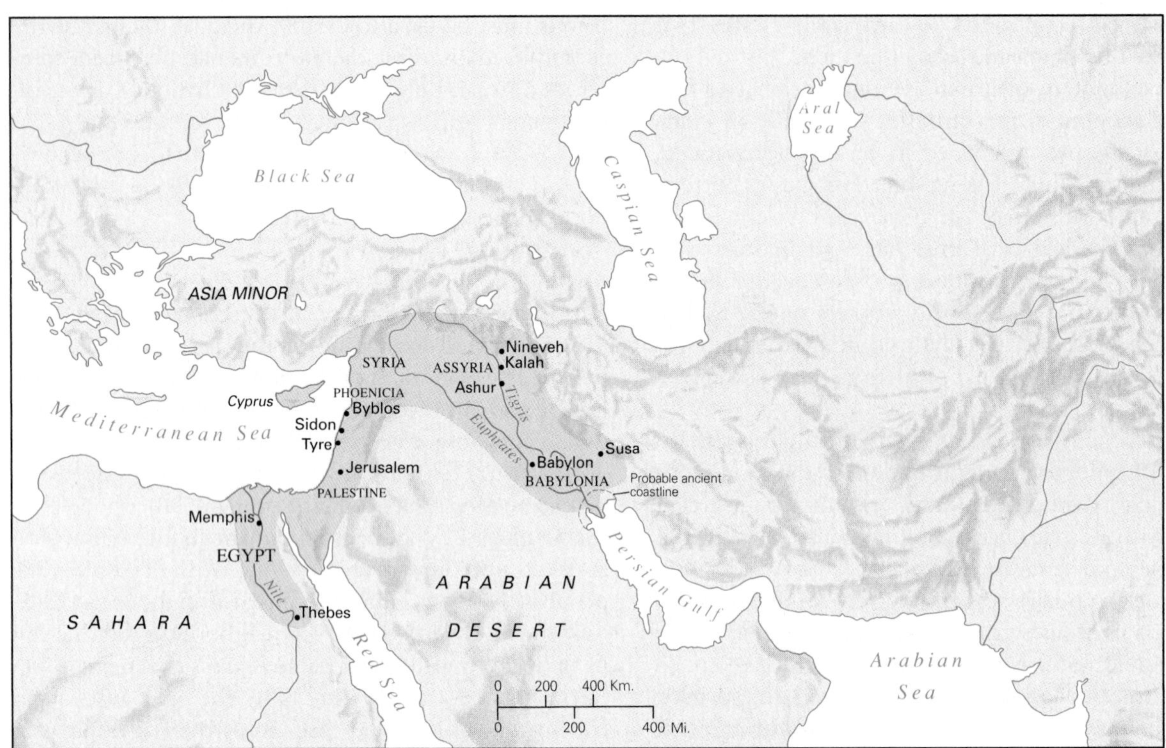

MAP 2.2 The Assyrian Empire The Assyrian Empire at its height (ca 650 B.C.) included almost all of the old centers of power in the ancient Near East. As Map 2.3 shows, however, its size was far smaller than that of the later Persian Empire.

kingdom of Judah, became subservient to the warriors from the Tigris. In 717 to 716 B.C., Sargon led his army in a sweeping attack along the Philistine coast, where he defeated the pharaoh, who suffered the further ignominy of paying tribute to the foreign conquerors. Sargon also lashed out at Assyria's traditional enemies to the north and then turned south against a renewed threat in Babylonia. By means of almost constant warfare, Tiglath-pileser III and Sargon carved out an Assyrian empire that stretched from east and north of the Tigris River to central Egypt (Map 2.2). Revolt against the Assyrians inevitably promised the rebels bloody battles; prolonged sieges accompanied by starvation, plague, and sometimes even cannibalism; and finally surrender followed by systematic torture and slaughter.

Though atrocity and terrorism struck unspeakable fear into Assyria's subjects, Assyria's success was actually due to sophisticated, farsighted, and effective military organization. By Sargon's time the Assyrians had invented the mightiest military machine the ancient Near East had ever seen. The mainstay of the Assyrian army, the soldier who ordinarily decided the outcome of battles, was the infantryman armed with spear and sword and protected by helmet and armor. The Assyrian army also featured archers, some on foot, others on horseback, still others in chariots—the latter ready to wield lances once they had expended their supply of arrows. Some infantry archers wore heavy armor. These soldiers served as a primitive field artillery, whose job was to sweep the enemy's walls of defenders so that others could storm the defenses. Slingers also served as artillery in pitched battles. For mobility on the battlefield, the Assyrians organized a corps of chariots.

Assyrian military genius was remarkable for the development of a wide variety of siege machinery and techniques, including excavation to undermine city walls and battering rams to knock down walls and gates. Never before in the Near East had anyone applied such technical knowledge to warfare. The Assyrians even invented the concept of a corps of engineers, who bridged rivers with pontoons or provided soldiers with inflatable skins for swimming. Furthermore, the Assyrians knew how to coordinate their efforts, both in open battle and in siege warfare. King Sennacherib's account of his siege of Jerusalem in 701 B.C. is a vivid portrait of the Assyrian war machine in action:

As to Hezekiah, the Jew, he did not submit to my yoke, I laid siege to 46 of his strong cities, walled forts and to the countless small villages in their vicinity, and conquered them by means of well-stamped earth-ramps, and battering rams brought thus near to the walls combined with the attack by foot soldiers, using mines, breaches as well as sapper work. . . . Himself I made prisoner in Jerusalem, his royal residence, like a bird in a cage. I surrounded him with earthwork in order to molest those who were leaving his city's gate.[6]

Assyrian Rule and Culture

Not only did the Assyrians know how to win battles, but they also knew how to use their victories. As early as the reign of Tiglath-pileser III, the Assyrian kings began to organize their conquered territories into an empire. The lands closest to Assyria became provinces governed by Assyrian officials. Kingdoms beyond the provinces were not annexed but became dependent states that followed Assyria's lead. The Assyrian king chose their rulers either by regulating the succession of native kings or by supporting native kings who appealed to him. Against more distant states the Assyrian kings waged frequent war in order to conquer them outright or make the dependent states secure.

In the seventh century B.C. Assyrian power seemed firmly established. Yet the downfall of Assyria was swift and complete. Babylon finally won its independence in 626 B.C. and joined forces with a newly aggressive people, the Medes, an Indo-European-speaking folk from Iran. Together the Babylonians and the Medes destroyed the Assyrian Empire in 612 B.C., paving the way for the rise of the Persians. The Hebrew prophet Nahum spoke for many when he asked: "Nineveh is laid waste: who will bemoan her?"[7] Their cities destroyed and their power shattered, the Assyrians disappeared from history, remembered only as a cruel people of the Old Testament who oppressed the Hebrews. Two hundred years later, when the Greek adventurer and historian Xenophon passed by the ruins of Nineveh, he

Siege of a City Art here serves to glorify horror. The Assyrian king Tiglath-pileser III launches an assault on a fortified city. The impaled bodies shown at center demonstrate the cruelty of Assyrian warfare. Also noticeable are the various weapons and means of attack used against the city. *(Courtesy of the Trustees of the British Museum)*

marveled at the extent of the former city but knew nothing of the Assyrians. The glory of their empire was forgotten.

Yet modern archaeology has brought the Assyrians out of obscurity. In 1839 the intrepid English archaeologist and traveler A. H. Layard began the most noteworthy excavations of Nineveh, then a mound of debris beside the Tigris. His findings electrified the world. In the course of a few years, Layard's discoveries shed remarkable new light on Assyrian history and had an equally stunning impact on the history of art. Layard's workers unearthed masterpieces, including monumental sculpted figures—huge winged bulls, human-headed lions, and sphinxes—as well as brilliantly sculpted friezes. Equally valuable were the numerous Assyrian cuneiform documents, which ranged from royal accounts of mighty military campaigns to simple letters by common people.

Royal Lion Hunt This relief from the palace of Ashurbanipal at Nineveh, which shows the king fighting a lion, is a typical representation of the energy and artistic brilliance of Assyrian sculptors. The lion hunt, portrayed in a series of episodes, was a favorite theme of Assyrian palace reliefs. *(Courtesy of the Trustees of the British Museum)*

Among the most renowned of Layard's finds were the Assyrian palace reliefs, whose number has been increased by the discoveries of twentieth-century archaeologists. Assyrian kings delighted in scenes of war, which their artists depicted in graphic detail. By the time of Ashurbanipal (r. 668–633 B.C.), Assyrian artists had hit on the idea of portraying a series of episodes—in fact, a visual narrative of events that had actually taken place. Scene followed scene in a continuous frieze, so that the viewer could follow the progress of a military campaign from the time the army marched out until the enemy was conquered.

Assyrian art is stark and often brutal in subject matter, yet marked by an undeniable strength and sophistication of composition. It often conveys both action and tension. Assyrian art fared better than Assyrian military power. The techniques of Assyrian artists influenced the Persians, who adapted them to gentler scenes.

In fact, many Assyrian innovations, military and political as well as artistic, were taken over wholesale by the Persians. Although the memory of Assyria was hateful throughout the Near East, the fruits of Assyrian organizational genius helped enable the Persians to bring peace and stability to the same regions where Assyrian armies had spread terror.

CHALDEAN BABYLONIA (626–539 B.C.)

The decline of Assyria allowed the Babylonians to create a new dynasty of kings and priests known as the Chaldeans. This period is marked by the restoration of past Babylonian greatness. The Chaldeans were Semitic-speaking tribes that settled in southern Mesopotamia, where they established their rule, later extending it farther north. They grew strong enough to overthrow Assyrian rule with the help of another new people, the Indo-European Medes, who had established themselves in modern western Iran (see page 52). Their most famous king, Nebuchadrezzar (r. 604–562 B.C.), thrust Babylonian power into Syria and Judah, and in the process destroyed the city of Jerusalem. He deported the captive population to Babylonia.

The Chaldeans were unaware of this development. Their attention was focused on solidifying their power and legitimizing their authority. Kings and priests consciously looked back to the great days of Hammurabi. They instituted a religious revival that included restoring old temples and sanctuaries, as well as creating new ones in the same tradition. Part of their effort was commercial, as they sought to revive the economy in order to resurrect the image of Babylonian greatness. In their hands Babylonia itself became one of the wonders of the ancient world. They preserved many basic aspects of Babylonian law, literature, and government. Yet they failed to bring peace and prosperity to Mesopotamia. Loss of important trade routes to the north and northeast, combined with catastrophic inflation, reduced actual income. Additional misfortune came in the form of famine and plague. The Chaldean kings had to some degree created a situation that ultimately led to their downfall. It would not come from internal rebellion, but rather from two groups of Iranian newcomers—the Medes and the Persians.

THE EMPIRE OF THE PERSIAN KINGS

Like the Hittites before them, the Iranians were Indo-Europeans from central Europe and southern Russia. They migrated into the land to which they have given their name, the area between the Caspian Sea and the Persian Gulf. Like the Hittites, they then fell under the spell of the more sophisticated cultures of their Mesopotamian neighbors. Yet the Iranians went on to create one of the greatest empires of antiquity, one that encompassed scores of peoples and cultures. The Persians, the most important of the Iranian peoples, had a far-sighted conception of empire. Though as conquerors they willingly used force to accomplish their ends, they normally preferred to depend on diplomacy to rule. They usually respected their subjects and allowed them to practice their native customs and religions. Thus the Persians gave the Near East both political unity and cultural diversity. Never before had Near Eastern people viewed empire in such intelligent and humane terms.

The Land of Mountains and Plateau

Persia—the modern country of Iran—is a stark land of towering mountains and flaming deserts, with a broad central plateau in the heart of the country (Map 2.3). Iran stretches from the Caspian Sea in the north to the Persian Gulf in the south. Between the Tigris-Euphrates Valley in the west and the Indus Valley in the east rises an immense plateau, surrounded on all sides by lofty mountains that cut off the interior from the sea.

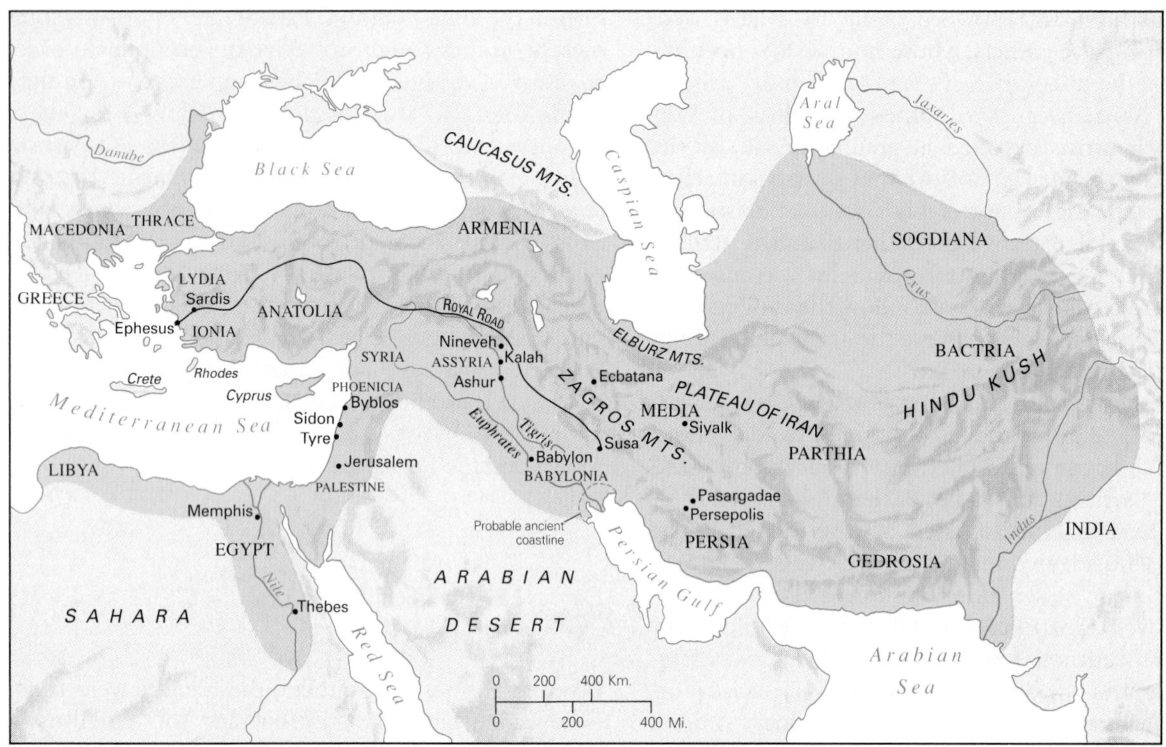

MAP 2.3 The Persian Empire By 513 B.C. the Persian Empire not only included more of the ancient Near East than had the Assyrian Empire but also extended as far east as western India. With the rise of the Medes and Persians, the balance of power in the Near East shifted east of Mesopotamia for the first time.

The central plateau is very high, a landscape of broad plains, scattered oases, and two vast deserts. The high mountains, which catch the moisture coming from the sea, generate ample rainfall for the plateau. This semitropical area is very fertile, in marked contrast to the aridity of most of Iran. The mountains surrounding the central plateau are dotted with numerous oases, often very fertile, which have from time immemorial served as havens for small groups of people.

At the center of the plateau lies an enormous depression—a forbidding region devoid of water and vegetation, so glowing hot in summer that it is virtually impossible to cross. This depression forms two distinct grim and burning salt deserts, perhaps the most desolate spots on earth.

Iran's geographical position and topography explain its traditional role as the highway between East and West. Throughout history wild, nomadic peoples migrating from the broad steppes of Russia and central Asia have streamed into Iran. The very harshness of the geography urged them to continue in search of new and more hospitable lands. Confronting the uncrossable salt deserts, most have turned either eastward or westward, moving on until they reached the advanced and wealthy urban centers of Mesopotamia and India. When cities emerged along the natural lines of East-West communication, Iran became the area where nomads met urban dwellers, a meeting ground of unique significance for the civilizations of both East and West.

The Coming of the Medes and Persians

The Iranians entered this land around 1000 B.C. They were part of the vast movement of Indo-European-speaking peoples whose wanderings led them into Europe, the Near East, and India in many successive waves (see page 28). These Iranians were nomads who migrated with their flocks and herds. Like their kinsmen the Aryans, who moved into India, they were also horse breeders, and the horse gave them a decisive military advantage over the prehistoric peoples of Iran. The Iranians rode into battle in horse-drawn chariots or on horseback and easily swept the natives before them. Yet, because the influx of Iranians went on for centuries, there continued to be constant cultural interchange between conquering newcomers and conquered natives.

The Iranians initially created a patchwork of tiny kingdoms, of which Siyalk was one. The chieftain or petty king was basically a warlord who depended on fellow warriors for aid and support. This band of noble warriors, like the Greek heroes of the *Iliad,* formed the fighting strength of the army. The king owned estates that supported him and his nobles; for additional income the king levied taxes, which were paid in kind and not in cash. He also demanded labor services from the peasants. Below the king and his warrior nobles were free people who held land and others who owned nothing. Artisans produced the various goods needed to keep society running. At the bottom of the social scale were slaves—probably both natives and newcomers—to whom fell the drudgery of hard labor and household service to king and nobles.

Rhyton This rhyton, or drinking cup, is a masterpiece of metalwork. The winged lion serves as the base, and the conical cup at its rear held the wine. This was a ceremonial piece, too big and heavy for any but grand official occasions. *(Courtesy, The National Museum of Iran)*

This early period saw some significant economic developments. The use of iron increased. By the seventh century B.C. iron farm implements had become widespread, leading to increased productivity, greater overall prosperity, and higher standards of living. At the same time Iranian agriculture saw the development of the small estate. Farmers worked small plots of land, and the general prosperity of the period bred a sturdy peasantry, people who enjoyed greater freedom than their contemporaries in Egypt and Mesopotamia.

Kings exploited Iran's considerable mineral wealth, and Iranian iron, copper, and lapis lazuli attracted Assyrian raiding parties. Even more important, mineral wealth and Iranian horse breeding stimulated brisk trade with the outside world. Kings found that merchants, who were not usually Iranians, produced large profits to help fill the kings' coffers. Overland trade also put the Iranians in direct contact with their Near Eastern neighbors.

Gradually two groups of Iranians began coalescing into larger units. The Persians had settled in Persia, the modern region of Fars, in southern Iran. Their kinsmen the Medes occupied Media, the modern area of Hamadan in the north, with their capital at Persepolis. The Medes were exposed to attack by nomads from the north, but their greatest threat was the frequent raids of the Assyrian army. Even though distracted by grave pressures from their neighbors, the Medes united under one king around 710 B.C. and extended their control over the Persians in the south. In 612 B.C. the Medes were strong enough to join the Babylonians in overthrowing the Assyrian Empire. With the rise of the Medes, the balance of power in the Near East shifted for the first time east of Mesopotamia.

The Creation of the Persian Empire

In 550 B.C. Cyrus the Great (r. 559–530 B.C.), king of the Persians and one of the most remarkable statesmen of antiquity, threw off the yoke of the Medes by conquering them and turning their country into his first *satrapy,* or province. In the space of a single lifetime, Cyrus created one of the greatest empires of antiquity. Two characteristics lift Cyrus above the common level

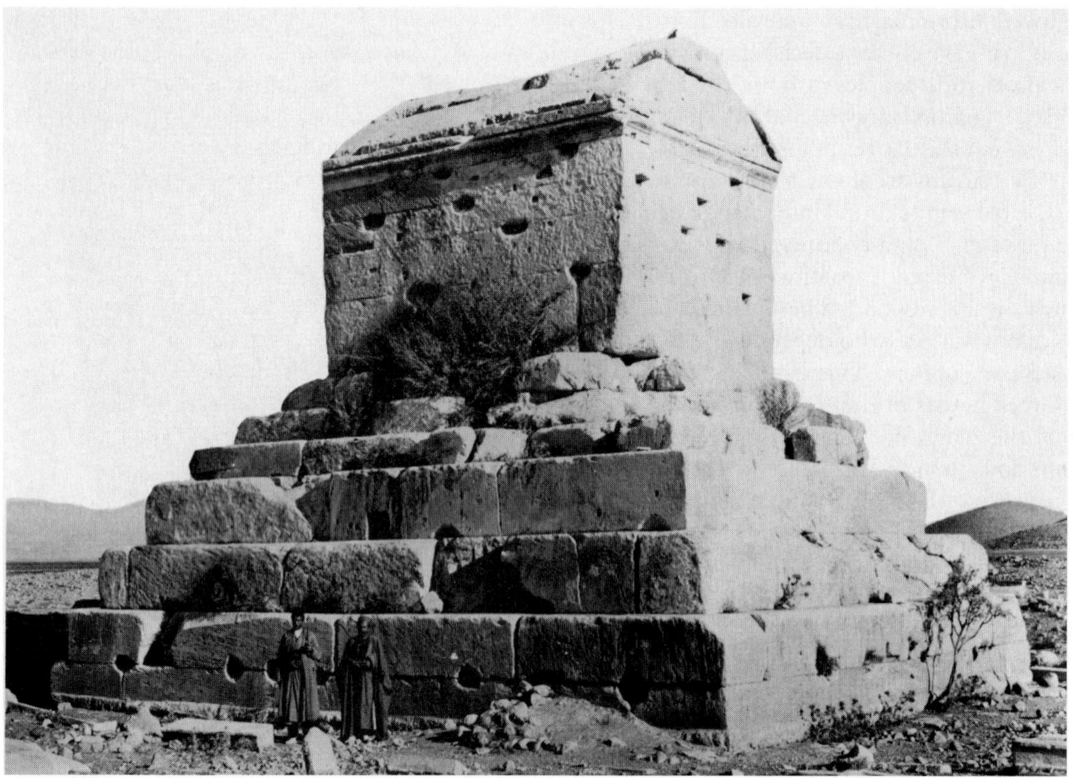

Tomb of Cyrus For all of his greatness Cyrus retained a sense of perspective. His tomb, though monumental in size, is rather simple and unostentatious. Greek writers reported that it bore the following epitaph: "O man, I am Cyrus the son of Cambyses. I established the Persian Empire and was king of Asia. Do not begrudge me my memorial." *(The Oriental Institute, University of Chicago)*

of warrior-kings. First, he thought of Iran, not just Persia and Media, as a state. His concept has survived a long, complex, and often turbulent history to play its part in the contemporary world.

Second, Cyrus held an enlightened view of empire. Many of the civilizations and cultures that fell to his armies were, he realized, far older, more advanced, and more sophisticated than his. Free of the narrow-minded snobbery of the Egyptians, the religious exclusiveness of the Hebrews, and the calculated cruelty of the Assyrians, Cyrus gave Near Eastern peoples and their cultures his respect, toleration, and protection. Conquered peoples continued to enjoy their institutions, religions, languages, and ways of life under the Persians. The Persian Empire, which Cyrus created, became a political organization sheltering many different civilizations. To rule such a vast area and so many diverse peoples demanded talent, intelligence, sensitivity, and a cosmopolitan view of the world. These qualities Cyrus and many of his successors possessed in abundance. Though the Persians were sometimes harsh, especially with those who rebelled against them, they were for the most part enlightened rulers. Consequently, the Persians gave the ancient Near East over two hundred years of peace, prosperity, and security.

Cyrus showed his magnanimity at the outset of his career. Once the Medes had fallen to him, Cyrus united them with his Persians. Persepolis became a Persian seat of power. Medes were honored with important military and political posts and thenceforth helped the Persians to rule the expanding empire. Cyrus's conquest of the Medes resulted not in slavery and slaughter but in the union of Iranian peoples.

With Iran united, Cyrus looked at the broader world. He set out to achieve two goals. First, he wanted to win control of the west and thus of the terminal ports of the great trade routes that crossed Iran and Anatolia. Second, Cyrus strove to secure eastern Iran from the pressure of nomadic invaders. In 550 B.C. neither goal was easy to accomplish. To the northwest was the young kingdom of Lydia in Anatolia, whose king Croesus was proverbial for his wealth. To the west was Babylonia, enjoying a new period of power now that the Assyrian Empire had been crushed. To the southwest was Egypt, still weak but sheltered behind its bulwark of sand and sea. To the east ranged tough, mobile nomads, capable of massive and destructive incursions deep into Iranian territory.

Cyrus turned first to Croesus's Lydian kingdom, which fell to him around 546 B.C. He established a garrison at Sardis, the capital of Lydia, and ordered his generals to subdue the Greek cities along the coast of Anatolia. Cyrus had thus gained the important ports that looked out to the Mediterranean world. In addition, for the first time the Persians came into direct contact with the Greeks, a people with whom their later history was to be intimately connected.

From Lydia, Cyrus next marched to the far eastern corners of Iran. In a brilliant campaign he conquered the regions of Parthia and Bactria. All of Iran was now Persian, from Mesopotamia in the west to the western slopes of the Hindu Kush in the east. In 540 B.C. Cyrus moved against Babylonia, now isolated from outside help. When Persian soldiers marched quietly into Babylon the next year, the Babylonians welcomed Cyrus as a liberator. Cyrus won the hearts of the Babylonians with humane treatment, toleration of their religion, and support of their efforts to refurbish their capital.

Cyrus was equally generous toward the Jews. He allowed them to return to Palestine, from which they had been deported by the Babylonians. He protected them, gave them back the sacred items they used in worship, and rebuilt the temple of Yahweh in Jerusalem. The Old Testament sings the praises of Cyrus, whom the Jews considered the shepherd of Yahweh, the lord's anointed. Rarely have conquered peoples shown such gratitude to their conquerors. Cyrus's benevolent policy created a Persian Empire in which the cultures and religions of its members were respected and honored. Seldom have conquerors been as wise, sensitive, and farsighted as Cyrus and his Persians.

Thus Spake Zarathustra

Iranian religion was originally simple and primitive. Ahuramazda, the chief god, was the creator and benefactor of all living creatures. Yet, unlike Yahweh, he was not a lone god. The Iranians were polytheistic. Mithra the sun-god, whose cult would later spread throughout the Roman Empire, saw to justice and redemption. Other Iranian deities personified the natural elements: moon, earth, water, and wind. As in ancient India, fire was a particularly important god. The sacred fire consumed the blood sacrifices that the early Iranians offered to all of their deities.

Early Iranian religion was close to nature and unencumbered by ponderous theological beliefs. A priestly class, the Magi, developed among the Medes to officiate at sacrifices, chant prayers to the gods, and tend the sacred flame. A description of this early worship comes from the German historian Eduard Meyer:

> *Iranian religion knew neither divine images nor temples. On a hilltop one called upon god and his manifestations—sun and moon, earth and fire, water and wind—and erected altars with their eternal fire. But in other appropriate places one could, without further preparation, pray to the deity and bring him his offerings, with the assistance of the Magi.*[8]

In time the Iranians built fire temples for these sacrifices. As late as the nineteenth century, fire was still worshiped in Baku, a major city on the Russian-Iranian border.

Around 600 B.C. the religious thinking of Zarathustra—Zoroaster, as he is better known—breathed new meaning into Iranian religion. So little is known of Zoroaster that even the date of his birth is unknown, but it cannot be earlier than around 1100 B.C. Whatever the exact dates of his life, his work endured long afterward. The most reliable information about Zoroaster comes from the *Zend Avesta,* a collection of hymns and poems, the earliest part of which treats Zoroaster and primitive Persian religion. Zoroaster preached a novel concept of divinity and human life. Life, he taught, is a constant battleground for two opposing forces, good and evil. Ahuramazda embodied good and truth but was opposed by Ahriman, a hateful spirit who stood for evil and falsehood. Ahuramazda and Ahriman were locked together in a cosmic battle for the human race, a battle that stretched over thousands of years.

Zoroaster emphasized the individual's responsibility to choose between good and evil. He taught that people possessed the free will to decide between Ahuramazda and Ahriman and that they must rely on their own conscience to guide them through life. Their decisions were crucial, Zoroaster warned, for there would be a time of reckoning. He promised that Ahuramazda would eventually triumph over evil and lies, and that at death each person would stand before the tribunal of good. Ahuramazda, like the Egyptian god Osiris, would judge whether the dead had lived righteously and on that basis would weigh their lives in the balance. In short, Zoroaster taught the concept of a Last Judgment at which Ahuramazda would decide each person's eternal fate.

In Zoroaster's thought the Last Judgment was linked to the notion of a divine kingdom after death for those who had lived according to good and truth. Liars and the wicked, denied this blessed immortality, would be condemned to eternal pain, darkness, and punishment. Thus Zoroaster preached a Last Judgment that led to a heaven or a hell.

Though tradition has it that Zoroaster's teachings originally met with opposition and coldness, his thought converted Darius (r. 521–486 B.C.), one of the most energetic men ever to sit on the Persian throne. The Persian royal family adopted Zoroastrianism but did not try to impose it on others. Under the protection of the Persian kings, Zoroastrianism swept through Iran, winning converts and sinking roots that sustained healthy growth for centuries. Zoroastrianism survived the fall of the Persian Empire to influence religious thought in the age of Jesus and to make a vital contribution to Manicheanism, a theology that was to spread through the Byzantine Empire and pose a significant challenge to Christianity. A handful of the faithful still follow the teachings of Zoroaster, whose vision of divinity and human life has transcended the centuries.

Persia's World Empire

Cyrus's successors rounded out the Persian conquest of the ancient Near East. In 525 B.C. Cyrus's son Cambyses (r. 530–522 B.C.) subdued Egypt. Darius (r. 521–486 B.C.) and his son Xerxes (r. 486–464 B.C.) invaded Greece but were forced to retreat (see pages 80–81); the Persians never won a permanent foothold in Europe. Yet Darius carried Persian arms into India.

Persian Nobles in Chariot Here two Persian nobles ride in a chariot pulled by four horses. The chariot is simple in construction but elegant in its ornamentation. The harness of the horses is worked in elaborate and accurate detail. This chariot was used for ceremonial purposes, not for warfare. *(Courtesy of the Trustees of the British Museum)*

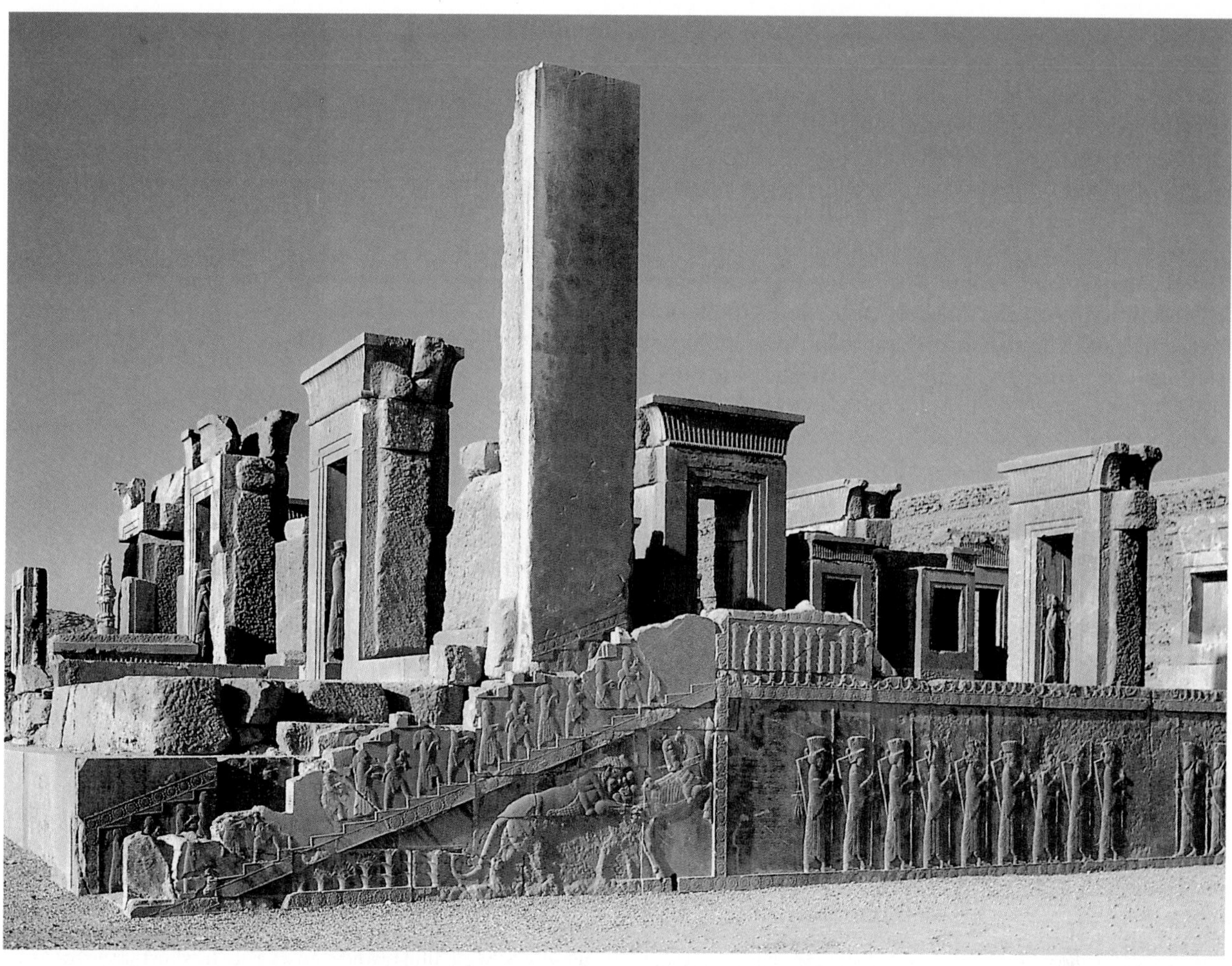

The Royal Palace at Persepolis King Darius began and King Xerxes finished building a grand palace worthy of the glory of the Persian Empire. Pictured here is the monumental audience hall, where the king dealt with ministers of state and foreign envoys. *(George Holton/Photo Researchers)*

Around 513 B.C. western India became the Persian satrapy of Hindush, which included the valley of the Indus River. Thus within thirty-seven years (550–513 B.C.) the Persians transformed themselves from a subject people to the rulers of an empire that included Anatolia, Egypt, Mesopotamia, Iran, and western India. They had created a "world empire" encompassing all of the oldest and most honored kingdoms and peoples of the ancient Near East. Never before had the Near East been united in one such vast political organization (see Map 2.3).

The Persians knew how to use the peace they had won on the battlefield. Unlike the Assyrians, they did not resort to royal terrorism to keep order. Like the Assyrians, however, they employed a number of bureaucratic techniques to bind the empire together. The sheer size of the empire made it impossible for one man to rule it effectively. Consequently, the Persians divided the empire into some twenty huge satrapies measuring hundreds of square miles apiece, many of them kingdoms in themselves. Each satrapy had a governor, usually drawn from the Median and Persian nobility and often a relative of the king; the governor, or *satrap,* was directly responsible to the king. Others were local dynasts subject to the Persian king. An army officer, also responsible to the king, commanded the military forces stationed in the satrapy. Still another official collected the taxes. Moreover, the king sent out royal inspectors to watch the satraps and other officials, a method of surveillance later used by the medieval king Charlemagne.

Effective rule of the empire demanded good communications. To meet this need the Persians established a network of roads. The main highway, known as the Royal Road, spanned some 1,677 miles from the Greek city of Ephesus on the coast of Asia Minor to Susa in western Iran. The distance was broken into 111 post stations, each equipped with fresh horses for the king's messengers. Other roads branched out to link all parts of the empire from the coast of Asia Minor to the valley of the Indus River. This system of communications enabled the Persian king to keep in intimate touch with his subjects and officials. He was able to rule efficiently, keep his ministers in line, and protect the rights of the peoples under his control.

SUMMARY

During the centuries following the Sea Peoples' invasions, Egypt was overrun by its African neighbors, but its long and rich traditions and culture, its firmly established religion, and its administrative techniques became the heritage of these conquerors. The defeat of Egypt also led to conditions that allowed the Hebrews to create their own state. A series of strong leaders fighting hard wars won the Hebrews independence and security. In this atmosphere Hebrew religion evolved and flourished, thanks to priests, prophets, and common piety among the people. Daily life involved the transition from nomad to farmer, and people's lives revolved around the religious and agricultural year.

In the eighth century B.C. the Hebrews and others in the ancient Near East fell to the onslaught of Assyria, a powerful Mesopotamian kingdom. The Assyrians combined administrative skills, economic acumen, and wealth with military organization to create an aggressive military state. Yet the Assyrians' military ruthlessness and cruelty raised powerful enemies against them. The most important of these enemies were the Iranians, who created the Persian Empire. The Persians had migrated into Iran, settled the land, and entered the cultural orbit of the Near East. The result was rapid progress in culture, economic prosperity, and increase in population, which enabled them to create the largest empire yet seen in the Near East. Unlike the Assyrians, however, they ruled mildly and gave the Near East a long period of peace.

NOTES

1. James H. Breasted, *Ancient Records of Egypt* (Chicago: University of Chicago Press, 1907), vol. 4, para. 398.
2. 2 Kings 23:3.
3. Jeremiah 3:12.
4. Psalms 128:3.
5. Proverbs 13:24.
6. J. B. Pritchard, ed., *Ancient Near Eastern Texts,* 3d ed. (Princeton, N.J.: Princeton University Press, 1969), p. 288.
7. Nahum 3:7.
8. E. Meyer, *Geschichte des Altertums,* 7th ed., vol. 4, pt. 1 (Darmstadt: Wissenschaftliche Buchgesellschaft, 1975), pp. 114–115. John Buckler is the translator of all uncited quotations from foreign languages in Chapters 1–6.

SUGGESTED READING

Although late Egyptian history is still largely a specialist's field, K. A. Kitchen, *The Third Intermediate Period in Egypt* (1973), is a sturdy synthesis of the period from 1100 to 650 B.C. D. B. Redford, *Egypt, Canaan, and Israel in Ancient Times* (1992), is an excellent study of relations among the three states. D. O'Connor, *Ancient Nubia* (1994), which is well illustrated, gives the freshest treatment of that region and points to its importance in African developments. G. Herm, *The Phoenicians* (1975), treats Phoenician seafaring and commercial enterprises. Similarly, M. Gil, *A History of Palestine* (1997), provides the most recent treatment of that region.

The Jews have been one of the best-studied people in the ancient world, so the reader can easily find many good treatments of Jewish history and society. A rewarding approach is J. Bartlett, ed., *Archaeology and Biblical Interpretation* (1997). More general is W. R. F. Browning, ed., *Oxford Dictionary of the Bible* (1996), which is very rich in a variety of topics. Similar is R. S. Zwi Werblowsky and G. Wigoder, eds., *The Oxford Dictionary of the Jewish Religion* (1997). For the Jews in Egypt, two good studies have appeared: J. K. Hoffmeier, *Israel in Egypt* (1997), which discusses the evidence for the authenticity of the tradition concerning the Exodus; and J. Assmann, *Moses the Egyptian* (1997), which is a study in monotheism. A broader interpretation of Jewish religious developments can be found in S. Niditch, *Ancient Israelite Religion* (1997). G. Alon, *The Jews in Their Land* (1989), covers the Talmudic age. H. Shanks, ed., *The Rise of Ancient Israel* (1991), is a collection of papers that treat numerous aspects of the period. R. Tappy, *The Archaeology of Israelite Samaria* (1993), studies the archaeological remains of the period. S. Niditch, *War in the Hebrew Bible* (1992), addresses the ethics of violence in the Bible. H. W. Attridge, ed., *Of Scribes and Scrolls* (1990), gives a fascinating study of the Hebrew Bible and of Christian origins. Turning to politics, M. Smith, *Palestinian Parties and Politics That Shaped the Old Testament,* 2d ed. (1987), takes a practical look at events. W. D. Davis et al., *The Cambridge History of Judaism,* vol. 1 (1984), begins an important new synthesis with work on Judaism in the Persian period. R. Hachlili, *Ancient Jewish Art and Archaeology in the Land of Israel* (1988), attempts to trace the development and meaning of Jewish art in its archaeological context.

The Assyrians, despite their achievements, have not attracted the scholarly attention that other Near Eastern peoples have. Even though woefully outdated, A. T. Olmstead, *History of Assyria* (1928), has the merit of being soundly based in the original sources. H. W. F. Saggs, *Everyday Life in Babylonia and Assyria,* rev. ed. (1987), offers a general and well-illustrated survey of Mesopotamian history from 3000 to 300 B.C. M. T. Larsen, *The Conquest of Assyria* (1996), gives a fascinating account of the modern discovery of the Assyrians. Those who appreciate the vitality of Assyrian art should start with the masterful work of R. D. Barnett and W. Forman, *Assyrian Palace Reliefs,* 2d ed. (1970), an exemplary combination of fine photographs and learned, but not difficult, discussion.

A comprehensive survey of Persian history is given by one of the leading scholars in the field, R. N. Frye, *History of Ancient Iran* (1984). I. Gershevitch, ed., *The Cambridge History of Iran*, vol. 2 (1985), provides the reader with a full account of ancient Persian history, but many of the chapters are out of date. E. Herzfeld, *Iran in the Ancient East* (1987), puts Persian history in a broad context. Most welcome is M. A. Dandamaev, *A Political History of the Achaemenid Empire* (1989), which discusses in depth the history of the Persians and the organization of their empire. Finally, M. Boyce, a leading scholar in the field, provides a sound and readable treatment of the essence of Zoroastrianism in her *Zoroastrianism* (1979).

LISTENING TO THE PAST

The Covenant Between Yahweh and the Hebrews

These passages from the Hebrew Bible address two themes important to Hebraic thinking. The first is the meaning of kingship; the second is the nature of the Covenant between the Hebrews and the Lord, Yahweh. The selection also raises the difficult question of how much of the Hebrew Bible can be accepted historically. As we discussed in this chapter, the Hebrew Bible is not a document that we may accept as literal truth, but it does tell us a great deal about the people who created it. From the following passages we may discern what the Hebrews thought about their own past and religion.

The background of the excerpt is a political crisis that has some archaeological support. The war with the Philistines put a huge strain on Hebrew society. The passage below describes one such incident when Nahash, the king of the Ammonites, threatens to destroy the Hebrews. A new and effective political and military leadership was needed to meet the situation. The elders of the tribes had previously chosen judges to lead the community only in times of crisis. The Hebrews, however, demanded that a kingship be established, even though Yahweh was their king. They turned to Samuel, the last of the judges, who anointed Saul as the first Hebrew king. In this excerpt Samuel reviews the political, military, and religious situation confronting the Hebrews, reminding them of their obligation to honor the Covenant and expressing hesitation in naming a king.

Then Nahash the Ammonite came up and encamped against Jabeshgilead: and all the men of Jabesh said unto Nahash, Make a covenant with us, and we will serve thee. And Nahash the Ammonite answered them, On this condition will I make a covenant with you, that I may thrust out all your right eyes, and lay it for a reproach upon all Israel. And the elders of Jabesh said unto him, Give us seven days' respite, that we may send messengers unto all the coasts of Israel: and then, if there be no man to save us, we will come out to thee.

Then came the messengers to Gibeah of Saul, and told the tidings in the ears of the people: and all the people lifted up their voices, and wept. And, behold, Saul came after the herd out of the field; and Saul said, What aileth the people that they weep? And they told him the tidings of the men of Jabesh. And the Spirit of God came upon Saul when he heard those tidings, and his anger was kindled greatly. And he took a yoke of oxen, and hewed them in pieces, and sent them throughout all the coasts of Israel by the hands of messengers, saying, Whosoever cometh not forth after Saul and after Samuel, so shall it be done unto his oxen. And the fear of the Lord fell on the people, and they came out with one consent. And when he numbered them in Bezek, the children of Israel were three hundred thousand, and the men of Judah thirty thousand. And they said unto the messengers that came, Thus shall ye say unto the men of Jabeshgilead, To morrow, by that time the sun be hot, ye shall have help. And the messengers came and shewed it to the men of Jabesh; and they were glad. Therefore the men of Jabesh said, To morrow we will come out unto you, and ye shall do with us all that seemeth good unto you. And it was so on the morrow, that Saul put the people in three companies; and they came into the midst of the host in the morning watch, and slew the Ammonites until the heat of the day: and it came to pass, that they which remained were scattered, so that two of them were not left together.

And the people said unto Samuel, Who is he that said, Shall Saul reign over us? bring the men, that we may put them to death. And Saul said, There shall not a man be put to death this day: for to day the Lord hath wrought salvation in Israel. Then said Samuel to the people, Come, and let us go to Gilgal, and renew the kingdom there. And all the people went to Gilgal; and there they made Saul king before the Lord in Gilgal; and there they sacrificed sacrifices of peace offerings before the Lord; and there Saul and all the men of Israel rejoiced greatly.

And Samuel said unto all Israel, Behold, I have hearkened unto your voice in all that you said to me, and have made a king over you. And now, behold, the king walks before you; and I am old and

Balkan Peninsula of Greece their homeland. All that can now safely be said is that by about 1650 B.C. Greeks had established themselves at the great city of Mycenae in the Peloponnesus and elsewhere in Greece. Before then, the area from Thessaly in the north to Messenia in the south was inhabited by small farming communities. Quite probably the Greeks merged with these natives, and from that union emerged the society that modern scholars call "Mycenaean," after Mycenae, the most important site of this new Greek-speaking culture.

Of this epoch later Greeks themselves remembered almost nothing. The *Iliad* and the *Odyssey,* Homer's magnificent epic poems (eighth century B.C.), retain some dim memory of this period but very little that is authentic. One of the sterling achievements of modern archaeology is the discovery of this lost past. In the nineteenth century Heinrich Schliemann, a German businessman, fell in love with the *Iliad* and decided to find the sites it mentioned. He excavated Troy in modern Turkey, Mycenae, and several other sites in Greece to discover the lost past of the Greek people. At the beginning of the twentieth century, the English archaeologist Sir Arthur Evans uncovered the remains of an entirely unknown civilization at Cnossus in Crete, and he gave it the name "Minoan" after the mythical Cretan king Minos. Scholars since then have further illuminated this long-lost era, and despite many uncertainties a reasonably clear picture of the Minoans and Mycenaeans has begun to emerge.

By about 1650 B.C. the island of Crete was the home of the flourishing and vibrant Minoan culture. The Minoans had occupied Crete from at least the Neolithic period. They had also developed a script, now called "Linear A" (and yet to be deciphered), to express their language in writing. Because Linear A is still a riddle, it is as yet worthless to historians as a literary source and can provide no information on the status of men and women in society and politics or any idea of the course of Minoan history. Only archaeology and art offer clues to Minoan life. The symbol of Minoan culture was the palace. Around 1650 B.C. Crete was dotted with palaces, such as those at Mallia on the northern coast and Kato Zakro on the eastern tip of the island. Towering above all others in importance was the palace at Cnossus. The palace was the political and economic center of Minoan society, which, like many ancient Near Eastern societies, was rigorously controlled from above. Few specifics are known about Minoan society except that at its head stood a king and his nobles, who governed the lives and toil of Crete's farmers, sailors, shepherds, and artisans. The implements of the Minoans, like those of the Mycenaeans, were bronze, so archaeologists have named this period the "Bronze Age." Minoan society was wealthy and, to judge from the absence of fortifications on the island, peaceful. Enthusiastic sailors and merchants, the Minoans traded with Egypt and the cities of the Levant, the area known today as the Middle East. Their ships also penetrated the Aegean Sea, throughout which they established trading posts. Their voyages in this direction brought them into contact with the Mycenaeans on the Greek peninsula.

MAP 3.1 Ancient Greece In antiquity the home of the Greeks included the islands of the Aegean and the western shore of Turkey as well as the Greek peninsula itself.

By about 1650 B.C. Greek-speakers were firmly settled at Mycenae, which became a major city and trading center. Later, other Mycenaean palaces and cities developed at Thebes, Athens, Tiryns, and Pylos. As in Crete, the political unit was the kingdom. The king and his warrior aristocracy stood at the top of society. The seat and symbol of the king's power and wealth was his palace, which was also the economic center of the kingdom. Within its walls royal craftsmen fashioned jewelry and rich ornaments, made and decorated fine pottery, forged weapons, prepared hides and wool for clothing, and manufactured the other goods needed by the king and his retainers. Palace scribes kept records in Greek with a script known as "Linear B," which was derived from Minoan Linear A. The scribes kept account of taxes and drew up inventories of the king's possessions. From the palace, as at Cnossus, the Mycenaean king directed the lives of his subjects. Little is known of the king's subjects except that they were the artisans, traders, and farmers of Mycenaean society. The Mycenaean economy was marked by an extensive division of labor, all tightly controlled from the palace. At the bottom of the social scale were the slaves, who were normally owned by the king and aristocrats but who also worked for ordinary craftsmen.

The Linear B tablets also held a surprise for those interested in Greek religion. Some of them recorded offerings to deities such as Zeus, Apollo, and Athena, the traditional Olympian gods. As late as 1995 Greek archaeologists in Thebes discovered over two hundred new Linear B tablets that are as yet unpublished. The excavators were gracious enough to allow foreign scholars to examine them before publication. These tablets, as well as those already known, prove that the Greeks

Minoan Naval Scene This fresco, discovered at Thera, probably depicts the homecoming of a Minoan fleet of warships. Though later Greeks thought that the Minoans had ruled the sea, fleets such as the one pictured here probably protected Minoan maritime interests and suppressed piracy. Despite its military nature, the scene displays a general air of festivity, characteristic of Minoan art. *(National Archaeological Museum, Athens/Ekdotike Athenon)*

brought their traditional deities with them on their journey to Greece.

Contacts between the Minoans and Mycenaeans were originally peaceful, and Minoan culture flooded the Greek mainland. But around 1450 B.C. the Mycenaeans attacked Crete, destroying many Minoan palaces and taking possession of the grand palace at Cnossus. For about the next fifty years the Mycenaeans ruled much of the island until a further wave of violence left Cnossus in ashes. These events are more disputed than understood, and the fate of Cnossus in particular has sparked controversy. Theories that Cnossus was destroyed by natural catastrophe have long since been disproved. Without a doubt, human beings were responsible for the conflagration. Archaeologists cannot, however, determine who was responsible—whether the Mycenaeans at Cnossus were attacked by other Mycenaeans or whether the conquered Minoans rose in revolt.

Whatever the answer, the Mycenaean kingdoms in Greece benefited from the fall of Cnossus and the collapse of its trade. Mycenaean commerce quickly expanded throughout the Aegean, reaching as far abroad as Anatolia, Cyprus, and Egypt. Throughout central and southern Greece Mycenaean culture flourished as never before. Palaces became grander, and citadels were often protected by mammoth stone walls. Prosperity, however, did not bring peace, and between 1300 and 1000 B.C. kingdom after kingdom suffered attack and destruction.

Later Greeks accused the Dorians, who spoke a particular dialect of Greek, of overthrowing the Mycenaean kingdoms. Yet some modern linguists argue that the Dorians dwelt in Greece during the Mycenaean period. Archaeologists generally conclude that the Dorians, if not already present, could have entered Greece only long after the era of destruction. Furthermore, not one alien artifact has been found on any of these sites; thus there is no archaeological evidence for outside invaders. Normally, foreign invaders leave traces of themselves—for example, broken pottery and weapons—that are different from those of the attacked.

PERIODS OF GREEK HISTORY

Period	Significant Events	Major Writers
Bronze Age **2000–1100 B.C.**	Arrival of the Greeks in Greece Rise and fall of the Mycenaean kingdoms	
Dark Age **1100–800 B.C.**	Greek migrations within the Aegean basin Social and political recovery Evolution of the polis Rebirth of literacy	Homer Hesiod
Lyric Age **800–500 B.C.**	Rise of Sparta and Athens Colonization of the Mediterranean basin Flowering of lyric poetry Development of philosophy and science in Ionia	Archilochus Sappho Tyrtaeus Solon Anaximander Heraclitus
Classical Period **500–338 B.C.**	Persian wars Growth of the Athenian Empire Peloponnesian War Rise of drama and historical writing Flowering of Greek philosophy Spartan and Theban hegemonies Conquest of Greece by Philip of Macedon	Herodotus Thucydides Aeschylus Sophocles Euripides Aristophanes Plato Aristotle

We can conclude, therefore, that no outside intrusion destroyed the Mycenaean world. In fact, the legends preserved by later Greeks told of grim wars between Mycenaean kingdoms and of the fall of great royal families. Apparently Mycenaean Greece destroyed itself in a long series of internecine wars, a pattern that later Greeks would repeat.

The fall of the Mycenaean kingdoms ushered in a period of such poverty, disruption, and backwardness that historians usually call it the "Dark Age" of Greece (ca 1100–800 B.C.). Even literacy, which was not widespread in any case, was a casualty of the chaos. Nonetheless, the Greeks survived the storm to preserve their culture and civilization. Greece remained Greek; nothing essential was swept away. Greek religious cults remained vital to the people, and basic elements of social organization continued to function effectively. It was a time of change and challenge, but not of utter collapse.

This period also saw a development of enormous importance for the course of Western civilization. The disruption of Mycenaean societies caused the widespread movement of Greek peoples. Some Greeks sailed to Crete, where they established new communities. The most important line of immigration was east to the shores of Asia Minor. The Greeks arrived during a time when the traditional states and empires had collapsed. Economic hardship was common, and various peoples wandered for years. The age saw both the displacement of peoples throughout the region and ethnic intermixing. Whereas the Sea Peoples (see page 31) had eventually dissolved into their various parts and gone their separate ways, the Greeks spread the culture of their homeland throughout the eastern Mediterranean.

Upon landing in Asia Minor, the Greeks encountered peoples who had been influenced by the older cultures of the region. Furthermore, the Greeks themselves had had long associations with these peoples. Thus they were hardly strangers, nor was Greek culture alien or unknown to the natives. By the end of the Dark Age of Greece, the Greeks had established a string of settlements along a coast already accustomed to them. Their arrival resulted in the spread of Greek culture throughout the area, not through force of arms but because of its freedom of ideas, the right of individuals to express them, and the vitality of Greek social life.

Homer, Hesiod, and the Heroic Past (1100–800 B.C.)

The Greeks, unlike the Hebrews, had no sacred book that chronicled their past. Instead they had Homer's *Iliad* and *Odyssey* to describe a time when gods still walked the earth. And they learned the origin and descent of the gods from the *Theogony,* an epic poem by Hesiod. Instead of authentic history, the poems of Homer and Hesiod offered the Greeks an ideal past, a largely legendary Heroic Age. In terms of pure history these poems contain scraps of information about the Bronze Age, much about the early Dark Age, and some about the poets' own era. Chronologically, then, the Heroic Age falls mainly in the period between the collapse of the Mycenaean world and the rebirth of literacy.

The *Iliad* recounts an expedition of Mycenaeans, whom Homer called "Achaeans," to besiege the city of Troy in Asia Minor. The heart of the *Iliad*, however, concerns the quarrel between Agamemnon, the king of Mycenae, and Achilles, the tragic hero of the poem, and how their quarrel brought suffering to the Achaeans. Only when Achilles put away his anger and pride did he consent to come forward, face, and kill the Trojan hero Hector. The *Odyssey*, probably composed later than the *Iliad,* narrates the adventures of Odysseus, one of the Achaean heroes who fought at Troy, during his voyage home from the fighting.

The splendor of these poems does not lie in their plots, although the *Odyssey* is a marvelous adventure story. Rather, both poems portray engaging but often flawed characters who are larger than life and yet typically human. Homer was also strikingly successful in depicting the great gods, who generally sit on Mount Olympus and watch the fighting at Troy like spectators at a baseball game, although they sometimes participate in the action. Homer's deities are reminiscent of Mesopotamian gods and goddesses. Hardly a decorous lot, the Olympians are raucous, petty, deceitful, and splendid. In short, they are human.

Homer at times portrayed the gods in a serious vein, but he never treated them in a systematic fashion, as did Hesiod, who lived somewhat later than Homer. Hesiod's epic poem the *Theogony* traces the descent of Zeus. Hesiod was influenced by Mesopotamian myths, which the Hittites had adopted and spread to the Aegean. Hesiod's poem claims that in the beginning there was chaos, the "yawning deep." From chaos came Gaea (Earth), who gave birth to Uranus (Heaven). Gaea and Uranus then gave birth to Cronus and Ocean (the deep-swelling waters). Cronus, the son of Earth and Heaven, like the Mesopotamian Enlil, separated the two and became king of the gods.

Like the Hebrews, Hesiod envisaged his cosmogony—his account of the way the universe developed—in moral terms. Zeus, the son of Cronus, defeated his evil father and took his place as king of the gods. He then sired Lawfulness, Right, Peace, and other powers of light and beauty. Thus, in Hesiod's conception, Zeus was the god of righteousness, who loved justice and hated wrongdoing.

In another epic poem, *Works and Days*, Hesiod wrote of his own time and his own village of Ascra in Boeotia, a scenic place set between beautiful mountains and fertile plains. In his will, Hesiod's father had divided his lands between Hesiod and his brother, Perses. Perses bribed the aristocratic authorities to give him the larger part of the inheritance and then squandered his wealth. Undaunted by the injustice of the powerful, Hesiod thundered back:

Bribe-devouring lords, make straight your decisions,
Forget entirely crooked judgments.
He who causes evil to another harms himself.
Evil designs are most evil to the plotter.[2]

The similarities are striking between the fictional Khunanup and Hesiod, both of whom were oppressed by the rich and powerful. Yet the differences are even more significant. Hesiod, unlike Khunanup, did not receive justice from the political authorities of the day, but he fully expected divine vindication. Hesiod's call for justice has gone ringing through the centuries, its appeal as fresh today as when he first uttered it more than two millennia ago. Hesiod spoke of Zeus as Jeremiah had spoken of Yahweh, warning that Zeus would see that justice was done and injustice punished. He cautioned his readers that Zeus was angered by those who committed adultery, harmed orphans, and offended the aged. Hesiod's ethical concepts and faith in divine justice were the products of his belief that the world was governed by the power of good.

Polis of Argos This view of modern Argos remarkably illustrates the structure of an ancient polis. Atop the hill in the background are the remains of the ancient acropolis. At its foot to the right are foundations of ancient public and private buildings, spreading beyond which are modern houses, situated where ancient houses were located. The trees and cut grain in the foreground were also major features of the *chora,* the agricultural basis of the polis. *(John Buckler)*

 THE POLIS

After the upheavals that ended the Mycenaean period and the slow recovery of prosperity during the Dark Age, the Greeks developed their basic political and institutional unit, the *polis.* The term *polis* is generally interpreted as "city-state," one of the worst possible translations of a word that is basically untranslatable. Despite its defects, however, *city-state* is at least a term generally understood and accepted. Two problems arise in an attempt to understand the polis. The first is how it developed, and the second is what it was. Even the Greeks took the polis for granted. Although they remembered a time when kings ruled over many parts of Greece, they did not know how the polis evolved from those legendary kingdoms. In his *Politics* (1.1.9) Aristotle describes the growth of the polis in terms that are as biological as they are political. For example, he states that "man is by nature a being of the polis." He means that people developed the polis as naturally as plants and animals themselves develop. The biological analogy is wrong, but the concept of political evolution is largely correct.

Recent archaeological expeditions and careful study have done much to clarify the origins of the polis. Even during the late Mycenaean period, towns had grown up around palaces. These towns and even smaller villages performed basically local functions. The first was to administer the ordinary political affairs of the community. The village also served a religious purpose in that no matter how small, each had its local cult to its own deity. The exchange of daily goods made these towns and villages economically important, if only on a small scale. These settlements also developed a social system that was particularly their own. They likewise had their own views of the social worth and status of their inhabitants and the nature of their public responsibilities. In short, they relied on custom and mutual agreement to direct their ordinary affairs.

When tumult overwhelmed the Mycenaean kingdoms, these towns and villages survived. The traditional aristocracy was intact, but at first it was somewhat weakened. Yet the concepts of community and membership in it endured, and in these ideas the polis took root. The basic concepts were kinship and a feeling that all people in the community were physically and socially related. In addition, the people all shared a common religion in which all participated. There was already a sense of union between people and the land. This relationship is sometimes difficult for the contemporary American to appreciate, owing to our mobility and ease of communication. Yet to these Greeks the land was a vital part of their heritage and their lives.

The coming of the Dorians did not significantly change this political evolution, but it had two effects. In some cases it disrupted the task of rebuilding and consolidating some of these developing communities. The Dorians at times carved out territory for themselves at the expense of the natives, but they also assimilated the culture around them. This process actually strengthened the sense of identity among the local people. The situation could have been cataclysmic, but for the most part it was not. The native inhabitants acknowledged their differences with the newcomers. They maintained their traditional religion, albeit sometimes in altered form, but they also accepted the religious validity of new cults. In addition, they looked upon the Dorians as fellow Greeks. Recent archaeological and historical studies reveal a picture of continuity and assimilation. The newcomers did not hinder the evolution of the polis; instead they readily embraced the new political and social structure.

When fully developed, each polis normally shared a surprisingly large number of features with other poleis. Physically a polis was a society of people who lived in a city *(asty)* and cultivated the surrounding countryside *(chora)*. The city's water supply came from public fountains, springs, and cisterns. By the fifth century B.C. the city was generally surrounded by a wall. The city contained a point, usually elevated, called the *acropolis* and a public square or marketplace called the *agora*. On the acropolis, which in the early period was a place of refuge, stood the temples, altars, public monuments, and various dedications to the gods of the polis. The agora was originally the place where the warrior assembly met, but it became the political center of the polis. In the agora were porticoes, shops, and public buildings and courts.

Until quite recently most scholars have concentrated their attention on the city. This focus is understandable, for the city was so adorned with monuments that it still inspires the imagination. The city provides a wealth of evidence on urban planning and daily life, and often yields public documents that illustrate the actual functioning of the polis. Nevertheless, the countryside was vital to the city and the polis in general for a variety of reasons. Previous pictures of life there depict a scene that is dull and backward: nothing happened in the country. Reality was very different. The traditional view overlooks the vitality and the basic importance of the village. The primary significance of the village and its surroundings was that it fed the city. Whether the village was a farming or a fishing community, it provided the basic resources that nurtured the city. This relationship united the village with the city in an indivisible unit.

A previously unappreciated aspect of the countryside was its religious significance. Today people normally think first of the great religious festivals celebrated in the city. Although they were indeed important, most Greek religious practices were rooted in the country. The sanctuaries there were a reflection of the cults of the deities that nurtured the polis. The sanctuaries themselves and the religious rites connected with them were means of appealing to the gods to protect the crops, animals, and people who depended on the earth for survival. The sanctuaries and other religious sites on the borders of the polis linked country and city dwellers in one religious unit. They also served as sources of identification of the polis in that sacred buildings, shrines, and altars were the physical symbols of a particular people, no matter where in the polis they lived. The religious dedications in them were the possessions not only of the gods but also of the polis itself. The permanent dedications made to the gods reflected the power and prestige of the polis.

The size of the polis varied according to geographical circumstances. Population figures for Greece are mostly guesswork, because most city-states were too small to need a census. The philosopher Plato thought that five thousand citizens constituted the ideal population of a polis. The intimacy of the polis was an important factor, one that is hard for modern city dwellers to imagine. The small population enabled Greeks to see how the in-

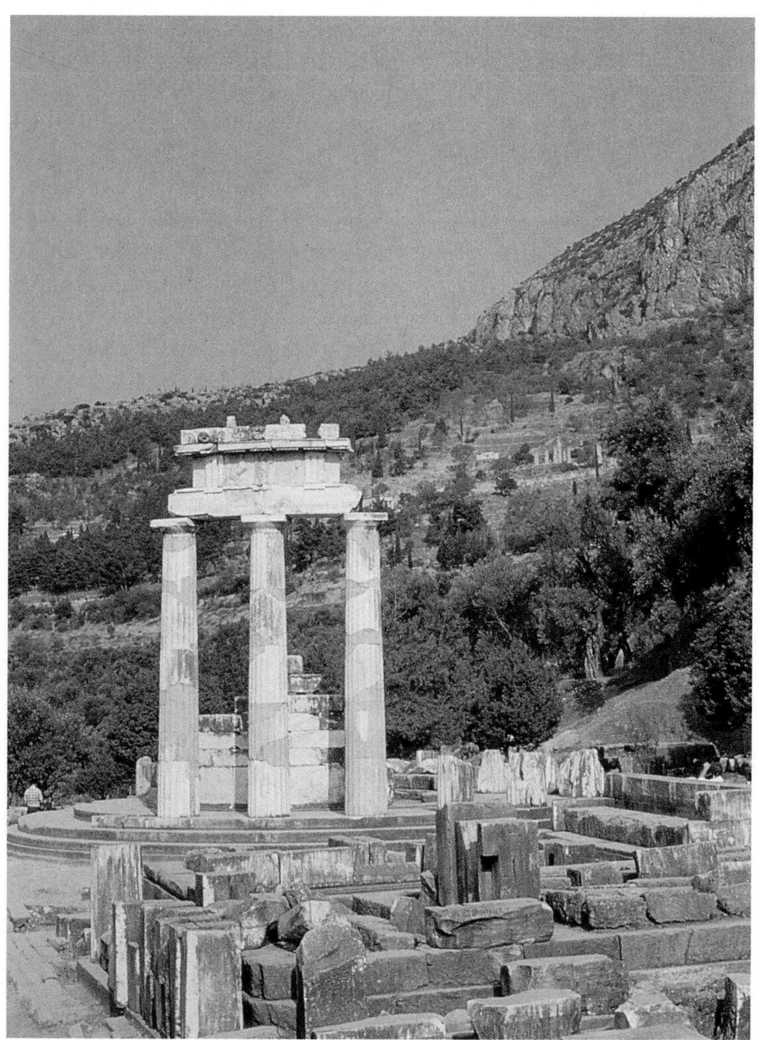

The Delphic Oracle The Marmaria, the sanctuary of Athena, is seen here against the backdrop of the mountains that surround the sanctuary of Apollo. Around the oracle clustered many temples to various deities, shrines, and other sacred buildings, all of them in a remote mountainous area especially chosen by Apollo to be his home and the place where he answered the supplications of the faithful. *(John Buckler)*

dividual fitted into the overall system—how the human parts made up the social whole.

The average polis did not have a standing army. Instead it relied on its citizens for protection. Very rich citizens often served as cavalry, which was, however, never as important as the heavily armed infantry, or *hoplites*. These were the backbone of the army. They wore metal helmets and body armor, carried heavy, round shields, and armed themselves with spears and swords. They provided their own equipment and were basically amateurs. In the classical period (ca 500–338 B.C.) they were generally wealthy landowners who were accustomed to outdoor labor. When in battle, they stood in several dense lines, in which cohesion and order became as valuable as courage. This effort also gave them a sense of comradeship and pride. Poor men made up the lightly armed infantry. Usually wielding only a javelin or two, they used their mobility in rough areas to harass hoplites. In some instances the citizens of a polis hired mercenaries to fight their battles. Mercenaries were expensive, untrustworthy, and willing to defect to a higher bidder. Even worse they sometimes seized control over the polis that had hired them.

Regardless of its size or wealth, the polis was fundamental to Greek life. The polis was far more than a political institution. Above all it was a community of citizens, and the affairs of the community were the concern of all. The customs of the community were at the same time the laws of the polis. Rome later created a single magnificent body of law, but the Greeks had as many law codes as they had city-states. Though the laws of one polis might be roughly similar to those of another, the law of any given polis was unique simply because the customs and the experience of each one had been unique.

The polis could be governed in any of several ways. First, it could be a *monarchy,* a term derived from the Greek for "the rule of one man." A king could represent the community, reigning according to law and respecting the rights of the citizens. Second, the *aristocracy* could govern the state. Third, the running of the polis could be the duty and prerogative of an *oligarchy,* which literally means "the rule of a few"—in this case a small group of wealthy citizens not necessarily of aristocratic birth. Or the polis could be governed as a *democracy,* through the rule of the people, a concept that in Greece meant that all citizens, without respect to birth or wealth, administered the workings of government. How a polis was governed depended on who had the upper hand. When the wealthy held power, they usually instituted oligarchies; when the people could break the hold of the rich, they established democracies. In any case no polis ever had an ironclad, unchangeable constitution. Still another form of Greek government was *tyranny.* Under tyranny the polis was ruled by a tyrant, a man who had seized power by unconstitutional means, generally by using his wealth to gain a political following that could topple the existing government.

The political structure of the polis was so flexible that it can be described but not precisely defined. The polis of Sparta was a collection of villages lacking a single, central city. By contrast Olynthus and Thebes, in northern and central Greece, respectively, were logically planned urban sites, with the city being the political focus of the community. Although the acropolis was planned, the asty developed somewhat haphazardly as the community prospered and grew. Corinth flourished because of its geographical and maritime advantages. It differed from the other poleis because it did not depend on the countryside for its economic health. The one thing that links all of these prominent city-states is that they all believed that the people made the polis.

Ironically, the very integration of the polis proved to be one of its weaknesses. Because the bonds that held the polis together were so intimate, Greeks were extremely reluctant to allow foreigners to share fully in its life. An alien, even someone Greek by birth, could almost never expect to be made a citizen. Nor could women play a political role. Women participated in the civic cults and served as priestesses, but the polis had no room for them in state affairs. Thus the exclusiveness of the polis doomed it to a limited horizon.

Although each polis was normally jealous of its independence, some Greeks banded together to create leagues of city-states. Here was the birth of Greek federalism, a political system in which several states formed a central government while remaining independent in their internal affairs. United in a league, a confederation of city-states was far stronger than any of its individual members and better able to withstand external attack.

Yet even federalism could not overcome the passionate individualism of the polis, which proved to be a serious weakness. The citizens of each polis were determined to remain free and autonomous. Rarely were the Greeks willing to unite in larger political bodies. The political result in Greece, as in Sumer, was almost constant warfare. The polis could dominate, but unlike Rome it could not incorporate.

The Lyric Age (800–500 B.C.)

The maturation of the polis coincided with one of the most vibrant periods of Greek history, an era of extraordinary expansion geographically, artistically, and politically. Greeks ventured as far east as the Black Sea and as far west as Spain (Map 3.2). With the rebirth of literacy, this period also witnessed a tremendous literary flowering as poets broke away from the heroic tradition and wrote about their own lives. Politically these were the years when Sparta and Athens—the two poles of the Greek experience—rose to prominence.

Overseas Expansion

During the years 1100–800 B.C. the Greeks not only recovered from the breakdown of the Mycenaean world but also grew in wealth and numbers. This new prosperity brought with it new problems. Greece is a small and not especially fertile country. The increase in population meant that many men and their families had very little land or none at all. Land hunger and the resulting social and political tensions drove many Greeks to seek new homes outside of Greece. Other factors, largely intangible, played their part as well: the desire for a new start, a love of excitement and adventure, and natural curiosity about what lay beyond the horizon.

MAP 3.2 Colonization of the Mediterranean Though the Greeks and Phoenicians colonized the Mediterranean basin at about the same time, the Greeks spread much farther.

The Mediterranean offered the Greeks an escape valve, for they were always a seafaring people. To them the sea was a highway, not a barrier. Through their commercial ventures they had long been familiar with the rich areas of the western Mediterranean. Moreover, the geography of the Mediterranean basin favored colonization. The land and climate of the Mediterranean region are remarkably uniform. Greeks could travel to new areas, whether to Cyprus in the east or to Malta in the west, and establish the kind of settlement they had known in Greece. They could also raise the same crops they had raised in Greece. The move to a new home was not a plunge into totally unknown conditions. Once the colonists had established themselves in new homes, they continued life essentially as in Greece.

From about 750 to 550 B.C., Greeks from the mainland and Asia Minor traveled throughout the Mediterranean and even into the Atlantic Ocean in their quest for new land. They sailed in the greatest numbers to Sicily and southern Italy, where there was ample space for expansion. They also sailed farther west to Sardinia, southern France and Spain, and even the Canary Islands. In Sicily they found the Sicels, who had already adopted many Carthaginian customs, including a nascent urban culture. Fiercely independent, they greeted the coming of the Greeks just as they had the arrival of the Carthaginians. They welcomed Greek culture but not Greek demands for their land. Nonetheless, the two peoples made a somewhat uneasy accommodation. There was enough land in Sicily for Greeks and Sicels alike, so both flourished, albeit not always peacefully.

In southern Italy the Greeks encountered a number of Indo-European peoples. They were for the most part rural and enjoyed few material comforts. Some of their villages were evolving into towns, but in the mountains looser tribal units prevailed. They both welcomed Greek culture, and the Greeks found it easy to establish prosperous cities without facing significant local hostility.

Some adventurous Greeks sailed to Sardinia and the southern coast of modern France. In Sardinia they established outposts that were originally trading stations, meant primarily for bartering with the natives. Commerce was so successful that some Greeks established permanent towns there. Greek influence, in terms of physical remains and the ideas that they reflect, was far stronger on the island than was recognized even a few years ago. From these new outposts Greek influence extended to southern France. The modern city of Marseilles began as a Greek colony and later sent settlers to southern Spain.

One of the most remarkable aspects of the sense of adventure of the Greeks is seen from their remains on the Canary Islands in the Atlantic Ocean. Their settlements on some of the islands took their culture beyond the Mediterranean for the first time. The presence of these pioneers widened the geographical and intellectual horizons of the Greek world. In the process, the Greeks of the Canary Islands introduced their culture to a part of Africa that had not even heard of them. This era of colonization not only spread Greek settlers over much of the western Mediterranean and beyond, but also passed on the Hellenic legacy to the rest of the Mediterranean and even to a part of western Africa.

Colonization changed the entire Greek world, both at home and abroad. When the Greeks came into contact with other peoples, they encountered new ideas and customs. They also established new economic links. As the eminent German scholar Walter Burkert has recently demonstrated, the Greeks grafted some foreign ideas and artistic styles from the Near East and Egypt onto their own culture. In vase painting the Greeks began to decorate their pots with exotic monsters derived from Eastern models, but they did so on existing types of vases. Something similar occurred with sculpture. The Egyptians had a long tradition of carving statues of people in a stylized position. The Greeks adapted that style to their own tradition of sculpture that blended realism and idealism. They then spread their increasingly cosmopolitan art and culture beyond the Aegean to Italy and Carthage in the west.

In economic terms the expansion of the Greeks created a much larger market for agricultural and manu-

Greek Influence Abroad This stunning gold comb is a remarkable combination of Greek and eastern details. The art is almost purely Greek. The mounted horseman is clothed with largely Greek armor, but he attacks an eastern enemy. The horseman's companion is also eastern. This splendid piece of art testifies to the exchange of artistic motifs and styles in the eastern Mediterranean basin. *(Hermitage, Leningrad)*

factured goods. From the east, especially from the northern coast of the Black Sea, came wheat in a volume beyond the capacity of Greek soil. In return flowed Greek wine and olive oil, which could not be produced in the harsher climate of the north. Greek-manufactured goods, notably rich jewelry and fine pottery, circulated from southern Russia to Spain. During this same period the Greeks adopted the custom of minting coins, which they apparently imported from Lydia. At first coinage was of little economic importance, and only later did it replace the common practice of barter. In the barter system one person simply exchanges one good for another without the use of money. Each person decides the value of the goods traded. Even today, especially in the backcountry of Greece, a surprisingly large number of economic transactions are done by barter. Thus Greek culture and economics, fertilized by the influences of other societies, spread throughout the Mediterranean basin.

Colonization presented the polis with a huge challenge, for it required organization and planning on an unprecedented scale. The colonizing city, called the *metropolis,* or mother city, first decided where to establish the colony, how to transport colonists to the site, and who would sail. Then the metropolis collected and stored the supplies that the colonists would need both to feed themselves and to plant their first crop. The metropolis also had to provide adequate shipping for the voyage. All preparations ready, a leader, called an *oikist*, ordered the colonists to sail. The oikist was then in full command of the band until the colony was established in its new site and capable of running its own affairs. A significant aspect of colonizing ventures was that colonists sailed as equals, and as equals they set about building a new life together.

Once the colonists landed, the oikist laid out the new polis, selected the sites of temples and public buildings, and established the government. Then he surrendered power to the new leaders. The colony was thereafter independent of the metropolis. For the Greeks, colonization had two important aspects. First, it demanded that the polis assume a much greater public function than ever before, thus strengthening the city-state's institutional position. Second, colonization spread the polis and its values far beyond the shores of Greece. Even more important, colonization on this scale had a profound impact on the course of Western civilization. It meant that the prevailing culture of the Mediterranean basin would be Greek, the heritage to which Rome would later fall heir.

One man can in many ways stand as the symbol of the vital and robust era of colonization. Archilochus, the bastard son of an aristocrat, was born on the island of Paros. He knew that because of his illegitimacy he would never inherit his father's land, and this knowledge seems to have made him self-reliant. He was also a poet of genius, the first of the lyric poets who left an indelible mark on this age. Unlike the epic poets, who portrayed the deeds of heroes, Archilochus sang of himself. He knew the sea, the dangers of sailing, and the price that the sea often exacted. He spoke of one shipwreck in grim terms and even treated the god of the sea with irony: "Of fifty men gentle Poseidon left one, Koiranos, to be saved from shipwreck."

Together with others from Paros he took part in the colonization of Thasos in the northern Aegean. He described the island in less than glowing terms: "Like the spine of an ass it stands, crowned to the brim with a wild forest." His opinion of his fellow colonists was hardly kinder: "So the misery of all Greece came together in Thasos." Yet at Thasos he fell in love with a woman named Neoboule. They did not marry because her father opposed the match. In revenge, Archilochus seduced Neoboule's younger sister, railed at the entire family, and left Thasos to live the life of a mercenary.

His hired lance took him to Euboea, and he left a striking picture of the fighting there:

Not many bows will be strung, nor slings be slung
When Ares begins battle in the plain.
There will be the mournful work of the sword:
For in this kind of battle are the spear-famed
Lords of Euboea experienced.[3]

Archilochus exemplifies the energy, restlessness, self-reliance, and sense of adventure that characterized this epoch. People like him broke old ties, faced homelessness and danger, and built new homes for themselves. They made the Mediterranean Greek.

Lyric Poets

Archilochus the colonist and adventurer is not nearly as important as Archilochus the lyric poet, whose individualism set a new tone in Greek literature. For the first time in Western civilization, men and women began to write of their own experiences. Their poetry reflected their belief that they had something precious to say about themselves. To them poetry did not belong only to the gods or to the great heroes on the plain of Troy. Some lyric poets used their literary talents for the good of their city-states. They stood forth as individuals and in their poetry urged their countrymen to be patriotic and just.

One of the most unforgettable of these writers is the poet Sappho. Unlike Archilochus, she neither braved the wilds nor pushed into the unknown, yet she was no less individual than he. Sappho was born in the seventh century B.C. on the island of Lesbos, a place of sun, sea, and rustic beauty. Her marriage produced a daughter, to whom she wrote some of her poems. Sappho's poetry is personal and intense. She delighted in her surroundings, which were those of aristocratic women, and celebrated the little things around her. Hers was a world of natural beauty, sacred groves, religious festivals, wedding celebrations, and noble companions. Sappho fondly remembers walks with a woman friend:

How we went to every hill, brook,
And holy place, and when early spring
Filled the woods with noises of birds
And a choir of nightingales—we two
In solitude were wandering there.[4]

Sappho is best known for erotic poetry, for she expressed her love frankly and without shame. She was bisexual, and much of her poetry deals with her homosexual love affairs. In one of her poems she remembers the words of her lover:

Sappho, if you do not come out,
I swear, I will love you no more.
O rise and free your lovely strength
From the bed and shine upon us.
Lifting off your Chian nightgown, and
Like a pure lily by a spring,
Bathe in the water.[5]

In antiquity Sappho's name became linked with female homosexual love. Today the English word *lesbian* is derived from Sappho's island home. The Greeks accepted bisexuality—that men and women could enjoy both homosexual and heterosexual lovemaking. Homosexual relationships normally carried no social stigma. In her mature years Sappho was courted by a younger man who wanted to marry her. By then she had already proclaimed her love for several girls, yet the young man was not troubled by these affairs. As it turned out, Sappho refused to marry because she was past childbearing age.

In their poetry Archilochus and Sappho reveal two sides of Greek life in this period. Archilochus exemplifies the energy and adventure of the age, while Sappho expresses the intensely personal side of life. The link connecting the two poets is their individualism, their faith in themselves, and their desire to reach out to other men and women in order to share their experiences, thoughts, and wisdom.

The Growth of Sparta

During the Lyric Age the Spartans expanded the boundaries of their polis and made it the leading power in Greece. Like other Greeks, the Spartans faced the problems of overpopulation and land hunger. Unlike other Greeks, the Spartans solved these problems by conquest, not by colonization. To gain more land the Spartans set out in about 735 B.C. to conquer Messenia, a rich, fertile region in the southwestern Peloponnesus. This conflict, the First Messenian War, lasted for twenty years and ended in a Spartan triumph. The Spartans appropriated Messenian land and turned the Messenians into *helots,* or state serfs.

In about 650 B.C. Spartan exploitation and oppression of the Messenian helots led to a helot revolt so massive and stubborn that it became known as the Second Messenian War. The Spartan poet Tyrtaeus, a contemporary of these events, vividly portrays the ferocity of the fighting:

For it is a shameful thing indeed
When with the foremost fighters
An elder falling in front of the young men
Lies outstretched,
Having white hair and grey beard,
Breathing forth his stout soul in the dust,
Holding in his hands his genitals
stained with blood.[6]

Confronted with such horrors, Spartan enthusiasm for the war waned. Finally, after some thirty years of fighting, the Spartans put down the revolt. Nevertheless, the political and social strain it caused led to a transformation of the Spartan polis.

It took the full might of the Spartan people, aristocrat and commoner alike, to win the Second Messenian War. After the victory the non-nobles, who had done much of the fighting, demanded rights equal to those of the nobility. They had taken their place in the battle line next to their aristocratic neighbors but lacked the social prestige and political rights of their noble companions. The agitation of these non-nobles disrupted society until the aristocrats agreed to remodel the state.

Spartan Hoplite This splendid bronze figurine portrays a Spartan hoplite, a heavily armed soldier, as seen about to strike an enemy. His massive bronze helmet with its full crest gives his head nearly complete protection, while a bronze corselet covers his chest and back and greaves protect his shins. In his right hand he carries a thrusting spear and in his left a large round shield. Hoplites were the backbone of all Greek armies. *(Staatliche Museen zu Berlin/Bildarchiv Preussischer Kulturbesitz)*

The "Lycurgan regimen," as these reforms were called after a legendary lawgiver, was a new political, economic, and social system. Political distinctions among the Spartans were eliminated, and all citizens became legally equal. Actual governance of the polis was in the hands of two kings, who were primarily military leaders. The kings and twenty-eight elders made up a council that deliberated on foreign and domestic matters and prepared legislation for the assembly, which consisted of all Spartan citizens. The real executive power of the polis was in the hands of five *ephors,* or overseers, elected from and by all the people. In effect the Lycurgan regime did nothing more than broaden the aristocracy, while at the same time setting limits on its size. Social mobility was for the most part abolished, and instead an aristocratic warrior class governed the polis.

To provide for their economic needs the Spartans divided the land of Messenia among all citizens. Helots worked the land, raised the crops, provided the Spartans with their living, and occasionally served in the army. The Spartans kept the helots in line by means of systematic terrorism, hoping to beat them down and keep them quiet. Spartan citizens were supposed to devote their time exclusively to military training.

In the Lycurgan system every citizen owed primary allegiance to Sparta. Suppression of the individual together with emphasis on military prowess led to a barracks state. Family life itself was sacrificed to the polis. Once Spartan boys reached the age of twelve, they were enrolled in separate companies with other boys their age. They slept outside on reed mats and underwent rugged physical and military training until age twenty-four, when they became frontline soldiers. For the rest of their lives, Spartan men kept themselves prepared for combat. Their military training never ceased, and the older men were expected to be models of endurance, frugality, and sturdiness to the younger men. In battle Spartans were supposed to stand and die rather than retreat. An anecdote about one Spartan mother sums up Spartan military values. As her son was setting off to battle, the mother handed him his shield and advised him to come back either victorious, carrying the shield, or dead, being carried on it. In the Lycurgan regimen Spartan men were expected to train vigorously, disdain luxury and wealth, do with little, and like it.

Similar rigorous requirements applied to Spartan women, who may have been unique in all of Greek society. They were prohibited from wearing jewelry or ornate clothes. They too exercised strenuously in the belief that hard physical training promoted the birth of healthy children. Yet they were hardly oppressed. They enjoyed a more active and open public life than most other Greek women, even though they could neither vote nor hold office. They were far more emancipated than many other Greek women in part because Spartan society felt that mothers and wives had to be as hardy as their sons and husbands. Sparta was not a place for weaklings, male or female. Spartan women saw it as their privilege to be the wives and mothers of victorious warriors, and on several occasions their own courage became legendary. They had a reputation for an independent spirit and self-assertion. This position stemmed from their genuine patriotism, but also from their title to much Spartan land. For all of these reasons, they shared a footing with Spartan men that most other Greek women lacked in their own societies.

Along with the emphasis on military values for both sexes, the Lycurgan regimen had another purpose as well: it served to instill in society the civic virtues of dedication to the state and a code of moral conduct. These aspects of the Spartan system were generally admired throughout the Greek world.

The Evolution of Athens

Like Sparta, Athens faced pressing social and economic problems during the Lyric Age, but the Athenian response was far different from that of the Spartans. Instead of creating an oligarchy, the Athenians extended to all citizens the right and duty of governing the polis. Indeed, the Athenian democracy was one of the most thoroughgoing in Greece.

The late seventh century B.C. was for Athens a time of turmoil, the causes for which are virtually unknown. In either 632 or 636 B.C. Cylon, an Athenian aristocrat, seized the Acropolis in an effort to become tyrant. Rushing immediately into the city, peasants foiled Cylon's attempt. In 621 B.C. Draco, an Athenian aristocrat, doubtless under pressure from the peasants, published the first law code of the Athenian polis. His code was thought harsh, but it nonetheless embodied the ideal that the law belonged to the citizens. Nevertheless, peasant unrest continued.

By the early sixth century B.C. social and economic conditions led to another explosive situation. The aristocracy still governed Athens as oppressively as the "bribe-devouring lords" of Boeotia against whom Hesiod had railed. The aristocrats owned the best land, met in an assembly to govern the polis, and interpreted the law. Noble landowners were forcing small farmers into economic dependence. Many families were sold into slavery; others were exiled and their land was pledged to the rich. Poor farmers who had borrowed from their wealthy neighbors had to put up their land as collateral. If a farmer was unable to repay the loan, his creditor put a stone on the borrower's field to signify his indebtedness and thereafter took one-sixth of the annual yield until the debt was paid. If the farmer had to borrow again, he pledged himself and sometimes his family. If he was again unable to repay the loan, he became the slave of his creditor. Because the harvests of the poor farmer were generally small, he could usually raise enough crops to live on but not enough to repay his loan.

In many other city-states conditions like those in Athens led to the rise of tyrants. One person who recognized these problems clearly was Solon, himself an aristocrat and poet, and a man opposed to tyrants. He was also the one man in Athens who enjoyed the respect of both aristocrats and peasants. Like Hesiod, Solon used his poetry to condemn the aristocrats for their greed and dishonesty. Solon recited his poems in the Athenian agora, where everyone could hear his relentless call for justice and fairness. The aristocrats realized that Solon was no crazed revolutionary, and the common people trusted him. Around 594 B.C. the nobles elected him *archon,* chief magistrate of the Athenian polis, and gave him extraordinary power to reform the state.

Solon immediately freed all people enslaved for debt, recalled all exiles, canceled all debts on land, and made enslavement for debt illegal. He also divided society into four legal groups on the basis of wealth. In the most influential group were the wealthiest citizens, but even the poorest and least powerful group enjoyed certain rights. Solon allowed them into the old aristocratic assembly, where they could take part in the election of magistrates.

In all his work Solon gave thought to the rights of the poor as well as the rich. He gave the commoners a place in government and a voice in the political affairs of Athens. His work done, Solon insisted that all swear to uphold his reforms. Then, because many were clamoring for him to become tyrant, he left Athens.

Although Solon's reforms solved some immediate problems, they did not bring peace to Athens. Some aristocrats attempted to make themselves tyrants, while others banded together to oppose them. In 546 B.C. Pisistratus, an exiled aristocrat, returned to Athens, defeated his opponents, and became tyrant. Pisistratus reduced the power of the aristocracy while supporting the common people. Under his rule Athens prospered, and his building program began to transform the city into one of the splendors of Greece. His reign as tyrant promoted the growth of democratic ideas by arousing in the Athenians rudimentary feelings of equality.

Athenian acceptance of tyranny did not long outlive Pisistratus, for his son Hippias ruled harshly, committing excesses that led to his overthrow. After a brief period of turmoil between factions of the nobility, Cleisthenes, a wealthy and prominent aristocrat, emerged triumphant in 508 B.C., largely because he won the support of the people. Cleisthenes created the Athenian democracy with the full knowledge and approval of the Athenian people. He reorganized the state completely but presented every innovation to the assembly for discussion and ratification. All Athenian citizens had a voice in Cleisthenes' work.

Cleisthenes created the *deme,* a local unit, to serve as the basis of his political system. Citizenship was tightly linked to the deme, for each deme kept the roll of those within its jurisdiction who were admitted to citizenship. Cleisthenes also created ten new tribes as administrative units. All the demes were grouped in tribes, which thus formed the link between the demes and the central government. The central government included an assembly of all citizens and a new council of five hundred members. Cleisthenes is often credited with the institution of *ostracism,* a vote of the Athenian people by which the man receiving the most votes went into exile. The goal of ostracism was to rid the state peacefully of a difficult or potentially dangerous politician.

The democracy functioned on the idea that all full citizens, the *demos,* were sovereign. Yet not all citizens could take time from work to participate in government. Therefore, they delegated their power to other citizens by creating various offices meant to run the democracy. The most prestigious of them was the board of ten archons, who were charged with handling legal and military matters. Six of them oversaw the Athenian legal system. They presided over courts, fixed dates for trials, and ensured that the laws of Athens were consistent. They were all elected for one year. After leaving office they entered the *Areopagus,* a select council of ex-archons who handled cases involving homicide, wounding, and arson.

Legislation was in the hands of two bodies, the *boule,* or council, composed of five hundred members, and the *ecclesia,* the assembly of all citizens. The boule, separate from the Areopagus, was perhaps the major institution of the democracy. By supervising the various committees of government and proposing bills to the assembly, it guided Athenian political life. It received foreign envoys and forwarded treaties to the assembly for ratification. It oversaw the granting of state contracts and was responsible for receiving many revenues. It held the democracy together. Nonetheless, the assembly had the final word. Open to all male citizens over eighteen years of age, it met at a specific place to vote on matters presented to it. The assembly could either accept, amend, or reject bills put before it. Every member could express his opinion on any subject on the agenda, and a simple majority vote was needed to pass or reject a bill.

Athenian democracy was to prove an inspiring ideal in Western civilization. It demonstrated that a large group of people, not just a few, could efficiently run the affairs of state. By heeding the opinions, suggestions, and wisdom of all its citizens, the polis enjoyed the maximum amount of good counsel. Because all citizens could speak their minds, they did not have to resort to rebellion or conspiracy to express their desires.

The nature of ancient Athenian democracy can easily be misunderstood by modern people. The rights and privileges of Athenian citizenship were the preserve of only a limited number of men. The rich and the wellborn had the financial resources and the social prestige to guide the state. They had the education and the leisure to learn the laws. They enjoyed the social status needed to represent the polis in diplomatic affairs. In return they received great prestige and exercised considerable influence in the actual workings of Athenian democracy.

Ordinary citizens played a more humble role in the democracy. They seldom served as magistrates or made the important decisions that determined the course of their lives. Yet they were not powerless. Although they usually voted in the assembly, they rarely stood up to speak against their social "betters." Nonetheless, their votes counted equally with those of the aristocrats in the assembly. Ordinary citizens made their greatest contributions to the running of the polis in the law courts. There they not only dealt with cases between individuals but also voted on the conduct of their leaders. Anyone could indict a public official for misconduct or incompetence in office. The jury could deliver its verdict and thereby make its voice heard. The Athenian concept of democracy bears little resemblance to that of modern America, but its very ideal has been a fertile, sturdy, and enduring contribution to the life and thought of Western civilization.

The Classical Period (500–338 B.C.)

In the years 500 to 338 B.C. Greek civilization reached its highest peak in politics, thought, and art. In this period the Greeks beat back the armies of the Persian Empire. Then, turning their spears against one another, they destroyed their own political system in a century of warfare. Some thoughtful Greeks felt prompted to record and analyze these momentous events; the result was the creation of history. This era saw the flowering of philosophy, as thinkers in Ionia on the western coast of Asia Minor and on the Greek mainland began to ponder the nature and meaning of the universe and human experience; they used their intellects to explain the world around them and to determine humanity's place in it. The Greeks invented drama, and the Athenian tragedians Aeschylus, Sophocles, and Euripides explored themes that still inspire audiences today. Greek architects reached the zenith of their art and created buildings whose very ruins still inspire awe. Because Greek intellectual and artistic efforts attained their fullest and finest expression in these years, this age is called the "classical period." Few periods in the history of Western society can match it in sheer dynamism and achievement.

The Persian Wars (499–479 B.C.)

One of the many ironies of Greek history is that the polis was enjoying the benefits of youthful vigor when it confronted its greatest external danger. In 499 B.C. the Ionian Greeks, with the feeble help of Athens, rebelled against the Persian Empire. In 490 B.C. the Persians struck back at Athens but were beaten off at the Battle of Marathon, a small plain in Attica (Map 3.3). This failure prompted the Persians to try again. In 480 B.C. the Persian king Xerxes led a mighty invasion force into Greece. Facing this emergency, many of the Greeks united and pooled their resources to repulse the invaders. The Spartans provided the overall leadership and commanded the Greek armies. The Athenians, led by the wily Themistocles, provided the heart of the naval forces.

The first confrontations between the Persians and the Greeks occurred at the pass of Thermopylae and in the waters off Artemisium, the northern tip of Euboea. At Thermopylae the Greek hoplites showed their mettle. Before the fighting began, a report came in that when the Persian archers shot their bows, the arrows darkened the sky. One gruff Spartan replied, "Fine, then we'll fight in the shade." The Greeks at Thermopylae fought heroically, but the Persians took the position. In 480 B.C. the Greek fleet, inspired by the energetic Themistocles, met the Persian armada at Salamis, an island just west of Athens. Though outnumbered by the Persians, the Greek navy won an overwhelming victory. The remnants of the Persian fleet retired, and with them went all hope of Persian victory. In the following year a coalition of Greek forces, commanded by the Spartan Pausanias with assistance from the Athenian Aristides, smashed the last Persian army at Plataea, a small polis in Boeotia. Greece remained free.

The victory of the Greeks was not a foregone conclusion. They were always outnumbered but managed to fight on fields or seas of their own choosing. More importantly many of the Greek states made a significant political decision when they decided to build a Pan-Hellenic alliance with recognized lines of command to determine strategy. This was the first time in Greek history that the individual states thought of all of Greece rather than their particular concerns. These were the days of which many contemporary and later Greeks were proudest. The stakes were high and the future of

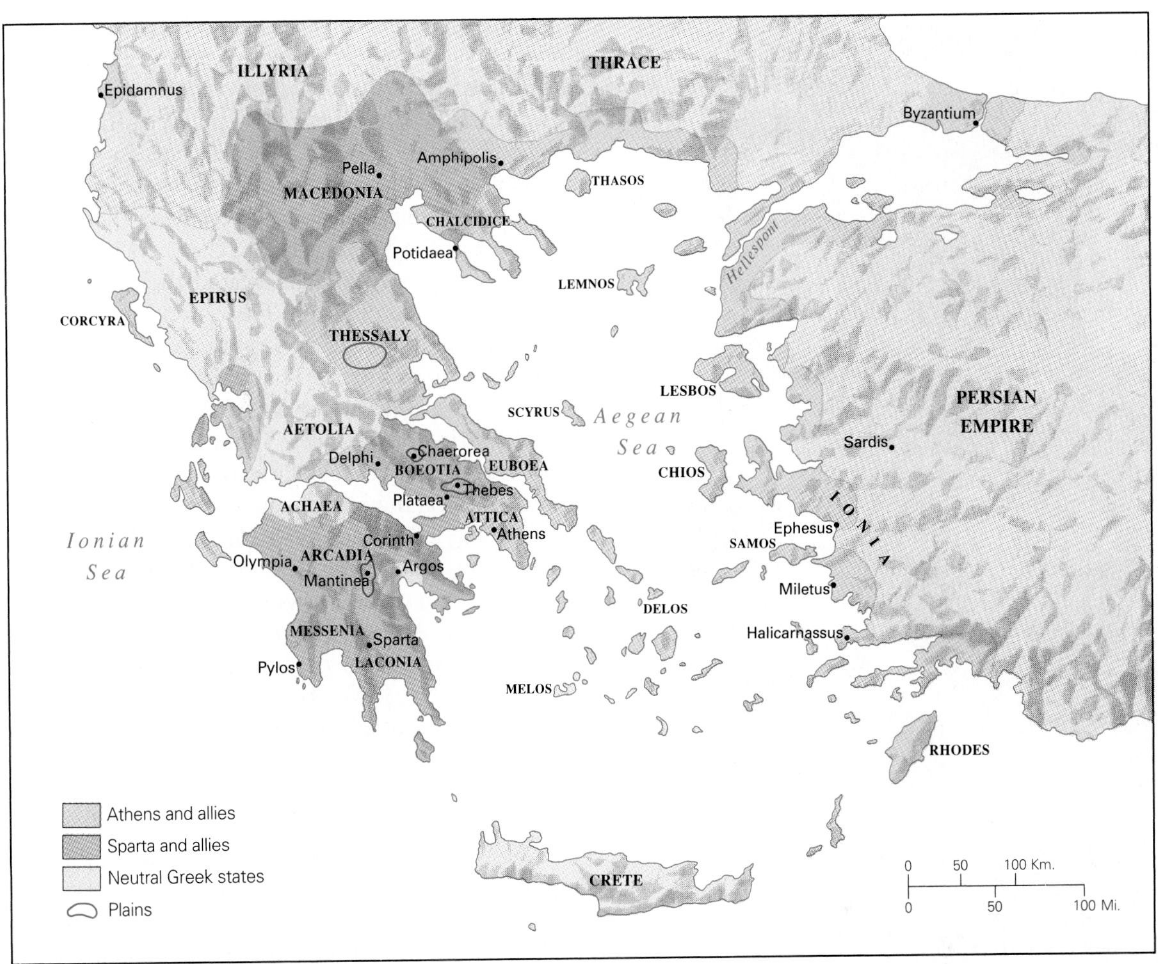

MAP 3.3 The Peloponnesian War This map, which shows the alignment of states during the Peloponnesian War, vividly illustrates the large scale of the war and its divisive impact.

Greek civilization depended on the outcome. By defeating the Persians, the Greeks ensured that oriental monarchy would not stifle Greek achievement. The Greeks were thus able to develop their particular genius free from outside interference. These decisive victories meant that Greek political forms and intellectual concepts would be the heritage of the West.

Growth of the Athenian Empire (478–431 B.C.)

For the Greeks the Persian wars were a beginning, not an end. Before them was a novel situation: the defeat of the Persians had created a power vacuum in the Aegean. The state with the strongest navy could turn the Aegean into its lake. In 478 B.C., to take advantage of this situation, the Athenians and their allies, again led by Aristides, formed the Delian League, a grand naval alliance aimed at liberating Ionia from Persian rule. The league took its name from the small island of Delos, on which stood a religious center sacred to all parties. The Delian League was intended as a free alliance under the leadership of Athens. Athenians provided most of the warships and crews and determined how many ships or how much money each member of the league should contribute to the allied effort.

The Athenians, supported by the Delian League and led by the young aristocrat Cimon, carried the war against Persia. Cimon, more than any other Athenian

The Persian Wars This vase dates to the early fifth century B.C. It depicts fighting between a heavily armed Greek hoplite on the left, carrying a shield and spear, against an Asian soldier who is less heavily armed. *(The Metropolitan Museum of Art, Rogers Fund, 1906 [06.1021.117]. Photograph © 1986 The Metropolitan Museum of Art)*

politician, turned the Delian League into an Athenian empire. His culture and social graces did not prevent him from exercising ruthless and cynical control over peoples who had but a few years before been Athenian allies. The Athenians sternly put down dissident or rebellious governments, replacing them with trustworthy puppets. Tribute was often collected by force, and the Athenians placed the economic resources of the Delian League under tighter and tighter control.

Athens justified its conduct by its successful leadership. In about 467 B.C. Cimon defeated a new and huge Persian force at the Battle of the Eurymedon River in Asia Minor, once again removing the shadow of Persia from the Aegean. But as the threat from Persia waned and the Athenians treated their allies more harshly, major allies such as Thasos revolted (ca 465 B.C.), requiring the Delian League to use its forces against its own members. The expansion of Athenian power and the aggressiveness of Athenian rule also alarmed Sparta and its allies. While relations between Athens and Sparta cooled, Pericles (ca 494–429 B.C.) became the leading statesman in Athens. Like the democracy he led, Pericles, an aristocrat of solid intellectual ability, was aggressive and imperialistic. At last, in 459 B.C., Sparta and Athens went to war over conflicts between Athens and some of Sparta's allies. Though the Athenians conquered Boeotia, Megara, and Aegina in the early stages of the war, they met with defeat in Egypt and later in Boeotia. The war ended in 445 B.C. with no serious damage to either side and nothing settled. But this war divided the Greek world between the two great powers.

During the 440s and 430s, Athens continued its severe policies toward its subject allies and came into conflict with Corinth, one of Sparta's leading supporters (see Map 3.3). In response the Spartans convened a meeting of their allies, whose complaints of Athenian aggression ended with a demand that Athens be stopped. Reluctantly the Spartans agreed to declare war. The real reason for war, according to the Athenian historian Thucydides, was very simple: "The truest explanation, though the one least mentioned, was the great growth of Athenian power and the fear it caused the Lacedaemonians [Spartans], which drove them to war."[7]

At the outbreak of this, the Peloponnesian War, the Spartan ambassador warned the Athenians: "This day will be the beginning of great evils for the Greeks." Few have ever spoken more prophetically. The Peloponnesian War lasted a generation (431–404 B.C.) and brought in its wake fearful plagues, famine, civil wars, widespread destruction, and huge loss of life. Thucydides described its cataclysmic effects:

For never had so many cities been captured and destroyed, whether by the barbarians or by the Greeks who were fighting each other. . . . Never had so many men been exiled or slaughtered, whether in the war or because of civil conflicts.[8]

As the war dragged on, older leaders like Pericles died and were replaced by men of the war generation. In Athens the most prominent of this new breed of politicians was Alcibiades (ca 450–404 B.C.), an aristocrat, a kinsman of Pericles, and a student of the philosopher Socrates (see page 95). Brilliant, handsome, charming, and popular with the people, Alcibiades was also self-seeking and egotistical and a shameless opportunist. His first thoughts were always for himself.

Alcibiades' schemes helped bring Athens down to defeat. Having planned an invasion of Sicily that ended in disaster, he deserted to the Spartans and plotted with the Persians, who had sided with Sparta, against his homeland. In the end all of Alcibiades' intrigues failed. The Spartans defeated the Athenian fleet in the Aegean and blockaded Athens by land and sea. Finally, in 404 B.C. the Athenians surrendered and watched helplessly while the Spartans and their allies destroyed the walls of Athens to the music of flute girls. The Peloponnesian War, which lasted twenty-seven years, dealt Greek civilization a serious blow.

The Birth of Historical Awareness

One positive development grew out of the Persian and Peloponnesian wars: the beginnings of historical writing. In his book *The Histories* Herodotus (ca 485–425 B.C.), known as the father of history, chronicled the rise of the Persian Empire, sketched the background of Athens and Sparta, and described the land and customs of the Egyptians and the Scythians, who lived in the region of the modern Crimea. The sheer scope of this work is awesome. Perhaps Herodotus's most striking characteristic was his curiosity. He diligently questioned everyone who could tell him anything about the Persian wars. The confrontation between East and West unfolds relentlessly in *The Histories.*

The outbreak of the Peloponnesian War prompted Thucydides (ca 460–ca 400 B.C.) to write a history of its course in the belief that it would be the greatest war in Greek history. An Athenian politician and general, Thucydides saw action in the war until he was exiled for a defeat. Exile gave him the time and opportunity to question eyewitnesses about the details of events and to visit battlefields.

Thucydides was intensely interested in human nature and how it manifested itself during the war. When a terrible plague struck Athens in 430 B.C., Thucydides described in the same clinical terms both the symptoms of the plague and the reactions of the Athenians. He portrayed the virtual breakdown of a society beset by war, disease, desperation, and despair. (See the feature "Listening to the Past: The Great Plague at Athens, 430 B.C." on pages 102–103.)

Athenian Arts in the Age of Pericles

In the last half of the fifth century B.C., Pericles turned Athens into the showplace of Greece. He appropriated Delian League funds to pay for a huge building program, planning temples and other buildings to honor Athena, the patron goddess of the city, and to display to all Greeks the glory of the Athenian polis. Pericles also pointed out that his program would employ many Athenians and bring economic prosperity to the city.

Thus began the undertaking that turned the Acropolis into a monument for all time. Construction of the Parthenon began in 447 B.C., followed by the Propylaea, the temple of Athena Nike (Athena the Victorious), and the Erechtheum (Map 3.4). Even the pollution of modern Athens, although it is destroying the ancient buildings, cannot rob them of their splendor and charm.

The planning of the architects and the skill of the workmen who erected these buildings were both very sophisticated. Visitors approaching the Acropolis first saw the Propylaea, the ceremonial gateway, a building of complicated layout and grand design whose Doric columns seemed to hold up the sky. On the right was the small temple of Athena Nike, whose dimensions harmonized with those of the Propylaea. The temple was built to commemorate the victory over the Persians, and the Ionic frieze above its columns depicted the struggle between the Greeks and the Persians. Here for all the world to see was a tribute to Athenian and Greek valor—and a reminder of Athens's part in the victory.

To the left of the visitors, as they passed through the Propylaea, stood the Erechtheum, an Ionic temple that housed several ancient shrines. On its southern side was the famous Portico of the Caryatids, a porch whose roof was supported by statues of Athenian maidens. The graceful Ionic columns of the Erechtheum provided a delicate relief from the prevailing Doric order of the massive Propylaea and Parthenon.

As visitors walked on, they obtained a full view of the Parthenon, thought by many to be the perfect Doric

Temple at Bassae The temple at Bassae sits in wild splendor in the mountains of Arcadia. It is an almost perfect Dorian temple, with its massive columns surrounding the cella, the inner room that contained the statue of Apollo. In such elevated, lonely places many Greeks felt that they entered a region dear to the gods. *(John Buckler)*

temple. The Parthenon was the chief monument to Athena and her city. The sculptures that adorned the temple portrayed the greatness of Athens and its goddess. The figures on the eastern pediment depicted Athena's birth, those on the west the victory of Athena over the god Poseidon in their struggle for the possession of Attica. Inside the Parthenon stood a huge statue of Athena, the masterpiece of the great sculptor Phidias.

In many ways the Athenian Acropolis is the epitome of Greek art and its spirit. Although the buildings were dedicated to the gods and most of the sculptures portrayed gods, these works nonetheless express the Greek fascination with the human and the rational. Greek deities were anthropomorphic, and Greek artists portrayed them as human beings. While honoring the gods, Greek artists were thus celebrating human beings. In the Parthenon sculptures it is visually impossible to distinguish the men and women from the gods and goddesses. The Acropolis also exhibits the rational side of Greek art. Greek artists portrayed action in a balanced, restrained, and sometimes even serene fashion, capturing the noblest aspects of human beings: their reason, dignity, and promise.

Other aspects of Athenian cultural life were as rooted in the life of the polis as were the architecture and sculpture of the Acropolis. The development of drama was tied to the religious festivals of the city. The polis sponsored the production of plays and required that wealthy citizens pay the expenses of their production. At the beginning of the year, dramatists submitted their

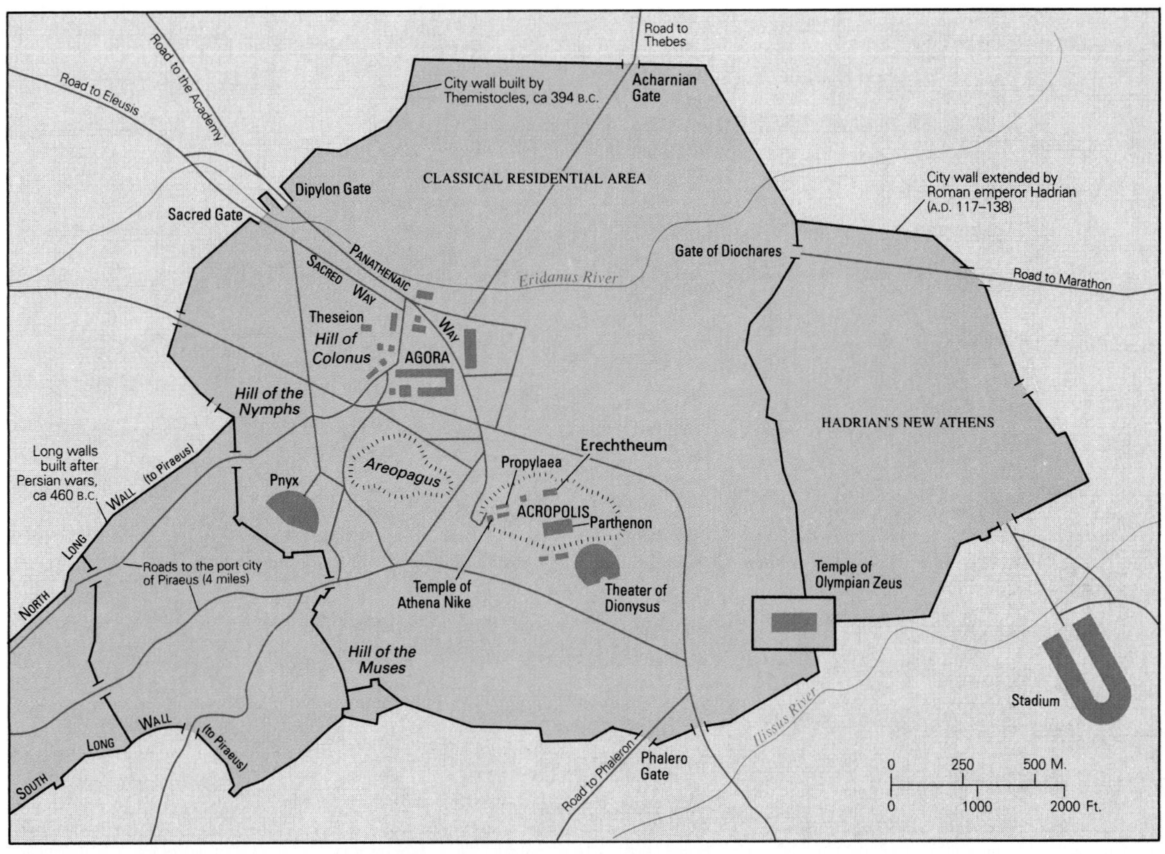

MAP 3.4 Ancient Athens By modern standards the city of Athens was hardly more than a town, not much larger in size than one square mile. Yet this small area reflects the concentration of ancient Greek life in the polis.

plays to the archon. He chose those he considered best and assigned a theatrical troupe to each playwright. Although most Athenian drama has perished, enough has survived to prove that the archons had superb taste. Many plays were highly controversial, but the archons neither suppressed nor censored them.

The Athenian dramatists were the first artists in Western society to examine such basic questions as the rights of the individual, the demands of society on the individual, and the nature of good and evil. Conflict is a constant element in Athenian drama. The dramatists used their art to portray, understand, and resolve life's basic conflicts.

Aeschylus (525–456 B.C.), the first of the great Athenian dramatists, was also the first to express the agony of the individual caught in conflict. In his trilogy of plays, *The Oresteia,* Aeschylus deals with the themes of betrayal, murder, and reconciliation, urging that reason and justice be applied to reconcile fundamental conflicts. The final play concludes with a prayer that civil dissension never be allowed to destroy the city and that the life of the city be one of harmony and grace.

Sophocles (496–406 B.C.) also dealt with matters personal and political. In *Antigone* he expresses the precedence of divine law over human defects and touches on the need for recognition of the law and adherence to it as a prerequisite for a tranquil state.

Sophocles' masterpieces have inspired generations of playwrights. Perhaps his most famous plays are *Oedipus the King* and its sequel, *Oedipus at Colonus. Oedipus the King* is the ironic story of a man doomed by the gods to kill his father and marry his mother. Try as he might to avoid his fate, Oedipus's every action brings him closer to its fulfillment. When at last he realizes that he has

The Athenian Acropolis This painting, though made only in the nineteenth century, gives a vivid impression of what the buildings and their entire setting looked like in antiquity. It demonstrates the artistic appeal of these buildings, both then and now, and proves what Plutarch wrote of them: "Each of them is always in bloom, maintaining its appearance as though untouched by time, as though an evergreen breath and undecaying spirit had been mixed in its construction." *(Neue Pinakothek, München)*

carried out the decree of the gods, Oedipus blinds himself and flees into exile. In *Oedipus at Colonus* Sophocles dramatizes the last days of the broken king, whose patient suffering and uncomplaining piety win him an exalted position. In the end the gods honor him for his virtue. The interpretation of these two plays has been hotly debated, but Sophocles seems to be saying that human beings should obey the will of the gods, even without fully understanding it, for the gods stand for justice and order.

Euripides (ca 480–406 B.C.), the last of the three great Greek tragic dramatists, also explored the theme of personal conflict within the polis and sounded the depths of the individual. With Euripides drama entered a new, in many ways more personal, phase. To him the gods were far less important than human beings. The essence of Euripides' tragedy is the flawed character—men and women who bring disaster on themselves and their loved ones because their passions overwhelm reason. Although Euripides' plays were less popular in his lifetime than were those of Aeschylus and Sophocles, Euripides was a dramatist of genius whose work later had a significant impact on Roman drama.

Writers of comedy treated the affairs of the polis bawdily and often coarsely. Even so, their plays also were performed at religious festivals. The comic playwrights dealt primarily with the political affairs of the polis and the conduct of its leading politicians. Best known are the comedies of Aristophanes (ca 445–386 B.C.), an ardent lover of his city and a merciless critic of cranks and quacks. He lampooned eminent generals, at times depicting them as morons. He commented snidely on Pericles, poked fun at Socrates, and hooted at Euripides. Like Aeschylus, Sophocles, and Euripides, Aristophanes used his art to dramatize his ideas on the right conduct of the citizen and the value of the polis.

Perhaps never were art and political life so intimately and congenially bound together as at Athens. Athenian art was the product of deep and genuine love of the polis. It was aimed at bettering the lives of the citizens and the quality of life in the state.

Daily Life in Periclean Athens

In sharp contrast with the rich intellectual and cultural life of Periclean Athens stands the simplicity of its material life. The Athenians—and in this respect they were typical of Greeks in general—lived very happily with comparatively few material possessions. In the first place, there were very few material goods to own. The thousands of machines, tools, and gadgets considered essential for modern life had no counterparts in Athenian life. The inventory of Alcibiades' goods, which the Athenians confiscated after his desertion, is enlightening. His household possessions consisted of chests,

Mosaic of the Muses This mosaic was recently discovered at Elis in Greece. Not found in a great or famous urban center, it nonetheless testifies to the wide dissemination of culture and art throughout Greece. The figures of the mosaic represent the nine Muses, goddesses of the arts. The harp of Apollo occupies the center, and Clio, the goddess of history, is represented by the scroll in the upper right of the harp. *(Professor Nicolas Yalouris, Former General Inspector of Antiquities, Athens)*

beds, couches, tables, screens, stools, baskets, and mats. Other common items in the Greek home included pottery, metal utensils for cooking, tools, luxury goods such as jewelry, and a few other things. These items the Greeks had to buy from craftsmen. Whatever else they needed, such as clothes and blankets, they produced at home.

The Athenian house was rather simple. Whether large or small, the typical house consisted of a series of rooms built around a central courtyard, with doors opening onto the courtyard. Many houses had bedrooms on an upper floor. Artisans and craftsmen often set aside a room to use as a shop or work area. The two principal rooms were the men's dining room and the room where the women worked wool. Other rooms included the kitchen and bathroom. By modern standards there was not much furniture. In the men's dining room were couches, a sideboard, and small tables. Cups and other pottery were often hung on the wall from pegs. Other household furnishings included items such as those confiscated from Alcibiades after his desertion.

In the courtyard were the well, a small altar, and a washbasin. If the family lived in the country, the stalls of the animals faced the courtyard. Country dwellers kept oxen for plowing, pigs for slaughtering, sheep for wool, goats for cheese, and mules and donkeys for transportation. Even in the city chickens and perhaps a goat or two roamed the courtyard together with dogs and cats.

Cooking, done over a hearth in the house, provided welcome warmth in the winter. Baking and roasting were done in ovens. Food consisted primarily of various grains, especially wheat and barley, as well as lentils, olives, figs, and grapes. Garlic and onion were popular garnishes, and wine was always on hand. These foods were stored at home in large jars; with them the Greek family sometimes ate fish, chicken, and vegetables. Women ground wheat into flour, baked it into bread, and on special occasions made honey or sesame cakes. The Greeks used olive oil for cooking, as families still do in modern Greece; they also used it as an unguent and as lamp fuel.

By American standards the Greeks did not eat much meat. On special occasions, such as important religious festivals, the family ate the animal sacrificed to the god and gave the god the exquisite delicacy of the thighbone wrapped in fat. The only Greeks who consistently ate meat were the Spartan warriors. They received a small portion of meat each day, together with the infamous Spartan black broth, a ghastly concoction of pork cooked in blood, vinegar, and salt. One Greek, after tasting the broth, commented that he could easily understand why the Spartans were so willing to die.

In the city a man might support himself as a craftsman—a potter, bronzesmith, sailmaker, or tanner—or he could contract with the polis to work on public buildings, such as the Parthenon and Erechtheum. Men without skills worked as paid laborers but competed with slaves for work. Slaves were usually foreigners and often barbarians. By "barbarians" the Greeks meant people whose native language was not Greek. Citizens, slaves, and barbarians were paid the same amount for their work.

Slavery was commonplace in Greece, as it was throughout the ancient world. In its essentials Greek slavery resembled Mesopotamian slavery. Slaves received some protection under the law and could buy their freedom. On the other hand, masters could mistreat or neglect their slaves, although killing them was illegal. Most slaves in Athens served as domestics and performed light labor around the house. Nurses for children, teachers of reading and writing, and guardians for young men were often slaves. The lives of these slaves were much like those of their owners. Other slaves were skilled workers, who could be found working on public buildings or in small workshops.

The importance of slavery in Athens must not be exaggerated. Athenians did not own huge gangs of slaves as did Roman owners of large estates. Slave labor competed with free labor and kept wages down, but it never replaced the free labor that was the mainstay of the Athenian economy.

Most Athenians supported themselves by agriculture, but unless the family was fortunate enough to possess holdings in a plain more fertile than most of the land, they found it difficult to reap a good crop from the soil. Many people must have consumed nearly everything they raised. Attic farmers were free and, though hardly prosperous, by no means destitute. They could usually expect yields of five bushels of wheat and ten of barley per acre for every bushel of grain sown. A bad harvest meant a lean year. In many places farmers grew more barley than wheat because of the nature of the soil. Wherever possible farmers also cultivated vines and olive trees.

The social condition of Athenian women has been the subject of much debate and little agreement. One of the difficulties is the fragmentary nature of the evidence. Women appear frequently in literature and art, often in idealized roles, but seldom in historical contexts of a wider and more realistic nature. This is due in part to the fact that most Greek historians of the time recounted primarily the political, diplomatic, and military events of the day, events in which women seldom played a notable part. Yet that does not mean that women were totally invisible in the life of the polis. It indicates instead that ancient sources provide only a glimpse of how women affected the society in which they lived. Greek wives, for example, played an important economic and social role by their management of the household. Perhaps the best way to describe the position of the free woman in Greek society is to use the anthropologist's term *liminal,* which means in this case that although women lacked official power, they nonetheless played a vital role in shaping the society in which they lived. The same situation had existed in Hammurabi's Babylonia, and it would later recur in the Hellenistic period. The mere fact that Athenian and other Greek women did not sit in the assembly does not mean that they did not influence public affairs.

The status of a free woman of the citizen class was strictly protected by law. Only her children, not those of foreigners or slaves, could be citizens. Only she was in charge of the household and the family's possessions. Yet the law protected her primarily to protect her husband's interests. Raping a free woman was a lesser crime than seducing her, because seduction involved the winning of her affections. This law was concerned not with the husband's feelings but with ensuring that he need not doubt the legitimacy of his children.

Women in Athens and elsewhere in Greece received a certain amount of social and legal protection from their dowries. Upon marriage, the bride's father gave the couple a gift of land or money, which the husband administered. However, it was never his; and in the rare cases of divorce, it returned to the wife's domain. The same is often true in Greece today among the upper class.

Ideally, respectable women lived a secluded life in which the only men they saw were relatives. How far this ideal was actually put into practice is impossible to say. At least Athenian women seem to have enjoyed a social circle of other women of their own class. They also attended public festivals, sacrifices, and funerals. Nonetheless, prosperous and respectable women probably spent much of their time in the house. A white complexion—a sign that a woman did not have to work in the fields—was valued highly.

Courtesans lived the freest lives of all Athenian women. Although some courtesans were simply prostitutes, others added intellectual accomplishments to physical beauty. In constant demand, cultured courtesans moved freely in male society. Their artistic talents and intellectual abilities appealed to men who wanted more than sex. The most famous of all courtesans was Aspasia, mistress of Pericles and supposedly a friend of Socrates. (See the feature "Individuals in Society: Aspasia.")

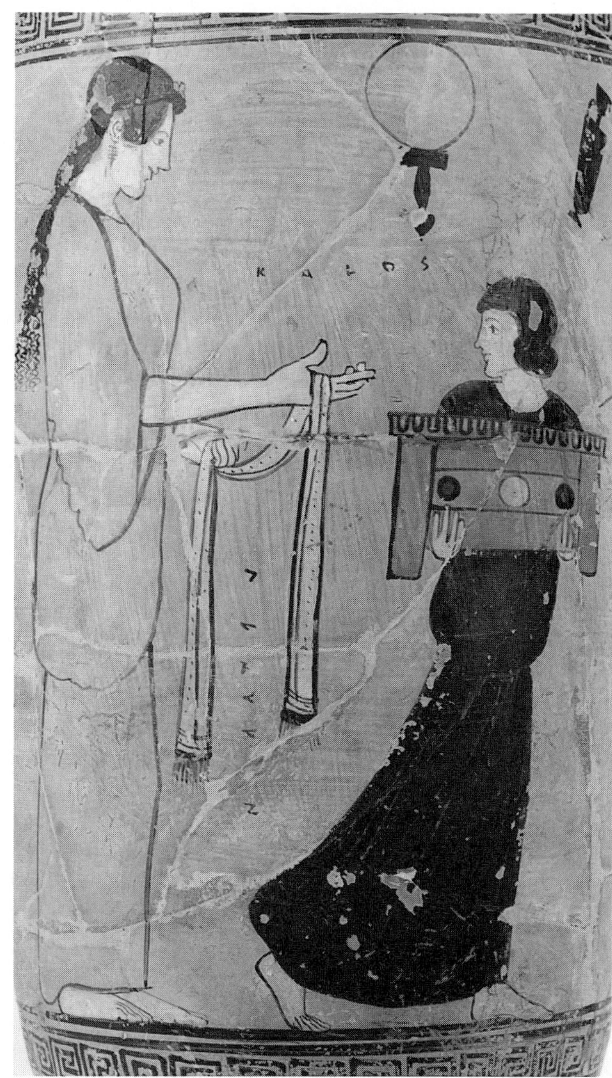

Mistress of the Household This domestic scene captures an ordinary moment in the life of an Athenian lady. She is putting the finishing touches on her attire, helped by a servant boy who holds a chest for her. Above them hang a mirror and a lekythos. *(Musées royaux d'Art et d'Histoire, Brussels)*

Individuals in Society

Aspasia

Idealized portrait of Aspasia. *(Alinari/Art Resource, NY)*

"If it is necessary for me indeed to speak of female virtues, to those of you who have now become widows, I shall explain the entire situation briefly. It is in your hands whether you will not fall below your nature. The greatest glory to you is to be least talked about by men, either for excellence or blame" (Thucydides 2.46). These warm-hearted words were reportedly uttered by Pericles to the widows at a public funeral honoring those killed during the first year of the Peloponnesian War. At the same time he was enjoying a long-standing affair with Aspasia, who was very much talked about by men and women. Whether Pericles actually said these words is for the most part irrelevant. Their significance is in their expression of the Athenian ideal of the role of the proper Athenian lady. In short, she should stay at home and limit her talents to her household. The broader world was beyond her.

Aspasia was born in the Greek city of Miletus and came to Athens in about 445 B.C. She is easily one of the most intriguing women of ancient history. Little is known about her life, but she played a role in Athenian society that was far more renowned than, and far different from, that allegedly proposed by Pericles. The irony of her life is that she became his mistress and enjoyed a very public career, exactly the opposite of the opinions attributed to Pericles in the Funeral Oration.

Once in Athens, Aspasia became a *hetaira,* which literally means "companion." The duties of a hetaira varied. She could be someone who accompanied men at dinners and drinking parties, but she could also be a prostitute. The comic poet Aristophanes specifically calls Aspasia a madam. The major attractions of a successful hetaira included beauty, intelligent conversation, and proper etiquette. In return she was paid for her charms. She also enjoyed the opportunity to become the mistress of a wealthy man. Although some have made much of the hetaira as a sexual partner of her client, she also filled an intellectual role not usually expected of a proper wife.

Aspasia fits into the category of a lovely and very intelligent companion. Ancient legend reports that she taught rhetoric, an essential tool for Athenian politicians. That meant that her pupils were necessarily men. She thus enjoyed a rare opportunity for a woman to influence the men who shaped the political life of Athens. Plutarch reports that Aspasia enjoyed the company of the foremost men in Athens. Their conversations included philosophy, and she is reputed to have taught Socrates the art of public speaking. The claim is probably false, but it at least points to her reputation as a very accomplished woman.

The great change in Aspasia's life came with her introduction to Pericles, who was reportedly taken with her rare political wisdom. More can be imagined. After Pericles divorced his wife, he took Aspasia as his mistress. She and Pericles produced a son, also named Pericles. Although it was illegal for the son of a foreign parent to be granted Athenian citizenship, the laws were waived in this case. That remarkable fact is testimony to the respect that a number of Athenians felt not only for the great statesman but also for Aspasia. Others ridiculed the connection and felt that Pericles was making a fool of himself. The majority thought otherwise, or the son would not have been granted citizenship.

Aspasia's achievements are clear. She lifted herself from a vulnerable to a respected position in Athenian society. It is not enough to ascribe this to her beauty. Her intelligence and her sense of culture were equally, if not more, important. Social mobility in classical Athens was rare, but Aspasia proves that it was possible.

Questions for Analysis

1. What talents enabled Aspasia to rise from companion or courtesan to generally respected person in society?
2. What made Aspasia's position in Athens precarious despite her obvious talents?

A woman's main functions were to raise the children, oversee the domestic slaves and hired labor, and together with her maids work wool into cloth. The women washed the wool in the courtyard and then brought it into the women's room, where the loom stood. They spun the wool into thread and wove the thread into cloth. They also dyed wool at home and decorated the cloth by weaving in colors and designs. The woman of the household either did the cooking herself or directed her maids. In a sense, poor women lived freer lives than did wealthier women. They performed manual labor in the fields or sold goods in the agora, going about their affairs much as men did.

A distinctive feature of Athenian life and of Greek life in general was acceptance of homosexuality. The Greeks accepted the belief that both homosexual and heterosexual practices were normal parts of life. They did not think that these practices created any particular problems for those who engaged in them.

No one has satisfactorily explained how the Greek attitude toward homosexual love developed or determined how common homosexual behavior was. Homosexuality was probably far more common among the aristocracy than among the lower classes. Even among the aristocracy attitudes toward homosexuality were complex and sometimes conflicting. Most people saw homosexual love affairs among the young as a stage in the development of a mature heterosexual life. Warrior aristocracies generally emphasized the physical side of the relationship in the belief that warriors who were also lovers would fight all the harder to impress and to protect each other. Whatever their intellectual content, homosexual love affairs were also overtly sexual.

Greek Religion

Greek religion is extremely difficult for modern people to understand, largely because of the great differences between Greek and modern cultures. In the first place, it is not even easy to talk about "Greek religion," since the Greeks had no uniform faith or creed. Although the Greeks usually worshiped the same deities—Zeus, Hera, Apollo, Athena, and others—the cults of these gods and goddesses varied from polis to polis. The Greeks had no sacred books such as the Bible, and Greek religion was often a matter more of ritual than of belief. Nor did cults impose an ethical code of conduct. Greeks did not have to follow any particular rule of life, practice certain virtues, or even live decent lives in order to participate. Unlike the Egyptians and Hebrews, the Greeks lacked a priesthood as the modern world understands the term. In Greece priests and priestesses existed to care for temples and sacred property and to conduct the proper rituals, but not to make religious rules or doctrines, much less to enforce them. In short, there existed in Greece no central ecclesiastical authority and no organized creed.

Although temples to the gods were common, they were unlike modern churches or synagogues in that they were not normally places where a congregation met to worship as a spiritual community. Instead, the individual Greek either visited the temple occasionally on matters of private concern or walked in a procession to a particular temple to celebrate a particular festival. In Greek religion the altar, which stood outside the temple, was important; when the Greeks sought the favor of the gods, they offered them sacrifices. Greek religious observances were generally cheerful. Festivals and sacrifices were frequently times for people to meet together socially, times of high spirits and conviviality rather than of pious gloom. By offering the gods parts of the sacrifice while consuming the rest themselves, worshipers forged a bond with the gods.

Besides the Olympian gods, each polis had its own minor deities, each with his or her own local cult. In many instances Greek religion involved the official gods and goddesses of the polis and their cults. The polis administered the cults and festivals, and all were expected to participate in this civic religion, regardless of whether they even believed in the deities being worshiped. Participating unbelievers, who seem to have been a small minority, were not considered hypocrites. Rather, they were seen as patriotic, loyal citizens who in honoring the gods also honored the polis. If this attitude seems contradictory, an analogy may help. Before baseball games Americans stand at the playing of the national anthem, whether they are Democrats, Republicans, or neither, and whether they agree or disagree with the policies of the current administration. They honor their nation as represented by its flag, in somewhat the same way an ancient Greek honored the polis and demonstrated solidarity with it by participating in the state cults.

Some Greeks turned to mystery religions like those of the Eleusinian mysteries in Attica and of Trophonios in Boeotia. These mystery religions in some ways foreshadowed aspects of early Christian practices by their rites of initiation, their acceptance of certain doctrines, and generally their promise of life after death. The basic concept of these cults was to unite individuals in an exclusive religious society with particular deities. Those

A Greek God Few pieces of Greek art better illustrate the conception of the gods as greatly superior forms of human beings than this magnificent statue, over six feet, ten inches in height. Here the god, who may be either Poseidon or Zeus, is portrayed as powerful and perfect but human in form. *(National Archaeological Museum, Athens/Archaeological Receipts Fund)*

who joined them went through a period of preparation in which they learned the essential beliefs of the cult and its necessary rituals. Once they had successfully undergone initiation, they were forbidden to reveal the secrets of the cult. Consequently, modern scholars know comparatively little about their tenets. Although the mystery religions were popular until the coming of Christianity in the Roman Empire, relatively few except the wealthy could afford the luxuries of time and money to join them.

For most Greeks religion was quite simple and close to nature. They believed in the supernatural and the primitive. The religion of the common people was a rich combination of myth, ritual, folklore, and cult. They believed in a world of deities who were all around them. The goddess Hestia oversaw the sanctity of the hearth, various nymphs resided at clear springs, and Pan, the lover of wild things and places, protected the herds and flocks. Deities and human beings shared their world so intimately that they could change places within it. An excellent example comes from the myth of Zeus, the Olympian god, who could change his shape into that of a bull in order to carry Europa, the daughter of a Phoenician king, to Crete. Having borne Zeus several children, she herself became a goddess, for whom the continent of Europe is named.

So much of popular religion was taken for granted that comparatively little of it is now known. An example, however, gives an idea of the nature of this religion, its bond with nature, and its sense of ethics and propriety. Probably no one today thinks much about wading across a stream, unless it is too deep. That attitude would have horrified the Boeotian farmer and poet Hesiod, who would have considered it sacrilegious. Instead, he advises the traveler who encounters a stream:

Never cross the beautifully flowing water of an overflowing river on foot,
until having looked into the lovely stream and having washed your hands in the very lovely, clear waters,
you offer a prayer. Whoever crosses a river and with hands unwashed of evil,
to him the gods will wreak vengeance and will give him pain.[9]

Though Greek religion in general was individual or related to the polis, the Greeks also shared some Pan-Hellenic festivals, the chief of which were held at Olympia in honor of Zeus and at Delphi in honor of Apollo. The festivities at Olympia included the famous games, athletic contests that have inspired the modern Olympic games. Held every four years, these games were for the glory of Zeus. They attracted visitors from all over the Greek world and lasted well into Christian times. The Pythian games at Delphi were also held every four years, but these contests differed from the Olympic games by including musical and literary contests. Both the Olympic and the Pythian games were unifying factors in Greek life, bringing Greeks together culturally as well as religiously.

The Flowering of Philosophy

The myths and epics of the Mesopotamians are ample testimony that speculation about the origin of the universe and of mankind did not begin with the Greeks. The signal achievement of the Greeks was the willingness of some to treat these questions in rational rather than mythological terms. Although Greek philosophy did not fully flower until the classical period, Ionian thinkers had already begun in the Lyric Age to ask what the universe was made of. These men are called the Pre-Socratics, for their work preceded the philosophical revolution begun by the Athenian Socrates. Though they were keen observers, the Pre-Socratics rarely undertook deliberate experimentation. Instead, they took individual facts and wove them into general theories. Despite appearances, they believed, the universe was actually simple and subject to natural laws. Drawing on their observations, they speculated about the basic building blocks of the universe.

The first of the Pre-Socratics, Thales (ca 600 B.C.), learned mathematics and astronomy from the Babylonians and geometry from the Egyptians. Yet there was an immense and fundamental difference between Near Eastern thought and the philosophy of Thales. The Near Eastern peoples considered such events as eclipses to be evil omens. Thales viewed them as natural phenomena that could be explained in natural terms. In short, he asked why things happened. He believed the basic element of the universe to be water. Although he was wrong, the way in which he had asked the question was momentous: it was the beginning of the scientific method.

Thales' follower Anaximander continued his work. Anaximander was the first of the Pre-Socratics to use general concepts, which are essential to abstract thought. One of the most brilliant of the Pre-Socratics, a man of striking originality, Anaximander theorized that the basic element of the universe is the "boundless" or "endless"—something infinite and indestructible. In his view the earth floats in a void, held in balance by its distance from everything else in the universe. Anaximander even concluded that mankind had evolved naturally from lower organisms: "In water the first animal arose covered with spiny skin, and with the lapse of time some crawled onto dry land and breaking off their skins in a short time they survived."[10] This remarkable speculation corresponds crudely to Darwin's theory of the evolution of species, although it predates Darwin by two and a half millennia.

An Ionian, Heraclitus (ca 500 B.C.), declared the primal element to be fire. He also declared that the world had neither beginning nor end: "This world, the world of all things, neither any god nor man made, but it always was and it is and it will be: an everlasting fire, measures kindling and measures going out."[11] Although the universe was eternal, according to Heraclitus, it changed constantly. An outgrowth of this line of speculation was the theory of Democritus that the universe was made of invisible, indestructible atoms. The culmination of Pre-Socratic thought was the theory that four simple substances make up the universe: fire, air, earth, and water.

Not all of these early philosophers devoted their attention to pure philosophy or natural science. Aesop (d. 564 B.C.) devoted his attention to ethics, the treatment of moral behavior. A slave endowed with a keen mind, Aesop made his points by using fables, which were as

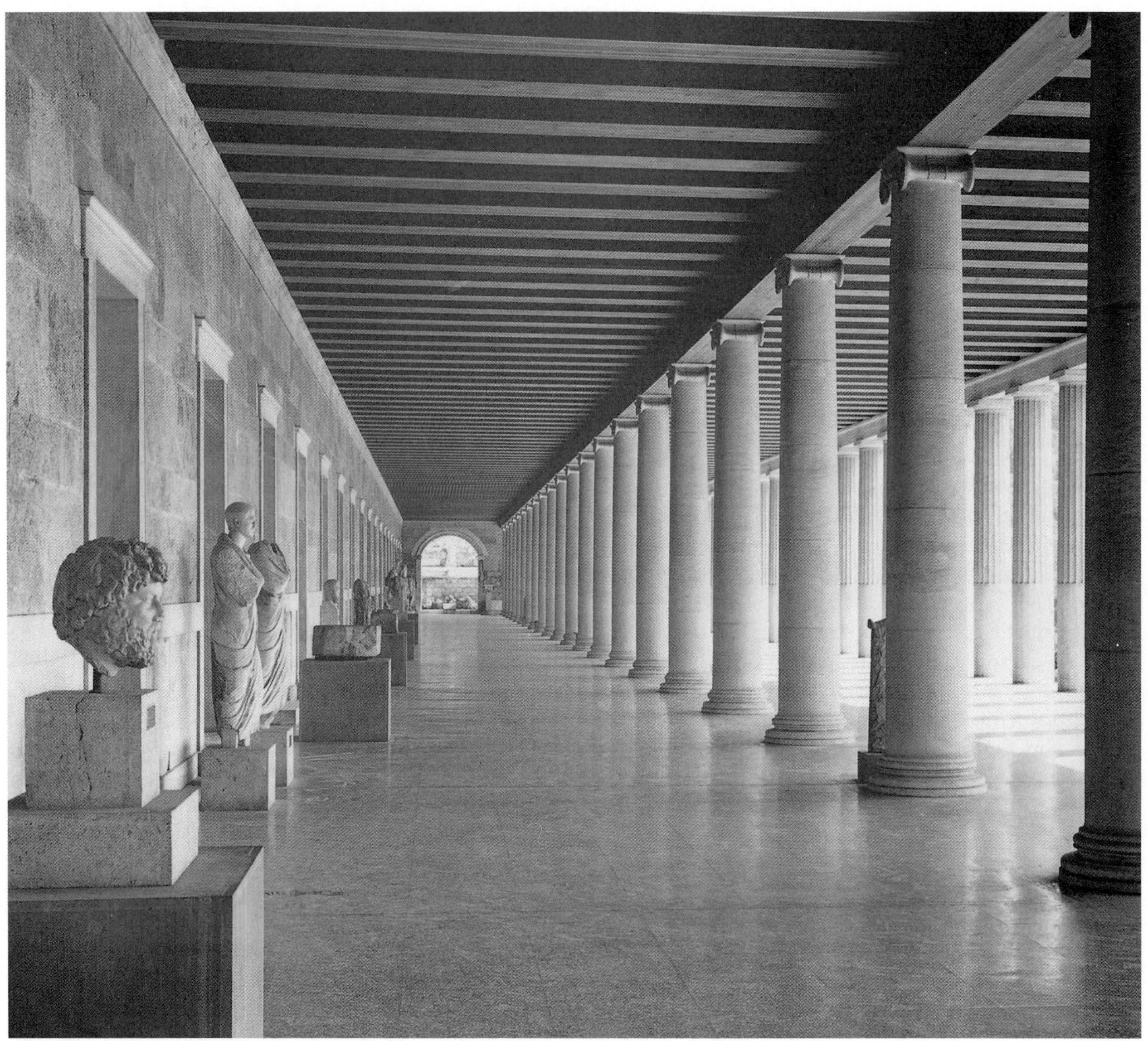

Stoa of Attalos in Athens The Greek stoa, or portico, was a long building divided along its center by a spacious roofed corridor that allowed people to walk while enjoying the air but avoiding the sun and rain. On the other side opened the rooms of various shops. Philosophers were fond of discussing their ideas while strolling along the spacious arcade. The philosophical school of Zeno received its name *Stoicism* because its adherents formulated their views in a stoa. *(Courtesy, American School of Classical Studies, Agora)*

popular in antiquity as they are today. Fables make their points metaphorically, often using animals instead of people as the main characters. His tales spread throughout Greece, survived in medieval and modern Europe, and not only can still be enjoyed in books today but also sometimes even form the plot line of Bugs Bunny cartoons. They are a reservoir of good sense and simple patterns of behavior. An example will illustrate Aesop's method of conveying his message. In one of his fables Aesop tells of a hungry fox who encounters sun-ripened grapes in a vineyard. Try as he might, he cannot reach them. In disgust he leaves, muttering that they are probably sour and wormy anyway, whence comes our expression "sour grapes." The moral is that all fools can criticize what they cannot get. Many people who never read the writings of philosophers learned from such fables as Aesop's something about life and ethics.

With this impressive heritage behind them, the philosophers of the classical period ventured into new areas of speculation. This development was partly due to the work of Hippocrates (second half of the fifth century B.C.), the father of medicine. Like Thales, Hippocrates sought natural explanations for natural phenomena. Basing his opinions on empirical knowledge, not on religion or magic, he taught that natural means could be employed to fight disease. In his treatise *On Airs, Waters, and Places,* he noted the influence of climate and environment on health. Hippocrates and his followers put forward a theory that was to prevail in medical circles until the eighteenth century. The human body, they declared, contains four humors, or fluids: blood, phlegm, black bile, and yellow bile. In a healthy body the four humors are in perfect balance; too much or too little of any particular humor causes illness. But Hippocrates broke away from the mainstream of Ionian speculation by declaring that medicine was a separate craft—just as ironworking was—that had its own set of principles.

The distinction between natural science and philosophy on which Hippocrates insisted was also promoted by the Sophists, who traveled the Greek world teaching young men. Despite differences of opinion on philosophical matters, the Sophists all agreed that human beings were the proper subject of study. They also believed that excellence could be taught, and they used philosophy and rhetoric to prepare young men for life in the polis. The Sophists put great emphasis on logic and the meanings of words. They criticized traditional beliefs, religion, rituals, and myth and even questioned the laws of the polis. In essence they argued that nothing is absolute, that everything is relative. Hence more traditional Greeks considered them wanton and harmful, men who were interested in "making the worse seem the better cause."

One of those who was thought to be a Sophist was Socrates (ca 470–399 B.C.). Socrates was an Athenian of pure blood, which conferred citizenship on him. He sprang from a traditional Athenian family of modest wealth, and he loyally served his polis on the battlefield during the Peloponnesian War and in the assembly at Athens. His major interests, however, were philosophical, not political. He was not strictly a Sophist, because he never formally taught or collected fees from anyone. He nonetheless shared the Sophists' belief that human beings and their environment were the essential subjects of philosophical inquiry. Like the Sophists, Socrates thought that excellence could be learned and passed on to others. His approach when posing ethical questions and defining concepts was to start with a general topic or problem and to narrow the matter to its essentials. He did so by continuous questioning, a running dialogue. Never did he lecture. Socrates thought that by constantly pursuing excellence, an essential part of which was knowledge, human beings could approach the supreme good and thus find true happiness. Yet in 399 B.C. Socrates was brought to trial, convicted, and executed on charges of corrupting the youth of the city and introducing new gods.

Socrates' student Plato (427–347 B.C.) carried on his master's search for truth. Unlike Socrates, Plato wrote down his thoughts and theories and founded a philosophical school, the Academy. Most people rightly think of Plato as a philosopher. Yet his writings were also literary essays of great charm. They drew out characters, locales, and scenes from ordinary life that would otherwise be lost to posterity. In addition, Plato used satire, irony, and comedy to relay his thoughts. Despite all the reverence that people normally pay to Plato, they can also read him for the sheer fun of it. Behind the elegance of his literary style, however, stand the profound thoughts of a brilliant mind that grappled with the problems of his own day and the eternal realities of life. The destruction and chaos of the Peloponnesian War prompted him to ask new and different questions about the nature of human society. He pondered where, why, and how the polis had gone wrong. Thus he gave serious thought to the very nature of the polis and what was the best form that it should take. In these considerations Plato was not only a philosopher but a political scientist and a utopian, a man who genuinely thought that he could create a form of government that would give people the most ethical and satisfying way of life possible. He spent his entire life trying to determine the ideal polis.

The ideal polis could exist only when its citizens were well educated. Plato tried to show that a life of ignorance was wretched. From education came the possibility of determining an all-comprising unity of virtues that would lead to an intelligent, moral, and ethical life. Yet can virtue be taught? Plato never satisfactorily answered his own question. He concluded that only divine providence could guide people to virtue. In his opinion divine providence was one intelligible and individualistic being. In short, he equated god with the concept of good. Plato's tool was mathematics as the servant of education. Human life is transitory, but ideas are permanent. If people could master the essential ideas, guided by mathematics, their souls would become immortal. Here is where the state helped people to reach this goal. It was the highest duty of true statesmen to educate their people in this regard.

Plato developed the theory that all visible, tangible things are unreal and temporary, copies of "forms" or "ideas" that are constant and indestructible. Only the mind, not the senses, can perceive eternal forms. In Plato's view the highest form is the idea of good. He discussed these ideas in two works. In *The Republic* Plato applied his theory of forms to politics in an effort to describe the ideal polis. His perfect polis was utopian; it aimed at providing the greatest good and happiness to all its members. Plato thought that the ideal polis could exist only if its rulers were philosophers. He divided society into rulers, guardians of the polis, and workers. The role of people in each category would be decided by the education, wisdom, and ability of the individual. In Plato's republic men and women would be equal to one another, and women could become rulers. The utopian polis would be a balance, with each individual doing what he or she could to support the state and with each receiving from the state his or her just due. In *The Laws,* however, he drew a more authoritarian picture of government and society, one not so very different from that of twentieth-century dictatorship. If Plato ultimately failed to realize his utopia, he at least introduced to others the concept that they could strive to shape an ideal society.

Aristotle (384–322 B.C.) carried on the philosophical tradition of Socrates and Plato. A student of Plato, Aristotle went far beyond him in striving to understand the universe. The range of Aristotle's thought is staggering. Everything in human experience was a fit subject for his inquiry. In *Politics* Aristotle followed Plato's lead by writing about the ideal polis. Yet Aristotle approached the question more realistically than Plato and criticized *The Republic* and Plato's other writings on many points. In his *Politics* and elsewhere, Aristotle stressed moderation, concluding that the balance of his ideal state depended on people of talent and education who could avoid extremes.

Aristotle also tried to understand the changes of nature—what caused them and where they led. Hence he was both a philosopher and a scientist. He became increasingly interested in the observation and explanation of natural phenomena. The range of his interests was stunning, embracing logic, dialectic, ethics, natural sciences, politics, poetry, and art. He used logic as his method of scientific discussion. His method was the syllogism, whereby he reasoned from a general statement to a particular conclusion. His thinking was so different from Plato's that he established his own school. He held lectures in a gymnasium and afterward discussed topics with students while walking under the eaves of the building. From that practice his school gained the name *Peripatos,* which literally means "to walk around" (and is related to our modern English word *peripatetic*).

Aristotle also attempted to bridge the gap that Plato had created between abstract truth and concrete perception. He argued that the universe is finite, spherical, and eternal. Here he discusses an immaterial being that is his conception of god. Yet his god neither created the universe nor guided it. The inconsistencies of Aristotle on these matters are obvious. His god is without purpose. Yet for him scientific endeavor, the highest attainable form of living, reaches the divine.

Aristotle expressed the heart of his philosophy in two masterful works, *Physics* and *Metaphysics*. In them he combined empiricism, or observation, and speculative method. In *Physics* he tried to explain all of nature to how natural physical phenomena worked on one another and how these actions lead to the results that people actually see around them daily. He postulated the four principles of matter, form, movement, and goal. A good analogy is a seed. It possesses both matter and an encoded form. Form determines whether the plant will be a rose or poison ivy. Growth represents movement, and the mature plant the goal of the seed. Although Aristotle considered nature impersonal, he also felt that it had its own purposes. In a sense, this is a rudimentary ancestor of the concept of evolution.

In *On the Heaven* Aristotle took up the thread of Ionian speculation. His theory of cosmology added ether to air, fire, water, and earth as building blocks of the universe. He concluded that the universe revolves and that it is spherical and eternal. He wrongly thought that the earth is the center of the universe, with the stars and planets revolving around it. The Hellenistic scientist Aristarchus of Samos later realized that the earth revolves around the sun, but Aristotle's view was accepted until the time of the sixteenth-century astronomer Nicolaus Copernicus.

Aristotle possessed one of the keenest and most curious philosophical minds of Western civilization. While rethinking the old topics explored by the Pre-Socratics, he also created whole new areas of study. In short, he tried to learn everything possible about the universe and everything in it. He did so in the belief that all

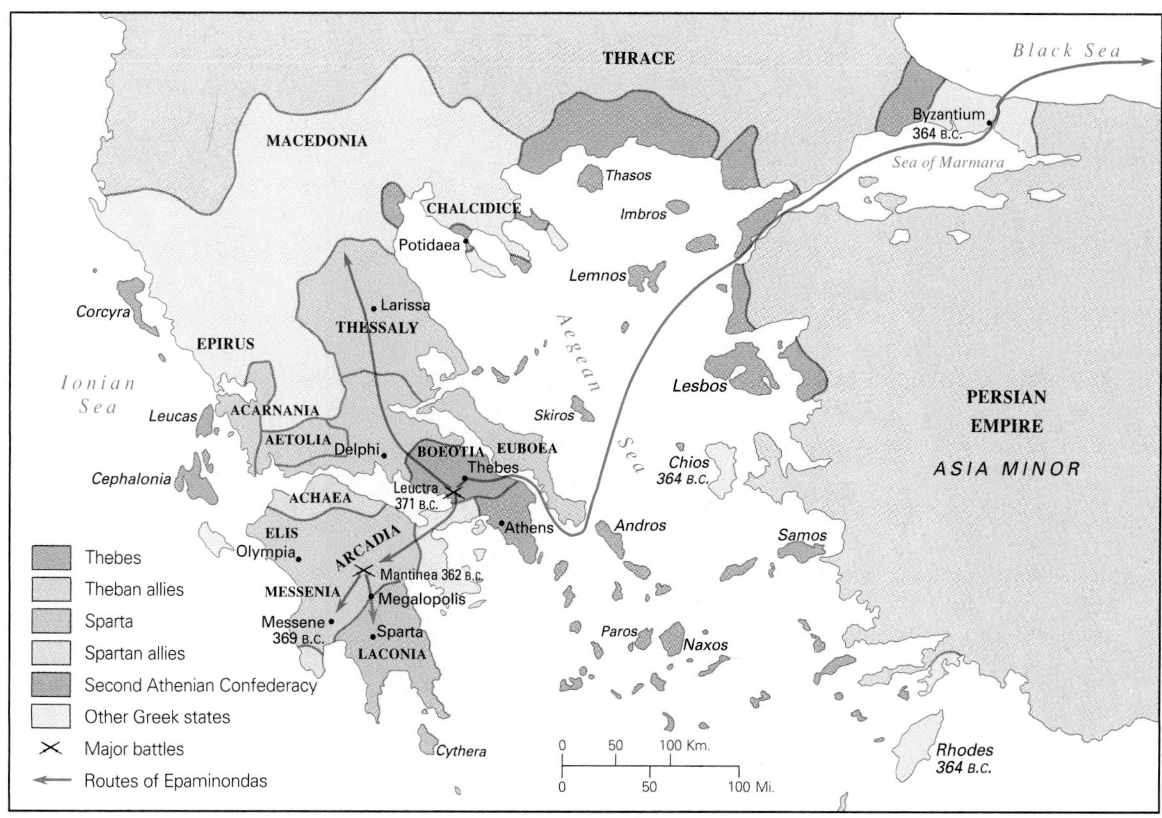

MAP 3.5 Greece at 362 B.C. The fourth century B.C. witnessed the rapid growth of Greek federalism as states sought allies to gain security from rival powers.

knowledge could be synthesized to produce a simple explanation of the universe and of humanity. Because he was such a popular and prolific writer, his works circulated widely throughout the Greek world. The Ptolemies, a line of Hellenistic kings (see page 115), accumulated as many of them as possible in their famous library at Alexandria. The mere fact that he put his thoughts into writing ensured their preservation.

The Final Act (404–338 B.C.)

The end of the Peloponnesian War only punctuated a century of nearly constant warfare that lasted from 421 to 338 B.C. The events of the fourth century demonstrated that no single Greek state possessed enough power and resources to dominate the others. There nevertheless ensued an exhausting struggle for hegemony among the great powers, especially Sparta, Athens, and Thebes (Map 3.5). Immediately after the Peloponnesian War, with Athens humbled, Sparta began striving for empire over the Greeks. The arrogance and imperialism of the Spartans turned their former allies against them. Even with Persian help Sparta could not maintain its hold on Greece. In 371 B.C. the Spartans met their match on the plain of Leuctra in Boeotia. A Theban army under the command of Epaminondas, one of Greece's most brilliant generals, destroyed the flower of the Spartan army on a single summer day. The victory at Leuctra left Thebes the most powerful state in Greece. Under Epaminondas the Thebans destroyed Sparta as a first-rank power and checked the ambitions of Athens, but they were unable to bring peace to Greece. In 362 B.C. Epaminondas was killed in battle, and a period of stalemate set in. The Greek states were virtually exhausted.

The Lion of Chaeronea This stylized lion marks the mass grave of nearly 300 elite Theban soldiers who valiantly died fighting the Macedonians at the Battle of Chaeronea. After the battle, when Philip viewed the bodies of these brave troops, he said: "May those who suppose that these men did or suffered anything dishonorable perish wretchedly." *(Caroline Buckler)*

The man who turned the situation to his advantage was Philip II, king of Macedonia (359–336 B.C.). Throughout most of Greek history Macedonia, which bordered Greece in the north, in modern Greece and Serbia, had been a backward, disunited kingdom, but Philip's genius, courage, and drive turned it into a major power. One of the ablest statesmen of antiquity, Philip united his powerful kingdom, built a redoubtable army, and pursued his ambition with drive and determination. His horizon was not limited to Macedonia, for he realized that he could turn the rivalry and exhaustion of the Greek states to his own purposes. By clever use of his wealth and superb army Philip won control of the northern Aegean and awakened fear in Athens, which had vital interests there. Demosthenes, an Athenian patriot and a fine orator, warned his fellow citizens against Philip. Others too saw Philip as a threat. A comic playwright depicted one of Philip's ambassadors warning the Athenians:

Do you know that your battle will be with men
Who dine on sharpened swords,
And gulp burning firebrands for wine?
Then immediately after dinner the slave

ble care being taken of them. As for a recognized method of treatment, it would be true to say that no such thing existed; what did good in some cases did harm in others. Those with naturally strong constitutions were no better able than the weak to resist the disease, which carried away all alike, even those who were treated and dieted with the greatest care. The most terrible thing of all was the despair into which people fell when they realized that they had caught the plague. Terrible, too, was the sight of people dying like sheep through having caught the disease as a result of nursing others. This indeed caused more deaths than anything else. For when people were afraid to visit the sick, then they died with no one to look after them. Indeed, there were many houses in which all the inhabitants perished through lack of attention. When, on the other hand, they did visit the sick, they lost their own lives, and this was particularly true of those who made it a point of honor to act properly. Such people felt ashamed to think of their own safety and went into their friends' houses at times when even the members of the household were so overwhelmed by the weight of their calamities that they had actually given up the usual practice of making laments for the dead. Yet still the ones who felt most pity for the sick and the dying were those who had had the plague themselves and had recovered from it. They knew what it was like and at the same time felt themselves to be safe, for no one caught the disease twice, or, if he did, the second attack was never fatal. . . .

A factor that made matters much worse than they were already was the removal of people from the country into the city, and this particularly affected the newcomers. There were no houses for them, and, living as they did during the hot season in badly ventilated huts, they died like flies. The bodies of the dying were heaped one on top of the other, and half-dead creatures could be seen staggering about in the streets or flocking around the fountains in their desire for water.

The catastrophe was so overwhelming that people, not knowing what would happen next to them, became indifferent to every rule of religion and law. Athens owed to the plague the beginnings of a state of unprecedented lawlessness. People now began openly to venture on acts of self-indulgence which before then they used to keep in the dark. Thus they resolved to spend their money quickly and to spend it on pleasure, since money and life alike seemed equally ephemeral. As for what is called honor, no one showed himself willing to abide by its laws, so doubtful was it whether one would survive to enjoy the name for it. It was

✣ Coin depicting the god Asclepius, represented by a snake, putting an end to urban plague. *(Bibliothèque Nationale, Paris)*

generally agreed that what was both honorable and valuable was the pleasure of the moment and everything that might conceivably contribute to that pleasure. No fear of god or law of man had a restraining influence. As for the gods, it seemed to be the same thing whether one worshiped them or not, when one saw the good and the bad dying indiscriminately. As for offenses against human law, no one expected to be punished. Instead, everyone felt that already a far heavier sentence had been passed on him and was hanging over him, and that before the time for its execution arrived, it was only natural to get some pleasure out of life.

This, then, was the calamity that fell upon Athens, and the times were hard indeed, with people dying inside the city and the land outside being laid waste.

Questions for Analysis

1. What does this account of the plague say about human nature when put in an extreme crisis?
2. Does popular religion offer any solace during such a catastrophe?
3. How did public laws and customs cope with such a disaster?

Source: R. Warner, trans., *Thucydides, History of the Peloponnesian War* (Penguin Books, 1972), pp. 152–156. Used by permission of Penguin UK.

CHAPTER

4 Hellenistic Diffusion

Wall painting from Pompeii: Pelias and his daughters. *(National Museum, Naples)*

Two years after his conquest of Greece, Philip of Macedon fell victim to an assassin's dagger. Philip's twenty-year-old son, historically known as Alexander the Great (r. 336–323 B.C.), assumed the Macedonian throne. This young man, one of the most remarkable personalities of Western civilization, was to have a profound impact on history. By overthrowing the Persian Empire and by spreading *Hellenism*—Greek culture, language, thought, and way of life—as far as India, Alexander was instrumental in creating a new era, traditionally called "Hellenistic" to distinguish it from the Hellenic. As a result of Alexander's exploits, the individualistic and energetic culture of the Greeks came into intimate contact with the venerable older cultures of the Near East.

The impact of Philip and Alexander was so enormous that the great German historian Hermann Bengtson has commented:

Philip and his son Alexander were the ones who opened the door of the world to the Macedonians and Greeks. With Macedonian imperialism was joined the diffusion of the Greek spirit, which permeated the entire ancient world. Without the achievement of these two kings, neither the Roman Empire nor the diffusion of Christianity would have been conceivable.[1]

- Is this estimation correct, or is it mere rhetoric?
- What did the spread of Hellenism mean to the Greeks and the peoples of the Near East?
- What did the meeting of West and East hold for the development of economics, religion, philosophy, women's concerns, science, and medicine?

These are the questions we will explore in this chapter.

Alexander and the Great Crusade

In 336 B.C. Alexander inherited not only Philip's crown but also his policies. After his victory at Chaeronea, Philip had organized the states of Greece into a huge league under his leadership and announced to the Greeks his plan to lead them and his Macedonians against the Persian Empire. Fully intending to carry out Philip's designs, Alexander proclaimed to the Greek world that the invasion of Persia was to be a great crusade, a mighty act of revenge for the Persian invasion of Greece in 480 B.C. It would also be the means by which Alexander would create an empire of his own in the East.

Despite his youth, Alexander was well prepared to lead the attack. Philip had groomed his son to become king and given him the best education possible. In 343 B.C. Philip invited the philosopher Aristotle to tutor his son. From Aristotle, Alexander learned to appreciate Greek culture and literature, and the teachings of the great philosopher left a lasting mark on him. Alexander must also have profited from Aristotle's practical knowledge, but he never accepted Aristotle's political theories. Philip appointed Alexander regent of Macedonia at the age of sixteen, and two years later at the Battle of Chaeronea Alexander helped defeat the Greeks. By 336 B.C. Alexander had acquired both the theoretical and the practical knowledge to rule peoples and lead armies.

In 334 B.C. Alexander led an army of Macedonians and Greeks into Asia Minor. With him went a staff of philosophers and poets, scientists whose job it was to map the country and study strange animals and plants, and the historian Callisthenes, who was to write an account of the campaign. Alexander intended not only a military campaign but also an expedition of discovery.

In the next three years Alexander won three major battles at the Granicus River, Issus, and Gaugamela. As Map 4.1 shows, these battle sites stand almost as road signs marking his march to the East. When Alexander reached Egypt, he quickly seized the land, honored the priestly class, and was proclaimed pharaoh, the legitimate ruler of the country. He next marched to the oasis of Siwah, west of the Nile Valley, to consult the famous oracle of Zeus-Amon. No one will ever know what the priest told him, but henceforth Alexander considered himself the son of Zeus. Next he marched into western Asia, where at Gaugamela he defeated the Persian army. After this victory the principal Persian capital of Persepolis easily fell to him. There he performed a symbolic act of retribution by burning the buildings of Xerxes, the invader of Greece. In 330 B.C. he took Ecbatana, the last Persian capital, and pursued the Persian king to his death.

The Persian Empire had fallen, and the war of revenge was over, but Alexander had no intention of stopping. He dismissed his Greek troops but permitted many of them to serve on as mercenaries. Alexander then began his personal odyssey. With his Macedonian

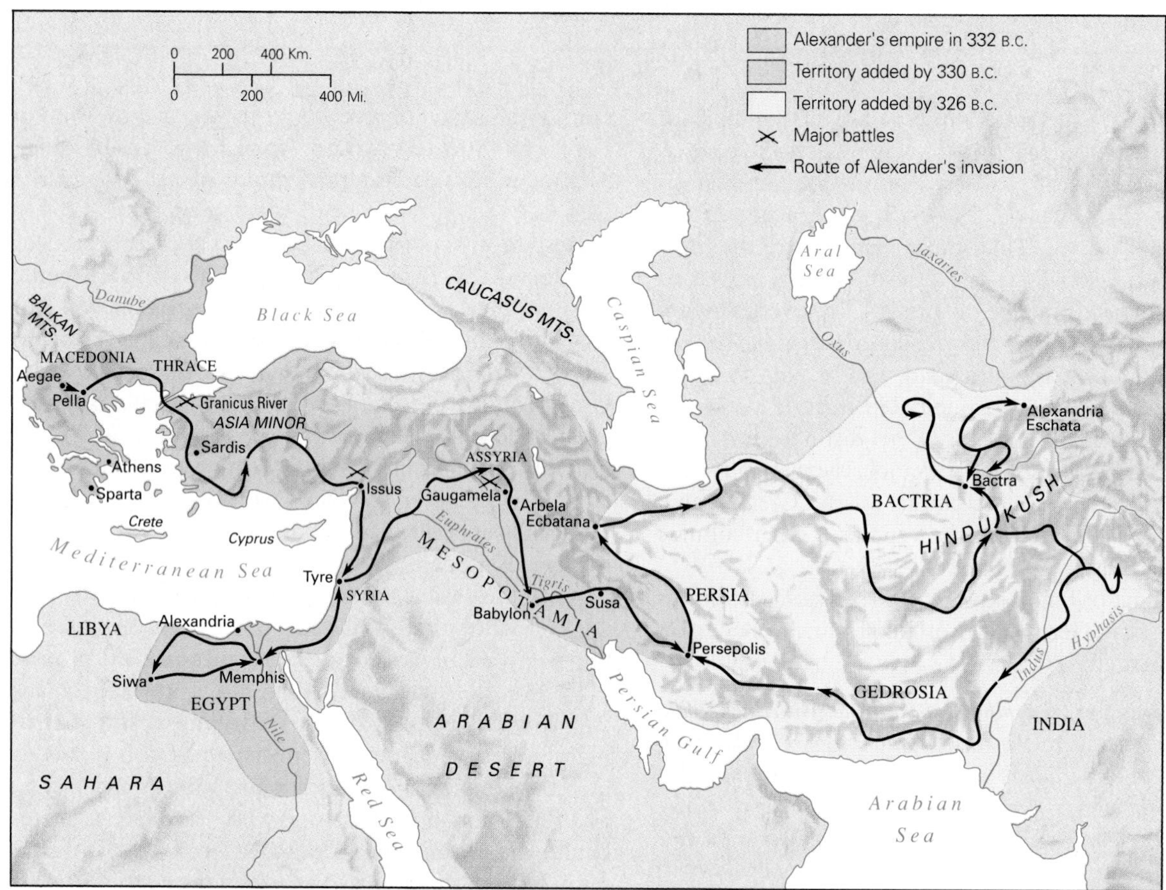

MAP 4.1 Alexander's Conquests This map shows the course of Alexander's invasion of the Persian Empire and the speed of his progress. More important than the great success of his military campaigns was his founding of Hellenistic cities in the East.

soldiers and Greek mercenaries, he set out to conquer the rest of Asia. He plunged deeper into the East, into lands completely unknown to the Greek world. Alexander's way was marked by bitter fighting and bloodshed. It took his soldiers four additional years to conquer Bactria and the easternmost parts of the now-defunct Persian Empire, but still Alexander was determined to continue his march.

In 326 B.C. Alexander crossed the Indus River and entered India. There, too, he saw hard fighting, and finally at the Hyphasis River his troops refused to go farther. Alexander was enraged by the mutiny, for he believed he was near the end of the world. Nonetheless, the army stood firm, and Alexander had to relent. Still eager to explore the limits of the world, Alexander turned south to the Arabian Sea. Though the tribes in the area did not oppose him, he waged a bloody, ruthless, and unnecessary war against them. After reaching the Arabian Sea and turning west, he led his army through the grim Gedrosian Desert. The army suffered fearfully, and many soldiers died along the way; nonetheless, in 324 B.C. Alexander reached his camp at Susa. The great crusade was over, and Alexander himself died the next year in Babylon.

Alexander's Legacy

Alexander so quickly became a legend during his lifetime that he still seems superhuman. That alone makes a reasoned interpretation of him very difficult. Some historians have seen him as a high-minded philosopher, and none can deny that he possessed genuine intellectual gifts. Others, however, have portrayed him as a bloody-minded autocrat, more interested in his own ambition than in any philosophical concept of the common good. Alexander is the perfect example of the need for the historian carefully to interpret the known facts.

The historical record shows that Alexander in a drunken brawl murdered the friend who had saved his life at the Battle of the Granicus River. Alexander also used his power to have several other trusted officials, who had done nothing to offend him, assassinated. Other uglier and grimmer facts argue against the view that Alexander was a humane and tolerant man. In eastern Iran and India he savagely and unnecessarily slaughtered peoples whose only crime was their desire to be left in peace.

The only rationale to support those who see Alexander as a philosopher-king comes from a banquet held in 324 B.C. at the end of his career of carnage. This event is very important for a variety of reasons. It came immediately on the heels of a major Macedonian mutiny. The veteran and otherwise loyal Macedonians resented Alexander's new policy of giving high offices to Persians, people whom they had conquered after great suffering. Alexander realized that his Macedonians were too few to administer his new empire and that he needed the ability and experience of the Persians. As a gesture of reconciliation and to end the mutiny, Alexander named the entire Macedonian army his kinsmen and held a vast banquet to heal wounds. He reserved the place of honor for the Macedonians, giving the Persians and others positions of lesser status. At the banquet Alexander offered a public prayer for harmony and partnership between the Macedonians and the Persians, and this prayer has been interpreted as an expression of deep philosophical views. But far from representing an ideal desire for the brotherhood of man, the gesture

Alexander at the Battle of Issus At left, Alexander the Great, bareheaded and wearing a breastplate, charges King Darius, who is standing in a chariot. The moment marks the turning point of the battle, as Darius turns to flee from the attack. *(National Museum, Naples/Alinari/Art Resource, NY)*

was a blatant call for Macedonians and Persians to form a superior union for the purpose of ruling his new empire. It is undeniably true that the concepts of universal harmony and the brotherhood of man became common during the Hellenistic period, but they were the creations of talented philosophers, not the battle-hardened king of Macedonia.

Alexander was instrumental in changing the face of politics in the eastern Mediterranean. His campaign swept away the Persian Empire, which had ruled the East for over two hundred years. In its place he established a Macedonian monarchy.

More important in the long run was his founding of new cities and military colonies, which scattered Greeks and Macedonians throughout the East. Thus the practical result of Alexander's campaign was to open the East to the tide of Hellenism.

The Political Legacy

In 323 B.C. Alexander the Great died at the age of thirty-two. The main question at his death was whether his vast empire could be held together. A major part of his legacy is what he had not done. Although he fathered a successor while in Bactria, his son was an infant at Alexander's death. The child was too young to assume the duties of kingship and was cruelly murdered. That meant that Alexander's empire was a prize for the taking by the strongest of his generals. Within a week of Alexander's death a round of fighting began that was to continue for forty years. No single Macedonian general was able to replace Alexander as emperor of his entire domain. In 301 B.C. many of Alexander's successors joined in battle at Ipsus, in central Phrygia. The battle was decisive only in that it determined that no one general would be able to maintain Alexander's vast empire. In effect, the strongest divided it among themselves. By 275 B.C. three officers had split the empire into large monarchies (Map 4.2). Antigonus Gonatas became king of Macedonia and established the Antigonid dynasty, which ruled until the Roman conquest in 168 B.C. Ptolemy, son of Lagus, made himself king of Egypt, and his descendants, the Ptolemies, assumed the powers and position of pharaohs. Seleucus, founder of the Seleucid dynasty, carved out a kingdom that stretched from the coast of Asia Minor to India. In 263 B.C. Eumenes, the Greek ruler of Pergamum, a city in western Asia Minor, won his independence from the Seleucids and created the Pergamene monarchy. Though the Seleucid kings soon lost control of their easternmost provinces, Greek influence in this area did not wane. In modern Turkestan and Afghanistan another line of Greek kings established the kingdom of Bactria and even managed to spread their power and culture into northern India.

The political face of Greece itself changed during the Hellenistic period. The day of the polis was over; in its place rose leagues of city-states. The two most powerful and extensive were the Aetolian League in western and central Greece and the Achaean League in the Peloponnesus. Once-powerful city-states like Athens and Sparta sank to the level of third-rate powers.

The political history of the Hellenistic period was dominated by the great monarchies and the Greek leagues. The political fragmentation and incessant warfare that marked the Hellenic period continued on an even wider and larger scale during the Hellenistic period. Never did the Hellenistic world achieve political stability or lasting peace. Hellenistic kings never forgot the vision of Alexander's empire, spanning Europe and Asia, secure under the rule of one man. Try though they did, they were never able to re-create it. In this respect Alexander's legacy fell not to his generals but to the Romans of a later era.

The Cultural Legacy

As Alexander waded ever deeper into the East, distance alone presented him with a serious problem: how was he to retain contact with the Greek world behind him? Communications were vital, for he drew supplies and reinforcements from Greece and Macedonia. Alexander had to be sure that he was never cut off and stranded far from the Mediterranean world. His solution was to plant cities and military colonies in strategic places. In these settlements Alexander left Greek mercenaries and Macedonian veterans who were no longer up to active campaigning. Besides keeping the road open to the West, these settlements served the purpose of dominating the countryside around them.

Their military significance apart, Alexander's cities and colonies became powerful instruments in the spread of Hellenism throughout the East. Plutarch described Alexander's achievement in glowing terms: "Having founded over 70 cities among barbarian peoples and having planted Greek magistracies in Asia, Alexander overcame its wild and savage way of life."[2] Alexander had indeed opened the East to an enormous wave of immigration, and his successors continued his policy by inviting Greek colonists to settle in their

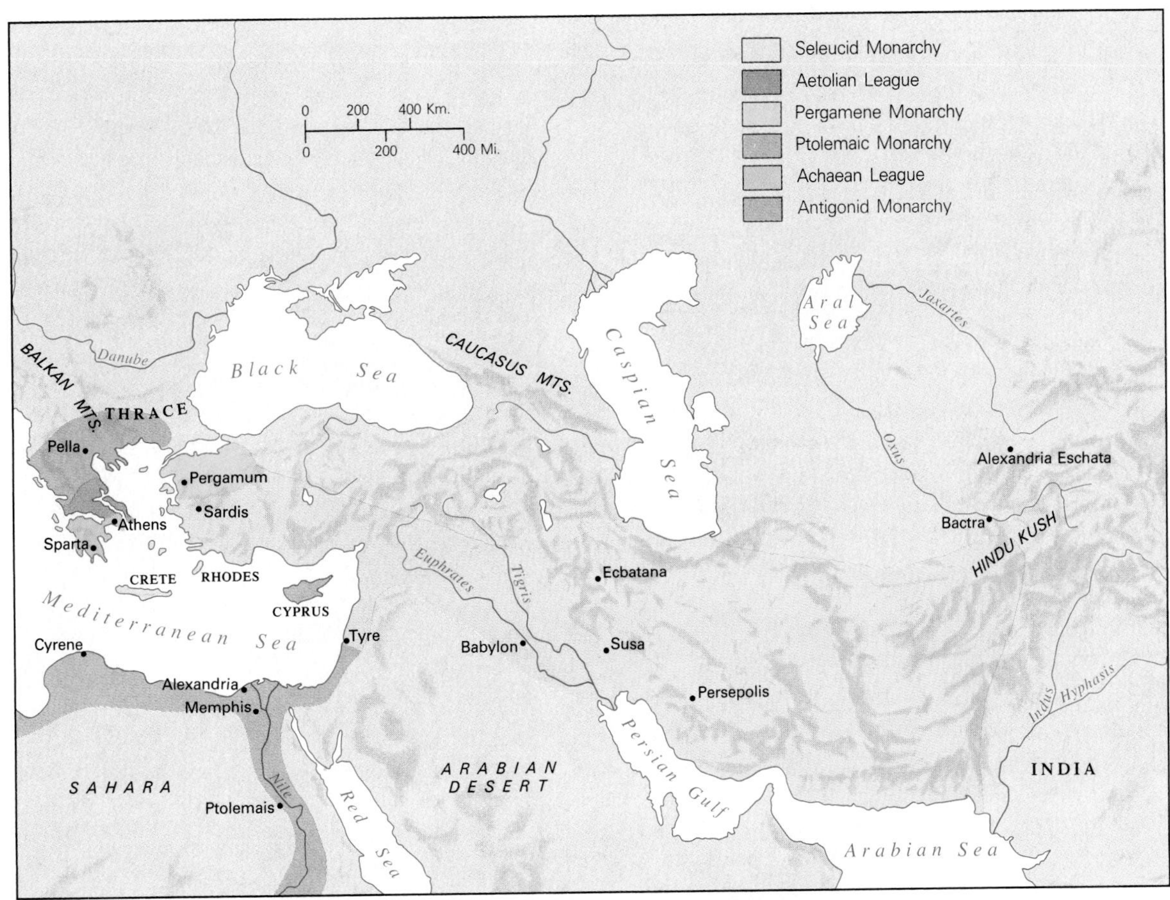

MAP 4.2 The Hellenistic World After Alexander's death, no single commander could hold his vast conquests together, resulting in the empire's breakup into several kingdoms and leagues.

realms. For seventy-five years after Alexander's death, Greek immigrants poured into the East. At least 250 new Hellenistic colonies were established. The Mediterranean world had seen no comparable movement of peoples since the days of Archilochus (see page 75), when wave after wave of Greeks had turned the Mediterranean basin into a Greek-speaking region.

One concrete and almost exotic example of these trends comes from the newly discovered Hellenistic city of Ay Khanoum. Situated on the borders of Russia and Afghanistan and not far from China, the city was predominantly Greek. It had the typical Greek trappings of a gymnasium, various temples, and administration buildings. It was not, however, purely Greek. It also contained an oriental temple and artistic remains that prove that the Greeks and the natives had already embraced aspects of each other's religions. One of the most curious discoveries was a long inscription written in Greek verse by Clearchus, a pupil of Aristotle. The inscription, carved in stone, was set up in a public place for all to see. Clearchus had simply copied the precepts of famous Greeks. The inscription was philosophy for the common people, a contribution to popular culture. It provided the Greeks with a link to their faraway homeland. It was also an easy way to make at least some of Greek culture available to natives.

The overall result of Alexander's settlements and those of his successors was the spread of Hellenism as far east as India. Throughout the Hellenistic period, Greeks and Easterners became familiar with and adapted themselves to each other's customs, religions, and ways of life. Although Greek culture did not completely conquer the

Ay Khanoum This view of a Greek palaestra was found at Ay Khanoum, a city located in modern Afghanistan. The palaestra and other buildings are mute evidence of how the Greeks took their culture with them no matter how far from home. *(French Archaeological Delegation, Afghanistan)*

East, it gave the East a vehicle of expression that linked it to the West. Hellenism became a common bond among the East, peninsular Greece, and the western Mediterranean. This pre-existing cultural bond was later to prove supremely valuable to Rome—itself heavily influenced by Hellenism—in its efforts to impose a comparable political unity on the known world.

The Spread of Hellenism

When the Greeks and Macedonians entered Asia Minor, Egypt, and the more remote East, they encountered civilizations older than their own. In some ways the Eastern cultures were more advanced than the Greek, in others less so. Thus this third great tide of Greek migration differed from preceding waves, which had spread over land that was uninhabited or inhabited by less-developed peoples.

What did the Hellenistic monarchies offer Greek immigrants politically and materially? More broadly, how did Hellenism and the cultures of the East affect one another? What did the meeting of East and West entail for the history of the world?

Cities and Kingdoms

One of the major developments of these new kingdoms was the resurgence of monarchy, which had many repercussions. For most Greeks monarchs were something out of the heroic past, something found in

Homer's *Iliad* but not in daily life. Furthermore, most Hellenistic kingdoms embraced numerous different peoples who had little in common. Hellenistic kings thus needed a new political concept to unite them. One solution was the creation of a ruler cult that linked the king's authority with that of the gods. Thus, royal power had divine approval and was meant to create a political and religious bond between the kings and their subjects. These deified kings were not considered gods as mighty as Zeus or Apollo, and the new ruler cults probably made little religious impact on those ruled. Nonetheless, the ruler cult was an easily understandable symbol of unity within the kingdom.

Monarchy also included royal women, who began to play an active part in political and diplomatic life. Some of them did so in their own right, others by manipulating their husbands. For the most part they served as examples that women too were capable of shouldering vast responsibilities and performing them successfully.

Although Alexander's generals created huge kingdoms, the concept of monarchy, even when combined with the ruler cult, never replaced the ideal of the polis. Consequently, the monarchies never won the deep emotional loyalty that Greeks had once felt for the polis. Hellenistic kings needed large numbers of Greeks to run their kingdoms. Otherwise royal business would grind to a halt, and the conquerors would soon be swallowed up by the far more numerous conquered population. Obviously, then, the kings had to encourage Greeks to immigrate and build new homes. The Hellenistic kings thus confronted the problem of making life in the new monarchies resemble the traditional Greek way of life. Since Greek civilization was urban, the kings continued Alexander's policy of establishing cities throughout their kingdoms in order to entice Greeks to immigrate. Yet the creation of these cities posed a serious political problem that the Hellenistic kings failed to solve.

To the Greeks civilized life was unthinkable without the polis, which was far more than a mere city. The Greek polis was by definition *sovereign*—an independent, autonomous state run by its citizens, free of any outside power or restraint. Hellenistic kings, however, refused to grant sovereignty to their cities. In effect, these kings willingly built cities but refused to build a polis.

Hellenistic monarchs gave their cities all the external trappings of a polis. Each had an assembly of citizens, a council to prepare legislation, and a board of magistrates to conduct the city's political business. Yet, however similar to the Greek polis they appeared, these cities could not engage in diplomatic dealings, make treaties, pursue their own foreign policy, or wage their own wars. None could govern its own affairs without interference from the king, who, even if he stood in the background, was the real sovereign. In the eyes of the king the cities were important parts of the kingdom, but the welfare of the whole kingdom came first. The cities had to follow royal orders, and the king often placed his own officials in the cities to see that his decrees were followed.

A new Hellenistic city differed from a Greek polis in other ways as well. The Greek polis had enjoyed political and social unity even though it was normally composed of citizens, slaves, and resident aliens. The polis had one body of law and one set of customs. In the Hellenistic city Greeks represented an elite citizen class. Natives and non-Greek foreigners who lived in Hellenistic cities usually possessed lesser rights than Greeks and often had their own laws. In some instances this disparity spurred natives to assimilate Greek culture in order to rise politically and socially. The Hellenistic city was not homogeneous and could not spark the intensity of feeling that marked the polis. (See the feature "Individuals in Society: Menander, a Playwright for a New World.")

In many respects the Hellenistic city resembled a modern city. It was a cultural center with theaters, temples, and libraries. It was a seat of learning, home of poets, writers, teachers, and artists. It was a place where people could find amusement. The Hellenistic city was also an economic center that provided a ready market for grain and produce raised in the surrounding countryside. The city was an emporium, scene of trade and manufacturing. In short, the Hellenistic city offered cultural and economic opportunities but did not foster a sense of united, integrated enterprise.

There were no constitutional links between city and king. The city was simply his possession. Its citizens had no voice in how the kingdom was run. The city had no rights except for those the king granted, and even those he could summarily take away. Ambassadors from the city could entreat the king for favors and petition him on such matters as taxes, boundary disputes, and legal cases. But the city had no right to advise the king on royal policy and enjoyed no political function in the kingdom.

Hellenistic kings tried to make the kingdom the political focus of citizens' allegiance. If the king could secure the frontiers of his kingdom, he could give it a geographical identity. He could then hope that his subjects would direct their primary loyalty to the kingdom

Theater of Stratos Excavation of this theater began only in 1994 in Stratos, a major city in northwestern Greece. Not a city in the mainstream of Greek affairs, Stratos nevertheless shared the love and appreciation of the arts that stamped all of Greek culture. Even in its partially excavated state, the theater boasts the remains of a stone building in the foreground, the orchestra, and behind it the seats. Beyond its many architectural refinements, the theater is of interest because most Greek plays were staged in small theaters such as this. *(John Buckler)*

rather than to a particular city. However, the kings' efforts to fix their borders led only to sustained warfare. Boundaries were determined by military power, and rule by force became the chief political principle of the Hellenistic world.

Border wars were frequent and exhausting. The Seleucids and Ptolemies, for instance, waged five wars for the possession of southern Syria. Other kings refused to acknowledge boundaries at all. They followed Alexander's example and waged wars to reunify his empire under their own authority. By the third century B.C. a weary balance of power was reached, but only as the result of stalemate. It was not based on any political principle.

Though Hellenistic kings never built a true polis, that does not mean that their urban policy failed. Rather, the Hellenistic city was to remain the basic social and political unit in the Hellenistic East until the sixth century A.D. Cities were the chief agents of Hellenization, and their influence spread far beyond their walls. These cities formed a broader cultural network in which Greek language, customs, and values flourished. Roman rule in the Hellenistic East would later be based on this urban culture, which facilitated the rise and spread of Christianity. In broad terms, Hellenistic cities were remarkably successful.

The Greeks and the Opening of the East

If the Hellenistic kings failed to satisfy the Greeks' political yearnings, they nonetheless succeeded in giving them unequaled economic and social opportunities. The ruling dynasties of the Hellenistic world were Macedonian, and Greeks filled all important political, military, and diplomatic positions. They constituted an upper class that sustained Hellenism in the barbarian

Individuals in Society

Menander, a Playwright for a New World

Bas relief (detail) of Menander from the end of the fourth century B.C. *(The Art Museum, Princeton University, Museum Purchase, Caroline G. Mather Fund)*

The triumph of Alexander the Great directly and sometimes indirectly changed the face of the ancient world. Greece was not immune to the change, and even the arts were affected. Sculpture, literature, and drama became more personal and generally less political than before. Nowhere can these changes be better seen than in the Athenian theater. During the heady days of the polis, poets such as Aristophanes used the stage to caricature political leaders and criticize policies of state. With the opening of the East, however, mainland Greece began to decline in political importance. This situation was particularly true of Athens. Though still respected, the Athens of the Hellenistic period had seen its greatest days. Attic theater reflected this change. The New Comedy, as it is known, was individualistic and began a literary tradition that continues to flourish today.

No one artist better exemplifies this development than Menander (342–291 B.C.). When five years old, the boy heard of the Macedonian conquest of Greece. Thus he learned of former Athenian greatness only from the tales and memories of his elders and the public monuments that he saw around him. He, like other Greeks, had to adapt to new developments. His education reflected the changed situation. He studied with Theophrastus, who had succeeded Aristotle as the leader of his school of philosophy. Theophrastus was an original thinker who explored human conduct and character. His influence on Menander cannot be determined, but both were interested in individuals.

When Menander performed his military service, he met Epicurus, the philosopher who formed his own school in Athens. The two men became friends, but philosophy played little role in Menander's plays. The link between the playwright and the philosopher was again their emphasis on individualism. Menander's later career in some ways reflects the fate of his native Athens. After Alexander's death, Athens fell to Cassander in 317 B.C., who appointed Demetrius of Phalarum to rule the city. Demetrius had also studied with Theophrastus, and he and Menander soon became friends. The Athenians considered Demetrius a foreign-supported tyrant, and his friendship with Menander endangered the poet's life. Despite his political affiliations, Menander's plays remained popular. The irony is that both men reflected the coming of the new Hellenistic period. Demetrius, the philosopher-politician under the control of the Macedonians, proved that Athens could not compete with the greater Macedonian powers. Menander, the poet, wrote plays that reflected the diminished importance of Athenian politics.

A remarkable aspect of Menander's art is that even though tumultuous events occurred during his lifetime, little trace of them appears in his plays. The world that he portrayed is rather ordinary. The plots normally involved domestic situations. Menander often introduced the theme of love and its complications, which sometimes comes off as being artificial but nonetheless amusing. He also wrote in a realistic style that made his plays more accessible to his audience. In short, he brought theater down to earth.

Most of Menander's plays were lost sometime during the seventh and eighth centuries A.D., but the sands of Egypt have preserved some of them for reading today. Menander also left a remarkable heritage to the culture of Rome. The playwrights Plautus and Terence translated his plays and freely adapted them for the Roman stage.

Menander was an early exponent of a changed Greek world, one in which the individual took precedence over the polis. By writing about ordinary people he achieved a universalism that still appeals to people continents away from Athens and centuries after he lived.

Questions for Analysis

1. How did Menander's approach to life and drama differ from that of classical dramatists and comedians?
2. How realistic are Menander's plays, and do they reflect the concerns of his day?

Old Shepherdess Daily life for the poor and elderly was as hard in the Hellenistic period as in other times. Here a tough, old, scantily clothed shepherdess brings a sheep to market. Such scenes were common during the period; but art, not written sources, has preserved them for posterity. *(Alinari/Art Resource, NY)*

East. Besides building Greek cities, Hellenistic kings offered Greeks land and money as lures to further immigration.

The opening of the East offered ambitious Greeks opportunities for well-paying jobs and economic success. The Hellenistic monarchy, unlike the Greek polis, did not depend solely on its citizens to fulfill its political needs. Talented Greeks could expect to rise quickly in the governmental bureaucracy. Appointed by the king, these administrators did not have to stand for election each year, as had many officials of a Greek polis. Since they held their jobs year after year, they had ample time to evolve new administrative techniques. Naturally they became more efficient than the amateur officials common in Hellenic Greek city-states. The needs of the Hellenistic monarchy and the opportunities it offered thus gave rise to a professional corps of Greek administrators.

Greeks and Macedonians also found ready employment in the armies and navies of the Hellenistic monarchies. Alexander had proved the Greco-Macedonian style of warfare to be far superior to that of the Easterners, and Alexander's successors, themselves experienced officers, realized the importance of trained Greek and Macedonian soldiers. Moreover, Hellenistic kings were extremely reluctant to arm the native populations or to allow them to serve in the army, fearing military rebellions among their conquered subjects. The result was the emergence of professional armies and navies consisting entirely of Greeks and Macedonians.

Greeks were able to dominate other professions as well. The kingdoms and cities recruited Greek writers and artists to create Greek literature, art, and culture on Asian soil. Architects, engineers, and skilled craftsmen found their services in great demand because of the building policies of the Hellenistic monarchs. If Hellenistic kingdoms were to have Greek cities, those cities needed Greek buildings—temples, porticoes, gymnasia, theaters, fountains, and houses. Architects and engineers were sometimes commissioned to design and build whole cities, which they laid out in checkerboard fashion and filled with typical Greek buildings. An enormous wave of construction took place during the Hellenistic period.

New opportunities opened for women as well, owing in part to the examples of the queens. Especially in social and economic pursuits women played an expanded role. More women than ever before received educations that enabled them to enter medicine and other professions. Literacy among women increased dramatically, and their options expanded accordingly. Some won fame as poets, while others studied with philosophers and contributed to the intellectual life of the age. As a rule, however, these developments touched only wealthier women, and not all of them. Although some poor women were literate, most were not.

The major reason for the new prominence of women was their increased participation in economic affairs. During the Hellenistic period some women took part in commercial transactions. They still lived under legal handicaps; in Egypt, for example, a Greek woman needed a male guardian to buy, sell, or lease land, to borrow money, and to represent her in other transactions. Yet often such a guardian was present only to fulfill the letter of the law. The woman was the real agent and handled the business being transacted. In Hellenistic Sparta, women accumulated large fortunes and vast amounts of land. As early as the beginning of the Hellenistic period, women owned two-fifths of the land of Laconia. Spartan women, however, were exceptional. In most other areas even women who were wealthy in their own right were formally under the protection of their male relatives.

Women also began to participate in politics on a limited basis. They served in civil capacities, for which they often received public acknowledgment. Women sometimes received honorary citizenship from foreign cities because of aid given in times of crisis. Few women achieved these honors, however, and those who did were from the upper classes.

Despite the opportunities they offered, the Hellenistic monarchies were hampered by their artificial origins. Their failure to win the political loyalty of their Greek subjects and their policy of wooing Greeks with lucrative positions encouraged a feeling of uprootedness and self-serving individualism among Greek immigrants. Once a Greek had left home to take service with, for instance, the army or the bureaucracy of the Ptolemies, he had no incentive beyond his pay and the comforts of life in Egypt to keep him there. If the Seleucid king offered him more money or a promotion, he might well accept it and take his talents to Asia Minor. Why not? In the realm of the Seleucids he, a Greek, would find the same sort of life and environment that the kingdom of the Ptolemies had provided him. Thus professional Greek soldiers and administrators were very mobile and apt to look to their own interests, not their kingdom's.

One result of these developments was that the nature of warfare changed. Except in the areas of Greece and to some extent Macedonia, Hellenistic soldiers were professionals. Unlike the citizen hoplites of classical Greece, these men were regular soldiers capable of intricate maneuvers. Hellenistic kings paid them well, often giving them land as an incentive to remain loyal. Only in Macedonia among the kingdoms was there a national army that was devoted to its land, homes, and monarchy. The loyalty, skill, and bravery of Macedonian soldiers made them the most formidable in the Hellenistic world.

As long as Greeks continued to replenish their professional ranks, the kingdoms remained strong. In the process they drew an immense amount of talent from the Greek peninsula, draining the vitality of the Greek homeland. However, the Hellenistic monarchies could not keep recruiting Greeks forever, in spite of their wealth and willingness to spend lavishly. In time the huge surge of immigration slowed greatly. Even then the Hellenistic monarchs were reluctant to recruit Easterners to fill posts normally held by Greeks. The result was at first the stagnation of the Hellenistic world and finally, after 202 B.C., its collapse in the face of the young and vigorous Roman republic.

Greeks and Easterners

The Greeks in the East were a minority, and Hellenistic cities were islands of Greek culture in an Eastern sea. But Hellenistic monarchies were remarkably successful in at least partially Hellenizing Easterners and spreading a uniform culture throughout the East, a culture to which Rome eventually fell heir. The prevailing institutions, laws, and language of the East became Greek. Indeed, the Near East had seen nothing comparable since the days when Mesopotamian culture had spread throughout the area.

Yet the spread of Greek culture was wider than it was deep. At best it was a veneer, thicker in some places than in others. Hellenistic kingdoms were never entirely unified in language, customs, and thought. Greek culture took firmest hold along the shores of the Mediterranean, but in the Far East, in Persia and Bactria, it eventually gave way to Eastern cultures.

The Ptolemies in Egypt made little effort to spread Greek culture, and unlike other Hellenistic kings they were not city builders. Indeed, they founded only the city of Ptolemais near Thebes. At first the native Egyptian population, the descendants of the pharaoh's people, retained their traditional language, outlook, religion, and way of life. Initially untouched by Hellenism, the natives continued to be the foundation of the state: they fed it by their labor in the fields and financed its operations with their taxes.

Under the pharaohs talented Egyptians had been able to rise to high office, but during the third century B.C. the Ptolemies cut off this avenue of advancement. They tied the natives to the land ever more tightly, making it nearly impossible for them to leave their villages. The bureaucracy of the Ptolemies was ruthlessly efficient, and the native population was viciously and cruelly exploited. Even in times of hardship the king's taxes came first, although payment might mean starvation for the natives. Their desperation was summed up by one Egyptian, who scrawled the warning: "We are worn out; we will run away."[3] To many Egyptians revolt or a life of brigandage was certainly preferable to working the land under the harsh Ptolemies.

Throughout the third century B.C. the Greek upper class in Egypt had little to do with the native population. Many Greek bureaucrats established homes in Alexandria and Ptolemais, where they managed finances, served as magistrates, and administered the law. Other Greeks settled in military colonies and supplied the monarchy with fighting men. But in the second century B.C. Greeks and native Egyptians began to intermarry and mingle their cultures. The language of the native population influenced Greek, and many Greeks adopted Egyptian religion and ways of life. Simultaneously, natives adopted Greek customs and language and began to play a role in the administration of the kingdom and even to serve in the army. While many Greeks and Egyptians remained aloof from each other, the overall result was the evolution of a widespread Greco-Egyptian culture.

Meanwhile the Seleucid kings established many cities and military colonies in western Asia Minor and along the banks of the Tigris and Euphrates Rivers in order to nurture a vigorous and large Greek population. Especially important to the Seleucids were the military colonies, for they needed Greeks to defend the kingdom. The Seleucids had no elaborate plan for Hellenizing the native population, but the arrival of so many Greeks was bound to have an impact. Seleucid military colonies were generally founded near native villages, thus exposing Easterners to all aspects of Greek life. Many Easterners found Greek political and cultural forms attractive and imitated them. In Asia Minor and Syria, for instance, numerous native villages and towns developed along Greek lines, and some of them became Hellenized cities. Farther east, the Greek kings who replaced the Seleucids in the third century B.C. spread Greek culture to their neighbors, even into the Indian subcontinent.

For Easterners the prime advantage of Greek culture was its very pervasiveness. The Greek language became the common speech of the East. A common dialect called *koine* even influenced the speech of peninsular Greece itself. Greek became the speech of the royal court, bureaucracy, and army. It was also the speech of commerce: any Easterner who wanted to compete in business had to learn it. As early as the third century B.C. some Greek cities were giving citizenship to Hellenized natives.

The vast majority of Hellenized Easterners, however, took only the externals of Greek culture while retaining the essentials of their own ways of life. Though Greeks and Easterners adapted to each other's ways, there was never a true fusion of cultures. Nonetheless, each found useful things in the civilization of the other, and the two fertilized each other. This fertilization, this mingling of Greek and Eastern elements, is what makes Hellenistic culture unique and distinctive.

Hellenism and the Jews

A prime illustration of how the East took what it wanted from Hellenism while remaining true to itself is the impact of Greek culture on the Jews. At first, Jews in Hellenistic cities were treated as resident aliens. As they grew more numerous, they received permission to form a political corporation, a *politeuma,* which gave them a great deal of autonomy. The politeuma allowed Jews to attend to their religious and internal affairs without interference from the Greek municipal government. The Jewish politeuma had its own officials, the leaders of the synagogue. In time the Jewish politeuma gained the special right to be judged by its own law and its own officials, thus becoming in effect a Jewish city within a Hellenistic city.

The Jewish politeuma, like the Hellenistic city, obeyed the king's commands, but there was virtually no royal interference with the Jewish religion. Indeed, the Greeks were always reluctant to tamper with anyone's religion. Only the Seleucid king Antiochus Epiphanes (175–ca 164 B.C.) tried to suppress the Jewish religion in Judaea. He did so not because he hated the Jews (who were a small part of his kingdom), but because he was trying to unify his realm culturally to meet the threat of Rome. To the Jews he extended the same policy that he applied to all subjects. Apart from this instance, Hellenistic Jews suffered no official religious

Tazza Farnese This exquisite detail of a cameo bowl from Hellenistic Egypt dates from about 125 B.C. The figure on the left represents the Nile pouring out the horn of plenty. The other figures represent the deities who gave Egypt its great richness. *(G. Dagli Orti)*

persecution. Some Jews were given the right to become full citizens of Hellenistic cities, but few exercised that right. Citizenship would have allowed them to vote in the assembly and serve as magistrates, but it would also have obliged them to worship the gods of the city—a practice few Jews chose to follow.

Jews living in Hellenistic cities often embraced a good deal of Hellenism. So many Jews learned Greek, especially in Alexandria, that the Old Testament was translated into Greek, and services in the synagogue came to be conducted in Greek. Jews often took Greek names, used Greek political forms, adopted Greek practice by forming their own trade associations, put inscriptions on graves as the Greeks did, and much else. Yet no matter how much of Greek culture or its externals Jews borrowed, they normally remained attached to their religion. Thus, in spite of Hellenistic trappings, Hellenized Jews remained Jews at heart. Their ideas and those of the Greeks were different. The exceptions were some Jews in Asia Minor and Syria who incorporated Greek or local Eastern cults into their worship. To some degree this development was due to the growing belief among Greeks and Easterners that all peoples, despite differences in cult and ritual, actually worshiped the same gods.

Developments in the Western Mediterranean

While Hellenism made new and broader strides in the East, far more complicated and imperfectly understood developments occurred in the western Mediterranean. A survey of the region reveals a wealth of peoples and cultures, some already settled in the area and others moving into it. One group of peoples usually called

Berbers were Libyans, Numidians, and Moors, who settled the area of modern Algeria, Morocco, and Tunisia. They also made contact with Sicily and Spain to the north. Even by today's standards the western Mediterranean was a small world. Into this world had come the Phoenicians from the east, planting trading stations and spreading their customs primarily along the coast. To the north the Iberians, Celtiberians, and Celts, all Indo-European-speakers, moved into modern Spain and Portugal. In the eighth century B.C. they began mining the rich mineral deposits of these regions, which soon attracted the Phoenicians and later the Greeks. In southern France Ligurian and Celto-Ligurian peoples arrived from the east, sometimes in organized confederations. As early as the seventh century B.C. they extended contact beyond their immediate neighbors to the Greeks in southern Italy.

In Italy a pre-Indo-European people first occupied the land, but little is known of them. The arrival of Italic folk, who spoke a variety of related dialects, occurred perhaps as early as 1000 B.C. They overwhelmed the native population and transformed the way of life of the peninsula. In the process they encountered the Etruscans, one of the most mysterious peoples of antiquity, and came into contact with the Greeks, who had long established themselves in the south. For historical purposes the importance of these social contacts can be best understood by treating them in the context of the rise of Rome (see Chapter 5). Here it is sufficient to recognize that even at this early period, the Mediterranean world was drawing closer together.

The Economic Scope of the Hellenistic World

Alexander's conquest of the Persian Empire not only changed the political face of the ancient world but also brought the East fully into the sphere of Greek economics. Yet the Hellenistic period did not see a revolution in the way people lived and worked. The material demands of Hellenistic society remained as simple as those of Athenian society in the fifth century B.C. Clothes and furniture were essentially unchanged, as were household goods, tools, and jewelry. The real achievement of Alexander and his successors was linking East and West in a broad commercial network. The spread of Greeks throughout the East created new markets and stimulated trade. The economic unity of the Hellenistic world, like its cultural bonds, would later prove valuable to the Romans.

Commerce

Alexander's conquest of the Persian Empire had immediate effects on trade. In the Persian capitals Alexander had found vast sums of gold, silver, and other treasure. This wealth financed the creation of new cities, the building of roads, and the development of harbors. Most of the great monarchies coined their money on the Attic standard, which meant that much of the money used in Hellenistic kingdoms had the same value. Traders were less in need of moneychangers than in the days when each major power coined money on a different standard. As a result of Alexander's conquests, geographical knowledge of the East increased dramatically, making the East far better known to the Greeks than previously. The Greeks spread their law and methods of transacting business throughout the East. Whole new fields lay open to Greek merchants, who eagerly took advantage of the new opportunities. Commerce itself was a leading area where Greeks and Easterners met on grounds of common interest. In bazaars, ports, and trading centers Greeks learned of Eastern customs and traditions while spreading knowledge of their own culture.

The Seleucid and Ptolemaic dynasties traded as far afield as India, Arabia, and sub-Saharan Africa. Overland trade with India and Arabia was conducted by caravan and was largely in the hands of Easterners. The caravan trade never dealt in bulk items or essential commodities; only luxury goods could be transported in this very expensive fashion. Once the goods reached the Hellenistic monarchies, Greek merchants took a hand in the trade.

Essential to the caravan trade from the Mediterranean to Afghanistan and India were the northern route to Dura on the Euphrates River and the southern route through Arabia. The desert of Arabia may seem at first unlikely and inhospitable terrain for a line of commerce, but to the east of it lies the plateau of Iran, from which trade routes stretched to the south and still farther east to China. Commerce from the East arrived at Egypt and the excellent harbors of Palestine, Phoenicia, and Syria. From these ports goods flowed to Greece, Italy, and Spain. The backbone of this caravan trade was the camel—shaggy, ill-tempered, but durable. Only its mother could consider it beautiful, but the camel is a splendid beast of burden, and few other animals could

Camels in the Caravan Trade Trade during the Hellenistic period was truly international. Merchants formed caravans in Syria in the West and China in the East, and between these long distances they exchanged goods such as spices, precious metals, and silk. An individual merchant seldom, if ever, traveled the entire distance. Here the artist has caught a Chinese merchant urging his heavily loaded camel reluctantly to its feet. Camels were the mainstay of the caravan trade. *(The Field Museum, Chicago [neg. #A98631])*

have endured the harsh heat and aridity of the caravan routes.

Over the caravan routes traveled luxury goods that were light, rare, and expensive. In time these luxury items became more of a necessity than a luxury. In part this development was the result of an increased volume of trade. In the prosperity of the period more people could afford to buy gold, silver, ivory, precious stones, spices, and a host of other easily transportable goods. Perhaps the most prominent goods in terms of volume were tea and silk. Indeed, the trade in silk gave the major route the name the Great Silk Road, for not only was this route prominent in antiquity, but it also was used in early modern times. In return the Greeks and Macedonians sent east manufactured goods, especially metal weapons, cloth, wine, and olive oil. Although these caravan routes can trace their origins to earlier times, they became far more prominent in the Hellenistic period. Business customs developed and became standardized, so that merchants from different nationalities communicated in a way understandable to all of them.

The durability and economic importance of these caravan routes are amply demonstrated by the fact that the death of Alexander, the ensuing wars of his successors, and the triumph of the Parthians in Iran had little effect on the trade. Numerous mercantile cities grew up along these distant tracks, places where native cultures combined with both Greco-Macedonian and Eastern cultures to create local but nonetheless cosmopolitan societies that were neither entirely Western nor entirely Eastern. The commercial contacts brought people together, even if sometimes indirectly. The merchants and the caravan cities were links in a chain that reached from the Mediterranean Sea at least to Afghanistan and Iran. Ideas passed along these routes as easily as, and probably more comfortably than, gold and ivory.

In the early Hellenistic period, the Seleucids and Ptolemies ensured that the caravan trade proceeded efficiently. Later in the period—a time of increased war and confusion—they left the caravans unprotected. Taking advantage of this situation, Palmyra in the Syrian Desert and Nabataean Petra in Arabia arose as caravan states. Such states protected the caravans from bandits and marauders and served as dispersal areas for caravan goods.

The Ptolemies discovered how to use monsoon winds to establish direct contact with India. One hardy merchant has left a firsthand account of sailing this important maritime route:

Hippalos, the pilot, observing the position of the ports and the conditions of the sea, first discovered how to sail across the ocean. Concerning the winds of the ocean in this region, when with us the Etesian winds begin, in India a wind between southwest and south, named for Hippalos, sets in from the open sea. From then until now some mariners set forth from Kanes and some from the Cape of Spices. Those sailing to Dimurikes [in southern India] throw the bow of the ship farther out to sea. Those bound for Barygaza and the realm of the Sakas [in northern India] hold to the land no more than three days; and if the wind remains favorable, they hold the same course through the outer sea, and they sail along past the previously mentioned gulfs.[4]

Although this sea route never replaced overland caravan traffic, it kept direct relations between East and West alive, stimulating the exchange of ideas as well as goods.

More economically important than this exotic trade were commercial dealings in essential commodities like raw materials, grain, and industrial products. The Hellenistic monarchies usually raised enough grain for their own needs as well as a surplus for export. For the cities of Greece and the Aegean this trade in grain was essential, because many of them could not grow enough. Fortunately for them, abundant wheat supplies were available nearby in Egypt and in the Crimea in southern Russia.

The large-scale wars of the Hellenistic period often interrupted both the production and the distribution of grain. This was especially true when Alexander's successors were trying to carve out kingdoms. In addition, natural calamities, such as excessive rain or drought, frequently damaged harvests. Throughout the Hellenistic period, famine or severe food shortage remained a grim possibility.

Most trade in bulk commodities was seaborne, and the Hellenistic merchant ship was the workhorse of the day. The merchant ship had a broad beam and relied on sails for propulsion. It was far more seaworthy than the contemporary warship, which was long, narrow, and built for speed. A small crew of experienced sailors could handle the merchant vessel easily. Maritime trade provided opportunities for workers in other industries and trades: sailors, shipbuilders, dockworkers, accountants, teamsters, and pirates. Piracy was always a factor in the Hellenistic world and remained so until Rome extended its power throughout the East.

The Greek cities paid for their grain by exporting olive oil and wine. When agriculture and oil production developed in Syria, Greek products began to encounter competition from the Seleucid monarchy. Later in the Hellenistic period, Greek oil and wine found a lucrative market in Italy. Another significant commodity was fish, which for export was either salted, pickled, or dried. This trade was doubly important because fish provided poor people with an essential element of their diet. Salt too was often imported, and there was some very slight trade in salted meat, which was a luxury item. Far more important was the trade in honey, dried fruit, nuts, and vegetables. Of raw materials, wood was high in demand, but little trade occurred in manufactured goods.

Slaves were a staple of Hellenistic trade. The wars provided prisoners for the slave market; to a lesser extent, so did kidnapping and capture by pirates. The number of slaves involved cannot be estimated, but there is no doubt that slavery flourished. Both old Greek states and new Hellenistic kingdoms were ready slave markets, as was Rome when it emerged triumphant from the Second Punic War (see page 146).

Throughout the Mediterranean world slaves were almost always in demand. Only the Ptolemies discouraged both the trade and slavery itself, and they did so only for economic reasons. Their system had no room for slaves, who would only have competed with free labor. Otherwise slave labor was to be found in the cities and temples of the Hellenistic world, in the factories and fields, and in the homes of wealthier people. In Italy and some parts of the East, slaves performed manual labor for large estates and worked the mines. They were vitally important to the Hellenistic economy.

Industry

Although demand for goods increased during the Hellenistic period, no new techniques of production appear to have developed. The discoveries of Hellenistic mathematicians and thinkers failed to produce any significant corresponding technological development. Manual labor, not machinery, continued to turn out the raw materials and few manufactured goods the Hellenistic world used. Human labor was so cheap and so abundant that kings had no incentive to encourage the invention and manufacture of laborsaving machinery.

Perhaps only one noteworthy technological innovation dates to the Hellenistic period—the Archimedean screw, a device used to pump water into irrigation ditches and out of mines. At Thoricus in Attica miners dug ore by hand and hauled it from the mines for processing. This was grueling work; invariably miners were slaves, criminals, or forced laborers. The conditions under which they worked were frightful. The Ptolemies ran their gold mines along the same harsh lines. One historian gives a grim picture of the miners' lives:

The kings of Egypt condemn [to the mines] those found guilty of wrong-doing and those taken prisoner in war, those who were victims of false accusations and were put into jail because of royal anger. . . . The condemned—and they are very many—all of them are put in chains, and they work persistently and continually, both by day and throughout the night, getting no rest, and carefully cut off from escape.[5]

The Ptolemies even condemned women and children to work in the mines. The strongest men lived and died swinging iron sledgehammers to break up the gold-bearing quartz rock. Others worked underground following the seams of quartz; laboring with lamps bound to their foreheads, they were whipped by overseers if they slacked off. Once the diggers had cut out blocks of quartz, young boys gathered up the blocks and carried them outside. All of them—men, women, and boys—worked until they died.

Apart from gold and silver, which were used primarily for coins and jewelry, iron was the most important metal and saw the most varied use. Even so, the method of its production never became very sophisticated. The Hellenistic Greeks did manage to produce a low-grade steel by adding carbon to iron.

Pottery remained an important commodity, and most of it was made locally. The pottery used in the kitchen, the coarse ware, did not change at all. Fancier

Stag Hunt This mosaic is of interest both for its vigorous hunting scene and for its composition in brilliantly colored pebbles. The artist's drawing is superb and the action vigorous but disciplined. *(National Museum, Pella/Archaeological Receipts Fund, Athens)*

pots and bowls, decorated with a shiny black glaze, came into use during the Hellenistic period. This ware originated in Athens, but potters in other places began to imitate its style, heavily cutting into the Athenian market. In the second century B.C. a red-glazed ware, often called Samian, burst on the market and soon dominated it. Athens still held its own, however, in the production of fine pottery. Despite the change in pottery styles, the method of production of all pottery, whether plain or fine, remained essentially unchanged.

Agriculture

Hellenistic kings paid special attention to agriculture. Much of their revenue was derived from the produce of royal land, rents paid by the tenants of royal land, and taxation of agricultural land. Some Hellenistic kings even sought out and supported agricultural experts. The Ptolemies, for instance, sponsored experiments on seed grain, selecting seeds that seemed hardy and productive and trying to improve their characteristics. Hellenistic authors wrote handbooks discussing how farms and large estates could most profitably be run. These handbooks described soil types, covered the proper times for planting and reaping, and discussed care of farm animals. Whether these efforts had any impact on the average farmer is difficult to determine.

The Ptolemies made the greatest strides in agriculture, and the reason for their success was largely political. Egypt had a strong tradition of central authority dating back to the pharaohs, which the Ptolemies inherited and tightened. They could decree what crops Egyptian farmers would plant and what animals would be raised, and they had the power to carry out their commands. The Ptolemies recognized the need for well-planned and constant irrigation, and much native labor went into the digging and maintenance of canals and ditches. The Ptolemies also reclaimed a great deal of land from the desert, including the Fayum, a dried lake bed near the Nile.

The centralized authority of the Ptolemies explains how agricultural advances occurred at the local level in Egypt. But such progress was not possible in any other Hellenistic monarchy. Despite royal interest in agriculture and a more studied approach to it in the Hellenistic period, there is no evidence that agricultural productivity increased. Whether Hellenistic agricultural methods had any influence on Eastern practices is unknown.

Religion in the Hellenistic World

In religion Hellenism gave Easterners far less than the East gave the Greeks. At first the Hellenistic period saw the spread of Greek religious cults throughout the East. When Hellenistic kings founded cities, they also built temples and established new cults and priesthoods for the old Olympian gods. The new cults enjoyed the prestige of being the religion of the conquerors, and they were supported by public money. The most attractive aspects of the Greek cults, at least to the Greeks, were their rituals and festivities, as they were at least familiar. Greek cults sponsored literary, musical, and athletic contests, which were staged in beautiful surroundings among impressive Greek buildings. In short, the cults offered bright and lively entertainment, both intellectual and physical. They fostered Greek culture and traditional sports and thus were a splendid means of displaying Greek civilization in the East.

Despite various advantages, Greek cults suffered from some severe shortcomings. They were primarily concerned with ritual. Participation in the civic cults did not even require belief (see pages 91–93). On the whole, the civic cults neither appealed to religious emotions nor embraced matters such as sin and redemption. Greek mystery religions helped fill this gap, but the centers of these religions were in old Greece. Although the new civic cults were lavish in pomp and display, they could not satisfy deep religious feelings or spiritual yearnings.

Even though the Greeks participated in the new cults for cultural reasons, they felt little genuine religious attachment to them. In comparison with the emotional and sometimes passionate religions of the East, the Greek cults seemed sterile. Greeks increasingly sought solace from other sources. Educated and thoughtful people turned to philosophy as a guide to life, while others turned to superstition, magic, or astrology. Still others might shrug and speak of *Tyche,* which meant "Fate" or "Chance" or "Doom"—a capricious and sometimes malevolent force.

In view of the spiritual decline of Greek religion, it is surprising that Eastern religions did not make more immediate headway among the Greeks. Although Hellenistic Greeks clung to their own cults as expressions of their Greekness rather than for any ethical principles, they did not rush to embrace native religions. Only in the second century B.C., after a century of exposure to Eastern religions, did Greeks begin to adopt them.

Religious Syncretism This relief was found at the Greek outpost of Dura-Europus, located on the Euphrates. In the center sits Zeus Olympius-Baalshamin, a combination of a Greek god and a Semitic god. The Eastern priest at the left is burning incense on an altar, while the figure on the right in Macedonian dress crowns the god. Both the religious sentiments and the style of art show the meeting of East and West. *(Yale University Art Gallery, Dura-Europos Collection)*

Nor did Hellenistic kings make any effort to spread Greek religion among their Eastern subjects. The Greeks always considered religion a matter best left to the individual. Greek cults were attractive only to those socially aspiring Easterners who adopted Greek culture for personal advancement. Otherwise Easterners were little affected by Greek religion. Nor did native religions suffer from the arrival of the Greeks. Some Hellenistic kings limited the power of native priesthoods, but they also subsidized some Eastern cults with public money. Alexander the Great actually reinstated several Eastern cults that the Persians had suppressed.

The only significant junction of Greek and Eastern religious traditions was the growth and spread of new "mystery religions," so called because they featured a body of ritual not to be divulged to anyone not initiated into the cult. These new mystery cults incorporated aspects of both Greek and Eastern religions and had broad appeal for both Greeks and Easterners who yearned for personal immortality. Since the Greeks were already familiar with old mystery cults, such as the Eleusinian mysteries in Attica, the new cults did not strike them as alien or barbarian. Familiar, too, was the concept of preparation for an initiation. Devotees of the Eleusinian mysteries and other such cults had to prepare themselves mentally and physically before entering the gods' presence. Thus the mystery cults fit well with Greek usage.

The new religions enjoyed one tremendous advantage over the old Greek mystery cults. Whereas old Greek mysteries were tied to particular places, such as Eleusis, the new religions spread throughout the Hellenistic world. People did not have to undertake long and expensive pilgrimages just to become members of the religion. In that sense the mystery religions came to the people, for temples of the new deities sprang up wherever Greeks lived.

The mystery religions all claimed to save their adherents from the worst that fate could do and promised life for the soul after death. They all had a single concept in common: the belief that by the rites of initiation devotees became united with the god, who had himself died and risen from the dead. The sacrifice of the god and his victory over death saved the devotee from eternal death. Similarly, all mystery religions demanded a period of preparation in which the convert strove to become holy, that is, to live by the religion's precepts. Once aspirants had prepared themselves, they went through an initiation in which they learned the secrets of the religion. The initiation was usually a ritual of great emotional intensity, symbolizing the entry into a new life.

The Eastern mystery religions that took the Hellenistic world by storm were the Egyptian cults of Serapis and Isis. Serapis, who was invented by King Ptolemy, combined elements of the Egyptian god Osiris with aspects of the Greek gods Zeus, Pluto (the prince of the underworld), and Asclepius. Serapis was believed to be the judge of souls, who rewarded virtuous and righteous people with eternal life. Like Asclepius, he was a god of healing. Serapis became an international god, and many Hellenistic Greeks thought of him as Zeus. Associated with Isis and Serapis was Anubis, the old Egyptian god who, like Charon in the Greek pantheon, guided the souls of initiates to the realm of eternal life. (See the feature "Listening to the Past: The Greeks Welcome the Egyptian God Serapis" on pages 132–133.)

The cult of Isis enjoyed even wider appeal than that of Serapis. Isis, wife of Osiris, claimed to have conquered Tyche and promised to save any mortal who came to her. She became the most important goddess of the Hellenistic world, and her worship was very popular among women. Her priests claimed that she had bestowed on humanity the gift of civilization and founded law and literature. She was the goddess of marriage, conception, and childbirth, and like Serapis she promised to save the souls of her believers.

There was neither conflict between Greek and Eastern religions nor wholesale acceptance of one or the other. Nonetheless, Greeks and Easterners noticed similarities among their respective deities and assumed that they were worshiping the same gods in different garb. These tendencies toward religious universalism and the desire for personal immortality would prove significant when the Hellenistic world came under the sway of Rome, for Hellenistic developments paved the way for the spread of Christianity.

Philosophy and the People

Philosophy during the Hellenic period was the exclusive province of the wealthy, for only they had leisure enough to pursue philosophical studies. During the Hellenistic period, however, philosophy reached out to touch the lives of more men and women than ever before. The reasons for this development were several. Since the ideal of the polis had declined, politics no longer offered people an intellectual outlet. Moreover, much of Hellenistic life, especially in the new cities of the East, seemed unstable and without venerable traditions. Greeks were far more mobile than they had ever been before, but their very mobility left them feeling uprooted. Many people in search of something permanent, something unchanging in a changing world, turned to philosophy. Another reason for the increased influence of philosophy was the decline of traditional religion and a growing belief in Tyche. To protect against the worst that Tyche could do, many Greeks looked to philosophy.

Philosophers themselves became much more numerous, and several new schools of philosophical thought emerged. In spite of their many differences, the major branches of philosophy agreed on the necessity of making people self-sufficient. They all recognized the need to equip men and women to deal successfully with Tyche. The major schools of Hellenistic philosophy all taught that people could be truly happy only when they had turned their backs on the world and focused full attention on one enduring thing. They differed chiefly on what that enduring thing was.

Cynics

Undoubtedly the most unusual of the new philosophers were the Cynics, who urged a return to nature. They advised men and women to discard traditional customs and conventions (which were in decline anyway) and live simply. The Cynics believed that by rejecting material things people would become free and that nature would provide all necessities.

The founder of the Cynics was Antisthenes (b. ca 440 B.C.), but it was Diogenes of Sinope (ca 412–323 B.C.), one of the most colorful men of the period, who spread the philosophy. Diogenes came to Athens to study philosophy and soon evolved his own ideas on the ideal life. He hit on the solution that happiness was possible only by living according to nature and forgoing luxuries. He attacked social conventions because he considered them contrary to nature. Throughout Greece he gained fame for the rigorous way in which he put his beliefs into practice.

Diogenes' disdain for luxury and social pretense became legendary. Once, when he was living at Corinth, he was supposedly visited by Alexander the Great: "While Diogenes was sunning himself . . . Alexander stood over him and said: 'Ask me whatever gift you like.' In answer Diogenes said to him: 'Get out of my sunlight.'"[6] The story underlines the essence of Diogenes' teachings: even a great, powerful, and wealthy conqueror such as Alexander could give people nothing of any real value. Nature had already provided them with everything essential.

Diogenes did not establish a philosophical school in the manner of Plato and Aristotle. Instead, he and his followers took their teaching to the streets and marketplaces. More than any other philosophical group, they tried to reach the common people. As part of their return to nature, they often did without warm clothing, sufficient food, or adequate housing, which they considered unnecessary. The Cynics also tried to break down political barriers by declaring that people owed no allegiance to any city or monarchy. They said all people are cosmopolitan—that is, citizens of the world. The Cynics reached across political boundaries to create a community of people, all sharing their humanity and living as close to nature as humanly possible. The Cynics set a striking example of how people could turn away from materialism. Although comparatively few men and women could follow such rigorous precepts, the Cynics influenced all the other major schools of philosophy.

Tyche This statue depicts Tyche as the city-goddess of Antioch, a new Hellenistic foundation of the Seleucid king Antiochus. Some Hellenistic Greeks worshiped Tyche in the hope that she would be kind to them. Philosophers tried to free people from her whimsies. Antiochus tried to win her favor by honoring her. *(Photo Vatican Museums)*

Epicureans

Epicurus (340–270 B.C.), who founded his own school of philosophy at Athens, based his view of life on scientific theories. Accepting Democritus's theory that the universe is composed of indestructible particles, Epicurus put forward a naturalistic theory of the universe. Although he did not deny the existence of the gods, he taught that they had no effect on human life. The essence of Epicurus's belief was that the principal good of human life is pleasure, which he defined as the absence of pain. He was not advocating drunken revels or sexual dissipation, which he thought actually caused pain. Instead, Epicurus concluded that any violent emotion is undesirable. Drawing on the teachings of the Cynics, he advocated mild self-discipline. Even poverty he considered good, as long as people had enough food, clothing, and shelter. Epicurus also taught that individuals can most easily attain peace and serenity by ignoring the outside world and looking into their personal feelings and reactions. Thus Epicureanism led to quietism.

Epicureanism taught its followers to ignore politics and issues, for politics led to tumult, which would disturb the soul. Although the Epicureans thought that the state originated through a social contract among individuals, they did not care about the political structure of the state. They were content to live in a democracy, oligarchy, monarchy, or any other form of government, and they never speculated about the ideal state. Their ideals stood outside all political forms.

Stoics

Opposed to the passivity of the Epicureans, Zeno (335–262 B.C.), a philosopher from Citium in Cyprus, advanced a different concept of human beings and the universe. When Zeno first came to Athens, he listened avidly to the Cynics. Concluding, however, that the Cynics were extreme, he stayed in Athens to form his own school, the Stoa, named after the building where he preferred to teach.

Stoicism became the most popular Hellenistic philosophy and the one that later captured the mind of Rome. Zeno and his followers considered nature an expression of divine will; in their view, people could be happy only when living in accordance with nature. They stressed the unity of man and the universe, stating that all men were brothers and obliged to help one another. Stoicism's science was derived from Heraclitus, but its broad and warm humanity was the work of Zeno and his followers.

Unlike the Epicureans, the Stoics taught that people should participate in politics and worldly affairs. Yet this idea never led to the belief that individuals should try to change the order of things. Time and again the Stoics used the image of an actor in a play: the Stoic plays an assigned part but never tries to change the play. To the Stoics the important question was not whether they achieved anything, but whether they lived virtuous lives. In that way they could triumph over Tyche, for Tyche could destroy achievements but not the nobility of their lives.

Though the Stoics evolved the concept of a world order, they thought of it strictly in terms of the individual. Like the Epicureans, they were indifferent to specific political forms. They believed that people should do their duty to the state in which they found themselves. The universal state they preached about was ethical, not political. The Stoics' most significant practical achievement was the creation of the concept of natural law. The Stoics concluded that as all men were brothers, partook of divine reason, and were in harmony with the universe, one law—a part of the natural order of life—governed them all.

The Stoic concept of a universal state governed by natural law is one of the finest heirlooms the Hellenistic world passed on to Rome. The Stoic concept of natural law, of one law for all people, became a valuable tool when the Romans began to deal with many different peoples with different laws. The ideal of the universal state gave the Romans a rationale for extending their empire to the farthest reaches of the world. The duty of individuals to their fellows served the citizens of the Roman Empire as the philosophical justification for doing their duty. In this respect, too, the real fruit of Hellenism was to ripen only under the cultivation of Rome.

HELLENISTIC SCIENCE

The area in which Hellenistic culture achieved its greatest triumphs was science. Here, too, the ancient Near East made contributions to Greek thought. The patient observations of the Babylonians, who for generations had scanned the skies, had provided the raw materials for Thales' speculations, which were the foundation of Hellenistic astronomy. The most notable of the Hellenistic astronomers was Aristarchus of Samos (ca 310–230 B.C.), who was educated in Aristotle's school. Aristarchus concluded that the sun is far larger than the earth and that the stars are enormously distant from the earth. He argued against Aristotle's view that the earth is the center of the universe. Instead, Aristarchus propounded the *heliocentric theory*—that the earth and planets revolve around the sun. His work is all the more impressive because he lacked even a rudimentary telescope. Aristarchus had only the human eye and brain, but they were more than enough.

Unfortunately, Aristarchus's theories did not persuade the ancient world. In the second century A.D. Claudius Ptolemy, a mathematician and astronomer in Alexandria, accepted Aristotle's theory of the earth as the center of the universe, and their view prevailed for fourteen hundred years. Aristarchus's heliocentric theory lay dormant until resurrected in the sixteenth century by the brilliant Polish astronomer Nicolaus Copernicus.

In geometry Hellenistic thinkers discovered little that was new, but Euclid (ca 300 B.C.), a mathematician who lived in Alexandria, compiled a valuable textbook of existing knowledge. His book *The Elements of Geometry* has exerted immense influence on Western civilization, for it rapidly became the standard introduction to geometry. Generations of students, from the Hellenistic period to the present, have learned the essentials of geometry from it.

The greatest thinker of the Hellenistic period was Archimedes (ca 287–212 B.C.), who was a clever inventor as well. He lived in Syracuse in Sicily and watched Rome emerge as a power in the Mediterranean. When the Romans laid siege to Syracuse in the Second Punic War, Archimedes invented a number of machines to thwart the armed forces. His catapults threw rocks large enough to sink ships and disrupt battle lines. His grappling devices lifted ships out of the water. Archimedes built such machines out of necessity, but they were of little real interest to him. In a more peaceful vein he invented the Archimedean screw and the compound pulley. Plutarch described Archimedes' dramatic demonstration of how easily his pulley could move huge weights with little effort:

A three-masted merchant ship of the royal fleet had been hauled on land by hard work and many hands. Archimedes put aboard her many men and the usual freight. He sat far away from her; without haste, but gently working a compound pulley with his hand, he drew her towards him smoothly and without faltering, just as though she were running on the surface of the sea.[7]

Tower of the Four Winds This remarkable building, which still stands in Athens, was built by an astronomer to serve as a sundial, water-clock, and weather vane. It is one of the few examples of the application of Hellenistic science to daily life. *(Ekdotike Athenon)*

Archimedes was far more interested in pure mathematics than in practical inventions. His mathematical research, covering many fields, was his greatest contribution to Western thought. In his book *On Plane Equilibriums* Archimedes dealt for the first time with the basic principles of mechanics, including the principle of the lever. He once said that if he were given a lever and a suitable place to stand, he could move the world. With his treatise *On Floating Bodies* Archimedes founded the science of hydrostatics. He concluded that whenever a solid floats in a liquid, the weight of the solid is equal to the weight of liquid displaced. The way he made his discovery has become famous:

When he was devoting his attention to this problem, he happened to go to a public bath. When he climbed down into the bathtub there, he noticed that water in the tub equal to the bulk of his body flowed out. Thus, when he observed this method of solving the problem, he did not wait. Instead, moved with joy, he sprang out of the tub, and rushing home naked he kept indicating in a loud voice that he had indeed discovered what he was seeking. For while running he was shouting repeatedly in Greek, "eureka, eureka" *("I have found it, I have found it.").*[8]

Archimedes was willing to share his work with others, among them Eratosthenes (285–ca 204 B.C.), a man of almost universal interests. From his native Cyrene in North Africa, Eratosthenes traveled to Athens, where he studied philosophy and mathematics. He refused to join any of the philosophical schools, for he was interested in too many things to follow any particular dogma. Around 245 B.C. King Ptolemy invited Eratosthenes to Alexandria. The Ptolemies had done much to make Alexandria an intellectual, cultural, and scientific center. Eratosthenes came to Alexandria to become librarian of the royal library, a position of great prestige.

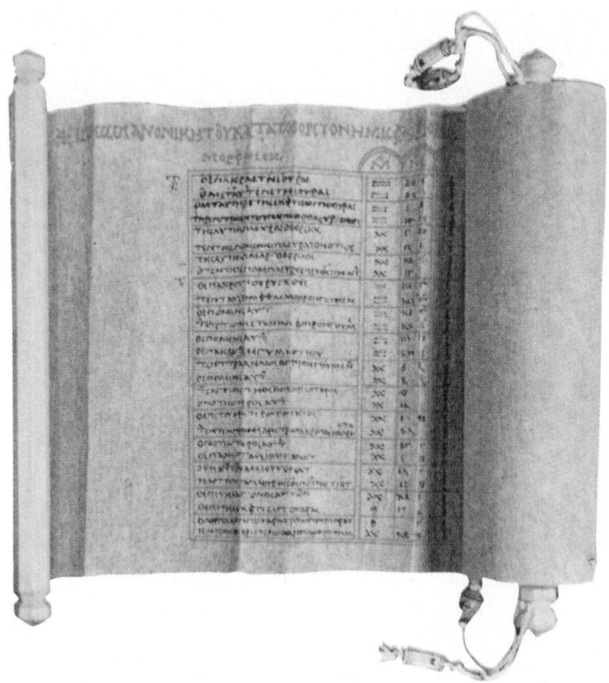

Alexandrian Scroll The famous library at Alexandria in Egypt was a storehouse of classical and Hellenistic learning. Works of various authors were kept on separate scrolls and catalogued for convenient use. The reader unrolled the scroll while reading the page. This reproduction of a scroll contains the text of the astronomer Ptolemy's table of the stars. *(Michaeljohn Harris/BBC Television)*

The library was a huge collection of Greek writings, including such classic works as the poems of Homer, the histories of Herodotus and Thucydides, and the philosophical works of Plato and Aristotle. The library became one of the foremost intellectual centers of the ancient world. Eratosthenes had the honor of becoming its head. While there he continued his mathematical work and by letter struck up a friendship with Archimedes.

Unlike Archimedes, Eratosthenes did not devote his life entirely to mathematics, although he never lost interest in it. He used mathematics to further the geographical studies for which he is most famous. He calculated the circumference of the earth geometrically, estimating it as about 24,675 miles. He was not wrong by much: the earth is actually 24,860 miles in circumference. Eratosthenes also concluded that the earth was a spherical globe, that the landmass was roughly four-sided, and that the land was surrounded by ocean. He discussed the shapes and sizes of land and ocean and the irregularities of the earth's surface. He drew a map of the earth and used his own system of explaining the divisions of the earth's landmass.

Using geographical information gained by Alexander the Great's scientists, Eratosthenes tried to fit the East into Greek geographical knowledge. Although for some reason he ignored the western Mediterranean and Europe, he declared that a ship could sail from Spain either around Africa to India or directly westward to India. Not until the great days of Western exploration did sailors such as Vasco da Gama and Magellan actually prove Eratosthenes' theories. Like Eratosthenes, other Greek geographers also turned their attention southward to Africa. During this period the people of the Mediterranean learned of the climate and customs of Ethiopia and gleaned some scant information about equatorial Africa.

In the Hellenistic period the scientific study of botany had its origin. Aristotle's pupil Theophrastus (ca 372–288 B.C.), who became head of the Lyceum, the school established by Aristotle, studied the botanical information made available by Alexander's penetration of the East. Aristotle had devoted a good deal of his attention to zoology, and Theophrastus extended his work to plants. He wrote two books on the subject, *History of Plants* and *Causes of Plants.* He carefully observed phenomena and based his conclusions on what he had actually seen. Theophrastus classified plants and accurately described their parts. He detected the process of germination and realized the importance of climate and soil to plants. Some of Theophrastus's work found its way into agricultural handbooks, but for the most part Hellenistic science did not carry the study of botany further.

Despite its undeniable brilliance, Hellenistic science suffered from a remarkable weakness almost impossible for practical-minded Americans to understand. Although scientists of this period invented such machines as the air gun, the water organ, and even the steam engine, they never used their discoveries as laborsaving devices. No one has satisfactorily explained why these scientists were so impractical, but one answer is quite possible: they and the rest of society saw no real need for machines. Slave labor was especially abundant, a fact that made the use of laborsaving machinery superfluous. Science was applied only to war. Even though Hellenistic science did not lead the ancient world to an industrial revolution, later Hellenistic thinkers preserved the knowledge of machines and the principles behind them. In so doing they saved the discoveries of Hellenistic science for the modern age.

HELLENISTIC MEDICINE

The study of medicine flourished during the Hellenistic period, and Hellenistic physicians carried the work of Hippocrates into new areas. Herophilus, who lived in the first half of the third century B.C., worked at Alexandria and studied the writings of Hippocrates. He accepted Hippocrates' theory of the four humors and approached the study of medicine in a systematic, scientific fashion. He dissected dead bodies and measured what he observed. He discovered the nervous system and concluded that two types of nerves, motor and sensory, existed.

Herophilus also studied the brain, which he considered the center of intelligence, and discerned the cerebrum and cerebellum. His other work dealt with the liver, lungs, and uterus. His younger contemporary Erasistratus also conducted research on the brain and nervous system and improved on Herophilus's work. Erasistratus too followed in the tradition of Hippocrates and preferred to let the body heal itself by means of diet and air.

Both Herophilus and Erasistratus were members of the Dogmatic school of medicine at Alexandria. In this school speculation played an important part in research. So, too, did the study of anatomy. To learn more about human anatomy, Herophilus and Erasistratus dissected corpses and even vivisected criminals whom King Ptolemy contributed for the purpose. The practice of vivisection seems to have been short-lived, although dissection continued. Better knowledge of anatomy led to improvements in surgery. These advances enabled the Dogmatists to invent new surgical instruments and techniques.

In about 280 B.C. Philinus and Serapion, pupils of Herophilus, led a reaction against the Dogmatists. Believing that the Dogmatists had become too speculative, they founded the Empiric school of medicine at Alexandria. Claiming that the Dogmatists' emphasis on anatomy and physiology was misplaced, they concentrated instead on the observation and cure of illnesses. They also laid heavier stress on the use of drugs and medicine to treat illnesses. Heraclides of Tarentum (perhaps first century B.C.) carried on the Empirical tradition and dedicated himself to observation and use of medicines. He discovered the benefits of opium and worked with other drugs that relieved pain. He also steadfastly rejected the relevance of magic to drugs and medicines.

Hellenistic medicine had its dark side, for many physicians were moneygrubbers, fools, and quacks. One of the angriest complaints comes from the days of the Roman Empire:

Of all men only a physician can kill a man with total impunity. Oh no, on the contrary, censure goes to him who dies and he is guilty of excess, and furthermore he *is blamed. . . . Let me not accuse their [physicians'] avarice, their greedy deals with those whose fate hangs in the balance, their setting a price on pain, and their demands for down payment in case of death, and their secret doctrines.*[9]

An Unsuccessful Delivery This funeral stele depicts a mother who has perhaps lost her own life as well as her baby's. Maternal and infant mortality were quite common in antiquity. A similar stele elsewhere bears the heartbreaking words attributed to the mother by her grieving family: "All my labor could not bring the child forth; he lies in my womb, among the dead." *(National Archaeological Museum, Athens/Archaeological Receipts Fund)*

Abuses such as these existed already in the Hellenistic period. As is true today, many Hellenistic physicians did not take the Hippocratic oath very seriously.

Besides incompetent and greedy physicians, the Hellenistic world was plagued by people who claimed to cure illnesses through incantations and magic. Their potions included such concoctions as blood from the ear of an ass mixed with water to cure fever, or the liver of a cat killed when the moon was waning and preserved in salt. Broken bones could be cured by applying the ashes of a pig's jawbone to the break. The dung of a goat mixed with old wine was good for healing broken ribs. One charlatan claimed that he could cure epilepsy by making the patient drink spring water, drawn at night, from the skull of a man who had been killed but not cremated. These quacks even claimed that they could cure mental illness. The treatment for a person suffering from melancholy was calf dung boiled in wine. No doubt the patient became too sick to be depressed.

Quacks who prescribed such treatments were very popular but did untold harm to the sick and injured. They and greedy physicians also damaged the reputation of dedicated doctors who honestly and intelligently tried to heal and alleviate pain. The medical abuses that arose in the Hellenistic period were so flagrant that the Romans, who later entered the Hellenistic world, developed an intense dislike and distrust of physicians. The Romans considered the study of Hellenistic medicine beneath the dignity of a Roman, and even as late as the time of the Roman Empire, few Romans undertook the study of Greek medicine. Nonetheless, the work of men like Herophilus and Serapion made valuable contributions to the knowledge of medicine, and the fruits of their work were preserved and handed on to the West.

SUMMARY

It can safely be said that Philip and Alexander broadened Greek and Macedonian horizons, but not in ways that they had intended. Although Alexander established Macedonian and Greek colonies across western and central Asia for military reasons, they resulted in the spread of Hellenism as a side effect. In the Aegean and Near East the fusion of Greek and Eastern cultures laid the social, intellectual, and cultural foundations on which the Romans would later build. In the heart of the old Persian Empire, Hellenism was only another new influence that was absorbed by older ways of thought and life. Yet overall, in the exchange of ideas and the opportunity for different cultures to learn about one another, a new cosmopolitan society evolved. That society in turn made possible such diverse advances as a wider extent of trade and agriculture, the creation of religious and philosophical ideas that paved the way for Christianity, and greater freedom for women. People of the Hellenistic period also made remarkable advances in science and medicine. They not only built on the achievements of their predecessors, but also produced one of the most creative intellectual eras of classical antiquity.

NOTES

1. H. Bengtson, *Philipp und Alexander der Grosse* (Munich: Callwey, 1985), p. 7. John Buckler is the translator of all uncited quotations from a foreign language in Chapters 1–6.
2. Plutarch, *Moralia* 328E.
3. Quoted in W. W. Tarn and G. T. Griffith, *Hellenistic Civilizations,* 3d ed. (Cleveland and New York: Meridian Books, 1961), p. 199.
4. *Periplous of the Erythraian Sea* 57.
5. Diodorus 3.12.2–3.
6. Diogenes Laertius 6.38.
7. Ibid., 14.13.
8. Vitruvius, *On Architecture* 9 Preface, 10.
9. Pliny the Elder, *Natural History* 29.8.18, 21.

SUGGESTED READING

General treatments of Hellenistic political, social, and economic history can be found in F. W. Walbank et al., *The Cambridge Ancient History,* 2d ed., vol. 7, pt. 1 (1984). Shorter is F. W. Walbank, *The Hellenistic World,* rev. ed. (1993), a fresh appraisal by one of the foremost scholars in the field. The undisputed classic in this area is M. Rostovtzeff, *The Social and Economic History of the Hellenistic World,* 3 vols. (1941). R. M. Errington, *A History of Macedonia* (English trans., 1990), places Macedonia clearly within a much broader Hellenistic context. A new examination of significant aspects of the period comes from R. W. Wallace and E. M. Harris, eds., *Transitions to Empire,* pt. 2 (1996). Good selections of primary sources in accurate and readable translation can be found in M. M. Austin, *The Hellenistic World from Alexander to the Roman Conquest* (1981); and S. M. Burstein, *The Hellenistic Age from the Battle of Ipsos to the Death of Kleopatra III* (1985).

Each year brings a new crop of biographies of Alexander the Great. Still the best is J. R. Hamilton, *Alexander the Great* (1973). Newer is N. G. L. Hammond, *Alexander the*

Great, 3d ed. (1994), which is, however, inferior to Hamilton's older book. Although many historians have idealized Alexander the Great, recent scholarship has provided a more realistic and unflattering view of him. The foremost expert on Alexander is E. Badian, who has reinterpreted Alexander's career in a variety of journal articles: *Historia* 7 (1958): 425–444; *Classical Quarterly* 52 (1958): 144–157; *Journal of Hellenic Studies* 81 (1961): 16–43; and *Greece and Rome* 12 (1965): 166–182. Badian's analysis of Alexander also appears in *The Cambridge History of Iran,* vol. 2 (1985), chap. 8. Recent political studies of the Hellenistic period include A. B. Bosworth, *Conquest and Empire* (1988), which sets Alexander's career in a broad context, and F. L. Holt, *Alexander the Great and Bactria* (1988), which discusses the formation of a Greco-Macedonian frontier in central Asia. Two new works deal with the Hellenization of much of the Mediterranean world: P. M. Frazer, *Cities of Alexander the Great* (1996); and, more broadly, G. M. Cohen, *The Hellenistic Settlements in Europe, the Islands, and Asia Minor* (1996), a welcome new contribution to the understanding of the impact of the Greeks on the world around them.

A. K. Bowman, *Egypt After the Pharaohs* (1986), is a readable account of the impact of the Greeks and Macedonians on Egyptian society. The same topic is treated by N. Lewis, a major scholar in the field, in his *Greeks in Ptolemaic Egypt* (1986). A brief, new study comes from the pen of another major scholar, A. E. Samuel, *The Shifting Sands of History: Interpretations of Ptolemaic Egypt* (1989), which deals with history and historiography. W. Heckel, *The Marshals of Alexander's Empire* (1992), treats the careers of the more than 130 men who were not actually Alexander's chief officers but nonetheless substantially shaped Hellenistic political history. S. Sherwin-White and A. Kuhrt, *From Samarkand to Sardis* (1992), offer a new study of the Seleucid monarchy that puts it in an Asian rather than a Greek perspective. J. D. Grainger, *Seleukos Nikator* (1990), examines how the Hellenistic king created his empire. R. A. Billows, *Antigone the One-Eyed and the Creation of the Hellenistic State* (1990), examines the career of the one man who most nearly reunited Alexander's empire. E. V. Hansen, *The Attalids of Pergamon,* 2d ed. (1971), though dated, is still the best treatment of that kingdom. B. Bar-Kochva, *Judas Maccabaeus* (1988), treats the Jewish struggle against the Seleucids and Hellenistic influences. A good portrait of one of the busiest ports in the Hellenistic world can be found in R. Garland, *Piraeus* (1987).

Much new work has focused on the spread of Hellenism throughout the Near East. Very extensive is A. Kuhrt and S. Sherwin-White, eds., *Hellenism in the East* (1988), which touches on a broad range of topics, including biblical studies, Christianity, and Islam. A. E. Samuel, *The Promise of the West* (1988), studies the connections among Greek, Roman, and Jewish culture and thought and their significance for Western history. P. McKechnie, *Outsiders in the Greek Cities of the Fourth Century* (1989), provides an interesting study of the social dislocation of the Greeks in the time of Philip II and Alexander the Great.

No specific treatment of women in the Hellenistic world yet exists, but two studies shed light on certain aspects of the topic. N. L. Goodrich, *Priestesses* (1989), examines the importance of priestesses in cults from the Near East to Ireland. S. B. Pomeroy, *Women in Hellenistic Egypt* (1984), studies women in the kingdom from which the most ancient evidence has survived.

Two general studies of religion in the Hellenistic world are F. Grant, *Hellenistic Religion: The Age of Syncretism* (1953), and H. J. Rose, *Religion in Greece and Rome* (1959). L. H. Feldman, *Jew and Gentile in the Ancient World* (1993), argues that the pagan response to Judaism within the Greco-Roman period was not as negative as often thought. R. van den Broek et al., eds., *Knowledge of God in the Graeco-Roman World* (1988), is a difficult but rewarding collection of essays that points out how similarly pagans, Hellenistic Jews, and Christians thought about human attempts to know God. R. E. Witt, *Isis in the Graeco-Roman World* (1971), an illustrated volume, studies the origins and growth of the Isis cult. More specifically, S. K. Heyob, *The Cult of Isis Among Women in the Graeco-Roman World* (1975), explores its popularity among women. The cult of Isis's consort Osiris is the subject of J. G. Griffiths, *The Origins of Osiris and His Cult* (1980). For the mystery cults in general, see W. Burkert, *Ancient Mystery Cults* (1987), written by one of the finest scholars in the field.

Hellenistic philosophy and science have attracted the attention of a number of scholars, and the various philosophical schools are especially well covered. A general treatment can be recommended because it deals with the broader question of the role of the intellectual in the classical and Hellenistic worlds: F. L. Vatai, *Intellectuals in Politics in the Greek World from Early Times to the Hellenistic Age* (1984). Broader is S. Blundell, *The Origin of Civilization in Greek and Roman Thought* (1986), a survey of classical political and social theories through a period of ten centuries, from Aristotle to the Stoics and their Roman successors. A. W. Bulloch et al., *Images and Ideologies* (1993), is a broad-ranging work that studies all the important intellectual aspects of Hellenistic history. Newer and also comprehensive is R. W. Sharples, *Stoics, Epicureans, Sceptics* (1996), which provides a good synthesis of these three major branches of Hellenistic philosophy. A good survey of Hellenistic science is G. E. R. Lloyd, *Greek Science After Aristotle* (1963), and specific studies of major figures can be found in T. L. Heath's solid work, *Aristarchos of Samos* (1920), still unsurpassed, and E. J. Dijksterhuis, *Archimedes,* rev. ed. (1987). Last, N. Zagagi, *The Comedy of Menander* (1995), traces the conventions of the Attic stage and Menander's original contributions to it.

LISTENING TO THE PAST

The Greeks Welcome the Egyptian God Serapis

Greek religion was generally tolerant of, indeed liberal toward and inclusive of, other religions. For instance, the Athenians set up an altar to the "Unknown God," in the belief that there were gods of whom they were unaware. Known or not, these gods should be honored. Easily the best example of this attitude comes from the meeting of the Greeks and the peoples of Egypt and western Asia. These Easterners had long-established and much-revered cults of their own, and they in turn were generally fascinated by Greek cults. The result was not hostility, but religious syncretism, *the attempt to unify or reconcile various religious ideas. In some instances, the Greeks simply adopted Eastern cults as they found them. One such case involves the Greek embrace of the cult of the Egyptian god Serapis. First originally recognized in Egypt, the cult quickly spread throughout the Hellenistic world. The following account by Tacitus tells of how the Hellenistic king Ptolemy I of Egypt formally established the cult of Serapis in his kingdom.*

King Ptolemy I, while he was providing Alexandria, which had recently been founded, with walls, temples, and cults, saw in a dream a young man of exceptional beauty and of more than human size, who instructed him to send his most trusted friends to the Black Sea to bring back his image. This would bring prosperity to his kingdom, and the home that welcomed him would be great and famous. At the same time the young man seemed to him to rise up in the sky enveloped in a mighty conflagration. Ptolemy was struck by the portent and the miracle, and revealed the night's apparition to the Egyptian priests who are accustomed to understanding prodigies of this kind. And since they knew too little about the Pontus [Black Sea] and the outside world, the king turned to Timotheus of Athens, a priest of the Eleusinian Mysteries, and asked him what was this cult and who was this deity. After searching for persons who had been to the Pontus, Timotheus learned that there was a city there, Sinope, with nearby a temple of Jupiter Dis which had long been famous among the local inhabitants and that next to the image of the god stood one of a woman generally called Proserpine or Demeter. But Ptolemy, as kings do, was quick to take fright; but when he had recovered a sense of security, he turned more to pleasure than to religion, gradually neglected the matter and turned his attention elsewhere, until the same apparition, but now more frightening and urgent, predicted doom for him and his kingdom if his orders were not carried out. Then Ptolemy ordered the sending of envoys with gifts to King Scydrothemis, who at that time ruled Sinope, and instructed the envoys as they were to depart to consult Pythian Apollo at Delphi. They journeyed safely by sea, and the answer of the oracle was clear: they must go and bring back the image of his father [i.e., Jupiter Dis], but leave that of his sister. When they reached Sinope they produced the gifts, the prayers and the instructions of the king to Scydrothemis, who hesitated, being at times fearful of the deity and at times terrified by the threats and the opposition of the people, and often he would be influenced by the gifts and the promises of the envoys. Three years elapsed and Ptolemy did not relax his zeal or his prayers, and kept increasing the dignity of his envoys, the number of ships and the amount of gold offered. Then Scydrothemis saw a threatening apparition which enjoined him not to delay any further the execution of the god's orders. As he still hesitated he was harassed by various calamities, by diseases, and clear signs of divine anger which increased every day. He summoned an assembly and recounted the orders of the deity, the visions he and Ptolemy had had, and the disasters that were falling on them. The crowd rebuffed the king, and was jealous of Egypt; they feared for themselves and surrounded the temple. This is what gave rise to the widespread report that the god himself had boarded the ships moored to the shore, and remarkably, three days later after crossing such a large expanse of sea, they landed at Alexandria. A temple commensurate with the size of the city was built in the district called Rhacotis where there had existed a small shrine dedicated from of old to Serapis and Isis. Such is the most widespread account of the origin and coming of the god. I [Tacitus] am well aware that there are some who say that he was brought from Seleucia, a city in Syria, in the reign of the third Ptolemy, while others relate that the same Ptolemy was responsible for introducing him from his ancient home of Memphis, a city formerly famous and a pillar of ancient Egypt. As for the god himself many liken him to Asclepius for his healing powers, some to Osiris, the most ancient deity of that people, many to Jupiter as lord of the universe, and the majority to Zeus-Dis because of his own obvious attributes or through elaborate interpretations.

Questions for Analysis

1. Were the origins of the cult of Serapis based on fact? Why were there so many versions of it?
2. Is it likely that Ptolemy needed to send envoys to Sinope, when the cult of Serapis was already well known in Egypt? If not, why the story?
3. What does this account tell of the expansion of the cult of Serapis before Ptolemy's adoption of it?

Source: Tacitus, *Histories* 4.83–84, in M. M. Austin, *The Hellenistic World from Alexander to the Roman Conquest* (Cambridge: Cambridge University Press, 1981), pp. 438–440 (adapted).

Bust of the Egyptian god Serapis depicted in Greek dress and with Greek hairstyle. *(Alinari/Art Resource, NY)*

CHAPTER

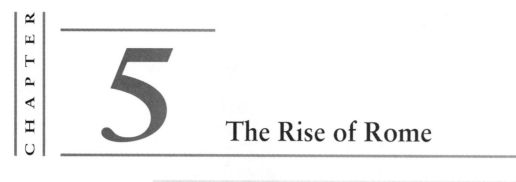

5 The Rise of Rome

Etruscan soldiers carrying a slain comrade, from the lid of a fourth-century B.C. bronze container. *(Scala/Art Resource, NY)*

Who is so thoughtless and lazy that he does not want to know in what way and with what kind of government the Romans in less than 53 years conquered nearly the entire inhabited world and brought it under their rule—an achievement previously unheard of?"[1] This question was first asked by Polybius, a Greek historian who lived in the second century B.C. With keen awareness Polybius realized that the Romans were achieving something unique in world history.

What was that achievement? Was it simply the creation of a huge empire? Hardly. The Persians had done the same thing. For that matter, Alexander the Great had conquered vast territories in a shorter time. Was it the creation of a superior culture? Even the Romans admitted that in matters of art, literature, philosophy, and culture they learned from the Greeks. Rome's achievement lay in the ability of the Romans not only to conquer peoples but to incorporate them into the Roman system. Rome succeeded where the Greek polis had failed. Unlike the Greeks, who refused to share citizenship, the Romans extended their citizenship first to the Italians and later to the peoples of the provinces. With that citizenship went Roman government and law. Rome created a world state that embraced the entire Mediterranean area and extended northward.

Nor was Rome's achievement limited to the ancient world. Rome's law, language, and administrative practices were a precious heritage to medieval and modern Europe. London, Paris, Vienna, and many other modern European cities began as Roman colonies or military camps. When the Founding Fathers created the American republic, they looked to Rome as a model. On the darker side, Napoleon and Mussolini paid their own tribute to Rome by aping its forms. Whether Founding Father or modern autocrat, all were acknowledging admiration for the Roman achievement.

Roman history is usually divided into two periods: the republic, the age in which Rome grew from a small city-state to ruler of an empire, and the empire, the period when the republican constitution gave way to constitutional monarchy.

- How did Rome rise to greatness?
- What effects did the conquest of the Mediterranean have on the Romans themselves?
- Finally, why did the republic collapse?

These are the questions we will explore in this chapter.

The Land and the Sea

To the west of Greece the boot-shaped peninsula of Italy, with Sicily at its toe, occupies the center of the Mediterranean basin. As Map 5.1 shows, Italy and Sicily thrust southward toward Africa: the distance between southwestern Sicily and the northern African coast is at one point only about a hundred miles. Italy and Sicily literally divide the Mediterranean into two basins and form the focal point between the halves.

Like Greece and other Mediterranean lands, Italy enjoys a genial, almost subtropical climate. The winters are rainy, but the summer months are dry. Because of the climate the rivers of Italy usually carry little water during the summer, and some go entirely dry. The low water level of the Arno, one of the principal rivers of Italy, once led Mark Twain to describe it as "a great historical creek with four feet in the channel and some scows floating around. It would be a very plausible river if they would pump some water into it."[2] The Arno at least is navigable. Most of Italy's other rivers are not. Clearly these small rivers were unsuitable for regular, large-scale shipping. Italian rivers, unlike Twain's beloved Mississippi, never became major thoroughfares for commerce and communication.

Geography encouraged Italy to look to the Mediterranean. In the north Italy is protected by the Apennine Mountains, which break off from the Alps and form a natural barrier. The Apennines hindered but did not prevent peoples from penetrating Italy from the north. Throughout history, in modern times as well as ancient, various invaders have entered Italy by this route. North of the Apennines lies the Po Valley, an important part of modern Italy. In antiquity this valley did not become Roman territory until late in the history of the republic. From the north the Apennines run southward the entire length of the Italian boot; they virtually cut off access to the Adriatic Sea, a feature that further induced Italy to look west to Spain and Carthage rather than east to Greece.

Even though most of the land is mountainous, the hill country is not as inhospitable as are the Greek highlands. In antiquity the general fertility of the soil provided the basis for a large population. Nor did the mountains of Italy so carve up the land as to prevent the development of political unity. Geography proved kinder to Italy than to Greece.

In their southward course the Apennines leave two broad and fertile plains, those of Latium and Campania. These plains attracted settlers and invaders from the time when peoples began to move into Italy. Among these peoples were the Romans, who established their city on the Tiber River in Latium.

This site enjoyed several advantages. The Tiber provided Rome with a constant source of water. Located at an easy crossing point on the Tiber, Rome stood astride the main avenue of communication between northern and southern Italy. The famous seven hills of Rome were defensible and safe from the floods of the Tiber. Rome was in an excellent position to develop the resources of Latium and maintain contact with the rest of Italy.

The Etruscans and Rome (750–509 B.C.)

In recent years archaeologists have found traces of numerous early peoples in Italy. The origins of these cultures and their precise relations with one another are not completely understood. In fact no totally coherent account of the prehistory of Italy is yet possible, but certain elements of this period are yearly coming into sharper focus. One fundamental fact is, however, indisputable: from about 1000 to 875 B.C. many peoples speaking Indo-European languages were moving into Italy from the north, probably in small groups. They were part of the awesome but imperfectly understood movement of peoples that spread the Indo-European languages from Spain to India.

Only with the coming of the Greeks does Italy enter into the light of history. Yet Italy had a long prehistory before the Greeks arrived. Old legends preserved a faint memory of past events, and modern archaeology has brought much of this distant past to light. The oldest developments in Italy are almost bewilderingly complex. The Greeks found that the Phoenicians from Tyre and Sidon had traded with peoples in Italy from at least the eleventh century B.C. In the eighth and seventh centuries B.C. their merchants had exchanged material goods with many peoples throughout the area. Phoenician influence, however, was not very significant, for they came to trade, not to settle. The Greeks also encountered the Etruscans, Celts, and Italians, all scattered along the peninsula and each independent of the other.

The Etruscans

Despite much uncertainty, a generally reliable outline of events can be sketched. Among the various peoples in Italy were the Etruscans, one of the most mysterious peoples of antiquity. Who they were and where they came from are topics still being argued. Earlier scholars have concluded either that they were newcomers from the north, part of the vast movement of peoples of the period, or that they had sailed from Lydia in the Near East. Recent work in archaeology and epigraphy—the study of inscriptions—suggests that they may have been a people indigenous to Italy. That means that they developed their culture and were one of the peoples who had been in Italy from time immemorial. Excavations have clearly demonstrated a continuity of settlement and culture that goes back at least to the eighth century B.C. There is no break in the archaeological record, no indication of the arrival of newcomers, and no dramatic and unexpected change in customs. In short, archaeology strongly suggests that the Etruscans evolved from earlier native folk.

Study of the Etruscan language proves that it is unrelated to any known language. This is precisely what one can expect of an indigenous people who developed their culture in isolation from the outside world. There is no evidence that they were even literate until about 700 B.C., when they adopted and adapted a western Greek alphabet in which to write their language. (As we saw in Chapter 3, the Greeks had done something similar by using the Semitic Phoenician alphabet to write their Indo-European language.)

Of greater importance than the question of the origins of the Etruscans is an understanding of their accomplishments. Once established as a major player in Italian life, they exported their rich mineral resources to pay for luxury goods imported from the eastern Mediterranean. They also played an important role in the wider Mediterranean world because of their contacts with their neighbors. In addition, they created an export market in olive oil and wine. Their society evolved cities that resembled Greek city-states, and their wealth, along with their political and military institutions, enabled them to form a loosely organized league of cities whose domination extended as far north

MAP 5.1 Italy and the City of Rome The geographical configuration of the Italian peninsula shows how Rome stood astride north-south communication routes and how the state that united Italy stood poised to move into Sicily and northern Africa.

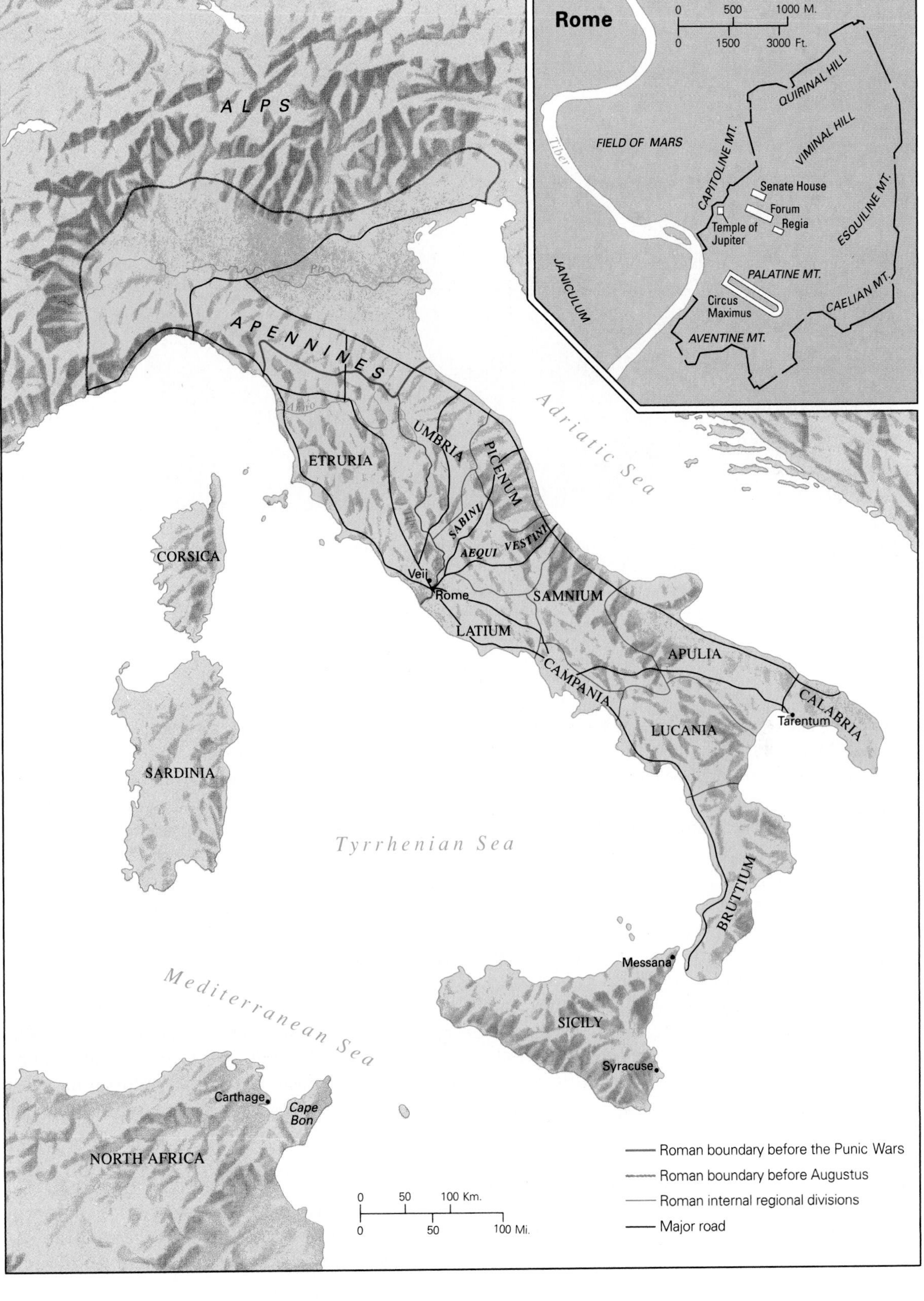
Rome
0 500 1000 M.
0 1500 3000 Ft.
QUIRINAL HILL
VIMINAL HILL
FIELD OF MARS
CAPITOLINE MT.
Tiber
Senate House
Forum
Regia
Temple of Jupiter
ESQUILINE MT.
JANICULUM
PALATINE MT.
Circus Maximus
CAELIAN MT.
AVENTINE MT.
ALPS
Po
APENNINES
Arno
Adriatic Sea
UMBRIA
PICENUM
ETRURIA
SABINI
AEQUI
VESTINI
CORSICA
Veii
Rome
SAMNIUM
LATIUM
APULIA
CAMPANIA
CALABRIA
Tarentum
LUCANIA
SARDINIA
Tyrrhenian Sea
BRUTTIUM
Messana
Mediterranean Sea
SICILY
Syracuse
Carthage
Cape Bon
NORTH AFRICA
0 50 100 Km.
0 50 100 Mi.
Roman boundary before the Punic Wars
Roman boundary before Augustus
Roman internal regional divisions
Major road

Sarcophagus of Lartie Seianti The woman portrayed on this lavish sarcophagus is the noble Etruscan Lartie Seianti. Although the sarcophagus is her place of burial, she is portrayed as in life, comfortable and at rest. The influence of Greek art on Etruscan is apparent on almost every feature of the sarcophagus. *(Archaeological Museum, Florence/Nimatallah/Art Resource, NY)*

as the Po Valley and as far south as Latium and Campania (see Map 5.1). In Latium they founded cities and took control of a small collection of villages subsequently called Rome. By the seventh century B.C. they had fully entered the cosmopolitan life of the Mediterranean world.

The Celts

Less needs to be said of the Celts than of the Etruscans, simply because most of them played a small role in Roman history. They first appeared in the thirteenth century B.C. in the upper Danube Valley. For the most part these Indo-European-speaking peoples spread westward across northern Europe and eastward into Asia Minor, notably the area of modern western Turkey. No one knows what prompted their migration, but by the eighth and seventh centuries B.C. they had reached the modern states of Spain, France, Great Britain, and Ireland. Although they had little permanent impact on Rome and were limited to northern Italy, they put down roots in the west, and their language, in modified form, is still spoken in Ireland, Scotland, Cornwall, and Brittany. They were fierce fighters, armed first with bronze and later with iron. The combination of personal valor, good equipment, and lack of organized opposition from the local populations opened the way of conquest for them.

In religious matters they were inspired by the Druids, a priestly fraternity that performed rites considered savage by the Romans. Yet the Druids also preserved the myths and traditions of the Celts. Since much of their knowledge was never written down, however, it was later lost. Some remnants have survived in remote parts of Ireland and Wales, where fragments of it were preserved. Although the Celts had little impact on the Mediterranean world, they were an important force in the development of western Europe north of the Alps.

The Romans

The Romans, as they have been called from antiquity to today, were part of the larger movements of Italic peoples. Archaeology places them on the site of modern

Rome in the eighth century B.C. The Etruscans found them settled on three of Rome's seven hills. The site of the future Forum Romanum, the famous public square and center of political life, was originally the cemetery of the small community. According to Roman legend, Romulus and Remus founded Rome in 753 B.C. Romulus built his settlement on the Palatine Hill, while Remus chose the Aventine (see inset, Map 5.1). Jealous of his brother's work, Remus ridiculed it by jumping over Romulus's unfinished wall. In a rage Romulus killed his brother and vowed, "So will die whoever else shall leap over my walls." In this instance legend preserves some facts. Archaeological investigation has confirmed that the earliest settlement at Rome was situated on the Palatine Hill and that it dates to the first half of the eighth century B.C. The legend also shows traces of Etruscan influence on Roman customs. The inviolability of Romulus's walls recalls the Etruscan concept of the *pomerium,* a sacred boundary intended to keep out anything evil or unclean.

During the years 753 to 509 B.C., the Romans embraced many Etruscan customs. They adopted the Etruscan alphabet, which the Etruscans themselves had adopted from the Greeks. The Romans later handed on this alphabet to medieval Europe and thence to the modern Western world. The Romans also adopted symbols of political authority from the Etruscans. The symbol of the Etruscan king's right to execute or scourge his subjects was a bundle of rods and an ax, called in Latin the *fasces,* which the king's retainer carried before him on official occasions. When the Romans expelled the Etruscan kings, they created special attendants called "lictors" to carry the fasces before their new magistrates, the consuls. Even the *toga,* the white woolen robe worn by the citizens, came from the Etruscans. In engineering and architecture the Romans adopted from the Etruscans the vault and the arch. Above all, it was thanks to the Etruscans that the Romans truly became urban dwellers.

Etruscan power and influence at Rome were so strong that Roman traditions preserved the memory of Etruscan kings who ruled the city. Under the Etruscans, Rome enjoyed contacts with the larger Mediterranean world, and the city began to grow. In the years 575 to 550 B.C. temples and public buildings began to grace the city. The Capitoline Hill became the religious center of the city when the temple of Jupiter Optimus Maximus (Jupiter the Best and Greatest) was built there. The Forum ceased to be a cemetery and began its history as a public meeting place, a development parallel to that of the Greek agora. Trade in metalwork became common, and the wealthier Roman classes began to import large numbers of fine Greek vases. The Etruscans had found Rome a collection of villages and made it a city.

THE ROMAN CONQUEST OF ITALY (509–290 B.C.)

Early Roman history is an uneven mixture of fact and legend. Roman traditions often contain an important kernel of truth, but that does not make them history. In many cases they are significant because they illustrate the ethics, morals, and ideals that Roman society considered valuable.

According to Roman tradition, the Romans expelled the Etruscan king Tarquin the Proud from Rome in 509 B.C. and founded the republic. In the years that followed, the Romans fought numerous wars with their neighbors on the Italian peninsula. They became soldiers, and the grim fighting bred tenacity, a prominent Roman trait. At an early date the Romans also learned the value of alliances and how to provide leadership for their allies. Alliances with the Latin towns around them provided them with a large reservoir of manpower. These alliances involved the Romans in still other wars and took them farther afield in the Italian peninsula.

The growth of Roman power was slow but steady. Not until roughly a century after the founding of the republic did the Romans drive the Etruscans entirely out of Latium. Around 390 B.C. the Romans suffered a major setback when a new people, the Celts—or "Gauls," as the Romans called them—swept aside a Roman army and sacked Rome. More intent on loot than on land, they agreed to abandon Rome in return for a thousand pounds of gold.

From 390 to 290 B.C. the Romans rebuilt their city and recouped their losses. They also reorganized their army to create the mobile legion, a flexible unit capable of fighting on either broken or open terrain. The Romans finally brought Latium and their Latin allies fully under their control and conquered Etruria (see Map 5.1). In 343 B.C. they grappled with the Samnites in a series of bitter wars for the possession of Campania and southern Italy. The Samnites were a formidable enemy and inflicted serious losses on the Romans. But the superior organization, institutions, and manpower of the Romans won out in the end. Although Rome had yet to subdue the whole peninsula, for the first time in history the city stood unchallenged in Italy.

Rome's success in diplomacy and politics was as important as its military victories. Unlike the Greeks, the Romans did not simply conquer and dominate. Instead, they shared with other Italians both political power and degrees of Roman citizenship. With many of their oldest allies, such as the Latin cities, they shared full Roman citizenship. In other instances they granted citizenship without the franchise (*civitas sine suffragio*). Allies who held this status enjoyed all the rights of Roman citizenship except that they could not vote or hold Roman offices. They were subject to Roman taxes and calls for military service but ran their own local affairs. The Latin allies were able to acquire full Roman citizenship by moving to Rome. A perhaps humble but very efficient means of keeping the Romans and their colonies together were the Roman roads, many of which were in use as late as the medieval period. These roads provided an easy route of communication between the capital and outlying areas, allowed for the quick movement of armies, and offered an efficient means of trade. They were the tangible sinews of unity.

By their willingness to extend their citizenship, the Romans took Italy into partnership. Here the political genius of Rome triumphed where Greece had failed. Rome proved itself superior to the Greek polis because it both conquered and shared the fruits of conquest with the conquered. Rome could consolidate where Greece could only dominate. The unwillingness of the Greek polis to share its citizenship condemned it to a limited horizon. Not so with Rome. The extension of Roman citizenship strengthened the state, gave it additional manpower and wealth, and laid the foundation of the Roman Empire.

The Roman State

The Romans summed up their political existence in a single phrase: *senatus populusque Romanus,* "the Roman senate and the people." The real genius of the Romans lay in the fields of politics and law. Unlike the Greeks, they did not often speculate on the ideal state or on political forms. Instead, they realistically met actual challenges and created institutions, magistracies, and legal concepts to deal with practical problems. Change was consequently commonplace in Roman political life, and the constitution of 509 B.C. was far simpler than that of 27 B.C. Moreover, the Roman constitution, unlike the American, was not a single written document. Rather, it was a set of traditional beliefs, customs, and laws.

In the early republic social divisions determined the shape of politics. Political power was in the hands of the aristocracy—the *patricians,* who were wealthy landowners. Patrician families formed clans, as did aristocrats in early Greece. They dominated the affairs of state, provided military leadership in time of war, and monopolized knowledge of law and legal procedure. The common people of Rome, the *plebeians,* had few of the patricians' advantages. Some plebeians formed their own clans and rivaled the patricians in wealth. Many plebeian merchants increased their wealth in the course of Roman expansion, but most plebeians were poor. They were the artisans, small farmers, and landless urban dwellers. The plebeians, rich and poor alike, were free citizens with a voice in politics. Nonetheless, they were overshadowed by the patricians.

Historians today still argue about the origins of these two groups and how they functioned both socially and politically within the state. The question of how the distinction between patrician and plebeian arose can probably never be answered definitely. No one now knows whether it existed before the coming of the Etruscans, whether the Etruscans introduced it in Rome, or whether it occurred at the creation of the republic. Despite all the contemporary research on the topic, only speculation is the result. In this area, as in many others, historians must possess the intelligence, the learning, and the humility to admit that they just do not know the answer. It is perfectly clear, however, that these two social groups determined the shape of Roman politics.

Perhaps the greatest institution of the republic was the senate, which had originated under the Etruscans as a council of noble elders who advised the king. During the republic the senate advised the consuls and other magistrates. Because the senate sat year after year, while magistrates changed annually, it provided stability and continuity. It also served as a reservoir of experience and knowledge. Technically, the senate could not pass legislation; it could only offer its advice. But increasingly, because of the senate's prestige, its advice came to have the force of law.

The Romans created several assemblies through which the people elected magistrates and passed legislation. The earliest was the *comitia curiata,* which had religious, political, and military functions. According to Roman tradition, King Servius Tullius (578–535 B.C.), who reorganized the state into 193 *centuries* for

The Roman Forum The forum was the center of Roman political life. From simple beginnings it developed into the very symbol of Rome's imperial majesty. *(Josephine Powell, Rome)*

military purposes, created the *comitia centuriata* as a political body to decide Roman policy. The comitia centuriata voted in centuries, which in this instance means political blocs. The patricians possessed the majority of centuries because they shouldered most of the burden of defense. Thus they could easily outvote the plebeians. In 471 B.C. the plebeians won the right to meet in an assembly of their own, the *concilium plebis,* and to pass ordinances. In 287 B.C. the bills passed in the concilium plebis were recognized as binding on the entire population.

The chief magistrates of the republic were the two consuls, elected for one-year terms. At first the consulship was open only to patricians. The consuls commanded the army in battle, administered state business, convened the comitia centuriata, and supervised financial affairs. In effect, they and the senate ran the state. The consuls appointed *quaestors* to assist them in their duties, and in 421 B.C. the quaestorship became an elective office open to plebeians. The quaestors took charge of the public treasury and prosecuted criminals in the popular courts.

In 366 B.C. the Romans created a new office, that of *praetor,* and in 227 B.C. the number of praetors was increased to four. When the consuls were away from Rome, the praetors could act in their place. The praetors dealt primarily with the administration of justice. When he took office, a praetor issued a proclamation declaring the principles by which he would interpret the law. These proclamations became very important because they usually covered areas where the law was vague and thus helped clarify the law.

Other officials included the powerful *censors,* created in 443 B.C., who had many responsibilities, the most important being supervision of public morals, the power to determine who lawfully could sit in the senate, the registration of citizens, and the leasing of public contracts. Later officials were the *aediles,* four in number, who supervised the streets and markets and presided over public festivals.

After the age of overseas conquest (see pages 143–146), the Romans divided the Mediterranean area into provinces governed by ex-consuls and ex-praetors. Because of their experience in Roman politics, they were well suited to administer the affairs of the provincials and to fit Roman law and custom into new contexts.

One of the most splendid achievements of the Romans was their development of law. Roman law began as a set of rules that regulated the lives and relations of citizens. This civil law, or *ius civile,* consisted of statutes, customs, and forms of procedure. Roman assemblies added to the body of law, and praetors interpreted it. The spirit of the law aimed at protecting the property, lives, and reputations of citizens, redressing wrongs, and giving satisfaction to victims of injustice.

As the Romans came into more frequent contact with foreigners, they had to devise laws to deal with disputes between Romans and foreigners and between foreigners under Roman jurisdiction. In these instances, where there was no precedent to guide the Romans, the legal decisions of the praetors proved of immense importance. The praetors adopted aspects of other legal systems and resorted to the law of equity—what they thought was right and just to all parties. Free, in effect, to determine law, the praetors enjoyed a great deal of flexibility. This situation illustrates the practicality and the genius of the Romans. By addressing specific, actual circumstances the praetors developed a body of law, the *ius gentium,* "the law of peoples," that applied to Romans and foreigners and that laid the foundation for a universal conception of law. By the time of the late republic, Roman jurists were reaching decisions on the basis of the Stoic concept of *ius naturale,* "natural law," a universal law that could be applied to all societies.

Social Conflict in Rome

Another important aspect of early Roman history was a great social conflict, usually known as the Struggle of the Orders, which developed between patricians and plebeians. What the plebeians wanted was real political representation and safeguards against patrician domination. The plebeians' efforts to obtain recognition of their rights is the crux of the Struggle of the Orders.

Rome's early wars gave the plebeians the leverage they needed: Rome's survival depended on the army, and the army needed the plebeians. The first showdown between plebeians and patricians came, according to tradition, in 494 B.C. To force the patricians to grant concessions, the plebeians seceded from the state; they literally walked out of Rome and refused to serve in the army. The plebeians' general strike worked. Because of it the patricians made important concessions. One of these was social. In 445 B.C. the patricians passed a law, the *lex Canuleia,* which for the first time allowed patricians and plebeians to marry one another. Furthermore, the patricians recognized the right of plebeians to elect their own officials, the *tribunes.* The tribunes in turn had the right to protect the plebeians from the arbitrary conduct of patrician magistrates. The tribunes brought plebeian grievances to the senate for resolution. The plebeians were not bent on undermining the state. Rather, they used their gains only to win full equality under the law.

The law itself was the plebeians' primary target. Only the patricians knew what the law was, and only they could argue cases in court. All too often they had used the law for their own benefit. The plebeians wanted the law codified and published. The result of their agitation was the Law of the Twelve Tables, so called because the laws, which covered civil and criminal matters, were inscribed on twelve large bronze plaques. Later still, the plebeians forced the patricians to publish legal procedures as well. The plebeians had broken the patricians' legal monopoly and henceforth enjoyed full protection under the law.

The decisive plebeian victory came with the passage of the Licinian-Sextian rogations (or laws) in 367 B.C. Licinius and Sextus were plebeian tribunes who led a ten-year fight for further reform. Rich plebeians, such as Licinius and Sextus themselves, joined the poor to mount a sweeping assault on patrician privilege. Wealthy plebeians wanted the opportunity to provide political leadership for the state. They demanded that the patricians allow them access to all the magistracies of the state. If they could hold the consulship, they could also sit in the senate and advise the senate on policy. The two tribunes won approval from the senate for a law that stipulated that one of the two annual consuls had to be a plebeian. Though decisive, the Licinian-Sextian rogations did not automatically end the Struggle of the Orders. That happened only in 287 B.C. with the passage of a law, the *lex Hortensia,* that gave the resolutions of the concilium plebis the force of law for patricians and plebeians alike.

The results of the compromise between the patricians and the plebeians were far-reaching. They secured economic reform and defined the access of all citizens to public land. The principal result was the definition of political leadership. Plebeians could now hold the consulship, which brought with it the consular title, places of honor in the senate, and such cosmetic privileges as wearing the purple toga, the symbol of aristocracy. Far more important, the compromise established a new nobility shared by the plebeians and the patricians. They were both groups of wealthy aristocrats who had simply agreed to share the great offices of power within the republic. This would lead not to major political reform but to an extension of aristocratic rule. Nevertheless, the patricians were wise enough to give the plebeians wider political rights than they had previously enjoyed. The compromise was typically Roman.

The Struggle of the Orders resulted in a Rome stronger and better united than before. It could have led to anarchy, but again certain Roman traits triumphed. The values fostered by their social structure predisposed the Romans to compromise, especially in the face of common danger. Resistance and confrontation in Rome never exploded into class warfare. Instead, both sides resorted to compromises to hammer out a realistic solution. Important, too, were Roman patience, tenacity, and a healthy sense of the practical. These qualities enabled both sides to keep working until they had resolved the crisis. The Struggle of the Orders ended in 287 B.C. with a new concept of Roman citizenship. All citizens shared equally under the law. Theoretically, all could aspire to the highest political offices. Patrician or plebeian, rich or poor, Roman citizenship was equal for all.

ROMAN EXPANSION

Once the Romans had settled their internal affairs, they were free to turn their attention to the larger world around them. As seen earlier, they had already come to terms with the Italic peoples in Latium. Only later did Rome achieve primacy over its Latin allies, partly because of successful diplomacy and partly because of overwhelming military power. In 282 B.C. Rome expanded even farther in Italy and extended its power across the seas to Sicily, Corsica, and Sardinia.

Italy Becomes Roman

In only twenty years, from 282 to 262 B.C., the Romans dramatically built on their earlier successes. Their energy was remarkable, and the results they achieved were not always due to warfare. They established a string of colonies throughout Italy, some of them populated by Romans and others by Latins. Here was an effective way of sharing their success with their Italian allies. These colonies spread from Ariminum to Cosa in the north, and along the coasts of the Adriatic and Tyrrhenian Seas. They stretched through central Italy as far south as Paestum and Brundisium. With the exception of some Greek cities in the extreme south, Italy belonged to the Romans and their Italian allies.

The genius of the Romans lay in bringing these various peoples into one political system. First the Romans divided the Italians into two broad classes. Those living closest to Rome were incorporated into the Roman state. They enjoyed the full franchise and citizenship that the Romans themselves possessed. The other class comprised those Italians who lived farther afield. They were bound by treaty with the Romans and were considered allies. Although they received lesser rights of active citizenship, the allies retained their right of local self-government. The link between the allies and Rome was as much social as political, as both were ruled by aristocrats.

These contacts—social, political, and legal—with their neighbors led the Romans to a better acquaintance with the heritage, customs, and laws of their fellow Italians. Rome and the rest of Italy began to share similar views of their common welfare. By including others in the Roman political and social system, Rome was making Italy Roman.

Overseas Conquest (282–146 B.C.)

In 282 B.C., when the Romans had reached southern Italy, they embarked upon a series of wars that left them the rulers of the Mediterranean world. The nature of these wars demands attention. Unlike the Italians or even the Etruscans, the Romans felt that they were dealing with foreigners, people not akin to them. They were also moving into areas largely unfamiliar to them. These wars became fiercer and were fought on a larger scale than those in Italy. Yet there was nothing ideological about them. Unlike Napoleon or Hitler, the

Roman holdings in 133 B.C.
Roman holdings added by 44 B.C.
Major battles
North Sea
Baltic Sea
BRITAIN
ATLANTIC OCEAN
Elbe
Vistula
Don
Volga
Dnieper
Rhine
GERMANY
Caspian Sea
GAUL
RAETIA
NORICUM
ALPS
Lyons
CRIMEA
CISALPINE GAUL
PANNONIA
DACIA
Rhône
Ebro
Po
Danube
Trebia River
Black Sea
NARBONENSIS
Ravenna
Narbo
Massilia
DALMATIA
FARTHER SPAIN
Metaurus
MOESIA
L. Trasimene
Tiber
Adriatic Sea
ARMENIA
THRACE
CORSICA
Byzantium
Rome
MACEDONIA
Saguntum
Cannae
PHRYGIA
CAPPADOCIA
NEARER SPAIN
SARDINIA
Misenum
Brundisium
PARTHIA
BALEARIC IS.
Tarentum
EPIRUS
Gades
Pharsalus
Pergamum
ASIA
Carrhae
Actium
Smyrna
Tarsus
Tigris
Euphrates
Mylae
Drepena
Messana
Athens
Corinth
CILICIA
Antioch
Ctesiphon
Mediterranean Sea
SICILY
Syracuse
Seleucia
MAURETANIA
Carthage
SYRIA
Zama
RHODES
CYPRUS
NUMIDIA
CRETE
Damascus
JUDAEA
Jerusalem
Cyrene
Petra
NORTH AFRICA
Alexandria
LIBYA
ARABIAN DESERT
EGYPT
0
200
400 Km.
0
200
400 Mi.
Nile
Red Sea
SAHARA

Romans did not map out grandiose strategies for world conquest. They had no idea of what lay before them. If they could have looked into the future, they would have stood amazed. In many instances the Romans did not even initiate action; they simply responded to situations as they arose. Nineteenth-century Englishmen were fond of saying, "We got our empire in a fit of absence of mind." The Romans could not go quite that far. Though they sometimes declared war reluctantly, they nonetheless felt the need to dominate, to eliminate any state that could threaten them.

Rome was imperialistic, and its imperialism took two forms. In the barbarian West, the home of fierce tribes, Rome resorted to bald aggression to conquer new territory. In areas such as Spain and later Gaul, the fighting was fierce and savage, and gains came slowly. In the civilized East, the world of Hellenistic states, Rome tried to avoid annexing territory. The East was already heavily populated, and those people would have become Rome's responsibility. New responsibilities meant new problems, and such headaches the Romans shunned. In the East the Romans preferred to be patrons rather than masters. Only when that policy failed did they directly annex land. But in 282 B.C. all this lay in the future.

The Samnite wars had drawn the Romans into the political world of southern Italy. In 282 B.C., alarmed by the powerful newcomer, the Greek city of Tarentum in southern Italy called for help from Pyrrhus, king of Epirus in western Greece. A relative of Alexander the Great and an excellent general, Pyrrhus won two furious battles but suffered heavy casualties—thus the phrase "Pyrrhic victory" for a victory involving severe losses. Roman bravery and tenacity led him to comment: "If we win one more battle with the Romans, we'll be completely washed up." Against Pyrrhus's army the Romans threw new legions, and in the end manpower proved decisive. In 275 B.C. the Romans drove Pyrrhus from Italy and extended their sway over southern Italy. Once they did, the island of Sicily became a key for them to block Carthaginian expansion northward.

Pyrrhus once described Sicily as a future "wrestling ground for the Carthaginians and Romans." The Phoenician city of Carthage in North Africa (Map 5.2) had for centuries dominated the western Mediterranean. Sicily had long been a Carthaginian target. Since Sicily is the steppingstone to Italy, the Romans could not let it fall to an enemy.

MAP 5.2 Roman Expansion During the Republic The main spurt of Roman expansion occurred between 264 and 133 B.C., when most of the Mediterranean fell to Rome, followed by the conquest of Gaul and the eastern Mediterranean by 44 B.C.

By 264 B.C. Carthage was the unrivaled power of the western Mediterranean. Since the second half of the eighth century B.C. it had built its wealth on trade in tin and precious metals. It commanded one of the best harbors on the northern African coast and was supported by a fertile hinterland. The Carthaginians were for the most part merchants, not soldiers, and they made contributions to geographical knowledge by exploring as far west as the Atlantic coasts of northern Africa and Spain. They soon dominated the commerce of the western Mediterranean. By the fourth century B.C. they were fully integrated into the Hellenistic economy, which now spread from Gibraltar to the Parthian empire.

Commercial ambitions led to political conflict. Expansion led to war with the Etruscans and Greeks, but the Carthaginians won control of parts of Sardinia, Spain, and Sicily. At the end of a long string of wars, the Carthaginians held control of only the western tip of Sicily but retained considerable influence farther to the west. In fact, the Carthaginians had created and defended a mercantile empire that stretched from western Sicily to beyond Gibraltar.

This in essence is the background of the First Punic War between Rome and Carthage, two powers expanding into the same area. The First Punic War lasted for twenty-three years (264–241 B.C.). The Romans quickly learned that they could not conquer Sicily unless they controlled the sea. Although they lacked a fleet and hated the sea as fervently as cats hate water, with grim resolution the Romans built a navy. They fought seven major naval battles with the Carthaginians, won six, and finally wore down the Carthaginians. In 241 B.C. the Romans took possession of Sicily, which became their first real province. Once again Rome's resources, manpower, and determination proved decisive.

The First Punic War was a beginning, not an end. Carthage was still a formidable enemy. After the war the Carthaginians expanded their power to Spain and turned the Iberian Peninsula into a rich field of operations. By 219 B.C. Carthage had found its avenger—Hannibal (ca 247–183 B.C.). In Spain Hannibal learned how to lead armies and to wage war on a large scale. A brilliant general, he realized the advantages of swift mobile forces, and he was an innovator in tactics.

In 219 B.C. Hannibal defied the Romans by laying siege to the small city of Saguntum in Spain. When the

Romans declared war the following year, he gathered his forces and led them on one of the most spectacular marches in ancient history. Hannibal carried the Second Punic War to the very gates of Rome. Starting in Spain, he led his troops—infantry, cavalry, and elephants—over the Alps and into Italy on a march of more than a thousand miles. Once in Italy he defeated one Roman army at the Battle of Trebia (218 B.C.) and another at the Battle of Lake Trasimene (217 B.C.). At the Battle of Cannae in 216 B.C. Hannibal inflicted some forty thousand casualties on the Romans. He spread devastation throughout Italy but failed to crush Rome's iron circle of Latium, Etruria, and Samnium. The wisdom of Rome's political policy of extending rights and citizenship to its allies showed itself in these dark hours. Italy stood solidly with Rome against the invader. And Rome fought back.

The Roman general Scipio Africanus (ca 236–ca 183 B.C.) copied Hannibal's methods of mobile warfare. Scipio gave his new army combat experience in Spain, which he wrested from the Carthaginians. Meanwhile the Roman fleet dominated the western Mediterranean and interfered with Carthaginian attempts to reinforce Hannibal. In 204 B.C. the Roman fleet landed Scipio in Africa, prompting the Carthaginians to recall Hannibal from Italy to defend the homeland. In 202 B.C., near the town of Zama (see Map 5.2), Scipio defeated Hannibal in one of the world's truly decisive battles. Scipio's victory meant that Rome's heritage would be passed on to the Western world.

The Second Punic War contained the seeds of still other wars. The Third Punic War ended in 146 B.C. when Scipio Aemilianus, grandson of Scipio Africanus, destroyed Carthage. As the Roman conqueror watched the death pangs of that great city, he turned to his friend Polybius with the words: "I fear and foresee that someday someone will give the same order about my fatherland." In 133 B.C., after years of brutal and ruthless warfare, Scipio Aemilianus finally conquered Spain.

During the dark days of the Second Punic War, the king of Macedonia made an alliance with Hannibal against Rome. Even while engaged in the West, the Romans turned east to settle accounts. When the Romans intervened in the Hellenistic East, they went from triumph to triumph. The kingdom of Macedonia fell to the Roman legions, as did Greece and the Seleucid monarchy. By 146 B.C. the Romans stood unchallenged in the eastern Mediterranean and had turned many states and kingdoms into provinces. In 133 B.C. the king of Pergamum in Asia Minor left his kingdom to the Romans in his will. The Ptolemies of Egypt meekly obeyed Roman wishes. East and West, the Mediterranean had become *mare nostrum,* "our sea."

Old Values and Greek Culture

Rome had conquered the Mediterranean world, but some Romans considered that victory a misfortune. The historian Sallust (86–34 B.C.), writing from hindsight, complained that the acquisition of an empire was the beginning of Rome's troubles:

> *But when through labor and justice our Republic grew powerful, great kings defeated in war, fierce nations and mighty peoples subdued by force, when Carthage the rival of the Roman people was wiped out root and branch, all the seas and lands lay open, then fortune began to be harsh and to throw everything into confusion. The Romans had easily borne labor, danger, uncertainty, and hardship. To them leisure, riches—otherwise desirable—proved to be burdens and torments. So at first money, then desire for power grew great. These things were a sort of cause of all evils.*[3]

Sallust was not alone in his feelings. At the time some senators had opposed the destruction of Carthage on the grounds that fear of their old rival would keep the Romans in check. In the second century B.C. the Romans learned that they could not return to what they fondly considered a simple life. They were world rulers. The responsibilities they faced were complex and awesome. They had to change their institutions, social patterns, and way of thinking to meet the new era. They were in fact building the foundations of a great imperial system. It was a daunting challenge, and there were failures along the way. Roman generals and politicians would destroy each other. Even the republican constitution would eventually be discarded. But in the end Rome triumphed here just as it had on the battlefield, for out of the turmoil would come the *pax Romana*—"Roman peace."

How did the Romans of the day meet these challenges? How did they lead their lives and cope with these momentous changes? Obviously there are as many answers to these questions as there were Romans. Yet two men represent the major trends of the second century B.C. Cato the Elder shared the mentality of those who longed for the good old days and idealized the traditional agrarian way of life. Scipio Aemilianus led those who embraced the new urban life, with its eager acceptance of Greek culture. Forty-nine years older than Scipio, Cato was a product of an earlier generation, one that confronted a rapidly changing world. Cato and Scipio were both aristocrats, and neither of them was typical, even of the aristocracy. But they do exemplify opposing sets of attitudes that marked Roman society and politics in the age of conquest.

Coin of Hannibal This Carthaginian coin bears one of the few profiles of Hannibal. The style of the profile is Roman, but the artist has captured the actual likeness of the archenemy of Rome. *(Courtesy of the Trustees of the British Museum)*

Cato and the Traditional Ideal

Marcus Cato (234–149 B.C.) was born a plebeian, but his talent and energy carried him to Rome's highest offices. He cherished the old virtues and consistently imitated the old ways. In Roman society ties within the family were very strong. In this sense Cato and his family were typical. Cato was *paterfamilias,* a term that meant far more than merely "father." The paterfamilias was the oldest dominant male of the family. He held nearly absolute power over the lives of his wife and children as long as he lived. He could legally kill his wife for adultery or divorce her at will. He could kill his children or sell them into slavery. He could force them to marry against their will. Until the paterfamilias died, his sons could not legally own property. At his death the wife and children of the paterfamilias inherited his property.

Despite his immense power, the paterfamilias did not necessarily act alone or arbitrarily. To deal with important family matters he usually called a council of the adult males. In this way the leading members of the family aired their views. They had the opportunity to give their support to the paterfamilias or to dissuade him from harsh decisions. In these councils the women of the family had no formal part, but it can safely be assumed that they played an important role behind the scenes. Although the possibility of serious conflicts between a paterfamilias and his grown sons is obvious, no one in ancient Rome ever complained about the institution. Perhaps in practice the paterfamilias preferred to be lenient rather than absolute.

Like most Romans, Cato and his family began the day early in the morning. The Romans divided the period of daylight into twelve hours and the darkness into another twelve. The day might begin as early as half past four in summer, as late as half past seven in winter. Because Mediterranean summers are invariably hot, the farmer and his wife liked to take every advantage of the cool mornings. Cato and his family, like modern Italians, ordinarily started the morning with a light breakfast, usually nothing more than some bread and cheese. After breakfast the family went about its work.

Because of his political aspirations, Cato often used the mornings to plead law cases. He walked to the marketplace of the nearby town and defended anyone who wished his help. He received no fees for these services but did put his neighbors in his debt. In matters of law and politics Roman custom was very strong. It demanded that Cato's clients give him their political support or their votes in repayment whenever he asked for them. These clients knew and accepted their obligations to Cato for his help.

Cato's wife (whose name is unknown) was the matron of the family, a position of authority and respect. The virtues expected of a Roman matron were fidelity, chastity, modesty, and dedication to the family. Cato's wife also followed the old ways. While he was in town, she ran the household. She spent the morning spinning and weaving wool for the clothes the family wore. She supervised the domestic slaves, planned the meals, and devoted a good deal of attention to her son. In wealthy homes during this period, the matron had begun to employ a slave as a wet nurse. Cato's wife refused to delegate maternal duties. Like most ordinary Roman women, she nursed her son herself and bathed and swaddled him daily. Later the boy was allowed to play with toys and terra-cotta dolls. Roman children, like children everywhere, kept pets. Dogs were especially

Scene of the Life of a Child This scene depicts the life of Marcus Cornelius from his infancy to his playing with his ponies to his death. The entire scene suggests a pleasant and loving, if brief, childhood. *(Giraudon/Art Resource, NY)*

popular and valuable as house guards. Children played all sorts of games, and games of chance were very common. Until the age of seven the child was under the matron's care. During this time the mother began to educate her daughter in the management of the household. After the age of seven, the son—and in many wealthy households the daughter too—began to undertake formal education.

In the country Romans like Cato continued to take their main meal at midday. This meal included either coarse bread made from the entire husk of wheat or porridge made with milk or water; it also included turnips, cabbage, olives, and beans. When Romans ate meat, they preferred pork. Unless they lived by the sea, the average farm family did not eat fish, an expensive delicacy. Cato once complained that Rome was a place where a fish could cost more than a cow. With the midday meal the family drank ordinary wine mixed with water. Afterward any Roman who could took a nap. This was especially true in the summer, when the Mediterranean heat can be fierce. Slaves, artisans, and hired laborers, however, continued their work. In the evening Romans ate a light meal and went to bed at nightfall.

The agricultural year followed the sun and the stars—the farmer's calendar. Like Hesiod in Boeotia, the Roman farmer looked to the sky to determine when to plant, weed, shear sheep, and perform other chores. Spring was the season for plowing. Roman farmers plowed their land at least twice and preferably three times. The third plowing was to cover the sown seed in ridges and to use the furrows to drain off excess water. The Romans used a variety of plows. Some had detachable shares. Some were heavy for thick soil, others light for thin, crumbly soil. Farmers used oxen and donkeys to pull the plow, collecting the dung of the animals for fertilizer. Besides spreading manure, some farmers fertilized their fields by planting lupines and beans; when they began to pod, farmers plowed them under. The main money crops, at least for rich soils, were wheat and flax. Forage crops included clover, vetch, and alfalfa. Prosperous farmers like Cato raised olive trees chiefly for the oil. They also raised grapevines for the production of wine. Cato and his neighbors harvested their cereal crops in summer and their grapes in autumn. Harvests varied depending on the soil, but farmers could usually expect yields of 5½ bushels of wheat or 10½ bushels of barley per acre.

An influx of slaves resulted from Rome's wars and conquests. Prisoners from Spain, Africa, and the Hellenistic East and even some blacks and other prisoners from Hannibal's army came to Rome as the spoils of war. The Roman attitude toward slaves and slavery had little in common with modern views. To the Romans slavery was a misfortune that befell some people, but it did not entail any racial theories. Races were not enslaved because the Romans thought them inferior. The black African slave was treated no worse—and no better—than the Spaniard. Indeed, some slaves were valued because of their physical distinctiveness: black Africans and blond Germans were particular favorites. For the talented slave the Romans always held out the hope of eventual freedom. *Manumission*—the freeing of individual slaves by their masters—became so common that it had to be limited by law. Not even Christians questioned the institution of slavery. It was just a fact of life.

Slaves were entirely their master's property and might be treated with great cruelty. Many Romans were practical enough to realize that they got more out of their slaves by kindness than by severity. Yet in Sicily slave owners treated their slaves viciously. They bought slaves in huge numbers, branded them for identification, put them in irons, and often made them go without food and clothing. In 135 B.C. these conditions gave rise to a major slave revolt, during which many of the most brutal masters died at their slaves' hands. Italy too had trouble with slave unrest, but conditions there were generally better than in Sicily.

For Cato and most other Romans, religion played an important part in life. Originally the Romans thought of the gods as invisible, shapeless natural forces. Only through Etruscan and Greek influence did Roman deities take on human form. Jupiter, the sky-god, and his wife, Juno, became equivalent to the Greek Zeus and Hera. Mars was the god of war but also guaranteed the fertility of the farm and protected it from danger. The gods of the Romans were not loving and personal. They were stern, powerful, and aloof. But as long as the Romans honored the cults of their gods, they could expect divine favor.

Along with the great gods the Romans believed in spirits who haunted fields, forests, crossroads, and even the home itself. Some of these deities were hostile; only magic could ward them off. (See the feature "Listening to the Past: Popular Roman Views of Religion and Magic" on pages 160–161.) The spirits of the dead, like ghosts in modern horror films, frequented places where they had lived. They too had to be placated but were ordinarily benign. As the poet Ovid (43 B.C.–A.D. 17) put it:

The spirits of the dead ask for little.
They are more grateful for piety than for an expensive gift—
Not greedy are the gods who haunt the Styx below.
A rooftile covered with a sacrificial crown,
Scattered kernels, a few grains of salt,
Bread dipped in wine, and loose violets—
These are enough.
Put them in a potsherd and leave them in the middle of the road.[4]

A good deal of Roman religion consisted of rituals such as those Ovid describes. These practices lived on long after the Romans had lost interest in the great gods. Even Christianity could not entirely wipe them out. Instead, Christianity was to incorporate many of these rituals into its own style of worship.

African Acrobat Conquest and prosperity brought exotic pleasure to Rome. Every feature of this sculpture is exotic. The young African woman and her daring gymnastic pose would catch anyone's attention. And to add to the spice of her act, she performs using a live crocodile as her platform. Americans would have loved it. *(Courtesy of the Trustees of the British Museum)*

Scipio Aemilianus: Greek Culture and Urban Life

The old-fashioned ideals that Cato represented came into conflict with a new spirit of wealth and leisure. The conquest of the Mediterranean world and the spoils of war made Rome a great city. Roman life, especially in the cities, was changing and becoming less austere. The spoils of war went to build baths, theaters, and other places of amusement. Romans and Italian townspeople began to spend more of their time in leisure pursuits. Simultaneously, the new responsibilities of governing the world produced in Rome a sophisticated society. Romans developed new tastes and a liking for Greek culture and literature. They began to learn the Greek language. It became common for an educated Roman to speak both Latin and Greek. Hellenism dominated the cultural life of Rome. Even diehards like Cato found a knowledge of Greek essential for political and diplomatic affairs. The poet Horace (64–8 B.C.) summed it up well: "Captive Greece captured her rough conqueror and introduced the arts into rustic Latium."

One of the most avid devotees of Hellenism and the new was Scipio Aemilianus, the destroyer of Carthage. Scipio realized that broad and worldly views had to replace the old Roman narrowness. The new situation called for new ways. Rome was no longer a small city on the Tiber; it was the capital of the world, and Romans had to adapt themselves to that fact. Scipio was ready to become an innovator in both politics and culture. He broke with the past in the conduct of his political career, choosing a more personal style of politics, one that reflected his own views and looked unflinchingly at the broader problems that the success of Rome brought to its people. He embraced Hellenism wholeheartedly. Perhaps more than anyone else of his day, Scipio represented the new Roman—imperial, cultured, and independent.

In his education and interests, too, Scipio broke with the past. As a boy he had received the traditional Roman training, learning to read and write Latin and becoming acquainted with the law. He mastered the fundamentals of rhetoric and learned how to throw the javelin, fight in armor, and ride a horse. But later Scipio also learned Greek and became a fervent Hellenist. As a young man he formed a lasting friendship with the historian Polybius, who actively encouraged him in his study of Greek culture and in his intellectual pursuits. In later life Scipio's love of Greek learning, rhetoric, and philosophy became legendary. Scipio also promoted the spread of Hellenism in Roman society. He became the center of the Scipionic Circle, a small group of Greek and Roman artists, philosophers, historians, and poets. Conservatives like Cato tried to stem the rising tide of Hellenism, but men like Scipio carried the day and helped make the heritage of Greece an abiding factor in Roman life.

The new Hellenism profoundly stimulated the growth and development of Roman art and literature. The Roman conquest of the Hellenistic East resulted in wholesale confiscation of Greek paintings and sculpture to grace Roman temples, public buildings, and private homes. Roman artists copied many aspects of Greek art, but their emphasis on realistic portraiture carried on a native tradition.

Fabius Pictor (second half of the third century B.C.), a senator, wrote the first *History of Rome* in Greek. Other Romans translated Greek classics into Latin. Still others, such as the poet Ennius (239–169 B.C.), the father of Latin poetry, studied Greek philosophy, wrote comedies in Latin, and adapted many of Euripides' tragedies for the Roman stage. Ennius also wrote a history of Rome in Latin verse. Plautus (ca 254–184 B.C.) specialized in rough humor. He too decked out Greek plays in Roman dress but was no mere imitator. Indeed, his play *Amphitruo* was itself copied eighteen hundred years later by the French playwright Molière and the English poet John Dryden. The Roman dramatist Terence (ca 195–159 B.C.), a member of the Scipionic Circle, wrote comedies of refinement and grace that owed their essentials to Greek models. His plays lacked the energy and the slapstick of Plautus's rowdy plays. All of early Roman literature was derived from the Greeks, but it managed in time to speak in its own voice and to flourish because it had something of its own to say.

The conquest of the Mediterranean world brought the Romans leisure, and Hellenism influenced how they spent their free time. During the second century B.C. the Greek custom of bathing became a Roman passion and an important part of the day. In the early republic Romans had bathed infrequently, especially in the winter. Now large buildings containing pools and exercise rooms went up in great numbers, and the baths became an essential part of the Roman city. Architects built intricate systems of aqueducts to supply the bathing establishments with water. Conservatives railed at this Greek custom, calling it a waste of time and an encouragement to idleness. They were correct in that bathing establishments were more than just places to take a bath. They included gymnasia, where men exercised and played ball. Women had places of their own to bathe, generally sections of the same baths used by men; for some reason, women's facilities lacked gymnasia. The baths contained hot-air rooms to induce a good sweat and pools of hot and cold water to finish the actual bathing. They also contained snack bars and halls where people chatted and read. The baths were socially important places where men and women went to see and be seen. Social climbers tried to talk to the right people and wangle invitations to dinner; politicians took advantage of the occasion to discuss the affairs of the day. Despite the protests of conservatives and moralists, the baths at least provided people—rich and poor—with places for clean and healthy relaxation.

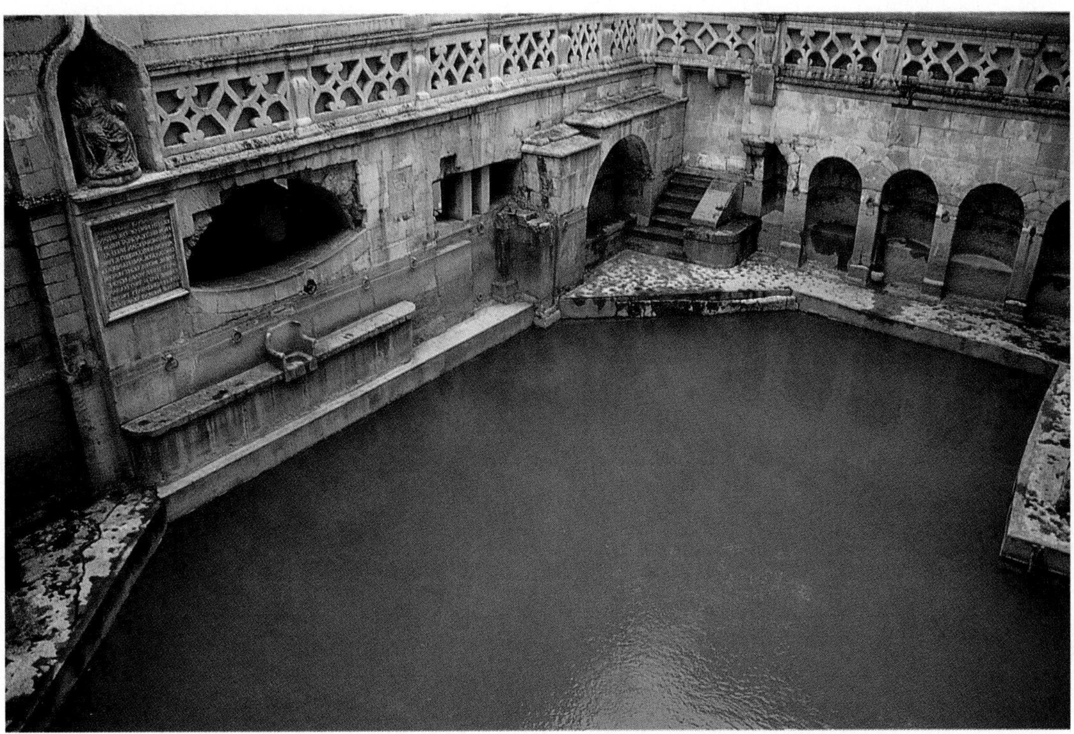

Roman Bath Once introduced into the Roman world, social bathing became a passion. These are the baths of Bath, England, to which they gave their name. A triumph of sophisticated engineering, they also demonstrate how Roman culture and institutions influenced life even on the perimeters of the Roman Empire. *(Horst Schafer/Peter Arnold Inc.)*

Did Hellenism and new social customs corrupt the Romans? Perhaps the best answer is this: the Roman state and the empire it ruled continued to exist for six more centuries. Rome did not collapse; the state continued to prosper. The golden age of literature was still before it. The high tide of its prosperity still lay in the future. The Romans did not like change but took it in stride. That was part of their practical turn of mind and their strength.

THE LATE REPUBLIC (133–31 B.C.)

The wars of conquest created serious problems for the Romans, some of the most pressing of which were political. The republican constitution had suited the needs of a simple city-state but was inadequate to meet the requirements of Rome's new position in international affairs (see Map 5.2). Sweeping changes and reforms were necessary to make it serve the demands of a state holding vast territory. A system of provincial administration had to be established. Officials had to be appointed to govern the provinces and administer the law. These officials and administrative organs had to find places in the constitution. Armies had to be provided for defense, and a system of tax collection had to be created.

Other political problems were equally serious. During the wars Roman generals commanded huge numbers of troops for long periods of time. Men such as Scipio Aemilianus were on the point of becoming too mighty for the state to control. Although Rome's Italian allies had borne much of the burden of the fighting, they received fewer rewards than did Roman officers and soldiers. Italians began to agitate for full Roman citizenship, including the right to vote.

Unrest in Rome and Italy

There were serious economic problems, too. Hannibal's operations and the warfare in Italy had left the countryside a shambles. The movements of numerous

Dressing of the Bride Preparations for a wedding was the occasion for fun and ceremony. On the night before the ceremony the bride tried on her wedding dress for a favorable omen. The next morning she was fastidiously dressed by her mother or under her mother's supervision. Here a sister or maid arranges the bride's hair, over which was later placed her veil, normally crowned with flowers that the girl had picked herself. *(Erich Lessing/Art Resource, NY)*

armies had disrupted agriculture. The prolonged fighting had also drawn untold numbers of Roman and Italian men away from their farms for long periods. The families of these soldiers could not keep the land under full cultivation. The people who defended Rome and conquered the world for Rome became impoverished for having done their duty.

These problems, complex and explosive, largely account for the turmoil of the closing years of the republic. The late republic was one of the most dramatic eras in Roman history. It produced some of Rome's most famous figures: the Gracchi, Marius, Sulla, Cicero, Pompey, and Julius Caesar, among others. In one way or another, each of these men attempted to solve Rome's problems. Yet they were also striving for the glory and honor that were the supreme goals of the senatorial aristocracy. Personal ambition often clashed with patriotism to create political tension throughout the period. (See the feature "Individuals in Society: Cicero.")

When the legionaries returned to their farms in Italy, they encountered an appalling situation. All too often their farms looked like the farms of people they had conquered. Two courses of action were open to them. They could rebuild as their forefathers had done, or they could take advantage of an alternative not open to their ancestors and sell their holdings. The wars of conquest had made some men astoundingly rich. These men wanted to invest their wealth in land. They bought up small farms to create huge estates, which the Romans called *latifundia.*

The purchase offers of the rich landowners appealed to the veterans for a variety of reasons. Many veterans had seen service in the East, where they had tasted the rich city life of the Hellenistic states. They were reluctant to return home and settle down to a dull life on the farm. Often their farms were so badly damaged that rebuilding hardly seemed worthwhile. Besides, it was hard to make big profits from small farms. Nor could the veterans supplement their income by working on the latifundia. Although the owners of the latifundia occasionally hired free men as day laborers, they preferred to use slaves. Slaves could not strike or be drafted into the army. Confronted by these conditions, veterans and their families opted to sell their land. They took what they could get for their broken farms and tried their luck elsewhere.

Most veterans migrated to the cities, especially to Rome. Although some found work, most did not. Industry and small manufacturing were generally in the hands of slaves. Even when work was available, slave labor kept the wages of free men low. Instead of a new start, veterans and their families encountered slum

Individuals in Society

Cicero

Bust of Cicero from the first century B.C. *(Alinari/Art Resource, NY)*

In republican Rome entry of a "new man" into the exalted rank of senator was possible but also difficult and infrequent. The families that had traditional hold on power in the senate formed an exclusive circle, jealous of their power and proud of their prestige. They provided the leadership of the republic and were very reluctant to allow social inferiors to join their ranks. Few men from the lower classes were admitted. Those few who were ultimately accepted into this rarefied air needed outstanding ability, wealth, a good education, social graces, and a noble patron. Cicero was one of those who possessed all of these advantages.

Marcus Tullius Cicero was born on January 3, 106 B.C., in Arpinum, southwest of Rome. He was of equestrian rank, which means that his social standing was inferior to that of the senators. Furthermore, not having been born in Rome, he was an outsider. Yet his father was intelligent, ambitious, and foresighted. He sent Cicero and his brother to Rome for an education. Rome was the place to make a reputation, and Cicero made good use of the opportunity. He studied philosophy and rhetoric there and laid the foundations of his later career.

From 90 to 89 B.C. he served in the Roman army, which gave him firsthand knowledge of military affairs. Although the dream of military glory remained with him always, his martial ability was that of a subordinate, not a leader.

After his military service Cicero turned to the study of law, which was a lucrative avenue to a political career. He won his first case in 81 B.C. and immediately earned a reputation for knowledge of the law, reasoned argument, and eloquent speaking. His victory may have annoyed Sulla, because it legally demonstrated the weakness of his dictatorship. In 79 B.C. Cicero traveled first to Athens and then to Rhodes to continue his study of philosophy and oratory. He was honing the skills that would establish his reputation and make his career.

Cicero returned to Rome to enter politics after Sulla's death in 78 B.C. Success was immediate. He became praetor of Sicily in 66 B.C., which gave him direct experience with Roman administration. He also earned a reputation as a man who honored Rome's traditional values. He was politically conservative and thus acceptable to many senators. The height of his political career came in 63 B.C., when he was elected consul. He was the first *novus homo* (new man) to be elected to the consulship in thirty-one years.

Cicero took no active part in the revolution that brought down the republic. Instead, he tried to stop it. He urged peace and a return to the traditional government, what he called "the concord of the orders," an attempt to reconcile the warring factions. His plan fell on deaf ears. Events had escalated beyond him, and now only politicians with armies could decide the fate of the republic. He took no part in Caesar's assassination but nonetheless made several influential enemies. One of them, Marc Antony, ordered his execution. Cicero made a halfhearted attempt to escape, but Roman soldiers caught him and murdered him on December 7, 43 B.C. He died with dignity and courage.

Cicero exhibited little military talent, fair but not brilliant administrative skills, and mediocre political abilities. Why does history remember him? Most Romans respected him for his dedication to Rome and its laws. Posterity has honored him for his writings, which have endured. He was a literary genius whose Latin prose was never equaled, even in antiquity. His essays on politics and philosophy explore the nature and functioning of proper, stable government and an attempt to understand the universe and people's place in it. The finest tribute to him was one he never heard. The emperor Augustus once called him "a learned man . . . and a lover of his country."

Questions for Analysis

1. Was Cicero's ideal of "the concord of the orders" a realistic ideal in his day?
2. For all of his fame and talent, how successful was Cicero in practical politics, and what did he achieve?

conditions that matched those of many modern American cities.

This trend held ominous consequences for the strength of Rome's armies. The Romans had always believed that only landowners should serve in the army, for only they had something to fight for. Landless men, even if they were Romans and lived in Rome, could not be conscripted into the army. These landless men may have been veterans of major battles and numerous campaigns; they may have won distinction on the battlefield. But once they sold their land, they became ineligible for further military service. A large pool of experienced manpower was going to waste. The landless ex-legionaries wanted a new start, and they were willing to support any leader who would provide it.

One man who recognized the plight of Rome's peasant farmers and urban poor was an aristocrat, Tiberius Gracchus (163–133 B.C.). Appalled by what he saw, Tiberius warned his countrymen that the legionaries were losing their land while fighting Rome's wars:

> *The wild beasts that roam over Italy have every one of them a cave or lair to lurk in. But the men who fight and die for Italy enjoy the common air and light, indeed, but nothing else. Houseless and homeless they wander about with their wives and children. And it is with lying lips that their generals exhort the soldiers in their battles to defend sepulchres and shrines from the enemy, for not a man of them has an hereditary altar, not one of all these many Romans an ancestral tomb, but they fight and die to support others in luxury, and though they are styled masters of the world, they have not a single clod of earth that is their own.*[5]

Until his death Tiberius Gracchus sought a solution to the problems of the veterans and the urban poor.

After his election as tribune of the people in 133 B.C., Tiberius proposed that public land be given to the poor in small lots. Although his reform enjoyed the support of some very distinguished and popular aristocrats, he immediately ran into trouble for a number of reasons. First, his reform bill angered many wealthy aristocrats who had usurped large tracts of public land for their own use. They had no desire to give any of it back, so they bitterly resisted Tiberius's efforts. This was to be expected, yet he unquestionably made additional problems for himself. He introduced his land bill in the concilium plebis without consulting the senate. When King Attalus III left the kingdom of Pergamum to the Romans in his will, Tiberius had the money appropriated to finance his reforms—another slap at the senate. As tribune he acted totally within his rights. Yet the way in which he proceeded was unprecedented. Many powerful Romans became suspicious of Tiberius's growing influence with the people, some even thinking that he aimed at tyranny. Others opposed him because of his unparalleled methods. After all, there were proper ways to do things in Rome, and he had not followed them. As a result, violence broke out when a large body of senators, led by the *pontifex maximus* (the chief priest), killed Tiberius in cold blood. It was a black day in Roman history. The very people who directed the affairs of state and administered the law had taken the law into their own hands. The death of Tiberius was the beginning of an era of political violence. In the end that violence would bring down the republic.

Although Tiberius was dead, his land bill became law. Furthermore, Tiberius's brother Gaius Gracchus (153–121 B.C.) took up the cause of reform. Gaius was a veteran soldier with an enviable record, but this fiery orator made his mark in the political arena. Gaius also became tribune and demanded even more extensive reform than his brother. To help the urban poor Gaius pushed legislation to provide them with cheap grain for bread. He defended his brother's land law and suggested other measures for helping the landless. He proposed that Rome send many of its poor and propertyless people out to form colonies in southern Italy. The poor would have a new start and lead productive lives. The city would immediately benefit because excess, nonproductive families would leave for new opportunities abroad. Rome would be less crowded, sordid, and dangerous.

Gaius went a step further and urged that all Italians be granted full rights of Roman citizenship. This measure provoked a storm of opposition, and reactionary senators rose against Gaius Gracchus and murdered him and three thousand of his supporters. Once again the cause of reform had met with violence. Once again it was Rome's leading citizens who flouted the law.

In 107 B.C. Gaius Marius, an Italian "new man" (a politician not from the traditional Roman aristocracy), became consul. A man of fierce vigor and courage, Marius saw the army as the tool of his ambition. To prepare for war in North Africa against Jugurtha, a rebellious Numidian king, Marius reformed the Roman army. He took the unusual but not wholly unprecedented step of recruiting an army by permitting the landless to serve in the legions. Marius thus tapped Rome's vast reservoir of idle manpower. His volunteer army was a professional force, not a body of draftees, and in 106 B.C. it handily defeated Jugurtha.

There was, however, a disturbing side to Marius's reforms, one that later would haunt the republic. To encourage enlistments, Marius promised land to his volunteers after the war. Poor and landless veterans flocked to him, but when Marius proposed a bill to grant land to his veterans, the senate refused to act, in effect turning its back on the soldiers of Rome. This was a disastrous mistake. Henceforth the legionaries expected their commanders—not the senate or the state—to protect their interests. By failing to reward the loyalty of Rome's troops, the senate set the stage for military rebellion and political anarchy.

Civil War

Marius's innovations had a huge impact on Roman soldiers and on the nature of the army. Until then Roman soldiers, like classical Greek hoplites, were citizen-soldiers with their roots in the land. They were essentially amateurs, a situation that changed during the Second Punic War and the wars of expansion. Having served long in the field, they became very proficient veteran troops. Marius gave them the opportunity to serve longer, even if they owned no property. What he and his successors Pompey and Caesar did was simply to create private armies that owed only nominal loyalty to Rome. This process was the predecessor of the creation of the professional armies of the empire.

In 88 B.C. there began a tumultuous series of events that would eventually result in the downfall of the Roman republic. The civil wars were not popular movements of the masses but purely the result of aristocratic ambition and rivalries. At first the principal protagonists were Marius and Sulla, a member of one of the oldest patrician families of the republic. Trouble began when the senate passed over Marius in favor of Sulla for the command of a major military expedition to restore order in Asia Minor, where peoples had taken advantage of Rome's difficulties to liberate themselves. Sulla accepted the assignment and began to collect soldiers in

The Orange Cadaster A cadaster is a register of property, this one named for Orange, France, where it was discovered. This fragment shows a piece of land divided by a river and an island. Parallel to the river run two roads. The land depicted is divided into various categories, which are indicated by the inscribed writing. *(By permission of the Musée Municipal d'Orange, Vaucluse [fragment 7 of Cadaster A])*

Roman Legionary A Roman legionary here has his hands full coping with hostile barbarians. The Roman wears a helmet and long cuirass and carries a long shield and sword. His opponents wear no armor and carry only a very long sword. Superior arms and training usually gave legionaries a decisive advantage over barbarians. *(Deutsches Archaeologisches Institut, Rome)*

southern Italy. Supporters of Marius forced the senate to strip Sulla of his command and give it instead to Marius. The move was constitutionally improper, and the timid acquiescence of the senate worsened an already dangerous situation. Still organizing his troops in Italy, Sulla led them instead against Rome itself, thus beginning the first civil war in Roman history.

Rome fell easily, and once there Sulla passed laws to strengthen the senate. Marius was able to escape, but instead of pursuing him Sulla launched his campaign in the East. Marius and his followers took advantage of Sulla's absence to return to Rome and immediately began to slaughter Sulla's supporters. This type of political and social outrage was new to the Romans. Although Marius died peacefully shortly after his successful rebellion, his followers maintained control of Rome. Only in 83 B.C. did Sulla return triumphantly to Italy, his work in Asia Minor done. The Roman aristocracy immediately flocked to his standard, and he quickly marched against his enemies. The following year Sulla defeated his enemies and began to massacre the leading survivors among Marius's supporters. He re-established constitutional government, but so much damage had been done that the old republic could not be restored. Violence had begun to replace law as the arbiter of Roman politics.

After the blood had dried, Sulla pursued a drastic program to restore the republican constitution. First he had himself declared dictator to carry through his reforms. He was apparently sincere, although this interpretation is still doubted by many historians. At any rate he did try to revive the dying constitution. He returned to the senate its traditional powers and opened public offices to many Italians who had previously been excluded. After an unprecedented three years as dictator, Sulla voluntarily resigned in the hope that his stern reforms would allow the republic again to function normally. Yet his dictatorship cast a long shadow over the late republic. Sulla the political reformer proved far less influential than Sulla the successful general and dictator. Civil war was to be the constant lot of Rome for the next fifty years, until the republican constitution gave way to the empire of Octavian, later named Augustus in 27 B.C. The republic was doomed.

Although the situation in Rome seemed settled and ordinary life could resume, unexpected trouble that had nothing to do with aristocratic quarrels broke out. The downfall of Sulla's constitution and the renewal of civil war resulted from a slave revolt led by Spartacus, a Thracian gladiator. In 73 B.C. Spartacus organized a huge slave army that ravaged large portions of southern Italy. Two years later Marcus Crassus, a former lieutenant of Sulla, collected an army and crushed Spartacus's forces. While Crassus rounded up the few slaves who had escaped the carnage, Pompey arrived to help the effort.

Pompey was a talented general without much political sense. What he lacked in ideas he made up in military skill and personal ambition. Crassus and Pompey led their armies on Rome, where they forced the senate to elect them consuls. Their act was the first official nail in the coffin of Sulla's constitution. Pompey especially began to assume greater powers that virtually put him above the law. The political life of Rome had reverted to the dark days of Marius and Sulla.

Julius Caesar This realistic bust of Caesar captures all of the power, intensity, and brilliance of the man. It is a study of determination and an excellent example of Roman portraiture. *(National Archaeological Museum, Naples/Alinari/Art Resource, NY)*

The Triumph of Julius Caesar

The man who had the greatest impact during this troubled period was Gaius Julius Caesar (100–44 B.C.). More than a mere soldier, Caesar was a cultivated man. Born of a noble family, he received an excellent education, which he furthered by studying in Greece with some of the eminent teachers of the day. He had serious intellectual interests, and his literary ability was immense. Caesar was a superb orator, and his affable personality and wit made him popular. He was also a shrewd politician of unbridled ambition. Since military service was an effective steppingstone to politics, Caesar launched his military career in Spain, where his courage won him the respect and affection of his troops. Personally brave and tireless, Caesar was a military genius who knew how to win battles and turn victories into permanent gains.

When he returned to Rome, he struck up a political alliance with Pompey and Crassus, usually known as the First Triumvirate, in which they agreed to advance one another's interests. This political agreement won Caesar the consulship in 59 B.C., after which he became governor of Cisalpine Gaul, or modern northern Italy. By 50 B.C. he had conquered all of Gaul, or modern France. Caesar's *Commentaries,* the account of his operations during the Gallic wars, became a classic in Western literature and a misery to most schoolchildren who read it in beginning Latin. By 49 B.C. the First Triumvirate had fallen apart.

The trouble had begun with the death of Crassus in 53 B.C. while he was fighting the Parthians in Mesopotamia. The result was severe strain and suspicion between Caesar and Pompey. From his command in Gaul, Caesar made the decision to march on Rome. In 50 B.C. he illegally crossed the Rubicon River, the boundary between Gaul and Roman territory. It is still thought-provoking today to look at the narrow and quiet Rubicon and to ponder the small but significant part that it played in Caesar's decision to seize supreme power in Rome. The result was a long and bloody civil war between Caesar and Pompey that raged from Spain to Greece and across northern Africa to Egypt. Although Pompey enjoyed the official support of the government, Caesar finally defeated his forces in 45 B.C. Caesar had overthrown the republic and made himself dictator.

Julius Caesar was not merely another victorious general. Politically brilliant, he was determined to make basic reforms, even at the expense of the old constitution. He took the first long step to break down the barriers between Italy and the provinces, extending citizenship to many of the provincials who had supported him. Caesar also took measures to cope with Rome's burgeoning population. By Caesar's day perhaps 750,000 people lived in Rome. Caesar drew up plans to send his veterans and some 80,000 of the poor and unemployed to colonies throughout the Mediterranean. He founded at least twenty colonies, most of which were located in Gaul, Spain, and North Africa. These colonies were important agents in spreading Roman culture in the western Mediterranean. A Roman empire composed of citizens, not subjects, was the result.

In 44 B.C. a group of conspirators assassinated Caesar and set off another round of civil war. Caesar had named his eighteen-year-old grandnephew, Octavian, as his heir. Octavian joined forces with two of Caesar's lieutenants, Marc Antony and Lepidus, in a pact known as the Second Triumvirate, and together they hunted down and defeated Caesar's murderers. In the process, however, Octavian and Antony came into conflict. Antony, "boastful, arrogant, and full of empty exultation and capricious ambition," proved to be the major threat to Octavian's designs.[6] In 33 B.C. Octavian branded Antony a traitor and rebel. He painted lurid pictures of Antony lingering in the eastern Mediterranean, a romantic and foolish captive of the seductive Cleopatra, queen of Egypt and bitter enemy of Rome. In 31 B.C., with the might of Rome at his back, Octavian met and defeated the army and navy of Antony and Cleopatra at the Battle of Actium in Greece. Octavian's victory put an end to an age of civil war that had lasted since the days of Sulla. In 27 B.C. the senate voted Octavian the name *Augustus* for his success in having ended the civil war. Ever since that day he has been known to history as Augustus.

SUMMARY

The rise of Rome to greatness resulted from many factors. At the outset the geographical position of Rome put it on good, natural lines of communication within Italy. The Italian peninsula itself was generally fertile, and the mountains did not prevent political unification. The Etruscans transformed the Roman settlements into a city. Once free of the Etruscans, the Romans used their political organization, their prosperity, and their population to conquer their neighbors. Yet instead of enslaving them, the Romans extended citizenship to the conquered. Having united Italy under them, the Romans became a major power that looked to the broader Mediterranean world. In a succession of wars with Carthage, in Spain, and in the Hellenistic East, Rome won an empire. These conquests not only prompted the Romans to invent a system to administer the empire but also brought them into the mainstream of Hellenistic civilization. The wealth derived from the empire meant that life for many Romans became richer. But there was also a dark side to these developments. Personal ambition, as well as defects in the Roman system of government, led some ambitious leaders to seize unprecedented power. Others resisted, throwing the republic into a series of civil wars. Finally, Caesar and his grandnephew Octavian restored order, but in the process the Roman republic had become a monarchy.

NOTES

1. Polybius, *The Histories* 1.1.5. John Buckler is the translator of all uncited quotations from a foreign language in Chapters 1–6.
2. Mark Twain, *The Innocents Abroad* (New York: Signet Classics, 1966), p. 176.
3. Sallust, *War with Catiline* 10.1–3.
4. Ovid, *Fasti* 2.535–539.
5. Plutarch, *Life of Tiberius Gracchus* 9.5–6.
6. Plutarch, *Life of Antony* 2.8.

SUGGESTED READING

H. H. Scullard gives a broad account of Roman history in *A History of the Roman World, 753–146 B.C.*, 4th ed. (1993), to which should be added T. Cornell, *The Beginnings of Rome* (1995), which covers the history of Rome from the Bronze Age to the Punic Wars. The Etruscans have inspired a great deal of work. M. Pallottino, *A History of Earliest Italy* (1991), addresses the tangled problem of the early relations among the Italic peoples. The best treatment of the subject is H. Barker and T. Rasmussen, *The Etruscans* (1997). O. J. Brendel, *Etruscan Art* (1995), discusses not only art itself but its relation to that of Greece and Rome. E. Gabba, *Dionysius and the History of Archaic Rome* (1991), is the study of the origins of Rome by an eminent scholar who also looks at how the Greeks perceived it. J. E. Stambaugh, *The Ancient Roman City* (1988), gives a full account of the topography of Rome and its institutions, all the more important because of the rapid growth of modern Rome. A great deal of recent work has been done on the importance of the Gauls and Celts, notably D. Rankin, *Celts and the Classical World* (1996). Similar is F. Funck-Bretano, *A History of Gaul* (1993), which treats the region from the prehistoric to the medieval period.

Roman expansion continues to attract attention. A new interpretation of Rome's dealings with the Latin League comes from R. Howarth, "Rome and the Latins" (Ph.D. diss., University of Illinois, 1997). More easily available is C. J. Smith, *Early Rome and Latium: Economy and Society, c. 1000 to 500 B.C.* (1996). Many studies deal with Roman expansion throughout the Mediterranean. In Italy itself D. J. Gargola, *Lands, Laws, and Gods* (1995), examines how the Roman magistrates regulated the public lands of Rome. Similar is N. Morley, *Metropolis and Hinterland* (1996), a study of how Romans and Italians integrated their economies between 200 B.C. and A.D. 200. J. Lazenby addresses Rome's conflict with Carthage in two books: *First Punic War* (1996) and *Hannibal's War* (1978), dealing with the Second Punic War. R. Kallet-Marx, *Hegemony to Empire* (1995), examines how Rome's power in the eastern Mediterranean became established between 148 and 62 B.C. S. L. Dyson, *The Creation of the Roman Frontier* (1985), deals with the process by which the Romans established their frontiers, and K. R. Bradley, *Slavery and Rebellion in the Roman World* (1989), analyzes the slave revolts of Spartacus and others.

One of the best studies of Rome's political evolution is A. N. Sherwin-White, *Roman Citizenship,* 2d ed. (1973), a classic work of enduring value. J. F. Gardner, *Being a Roman Citizen* (1993), is a broad work that includes material on ex-slaves, the lower classes, and much else. E. S. Gruen explores the effects of the introduction of Greek ideas, literature, and learning into central aspects of Roman life in two books: *Culture and National Identity in Republican Rome* (1992) and *Studies in Greek Culture and Roman Policy* (1996). The topic of Roman intellectual and cultural growth is one of the most studied aspects of republican history. G. B. Conte, *Latin Literature* (1994), is a comprehensive work that begins with the origins of Latin literature and continues into the early medieval period. E. Fantham, *Roman Literary Culture* (1996), answers the question of who in Rome read the books that helped shape Roman culture.

The great figures and events of the late republic have been the object of much work. E. S. Gruen, *The Last Generation of the Roman Republic* (1974), treats the period as a whole. Very important are the studies of E. Badian, *Roman Imperialism in the Late Republic* (1968) and *Publicans and Sinners* (1972). R. Syme, *The Roman Revolution,* rev. ed. (1952), is a classic. Valuable also are P. A. Brunt, *Social Conflicts in the Roman Republic* (1971); A. W. Lintott, *Violence in the Roman Republic* (1968); and J. K. Evans, *War, Women and Children in Ancient Rome* (1991).

Many works deal with individual Romans who left their mark on this period. H. C. Boren, *The Gracchi* (1968), treats the work of the two brothers, and A. M. Eckstein's *Senate and Generals* (1987) discusses how the decisions of individual generals affected both the senate and Roman foreign relations. A. Keaveney, *Sulla: The Last Republican* (1983), is a study of a man who thought of himself as a reformer. A. E. Astin has produced two works that are far more extensive than their titles indicate: *Scipio Aemilianus* (1967) and *Cato the Censor* (1978). J. Leach, *Pompey the Great* (1978), surveys the career of this politician, and B. Rawson, *The Politics of Friendship: Pompey and Cicero* (1978), treats both figures in their political environment. M. Gelzer, *Caesar, Politician and Statesman* (English trans., 1968), is easily the best study of one of history's most significant figures. N. Wood, *Cicero's Social and Political Thought* (1991), is an original study of Cicero's thought about the Rome of his day. E. G. Huzar, *Marc Antony* (1987), offers a new assessment of the career of the man who challenged Octavian for control of the Roman world. Caesar's onetime colleague Marcus Crassus is studied in B. A. Marshall, *Crassus: A Political Biography* (1976), and A. Ward, *Marcus Crassus and the Late Roman Republic* (1977). R. S. Weigel, *Lepidus* (1992), covers the career of the third member of the Second Triumvirate.

K. D. White, *Roman Farming* (1970), deals with agriculture. Greek cultural influence on Roman life is the subject of A. Wardman, *Rome's Debt to Greece* (1976). F. Schulz, *Classical Roman Law* (1951), is a useful introduction to an important topic. H. H. Scullard, *Festivals and Ceremonies of the Roman Republic* (1981), gives a fresh look at religious practices. Work on Roman social history has advanced in several areas. G. Alfoeldy, a major scholar, has written *The Social History of Rome* (1985), an ambitious undertaking. D. S. Levene, *Religion in Livy* (1993), traces the influence of religion on the foremost historian of Rome. S. Dixon, *The Roman Mother* (1988), focuses on women's role as mothers within the Roman family. A wealth of other research on the Roman family and related topics has newly appeared, including K. R. Bradley, *Discovering the Roman Family* (1990), a series of essays on Roman social history; S. Dixon, *The Roman Family* (1992); S. Treggiari, *Roman Marriage* (1991); and R. A. Baumann, *Women and Politics in Ancient Rome* (1992). A novel work is E. Eyben, *Restless Youth in Ancient Rome* (1993), which explores the mores of youth of the upper class.

LISTENING TO THE PAST

Popular Roman Views of Religion and Magic

Magic and enchantment have been constant factors wherever people have lived. Rome was no exception. A common aspect of Roman popular culture was the curse tablet. When people were particularly angry with others, they often went to professional sorcerers, who listened to their clients' complaints. Then they wrote the clients' curses on thin lead tablets and wrapped them around nails. The curses were considered binding, and the various gods invoked were expected to carry them out. In return the gods received payment for having inflicted the curse.

Often people called down the wrath of the gods on troublesome neighbors or commercial rivals. Many other tablets involved love gone wrong. The first of the following three examples is one of them. For reasons that are left unstated, a woman calls down all sorts of catastrophes on her husband or lover, Plotius. The aggrieved party in this case makes it dramatically clear what she expects from Proserpina, the wife of Pluto, both gods of the underworld. The woman includes in her curse Cerberus, the hound that guarded the gates of Hades. We do not know the fate of her lover.

O wife of Pluto, good and beautiful Proserpina (unless I ought to call you Salvia), pray tear away from Plotius health, body, complexion, strength, faculties. Consign him to Pluto your husband. May he be unable to avoid this by devices of his. Consign that man to the fourth-day, the third-day, the every-day fever [malaria]. May they wrestle and wrestle it out with him, overcome and overwhelm him unceasingly until they tear away his life. So I consign him as victim to you Proserpina, unless, O Proserpina, unless I ought to call you Goddess of the Lower World. Send, I pray, someone to call up the three-headed dog [Cerberus] with request that he may tear out Plotius' heart. Promise Cerberus that you will give him three offerings—dates, dried figs, and a black pig—if he has fulfilled his task before the month of March. All these, Proserpina Salvia, will I give you when you have made me master of my wish. I give you the head of Plotius, slave of Avonia. O Proserpina Salvia, I give you Plotius' forehead. Proserpina Salvia, I give you Plotius' eyebrows. Proserpina Salvia, I give you Plotius' eyelids. Proserpina Salvia, I give you Plotius' eye-pupils. Proserpina Salvia, I give you Plotius' nostrils, his ears, nose, and his tongue and teeth so that Plotius may not be able to utter what it is that gives him pain; his neck, shoulders, arms, fingers, so that he may not be able to help himself at all; his chest, liver, heart, lungs, so that he may not be able to feel what gives him pain; his abdomen, belly, navel, sides, so that he may not be able to sleep; his shoulder blades, so that he may not be able to sleep well; his sacred part, so that he may not be able to make water; his buttocks, vent, thighs, knees, legs, shins, feet, ankles, soles, toes, nails, that he may not be able to stand by his own aid. Should there so exist any written curse, great or small—in what manner Plotius has, according to the laws of magic, composed any curse and entrusted it to writing, in such manner I consign, hand over to you, so that you may consign and hand over that fellow, in the month of February. Blast him! damn him! blast him utterly! Hand him over, consign him, that he may not be able to behold, see, and contemplate any month further!

Curses and enchantments were not limited to love affairs. The following one concerns the next day's chariot race in Rome. The person invoking the curse was certainly not betting on Eucherius the charioteer and his horses.

I conjure you up, holy beings and holy names; join in aiding this spell, and bind, enchant, thwart, strike, overturn, conspire against, destroy, kill, break, Eucherius, the charioteer, and all his horses tomorrow in the circus at Rome. May he not leave the barriers well; may he not be quick in the contest; may he not outstrip anyone; may he not make the turns well; may he not win any prizes; and if he has pressed someone hard, may he not come off the victor; and if he follows someone from behind, may he not overtake him; but may he meet with an accident; may he be bound; may he be broken; may he be dragged along by your power, in the morning and afternoon races. Now! Now! Quickly! Quickly!

The next curse is that of an outraged person who was the victim of a thief. The person calls on Hermes and other deities to catch the thief. Note that the text is filled with many unintelligible words—"mumbo jumbo"—which supposedly have magical powers.

I call you, Hermes, immortal god, who cuts a furrow down Olympus, and who [presides over] the sacred boat, O light-bringer Iao, the great ever-living, terrible to behold and terrible to hear, give up the thief whom I seek. Aberamentho oulerthe xenax sonelueothenemareba. This spell is to be said twice at the purification. The spell of bread and cheese. Come to me, lisson maternamau, erte, preptektioun, intiki, ous, olokotous, periklusai, bring to me that which is lost, and make the thief manifest on this very day. And I invoke Hermes, the discoverer of thieves, and the sun and the eye-pupils of the sun, the two bringers-to-light of unlawful deeds, and Justice, and Errinys, and Ammon, and Parammon, to seize the throat of the thief and to manifest him this very day, at the present hour. The ceremony: the same spell [as that] pronounced at the purification. Take a flush-green vessel and put water in it and myrrh, and the herb cynocephalium, and dipping in it a branch of laurel, sprinkling each person with the water, take a tripod and place it upon an altar of earth. . . . Offer myrrh and frankincense and a frog's tongue, and taking some unsalted winter wheat and goat's cheese, give these to each, pronouncing the spell at length. "Lord Iao, light-bearer, give up the thief whom I seek." And if any of them does not swallow what was given him, that one is the thief.

✣ Curse tablet from the Roman temple at Uley in Gloucestershire, England. *(Courtesy of the Trustees of the British Museum)*

Questions for Analysis

1. Given the many forms of curses and the common use of these tablets, what social functions did such curse tablets serve in Roman society?
2. Since Romans resorted to these curses, does it mean that they considered magic more powerful than formal religion? Why or why not?
3. What do the tablets tell us about the common culture of the Romans?

Source: Slightly adapted from N. Lewis and M. Reinhold, *Roman Civilization,* 2 vols. Copyright © 1966 by Columbia University Press, New York. Reprinted with permission of the publisher.

CHAPTER

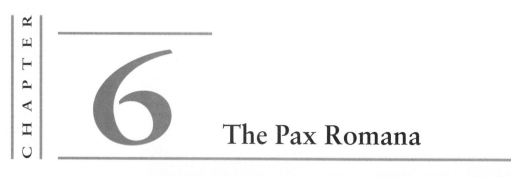

6 The Pax Romana

Hadrian's Wall. *(D. J. Ball/Tony Stone Images)*

Had the Romans conquered the entire Mediterranean world only to turn it into their battlefield? Would they, like the Greeks before them, become their own worst enemies, destroying one another and wasting their strength until they perished? At Julius Caesar's death in 44 B.C. it must have seemed so to many. Yet finally, in 31 B.C., Augustus restored peace to a tortured world, and with peace came prosperity, new hope, and a new vision of Rome's destiny. The Roman poet Virgil expressed this vision most nobly:

You, Roman, remember—these are your arts:
To rule nations, and to impose the ways of peace,
To spare the humble and to war down the proud.[1]

In place of the republic, Augustus established what can be called a constitutional monarchy. He attempted to achieve lasting cooperation in government and balance among the people, magistrates, senate, and army. His efforts were not always successful. His settlement of Roman affairs did not permanently end civil war. Yet he carried on Caesar's work. It was Augustus who created the structure that the modern world calls the "Roman Empire." He did his work so well and his successors so capably added to it that Rome realized Virgil's hope. For the first and second centuries A.D. the lot of the Mediterranean world was the Roman peace—the *pax Romana,* a period of security, order, harmony, flourishing culture, and expanding economy. It was a period that saw the wilds of Gaul, Spain, Germany, eastern Europe, and western Africa introduced to Greco-Roman culture. By the third century A.D., when the empire began to give way to the medieval world, the greatness of Rome and its culture had left an indelible mark on the ages to come.

- How did the Roman emperors govern the empire, and how did they spread Roman influence into northern Europe?
- What were the fruits of the pax Romana?
- Why did Christianity, originally a minor local religion, sweep across the Roman world to change it fundamentally?
- Finally, how did the Roman Empire meet the grim challenge of barbarian invasion and subsequent economic decline?

These are the main questions we will consider in this chapter.

Augustus's Settlement (31 B.C.–A.D. 14)

When Augustus put an end to the civil wars that had raged since 88 B.C., he faced monumental problems of reconstruction. Sole ruler of the entire Mediterranean world as no Roman had ever been before, he had a rare opportunity to shape the future. But how?

Augustus could easily have declared himself dictator, as Caesar had, but the thought was repugnant to him. Augustus was neither an autocrat nor a revolutionary. His solution, as he put it, was to restore the republic. But was that possible? Some eighteen years of anarchy and civil war had shattered the republican constitution. It could not be rebuilt in a day. Augustus recognized these problems but did not let them stop him. From 29 to 23 B.C. he toiled to heal Rome's wounds. The first problem facing him was to rebuild the constitution and the organs of government. Next he had to demobilize much of the army yet maintain enough soldiers in the provinces of the empire to meet the danger of barbarians at Rome's European frontiers. Augustus was highly successful in meeting these challenges. His gift of peace to a war-torn world sowed the seeds of a literary flowering that produced some of the finest fruits of the Roman mind.

The Principate and the Restored Republic

Augustus claimed that in restoring constitutional government he was also restoring the republic. Typically Roman, he preferred not to create anything new; he intended instead to modify republican forms and offices to meet new circumstances. Augustus planned for the senate to take on a serious burden of duty and responsibility. He expected it to administer some of the provinces, continue to be the chief deliberative body of the state, and act as a court of law. Yet he did not give the senate enough power to become his partner in government. As a result, the senate could not live up to the responsibilities that Augustus assigned. Many of its prerogatives shifted to Augustus and his successors by default.

Augustus's own position in the restored republic was something of an anomaly. He could not simply surrender the reins of power, for someone else would only have seized them. But how was he to fit into a republican constitution? Again Augustus had his own answer.

He became *princeps civitatis,* "First Citizen of the State." This prestigious title carried no power; it indicated only that Augustus was the most distinguished of all Roman citizens. In effect, it designated Augustus as the first among equals, a little "more equal" than anyone else in the state. Clearly, much of the *principate,* as the period of First Citizen is known, was a legal fiction. Yet that need not imply that Augustus, like a modern dictator, tried to clothe himself with constitutional legitimacy. In an inscription known as *Res Gestae* (The Deeds of Augustus), Augustus described his constitutional position:

In my sixth and seventh consulships [28–27 B.C.*], I had ended the civil war, having obtained through universal consent total control of affairs. I transferred the Republic from my power to the authority of the Roman people and the senate. . . . After that time I stood before all in rank, but I had power no greater than those who were my colleagues in any magistracy.*[2]

What is to be made of Augustus's constitutional settlement? Despite his claims to the contrary, Augustus had not restored the republic. Augustus had created a constitutional monarchy, something completely new in Roman history. The title *princeps,* First Citizen, came to mean in Rome, as it does today, "prince" in the sense of a sovereign ruler.

Augustus was not exactly being a hypocrite, but he carefully kept his real military power in the background. As consul he had no more constitutional and legal power than his fellow consul. Yet in addition to the consulship Augustus had many other magistracies, which his fellow consul did not. Constitutionally, his ascendancy within the state stemmed from the number of magistracies he held and the power granted him by the senate. At first he held the consulship annually; then the senate voted him proconsular power on a regular basis. The senate also voted him *tribunicia potestas*—the "full power of the tribunes." Tribunician power gave Augustus the right to call the senate into session, present legislation to the people, and defend their rights. He held either high office or the powers of chief magistrate year in and year out. No other magistrate could do the same. In 12 B.C. he became *pontifex maximus,* the chief priest of the state. By assuming this position of great honor, Augustus also became chief religious official. Without specifically saying so, he had created the office of emperor, which included many traditional powers separated from their traditional offices.

The main source of Augustus's power was his position as commander of the Roman army. His title *imperator,* with which Rome customarily honored a general after a major victory, came to mean "emperor" in the modern sense of the term. Augustus governed the provinces where troops were needed for defense. The frontiers were his special concern. There Roman legionaries held the German barbarians at arm's length. The frontiers were also areas where fighting could be expected to break out. Augustus made sure that Rome went to war only at his command. He controlled deployment of the Roman army and paid its wages. He granted it bonuses and gave veterans retirement benefits. Thus he avoided the problems with the army that the old senate had created for itself. Augustus never shared control of the army, and no Roman found it easy to defy him militarily.

Augustus made a momentous change in the army by making it a permanent, professional force. This was Rome's first standing army. Soldiers received regular and standard training under career officers who advanced in rank according to experience, ability, valor, and length of service. Legions were transferred from place to place, as the need arose. They had no regular barracks. In that respect they were like American army divisions. In later years of the empire soldiers could live with their families in the camps themselves. By making the army professional, Augustus forged a reliable tool for the defense of the empire. The army could also act against the central authority, much as Marius's army had earlier. Yet the mere fact that men could make a career of the army meant that it became a recognized institution of government and that its soldiers had the opportunity to achieve a military effectiveness superior to that of most of its enemies.

The very size of the army was a special problem for Augustus. Rome's legions numbered thousands of men, far more than were necessary to maintain peace. What was Augustus to do with so many soldiers? This sort of problem had constantly plagued the late republic, whose leaders never found a solution. Augustus gave his own answer in the *Res Gestae:* "I founded colonies of soldiers in Africa, Sicily, Macedonia, Spain, Achaea, Gaul, and Pisidia. Moreover, Italy has 28 colonies under my auspices."[3] At least forty new colonies arose, most of them in the western Mediterranean. Augustus's veterans took abroad with them their Roman language and culture. His colonies, like Julius Caesar's, were a significant tool in the spread of Roman culture throughout the West.

Roman colonies were very different from earlier Greek colonies. Greek colonies were independent. Once founded, they went their own way. Roman colonies were part of a system—the Roman Empire—that linked East with West in a mighty political, social, and economic network. The glory of the Roman Empire was its great success in uniting the Mediterranean world and spreading Greco-Roman culture throughout it. Roman colonies played a crucial part in that process, and Augustus deservedly boasted of the colonies he founded.

Augustus, however, also failed to solve a momentous problem. He never found a way to institutionalize his position with the army. The ties between the princeps and the army were always personal. The army was loyal to the princeps but not necessarily to the state. The Augustan principate worked well at first, but by the third century A.D. the army would make and break emperors at will. Nonetheless, it is a measure of Augustus's success that his settlement survived as long and as well as it did.

Augustus as Imperator Here Augustus, dressed in breastplate and uniform, emphasizes the imperial majesty of Rome and his role as *imperator.* The figures on his breastplate represent the restoration of peace, one of Augustus's greatest accomplishments and certainly one that he frequently stressed. *(Alinari/Art Resource, NY)*

Augustus's Administration of the Provinces

To gain an accurate idea of the total population of the empire, Augustus ordered a census to be taken in 28 B.C. In Augustus's day the population of the Roman Empire was between 70 million and 100 million people, fully 75 percent of whom lived in the provinces. In the areas under his immediate jurisdiction, Augustus put provincial administration on an ordered basis and improved its functioning. Believing that the cities of the empire should look after their own affairs, he encouraged local self-government and urbanism. Augustus respected local customs and ordered his governors to do the same.

As a spiritual bond between the provinces and Rome, Augustus encouraged the cult of Roma, goddess and guardian of the state. In the Hellenistic East, where king-worship was an established custom, the cult of *Roma et Augustus* grew and spread rapidly. Augustus then introduced it in the West. By the time of his death in A.D. 14, nearly every province in the empire could boast an altar or a shrine to *Roma et Augustus.* In the West it was not the person of the emperor who was worshiped but his *genius*—his guardian spirit. In praying for the good health and welfare of the emperor, Romans and provincials were praying for the empire itself. The cult became a symbol of Roman unity.

Roman Expansion into Northern and Western Europe

For the history of Western civilization one of the most momentous aspects of Augustus's reign was Roman expansion into the wilderness of northern and western Europe (Map 6.1). In this respect Augustus was following in Julius Caesar's footsteps. Carrying on Caesar's work, Augustus pushed Rome's frontier into the region of modern Germany.

Augustus began his work in the west and north by completing the conquest of Spain. In Gaul, apart from minor campaigns, most of his work was peaceful. He founded twelve new towns, and the Roman road system linked new settlements with one another and with Italy. But the German frontier, along the Rhine River, was the scene of hard fighting. In 12 B.C. Augustus ordered a major invasion of Germany beyond the Rhine. Roman legions advanced to the Elbe River, and a Roman fleet explored the North Sea and Jutland. The area north of

Major battle
Roman Empire under Augustus
Territory added by the time of Hadrian
North Sea
JUTLAND
Baltic Sea
BRITAIN
ATLANTIC OCEAN
Teutoburger Forest
Cologne
BELGIUM
GERMANY
Elbe
Rhine
Don
Volga
Dnieper
Caspian Sea
AUSTRIA
GAUL
RAETIA
NORICUM
CRIMEA
Lyons
Milan
CISALPINE GAUL
Po
PANNONIA
Danube
DACIA
Black Sea
Rhône
Ebro
NARBONENSIS
Ravenna
DALMATIA
Massilia
FARTHER SPAIN
Arrentium
Tiber
MOESIA
ARMENIA
CORSICA
Adriatic Sea
THRACE
Rome
Byzantium
NEARER SPAIN
Capua
Brundisium
PHRYGIA
CAPPADOCIA
PARTHIA
SARDINIA
MACEDONIA
BALEARIC IS.
LYDIA
Gades
Pergamum
ASIA
PISIDIA
MESOPOTAMIA
Tarsus
Tigris
Athens
Ephesus
CILICIA
Euphrates
Corinth
ACHAEA
Antioch
Mediterranean Sea
SICILY
Syracuse
Ctesiphon
Seleucia
MAURETANIA
Carthage
SYRIA
RHODES
CYPRUS
NUMIDIA
CRETE
Damascus
JUDAEA
Jerusalem
Cyrene
Petra
NORTH AFRICA
Alexandria
LIBYA
ARABIAN DESERT
0 200 400 Km.
0 200 400 Mi.
EGYPT
Nile
SAHARA
Red Sea

Boscoreale Cup The central scene lavishly depicted on the side of a silver cup shows Augustus seated in majesty. In his right hand he holds an orb that represents his position as master of the world. The scroll in his left hand symbolizes his authority as lawgiver. On his right is a group of divinities who support his efforts, on his left a group of barbarians who have submitted to Rome. *(© Musée du Louvre)*

the Main River and west of the Elbe was on the point of becoming Roman. But in A.D. 9 Augustus's general Varus lost some twenty thousand troops at the Battle of the Teutoburger Forest. Thereafter the Rhine remained the Roman frontier.

Meanwhile more successful generals extended the Roman standards as far as the Danube. Roman legions penetrated the area of modern Austria, southern Bavaria, and western Hungary. The regions of modern Serbia, Bulgaria, and Romania fell. Within this area the legionaries built fortified camps. Roads linked these camps with one another, and settlements grew up around the camps. Traders began to frequent the frontier and to traffic with the barbarians. Thus Roman culture—the rough-and-ready kind found in military camps—gradually spread into the northern wilderness.

One excellent example of this process comes from the modern French city of Lyons. The site was originally the capital of a native tribe; and after his conquest of Gaul, Caesar made it a Roman military settlement. Augustus took an important step toward Romanization and conciliation in 12 B.C., when he made it a political and religious center, with responsibilities for administering the area and for honoring the gods of the Romans and Gauls. Physical symbols of this fusion of two cultures can still be seen today. For instance, the extensive remains of the amphitheater and other buildings at Lyons testify to the fact that the Gallo-Roman city was prosperous enough to afford expensive Roman buildings and the style of life that they represented. Second, the buildings show that the local population appreciated Roman culture and did not find it alien. At Lyons, as at many other of these new cities, there emerged a culture that was both Roman and native. Many such towns were soon granted Roman citizenship for their embrace of Roman culture, government, and their importance to the Roman economy. (See the feature "Listening to the Past: Rome Extends Its Citizenship" on pages 196–197.)

Although Lyons is typical of the success of Romanization in new areas, the arrival of the Romans often provoked resistance from barbarian tribes that simply wanted to be left alone. In other cases the prosperity and wealth of the new Roman towns lured barbarians eager for plunder. The Romans maintained peaceful relations with the barbarians whenever possible, but Roman legions remained on the frontier to repel hostile barbarians. The result was the evolution of a consistent, systematic frontier policy.

MAP 6.1 Roman Expansion Under the Empire Following Roman expansion during the republic, Augustus added vast tracts of Europe to the Roman Empire, which the emperor Hadrian later enlarged by assuming control over parts of central Europe, the Near East, and North Africa.

Pont du Gard Long after the Roman Empire gave way to the medieval world, this aqueduct still stands in France, where until recently it still carried water to Nîmes. The aqueduct is not only a splendid feat of Roman engineering but also a work of art. *(Vanni/Art Resource, NY)*

Literary Flowering

The Augustan settlement's gift of peace inspired a literary flowering unparalleled in Roman history. With good reason this period is known as the golden age of Latin literature. Augustus and many of his friends actively encouraged poets and writers. Horace, one of Rome's finest poets, offered his own opinion of Augustus and his era:

With Caesar [Augustus] the guardian of the state
Not civil rage nor violence shall drive out peace,
Nor wrath which forges swords
And turns unhappy cities against each other.[4]

These lines are not empty flattery, despite Augustus's support of many contemporary Latin writers. To a generation that had known only vicious civil war, Augustus's settlement was an unbelievable blessing.

The tone and ideal of Roman literature, like that of the Greeks, was humanistic and worldly. Roman poets and prose writers celebrated the dignity of humanity and the range of its accomplishments. They stressed the physical and emotional joys of a comfortable, peaceful life. Their works were highly polished, elegant in style, and intellectual in conception. Roman poets referred to the gods often and treated mythological themes, but always the core of their work was human, not divine.

Virgil (70–19 B.C.), Rome's greatest poet, celebrated the new age in the *Georgics,* a poetic work on agriculture in four books. Virgil delighted in his own farm, and his poems sing of the pleasures of peaceful farm life. The poet also tells how to keep bees, grow grapes and olives, plow, and manage a farm. Throughout the *Georgics* Virgil writes about things he himself has seen, rather than drawing from the writings of others. Virgil could be vivid and graphic as well as pastoral. Even a small event could be a drama for him. The death of a bull while plowing is hardly epic material, yet Virgil captures the sadness of the event in the image of the farmer unyoking the remaining animal:

Look, the bull, shining under the rough plough,
falls to the ground
and vomits from his mouth blood mixed with foam,
and releases his dying groan.
Sadly moves the ploughman, unharnessing the
young steer grieving for the death of his brother
and leaves in the middle of the job
the plough stuck fast.[5]

Virgil's poetry is robust yet graceful. A sensitive man who delighted in simple things, Virgil left in his *Georgics* a charming picture of life in the Italian countryside during a period of peace.

Virgil's masterpiece is the *Aeneid,* an epic poem that is the Latin equivalent of the Greek *Iliad* and *Odyssey.* In the *Aeneid* Virgil expressed his admiration for Augustus's work by celebrating the shining ideal of a world blessed by the pax Romana. Virgil's account of the founding of Rome and the early years of the city gave final form to the legend of Aeneas, the Trojan hero who escaped to Italy at the fall of Troy. The principal Roman tradition held that Romulus was the founder of Rome, but the legend of Aeneas was known as early as the fifth century B.C. Virgil linked the legends of Aeneas and Romulus and preserved them both; in so doing he connected Rome with Greece's heroic past. He also mythologized later aspects of Roman history. Recounting the story of Aeneas and Dido, the queen of Carthage, Virgil made their ill-fated love affair the cause of the Punic Wars. But above all the *Aeneid* is the expression of Virgil's passionate belief in Rome's greatness. It is a vision of Rome as the protector of the good and noble against the forces of darkness and disruption.

The poet Ovid shared Virgil's views of the simple pleasures of life and also celebrated the popular culture of the day. In his *Fasti* (ca A.D. 8) he takes a personal approach to discuss and explain the ordinary festivals of the Roman year, festivals that most Romans took for granted. Without his work the modern world would be much the poorer in its knowledge of the popular religion of imperial Rome. For instance, he tells his readers that on a journey to Rome he encountered a white-robed crowd in the middle of the road. A priest and farmers were performing an annual festival. Ovid stopped to ask the priest what was happening. The priest explained that they were sacrificing to Mildew, not a farmer's favorite goddess. By burning the offerings the priest and his friends asked the goddess to be so content with them that she would not attack the crops. He further asked her not to attack the farmers' tools but to be satisfied with swords and other weapons of iron. He reminded her that "there is no need for them; the world lives in peace."[6] In his poetry Ovid, like Virgil, celebrates the pax Romana, while giving a rare glimpse of ordinary Roman life.

In its own way Livy's history of Rome, titled simply *Ab Urbe Condita* (From the Founding of the City), is the prose counterpart of the *Aeneid.* Livy (59 B.C.–A.D. 17) received training in Greek and Latin literature, rhetoric, and philosophy. He even urged the future emperor Claudius to write history. Livy loved and admired the heroes and great deeds of the republic, but he was also a friend of Augustus and a supporter of the principate. He especially approved of Augustus's efforts to restore republican virtues. Livy's history began with the legend of Aeneas and ended with the reign of Augustus. His theme of the republic's greatness fitted admirably with Augustus's program of restoring the republic. Livy's history was colossal, consisting of 142 books, and only a quarter of it still exists. Livy was a sensitive writer and something of a moralist. Like Thucydides, he felt that history should be applied to the present. His history later became one of Rome's legacies to the

Virgil and the *Aeneid* Virgil's great epic poem, the *Aeneid,* became a literary classic immediately on its appearance and has lost none of its power since. The Roman world honored Virgil for his poetic genius not only by treasuring his work but also by portraying him in art. Here two muses, who inspired artists, flank the poet while he writes his epic poem. *(C. M. Dixon)*

Ara Pacis This scene from the Ara Pacis, the Altar of Peace, celebrates Augustus's restoration of peace and the fruits of peace. Here Mother Earth is depicted with her children. The cow and the sheep under the goddess represent the prosperity brought by peace, especially the agricultural prosperity so highly cherished by Virgil. *(Art Resource, NY)*

modern world. During the Renaissance *Ab Urbe Condita* found a warm admirer in the poet Petrarch and left its mark on Machiavelli, who read it avidly.

The poet Horace (65–8 B.C.) rose from humble beginnings to friendship with Augustus. The son of an ex-slave and tax collector, Horace nonetheless received an excellent education. He loved Greek literature and finished his education in Athens. After Augustus's victory he returned to Rome and became Virgil's friend. Horace happily turned his pen to celebrating Rome's newly won peace and prosperity. One of his finest odes commemorates Augustus's victory over Cleopatra at Actium in 31 B.C. Cleopatra is depicted as a frenzied queen, drunk with desire to destroy Rome. Horace saw in Augustus's victory the triumph of West over East, of simplicity over oriental excess. One of the truly moving aspects of Horace's poetry, like Virgil's and Ovid's, is his deep and abiding gratitude for the pax Romana.

The solidity of Augustus's work became obvious at his death in A.D. 14. Since the principate was not technically an office, Augustus could not legally hand it to a successor. Augustus recognized this problem and long before his death had found a way to solve it. He shared his consular and tribunician powers with his adopted son, Tiberius, thus grooming him for the principate. In his will Augustus left most of his vast fortune to Tiberius, and the senate formally requested Tiberius to assume the burdens of the principate. Formalities apart, Augustus had succeeded in creating a dynasty.

 The Coming of Christianity

During the reign of the emperor Tiberius (A.D. 14–37), perhaps in A.D. 29, Pontius Pilate, prefect of Judaea, the Roman province created out of the Jewish kingdom of Judah, condemned Jesus of Nazareth to death. At the time a minor event, this has become one of the best-known moments in history. How did these two men come to their historic meeting? The question is not idle, for Rome was as important as Judaea to Christianity. Jesus was born in a troubled time, when Roman rule aroused hatred and unrest among the Jews. This climate of hostility affected the lives of all who lived in Judaea, Roman and Jew alike. It formed the backdrop of Jesus' life, and it had a fundamental impact on his ministry. Without an understanding of this age of anxiety in Judaea, Jesus and his followers cannot be fully appreciated.

Unrest in Judaea

The entry of Rome into Jewish affairs was anything but peaceful. The civil wars that destroyed the republic wasted the prosperity of Judaea and the entire eastern Mediterranean world. Jewish leaders took sides in the fighting, and Judaea suffered its share of ravages and military confiscations. Peace brought little satisfaction to the Jews. Although Augustus treated Judaea generously, the Romans won no popularity by making Herod king of Judaea (ca 37–4 B.C.). King Herod gave Judaea prosperity and security, but the Jews hated his acceptance of Greek culture. He was also a bloodthirsty prince who murdered his own wife and sons. At his death the Jews in Judaea broke out in revolt. For the next ten years Herod's successor waged almost constant war against the rebels. Added to the horrors of civil war were years of crop failure, which caused famine and plague. Men calling themselves prophets proclaimed the end of the world and the coming of the Messiah, the savior of Israel.

At length the Romans intervened to restore order. Augustus put Judaea under the charge of a prefect answerable directly to the emperor. Religious matters and local affairs became the responsibility of the *Sanhedrin,* the highest Jewish judicial body. Although many prefects tried to perform their duties scrupulously and conscientiously, many others were rapacious and indifferent to Jewish culture. Often acting from fear rather than cruelty, some prefects fiercely stamped out any signs of popular discontent. Pontius Pilate, prefect from A.D. 26 to 36, is typical of such incompetent officials. Although eventually relieved of his duties in disgrace, Pilate brutally put down even innocent demonstrations. Especially hated were the Roman tax collectors, called "publicans," many of whom pitilessly gouged the Jews. *Publicans* and *sinners*—the words became synonymous. Clashes between Roman troops and Jewish guerrillas inflamed the anger of both sides.

In A.D. 40 the emperor Caligula undid part of Augustus's good work by ordering his statue erected in the temple at Jerusalem. The order, though never carried out, further intensified Jewish resentment. Thus the Jews became embittered by Roman rule because of taxes, sometimes unduly harsh enforcement of the law, and misguided religious interference.

Among the Jews two movements spread. First was the rise of the Zealots, extremists who worked and fought to rid Judaea of the Romans. Resolute in their worship of Yahweh, they refused to pay any but the tax levied by the Jewish temple. Their battles with the Roman legionaries were marked by savagery on both sides. As usual the innocent caught in the middle suffered grievously. As Roman policy grew tougher, even moderate Jews began to hate the conquerors. Judaea came more and more to resemble a tinderbox, ready to burst into flames at a single spark.

The second movement was the growth of militant apocalyptic sentiment—the belief that the coming of the Messiah was near. This belief was an old one among the Jews. But by the first century A.D. it had become more widespread and fervent than ever before. Typical was the Apocalypse of Baruch, which foretold the destruction of the Roman Empire. First would come a period of great tribulation, misery, and injustice. At the worst of the suffering, the Messiah would appear. The Messiah would destroy the Roman legions and all the kingdoms that had ruled Israel. Then the Messiah would inaugurate a period of happiness and plenty for the Jews.

This was no abstract notion among the Jews. As the ravages of war became widespread and conditions worsened, more and more people prophesied the imminent coming of the Messiah. One such was John the Baptist, "the voice of one crying in the wilderness, Prepare ye the way of the lord."[7] Many Jews did just that. The sect described in the Dead Sea Scrolls readied itself for the end of the world. Its members were probably Essenes, and their social organization closely resembled that of early Christians. Members of this group shared possessions, precisely as John the Baptist urged people to do. Yet this sect, unlike the Christians, also made military preparations for the day of the Messiah.

Jewish religious aspirations were only one part of the story. What can be said of the pagan world of Rome and its empire, into which Christianity was shortly to be born? To answer that question one must first explore the spiritual environment of the pagans, many of whom would soon be caught up in the new Christian religion. The term *pagans* refers to all those who believed in the

Greco-Roman gods. Paganism at the time of Jesus' birth can be broadly divided into three spheres: the official state religion of Rome, the traditional Roman cults of hearth and countryside, and the new mystery religions that flowed from the Hellenistic East. The official state religion and its cults honored the traditional deities: Jupiter, Juno, Mars, and such newcomers as Isis (see page 124). This very formal religion was conducted on an official level by socially prominent state priests. It was above all a religion of ritual and grand spectacle, but it provided little emotional or spiritual comfort for the people. The state cults were a bond between the gods and the people, a religious contract to ensure the well-being of Rome. Most Romans felt that the official cults must be maintained, despite their lack of spiritual content, simply for the welfare of the state. After all, observance of the traditional official religion had brought Rome victory, empire, security, and wealth.

For emotional and spiritual satisfaction, many Romans observed the old cults of home and countryside, the same cults that had earlier delighted Cato the Elder (see page 149). These traditional cults brought the Romans back in touch with nature and with something elemental to Roman life. Particularly popular was the rustic shrine—often a small building or a sacred tree in an enclosure—to honor the native spirit of the locality. Though familiar and simple, even this traditional religion was not enough for many. They wanted something more personal and immediate. Many common people believed in a supernatural world seen dimly through dreams, magic, miracles, and spells. They wanted some sort of revelation about this supernatural world and security in it after death. Some people turned to astrology in the belief that they could read their destiny in the stars. But that was cold comfort, since they could not change what the stars foretold.

Many people in the Roman Empire found the answer to their need for emotionally satisfying religion and spiritual security in the various Hellenistic mystery cults. Such cults generally provided their adherents with an emotional outlet. For example, the cult of Bacchus was marked by wine drinking and often by drunken frenzy. The cult of the Great Mother, Cybele, was celebrated with emotional and even overwrought processions, and it offered its worshipers the promise of immortality. The appeal of the mystery religions was not simply that they provided emotional release. They gave their adherents what neither the traditional cults nor philosophy could—above all, security. Yet the mystery religions were by nature exclusive, and none was truly international, open to everyone.

The Life and Teachings of Jesus

Into this climate of Roman religious yearning, political severity, fanatical Zealotry, and Messianic hope came Jesus of Nazareth (ca. 5 B.C.–A.D. 29). He was raised in Galilee, stronghold of the Zealots. It was also a fertile region in which a variety of Semitic peoples and others mingled. Galilee had been influenced by Hellenism, and most people in the southern part spoke Greek as well as their native language. Through Galilee passed major trade routes, which means that it was hardly a backwater or isolated region. Ideas moved as easily as merchandise along these routes.

Much contemporary scholarship has attempted to understand who Jesus was and what he meant by his teachings. Views vary widely. Some see him as a visionary and a teacher, others as a magician and a prophet, and still others as a rebel and a revolutionary. The search for the historical Jesus is complicated by many factors. One is the difference between history and faith. History relies on proof for its conclusions; faith depends on belief. The burden of history is not only to establish the facts whenever possible but also to interpret them properly. Whether or not historians believe in Jesus' divinity is irrelevant. Their duty is to understand him in his religious, cultural, social, and historical context.

To sort out these various, but not necessarily conflicting, interpretations historians must begin with the sources. The principal evidence for the life and deeds of Jesus is the four Gospels of the New Testament. They are called the canonical Gospels because early Christians accepted them as authentic. These gospels are neither biographies of Jesus nor histories of his life. They are records of his teachings and religious doctrines with certain details of his life. The aim was to build a community of faith that believed that Jesus represented the culmination of the Messianic tradition. They were written some seventy-five years after his death, and modern biblical scholars have used literary analysis to detect a number of discrepancies among the four. For that matter, so did ancient writers, both pagan and Christian. These discrepancies are not the result of the authors having had different memories of the events of Jesus' life and mission. Instead, the writers all gave their own theological interpretations of them. As if the topic needs further complication, more gospels existed in antiquity than are now found in the New Testament.

There is no simple solution to this complex historical problem. Perhaps the wisest perspective is that of Helmut Koester, who masterfully evaluates the matter: "In the first century and early second century the number of gospels in circulation must have been much larger, at least a good dozen of which we at least have some pieces, and everybody could and did rewrite, edit, revise, and combine however he saw fit."[8] That point is at the heart of the textual problems of the tradition of Jesus' life.

What can reasonably be said of Jesus, based on the evidence, is that he preached a heavenly kingdom, one of eternal happiness in a life after death. His teachings were essentially Jewish. His orthodoxy enabled him to preach in the synagogue and the temple. His major deviation from orthodoxy was his insistence that he taught in his own name, not in the name of Yahweh. Was he then the Messiah? A small band of followers thought so, and Jesus claimed that he was. Yet Jesus had his own conception of the Messiah. Unlike the Messiah of the Apocalypse of Baruch, Jesus would not destroy the Roman Empire. He told his disciples flatly that they were to "render unto Caesar the things that are Caesar's." Jesus would establish a spiritual kingdom, not an earthly one. He told his disciples that his kingdom was "not of this world."

Of Jesus' life and teachings the prefect Pontius Pilate knew little and cared even less. All that concerned him was the maintenance of peace and order. The crowds following Jesus at the time of the Passover, a highly emotional time in the Jewish year, alarmed Pilate, who faced a volatile situation. Some Jews believed that Jesus was the long-awaited Messiah. Others were disappointed because he refused to preach rebellion against Rome. Still others who hated and feared Jesus wanted

Pontius Pilate and Jesus This Byzantine mosaic from Ravenna illustrates a dramatic moment in Jesus' trial and crucifixion. Jesus stands accused before Pilate, but Pilate symbolically washes his hands of the whole affair. *(Scala/Art Resource, NY)*

to be rid of him. The last thing Pilate wanted was a riot on his hands. Christian tradition has made much of Pontius Pilate. In the medieval West he was considered a monster. In the Ethiopian church he is considered a saint. Neither monster nor saint, Pilate was simply a hard-bitten Roman official who did his duty, at times harshly. In Judaea his duty was to enforce the law and keep the peace. These were the problems on his mind when Jesus stood before him. Jesus as king of the Jews did not worry him. The popular agitation surrounding Jesus did. To avert riot and bloodshed, Pilate condemned Jesus to death. It is a bitter historical irony that such a gentle man died such a cruel death. After being scourged, he was hung from a cross until he died in the sight of family, friends, enemies, and the merely curious.

Once Pilate's soldiers had carried out the sentence, the entire matter seemed to be closed. Yet on the third day after Jesus' crucifixion, an odd rumor began to circulate in Jerusalem. Some of Jesus' followers were saying he had risen from the dead, while others accused them of having stolen his body. For the earliest Christians and for generations to come, the resurrection of Jesus became a central element of faith—and more than that, a promise: Jesus had triumphed over death, and his resurrection promised all Christians immortality. In Jerusalem, meanwhile, the tumult subsided. Jesus' followers lived quietly and peacefully, unmolested by Roman or Jew. Pilate had no quarrel with them, and Judaism already had many minor sects.

The memory of Jesus and his teachings sturdily survived. Believers in his divinity met in small assemblies or congregations, often in one another's homes, to discuss the meaning of Jesus' message. These meetings always took place outside the synagogue. They included such orthodox Jews as the Pharisees. These earliest Christians were clearly defining their faith to fit the life of Jesus into an orthodox Jewish context. Only later did these congregations evolve into what can be called a church with a formal organization and set of beliefs. One of the first significant events occurred in Jerusalem on the Jewish festival of Pentecost, when Jesus' followers assembled. They were joined by Jews from many parts of the world, including some from as far away as Parthia to the east, Crete to the west, Rome, and Ethiopia. These early followers were Hellenized Jews, many of them rich merchants. They were in an excellent position to spread the word throughout the known world.

The catalyst in the spread of Jesus' teachings and the formation of the Christian church was Paul of Tarsus, a Hellenized Jew who was comfortable in both the Roman and Jewish worlds. He had begun by persecuting the new sect, but on the road to Damascus he was converted to belief in Jesus. He was the single most important figure responsible for changing Christianity from a Jewish sect into a separate religion. Paul was familiar with Greek philosophy, and he had actually discussed the tenets of the new religion with Epicurean and Stoic philosophers in Athens. Indeed, one of his seminal ideas may have stemmed from the Stoic concept of the unity of mankind. He proclaimed that the mission of Christianity was "to make one of all the folk of men."[9] His vision was to include all the kindred of the earth. That concept meant that he urged the Jews to include non-Jews in the faith. He was the first to voice a universal message of Christianity.

Paul's vision was both bold and successful. When he traveled abroad, he first met with the leaders of the local synagogue, then went among the people. He applied himself especially to the Greco-Romans, whom he did not consider common or unclean because they were not Jews. He went so far as to say that there were no differences between Jews and Gentiles, which in orthodox Jewish thought was not only revolutionary but also heresy. Paul found a ready audience among the Gentiles, who converted to the new religion with surprising enthusiasm. A significant part of this process was the acceptance of Gentile women into the faith. The reasons for this were several. First, intermarriage between Greeks and Jews was common. More important, Christianity gave women more rights than they could expect from either paganism or Judaism. For women Christianity was a source of liberation.

Surprisingly the Gentile response pleased the Jews in Jerusalem. The inclusion of Gentiles led to a growing distinction between Christians and Jews. Paul went so far as to say that Christian baptism was different from the Jewish baptism practiced by John the Baptist. The break came when Paul told the Jews that because they would not believe in Jesus' mission to them, he would teach that the salvation of God was sent to the Gentiles, who would listen to the Word. Christianity was no longer a Jewish sect.

Christianity appealed to common people and to the poor. Its communal celebration of the Lord's Supper gave men and women a sense of belonging. Christianity also offered its adherents the promise of salvation. Christians believed that Jesus on the cross had defeated evil and that he would reward his followers with eternal life after death. Christianity also offered the possibility of forgiveness. Human nature was weak, and even the best Christians would fall into sin. But Jesus loved sinners and forgave those who repented. In its doctrine of salvation and forgiveness alone, Christianity had a powerful ability to give solace and strength to believers.

Christianity was attractive to many because it gave the Roman world a cause. Hellenistic philosophy had attempted to make men and women self-sufficient: people who became indifferent to the outside world could no longer be hurt by it. That goal alone ruled out any cause except the attainment of serenity. The Romans, never innovators in philosophy, merely elaborated this lonely and austere message. Instead of passivity, Christianity stressed the ideal of striving for a goal. Every Christian, no matter how poor or humble, supposedly worked to realize the triumph of Christianity on earth. This was God's will, a sacred duty for every Christian. By spreading the word of Christ, Christians played their part in God's plan. No matter how small, the part each Christian played was important. Since this duty was God's will, Christians believed that the goal would be achieved. The Christian was not discouraged by temporary setbacks, believing Christianity to be invincible.

Christianity gave its devotees a sense of community. No Christian was alone. All members of the Christian community strove toward the same goal of fulfilling God's plan. Each individual community was in turn a member of a greater community. And that community, the Church General, was indestructible. After all, Jesus himself had reportedly promised, "Thou art Peter, and upon this rock I will build my church; and the gates of hell shall not prevail against it."[10]

So Christianity's attractions were many, from forgiveness of sin to an exalted purpose for each individual. Its insistence on the individual's importance gave solace and encouragement, especially to the poor and meek. Its claim to divine protection fed hope in the eventual success of the Christian community. Christianity made participation in the universal possible for everyone. The ultimate reward promised by Christianity was eternal bliss after death.

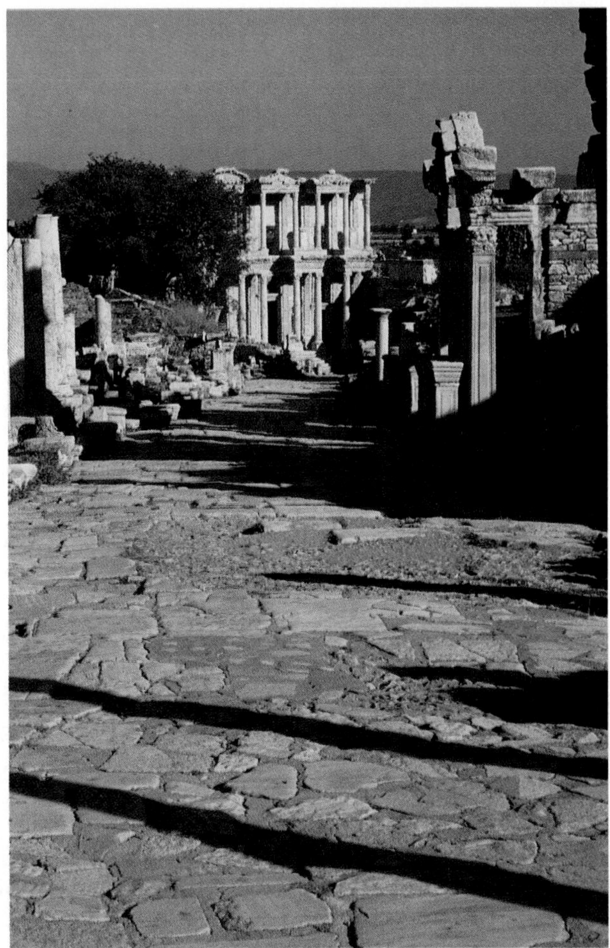

Arkadiana This beautiful paved street, the Arkadiana in Ephesus, Turkey, is still lined with the remains of columns, statues, and altars. Opening onto the Arkadiana were shops where people could make their purchases under the protection of the colonnade. The Apostle Paul often strolled along the Arkadiana and its neighboring streets. *(Robert Frerck/Woodfin Camp & Associates)*

THE JULIO-CLAUDIANS AND THE FLAVIANS (27 B.C.–A.D. 96)

For fifty years after Augustus's death the dynasty that he established—known as the Julio-Claudians because they were all members of the Julian and Claudian clans—provided the emperors of Rome. Some of the Julio-Claudians, such as Tiberius and Claudius, were sound rulers and able administrators. Others, including Caligula and Nero, were weak and frivolous men who exercised their power stupidly and brought misery to the empire. Writers such as the biting and brilliant historian Tacitus (ca A.D. 55–ca 116) and the gossipy Suetonius (ca A.D. 75–150) have left unforgettable—and generally hostile—portraits of these emperors. Yet the venom of Tacitus and Suetonius cannot obscure the fact that the Julio-Claudians were responsible for some notable achievements. During their reigns the empire largely prospered.

One of the most momentous achievements of the Julio-Claudians was Claudius's creation of an imperial bureaucracy composed of professional administrators. Even the most energetic emperor could not run the empire alone. The numerous duties and immense responsibilities of the emperor prompted Claudius to delegate power. He began by giving the freedmen of his household official duties, especially in finances. It was a simple, workable system. Claudius knew his ex-slaves well and could discipline them at will. The effect of Claudius's innovations was to enable the emperor to rule the empire more easily and efficiently.

One of the worst defects of Augustus's settlement—the army's ability to interfere in politics—became obvious during the Julio-Claudian period. Augustus had created a special standing force, the Praetorian Guard, as an imperial bodyguard. In A.D. 41 one of the Praetorians murdered Caligula while others hailed Claudius as the emperor. Under the threat of violence, the senate ratified the Praetorians' choice. It was a story repeated frequently. During the first three centuries of the empire, the Praetorian Guard all too often murdered emperors they were supposed to protect and saluted emperors of their own choosing.

In A.D. 68 Nero's inept rule led to military rebellion and his death, thus opening the way to widespread disruption. In A.D. 69, the "Year of the Four Emperors," four men claimed the position of emperor. Roman armies in Gaul, on the Rhine, and in the East marched on Rome to make their commanders emperor. The man who emerged triumphant was Vespasian, commander of the eastern armies, who entered Rome in 70 and restored order. Nonetheless, the Year of the Four Emperors proved that the Augustan settlement had failed to end civil war.

Not a brilliant politician, Vespasian did not institute sweeping reforms, as had Augustus, or solve the problem of the army in politics. To prevent usurpers from claiming the throne, Vespasian designated his sons Titus and Domitian as his successors. By establishing the Flavian dynasty (named after his clan), Vespasian turned the principate into an open and admitted monarchy. He also expanded the emperor's power by increasing the size of the budding bureaucracy Claudius had created.

One of Vespasian's first tasks was to suppress rebellions that had erupted at the end of Nero's reign. The most famous had taken place in Judaea, which still seethed long after Jesus' crucifixion. Long-standing popular unrest and atrocities committed by Jews and Romans alike sparked a massive revolt in A.D. 66. Four years later a Roman army reconquered Judaea and reduced Jerusalem by siege. The Jewish survivors were enslaved, their state destroyed. The mismanagement of Judaea was one of the few—and worst—failures of Roman imperial administration.

The Flavians carried on Augustus's work on the frontiers. Domitian, the last of the Flavians, won additional territory in Germany and consolidated it in two new provinces. He defeated barbarian tribes on the Danube frontier and strengthened that area as well. Even so, Domitian was one of the most hated of Roman emperors because of his cruelty, and he fell victim to an assassin's dagger. Nevertheless, the Flavians had given the Roman world peace and had kept the legions in line. Their work paved the way for the era of the "five good emperors," the golden age of the empire.

THE AGE OF THE "FIVE GOOD EMPERORS" (A.D. 96–180)

In the second century of the Christian era, the Empire of Rome comprehended the fairest part of the earth, and the most civilised portion of mankind. The frontiers of that extensive monarchy were guarded by ancient renown and disciplined valor. The gentle but powerful influence of laws and manners had gradually cemented the union of the provinces. Their peaceful inhabitants enjoyed and abused the advantages of wealth and luxury. The image of a free constitution was preserved with decent reverence: the Roman senate appeared to possess the sovereign authority, and devolved on the emperors all the executive powers of government. During a happy period [A.D. 96–180] of more than fourscore years, the public administration was conducted by the virtue and abilities of Nerva, Trajan, Hadrian, and the two Antonines.[11]

Thus Edward Gibbon (1737–1794) began his monumental *History of the Decline and Fall of the Roman Empire.* Gibbon saw the era of Nerva, Trajan, Hadrian, Antoninus Pius, and Marcus Aurelius—the "five good emperors"—as the happiest in human history, a last burst of summer before an autumn of failure and barbarism. Gibbon recognized a great truth: the age of the Antonines, as the five good emperors are often called, was one of almost unparalleled prosperity for the empire. The Romans were generally victorious in war, which was confined to the frontiers. Even the serenity of Augustus's day seemed to pale in comparison. These emperors were among the noblest, most dedicated, ablest men in Roman history. Yet fundamental political and military changes had taken place since the time of Augustus's rule.

Scene from Trajan's Column From 101 to 107 Trajan fought the barbarian tribes along the Danube. With remarkable realism, a feature of Roman art, this scene portrays Roman soldiers building field-works outside of a city. *(Ancient Art & Architecture Collection)*

The Antonine Monarchy

Augustus had claimed that his influence arose from the collection of offices the senate had bestowed on him. However, there was in law no such office as emperor. Augustus was merely the First Citizen. Under the Flavians the principate became a full-blown monarchy, and by the time of the Antonines the principate was an office with definite rights, powers, and prerogatives. In the years between Augustus and the Antonines, the emperor had become an indispensable part of the imperial machinery. In short, without the emperor the empire would quickly fall to pieces. Augustus had been monarch in fact but not in theory; during their reigns, the Antonines were monarchs in both.

The five good emperors were not power-hungry autocrats. The concentration of power was the result of empire. The easiest and most efficient way to run the Roman Empire was to invest the emperor with vast powers. Furthermore, Roman emperors on the whole proved to be effective rulers and administrators. As capable and efficient emperors took on new tasks and functions, the emperor's hand was felt in more areas of life and government. Increasingly the emperors became the source of all authority and guidance in the empire. The five good emperors were benevolent and exercised their power intelligently, but they were absolute kings all the same. Lesser men would later throw off the façade of constitutionality and use this same power in a despotic fashion.

Typical of the five good emperors is the career of Hadrian, who became emperor in A.D. 117. He was born in Spain, a fact that illustrates the importance of the provinces in Roman politics. Hadrian received his education at Rome and became an ardent admirer of Greek culture. He caught the attention of his elder

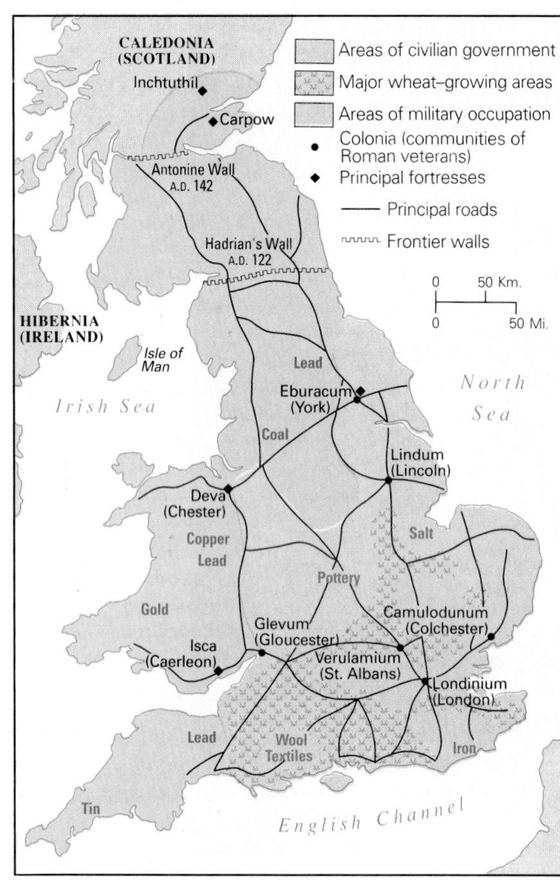

MAP 6.2 Roman Britain Though the modern state of Great Britain plays a major role in international affairs, it was a peripheral part of the Roman Empire, a valuable area but nonetheless definitely on the frontier.

cousin Trajan, the future emperor, who started him on a military career. At age nineteen Hadrian served on the Danube frontier, where he learned the details of how the Roman army lived and fought and saw for himself the problems of defending the frontiers. When Trajan became emperor in A.D. 98, Hadrian was given important positions in which he learned how to defend and run the empire. At Trajan's death in 117 Hadrian assumed power.

Roman government had changed since Augustus's day. One of the most significant changes was the enormous growth of the imperial bureaucracy created by Claudius. Hadrian reformed this system by putting the bureaucracy on an organized, official basis. He established imperial administrative departments to handle the work formerly done by imperial freedmen. Hadrian also separated civil service from military service. Men with little talent or taste for the army could instead serve the state as administrators. Hadrian's bureaucracy demanded professionalism from its members. Administrators made a career of the civil service. These innovations made for more efficient running of the empire and increased the authority of the emperor—the ruling power of the bureaucracy.

Changes in the Army

The Roman army had also changed since Augustus's time. The Roman legion had once been a mobile unit, but its duties under the empire no longer called for mobility. The successors of Augustus generally called a halt to further conquests. The army was expected to defend what had already been won. Under the Flavian emperors (A.D. 69–96) the frontiers became firmly fixed, except for a brief period under Trajan, who attempted to expand the empire. Forts and watch stations guarded the borders. Behind the forts the Romans built a system of roads that allowed the forts to be quickly supplied and reinforced in times of trouble. The army had evolved into a garrison force, with legions guarding specific areas for long periods.

The personnel of the legions was changing, too. Italy could no longer supply all the recruits needed for the army. Increasingly only the officers came from Italy and from the more Romanized provinces. The legionaries were mostly drawn from the less civilized provinces, especially the ones closest to the frontiers. A major trend was already obvious in Hadrian's day: fewer and fewer Roman soldiers were really Roman. In the third century A.D. the barbarization of the army would result in an army indifferent to Rome and its traditions. In the age of the five good emperors, however, the army was still a source of economic stability and a Romanizing agent (Map 6.2). Men from the provinces and even barbarians joined the army to learn a trade and to gain Roman citizenship. Even so, the signs were ominous. Veterans from Julius Caesar's campaigns would hardly have recognized Hadrian's troops as Roman legionaries. (See the feature "Individuals in Society: Bithus, a Typical Roman Soldier.")

 LIFE IN THE "GOLDEN AGE"

Many people, both ancient and modern, have considered these years one of the happiest epochs in Western history. But popular accounts have also portrayed Rome as already decadent by the time of the five good emperors. If Rome was decadent, who kept the empire running? For that matter, can life in Rome itself be taken as representative of life in other parts of the empire? Rome was unique and must be seen as such. Surely Rome no more resembled a provincial city like Cologne than New York could possibly resemble Keokuk, Iowa. Only when the uniqueness of Rome is understood in its own right can one turn to the provinces to obtain a full and reasonable picture of the empire under the Antonines.

Imperial Rome

Rome was truly an extraordinary city, especially by ancient standards. It was also enormous, with a population somewhere between 500,000 and 750,000. Although it could boast of stately palaces, noble buildings, and beautiful residential areas, most people lived in jerrybuilt apartment houses. Fire and crime were perennial problems, even after Augustus created fire and urban police forces. Streets were narrow and drainage was inadequate. During the republic sanitation had been a common problem. Numerous inscriptions record prohibitions against dumping human refuse and even cadavers on the grounds of sanctuaries and cemeteries. Under the empire this situation improved. By comparison with medieval and early modern European cities, Rome was a healthy enough place to live.

Rome was such a huge city that the surrounding countryside could not feed it. Because of the danger of starvation, the emperor, following republican practice, provided the citizen population with free grain for bread and, later, oil and wine. By feeding the citizenry the emperor prevented bread riots caused by shortages and high prices. For the rest of the urban population who did not enjoy the rights of citizenship, the emperor provided grain at low prices. This measure was designed to prevent speculators from forcing up grain prices in times of crisis. By maintaining the grain supply the emperor kept the favor of the people and ensured that Rome's poor and idle did not starve.

The emperor also entertained the Roman populace, often at vast expense. The most popular forms of public entertainment were gladiatorial contests and chariot racing. Gladiatorial fighting was originally an Etruscan funerary custom, a blood sacrifice for the dead. Even a humane man like Hadrian staged extravagant contests. In A.D. 126 he sponsored six days of such combats, during which 1,835 pairs of gladiators dueled, usually with swords and shields. Many gladiators were criminals, some of whom were sentenced to be slaughtered in the arena. These convicts were given no defensive weapons and stood little real chance of survival. Other criminals were sentenced to fight in the arena as fully armed gladiators. Some gladiators were the slaves of gladiatorial trainers; others were prisoners of war. Still others were free men who volunteered for the arena. Even women at times engaged in gladiatorial combat. What drove these men and women? Some obviously had no other choice. For a criminal condemned to die, the arena was preferable to the imperial mines, where convicts worked digging ore and died under wretched conditions. At least in the arena the gladiator might fight well enough to win freedom. Others no doubt fought for the love of danger or for fame. Although some Romans protested gladiatorial fighting, most delighted in it—one of their least attractive sides. Not until the fifth century did Christianity put a stop to it.

The Romans were even more addicted to chariot racing than to gladiatorial shows. Under the empire four permanent teams competed against one another. Each had its own color—red, white, green, or blue. Some Romans claimed that people cared more about their favorite team than about the race itself. Two-horse and four-horse chariots ran a course of seven laps, about five miles. A successful driver could be the hero of the hour. One charioteer, Gaius Appuleius Diocles, raced for twenty-four years. During that time he drove 4,257 starts and won 1,462 of them. His admirers honored him with an inscription that proclaimed him champion of all charioteers.

But people like the charioteer Diocles were no more typical of the common Roman than Babe Ruth was of the average American. Ordinary Romans left their mark in the inscriptions that grace their graves. They were proud of their work and accomplishments, affectionate toward their families and friends, and eager to be remembered after death. Typical Romans did not spend their entire lives in idleness, watching gladiators or chariot races; instead, they had to make a living. They dealt with everyday problems and rejoiced over small pleasures. An impression of them and their cares can be gained from their epitaphs. The funerary inscription of Paprius Vitalis to his wife is particularly engaging: "If there is anything good in the lower regions—I, however, finish a poor life without you—be happy there too, sweetest Thalassia . . . married to me for 40 years."[12]

Even the personal philosophies of typical Romans have come down from antiquity. Marcus Antonius Encolpus erected a funerary inscription to his wife that reads in part:

Do not pass by my epitaph, traveler.
But having stopped, listen and learn, then go your way.
There is no boat in Hades, no ferryman Charon,

Chariot Racing This brilliant mosaic found near Lyons, France, gives in almost a snapshot view a typical chariot race. In the center around which the chariots raced was a decorative pond with gushing water, dolphins, and egg-shaped spheres. *(Cliché Musée de la Civilisation Gallo-romaine de Lyon)*

no caretaker Aiakos, no dog Cerberus.
All we who are dead below
have become bones and ashes, but nothing else.
I have spoken to you honestly, go on, traveler,
lest even while dead I seem loquacious to you.[13]

Others put it more simply: "I was, I am not, I don't care." "To each his own tombstone." These Romans went about their lives as people have always done.

Rome and the Provinces

The question of how much Roman civilization influenced life in the provinces is impossible to answer, despite the great amount of new material that has been discovered in recent years. The problem, as usual, depends on the surviving sources. The rural population throughout the empire left few records, and despite the political domination of Rome, the majority of native inhabitants of the provinces continued to speak their own languages. They used Greek and Latin mostly for official purposes. Urban centers across the empire attracted wealthy and talented people who embraced the Roman system of governance, commerce, and culture and the Latin and Greek languages. The principal distinction was not, therefore, between Romans and provincials, but between urban and rural.

A brief survey of the provinces proves the point. For instance, in Gaul country people retained their ancestral gods, and there was not much difference in many parts of the province between the original Celtic villages and their Roman successors. Life along the Rhine River is likewise illustrative of the interaction between natives and newcomers. The distinction came with the growth of Roman military colonies along the river, which fostered a life quite different from that of the countryside around them. On the western bank the villages remained largely Celtic in cultural, social, and political organization. Roman influence in this region lay more in methods of production than in cultural innovations. Yet the very success of Roman merchants transformed the economy of the area.

This region provides an excellent illustration of how Romanization of the provinces actually worked. The Romans provided the capital for commerce, agricultural development of the land, and large-scale building. Roman merchants also became early bankers, who loaned money to the natives and often brought them under financial control. The native inhabitants formed the labor force. They normally lived in villages and huts near the villas of successful merchants. Thus contact between the two groups was generally as much economic as social and cultural. Although Roman ideas spread and there was a good deal of cultural blending, native

Individuals in Society

Bithus, a Typical Roman Soldier

Few people think of soldiers as missionaries of culture, but they often are. The culture that they spread is seldom of high intellectual or artistic merit, but they expose others to their own traditions, habits, and ways of thinking. A simple modern example may suffice. In World War II American GIs in Italy taught children there how to play baseball. From their very presence the young Americans taught their Italian friends many other things about the United States and themselves learned a great deal about Italian life and values. Even today a stranger can wander around an Italian town and see the results of this meeting of two cultures.

The same was true of the armies of the Roman Empire. The empire was so vast even by modern standards that soldiers were recruited from all parts of it to serve in distant places. A soldier from Syria might find himself keeping watch on Hadrian's Wall in Britain. He brought with him the ideas and habits of his birthplace and soon realized that others lived life differently. Yet they all lived in the same empire. Despite their ethnic differences, they were united by many commonly shared beliefs and opinions. Although the Roman Empire never became totally Romanized, soldiers, like officials and merchants, played their part in disseminating Roman ideas of government, religion, and way of life.

One such person was the infantryman Bithus, who was a native of Thrace, the modern region of northeastern Greece. His career was eventful but not particularly distinguished. He is, however, typical of many others who also served in the legions. Bithus's military life took him far from his native Thrace. He was stationed largely in Syria, where he mingled with other soldiers from throughout the empire. He came into contact with people from as far west as Gaul and Spain, from western Africa, and from the modern Middle East. Unlike many other cohorts that were shifted periodically, he saw service in one theater. After twenty-five years of duty, he received his reward on November 7, 88. Upon his mustering out of the army, he received the grant of Roman citizenship for himself and his family. In his civilian life the veteran enjoyed a social status that granted him honor and privileges accorded only to Romans. From his military record, there is no reason to conclude that Bithus had even seen Rome, but because of his service to it, he became as much a Roman as anyone born near the Tiber.

The example of Bithus is important because it is typical of thousands of other people who voluntarily supported the empire. One of the rewards of their service was that in the process they learned about the nature of the empire, and they exchanged experiences with other soldiers and the local population that helped shape a sense that the empire was a human as well as a political unit.

Idealized statue of a Roman soldier. *(Deutsches Archaeologisches Institut, Rome)*

Questions for Analysis

1. What did Bithus gain from his twenty-five years of service in the Roman army?
2. What effect did soldiers such as Bithus have on the various parts of the Roman Empire where they served, both in their way of seeing new cultures and in their way of sharing new experiences?

Source: Corpus Inscriptionum Latinarum, vol. 16 (Berlin: G. Reimer, 1882), no. 35.

ROMAN HISTORY AFTER AUGUSTUS

Period	Important Emperors	Significant Events
Julio-Claudians **27 B.C.–A.D. 68**	Augustus, 27 B.C.–A.D. 14 Tiberius, 14–37 Caligula, 37–41 Claudius, 41–54 Nero, 54–68	Augustan settlement Beginning of the principate Birth and death of Jesus Expansion into northern and western Europe Creation of the imperial bureaucracy
Year of the Four Emperors **69**	Nero Galba Otho Vitellius	Civil war Major breakdown of the concept of the principate
Flavians **69–96**	Vespasian, 69–79 Titus, 79–81 Domitian, 81–96	Growing trend toward the concept of monarchy Defense and further consolidation of the European frontiers
Antonines **96–192**	Nerva, 96–98 Trajan, 98–117 Hadrian, 117–138 Antoninus Pius, 138–161 Marcus Aurelius, 161–180 Commodus, 180–192	The "golden age"—the era of the "five good emperors" Economic prosperity Trade and growth of cities in northern Europe Beginning of barbarian menace on the frontiers
Severi **193–235**	Septimius Severus, 193–211 Caracalla, 198–217 Elagabalus, 218–222 Severus Alexander, 222–235	Military monarchy All free men within the empire given Roman citizenship
"Barracks Emperors" **235–284**	Twenty-two emperors in forty-nine years	Civil war Breakdown of the empire Barbarian invasions Severe economic decline
Tetrarchy **284–337**	Diocletian, 284–305 Constantine, 306–337	Political recovery Autocracy Legalization of Christianity Transition to the Middle Ages in the West Birth of the Byzantine Empire in the East

customs and religions continued to thrive. The Romans also learned about and began to respect native gods. Worship of them became popular among the Romans and the Greeks, which encouraged local peoples to preserve their religions.

The situation on the eastern bank of the Rhine was also typical of life on the borders, but it demonstrates the rawer features of frontier life. To this troubled land the Romans brought peace and stability, first by building forts and roads and then by opening the rivers to navigation. Around the forts grew native villages, and peace encouraged more intensive cultivation of the soil. The region became more prosperous than ever before, and prosperity attracted Roman settlers. In this rough

Rowing Barge Rowing barges and other river boats plied the rivers of northern Europe, transporting goods in bulk. Here a barge loaded with four large barrels of wine rows down the Mosselle River. The boat has a crew of eight, six of whom are rowers. A steersman sits in the stern, steering the boat with a long sweep. A helmsman in the bow keeps time for the rowers by clapping his hands. *(Landesmuseum, Trier)*

and often unforeseen manner there developed a pattern of farms and agricultural estates, where Roman veterans mingled with the Celtic aristocracy. The villa, not the city, was the primary unit of organized political life. This pattern of life differed from that of the Mediterranean, but it prefigured that of the early Middle Ages. The same was true in Britain, where the normal social and economic structures were farms and agricultural villages. Very few cities were to be found, and many native Britons were largely ignorant of Greco-Roman culture.

Across eastern Europe the pattern was much the same. In the Alpine provinces north of Italy, Romans and native Celts came into contact in the cities, but native cultures flourished in the countryside. In Illyria and Dalmatia, the regions of modern Albania and the former Yugoslavia, the native population never widely embraced either Roman culture or urban life. Similarly, the Roman soldiers who increasingly settled parts of these lands made little effort to absorb the natives or to Romanize them. To a certain extent Romanization occurred simply because these peoples lived in such close proximity.

The same situation existed in Asia Minor and Africa. The Romans built on earlier Greek achievements, but they apparently never tried to change the lives of the peoples who lived there. They concentrated their attention on the cities, which were the administrative, political, and economic centers of the countryside surrounding them. This was especially true of Syria, Judaea, and Egypt, where life outside the cities proceeded in traditional ways. The Romans, like the Greeks before them, largely ignored Nubia, the homeland of the Ethiopians. The destruction of Ethiopia at the end of the third century was due to its African neighbors, not the Romans.

Only in western Africa did the Romans make a lasting impression on both urban and rural societies. There the large number of colonies of Roman veterans spread their culture over a wider spectrum than elsewhere. Nonetheless, this pattern was largely limited to the new cities established in the region. If western Africa was more Romanized than many other provinces, it was simply because there were more Romans there. The local populace learned to read and write a little Greek and Latin, and probably spoke more, but they never abandoned their traditional ways.

Obviously the Romans went to no great lengths to spread their culture. Their chief aim was political stability. As long as the empire prospered and the revenues reached the imperial coffers, the Romans were willing to live and let live.

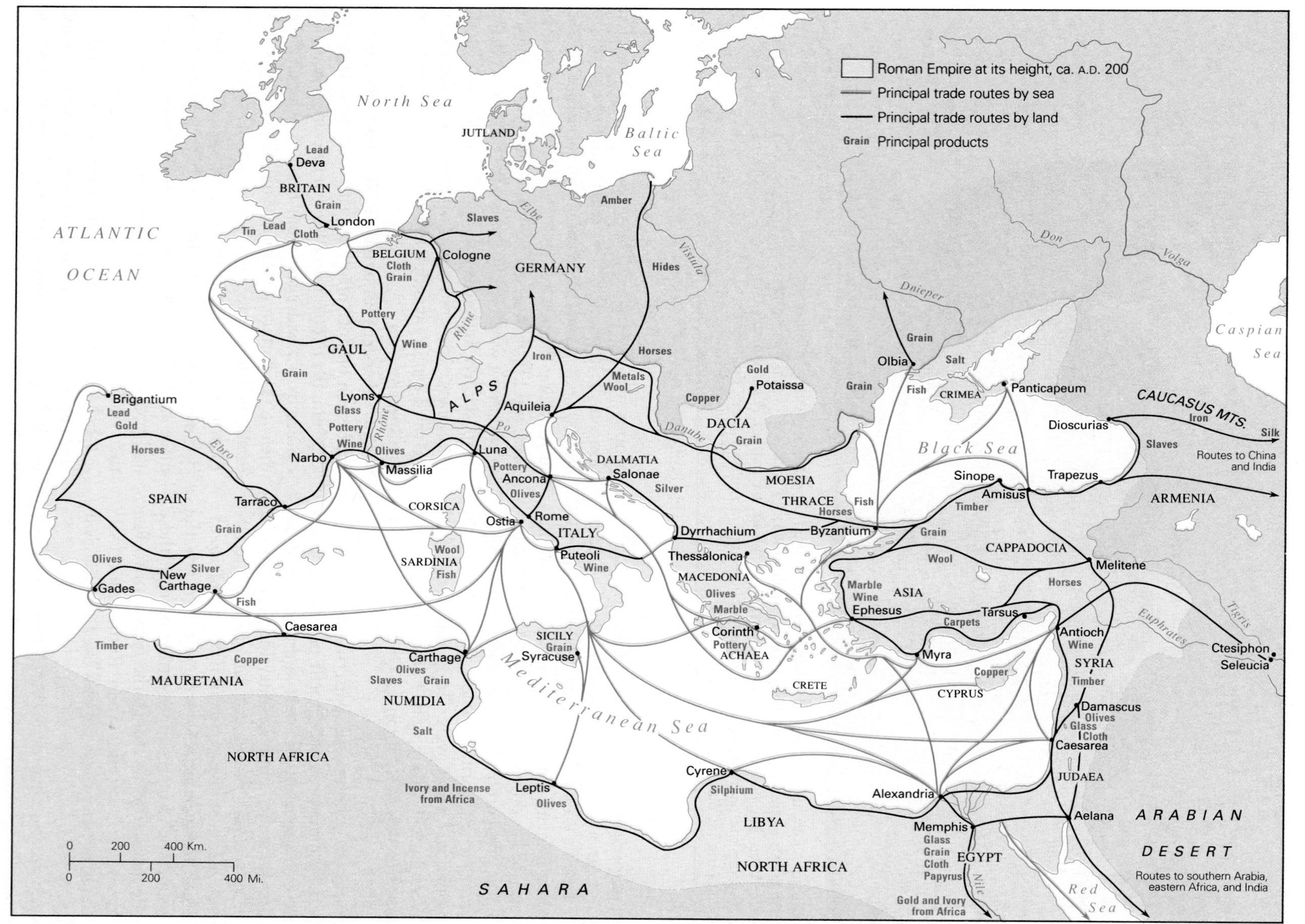
Roman Empire at its height, ca. A.D. 200
Principal trade routes by sea
Principal trade routes by land
Grain Principal products
ATLANTIC OCEAN
North Sea
Baltic Sea
Black Sea
Caspian Sea
Mediterranean Sea
Red Sea
BRITAIN
Deva
London
Lead
Grain
Cloth
Tin
JUTLAND
GERMANY
BELGIUM
Cloth
Grain
Cologne
Slaves
Amber
Hides
Horses
GAUL
Lyons
Glass
Pottery
Wine
Narbo
Massilia
Olives
ALPS
Iron
SPAIN
Brigantium
Gold
Horses
Tarraco
New Carthage
Silver
Gades
Olives
Timber
Fish
CORSICA
SARDINIA
Wool
Fish
ITALY
Rome
Ostia
Puteoli
Luna
Ancona
Aquileia
Metals
Wool
SICILY
Syracuse
DALMATIA
Salonae
Silver
DACIA
Potaissa
Gold
Copper
MOESIA
THRACE
Byzantium
Dyrrhachium
Thessalonica
MACEDONIA
Corinth
ACHAEA
Pottery
Marble
CRETE
ASIA
Ephesus
Marble
Wine
Wool
Grain
Myra
Tarsus
Carpets
CYPRUS
Copper
CAPPADOCIA
Horses
Sinope
Amisus
Timber
Trapezus
Dioscurias
Panticapeum
CRIMEA
Salt
Fish
Olbia
CAUCASUS MTS.
Iron
Slaves
Silk
Routes to China and India
ARMENIA
Melitene
Antioch
Wine
SYRIA
Timber
Damascus
Olives
Glass
Cloth
Caesarea
JUDAEA
Aelana
Ctesiphon
Seleucia
ARABIAN DESERT
Routes to southern Arabia, eastern Africa, and India
EGYPT
Memphis
Alexandria
Glass
Grain
Cloth
Papyrus
Gold and Ivory from Africa
LIBYA
Cyrene
Silphium
NORTH AFRICA
Leptis
Olives
Ivory and Incense from Africa
Carthage
Olives
Slaves
Grain
NUMIDIA
Salt
Caesarea
Copper
MAURETANIA
SAHARA
Rhine
Rhône
Elbe
Vistula
Danube
Po
Ebro
Dnieper
Don
Volga
Tigris
Euphrates
Nile
0 200 400 Km.
0 200 400 Mi.

Despite the fact that cultural relations were often limited, one of the most striking features of this period was the growth of industry in the provinces (Map 6.3). Cities in Gaul and Germany eclipsed the old Mediterranean manufacturing centers. Italian cities were particularly hard hit by this development. Cities like Arretium and Capua had dominated the production of glass, pottery, and bronze ware. Yet in the second century A.D. Gaul and Germany took over the pottery market. Lyons in Gaul became the new center of the glassmaking industry. The technique of glass blowing spread to Britain and Germany, and later in the second century Cologne replaced Lyons in glass production. The cities of Gaul were nearly unrivaled in the manufacture of bronze and brass. Gallic craftsmen invented a new technique of tin-plating and decorated their work with Celtic designs. Their wares soon drove Italian products out of the northern European market. For the first time in history, northern Europe was able to rival the Mediterranean as a producer of manufactured goods. Europe had entered fully into the economic and cultural life of the Mediterranean world.

The age of the five good emperors was generally one of peace, progress, and prosperity. The work of the Romans in northern and western Europe was a permanent contribution to the history of Western society. This period was also one of consolidation. Roads and secure sea-lanes linked the empire in one vast web. The empire had become a commonwealth of cities, and urban life was its hallmark.

CIVIL WARS AND INVASIONS IN THE THIRD CENTURY

The age of the five good emperors gave way to a period of chaos and stress. During the third century A.D. the empire was stunned by civil wars and barbarian invasions. By the time peace was restored, the economy was shattered, cities had shrunk in size, and agriculture was becoming manorial (see page 189). In the disruption of the third century and the reconstruction of the fourth, the medieval world had its origins.

MAP 6.3 The Economic Aspect of the Pax Romana
The Roman Empire was not merely a political and military organization but also an intricate economic network through which goods from Armenia and Syria were traded for Western products from as far away as Spain and Britain.

After the death of Marcus Aurelius, the last of the five good emperors, his son Commodus, a man totally unsuited to govern the empire, came to the throne. His misrule led to his murder and a renewal of civil war. After a brief but intense spasm of fighting, the African general Septimius Severus defeated other rival commanders and established the Severan dynasty (A.D. 193–235). Although Septimius Severus was able to stabilize the empire, his successors proved incapable of disciplining the legions. When the last of the Severi was killed by one of his own soldiers, the empire plunged into still another grim, destructive, and this time prolonged round of civil wars.

Over twenty different emperors ascended the throne in the forty-nine years between 235 and 284, and many rebels died in the attempts to seize power. At various times parts of the empire were lost to rebel generals, one of whom, Postumus, set up his own empire in Gaul for about ten years (A.D. 259–269). Yet other men, like the iron-willed Aurelian (A.D. 270–275), dedicated their energies to restoring order. So many military commanders ruled that the middle of the third century has become known as the age of the "barracks emperors." The Augustan principate had become a military monarchy, and that monarchy was nakedly autocratic.

Barbarians on the Frontiers

The first and most disastrous result of the civil wars was trouble on the frontiers. It was Rome's misfortune that this era of anarchy coincided with immense movements of barbarian peoples. Historians still dispute the precise reason for these migrations, though their immediate cause was pressure from tribes moving westward across Asia. In the sixth century A.D. Jordanes, a Christianized Goth, preserved the memory of innumerable wars among the barbarians in his *History of the Goths.* Goths fought Vandals; Huns fought Goths. Steadily the defeated and displaced tribes moved toward the Roman frontiers. Finally, like "a swarm of bees"—to use Jordanes's image—the Goths, one such people, burst into Europe in A.D. 258.

When the barbarians reached the Rhine and Danube frontiers, they often found huge gaps in the Roman defenses. Typical is the case of Decius, a general who guarded the Danube frontier in Dacia (modern Romania). In A.D. 249 he revolted and invaded Italy in an effort to become emperor. Decius left the frontier deserted, and the Goths easily poured through, looking for new homes. During much of the third century A.D., bands of Goths devastated the Balkans as far south as

Greece. They even penetrated Asia Minor. The Alamanni, a Germanic people, swept across the Danube. At one point they entered Italy and reached Milan before they were beaten back. Meanwhile the Franks, still another Germanic folk, hit the Rhine frontier. The Franks then invaded eastern and central Gaul and northeastern Spain. Saxons from Scandinavia sailed into the English Channel in search of loot. In the East the Sassanids overran Mesopotamia. If the army had been guarding the borders instead of creating and destroying emperors, none of these invasions would have been possible. The barracks emperors should be credited with one accomplishment, however: they fought barbarians when they were not fighting each other. Only that kept the empire from total ruin.

Turmoil in Farm and Village Life

How did the ordinary people cope with this period of iron and blood? What did it mean to the lives of men and women on farms and in villages? How did local officials continue to serve their emperor and neighbors? Some people became outlaws. Others lived more prosaically. Some voiced their grievances to the emperor, thereby leaving a record of the problems they faced.

In a surprising number of cases barbarians were less of a problem than lawless soldiers, imperial officials, and local agents. For many ordinary people official corruption was the tangible and immediate result of the breakdown of central authority. In one instance some tenant farmers in Lydia (modern Turkey) complained to the emperor about arbitrary arrest and the killing of prisoners. They claimed that police agents had threatened them and prevented them from cultivating the land. Tenant farmers in Phrygia (also in modern Turkey) voiced similar complaints. They suffered extortion at the hands of public officials. Military commanders, soldiers, and imperial agents requisitioned their livestock and compelled the farmers to forced labor. The farmers were becoming impoverished, and many people deserted the land to seek safety elsewhere. The inhabitants of an entire village in Thrace (modern Bulgaria) complained that they were being driven from their homes. From imperial and local officials they suffered insolence and violence. Soldiers demanded to be quartered and given supplies. Many villagers had already abandoned their homes to escape. The remaining villagers warned the emperor that, unless order was restored, they too would flee.

Local officials were sometimes unsympathetic or violent toward farmers and villagers because of their own plight. They were responsible for the collection of imperial revenues. If their area could not meet its tax quota, they paid the deficit from their own pockets. Because the local officials were themselves so hard-pressed, they squeezed whatever they could from the villagers and farmers.

Reconstruction Under Diocletian and Constantine (A.D. 284–337)

At the close of the third century A.D. the emperor Diocletian (r. 284–305) put an end to the period of turmoil. Repairing the damage done in the third century was the major work of the emperor Constantine (r. 306–337) in the fourth. But the price was high.

Under Diocletian, Augustus's polite fiction of the emperor as first among equals gave way to the emperor as absolute autocrat. The princeps became *dominus*—"lord." The emperor claimed that he was "the elect of God"—that he ruled because of God's favor. Constantine even claimed to be the equal of Jesus' first twelve followers. To underline the emperor's exalted position, Diocletian and Constantine adopted the gaudy court ceremonies and trappings of the Persian Empire. People entering the emperor's presence prostrated themselves before him and kissed the hem of his robes. Constantine went so far as to import Persian eunuchs to run the palace. The Roman emperor had become an oriental monarch.

No mere soldier, but rather an adroit administrator, Diocletian gave serious thought to the empire's ailments. He recognized that the empire and its difficulties had become too great for one man to handle. He also realized that during the third century provincial governors had frequently used their positions to foment or participate in rebellions. To solve the first of these problems, Diocletian divided the empire into a western and an eastern half (Map 6.4). Diocletian assumed direct control of the eastern part; he gave the rule of the western part to a colleague, along with the title *augustus,* which had become synonymous with emperor. Diocletian and his fellow augustus further delegated power by appointing two men to assist them. Each man was given the title of *caesar* to indicate his exalted rank. Although this system is known as the *Tetrarchy* because four men ruled the empire, Diocletian was clearly the senior partner and final source of authority.

Each half of the empire was further split into two prefectures, each governed by a prefect responsible to an augustus. Diocletian reduced the power of the old provincial governors by dividing provinces into smaller units. He organized the prefectures into small administrative units called *dioceses,* which were in turn subdivided into small provinces. Provincial governors were also deprived of their military power, leaving them only civil and administrative duties.

Diocletian's political reforms were a momentous step. The Tetrarchy soon failed, but Diocletian's division of the empire into two parts became permanent. Constantine and later emperors tried hard but unsuccessfully to keep the empire together. Throughout the fourth century A.D. the eastern and the western sections drifted apart. In later centuries the western part witnessed the fall of Roman government and the rise of barbarian kingdoms, while the eastern empire evolved into the majestic Byzantine Empire.

The most serious immediate matters confronting Diocletian and Constantine were economic, social, and religious. They needed additional revenues to support the army and the imperial court. Yet the wars and the barbarian invasions had caused widespread destruction and poverty. The fighting had struck a serious blow to Roman agriculture, which the emperors tried to revive. Christianity had become too strong either to ignore or to crush. The responses to these problems by Diocletian, Constantine, and their successors helped create the economic and social patterns that medieval Europe inherited.

Diocletian's Tetrarchy The emperor Diocletian's attempt to reform the Roman Empire by dividing rule among four men is represented in this piece of sculpture, which in many features illustrates the transition from ancient to medieval art. Here the four tetrarchs demonstrate their solidarity by clasping one another on the shoulder. Nonetheless each man has his other hand on his sword—a gesture that proved prophetic when Diocletian's reign ended and another struggle for power began. *(Alinari/Art Resource, NY)*

Inflation and Taxes

The barracks emperors had dealt with economic hardship by depreciating the currency, cutting the silver content of coins until money was virtually worthless. As a result, the entire monetary system fell into ruin. In Egypt governors had to order bankers to accept imperial money. The immediate result was crippling inflation throughout the empire.

The empire was less capable of recovery than in earlier times. Wars and invasions had disrupted normal commerce and the means of production. Mines were exhausted in the attempt to supply much-needed ores, especially gold and silver. The turmoil had hit the cities especially hard. Markets were disrupted, and travel became dangerous. Craftsmen, artisans, and traders rapidly left devastated regions. The prosperous industry and commerce of Gaul and the Rhineland declined markedly. Those who owed their prosperity to commerce and the needs of urban life likewise suffered. Cities were no longer places where trade and industry thrived. The devastation of the countryside increased the difficulty of feeding and supplying the cities. The destruction was so extensive that many wondered whether the ravages could be repaired at all.

The response of Diocletian and Constantine to these problems was marked by compulsion, rigidity, and loss of individual freedom. Diocletian's attempt to curb inflation illustrates the methods of absolute monarchy. In a move unprecedented in Roman history, he issued an

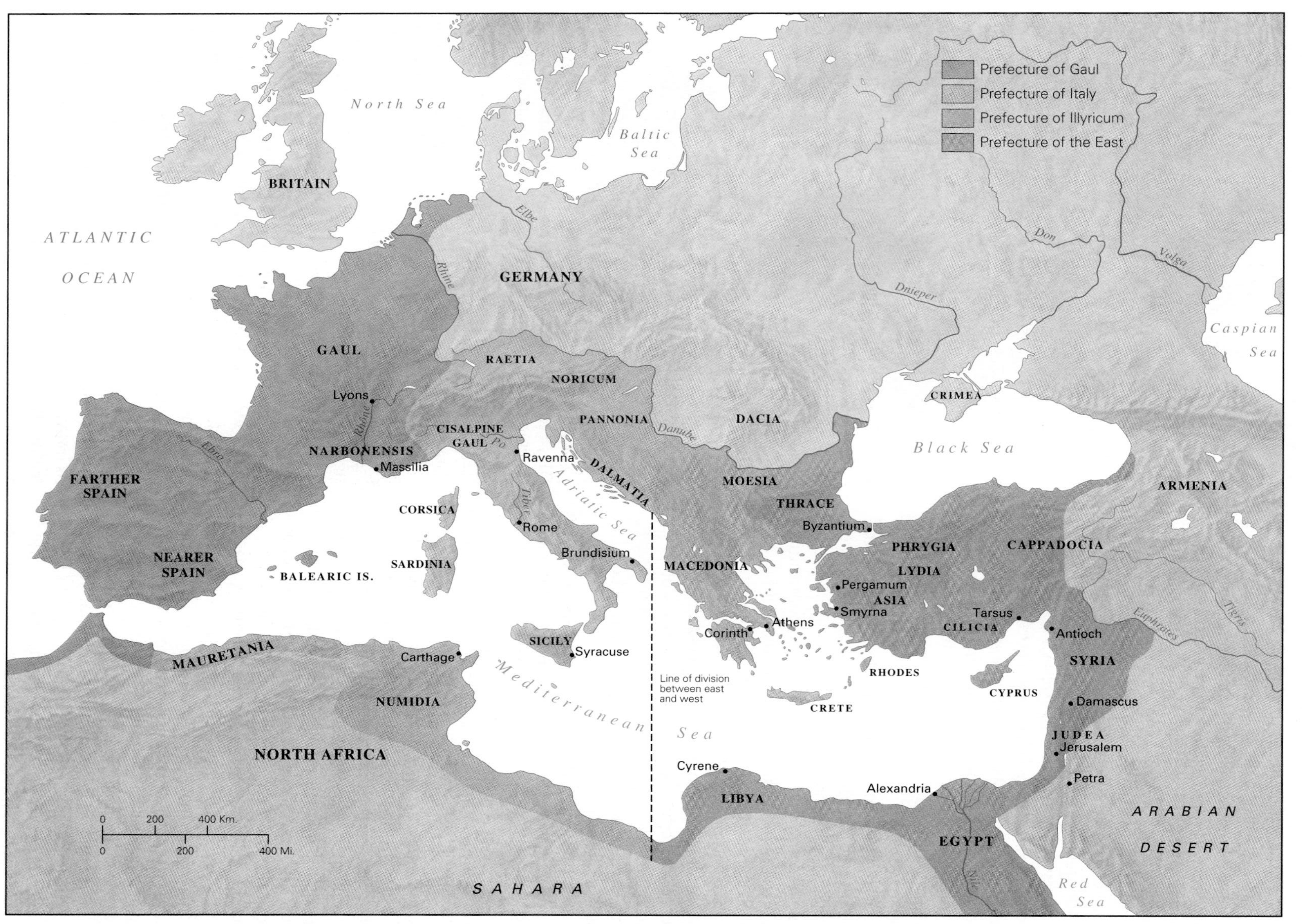

Prefecture of Gaul
Prefecture of Italy
Prefecture of Illyricum
Prefecture of the East
North Sea
Baltic Sea
BRITAIN
ATLANTIC OCEAN
Elbe
Rhine
GERMANY
Don
Volga
Dnieper
Caspian Sea
GAUL
RAETIA
NORICUM
Lyons
Rhône
PANNONIA
Danube
DACIA
CRIMEA
Black Sea
CISALPINE GAUL
Po
Ebro
NARBONENSIS
Massilia
Ravenna
DALMATIA
Adriatic Sea
FARTHER SPAIN
CORSICA
Tiber
Rome
MOESIA
THRACE
ARMENIA
Byzantium
PHRYGIA
CAPPADOCIA
NEARER SPAIN
BALEARIC IS.
SARDINIA
Brundisium
MACEDONIA
LYDIA
Pergamum
ASIA
Smyrna
Tarsus
CILICIA
Antioch
Euphrates
Tigris
Athens
Corinth
SICILY
Syracuse
MAURETANIA
Carthage
Mediterranean Sea
SYRIA
RHODES
Line of division between east and west
CYPRUS
CRETE
NUMIDIA
Damascus
JUDEA
Jerusalem
Petra
NORTH AFRICA
Cyrene
LIBYA
Alexandria
ARABIAN DESERT
0 200 400 Km.
0 200 400 Mi.
EGYPT
Nile
Red Sea
SAHARA

edict that fixed maximum prices and wages throughout the empire. The measure proved a failure because it was unrealistic as well as unenforceable.

The emperors dealt with the tax system just as strictly and inflexibly. As in the past, local officials bore the responsibility of collecting imperial taxes. Constantine made these officials into a hereditary class; son followed father whether he wanted to or not. In this period of severe depression many localities could not pay their taxes. In such cases these local officials had to make up the difference from their own funds. This system soon wiped out a whole class of moderately wealthy people. It was a bad policy for everyone involved.

With the monetary system in ruins, most imperial taxes became payable in kind—that is, in goods or produce instead of money. The major drawback of payment in kind is its demands on transportation. Goods have to be moved from where they are grown or manufactured to where they are needed. Accordingly, the emperors locked into their occupations all those involved in the growing, preparation, and transportation of food and essential commodities. A baker or shipper could not go into any other business, and his son took up the trade at his death. The late Roman Empire had a place for everyone, and everyone had a place.

The Decline of Small Farms

The late Roman heritage to the medieval world is most obvious in agriculture. Because of worsening conditions, free tenant farmers were reduced to serfdom. During the third century A.D. many were killed, fled the land to escape the barbarians, or abandoned farms ravaged in the fighting. Consequently, large tracts of land lay deserted. Great landlords with ample resources began at once to reclaim as much of this land as they could. The huge estates that resulted were the forerunners of medieval manors. Like manors, these villas were self-sufficient. Because they often produced more than they consumed, they successfully competed with the declining cities by selling their surplus in the countryside. They became islands of stability in an unsettled world.

While the villas were growing, the small farmers who remained on the land barely held their own. They were too poor and powerless to stand against the tide of chaos. They were exposed to the raids of barbarians or brigands and to the tyranny of imperial officials. For relief they turned to the great landlords. After all, the landowners were men of considerable resources, lords in their own right. They were wealthy and had many people working their land. They were independent and capable of defending themselves. If need be, they could—and at times did—field a small force of their own. Already influential, the landowning class united in protest against the demands of imperial officials.

In return for the protection and security landlords could offer, the small landholders gave over their lands. Free men and their families became clients of the landlords and lost much of their freedom. To guarantee a steady supply of labor, the landlords bound them to the soil. They could no longer decide to move elsewhere. Henceforth they and their families worked their patrons' land, not their own. Free men and women were in effect becoming serfs.

MAP 6.4 The Roman World Divided Under Diocletian, the Roman Empire was first divided into a western and an eastern half, a development that foreshadowed the medieval division between the Latin West and the Byzantine East.

The Acceptance of Christianity

In religious affairs Constantine took the decisive step of recognizing Christianity as a legitimate religion. No longer would Christians suffer persecution for their beliefs as they had occasionally experienced earlier. Constantine himself died a Christian in 337. Why had the pagans persecuted Christians in the first place? Polytheism is by nature tolerant of new gods and accommodating in religious matters. Why was Christianity singled out for violence? Such questions as these are still matters of scholarly debate to which some broad answers can be given.

A splendid approach to these problems has come from the eminent Italian scholar Marta Sordi.[14] Confronting a very complicated topic, she distinguishes among many different phases in the relationship between Christianity and official Roman acceptance of it. The Christians exaggerated the degree of pagan hostility to them, and most of the gory stories about the martyrs are fictitious. There were indeed some cases of pagan persecution of the Christians, but with few exceptions they were local and sporadic in nature. Even Nero's notorious persecution was temporary and limited to Rome. No constant persecution of Christians occurred. Instead, pagans and Christians alike enjoyed long periods of tolerance and even friendship. Nonetheless, some pagans thought that Christians were atheists because they scorned the traditional pagan gods. Christians in fact either denied the existence of pagan gods or called them evil spirits. They went so far as to urge people not to worship pagan gods. In turn pagans, who believed in their gods as fervently as the Christians theirs, feared that the gods would withdraw their favor from the Roman Empire because of Christian blasphemy.

At first many pagans genuinely misunderstood Christian practices and rites. Even educated and cultured people like the historian Tacitus opposed Christianity because they saw it as a bizarre new sect. Tacitus believed that Christians hated the whole human race. As a rule early Christians kept to themselves. Romans distrusted and feared their exclusiveness, which seemed unsociable and even subversive. They thought that such secret rites as the Lord's Supper, at which Christians said that they ate and drank the body and blood of Jesus, were acts of cannibalism. Pagans also thought that Christians indulged in immoral and indecent rituals. They considered Christianity one of the worst of the oriental mystery cults, for one of the hallmarks of many of those cults was disgusting rituals.

Another source of misunderstanding was that the pagans did not demand that Christians *believe* in pagan gods. Greek and Roman religion was never a matter of belief or ethics. It was purely a religion of ritual. One of the clearest statements of pagan theological attitudes comes from the Roman senator Symmachus in the late fourth century A.D.:

> *We watch the same stars; heaven is the same for us all; the same universe envelops us: what importance is it in what way anyone looks for truth? It is impossible to arrive by one route at such a great secret.*[15]

Yet Roman religion was inseparable from the state. An attack on one was an attack on the other. The Romans were being no more fanatical or intolerant than the eighteenth-century English judge who declared the Christian religion part of the law of the land. All the pagans expected was performance of the ritual act, a small token of sacrifice. Those Christians who sacrificed went free, no matter what they personally believed.

As time went on, pagan hostility decreased. Pagans realized that Christians were not working to overthrow the state and that Jesus was no rival of Caesar. The emperor Trajan forbade his governors to hunt down Christians. Trajan admitted that he thought Christianity an abomination, but he preferred to leave Christians in peace.

The stress of the third century, however, seemed to some emperors the punishment of the gods. What else could account for such anarchy? With the empire threatened on every side, a few emperors thought that one way to appease the gods was by offering them the proper sacrifices. Such sacrifices would be a sign of loyalty to the empire, a show of Roman solidarity and religious piety. Consequently, a new wave of persecutions began out of desperation. Although the Christians depicted the emperor Diocletian as a fiend, he persecuted them in the hope that gods would restore their blessings on Rome. Yet even these persecutions were never very widespread or long-lived; most pagans were not greatly sympathetic to the new round of persecutions. By the late third century, pagans had become used to Christianity. Constantine's acceptance of Christianity can be seen as the pagans' alliance with the strongest god of them all. Pagan and Christian alike must have been relieved when Constantine legalized the Christian religion.

In time the Christian triumph would be complete. In 380 the emperor Theodosius made Christianity the official religion of the Roman Empire. At that point Christians began to persecute the pagans for their beliefs. History had come full circle.

The Construction of Constantinople

The triumph of Christianity was not the only event that made Constantine's reign a turning point in Roman history. Constantine took the bold step of building a new capital for the empire. Constantinople, the New Rome, was constructed on the site of Byzantium, an old Greek city on the Bosporus. Throughout the third century emperors had found Rome and the West hard to defend. The eastern part of the empire was more easily defensible and escaped the worst of the barbarian devastation. It was wealthy and its urban life still vibrant. Moreover Christianity was more widespread in the East than in the West, and the city of Constantinople was intended to be a Christian center.

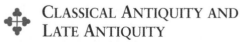

Classical Antiquity and Late Antiquity

Historians commonly divide long time spans into smaller, more workable periods with distinguishing features. The process is called periodization. While traditional students have labeled the thousand years from about 500 B.C. to about A.D. 500 as "classical civilization" or "classical antiquity," some recent scholars have broken that millennium into sections and called the

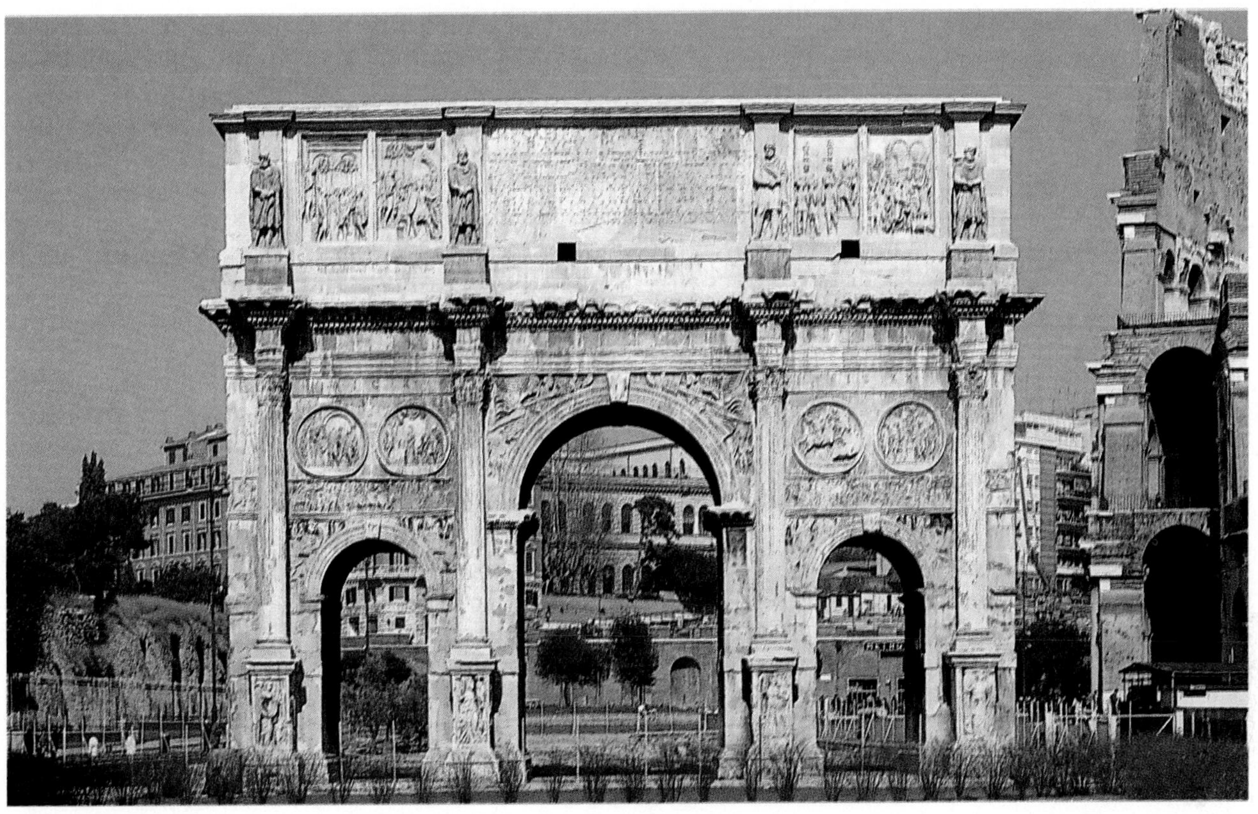

The Arch of Constantine To celebrate the victory that made him emperor, Constantine built his triumphal arch in Rome. Rather than decorate the arch with the inferior work of his own day, Constantine plundered other Roman monuments, including those of Trajan and Marcus Aurelius. *(C. M. Dixon)*

period around A.D. 200 to 700 "late antiquity." During later centuries the Mediterranean world witnessed tremendous religious, social, political, and intellectual ferment. Some features of that period, such as the development of Christian monasticism, the continuation of the eastern Roman (Byzantine) Empire, and the rise and expansion of Islam, are discussed in Chapter 7. As we try to understand late antiquity, several questions come to mind: How did the world of late antiquity differ from the world of the pax Romana? Why did Christianity gradually replace the pagan religious cults? How was imperial rule affected by Christianity? How did the spread of Christianity affect the intellectual elites of the time?

The Roman world of the pax Romana, over which Augustus had extended order, harmony, and security, clustered around the Mediterranean Sea. An aristocracy of uniform culture, taste, and language governed that world. The educated oligarchies that held power in Alexandria, Antioch, and Jerusalem in the East, and the senatorial elites that governed Italy, northern Africa, Gaul, and the Ebro and Guadalquivir regions of the Iberian Peninsula in the West, were bilingual, passing easily from Greek to Latin. A common urbane culture bound together the entire region. By about A.D. 500, however, a clear political, geographical, and cultural division existed between East and West. The East remained Mediterranean centered, ruled by a Roman—that is, Byzantine—emperor. It was primarily urban, and in its populous cities local and long-distance trade played a large role in maintaining a sophisticated and cosmopolitan way of life. In the West Roman imperial power had decayed, as had cities where commerce declined. Economic life meant agriculture, and the increasingly isolated rural villa was becoming the typical form of organized life.

An enormous and widening gulf between rich and poor was probably the most important socioeconomic feature of late antiquity. The western senatorial aristocracy, although a fluid society relatively open to talent from below, possessed five times more wealth than had first-century senators. In the vibrant cities of the eastern parts of the Roman world, the rich enjoyed a lavish way of life. Constantinople, founded in 324, had 4,388 private mansions just a century later. The annual income of a Roman senator in Constantinople might have been 120,000 gold pieces, that of a merchant 200, and that of a peasant only 5.[16] An oppressive and inequitable system of taxation ate up the farmers' produce, forcing many to sell their small plots to the local aristocracy. Sometimes local aristocrats protected the poor from the tax collectors, and since the imperial government could not render justice to the lowest social ranks, that responsibility fell to local elites.

The composition of the Roman army in A.D. 500 was very different from that in 200. In 200 Roman aristocrats led an army of Italian or Mediterranean-born legions. By 500 assimilated Germans (see pages 205–207) held commissions over soldiers from various Germanic tribes.

How did Christianity differ from the official state religion and the oriental cults of second-century Rome, and why did it eventually replace those religions? Christianity was inclusive and egalitarian, and its requirements were explicit. The Roman state religion was a matter of social ritual in which one participated as a matter of civic duty. So long as a person did his or her formal religious duty, neither the state religion nor the oriental cults opposed participation in other religious observances. The Eastern cults and the Roman state practiced what we would call toleration. Christianity, however, demanded conversion, a conscious turning toward and acceptance of the teachings of Jesus and an attempt to live one's life according to those teachings. In its intolerance of other faiths and cults Christianity was thoroughly exclusive: it denied or forbade any involvement in the rites of other religions. Intermittent persecution of Christians, leading to the creation of *martyrs,* or witnesses to Christian belief, backfired and served to attract more Christian converts.

Christians professed, and according to the evidence of the Acts of the Apostles lived, an egalitarian life. Paul had told the Christians of Galatia in central Anatolia (modern Turkey): "There does not exist among you Jew or Greek, slave or freeman, male or female. You are all one in Christ Jesus."[17] A pagan aristocrat might have found such an idea ludicrous and subversive of the social order, but to the half-starving masses of Jerusalem or Rome, Christian living seemed a remarkable social experience. Christians offered a strong sense of community by maintaining their prayer and Eucharistic services during the third century when Roman public ceremonies and processions were declining; offering spiritual support and encouragement to people who felt lonely or isolated in large urban environments; and financially assisting not only local but also distant Christian communities, as the churches of Rome and Carthage did for fellow believers in Cappadocia and Africa in 256.[18] Community, an idea adopted from the Jews, had strong appeal.

Christianity began and spread as an urban religion. Between 200 and 500, as Roman civic officials neglected or were unable to perform their duties, or as they retreated from the cities to live leisurely lives on their country estates, Christian bishops or ecclesiastical officials assumed public responsibilities. When imperial authorities failed to repair pipes or aqueducts, essential for the supply of drinking water, Christian bishops took over that secular function. When flood, drought, or crop failure threatened famine, bishops executed measures for public relief. For example, in 535–536 Bishop Datius of Milan arranged for the distribution of grain and set prices for other necessities. When the Tiber River overflowed its banks in Rome because urban authorities had put off repairs, bishops such as Pope Gregory I (590–604) repaired the banks. In 340, when German chieftains threatened to attack Nisibis (modern southeastern Turkey), Bishop Jacob organized the city's defenses. Likewise when the Huns menaced Rome in the fifth century, Pope Leo I (440–461) successfully negotiated with the enemy. These public activities of Christian officials enhanced their prestige and that of the people they represented. Such actions also reflect the shift of public power between A.D. 200 and 500 from imperial authorities to Christian bishops.[19]

Finally, in the intellectual sphere a sharp boundary between the urbane, bilingual, "high culture" of the educated aristocrat and the "popular culture" of the broad masses existed in the Mediterranean world of classical antiquity. The aristocratic ideal was *otium,* or "leisure," in which to develop the mind. The aristocratic Roman enjoyed a "secular" culture independent of any government supervision, was tolerant of or indifferent to religious differences, and considered reflection on such philosophical questions as "What is truth?" and "What is beauty?" to be the goal of a civilized life. In this world around A.D. 200 Christians were a small and insignificant minority.

By about 600, however, not only was Christianity the dominant religion, but society was almost totally Christian. The pagan, senatorial, educated elite had either disappeared or, like Bishop Ambrose of Milan (374–397), become Christians and even bishops. Bishops were busy men with scant time for leisurely thought. About 600 a Roman priest wrote, "We think no one nowadays can boast much learning. Here the fury of the barbarians burns daily. . . . Our whole life is taken up in cares, and all our efforts go to beating back the war bands that surround us." What they needed was not cultivated leisure but simple, basic literacy. Even if church officials had the time, they neither wanted to study pagan writers nor allowed their people to do so, as the bishops feared that the people would learn pagan superstitions. Bishop Caesarius of Arles (502–542) in southeastern France looked with deep hostility on non-Christian literature and pagan practices. In the East, where ancient Greek texts remained accessible, small circles of intellectuals sometimes were allowed to continue, provided they posed no threat to the church. In 529 the emperor Justinian (see pages 226–230) issued a decree prohibiting pagans from holding positions in public education. This led to the closing of the Academy of Athens, for a millennium a major center for the education of bright young men of the eastern Mediterranean. Justinian's purpose was to make the schools of Constantinople superior and to substitute Christian doctrine for Greek philosophy in the curriculum. In the West very few people knew or cared about Greek learning, and churchmen were very suspicious of "wisdom from outside"; they preferred the revealed truths of Scripture.[20]

By about 600 people generally identified themselves by their Christian religion: "He did not owe allegiance to a state; he belonged to a religious community."[21] (In Chapter 7 we will see that Muslims had an identical attitude.) The religious leaders provided the culture. What of the pagan nonbeliever or the Jew? Whereas classical culture had displayed an urbane tolerance, by the sixth century anyone outside Christianity was virtually an outlaw. In Spain, Byzantium, and North Africa this atmosphere of intolerance led to the savage persecution of Jews and the few remaining pagans. Once the Christian church was able to direct the religious life of the old Roman world, it adapted or severely restricted Roman culture.

SUMMARY

The Roman emperors expanded the provincial system established during the republic. They gave it more definite organization, both militarily to defend it and bureaucratically to administer it. The result was the pax Romana, a period of peace and prosperity for the empire. Into this climate came Christianity, which was able to spread throughout the Roman world because peace and security made communication within the empire safe and easy. Christianity satisfied people's emotional and spiritual needs in ways that traditional pagan religions did not. Although other mystery religions existed, they were normally exclusive in one way or another. Christianity was open to all, rich and poor, men and women. Paul of Tarsus was the first of many talented Christians to spread the new religion throughout the receptive world. But that world was disrupted in the third century by a combination of barbarian invasions, civil wars, and economic decline. The bonds that held the empire together weakened, and only the herculean efforts of the emperors Diocletian and Constantine restored order. Those emperors repulsed the barbarians, defeated rebellious generals, and reformed the economy in a restrictive way. The result was an empire very changed from the time of the Augustan peace, but one that left an enduring legacy for later generations.

NOTES

1. Virgil, *Aeneid* 6.851–853. John Buckler is the translator of all uncited quotations from a foreign language in Chapters 1–6.
2. Augustus, *Res Gestae* 6.34.
3. Ibid., 5.28.
4. Horace, *Odes* 4.15.
5. Virgil, *Georgics* 3.515–519.
6. Ovid, *Fasti* 4.925.
7. Matthew 3:3.
8. Helmut Koester, in *Colloquy on New Testament Studies*, ed. B. Corley (Macon, Ga.: Mercer University Press, 1983), p. 77.
9. Acts 17:26.
10. Matthew 16:18.
11. Edward Gibbon, *The History of the Decline and Fall of the Roman Empire* (New York: Modern Library, n.d.), 1.1.
12. *Corpus Inscriptionum Latinarum*, vol. 6 (Berlin: G. Reimer, 1882), no. 9792.
13. Ibid., vol. 6, no. 14672.
14. See Marta Sordi, *The Christians and the Roman Empire* (London: Croom Helm, 1986).
15. Symmachus, *Relations* 3.10.
16. See Peter Brown, *The World of Late Antiquity, A.D. 150–750* (New York: W. W. Norton, 1989), pp. 34–36. This section leans on Brown's rich study.
17. Galatians 3:28.
18. Brown, *World of Late Antiquity*, p. 67.

19. See Judith Herrin, *The Formation of Christendom* (Princeton, N.J.: Princeton University Press, 1987), pp. 72–75.
20. Ibid., p. 76.
21. Brown, *World of Late Antiquity,* p. 186.

Suggested Reading

Some good general treatments of the empire include P. Garnsey and R. Saller, *The Roman Empire* (1987); and J. Wacher, ed., *The Roman World,* 2 vols. (1987), which attempts a comprehensive survey of the world of the Roman Empire. A recent general statement comes from M. Goodman, *The Roman World, 44 B.C.–A.D. 180* (1997). C. M. Wells, *The German Policy of Augustus* (1972), uses archaeological findings to illustrate Roman expansion into northern Europe. H. Schutz, *The Romans in Central Europe* (1985), treats Roman expansion, its problems, and its successes in a vital area of the empire. C. R. Wittaker, *Frontiers of the Roman Empire* (1994), is a social and economic account of how Roman expansion on the frontiers affected life there. How the Romans kept in touch with their empire is the theme of N. J. E. Austin, *Exploratio* (1995), a study of Roman military and political intelligence. H. Parkins, ed., *Roman Urbanism* (1997), demonstrates that Rome was more than a city of consumers and illustrates Rome's links to the world around it. J. Lendon, *Empire of Honour* (1997), explores how the imperial government used art to glorify Roman rule. Two new studies shed light on ordinary social history: B. J. Brooten, *Love Between Women* (1996), examines early Christian responses to lesbianism; J. M. C. Toynbee, *Death and Burial in the Roman World* (1996), comprehensively examines all aspects of Roman religious practices and beliefs in an afterlife. In *The Augustan Aristocracy* (1985), one of the great Roman historians of this century, R. Syme, studies the new order that Augustus created to help him administer the empire. Rather than study the Augustan poets individually, see D. A. West and A. J. Woodman, *Poetry and Politics in the Age of Augustus* (1984).

Even though Augustus himself still remains an enigma, F. Millar and E. Segal, eds., *Caesar Augustus: Seven Aspects* (1984), is an interesting volume of essays that attempts, not always successfully, to penetrate the official façade of the emperor. Several books examine the reigns of some supposedly unpopular emperors. D. Shotter, *Tiberius Caesar* (1993), presents the most recent biography of this controversial emperor. Shotter continues his work on the emperors in *Nero* (1997). A. Ferrill does the same for his subject in *Caligula, Emperor of Rome* (1992). B. W. Jones, *The Emperor Domitian* (1992), is an attempt to understand this often hated emperor.

Work on the Roman army includes M. Speidel, *Roman Army Studies,* vol. 1 (1984), and L. Keppie, *The Making of the Roman Army from Republic to Empire* (1984). The army that carried out the emperor's strategy is the subject of G. Webster, *The Roman Imperial Army* (1969). R. MacMullen, *Enemies of the Roman Order* (1993), treats the ways in which the Romans dealt with alien and sometimes hostile behavior within the empire. More specific is V. Rudich, *Political Dissidence Under Nero* (1993), an unorthodox treatment of the subject that examines the reasons behind some popular rejections of official policy. D. J. Breeze and B. Dobson, *Roman Officers and Frontiers* (1993), analyzes the careers of officers and how they defended the frontiers.

The commercial life of the empire is the subject of K. Greene, *The Archaeology of the Roman Economy* (1986), which offers an intriguing way to picture the Roman economy through physical remains. The classic treatment, which ranges across the empire, is M. Rostovtzeff, *The Economic and Social History of the Roman Empire* (1957). P. W. de Neeve, *Colonies: Private Farm-Tenancy in Roman Italy* (1983), covers agriculture and the styles of landholding from the republic to the early empire. J. Rich, *The City in Late Antiquity* (1992), traces the influence of late Roman cities on their medieval successors. J. D. Deiss, *Herculaneum* (1989), describes one of the most important sites in Italy and reconstructs the lives of its people.

Social aspects of the empire are the subject of R. MacMullen, *Roman Social Relations, 50 B.C. to A.D. 284* (1981). Another contribution is L. A. Thompson, *Romans and Blacks* (1989). An important feature of Roman history is addressed in R. P. Saller, *Personal Patronage Under the Early Empire* (1982). J. Humphrey, *Roman Circuses and Chariot Racing* (1985), treats a topic very dear to the hearts of ancient Romans. C. A. Barton, *The Sorrows of the Ancient Romans* (1993), is an intriguing and daring attempt to understand the Roman fascination for gladiatorial games. K. R. Bradley, *Slaves and Masters in the Roman Empire* (1988), discusses social controls in a slaveholding society. Last, B. Cunliffe, *Greeks, Romans and Barbarians* (1988), uses archaeological and literary evidence to discuss the introduction of Greco-Roman culture into western Europe.

A veritable explosion has taken place in the related topics of the identity of Jesus, the history of early Christianity, its relationship to contemporary Judaism, and the role that paganism played in these developments. J. D. Crossan, *The Historical Jesus* (1992), puts Jesus in the garb of a Mediterranean Jewish peasant, not in a disrespectful way but in the context of his environment. Related are J. Meier, *A Marginal Jew* (1992); and P. Fredriksen, *From Jesus to Christ* (1988), which studies the images of Jesus in the New Testament. J. E. Powell, *The Evolution of the Gospel* (1994), examines the Gospel of Matthew and argues that it was the first Gospel written. Perhaps more challenging is B. L. Mack, *The Lost Gospel of Q* (1993), which traces the earliest elements of the Gospels. Both S. G. Burnett, *From Christian Hebraism to Jewish Studies*

(1996), and J. H. Hexter, *The Judaeo-Christian Tradition,* 2d ed. (1995), deal with Judaism and Christianity in their mutual impact. Social history of early Christianity includes H. Y. Gamble, *Books and Readers in the Early Christian Church* (1995), which examines the extent of the dissemination of the Christian message and its importance to early Christian communities. H. G. Kee, *Who Are the People of God?* (1994), explores early Christian origins in the context of Jewish culture. Also helpful is H. Moxnes, ed., *Constructing Early Christian Families* (1997). A new approach to early Christian society is D. F. Sawyer, *Women and Religion in the First Christian Centuries* (1996). F. R. Trombley, *Hellenic Religion and Christianization, c. 370–529,* 2 vols. (1993), is an excellent examination of how Greek religion influenced the development of Christianity in the eastern parts of the later Roman Empire.

Convenient surveys of Roman literature are J. W. Duff, *Literary History of Rome from the Origins to the Close of the Golden Age* (1953) and *Literary History of Rome in the Silver Age,* 3d ed. (1964). New treatments of two of the most important Augustan poets are C. Kallendorf, ed., *Virgil* (1993); and W. S. Anderson, ed., *Ovid* (1993).

Ever since E. Gibbon's *History of the Decline and Fall of the Roman Empire,* one of the masterpieces of English literature, the decline of the empire has been a fertile field of investigation. J. Bennett, *Trajan, Optimus Princeps* (1997), gives an account of the emperor who sought to expand the empire. S. Perowne, *Hadrian* (1987), explores the emperor who tried to stabilize the military situation. Broader are A. M. H. Jones, *The Decline of the Ancient World* (1966); and F. W. Walbank, *The Awful Revolution* (1969). S. N. C. Lieu and M. Dodgeon, *Rome's Eastern Frontier, A.D. 226–363* (1988), relies primarily on documents to trace Rome's policy in the East during this difficult period. Two studies analyze the attempts at recovery from the breakdown of the barracks emperors: T. D. Barnes, *The New Empire of Diocletian and Constantine* (1982), which, as its title indicates, focuses on the necessary innovations made by the two emperors; and, more narrowly, S. Williams, *Diocletian and the Roman Recovery,* rev. ed. (1996). A. Ferrill, *The Fall of the Roman Empire* (1986), with plans and illustrations, offers a military explanation for the "fall." R. MacMullen, *Constantine* (1988), provides a broad and lucid interpretation of Constantine and the significance of his reign. MacMullen is a leading scholar in the field. A more recent study is H. A. Pohlsander, *The Emperor Constantine* (1997).

LISTENING TO THE PAST

Rome Extends Its Citizenship

One of the most dramatic achievements of the pax Romana was the extension of citizenship throughout the Roman Empire. People who had never visited Rome, and perhaps had never even seen a provincial governor, became members, not subjects, of their government. By granting citizenship to most people in the empire, the Roman government in effect took them into partnership.

Yet various emperors went even further by viewing Rome not only as a territorial but also as a political concept. In their eyes Rome was a place and *an idea. Not every Roman agreed with these cosmopolitan views. Emperor Claudius (41–54) took the first major step in this direction by allowing Romanized Gauls to sit in the senate. He was roundly criticized by some Romans, but in the damaged stone inscription that follows, he presents his own defense.*

Surely both my great-uncle, the deified Augustus, and my uncle, Tiberius Caesar, were following a new practice when they desired that all the flower of the colonies and the municipalities everywhere—that is, the better class and the wealthy men—should sit in this senate house. You ask me: Is not an Italian senator preferable to a provincial? I shall reveal to you in detail my views on this matter when I come to obtain approval for this part of my censorship [a magistracy that determined who was eligible for citizenship and public offices]. But I think that not even provincials ought to be excluded, provided that they can add distinction to this senate house.

Look at that most distinguished and most flourishing colony of Vienna [the modern Vienne in France], how long a time already it is that it has furnished senators to this house! From that colony comes that ornament of the equestrian order—and there are few to equal him—Lucius Vestinus, whom I cherish most intimately and whom at this very time I employ in my affairs. And it is my desire that his children may enjoy the first step in the priesthoods, so as to advance afterwards, as they grow older, to further honors in their rank. . . . I can say the same of his brother, who because of this wretched and most shameful circumstance cannot be a useful senator for you.

The time has now come, Tiberius Caesar Germanicus [Claudius himself], now that you have reached the farthest boundaries of Narbonese Gaul, for you to unveil to the members of the senate the import of your address. All these distinguished youths whom I gaze upon will no more give us cause for regret if they become senators than does my friend Persicus, a man of most noble ancestry, have cause for regret when he reads among the portraits of his ancestors the name Allobrogicus. But if you agree that these things are so, what more do you want, when I point out to you this single fact, that the territory beyond the boundaries of Narbonese Gaul already sends you senators, since we have men of our order from Lyons and have no cause for regret. It is indeed with hesitation, members of the senate, that I have gone outside the borders of the provinces with which you are accustomed and familiar, but I must now plead openly the cause of Gallia Comata [a region in modern France]. And if anyone, in this connection, has in mind that these people engaged the deified Julius in war for ten years, let him set against that the unshakable loyalty and obedience of a hundred years, tested to the full in many of our crises. When my father Drusus was subduing Germany, it was they who by their tranquility afforded him a safe and securely peaceful rear, even at a time when he had been summoned away to the war from the task of organizing the census which was still new and unaccustomed to the Gauls. How difficult such an operation is for us at this precise moment we are learning all too well from experience, even though the survey is aimed at nothing more than an official record of our resources. [The rest of the inscription is lost.]

Only later, in A.D. 212, did the emperor Caracalla (198–217) extend Roman citizenship to all freeborn men with the exception of those called dediticii, *whose identity remains a source of controversy. Caracalla claimed that he made this proclamation because the gods had saved him from a plot on his life. Some modern scholars, however, have suggested that he wanted more citizens to tax. Whatever the truth, Caracalla continued the work of Augustus (27 B.C.–A.D. 14) and Claudius. The Romans succeeded where the Greeks had failed: they built an empire of citizens. The following is a damaged copy of Caracalla's edict.*

The Emperor Caesar Marcus Aurelius Serverus Antoninus Augustus [Caracalla] declares: . . . I may show my gratitude to the immortal gods for preserving me in such [circumstances?]. Therefore I consider that in this way I can . . . rend proper service to their majesty . . . by bringing with me to the worship [?] of the gods all who enter into the number of my people. Accordingly, I grant Roman citizenship to all aliens, throughout the world, with no one remaining outside the citizen bodies except the *dediticii.* For it is proper that the multitude should not only help carry [?] all the burdens but should also now be included in my victory.

Citizenship was often granted to soldiers who had fought in the Roman army. The usual reasons were conspicuous bravery or wounds suffered in the course of duty. The emperor Trajan (98–117) made such a grant of citizenship in 106 to British soldiers who had served in the campaign in Dacia, a southern region of the former Yugoslavia. These men were also honored for their valor with an early discharge.

The Emperor Trajan . . . has granted Roman citizenship before completion of military service to the infantrymen and cavalrymen whose names appear below, serving in the First British Thousand-Man Ulpian Decorated Loyal Fortunate Cohort composed of Roman citizens, which is on duty in Dacia under Decimus Terentius Scaurianus, for having dutifully and faithfully discharged the Dacian campaign.

✣ *Provocatio,* the right of appeal, was considered a fundamental element of Roman citizenship. (*Courtesy of the Trustees of the British Museum*)

Questions for Analysis

1. What was the basic justification underlying Claudius's decision to allow Gallic nobles to sit in the senate? Did he see them as debasing the quality of the senate?
2. What do his words tell us about the changing nature of the Roman Empire?
3. What was the significance of Caracalla's extension of Roman citizenship to all freeborn men?
4. Notice that the Roman government did not extend citizenship to women. Speculate about the practical and ideological reasons for women's exclusion from political power.

Source: Slightly adapted and abbreviated from N. Lewis and M. Reinhold, *Roman Civilization,* 2 vols. Copyright © 1966 by Columbia University Press, New York. Reprinted with permission of the publisher.

CHAPTER

7 The Making of Europe

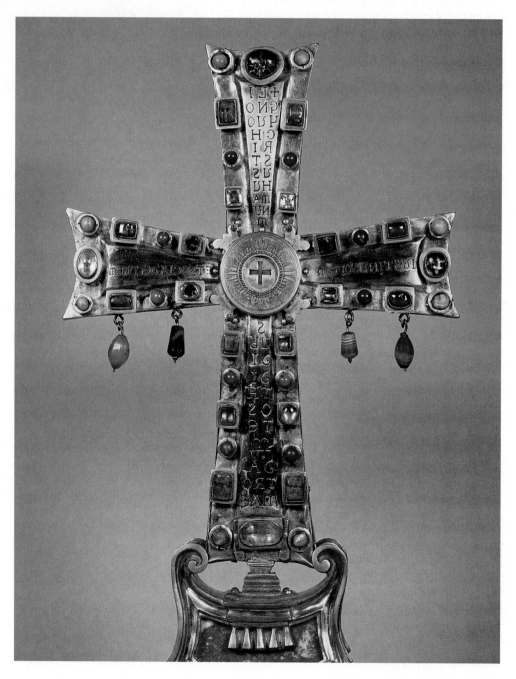

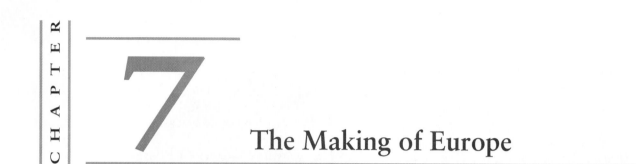

Byzantine cross. Justin II gave this cross to Pope John III; it was one of very few not destroyed in the sack of Rome in 1527. *(Scala/Art Resource, NY)*

The centuries between approximately 400 and 900 present a paradox. On the one hand, they witnessed the disintegration of the western Roman Empire, which had been one of humanity's great political and cultural achievements. On the other hand, these five centuries were a creative and seminal period, during which Europeans laid the foundations for medieval and modern Europe. It is not too much to say that this period saw the making of Europe.

The idea of Europe—with the geographical and cultural implications that we in the late twentieth century attach to the word—is actually a fairly recent notion. Classical geographers used the term *Europe* to distinguish it from Africa and Asia, the only other landmasses they knew, and medieval scholars imitated and followed the ancients. Only in the sixteenth century did the word *Europe* enter the common language of educated peoples living in the western parts of the European landmass and did the continent we call Europe gain a map-based frame of reference.[1] The vision of almost everyone else was provincial, limited by the boundaries of their province or even village. While the peoples living there did not define themselves as European for centuries, a European identity began to be forged in late antiquity and the early medieval period.

The basic ingredients that went into the making of a distinctly European civilization were the cultural legacy of Greece and Rome, the customs and traditions of the Germanic peoples, and the Christian faith. The most important of these was Christianity, because it absorbed and assimilated the other two. It reinterpreted the classics in a Christian sense. It instructed the Germanic peoples and gave them new ideals of living and social behavior. Christianity became the cement that held European society together. One of the burdens of this chapter is to explore how people's understanding of themselves shifted from a social or political one (Germanic or Celtic tribal, Roman citizen) to a religious one.

During this period, the Byzantine Empire, centered at Constantinople, served as a protective buffer between Europe and peoples to the east. The Byzantine Greeks preserved the philosophical and scientific texts of the ancient world, which later formed the basis for study in science and medicine, and produced a great synthesis of Roman law, the Justinian *Code.* In the urbane and sophisticated life led at Constantinople, the Greeks set a standard far above the primitive existence of the West.

In the seventh and eighth centuries, Arabic culture spread around the southern fringes of Europe—to Spain, Sicily, and North Africa, and to Syria, Palestine, and Egypt. The Arabs translated the works of such Greek thinkers as Euclid, Hippocrates, and Galen and made important contributions in mathematics, astronomy, and physics. In Arabic translation, Greek texts trickled to the West, and most later European scientific study rested on the Arabic work.

The civilization later described as European resulted from the fusion of the Greco-Roman heritage, Germanic traditions, the Christian faith, and significant elements of Islamic culture.

- How did these components act on one another?
- How did they lead to the making of Europe?
- What influence did the Byzantine and Islamic cultures have on the making of Europe?

This chapter will focus on these questions.

THE GROWTH OF THE CHRISTIAN CHURCH

Although Christianity had explicit requirements and preached social egalitarianism (see pages 192–193), in doctrine Christianity was a syncretic faith. It absorbed and adopted many of the religious ideas of the eastern Mediterranean world. From Judaism came the concept, unique in the ancient world, of monotheism, belief in one God, together with the rich ethical and moral precepts of the Old Testament Scriptures. From Orphism, a set of sixth-century B.C. religious ideas, came the belief that the body is the prison of the soul. From Hellenistic thought derived the notion of the superiority of spirit over matter. Likewise, scholars have noticed the similarity between the career of Jesus and that of the gods of Eastern mystery cults such as Mithra, who died and rose from the dead, and whose followers had a ceremony of communion in which the god's flesh was symbolically eaten. All of these ideas played a part in the formulation of Christian doctrine and in attracting people to it.

While many elements of the Roman Empire disintegrated, the Christian church survived and grew. What is the church? Scriptural scholars tell us that the earliest use of the word *church,* assembly or congregation (in

Greek, *ekklesia*), in the New Testament appears in Saint Paul's Letter to the Christians of Thessalonica in northern Greece, written about A.D. 51. By *ekklesia* Paul meant the local community of Christian believers. In Paul's later letters, the term *church* refers to the entire Mediterranean-wide assembly of Jesus' followers. After the legalization of Christianity by the emperor Constantine (see page 189) and the growth of institutional offices and officials, the word *church* was sometimes applied to those officials—much as we use the terms *the college* or *the university* when referring to academic administrators.

Roman bishops used the text known as the Petrine Doctrine (see page 201) to support their assertions of authority over the bishops in the church. Thus the popes maintained that they represented "the church." The word *church,* therefore, has several connotations. Although modern Catholic theology frequently defines the church as "the people of God" and identifies it with local and international Christian communities, in the Middle Ages the institutional and monarchial interpretations tended to be stressed.

Having gained the support of the fourth-century emperors, the church gradually adopted the Roman system of organization. Christianity had a dynamic missionary policy, and the church slowly succeeded in assimilating—that is, adapting—pagan peoples, both Germans and Romans, to Christian teaching. Moreover, the church possessed able administrators and leaders and highly literate and creative thinkers. These factors help to explain the survival and growth of the Christian church in the face of repeated Germanic invasions.

The Church and the Roman Emperors

The church benefited considerably from the emperors' support. In return, the emperors expected the support of the Christian church in maintaining order and unity. Constantine had legalized the practice of Christianity within the empire in 312. Although he was not baptized until he was on his deathbed, Constantine encouraged Christianity throughout his reign. He freed the clergy from imperial taxation. At churchmen's request, he helped settle theological disputes and thus preserved doctrinal unity within the church. Constantine generously endowed the building of Christian churches, and one of his gifts—the Lateran Palace in Rome—remained the official residence of the popes until the fourteenth century. Constantine also declared Sunday a public holiday, a day of rest for the service of God. As the result of its favored position in the empire, Christianity slowly became the leading religion.

In 380 the emperor Theodosius went further than Constantine and made Christianity the official religion of the empire. Theodosius stripped Roman pagan temples of statues, made the practice of the old Roman state religion a treasonable offense, and persecuted Christians who dissented from orthodox doctrine. Most significant, he allowed the church to establish its own courts. Church courts began to develop their own body of law, called "canon law." These courts, not the Roman government, had jurisdiction over the clergy and ecclesiastical disputes. At the death of Theodosius, the Christian church was considerably independent of the Roman state. The foundation for the medieval church's power had been laid.

What was to be the church's relationship to secular powers? How was the Christian to render unto Caesar the things that were Caesar's while returning to God what was due to God? This problem had troubled the earliest disciples of Christ. The toleration of Christianity and the coming to power of Christian emperors in the fourth century did not make it any easier.

In the fourth century, theological disputes frequently and sharply divided the Christian community. Some disagreements had to do with the nature of Christ. For example, Arianism, which originated with Arius (ca 250–336), a priest of Alexandria, denied that Christ was divine and co-eternal with God the Father—two propositions of orthodox Christian belief. Arius held that God the Father was by definition uncreated and unchangeable. Jesus, however, was born of Mary, grew in wisdom, and suffered punishment and death. Therefore, Arius reasoned, Jesus the Son must be less or inferior to the Unbegotten Father, who was incapable of suffering and did not die. Jesus was created by the will of the Father and thus was not co-eternal with the Father. This argument implies that Jesus must be somewhere between God the Creator and humanity in need of redemption. Orthodox theologians branded Arius's position a heresy—denial of a basic doctrine of faith.

Arianism enjoyed such popularity and provoked such controversy that Constantine, to whom religious disagreement meant civil disorder, interceded. He summoned a council of church leaders to Nicaea in Asia Minor and presided over it personally. The council produced the Nicene Creed, which defined the orthodox position that Christ is "eternally begotten of the Father" and of the same substance as the Father. Arius and those who refused to accept the creed were banished, the first case of civil punishment for heresy. This participation of the emperor in a theological dispute within the church paved the way for later emperors to claim that they could do the same.

So active was the emperor Theodosius's participation in church matters that he was eventually at loggerheads with Bishop Ambrose of Milan (339–397). Theodosius ordered Ambrose to hand over his cathedral church to the emperor. Ambrose's response had important consequences for the future:

At length came the command, "Deliver up the Basilica"; I reply, "It is not lawful for us to deliver it up, nor for your Majesty to receive it. By no law can you violate the house of a private man, and do you think that the house of God may be taken away? It is asserted that all things are lawful to the Emperor, that all things are his. But do not burden your conscience with the thought that you have any right as Emperor over sacred things. Exalt not yourself, but if you would reign the longer, be subject to God. It is written, God's to God and Caesar's to Caesar. The palace is the Emperor's, the churches are the Bishop's. To you is committed jurisdiction over public, not over sacred buildings."[2]

Ambrose's statement was to serve as the cornerstone of the Christian theory of civil-ecclesiastical relations throughout the Middle Ages. Ambrose insisted that the church was independent of the state's jurisdiction and that, in matters relating to the faith or the church, the bishops were to be the judges of emperors, not the other way around. In a Christian society, harmony and peace depended on agreement between the bishop and the secular ruler. But if disagreement developed, the church was ultimately the superior power because the church was responsible for the salvation of all (including the emperor). In a letter to the emperor Anastasius I, Pope Gelasius I (492–496) put this idea another way. Gelasius stated that both authorities, the civil and the religious, were created by God and essential to a well-ordered Christian society. Each was supreme in its own domain—the church in the spiritual, the civil in the secular—and cooperation in building a Christian society was their mutual responsibility. In later centuries, theologians, canonists, and propagandists repeatedly cited Ambrose's and Gelasius's position as the basis of relations between the two powers.

Inspired Leadership

The early Christian church benefited from the brilliant administrative abilities of some church leaders and from identification of the authority and dignity of the bishop of Rome with the imperial traditions of the city. Some highly able Roman citizens accepted baptism and applied their intellectual powers and administrative skills to the service of the church rather than the empire. With the empire in decay, educated people joined and worked for the church in the belief that it was the one institution able to provide leadership. Bishop Ambrose, for example, the son of the Roman prefect of Gaul, was a trained lawyer and governor of a province. He is typical of those Roman aristocrats who held high public office, were converted to Christianity, and subsequently became bishops. Such men later provided social continuity from Roman to Germanic rule. As bishop of Milan, Ambrose himself exercised responsibility in the temporal as well as the ecclesiastical affairs of northern Italy.

During the reign of Diocletian (284–305), the Roman Empire had been divided for administrative purposes into geographical units called dioceses. Gradually the church made use of this organizational structure. Christian bishops—the leaders of early Christian communities elected by the Christian people—established their headquarters, or sees, in the urban centers of the old Roman dioceses. Their jurisdiction extended throughout the diocese. The center of the bishop's authority was his cathedral (the word derives from the Latin *cathedra,* meaning "chair"). Thus church leaders capitalized on the Roman imperial method of organization and adapted it to ecclesiastical purposes. The bishops of Rome— known as "popes," from the Latin word *papa,* meaning "father"—claimed to speak and act as the source of unity for all Christians. The popes claimed to be the successors of Saint Peter and heirs to his authority as chief of the apostles, on the basis of Jesus' words:

You are Peter, and on this rock I will build my church, and the jaws of death shall not prevail against it. I will entrust to you the keys of the kingdom of heaven. Whatever you declare bound on earth shall be bound in heaven; whatever you declare loosed on earth shall be loosed in heaven.[3]

Theologians call this statement the Petrine Doctrine.

After the removal of the capital and the emperor to Constantinople (see page 190), the bishop of Rome exercised considerable influence in the West because he had no real competitor there. The bishops of Rome stressed that Rome had been the capital of a worldwide empire and emphasized the special importance of Rome in the framework of that empire. Successive bishops of Rome reminded Christians in other parts of the world that Rome was the burial place of Saint Peter and Saint

Pope Gregory I (590–604) and Scribes One of the four "Doctors" (or Learned Fathers) of the Latin Church, Gregory is shown in this tenth-century ivory book cover writing at his desk while the Holy Spirit in the form of a dove whispers in his ear. Below, scribes copy Gregory's works. *(Kunsthistorisches Museum, Vienna)*

Paul. Moreover, according to tradition, Saint Peter, the chief of Christ's first twelve followers, had lived and been executed in Rome. No other city in the world could make such claims. Hence the bishop of Rome was called "Patriarch of the West." In the East, the bishops of Antioch, Alexandria, Jerusalem, and Constantinople, because of the special dignity of their sees, also gained the title of patriarch. Their jurisdictions extended over lands adjoining their sees; they consecrated bishops, investigated heresy, and heard judicial appeals.

In the fifth century, the bishops of Rome began to stress their supremacy over other Christian communities and to urge other churches to appeal to Rome for the resolution of disputed doctrinal issues. Thus Pope Innocent I (401–417) wrote to the bishops of Africa:

We approve your action in following the principle that nothing which was done even in the most remote and distant provinces should be taken as finally settled unless it came to the notice of this See, that any just pronouncement might be confirmed by all the authority of this See, and that the other churches might from thence gather what they should teach.[4]

The prestige of Rome and the church as a whole was also enhanced by the courage and leadership of the Roman bishops. As described in Chapter 6 (see page 192), church officials played important roles in addressing civil problems previously handled by Roman imperial authorities. The fact that it was Christian leaders, rather than imperial administrators, who responded to dire urban needs could not help but increase the prestige and influence of the church.

Although Popes Innocent I and Leo I (440–461) strongly asserted the primacy of the Roman papacy, those assertions were not everywhere accepted. Local Christian communities and their leaders often exercised the decisive authority over their churches. Particular social and political situations determined the actual power of the bishop of Rome in a given circumstance. The importance of arguments for the Roman primacy rests in the fact that they served as precedents for later appeals.

Missionary Activity

The word *catholic* derives from a Greek word meaning "general," "universal," or "worldwide." Christ had said that his teaching was for all peoples, and Christians sought to make their faith catholic—that is, believed everywhere. This could be accomplished only through missionary activity. As Saint Paul had written to the Christian community at Colossae in Asia Minor, "there is no room for distinction between Greek and Jew, between the circumcised or the uncircumcised, or between barbarian or Scythian, slave and free man. There is only Christ; he is everything and he is in everything."[5] Paul urged Christians to bring the "good news" of Christ to all peoples. The Mediterranean served as the highway over which Christianity spread to the cities of the empire.

During the Roman occupation, Christian communities were scattered throughout Gaul and Britain. The effective beginnings of Christianity in Gaul can be traced to Saint Martin of Tours (ca 316–397), a Roman soldier who, after giving away half his cloak to a naked beggar, had a vision of Christ and was baptized. Martin founded the monastery of Ligugé, the first in Gaul, which became a center for the evangelization of the country districts. In 372 he became bishop of Tours and introduced a rudimentary parish system. The Christianization of rural areas followed a different pattern from that of the cities.

Religion was not a private or individual matter; it was a social affair, and the religion of the chieftain or king determined the religion of the people. Thus missionaries concentrated their initial efforts not on the people, but on kings or tribal chieftains. According to custom, kings negotiated with all foreign powers, including the gods. Because the Christian missionaries represented a "foreign" power (the Christian God), the king dealt with them. Germanic kings accepted Christianity because they believed the Christian God was more powerful than pagan ones and the Christian God would deliver victory in battle; or because Christianity taught obedience to (kingly) authority; or because Christian priests possessed knowledge and a charisma that could be associated with kingly power. Missionaries, therefore, focused their attention on kings. Kings who converted, such as Ethelbert of Kent and the Frankish chieftain Clovis, sometimes had Christian wives. Besides the personal influence a Christian wife exerted on her husband, conversion may have indicated that barbarian kings wanted to enjoy the cultural advantages that Christianity brought, such as literate assistants and an ideological basis for their rule.

Tradition identifies the conversion of Ireland with Saint Patrick (ca 385–461). Born in western England to a Christian family of Roman citizenship, Patrick was captured and enslaved by Irish raiders and taken to Ireland, where he worked for six years as a herdsman. He escaped and returned to England, where a vision urged him to Christianize Ireland. In preparation, Patrick studied in Gaul and in 432 was consecrated a bishop. He landed in Ireland, and at Tara in present-day County Meath—seat of the high kings of Ireland—he made his first converts. Patrick's missionary activities followed the existing social pattern: he converted the Irish tribe by tribe, first baptizing the king. In 445, with the approval of Pope Leo I, Patrick established his see in Armagh. The ecclesiastical organization that Patrick set up, however, differed in a fundamental way from church structure on the continent: Armagh was a monastery, and the monastery, rather than the diocese, served as the center of ecclesiastical organization. Local tribes and the monastery were interdependent, with the clan supporting the monastery economically and the monastery providing religious and educational services for the tribe. By the time of Patrick's death, the majority of the Irish people had received Christian baptism. In his missionary work, Patrick had the strong support of Bridget of Kildare (ca 450–ca 528), daughter of a wealthy chieftain and one of his concubines, who defied parental pressure to marry and became a nun. Bridget and the nuns at Kildare instructed relatives and friends in basic Christian doctrine, made religious vestments for churches, copied books, taught children, and above

Celtic Crucifixion This eighth-century cast-bronze was probably modeled on a ceremonial or reliquary cross used to hold sacred relics. The figure's chest is covered with spirals, and the skirt has spirals and geometric patterns—both characteristic of Celtic art. *(National Museum of Ireland, Dublin)*

MAP 7.1 Anglo-Saxon England The seven kingdoms of the Heptarchy—Northumbria, Mercia, East Anglia, Essex, Kent, Sussex, and Wessex—dominated but did not subsume Britain. Scotland remained a Pict stronghold, while the Celts resisted invasion of their native Wales by Germanic tribes.

all set a religious example by their lives of prayer. In Ireland and later in continental Europe, women shared fully in the process of conversion.

A strong missionary fervor characterized Irish Christianity. Perhaps the best representative of Irish-Celtic zeal was Saint Columba (ca 521–597), who established the monastery of Iona on an island in the Inner Hebrides off the west coast of Scotland. Iona served as a base for converting the pagan Picts of Scotland. Columba's proselytizing efforts won him the title "Apostle of Scotland," and his disciples carried the Christian Gospel to the European continent.

The Christianization of the English really began in 597, when Pope Gregory I (590–604) sent a delegation of monks under the Roman Augustine to Britain to convert the English. Augustine's approach, like Patrick's, was to concentrate on converting the king. When he succeeded in converting Ethelbert, king of Kent, the baptism of Ethelbert's people took place as a matter of course. Augustine established his headquarters, or see, at Canterbury, the capital of Kent.

In the course of the seventh century, two Christian forces competed for the conversion of the pagan Anglo-Saxons: Roman-oriented missionaries traveling north from Canterbury and Celtic monks from Ireland and northwestern Britain. Monasteries were established at Iona, Lindisfarne, Jarrow, and Whitby (Map 7.1).

The Roman and Celtic traditions differed completely in their forms of church organization, types of monastic life, and methods of arriving at the date of the central feast of the Christian calendar, Easter. Through the influence of King Oswiu of Northumbria, the Synod (ecclesiastical council) of Whitby in 664 opted to follow the Roman practices. The conversion of the English and the close attachment of the English church to Rome had far-reaching consequences because Britain later served as a base for the Christianization of the continent (Map 7.2).

Between the fifth and tenth centuries, the great majority of peoples living on the European continent and the nearby islands accepted the Christian religion—that is, they received baptism, though baptism in itself did not automatically transform people into Christians. Once a ruler had marched his people to the waters of baptism, the work of Christianization had only begun. Baptism meant either sprinkling the head or immersing the body in water. Conversion meant mental and heartfelt acceptance of the beliefs of Christianity. What does it mean to be a Christian? This question has troubled sincere people from the time of Saint Paul to the present. The problem rests in part in the basic teaching of Jesus in the Gospel:

> *Then fixing his eyes on his disciples he said: . . . "Happy are you when people hate you, drive you out, abuse you, denounce your name as criminal, on account of the Son of Man. Rejoice when that day comes and dance for joy, then your reward will be great in heaven.*
>
> *"But I say this to you who are listening: Love your enemies, do good to those who hate you, bless those who curse you, pray for those who treat you badly. . . . Treat others as you would like them to treat you."*[6]

These ideas are among the most radical and revolutionary the world has heard.

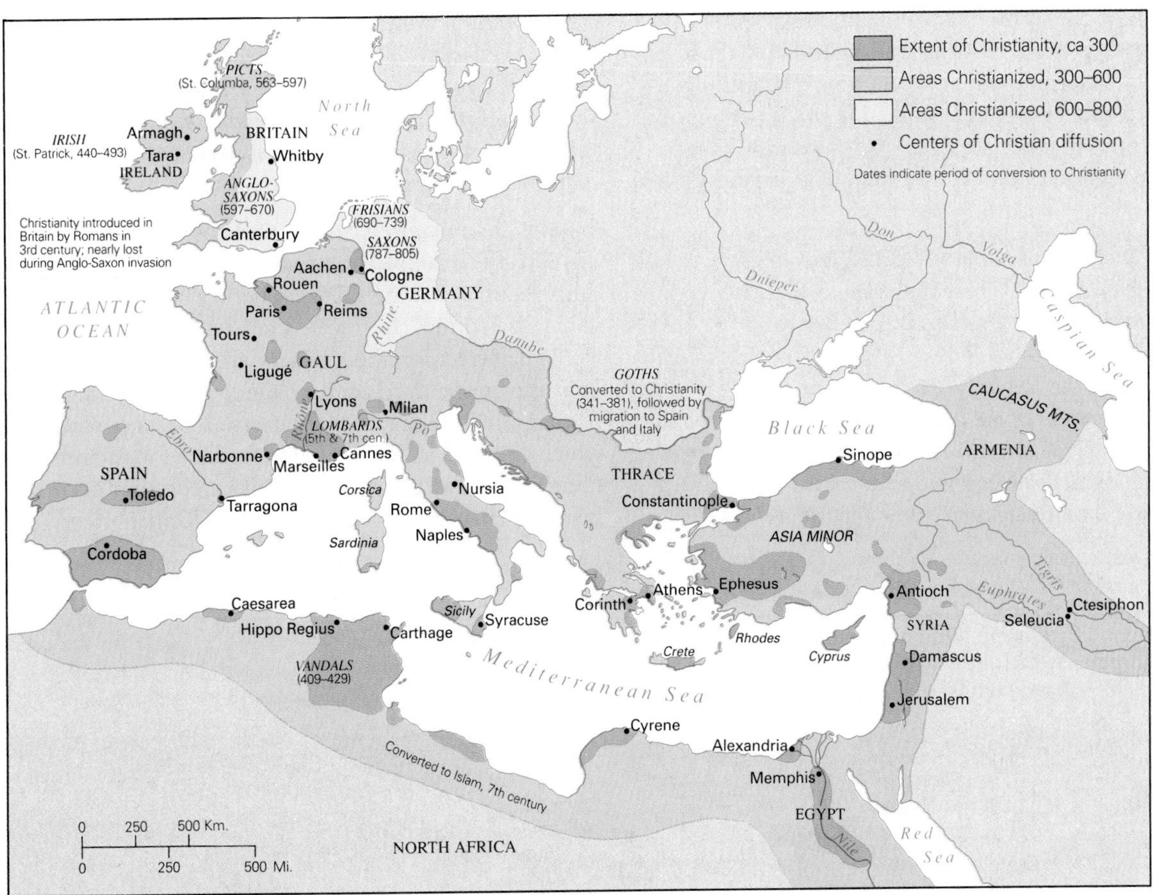

MAP 7.2 The Spread of Christianity Originating in Judaea, the southern part of modern Israel and Jordan, Christianity spread throughout the Roman world. Roman sea lanes and Roman roads facilitated the expansion.

The German people were warriors who idealized the military virtues of physical strength, ferocity in battle, and loyalty to the leader. Victors in battle enjoyed the spoils of success and plundered the vanquished. The greater the fighter, the more trophies and material goods he collected. Thus the Germans had trouble accepting the Christian precepts of "love your enemies" and "turn the other cheek."

The Germanic tribes found the Christian notions of sin and repentance virtually incomprehensible. Sin in Christian thought meant disobedience to the will of God as revealed in the Ten Commandments and the teaching of Christ. "Moral" behavior to the barbarians meant the observance of tribal customs and practices. Dishonorable behavior caused social ostracism. The inculcation of Christian ideals took a very long time.

Conversion and Assimilation

In Christian theology, conversion involves a turning toward God—that is, a conscious effort to live according to the Gospel message. How did missionaries and priests get masses of pagan and illiterate peoples to understand and live by Christian ideals and teachings? Through preaching, assimilation, and the penitential system. Preaching aimed at instruction and edification. Instruction presented the basic teachings of Christianity. Edification was intended to strengthen the newly baptized in their faith through stories about the lives of Christ and the saints. But deeply ingrained pagan customs and practices could not be stamped out by words alone or even by imperial edicts. Christian missionaries often pursued a policy of assimilation, easing the conversion of pagan men and women by stressing similarities between their customs and beliefs and those of Christianity. A letter from Pope Gregory I beautifully illustrates this policy. Sent to Augustine of Canterbury in Britain in 601, it expresses the pope's intention that pagan buildings and practices be given a Christian significance:

To our well beloved son Abbot Mellitus: Gregory servant of the servants of God. . . . Therefore, when by God's help you reach our most reverent brother, Bishop Augustine, we wish you to inform him that we have been giving careful thought to the affairs of the English, and have come to the conclusion that the temples of the idols among that people should on no account be destroyed. The idols are to be destroyed, but the temples themselves are to be aspersed with holy water, altars set up in them, and relics deposited there. For if these temples are well-built, they must be purified from the worship of demons and dedicated to the service of the true God. In this way we hope that the people, seeing that their temples are not destroyed, may abandon their error and, flocking more readily to their accustomed resorts, may come to know and adore the true God.[7]

How assimilation works is perhaps best appreciated through the example of a festival familiar to all Americans, Saint Valentine's Day. There were two Romans named Valentine. Both were Christian priests, and both were martyred for their beliefs around the middle of February in the third century. Since about 150 B.C., the Romans had celebrated the festival of Lupercalia, at which they asked the gods for fertility for themselves, their fields, and their flocks. This celebration occurred in mid-February, shortly before the Roman New Year

The Pantheon (Interior) Originally a temple for the gods, the Pantheon later served as a Christian church. As such, it symbolizes the adaptation of pagan elements to Christian purposes. *(Alinari/Art Resource, NY)*

and the arrival of spring. Thus the early church "converted" the old festival of Lupercalia into Saint Valentine's Day. (Nothing in the lives of the two Christian martyrs connects them with lovers or the exchange of messages and gifts. That practice began in the later Middle Ages.) The fourteenth of February was still celebrated as a festival, but it had taken on Christian meaning.

A process that had an equally profound, if gradual, impact on the conversion of the pagan masses was the rite of reconciliation in which the sinner revealed his or her sins in order to receive God's forgiveness. In the early Church, "confession" meant that the sinner publicly acknowledged charges laid against him or her and publicly carried out the penitential works prescribed by the priest or bishop. For example, the adulterer might have to stand outside the church before services wearing a sign naming his or her sin and asking the prayers of everyone who entered.

Beginning in the late sixth century, however, Irish and English missionaries brought the more private penitential system to continental Europe. Penitentials were manuals for the examination of conscience. The penitent knelt before the priest, who questioned the penitent about the sins he or she might have committed. A penance was then imposed. Penance usually meant fasting for a period of time on bread and water, which was intended as a medicine for the soul. Here is a section of the penitential prepared by Archbishop Theodore of Canterbury (668–690), which circulated widely at the time:

If anyone commits fornication with a virgin he shall do penance for one year. If with a married woman, he shall do penance for four years.

A male who commits fornication with a male shall do penance for three years.

If a woman practices vice with a woman, she shall do penance for three years.

Whoever has often committed theft, seven years is his penance, or such a sentence as his priest shall determine, that is, according to what can be arranged with those whom he has wronged. . . .

Women who commit abortion before [the fetus] has life, shall do penance for one year or for the three forty-day periods or for forty days, according to the nature of the offense; and if later, that is, more than forty days after conception, they shall do penance as murderesses.

If a poor woman slays her child, she shall do penance for seven years. In the canon it is said that if it is a case of homicide, she shall do penance for ten years.[8]

Penitentials provide considerable information about the ascetic ideals of early Christianity and about the crime-ridden realities of Celtic and Germanic societies. Penitentials also reveal the ecclesiastical foundations of some modern attitudes toward sex, birth control, and abortion. Unlike the earlier public penances, Celtic forms permitted the repeated reconciliation of the same sinner in a private situation involving only the priest and penitent. We do not know whether these severe penances were actually enforced; some scholars believe they were not. In any case, the penitential system contributed to the gradual growth of a different attitude toward religion: formerly public, corporate, and social, religious observances slowly became private, personal, and individual.[9]

Christian Attitudes Toward Classical Culture

Probably the major dilemma the early Christian church faced concerned Greco-Roman culture. The Roman Empire as a social, political, and economic force gradually disintegrated. Its culture, however, survived. In Greek philosophy, art, and architecture, in Roman law, literature, education, and engineering, the legacy of a great civilization continued. The Christian religion had begun and spread within this intellectual and psychological milieu. What was to be the attitude of Christians to the Greco-Roman world of ideas?

Adjustment

Christians in the first and second centuries believed that the end of the world was near. Christ had promised to return, and Christians expected to witness that return. Therefore, they considered knowledge useless and learning a waste of time. The important duty of the Christian was to prepare for the Second Coming of the Lord. Good Christians who sought the Kingdom of Heaven through the imitation of Christ believed they had to disassociate themselves from the "filth" that Roman culture embodied.

As Saint Paul wrote, "The wisdom of the world is foolishness, we preach Christ crucified." Tertullian (ca 160–220), an influential African church father and writer, condemned all secular literature as foolishness in the eyes of God. He called the Greek philosophers, such as Aristotle, "hucksters of eloquence" and compared them to "animals of self-glorification." "What has

Athens to do with Jerusalem," he demanded, "the Academy with the Church? We have no need for curiosity since Jesus Christ, nor for inquiry since the gospel." Tertullian insisted that Christians would find in the Bible all the wisdom they needed.

On the other hand, Christianity encouraged adjustment to the ideas and institutions of the Roman world. Some biblical texts urged Christians to accept the existing social, economic, and political establishment. Specifically addressing Christians living among non-Christians in the hostile environment of Rome, the author of the First Letter of Peter had written about the obligations of Christians:

Always behave honorably among pagans, so that they can see your good works for themselves and, when the day of reckoning comes, give thanks to God for the things which now make them denounce you as criminals. . . .

For the sake of the Lord, accept the authority of every social institution: the emperor, as the supreme authority, and the governors as commissioned by him to punish criminals and praise good citizenship. God wants you to be good citizens. . . . Have respect for everyone and love for your community; fear God and honour the emperor.[10]

Christians really had little choice. While the ancient world had many diverse cultures, Christianity emerged within Jewish and Greco-Roman milieus; they were the only cultures the first Christians knew. Many early Christians had grown up as pagans, been educated as pagans, and been converted only as adults.

Even had early Christians wanted to give up Greco-Roman ideas and patterns of thought, they would have had great difficulty doing so. Therefore, they had to adapt their Roman education to their Christian beliefs. Saint Paul himself believed there was a good deal of truth in pagan thought, as long as it was correctly interpreted and understood.

The result was a compromise. Christians gradually came to terms with Greco-Roman culture. Saint Jerome (340–419), a distinguished theologian and linguist, remains famous for his translation of the Old and New Testaments from Hebrew and Greek into vernacular Latin. Called the "Vulgate," his edition of the Bible served as the official translation until the sixteenth century; even today, scholars rely on it. Familiar with the writings of classical authors, Saint Jerome also believed that Christians should study the best of ancient thought because it would direct their minds to God. Jerome maintained that the best ancient literature should be interpreted in light of the Christian faith.

Christian attitudes toward women and toward homosexuality illustrate the ways early Christians adopted the views of their contemporary world.

Jesus, whom Christians accept as the Messiah, considered women the equal of men in his plan of salvation. He attributed no disreputable qualities to women, made no comment on the wiles of women, no reference to them as inferior creatures. On the contrary, women were among his earliest and most faithful converts. He discussed his mission with them (John 4:21–25); he accepted the ministrations of a reformed prostitute; and women were the first persons to whom he revealed himself after his resurrection (Matthew 28:9–10). Jewish and Christian writers, however, not Jesus, had a greater influence on the formation of medieval (and modern) attitudes toward women.

Jesus' message emphasized love for God and one's fellow human beings; later writers tended to stress Christianity as a religion of renunciation and asceticism. Their views derive from Platonic-Hellenistic ideas of the contemporary Mediterranean world. The Hellenistic Jewish philosopher Philo of Alexandria (ca 20 B.C.–ca A.D. 50), for example, held that since the female represented sense perception and the male the higher, rational soul, the female was inferior to the male. Pnilo accepted the biblical command to increase and multiply but argued that the only good of marriage was the production of children for the continuation of the race. Female beauty may come from God, who created everything, the African church father Tertullian wrote, but it should be feared. Women should wear veils, or men will be endangered by the sight of them. While early Christian writers repeated such statements, perhaps the most revolting image of women comes from Saint John Chrysostom (347–407), patriarch of Constantinople, a ruthless critic of contemporary morals. Commenting on female beauty, he wrote that

if a man consider what is stored up inside those beautiful eyes and that straight nose, and the mouth and the cheeks, you will affirm the well-shaped body to be nothing else than a white sepulchre; the parts within are full of so much uncleanliness. Moreover, when you see a rag with any of these things on it, such as phlegm or spittle, you cannot bear to touch it, with even the tips of your fingers, nay you cannot even endure looking at it; yet you are in a flutter of excitement about the storehouses and depositories [women] of these things.[11]

The church fathers acknowledged that God had established marriage for the generation of children, but they believed it was a concession to weak souls who could not bear celibacy. God had clearly sanctioned marriage, and coitus was theoretically good since it was created by God. But in daily life, every act of intercourse was evil; the child was conceived by a sinful act and came into the world tainted with "original sin" (see page 210). Celibacy was the highest good, intercourse little more than animal lust.

Because women were considered incapable of writing on the subject, we have none of their views. The church fathers, by definition, were all males. Since many of them became aware of their physical desires when in the presence of women, misogyny (hatred of women) entered Christian thought. Although early Christian writers believed women the spiritual equals of men, and although some women, such as Saints Melania and Scholastica (see page 215), exercised influence as teachers and charismatic leaders, Christianity became a male-centered and sex-negative religion.[12] Until perhaps very recently, this attitude dominated Western thinking on human sexuality.

Toward homosexuality, according to a controversial study, Christians of the first three or four centuries simply imbibed the attitude of the world in which they lived. Like the Greeks, many Romans indulged in homosexual activity, and contemporaries did not consider such behavior (or inclinations to it) any more immoral, bizarre, or harmful than heterosexual behavior. Several emperors were openly homosexual, and homosexuals participated freely in all aspects of Roman life and culture. Early Christians, too, considered homosexuality a conventional expression of physical desire and were no more susceptible to antihomosexual prejudices than pagans were. Some prominent Christians experienced loving same-gender relationships that probably had a sexual element. What eventually led to a change in public and Christian attitudes toward homosexual behavior was the shift from the sophisticated urban culture of the Greco-Roman world to the rural culture of medieval Europe.[13]

The Marys at the Sepulcher This late fourth-century ivory panel tells the story (Matthew 28:1–6) of Mary Magdalene and another Mary (lower) who went to Jesus' tomb to discover the stone at the entrance rolled away; that an angel had descended from heaven; and in shock the guards assigned (upper) to watch the tomb "trembled and became like dead men." The angel told the women that Jesus had risen. The blend of Roman artistic style—in spacing, drapery, men's hair fashion—and Christian subject matter shows the assimilation of classical form and Christian teaching. *(Castello Sforzesco/Scala/Art Resource, NY)*

Synthesis: Saint Augustine

The finest representative of the blending of classical and Christian ideas, and indeed one of the most brilliant thinkers in the history of the Western world, was Saint Augustine of Hippo (354–430). Saint Augustine was born into an urban family in what is now Algeria in North Africa. His father was a pagan; his mother, Monica, a devout Christian. Because his family was poor—his father was a minor civil servant—the only avenue to success in a highly competitive world was a classical education.

Augustine's mother believed that a good classical education, though pagan, would make her son a better Christian, so Augustine's father scraped together the money to educate him. The child received his basic education in the local school. By modern and even medieval standards, that education was extremely narrow: textual study of the writings of the poet Virgil, the orator-politician Cicero, the historian Sallust, and the playwright Terence. At that time, learning meant memorization. Education in the late Roman world aimed at appreciation of words, particularly those of renowned and eloquent orators.

At the age of seventeen, Augustine went to nearby Carthage to continue his education. There he took a mistress with whom he lived for fifteen years. At Carthage Augustine entered a difficult psychological phase and began an intellectual and spiritual pilgrimage that led him through experiments with several philosophies and heretical Christian sects. In 383 he traveled to Rome, where he endured not only illness but also disappointment in his teaching: his students fled when their bills were due.

Finally, in Milan in 387, through the insights he gained from reading Saint Paul's Letter to the Romans, Augustine received Christian baptism. He later became bishop of the seacoast city of Hippo Regius in his native North Africa. He was a renowned preacher to Christians there, a vigorous defender of orthodox Christianity, and the author of over ninety-three books and treatises.

Augustine's autobiography, *The Confessions,* is a literary masterpiece and one of the most influential books in the history of Europe. Written in the form of a prayer, *The Confessions* describes Augustine's moral struggle, the conflict between his spiritual and intellectual aspirations and his sensual and material self.

Great are thou, O Lord, and exceedingly to be praised: great is thy power and of thy wisdom there is no reckoning. And man, indeed, one part of thy creation, has the will to praise thee: yea, man, though he bears his mortality about with him . . . even man, a small portion of thy creation, has the will to praise thee. Thou dost stir him up, that it may delight him to praise thee, for thou hast made us for thyself and our hearts are restless till they find repose in thee.[14]

The Confessions reveals the change and development of a human mind and personality steeped in the philosophy and culture of the ancient world. Many Greek and Roman philosophers had taught that knowledge and virtue are the same: a person who really knows what is right will do what is right. Augustine rejected this idea. He believed that a person may know what is right but fail to act righteously because of the innate weakness of the human will. People do not always act on the basis of rational knowledge. Here Augustine made a profound contribution to the understanding of human nature: he demonstrated that a learned person can also be corrupt and evil. *The Confessions,* written in the rhetorical style and language of late Roman antiquity, marks the synthesis of Greco-Roman forms and Christian thought.

Augustine's ideas on sin, grace, and redemption became the foundation of all subsequent Christian theology, Protestant as well as Catholic. He wrote that the basic or dynamic force in any individual is the will, which he defined as "the power of the soul to hold on to or to obtain an object without constraint." The end or goal of the will determines the moral character of the individual. When Adam ate the fruit forbidden by God in the Garden of Eden (Genesis 3:6), he committed the "original sin" and corrupted the will; by concupiscence, or sexual desire, which all humans have, Adam's sin was passed on by hereditary transmission through the flesh to all humanity. Original sin thus became a common social stain. Because Adam disobeyed God and fell, so all human beings have an innate tendency to sin: their will is weak. But according to Augustine, God restores the strength of the will through grace, which is transmitted through the sacraments.

Augustine also contributed to the discussion on the nature of the church sparked by the Donatist heretical movement. Promoted by the North African bishop of Carthage, Donatus (313–347), Donatism denied the value of sacraments administered by priests or bishops who had denied their faith under persecution or had committed grave sin. For the Donatists, the holiness of the minister was as important as the sacred rites he performed. Donatists viewed themselves as a separate "chosen people" that had preserved its purity and identity in a corrupt world. The true church, therefore, consisted of a small spiritual elite that was an alternative to society. Augustine responded with extensive preaching and the treatise *On Baptism and Against the Donatists* (A.D. 400). He argued that, through God's action, the rites of the church have an objective and permanent validity, regardless of the priest's spiritual condition. Being a Christian and a member of the church, Augustine maintained, meant striving for holiness; rather than seeing themselves as apart from society, Christians must live in and transform society. The notion of the church as a special spiritual elite, distinct from and superior to the rest of society, recurred many times in the Middle Ages. Each time it was branded a heresy, and Augustine's arguments were marshaled against it.

When the Visigothic chieftain Alaric conquered Rome in 410, horrified pagans blamed the disaster on the Christians. In response, Augustine wrote *City of God.* This profoundly original work contrasts Christianity with the secular society in which it existed. *City of God* presents a moral interpretation of the Roman government—in fact, of all history. Filled with references to ancient history and mythology, it remained for centuries the standard statement of the Christian philosophy of history.

According to Augustine, history is the account of God acting in time. Human history reveals that there are two kinds of people: those who live according to the flesh in the City of Babylon and those who live according to the spirit in the City of God. The former will endure eternal hellfire; the latter enjoy eternal bliss.

Augustine maintained that states came into existence as the result of Adam's fall and people's inclination to sin. The state is a necessary evil, but it can work for the good by providing the peace, justice, and order that Christians need in order to pursue their pilgrimage to the City of God. The particular form of government—whether monarchy, aristocracy, or democracy—is basically irrelevant. Any civil government that fails to provide justice is no more than a band of gangsters.

Although the state results from moral lapse—from sin—neither is the church (the Christian community) entirely free from sin. The church is certainly not equivalent to the City of God. But the church, which is concerned with salvation, is responsible for everyone, including Christian rulers. Churches in the Middle Ages used Augustine's theory to defend their belief in the ultimate superiority of the spiritual power over the temporal. This remained the dominant political theory until the late thirteenth century.

CHRISTIAN MONASTICISM

Christianity began and spread as a city religion. Since the first century, however, some especially pious Christians had felt that the only alternative to the decadence of urban life was complete separation from the world. All-consuming pursuit of material things, gross sexual promiscuity, and general political corruption disgusted them. They believed that the Christian life as set forth in the Gospel could not be lived in the midst of such immorality. They rejected the values of Roman society and were the first real nonconformists in the church.

The fourth century witnessed a significant change in the relationship of Christianity and the broader society. Until Constantine's legalization of Christianity, Christians were a persecuted minority. People were tortured and killed for their faith. Christians greatly revered these martyrs, the men and women who, like Jesus, suffered and died for their faith. The martyrs were the great heroes of the early church. When Christianity was legalized and the persecutions ended, a new problem arose. Whereas Christians had been a suffering minority, now they came to be identified with the state: non-Christians could not advance in the imperial service. And if Christianity had triumphed, so had "the world," since secular attitudes and values pervaded the church. The church of martyrs no longer existed, and some scholars believe the monasteries provided a way of life for those Christians who wanted to make a total response to Christ's teachings, people who wanted more than a lukewarm Christianity. The monks became the new martyrs. Saint Anthony of Egypt (251?–356), the earliest monk for whom there is concrete evidence and the person later considered the father of monasticism, went to Alexandria during the last persecution in the hope of gaining martyrdom. Christians believed that monks, like the martyrs before them, could speak to God and that their prayers had special influence with him.

Western Monasticism

Monasticism began in Egypt in the third century. At first individuals and small groups withdrew from cities and organized society to seek God through prayer in caves and shelters in the desert or mountains. Gradually large colonies of monks emerged in the deserts of Upper Egypt. They were called hermits, from the Greek word *eremos,* meaning "desert." Many devout women also were attracted to the monastic life. We have no way of knowing how many hermits there were in the fourth and fifth centuries because their conscious aim was a hidden life known only to God. Although monks (and nuns) led isolated lives and the monastic movement represented the antithesis of the ancient ideal of an urban social existence, ordinary people soon recognized the monks and nuns as holy people and sought them as spiritual guides.

When monasticism spread to western Europe, several factors worked against the continuation of the eremitical form. The cold, snow, ice, and fog that covered much of northern Europe for many months of the year discouraged isolated living. Dense forests filled with wild animals and wandering Germanic tribes presented obvious dangers. Also, church leaders did not really approve of eremitical life. Hermits sometimes claimed to have mystical experiences, direct communications with God. No one could verify these experiences. If hermits could communicate directly with the Lord, what need had they for the priest and the institutional church? Saint Basil (329?–379), the scholarly bishop of Caesarea in Cappadocia in Asia Minor, opposed the eremitical life on other grounds: the impossibility of material self-sufficiency; the danger of excessive concern with the self; and the fact that the eremitical life did not provide the opportunity for the exercise of charity, the first virtue of any Christian. The Egyptian ascetic Pachomius (290–346?) had organized communities of men and women at his coenobitic monastery at Tabennisi on the Upper Nile drawing thousands of recruits. Saint Basil and the church hierarchy encouraged *coenobitic monasticism,* communal living in monasteries. Communal living, they felt, provided an environment for training the aspirant in the virtues of charity, poverty, and freedom from self-deception.

In the fourth, fifth, and sixth centuries, Bishop Athanasius of Alexandria's *Life of St. Anthony,* the monk John Cassian's *Conferences,* which is based on his conversations with Egyptian monks, and other information about Egyptian monasticism came to the West. The literature of the Egyptian monastic experience led to a flood of converts. Many experiments in communal monasticism were made in Gaul, Italy, Spain, England, and Ireland. While at Rome, Saint Jerome attracted a group of aristocratic women, whom he instructed in the Scriptures and the ideals of ascetic life. After studying both eremitical and coenobitic monasticism in Egypt and Syria, John Cassian established two monasteries near Marseilles in Gaul around 415. One of his books, *Conferences,* discussed the dangers of the isolated hermit's life. The abbey of Lérins on the Mediterranean Sea near Cannes (ca 410) also had significant contacts with monastic centers in western Asia and North Africa. Lérins encouraged the severely penitential and extremely ascetic behavior common in the East, such as long hours of prayer, fasting, and self-flagellation. It was this tradition of harsh self-mortification that the Roman-British monk Saint Patrick carried from Lérins to Ireland in the fifth century.

Around 540 the Roman senator Cassiodorus retired from public service and established a monastery, the Vivarium, on his estate in Italy. Cassiodorus wanted the Vivarium to become an educational and cultural center and enlisted highly educated and sophisticated men for it. He set the monks to copying both sacred and secular manuscripts, intending this to be their sole occupation. Cassiodorus started the association of monasticism with scholarship and learning. That developed into a great tradition in the medieval and modern worlds. But Cassiodorus's experiment did not become the most influential form of monasticism in European society. The fifth and sixth centuries witnessed the appearance of many other monastic lifestyles.

The Rule of Saint Benedict

In 529 Benedict of Nursia (480–543), who had experimented with both the eremitical and the communal forms of monastic life, wrote a brief set of regulations for the monks who had gathered around him at Monte Cassino between Rome and Naples. Recent research has shown that Benedict's *Rule* derives from a longer, repetitious, and sometimes turgid document called *The Rule of the Master.* Benedict's guide for monastic life proved more adaptable and slowly replaced all others. *The Rule of Saint Benedict* has influenced all forms of organized religious life in the Roman church.

Saint Benedict conceived of his *Rule* as a simple code for ordinary men. It outlined a monastic life of regularity, discipline, and moderation in an atmosphere of silence. Each monk had ample food and adequate sleep. Self-destructive acts of mortification were forbidden. The monk spent part of each day in formal prayer, which Benedict called the *Opus Dei* (Work of God) and Christians later termed the divine office, the public prayer of the church. This consisted of chanting psalms and other prayers from the Bible in that part of the monastery church called the "choir." The rest of the day was passed in manual labor, study, and private prayer. After a year of testing or probation, the novice (newcomer) made three vows.

First, he vowed stability: he promised to live his entire life in the monastery of his profession. The vow of stability was Saint Benedict's major contribution to Western monasticism; his object was to prevent the wandering so common in his day. Second, the monk vowed conversion of manners—that is, to strive to improve himself and to come closer to God. Third, he promised obedience, the most difficult vow because it meant the complete surrender of his will to the abbot, or head of the monastery.

The Rule of Saint Benedict expresses the assimilation of the Roman spirit into Western monasticism. It reveals the logical mind of its creator and the Roman concern for order, organization, and respect for law. Its spirit of moderation and flexibility is reflected in the patience, wisdom, and understanding with which the abbot is to govern and, indeed, with which life is to be led. The

Saint Benedict Holding his *Rule* in his left hand, the seated and cowled patriarch of Western monasticism blesses a monk with his right hand. His monastery, Monte Cassino, is in the background. *(Biblioteca Apostolica Vaticana)*

Rule could be used in vastly different physical and geographical circumstances, in damp and cold Germany as well as in warm and sunny Italy. The *Rule* was quickly adapted for women, and many convents of nuns were established in the early Middle Ages.

Saint Benedict's *Rule* implies that a person who wants to become a monk or nun need have no previous ascetic experience or even a particularly strong bent toward the religious life. Thus it allowed for the admission of newcomers with different backgrounds and personalities. From Chapter 59, "The Offering of Sons by Nobles or by the Poor," and from Benedict's advice to the abbot—"The abbot should avoid all favoritism in the monastery. . . . A man born free is not to be given higher rank than a slave who becomes a monk" (Chapter 2)—we know that men of different social classes belonged to his monastery. This flexibility helps to explain the attractiveness of Benedictine monasticism throughout the centuries.

At the same time, the *Rule* no more provides a picture of actual life in a Benedictine abbey of the seventh or eighth (or twentieth) century than the American Constitution of 1789 describes living conditions in the United States today. A code of laws cannot do that. Monasteries were composed of individuals, and human beings defy strict classification according to rules, laws, or statistics. *The Rule of Saint Benedict* had one fundamental purpose: the exercises of the monastic life were designed to draw the individual slowly but steadily away from attachment to the world and love of self and toward the love of God.

Why did the Benedictine form of monasticism eventually replace other forms of Western monasticism? The answer lies partly in its spirit of flexibility and moderation and partly in the balanced life it provided. Early Benedictine monks and nuns spent part of the day in prayer, part in study or some other form of intellectual activity, and part in manual labor. The monastic life as conceived by Saint Benedict did not lean too heavily in any one direction; it struck a balance between asceticism and activity. It thus provided opportunities for persons of entirely different abilities and talents—from mechanics to gardeners to literary scholars. Benedict's *Rule* contrasts sharply with Cassiodorus's narrow concept of the monastery as a place for aristocratic scholars and bibliophiles.

Benedictine monasticism also suited the social circumstances of early medieval society. The German invasions had fragmented European life: the self-sufficient rural estate replaced the city as the basic unit of civilization. A monastery, too, had to be economically self-sufficient. It was supposed to produce from its lands and properties all that was needed for food, clothing, shelter, and liturgical service of the altar. The monastery fitted in—indeed, represented—the trend toward localism. The Benedictine form of religious life also proved congenial to women. Five miles from Monte Cassino at Plombariola, Benedict's twin sister Scholastica (480–543) adapted the *Rule* for the use of her community of nuns. The adoption of Benedict's *Rule* by houses of women paralleled that in houses of men.

Benedictine monasticism also succeeded partly because it was so materially successful. In the seventh and eighth centuries, monasteries pushed back forests and wastelands, drained swamps, and experimented with crop rotation. For example, the abbey of Saint Wandrille, founded in 645 near Rouen in northwestern Gaul, sent squads of monks to clear the forests that surrounded it. Within seventy-five years, the abbey was immensely wealthy. Such Benedictine houses made a significant contribution to the agricultural development of Europe. The communal nature of their organization, whereby property was held in common and profits were pooled and reinvested, made this contribution possible.

Finally, monasteries conducted schools for local young people. Some learned about prescriptions and herbal remedies and went on to provide medical treatment for their localities. A few copied manuscripts and wrote books. This training did not go unappreciated in a society desperately in need of it. Local and royal governments drew on the services of the literate men and able administrators the monasteries produced. This was not what Saint Benedict had intended, but the effectiveness of the institution he designed made it perhaps inevitable.

Eastern Monasticism

From Egypt, Christian monasticism also spread to the Greek provinces of Syria and Palestine and to Constantinople itself. Saint Basil (see page 212) composed a set of regulations that considerably influenced Eastern monasticism. Called the *Long Rules,* Basil's regulations recommended communities of economically self-sufficient monks (or nuns) who lived lives of moderation. Basil discouraged the severe asceticism that was so common in Egypt and also supported the establishment of urban monasteries.

With financial assistance from the emperor Justinian I (527–565) and from wealthy nobles, monasteries soon spread throughout the empire, with seventy abbeys erected in Constantinople alone. Justinian granted the monks the right to inherit property from private citizens and the right to receive *solemnia,* or annual gifts, from the imperial treasury or from the taxes of certain provinces, and he prohibited lay confiscation of monastic estates. Beginning in the tenth century, the monasteries acquired fields, pastures, livestock, mills, saltworks, and urban rental properties, as well as cash and precious liturgical vessels. The exemption of Byzantine monasteries from state taxes also served to increase monastic wealth.

What did the monasteries do with their revenues? Did the Greek monasteries have an impact on the broader society? Implementing Saint Basil's belief that *philanthropia,* active love for humankind, was a central part of the monastic vocation, monasteries performed important social services: they distributed food, clothing, and money to the poor and needy. Many monasteries contained within their compounds hospitals for the sick (see pages 230, 327); homes for the destitute elderly, staffed by monks or nuns; and inns for travelers, where food and lodging were free. Orphans, handicapped people, the mentally ill, and battered women also found temporary or permanent refuges in the monasteries of monks or nuns. The Byzantine scholar Norman Baynes has written, "The Byzantine in his hour of need turned instinctively to the ascete (monk) in the full assurance of his sympathy and succor." A few monks undertook evangelical work. For example, Saint Nikon (ca 930–1000) reconverted the people of Crete after the Muslim occupation and preached among the pagan Slavs of the Peloponnesus. The Christian East, however, never regarded missionary or charitable work as the primary work of monasticism.

The main duty of monks or nuns was to pray. They served the world not so much by what they *did* as by what they *were:* people of prayer. The monastery was the scene of the daily and continuous ritual of the divine office; the monks and nuns spent heavily on the sacred vestments and vessels used in their liturgies, which in the course of the centuries became famous for their elaborateness and splendor. The holy and charismatic elder (or *starets* in Slavonic) became a characteristic figure in orthodox monasticism: he or she was the spiritually mature physician capable of guiding others and healing their souls. Thus Saint Melania (383–439), abbess of a community of nuns at the Mount of Olives in Jerusalem, guided Evagrius of Pontus (ca 345–ca 399), a Syrian who later served as the spiritual father of many of the Egyptian monks at Nitria and Kellia in Upper Egypt.

Monasticism in the Greek Orthodox world differed in fundamental ways from the monasticism that evolved in western Europe. First, while *The Rule of Saint Benedict* gradually became the universal guide or constitution for all western European monasteries, each individual house in the Byzantine world developed its own *typikon,* or set of rules for organization and behavior. The *typika* contain regulations about novitiate, diet, clothing, liturgical functions, commemorative services for benefactors, and the election of officials, such as the *hegoumenos,* or superior of the house. Second, while stability in the monastery eventually characterized Western monasticism, many Orthodox monks, especially those with a reputation for holiness, "moved frequently from one monastery to another or alternated between a coenobitic monastery and a hermit's kellion [cell]."[15] Finally, unlike the West, where monasteries often established schools for the education of the youth of the neighborhood, education never became a central feature of the Greek houses. Monks and nuns had to be literate to perform the services of the choir, and children destined for the monastic life were taught to read and write. In the monasteries where monks or nuns devoted themselves to study and writing, their communities sometimes played important roles in the development of theology and in the intellectual life of the empire. But those houses were very few, and no monastery assumed responsibility for the general training of the local young. Since bishops and patriarchs of the Greek church were recruited only from the monasteries, Greek houses did, however, exercise a cultural influence.

THE MIGRATION OF THE GERMANIC PEOPLES

The migration of peoples from one area to another has been a dominant and continuing feature of Western history. Mass movements of Europeans occurred in the fourth through sixth centuries, in the ninth and tenth centuries, and in the twelfth and thirteenth centuries. From the sixteenth century to the present, such movements have been almost continuous, involving not just the European continent but the entire world. The causes of early migrations varied and are not thoroughly understood by scholars. But there is no question that they profoundly affected both the regions to which peoples moved and the ones they left behind.

As Julius Caesar advanced through Gaul between 58 and 50 B.C. (see page 157), he encountered Celts and Germans. To the Romans, all peoples living beyond the Roman Empire were "barbarians," for the Romans a word carrying political and cultural connotations. Modern historians have tended to use the terms *German* and *Celt* in a racial sense, but anthropologists insist that race is a difficult and unworkable concept, because different peoples have many similarities. Recent research stresses that *Celt* and *German* are linguistic terms, a Celt being one who spoke a Celtic language and a German one who spoke German. Celts and Germans displayed many similarities. Both were Indo-European peoples. In the first century A.D., the Celts lived east of the Rhine River in an area bounded by the Main Valley and extending westward to the Somme River. Germans were more numerous along the North and Baltic Seas. Both Germans and Celts used a wheeled plow and a three-field system of crop rotation (see page 221). The Celts had developed iron manufacturing, using shaft furnaces as sophisticated as those of the Romans. The Celts' use of iron swords and spears suggests that they were not the "peaceful" people historians have long described them to be. There were probably many Celtic peoples with differing cultural traditions. By the fourth century B.C., under pressure from the Germans, the Celts had moved westward, settling in Brittany (modern northwestern France) and throughout the British Isles (England, Wales, Scotland, and Ireland). By the third century A.D., the Picts of Scotland, as well as the Welsh, Britons, and Irish, were peoples of Celtic descent.

The migrations of the Germanic peoples were important in the decline of the western Roman Empire and in the making of European civilization. Many twentieth-century scholars have tried to explain who the Germans were and why they migrated, but historians and sociologists are only beginning to provide satisfactory explanations. The present consensus, based on the study of linguistic and archaeological evidence, is that there were not one but many Germanic peoples with very different cultural traditions. The largest Germanic tribe was a polyethnic group consisting of perhaps 15,000 to 20,000 warriors, which with women and children amounted to 100,000 people. It was supplemented by slaves, coloni, peoples who, because of their desperate situation under Roman rule, joined the Goths during their migrations.[16] Archaeological remains—bone fossils, cooking utensils, jewelry, weapons of war, and other artifacts—combined with linguistic data suggest three broad groupings of Germanic peoples. One group lived along the North and Baltic Seas in the regions of present-day northern Germany, southern Sweden, and Denmark. A second band inhabited the area between the Elbe and Oder Rivers. A third group lived along the Rhine and Weser Rivers, closest to the Roman frontier. Although these groupings sometimes showed cultural affiliation, they were very fluid and did not possess political, social, or ethnic solidarity.

Since about 150, Germanic tribes had pressed along the Rhine-Danube frontier of the Roman Empire. Some tribes, such as the Visigoths and Ostrogoths, led a settled existence, engaged in agriculture and trade, and accepted Arian Christianity. Tribes such as the Angles, Saxons, and Huns led a nomadic life unaffected by Roman influences. Scholars do not know exactly when the Mongolian tribe called the Huns began to move westward from China, but about 376 they pressured the Goths along the Rhine-Danube frontier.

Why did the Germans migrate? Recent scholarship suggests that their movements were *not* due to overpopulation, as scholars have long believed. Rather, movements may have occurred because barbarian societies were in a constant state of war. Or possibly "the primary stimulus for this gradual migration was the Roman frontier, which increasingly offered service in the (Roman) army and work for pay around the camps."[17]

Romanization and Barbarization

The Roman Empire, it should be remembered, centered on the Mediterranean. Italy, Spain, and North Africa were the areas most vital to it. Aside from Rome, obviously, Alexandria, Antioch, Ephesus, and later Constantinople represented the great economic, cultural, and population centers. North of Italy, in Gaul, Germany, and Britain, Celtic and Germanic peoples had long predominated. The Roman army had spread a veneer of Roman culture in the territories it controlled, but from the third to the sixth century, as Roman influence declined, native Germanic traditions reasserted themselves.

The Roman army had been the chief means of Romanization throughout the empire (see Chapter 6). But from the third century, the army became the chief agent of barbarization. How? In the third and fourth centuries, increasing pressures on the frontiers from the east and north placed greater demands on military

Helmet of King Agiluf German chieftains wanted to be portrayed as Roman-style rulers, so that the representation would convey Roman ideals of power. On this plaque for the helmet of Lombard king Agiluf, the king sits enthroned in majesty flanked by bodyguards, while subject cities bring tribute. *(Scala/Art Resource, NY)*

manpower, which plague and a declining birthrate had reduced. Therefore, Roman generals recruited barbarians to fill the ranks. They bribed Germanic chiefs with treaties and gold, the masses with grain. By the late third century, a large percentage of military recruits came from the Germanic peoples.

Besides army recruits, several types of barbarian peoples entered the empire and became affiliated with Roman government. The *laeti,* refugees or prisoners of war, were settled with their families in areas of Gaul and Italy under the supervision of Roman prefects and landowners. Generally isolated from the local Roman population, the laeti farmed regions depopulated by plague. The men had to serve in the Roman army. Free barbarian units called *foederati,* stationed near major provincial cities, represented a second type of affiliated barbarian group. Recent research has suggested that rather than giving them land, the Romans assigned the foederati shares of the tax revenues from the region.[18] Living in close proximity to Roman communities, the foederati quickly assimilated into Roman culture. In fact, in the fourth century, some foederati rose to the highest ranks of the army and moved in the most cultured and aristocratic circles. Third, the arrival of the Huns in the west in 376 precipitated the entry of entire peoples, the *gentes,* into the Roman Empire. Pressured by defeat in battle, starvation, or the movement of other peoples, tribes such as the Ostrogoths and Visigoths entered in large numbers.[19] Under the pro-Roman general Fritigern, the Visigoths petitioned the emperor Valens to admit them to the empire. Seeing in the hordes of warriors the solution to his manpower problem, Valens agreed. Once the Visigoths were inside the empire, Roman authorities exploited their hunger by forcing them to sell their own people as slaves in exchange for dog flesh: "the going rate was one dog for one Goth." Still, the Visigoths sought peace. Fritigern offered himself as a friend and ally of Rome, if Rome would grant his people the province of Thrace—land, crops, and livestock. With a Roman army of between thirty thousand and forty thousand men, against about ten thousand Goths, Valens did not take the offer seriously, and his council voted for battle. When the two armies met on August 9, 378, near Adrianople, a lightning-quick attack by the Gothic cavalry easily broke the Roman battle lines and surrounded the imperial forces. The Visigoths slashed down the army, including thirty-five high-ranking officers and the emperor Valens himself. But the Goths had neither the equipment nor the tactical skill to take the city of Adrianople. The Battle of Adrianople marks no notable change in the military or political history of the Roman Empire. As the Visigoths migrated into Thrace and the Balkans, however, they forced the Romans to change imperial policy toward the barbarians. That policy alternated between official recognition by treaty and enmity. Alaric I's invasion of Italy and sack of Rome in 410 represents the culmination of hostility between the Visigoths and the Romans, but a year later Alaric died, and his successor led his people into Gaul.[20]

Except for the Lombards, whose conquests of Italy persisted into the mid-eighth century, the movements of Germanic peoples on the continent ended about 600 (Map 7.3). Between 450 and 565, the Germans established a number of kingdoms, but none except the Frankish kingdom lasted very long. Since the German kingdoms did not have definite geographical boundaries, their locations are approximate. The Visigoths overran much of southwestern Gaul. Establishing their headquarters at Toulouse, they exercised a weak domination over Spain until a Muslim victory at Guadalete in 711 ended Visigothic rule. The Vandals, whose destructive ways are commemorated in the word *vandal,* settled in North Africa. In northern and western Europe in the sixth century, the Burgundians ruled over lands roughly circumscribed by the old Roman army camps at Lyons, Besançon, Geneva, and Autun.

In northern Italy, the Ostrogothic king Theodoric (r. 471–526) established his residence at Ravenna and gradually won control of all Italy, Sicily, and the territory north and east of the upper Adriatic. Although attached to the customs of his people, Theodoric pursued a policy of assimilation between Germans and Romans. He maintained close relations with the emperor at Constantinople and attracted to his administration able scholars such as Cassiodorus (see page 212). Theodoric's accomplishments were significant, but after his death his administration fell apart.

The kingdom established by the Franks in the sixth century, in spite of later civil wars, proved to be the most powerful and enduring of all the barbarian kingdoms. The Franks were a confederation of peoples who originated in the marshy lowlands north and east of the northernmost part of the Rhine frontier of the Roman Empire. They spoke a Germanic language. In the fourth and fifth centuries, they settled within the empire and allied with the Romans, some attaining high military and civil positions. In the sixth century one group, the Salian Franks, issued a law code called the Salic Law, the earliest description of Germani Chlodio (fifth century) is the first member of t ish dynasty for whom evidence survives. Acc

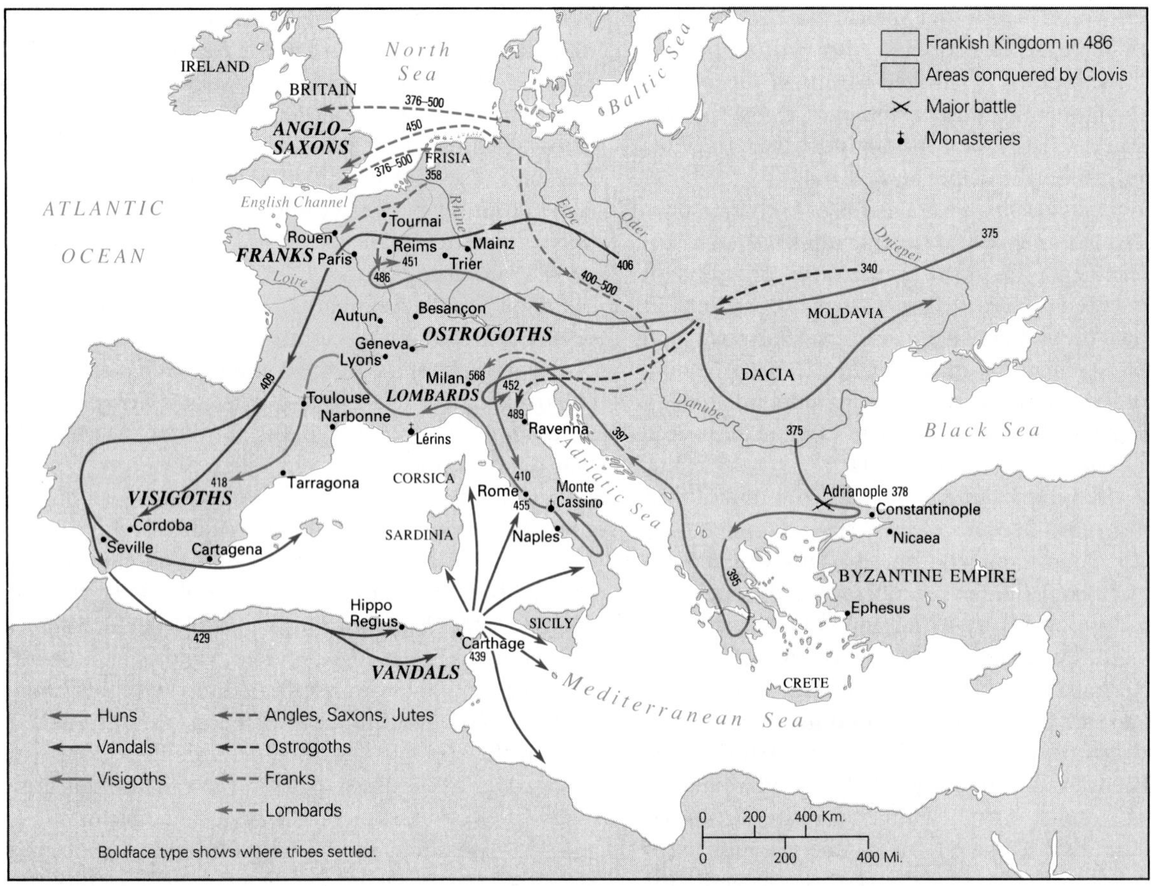

MAP 7.3 The Germanic Migrations The Germanic tribes infiltrated and settled in all parts of western Europe. The Huns, who were not German ethnically, originated in central Asia. The Huns' victory over the Ostrogoths led the emperor to allow the Visigoths to settle within the empire, a decision that proved disastrous for Rome.

legend, Chlodio's wife went swimming, encountered a sea monster, and conceived Merovech. The Franks believed that Merovech, a man of supernatural origins, founded the Merovingian dynasty.

The reign of Clovis (ca 481–511) marks the decisive period of the development of the Franks as a unified people. Through military campaigns, Clovis acquired the central provinces of Roman Gaul. While the Franks attributed their success to divine favor, modern scholars hold that this Frankish acquisition of "the wealthy and geographically central provinces of Roman Gaul," with their administrative machinery intact, laid the foundation of Frankish importance in European history. The next two centuries witnessed the steady assimilation of Franks and Gallo-Romans, as many Franks adopted the Latin language and Roman ways, and Gallo-Romans copied Frankish customs and Frankish personal names. These centuries also saw Frankish acquisition of the Burgundian kingdom and of territory held by the Goths in Provence.[21]

Many writers have debated the issue of Clovis's conversion from Arian to Roman Christianity. His near-contemporary Gregory, bishop of Tours, attributed Clovis's conversion to the influence of his Catholic wife, Chlotilde (which a modern scholar interprets as the "pressure of a nagging wife"). Another contemporary writer holds that in his war with the Alamans (ca 496), Clovis prayed to the Christian god; in thanksgiving for his victory, he accepted baptism. A third contemporary witness believed that the conversion was "the personal choice of an intelligent monarch." A recent student of the Franks argues that Clovis was baptized in 508 (and not in 496, as has been traditionally believed), at the time he was at war in southwestern

Gaul with the Visigothic king Alaric II, and that there was propaganda value to be gained by appearing as the defender of Catholicism against Arianism.[22] Certainly conversion brought Clovis the crucial support of the papacy and of the bishops of Gaul. (See the feature "Listening to the Past: The Conversion of Clovis" on pages 240–241.)

GERMANIC SOCIETY

Germanic society had originated with Iron Age peoples (800–500 B.C.) in the northern parts of central Europe and the southern regions of Scandinavia. After the Germans replaced the Romans, re-establishing their rule over most of the European continent, German customs and traditions formed the basis of European society for centuries. What patterns of social, political, and economic life characterized the Germans?

Scholars are hampered in answering such questions because the Germans did not write and thus kept no written records before their conversion to Christianity. The earliest information about them comes from moralistic accounts by such Romans as the historian Tacitus, who was acquainted only with the tribes living closest to the borders of the empire. Furthermore, Tacitus imposed Greco-Roman categories of tribes and nations on the German peoples he described, ethnographic classifications that have dominated scholarly writing until very recently. Only in the past few decades have anthropologists begun to study early German society on its own terms.

Kinship, Custom, and Class

The Germans had no notion of the state as we in the twentieth century use the term; they thought in social, not political, terms. The basic Germanic social unit was the tribe, or *folk.* Members of the folk believed that they were all descended from a common ancestor. Blood united them. Kinship protected them. Law was custom—unwritten, preserved in the minds of the elders of the tribe, and handed down by word of mouth from generation to generation. Custom regulated everything. Every tribe had its customs, and every member of the tribe knew what they were. Members were subject to their tribe's customary law wherever they went, and friendly tribes respected one another's laws.

In the second and third centuries, Germanic peoples experienced continued stress and pressures from other peoples. A radical restructuring of tribes occurred as tribal groups splintered, some disappeared, and new tribes were formed. What bound a tribe, at least temporarily, was a shared peace—peace among those peoples who considered themselves part of a tribe.

Germanic tribes were led by kings, or tribal chieftains. The chief was that member of the folk recognized as the strongest and bravest in battle, elected from among the male members of the strongest family. He led the tribe in war, settled disputes among its members, conducted negotiations with outside powers, and offered sacrifices to the gods. The period of migrations and conquests of the western Roman Empire witnessed the strengthening of kingship among the Germanic tribes. Tribes that did not migrate did not develop kings.

Closely associated with the king in some southern tribes was the *comitatus,* or "war band." Writing at the end of the first century, Tacitus described the war band as the bravest young men in the tribe. They swore loyalty to the chief, fought with him in battle, and were not supposed to leave the battlefield without him; to do so implied cowardice, disloyalty, and social disgrace. A social egalitarianism existed among members of the war band. The comitatus had importance for the later development of feudalism.

During the migrations of the third and fourth centuries, however, and as a result of constant warfare, the war band was transformed into a system of stratified ranks. For example, among the Ostrogoths a warrior-nobility and several other nobilities evolved. Contact with the Romans, who produced such goods as armbands for trade with the barbarians, stimulated demand for armbands. Thus armbands, especially the gold ones reserved for the "royal families," promoted the development of hierarchical ranks within war bands. During the Ostrogothic conquest of Italy under Theodoric, warrior-nobles also sought to acquire land, both as a mark of prestige and as a means to power. As land and wealth came into the hands of a small elite class, social inequalities emerged and gradually grew stronger.[23] These inequalities help to explain the origins of the European noble class (see pages 222, 244).

Law

As long as custom determined all behavior, the early Germans had no need for written law. Beginning in the late sixth century, however, German tribal chieftains began to collect, write, and publish lists of their customs. Why then? The Christian missionaries who were slowly converting the Germans to Christianity wanted to know the tribal customs and encouraged German rulers to set down their customs in written form. Churchmen wanted to read about German ways in order to assimilate the tribes to Christianity. Augustine of Canterbury, for example, persuaded King Ethelbert of Kent to have his folk laws written down: these *Dooms of Ethelbert* date from between 601 and 604, roughly five years after Augustine's arrival in Britain. Moreover, by the sixth century the German kings needed regulations for the Romans under their jurisdiction as well as for their own people.

King Lhodari of the Alemanni The Alemanni occupied territory in southwestern Germany and Switzerland in the fifth century but didn't accept Christianity until the late seventh or early eighth century. King Lhodari had Alemanni law (hitherto transmitted orally) written down in Latin. (In French speech the name Allemands came to signify all Germans.) Here the ninth-century artist portrays Lhodari in Roman military garb. *(Bibliothèque Nationale, Paris)*

Today, if a person holds up a bank, American law maintains that the robber attacks both the bank and the state in which it exists—a sophisticated notion involving the abstract idea of the state. In early German law, all crimes were regarded as crimes against a person.

According to the code of the Salian Franks, every person had a particular monetary value to the tribe. This value was called the *wergeld,* which literally means "man-money" or "money to buy off the spear." Men of fighting age had the highest wergeld, then women of childbearing age, children, and finally the aged. Everyone's value reflected his or her potential military worthiness. If a person accused of a crime agreed to pay the wergeld and if the victim and his or her family accepted the payment, there was peace (hence the expression "money to buy off the spear"). If the accused refused to pay the wergeld or if the victim's family refused to accept it, a blood feud ensued. Individuals depended on their kin for protection, and kinship served as a force of social control.

Historians and sociologists have difficulty interpreting the early law codes, partly because they are patchwork affairs studded with additions made in later centuries. Yet much historical information can be gleaned from these codes. For example, the Salic Law (see page 217) offers a general picture of Germanic life and problems in the early Middle Ages and is typical of the law codes of other tribes, such as the Visigoths, Burgundians, Lombards, and Anglo-Saxons.

The Salic Law lists the money fines to be paid to the victim or the family for such injuries as theft, rape, assault, arson, and murder:

> *If any person strike another on the head so that the brain appears, and the three bones which lie above the brain shall project, he shall be sentenced to 1200 denars, which make 300 shillings. . . .*
>
> *If any one have killed a free woman after she has begun bearing children, he shall be sentenced to 2400 denars, which make 600 shillings. . . .*
>
> *If any one shall have drawn a harrow through another's harvest after it has sprouted, or shall have gone through it with a wagon where there was no road, he shall be sentenced to 120 denars, which make 30 shillings.*[24]

This is not a systematic statement of a body of law, but a list of fines for particular offenses. German law aimed at the prevention or reduction of violence. It was not concerned with abstract justice.

Vandal Landowner The adoption of Roman dress—short tunic, cloak, and sandals—reflects the way the Germanic tribes accepted Roman lifestyles. Likewise both the mosaic art form and the man's stylized appearance show the Germans' assimilation of Roman influences. (Notice that the rider has a saddle but not stirrups.) *(Courtesy of the Trustees of the British Museum)*

At first, Romans had been subject to Roman law and Germans to Germanic custom. As German kings accepted Christianity and as Romans and Germans increasingly intermarried, the distinction between the two laws blurred and, in the course of the seventh and eighth centuries, disappeared. The result would be the new feudal law, to which Romans and Germans were subject alike.

German Life

The Germans usually resided in small villages where climate and geography determined the basic patterns of agricultural and pastoral life. In the flat or open coastal regions, German males engaged in animal husbandry, especially cattle raising. They also domesticated pigs, sheep, goats, horses, chickens, and geese. Many tribes lived in small settlements on the edges of clearings where they raised barley, wheat, oats, peas, and beans. They tilled their fields with a simple wooden scratch plow and harvested their grains with a small iron sickle. The kernels of grain were ground with a grindstone, and the resulting flour was made into a dough that was baked on clay trays into flat cakes. Much of the grain was fermented into a strong, thick beer. Women performed the heavy work of raising, grinding, and preserving cereals, a mark, some scholars believe, of their low status in a male-dominated society. Women also had responsibility for weaving and spinning the thread that went into the manufacture of clothing and all textiles.

Within the small villages, there were great differences in wealth and status. Free men constituted the largest class. The number of cattle a man possessed indicated his wealth and determined his social status. "Cattle were so much the quintessential indicator of wealth in traditional society that the modern English term 'fee' (meaning cost of goods or services), which developed from the medieval term 'fief,' had its origin in the Germanic term *fihu* . . . , meaning cattle, chattels, and hence, in general, wealth."[25] Free men also shared in tribal warfare. Slaves (prisoners of war) worked as farm laborers, herdsmen, or household servants.

German society was patriarchal: within each household the father had authority over his wives, children, and slaves. The Germans practiced polygamy, and men who could afford them had more than one wife.

Did the Germans produce goods for trade and exchange? Ironworking represented the most advanced craft of the Germanic peoples. Much of northern Europe had iron deposits at or near the earth's surface, and the dense forests provided wood for charcoal. Most villages had an oven and smiths who produced agricultural tools and instruments of war—one-edged swords, arrowheads, and shields. In the first two centuries A.D., the quantity and quality of German goods increased dramatically, and the first steel swords were superior to the weapons of Roman troops. But German goods were produced for war and the subsistence economy, not for trade. Goods were also used for gift giving, a major social custom. Gift giving conferred status on the giver, who, in giving, showed his higher (economic) status, cemented friendship, and placed the receiver in the giver's debt.[26] Goods that could not be produced in the village were acquired by raiding and warfare rather than by commercial exchanges. Warfare constituted the main characteristic of Germanic society. Raids between tribes brought the victors booty; the cattle and slaves captured were traded or given as gifts. Warfare determined the economy and the individual's status within the Germanic society.

What was the position of women in Germanic society? The law codes provide the best evidence. The codes show societies that regarded women as family property. A marriageable daughter went to the highest bidder. A woman of childbearing years had a very high wergeld. The codes also protected the virtue of women. For example, the Salic Law of the Franks fined a man the large amount of 15 solidi (from *solidus,* a coin originally minted by Constantine and later the basis of much European currency, such as the English shilling) if he pressed the hand of a woman, 35 if he touched her above the elbow. On the other hand, heavy fines did not stop injury, rape, or abduction. Widows were sometimes seized on the battlefields where their dead husbands lay and forced to marry the victors. The sixth-century queen Radegund was forced to marry Chlotar I, the murderer of several of her relatives. Radegund later escaped her polygamous union and lived out her life in a convent. Still, the very high fine of 600 solidi for the murder of a woman of childbearing years—the same value attached to military officers of the king, priests, and boys preparing to become warriors—suggests the considerable status of women in Frankish society.

The authority of a father over his daughter or of a husband over his wife was almost absolute: he managed her property and represented her in court. However, once a widow (and there must have been many widows in such a violent, warring society), a woman assumed her husband's rights. She completely controlled their property and held the guardianship of their children. Religious writers and prelates doubted the spiritual equality of women with men. For those writers, women demonstrated their spiritual worth by converting their husbands, raising pious children, endowing churches and monasteries, and dispensing charity to the poor.

A few slaves and peasant women used their beauty and their intelligence to advance their positions. The slave Fredegunda, for whom King Chilperic murdered his Visigothic wife, became a queen and held her position after her husband's death. Another slave, Balthilda, became the wife of Clovis II. During her sons' minority, she worked to alleviate the evils of the slave trade.[27]

In monasteries and convents, women found outlets for their talents as writers, copyists, artists, embroiderers, and teachers. Some houses of religious women, such as Mauberge in Northern Francia under Abbess Aldegund (ca 661), produced important scholarship. Women also used their economic abilities as managers of abbatial estates.[28] The dowry required for entrance to convents restricted admission to upper-class women.

Anglo-Saxon England

The island of Britain, conquered by Rome during the reign of Claudius, shared fully in the life of the Roman Empire during the first four centuries of the Christian era. A military aristocracy governed, and the official religion was the cult of the emperor. Towns were planned in the Roman fashion, with temples, public baths, theaters, and amphitheaters. In the countryside, large manors controlled the surrounding lands. Roman merchants brought Eastern luxury goods and Eastern religions—including Christianity—into Britain. The Celts with their iron spears had posed the greatest threat to Roman rule, and the Romans had suppressed the Celtic chieftains. In the course of the second and third centuries, the Celts assimilated to Roman culture.

The Roman army in Britain, as elsewhere, consisted largely of barbarian troops allowed to settle there as foederati (see page 217), in return for the responsibility of military defense. In 407 the emperor Honorius (r. 395–423), faced with the Visigothic army under Alaric, was forced to withdraw imperial troops from Britain. The Picts from Scotland continued to harass the north. According to the eighth-century historian Bede (see page 251), the Celtic king Vortigern invited the Saxons from Denmark to help him against his rivals in Britain. Teutonic tribes from modern-day Norway, Sweden, and Denmark—the Angles, Saxons, and Jutes—stepped up their assaults, attacking in a hit-and-run fashion. Their goal was plunder, and at first their invasions led to no permanent settlements. As more Germans arrived, however, they took over the best lands and humbled the Britons. Increasingly, the Britons fled to Wales in the west and across the English Channel to Brittany. The sporadic raids continued for over a century and led to Germanic control of most of Britain. Historians have labeled the period 500 to 1066, the year of the Norman Conquest, "Anglo-Saxon."

Except for the Jutes, who probably came from Jutland (modern Denmark), the Teutonic tribes came from the least Romanized and least civilized parts of Europe. The Germans destroyed Roman culture in Britain. Tribal custom superseded Roman law.

The Anglo-Saxon invasion gave rise to a rich body of Celtic mythology, based on the writings of the ninth-century Welsh scholar Nennius; the mythology became known as the Arthurian legends. When Arthur, the illegitimate son of the king of Britain, successfully drew a sword from a stone, Merlin, the court magician, revealed Arthur's royal parentage. Arthur won recognition as king, and the mysterious Lady of the Lake gave him the invincible sword Excalibur, with which he fought many battles against the Saxon invaders. Arthur held his court at Camelot, with his knights seated at the Round Table (to avoid quarrels over precedence). Those knights—including Sir Tristan, Sir Lancelot, Sir Galahad, and Sir Percival (Parsifal), who came to represent the ideal of medieval knightly chivalry—played a large role in later medieval and modern literature.

The Arthurian legends represent Celtic hostility to the Anglo-Saxon invaders. The beginnings of the Germanic kingdoms in Britain are very obscure, but scholars suspect they came into being in the seventh and eighth centuries. The scholar Bede described seven kingdoms: the Jutish kingdom of Kent; the Saxon kingdoms of the East Saxons (Essex), South Saxons (Sussex), and West Saxons (Wessex); and the kingdoms of the Angles, Mercians, and Northumbrians (see Map 7.1). The names imply that these peoples thought of themselves in tribal rather than geographical terms. They referred to the kingdom of the West Saxons, for example, rather than simply to Wessex. Because of Bede's categorization, scholars often refer to the Heptarchy, or seven kingdoms, of Anglo-Saxon Britain. The suggestion of total Anglo-Saxon domination, however, is not entirely accurate. Germanic tribes never subdued Scotland, where the Picts remained strong, or Wales, where the Celts and native Britons continued to put up stubborn resistance.

Thus Anglo-Saxon England was divided along ethnic and political lines. The Teutonic kingdoms in the south, east, and center were opposed by the Britons in the west, who wanted to get rid of the invaders. The Anglo-Saxon kingdoms also fought among themselves, causing boundaries to shift constantly. Finally, in the ninth century, under pressure of the Danish, or Viking, invasions, the Britons and the Germanic peoples were molded together under the leadership of King Alfred of Wessex (r. 871–899).

THE BYZANTINE EAST (CA 400–788)

Constantine had tried to maintain the unity of the Roman Empire, but during the fifth and sixth centuries the western and eastern halves drifted apart. Later emperors worked to hold the empire together. Justinian (r. 527–565) waged long and hard-fought wars against the Ostrogoths and temporarily regained Italy and North Africa. But his conquests had disastrous consequences. Justinian's wars exhausted the resources of the Byzantine state, destroyed Italy's economy, and killed a large part of Italy's population. The wars paved the way for the easy conquest of Italy by another Germanic tribe, the Lombards, shortly after Justinian's death. In the late sixth century, the territory of the western Roman

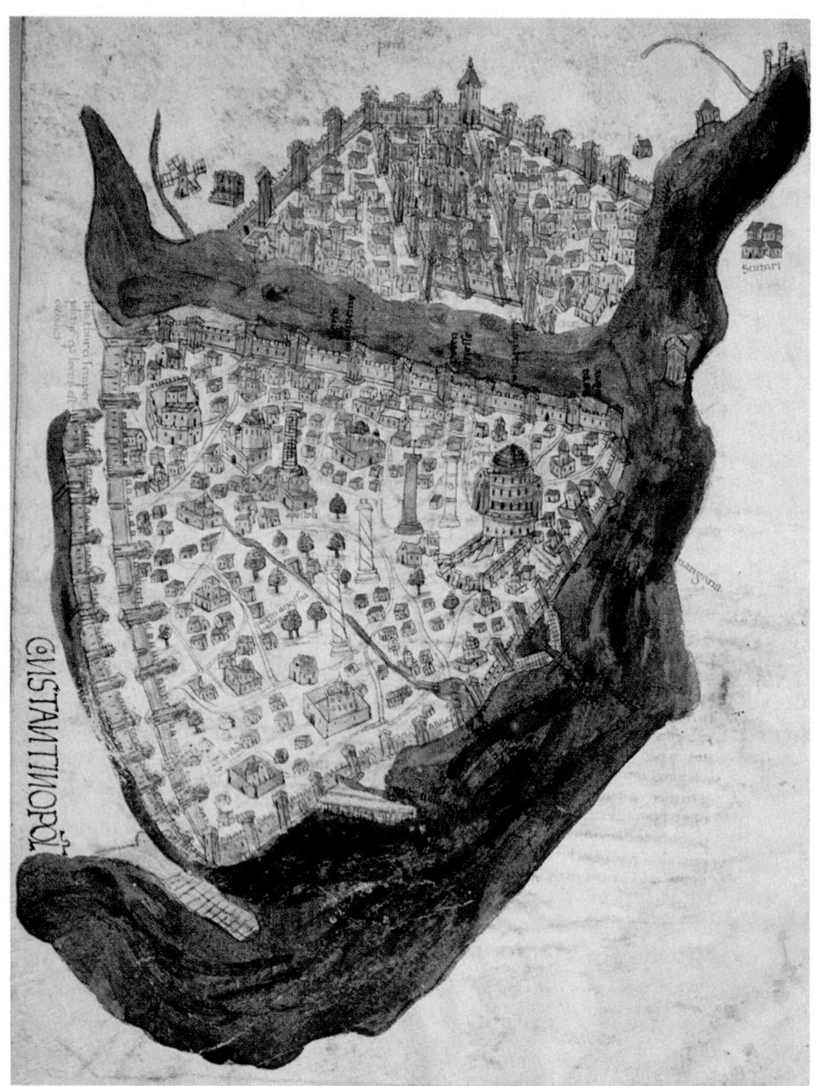

Map of Constantinople This early fifteenth-century map of Constantinople shows the Sea of Marmora (bottom), the inlet of the Golden Horn (center), two lines of city walls (left), and the domed Sancta Sophia. The U-shaped walls below the church contain the Hippodrome, site of the games, triumphs, and circuses. *(Bibliothèque Nationale, Paris)*

Empire came under Germanic sway, while in the East the Byzantine Empire continued the traditions and institutions of the caesars.

While the western parts of the Roman Empire gradually succumbed to Germanic invaders, the eastern or Roman-Byzantine Empire survived Germanic, Persian, and Arab attacks. In 540 the Huns and Bulgars crossed the Danube and raided the Balkans as far south as the Isthmus of Corinth. In 559 a force of Huns and Slavs reached the gates of Constantinople. In 583 the Avars, a mounted Mongol people who had swept across Russia and southeastern Europe, seized Byzantine forts along the Danube and also reached the walls of Constantinople. Between 572 and 630, the Sasanid Persians posed a formidable threat, and the Greeks were repeatedly at war with them. Beginning in 632, the Arabs pressured the Greek empire (see page 230). Why didn't one or a combination of these enemies capture Constantinople, as the Germans had taken Rome?

The answer lies in the strong military leadership the Greeks possessed, and even more in the city's location and its excellent fortifications. Under the skillful leadership of General Priskos (d. 612), Byzantine armies inflicted a severe defeat on the Avars in 601. Then, after a long war, the well-organized emperor Heraclius I (r. 610–641), helped by dynastic disputes among the Persians and Muslim pressures on them, crushed the Persians at Nineveh in Iraq. The Muslim Arabs now posed the greatest threat to the Byzantines. Why didn't they conquer the city? As a recent scholar explains, "If in the fourth century Constantine had chosen Antioch, Alexandria or Palestinian Caesarea as a capital there can be little doubt that the Roman empire would have gone as swiftly (to the Muslims) as the Persian."[29] The site of Constantinople was not absolutely impregnable—as the Venetians demonstrated in 1204 (see pages 284, 358) and as the Ottoman Turks did in 1453. But it was almost so. By land, the 750-mile distance between Damascus, the Muslim capital, and Constantinople, some of it mountainous terrain, posed greater geographical and logistical problems than a seventh- or eighth-century government could solve. Even if an army could be brought so far, how would it be fed and supplied? By sea, aside from the perils of navigation and the dangerous wind patterns in the eastern Mediterranean, Constantinople had the most powerful defenses in the ancient world. Massive triple walls, built by Constantine and Theodosius II (408–450) and kept in good repair, protected the city from sea invasion. Within the walls huge cisterns provided water, and vast gardens and grazing areas supplied vegetables and meat. Such strong fortifications and provisions meant that if attacked by sea, a defending people could hold out far longer than a besieging army.

The site chosen for the imperial capital in the fourth century and the thick and extensive walls built around it in the fifth century enabled Constantinople to survive in the eighth century. Because the city survived, the empire, though reduced in territory, endured.[30]

The Byzantine Empire maintained a high standard of living, and for centuries the Greeks were the most civilized people in the Western world. Most important, however, is the role of Byzantium as preserver of the wisdom of the ancient world. Byzantium protected and then handed on to the West the intellectual heritage of Greco-Roman civilization.

Byzantine East and Germanic West

As imperial authority disintegrated in the West during the fifth century, civic functions were performed first by church leaders and then by German chieftains. Meanwhile, in the East, the Byzantines preserved the forms and traditions of the old Roman Empire and even called themselves Romans. Byzantine emperors traced their lines back past Constantine to Augustus. The senate that sat in Constantinople carried on the traditions and preserved the glory of the old Roman senate. The army that defended the empire was the direct descendant of the old Roman legions. Even the chariot factions of the Roman Empire lived on under the Byzantines, who cheered their favorites as enthusiastically as had the Romans of Hadrian's day.

The position of the church differed considerably in the Byzantine East and the Germanic West. The fourth-century emperors Constantine and Theodosius I had wanted the church to act as a unifying force within the empire, but the Germanic invasions made that impossible. The bishops of Rome repeatedly called on the emperors at Constantinople for military support against the invaders, but rarely could the emperors send it. The church in the West steadily grew away from the empire and became involved in the social and political affairs of Italy and the West. Nevertheless, until the eighth century, the popes, who were often selected by the clergy of Rome, continued to send announcements of their elections to the emperors at Constantinople—a sign that the Roman popes long thought of themselves as bishops of the Roman Empire. Most church theology in the West came from the East, and the overwhelming majority of popes were themselves of Eastern origin.

Tensions occasionally developed between church officials and secular authorities in the West. The dispute between Bishop Ambrose of Milan and the emperor Theodosius (see page 200) is a good example. A century later, Pope Gelasius I (492–496) insisted that bishops, not civil authorities, were responsible for the administration of the church. Gelasius maintained that two powers governed the world: the sacred authority of popes and the royal power of kings. Because priests had to answer to God even for the actions of kings, the sacred power was the greater.

Students traditionally used the term *caesaropapism* to describe the supposedly unlimited power the emperor had over the church, even in doctrinal matters. According to this theory, the Orthodox church, in contrast to the Western church, lost its independence and was a branch of the Byzantine state. Recent scholars reject this idea as too simple. On the one hand, emperors appointed the highest officials of the church hierarchy, including the patriarchs; the emperors or their representatives presided at ecumenical councils; and the emperors controlled some of the material resources of the church—land, rents, dependent peasantry. On the other hand, the emperors performed few liturgical functions and rarely tried to impose their views in theological disputes; Greek churchmen vigorously defended the church's independence, and some even asserted the superiority of the bishop's authority over the emperor; and the church possessed such enormous economic wealth and influence over the population that it could block governmental decisions.[31] Caesaropapism, therefore, exaggerates the degree of control the emperors had over the church.

The steady separation of the Byzantine East and the Germanic West rests partly on the ways Christianity and classical culture were received in the two parts of the Roman Empire. In the West, Christians initially constituted a small, alien minority within the broad Roman culture; they kept apart from the rest of society. Roman society and classical culture were condemned, avoided, and demystified. In Byzantium, by contrast, most Greeks were Christian. *Apologists,* or defenders, of Christianity insisted on harmony between Christianity and classical culture: they used Greek philosophy to buttress Christian tenets. Politically, as we have seen, emperors beginning with Constantine worked for the unanimity of church and state.

The expansion of the Arabs in the Mediterranean in the seventh and eighth centuries furthered the separation of the Western and Eastern churches by dividing the two parts of Christendom. Separation bred isolation. Isolation, combined with prejudice on both sides, bred hostility. Finally, in 1054, a theological disagreement led the bishop of Rome and the patriarch of Constantinople to excommunicate each other. The outcome was a permanent *schism,* or split, between the Roman Catholic and Greek Orthodox churches. The Byzantine church claimed to be *orthodox,* that is, that it always possessed right doctrine.

Despite religious differences, the Byzantine Empire served as a bulwark for the West, protecting it against invasions from the East. The Greeks stopped the Persians in the seventh century. They blunted but could not stop Arab attacks in the seventh and eighth centuries, and they fought courageously against Turkish invaders until the fifteenth century, when they were finally overwhelmed. Byzantine Greeks slowed the impetus of Slavic incursions in the Balkans and held the Russians at arm's length.

Turning from war to peace, the Byzantines set about civilizing the Slavs, both in the Balkans and in Russia. Byzantine missionaries spread the word of Christ, and one of their triumphs was the conversion of the Russians in the tenth century. The Byzantine missionary Cyril invented a Slavic alphabet using Greek characters, and this script (called the "Cyrillic alphabet") is still in use today. Cyrillic script made possible the birth of Russian literature. Similarly, Byzantine art and architecture became the basis and inspiration of Russian forms. The Byzantines were so successful that the Russians claimed to be the successors of the Byzantine Empire. For a time, Moscow was even known as the "Third Rome" (the second Rome being Constantinople).

The Law Code of Justinian

One of the most splendid achievements of the Byzantine emperors was the preservation of Roman law for the medieval and modern worlds. Roman law had developed from many sources—decisions by judges, edicts of the emperors, legislation passed by the senate, and the opinions of jurists expert in the theory and practice of law. By the fourth century, Roman law had become a huge, bewildering mass. Its sheer bulk made it almost unusable. Some laws had become outdated; some repeated or contradicted others.

Sweeping and systematic codification took place under the emperor Justinian. He appointed a committee of eminent jurists to sort through and organize the laws. The result was the *Code,* which distilled the legal genius of the Romans into a coherent whole, eliminated outmoded laws and contradictions, and clarified the law itself. Not content with the *Code,* Justinian set about bringing order to the equally huge body of Roman *jurisprudence,* the science or philosophy of law.

During the second and third centuries, the foremost Roman jurists, at the request of the emperors, had expressed learned opinions on complex legal problems, but often these opinions differed from one another. To harmonize this body of knowledge, Justinian directed his jurists to clear up disputed points and to issue definitive rulings. Accordingly, in 533 his lawyers published the *Digest,* which codified Roman legal thought. Finally, Justinian's lawyers compiled a handbook of civil law, the *Institutes.* These three works—the *Code, Digest,* and *Institutes*—are the backbone of the *corpus juris civilis,* the "body of civil law," which is the foundation of law for nearly every modern European nation.

The following excerpts on marriage and adultery from the corpus juris civilis provide valuable information on the status of women in Roman and Byzantine law:

—Roman citizens unite in legal marriage when they are joined according to the precepts of the law, and males have attained the age of puberty and the females are capable of childbirth . . . [they must] if the latter have also the consent of the relatives under whose authority they may be, for this should be obtained and both civil and natural law require that it should be secured.

—The lex Julia ("Julian law," dating from 18 B.C.) declares that wives have no right to bring criminal accusations for adultery against their husbands, even though they may desire to complain of the violation of the marriage vow, for while the law grants this privilege to men it does not concede it to women.[32]

Justinian and His Attendants This mosaic detail is composed of thousands of tiny cubes of colored glass or stone called *tessarae,* which are set in plaster against a blazing golden background. Some attempt has been made at naturalistic portraiture. *(Scala/Art Resource, NY)*

Byzantine Intellectual Life

Among the Byzantines, education was highly prized, and because of them many masterpieces of ancient Greek literature survived to influence the intellectual life of the modern world. The literature of the Byzantine Empire was predominantly Greek, although Latin was long spoken among top politicians, scholars, and lawyers. Indeed, Justinian's *Code* was first written in Latin. Among the large reading public, history was a favorite subject. Generations of Byzantines read the historical works of Herodotus, Thucydides, and others. Some Byzantine historians abbreviated long histories, such as those of Polybius, while others wrote detailed narratives of their own days.

The most remarkable Byzantine historian was Procopius (ca 500–ca 562), who left a rousing account praising Justinian's reconquest of North Africa and Italy. Proof that the wit and venom of ancient writers such as Archilochus and Aristophanes lived on in the Byzantine era can be found in Procopius's *Secret History,* a vicious and uproarious attack on Justinian and his wife, the empress Theodora. (See the feature "Individuals in Society: Theodora of Constantinople.") Witness Procopius's description of Justinian's character:

> *For he was at once villainous and amenable; as people say colloquially, a moron. He was never truthful with anyone, but always guileful in what he said and did, yet easily hoodwinked by any who wanted to deceive him. His nature was an unnatural mixture of folly and wickedness.*[33]

How much of this is true, how much the hostility of a sanctimonious hypocrite relishing the gossip he spreads,

Individuals in Society

Theodora of Constantinople (ca 497–548)

The most notorious woman in Byzantine history, daughter of a circus bear trainer in the hippodrome, Theodora grew up in what contemporaries considered a morally corrupt atmosphere. Heredity gave her intelligence, wit, charm, and beauty, which she put to use as a striptease artist and actress. Modern scholars question the tales spread by the historian Procopius's *Secret History* (ca 550) about Theodora's insatiable sexual appetites, but the legend of her sensuality has often influenced interpretations of her.

Theodora gave up her stage career and passed her time spinning wool and discussing theological issues. When Justinian first saw her, he was so impressed by her beauty and wit, he brought her to the court, raised her to the *patriciate* (high nobility), and in 525 married her. When he was proclaimed co-emperor with his uncle Justin on April 1, 527, Theodora received the rare title of *augusta,* empress. Thereafter her name was always linked with Justinian's in the exercise of imperial power.

We know a fair amount about Theodora's public life. With four thousand attendants, she processed through the streets of Constantinople to attend Mass and celebrations thanking God for deliverance from the plague. She presided at imperial receptions for Arab sheiks, Persian ambassadors, Gothic princesses from the West, and barbarian chieftains from southern Russia. Her endowment of hospitals, orphanages, houses for the rehabilitation of prostitutes, and Monophysite churches gave her a reputation for piety and charity. But her private life remains hidden. She spent her days in the silken luxury of the *gynaceum* (women's quarters) among her female attendants and eunuch guards. She took the waters at the sulfur springs in Bithynia, and spent the hot summer months at her palace at Hieron, a small town on the Asiatic shore of the Bosporus. Justinian is reputed to have consulted her every day about all aspects of state policy.

One conciliar occasion stands out. In 532 various elements combined to provoke a massive revolt against the emperor. Shouting N-I-K-A (Victory), rioters swept through the city burning and looting. Justinian's counselors urged flight, but Theodora rose and declared:

For one who has reigned, it is intolerable to be an exile. . . . If you wish, O Emperor, to save yourself, there is no difficulty: we have ample funds and there are the ships. Yet reflect whether, when you have once escaped to a place of security, you will not prefer death to safety. I agree with an old saying that the purple is a fair winding sheet.

The Empress Theodora, with a halo—symbolic of power in Eastern art. *(Scala/Art Resource, NY)*

Justinian rallied, had the rioters driven into the hippodrome, and ordered between thirty-five thousand and forty thousand men and women executed. The revolt was crushed. When the bubonic plague hit Justinian in 532, Theodora took over his duties. Her influence over her husband and her power in the Byzantine state continued until she died of cancer.

How do we assess this highly complicated woman who played so many roles, who could be ruthless and merciless, political realist and yet visionary, totally loyal to those she loved? As striptease artist? Actress? Politician? Pious philanthropist? Did she learn survival in the brutal world of the hippodrome? To jump from striptease artist and the stage all the way to the imperial throne suggests enormous intelligence. Is Theodora a symbol of that manipulation of beauty and cleverness by which some women (and men) in every age have attained position and power? Were her many charitable works, especially the houses for the rehabilitation of prostitutes, the result of compassion for a profession she knew well? Or were those benefactions only what her culture expected of the rich and famous? With twenty years service to Justinian and the state, is it fair to brand her as "notorious" for what may only have been youthful indiscretions?

Questions for Analysis

1. How would you assess the importance of ceremony in Byzantine life?
2. Since Theodora's name was always linked with Justinian's, was she a co-ruler?

thinkers expressed both their own ideals and religious doctrines and the laws and customs of the Germanic peoples. Christian missionaries preached the Gospel to the Germanic peoples, instructed them in the basic tenets of the Christian faith, and used penitentials to give them a sense of right moral behavior. Monasteries provided a model of Christian living, a pattern of agricultural development, and a place for education and learning. Christianity, because it energetically and creatively fashioned the Germanic and classical legacies, proved the most powerful agent in the making of Europe.

Islam and Byzantium also made contributions. As the ancient world declined, religious faith, rather than imperial rule, became the core of social identity. Each area came to define its world in religious terms. Christians called their world *ecumenical,* meaning universal. Muslims divided the world into two fundamental sections: the House of Islam, which consisted of all those regions where the law of Islam prevailed, and the House of War, which was the rest of the world. By the logic of Islamic law, no political entity outside of Islam could exist permanently: "As there is one God in heaven, so there can be only one ruler on earth." Islam and Christianity thus each fused the social and political aspects of culture into a self-contained system.

Byzantium could not confine Islam to Arabia, but it thwarted the Muslim challenge to Christianity by restricting Arab expansion. This Byzantine check permitted a separate medieval Christendom to rise in the West. In the eighth century, spiritual loyalty to Rome enabled the papacy to develop into a supranational authority virtually independent of a secular power. The goals and energy of the bishops of Rome, combined with the military strength of the Frankish rulers, built a strong Christian faith in the Latin West.[45]

NOTES

1. See J. Hale, *The Civilization of Western Europe in the Renaissance* (New York: Atheneum, 1994), pp. xix, 3–5.
2. R. C. Petry, ed., *A History of Christianity: Readings in the History of Early and Medieval Christianity* (Englewood Cliffs, N.J.: Prentice-Hall, 1962), p. 70.
3. Matthew 16:18–19.
4. H. Bettenson, ed., *Documents of the Christian Church* (Oxford: Oxford University Press, 1947), p. 113.
5. Colossians 3:9–11.
6. Luke 6:20–31.
7. L. Sherley-Price, trans., *Bede: A History of the English Church and People* (Baltimore: Penguin Books, 1962), pp. 86–87.
8. J. T. McNeill and H. Gamer, trans., *Medieval Handbooks of Penance* (New York: Octagon Books, 1965), pp. 184–197.
9. L. White, "The Life of the Silent Majority," in *Life and Thought in the Early Middle Ages,* ed. R. S. Hoyt (Minneapolis: University of Minnesota Press, 1967), p. 100.
10. Peter 2:11–20.
11. V. L. Bullough, *The Subordinate Sex: A History of Attitudes Toward Women* (Urbana: University of Illinois Press, 1973), pp. 118–119.
12. Ibid.
13. See J. Boswell, *Christianity, Social Tolerance, and Homosexuality: Gay People in Western Europe from the Beginning of the Christian Era to the Fourteenth Century* (Chicago: University of Chicago Press, 1980), chaps. 3 and 5, esp. pp. 87, 127–131.
14. F. J. Sheed, trans., *The Confessions of St. Augustine* (New York: Sheed & Ward, 1953), bk. 1, pt. 3.
15. A. Talbot, "Monasteries," in *The Oxford Dictionary of Byzantium,* ed. A. P. Kazhdan, vol. 2 (New York: Oxford University Press, 1991), p. 1393.
16. H. Wolfram, *History of the Goths* (Berkeley: University of California Press, 1988), pp. 6–10.
17. Ibid., p. 7. See also T. Burns, *A History of the Ostrogoths* (Bloomington: University of Indiana Press, 1984), pp. 18, 21.
18. See W. Goffart, *Barbarians and Romans: The Techniques of Accommodation* (Princeton, N.J.: Princeton University Press, 1980), chap. 3 and esp. Conclusion, pp. 211–230.
19. See P. J. Geary, *Before France and Germany: The Creation and Transformation of the Merovingian World* (New York: Oxford University Press, 1988), pp. 18–25.
20. Wolfram, *History of the Goths,* pp. 125–131.
21. E. James, *The Franks* (New York: Basil Blackwell, 1988), pp. 3, 7–10, 58.
22. I. Wood, *The Merovingian Kingdoms, 450–751* (New York: Longman, 1994), pp. 41–45.
23. Geary, *Before France and Germany,* pp. 108–112.
24. E. F. Henderson, ed., *Select Historical Documents of the Middle Ages* (London: G. Bell & Sons, 1912), pp. 176–189.
25. Geary, *Before France and Germany,* p. 46.
26. Ibid., p. 50.
27. See S. F. Wemple, "Sanctity and Power: The Dual Pursuit of Early Medieval Women," in *Becoming Visible: Women in European History,* ed. R. Bridenthal et al., 2d ed. (Boston: Houghton Mifflin, 1987), pp. 133–136.
28. See S. F. Wemple, *Women in Frankish Society: Marriage and the Cloister, 500–900* (Philadelphia: University of Pennsylvania Press, 1981), pp. 28–31, 175–187.
29. Mark Whittow, *The Making of Byzantium, 600–1025* (Berkeley: University of California Press, 1996), p. 99.
30. Ibid., pp. 99–103.
31. See A. Papadakis and A. P. Kazhdan, "Caesaropapism," in *The Oxford Dictionary of Byzantium,* ed. A. P. Kazh-

dan, vol. I (New York: Oxford University Press, 1991), pp. 364–365.

32. Quoted in J. B. Bury, *History of the Latter Roman Empire,* vol. 1 (New York: Dover, 1958), pp. 233–234.
33. R. Atwater, trans., *Procopius: The Secret History* (Ann Arbor: University of Michigan Press, 1963), bk. 8.
34. W. H. McNeill, *Plagues and Peoples* (New York: Doubleday, 1976), pp. 127–128.
35. J. L. Esposito, *Islam: The Straight Path* (New York: Oxford University Press, 1988), p. 15; see also pp. 6–17.
36. F. E. Peters, *A Reader on Classical Islam* (Princeton: Princeton University Press, 1994), pp. 208–209.
37. J. O'Faolain and L. Martines, eds., *Not in God's Image: Women in History from the Greeks to the Victorians* (New York: Harper & Row, 1973), pp. 108–114.
38. T. F. Glick, *Islamic and Christian Spain in the Early Middle Ages* (Princeton, N.J.: Princeton University Press, 1979), pp. 77–78.
39. See R. W. Brauer, *Boundaries and Frontiers in Medieval Muslim Geography* (Philadelphia: American Philosophical Society, 1995), p. 41.
40. Ibid., p. 69.
41. Ibid., pp. 12–13.
42. See Esposito, *Islam,* p. 40; Peters, *A Reader on Classical Islam,* p. 154.
43. See Jo Ann Hoeppner Moran Cruz, "Popular Attitudes Towards Islam in Medieval Europe" (forthcoming).
44. See B. Lewis, *The Muslim Discovery of Europe* (New York: W. W. Norton, 1982), pp. 296–297.
45. See J. Herrin, *The Formation of Christendom* (Princeton, N.J.: Princeton University Press, 1987), pp. 7–8, 477, passim.

SUGGESTED READING

Students seeking information on the early Christian church will find sound material in the following reference works: Angelo Di Berardino, ed., *Encyclopedia of the Early Church,* trans. A. Walford, 2 vols. (1992); J. F. Kelly, *The Concise Dictionary of Early Christianity* (1992); J. McManners, ed., *The Oxford Illustrated History of Christianity* (1990); and A. P. Kazhdan, ed., *The Oxford Dictionary of Byzantium* (1991).

J. Herrin, *The Formation of Christendom* (1987), is the best recent synthesis of the history of the early Middle Ages; it also contains an excellent discussion of Byzantine, Muslim, and Western art. In addition to the other studies listed in the Notes, students may consult the following works for a more detailed treatment of the early Middle Ages. P. Brown, *The World of Late Antiquity,* A.D. *150–750,* rev. ed. (1989), stresses social and cultural change, is lavishly illustrated, and has lucidly written introductions to the entire period. J. Pelikan, *The Excellent Empire: The Fall of Rome and the Triumph of the Church* (1987), describes how interpretations of the fall of Rome have influenced our understanding of Western culture.

J. Pelikan, *Jesus Through the Centuries: His Place in the History of Culture* (1985), discusses the image of Jesus held by various cultures over the centuries and its function in the development of these cultures. W. Meeks, *The First Urban Christians: The Social World of the Apostle Paul* (1983), shows that the early Christians came from all social classes. For a solid appreciation of Christian life in a non-Christian society, see M. Mullin, *Called to Be Saints: Christian Living in First Century Rome* (1992). J. Richards, *Consul of God: The Life and Times of Gregory the Great* (1980), is the first significant study in seventy years of this watershed pontificate. P. Brown, *The Cult of the Saints: Its Rise and Function in Latin Christianity* (1982), describes the significance of the saints in popular religion. Students seeking to understand early Christian attitudes on sexuality and how they replaced Roman ones should consult the magisterial work P. Brown, *The Body and Society: Men, Women, and Sexual Renunciation in Early Christianity* (1988). R. Macmullen, *Christianity and Paganism in the Fourth to Eighth Centuries* (1998) explores the influences of Christianity and paganism on each other.

The best biography of Saint Augustine is P. Brown, *Augustine of Hippo* (1967), which treats him as a symbol of change. J. B. Russell, *Dissent and Order in the Middle Ages: The Search for Legitimate Authority* (1992), offers a provocative discussion of religious orthodoxy and heresy in the church.

The phenomenon of monasticism has attracted interest throughout the centuries. The best modern edition of the Benedictine *Rule* is T. Fry et al., eds., *RB 1980: The Rule of St. Benedict in Latin and English with Notes* (1981), which contains a history of Western monasticism and a scholarly commentary on the *Rule.* L. Eberle, trans., *The Rule of the Master* (1977), offers the text of and a commentary on Benedict's major source. C. H. Lawrence, *Medieval Monasticism: Forms of Religious Life in Western Europe in the Middle Ages* (1988), provides a good general sketch and a helpful glossary of terms, though it confuses the monastic and the mendicant orders. Two beautifully illustrated syntheses by leading authorities are D. Knowles, *Christian Monasticism* (1969), which sketches monastic history through the middle of the twentieth century; and G. Zarnecki, *The Monastic Achievement* (1972), which focuses on the medieval centuries. For women in monastic life, see S. F. Wemple, *Women in Frankish Society: Marriage and the Cloister, 500–900* (1981), an important book with a good bibliography; and the magisterial achievement of J. K. McNamara, *Sisters in Arms: Catholic Nuns Through Two Millennia* (1996).

For Byzantium and the Arabs, see J. J. Norwich, *Byzantium: The Early Centuries* (1989), an elegantly written sketch; E. Patlagean, "Byzantium in the Tenth and Eleventh Centuries," in *A History of Private Life.* Vol. 1: *From Pagan Rome to Byzantium* (1987); J. Hussey, *The*

Byzantine World (1961); S. Runciman, *Byzantine Civilization* (1956); and A. Bridge, *Theodora: Portrait in a Byzantine Landscape* (1984), a romantic and amusing biography of the courtesan who became empress. A. Harvey, *Economic Expansion in the Byzantine Empire, 900–1200* (1989), should prove useful for research on social and economic change. J. L. Esposito, *Islam: The Straight Path* (1988), is an informed and balanced work based on the best modern scholarship, but the older study of M. Rodinson, *Mohammed* (1974), is still useful. R. Collins, *The Arab Conquest of Spain, 710–797* (1994), assesses the cultural impact of Arab rule, and D. J. Wasserstein, *The Caliphate in the West: An Islamic Political Institution in the Iberian Peninsula* (1993), studies the major political institution. The articles in B. Lewis, *Islam and the West* (1993), especially "The Encounter of Europe and Islam" and "The Shi'a in Islamic History," offer a provocative treatment of some of the themes of this chapter. L. Ahmed, *Women and Gender in Islam: Historical Roots of a Modern Debate* (1992), is a most important contribution and the starting point for all research on Islam and gender, while N. R. Keddie and B. Brown, eds., *Women in Middle Eastern History: Shifting Boundaries in Sex and Gender* (1992), provides a variety of perspectives on women's roles.

LISTENING TO THE PAST

The Conversion of Clovis

Modern Christian doctrine holds that conversion is a process, the gradual turning toward Jesus and the teachings of the Christian Gospels. But in the early medieval world, conversion was perceived more as a one-time event determined by the tribal chieftain. If he accepted baptism, the mass conversion of his people followed. The selection here about the Frankish king Clovis is from the History of the Franks *by Gregory, bishop of Tours (ca 504–594), written about a century after the events it describes.*

The first child which Clotild bore for Clovis was a son. She wanted to have her baby baptized, and she kept urging her husband to agree to this. "The gods whom you worship are no good," she would say. "They haven't even been able to help themselves, let alone others. . . . Take your Saturn, for example, who ran away from his own son to avoid being exiled from his kingdom, or so they say; and Jupiter, that obscene perpetrator of all sorts of mucky deeds, who couldn't keep his hands off other men, who had his fun with all his female relatives and couldn't even refrain from intercourse with his own sister. . . .

"You ought instead to worship Him who created at a word and out of nothing heaven, and earth, the sea and all that therein is, who made the sun to shine, who lit the sky with stars, who peopled the water with fish, the earth with beasts, the sky with flying creatures, by whose hand the race of man was made, by whose gift all creation is constrained to serve in deference and devotion the man He made." However often the Queen said this, the King came no nearer to belief. . . .

The Queen, who was true to her faith, brought her son to be baptized. . . . The child was baptized; he was given the name Ingomer; but no sooner had he received baptism than he died in his white robes. Clovis was extremely angry. He began immediately to reproach his Queen. "If he had been dedicated in the name of my gods," he said, "he would have lived without question; but now that he has been baptized in the name of your God he has not been able to live a single day!"

"I give thanks to Almighty God," replied Clotild, "the Creator of all things who has not found me completely unworthy, for He has deigned to welcome into his Kingdom a child conceived in my womb. . . ."

Some time later Clotild bore a second son. He was baptized Chlodomer. He began to ail and Clovis said, "What else do you expect? It will happen to him as it happened to his brother: no sooner is he baptized in the name of your Christ than he will die!" Clotild prayed to the Lord and at His commands the baby recovered.

Queen Clotild continued to pray that her husband might recognize the true God and give up his idol-worship. Nothing could persuade him to accept Christianity. Finally war broke out against the Alamanni and in this conflict he was forced by necessity to accept what he had refused of his own free will. It so turned out that when the two armies met on the battlefield there was a great slaughter and the troops of Clovis were rapidly being annihilated. He raised his eyes to heaven when he saw this, felt compunction in his heart and was moved to tears. "Jesus Christ," he said, "you who Clotild maintains to be the Son of the living God, you who deign to give help to those in travail and victory to those who trust in you, in faith I beg the glory of your help. If you will give me victory over my enemies, and if I may have evidence to that miraculous power which the people dedicated to your name say that they have experienced, then I will believe in you and I will be baptized in your name. I have called upon my own gods, but, as I see only too clearly, they have no intention of helping me. I therefore cannot believe that they possess any power for they do not come to the assistance of those who trust them. I now call upon you. I want to believe in you, but I must first be saved from my enemies." Even as he said this the Alamanni turned their backs and began to run away. As soon as they saw that their King was killed, they submitted to Clovis. "We beg you," they said, "to put an end to this slaughter. We are prepared to obey you." Clovis stopped the war. He made a speech in which he called for peace. Then he went home. He told the Queen how he had won a victory by calling on the name of Christ. This happened in the fifteenth year of his reign (496).

The Queen then ordered Saint Remigius, Bishop of the town of Rheims, to be summoned in secret. She begged him to impart the word of salvation to the King. The Bishop asked Clovis to meet him in private and began to urge him to believe in the true God, Maker of heaven and earth, and to forsake his idols, which were powerless to help him or anyone else. The King replied: "I have listened to you willingly, holy father. There remains one obstacle. The people under my command will not agree to forsake their gods. I will go and put to them what you have just said to me." He arranged a meeting with this people, but God in his power had preceded him, and before he could say a word all those present shouted in unison: "We will give up worshipping our mortal gods, pious King, and we are prepared to follow the immortal God about whom Remigius preaches." This news was reported to the Bishop. He was greatly pleased and he ordered the baptismal pool to be made ready. . . . The baptistry was prepared, sticks of incense gave off clouds of perfume, sweet-smelling candles gleamed bright and the holy place of baptism was filled with divine fragrance. God filled the hearts of all present with such grace that they imagined themselves to have been transported to some perfumed paradise. King Clovis asked that he might be baptized first by the Bishop. Like some new Constantine he stepped forward to the baptismal pool, ready to wash away the sores of his old leprosy and to be cleansed in flowing water from the sordid stains which he had borne so long.

King Clovis confessed his belief in God Almighty, three in one. He was baptized in the name of the Father, the Son and the Holy Ghost, and marked in holy chrism [an anointing oil] with the sign of the Cross of Christ. More than three thousand of his army were baptized at the same time.

✣ Ninth-century ivory carving showing Clovis being baptized by Saint Remi. *(Musée Condé, Chantilly/Laurie Platt Winfrey, Inc.)*

Questions for Analysis

1. Who took the initiative in urging Clovis's conversion? What can we deduce from that?
2. According to this account, why did Clovis ultimately accept Christianity?
3. For the Salian Franks, what was the best proof of divine power?
4. On the basis of this selection, do you consider the *History of the Franks* reliable history? Why or why not?

Sources: L. Thorpe, trans., *The History of the Franks by Gregory of Tours* (Harmondsworth, England: Penguin, 1974), p. 159; P. J. Geary, ed., *Readings in Medieval History* (Peterborough, Ontario: Broadview Press, 1991), pp. 165–166.

CHAPTER 8

The Carolingian World: Europe in the Early Middle Ages

Cover of codex Aureus of Saint Emmeram, ca 870. *(Stadtsbibliothek, Munich)*

The Frankish chieftain Charles Martel defeated Muslim invaders in 732 at the Battle of Poitiers in central France.[1] Muslims and Christians have interpreted the battle differently. To the Muslims, it was only a minor skirmish, won by the Franks because of Muslim difficulties in maintaining supply lines over long distances and the distraction of ethnic conflicts and unrest in Islamic Spain. For Christians, the Frankish victory has been perceived as one of the great battles of history: it halted Muslim expansion in Europe. A century after this victory, in 843, Charles Martel's three great-great-grandsons concluded the Treaty of Verdun, which divided the European continent among themselves.

Between 732 and 843, a distinctly European society emerged. A new kind of social and political organization, later called "feudalism," appeared. And for the first time since the collapse of the Roman Empire, most of western Europe was united under one government. That government reached the peak of its development under Charles Martel's grandson, Charlemagne. Christian missionary activity among the Germanic peoples continued, and strong ties were forged with the Roman papacy. A revival of study and learning, sometimes styled the "Carolingian Renaissance," occurred under Charlemagne.

- How did Merovingian and Carolingian rulers govern their kingdoms and empire?
- What was the significance of the relations between Carolingian rulers and the church?
- The culture of the Carolingian Empire has been described as the "first European civilization." What does this mean?
- What factors contributed to the disintegration of the Carolingian Empire?
- In a society wracked with constant war and violence, what medical care was available?
- Consider some of the historiographical problems related to the word *feudalism.*
- How did Viking expansion lead to the establishment of the Kievan principality?

These are among the questions that this chapter will explore.

The Frankish Kingdom and the Emergence of the Carolingians

The success of the Frankish king Clovis, as we have seen (see pages 218–219), rested on three major developments: Clovis's series of military victories over other Germanic tribes; his acquisition of the wealthy provinces of Roman Gaul with their administrative machinery intact; and, after Clovis's conversion to orthodox Christianity, the ideological support of the Roman papacy and of the bishops of Gaul. By selecting as his capital Paris—legendary scene of the martyrdom of Saint Denis, believed to be a disciple of Saint Paul—Clovis identified himself with the cult of Saint Denis and used it to strengthen his rule. The Frankish kingdom included much of what is now France and a large section of southwestern Germany.

When he died, following Frankish custom, Clovis divided his kingdom among his four sons, a partition not according to strict acreage but in portions yielding roughly equal revenues.[2] Historians have long described Merovingian Gaul in the sixth and seventh centuries as wracked by civil wars, chronic violence, and political instability as Clovis's descendants fought among themselves. So brutal and destructive were these wars and so violent the ordinary conditions of life that the term *Dark Ages* came to designate the entire Merovingian period. Recent research has presented a more complex picture. The civil wars were indeed destructive but they "did not pose a threat to the survival of the kingdom. Indeed, in a sense, they were a unifying part of the structure of the Frankish state in the sixth century and for most of the seventh."[3]

What caused the civil wars? First, the death or even reported death of a king triggered crisis and war. Lacking a clear principle of succession, any male of Merovingian blood could claim the throne, and within the Merovingian family there were often many possibilities. A prince-claimant had to prove himself worthy on the battlefield. Second, the desire for new lands provoked conflict. Royal officials and warriors had a similar desire for new estates, and they sold their support to the prince who would promise them more lands. Royal armies also wanted war because war meant booty and plunder. Sometimes a Merovingian king's great warriors urged him, even against his better judgment, to make war so that they could profit economically. No one disputed the Merovingian family's right to rule: it alone possessed the blood and charisma. The issue was which member. Thus the royal family and the royal court served as the focus around which conflicts arose, and in this sense the civil wars actually held the kingdom together.[4]

Merovingian politics provided royal women with opportunities, and some queens not only influenced but occasionally dominated events. The theoretical status of a princess or queen rested on her diplomatic importance, with her marriage sealing or divorce breaking an alliance; on her personal relationship with her husband and her ability to give him sons and heirs; on her role as the mother and guardian of princes who had not reached legal adulthood; and on her control of the royal treasury. For example, when King Chilperic I (561–584) was murdered, his wife Fredegunda controlled a large state treasury. The historian Fredegar alleges that Queen Brunhilda (d. 613), wife of King Sigebert of the East Frankish kingdom, killed twelve kings in pursuit of her political goals, including Sigebert, her grandchildren, and their offspring. When her sister Galswintha was found strangled to death in bed shortly after her marriage to Chilperic, ruler of the West Frankish kingdom, Brunhilda suspected Chilperic of the murder—so that he could marry his then mistress, Fredegunda. Brunhilda instigated war between the two kingdoms. After 592 she was the real power behind her sons' and grandsons' shaky thrones, and she also ruled Burgundy, which her maneuvers had united to the East Frankish kingdom. Contemporaries may have exaggerated Brunhilda's murders, but her career reflects both the domestic violence of the Merovingian royal family and the fierce determination of some queens to exercise power.

How did Merovingian rulers govern? What were their sources of income? How did they communicate with their peoples? While local administration probably varied somewhat according to regional tradition, the *civitas*—the city and surrounding territory—served as the basis of the administrative system in the Frankish kingdom. A *comites*—senior official or royal companion, later called a count—presided over the civitas. He collected royal revenue, heard lawsuits, enforced justice, and raised troops. To receive his tax revenues, a Frankish king had to be sure of the comites' loyalty. Rebellion led to confiscation of the comites' lands. A ruler's general sources of income were revenues from the royal estates, especially large in the north; the right to hospitality when he visited an area (with wives, children, servants, court officials, and several hundred warriors, plus all their horses, hospitality could be a severe drain on the resources of a region); the conquest and confiscation of new lands, which replenished lands given as monastic or religious endowments; and the "gifts" of subject peoples, such as plunder and tribute paid by peoples east of the Rhine River. Specific income derived from a land tax paid by all free landowners, originally collected by the Romans and continued by the Franks. In the course of the seventh century, the value of this tax declined as all Franks gradually gained immunity from it. In fact, the term *frank* began to be associated with freedom from taxation, which may have been an incentive for Gallo-Romans to shift their ethnic allegiance to the Franks. Fines imposed for criminal offenses and tolls and customs duties on roads, bridges, and waterways (and the goods transported over them) also yielded income. As with the Romans, the minting of coins was a royal monopoly, with drastic penalties for counterfeiting. For all this, the comites had responsibility.[5]

Merovingian, Carolingian (see page 245), and later medieval rulers led peripatetic lives, traveling constantly to check up on local administrators and peoples. Merovingian kings also relied on the comites and bishops to gather and send local information to them. Gallo-Roman by descent, bishops and comites were usually native to the regions they administered and knew their areas well. A bishop, for example, might report injustices done by secular officials. Frankish royal administration involved a third official, the *dux* (duke). He was a military leader, commanding troops in the territory of several civitas, and thus responsible for all defensive and offensive strategies. Kings seem to have appointed only Franks to this position.

Clovis and his descendants in the sixth and seventh centuries also issued *capitularies,* administrative and legislative orders divided into *capitula,* chapters or articles. These laws attempted to regulate a variety of matters: for example, protecting priests, monks, nuns, and church property from violence; defining ownership and inheritance; punishing drunkenness, robbery, arson, rape, and murder. Apart from the violent and crime-ridden realities of Merovingian society, capitularies show the strong influence of Roman law. They also reveal Merovingian kings trying to maintain law and order, holding courts, and being actively involved in exercising judicial authority. The Roman idea, strengthened by political Augustinianism began to take root: a good or effective king maintained peace and gave his people justice.

The court or household of Merovingian kings also included scribes who kept records, legal officials who advised the king on matters of law, and treasury agents responsible for aspects of royal finance. These officials

Merovingian Army This sixth- or seventh-century ivory depicts a nobleman in civilian dress followed by seven warriors. Note that the mounted men do not have stirrups and that they seem to have fought with spears and bows and arrows. The power of the Frankish aristocracy rested on these private armies. *(Landesmuseum, Trier)*

could all read and write Latin. Over them all presided the mayor of the palace, the most important secular figure in the kingdom. Usually a leader of one of the great aristocratic families, the mayor governed the palace and the kingdom in the king's absence.[6]

Kings also consulted regularly with the leaders of the aristocracy. This class represented a fusion of Franks and the old Gallo-Roman leadership. It possessed landed wealth, villas over which it exercised lordship, dispensing local customary, not royal, law; and it often led a rich and lavish lifestyle. Members of this class constituted, when they were with the king, the royal court, those around the king at a given time. If he consulted them and they were in agreement, there was peace. Failure to consult could mean resentment and the potential for civil war.

From this aristocracy there gradually emerged in the eighth century one family that replaced the Merovingian dynasty. The emergence of the Carolingians—whose name comes from the Latin *Carolus,* or Charles—rests on several factors. First, beginning with Pippin I (d. 640), the head of the family acquired and held on to the powerful position of mayor of the palace. Second, a series of advantageous marriage alliances brought the family estates and influence in different parts of the Frankish world. Thus Pippin II (d. 714), through his first marriage, won influence in the territory around Echternach (modern Luxembourg) and, by his second wife, estates in the Meuse Valley. The landed wealth and treasure acquired by Pippin II, Charles Martel (r. 714–741), and Pippin III (r. 751–768) formed the basis of Carolingian power.[7] Although Pippin II and his son Charles Martel possessed more lands than any other single aristocratic family, and although they held the positions of mayor of the palace and duke, their ultimate supremacy was by no means certain. Other dukes rallied to the support of the Merovingians, and Pippin devoted much energy to fighting these magnates. Only his victory over them and King Theuderich at Tertry in 687 ensured his dominance. Such victories gave the family a reputation for military strength. Charles Martel's successful wars against the Saxons, Frisians, Alamans, and Bavarians, as well as his defeat of the Arabs near Poitiers in 732, further enhanced the family's prestige, while also adding distinction as defenders of Christendom against the Muslims.

The early Carolingians also acquired the support of the church, perhaps the decisive asset. Irish, Frankish, and Anglo-Saxon missionaries, of whom the Englishman Boniface (680–754) is the most famous, preached

Christianity to pagan peoples and worked to reorganize the Frankish church. Boniface's courage in chopping down the oak of Thor at Geismar, near Fritzlar, the center of a large pagan cult, won him many converts. With close ties to the Roman papacy, Boniface participated in establishing the abbey of Fulda and the archdiocese of Mainz, held church councils, and promoted *The Rule of Saint Benedict* in all monasteries. (In the latter, Boniface was not successful. Many monasteries preferred to be guided by several monastic directives.) The Carolingian mayors of the palace, Charles Martel and Pippin III, fully supported this evangelizing activity, as missionaries also preached obedience to secular authorities as a religious duty.

As mayor of the palace, Charles Martel had exercised the power of king of the Franks. His son Pippin III aspired to the title as well. Against the background of collaboration between missionaries and the Frankish mayors, Pippin sent delegates to Pope Zacharias asking him whether the man who held the power should also have the title of king. Pippin's ambassadors reached Rome at a diplomatically opportune moment. In the eighth century, the Lombards severely threatened the papacy, which, being subject to the Byzantine emperor, looked to Constantinople for support. But Byzantium, pressured from the outside by attacks from the Arabs and the Avars and wracked internally by the dispute over the veneration of icons, known as iconoclasm, was in no position to send help to the West. Pope Zacharias therefore shifted his allegiance from the Greeks to the Franks and told Pippin that "it was better to call him king who had the royal power 'in order to prevent provoking civil war in Francia'" and that Zacharias "by virtue of his apostolic authority commanded that Pippin should be made king."[8] Chilperic, the last Merovingian ruler, was consigned to a monastery. An assembly of Frankish magnates elected Pippin king, and he was anointed by Boniface at Soissons. When, in 754, Lombard expansion again threatened the papacy, Pope Stephen II journeyed to the Frankish kingdom seeking help. On this occasion, he personally anointed Pippin and gave him the title "Patrician of the Romans." Pippin promised restitution of the papal lands.

Thus an important alliance had been struck between the papacy and the Frankish monarchs. On a successful campaign in Italy in 756, Pippin made a large donation

Christ as a War Leader To capture the imagination of the Germanic warriors for Christianity, artists sometimes portrayed Christ as a military figure, as in this seventh-century funerary plaque where he appears holding a lance and wearing a battle-axe, but treading on a snake—symbolizing his triumph over evil and death. *(University Library, Utrecht)*

to the papacy. The gift consisted of estates in central Italy that technically belonged to the Byzantine emperor. Because of his anointment, Pippin's kingship took on a special spiritual and moral character. Before Pippin, only priests and bishops had received anointment. Pippin became the first to be anointed with the sacred oils and acknowledged as *rex et sacerdos* (king and priest). Anointment, rather than royal blood, set the Christian king apart. Pippin also cleverly eliminated possible threats to the Frankish throne, and the pope promised him support in the future. When Pippin died, his son Charles, generally known as Charlemagne, succeeded him.

When Charlemagne went to Rome in 800, Pope Leo III showed him the signs of respect due only to the emperor. The Carolingian family thus received official recognition from the leading spiritual power in Europe, and the papacy gained a military protector. The Greeks regarded the papal acts as rebellious and Charlemagne as a usurper. The imperial coronation marks a decisive break between Rome and Constantinople.

The Imperial Coronation of Charlemagne

In the autumn of the year 800, Charlemagne paid a momentous visit to Rome. Charlemagne's secretary and biographer, Einhard, gives this account of what happened:

His last journey there [to Rome] was due to another factor, namely that the Romans, having inflicted many injuries on Pope Leo—plucking out his eyes and tearing out his tongue, he had been compelled to beg the assistance of the king. Accordingly, coming to Rome in order that he might set in order those things which had exceedingly disturbed the condition of the Church, he remained there the whole winter. It was at the time that he accepted the name of Emperor and Augustus. At first he was so much opposed to this that he insisted that although that day was a great [Christian] feast, he would not have entered the Church if he had known beforehand the pope's intention. But he bore very patiently the jealousy of the Roman Emperors [that is, the Byzantine rulers] who were indignant when he received these titles. He overcame their arrogant haughtiness with magnanimity, a virtue in which he was considerably superior to them, by sending frequent ambassadors to them and in his letters addressing them as brothers.[9]

For centuries scholars have debated the significance of the imperial coronation of Charlemagne. Did Charlemagne plan the ceremony in Saint Peter's on Christmas Day, or did he merely accept the title of emperor? What did he have to gain from it? If, as Einhard implies, the coronation displeased Charlemagne, did that displeasure rest on Pope Leo's role in the ceremony, which, on the principle that he who gives can also take away, placed the pope in a higher position than the emperor? Did Pope Leo arrange the coronation in order to identify the Frankish monarchy with the papacy and papal policy?

Though final answers will probably never be found, several things seem certain. First, Charlemagne gained the imperial title of Holy Roman emperor and considered himself a Christian king ruling a Christian people. His motto, *Renovatio romani imperi* (Revival of the Roman Empire), "implied a revival of the Western Empire in the image of Augustinian political philosophy."[10] Charlemagne was consciously perpetuating old Roman imperial notions, while at the same time identifying with the new Rome of the Christian church. Charlemagne and his government represented a combination of Frankish practices and Christian ideals, the two basic elements of medieval European society. Second, later German rulers were anxious to gain the imperial title and to associate themselves with the legends of Charlemagne and ancient Rome. They wanted to use the ideology of imperial Rome to strengthen their positions. Finally, ecclesiastical authorities continually cited the event as proof that the dignity of the imperial crown could be granted only by the pope. The imperial coronation of Charlemagne, whether planned by the Carolingian court or by the papacy, was to have a profound effect on the course of German history and on the later history of Europe.

THE EMPIRE OF CHARLEMAGNE

Charles the Great (r. 768–814), known as Charlemagne, built on the military and diplomatic foundations of his ancestors and on the administrative machinery of the Merovingian kings. Einhard wrote a lengthy idealization of this warrior-ruler. It has serious flaws, partly because it is modeled directly on the Roman author Suetonius's *Life of the Emperor Augustus.* Still, it is the earliest medieval biography of a layman, and historians consider it generally accurate:

Charles was large and strong, and of lofty stature, though not disproportionately tall . . . the upper part of his head was round, his eyes very large and animated, nose a little long, hair fair, and face laughing and merry. Thus his appearance was always stately and dignified . . . although his neck was thick and somewhat short, and his belly rather

Charlemagne in the Twelfth Century The image of a stern, slender Charles in classical Roman garb reflects twelfth-century physical and political ideals, not the squat, pot-bellied ruler described by his contemporary Einhard. Charles wears a crown or helmet, symbol of his duty to protect and defend his people. In his right hand he carries an orb surmounted by a cross, representing universal power and his obligation to give justice under God; his left hand bears the scepter, emblem of authority. The statue shows the fusion of legend and history in early medieval culture. *(Ann Münchow, Aachen, Courtesy of Domkapital)*

prominent; but the symmetry of the rest of his body concealed these defects. His gait was firm, his whole carriage manly and his voice clear, but not so strong as his size led one to expect. His health was excellent, except during the four years preceding his death. . . .

In accordance with the national custom, he took frequent exercise on horseback and in the chase. . . . He . . . often practiced swimming, in which he was such an adept that none could surpass him. . . . He used not only to invite his sons to his bath, but his nobles and friends, and now and then a troop of his retinue or bodyguard.[11]

Though crude and brutal, Charlemagne was a man of enormous intelligence. He appreciated good literature, such as Saint Augustine's *City of God,* and Einhard considered him an unusually effective speaker. Recent scholarship disputes Einhard's claim that Charlemagne could not write.

The security and continuation of his dynasty and the need for diplomatic alliances governed Charlemagne's complicated marriage pattern. The high rate of infant mortality required many sons. Married first to the daughter of Desiderius, king of the Lombards, Charlemagne divorced her either because she failed to produce a child within a year or for diplomatic reasons. His second wife, Hildegard, produced nine children in twelve years. When she died, Charlemagne married Fastrada, daughter of an East Frankish count whose support he needed in his campaign against the Saxons. Charlemagne had a total of four legal wives and six concubines, and even after the age of sixty-five, he continued to sire children. Though three sons reached adulthood, only one outlived him. Four surviving grandsons ensured perpetuation of the family.[12] The most striking feature of Charlemagne's character was his phenomenal energy, which helps to explain his great military achievements.

Territorial Expansion

Continuing the expansionist policies of his ancestors, Charlemagne fought more than fifty campaigns and became the greatest warrior of the early Middle Ages. He subdued all of the north of modern France. In the south, the lords of the mountainous ranges of Aquitaine fought off his efforts at total conquest. The Muslims in northeastern Spain were checked by the establishment of strongly fortified areas known as *marches.*

Charlemagne's greatest successes were in today's Germany. There his concerns were basically defensive. In the course of a thirty-year war against the Saxons, he added most of the northwestern German tribes to the Frankish kingdom. Because of their repeated rebellions, Charlemagne ordered, according to Einhard, more than four thousand Saxons slaughtered in one day.

To the south, he also achieved spectacular results. In 773 to 774, the Lombards in northern Italy again threatened the papacy. Charlemagne marched south, overran fortresses at Pavia and Spoleto, and incorporated Lombardy into the Frankish kingdom. To his title king of the Franks he added king of the Lombards. Charlemagne also ended Bavarian independence and defeated the nomadic Avars, opening the Danubian plain for later settlement. He successfully fought the Byzantine Empire for Venetia (excluding the city of Venice itself), Istria, and Dalmatia and temporarily annexed those areas to his kingdom.

Charlemagne also tried to occupy Basque territory in northwestern Spain. When his long siege of Saragossa proved unsuccessful and the Saxons on his northeastern borders rebelled, Charlemagne decided to withdraw, but the Basques annihilated his rear guard under Count Roland at Roncesvalles (778), near Pamplona in the Pyrenees. This attack represented Charlemagne's only defeat, and he forbade people to talk about it. However, the expedition inspired the great medieval epic *The Song of Roland.* Based on legend and written down about 1100 at the beginning of the European crusading movement, the poem portrays Roland as the ideal chivalric knight and Charlemagne as exercising a sacred kind of kingship. Although many of the epic's details differ from the historical evidence, *The Song of Roland* is important because it reveals the popular image of Charlemagne in later centuries.

By around 805, the Frankish kingdom included all of northwestern Europe except Scandinavia (Map 8.1). Not since the third century A.D. had any ruler controlled so much of the Western world.

The Government of the Carolingian Empire

Charlemagne ruled a vast rural world dotted with isolated estates and small villages and characterized by constant warfare. According to the chroniclers of the time, between 714 and 814 only seven years were peaceful. Charlemagne's empire was not a state as people today understand that term; it was a collection of peoples and tribes. Apart from a small class of warrior-aristocrats and clergy, and a very tiny minority of Jews, almost everyone engaged in agriculture. Trade and commerce played a small part in the general economy. Towns served as the headquarters of bishops, as ecclesiastical centers. The Carolingians inherited the office and the administrative machinery of the Merovingian kings and the functions of the mayor of the palace. The Carolingians relied heavily on the personality and energy of the monarchs. The scholar-adviser Alcuin (see pages 255–256) wrote that "a king should be strong against his enemies, humble to Christians, feared by pagans, loved by the poor and judicious in counsel and maintaining justice."[13] Charlemagne worked to realize that ideal. By military expeditions that brought wealth—lands, booty, slaves, and tribute—and by peaceful travel, personal appearances, and the sheer force of his personality, Charlemagne sought to awe newly conquered peoples and rebellious domestic enemies with his fierce presence and terrible justice. By confiscating the estates of great territorial magnates, he acquired lands and goods with which to gain the support of lesser lords, further expanding the territory under his control.

The political power of the Carolingians rested on the cooperation of the dominant social class, the Frankish aristocracy. By the seventh century, through mutual cooperation and frequent marriage alliances, these families exercised great power that did not derive from the Merovingian kings. The Carolingians themselves had emerged from this aristocracy, and the military and political success that Carolingians such as Pippin II achieved depended on the support of the nobility. The lands and booty with which Charles Martel and Charlemagne rewarded their followers in these families enabled the nobles to improve their economic position, but it was only with noble help that the Carolingians were able to wage wars of expansion and suppress rebellions. In short, Carolingian success was a matter of reciprocal help and reward.[14]

For administrative purposes, Charlemagne divided his entire kingdom into *counties,* based closely on the old Merovingian civitas (see page 244). Each of the approximately six hundred counties was governed by a count (or in his absence, a viscount), who published royal orders, held courts and resolved legal cases, collected taxes and tolls, raised troops for the army, and supervised maintenance of roads and bridges. Counts were at first sent out from the royal court; later someone native to the region was appointed. As a link between local authorities and the central government, Charlemagne appointed officials called *missi dominici,* "agents of the lord king." The empire was divided into visitorial districts. Each year, beginning in 802, two missi, usually a count and a bishop or abbot, visited assigned districts. They held courts and investigated the district's judicial, financial, and clerical activities. They organized commissions to regulate crime, moral conduct, the clergy, education, the poor, and many other matters. The missi checked up on the counts. In the *marches,* especially in unstable or threatened areas such as along the Spanish or Danish frontiers, officials called *margraves* had extensive powers to govern.

A modern state has institutions of government, such as a civil service, courts of law, financial agencies for collecting and apportioning taxes, and police and military powers with which to maintain order internally and defend against foreign attack. These simply did not exist in Charlemagne's empire. Instead, society was held together by dependent relationships cemented by oaths promising faith and loyalty.

Although the empire lacked viable institutions, some Carolingians involved in governing did have vigorous political ideas. The abbots and bishops who served as

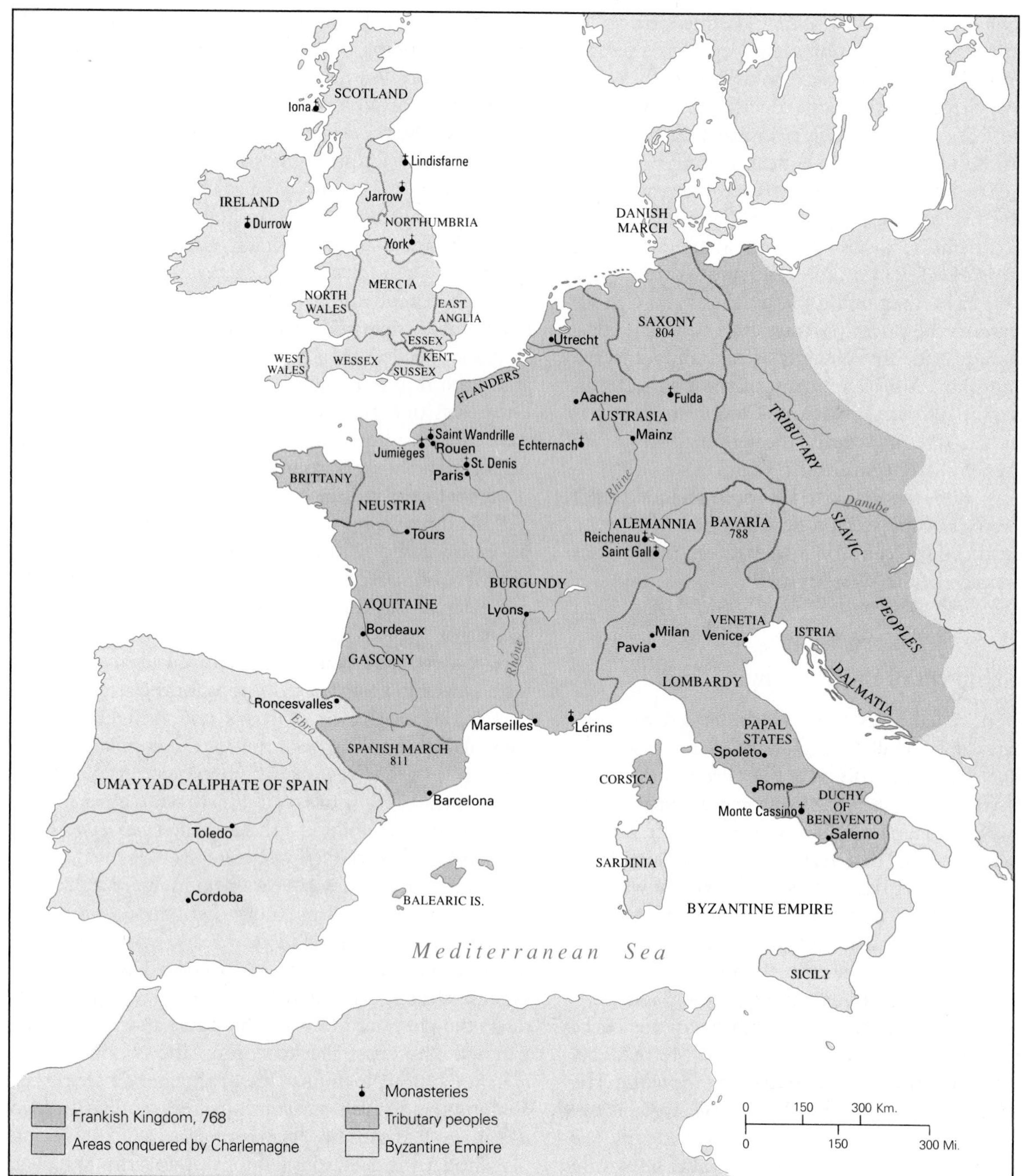

MAP 8.1 The Carolingian World The extent of Charlemagne's nominal jurisdiction was extraordinary: it was not equaled until the nineteenth century.

Charlemagne's advisers worked out what was for their time a sophisticated political ideology. In letters and treatises, they set before their ruler high ideals of behavior and government. They wrote that a ruler may hold power from God but is responsible to the law. Just as all subjects of the empire were required to obey him, he, too, was obliged to respect the law. They envisioned a unified Christian society presided over by a king who was responsible for maintaining peace, law, and order and doing justice, without which neither the ruler nor the kingdom had any justification. These views derived largely from Saint Augustine's theories of kingship. Inevitably, they could not be realized in an illiterate, preindustrial society. But they were the seeds from which medieval and even modern ideas of government were to develop.

The Carolingian Intellectual Revival

It is perhaps ironic that Charlemagne's most enduring legacy was the stimulus he gave to scholarship and learning. Barely literate himself, preoccupied with the control of vast territories, much more a warrior than an intellectual, he nevertheless set in motion a cultural revival that had widespread and long-lasting consequences. The revival of learning associated with Charlemagne and his court at Aachen drew its greatest inspiration from seventh- and eighth-century intellectual developments in the Anglo-Saxon kingdom of Northumbria, situated at the northernmost tip of the old Roman world.

Northumbrian Culture

Despite the victory of the Roman forms of Christian liturgy at the Synod of Whitby in 664 (see page 204), Irish-Celtic culture permeated the Roman church in Britain and resulted in a flowering of artistic and scholarly activity. Northumbrian creativity owes a great deal to the intellectual curiosity and collecting zeal of Saint Benet Biscop (ca 628–689). The manuscripts and other treasures he brought back from Italy formed the library on which much later study rested. (See the feature "Individuals in Society: Saint Benet Biscop of Wearmouth and Jarrow.")

Northumbrian monasteries produced scores of books: *missals* (used for the celebration of the Mass), *psalters* (which contained the 150 psalms and other prayers used by the monks in their devotions), commentaries on the Scriptures, illuminated manuscripts, law codes, and collections of letters and sermons. The finest product of Northumbrian art is probably the Gospel book produced at Lindisfarne around 700. The incredible expense involved in the publication of such a book—for vellum (calfskin or lambskin specially prepared for writing), coloring, and gold leaf—represents in part an aristocratic display of wealth. The script, *uncial,* is a Celtic version of contemporary Greek and Roman handwriting. The illustrations have a strong Eastern quality, combining the abstract, nonrepresentational style of the Christian Middle East and the narrative (storytelling) approach of classical Roman art. Likewise, the use of geometrical decorative designs shows the influence of Syrian art. Many scribes, artists, and illuminators must have participated in the book's preparation.

In Gaul and Anglo-Saxon England, women shared with men in the work of evangelization and in the new Christian learning. Kings and nobles, seeking suitable occupations for daughters who did not or would not marry, founded monasteries for nuns, some of which were *double monasteries.* A double monastery housed both men and women in two adjoining establishments and was governed by one superior, an *abbess.* Double monasteries provided women of the ruling class with something to rule. Nuns and monks worked together. Nuns looked after the children given to the monastery as *oblates* (offerings), the elderly who retired at the monastery, and travelers who needed hospitality. Monks provided protection, since in a violent age an isolated house of women invited attack. Monks also did the heavy work on the land. Perhaps the most famous abbess of the Anglo-Saxon period was Saint Hilda (d. 680). A noblewoman of considerable learning and administrative ability, she ruled the double monastery of Whitby on the Northumbrian coast, advised kings and princes, hosted the famous synod of 664, and encouraged scholars and poets. "She compelled those under her direction to devote time to the study of the Holy Scriptures, and to exercise themselves in works of justice," with the result that five monks from Whitby became bishops. Several generations after Hilda, Saint Boniface (see page 245) wrote many letters to Whitby and other houses of nuns, pleading for copies of books; these attest to the nuns' intellectual reputations.[15]

The finest representative of Northumbrian, and indeed all Anglo-Saxon, scholarship is the Venerable Bede (ca 673–735). At the age of seven, he was given by his parents as an oblate to Benet Biscop's monastery at Wearmouth. Later he was sent to the new monastery at Jarrow five miles away. Surrounded by the books Benet Biscop had brought from Italy, Bede spent the rest of his life there.

The author of learned commentaries on the Scriptures, Bede also devoted himself to other scholarly fields. Modern scholars praise him for his *Ecclesiastical History of the English People.* Broader in scope than the title suggests, the work is the chief source of information about early Britain. Bede searched far and wide for his information, discussed the validity of his evidence, compared various sources, and exercised a rare critical judgment. For these reasons, he has been called "the

Individuals in Society

Saint Benet Biscop of Wearmouth and Jarrow

The facts of Benet Biscop's multifaceted life derive from one source, the biographical sketch written by his younger contemporary, Bede. Descended from the "noble lineage of the Angles," Benet (ca 628– 689) became a warrior and official at the court of King Oswiu of Northumbria. About age twenty-five, he decided to visit the tombs of the Apostles Peter and Paul at Rome. On a second visit, he studied in Rome, then entered the monastery of Saint Honorat at Lérins off the southeastern coast of France, near Nice. He spent two years there, received the monastic tonsure, and took monastic vows. Benet then went back to Rome, where the pope ordered him to serve as guide and interpreter in England for a new archbishop of Canterbury, Theodore of Tarsus (r. 668–690). Theodore appointed Benet abbot of Saint Augustine's abbey at Canterbury, but he decided to found his own monastery.

With the support of King Egfrith of Northumbria, who gave him seventy hides of land (roughly eight thousand acres), Benet established the abbey of Wearmouth in 674. He imported Frankish stonemasons and, while himself serving as architect (or master mason, as medieval people would say), supervised the construction of a Romanesque church. Within a year, the walls were up, the roof was on, and the church was dedicated to Saint Peter. Benet's agents soon brought from Gaul glassmakers who built windows for the church and monastery. Books brought from Rome formed the basis of a library, and Benet devised a rule, probably based on that of Benedict (see page 212) and the other monasteries he had visited for the government of the community. On a fifth journey to Rome, Benet Biscop secured pictures to adorn the church, more books and relics, and vestments and religious vessels for the liturgical services. He brought John, the choir director of Saint Peter's in Rome, back to England to instruct the monks in the Roman style of chanting.

So impressed was King Egfrith with all that Benet Biscop had accomplished, and so rapidly, that the king gave him forty more hides of land. With this Benet built a second house at Jarrow dedicated to Saint Paul, with the stipulation that the two monasteries were to be permanently united under the names of Saints Peter and Paul. In 685, on a last visit to Rome, he returned with more books, sacred images for wall decorations, and vestments. When he died of paralysis in 689, he urged the monks to keep the library intact and in good repair.

Cover page for the Lindisfarne Gospels, an example of Northumbrian culture from the same time as Benet Biscop. *(British Library)*

What did he look like and what were the chief features of his personality? Bede tells us that he was a man "of great physical strength, (with) a pleasant tone of voice, of a kind disposition, and fair to look on." As a monk he shared fully in the manual labor of the house—plowing the fields, milking cows and ewes, threshing and winnowing grain, helping in the kitchen. Bede says that although he was of noble birth, Benet Biscop did not make that "like some men, a cause of boasting . . . but a motive for exercising nobility of mind . . . as he became a servant of the Lord." Soldier and royal official, monk, European traveler at a time when travel was difficult and dangerous, guide and interpreter, fundraiser, architect, book and art collector, governing abbot—Benet was all of these. A great nineteenth-century historian wrote:

> *The debt which England owes to Benet Biscop is a very great one, and has scarcely ever been fairly recognized . . . [as] the civilization and learning of the 8th century rested on the monastery which he founded, which produced Bede and through him the school of York, Alcuin, and the Carolingian school, on which the culture of the Middle Ages was based.*[1]

Questions for Analysis

1. How does the career of Benet Biscop fit your understanding of the monastic life?
2. Consider Benet Biscop's relationship with King Egfrith of Northumbria.

1. William Stubbs, *Dictionary of Christian Biography,* vol. 1, p. 309, as quoted in E. Fletcher, "Benedict Biscop," in *Jarrow Lecture* (1981), p. 3.

Saint Hilda The superior of a mixed monastery of men and women at Whitby in Northumbria, Saint Hilda (614–680) here receives a copy of the scholar Aldhelm's treatise *In Praise of Holy Virgins.* The simple drapery of the nuns' clothing with its nervous quality is characteristic of the eleventh-century Anglo-Saxon scriptoria. *(His Grace the Archbishop of Canterbury and the Trustees of Lambeth Palace Library)*

first scientific intellect among the Germanic peoples of Europe."[16]

Bede was probably the greatest master of chronology in the Middle Ages. He also popularized the system of dating events from the birth of Christ, rather than from the foundation of the city of Rome, as the Romans had done, or from the regnal years of kings, as the Germans did. Bede introduced the term *anno Domini*, "in the year of the Lord," abbreviated A.D. He fitted the entire history of the world into this new dating method. (The reverse dating system of B.C., "before Christ," does not seem to have been widely used before 1700.) Saint Boniface introduced this system of reckoning time throughout the Frankish empire of Charlemagne.

At about the time that monks at Lindisfarne were producing their Gospel book and Bede at Jarrow was writing his *History,* another Northumbrian monk was at work on a nonreligious epic poem that provides considerable information about the society that produced it. In contrast to the works of Bede, which were written in Latin, the poem *Beowulf* was written in the vernacular Anglo-Saxon. Although *Beowulf* is the only native English heroic epic, all the events of the tale take place in Denmark and Sweden, suggesting the close relationship between England and the continent in the eighth century. Scholars have hailed it as a masterpiece of Western literature.

The physical circumstances of life in the seventh and eighth centuries make Northumbrian cultural achievements like the Lindisfarne Gospel book and *Beowulf* all the more remarkable. Learning was pursued under terribly difficult conditions. Monasteries such as Jarrow and Lindisfarne stood on the very fringes of the European world. The barbarian Picts, just an afternoon's walk from Jarrow, were likely to attack at any time.

Food was not that big a problem. The North Sea and nearby rivers, the Tweed and the Tyne, yielded abundant salmon and other fish, which could be salted or smoked for winter, a nutritious if monotonous diet. Climate was another matter. Winter could be extremely harsh. In 664, for example, deep snow was hardened by frost from early winter until mid-spring. When it melted away, many animals, trees, and plants were found dead. To make matters worse, disease could take terrible tolls.

Model of the Abbey of Saint Gall This is a ninth-century architectural model for a self-supporting monastic community of 270 members. The monks' lives focused on the church and the cloister, which appear in the center of the model. To the left stand guest house, abbot's house, a physician's room, and at front left are extensive herbal gardens from which the monks prepared prescriptions and medications for the sick. This ideal monastery was never actually built. *(Wim Cox, Cologne)*

Bede described events in the year 664:

In the same year of our Lord 664 there was an eclipse of the sun on the third day of May at about four o'clock in the afternoon. Also in that year a sudden pestilence first depopulated the southern parts of Britain and then attacked the kingdom of the Northumbrians as well. Raging far and wide for a long time with cruel devastation it struck down a great multitude of men. . . . This same plague oppressed the island of Ireland with equal destruction.[17]

Damp cold with bitter winds blowing across the North Sea must have pierced everything, even stone monasteries. Inside, only one room, the *calefactory,* or "warming room," had a fire. Scribes in the *scriptorium,* or "writing room," had to stop frequently to rub circulation back into their numb hands. These monk-artists and monk-writers paid a high physical price for what they gave to posterity.

Had they remained entirely insular, Northumbrian cultural achievements would have been of slight significance. But an Englishman from Northumbria played a decisive role in the transmission of English learning to the Carolingian Empire and continental Europe.

The Carolingian Renaissance

In Roman Gaul through the fifth century, the general culture rested on an education that stressed grammar; the works of the Greco-Roman orators, poets, dramatists, and historians; and the legal and medical treatises of the Roman world. Beginning in the seventh and eighth centuries, a new cultural tradition common to Gaul, Italy, the British Isles, and to some extent Spain emerged. This culture was based primarily on Christian sources. Scholars have called this new Christian and ecclesiastical culture, and the educational foundation on which it was based, the "Carolingian Renaissance," because Charlemagne was its major patron.

In a letter addressed to the abbot of Fulda, with copies sent to every monastery and bishopric in his kingdom, Charlemagne directed that the monasteries "should cultivate learning and educate the monks and secular clergy so that they might have a better understanding of the Christian writings." Likewise, in a "General Admonition" to all the leading clergy, Charles urged the establishment of cathedral and monastic schools, where boys might learn to read and to pray properly. Thus the main purpose of this rebirth of learning was to promote an understanding of the Scriptures and of Christian writers, to instruct people to pray and to praise God in the correct manner. The education required was to be a Christian one.[18]

At his court at Aachen, Charlemagne assembled learned men from all over Europe. The most important scholar and the leader of the palace school was the Northumbrian Alcuin (ca 735–804). From 781 until his death, Alcuin was the emperor's chief adviser on religious and educational matters. An unusually prolific scholar, Alcuin prepared some of the emperor's official documents and wrote many moral *exempla,* or "models," which set high standards for royal behavior and constitute a treatise on kingship. Alcuin's letters to Charlemagne set forth political theories on the authority, power, and responsibilities of a Christian ruler.

Aside from Alcuin's literary efforts, what did the scholars at Charlemagne's court do? They copied books and manuscripts and built up libraries. They used the beautifully clear handwriting known as "caroline minuscule," from which modern Roman type is derived. (This script is called "minuscule" because unlike the Merovingian majuscule, which had letters of equal size, minuscule had both upper- and lowercase letters.) Caroline minuscule improved the legibility of texts and meant that a sheet of vellum could contain more words and thus be used more efficiently. With the materials at hand, many more manuscripts could be copied. Book production on this scale represents a major manifestation of the revival of learning.

Caroline minuscule illustrates the way a seemingly small technological change has broad cultural consequences. Cathedral and monastic schools placed great emphasis on the education of priests, trying to make all priests at least able to read, write, and do simple arithmetic. Their greatest contribution was not so much the originality of their ideas as their hard work of salvaging and preserving the thoughts and writings of the ancients. Although hardly widespread by later standards, basic literacy was established among the clergy and even among some of the nobility.

Although scholars worked with Latin, exchanged books between monasteries, and generally collaborated in book production, the common people spoke their local or vernacular languages. The Bretons, for example, retained their local dialect, and the Saxons and Bavarians could not understand each other. Some scholars believe that Latin words and phrases gradually penetrated the various vernacular languages, facilitating communication among diverse peoples.

Once basic literacy was established, monastic and other scholars went on to more difficult work. By

Saint Luke from the Ada Gospels (late eighth to early ninth century) After the cross, the most famous early Christian symbols were representations of the four evangelists: Matthew (man), Mark (lion), Luke (a winged ox), and John (eagle), based on the text in Revelations 4:7. The "Ada School" of painting was attached to the court of Charlemagne, and gets its name from Ada, a sister of Charlemagne who commissioned some of the school's work. In this lavishly illuminated painting, a statuesque Saint Luke sits enthroned, his draperies falling in nervous folds reminiscent of Byzantine art, and surrounded by an elaborate architectural framework. A splendid example of Carolingian Renaissance art. *(Municipal Library, Trier)*

the middle years of the ninth century, there was a great outpouring of more sophisticated books. Ecclesiastical writers, imbued with the legal ideas of ancient Rome and the theocratic ideals of Saint Augustine, instructed the semibarbaric rulers of the West. And it is no accident that medical study in the West began at Salerno in southern Italy in the late ninth century, *after* the Carolingian Renaissance.

Alcuin completed the work of his countryman Boniface—the Christianization of northern Europe. Latin Christian attitudes penetrated deeply into the consciousness of European peoples. By the tenth century, the patterns of thought and lifestyles of educated western Europeans were those of Rome and Latin Christianity. Even the violence and destruction of the great invasions of the late ninth and tenth centuries could not destroy the strong foundations laid by Alcuin and his colleagues.

Health and Medical Care in the Early Middle Ages

Scholars' examination of medical treatises, prescription (or herbal) books, manuscript illustrations, and archaeological evidence has revealed a surprising amount of information about medical treatment in the early Middle Ages. In a society devoted to fighting, warriors and civilians alike stood a strong chance of wounds from sword, spear, battle-ax, or blunt instrument. Trying to eke a living from poor soil with poor tools, perpetually involved in pushing back forest and wasteland, the farmer and his family daily ran the risk of accidents. Poor diet weakened everyone's resistance to disease. People bathed rarely, and low standards of personal hygiene increased the danger of infection. This being the case, what medical attention was available to medieval people?

Medical practice consisted primarily of drug and prescription therapy. Through the monks' efforts and recovery of Greek and Arabic manuscripts, a large body of the ancients' prescriptions was preserved and passed on. For almost any ailment, several recipes were likely to exist in the prescription lists. Balsam was recommended for coughs. For asthma, an ointment combining chicken, wormwood, laurel berries, and oil of roses was to be rubbed on the chest. The scores of prescriptions to rid the body of lice, fleas, and other filth reflect frightful standards of personal hygiene. The large number of prescriptions for eye troubles suggests that they, too, must have been common. This is understandable, given the widespread practice of locating the fireplace in the center of the room. A lot of smoke and soot filtered into the room, rather than going up the chimney. One remedy calls for bathing the eyes in a solution of herbs mixed with honey, balsam, rainwater, salt water, or wine.

Poor diet caused frequent stomach disorders and related ailments such as dysentery, constipation, and diarrhea. The value of dieting and avoiding greasy foods was recognized. Charlemagne's biographer tells us that the emperor's doctors urged him to avoid roasts and greasy meats and to eat boiled meat instead. For poor circulation, a potion of meadow wort, oak rind, and lustmock was recommended. Pregnant women were advised to abstain from eating the flesh of almost all male animals, because such meat might deform the child. Men with unusually strong sexual appetites were advised to fast and to drink at night the juice of agrimony (an herb of the rose family) boiled in ale. If a man suffered from lack of drive, the same plant boiled in milk gave him "courage."

Because of the need for agricultural laborers in the peasant classes and for male heirs in all classes, early medieval people placed a high priority on procreation. Pregnancy and childbirth, however, posed grave threats of infection for both mother and child. Also, heavy field work could cause miscarriages. Some recent scholars have argued that midwives possessed a store of pharmaceutical information deriving from the Romans about fertility, contraception, pregnancy, and childbirth. (Men had no experience in these matters because modesty forbade their presence at a baby's birth. Thus everything associated with childbirth was entirely in the female domain.) The weight of present evidence on pre- and postnatal matters, however, is that midwives and matrons actually knew very little about drugs to increase contractions, episiotomy (surgical incision of the perineum to allow birth), or the use of forceps (a seventeenth-century invention) during childbirth. The result was a staggeringly high death rate for mothers and newborns. Recent research on the village of Frénouville in Normandy for the fifth to eighth centuries reveals a 45 percent infant mortality rate; in addition, many mothers died of puerperal fever, an illness resulting from postpartum infection. However, some parts of the Carolingian Empire, such as the estates of the abbey of Saint Victor near Marseilles, showed surges in the birthrate, with 38 percent of the population composed of young unmarried people.[19]

Physicians, or "leeches," as they were known in Anglo-Saxon England, were not concerned with the treatment of specific illnesses. They did not examine pa-

Bone-Setting of Jaw Byzantine physicians relied on classical medical treatises, especially those of Hippocrates and Galen; they did not simply parrot their sources, but rearranged and supplemented them with contemporary experimentation. A ninth-century Greek physician added this illustration to his commentary on a first-century manuscript. With the patient sitting on a stool and an assistant holding his head, the doctor takes the dislocated jaw between his fingers and puts it back into place. By medieval standards, Byzantine practical medicine was on a high level. *(Biblioteca Medicea Laurenziana, Florence/ Scandigli, photographer)*

tients, but treated only what they could see or deduce from obvious symptoms. Physicians knew little about the pathology of disease or physiological functions. They had no accurate standards of weights and measures. Prescriptions called for "a pinch" or "a handful" or "an eggshell full."

All wounds and open injuries invited infection, and infection invited gangrene. Several remedies were known for wounds. Physicians appreciated the antiseptic properties of honey, and prescriptions recommended that wounds be cleaned with it. When an area or a limb had become gangrenous, a good technique of amputation existed. The physician was instructed to cut above the diseased flesh—that is, to cut away some healthy tissue and bone—in order to hasten cure. The juice of white poppy plants—the source of heroin—could be added to wine and drunk as an anesthetic. White poppies, however, grew only in southern Europe and North Africa. If a heavy slug of wine was not enough to dull the patient, he or she had to be held down forcibly while the physician cut. Egg whites, which have a soothing effect, were prescribed for burns.

Teeth survive long periods of burial and give reasonably good information about disease. Evidence from early medieval England shows that the incidence of tooth decay was very low. In the adult population, the rate of cavities was only one-sixth that of today. Cavities below the gum line, however, were very common, because of the prevalence of carbohydrates in the diet. The result was abscesses of the gums. These and other forms of periodontal disease were widespread after the age of thirty.[20]

The spread of Christianity in the Carolingian era had a beneficial effect on medical knowledge and treatment. Several of the church fathers expressed serious interest in medicine. Some of them even knew something about it. The church was deeply concerned about human suffering, whether physical or mental. Christian teaching vigorously supported concern for the poor, sick, downtrodden, and miserable. Churchmen taught that, while all knowledge came from God, He had supplied it so that people could use it for their own benefit.

The foundation of a school at Salerno in southern Italy sometime in the ninth century gave a tremendous impetus to medical study by laypeople. The school's location attracted Arabic, Greek, and Jewish physicians from all over the Mediterranean region. Students flocked there from northern Europe. The Jewish physician Shabbathai Ben Abraham (931–982) left pharmacological notes that were widely studied in later centuries.

By the eleventh century, the medical school at Salerno enjoyed international fame. Its most distinguished professor then was Constantine the African, a native of Carthage who had studied medicine throughout western Asia. Because of his thorough knowledge of oriental languages, he served as an important transmitter of Arabic culture to the West. Constantine taught and practiced medicine at Salerno for some years before becoming a monk at Monte Cassino.

As in ancient China, local folk medicine practiced by nonprofessionals and based on herbal remedies provided such help as people could get. Physicians were few in the early Middle Ages. They charged a fee that only the rich could afford. Apparently most illnesses simply took their course. People had to develop a stoical attitude. Death came early. A person aged forty was considered old. People's vulnerability to ailments for which there was no probable cure contributed to a fatalistic acceptance of death at an early age. Early medical literature shows that attempts to relieve pain were crude; even so, attempts *were* made.

Aristocratic Resurgence

Charlemagne left his vast empire to his sole surviving son, Louis the Pious (r. 814–840). Initially, Louis proved as tough and ruthless as his father. He banished from the court real or potential conspirators, crushed rebellions, and blinded his enemies or consigned them to monasteries. For these actions, Louis's biographers highly praised him. Then, in 821, Louis seems to have undergone some sort of change. He pardoned the conspirators implicated in earlier revolts, allowed some to return from exile, and promoted others to high ecclesiastical positions. Perhaps the emperor felt secure enough that he could now be generous. He was not. In pardoning dissident magnates, Louis showed that he underestimated them; they fomented jealousy among his sons and plotted to augment their wealth and power.

At Aachen in 817, Louis drew up the *Arrangement of the Empire,* in which he divided his territories among his three sons but stressed the importance of the unity of the empire. The eldest son, Lothar, received at once the imperial title as co-ruler with his father and was to be heir to the empire after Louis's death. The younger sons were given vast lands and powers, but they were to be subordinate to Lothar and to meet him annually to resolve mutual problems and to promote friendship. Dissatisfied with their portions, anxious to gain the imperial title, and incited by disaffected magnates, Louis's sons fought bitterly among themselves. Finally, in the Treaty of Verdun of 843, the brothers reached an agreement (Map 8.2).

Lothar retained the title of emperor and the "middle kingdom," the territories bordered by the Meuse, Saône, and Rhône Rivers in the west and the Rhine River in the east, plus the kingdom of Italy. The eastern and most Germanic part of the Carolingian Empire passed to Louis the German. This "eastern kingdom" achieved the greatest relative level of stability, partly because Louis avoided being dependent on any one aristocratic faction, partly because he successfully focused on expansion against the Slavs to the east. The "western kingdom" went to Charles the Bald (r. 843–877); it included the provinces of Aquitaine and Gascony and later formed the basis of medieval and modern France. Harassed on his northern and western frontiers by the Vikings (see page 262) and continually pressured by his magnates for lands and honors, Charles the Bald spent most of his reign at war.

Older scholarship has stressed the fratricidal wars among Louis the Pious's sons and grandsons as the major cause of the disintegration of the Carolingian Empire. Recent and better-informed research emphasizes the conspiracies and revolts of greedy magnates. Why? Perhaps they had never been fully reconciled to Carolingian rule. Perhaps they harbored personal grudges against Louis the Pious or one of his sons. Perhaps some counts and magnates, having acquired great lands and powers, lusted for more. In any case, from 830 (before the death of Louis the Pious) and extending through the later ninth century, "the growing strength and self-interest of the magnates" was the major cause of civil war and imperial weakness.[21] Nobles frequently worked through a disaffected member of the royal family, as the case of Carloman illustrates. Determined to prevent the partition of his kingdom, Charles the Bald used the strategy of placing his younger sons in the church, thereby removing them from the succession. His youngest boy, Carloman, was tonsured (crown of the head shaven, symbolic of entry into the clergy) at age five, ordained a deacon at eleven, and heaped with abbacies and ecclesiastical preferments. But Carloman resented being a cleric, and "gathering around him many accomplices and sons of Belial [the biblical name of the devil]," as *The Annals of St-Bertin* describes them,[22] revolted against his father. Carloman and his noble allies did considerable damage before he was captured, tried for treason, and blinded. (Like the Byzantine emperors, a Frankish king had to possess all his faculties; the loss of sight or reproductive powers effectively removed candidacy for the monarchy.)

While Charlemagne had worked to prevent the office of count from becoming hereditary in one family, in the ninth century counties passed from father to son in dynastic succession. Some magnates acquired several counties. For example, Robert the Strong held the counties of Angers, Blois, Tours, Autun, Auxerre, and Nevers, and Bernard Hairyfeet became count of Toulouse, Narbonne, Auvergne, and Limousin.[23] In the West Frankish kingdom, Charles the Bald's efforts to gain support with gifts of lands and comital offices weakened him. Some families of counts had such conglomerations of lands that they were able to deny the king's authority and effectively to resist him. The administration system built by Pippin III and Charlemagne survived, but imperial authority weakened. Actual power passed into the hands of local magnates.

MAP 8.2 Division of the Carolingian Empire, 843 The Treaty of Verdun (843), which divided the empire among Charlemagne's grandsons, is frequently taken as the start of the separate development of Germany, France, and Italy. The "middle kingdom" of Lothar, however, lacking defensive borders and any political or linguistic unity, quickly broke up into numerous small territories.

FEUDALISM AND THE HISTORIANS

The great English legal historian Frederic William Maitland used to amuse his classes at Cambridge University at the start of the twentieth century by telling them that feudalism was introduced into England in the seventeenth century. By that he meant that the word *feudalism* was not a medieval term. It was invented by scholars in the seventeenth century and popularized by French political philosophers in the eighteenth century, especially Montesquieu in *The Spirit of the Laws* (1748). In the ancien régime of late-eighteenth-century France, feudalism was identified with the privileges of the aristocratic nobility, privileges that provoked the wrath of the bourgeoisie. Thus feudalism was initially applied in a pejorative or condescending sense. From the radicals of revolutionary Europe (ca 1789–1815), the word was adopted by the communist writer Karl Marx (1818–1883) to mean all of precapitalistic society. The term *feudalism* did not come into general English usage until 1828. From the mid-nineteenth century down to the present, some of the ablest scholars in Europe and North America have tried to work out an accurate definition of *feudalism* applicable to the time period we call the Middle Ages (ca 700–1500). Those scholars have not been successful, as confusion and inaccuracy still surround the word.

Feudalism draws attention to just one aspect of a very complicated society—the *feud,* or "fief," an estate in land or money granted by a superior on condition of rendering him (or her) services. We have called the person who grants the fief the "lord" and the recipient of the fief the *vassus* (vassal) or *homo* (man) of the lord, but medieval people used those Latin words in very different contexts and with different meanings. The significance of the words varied from place to place and from time to time. Therefore, it is not only imprecise but inaccurate to use the terms *fief* and *vassal* in a discussion of the entire period we call the Middle Ages. Likewise, the form and pattern of feudalism changed considerably between the ninth and fifteenth centuries in France, Germany, Italy, and England. The feudalism of Norman England in 1100, for example, differed greatly from that of Capetian France, scarcely fifty miles away, at the same time. Modern historians have casually applied the technical definitions of seventeenth-century lawyers or nineteenth-century lexicographers to ninth-, eleventh-, and thirteenth-century circumstances. As an expert recently reminded us,

> *Fiefs and vassalage are post-medieval constructs, though rather earlier than the construct of feudalism. . . . Even when historians follow the terminology of the documents . . . they tend to fit their findings into a framework of interpretation that was devised in the sixteenth century and elaborated in the seventeenth or eighteenth. We cannot understand medieval society and its property relations if we see it through seventeenth or eighteenth century spectacles.*[24]

Then why have historians clung to this terminology? Why have they, in another scholar's words, "been tyrannized by a construct"?[25] The answer is that they have not been able to come up with a better alternative.

Interpretations of Feudalism

No current explanation of feudalism is entirely satisfactory. But to begin to understand the ideas and issues involved and historians' frames of reference, we have to gain some awareness of the general approaches to the problem. Two broad interpretations have conditioned medievalists' thinking. In 1940, the great French economic and social historian Marc Bloch published *Feudal Society*. Bloch regarded feudalism as a whole system of life—not only economic, but political, cultural, and ecclesiastical—centered on lordship. He saw feudalism as a political system, an economic system, and a system of values. Bloch described a feudal economy, a feudal literature, and a feudalized church in much the way we use the word *capitalistic* to mean not only a certain kind of production and exchange but also government, thought, or capitalistic spirit. Bloch's view of feudalism came close to that of Karl Marx and his followers, but Bloch differed from Marx in one fundamental way: Marxists insist that only the producers, the laborers, contribute anything to society, and Marxist historians tend to focus their research entirely on the peasants, unfree or free. Bloch did not do that; he did not make manorialism (see page 261) the sole aspect of feudalism.

The major alternative interpretation explains feudalism largely in political and legal terms. It holds that the feudalism that emerged in western Europe in the ninth century was a type of government "in which political power was treated as a private possession and was divided among a large number of lords."[26] This kind of government characterized most parts of western Europe from about 900 to 1300. Feudalism actually existed at two social levels: first, at the level of armed retainers who became knights; and second, at the level of royal officials, such as counts, who ruled great feudal principalities. A wide and deep gap in social standing and political function separated these social levels. (See the feature "Listening to the Past: Feudal Homage and Fealty" on pages 270–271.)

The Origins of Feudalism

Scholars have debated two theories about the origins of feudalism. According to the older explanation, in the early eighth century, the Carolingian kings and other powerful men needed bodyguards and retainers, armed men who could fight effectively on horseback. Around this time, the arrival in western Europe of a Chinese technological invention, the stirrup, revolutionized warfare. While an unstirruped rider had difficulty impaling an enemy, a horseman in stirrups could utilize the galloping animal's force to strike and damage his enemy. Charles Martel recognized the potential of an effective cavalry; thus the availability of stirrups increased his need for large numbers of retainers. Horses and armor were terribly expensive, and few could afford them. It also took considerable time to train an experienced cavalryman. As a result, the value of retainers increased. Therefore, Charles and other powerful men bound their retainers by oaths of loyalty and ceremonies of homage.

The other, more recent theory of the origin of feudalism does not give much importance to the stirrup. According to this interpretation, the stirrup did not lead to the wide use of mounted troops, since most warfare in the Carolingian period was siege warfare conducted by infantry. Rather, Charles Martel, using techniques common among his Merovingian predecessors, purchased the support and loyalty of his followers with grants of land or estates taken from churchmen or laymen, or with movable wealth such as weapons or jewelry, captured in battle.[27] Personal ties of loyalty cemented the relationship between lord and retainer; in exchange for the promise of service and loyalty, the lord distributed land or some other means of material support, such as cash.

These retainers became known as *vassals,* from a Celtic term meaning "servant." Since lesser vassals or knights were not involved in any governmental activity, and since only men who exercised political power were considered noble, knights were not part of the noble class. Instead, down to the eleventh century, political power was concentrated in a small group of counts.

Counts, descended from the Frankish aristocracy (see page 245), constituted the second level of feudalism. Under Charles Martel and his heirs, counts monopolized the high offices in the Carolingian Empire. While countships were not at first hereditary in the eighth century, they tended to remain within the same family. In the ninth century, regional concentrations of power depended on family connections and political influence at the king's court. The weakening of the Carolingian Empire, however, served to increase the power of regional authorities. Civil wars weakened the power and prestige of kings, because there was little they could do about domestic violence. Likewise, the great invasions of the ninth century, especially the Viking invasions (see pages 262–265), weakened royal authority. The West Frankish kings could do little to halt the invaders, and the aristocracy had to assume responsibility for defense. Common people turned for protection to the strongest local power, the counts, whom they considered their rightful rulers. Thus, in the ninth and tenth centuries, great aristocratic families increased their authority in the regions of their vested interests. They governed virtually independent territories in which distant and weak kings could not interfere. "Political power had become a private, heritable property for great counts and lords."[28] This is feudalism as a form of government.

Homage and Fealty Although the rite of entering a feudal relationship varied widely across Europe and sometimes was entirely verbal, we have a few illustrations of it. Here the vassal kneels before the lord, places his clasped hands between those of the lord, and declares, "I become your man." Sometimes the lord handed over a clump of earth, representing the fief, and the ceremony concluded with a kiss, symbolizing peace between them. *(Osterreichische Nationalbibliothek)*

Because feudal society was a military society, men held the dominant positions in it. A high premium was put on physical strength, fighting skill, and bravery. The legal and social position of women was not as insignificant as might be expected, however. Charters recording gifts to the church indicate that women held land in many areas. Women frequently endowed monasteries, churches, and other religious establishments. The possession of land obviously meant economic power. Moreover, women inherited fiefs, or landed estates. In southern France and Catalonia in Spain, women inherited feudal property as early as the tenth century. Other kinds of evidence attest to women's status. In parts of northern France, children sometimes identified themselves in legal documents by their mother's name rather than their father's, indicating that the mother's social position in the community was higher than the father's.

In a treatise he wrote in 822 on the organization of the royal household, Archbishop Hincmar of Reims placed the queen directly above the treasurer. She was responsible for giving the knights their annual salaries. She supervised the manorial accounts. Thus, in the management of large households with many knights to oversee and complicated manorial records to supervise, the lady of the manor had highly important responsibilities. With such responsibilities went power and influence.

Manorialism

Feudalism concerned the rights, powers, and lifestyle of the military elite; *manorialism* involved the services and obligations of the peasant classes. The economic power of the warring class rested on landed estates, which were worked by peasants. Hence feudalism and manorialism were inextricably linked. Peasants needed protection, and lords demanded something in return for that protection. Free peasants surrendered themselves and their lands to the lord's jurisdiction. The land was given back, but the peasants became tied to the land by various kinds of payments and services. In France, England, Germany, and Italy, local custom determined precisely what those services were, but certain practices became common everywhere. The peasant was obliged to turn over to the lord a percentage of the annual harvest, usually in produce, sometimes in cash. The peasant paid a fee to marry someone from outside the lord's estate. To inherit property, the peasant paid a fine, often the best beast the person owned. Above all, the peasant became part of the lord's permanent labor force. With vast stretches of uncultivated virgin land and a tiny labor population, lords encouraged population growth and immigration. The most profitable form of capital was not land but laborers.

In entering into a relationship with a feudal lord, free farmers lost status. Their position became servile, and they became *serfs*. That is, they were bound to the land and could not leave it without the lord's permission. They were also subject to the jurisdiction of the lord's court in any dispute over property and in any case of suspected criminal behavior.

The transition from freedom to serfdom was slow; its speed was closely related to the degree of political order in a given region. In the late eighth century, there were still many free peasants. And within the legal category of serfdom there were many economic levels, ranging from the highly prosperous to the desperately poor. Nevertheless, a social and legal revolution was taking place. By the year 800, perhaps 60 percent of the population of western Europe—completely free a century before—had been reduced to serfdom. The ninth-century Viking assaults on Europe created extremely unstable conditions and individual insecurity, leading to additional loss of personal freedom. (Chapter 10 details the lives of the peasants. As it shows, the later Middle Ages witnessed considerable upward social mobility.)

Great Invasions of the Ninth Century

After the Treaty of Verdun (843), continental Europe presented an easy target for foreign invaders. All three kingdoms controlled by Louis the Pious's sons (see page 258) were torn by domestic dissension and disorder. No European political power was strong enough to put up effective resistance to external attacks. The frontier and coastal defenses erected by Charlemagne and maintained by Louis the Pious were neglected. Three groups attacked Europe: Vikings from Scandinavia, representing the final wave of Germanic migrants; Muslims from the Mediterranean; and Magyars, Asiatic nomads forced westward by other peoples (Map 8.3). The combination of their assaults hastened the collapse of the Carolingian Empire.

Assaults on Western Europe

From the moors of Scotland to the mountains of Sicily, there arose in the ninth century the prayer, "Save us, O God, from the violence of the Northmen." The Northmen, also known as Normans or Vikings, were Germanic peoples from Norway, Sweden, and Denmark who had remained beyond the sway of the Christianizing and civilizing influences of the Carolingian Empire. Some scholars believe that the name *Viking* derives from the old Norse word *vik,* meaning "creek." A Viking, then, was a pirate who waited in a creek or bay to attack passing vessels.

The Vikings were superb seamen. Their advanced methods of boat building gave them great speed and maneuverability. Propelled either by oars or by sails, deckless, and about sixty-five feet long, a Viking ship could carry between forty and sixty men—quite enough to harass an isolated monastery or village. These ships, navigated by thoroughly experienced and utterly fearless sailors, moved through the most complicated rivers, estuaries, and waterways in Europe. The Carolingian Empire, with no navy and no notion of the importance of sea power, was helpless. The Vikings moved swiftly, attacked, and escaped to return again.

Scholars disagree about the reasons for Viking attacks and migrations. Recent research asserts that a very unstable Danish kingship and disputes over the succession led to civil war and disorder, which drove warriors abroad in search of booty and supporters. Older students hold that overpopulation on top of poor climatic conditions and crop failures forced migrations. Still other writers insist that the Vikings were looking for trade and new commercial contacts. What better targets for plunder than the mercantile centers of Francia and Frisia?

Viking attacks were very savage. The Vikings burned, looted, and did extensive short-term property damage, but there is little evidence that they caused long-term destruction—perhaps because, arriving in small bands, they lacked the manpower to do so. Nor is there much

MAP 8.3 The Great Invasions of the Ninth Century Note the Viking penetration of eastern Europe and their probable expeditions to North America. What impact did their various invasions have on European society?

evidence to show that the Vikings sought slaves in the Frankish kingdoms. Rather, they seized magnates and high churchmen and held them for ransom; they also demanded tribute from kings. In 844–845 Charles the Bald had to raise 7,000 pounds of silver,[29] and across the English Channel Anglo-Saxon rulers collected a land tax, the Danegeld, to buy off the Vikings. The Vikings exploited conflicts among the Carolingians, as in 841, when they sailed up the Seine and sacked Rouen, knowing that Charles the Bald had crushed a revolt of nobles there just a few weeks before and the region was vulnerable. The Carolingians also manipulated the Vikings, as Lothar "used his Viking ally Harald against his brothers in Frisia."[30] In the Seine and

Animal Headpost from Viking Ship Skilled woodcarvers produced ornamental headposts for ships, sledges, wagons, and bedsteads; the fearsome quality of many carvings suggests that they were intended to ward off evil spirits and to terrify. *(University Museum of National Antiquities, Oslo, Norway. Neg. Nr. 0.874. From Oseberg, Tonsberg in Vestfold)*

Loire Valleys, the frequent presence of Viking war bands seems to have had economic consequences, stimulating the production of food and wine and possibly the manufacture (for sale) of weapons and the breeding of horses. During the tenth century, as the Vikings settled down and adopted Frankish customs and military practices, considerable assimilation occurred among the two peoples.

Between 876 and 954, Viking control extended from Dublin across the Irish Sea to Britain, across northern Britain between the Dee and the Solway Rivers, and then across the North Sea to the Vikings' Scandinavian homelands. These invaders also overran a large part of northwestern France and called the territory "Norsemanland," from which the word *Normandy* derives. In the East, they pierced the rivers of Russia as far as the Black Sea (Map 8.4). In the West, they sailed as far as Iceland, Greenland, and even the coast of North America, perhaps as far south as Long Island Sound (New York).

Scarcely had the savagery of the Viking assaults begun to subside when Europe was hit from the east and south. Beginning about 890, Magyar tribes crossed the Danube and pushed steadily westward. (Since people thought of them as returning Huns, the Magyars came to be known as "Hungarians.") They subdued northern Italy, compelled Bavaria and Saxony to pay tribute, and penetrated even into the Rhineland and Burgundy. These roving bandits attacked isolated villages and monasteries, taking prisoners and selling them in the Eastern slave markets. The Magyars were not colonizers; their sole object was booty and plunder.

The Vikings and Magyars depended on fear. In their initial attacks on isolated settlements, many people were put to the sword. From the British Isles and territories along the Baltic Sea, the Vikings took *thralls* (slaves) for the markets of Magdeburg on the Elbe River and Regensburg in Bavaria on the Danube, for the fairs of Lyons on the Rhône River, and to supply the huge demand for slaves in the Muslim world. The slave trade represented an important part of Viking commerce. The Icelander Hoskuld Dala-Kolsson of Laxardal paid 3 marks of silver, three times the price of a common concubine, for a pretty Irish girl; she was one of twelve offered by a Viking trader. No wonder many communities bought peace by paying tribute.

From the south, the Muslims also began new encroachments, concentrating on the two southern peninsulas, Italy and Spain. Seventh- and early-eighth-century Islamic movements (see pages 233–234) had been for purposes of conquest and colonization, but the goal of ninth- and tenth-century incursions was plunder; these later raids were essentially piratical attacks. In Italy the monks of Monte Cassino were forced to flee. The Muslims drove northward and sacked Rome in 846. Expert seamen, they sailed around the Iberian Peninsula, braved the notoriously dangerous shoals and winds of the Atlantic coast, and attacked the Mediterranean settlements along the coast of Provence. But Muslim attacks on the European continent in the ninth

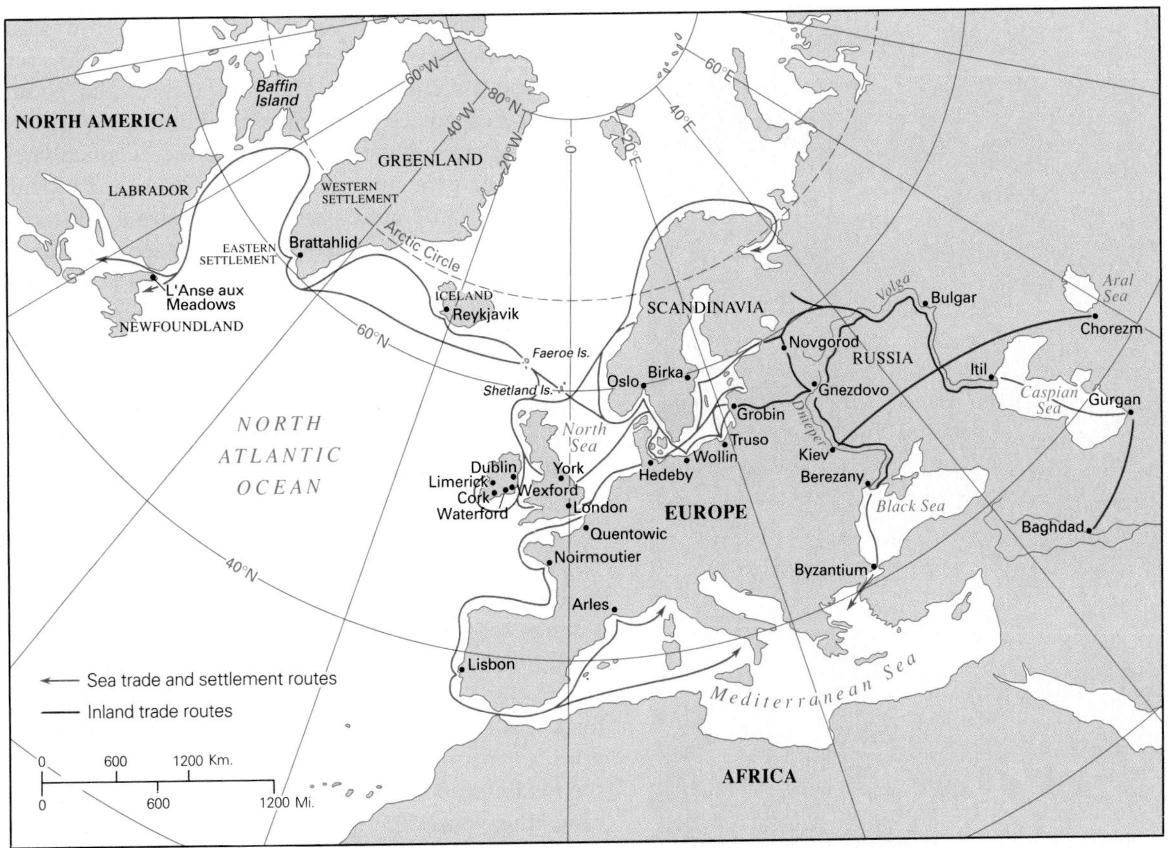

MAP 8.4 Viking Settlement and Trade Routes Viking trade and settlements extended from Newfoundland and Greenland to deep in Russia.

and tenth centuries were less destructive than Viking and Magyar assaults. Compared to the rich, sophisticated culture of the Arab capitals, northern Europe was primitive and backward and offered little.

What was the effect of these invasions on the structure of European society? Viking, Magyar, and Muslim attacks accelerated the fragmentation of political power. Lords capable of rallying fighting men, supporting them, and putting up resistance to the invaders did so. They also assumed political power in their territories. Weak and defenseless people sought the protection of local strongmen. Free peasants sank to the level of serfs.

The ninth-century invaders also left significant traces of their own cultures. The Vikings, for example, made positive contributions to the areas they settled. They carried everywhere their unrivaled knowledge of shipbuilding and seamanship. The northeastern and central parts of England where the Vikings settled became known as the *Danelaw* because Danish law and customs, not English, prevailed there. Scholars believe that some legal institutions, such as the ancestor of the modern grand jury, originated in the Danelaw. York in northern England, once a Roman army camp and then an Anglo-Saxon town, became a thriving center of Viking trade with Scandinavia. At Dublin on the east coast of Ireland, Viking iron- and steelworkers and combmakers established a center for trade with the Hebrides, Iceland, and Norway. The Irish cities of Limerick, Cork, Wexford, and Waterford trace their origins to Viking trading centers.

The Vikings and the Kievan Principality

In antiquity the Slavs lived as a single people in central Europe. With the start of the mass migrations of the late Roman Empire, the Slavs moved in different directions and split into three groups. The group later labeled the West Slavs included the Poles, Czechs, Slovaks,

Vikings Invade Britain In this twelfth-century representation of the Viking invasions, warriors appear to be armed with helmets, spears, and shields. Crossing the rough North Sea and English Channel in open, oar-propelled boats, they had great courage. *(The Pierpont Morgan Library/Art Resource, NY)*

and Wends. The South Slavs, comprising peoples who became the Serbs, Croats, Slovenes, Macedonians, and Bosnians, migrated southward into the Balkans and eventually achieved a relatively high degree of political development before being absorbed by the Ottoman Turks in the fourteenth and fifteenth centuries. Between the fifth and ninth centuries, the eastern Slavs, from whom the Ukrainians, Russians, and White Russians descend, moved into the vast and practically uninhabited area of present-day European Russia and the Ukraine.

This enormous area consisted of an immense virgin forest to the north, where most of the eastern Slavs settled, and an endless prairie grassland to the south. Probably organized as tribal communities, the eastern Slavs, like many North American pioneers much later, lived off the great abundance of wild game and a crude "slash and burn" agriculture. After clearing a piece of the forest to build log cabins, they burned the stumps and brush. The ashes left a rich deposit of potash and lime, and the land produced several good crops before it was exhausted. The people then moved on to another, untouched area and repeated the process.

In the ninth century, the Vikings appeared in the lands of the eastern Slavs. Called "Varangians" in the old Russian chronicles, the Vikings were interested primarily in international trade, and the opportunities were good, since the Muslim conquests of the eighth century had greatly reduced Christian trade in the Mediterranean. Moving up and down the rivers, the Vikings soon linked Scandinavia and northern Europe to the Black Sea and to the Byzantine Empire with its capital at Constantinople. They built a few strategic forts along the rivers, from which they raided the neighboring Slavic tribes and collected tribute. Slaves were the most important article of tribute, and *Slav* even became the word for "slave" in several European languages.

In order to increase and protect their international commerce, the Vikings declared themselves the rulers of the eastern Slavs. According to tradition, the semilegendary chieftain Ruirik founded a princely dynasty about 860. In any event, the Varangian ruler Oleg (r. 878–912) established his residence at Kiev. He and his successors ruled over a loosely united confederation of Slavic territories—the Kievan state—until 1054. The Viking prince and his clansmen quickly became assimilated into the Slavic population, taking local wives and emerging as the noble class.

Assimilation was accelerated by the conversion of the Vikings and local Slavs to Eastern Orthodox Christianity by missionaries of the Byzantine Empire. The written language of these missionaries, an early form of Slavic now known as Old Church Slavonic, was subsequently used in all religious and nonreligious documents in the Kievan principality. Thus the rapidly Slavified Vikings left two important legacies for the future: they created a loose unification of Slavic territories under a single ruling prince and a single ruling dynasty, and they imposed a basic religious unity by accepting Orthodox Christianity, as opposed to Roman Catholicism, for themselves and the eastern Slavs.

Even at its height under Great Prince Iaroslav the Wise (r. 1019–1054), the unity of the Kievan principality was extremely tenuous. Trade, rather than government, was the main concern of the rulers. Moreover, the Slavified Vikings failed to find a way of peacefully transferring power from one generation to the next. In medieval western Europe, this fundamental problem of government was increasingly resolved by resorting to the principle of primogeniture: the king's eldest son received the crown as his rightful inheritance when his father died. Civil war was thus averted; order was preserved. In early Kiev, however, there were apparently no fixed rules, and much strife accompanied each succession.

Possibly to avoid such chaos, Great Prince Iaroslav, before his death in 1054, divided the Kievan principality among his five sons, who in turn divided their properties when they died. Between 1054 and 1237, Kiev disintegrated into more and more competing units, each ruled by a prince claiming to be a descendant of Ruirik. Even when only one prince claimed to be the great prince, the whole situation was very unsettled.

The princes divided their land like private property because they thought of it as private property. A given prince owned a certain number of farms or landed estates and had them worked directly by his people, mainly slaves, called *kholops* in Russian. Outside of these estates, which constituted the princely domain, the prince exercised only very limited authority in his principality. Excluding the clergy, two kinds of people lived there: the noble *boyars* and the commoner peasants.

The boyars were the descendants of the original Viking warriors, and they also held their lands as free and clear private property. Although the boyars normally fought in princely armies, the customary law declared that they could serve any prince they wished. The ordinary peasants were also truly free. They could move at will wherever opportunities were greatest. In the touching phrase of the times, theirs was "a clean road, without boundaries."[31] In short, fragmented princely power, private property, and personal freedom all went together.

SUMMARY

Building on the military and diplomatic foundations of his ancestors, Charlemagne waged constant warfare to expand his kingdom. His wars with the Saxons in northwestern Germany and with the Lombards in northern Italy proved successful, and his kingdom ultimately included most of continental Europe. He governed this vast territory through a military elite, the Frankish counts, who exercised political, economic, and judicial authority at the local level.

The culture that emerged in Europe between 732 and 843 has justifiably been called the "first" European civilization. That civilization had definite characteristics: it was Christian, feudal, and infused with Latin ideas and models. Almost all people were baptized Christians. Latin was the common language—written as well as spoken—of educated people everywhere. This culture resulted from the mutual cooperation of civil and ecclesiastical authorities. Kings and church leaders supported each other's goals and utilized each other's prestige and power. Kings encouraged preaching and publicized church doctrines, such as the stress on monogamous marriage. In return, church officials urged obedience to royal authority. The support that Charlemagne gave to education and learning, the intellectual movement known as the Carolingian Renaissance, proved his most enduring legacy.

The resurgence of an ambitious aristocracy composed of greedy magnates who pressured later Carolingian kings for ever more lands; the growth of hereditary and semi-independent countships; and the invasions of the Vikings, Magyars, and Muslims—these factors all contributed to the empire's disintegration. As the empire broke down, a new form of decentralized government, later known as feudalism, emerged. In a feudal society, public and political power was held by a small group of military leaders. No civil or religious authority could maintain a stable government over a very wide area. Local strongmen provided what little security existed. Commerce and long-distance trade were drastically reduced. Because of their agricultural and commercial impact, the Viking and Muslim invaders represent the most dynamic and creative forces of the period. By the twelfth century, the Kievan principality—Slavic in ethnicity, Greek Orthodox in religion, and the center of considerable trade with the Chinese and Muslim worlds—constituted a loose collection of territories without a strong central government.

NOTES

1. The sources, both Muslim and Christian, dispute both the date (732) and the place of the battle (Poitiers or Tours). I. Wood, *The Merovingian Kingdoms, 450–751* (New York: Longman, 1994), pp. 282–286, provides a careful analysis of all the documentary evidence.

2. Wood, *The Merovingian Kingdoms,* p. 60.
3. Ibid., p. 101.
4. See ibid., chap. 6.
5. Ibid., pp. 60–66; and E. James, *The Franks* (New York: Basil Blackwell, 1988), pp. 191–194.
6. Wood, *The Merovingian Kingdoms,* pp. 102–119.
7. See R. McKitterick, *The Frankish Kingdoms and the Early Carolingians 751–987* (New York: Longman, 1983), pp. 36–37.
8. Quoted ibid., p. 34.
9. Quoted in B. D. Hill, ed., *Church and State in the Middle Ages* (New York: John Wiley & Sons, 1970), pp. 46–47.
10. P. Geary, "Carolingians and the Carolingian Empire," in *Dictionary of the Middle Ages,* ed. J. R. Strayer, vol. 3 (New York: Charles Scribner's Sons, 1983), p. 110.
11. Einhard, *The Life of Charlemagne,* with a foreword by S. Painter (Ann Arbor: University of Michigan Press, 1960), pp. 50–51.
12. P. Stafford, *Queens, Concubines, and Dowagers: The King's Wife in the Early Middle Ages* (Athens: University of Georgia Press, 1983), pp. 60–62.
13. Quoted in McKitterick, *The Frankish Kingdoms,* p. 77.
14. See K. F. Werner, "Important Noble Families in the Kingdom of Charlemagne," in T. Reuter, ed. and trans., *The Medieval Nobility: Studies on the Ruling Class of France and Germany from the Sixth to the Twelfth Century* (New York: North-Holland, 1978), pp. 174–184.
15. J. Nicholson, "Feminae Glorisae: Women in the Age of Bede," in *Medieval Women,* ed. D. Baker (Oxford: Basil Blackwell, 1978), pp. 15–31, esp. p. 19; and C. Fell, *Women in Anglo-Saxon England and the Impact of 1066* (Bloomington: Indiana University Press, 1984), p. 109.
16. R. W. Southern, *Medieval Humanism and Other Studies* (Oxford: Basil Blackwell, 1970), p. 3.
17. L. Sherley-Price, trans., *Bede: A History of the English Church and People* (Baltimore: Penguin Books, 1962), bk. 3, chap. 27, p. 191.
18. McKitterick, *The Frankish Kingdoms,* p. 145.
19. C. Klapisch-Zuber, ed., *A History of Women.* Vol. 2: *Silences of the Middle Ages* (Cambridge, Mass.: Harvard University Press, 1992), pp. 289–290.
20. See S. Rubin, *Medieval English Medicine* (New York: Barnes & Noble, 1974).
21. McKitterick, *The Frankish Kingdoms,* pp. 134–136, 169.
22. J. L. Nelson, trans., *The Annals of St-Bertin* (New York: Manchester University Press, 1991); and J. L. Nelson, *Charles the Bald* (New York: Longman, 1992), pp. 225–227.
23. McKitterick, *The Frankish Kingdoms,* pp. 182–183.
24. S. Reynolds, *Fiefs and Vassals: The Medieval Evidence Reconsidered* (Oxford: Clarendon Press, 1996), pp. 2–3.
25. E. A. R. Brown, "The Tyranny of a Construct: Feudalism and Historians of Medieval Europe," *American Historical Review* 79 (1974): 1060–1088.
26. J. R. Strayer, "The Two Levels of Feudalism," in *Medieval Statecraft and the Perspectives of History* (Princeton, N.J.: Princeton University Press, 1971), p. 63.
27. See B. S. Bachrach, "Charles Martel, Mounted Shock Combat, the Stirrup, and Feudalism," *Studies in Medieval and Renaissance History* 7 (1970): 49–75, esp. 66–75.
28. Strayer, "The Two Levels," pp. 66–76, esp. p. 71.
29. Nelson, *Charles the Bald,* p. 151.
30. Ibid., p. 39.
31. Quoted in R. Pipes, *Russia Under the Old Regime* (New York: Charles Scribner's Sons, 1974), p. 48.

SUGGESTED READING

For the Merovingians, the best general treatment is I. Wood, *The Merovingian Kingdoms, 450–751* (1994). For the Carolingians, see R. McKitterick, *The Frankish Kingdoms Under the Carolingians, 751–987* (1983). The scholarship of these books supersedes all previous work. R. McKitterick, *The Carolingians and the Written Word* (1989), will prove essential for many aspects of the Carolingian Renaissance, as will R. McKitterick, ed., *The Uses of Literacy in Early Medieval Europe* (1990), which includes essays on Ireland, Anglo-Saxon England, Merovingian Gaul, Muslim Spain, and Byzantium. J. L. Nelson, *Charles the Bald* (1992), is broader in scope than the biographical title would imply, since it contains excellent new material on the entire late Carolingian period. J. L. Nelson, *The Frankish World, 750–900* (1996), has useful articles on literacy, knighthood, and women.

Einhard's *Life of Charlemagne,* cited in the Notes, is a good starting point for study of the great chieftain. The best general biography of Charlemagne is D. Bullough, *The Age of Charlemagne* (1965). P. Riche, *Daily Life in the World of Charlemagne,* trans. J. McNamara (1978), is a detailed study of many facets of Carolingian society. P. Riche, *Education and Culture in the Barbarian West: From the Sixth Through the Eighth Century,* trans. J. J. Contreni (1976), provides a good treatment of intellectual activity. For agricultural and economic life, G. Duby, *The Early Growth of the European Economy: Warriors and Peasants from the Seventh to the Twelfth Century* (1978), relates economic behavior to other aspects of human experience in a thoroughly readable style. The importance of technological developments in the Carolingian period is described in L. White, *Medieval Technology and Social Change* (1962), now a classic work. As the title implies, G. Barraclough, *The Crucible of Europe: The Ninth and Tenth Centuries in European History* (1976), sees those centuries as crucial in the formation of European civilization. E. James, *The Origins of France: From Clovis to the Capetians, 500–1000* (1982), is a solid introductory survey of early French history, with an emphasis on family relationships.

In addition to L. Sherley-Price's translation *Bede,* cited in the Notes, see D. Wright, trans., *Beowulf* (1957), and D. L. Sayers, trans., *The Song of Roland* (1957). The latter provides an excellent key, in epic form, to the values and lifestyles of the feudal classes. P. H. Blair, *Northumbria in the Days of Bede* (1976), is also highly recommended.

For the development of the Christian church as an institution and its impact on pagan Germanic peoples, see the monumental work F. Kempf et al., *The Church in the Age of Feudalism,* trans. A. Biggs (1980), vol. 3 of the *History of the Church* series edited by H. Jedin and J. Dolan. For a nuanced account of the relations between the Roman papacy and the Frankish monarchs, see T. F. X. Noble, *The Republic of Saint Peter: The Birth of the Papal State* (1984). N. Brooks, "The Anglo-Saxon Cathedral Community 597–1070," in *A History of Canterbury Cathedral,* ed. P. Collinson et al. (1995), while focused on the cathedral, has interesting material on the entire Anglo-Saxon church. The scope of G. Tellenbach, *The Church in Western Europe from the Tenth to the Early Twelfth Century,* trans. T. Reuter (1993), is indicated by its title. F. Paxton, *Christianizing Death: The Creation of Ritual Process in Early Medieval Europe* (1990), and T. Head, *Hagiography and the Cult of the Saints* (1990), are valuable books dealing with specialized topics.

Those interested in women and children in early medieval society should see the title by Klapisch-Zuber cited in the Notes; D. Herlihy, "Land, Family, and Women in Continental Europe, 701–1200," in *Women in Medieval Society,* ed. S. M. Stuard (1976); and S. F. Wemple, *Women in Frankish Society: Marriage and the Cloister, 500–900* (1981), a fundamental work.

The following studies are also important and useful: J. McNamara, "A Legacy of Miracles: Hagiography and Nunneries in Merovingian Gaul," in *Women of the Medieval World: Essays in Honor of John H. Mundy,* ed. J. Kirshner and S. Wemple (1985); A. Warren, *Anchorites and Their Patrons in Medieval England* (1985); and the books by Stafford and Fell cited in the Notes.

For health and medical treatment, the curious student should consult W. H. McNeill, *Plagues and Peoples* (1976); J. F. Benton, "Trotula, Women's Problems, and the Professionalization of Medicine in the Middle Ages," *Bulletin of the History of Medicine* 59 (1985); Rubin's book cited in the Notes, esp. pp. 97–149; and J. M. Riddle, "Theory and Practice in Medieval Medicine," *Viator* 5 (1974), which is broader than the title implies. J. C. Russell, *The Control of Late Ancient and Medieval Population* (1985), discusses diet, disease, and demography.

For feudalism and manorialism see, in addition to the references given in the Notes, especially those by Reynolds and Brown, F. L. Ganshof, *Feudalism* (1961); and J. R. Strayer, "Feudalism in Western Europe," in *Feudalism in History,* ed. R. Coulborn (1956). M. Bloch, *Feudal Society,* trans. L. A. Manyon (1961), remains important. The more recent treatments of G. Duby, mentioned earlier, and P. Anderson, *Passages from Antiquity to Feudalism* (1978), stress the evolution of social structures and mental attitudes. For the significance of the ceremony of vassalage, see J. Le Goff, "The Symbolic Ritual of Vassalage," in *Time, Work, and Culture in the Middle Ages,* trans. A. Goldhammer (1982), a collection of provocative but difficult essays that includes "The Peasants and the Rural World in the Literature of the Early Middle Ages." The best broad treatment of peasant life and conditions is G. Duby, *Rural Economy and Country Life in the Medieval West,* trans. C. Postan (1968).

The Oxford Illustrated History of the Vikings (1997), ed. P. Sawyer, provides a sound account of the Vikings by an international team of scholars. J. Brondsted, *The Vikings* (1960), is an excellently illustrated study of many facets of Viking culture. G. Jones, *A History of the Vikings,* rev. ed. (1984), provides a comprehensive survey of the Viking world based on the latest archaeological findings and numismatic evidence, while P. H. Sawyer, *Kings and Vikings: Scandinavia and Europe, A.D. 700–1100* (1983), relies heavily on the literary evidence.

LISTENING TO THE PAST

Feudal Homage and Fealty

Feudalism was a social and political system held together by bonds of kinship, homage, and fealty and by grants of benefices—lands or estates given by king, lay lord, or ecclesiastical officer (bishop or abbot) to another member of the nobility or to a knight. In return for the benefice, or fief, the recipient became the vassal of the lord and agreed to perform certain services, usually military ones. Feudalism developed in the ninth century during the disintegration of the Carolingian Empire because rulers needed fighting men and officials. In a society that lacked an adequate government bureaucracy, a sophisticated method of taxation, or even the beginnings of national consciousness, personal ties provided some degree of cohesiveness.

In the first document, a charter dated 876, the emperor Charles the Bald (r. 843–877), Charlemagne's grandson, grants a benefice. In the second document, dated 1127, the Flemish notary Galbert of Bruges describes homage and fealty before Count Charles the Good of Flanders (r. 1119–1127). The ceremony consists of three parts: the act of homage; the oath of fealty, intended to reinforce the act; and the investiture (apparently with property). Because all three parts are present, historians consider this evidence of a fully mature feudal system.

In the name of the holy and undivided Trinity. Charles by the mercy of Almighty God august emperor . . . let it be known to all the faithful of the holy church of God and to our now, present and to come, that one of our faithful subjects, by name of Hildebertus, has approached our throne and has beseeched our serenity that through this command of our authority we grant to him for all the days of his life and to his son after him, in right of usufruct and benefice, certain estates which are . . . called Cavaliacus, in the county of Limoges. Giving assent to his prayers for reason of his meritorious service, we have ordered this charter to be written, through which we grant to him the estates already mentioned, in all their entirety, with lands, vineyards, forests, meadows, pastures, and with the men living upon them, so that, without causing any damage through exchanges or diminishing or lessening the land, he for all the days of his life and his son after him, as we have said, may hold and possess them in right of benefice and usufruct. . . .

Done of the sixteenth kalends of August [July 15th] the thirty-seventh year of the reign of Charles most glorious emperor in France . . . at Ponthion in the palace of the emperor. In the name of God, happily. Amen.

On Thursday, the seventh of the ides of April [April 7, 1127], acts of homage were again made to the count, which were brought to a conclusion through this method of giving faith and assurance. First, they performed homage in this fashion: the count inquired if [the prospective vassal] wished completely to become his man. He replied, "I do wish it," and with his hands joined and covered by the hands of the count, the two who were united by a kiss. Second, he who had done the homage gave faith to the representative of the count in these words: "I promise in my faith that I shall henceforth be faithful to Count William, and I shall fully observe the homage owed him against all men, in good faith and without deceit." Third, he took an oath on the relics of the saints. Then the count, with the rod which he had in his right hand, gave investiture to all those who by this promise had given assurance and due homage to the count, and had taken the oath.

✣ Charles the Bald and Roman attributes of rule, from a Bible, ca 846 A.D. (*Bibliothèque Nationale, Paris*)

Questions for Analysis

1. Why was the charter drawn up? Why did Charles grant the benefice?
2. Who were the "men living on it," and what economic functions did they perform?
3. What did the joined hands of the prospective vassal and the kiss symbolize?
4. In the oath of fealty, what was meant by the phrase "in my faith"? Why did the vassal swear on relics of the saints? What were these, and why were they used?
5. What does this ceremony tell us about the society that used it?

Source: The History of Feudalism by David Herlihy, ed.

CHAPTER

9 Revival, Recovery, Reform, and Expansion

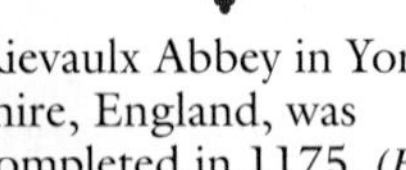

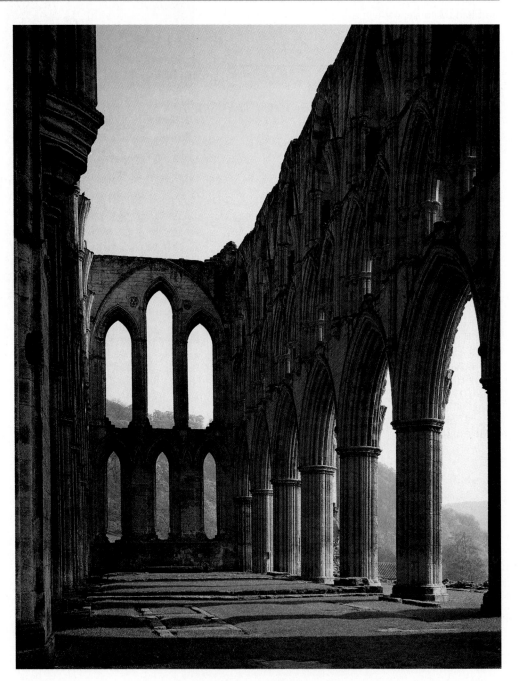

Rievaulx Abbey in Yorkshire, England, was completed in 1175. *(Eric Crichton/Bruce Coleman Ltd.)*

Beginning in the last half of the tenth century, after a long winter of discontent, Latin Christendom—that area of western Europe "that recognized papal authority and celebrated the Latin liturgy"[1]—saw the first hints of spring. The European springtime lasted from the middle of the eleventh century to the end of the thirteenth. This period from about 1050 to 1300 has been called the "High Middle Ages" or the "Central Middle Ages." Either term designates a time of change, growth, and cultural achievement between two eras of economic, political, and social crisis. These centuries also witnessed the expansion of Latin Christian culture into frontier zones, "border regions and regions of warfare"[2]—the Baltic, Scandinavia, eastern Europe, and Spain—through conquest and colonization.

- What were the ingredients of revival, and how did they come about?
- How did political revival affect the reform of the church? How, in turn, did religious reform influence secular developments?
- How did the reform of the Christian church come to affect relations between the church and civil authorities?
- What were the Crusades, and how did they manifest the influence of the church and the ideals of medieval society?
- What were the means of Latin Christian penetration into pagan and Muslim regions, and how did that penetration bring about change?

These are the questions that will frame the discussion in this chapter.

Political Revival

The eleventh century witnessed the beginnings of new political stability. Rulers in France, England, and Germany worked to reduce private warfare and civil anarchy. Domestic disorder subsided, and external invasions from the Vikings, Muslims, and Magyars (see page 274) gradually declined. These developments gave people security in their persons and property. Political order and stability provided the foundation for economic recovery and contributed to a slow increase in population.

The Decline of Invasion and Civil Disorder

In the tenth century, Charlemagne's descendants continued to hold the royal title in the West Frankish kingdom, but they exercised no effective control over the great feudal lords. Research on medieval France has focused on regions and principalities, emphasizing the diversity of languages and cultures, the differences in social structures, and the division of public authority. Northern French society, for example, had strong feudal elements, but the fief and vassalage were almost unknown in the south. The southern territories used Roman law, while the northern counties and duchies relied on customary law that was not formally codified until the thirteenth century. Thus broad generalizations about France, or indeed any single part of Europe, are very dangerous.[3]

Five counties dominated northern France: Anjou, Blois-Chartres, Brittany, Flanders, and Normandy. In the early eleventh century, all five experienced considerable internal disorder, and all were aggressively expansionist. But Normandy gradually emerged as the strongest territory with the greatest relative level of peace.

The territory that we call Normandy takes its name from the Northmen, or Vikings, who settled there in the tenth century. In 911 the West Frankish ruler Charles the Simple, unable to oust the Vikings, officially recognized their leader, Rollo, and later invested him with more lands; in return, Rollo gave allegiance and agreed to hold the region as a barrier against future Viking attacks. Rollo and his men were baptized as Christians and supported the West Frankish ruler when he needed their help. Although additional Northmen arrived, they were easily pacified. The late tenth and early eleventh centuries saw the assimilation of Norman and French, and major assaults on France ended.

During the minority of Rollo's descendant Duke William I (r. 1035–1089), however, rebellious lords ignored ducal authority, built private castles, and engaged in private warfare—with general instability the result. The alliance of Count Geoffrey Martel of Anjou and King Henry I of France posed a dire threat to ducal authority until 1054, when William defeated them. This victory turned the tide. Beginning in 1060, William united the Norman nobility under threat of external aggression from the counts of Blois and Maine and defended his frontier with a circle of castles. William also made feudalism work as a system of government. He insisted on the homage of his vassals, attached specific quotas of knight service to the lands he distributed, swiftly executed vassals who defaulted on their obligations, limited private warfare, and forbade the construction of private castles, always the symbol of feudal independence. The duke controlled the currency and supervised the church by participating in the selection of all bishops and abbots. By 1066 the Norman frontiers were stable, and the duchy possessed a feudal hierarchy. By the standards of the time, Normandy was an orderly and well-controlled principality.

Following the death of the last Carolingian ruler in 987, an assembly of nobles met to choose a successor. Accepting the argument of the archbishop of Reims that the French monarchy was elective, not hereditary, the nobles selected Hugh Capet, dux Francorum, duke of the Franks and head of a powerful clan in the West Frankish kingdom. Soon after his own coronation, Hugh crowned his son Robert to ensure the succession and prevent disputes after his (Hugh's) death and to weaken the feudal principle of elective kingship. The Capetian kings (so called from the *cope,* or cloak, Hugh wore as abbot of Saint-Denis) subsequently saved France from further division, but this was hardly apparent in 987. Compared with the duke of Normandy, the first Capetians were weak. By hanging on to what they had, however, they laid the foundation for later political stability.

Aquitaine, to the south, was the largest duchy in France geographically, and few lords in the north could match the power of Duke William V (995–1030). His authority extended from the Loire to the Garonne. Although scholars dispute the meaning of the term *vassal* in Aquitaine and whether William's knights actually performed their military service, he seems to have maintained their loyalty.[4] The export of wine and salt brought the duke wealth; the German emperor and the kings of Navarre, Aragon, and England sent him gifts; and William influenced the election of bishops in the duchy. All these suggest a relatively high level of political stability, and a contemporary chronicler said that the duke was thought to be more a king than a duke.[5]

Recovery followed a different pattern in Anglo-Saxon England. The Vikings had made a concerted effort to conquer and rule the whole island, and probably no part of Europe suffered more. Before the Viking invasions, England had never been united under a single ruler, and in 877 only parts of the kingdom of Wessex survived. The victory of the remarkable Alfred, king of the West Saxons (or Wessex), over Guthrun the Dane at Edington in 878 inaugurated a great political revival. Alfred and his immediate successors built a system of local defenses and slowly extended royal rule beyond Wessex to other Anglo-Saxon peoples until one law, royal law, replaced local custom. Alfred and his successors also laid the foundation for an efficient system of local government responsible directly to the king. Under the pressure of the Vikings, England was gradually united under one ruler.

In 1013 the Danish ruler Swen Forkbeard invaded England. His son Canute completed the subjugation of the island. King of England (1016–1035) and after 1030 king of Norway as well, Canute made England the center of his empire. He promoted a policy of assimilation and reconciliation between Anglo-Saxons and Vikings. Slowly the two peoples were melded together. The assimilation of Anglo-Saxon and Viking was personified by King Edward the Confessor (r. 1042–1066), the son of an Anglo-Saxon father and a Norman mother who had taken Canute as her second husband.

In the east, the German King Otto I (r. 936–973) inflicted a crushing defeat on the Hungarians on the banks of the Lech River in 955. This battle halted the Magyars' threat to Germany and made Otto a great hero to the Germans. It also signified the revival of the German monarchy and demonstrated that Otto was a worthy successor to Charlemagne.

When chosen king, Otto had selected Aachen as the site of his coronation to symbolize his intention to continue the tradition of Charlemagne. The basis of his power was alliance with and control of the church. Otto asserted the right to control ecclesiastical appointments. Before receiving religious consecration and being invested with the staff and ring symbolic of their offices, bishops and abbots had to perform feudal homage for the lands that accompanied the church office. (This practice, later known as "investiture," was to create a grave crisis in the eleventh century [see pages 280–282].)

Otto realized that he had to use the financial and military resources of the church to halt feudal anarchy. He used the higher clergy extensively in his administration, and the bulk of his army came from monastic and other church lands. Between 936 and 955, Otto succeeded in breaking the territorial power of the great German dukes.

Some of our knowledge of Otto derives from *The Deeds of Otto,* a history of his reign in heroic verse written by a nun, Hrotswitha of Gandersheim (ca 935–ca 1003). A learned poet, she also produced six verse plays, and she is considered the first dramatist after the fall of the ancient classical theater. Hrotswitha's literary productions give her an important place in the mainstream of tenth-century civilization.

Otto's coronation by the pope in 962 revived the imperial dignity and laid the foundation for what was later called the Holy Roman Empire. Further, the coronation showed that Otto had the support of the church in Germany and Italy. The uniting of the kingship with the imperial crown advanced German interests. Otto filled a power vacuum in northern Italy and brought peace among the great aristocratic families. The level of order there improved for the first time in over a century.

Peace and political stability in turn promoted the revival of northern Italian cities. Although plague, climatic deterioration that reduced agricultural productivity, and invasions had drastically reduced the population throughout Italy, most of the northern cities had survived the disorders of the early Middle Ages. By the ninth century, some of these cities showed considerable economic dynamism, in particular Venice, which won privileged access to Byzantine markets and imported silks, textiles, cosmetics, and Crimean slaves to sell to Padua and other cities. By the eleventh century, Venetian commerce had stimulated economic growth in Milan and Cremona, with those cities and Sicily supplying Venice with food in exchange for luxury goods from the East. The rising economic importance of Venice and later of Genoa, Pisa, and other cities became a central factor in the struggle between the papacy and the German Empire.

Christ Enthroned with Saints and the Emperor Otto I (tenth century) Between 933 and 973, Emperor Otto I founded the church of Saint Mauritius in Magdeburg. As a memorial to the event, Otto commissioned the production of this ivory plaque showing Christ accepting a model of the church from the emperor. Ivory was a favorite medium of Ottonian artists, and squat figures in a simple geometrical pattern characterize their work. *(The Metropolitan Museum of Art, Bequest of George Blumenthal, 1941 [41.100.157]. Photograph © 1986 The Metropolitan Museum of Art)*

Population, Climate, and Mechanization

A steady growth of population also contributed to Europe's general recovery. The decline of foreign invasions and internal civil disorder reduced the number of people killed and maimed. Feudal armies in the eleventh through thirteenth centuries continued their destruction, but they were very small by modern standards and fought few pitched battles. Most medieval conflicts consisted of sieges directed at castles or fortifications. As few as twelve men could defend a castle. With sufficient food and an adequate water supply, they could hold out for a long time. Monastic chroniclers, frequently bored and almost always writing from hearsay, tended to romanticize medieval warfare (as long as it was not in their own neighborhoods). Most conflicts were petty skirmishes with slight loss of life. The survival of more young people—those most often involved in war and usually the most sexually active—meant a population rise.

Nor was there any "natural," or biological, hindrance to population expansion. Between the tenth and fourteenth centuries, Europe was not hit by any major plague or other medical scourge, though leprosy and malaria did strike down some people. Leprosy, caused by a virus, was not very contagious, and it worked slowly. Lepers presented a frightful appearance: the victim's arms and legs rotted away, and gangrenous sores emitted a horrible smell. Physicians had no cure. For these reasons, and because of the command in the thirteenth chapter of Leviticus that lepers be isolated, medieval lepers were eventually segregated in hospitals called *leprosaria*.

Crop failure and the ever-present danger of starvation were much more pressing threats. The weather cooperated with the revival. Meteorologists believe that a slow but steady retreat of polar ice occurred between the ninth and eleventh centuries. A significant warming trend continued until about 1200. The century between 1080 and 1180 witnessed exceptionally clement weather in England, France, and Germany, with mild winters and dry summers. Good weather helps to explain advances in population growth, land reclamation, and agricultural yield. Increased agricultural output had a profound impact on society: it affected Europeans' health, commerce, industry, and general lifestyle. A better diet had an enormous impact on women's lives: it meant increased body fat, which increased fertility; also, more iron in the diet meant that women were less anemic and less subject to opportunistic diseases. Some researchers believe that it was in the High Middle Ages that Western women began to outlive men.

The tenth and eleventh centuries also witnessed a remarkable spurt in mechanization, especially in the use of energy. The increase in the number of water mills was spectacular. An ancient water mill unearthed near Monte Cassino could grind about 1.5 tons of grain in 10 hours, a quantity that would formerly have required the exertions of 40 slaves. The abundance of slave labor in the ancient world had retarded the development of mills, but by the mid-ninth century, on the lands of the abbey of Saint-Germaine-des-Prés near Paris, there were 59 water mills. Succeeding generations saw a continued increase. Thus, on the Robec River near Rouen, there were 2 mills in the tenth century, 4 in the eleventh, 10 in the thirteenth, and 12 in the fourteenth. *Domesday Book,* William the Conqueror's great survey of English economic resources in the late eleventh century (see page 336), recorded 5,624 water mills. On the 9,250 manors in England at that time, 3,463 had at least one mill. One scholar has calculated that on average each mill supplied 50 households. Besides grinding wheat or other grains to produce flour, water mills became essential in *fulling,* the process of scouring, cleansing, and thickening cloth. Rather than men or women trampling cloth in a trough, wooden hammers were raised and dropped on the cloth by means of a revolving drum connected to the spindle of a water wheel. Water mills revolutionized the means of grinding and fulling by using natural, rather than human, energy.

Successful at adapting waterpower to human needs, medieval engineers soon harnessed wind power. They replaced the wheels driven by water with sails. But while water always flows in the same direction, wind can blow from many directions. Windmill engineers solved this problem very ingeniously by mounting the framed wooden body, which contained the machinery and carried the sails, on a massive upright post free to turn in the wind.[6]

Revival and Reform in the Christian Church

The eleventh century also witnessed the beginnings of a remarkable religious revival. Monasteries, always the leaders in ecclesiastical reform, remodeled themselves under the leadership of the Burgundian abbey of Cluny. Subsequently, new religious orders, such as the Cistercians, were founded and became a broad spiritual movement.

The papacy itself, after a century of corruption and decadence, was cleaned up. The popes worked to clarify church doctrine and codify church law. They and their officials sought to communicate with all the clergy and peoples of Europe through a clearly defined, obedient hierarchy of bishops. The popes wanted the basic loyalty of all members of the clergy. Pope Gregory VII's strong assertion of papal power led to profound changes and serious conflict with secular authorities. The revival

Windmill The mill was constructed on a pivot, so that it could turn in the direction of the wind. Used primarily to grind grain, as shown here with a man carrying a sack of grain to be ground into flour, windmills were also used to process cloth, brew beer, drive saws, and provide power for iron forges. *(Bodleian Library, Oxford)*

of the church was manifested in the twelfth and thirteenth centuries by a flowering of popular piety, reflected in the building of magnificent cathedrals.

Monastic Revival

In the early Middle Ages, the best Benedictine monasteries had been citadels of good monastic observance and centers of learning. Between the seventh and ninth centuries, religious houses such as Bobbio in northern Italy, Luxeuil in France, and Jarrow in England copied and preserved manuscripts, maintained schools, and set high standards of monastic observance. Charlemagne had encouraged and supported these monastic activities, and the collapse of the Carolingian Empire had disastrous effects.

The Viking, Magyar, and Muslim invaders attacked and ransacked many monasteries across Europe. Some communities fled and dispersed. In the period of political disorder that followed the disintegration of the Carolingian Empire, many religious houses fell under the control and domination of local feudal lords. Powerful laymen appointed themselves or their relatives as abbots, while keeping their wives or mistresses. They took for themselves the lands and goods of monasteries, spending monastic revenues and selling monastic offices. Temporal powers all over Europe dominated the monasteries. The level of spiritual observance and intellectual activity declined.

Since the time of Charlemagne, secular powers had selected church officials and compelled them to become their vassals. Abbots, bishops, and archbishops thus had military responsibilities that required them to fight with their lords, or at least to send contingents of soldiers when called on to do so. Church law forbade clerics to shed blood, but many prelates found the excitement of battle too great to resist. In the ninth century, Abbot Lupus of Ferrières wrote his friend Abbot Odo of Corbie:

> *I am often most anxious about you, recalling your habit of heedlessly throwing yourself, all unarmed, into the thick of battle whenever your youthful energy is overcome with the greedy desire to conquer. . . . I, as you know, have never learned how to strike an enemy or to avoid his blows. Nor do I know how to execute all the other obligations of military service on foot or horseback.*

Lupus preferred the quiet of his scriptorium to the noise of the battlefield.[7] In the twelfth and thirteenth centuries, ecclesiastical barons owed heavy contingents of knight service; some prelates actually fought with the king. For example, in twelfth-century England, the abbot of Peterborough owed the king the service of sixty knights, the abbot of Bury Saint Edmunds forty knights, and the archbishop of Canterbury the huge service of five hundred knights, though after 1166 the service was usually commuted into a cash payment.[8] As feudal lords, ecclesiastical officials also had judicial authority over the knights, whose cases prelates tried in their feudal courts, and peasants, whose disputes they resolved in the manorial courts. For some prelates, the conflict between their religious duties on the one hand, and their judicial and military obligations on the other, posed a serious dilemma.

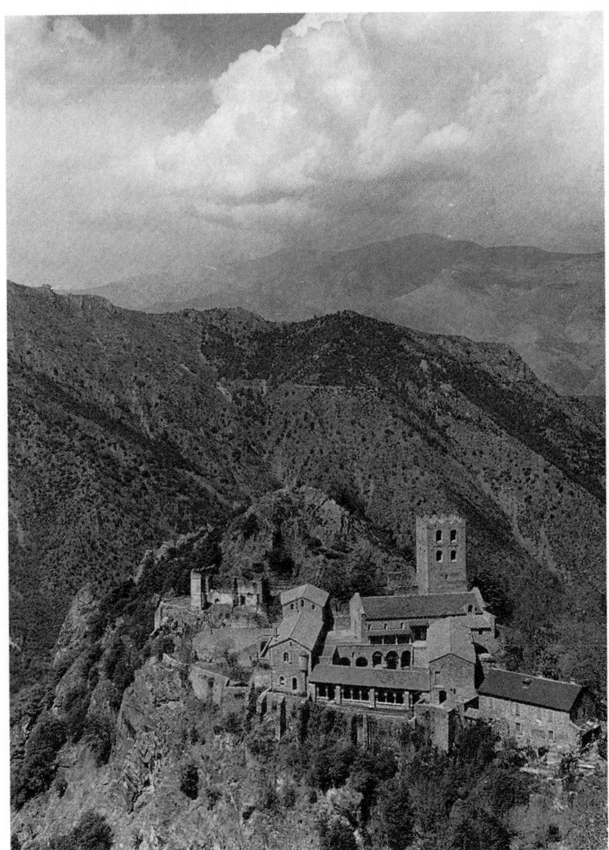

Monastery of Saint Martin de Canigou, in the eastern Pyrenees, was constructed in the early eleventh century in the new Romanesque style. With its thick walls and strategic position, it served as a Christian defensive fortress against the Muslims. *(Jean Dieuzaide)*

In 909 William the Pious, duke of Aquitaine, established the abbey of Cluny near Macon in Burgundy. This was to be a very important event. In his charter of endowment, Duke William declared that Cluny was to enjoy complete independence from all feudal (or secular) and episcopal lordship. The new monastery was to be subordinate only to the authority of Saints Peter and Paul as represented by the pope. The duke then renounced his own possession of and influence over Cluny.

This monastery and its foundation charter came to exert vast religious influence. The first two abbots of Cluny, Berno (910–927) and Odo (927–942), set very high standards of religious behavior. They stressed strict observance of *The Rule of Saint Benedict,* the development of a personal spiritual life by the individual monk, and the importance of the liturgy. Cluny gradually came to stand for clerical celibacy and the suppression of *simony* (the sale of church offices). In the eleventh century, Cluny was fortunate in having a series of highly able abbots who ruled for a long time. These abbots paid careful attention to sound economic management. In a disorderly world, Cluny gradually came to represent religious and political stability. Therefore, laypersons placed lands under its custody and monastic priories (a priory is a religious house, usually smaller in number than an abbey, governed by a prior) under its jurisdiction for reform. Benefactors wanted to be associated with Cluniac piety. Moreover, properties and monasteries under Cluny's jurisdiction enjoyed special protection, at least theoretically, from violence.[9] In this way, hundreds of monasteries, primarily in France and Spain, came under Cluny's authority.

Cluny was not the only center of monastic reform. The abbey of Gorze in Lotharingia (modern Lorraine) exercised a correcting influence on German religious houses. With royal support and through such abbeys as Saint Emmeran at Regensburg, Gorze directed a massive reform of monasteries in central Europe. Gorze and Cluny represented two different monastic traditions. Gorze became a center of literary culture, Cluny of liturgical ceremony. Gorze personified the simple lifestyle, Cluny the elaborate. Gorze accepted lay authority over monasteries; Cluny did not. Gorze served the empire, Cluny the Gregorian reformers (see pages 280–282). In some ways, Gorze stood for the German East, Cluny for the French West.[10]

Deeply impressed laypeople showered gifts on monasteries with good reputations. Jewelry, rich vestments, elaborately carved sacred vessels, even lands and properties poured into some houses. But with this wealth came lay influence. As the monasteries became richer, the lifestyle of the monks grew increasingly luxurious. Monastic observance and spiritual fervor declined. Soon fresh demands for reform were heard, and the result was the founding of new religious orders in the late eleventh and early twelfth centuries. The Cistercians, because of their phenomenal expansion, and the great economic, political, and spiritual influence they exerted, are the best representatives of the new reforming spirit.

In 1098 a group of monks left the rich abbey of Molesmes in Burgundy and founded a new house in the swampy forest of Cîteaux. They had specific goals and high ideals. They planned to avoid all involvement with secular feudal society. They decided to accept only uncultivated lands far from regular habitation. They intended to refuse all gifts of mills, serfs, tithes, and ovens—the traditional manorial sources of income. The early Cistercians determined to avoid elaborate liturgy and ceremony and to keep their chant simple. Finally, they refused to allow the presence of powerful laypeople in their monasteries, because they knew that such influence was usually harmful to careful observance.

The first monks at Cîteaux experienced sickness, a dearth of recruits, and terrible privations. But their obvious sincerity and high ideals eventually attracted attention. In 1112 a twenty-three-year-old nobleman called Bernard joined the community at Cîteaux, together with some of his brothers and other noblemen. Three years later, Bernard was appointed founding abbot of Clairvaux in Champagne. From this position, he conducted a vast correspondence, attacked the theological views of Peter Abelard (see page 361), intervened in the disputed papal election of 1130, drafted a constitution for the Knights Templars (see page 288), and preached the Second Crusade. For his learning, charm, and deep spiritual charisma, Bernard of Clairvaux exercised great influence on many aspects of twelfth-century culture. This reforming movement gained impetus. Cîteaux founded 525 new monasteries in the course of the twelfth century, and its influence on European society was profound. Unavoidably, however, Cistercian success brought wealth, and wealth brought power. By the later twelfth century, economic prosperity and political power had begun to compromise the original Cistercian ideals.

Reform of the Papacy

Some scholars believe that the monastic revival spreading from Cluny influenced reform of the Roman papacy and eventually of the entire Christian church. Certainly Abbot Odilo of Cluny (994–1048) was a close friend of the German emperor Henry III, who promoted reform throughout the empire. Pope Gregory VII, who carried the ideals of reform to extreme lengths, had spent some time at Cluny. And the man who consolidated the reform movement and strengthened the medieval papal monarchy, Pope Urban II (1088–1099),

What kinds of appeals came to the Roman curia? The majority of cases related to disputes over church property or ecclesiastical elections and above all to questions of marriage and annulment. Since the fourth century, Christian values had influenced the administration of the law, and bishops frequently sat in courts that heard marriage cases. Beginning in the tenth and eleventh centuries, church officials began to claim that they had exclusive jurisdiction over marriage. Appeals to an ecclesiastical tribunal, rather than to a civil court, or appeals from a civil court to a church court implied the acceptance of the latter's jurisdiction. Moreover, most of the popes in the twelfth and thirteenth centuries were canon lawyers who pressed the authority of church courts. The most famous of them, the man whose pontificate represented the height of medieval papal power, was Innocent III (1198–1216).

Innocent judged a vast number of cases. He compelled King Philip Augustus of France to take back his wife, Ingeborg of Denmark. He arbitrated the rival claims of two disputants to the imperial crown of Germany. He forced King John of England to accept as archbishop of Canterbury a man John did not want.

By the early thirteenth century, papal efforts at reform begun more than a century before had attained phenomenal success. The popes themselves were men of high principles and strict moral behavior. The frequency of clerical marriage and the level of violence had declined considerably. The practice of simony was much more the exception than the rule.

Yet the seeds of future difficulties were being planted. As the volume of appeals to Rome multiplied, so did the size of the papal bureaucracy. As the number of lawyers increased, so did concern for legal niceties and technicalities, fees, and church offices. As early as the mid-twelfth century, John of Salisbury, an Englishman working in the papal curia, had written that the people condemned the curia for its greed and indifference to human suffering. Nevertheless, the power of the curia continued to grow, as did its bureaucracy.

Thirteenth-century popes devoted their attention to the bureaucracy and their conflicts with the German emperor Frederick II. Some, like Gregory IX (1227–1241), abused their prerogatives to such an extent that their moral impact was seriously weakened. Even worse, Innocent IV (1243–1254) used secular weapons, including military force, to maintain his leadership. These popes badly damaged papal prestige and influence. By the early fourteenth century, the seeds of disorder would grow into a vast and sprawling tree, and once again cries for reform would be heard.

THE CRUSADES

The Crusades of the eleventh and twelfth centuries were the most obvious manifestation of the papal claim to the leadership of Christian society. The enormous popular response to papal calls for crusading reveals the influence of the reformed papacy. The Crusades also reflect the church's new understanding of the noble warrior class. A distinguished scholar of the Crusades wrote:

At around the turn of the millennium [the year 1000], the attitude of the church toward the military class underwent a significant change. The contrast between militia Christi [war for Christ] and militia saecularis [war for worldly purposes] was overcome and just as rulership earlier had been Christianized . . . , so now was the military profession; it acquired a direct ecclesiastical purpose, for war in the service of the church or for the weak came to be regarded as holy and was declared to be a religious duty not only for the king but also for every individual knight.[16]

Crusades in the late eleventh and early twelfth centuries were holy wars sponsored by the papacy for the recovery of the Holy Land from the Muslims. They grew out of the long conflict between Christians and Muslims in Spain, where by about 1250 Christian kings had regained roughly 90 percent of the peninsula. Although people of all ages and classes participated in the Crusades, so many knights did so that crusading became a distinctive feature of the upper-class lifestyle. In an aristocratic, military society, men coveted reputations as Crusaders; the Christian knight who had been to the Holy Land enjoyed great prestige. The Crusades manifested the religious and chivalric ideals—as well as the tremendous vitality—of medieval society.

The Roman papacy supported the holy war in Spain and by the late eleventh century had strong reasons for wanting to launch an expedition against Muslim infidels in the East as well. The papacy had been involved in the bitter struggle over investiture with the German emperors. If the pope could muster a large army against the enemies of Christianity, his claim to be leader of Christian society in the West would be strengthened. Moreover, in 1054 a serious theological disagreement had split the Greek church of Byzantium and the Roman church of the West. The pope believed that a crusade would lead to strong Roman influence in Greek territories and eventually the reunion of the two churches.

In 1071 at Manzikert in eastern Anatolia, Turkish soldiers defeated a Greek army and occupied much of Asia Minor. The emperor at Constantinople appealed to the West for support. Shortly afterward, the holy city of Jerusalem, the scene of Christ's preaching and burial, fell to the Turks. Pilgrimages to holy places in the Middle East became very dangerous, and the papacy claimed to be outraged that the holy city was in the hands of unbelievers. Since the Muslims had held Palestine since the eighth century, the papacy actually feared that the Seljuk Turks would be less accommodating to Christian pilgrims than the previous Muslim rulers of the areas had been.

In 1095 Pope Urban II journeyed to Clermont in France and on November 27 called for a great Christian holy war against the infidels. Urban's appeal at Clermont represents his policy of *rapprochement,* or reconciliation, with Byzantium, with church union his ultimate goal. (Mutual ill will, quarrels, and the plundering of Byzantine property by undisciplined westerners were to frustrate this hope.) He stressed the sufferings and persecution of Christians in Jerusalem. He urged Christian knights who had been fighting one another to direct their energies against the true enemies of God, the Muslims. Urban proclaimed an *indulgence,* or remission of the temporal penalties imposed by the church for sin, to those who would fight for and regain the holy city of Jerusalem. Few speeches in history have had such a dramatic effect as Urban's call at Clermont for the First Crusade.

Godfrey of Bouillon, Raymond of Toulouse, and other great lords from northern France immediately had the cross of the Crusader sewn on their tunics. Encouraged by popular preachers such as Peter the Hermit and by papal legates in Germany, Italy, and England, thousands of people of all classes joined the crusade. Although most of the Crusaders were French, pilgrims from many regions streamed southward from the Rhineland, through Germany and the Balkans. Of all of the developments of the High Middle Ages, none better reveals Europeans' religious and emotional fervor and the influence of the reformed papacy than the extraordinary outpouring of support for the First Crusade. (See the feature "Listening to the Past: An Arab View of the Crusades" on pages 298–299.)

Religious convictions inspired many, but mundane motives were also involved. For the curious and the adventurous, the crusade offered foreign travel and excitement. It provided kings, who were trying to establish order and build states, the perfect opportunity to get rid of troublemaking knights. It gave land-hungry younger sons a chance to acquire fiefs in the Middle East. Even some members of the middle class who stayed at home profited from the crusade. Nobles often had to borrow money from the burghers to pay for their expeditions, and they put up part of their land as security. If a noble did not return home or could not pay the interest on the loan, the middle-class creditor took over the land.

The Crusades also brought to the surface latent Christian prejudice against the Jews. Between the sixth and tenth centuries, descendants of Sephardic (from the modern Hebrew word *Separaddi,* meaning Spanish or Portuguese) Jews had settled along the trade routes of western Europe; in the eleventh century, they played a major role in the international trade between the Muslim Middle East and the West. Jews also lent money to peasants, townspeople, and nobles. Because the Jews performed these useful economic services, kings and lords protected them. When the First Crusade was launched, many poor knights had to borrow from Jews to equip themselves for the expedition. Debt bred resentment. (See the feature "Individuals in Society: The Jews of Speyer: A Collective Biography.")

The First Crusade was successful, mostly because of the dynamic enthusiasm of the participants. The Crusaders had little more than religious zeal. They knew nothing about the geography or climate of the Middle East. Although there were several counts with military experience among the host, the Crusaders could never agree on a leader, and the entire expedition was marked by disputes among the great lords. Lines of supply were never set up. Starvation and disease wracked the army, and the Turks slaughtered hundreds of noncombatants. Nevertheless, convinced that "God wills it," the war cry of the Crusaders, the army pressed on and in 1099 captured Jerusalem. Although the Crusaders fought bravely, Arab disunity was a chief reason for their victory. At Jerusalem, Edessa, Tripoli, and Antioch, Crusader kingdoms were founded on the Western feudal model (Map 9.1).

Between 1096 and 1270, the crusading ideal was expressed in eight papally approved expeditions to the East. Despite the success of the First Crusade, none of the later ones accomplished very much. The Third Crusade (1189–1192) was precipitated by the recapture of Jerusalem by the sultan Saladin in 1187. Frederick Barbarossa of the Holy Roman Empire, Richard the Lion-Hearted of England, and Philip Augustus of France participated, and the Third Crusade was better financed than previous ones. But disputes among the leaders and strategic problems prevented any lasting results.

During the Fourth Crusade (1202–1204), careless preparation and inadequate financing had disastrous consequences for Latin-Byzantine relations. In April 1204, the Crusaders and Venetians stormed Constantinople; sacked the city, destroying its magnificent library; and

Individuals in Society

The Jews of Speyer: A Collective Biography

An engraving (18th cent.) of the mass suicide of the Jews of Worms in 1096, when they were overwhelmed by Crusaders (with shields). *(Bildarchiv Preussischer Kulturbesitz)*

In the winter of 1095–1096, news of Pope Urban II's call for a crusade spread. In spring 1096, the Jews of northern France, fearing that a crusade would arouse anti-Semitic hostility, sent a circular letter to the Rhineland Jewry seeking its prayers. Jewish leaders in Mainz responded, "All the (Jewish) communities have decreed a fast. . . . May God save us and save you from all distress and hardship. We are deeply fearful for you. We, however, have less reason to fear (for ourselves), for we have heard not even a rumor of the crusade."[1] Ironically, French Jewry survived almost unscathed, while the Rhenish Jewry suffered frightfully.

Beginning in the late tenth century Jews trickled into Speyer—partly through Jewish perception of opportunity and partly because of the direct invitation of the bishop of Speyer. The bishop's charter meant that Jews could openly practice their religion, could not be assaulted, and could buy and sell goods. But they could not proselytize their faith, as Christians could. Jews also extended credit on a small scale, and, in an expanding economy with many coins circulating, determined the relative value of currencies. Unlike their Christian counterparts, many Jewish women were literate and acted as moneylenders. Jews also worked as skilled masons, carpenters, and jewelers. As the bishop had promised, the Jews of Speyer lived apart from Christians in a walled enclave where they exercised autonomy: they maintained law and order, raised taxes, and provided religious, social, and educational services for their community. (This organization lasted in Germany until the nineteenth century.) Jewish immigration to Speyer accelerated; everyday relations between Jews and Christians were peaceful.

But Christians resented Jews as newcomers, outsiders, and aliens; for enjoying the special protection of the bishop; and for providing economic competition. Anti-Semitic ideology had received enormous impetus from the virulent anti-Semitic writings of Christian apologists in the first six centuries A.D. Jews, they argued, were *deicides* (Christ-killers); worse, Jews could understand the truth of Christianity but deliberately rejected it; thus, they were inhuman. By the late eleventh century, anti-Semitism was an old and deeply rooted element in Western society.

Late in April 1096, Emich of Leisingen, a petty Rhineland lord who had the reputation of being a lawless thug, approached Speyer with a large band of Crusaders. Joined by a mob of burghers, they planned to surprise the Jews in their synagogue on Saturday morning, May 3, but the Jews prayed early and left before the attackers arrived. Furious, the mob randomly murdered eleven Jews. The bishop took the entire Jewish community into his castle, arrested some of the burghers, and cut off their hands. News of these events raced up the Rhine to Worms, creating confusion in the Jewish community. Some took refuge with Christian friends; others sought the bishop's protection. A combination of Crusaders and burghers killed a large number of Jews, looted and burned synagogues and desecrated the Torah (see page 47) and other books. Proceeding on to the old and prosperous city of Mainz, Crusaders continued attacking Jews. Facing overwhelming odds, eleven hundred Jews killed their families and themselves. Crusaders and burghers vented their hatred by inflicting barbaric tortures on the wounded and dying. The Jews were never passive; everywhere they put up resistance. If the Crusades had begun as opposition to Islam, after 1096 that hostility extended to those Christians saw as enemies of society—lepers, Jews, and homosexuals (see pages 348–349). But Jews continued to move to the Rhineland and to make important economic and intellectual contributions. Crusader-burgher attacks served as harbingers of events to come in the later Middle Ages and well into modern times.

Questions for Analysis

1. How do you explain Christian attacks on the Jews of Speyer? Were they defenses of faith?
2. What is meant by the term *dehumanization of the enemy?* Can you give other examples?

1. Quoted in R. Chazan, *In the Year 1096: The First Crusade and the Jews* (Philadelphia: Jewish Publication Society, 1996), p. 28.

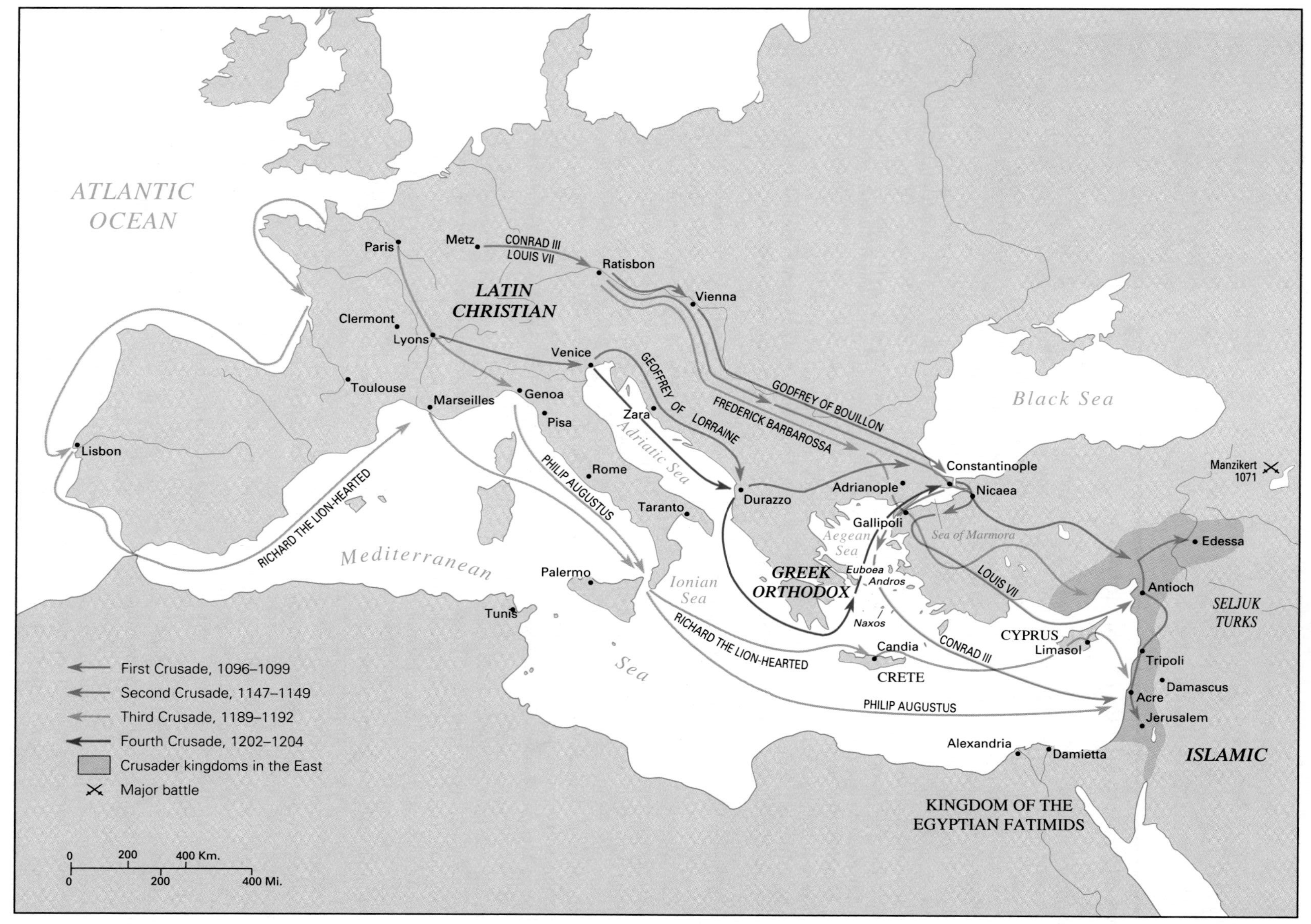

ATLANTIC OCEAN
Black Sea
Sea of Marmora
Aegean Sea
Adriatic Sea
Ionian Sea
Mediterranean Sea
LATIN CHRISTIAN
GREEK ORTHODOX
ISLAMIC
SELJUK TURKS
KINGDOM OF THE EGYPTIAN FATIMIDS
Paris
Metz
Ratisbon
Vienna
Clermont
Lyons
Toulouse
Marseilles
Genoa
Pisa
Venice
Zara
Rome
Taranto
Palermo
Tunis
Lisbon
Durazzo
Adrianople
Constantinople
Nicaea
Gallipoli
Euboea
Andros
Naxos
Candia
CRETE
CYPRUS
Limasol
Manzikert 1071
Edessa
Antioch
Tripoli
Damascus
Acre
Jerusalem
Alexandria
Damietta
CONRAD III
LOUIS VII
GODFREY OF BOUILLON
FREDERICK BARBAROSSA
GEOFFREY OF LORRAINE
PHILIP AUGUSTUS
RICHARD THE LION-HEARTED
First Crusade, 1096–1099
Second Crusade, 1147–1149
Third Crusade, 1189–1192
Fourth Crusade, 1202–1204
Crusader kingdoms in the East
Major battle
0 200 400 Km.
0 200 400 Mi.

The Capture of Jerusalem in 1099 As engines hurl stones to breach the walls, Crusaders enter on scaling ladders. Scenes from Christ's passion (above) identify the city as Jerusalem. *(Bibliothèque Nationale, Paris)*

MAP 9.1 The Routes of the Crusades The Crusades led to a major cultural encounter between Muslim and Christian values. What significant intellectual and economic effects resulted?

grabbed thousands of relics, which were later sold in Europe. (See the feature "Individuals in Society: Enrico Dandolo" on page 358.) The Byzantine Empire, as a political unit, never recovered from this destruction. Although the Crusader Baldwin IX of Flanders was chosen emperor, the empire splintered into three parts and soon consisted of little more than the city of Constantinople. Moreover, the assault of one Christian people on another—when one of the goals of the crusade was reunion of the Greek and Latin churches—made the split between the churches permanent. It also helped to discredit the entire crusading movement. In 1208, in one of the most memorable episodes, two expeditions of children set out on a crusade to the Holy Land. One contingent turned back; the other was captured and sold into slavery. Two later crusades against the Muslims, undertaken by King Louis IX of France, added to his prestige as a pious ruler. The last of the official crusades accomplished nothing at all.

Crusades were also mounted against groups within Europe that were perceived as heretical, political, or pagan threats. In 1208 Pope Innocent III proclaimed a crusade against the Albigensians, a heretical sect. The Albigensians, whose name derived from the southern French town of Albi where they were concentrated, rejected orthodox doctrine on the relationship of God and man, the sacraments, and clerical hierarchy. Fearing that religious division would lead to civil disorder, the French monarchy joined the crusade against the Albigensians. Under Count Simon de Montfort, the French inflicted a savage defeat on the Albigensians at Muret in 1213; the county of Toulouse passed to the authority of the French crown. Fearful of encirclement by imperial territories, the popes also promoted crusades against Emperor Frederick II in 1227 and 1239. This use of force backfired, damaging papal credibility as the sponsor of peace.

The Crusades also inspired the establishment of new religious orders. For example, the Knights Templars, founded in 1118 with the strong backing of Saint Bernard of Clairvaux, combined the monastic ideals of obedience and self-denial with the crusading practice of military aggression. The Templars waged wars against the pagan Prussians in the Baltic region. After 1230, and from a base in Poland, they established a new territory, Christian Prussia, and gradually the entire eastern shore of the Baltic came under their hegemony. Military orders such as the Templars served to unify Christian Europe.

In the entire crusading movement, fewer women than men participated directly, since the Crusades were primarily military expeditions and all societies have perceived war as a masculine enterprise. Given the aristocratic bias of the chroniclers, we have more information about royal and noble ladies who went to the Holy Land than about middle-class and peasant women, though the latter groups contributed the greater numbers. Eleanor of Aquitaine (1122?–1204) accompanied her husband, King Louis VII, on the Second Crusade (1147–1149), and the thirteenth-century English chronicler Matthew Paris says that large numbers of women went on the Seventh Crusade (1248–1254) so that they could obtain the crusading indulgence. The Crusades illustrate that women in feudal society exercised considerable power. Women who stayed home assumed their husbands' responsibilities in the management of estates, the dispensation of justice to vassals and serfs, and the protection of property from attack. Since Crusaders frequently could finance the expedition only by borrowing, it fell to their wives to repay the loans. These heavy responsibilities brought women power. The many women who operated inns and shops in the towns through which crusading armies passed profited from the rental of lodgings and the sale of foodstuffs, clothing, arms, and fodder for animals. For prostitutes, also, crusading armies offered business opportunities.

The Crusades introduced some Europeans to Eastern luxury goods, but their overall cultural impact on the West remains debatable. By the late eleventh century, strong economic and intellectual ties with the East had already been made. The Crusades testify to the religious enthusiasm of the High Middle Ages, but Steven Runciman, a distinguished scholar of the Crusades, concludes in his three-volume history:

> *The triumphs of the Crusades were the triumphs of faith. But faith without wisdom is a dangerous thing. . . . In the long sequence of interaction and fusion between orient and occident out of which our civilization has grown, the Crusades were a tragic and destructive episode. . . . High ideals were besmirched by cruelty and greed, enterprise and endurance by a blind and narrow self-righteousness; and the Holy War itself was nothing more than a long act of intolerance in the name of God, which is the sin against the Holy Ghost.*[17]

Along the Syrian and Palestinian coasts, the Crusaders set up a string of feudal states that managed to survive for about two centuries before the Muslims reconquered them. The Crusaders left two more permanent legacies in the Middle East that continue to affect us today. First, the long struggle between Islam and Christendom, and the example of persecution set by Christian kings and prelates, left an inheritance of deep bitterness; relations between Muslims and their Christian and Jewish subjects worsened. Second, European merchants, primarily Italians, had established communities in the Crusader states. After those kingdoms collapsed, Muslim rulers still encouraged trade with European businessmen. Commerce with the West benefited both Muslims and Europeans, and it continued to flourish.[18]

THE EXPANSION OF LATIN CHRISTENDOM

The period after the millennial year 1000 witnessed great migrations and cross-regional contacts. The movement of peoples and ideas from western France, the heartland of Christendom, and from western Germany into frontier regions—Ireland, Scandinavia, the Baltic lands, eastern Europe, and Spain—had, by about 1300, profound cultural consequences for those fringe territories. Wars of expansion, the establishment of new Christian bishoprics, and the vast migration of colonists, together with the papal emphasis on a unified Christian world, brought about the gradual Europeanization of the frontier (Map 9.2).

The Crusades provided the means for what a recent scholar has called "the aristocratic diaspora," the movement of knights from their homes in France to areas then on the frontiers of Christian Europe.[19] Wars of foreign conquest had occurred before the Crusades, as the Norman Conquest of England in 1066 (see page 223) illustrates, but for many knights "migration began with the taking of the cross." We have already seen how restless, ambitious knights, many of them younger sons with no prospects, left on crusade to the Holy Land. Some of them were able to carve out lordships in Palestine, Syria, and Greece. Others went to northwestern, eastern, and southern Europe.

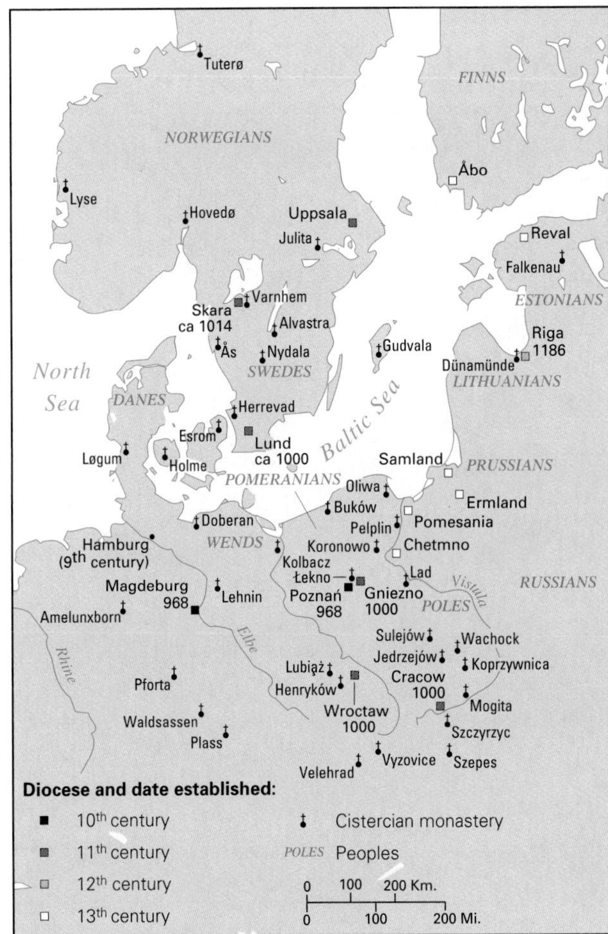

MAP 9.2 Christianization of the Baltic Region Dioceses and monasteries served as the means by which pagan Baltic peoples were Christianized and brought into the framework of Latin Christian culture. *(Source: Some data from R. Bartlett,* The Making of Europe: Conquest, Colonization and Cultural Change, 950–1350 *[Princeton, N.J.: Princeton University Press, 1993], pp. 16 and 259.)*

Northern and Eastern Europe

In 1177 John de Courcy, member of a Norman family with small estates in Somerset (southwestern England), with twenty-two knights and three hundred foot soldiers crossed the Irish Sea and raided Ulcad in the province of Ulster. John easily defeated the local ruler, Rory MacDunlevy, seized the town of Downpatrick, and with this foothold built himself a sizable lordship. Other Anglo-Norman settlers followed. Ireland had technically been Christian since the days of Saint Patrick (see page 203), but John de Courcy's intervention led to the remodeling of the Irish church from a monastic structure to an episcopal one with defined territorial dioceses. The Anglo-Norman invasion also meant the introduction of the fief, feudal cavalry, and Anglo-Norman landlords, as well as the beginnings of chartered towns on an English pattern. Similarly, Anglo-Norman, Anglo-French, and Flemish knights poured into Scotland in the twelfth century, bringing the fief and the language of feudalism. In 1286 the descendants of twelfth-century colonists held five of the thirteen Scottish earldoms. Scottish feudalism closely resembled that of western France, and immigrant knights transformed Scottish society.

Latin Christian influences entered Scandinavian and Baltic regions primarily through the erection of dioceses. As an easily identifiable religious figure, as judge, and as the only person who could ordain priests and

Saint Hedwig (1174–1243) of Bavaria was married to Henry, duke of Saxony, by whom she had seven children and from whom she suffered great abuse. She ruled Silesia (today partly in the Czech Republic, partly in Poland) when her husband was away at war; conducted diplomatic negotiations; and founded monasteries, including Trebnitz, the first Cistercian house for women. Hedwig and her niece Saint Elizabeth of Hungary (1207–1231) illustrate the powerful influence of women in the spread of Christianity in central and eastern Europe. In a manuscript commissioned by her fourteenth-century descendants (shown in small-scale donor portraits), Hedwig carries a book, rosary, and tiny statue of the Virgin Mary, references to her devout character. *(The John Paul Getty Museum, Los Angeles, Court Atelier of Duke Ludwig I of Liegnitz and Brieg [illuminator],* Vita beatae Hedwigis, *1353. Tempera colors, colored washes and ink bound between wood boards covered with red-stained pigskin, 34.1 × 24.8 cm)*

confirm laypeople, the bishop was the essential instrument in the spread of Christianity. Otto I (see page 274) established the first Scandinavian sees—Schleswig, Ribe, and Århus in Denmark—between 948 and 965. In 1060 a network of eight bishoprics was organized, and in 1103–1104 the Danish kingdom received its first archbishopric, Lund, in Scania (now part of Sweden). Royal power advanced institutional Christianity in Denmark; because that power was weaker in Sweden, Norway, and Iceland, Christianity progressed much more slowly in those lands. In the 1060s, however, two dioceses were set up in Norway and six in Sweden, and in 1164 Uppsala in Sweden, long a center of the pagan cults of Thor and Odin, became a Catholic archdiocese.

In the lands between the Oder River in the east and the Elbe and Saale Rivers in the west lived the Wends, a West Slavic people, and their linguistic cousins, the Balts (Prussians, Lithuanians, Latvians, Livonians, Estonians, and Finns). These peoples clung tenaciously to paganism in spite of extensive Christian missionary activity. Nevertheless, Otto I established a string of dioceses along his northern and eastern frontiers to pacify newly conquered Slavic lands and to Christianize. Among these were the archdiocese of Magdeburg, intended for "all the people of the Slavs beyond the Elbe and Saale, lately converted and to be converted to God,"[20] and the dioceses of Brandenburg, Schwerin, and Lübeck, all filled with German bishops. Repeated Slavic revolts, illustrating ethnic opposition to German lords and German bishops, indicate that the new faith did not easily penetrate the Baltic region. Only the ruthless tactics of Albert the Bear (d. 1170) pacified the region and forced the incorporation of the eastern and northern bishoprics into the structure of the Latin church.

A member of the highest Saxon nobility, with extensive experience in border warfare against the Slavs, Albert the Bear reconquered the town of Brandenburg on June 11, 1157. With this base, Albert declared himself margrave of Brandenburg and founded a dynasty that ruled there for seven generations. To support his *Ostiedlung* (orientation to the East), Albert proclaimed a German crusade against the Slavs. He invited Dutch, Flemish, and German knights from the Rhineland to colonize conquered territories. To keep the region as far as the Oder pacified, he built castles manned by these newly recruited knights. Slav revolts were ruthlessly crushed. Meantime, German knights from Saxony also moved into Esturia on the Gulf of Finland, into Silesia along the Oder, and into Bohemia and Hungary. Duke Boleslaw I of Silesia (1163–1201) invited German knights and German Cistercian monks to settle in

Hildebert Disturbed by a Mouse In the twelfth century, German art, especially that of Cologne, had a strong impact in Bohemia. In a copy of Saint Augustine's *City of God* (see page 211), the humorous Bohemian scribe Hildebert gives a self-portrait: While working at his drawing board (held up by a lion), he notices a mouse eating his dinner. The mouse has knocked the chicken off the table and is nibbling the cheese. Hildebert is about to throw a rock at the mouse. His assistant Erwinus (below) continues work unconcerned. The lines of Hildebert's gown suggest that he had studied in Cologne or under a Cologne master. *(Metropolitan Chapter Library of Saint Vitus, Prague)*

Silesia, thereby contributing to the political stability and agricultural development of his lands.[21]

Along with German knights, German (or Roman) ecclesiastical influences entered other parts of eastern Europe in the tenth and eleventh centuries. Prague in Bohemia became a bishopric in 973; from Prague missionaries set out to convert the Poles. The first diocese in Poland, Poznan, was erected in 968. The German emperor Otto I established an archdiocese at Gniezno in central Poland in 1000, with Poznan and several other sees subordinate to it. Likewise in Hungary, Esztergom became a diocese in 1001, and during the eleventh century Hungarian rulers established new ecclesiastical centers along the Danube and eastward into Transylvania (modern central Romania). In the twelfth and thirteenth centuries, tens of thousands of German settlers poured into eastern Europe, Silesia, Mecklenburg, Bohemia, Poland, Hungary, and Transylvania. But these settlers did *not* come to an empty frontier. In Poland, for example, towns had emerged after about 700 as fortress settlements, centers for safety from external threats. These early towns contained the residence of the military leader of the region, the duke, and his servants and knights. The Christian baptism of Duke Mieszko (d. 992) and his court in 966 at Gniezno led to the construction of a cathedral, the arrival of churchmen, and the building of churches and monasteries for monks and nuns. All these people represented a demand for goods and services. Centers such as Gniezno, Cracow, Wroclaw, and Plock attracted craftsmen and merchant immigrants seeking business opportunities.[22] With urbanization came Germanization. "When Queen Konstanze of Bohemia gave urban privileges to Hodonin (Göding) in southern Moravia in 1228, she announced in her charter: 'we have summoned worthy Germans and settled them in the city.'" Likewise, Duke Boleslaw of Poland's charter for his new city of Cracow stated "the city of Cracow was converted to German law and the site of the market, the houses and the courtyards was changed by the duke's

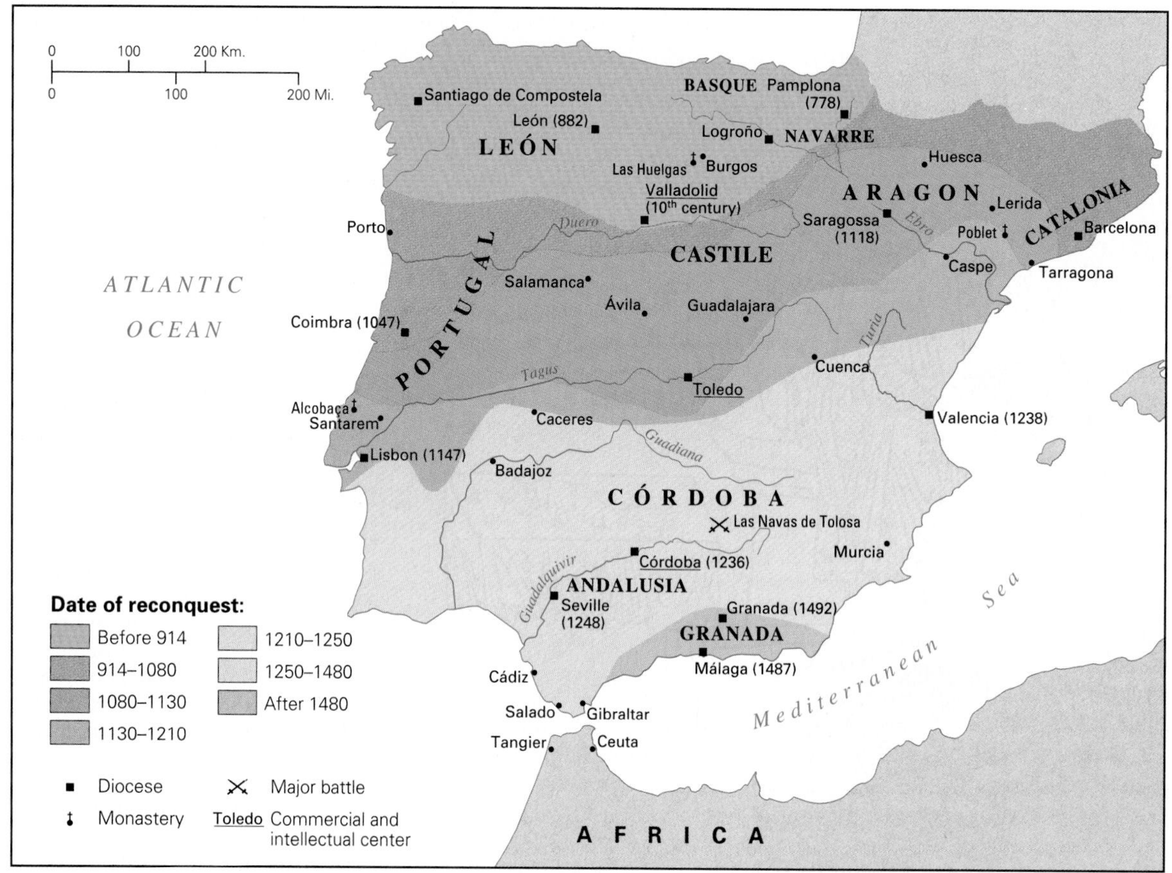

MAP 9.3 The Reconquista The Christian conquest of Muslim Spain was followed by ecclesiastical reorganization, with the establishment of dioceses, monasteries, and the Latin liturgy, which gradually tied the peninsula to the heartland of Christian Europe and to the Roman papacy. *(Source: Adapted from David Nicholas,* The Evolution of the Medieval World. *Copyright © 1992. Used by permission of Addison Wesley Longman Ltd..)*

officials."[23] Boleslaw specifically excluded Polish peasants from becoming burgesses, because he feared the depopulation of his estates. Again, when Bishop Albert of Livonia decided to found a new cathedral at Riga that would attract merchants from Lübeck and Gotland, he granted burgher-immigrants rights, declaring that they be judged according to "Gotland law," the law of the German burgesses of Visby, the chief city of Gotland. New immigrants were German in descent, name, language, and law. Towns such as Cracow and Riga engaged in long-distance trade and gradually grew into large urban centers. But there were also hundreds of small market towns populated by German immigrants, such as Kröpelin in Mecklenburg, which supplied the needs of the rural countryside. The townspeople, though living in Slavic regions, were German in language and culture and considered themselves German.

Spain

About 950 Caliph Abd al-Rahman III (912–961) of the Umayyad dynasty of Córdoba (see pages 233–234) ruled most of the Iberian Peninsula from the Mediterranean in the south to the Ebro River in the north. Christian Spain consisted of the kingdoms of Castile, León, Catalonia, Aragon, Navarre, and Portugal; the Almoravid dynasty (successor to the Umayyads) governed through the caliphate of Córdoba (Map 9.3). The civil wars that erupted among Rahman III's descendants had two important consequences: they divided the peninsula into small Muslim territories, and they made the Christian reconquest easier.

Fourteenth-century clerical propagandists called the movement to expel the Muslims the *reconquista* (reconquest)—a sacred and patriotic crusade to wrest the country from "alien" Muslim hands. This religious myth became part of Spanish political history and of the national psychology. In 1085 King Alfonso VI of Castile and León captured Toledo on the Tagus River in central Spain, center of the old Visigothic kingdom. He immediately named Bernard, a monk of Cluny in Burgundy, as archbishop of Toledo. Alfonso, who had married a Frenchwoman, invited French knights to settle in the *meseta,* the central plateau of Spain, a region well suited for sheep farming, viticulture, and cereal agriculture. His successor, Alfonso VIII (1158–1214), aided by the kings of Aragon, Navarre, and Portugal, crushed the Muslims at *Las Navas de Tolosa* in 1212, accelerating the Christian push southward. James the Conqueror of Aragon (1213–1215) captured Valencia on the Mediterranean coast in 1233, immediately turning the chief mosque into a cathedral. In 1236 Ferdinand of Castile and León captured the great Muslim industrial and intellectual center of Córdoba in the heart of Andalusia. The city's mosque became a Christian cathedral, and the city itself served thereafter as the main military base against Granada. When Seville fell to Ferdinand's Castilians in 1248 after a long siege, Christians controlled the entire Iberian Peninsula, save for the small state of Granada. Once in Seville, Ferdinand's heart "was full of joy at the great reward God had given him for his labours. . . . His mother (wanted) to revive the archiepiscopal see which had of old been abandoned, despoiled (by the Muslims) . . . and a worthy foundation was established in honor of Saint Mary."[24] Ferdinand's mother thus inspired the use of the chief

Almohad Banner At Las Navas de Tolosa in 1212, King Alfonso VIII of Castile won a decisive victory over the Almohads, a puritanical Muslim sect from North Africa that had ruled most of Spain in the twelfth century. The Spanish victory marked the beginning of Muslim decline. *(Institut Amatller d'Art Hispanic)*

mosque as the diocesan cathedral. (Since religious buildings serve as windows into the broader culture, with valuable social, intellectual, and economic information, scholars in many fields have deplored this assimilation of mosques at Córdoba, Valencia, and Seville to Christian religious use, as it involved the destruction of Muslim art. Just as the Muslims, when they conquered Spain in the eighth century, had desecrated ancient pagan shrines for the erection of their mosques, so Christians in the reconquista followed suit on Muslim buildings.)

By the end of the thirteenth century, Spain had fifty-one bishoprics: the reconquista meant the establishment of a Roman ecclesiastical structure. As in eastern Europe, new monasteries aided the growth of Christian culture. As Spanish ruler-kings of the reconquista pushed southward, they established Cistercian monasteries for the military, as well as the religious and cultural, integrity of the conquered areas. As a fortress and base for regional tactical operations, these abbeys served royal needs, though such were hardly the ideals of the Cistercian founders. Thus Ramón Berenguer IV, count of Barcelona (1131–1162) and prince of Aragon (1137–1162), founded Poblet in Catalonian Aragon in 1149; Poblet subsequently developed into a great banking center. In 1187 Alfonso VIII and his wife, Eleanor, sponsored the foundation of Los Huelgas in Burgos, the only Cistercian house of women. Its abbess was always a royal princess, and its nuns were recruited from the highest aristocracy. Alcobaça, founded in 1158 between Coimbra and Lisbon in Portugal, became a great intellectual center. These Iberian houses had distinctive features. First, all were Cistercian, established during the great wave of Cistercian expansion (see page 278). Second, they were royal monasteries: the inspiration for their foundation came from royal princes who endowed them as religious supports for their political power, resided in them, and were buried in the tombs attached to the abbey churches. These abbeys came to exercise a broad cultural, military, political, and economic influence, as well as a religious one, in the areas where they existed.[25]

In the early years of the reconquista, Spanish princes used the fighting skills of French knights. With Spanish victories, those knights were rewarded with Spanish lands. For example, the former crusader Gaston V of Béarn fought in Aragon and received the lordship of Uncastillo and the governorship of Saragossa. As the pace of the reconquista quickened in the thirteenth century and the resettlement of gigantic amounts of land acquired from the Muslims (perhaps 150,000 square miles) preoccupied the rulers, a few knights trickled down from north of the Pyrenees, such as William of Condom, Martin of Toulouse, and Richard of Cahors, whose names indicate their ancestry. But French aristocratic involvement in Spain declined. Most settlers came from within the peninsula. French feudalism left a small imprint on Spain.

Foreign business people, however, did come to northern Spain in the eleventh century. Muslim Spain had had more cities than any other country in Europe, so Christian Spain became the most urbanized part of the continent. Towns along the Pyrenees or on the pilgrimage route to the shrine of Saint James at Compostela had received a stream of French immigrants, invited by the kings. One example was the town of Logroño. King Alfonso VI decreed

that a town should be established there, assembling from all parts of the world burgesses of many different trades . . . Gaston, Bretons, English, Burgundians, Normans, Toulousains, Provençals and Lombards, and many other traders of various nations and foreign tongues; and thus he populated a town of no mean size.[26]

After decades of warfare during the reconquista, these towns needed settlers to revive. Moreover, victorious Spanish rulers had expelled the Muslims, leaving the towns with a population shortage. The new lords of Spain recruited immigrants from Old Catalonia, Castile, and León. The thirteenth century thus witnessed a huge migration of peoples from the north to the central and southern parts of the peninsula, into the depopulated cities of the reconquista.

Toward a Christian Society

It was one matter for Western institutions, such as French feudalism and a diocesan pattern of ecclesiastical organization, to penetrate the borderlands of continental Europe, including the Celtic fringe of Wales, Scotland, and Ireland; the Scandinavian fringe of Denmark, Sweden, and Norway; the Baltic fringe of Prussia and Lithuania; the Slavic fringe of Silesia, Bohemia, Poland, and Hungary; and the Iberian fringe of Spain and Portugal. Achieving a cultural unity between these frontier regions and the European heartland, however, presented a more difficult problem. Yet by about 1300, the geographical area that we now call Europe possessed a broad cultural uniformity. How did this unity, or homogeneity, come about?

Papal pressure for uniformity of religious worship and a growing loyalty to the institution of the Roman papacy promoted this homogeneity. Beginning with the reform movement of the eleventh century (see page

278), real papal power increased. Reverence in the broad public consciousness for Saint Peter and his successors in Rome meant obedience to the pope. Obedience to the pope meant a local commitment—whether in Scotland, Spain, or Silesia—to the Roman liturgy, the form of worship practiced in Rome. Pope Gregory VII and his successors in the twelfth century, through their letters and their legates, campaigned continually for one religious rite, the Roman rite, in all countries and places.

The period between 1075 and 1125 witnessed the establishment of new and regular contacts between the papacy, eastern Europe, and Celtic and Iberian lands. Gregory denied permission for a vernacular liturgy in Bohemia; he insisted on the Latin rite. He pressed for the abolition of a special rite in Spain, partly because it was believed to contain Arabic elements, partly because it differed from the Roman Latin rite. In 1081, Gregory wrote triumphantly to King Alfonso VI of Castile and León: "Most dearly beloved, know that one thing pleases us greatly . . . namely, that in the churches of your realm, you have caused the order of the Mother of all, the holy Roman church, to be received and celebrated in the ancient way."[27] In 1125, Pope Honorius II (1124–1130) sent his legate John of Cremona to Wales and Scotland to check on the moral condition of the clergy and the proper observance of the liturgy in those countries. By the time of Pope Innocent III (see page 283)—when papal directives and papal legates flowed to all parts of Europe; when twelve hundred prelates obediently came to Rome from the borderlands as well as the heartland for the Fourth Lateran Council of 1215; and when the same religious service was celebrated everywhere—the papacy was recognized as the nerve center of a homogeneous Christian society. Europeans identified themselves first and foremost as Christians and even described themselves as belonging to "the Christian race."[28] As in the Islamic world, religion had replaced tribal, political, and ethnic structures as the essence of culture. Whether Europeans were Christian in their observance of the Gospels remains another matter.

SUMMARY

The end of the great invasions signaled the beginning of profound changes in European society—social, political, and ecclesiastical. In the year 1000, having enough to eat was the rare privilege of a few nobles, priests, and monks. By the eleventh century, however, manorial communities were slowly improving their agricultural output through increased mechanization, especially the use of waterpower and wind power; these advances, aided by warmer weather, meant more food and increasing population.

Also in the eleventh century, rulers and local authorities gradually imposed some degree of order within their territories. Peace and domestic security contributed to the rise in population, bringing larger crops for the peasants and improving trading conditions for the townspeople. The church overthrew the domination of lay influences, and the spread of the Cluniac and Cistercian orders marked the ascendancy of monasticism. The Gregorian reform movement, with its stress on "the freedom of the church," led to a grave conflict with kings over lay investiture. The papacy achieved a technical success on the religious issue, but in Germany the greatly increased power of the nobility, at the expense of the emperor, represents the significant social consequence. Having put its own house in order, the Roman papacy in the twelfth and thirteenth centuries built the first strong government bureaucracy. In the High Middle Ages, the church exercised general leadership of European society. The Crusades exhibited that leadership, though their consequences for Byzantine-Western and for Christian-Muslim relations proved disastrous.

These centuries also saw the penetration of Latin Christian culture into frontier regions. Through the spread of Cluniac and Cistercian monasteries; through the use of military force against Muslim and pagan peoples; through the activities of new religious orders, such as the Knights Templars, who combined piety and aggression; and through the immigration of tens of thousands of settlers, border regions became incorporated into the Christian faith and Latin culture of the western European heartland. Christianization was the impulse for this incorporation. The Latin liturgy and loyalty to the Roman pontiff gradually bound all these regions together.

NOTES

1. R. Bartlett, *The Making of Europe: Conquest, Colonization and Cultural Change, 950–1350* (Princeton, N.J.: Princeton University Press, 1993), p. 6. The last section of this chapter leans on this important and seminal work.
2. See R. I. Burns, "The Significance of the Frontier in the Middle Ages," in *Medieval Frontier Societies,* ed. R. Bartlett and A. MacKay (Oxford: Clarendon Press, 1989), p. 322.
3. See E. M. Hallam, *Capetian France, 987–1328* (New York: Longman, 1980), pp. 12–43.

4. S. Reynolds, *Fiefs and Vassals: The Medieval Evidence Reconsidered* (Oxford: Clarendon Press, 1996), pp. 126–128, 174.
5. E. James, *The Origins of France: From Clovis to the Capetians, 500–1000* (New York: St. Martin's Press, 1982), pp. 190–191.
6. J. Gimpel, *The Medieval Machine: The Industrial Revolution of the Middle Ages* (New York: Penguin Books, 1976), pp. 10–15.
7. Quoted in P. Riche, *Daily Life in the World of Charlemagne,* trans. JoAnn McNamara (Philadelphia: University of Pennsylvania Press, 1978), p. 86.
8. See D. Knowles, *The Monastic Order in England,* rev. ed. (Cambridge: Cambridge University Press, 1950), p. 712.
9. See B. Rosenwein, *Rhinoceros Bound: Cluny in the Tenth Century* (Philadelphia: University of Pennsylvania Press, 1982), chap. 2.
10. See K. Hallinger, *Gorze-Kluny: Studien zu den monastichen Lebensformen und Gegensätzen im Hochmittelalter,* Studia Anselmiana xxii–v (Rome: Herder, 1950–1951), esp. p. 40.
11. I. S. Robinson, *The Papacy, 1073–1198: Continuity and Innovation* (New York: Cambridge University Press, 1990), p. 295.
12. B. D. Hill, ed., *Church and State in the Middle Ages* (New York: John Wiley & Sons, 1970), p. 68.
13. Robinson, *The Papacy,* p. 403.
14. Ibid., p. 405.
15. See J. B. Freed, *The Counts of Falkenstein: Noble Self-consciousness in Twelfth-Century Germany,* Transactions of the American Philosophical Society, vol. 74, pt. 6 (Philadelphia, 1984), pp. 9–11.
16. C. Erdmann, *The Origin of the Idea of the Crusade,* trans. M. Baldwin and W. Goffart (Princeton, N.J.: Princeton University Press, 1977), p. 57.
17. S. Runciman, *A History of the Crusades.* Vol. 3: *The Kingdom of Acre* (Cambridge: Cambridge University Press, 1955), p. 480.
18. See B. Lewis, *The Muslim Discovery of Europe* (New York: W. W. Norton, 1982), pp. 23–25.
19. Bartlett, *The Making of Europe,* p. 24.
20. Ibid., p. 8.
21. Ibid., pp. 34–35.
22. See P. Knoll, "Economic and Political Institutions on the Polish-German Frontier in the Middle Ages: Action, Reaction, Interaction," in *Medieval Frontier Societies,* ed. R. Bartlett and A. MacKay (Oxford: Clarendon Press, 1989), pp. 151–159.
23. Quoted in Bartlett, *The Making of Europe,* pp. 179–180.
24. Ibid., p. 13.
25. See B. D. Hill, "Poblet," in *Encyclopedia of Medieval Iberia* (forthcoming).
26. Bartlett, *The Making of Europe,* p. 178.
27. Quoted ibid., p. 249.
28. Ibid., pp. 250–255.

SUGGESTED READING

F. Barlow, *William I and the Norman Conquest* (1965), provides a sound and highly readable introduction to issues related to the Norman Conquest. Advanced students will find in M. Strickland, *War and Chivalry: The Conduct and Perception of War in England and Normandy, 1066–1217* (1996), a sophisticated treatment of military history and a detailed study of the aristocracy that fought. Two studies by G. M. Spiegel—"The Cult of Saint-Denis and Capetian Kingship," *Journal of Medieval History* 1 (April 1975), and *The Chronicle Tradition of Saint-Denis* (1978)—treat the close relationship between the Capetian dynasty and the royal abbey of Saint-Denis. For central and eastern Europe, see, in addition to the studies by Burns and Knoll cited in the Notes, J. W. Bernhardt, *Itinerant Kingship and Royal Monasteries in Early Medieval Germany* (1993), which describes how tenth- and eleventh-century German kings founded monasteries and used them for the implementation of royal policy; and P. Gorecki, *Economy, Society, and Lordship in Medieval Poland* (1992), which has articles on aspects of economic and social life. The older studies of G. Barraclough—*The Origins of Modern Germany* (1963) and *The Crucible of Europe: The Ninth and Tenth Centuries in European History* (1976)—are still helpful, if tinged with a Marxist ideology. For Spain, R. Fletcher, *The Quest for El Cid* (1990), provides an excellent introduction to Spanish social and political conditions through a study of Rodrigo Dias, the eleventh-century soldier of fortune who became the Spanish national hero. R. Fletcher, *Moorish Spain* (1992), is a highly readable sketch of the history of Islamic Spain from the eighth to the seventeenth century. O. R. Constable, *Trade and Traders in Muslim Spain: The Commercial Realignment of the Iberian Peninsula, 900–1500* (1996), surveys Iberian "international" trade and treats the impact of Christian conquest on that trade. For the developing social and economic importance of the Flemish towns, see D. Nicholas, *Medieval Flanders* (1992).

For monastic reform, the papacy, and ecclesiastical developments, see B. Rosenwein, *To Be the Neighbor of Saint Peter: The Social Meaning of Cluny's Property, 909–1049* (1989), and the same scholar's earlier study, *Rhinoceros Bound: Cluny in the Tenth Century* (1982), which offer up-to-date interpretations of Cluny. C. B. Bouchard's *Sword, Miter, and Cloister: Nobility and the Church in Burgundy* (1987) and *Holy Entrepreneurs: Cistercians, Knights, and Economic Exchange in Twelfth-Century Burgundy* (1991) are basic for study of the Cistercian economy. C. H. Berman, *Medieval Agriculture, the Southern French Countryside, and the Early Cistercians: A Study of Forty-three Monasteries* (1986), presents an important revisionist interpretation of some French Cistercian houses. For the legal, social, and liturgical significance of property gifts to monasteries, see S. D. White, *Custom, Kinship, and Gifts to Saints: The Laudatio Parentum in Western France, 1050–1150* (1988). The relationship of the monks to the ecclesiastical crisis of the late eleventh century is discussed in N. F. Cantor, "The Crisis of Western Monasticism," *American Historical Review* 66 (1960), but see also J. Van Engen, "The 'Crisis of Cenobitism' Reconsidered: Benedictine Monasticism in the Years 1050–1150," *Speculum* 61 (1986). I. S. Robinson, *The Papacy, 1073–1198: Continuity and Innovation* (1990), explores the changing role of the papacy in the eleventh and twelfth centuries and the development of the new model of papal government. G. Tellenbach, *Church, State, and Christian Society at the Time of the Investiture Contest* (1959), emphasizes the revolutionary aspects of the Gregorian reform program; G. Tellenbach, *The Church in Western Europe from the Tenth to the Twelfth Century* (1993), is a fine survey of the period. Using the insights of modern anthropological theory, J. Lynch, *Godparents and Kinship in Early Medieval Europe* (1986), explores the relationships created by the baptismal sponsorship of children and adults.

The best recent works on the Crusades are J. France, *Victory in the East: A Military History of the First Crusade* (1997), which studies the expedition as a military campaign; J. Riley-Smith, *The First Crusade and the Idea of Crusading* (1986), which explores many facets of the First Crusade; and M. C. Lyons, *Saladin: The Politics of the Holy War* (1997), which treats the political issues of the Third Crusade. K. Armstrong, *Holy War: The Crusades and Their Impact on Today's World* (1991), is a readable popular account that focuses on the Crusades' effects on the modern world. For the Knights Templars, see M. Barber, *The New Knighthood: A History of the Order of the Temple* (1995); and J. J. Robinson, *Dungeon, Fire and Sword: The Knights Templar in the Crusades* (1992), which tells an exciting story but is less reliable than Barber. There are sound articles on many facets of the Crusades, including "The Children's Crusade," "Crusade Propaganda," "Crusader Art and Architecture," and "The Political Crusades," all written by authorities and based on sound research, in *The Dictionary of the Middle Ages,* ed. J. R. Strayer, vol. 4 (1984). These articles contain good bibliographies. For the Fourth Crusade, see the excellent study by D. E. Queller, *The Fourth Crusade: The Capture of Constantinople* (1977), which gives an important revisionist interpretation. C. M. Brand, *Byzantium Confronts the West, 1180–1204* (1968), provides the Greek perspective on the Crusades, while B. Lewis, *The Muslim Discovery of Europe* (1982), gives the Muslim point of view. H. Kennedy, *Crusader Castles* (1994), explores the evolution of castle styles, siege techniques, and the defensive technologies of castles in the Middle East. For the many issues related to Jews and the Crusades, see R. Chazan, *In the Year 1096: The First Crusade and the Jews* (1996); B. Netanyahu, *The Origins of the Inquisition in Fifteenth Century Spain* (1995), a magisterial work that is much broader in scope than the title would imply; R. Gay, *The Jews of Germany: A Historical Portrait* (1992), a nicely illustrated study; G. Langmuir, *History, Religion, and Anti-Semitism* (1990), a very sophisticated study with a nuanced distinction drawn between anti-Semitic and anti-Judaic; and P. Johnson, *A History of the Jews* (1988), a sweeping general survey.

For the expansion of Latin Christendom into northern and eastern Europe, see the title by Bartlett cited in the Notes, and L. R. Johnson, *Central Europe: Enemies, Neighbors, Friends* (1996). For the Spanish reconquista, see the titles by Fletcher cited above.

Serious students will eventually want to consult the multivolume work K. M. Setton, gen. ed., *A History of the Crusades* (1955–1977). C. Tyerman, *England and the Crusades, 1095–1588* (1988), discusses the financial, political, and social implications of the Crusades.

Two broad surveys, D. Nicholas, *The Evolution of the Medieval World: Society, Government and Thought in Europe, 312–1500* (1992), and G. Holmes, ed., *The Oxford History of Medieval Europe* (1992), contain useful, up-to-date material.

LISTENING TO THE PAST

An Arab View of the Crusades

The Crusades helped shape the understanding that Arabs and Europeans had of each other and all subsequent relations between the Christian West and the Arab world. To medieval Christians, the Crusades were papally approved military expeditions for the recovery of holy places in Palestine; to the Arabs, these campaigns were "Frankish wars" or "Frankish invasions" for the acquisition of territory.

Early in the thirteenth century, Ibn Al-Athir (1160–1223), a native of Mosul, an important economic and cultural center in northern Mesopotamia (modern Iraq), wrote a history of the First Crusade. He relied on Arab sources for the events he described. Here is his account of the Crusaders' capture of Antioch.

The power of the Franks first became apparent when in the year 478/1085–86[1] they invaded the territories of Islam and took Toledo and other parts of Andalusia. Then in 484/1091 they attacked and conquered the island of Sicily and turned their attention to the African coast. Certain of their conquests there were won back again but they had other successes, as you will see.

In 490/1097 the Franks attacked Syria. This is how it all began: Baldwin, their King, a kinsman of Roger the Frank who had conquered Sicily, assembled a great army and sent word to Roger saying: "I have assembled a great army and now I am on my way to you, to use your bases for my conquest of the African coast. Thus you and I shall become neighbors."

Roger called together his companions and consulted them about these proposals. "This will be a fine thing for them and for us!" they declared, "for by this means these lands will be converted to the Faith!" At this Roger raised one leg and farted loudly, and swore that it was of more use than their advice. "Why?" "Because if this army comes here it will need quantities of provisions and fleets of ships to transport it to Africa, as well as reinforcements from my own troops. Then, if the Franks succeed in conquering this territory they will take it over and will need provisioning from Sicily. This will cost me my annual profit from the harvest. If they fail they will return here and be an embarrassment to me here in my own domain." . . .

He summoned Baldwin's messenger and said to him: "If you have decided to make war on the Muslims your best course will be to free Jerusalem from their rule and thereby win great honor. I am bound by certain promises and treaties of allegiance with the ruler of Africa." So the Franks made ready to set out to attack Syria.

Another story is that the Fatimids of Egypt were afraid when they saw the Seljuqids extending their empire through Syria as far as Gaza, until they reached the Egyptian border and Atsiz invaded Egypt itself. They therefore sent to invite the Franks to invade Syria and so protect Egypt from the Muslims.[2] But God knows best.

When the Franks decided to attack Syria they marched east to Constantinople, so that they could cross the straits and advance into Muslim territory by the easier, land route. When they reached Constantinople, the Emperor of the East refused them permission to pass through his domains. He said: "Unless you first promise me Antioch, I shall not allow you to cross into the Muslim empire." His real intention was to incite them to attack the Muslims, for he was convinced that the Turks, whose invincible control over Asia Minor he had observed, would exterminate every one of them. They accepted his conditions and in 490/1097 they crossed the Bosphorus at Constantinople. . . . They . . . reached Antioch, which they besieged.

When Yaghi Siyan, the ruler of Antioch, heard of their approach, he was not sure how the Christian people of the city would react, so he made the Muslims go outside the city on their own to dig trenches, and the next day sent the Christians out alone to continue the task. When they were ready to return home at the end of the day he refused to allow them. "Antioch is yours," he said, "but you will have to leave it to me until I see what happens between us and the Franks." "Who will protect our children and our wives?" they said. "I shall look after them for you." So they resigned themselves to their fate, and lived in the Frankish camp for nine months, while the city was under siege.

Yaghi Siyan showed unparalleled courage and wisdom, strength and judgment. If all the Franks who died had survived they would have overrun all the lands of Islam. He protected the families of the Christians in Antioch and would not allow a hair of their heads to be touched.

After the siege had been going on for a long time the Franks made a deal with . . . a cuirass-maker called Ruzbih whom they bribed with a fortune in money and lands. He worked in the tower that stood over the riverbed, where the river flowed out of the city into the valley. The Franks sealed their pact with the cuirass-maker, God damn him! and made their way to the water-gate. They opened it and entered the city. Another gang of them climbed the tower with their ropes. At dawn, when more than 500 of them were in the city and the defenders were worn out after the night watch, they sounded their trumpets. . . . Panic seized Yaghi Siyan and he opened the city gates and fled in terror, with an escort of thirty pages. His army commander arrived, but when he discovered on enquiry that Yaghi Siyan had fled, he made his escape by another gate. This was of great help to the Franks, for if he had stood firm for an hour, they would have been wiped out. They entered the city by the gates and sacked it, slaughtering all the Muslims they found there. This happened in jumada I (491/April/May 1098). . . .

It was the discord between the Muslim princes . . . that enabled the Franks to overrun the country.

✣ Miniature showing heavily armored knights fighting (Muslims). *(Bibliothèque Nationale, Paris)*

Questions for Analysis

1. From the Arab perspective, when did the Crusade begin?
2. How did Ibn Al-Athir explain the Crusaders' expedition to Syria?
3. Why did Antioch fall to the Crusaders?
4. The use of dialogue in historical narrative is a very old device dating from the Greek historian Thucydides (fifth century B.C.). Assess the value of Ibn Al-Athir's dialogues for the modern historian.

1. Muslims traditionally date events from Muhammad's hegira, or emigration, to Medina, which occurred in 622 according to the Christian calendar.

2. Although Muslims, Fatimids were related doctrinally to the Shi'ites, but the dominant Sunni Muslims considered the Fatimids heretics.

Sources: P. J. Geary, ed., *Readings in Medieval History* (Peterborough, Ontario: Broadview Press, 1991), pp. 443–444; E. J. Costello, trans., *Arab Historians of the Crusades* (Berkeley and Los Angeles: University of California Press, 1969).

CHAPTER

10 Life in Christian Europe in the High Middle Ages

Allegorical harvesting scenes from a German manuscript, *Speculum Virginum,* ca 1190. *(Rheinisches Landesmuseum, Bonn)*

In one of the writings produced at the court of the late-ninth-century Anglo-Saxon king Alfred, Christian society is described as composed of those who pray (the monks), those who fight (the nobles), and those who work (the peasants). Close links existed between educated circles on both sides of the English Channel; in France, Bishop Adalbero of Laon used the same device in a poem written about 1028. This image of the structure of society, in which function determined social classification,[1] gained wide circulation in the High Middle Ages. These social divisions, however, do not exactly reflect reality: in the eleventh and twelfth centuries, most monks descended from the noble class and as monks retained aristocratic attitudes and values; the lay brothers who did most of the agricultural work on many monastic estates, though legally monks, derived from the peasant classes. Moreover, this tripartite plan entirely omits the parish clergy, who usually were not monks. The division of society into fighters, monks, and peasants also presents too static a view of a world in which there was considerable social mobility. (See the feature "Listening to the Past: From Merchant to Monk" on pages 332–333.) Moreover, such a social scheme does not take into consideration townspeople and the emerging commercial classes (see pages 359–360). Traders and other city dwellers were not typical of medieval society, however. Medieval people were usually contemptuous (at least officially) of profit-making activities, and even after the appearance of urban commercial groups, the ideological view of medieval Christian society remained the one formulated in the ninth century. The most representative figures of Christian society in the High Middle Ages were peasants, nobles, and monks. The use of these sociological divisions provides insight into the medieval mind.

- How did these people actually live?
- What were their preoccupations and lifestyles?
- To what extent was social mobility possible for them?

These are some questions that this chapter will explore.

Those Who Work

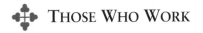

The largest and economically most productive group in medieval European society was the peasants. "Peasants were rural dwellers who possess (if they do not own) the means of agricultural production." Some peasants worked continuously on the land; others supplemented their ordinary work as brewers, carpenters, tailors, or housemaids with wage labor in the field. In either case, all peasants supported lords, clergy, and townspeople, as well as themselves.[2] The men and women who worked the land in the twelfth and thirteenth centuries made up the overwhelming majority of the population, probably more than 90 percent. Yet it is difficult to form a coherent picture of them. The records that serve as historical sources were written by and for the aristocratic classes. Since peasants did not perform what were considered "noble" deeds, the aristocratic monks and clerics did not waste time or precious writing materials on them. When peasants were mentioned, it was usually with contempt or in terms of the services and obligations they owed.

Usually—but not always. In the early twelfth century, Honorius, a monk and teacher at Autun, wrote: "What do you say about the agricultural classes? Most of them will be saved because they live simply and feed God's people by means of their sweat."[3] This sentiment circulated widely. Honorius's comment suggests that peasant workers may have been appreciated and respected more than modern students have generally believed.

In the past twenty-five years, historians have made remarkable advances in their knowledge of the medieval European peasantry. They have been able to do so by bringing fresh and different questions to old documents, by paying greater attention to such natural factors as geography and climate, and by studying demographic changes over time. Nevertheless, this new information raises additional questions, and a good deal remains unknown.

In 1932 a distinguished economic historian wrote, "The student of medieval social and economic history who commits himself to a generalization is digging a pit into which he will later assuredly fall and nowhere does the pit yawn deeper than in the realm of rural history."[4] Although recent decades have seen an explosion of literature on agrarian change, this statement retains some validity. It is therefore important to remember that peasants' conditions varied widely across Europe, that geographical and climatic features as much as human initiative and local custom determined the peculiar quality of rural life. The problems that faced the farmer in Yorkshire, England, where the soil was rocky and the climate rainy, were very different from those of the Italian peasant in the sun-drenched Po Valley.

Another difficulty has been historians' tendency to group all peasants into one social class. That is a serious mistake. It is true that medieval theologians lumped everyone who worked the land into the category of "those who work." In fact, however, there were many levels of peasants, ranging from complete slaves to free and very rich farmers. The period from 1050 to 1275 was one of considerable fluidity with significant social mobility. The status of the peasantry fluctuated widely all across Europe.

Slavery, Serfdom, and Upward Mobility

Slaves were found in western Europe in the High Middle Ages, but in steadily declining numbers. That the word *slave* derives from *Slav* attests to the widespread trade in men and women from the Slavic areas in the early Middle Ages. Around the year 1200, there were in aristocratic and upper-middle-class households in Provence, Catalonia, Italy, and Germany a few slaves—Slavs from the Baltic, Syrians, and blacks from sub-Saharan Africa.

Since ancient times, it had been a universally accepted practice to enslave conquered peoples. The Christian Gospels contain no explicit teaching on slavery, but they do stress the spiritual equality of all as children of the same God, the golden rule, and Jesus' affection for the oppressed. Saint Paul did not condemn slavery, but he tried to imbue both masters and slaves with the spirit of charity, which, over many centuries, was to reduce drastically the practice. But since slavery remains widespread in parts of the world today, it has never completely disappeared.

In western Europe during the Middle Ages, legal language differed considerably from place to place, and the distinction between slave and serf was not always clear. Both lacked freedom—the power to do as one wished—and both were subject to the arbitrary will of one person, the lord. A serf, however, could not be bought and sold like an animal or an inanimate object, as a slave could.

The serf was required to perform labor services on the lord's land. The number of workdays varied, but it was usually three days a week except in the planting or harvest seasons, when it would be more. Serfs frequently had to pay arbitrary levies. When a man married, he had to pay his lord a fee. When he died, his son or heir had to pay an inheritance tax to inherit his parcels of land. The precise amounts of tax paid to the lord on these important occasions depended on local custom and tradition. Every manor had its particular obligations. A free person had to do none of these things. For his or her landholding, rent had to be paid to the lord, and that was often the sole obligation. A free person could move and live as he or she wished.

Serfs were tied to the land, and serfdom was a hereditary condition. A person born a serf was likely to die a serf, though many did secure their freedom. About 1187 Glanvill, an official of King Henry II and an expert on English law, described how *villeins* (literally, "inhabitants of small villages")—as English serfs were called—could be made free:

> *A person of villein status can be made free in several ways. For example, his lord, wishing him to achieve freedom from the villeinage by which he is subject to him, may quit-claim [release] him from himself and his heirs; or he may give or sell him to another with intent to free him. It should be noted, however, that no person of villein status can seek his freedom with his own money, for in such a case he could, according to the law and custom of the realm, be recalled to villeinage by his lord, because all the chattels of a villein are deemed to such an extent the property of his lord that he cannot redeem himself from villeinage with his own money, as against his lord. If, however, a third party provides the money and buys the villein in order to free him, then he can maintain himself for ever in a state of freedom as against his lord who sold him. . . . If any villein stays peaceably for a year and a day in a privileged town and is admitted as a citizen into their commune, that is to say, their gild, he is thereby freed from villeinage.*[5]

Thus a serf could not buy his freedom with his own money, since technically all his chattels belonged to his lord. But he could give money to a third party, who could buy him in order to free him. Many energetic and hard-working serfs acquired their freedom in the High Middle Ages. More than anything else, the economic revival that began in the eleventh century (see pages 349–360) advanced the cause of individual liberty. The revival saw the rise of towns, increased land productivity, the growth of long-distance trade, and the development of a money economy. With the advent of a money economy, serfs could save money and, through a third-person intermediary, buy their freedom.

Another opportunity for increased personal freedom, or at least for a reduction in traditional manorial obligations and dues, was provided by the reclamation of waste and forest land in the eleventh and twelfth centuries. Resettlement on newly cleared land offered unusual possibilities for younger sons and for those living in areas of acute land shortage or on overworked, exhausted soil. Historians still do not know much about

The Three Classes Medieval people believed that their society was divided among warriors, clerics, and workers, here represented by a monk, a knight, and a peasant. The new commercial class had no recognized place in the agrarian military world. *(The British Library)*

this movement: how the new frontier territory was advertised, how men were recruited, how they and their households were transported, and how the new lands were distributed. It is certain, however, that there was significant migration and that only a lord with considerable authority over a wide territory could sponsor such a movement. Great lords supported the fight against the marshes of northern and eastern Germany and against the sea in the Low Countries. For example, in the twelfth century the invitation of German rulers led to peasant settlements in "the territory between the Saale and the upper Elbe" Rivers.[6] The thirteenth century witnessed German peasant migrations into Brandenburg, Pomerania, Prussia, and the Baltic States.

In the thirteenth century, the noble class frequently needed money to finance crusading, building, or other projects. For example, in 1240 when Geoffrey de Montigny became abbot of Saint-Pierre-le-Vif in the Sénonais region of France, he found the abbey church in disrepair. Geoffrey also discovered that the descendants of families who had once owed the abbey servile obligations now refused to recognize their bondage. Some of these peasants had grown wealthy. When the abbot determined to reclaim these peasants in order to get the revenues to rebuild his church, a legal struggle ensued. In 1257 a compromise was worked out whereby Geoffrey manumitted 366 persons who in turn agreed to pay him 500 pounds a year over a twelve-year period.[7] (See the feature "Individuals in Society: Jean Mouflet of Sens.")

As land long considered poor was brought under cultivation, there was a steady nibbling away at the wasteland on the edges of old villages. Clearings were made in forests. Marshes and fens were drained and slowly made arable. This type of agricultural advancement frequently improved the peasants' social and legal condition. A serf could clear a patch of fen or forestland, make it productive, and, through prudent saving, buy more land and eventually purchase freedom. In the thirteenth century there were many free tenants on the lands of the bishop of Ely in eastern England, tenants who had moved into the area in the twelfth century and drained the fens. Likewise, settlers on the lowlands of the abbey of Bourbourg in Flanders, who had erected

Individuals in Society

Jean Mouflet of Sens

Throughout most of Western history, the vast majority of people left little behind that identifies them as individuals. Baptismal, marriage, and death records; wills; grants for memorial masses; and, after the eighteenth century, brief census information collected by governments—these forms of evidence provide exciting information about groups of people but little about individuals. Before the nineteenth century, most people were illiterate; the relative few who could write, such as business people, used such literary skills as they had in matters connected with their work. The historian, therefore, has great difficulty reconstructing the life of an "ordinary" person. An exception occurs when a person committed a crime in a society that kept judicial records or when he or she made a legal agreement that was preserved. Such is the case of Jean Mouflet of Sens.[1]

We know little about him except what is revealed in a document granting what was probably the central desire of his life—his personal freedom. His ancestors had been serfs on the lands of the abbey of Saint-Pierre-le-Vif in the Sénonais region of France. There a serf was subject to legal disabilities that debased his dignity and implied inferior status. Work required on the lord's land bred resentment, because work was simultaneously needed on the rustic's own land. At death a peasant gave the lord a token, or not so token, gift—his best beast. Marriage presented another disability, first because one partner had to change dwelling and to do so had to gain the lord's permission; second because it raised the question of children: whose dependents did they become? Special "gifts" to the lord "encouraged" him to resolve these issues. Again, an unfree person, even if he or she possessed the expected dowry, could not become a monk or nun or enter holy orders without the lord's permission, because the lord stood to lose labor services. Finally, residence in a town for a year and a day did not always ensure freedom; years after the person settled there, the lord could claim him or her as a dependent.

In 1249 Jean Mouflet made an agreement with the abbot: in return for an annual payment, the monastery would recognize Jean as a "citizen of Sens." With a stroke of his quill, the abbot manumitted Jean and his heirs, ending centuries of servile obligations.

The customary form of manumission, *not* the manner in which Jean Mouflet gained his freedom. *(British Library)*

The agreement describes Jean as a leather merchant. Other evidence reveals that he had a large leather shop in the leather goods section of town[2] that he leased for the very high rent of fifty shillings a year. If not "rich," Jean was certainly well-to-do. Circumstantial evidence suggests that Jean's father had originally left the land to become a leatherworker and taught his son the trade. The agreement was witnessed by Jean's wife, Douce, daughter of a wealthy and prominent citizen of Sens, Félis Charpentier. To have been a suitable candidate for Douce, Jean would have to have been extremely industrious, very lucky, and accepted as a "rising young man" by the grudging burghers of the town. Such a giant step upward in one generation seems unlikely.

In addition to viticulture (the cultivation of grapes), the Sénonais was well suited for cereal production and for animal grazing. Jean undoubtedly bought hides from local herders and manufactured boots and shoes; saddles, bridles, and reins for horses; and belts and purses. He may also have made wineskins for local vintners or for those of Champagne. It is also fair to assume that the wealthy cathedral clergy, the townspeople, and, if his goods were of sufficiently high quality, the merchants of the nearby fairs of Champagne were his customers.

By private agreements with lords, servile peasants gained the most basic of human rights—freedom.

Questions for Analysis

1. What is human freedom?
2. How did trade and commerce contribute to the development of individual liberty?

1. This essay rests on the fine study of W. C. Jordan, *From Servitude to Freedom: Manumission in the Sénonais in the Thirteenth Century* (Philadelphia: University of Pennsylvania Press, 1986).
2. As in all medieval towns, merchants in particular trades—butchers, bakers, leatherworkers—had shops in one area. In 1990 Sens was still a major French leather-tanning center.

dikes and extended the arable lands, possessed hereditary tenures by 1159. They secured personal liberty and owed their overlord only small payments.

Peasants who remained in the villages of their birth often benefited because landlords, threatened with the loss of serfs, relaxed ancient obligations and duties. While it would be unwise to exaggerate the social impact of the settling of new territories, frontier lands in the Middle Ages did provide opportunities for upward mobility.

The Manor

In the High Middle Ages, most European peasants, free and unfree, lived on estates called "manors." The word *manor* derives from a Latin term meaning "dwelling," "residence," or "homestead." In the twelfth century it meant the estate of a lord and his dependent tenants.

The manor was the basic unit of medieval rural organization and the center of rural life. All other generalizations about manors and manorial life have to be limited by variations in the quality of the soil, local climatic conditions, and methods of cultivation. Manors varied from several thousand to as little as 120 acres. Recent evidence suggests that a manor might include several villages, a village whose produce was divided among several lords, or an isolated homestead.

The arable land of the manor was divided into two sections. The *demesne,* or home farm, was cultivated for the lord. The other part was held by the peasantry. Usually the peasants' portion was larger, held on condition that they cultivate the lord's demesne. All the arable land, both the lord's and the peasants', was divided into strips, and the strips belonging to any given individual were scattered throughout the manor. If one strip yielded little, other strips (of better soil) might be more bountiful. All peasants cooperated in the cultivation of the land, working it as a group. This meant that all shared in any disaster as well as any large harvest.

A manor usually held pasture or meadowland for the grazing of cattle, sheep, and sometimes goats. Often the manor had some forestland as well. Forests had enormous economic importance. They were the source of wood for building and resin for lighting; ash for candles, and ash and lime for fertilizers and all sorts of sterilizing products; wood for fuel and bark for the manufacture of rope. From the forests came wood for the construction of barrels, vats, and all sorts of storage containers. Last but hardly least, the forests were used for feeding pigs, cattle, and domestic animals on nuts, roots, and wild berries. If the manor was intersected by a river, it had a welcome source of fish and eels.

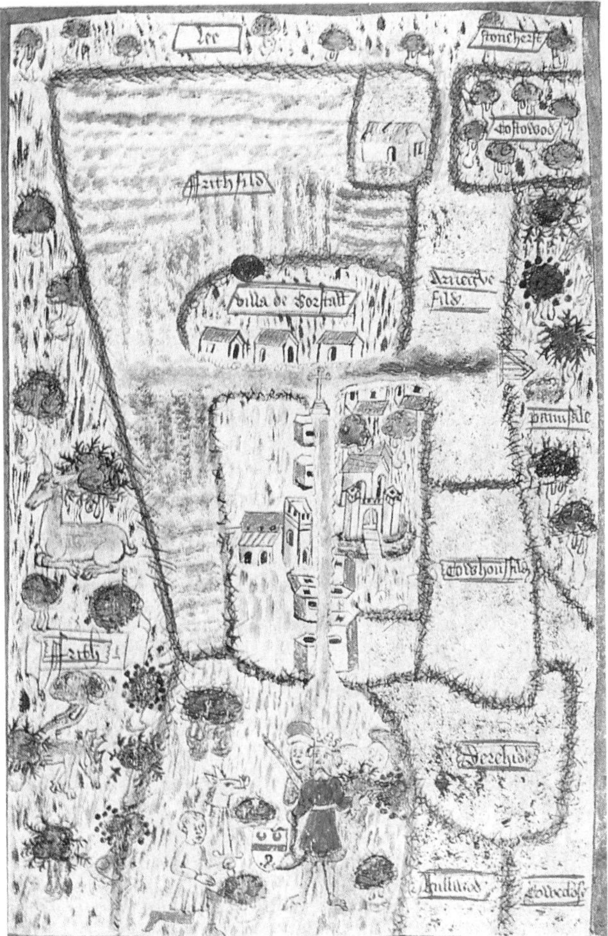

Boarstall Manor, Buckinghamshire In 1440, Edmund Rede, lord of this estate, had a map made showing his ancestor receiving the title from King Edward I (lower field). Note the manor house, church, peasants' cottages along the central road. In the common fields, divided by hedges, peasants cultivated on a three-year rotation cycle: winter wheat, spring oats, a year fallow. Peasants' pigs grazed freely in the woods, indicated by trees; we don't know whether they could hunt the deer. *(Buckinghamshire Record Office, Aylesbury)*

Agricultural Methods

According to the method historians have called the "open-field system," the arable land of a manor was divided into two or three fields without hedges or fences to mark the individual holdings of the lord, serfs, and freemen. On the premise that all should share in the poor as well as the good soil, the holdings of individual peasants were scattered in strips throughout the fields. Beginning in the eleventh century in those parts of France, England, and Germany where the quality of the soil permitted intensive cultivation, peasants divided all the arable land into three large fields, two of which in any one year were cultivated, while the third lay fallow. One part of the land was sown with winter cereals such as rye and wheat, the other with spring crops such as peas, beans, and barley. What was planted in a particular field varied each year as the crops were rotated.

Local needs, the fertility of the soil, and dietary customs determined what was planted and the method of crop rotation. Where one or several manors belonged to a great aristocratic establishment, such as the abbey of Cluny, which needed large quantities of oats for horses, more of the arable land would be planted in oats than in other cereals. Where the land was extremely fertile, such as in the Alsace region of Germany, a biennial cycle was used: one crop of wheat was sown and harvested every other year, and in alternate years all the land lay fallow. The author of an English agricultural treatise advised his readers to stick to a two-field method of cultivation and insisted that a rich harvest every second year was preferable to two mediocre ones every three years.

Farmers knew the value of animal fertilizers. Chicken manure, because of its high nitrogen content, was the richest but was limited in quantity. Sheep manure was also valuable. Gifts to English Cistercian monasteries (see page 326) were frequently given on condition that the monks' sheep be allowed to graze at certain periods on the benefactor's demesne. Because cattle were fed on the common pasture and were rarely stabled, gathering their manure was laborious and time-consuming. Nevertheless, whenever possible, animal manure was gathered and thinly spread. So also was house garbage—eggshells, fruit cores, onion skins—that had disintegrated in a compost heap.

Tools and farm implements are often shown in medieval manuscripts. But accepting such representations at face value is misleading. Rather than going out into a field to look at a tool, medieval artists simply copied drawings from classical and other treatises. Thus a plow or harrow pictured in a book written in the Île-de-France may actually have been used in England or Italy a half century before.

In the early twelfth century, the production of iron increased greatly. There is considerable evidence for the manufacture of iron plowshares (the part of the plow that cuts the furrow and grinds up the earth). In the thirteenth century, the wooden plow continued to be the basic instrument of agricultural production, but its edge was strengthened with iron. Only after the start of the fourteenth century, when lists of manorial equip-

Late Medieval Wheelless Plow This plow has a sharp-pointed colter, which cut the earth while the attached mold-board lifted, turned, and pulverized the soil. As the man steers the plow, his wife prods the oxen. The caption reads, "God speed the plow, and send us corn (wheat) enough." *(Trinity College Library, Cambridge)*

ment began to be kept, is there evidence for pitchforks, spades, axes, and harrows. The harrow, a cultivating instrument with heavy teeth, broke up and smoothed the soil. While the modern harrow has steel teeth (or disks), medieval ones were wooden and weighed down with stones to force a deep cut in the earth.

Plow and harrow were increasingly drawn by horses. The development of the padded horse collar, resting on the horse's shoulders and attached to the load by shafts, led to an agricultural revolution. The horse collar meant that the animal could put its entire weight into the task of pulling. The use of horses, rather than oxen, spread in the twelfth century, because horses' greater strength brought greater efficiency to farming and reduced the amount of human labor involved. The quality of the soil and the level of rainfall in the area seem to have determined whether peasants shifted from ox teams to horses. Horses worked best on light, dry, and easily tilled soil, but they had difficulties plowing through clay soils and in places where heavy moisture caused earth to cling to the plow. Oxen, on the other hand, worked well on heavy, muddy, or clay soil, but they slipped and suffered hoof damage on dry, stony land. Thus, in England, horses were employed in the light soils of Norfolk on the northeastern coast and on the stony lands of Yorkshire, while oxen remained common in the Midlands until the late sixteenth century.[8] At the same time, horses were an enormous investment, perhaps comparable to a modern tractor. They had to be shod (another indication of increased iron production), and the oats they ate were costly. Although horses represent a crucial element in the improvement of husbandry, students of medieval agriculture remain uncertain as to whether the greater use of horses increased crop yields.

The thirteenth century did, however, witness a tremendous spurt in the use of horses to haul carts to market. Large and small farmers increasingly relied on horses to pull wagons because they could travel much faster than oxen. Consequently, goods reached market faster, and the number of markets to which the peasant had access increased. The opportunities and temptations for consumer spending on nonagricultural goods multiplied.[9]

Agricultural yields varied widely from place to place and from year to year. Even with good iron tools, horsepower, and careful use of seed and fertilizer, medieval peasants were at the mercy of the weather. Even today lack of rain or too much rain can cause terrible financial loss and extreme hardship. How much more vulnerable was the medieval peasant with his primitive tools! By twentieth-century standards, medieval agricultural yields were very low. Inadequate soil preparation, poor seed selection, lack of manure—all made this virtually inevitable.

Yet there was striking improvement over time. Between the ninth and early thirteenth centuries, it appears that yields of cereals approximately doubled, and on the best-managed estates, for every bushel of seed planted, the farmer harvested five bushels of grain. This is a tentative conclusion. Because of the scarcity of manorial inventories before the thirteenth century, the student of medieval agriculture has great difficulty determining how much the land produced. The author of a treatise on land husbandry, Walter of Henley, who lived in the mid-thirteenth century, wrote that the land should yield three times its seed; that amount was necessary for sheer survival. The surplus would be sold to grain merchants in the nearest town. Townspeople were wholly dependent on the surrounding countryside for food, which could not be shipped a long distance. A poor harvest meant that both town and rural people suffered.

Grain yields were probably greatest on large manorial estates, where there was more professional management. For example, the estates of Battle Abbey in Sussex, England, enjoyed a very high yield of wheat, rye, and oats in the century and a half between 1350 and 1499. This was due to heavy seeding, good crop rotation, and the use of manure from the monastery's sheep flocks. Battle Abbey's yields seem to have been double those of smaller, less efficiently run farms. A modern Illinois farmer expects to get 40 bushels of soybeans, 150 bushels of corn, and 50 bushels of wheat for every bushel of seed planted. Of course, modern costs of production in labor, seed, and fertilizer are quite high, but this yield is at least ten times that of the farmer's medieval ancestor. While some manors may have achieved a yield of 12 or even 15 to 1, the *average* manor probably got a yield of only 5 to 1 in the thirteenth century.[10] As low as that may seem by current standards, it marked a rise in productivity equal to that of the years just before the start of the great agricultural revolution of the eighteenth century.

Life on the Manor

Life for most people in medieval Europe meant country life. A person's horizons were largely restricted to the manor on which he or she was born. True, peasants who colonized such sparsely settled regions as eastern Germany must have traveled long distances. But most people rarely traveled more than twenty-five miles beyond their villages. Everyone's world was small, narrow, and provincial in the original sense of the word: limited by the boundaries of the province. This way of life did not have entirely unfortunate results. A farmer had a strong sense of family and the certainty of its support and help in time of trouble. People knew what their life's work would be—the same as their mother's or father's. They had a sense of place, and pride in that place was reflected in adornment of the village church. Religion and the village gave people a sure sense of identity and with it psychological peace. Modern people—urban, isolated, industrialized, rootless, and thoroughly secularized—have lost many of these reinforcements.

On the other hand, even aside from the unending physical labor, life on the manor was dull. Medieval men and women must have had a crushing sense of frustration. Often they sought escape in heavy drinking. English judicial records of the thirteenth century reveal a surprisingly large number of "accidental" deaths. Strong, robust, commonsensical farmers do not ordinarily fall on their knives and stab themselves, or slip out of boats and drown, or get lost in the woods on a winter's night, or fall from horses and get trampled. They were probably drunk. Many of these accidents occurred, as the court records say, "coming from an ale." Brawls and violent fights were frequent at taverns.

Scholars have recently spent much energy investigating the structure of medieval peasant households. Because little concrete evidence survives, conclusions are very tentative. It appears, however, that a peasant household consisted of a simple nuclear family: a married couple alone, a couple with children, or widows or widowers with children. Peasant households were *not* extended families containing grandparents or married sons and daughters and their children. The simple family predominated in thirteenth-century England, in northern France in the fourteenth century, and in fifteenth-century Tuscany. Before the first appearance of the Black Death, perhaps 94 percent of peasant farmers married, and bride and groom were both in their early twenties. The typical household numbered about five people, the parents and three children.[11]

Women played a significant role in the agricultural life of medieval Europe. They worked with men in wheat and grain cultivation, in the vineyards, and in the harvest and preparation of crops needed by the textile industry—flax and plants used for dyeing cloth, such as madder (which produces shades of red) and woad (which yields blue dye). Especially at harvest time women shared with their fathers and husbands the backbreaking labor in the fields, work that was probably more difficult for them because of frequent pregnancies. Lords of great estates commonly hired female day laborers as well as men to shear sheep, pick hops (used in the manufacture of beer and ale), tend gardens, and do household chores such as cleaning, laundry, and baking; servant girls in the country considered their hired status as temporary, until they married. Thrifty farm wives contributed to the family income by selling for cash the produce of their gardens or kitchen: butter, cheese, eggs, fruit, soap, mustard, cucumbers. The adage from the Book of Proverbs—"Houses and riches are the inheritance of fathers; but a prudent wife is from the Lord"—was seldom more true than in an age when careful management was often all that separated a household from starvation in a year of crisis. And starvation was a very real danger to the peasantry down to the eighteenth century.

Women managed the house. The size and quality of peasants' houses varied according to their relative prosperity, and that prosperity usually depended on the amount of land held. Poorer peasants lived in windowless cottages built of wood and clay or wattle (poles interwoven with branches or reeds) and thatched with straw. These cottages consisted of one large room that served as the kitchen and living quarters for all. Everyone slept there. The house had an earthen floor and a fireplace. The lack of windows meant that the room was very sooty. A trestle table, several stools, one or two beds, and a chest for storing clothes constituted the furniture. A shed attached to the house provided storage for tools and shelter for animals. Prosperous peasants added rooms and furniture as they could be afforded, and some wealthy peasants in the early fourteenth century had two-story houses with separate bedrooms for parents and children.

Every house had a small garden and an outbuilding. Onions, garlic, turnips, and carrots were grown and stored through the winter in the main room of the dwelling or in the shed attached to it. Cabbage was raised almost everywhere and, after being shredded, salted, and packed in vats in hot water, was turned into kraut. Peasants ate vegetables not because they appreciated their importance for good health but because there was usually little else. Some manors had fruit trees—apple, cherry, and pear in northern Europe; lemon, lime, and olive in the south. But because of the high price of sugar, when it was available, fruit could not be preserved. Preserving and storing other foods were the basic responsibility of the women and children.

Women dominated in the production of ale for the community market. This industry required an initial investment in large vessels and knowledge of the correct proportions of barley, water, yeast, and hops. Women found brewing hard and dangerous work: it involved carrying twelve-gallon vats of hot liquid. Records of

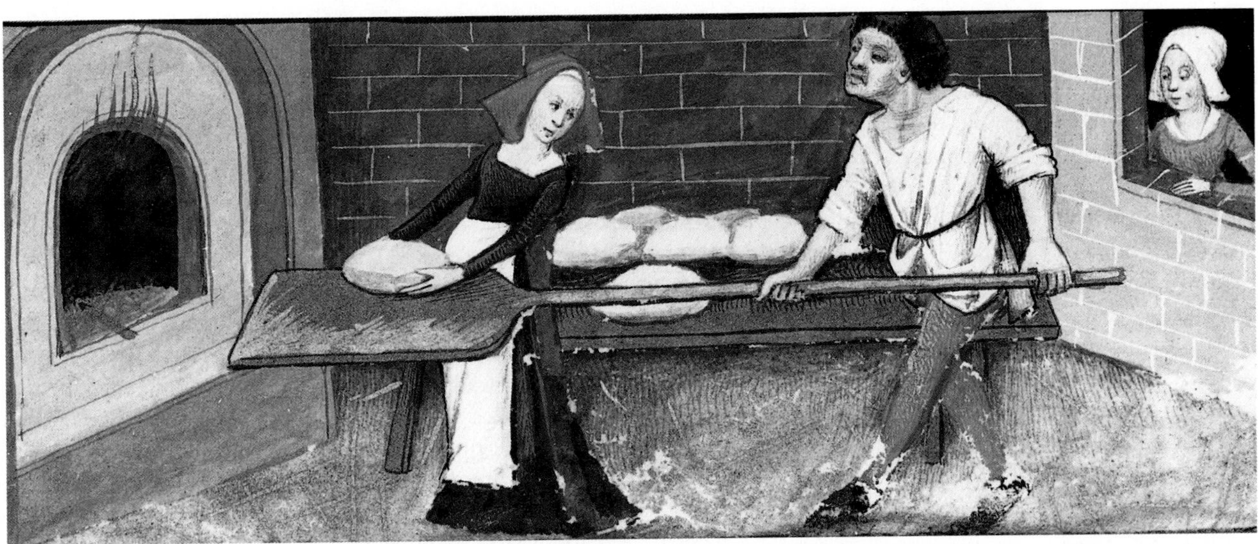

Baking Bread Bread and beer or ale were the main manorial products for local consumption. While women dominated the making of ale and beer, men and women cooperated in the making and baking of bread—the staple of the diet at the communal manorial oven, which, like a modern pizza oven, could bake several loaves at once. *(Bibliothèque Nationale, Paris)*

the English coroners' courts reveal that 5 percent of women who died lost their lives in brewing accidents, by falling into the vats of boiling liquid.[12] Ale was the universal drink of the common people in northern Europe. By modern American standards the rate of consumption was heroic. Each monk of Abingdon Abbey in twelfth-century England was allotted three gallons a day, and a man working in the fields for ten hours probably drank much more.[13]

The mainstay of the diet for peasants everywhere—and for all other classes—was bread. It was a hard, black substance made of barley, millet, and oats, rarely of expensive wheat flour. The housewife usually baked the household supply once a week. Where sheep, cows, or goats were raised, she also made cheese. In places like the Bavarian Alps of southern Germany, where hundreds of sheep grazed on the mountainsides,[14] or at Cheddar in southwestern England, cheese was a staple.

The diet of those living in an area with access to a river, lake, or stream would be supplemented with fish, which could be preserved by salting; people living close to the sea could gather shellfish such as oysters, mussels, and whelks. In many places there were severe laws against hunting and trapping in the forests. Deer, wild boars, and other game were strictly reserved for the king and nobility. These laws were flagrantly violated, however, and stolen rabbits and wild game often found their way to the peasants' tables. Woods and forests also provided nuts, which housewives and small children would gather in the fall.

Lists of peasant obligations and services to the lord, such as the following from Battle Abbey, commonly included the payment of chickens and eggs: "John of Coyworth holds a house and thirty acres of land, and owes yearly 2 p at Easter and Michaelmas; and he owes a cock and two hens at Christmas, of the value of 4 d."[15] Chickens and eggs must have been highly valued in the prudently managed household. Except for the rare chicken or illegally caught wild game, meat appeared on the table only on the great feast days of the Christian year: Christmas, Easter, and Pentecost. Then the meat was likely to be pork from the pig slaughtered in the fall and salted for the rest of the year. Some scholars believe that, by the mid-thirteenth century, there was an increase in the consumption of meat generally. If so, this improvement in diet is further evidence of an improved standard of living.

Breakfast, eaten at dawn before people departed for their farmwork, might well consist of bread, an onion (easily stored through the winter months), and a piece of cheese, washed down with milk or ale. Farmers, then as now, ate their main meal around noon. This was often soup—a thick *potage* of boiled cabbage, onions, turnips, and peas, seasoned with a bone or perhaps a sliver of meat. The evening meal, taken at sunset, consisted of leftovers from the noon meal, perhaps with bread, cheese, milk, or ale.

Once children were able to walk, they helped their parents in the hundreds of chores that had to be done. Small children were set to collecting eggs, if the family had chickens, or gathering twigs and sticks for firewood. As they grew older, children had more responsible tasks, such as weeding the family vegetable garden, milking the cows, shearing the sheep, cutting wood for fires, helping with the planting or harvesting, and assisting their mothers in the endless tasks of baking, cooking, and preserving. Because of poor diet, terrible sanitation, and lack of medical care, the death rate among children was phenomenally high.

Health Care

What of health care? What medical attention was available to the sick person in western Europe from the mid-eleventh century to the beginning of the fourteenth? Scholars are only beginning to explore these questions, and there are many aspects of public health that we know little about. The steady rise in population in these centuries, usually attributed to the beginnings of political stability and the reduction of violence and to the great expansion of land put under cultivation and thus the increased food supply, may also be ascribed partly to better health care. Survival to adulthood probably meant a tough people. A recent study of skeletal remains in the village of Brandes in Burgundy showed that peasants enjoyed very good health: they were well built, had excellent teeth, and their bones revealed no signs of chronic disease. Obviously we cannot generalize about the health of all people on the basis of evidence of one village, but preliminary research confirms the picture in romantic literature: in the prime of life the average person had a raw vitality that enabled him or her to eat, drink, work, and make love with great gusto.[16]

In recent years scholars have produced some exciting information relating to the natural processes of pregnancy and childbirth. But the acquisition of information has not been easy, because modesty forbade the presence of men at the birth of a child (hence very

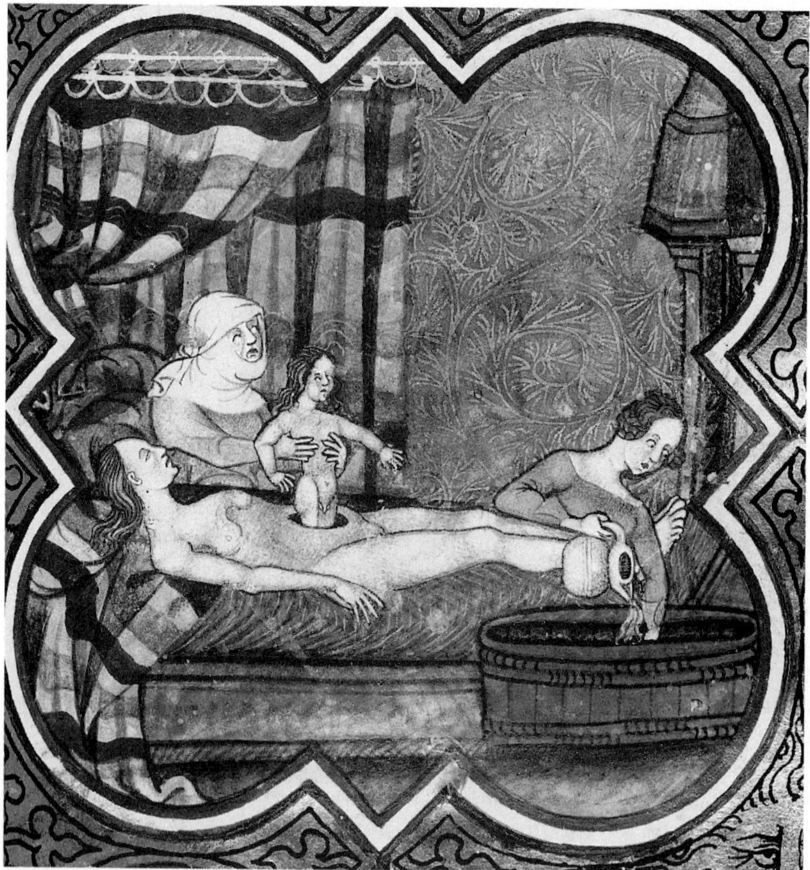

A Caesarean Birth, unlike a normal one, was a surgical procedure; as such, male physicians in the fourteenth century gradually marginalized women in the field of obstetrics, which they had always dominated. Here the midwife (identifiable from her headdress) lifts a male child from the abdominal opening in the mother's dead body. Her helper prepares the tub of water to bathe the child. Since few infants survived the procedure, midwives needed witnesses to assert that they had not bungled the birth or deliberately killed the infant. *(British Library)*

tainly could not reason out the increasingly sophisticated propositions of clever theologians. Still, Scriptural references and proverbs dotted everyone's language. The English "good-bye," the French "adieu," and the Spanish "adios" all derive from words meaning "God be with you." Christianity was a basic element in the common people's culture; indeed, it was the foundation of their culture.

Christians had long had special reverence and affection for the Virgin Mary, as the Mother of Christ. In the eleventh century, theologians began to emphasize the depiction of Mary at the Crucifixion in the Gospel of John: "When Jesus saw his mother and the disciple whom he loved standing near, he said to his mother, 'Woman, behold, your son!' Then he said to the disciple, 'Behold, your mother!'" Medieval scholars interpreted this passage as expressing Christ's compassionate concern for all humanity and Mary's spiritual motherhood of all Christians. The huge outpouring of popular devotions to Mary concentrated on her role as Queen of Heaven and, because of her special relationship to Christ, as all-powerful intercessor with him. Masses on Saturdays specially commemorated her, sermons focused on her unique influence with Christ, and hymns and prayers to her multiplied. The most famous prayer, "Salve Regina," perfectly expresses medieval people's confidence in Mary, their advocate with Christ:

Hail, holy Queen, Mother of Mercy! Our life, our sweetness, and our hope. To thee we cry, poor banished children of Eve; to thee we send up our sighs, mourning and weeping in this valley of tears. Turn, then, most gracious advocate, thy merciful eyes upon us; and after this our exile show us the blessed fruit of thy womb, Jesus. O merciful, O loving, O sweet Virgin Mary!

Peasants had a strong sense of the presence of God. They believed that God intervened directly in human affairs and could reward the virtuous with peace, health, and material prosperity. They believed that God punished men and women for their sins with disease, poor harvests, and war. Sin was caused by the Devil, who lurked everywhere. The Devil constantly incited people to evil deeds and sin, especially sins of the flesh. Sin frequently took place in the dark. Thus evil and the Devil were connected in the peasant's mind with darkness or blackness. In some medieval literature the Devil is portrayed as black, an identification that has had a profound and sorry impact on Western racial attitudes.

For peasants life was not only hard but short. Few lived beyond the age of forty. They had a great fear of nature: storms, thunder, and lightning terrified them. They had a terror of hell, whose geography and awful tortures they knew from sermons. And they certainly saw that the virtuous were not always rewarded but sometimes suffered considerably on earth. These things, which they could not explain, bred a deep pessimism.

Belief in an afterlife where the dead were rewarded or punished according to how they had lived on earth was a central principle of medieval people's faith. The clergy taught the immortality of the soul after the death of the body. The deceased, however, did not go immediately to heaven or hell. Rather, people believed that the recently deceased returned to the places they had frequented during their lives and either sought the prayers of the living or settled accounts with them. Hence the widespread belief in ghosts who haunted their former houses and frightened relatives and friends. Late in the twelfth century, to free houses and people of the haunting presence of the dead, the church affirmed the existence of *purgatory,* a temporary place where distressed souls made amends for their earthly sins before being assigned one of the eternal places, hell or heaven.[28] Prayers and masses helped those in purgatory. So did *indulgences,* documents bearing the pope's name that released the souls from purgatory. (Indulgences, it was believed, also relieved the living of those penalties imposed by the priest in confession for serious sins.) Indulgences could be secured for a small fee. People came to believe that indulgences and pilgrimages to the shrines of saints "promised" salvation. Vast numbers embarked on pilgrimages to the shrines of Saint James at Compostella in Spain, Saint Thomas Becket at Canterbury, Saint-Gilles de Provence, and Saints Peter and Paul at Rome.

Those Who Fight

The nobility, though a small fraction of the total population, strongly influenced all aspects of medieval culture—political, economic, religious, educational, and artistic. For that reason, European society in the twelfth and thirteenth centuries may be termed aristocratic. Despite political, scientific, and industrial revolutions, the nobility continued to hold real political and social power in Europe down to the nineteenth century. In order to account for this continuing influence, it is important to understand its development in the High Middle Ages. How did the social status and lifestyle of the nobility in the twelfth and thirteenth centuries differ from their tenth-century forms? What political and economic role did the nobility play?

First, in the tenth and eleventh centuries, the social structure in different parts of Europe varied considerably. There were distinct regional customs and social patterns. Broad generalizations about the legal and social status of the nobility, therefore, are dangerous, because they are not universally applicable. For example, in Germany until about 1200, approximately one thousand families, descended from the Carolingian imperial aristocracy and perhaps from the original German tribal nobility, formed the ruling social group. Its members intermarried and held most of the important positions in church and state.[29] Rigid distinctions existed between free and nonfree individuals, preventing the absorption of those of servile birth into the ranks of the nobility. Likewise, in the region around Paris from the tenth century on, a group of great families held public authority, was self-conscious about its ancestry and honorable status, was bound to the royal house, and was closed to the self-made man. From this aristocracy descended the upper nobility of the High Middle Ages.[30] To the west, however, in the provinces of Anjou and Maine, men of fortune who gained wealth and power became part of the closely related web of noble families by marrying into those families; in these regions, considerable upward mobility existed. Some scholars argue that before the thirteenth century the French nobility was an open caste.[31] Across the English Channel, the English nobility in the High Middle Ages derived from the Norman, Breton, French, and Flemish warriors who helped Duke William of Normandy defeat the Anglo-Saxons at the Battle of Hastings in 1066. In most places, for a son or daughter to be considered a noble, both parents had to be noble. Non-noble women could not usually enter the nobility through marriage, though evidence from Germany shows that some women were ennobled because they had married nobles. There is no evidence of French or English women being raised to the nobility.

Members of the nobility enjoyed a special legal status. A nobleman was free personally and in his possessions. He had immunity from almost all outside authorities. He was limited only by his military obligation to king, duke, or prince. As the result of his liberty, he had certain rights and responsibilities. He raised troops and commanded them in the field. He held courts that dispensed a sort of justice. Sometimes he coined money for use within his territories. He conducted relations with outside powers. He was the political, military, and judicial lord of the people who settled on his lands. He made political decisions affecting them, resolved disputes among them, and protected them in time of attack. The liberty of the noble meant that he possessed special privileges that were inheritable, perpetuated by blood and not by wealth alone.

The nobleman was a professional fighter. His social function, as churchmen described it, was to protect the weak, the poor, and the churches by arms. He possessed a horse and a sword. These, and the leisure time in which to learn how to use them in combat, were the visible signs of his nobility. He was encouraged to display chivalric virtues. Chivalry was a code of conduct originally devised by the clergy to transform the crude and brutal behavior of the knightly class. A knight was supposed to be brave, anxious to win praise, courteous, loyal to his commander, generous, and gracious. Above all, he was to be loyal to his lord and brave in battle. In a society lacking strong institutions of government, loyalty was the cement that held aristocratic society together. That is why the greatest crime was called a "felony," which meant treachery to one's lord. The medieval nobility developed independently of knighthood and preceded it; all nobles were knights, but not all knights were noble.[32]

During the eleventh century, the term *chevalier,* meaning "horseman" or "knight," gained wide currency in France. Non-French people gradually adopted it to refer to the nobility, "who sat up high on their warhorses, looking down on the poor masses and terrorizing the monks."[33] In France and England by the twelfth century, the noble frequently used the Latin term *miles,* or "knight." By this time the word connotated moral values, a consciousness of family, and participation in a superior hereditary caste. Those who aspired to the aristocracy desired a castle, the symbol of feudal independence and military lifestyle. Through military valor, a fortunate marriage, or outstanding service to king or lord, poor knights could and did achieve positions in the upper nobility. In Germany there also existed a large class of unfree knights, or *ministerials.* Recruited from the servile dependents of great lords, ministerials fought as warriors or served as stewards who managed nobles' estates or households. In the twelfth century, ministerials sometimes acquired fiefs and wealth. The most important ministerials served the German kings and had significant responsibilities. Legally, however, they remained of servile status: they were not noble.[34] Consequently, in southeastern Germany the term *knight* applied to the servile position of a ministerial.

Infancy and Childhood

Very exciting research has been done on childbirth in the Middle Ages. Most of the information comes from manuscript illuminations, which depict the birth process

Monastic Entrance In a world that had few career opportunities for "superfluous children," monasteries served a valuable social function. Because a dowry was expected, monastic life was generally limited to the children of the affluent. Advising his son to be obedient, a father, with a bag of coins in his left hand, hands his son over to the abbot. The boy does not look very enthusiastic. *(Bibliothèque Municipale de Troyes)*

from the moment of coitus through pregnancy to delivery. An interesting thirteenth-century German miniature from Vienna shows a woman in labor. She is sitting on a chair or stool surrounded by four other women, who are present to help her in the delivery. They could be relatives, neighbors, or midwives.

The rate of infant mortality (the number of babies who would die before their first birthday) in the High Middle Ages must have been staggering. Such practices as jolting the pregnant woman up and down to speed delivery surely contributed to the death rate of both the newborn and the mother. Natural causes—disease and poor or insufficient food—also resulted in many deaths. Infanticide, however, which was common in the ancient world, seems to have declined in the High Middle Ages. Ecclesiastical pressure worked steadily against it. Infanticide in medieval Europe is an indication of the slow, imperfect Christianization of European peoples.

On the other hand, the abandonment of infant children seems to have been the most favored form of family limitation, widely practiced throughout the entire Middle Ages. Abandonment was "the voluntary relinquishing of control over children by their natal parents or guardians, whether by leaving them somewhere, selling them, or legally consigning authority to some other person or institution."[35] Why did parents do this? What became of the children? What attitudes did medieval society have toward this practice?

Poverty or local natural disaster led some parents to abandon their children because they could not support them. Before the eleventh century, food was so scarce that few parents could feed themselves, let alone children. Thus Saint Patrick wrote that, in times of famine, fathers would sell their sons and daughters so that the children could be fed. Parents sometimes gave children away because they were illegitimate or the result of incestuous unions. An eighth-century penitential collection describes the proper treatment for a woman who exposes her unwanted child—that is, leaves it in the open to die—because she has been raped by an enemy or is unable to nourish it. She is not to be blamed, but she should do penance.[36]

Sometimes parents believed that someone of greater means or status might find the child and bring it up in better circumstances than the natal parents could provide. Disappointment in the sex of the child, or its physical weakness or deformity, might have also led parents to abandon it. Finally, some parents were indifferent—they "simply could not be bothered" with the responsibilities of parenthood.[37]

The Christian Middle Ages witnessed a significant development in the disposal of superfluous children: they were given to monasteries as *oblates*. The word *oblate* derives from the Latin *oblatio,* meaning "offering." Boys and girls were given to monasteries or convents as permanent gifts. Saint Benedict (see pages 212–214), in the fifty-ninth chapter of his *Rule,* takes oblation as a normal method for entrance into the monastic life. By the seventh century, church councils and civil codes had defined the practice: "Parents of any social status could donate a child, of either sex, at least up to the age of ten." Contemporaries considered oblation a religious act, since the child was offered to God often in recompense for parental sin. But oblation also served social and economic functions. The monastery nurtured and educated the child in a familial atmosphere, and it provided career opportunities for the mature monk or nun whatever his or her origins. Oblation has justifiably been described as "in many ways the most humane form of abandonment ever devised in the West."[38]

The fragmentary medieval evidence prevents the modern student from gaining precise figures on the rate of abandonment. Recent research suggests, however, that abandonment was very common among the poor until about the year 1000. The next two hundred years, which saw great agricultural change and relative prosperity, witnessed a low point in the abandonment of poor children. On the other hand, in the twelfth and thirteenth centuries, the incidence of noble parents giving their younger sons and daughters to religious houses increased dramatically; nobles wanted to preserve the estate intact for the eldest son. Consequently, oblates composed a high percentage of monastic populations. At Winchester in England, for example, 85 percent of the new monks between 1030 and 1070 were oblates. In the early thirteenth century, the bishop of Paris observed that children were ". . . cast into the cloister by parents and relatives just as if they were kittens or piglets whom their mothers could not nourish; so that they may die to the world not spiritually but . . . civilly, that is—so that they may be deprived of their hereditary position and that it may devolve on those who remain in the world." The abandonment of children remained a socially acceptable institution. Ecclesiastical and civil authorities never legislated against it.[39]

In addition to abandonment, nobles used other family-planning strategies to preserve family estates, but scholars disagree about the nature of these methods. According to one authority, "The struggle to preserve family holdings intact led them to primogeniture [the exclusive right of the first-born son to inherit]. . . ."[40] Another student has argued persuasively that nobles deliberately married late or limited the number of their children who could marry by placing them in the church or forbidding them to marry while still laypersons. Nobles may also have practiced birth control. The counts of Falkenstein, who held lordships in Upper Bavaria and Lower Austria, adopted the strategy of late marriages for men and few children. This custom plus a violent lifestyle ultimately backfired and extinguished the dynasty.[41] Another student, using evidence from tenth-century Saxony, maintains that parents during their lifetimes commonly endowed their sons with estates. This practice allowed sons to marry at a young age and to demonstrate their military prowess.[42] Until we know more about family size and local customs in the High Middle Ages, we cannot generalize about universal practices.

For children of aristocratic birth, the years from infancy to around the age of seven or eight were primarily years of play. Infants had their rattles, as the twelfth-century monk Guibert of Nogent reports, and young children their special toys. Of course, then as now, children would play with anything handy—balls, rings, pretty stones, horns, any small household object. Gerald of Wales, who later became a courtier of King Henry II, describes how as a child he built monasteries and churches in the sand while his brothers were making castles and palaces. Vincent of Beauvais, who composed a great encyclopedia around 1250, recommended that children be bathed twice a day, fed well, and given ample playtime.

Guibert of Nogent speaks in several places in his autobiography of "the tender years of childhood"—the years from six to twelve. Describing the severity of the tutor whom his mother assigned to him, Guibert wrote:

Placed under him, I was taught with such purity and checked with such honesty from the vices which commonly spring up in youth that I was kept from ordinary games and never allowed to leave my master's company, or to eat anywhere else than at home, or to accept gifts from anyone without his leave; in everything I had to show self-control in word, look, and deed, so that he seemed to require of me the conduct of a monk rather than a clerk. While others of my age wandered everywhere at will and were unchecked in the indulgence of such inclinations as were natural at their age, I, hedged in with constant restraints and dressed in my clerical garb, would sit and look at the troops of players like a beast awaiting sacrifice. Even on Sundays and saints' days I had to submit to the severity of school exercises.[43]

Guibert's mother had intended him for the church. Other boys and girls had much more playtime and freedom.

At about the age of seven, a boy of the noble class who was not intended for the church was placed in the household of one of his father's friends or relatives. There he became a servant to the lord and received his formal training in arms. He was expected to serve the lord at the table, to assist him as a private valet when called on to do so, and, as he gained experience, to care for the lord's horses and equipment. The boy might have a great deal of work to do, depending on the size of the household and the personality of the lord. The work children did, medieval people believed, gave them experience and preparation for later life.

Training was in the arts of war. The boy learned to ride and to manage a horse. He had to acquire skill in wielding a sword, which sometimes weighed as much as twenty-five pounds. He had to be able to hurl a lance, shoot with a bow and arrow, and care for armor and other equipment. Increasingly, in the eleventh and twelfth centuries, noble youths learned to read and write some Latin. Still, on thousands of charters from that period, nobles signed with a cross (+) or some other mark. Literacy for the nobility became more common in the thirteenth century. Formal training was concluded around the age of twenty-one with the ceremony of knighthood. The custom of knighting, though never universal, seems to have been widespread in France and England but not in Germany. The ceremony of knighthood was one of the most important in a man's life. Once knighted, a young man was supposed to be courteous and generous and to follow the chivalric ideals described earlier.

A Knightly Tournament or the Battle of the Sexes The lid of this exquisitely carved French ivory casket shows ladies and gentlemen on a balcony watching a tournament among mounted knights, while men storm the castle of love (left) and a lady and knight tilt with branches of flowers (right). *(Walters Art Gallery, Baltimore)*

Youth

Knighthood did not necessarily mean adulthood, power, and responsibility. Sons were completely dependent on their fathers for support. Unless a young man's father was dead, he was still considered a youth. He remained a youth until he was in a financial position to marry—that is, until his father died. That might not happen until he was in his late thirties, and marriage at forty was not uncommon. A famous English soldier of fortune, William Marshal, had to wait until he was forty-five to take a wife. One factor—the inheritance of land and the division of properties—determined the lifestyle of the aristocratic nobility. The result was tension, frustration, and sometimes violence.

Once knighted, the young man traveled. His father selected a group of friends to accompany, guide, and protect him. The band's chief pursuit was fighting. They meddled in local conflicts, sometimes departed on Crusades, hunted, and did the tournament circuit. The *tournament,* in which a number of men competed from horseback (in contrast to the *joust,* which involved only two competitors), gave the bachelor knight experience in pitched battle. Since the horses and equipment of the vanquished were forfeited to the victors, the knight could also gain a reputation and a profit. Young knights took great delight in spending money on horses, armor, gambling, drinking, and women. Everywhere they went they stirred up trouble. It is no wonder that kings supported the Crusades to rid their countries of the violence caused by bands of footloose young knights.

The period of traveling lasted two or three years. Although some young men met violent death and others were maimed or injured, many returned home, still totally dependent on their fathers for support. Serious trouble frequently developed at this stage, for the father was determined to preserve intact the properties of the lordship and to maintain his power and position in the family.

Parents often wanted to settle daughters' futures as soon as possible. Men, even older men, tended to prefer young brides. A woman in her late twenties or thirties would have fewer years of married fertility, limiting the number of children she could produce and thus threatening the family's survival. Therefore, aristocratic girls in the High Middle Ages were married at around the age of sixteen.

The future of many young women was not enviable. For a girl of sixteen, marriage to a man in his thirties was not the most attractive prospect, and marriage to a widower in his forties and fifties was even less so. If there were a large number of marriageable young girls in a particular locality, their "market value" was reduced. In the early Middle Ages, it had been the custom for the groom to present a dowry to the bride and her family, but by the late twelfth century the process was reversed. Thereafter, the size of the marriage portions offered by brides and their families rose higher and higher.

Within noble families and medieval society as a whole, paternal control of the family property and wealth led to serious difficulties. Because marriage was long delayed for men, a considerable age difference existed between husbands and wives and between fathers and sons. Because of this generation gap, as one scholar has written, "the father became an older, distant, but still powerful figure. He could do favors for his sons, but his very presence, once his sons had reached maturity, blocked them in the attainment and enjoyment of property and in the possession of a wife."[44] Consequently, disputes between the generations were common in the twelfth and thirteenth centuries. Older men held on to property and power. Younger sons wanted a "piece of the action." The conflicts and rebellions in the years 1173 to 1189 involving Henry II of England and his sons Henry, Geoffrey, and John were quite typical.

The relationship between the mother and her sons was also affected. Closer in years to her children than her husband, she seemed better able to understand their needs and frustrations. She often served as a mediator between conflicting male generations. One authority on French epic poetry has written, "In extreme need, the heroes betake themselves to their mother, with whom they always find love, counsel and help. She takes them under her protection, even against their father."[45]

When society included so many married young women and unmarried young men, sexual tensions also arose. The young male noble, unable to marry for a long time, could satisfy his lust with peasant girls or prostitutes. But what was a young woman unhappily married to a much older man to do? The literature of courtly love is filled with stories of young bachelors in love with young married women. How hopeless their love was is not known. The cuckolded husband is also a stock figure in such masterpieces as *The Romance of Tristan and Isolde,* Chaucer's *The Merchant's Tale,* and Boccaccio's *Fiammetta's Tale.*

Power and Responsibility

A male member of the nobility became an adult when he came into the possession of his property. He then acquired vast authority over lands and people. With it went responsibility. In the words of Honorius of Autun:

Soldiers: You are the arm of the Church, because you should defend it against its enemies. Your duty is to aid the oppressed, to restrain yourself from rapine and fornication, to repress those who impugn the Church with evil acts, and to resist those who are rebels against priests. Performing such a service, you will obtain the most splendid of benefices from the greatest of Kings.[46]

Nobles rarely lived up to this ideal, and there are countless examples of nobles attacking the church. In the early thirteenth century, Peter of Dreux, count of Brittany, spent so much of his time attacking the church that he was known as the "Scourge of the Clergy."

The nobles' conception of rewards and gratification did not involve the kind of postponement envisioned by the clergy. They wanted rewards immediately. Since by definition a military class is devoted to war, those rewards came through the pursuit of arms. When nobles were not involved in local squabbles with neighbors—usually disputes over property or over real or imagined slights—they participated in tournaments.

Complete jurisdiction over properties allowed the noble, at long last, to gratify his desire for display and lavish living. Since his status in medieval society depended on the size of his household, he would be anxious to increase the number of his household retainers. The elegance of his clothes, the variety and richness of his table, the number of his horses and followers, the freedom with which he spent money—all were public indications of his social standing. The aristocratic lifestyle was luxurious and extravagant. To maintain it, nobles often borrowed from financiers or wealthy monasteries.

At the same time, nobles had a great deal of work to do. The responsibilities of a noble in the High Middle Ages depended on the size and extent of his estates, the number of his dependents, and his position in his territory relative to others of his class and to the king. As a vassal he was required to fight for his lord or for the king when called on to do so. By the mid-twelfth century, this service was limited in most parts of western Europe to forty days a year. The noble might have to perform guard duty at his lord's castle for a certain number of days a year. He was obliged to attend his lord's court on important occasions when the lord wanted to put on great displays, such as at Easter, Pentecost, and Christmas. When the lord knighted his eldest son or married off his eldest daughter, he called his vassals to his court. They were expected to attend and to present a contribution known as a "gracious aid."

Throughout the year, a noble had to look after his own estates. He had to appoint prudent and honest overseers and make sure that they paid him the customary revenues and services. Since a great lord's estates were usually widely scattered, he had to travel frequently.

Until the late thirteenth century, when royal authority intervened, a noble in France or England had great power over the knights and peasants on his estates. He maintained order among them and dispensed justice to them. Holding the manorial court, which punished criminal acts and settled disputes, was one of his gravest obligations. The quality of justice varied widely: some lords were vicious tyrants who exploited and persecuted their peasants; others were reasonable and evenhanded. In any case, the quality of life on the manor and its productivity were related in no small way to the temperament and decency of the lord—and his lady.

Women played a large and important role in the functioning of the estate. They were responsible for the practical management of the household's "inner economy"—cooking, brewing, spinning, weaving, caring for yard animals. The lifestyle of the medieval warrior-nobles required constant travel, both for purposes of war and for the supervision of distant properties. When the lord was away for long periods, the women frequently managed the herds, barns, granaries, and outlying fields as well.

Frequent pregnancies and the reluctance to expose women to hostile conditions kept the lady at home and therefore able to assume supervision of the family's fixed properties. When a husband went away on crusade—and this could last anywhere from two to five years, if he returned at all—his wife often became the sole manager of the family properties. When her husband went to the Holy Land between 1060 and 1080, the lady Hersendis was the sole manager of her family's properties in northern France.

Nor were women's activities confined to managing households and estates in their husbands' absence. Medieval warfare was largely a matter of brief skirmishes, and few men were killed in any single encounter. But altogether the number slain ran high, and there were many widows. Aristocratic widows frequently controlled family properties and fortunes and exercised great authority. Although the evidence is scattered and sketchy, there are indications that women performed many of the functions of men. In Spain, France, and Germany they bought, sold, and otherwise transferred property. Gertrude, labeled "Saxony's almighty widow" by the chronicler Ekkehard of Aura, took a leading role in conspiracies against the emperor Henry V. And Eilika

Women Defending Castle As in virtually every other kind of activity, women shared with men the difficulties and dangers of defending castles. Armed with rocks, bows, and arrows, even a finger poked through the chain-mail helmet into the eye of a knight scaling the walls on a ladder, these noble ladies try to fight off attackers. *(Bibliothèque royale Albert Ier, Brussels)*

Billung, widow of Count Otto of Ballenstedt, built a castle at Burgwerben on the Saale River and, as advocate of the monastery of Goseck, removed one abbot and selected his successor. From her castle at Bernburg, the countess Eilika was also reputed to ravage the countryside.

Throughout the High Middle Ages, fighting remained the dominant feature of the noble lifestyle. The church's preachings and condemnations reduced but did not stop violence. Lateness of inheritance, depriving the nobility of constructive outlets for their energy, together with the military ethos of their culture, encouraged petty warfare and disorder. The nobility thus represented a constant source of trouble for the monarchy. In the thirteenth century, kings drew on the financial support of the middle classes to build the administrative machinery that gradually laid the foundations for strong royal government. The Crusades relieved the rulers of France, England, and the German Empire of some of their most dangerous elements. Complete royal control of the nobility, however, came only in modern times.

Those Who Pray

Medieval people believed that monks performed an important social service, prayer. In the Middle Ages, prayer was looked on as a vital service, one as crucial as the labor of peasants and the military might of nobles. Just as the knights protected and defended society with the sword and the peasants provided sustenance through their toil, so the monks with their prayers and chants worked to secure God's blessing for society.

Monasticism represented some of the finest aspirations of medieval civilization. The monasteries produced the educated elite that was continually drawn into the administrative service of kings and great lords. Monks kept alive the remains of classical culture and experimented with new styles of architecture and art. They introduced new techniques of estate management and land reclamation. Although relatively few in number in the High Middle Ages, the monks played a significant role in medieval society.

Recruitment

Toward the end of his *Ecclesiastical History,* when he was well into his sixties, Orderic Vitalis, a monk of the Norman abbey of Saint Evroul, interrupted his narrative to explain movingly how he happened to become a monk:

And so, O glorious God, you didst inspire my father Odeleric to renounce me utterly and submit me in all things to thy governance. So, weeping, he gave me, a weeping child, into the care of the monk Reginald, and sent me away into exile for love of thee, and never saw me again. And I, a mere boy, did not presume to oppose my father's wishes, but obeyed him in all things, for he promised me for his part that if I became a monk I should taste of the joys of Heaven with the Innocents after my death. . . . And so, a boy of ten, I crossed the English channel and came into Normandy as an exile, unknown to all, knowing no one. Like Joseph in Egypt I heard a language which I could not understand. But thou didst suffer me through thy grace to find nothing but kindness among strangers. I was received as an oblate in the abbey of St. Evroul by the venerable ab-

bot Mainier in the eleventh year of my life. . . . The name of Vitalis was given me in place of my English name, which sounded harsh to the Normans.[47]

Orderic Vitalis (ca 1075–ca 1140) was one of the leading scholars of his time. As such, he is not a representative figure or even a typical monk. Intellectuals, those who earn their living or spend most of their time working with ideas, are never typical figures of their times. In one respect, however, Orderic was quite representative of the monks of the High Middle Ages: although he had no doubt that God wanted him to be a monk, the decision was actually made by his parents, who gave him to a monastery as a child-oblate. Orderic was the son of Odelerius, a Norman priest of the household of Earl Roger of Montgomery and (after the Conquest of 1066) Shrewsbury, and an Englishwoman. The law requiring a celibate priesthood was not yet operative in England, but qualms of conscience may have led him to place his son in a Norman monastery.[48]

Medieval monasteries were religious institutions whose organization and structure fulfilled the social needs of the feudal nobility. The monasteries provided noble children with both an honorable and aristocratic life and opportunities for ecclesiastical careers.[49] Some men did become monks as adults, apparently for a wide variety of reasons: belief in a direct call from God, disgust with the materialism and violence of the secular world, the encouragement and inspiration of others, economic failure or lack of opportunity, poverty, sickness, fear of hell. However, most men who became monks, until about the early thirteenth century, seem to have been given as child-oblates by their parents.

In the thirteenth century, the older Benedictine and Cistercian orders had to compete with new orders of friars—the Franciscans and Dominicans. More monks had to be recruited from the middle class, that is, from small landholders or traders in the district near the abbey. As medieval society changed economically, and as European society ever so slowly developed middle-class traits, the monasteries almost inevitably drew their manpower, when they were able, from the middle classes. Until that time, they were preserves of the aristocratic nobility.

The Nuns

Throughout the Middle Ages, social class also defined the kinds of religious life open to women. Kings and nobles usually established convents for their daughters, sisters, aunts, or aging mothers. Entrance was restricted to women of the founder's class. Since a wellborn lady could not honorably be apprenticed to a tradesperson, and since her dignity did not permit her to do any kind of manual labor, the sole alternative to life at home was the religious life.

The founder's endowment and support greatly influenced the later social, economic, and political status of the convent. Social and religious bonds between benefactors and communities of nuns frequently continued over many generations. A few convents received large endowments and could accept many women. Amesbury Priory in Wiltshire, England, for example, received a handsome endowment from King Henry II in 1177, and his successors Henry III and Edward I also made lavish gifts. In 1256 Amesbury supported a prioress and 76 nuns, 7 priests, and 16 lay brothers. It owned 200 oxen, 23 horses, 7 cows, 4 calves, 300 pigs, and 4,800 sheep. The convent raised 100 pounds in annual rents and 40 pounds from the wool clip, very large sums at the time. The entrance of such highborn ladies as the dowager queen Eleanor (widow of Henry III), Edward I's daughter Mary, and his niece Isabella of Lancaster stimulated the gift of additional lands and privileges. By 1317 Amesbury had 177 nuns.[50] Most houses of women, however, possessed limited resources and remained small in numbers.

The office of abbess or prioress, the house's superior, customarily went to a nun of considerable social standing. Thus William the Conqueror's daughter Cecelia became abbess of her mother's foundation, Holy Trinity Abbey in Caen, and Henry II's daughter became abbess of Barking. Since an abbess or prioress had responsibility for governing her community and for representing it in any business with the outside world, she was a woman of local power and importance. Sometimes her position brought national prominence. In 1306 Edward I of England summoned several abbesses to Parliament; he wanted their financial support for the expenses connected with knighting his eldest son.

What kind of life did the nuns lead? Religious duties held prime importance. Then there were business responsibilities connected with lands, properties, and rents that preoccupied those women of administrative ability. Sewing, embroidery, and fine needlework were considered the special pursuits of gentlewomen. Nuns in houses with an intellectual tradition copied manuscripts. Although the level of intellectual life in the women's houses varied widely, the careers of two nuns—Hildegard of Bingen and Isabella of Lancaster—suggest the activities of some nuns in the High Middle Ages.

The tenth child of a lesser noble family, Hildegard (1098–1179) was given when eight years old as an oblate to an abbey in the Rhineland, where she learned Latin and received a good education. Obviously possessed of leadership and administrative talents, Hildegard went in 1147 to found the convent of Rupertsberg near Bingen. There she produced a body of writings including the *Scivias* (Know the Ways), a record of her mystical visions that incorporates vast theological learning; the *Physica* (On the Physical Elements), a classification of the natural elements, such as plants, animals, metals, and the movements of the heavenly bodies; a mystery play; and a medical work that led a distinguished twentieth-century historian of science to describe Hildegard as "one of the most original writers of the Latin West in the twelfth century." At the same time, she carried on a vast correspondence with scholars, prelates, and ordinary people and had such a reputation for wisdom that a recent writer has called her "the Dear Abby of the twelfth century to whom everyone came or wrote for advice or comfort."[51] An exceptionally gifted person, Hildegard represents the Benedictine ideal of great learning combined with a devoted monastic life.

As with monks, however, intellectual nuns were not typical of the era. The life of the English nun Isabella of Lancaster better exemplifies the careers of highborn women who became nuns. The niece of King Edward I, she was placed at Amesbury Priory in early childhood, grew up there, made her profession of commitment to the convent life, and became abbess in 1343. Isabella seems to have been a conventional but not devout nun. She traveled widely, spent long periods at the royal court, and with the support of her wealthy relations maintained a residence apart from the priory. She was, however, an able administrator who handled the community finances with prudent skill. Amesbury lacked the intellectual and spiritual standards of Bingen. Isabella's interests were secular, and her own literary production was a book of romances.

Prayer and Other Work

In medieval Europe the monasteries of men greatly outnumbered those of women. The pattern of life within individual monasteries varied widely from house to house and from region to region. Each monastic community was shaped by the circumstances of its foundation and endowment, by tradition, by the interests of its abbots and members, and by local conditions. It would therefore be a mistake to think that Christian monasticism in the High Middle Ages was everywhere the same. One central activity, however—the work of God—was performed everywhere. Daily life centered on the liturgy.

Seven times a day and once during the night, the monks went to choir to chant the psalms and other prayers prescribed by Saint Benedict. Prayers were offered for peace, rain, good harvests, the civil authorities, the monks' families, and their benefactors. Monastic patrons in turn lavished gifts on the monasteries, which often became very wealthy.

Prayer justified the monks' spending a large percentage of their income on splendid objects to enhance the liturgy; monks praised God, they believed, not only in prayer but in everything connected with prayer. They sought to accumulate priestly vestments of the finest silks, velvets, and embroideries, as well as sacred vessels of embossed silver and gold. Thuribles containing sweet-smelling incense brought at great expense from the Orient were used at the altars, following ancient Jewish ritual. The pages of Gospel books were richly decorated with gold leaf, and the books' bindings were ornamented and bejeweled. Every monastery tried to acquire the relics of its patron saint, which necessitated the production of a beautiful reliquary to house the relics. The liturgy, then, inspired a great deal of art, and the monasteries became the crucibles of art in Western Christendom.

It was generally agreed that monks could best fulfill their duty of praying if they were not distracted by worldly needs. Thus great and lesser lords gave the monasteries lands that would supply the community with necessities. Each manorial unit was responsible for provisioning the abbey for a definite period of time.

The administration of the abbey's estates and properties consumed considerable time. The operation of a large establishment, such as Cluny in Burgundy or Bury Saint Edmunds in England, which by 1150 had several hundred monks, involved planning, prudence, and wise management. Although the abbot or prior had absolute authority in making assignments, common sense advised that tasks be allotted according to the talents of individual monks.

The usual method of economic organization was the manor. Many monastic manors were small enough and close enough to the abbey to be supervised directly by the abbot. But if a monastery held and farmed vast estates, the properties were divided into administrative units under the supervision of one of the monks of the house. The lands of the German abbey of Saint Emmeran at Regensburg, for example, were divided into thirty-three manorial centers.

Because the *choir monks* were aristocrats, they did not till the land themselves. In each house one monk, the *cellarer,* or general financial manager, was responsible for supervising the peasants or lay brothers who did the actual agricultural labor. *Lay brothers* were vowed religious drawn from the servile classes, with simpler religious and intellectual obligations than those of the choir monks. The cellarer had to see to it that the estates of the monastery produced enough income to cover its expenses. Another monk, the *almoner,* was responsible for feeding and caring for the poor of the neighborhood. At the French abbey of Saint-Requier in the eleventh century, 110 persons were fed every day. At Corbie fifty loaves of bread were distributed daily to the poor.

The *precentor* or *cantor* was responsible for the library and the careful preservation of books. The *sacristan* of the abbey had in his charge all the materials and objects connected with the liturgy—vestments, candles, incense, sacred vessels, altar cloths, and hangings. The *novice master* was responsible for the training of recruits, instructing them in the *Rule,* the chant, the Scriptures, and the history and traditions of the house. For some monks work was some form of intellectual activity, such as the copying of books and manuscripts, the preparation of manuals, and the writing of letters. Historians usually work from written records, and modern monastic studies derive from the products of the scriptoria. The efficient operation of a monastic house, however, required the services of cooks, launderers, gardeners, tailors, mechanics, blacksmiths, pharmacists, and others whose essential work left, unfortunately, no written trace.

Although several orders forbade monks to study law and medicine, that rule was often ignored. In the twelfth and thirteenth centuries, many monks gained considerable reputations for their knowledge and experience in the practice of both the canon law of the church and the civil law of their countries. For example, the Norman monk Lanfranc, because of his legal knowledge and administrative ability, became the chief adviser of William the Conqueror as archbishop of Canterbury.

Although knowledge of medicine was primitive by twentieth-century standards, monastic practitioners were less ignorant than one would suspect. Long before 1066, a rich medical literature had been produced in England. The most important of these treatises was *The Leech Book of Bald* (*leech* means "medical"). This work exhibits a wide knowledge of herbal prescriptions, ancient authorities, and empirical practice. Bald discusses diseases of the lungs and stomach, together with their remedies, and demonstrates his acquaintance with surgery. Medical knowledge was sometimes rewarded. King Henry I of England enriched several of his physicians, and Henry

Synagogue Hildegard of Bingen, the first major German mystic, developed a rich theology on the basis of visions she received. Here Synagogue is portrayed as a tall woman commanded by God to prepare humanity for the coming of Christ. In her arms Moses holds up the stone tablets of the commandments, in her lap the patriarchs and prophets who foretold the birth of Christ. The headband symbolizes the Virgin Mary: because Mary gave the world the savior, Hildegard makes Synagogue the Mother of the Incarnation. *(Rheinische Bildarchiv)*

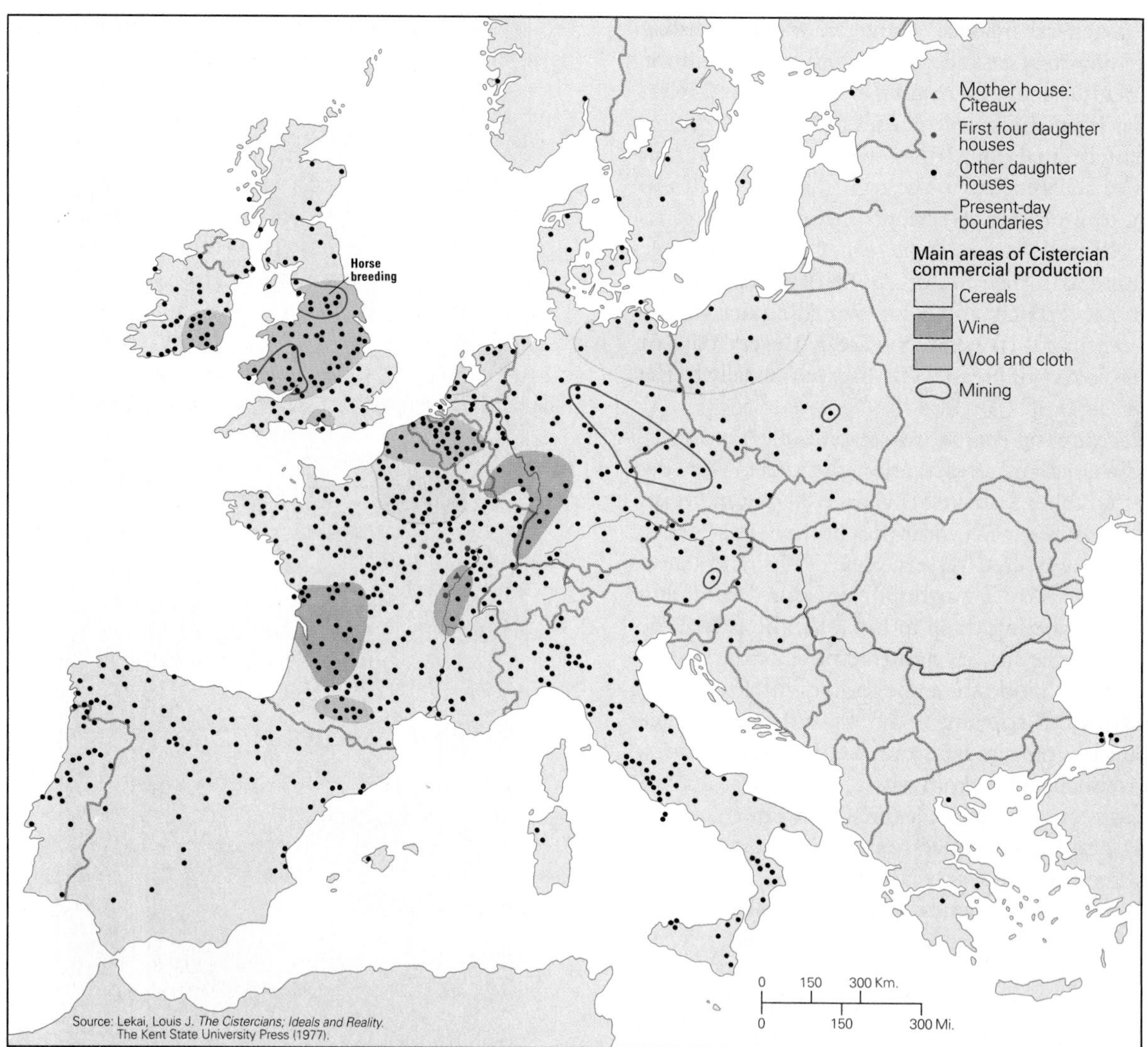

MAP 10.1 Cistercian Expansion The rapid expansion of the Cistercian order in the twelfth century reflects the spiritual piety of the age and its enormous economic vitality. The White Monks (so called because of their white robes) took advantage of whatever economic opportunities their locales offered: coal, iron, and silver mining, sheep farming, cereal growing, wine producing, and horse breeding.

II made his medical adviser, the monk Robert de Veneys, abbot of Malmesbury.

The religious houses of medieval Europe usually took full advantage of whatever resources and opportunities their location offered. For example, the raising of horses could produce income in a world that depended on horses for travel and for warfare. Some monasteries, such as the Cistercian abbey of Jervaulx in Yorkshire, became famous for and quite wealthy from their production of prime breeds. In the eleventh and twelfth centuries, a period of considerable monastic expansion, large tracts of swamp, fen, forest, and wasteland were brought under cultivation—principally by the Cistercians (Map 10.1).

The Cistercians, whose constitution insisted that they accept lands far from human habitation and forbade them to be involved in the traditional feudal-manorial structure, were ideally suited to the agricultural needs and trends of their times. In the Low Countries (present-day Holland, Belgium, and French Flanders) they built dikes to hold back the sea, and the reclaimed land was put to the production of cereals. In the eastern parts of Germany—Silesia, Mecklenburg, and Pomerania—they took the lead in draining swamps and cultivating wasteland. Because of a labor shortage, they advertised widely across Europe for monks and brothers. As a result of their efforts, the rich, rolling land of French Burgundy was turned into lush vineyards. In northern and central England, the rocky soil and damp downs of Lincolnshire, poorly suited to agriculture, were turned into sheep runs. By the third quarter of the twelfth century, the Cistercians were raising sheep and playing a large role in the production of England's staple crop, wool.

Some monasteries got involved in iron and lead mining. In 1291 the Cistercian abbey of Furness operated at least forty forges. The German abbeys of Königsbronn, Waldsassen, and Saabergen also mined iron in the thirteenth century. The monks entered this industry first to fill their own needs, but in an expanding economy they soon discovered a large market. Iron had hundreds of uses. Nails, hammers, plows, armor, spears, axes, stirrups, horseshoes, and many weapons of war were all made from this basic metal. When King Richard of England was preparing to depart on crusade in 1189, he wanted to take fifty thousand horseshoes with him. Lead also had a great variety of uses. It could be used for roofing; as an alloy for strengthening silver coinage; for framing pane-glass windows in parish, monastery, and cathedral churches; even for lavatory drainpipes.

Some monasteries lent their surplus revenues to the local nobility and peasantry. In the twelfth century the abbey of Savigny in Normandy, for example, acted as a banking house, providing loans at interest to many noble families of Normandy and Brittany. Although church law opposed usury, or lending at interest, one reliable scholar has recently written that "it was clerics and ecclesiastical institutions (monasteries and nunneries) that constituted the main providers of credit."[52]

Whatever work particular monks did and whatever economic activities individual monasteries were involved in, monks also performed social services and exerted an influence for the good. Monasteries often ran schools that gave primary education to young boys. Abbeys like Saint Albans, situated north of London on a busy thoroughfare, served as hotels and resting places for travelers. Monasteries frequently operated "hospitals" and leprosaria, which provided care and attention to the sick, the aged, and the afflicted—primitive care, it is true, but often all that was available. In short, monasteries performed a variety of social services in an age when there was no "state" and no conception of social welfare as a public responsibility.

Economic Difficulties

In the twelfth century, expenses in the older Benedictine monastic houses increased more rapidly than did income, leading to a steadily worsening economic situation. Cluny is a good example. Life at Cluny was lavish and extravagant. There were large quantities of rich food. The monks' habits were made of the best cloth available. Cluny's abbots and priors traveled with sizable retinues, as great lords were required to do. The

Monastic Hospitality Saint Benedict wrote that a monastery would never lack for guests (see page 212), and down to the present his words have proved prophetic. Hospitality, especially in an age before public accommodations, could be a heavy drain on a monastery's time and resources. *(British Library)*

Bee Keeping at Monte Cassino Because of the scarcity and expense of sugar, honey was the usual sweetener for pastries and liquids throughout the Middle Ages. This illustrator had never actually seen the process: without veils, nets, and gloves, the bee keepers would be badly stung. *(Biblioteca Apostolica Vaticana)*

abbots worked to make the liturgy ever more magnificent, and large sums were spent on elaborate vestments and jeweled vessels. Hugh, the sixth abbot (1049–1109), embarked on an extraordinarily expensive building program. He rebuilt the abbey church, and when Pope Urban II consecrated it in 1095, it was the largest church in Christendom. The monks lived like lords, which in a sense they were.

Revenue came from the hundreds of monasteries scattered across France, Italy, Spain, and England that Cluny had reformed in the eleventh century; each year they paid Cluny a cash sum. Novices were expected to make a gift of land or cash when they entered. For reasons of security, knights departing on crusade often placed their estates under Cluny's authority. Still this income was not enough. The management of Cluny's manors across Europe was entrusted to bailiffs or wardens who were not monks and were given lifetime contracts. Frequently these bailiffs were poor managers and produced no profits. But they could not be removed and replaced. In order to meet expenses, Cluny had to rely on cash reserves. For example, Cluny's estates produced only a small percentage of needed food supplies; the rest had to be paid for from cash reserves.

Cluny had two basic alternatives—improve management to cut costs or borrow money. The abbey could have placed the monastic manors under the jurisdiction of monks, rather than hiring bailiffs who would grow rich as middlemen. It could have awarded annual rather than lifetime contracts, supervised all revenues, and tried to cut costs within the monastery. But Cluny chose the second alternative—borrowing. The abbey spent hoarded reserves of cash and fell into debt.

In contrast to the abbot of Cluny, Suger, the superior of the royal abbey of Saint-Denis near Paris from 1122 to 1151, was a shrewd manager. Though he too spared no expense to enhance the beauty of his monastery and church, Suger kept an eye on costs and made sure that his properties were soundly managed. But the management of Saint-Denis was unusual. Far more typical was the economic mismanagement at Cluny. By the early thirteenth century, small and great monasteries were facing comparable financial difficulties.

The agricultural recession of the fourteenth century (see pages 379–380) forced the lay nobility to reduce their endowment of monasteries. This development, combined with internal mismanagement, compelled the older Benedictine houses to restrict the number of recruits so that they could live within their incomes. Since the nobility continued to send their children to monasteries, there was no shortage of applicants for the limited number of places. Widespread relaxation in the observance of the Benedictine *Rule* and the weakening of community life, however, meant that the atmosphere in many monasteries resembled that of a secular college offering comfort and security. Adult candidates with ascetic fervor and those seeking a spiritual challenge turned to the austere Cistercians or the preaching friars serving the needs of the townspeople[53] (see pages 369–370).

SUMMARY

Generalizations about peasant life in the High Middle Ages must always be qualified according to manorial customs, the weather and geography, and the personalities of local lords. Everywhere, however, the performance of agricultural services and the payment of rents preoccupied peasants. Though peasants led hard lives, the reclamation of wastelands and forestlands, migration to frontier territory, or manumission (see the "Individuals in Society" feature on page 304 and Chapter 11) offered means of social mobility. The Christian faith, though perhaps not understood at an intellectual level, provided strong emotional and spiritual solace.

By 1100 the knightly class was united in its ability to fight on horseback, its insistence that each member was descended from a valorous ancestor, its privileges, and its position at the top of the social hierarchy. The nobility possessed a strong class consciousness. Aristocratic values and attitudes shaded all aspects of medieval culture. Trained for war, nobles often devoted considerable time to fighting, and intergenerational squabbles were common. Yet a noble might have shouldered heavy judicial, political, and economic responsibilities, depending on the size of his estates.

The monks and nuns exercised a profound influence on matters of the spirit. In their prayers, monks and nuns battled for the Lord, just as the chivalrous knights did on the battlefield. In their chants and rich ceremonials, in their architecture and literary productions, and in the example of many monks' lives, the monasteries inspired Christian peoples to an incalculable degree. As the crucibles of sacred art, the monasteries became the cultural centers of Christian Europe.

Improved agricultural technology that brought larger crop yields, which in turn led to population growth; the movement from servile to free social status; the use of free, instead of servile, labor; the recruitment of nuns and monks from the upper middle rather than the aristocratic classes—these changes represent the enormous dynamism of the High Middle Ages.

NOTES

1. G. Duby, *The Chivalrous Society,* trans. C. Postan (Berkeley: University of California Press, 1977), pp. 90–93.
2. B. A. Hanawalt, *The Ties That Bound: Peasant Families in Medieval England* (New York: Oxford University Press, 1986), p. 5.
3. Honorius of Autun, "Elucidarium sive Dialogus de Summa Totius Christianae Theologiae," in *Patrologia Latina,* ed. J. P. Migne (Paris: Garnier Brothers, 1854), vol. 172, col. 1149.
4. E. Power, "Peasant Life and Rural Conditions," in J. R. Tanner et al., *The Cambridge Medieval History,* vol. 7 (Cambridge: Cambridge University Press, 1958), p. 716.
5. Glanvill, "De Legibus Angliae," bk. 5, chap. 5, in *Social Life in Britain from the Conquest to the Reformation,* ed. G. G. Coulton (London: Cambridge University Press, 1956), pp. 338–339.
6. J. B. Freed, *The Friars and German Society in the Thirteenth Century* (Cambridge, Mass.: Medieval Academy of America, 1977), p. 55.
7. See W. C. Jordan, *From Servitude to Freedom: Manumission in the Sénonais in the Thirteenth Century* (Philadelphia: University of Pennsylvania Press, 1986), esp. chap. 3, pp. 37–58.
8. J. Langdon, *Horses, Oxen, and Technological Innovation: The Use of Draught Animals in English Farming, 1066–1500* (Cambridge: Cambridge University Press, 1986), p. 256.
9. Ibid., pp. 254–270.
10. G. Duby, *The Early Growth of the European Economy: Warriors and Peasants from the Seventh to the Twelfth Century* (Ithaca, N.Y.: Cornell University Press, 1978), pp. 213–219.
11. Hanawalt, *The Ties That Bound,* pp. 90–100.
12. Ibid., p. 149.
13. On this quantity and medieval measurements, see D. Knowles, "The Measures of Monastic Beverages," in *The Monastic Order in England* (Cambridge: Cambridge University Press, 1962), p. 717.
14. G. Duby, *Rural Economy and Country Life in the Medieval West,* trans. C. Postan (London: Edward Arnold, 1968), pp. 146–147.
15. S. R. Scargill-Bird, ed., *Custumals of Battle Abbey in the Reigns of Edward I and Edward II* (London: Camden Society, 1887), pp. 213–219.
16. G. Duby, ed., *A History of Private Life,* vol. 2: *Revelations of the Middle Ages* (Cambridge, Mass.: Harvard University Press, 1988), p. 585.
17. Cited in E. Amt, ed., *Women's Lives in the Middle Ages: A Sourcebook* (New York: Routledge, 1992), pp. 103–104.
18. See C. Klapisch-Zuber, ed., *A History of Women.* Vol. 2: *Silences of the Middle Ages* (Cambridge, Mass.: Harvard University Press, 1992), p. 289 et seq.

19. See R. Blumenfeld-Kosinski, *Not of Woman Born: Representations of Caesarian Birth in Medieval and Renaissance Culture* (Ithaca, N.Y.: Cornell University Press, 1990), p. 27.
20. Ibid., p. 47.
21. E. J. Kealey, *Medieval Medicus: A Social History of Anglo-Norman Medicine* (Baltimore: The Johns Hopkins University Press, 1981), p. 102.
22. Ibid., pp. 88–97.
23. Klapisch-Zuber, *A History of Women,* vol. 2, p. 299.
24. See A. Gurevich, *Medieval Popular Culture: Problems of Belief and Perception,* trans. J. M. Bak and P. A. Hollingsworth (New York: Cambridge University Press, 1990), chap. 2, pp. 39–77, esp. p. 76.
25. Ibid.
26. See M. Rubin, *Corpus Christi: The Eucharist in Late Medieval Culture* (New York: Cambridge University Press, 1992), p. 13 et seq.
27. A. Vauchez, *The Laity in the Middle Ages: Religious Beliefs and Devotional Practices,* ed. D. E. Bornstein, trans. M. J. Schneider (Notre Dame, Ind.: University of Notre Dame Press, 1993), pp. 99–102.
28. Ibid., pp. 85–87.
29. J. B. Freed, "The Origins of the European Nobility: The Problem of the Ministerials," *Viator* 7 (1976): 213.
30. Duby, *The Chivalrous Society,* pp. 104–105.
31. See C. Bouchard, "The Origins of the French Nobility," *American Historical Review* 86 (1981): 501–532.
32. Duby, *The Chivalrous Society,* p. 98.
33. G. Duby, *The Age of the Cathedrals: Art and Society 980–1420,* trans. E. Levieux and B. Thompson (Chicago: University of Chicago Press, 1981), p. 38.
34. Freed, "The Origins of the European Nobility," p. 214.
35. J. Boswell, *The Kindness of Strangers: The Abandonment of Children in Western Europe from Late Antiquity to the Renaissance* (New York: Pantheon Books, 1989), p. 24. This section relies heavily on this important work.
36. Ibid., pp. 214, 223.
37. Ibid., pp. 428–429.
38. Ibid., pp. 238–239.
39. Ibid., pp. 297, 299, and the Conclusion.
40. J. C. Russell, *Late Ancient and Medieval Population Control* (Philadelphia: American Philosophical Society, 1985), p. 180.
41. See J. B. Freed, *The Counts of Falkenstein: Noble Self-Consciousness in Twelfth-Century Germany,* Transactions of the American Philosophical Society, vol. 74, pt. 6 (Philadelphia, 1984), pp. 163–167.
42. R. J. Leyser, *Rule and Conflict in an Early Medieval Society: Ottonian Saxony* (Bloomington: Indiana University Press, 1979), pp. 49, 59.
43. J. F. Benton, ed. and trans., *Self and Society in Medieval France: The Memoirs of Abbot Guibert of Nogent* (New York: Harper & Row, 1970), p. 46.
44. D. Herlihy, "The Generation Gap in Medieval History," *Viator* 5 (1974): 360.
45. Quoted ibid., p. 361.
46. Honorius of Autun, "Elucidarium sive Dialogus," vol. 172, col. 1148.
47. M. Chibnall, ed. and trans., *The Ecclesiastical History of Ordericus Vitalis* (Oxford: Oxford University Press, 1972), 2.xiii.
48. See M. Chibnall, *The World of Ordericus Vitalis: Norman Monks and Norman Knights* (Woodbridge, England: Boydell Press, 1996), p. 8.
49. R. W. Southern, *Western Society and the Church in the Middle Ages* (Baltimore: Penguin Books, 1970), pp. 224–230, esp. p. 228.
50. See M. W. Labarge, *A Small Sound of the Trumpet: Women in Medieval Life* (Boston: Beacon Press, 1986), pp. 104–105.
51. J. M. Ferrante, "The Education of Women in the Middle Ages in Theory, Fact, and Fantasy," in *Beyond Their Sex: Learned Women of the European Past,* ed. P. H. Labalme (New York: New York University Press, 1980), pp. 22–24.
52. W. C. Jordan, *Women and Credit in Pre-Industrial and Developing Societies* (Philadelphia: University of Pennsylvania Press, 1993), p. 61.
53. See C. H. Lawrence, *Medieval Monasticism: Forms of Religious Life in Western Europe in the Middle Ages* (New York: Longman, 1988), pp. 221–223.

Suggested Reading

Students seeking further elaboration of the material of this chapter will find the titles by Amt, Boswell, Duby, Hanawalt, Jordan, Langdon, and Vauchez cited in the Notes especially valuable. For a broad treatment of frontier regions, see R. Bartlett, *The Making of Europe: Conquest, Colonization and Cultural Change, 950–1350* (1993).

The student interested in aspects of medieval slavery, serfdom, or the peasantry should begin with M. Bloch, "How Ancient Slavery Came to an End" and "Personal Liberty and Servitude in the Middle Ages, Particularly in France," in *Slavery and Serfdom in the Middle Ages: Selected Essays,* trans. W. R. Beer (1975), but see also P. Bonnassie, *From Slavery to Feudalism* (1991); and P. Freedman, *The Origins of Peasant Servitude in Medieval Catalonia* (1991). There is an excellent discussion of these problems in the magisterial work of G. Duby, *Rural Economy and Country Life in the Medieval West,* trans. C. Postan (1968); and in the highly important work of W. C. Jordan, *From Servitude to Freedom: Manumission in the Sénonais in the Thirteenth Century* (1986). G. C. Homans, *English Villagers of the Thirteenth Century* (1975), has a good combination of sociological and historical scholarship. E. L. Ladurie, *Montaillou: Cathars and Catholics in a French Village, 1294–1324,* trans. B. Bray (1978), is a fascinating glimpse of village life. G. Duby, *The Early Growth of the European*

Economy (1978), is a superb synthesis by a leading authority. Advanced students should see the same author's *The Three Orders: Feudal Society Imagined* (1980), a brilliant but difficult book.

For the religion of the people, in addition to the works by Vauchez and Gurevich cited in the Notes, two studies are recommended: R. and C. Brooke, *Popular Religion in the Middle Ages* (1984), a readable synthesis; and T. J. Heffernan, *Sacred Biography: Saints and Their Biographers in the Middle Ages* (1992), a study of the goals, assumptions, and audiences of saints' lives, an important and scholarly study.

For the origins and status of the nobility in the High Middle Ages, students are strongly urged to see the studies by Bouchard, Duby, and Freed cited in the Notes. See, in addition, L. Genicot, "The Nobility in Medieval Francia: Continuity, Break, or Evolution?"; A. Borst, "Knighthood in the High Middle Ages: Ideal and Reality"; and two studies by G. Duby, "The Nobility in Eleventh and Twelfth Century Maconnais" and "Northwestern France: The 'Youth' in Twelfth Century Aristocratic Society." All these articles appear in F. L. Cheyette, ed., *Lordship and Community in Medieval Europe: Selected Readings* (1968). C. A. Newman, *The Anglo-Norman Nobility in the Reign of Henry I* (1988), examines the economic, political, and religious network of noble relationships in twelfth-century England, while P. R. Coss, *Lordship, Knighthood and Locality: A Study in English Society, c. 1180–1280* (1991), also focuses on English social conditions. Social mobility among both aristocracy and peasantry is discussed in T. Evergates, *Feudal Society in the Bailliage of Troyes Under the Counts of Champagne, 1152–1284* (1976). K. F. Bosl, "Kingdom and Principality in Twelfth-Century France," and the same author's "'Noble Unfreedom': The Rise of the Ministerials in Germany," in T. Reuter, ed., *The Medieval Nobility: Studies on the Ruling Classes of France and Germany from the Sixth to the Twelfth Century* (1978), are also useful. The career of the man described by contemporaries as "the greatest of knights" is celebrated in G. Duby, *William Marshal: The Flowering of Chivalry,* trans. R. Howard (1985), a rags-to-riches story.

There is no dearth of good material on the monks in medieval society. The titles listed in the Suggested Reading for Chapter 7 represent a good starting point for study. B. D. Hill's articles "Benedictines" and "Cistercian Order," in J. R. Strayer, ed., *Dictionary of the Middle Ages,* vols. 2 and 3 (1982 and 1983), provide broad surveys of the premier monastic orders and contain useful bibliographies. B. Harvey, *Living and Dying in England: The Monastic Experience, 1100–1540* (1993), has valuable material on monastic diet, clothing, routine, sickness, and death. L. J. Lekai, *The Cistercians: Ideals and Reality* (1977), synthesizes research on the white monks and carries their story down to the twentieth century. P. D. Johnson, *Prayer, Patronage, and Power: The Abbey of La Trinité, Vendome, 1032–1187* (1981), examines one important French monastery in its social environment; this book is a valuable contribution to medieval local history. For a sound study of a uniquely English monastic order, see B. Golding, *Gilbert of Sempringham and the Gilbertine Order, c. 1130–1300* (1995). J. Burton, *Monastic and Religious Orders in Britain, 1000–1300* (1995), treats many often neglected issues. B. P. McGuire, *Friendship and Community: The Monastic Experience, 350–1250* (1988), explores monastic friendships within the context of religious communities. Both W. Braunfels, *Monasteries of Western Europe: The Architecture of the Orders* (1972), and C. Brooke, *The Monastic World* (1974), have splendid illustrations and good bibliographies. The best study of medieval English Cistercian architecture is P. Fergusson, *Architecture of Solitude: Cistercian Abbeys in Twelfth Century England* (1984).

For women and children, in addition to the titles by Labarge and Boswell cited in the Notes, see Hanawalt, *Growing Up in Medieval London: The Experience of Childhood in History* (1993), which has exciting material on class and gender, apprenticeship, and the culture of matrimony; D. Herlihy, *Medieval Households* (1985), which treats marriage patterns, family size, sexual relations, and emotional life; and C. Brooke, *The Medieval Idea of Marriage* (1991), which draws on a wide variety of evidence to answer his question, "What is marriage and what sets it apart from other human relationships?" J. M. Bennett, *Women in the Medieval English Countryside* (1987), is an important and pioneering study of women in rural, preindustrial society. Also useful are A. Macfarlane, *Marriage and Love in England, 1300–1840* (1987); J. McNamara and S. F. Wemple, "Sanctity and Power: The Dual Pursuit of Medieval Women," in *Becoming Visible: Women in European History,* ed. R. Bridenthal and C. Koonz (1987); B. Hanawalt, ed., *Women and Work in Preindustrial Europe* (1986), which describes the activities of women as alewives, midwives, businesswomen, nurses, and servants; and D. Baker, ed., *Medieval Women* (1978), which contains articles on many facets of women's history.

For further treatment of nuns, see J. K. McNamara, *Sisters in Arms* (1996), a broad survey tracing the lives of religious women from the mothers of the Egyptian desert to the twentieth century; and M. Schmitt and L. Kulzer, eds., *Medieval Women Monastics: Wisdom's Wellsprings* (1996), which focuses on women mystics. In addition to the titles by Lekai cited earlier, see B. Newman, *Sister of Wisdom: St. Hildegard's Theology of the Feminine* (1987), a learned and lucidly written study; S. Elkins, *Holy Women in Twelfth-Century England* (1985); C. Bynum, *Jesus as Mother: Studies in the Spirituality of the High Middle Ages* (1984), which contains valuable articles on facets of women's religious history and an excellent contrast of the differing spirituality of monks and nuns; and C. Bynum, *Holy Feast and Holy Fast* (1987), which treats the significance of food for nuns and others in medieval society. For health and medical care, B. Rowland, *Medieval Woman's Guide to Health* (1981), makes very interesting reading.

LISTENING TO THE PAST

From Merchant to Monk

Godric of Finchdale (1069?–1170) was born a serf on a manor in Norfolk, England. He fled the manor, got a financial start peddling small goods throughout Lincolnshire, and then became a sea merchant trading bulk goods to Flanders, Denmark, Scotland, and England. His business brought him considerable wealth, along with a reputation for dishonest business methods. Around 1105, after pilgrimages to Saint James at Compostela (see Map 9.3 on page 292), Jerusalem, and Rome, Godric sold his business and disposed of all his wealth. He resolved to become a hermit and eventually settled in a hut at Finchdale near Durham (northern England), doing penance for his sexual sins as a sailor and his dishonesty as a merchant. His holiness and prophetic gifts attracted many people, and public opinion acclaimed him a saint. The excerpt below comes from a contemporary biography.

When the boy had passed his childless years quietly at home, then, as he began to grow to manhood, he began to follow more prudent ways of life, and to learn carefully and persistently the teachings of worldly forethought. Wherefore he chose not to follow the life of a husbandman [farmer] but rather to study, learn, and exercise the rudiments of more subtle conceptions. For this reason, aspiring to the merchant's trade, he began to follow the chapman's [peddler] way of life, first learning how to gain in small bargains and things of insignificant price; and thence, while yet a youth, his mind advanced little by little to buy and sell and gain from things of greater expense. For, in his beginnings, he was wont to wander with small wares around the villages and farmsteads of his own neighbourhood; but, in process of time, he gradually associated himself by compact with city merchants. Hence, within a brief space of time, the youth who had trudged for many weary hours from village to village, from farm to farm, did so profit by his increase of age and wisdom as to travel with associates of his own age through towns and boroughs, fortresses and cities, to fairs and to all the various booths of the market-place, in pursuit of his public chaffer [bargaining]. He went along the highway, neither puffed up by the good testimony of his conscience nor downcast in the nobler part of his soul by the reproach of poverty. . . .

Yet in all things he walked with simplicity; and, in so far as he yet knew how, it was ever his pleasure to follow in the footsteps of the truth. For, having learned the Lord's Prayer and the Creed from his very cradle, he oftentimes turned them over in his mind, even as he went alone on his longer journeys; and, in so far as the truth was revealed to his mind, he clung thereunto most devoutly in all his thoughts concerning God. At first, he lived as a chapman [peddler] for four years in Lincolnshire, going on foot and carrying the smallest wares; then he travelled abroad, first to St. Andrews in Scotland and then for the first time to Rome. On his return, having formed a familiar friendship with certain other young men who were eager for merchandise, he began to launch upon bolder courses and to coast frequently by sea to the foreign lands that lay around him. Thus, sailing often to and fro between Scotland and Britain, he traded in many divers wares and, amid these occupations, learned much worldly wisdom. . . .

Then he purchased the half of a merchant-ship with certain of his partners in the trade; and again by his prudence he bought the fourth part of another ship. At length, by his skill in navigation, wherein he excelled all his fellows, he earned promotion to the post of steersman. . . .

For he was vigorous and strenuous in mind, whole of limb and strong in body. He was of middle stature, broad-shouldered and deep-chested, with a long face, grey eyes most clear and piercing, bushy brows, a broad forehead, long and open nostrils, a nose of comely curve, and a pointed chin. His beard was thick, and longer than the ordinary, his mouth well-shaped, with lips of moderate thickness; in youth his hair was black, in age as white as snow; his neck was short and thick, knotted with veins and sinews; his legs were somewhat slender, his instep high, his knees hardened and horny with frequent kneeling; his whole skin rough beyond the ordinary, until all this roughness was softened by old age. . . .

And now he had lived sixteen years as a merchant, and began to think of spending on charity, to God's honour and service, the goods which he had so laboriously acquired. He therefore took the cross as a pilgrim to Jerusalem, and having visited the Holy Sepulchre, came back to England by way of St. James [of Compostela]. Not long afterwards he became steward to a certain rich man of his own country, with the care of his whole house and household. But certain of the younger household were men of iniquity, who stole their neighbours' cattle and thus held luxurious feasts, whereas Godric, in his ignorance, was sometimes present. Afterwards, discovering the truth, he rebuked and admonished them to cease; but they made no account of his warnings; wherefore he concealed not their iniquity, but disclosed it to the lord of the household, who, however, slighted his advice. Wherefore he begged to be dismissed and went on a pilgrimage, first to St. Gilles and thence to Rome the abode of the Apostles, that thus he might knowingly pay the penalty for those misdeeds wherein he had ignorantly partaken. I have often seen him, even in his old age, weeping for this unknowing transgression. . . .

Godric, when he had restored his mother safe to his father's arms, abode but a brief while at home; for he was now already firmly purposed to give himself entirely to God's service. Wherefore, that he might follow Christ the more freely, he sold all his possessions and distributed them among the poor. Then, telling his parents of this purpose and receiving their blessing, he went forth to no certain abode, but whithersoever the Lord should deign to lead him; for above all things he coveted the life of a hermit.

✣ Godric of Finchdale got his business start carrying small goods and trinkets in a shoulder pack as he walked from place to place exchanging his wares for others in a barter economy. *(Royal Commission on the Historical Monuments of England, © Crown copyright)*

Questions for Analysis

1. How would you characterize Godric's life? To what social category did he belong?
2. What does his career tell us about the tripartite view of society expressed in monastic writings?
3. What values do Godric's life and career reveal?

Source: Reginald of Durham, "Life of Godric of Finchdale," in *Social Life in Britain from the Conquest to the Reformation,* ed. G. G. Coulton (Cambridge: Cambridge University Press, 1918), pp. 415–420.

CHAPTER

11 The Creativity and Vitality of the High Middle Ages

Students in a lecture, University of Bologna. Detail of the Tomb of Giovanni de Legnano, 14th century. *(Scala/Art Resource, NY)*

The High Middle Ages witnessed some of the most remarkable achievements in the entire history of Western society. Europeans displayed tremendous creativity and vitality in many facets of culture. Political rulers tried to establish contact with all their peoples, developed new legal and financial institutions, and slowly consolidated power in the hands of the monarchy. The kings of France and England succeeded in laying the foundations of modern national states. The German emperors achieved a reduction of violence and disorder through alliances with the princes. The European economy underwent a remarkable recovery, as evidenced by the growth and development of towns and the revival of long-distance trade. Some towns and urbanized areas saw the growth of heretical movements. The university, a uniquely Western contribution to civilization and a superb expression of medieval creativity, came into being at the same time. The Gothic cathedral manifested medieval people's deep Christian faith and their appreciation for the worlds of nature, humanity, and God.

- How did medieval rulers in England, France, and Germany work to solve their problems of government, thereby laying the foundations of the modern state?
- How did medieval towns originate, and how do they reveal the beginnings of radical change in medieval society?
- Why did towns become the center of religious heresy, and what was the church's response?
- How did universities evolve, and what needs of medieval society did they serve?
- What do the Gothic cathedral and troubadour poetry reveal about the ideals, attitudes, and interests of medieval people?

This chapter will focus on these questions.

Medieval Origins of the Modern State

Rome's great legacy to Western civilization had been the concepts of the state and the law, but for almost five hundred years after the disintegration of the Roman Empire in the West, the state as a reality did not exist. Political authority was completely decentralized. Power was spread among many lords, who gave their localities such protection and security as their strength allowed. The fiefdoms, kingdoms, and territories that covered the continent of early medieval Europe did not have the characteristics or provide the services of a modern state. They did not have jurisdiction over many people, and their laws affected a relative few. There existed many frequently overlapping layers of authority—earls, counts, barons, knights—between a king and the ordinary people.

In these circumstances, medieval rulers had common goals. The rulers of England, France, and Germany wanted to strengthen and extend royal authority within their territories. They wanted to establish an effective means of communication with all peoples, in order to increase public order. They wanted more revenue and efficient bureaucracies. The solutions they found to these problems laid the foundations for modern national states.

The modern state is an organized territory with definite geographical boundaries that are recognized by other states. It has a body of law and institutions of government. If the state claims to govern according to law, it is guided in its actions by the law. The modern national state counts on the loyalty of its citizens, or at least of a majority of them. In return, it provides order so that citizens can go about their daily work and other activities. It protects its citizens in their persons and property. The state tries to prevent violence and to apprehend and punish those who commit it. It supplies a currency or medium of exchange that permits financial and commercial transactions. The state conducts relations with foreign governments. In order to accomplish even these minimal functions, the state must have officials, bureaucracies, laws, courts of law, soldiers, information, and money. By the twelfth century, medieval kingdoms and some lesser lordships possessed these attributes, at least to the extent that most modern states have them.[1]

Unification and Communication

Political developments in England, France, and Germany provide good examples of the beginnings of the national state in the High Middle Ages. These developments took a different course in southern Europe. In

Italy independent city-states evolved. In Spain the reconquest of the peninsula, which was under Muslim control, preoccupied the rulers of the Christian kingdoms. Spain and Italy will be discussed in Chapter 13. England, France, and Germany are discussed here.

Under the pressure of the Danish (or Viking) invasions of the ninth and tenth centuries, the seven kingdoms of Anglo-Saxon England united under one king (see page 274). At the same time, England was divided into local units called "shires," or counties, each under the jurisdiction of a sheriff appointed by the king. The Danish king Canute (r. 1016–1035) and his successor, Edward the Confessor (r. 1042–1066), exercised broader authority than any contemporary ruler on the continent. All the English *thegns,* or local chieftains, recognized the central authority of the kingship. The kingdom of England, therefore, had a political head start on the rest of Europe.

When Edward the Confessor died, his cousin Duke William of Normandy—known in English history as William the Conqueror—claimed the English throne and in 1066 defeated the Anglo-Saxon claimant on the battlefield of Hastings. Pre-Conquest Normandy, with clearly defined frontiers marked by rivers, with uniform legal customs, and with strong ducal government, possessed a political coherence and autonomy "unmatched elsewhere in feudal Europe."[2] Normandy already showed attributes of a modern state. As William subdued the rest of England, he distributed lands to his Norman followers and assigned specific military quotas to each estate. He also required all feudal lords to swear an oath of allegiance to him as king.

William the Conqueror (r. 1066–1087) preserved the Anglo-Saxon institution of sheriffs representing the king at the local level but replaced Anglo-Saxon sheriffs with Normans. A sheriff had heavy duties. He maintained order in the shire. He caught criminals and had them tried in the hundred court, over which his deputy, the undersheriff, presided. He collected taxes and, when the king ordered him to do so, raised an army of foot soldiers. Continuing an Anglo-Saxon practice, the sheriff also organized adult males in groups of ten, with each member liable for the good behavior of the others. The Conqueror thus made local people responsible for order in their communities. For all his efforts, the sheriff received no pay. This system, whereby unpaid officials governed the county, served as the basic pattern of English local government for many centuries. It cost the Crown nothing, but it restricted opportunities for public service to the well-to-do.

William also retained another Anglo-Saxon device, the *writ.* This brief administrative order, written in the vernacular (Anglo-Saxon) by a government clerk, was the means by which the central government communicated with people at the local level. Sheriffs were empowered to issue writs relating to matters in their counties.

The Conqueror introduced into England a major innovation, the Norman inquest. At his Christmas court in 1085, William discussed the state of the kingdom with his vassals and decided to conduct a systematic investigation of the entire country. The survey was to be made by means of *inquests,* or general inquiries, held throughout England. William wanted to determine how much wealth there was in his new kingdom, who held what land, and what land had been disputed among his vassals since the Conquest of 1066. Groups of royal officials or judges were sent to every part of the country. In every village and farm, the priest and six local people were put under oath to answer the questions of the king's commissioners truthfully. In the words of a contemporary chronicler:

He sent his men over all England into every shire and had them find out how many hundred hides there were in the shire [a hide was a measure of land large enough to support one family], or what land and cattle the king himself had, or what dues he ought to have in twelve months from the shire. Also . . . what or how much everybody had who was occupying land in England, in land or cattle, and how much money it was worth. So very narrowly did he have it investigated, that there was no single hide nor yard of land, nor indeed . . . one ox nor one cow nor one pig was there left out, and not put down in his record: and all these records were brought to him afterwards.[3]

The resulting record, called *Domesday Book* from the Anglo-Saxon word *doom* meaning "judgment," still survives. It is an invaluable source of social and economic information about medieval England (Map 11.1).

The Conqueror's scribes compiled *Domesday Book* in less than a year. *Domesday Book,* a unique document, provided William and his descendants with information vital for the exploitation and government of the country. Knowing the amount of wealth every area possessed, the king could tax accordingly. Knowing the amount of land his vassals had, he could allot knight service fairly. The inclusion of material covering England helped English kings to regard their country as one unit.

In 1128 the Conqueror's granddaughter Matilda was married to Geoffrey of Anjou. Their son, who became Henry II of England and inaugurated the Angevin (from Anjou, his father's county) dynasty, inherited the

The Bayeux Tapestry Measuring 231 feet by 19½ inches, the Bayeux Tapestry gives a narrative description of the events surrounding the Norman Conquest of England. The tapestry provides an important historical source for the clothing, armor, and lifestyles of the Norman and Anglo-Saxon warrior class. *(Tapisserie de Bayeux et avec autorisation spéciale de la Ville de Bayeux)*

French provinces of Normandy, Anjou, Maine, and Touraine in northwestern France. When Henry married the great heiress Eleanor of Aquitaine in 1152, he claimed lordships over Aquitaine, Poitou, and Gascony in southwestern France (Map 11.2). Each of these provinces had a separate administration made up of men native to the region; the provinces constituted a loose conglomeration of client territories linked together by dynastic law and personal oaths. There was no unity among them.[4] But the histories of England and France in the High Middle Ages were closely intertwined, leading to disputes and conflicts down to the fifteenth century.

In the early twelfth century, France consisted of a number of virtually independent provinces. Each was governed by its local ruler; each had its own laws and customs, coinage, and dialect. Unlike the king of England, the king of France had jurisdiction over a very small area. Chroniclers called King Louis VI (r. 1108–1137) *roi de Saint-Denis,* king of Saint-Denis, because the territory he controlled was limited to Paris and the Saint-Denis area surrounding the city (see Map 11.2). This region, called the *Île-de-France,* or royal domain, became the nucleus of the French state. The clear goal of the medieval French king was to increase the royal domain and extend his authority.

The term *Saint-Denis* had political and religious charisma, which the Crown exploited. Following the precedent of the Frankish chieftain Clovis (see page 218), Louis VI and his Capetian successors strongly supported and identified with the cult of Saint Denis, a deeply revered saint whom the French believed protected the country from danger. Under Saint Denis's banner, the oriflamme, French kings fought their battles and claimed their victories. The oriflamme rested in the abbey of Saint-Denis, which was richly endowed by the Crown and served as the burial place of the French kings. The Capetian kings identified themselves with the cult of Saint Denis in order to tap popular devotion to him and tie that devotion and loyalty to the monarchy.[5]

The work of unifying France began under Louis VI's grandson Philip II (r. 1180–1223). Rigord, Philip's biographer, gave him the title "Augustus" (from a Latin word meaning "to increase") because he vastly enlarged the territory of the kingdom of France. By defeating a baronial plot against the Crown, Philip Augustus acquired the northern counties of Artois and Vermandois.

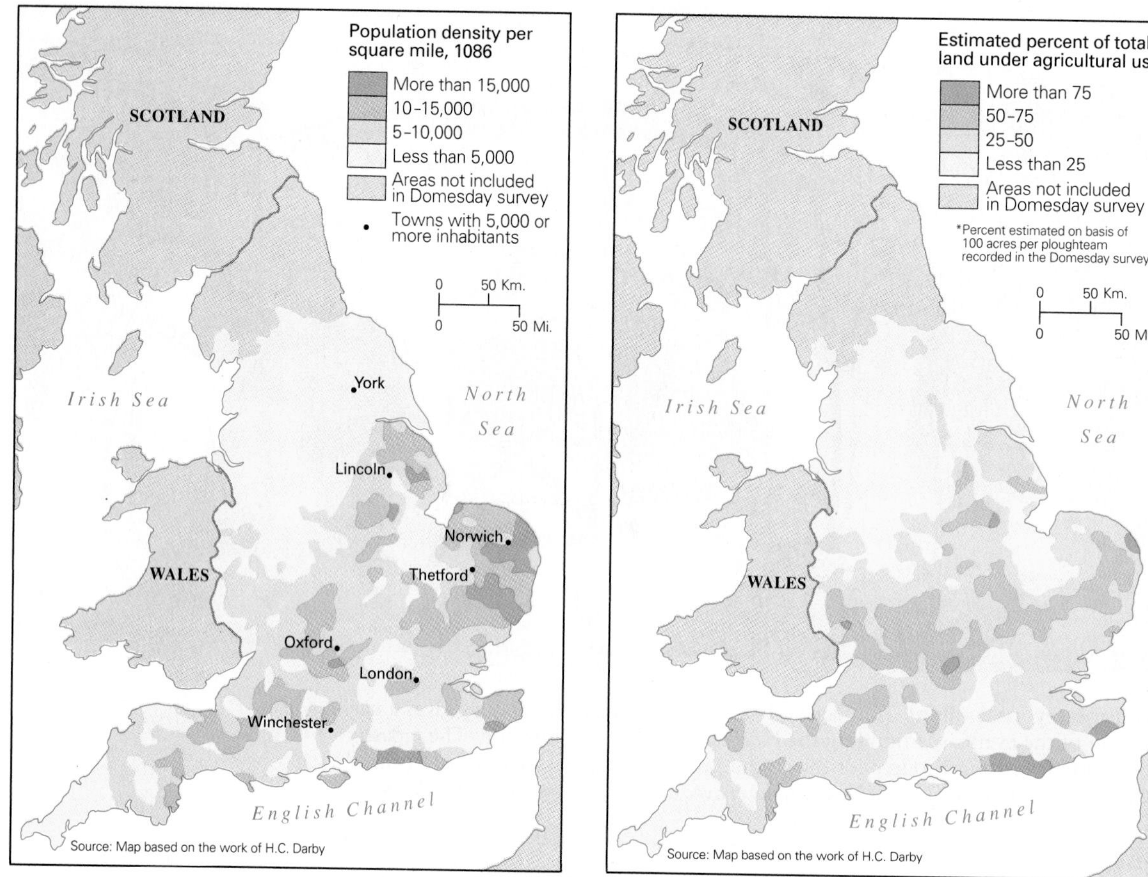

MAP 11.1 Domesday Population and Agriculture, 1086 The incomparably rich evidence of *Domesday Book* enables modern demographers and historians to calculate the English population and land under cultivation in the eleventh century.

When King John of England, who was Philip's vassal for the rich province of Normandy, defaulted on his feudal obligation to come to the French court, Philip declared Normandy forfeit to the French crown. He enforced his declaration militarily, and in 1204 Normandy fell to the French. Within two years Philip also gained the farmlands of Maine, Touraine, and Anjou. By the end of his reign Philip was effectively master of northern France.

In the thirteenth century, Philip Augustus's descendants acquired important holdings in the south. Louis VIII (r. 1223–1226) added the county of Poitou to the kingdom of France by war. Louis IX (r. 1226–1270) gained a vital interest in the Mediterranean province of Provence through his marriage to Margaret of Provence. Louis's son Philip III (r. 1270–1285) secured Languedoc through inheritance. By the end of the thirteenth century, most of the provinces of modern France had been added to the royal domain through diplomacy, marriage, war, and inheritance. The king of France was stronger than any group of nobles who might try to challenge his authority.

Philip Augustus devised a method of governing the provinces and providing for communication between the central government in Paris and local communities. Philip decided that each province would retain its own institutions and laws. But royal agents, called *baillis* in the north and *seneschals* in the south, were sent from Paris into the provinces as the king's official representatives with authority to act for him. Often middle-class lawyers, these men possessed full judicial, financial, and military jurisdiction in their districts. The baillis and seneschals were appointed by, paid by, and responsible to the king. Unlike the English sheriffs, they were never natives of the provinces to which they were assigned, and they could not own land there. This policy reflected the fundamental principle of French administration that royal interests superseded local interests.

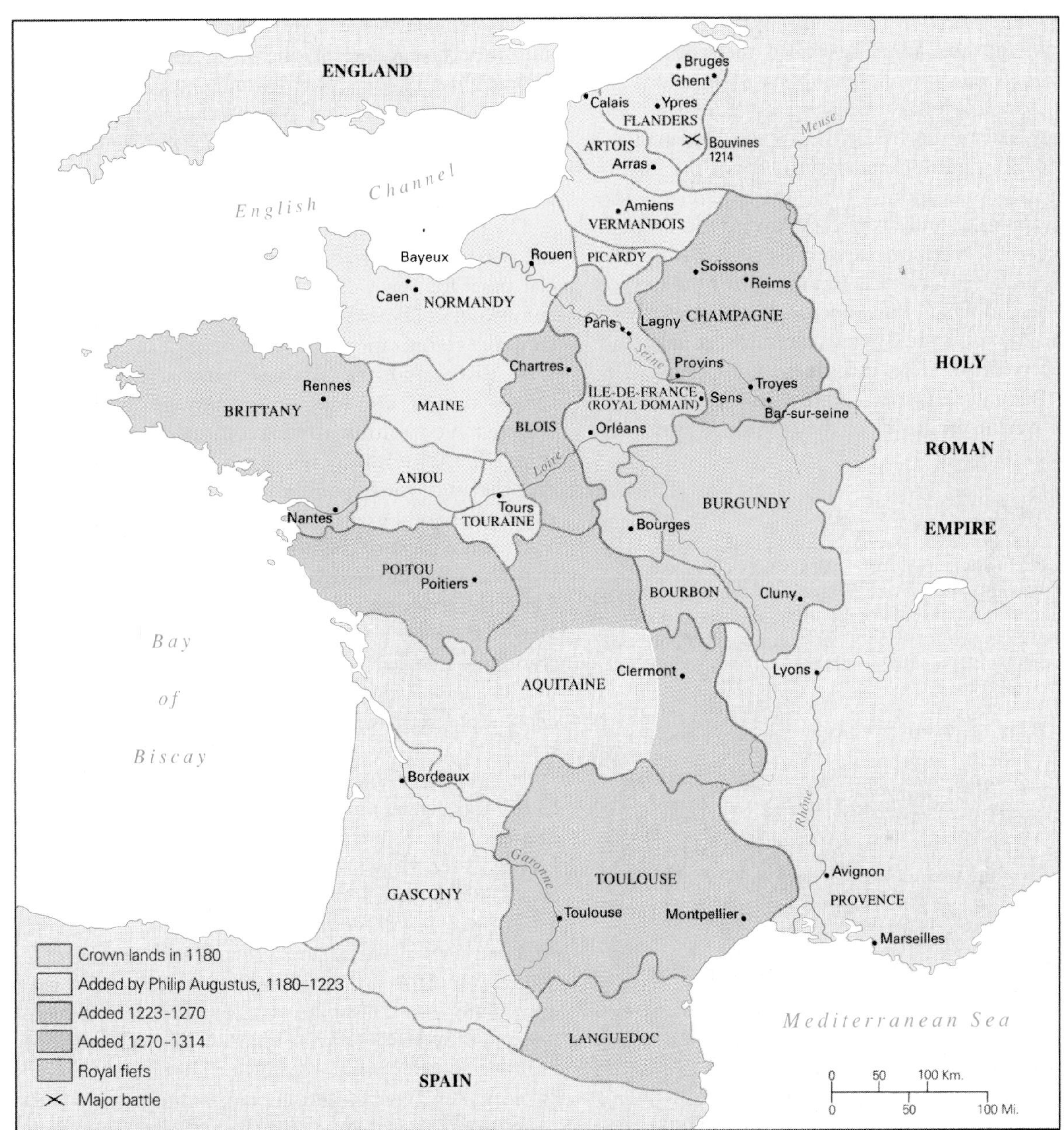

MAP 11.2 The Growth of the Kingdom of France Some scholars believe that Philip II received the title "Augustus" (from a Latin word meaning "to increase") because he vastly expanded the territories of the kingdom of France.

In the High Middle Ages, the political and institutional history of Germany evolved in a course different from that of France and England. Those western countries witnessed the beginnings of the nation-state, while Germany experienced the development of *territorial lordship.* In the period from about 1050 to about 1400 and down to 1871, German history is regional history. Why did Germany move in the direction of multiple independent principalities? What were the relations between the princes and the German monarchy?

As large entities, the German duchies such as Bavaria, Saxony, Swabia, Thuringia, and Lotharingia emerged from the East Frankish kingdom (see Chapter 8) in the tenth century as defensive units against Magyar and

Slavic invaders. The four great archbishoprics—Mainz, Trier, Cologne, and Salzburg—trace their origins to Charlemagne's reign, while Hamburg-Bremen was established for missionary work in Scandinavia, and Magdeburg was set up by Otto I for the Christianization of the Slavs. Although the authority of the imperial crown increased under Otto I, his empire was too vast geographically, and his resources were too limited, to be governable from one center. To hold it together, a kind of confederacy (a weak union of strong states, or principalities) in which the emperor shared power with the princes, dukes, archbishops, margraves, counts, and bishops developed. The investiture controversy between the German emperor and the Roman papacy solidified power in the hands of the territorial lords (see page 282).

Frederick Barbarossa A thirteenth-century chronicler portrayed the German emperor in classical Roman garb, but with the sign of the Crusader on his chest and shield. His left hand holds an orb, symbol of his (theoretically) universal sovereignty, while a tonsured monk holds up the Scriptures. *(Biblioteca Apostolica Vaticana)*

Between 1000 and 1300, regionally based princely authority emerged in the duchies as dynasties that had a strong sense of local identity and traced their descent through the paternal line. Newly constructed stone castles bearing the family name symbolized the dynasty's power and served as the center of its lands and rights—that is, its *Landesherrschaft,* or territorial lordship.

The enormous expansion of the German economy in the twelfth and thirteenth centuries supplied the financial basis for the wealth and power of the princes as landowners. The exploitation of vast tracts of forestland, the colonization and settlement of land east of the Elbe River, and the establishment of new markets, towns, manors, and monasteries brought local princes considerable wealth with which to maintain their lordships. The Wittelsbach dynasty in the duchy of Bavaria and the Ludowing family in the landgraviate of Thuringia are typical examples of territorial lordships.[6]

Through most of the first half of the twelfth century, civil war wracked Germany. When Conrad III died in 1152, the resulting anarchy was so terrible that the *electors*—the seven princes responsible for choosing the emperor—decided that the only alternative to continued chaos was the selection of a strong ruler. They chose Frederick Barbarossa of the house of Hohenstaufen.

Frederick Barbarossa (r. 1152–1190) tried valiantly to bring peace to the empire. Just as the French rulers branched out from their compact domain in the Île-de-France, Frederick tried to use his family duchy of Swabia in southwestern Germany as a power base (Map 11.3). Just as William the Conqueror had done, Frederick required all vassals in Swabia to take an oath of allegiance to him as emperor, no matter who their immediate lord might be. He appointed ministerials (see page 316) to exercise the full imperial authority over the administrative districts of Swabia. Ministerials linked the emperor and local communities.

To promote peace and increase order, the monarchy itself supported princely territorial power and jurisdiction. From Carolingian times, regional wars and feuds among lords represented a traditional feature of German aristocratic society. In 1158 Frederick Barbarossa forbade private warfare and ordered severe penalties for violations of the peace. But imperial orders alone did

MAP 11.3 The Holy Roman Empire, ca 1200 Frederick Barbarossa tried to use the feudal bond to tie the different provinces to the imperial monarchy.

0 100 200 300 Km.
0 100 200 300 Mi.
Lübeck
HOLSTEIN
POMERANIA
Bremen
BRANDENBURG
FRISIA
Brandenburg
SAXONY
POLAND
LUSATIA
Goslar
LOWER LORRAINE
Cologne
THURINGIA
MEISSEN
Aix-la-Chapelle
FRANCONIA
Prague
Mainz
Trier
BOHEMIA
MORAVIA
Worms
Verdun
UPPER LORRAINE
AUSTRIA
Toul
Augsburg
BAVARIA
SWABIA
Salzburg
FRANCE
STYRIA
Besançon
CARINTHIA
HUNGARY
CARNIOLA
VERONA
BURGUNDY-ARLES
Legnano 1176
Milan
Venice
LOMBARDY
Pavia
REPUBLIC OF VENICE
Roncaglia
Avignon
Florence
Arles
PAPAL STATES
TUSCANY
Marseilles
CORSICA
Rome
Capua
APULIA
Naples
Salerno
SARDINIA
KINGDOM OF SICILY
Major battle
Holy Roman Empire, ca 1200
Kingdom of Sicily
Republic of Venice
Messina
Palermo
SICILY

not bring peace. In 1179 he announced, "Out of duty to the imperial office, we are held of necessity and by the state of the provinces to ordain peace throughout our Empire and to confirm the ordinance by our authority." His solution was *Landfrieden,* sworn peace associations with the princes of various regions. In 1179 Landfrieden were issued for Franconia, and in 1223 Landfrieden were reissued for Saxony. They had already been established in the dioceses of Cologne and Bamberg. These peace associations had the judicial authority to punish breaches of the peace and criminals. Penalties for serious crimes, such as incendiary conduct during a conflict, increased from maiming to execution. German kings traveled continually and extensively, and the royal court could mete out justice anywhere. The presence of the royal court in an area temporarily superseded local jurisdiction, but in practice legal jurisdiction in the German Empire "meant the courts of counts, dukes, margraves, bishops and ecclesiastical advocates for serious cases and seigneurial or manorial courts for lesser misdemeanors." German monarchs regarded the local authority of the princes as traditional, legitimate, and essentially to the Crown's own benefit. As the emperor Frederick II put it in 1232,

The sublime throne of our Empire is exalted, and the governing powers of the Empire we dispose in full justice and peace, when we look ahead with due provisions for the rights of our princes and magnates in whom, as the head rests upon honorable limbs, our imperial rule is invigorated and strengthened, for the edifice of Caesar's magnitude so far directs and elevates those upon whose shoulders it is founded and carried.[7]

In the eleventh and twelfth centuries, the northern Italian cities had grown rich on trade, and Frederick Barbarossa wanted to cash in on Italian wealth. Frederick saw that, although the Italian cities were populous and militarily strong, they lacked stable governments and were often involved in struggles with one another.

Between 1154 and 1188, Frederick made six expeditions into Italy. His scorched-earth policy was successful at first, making for significant conquests in the north. The brutality of his methods, however, provoked revolts, and the Italian cities formed an alliance with the papacy. In 1176 Frederick suffered a defeat at Legnano (see Map 11.3). This battle marked the first time a feudal cavalry of armed knights was decisively defeated by bourgeois infantrymen. Frederick was forced to recognize the municipal autonomy of the northern Italian cities. Germany and Italy remained separate and followed separate courses of development.

Finance

As medieval rulers expanded territories and extended authority, they required more officials, larger armies, and more money. Officials and armies had to be paid, and kings had to find ways to raise revenue.

In England William the Conqueror's son Henry I (r. 1100–1135) established a bureau of finance called the "Exchequer" (for the checkered cloth at which his officials collected and audited royal accounts). Henry's income came from a variety of sources: from taxes paid by peasants living on the king's estates; from the *Danegeld,* an old tax originally levied to pay tribute to the Danes; from the *dona,* an annual gift from the church; from money paid to the Crown for settling disputes; and from fines paid by people found guilty of crimes. Henry also received income because of his position as feudal lord. If, for example, one of his vassals died and the son wished to inherit the father's properties, the heir had to pay Henry a tax called *relief.* From the knights Henry took *scutage,* money paid in lieu of the performance of military service. With the scutage collected, Henry could hire mercenary troops. The sheriff in each county was responsible for collecting all these sums and paying them twice a year to the king's Exchequer. Henry, like other medieval kings, made no distinction between his private income and state revenues.

An accurate record of expenditures and income is needed to ensure a state's solvency. Henry assigned a few of the barons and bishops at his court to keep careful records of the monies paid into and out of the royal treasury. These financial officials, called "barons of the Exchequer," gradually developed a professional organization with its own rules, procedures, and esprit de corps. The Exchequer, which by 1170 sat at Westminster, became the first institution of the governmental bureaucracy of England. Because of its work, an almost complete series of financial records for England dating back to 1130 survives; after 1154 the series is complete.

The development of royal financial agencies in most continental countries lagged behind the English Exchequer. Twelfth-century French rulers derived their income from their royal estates in the Île-de-France. As Philip Augustus and his successors added provinces to the royal domain, the need for money became increasingly acute. Philip made the baillis and seneschals responsible for collecting taxes in their districts. This income came primarily from fines and confiscations imposed by the courts. Three times a year the baillis and seneschals reported to the king's court with the money they had collected.

Limoges Casket The principal city of the Limousin in west central France, Limoges was famous for the superb work of its enamelers and goldsmiths. This casket, or chest, showing Thomas Becket's execution (lower panel) and burial (upper panel) was used to preserve his relics. The two scenes are done on gilded copper plaques nailed over wood. *(British Rail Pension Fund)*

ries from France and also strengthened the barons' opposition to John. On top of his heavy taxation, his ineptitude as a soldier in a society that idealized military glory was the final straw. Rebellion begun by northern barons eventually grew to involve many of the English nobility, including the archbishop of Canterbury and the earl of Pembroke, the leading ecclesiastical and lay peers. After lengthy negotiations, John met the barons at Runnymede, a meadow along the Thames River. There he was forced to approve and to attach his seal to the peace treaty called Magna Carta, "Magna" (great or large) simply because it was so long and detailed.

For contemporaries, Magna Carta was intended to redress the greviances that particular groups—the barons, the clergy, the merchants of London—had against King John. Charters were not unusual: many kings and lords at the time issued them. But because every English king between 1215 and 1485, as evidence of his promise to observe the law, reissued Magna Carta, this charter alone acquired enduring importance. It came to signify the principle that everyone, including the king and the government, must obey the law. As the royal justice Henry of Bracton (d. 1268) put it, the English shall be *"Non sub homine sed sub Deo et lege"* (Not under man but under God and the law), a motto that appears over the Harvard Law School. Drawn up to protect baronial interests, the document was used in later centuries to protect the interests of widows, orphans, townspeople, free men, and the church. Some clauses contain the germ of the ideas of due process of law and of the right to a fair and speedy trial. Because later generations referred to Magna Carta as a written statement of English liberties, it gradually came to have an almost sacred importance as a guarantee of law and justice.

In the thirteenth century, the judicial precedents set under Henry II slowly evolved into permanent institutions. The king's judges asserted the royal authority and applied the same principles everywhere in the country. English people found the king's justice more rational and evenhanded than the justice meted out in the baronial courts. Respect for the king's law and courts promoted loyalty to the Crown. By the time of Henry's great-grandson Edward I (r. 1272–1307), one law, the common law, operated all over England.

In the German empire of the thirteenth century, justice was administered at two levels. The manorial or seigneurial court, presided over by the lay or ecclesiastical lord, dealt with matters such as damage to crops and fields, trespass, boundary disputes, and debt—common conflicts at a time when princes were expanding their colonial jurisdictions over forestland and wasteland and receiving thousands of new settlers. Dukes, counts, margraves, bishops, and abbots possessed an authority called *Landgericht,* or regional magistracies. With this power, the lord's agents, or representatives, dispensed justice in serious criminal cases involving theft, arson, assault with a weapon, rape, and homicide. Regional magistrates held powers of high justice, that is, the right to execute a criminal; the imposition of the death penalty by hanging was the distinctive feature of this court. In the early Middle Ages, society perceived of major crimes as acts against an individual, and they were settled by the accused making a cash payment to the victim or his or her kindred. In the later Middle Ages, suspects were pursued and punished for acting against the *public* interest. Punishments varied from province to province, but almost everywhere the German ruling aristocracy made a concerted effort to punish violent crimes. One-third of all fines imposed went to the lord.[9]

In the later Middle Ages, the English common law developed features that differed strikingly from the system of Roman law operative in continental Europe. The common law relied on precedents: a decision in an important case served as an authority for deciding similar cases. By contrast, continental judges, trained in Roman law, used the fixed legal maxims of the Justinian *Code* (see page 226) to decide their cases. Thus the common-law system evolved according to the changing experience of the people, while the Roman-law tradition tended toward a more rigid or static approach. In countries influenced by the common law, such as Canada and the United States, the court is open to the public; in countries with Roman-law traditions, such as France and the Latin American nations, courts need not be public. Under the common law, people accused in criminal cases have a right to access to the evidence against them; under the other system, they need not. The common law urges judges to be impartial; in the Roman-law system, judges interfere freely in activities in their courtrooms. Finally, whereas torture is foreign to the common-law tradition, it was once widely used in the Roman legal system as a method of securing evidence or proof.

The extension of law and justice led to a phenomenal amount of legal codification all over Europe. The English judge Henry of Bracton wrote the *Treatise on the Laws and Customs of England;* the French jurist Philippe de Beaumanoir (1250–1296) produced the *Customs of Beaumanoir;* the German scholar Eike von Repgow compiled the *Sachsenspiegel* (ca 1225); and Pope Gregory IX (1227–1241) published a codification of ecclesiastical law, the *Liber extra,* the main source of canon law until 1917. Legal texts and encyclopedias exalted royal authority, consolidated royal power, and emphasized political and social uniformity. The pressure for social conformity in turn contributed to a rising hostility toward minorities, Jews, and homosexuals.

By the late eleventh century, many towns in western Europe had small Jewish populations. Jews had emigrated in post-Roman times from the large cities of the Mediterranean region to France, the Rhineland, and Britain. (See the feature "Individuals in Society: The Jews of Speyer" on page 285.) The laws of most countries forbade Jews to own land, though they could hold land pledged to them for debts. By the twelfth century, many Jews were usurers: they lent to consumers but primarily to new or growing business enterprises. New towns and underdeveloped areas where cash was scarce welcomed Jewish settlers. Like other business people, the Jews preferred to live near their work; they also settled close to their synagogue or school. Thus originated the Jews' street or quarter or ghetto. Such neighborhoods gradually became legally defined sections where Jews were required to live.

Jews had been generally tolerated and had become important parts of the urban economies through trade and finance. Some Jews had risen to positions of power and prominence. Through the twelfth century, for example, Jews managed the papal household. The later twelfth and entire thirteenth centuries, however, witnessed increasingly ugly anti-Semitism. Why? Present scholarship does not provide completely satisfactory answers, but we have some clues. Shifting agricultural and economic patterns aggravated social tensions. The indebtedness of peasants and nobles to Jews in an increasingly cash-based economy; the xenophobia that accompanied and followed the Crusades; Christian merchants' and financiers' resentment of Jewish business competition; the spread of vicious accusations of ritual murders or sacrileges against Christian property and persons; royal and papal legislation aimed at social conformity—these factors all contributed to rising anti-Semitism. Thus, from 1180 to 1182, Philip Augustus of France used hostility to Jews as an excuse to imprison them and then to demand heavy ransom for their release. The Fourth Lateran Council of 1215 forbade Jews to hold public office, restricted their financial activities, and required them to wear distinctive clothing. In 1290 Edward I of England capitalized on mercantile and other resentment of Jews to expel them from the country in return for a large parliamentary grant. In

The Jews Demonized The Fourth Lateran Council of 1215 required that Jews wear distinctive clothing—special caps and the star of David—so that they could be distinguished from Christians. In this caricature from an English treasury record for 1233, Isaac of Norwich (top center), reputedly the richest Jew in England, wears a crown implying his enormous influence and power. The figure at left (holding scales) suggests the Jewish occupation of moneylending. At right Satan leads Jews to hell. *(Public Record Office, London. Photo: Acehigh Photography)*

1306 Philip IV of France followed suit by expelling the Jews from his kingdom and confiscating their property.

Early Christians, as we have seen (page 209), displayed no special prejudice against homosexuals. While some of the church fathers, such as Saint John Chrysostom (347–407), preached against them, a general indifference to homosexual activity prevailed throughout the early Middle Ages. In the early twelfth century, a large homosexual literature circulated. Publicly known homosexuals such as Ralph, archbishop of Tours (1087–1118), and King Richard I of England held high ecclesiastical and political positions.

Beginning in the late twelfth century, however, a profound change occurred in public attitudes toward homosexual behavior. Why did this happen if prejudice against homosexuals cannot be traced to early Christianity? Scholars have only begun to investigate this question, and the root cause of intolerance rarely yields to easy analysis. In the thirteenth century, a fear of foreigners, especially Muslims, became associated with the crusading movement. Heretics were the most despised minority in an age that stressed religious and social uniformity. The notion spread that both Muslims and heretics, the great foreign and domestic menaces to the security of Christian Europe, were inclined to homosexual relations. Finally, the systematization of law and the rising strength of the state made any religious or sexual distinctiveness increasingly unacceptable. Whatever the precise cause, by 1300 homosexuality became illegal in most of Europe—and the most common penalty for conviction was death.[10] Most of these laws remained on statute books until the twentieth century. Anti-Semitism and hostility to homosexuals reflect a dark and evil side of high medieval culture, not the general creativity and vitality of the period.

 Towns and Economic Revival

A salient manifestation of Europe's recovery after the tenth-century disorders and of the vitality of the High Middle Ages was the rise of towns and the development of a new business and commercial class. This development was to lay the foundations for Europe's transformation, centuries later, from a rural agricultural society into an industrial urban society—a change with global implications.

Why did these developments occur when they did? What is known of town life in the High Middle Ages? What relevance did towns have for medieval culture? Part of the answer to these questions has already been given. Without increased agricultural output, there would not have been an adequate food supply for new town dwellers. Without a rise in population, there would have been no one to people the towns. Without a minimum of peace and political stability, merchants could not have transported and sold goods.

The Rise of Towns

Early medieval society was traditional, agricultural, and rural. The emergence of a new class that was none of these constituted a social revolution. The new class—artisans and merchants—came from the peasantry. They were landless younger sons of large families, driven away by land shortage. Or they were forced by war and famine to seek new possibilities. Or, as in central Europe and Spain after the reconquista (see page 293), they were immigrants colonizing newly conquered lands. Or they were unusually enterprising and adventurous, curious and willing to take a chance.

Historians have proposed three basic theories to explain the origins of European towns. Some scholars believe towns began as *boroughs*—that is, as fortifications erected during the ninth-century Viking invasions. According to this view, towns were at first places of defense, into which farmers from the surrounding countryside moved when their area was attacked. Later, merchants were attracted to the fortifications because they had something to sell and wanted to be where customers were. But most residents of early towns made their living by farming outside the towns.

Belgian historian Henri Pirenne maintained that towns sprang up when merchants who engaged in long-distance trade gravitated toward attractive or favorable spots, such as a fort. Usually traders settled just outside the walls, in the *faubourgs* or *suburbs*—both of which mean "outside" or "in the shelter of the walls." As their markets prospered and as their number outside the walls grew, the merchants built a new wall around themselves every century or so. According to Pirenne, a medieval town consisted architecturally of a number of concentric walls, and the chief economic pursuit of its residents was trade and commerce.

A third explanation focuses on the great cathedrals and monasteries, which represented a demand for goods and services. Cathedrals such as Notre Dame in Paris conducted schools, which drew students from far and wide. Consequently, traders and merchants settled near religious establishments to cater to the residents' economic needs. Concentrations of people accumulated, and towns came into being.

All three theories have validity, though none of them explains the origins of *all* medieval towns. Few towns of the tenth and eleventh centuries were "new" in the sense that American towns and cities were new in the seventeenth and eighteenth centuries, carved out of forest and wilderness. Some medieval towns that had become flourishing centers of trade by the mid-twelfth century had originally been Roman army camps. York in northern England, Bordeaux in west-central France, and Cologne in west-central Germany are good examples of ancient towns that underwent revitalization in the eleventh century. Some Italian seaport cities, such as Venice, Pisa, and Genoa, had been centers of shipping and commerce in earlier times. Muslim attacks and domestic squabbles had cut their populations and drastically reduced the volume of their trade in the early Middle Ages, but trade with Constantinople and the East had never stopped entirely. The restoration of order and political stability promoted rebirth and new development. Pirenne's interpretation accurately describes the Flemish towns of Ghent, Bruges, and Ypres. It does not fit the course of development in the Italian cities or in such centers as London. Nor does the Pirenne thesis take into account the significance of local trade and markets in the growth of towns. Moreover, the twelfth century witnessed the foundation of completely new towns, such as Lübeck, Berlin, and Munich.

Whether evolving from a newly fortified place or an old Roman army camp, from a cathedral site or a river junction or a place where several overland routes met, medieval towns had a few common characteristics. Walls enclosed the town. (The terms *burgher* and *bourgeois* derive from the Old English and Old German words *burg, burgh, borg,* and *borough* for "a walled or fortified place." Thus a burgher or bourgeois was originally a person who lived or worked inside the walls.) The town had a marketplace. It often had a mint for the coining of money and a court to settle disputes.

In each town, many people inhabited a small, cramped area. As population increased, towns rebuilt their walls, expanding the living space to accommodate growing numbers. Through an archaeological investigation of the amount of land gradually enclosed by walls, historians have gained a rough estimate of medieval town populations. For example, the walled area of the German city of Cologne equaled 100 hectares in the tenth century (1 hectare = 2.471 acres), about 185 hectares in 1106, about 320 in 1180, and 397 hectares in the fourteenth century. In 1180 Cologne's population was at least 32,000; in the mid-fourteenth century, perhaps 40,000.[11] The concentration of the textile industry in the Low Countries brought into being the most populous cluster of cities in western Europe: Ghent with about 56,000 people, Bruges with 27,000, Tournai and Brussels each with perhaps 20,000.[12] Paris, together with Milan, Venice, and Florence, each with about 80,000 people, led all Europe in population (Map 11.4).

In their backgrounds and abilities, townspeople represented diversity and change. They constituted an en-

Carcassonne, a town in Languedoc (southern France), originated in pre-Roman times. Its thick double walls provide an excellent example of the fortified medieval town. *(Jonathan Blair/Woodfin Camp & Associates)*

tirely new element in medieval society. They fit into none of the traditional categories. Their occupations, their preoccupations, were different from those of the feudal nobility and the laboring peasantry. Though townspeople derived originally from the peasantry, and though rural people profited from the sale of foodstuffs to the towns, farmers resented what they perceived as an easier, more luxurious lifestyle. Nor did the new commercial class make much sense initially to churchmen. The immediate goal of the middle class was obviously not salvation. It was to be a long while before churchmen developed a theological justification for the new class.

Town Liberties

In the words of the Greek poet Alcaeus, "Not houses finely roofed or well built walls, nor canals or dockyards make a city, but men able to use their opportunity."[13] People and opportunity. That is fundamentally what medieval towns meant—concentrations of people and varieties of chances. No matter where groups of traders congregated, they settled on someone's land and had to secure from king or count, abbot or bishop, permission to live and trade. Aristocratic nobles and churchmen were suspicious of and hostile to the middle class. They soon realized, however, that profits and benefits flowed to them and their territories from the markets set up on their land.

The history of towns in the eleventh through thirteenth centuries consists largely of merchants' efforts to acquire liberties. In the Middle Ages, *liberties* meant special privileges. For the town dweller, liberties included the privilege of living and trading on the lord's land. The most important privilege a medieval townsperson could gain was personal freedom. It gradually developed that an individual who lived in a town for a year and a day, and was accepted by the townspeople, was free of servile obligations and status. (Usually, but not always, as we saw in the case of Jean Mouflet on page 304, lords sometimes attempted to regain runaway serfs, even after a generation. How widespread this practice was remains to be investigated.) More than

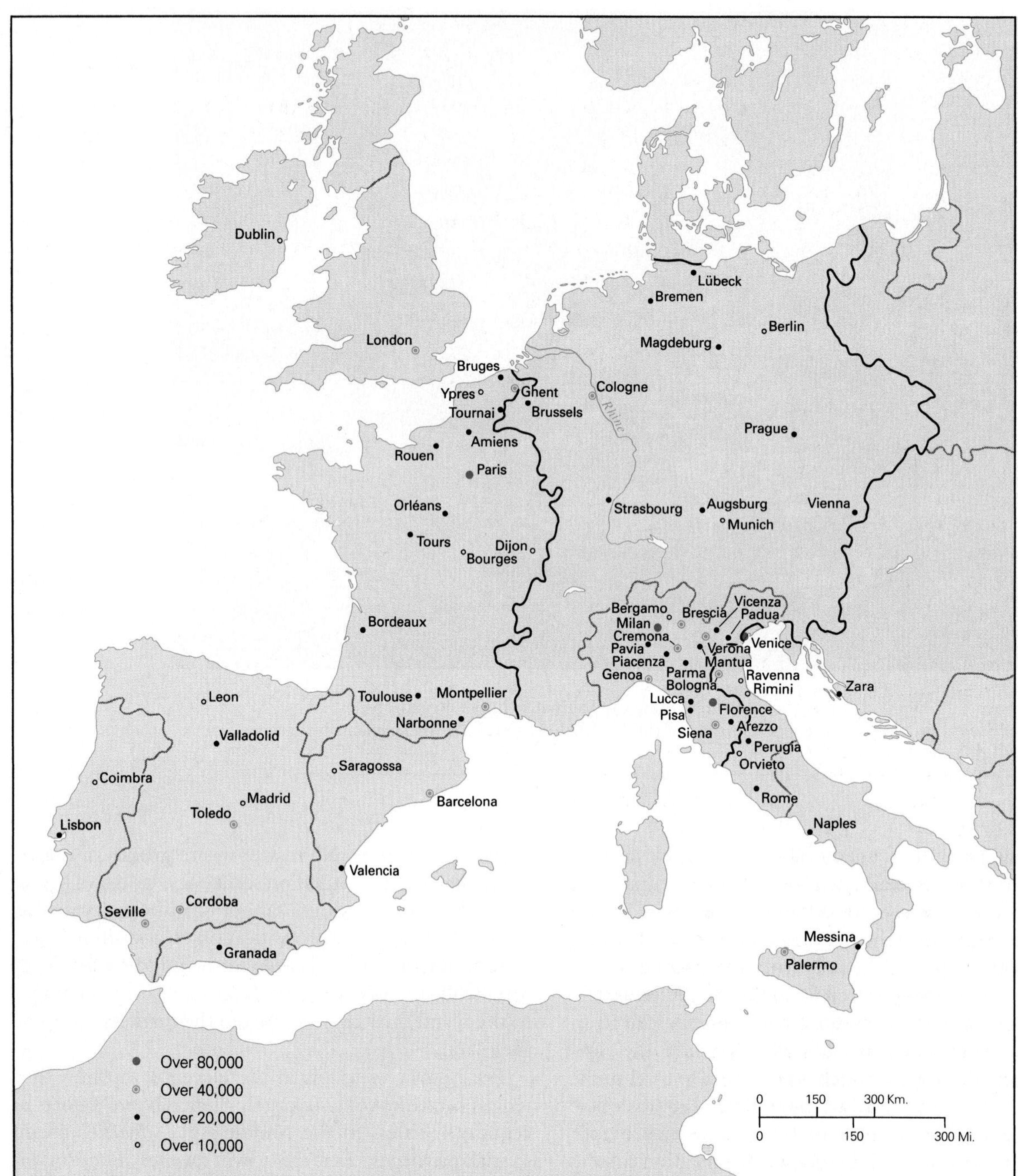

MAP 11.4 Population of European Urban Areas, ca Late Thirteenth Century Though there were scores of urban centers in the thirteenth century, the Italian and Flemish towns had the largest concentrations of people. By modern standards, Paris was Europe's only real city.

anything else, perhaps, the liberty of personal freedom that came with residence in a town contributed to the emancipation of the serfs in the High Middle Ages. Liberty meant citizenship, and citizenship in a town implied the right to buy and sell goods there. Unlike foreigners and outsiders of any kind, the full citizen did not have to pay taxes and tolls in the market. Obviously, this increased profits.

In the twelfth and thirteenth centuries, towns fought for, and slowly gained, legal and political rights. Since the tenth century, some English boroughs had held courts with jurisdiction over members of the town in civil and criminal matters. In the twelfth century, such English towns as London and Norwich developed courts that applied a special kind of law, called "law merchant." It dealt with commercial transactions, debt, bankruptcy, proof of sales, and contracts. Law merchant was especially suitable to the needs of the new bourgeoisie. Gradually, towns across Europe acquired the right to hold municipal courts that alone could judge members of the town. In effect, this right gave them judicial independence.[14]

In the acquisition of full rights of self-government, the *merchant guilds* played a large role. Medieval people were long accustomed to communal enterprises. In the late tenth and early eleventh centuries, those who were engaged in foreign trade joined together in merchant guilds; united enterprise provided them greater security and less risk of losses than did individual action. At about the same time, the artisans and craftsmen of particular trades formed their own guilds. Members of the *craft guilds* determined the quality, quantity, and price of the goods that they produced and the number of apprentices and journeymen that could be affiliated with the guild.

Recent research indicates that, by the fifteenth century, women composed the majority of the adult urban population. Many women were heads of households.[15] They engaged in every kind of urban commercial activity, both as helpmates to their husbands and independently. In many manufacturing trades women predominated, and in some places women were a large percentage of the labor force. In fourteenth-century Frankfurt, for example, about 33 percent of the crafts and trades were entirely female, about 40 percent wholly male, and the remaining crafts roughly divided between the sexes. Craft guilds provided greater opportunity for women than did merchant guilds. In late-twelfth-century Cologne, women and men had equal rights in the turners guild (the guild for those who made wooden objects on a lathe). Most members of the Paris silk and woolen trades were women, and some achieved the mastership. Widows frequently followed their late husbands' professions, but if they remarried outside the craft, they lost the mastership. Between 1254 and 1271, the chief magistrate of Paris drew up the following regulations for the silk industry. Any woman who wishes to be a silk spinster (woman who spins) on large spindles in the city of Paris—that is, reeling, spinning, doubling, and retwisting—may freely do so, provided she observe the following customs and usages of the crafts:

> *No spinster on large spindles may have more than three apprentices, unless they be her own or her husband's children born in true wedlock; nor may she contract with them for an apprenticeship of less than seven years or for a fee of less than 20 Parisian sols to be paid to her, their mistress. . . . If a working woman comes from outside Paris and wishes to practice the said craft in the city, she must swear before the guardians of the craft that she will practice it well and loyally and conform to its customs and usages. . . . No man of this craft who is without a wife may have more than one apprentice; . . . if, however, both husband and wife practice the craft, they may have two apprentices and as many journeymen as they wish.*[16]

Guild records show that women received lower wages than men for the same work, on the grounds that they needed less income.

Recent research also demonstrates that women with ready access to cash, such as female innkeepers, alewives, and women in trade, "extended credit on purchases, gave cash advances to good customers or accepted articles on pawn . . . and many widows supplemented their earnings from their late husbands' businesses or homesteads by putting out cash at interest." Likewise, Christian noblewomen, nuns, and Jewish businesswomen participated in money lending. In every part of Europe where Jews lived, Jewish women were active moneylenders: England, Flanders, northern France (where in the thirteenth century Jewish women constituted one-third of all Jewish lenders), the German-speaking parts of Europe, Navarre, Catalonia, and throughout Italy. Loans made by all women tended to be very small (in comparison to those extended by men), for domestic consumption (to "tide over" a household in some emergency, in contrast to productive loans such as those to repair or replace a piece of farm equipment), and for short terms (a few weeks or a month).[17]

By the late eleventh century, especially in the towns of the Low Countries and northern Italy, the leaders of the merchant guilds were quite rich and powerful. They constituted an oligarchy in their towns, controlling economic life and bargaining with kings and lords for political independence. Full rights of self-government included the right to hold a town court, the right to select the mayor and other municipal officials, and the right to tax and collect taxes. Kings often levied on their serfs and unfree townspeople the arbitrary tax, tallage. Such a tax (also known as "customs") called attention to the fact that men were not free. Citizens of a town much preferred to levy and collect their own taxes.

A charter that King Henry II of England granted to the merchants of Lincoln around 1157 nicely illustrates the town's rights. The quoted passages clearly suggest that the merchant guild had been the governing body in the city for almost a century and that anyone who lived in Lincoln for a year and a day was considered free:

Henry, by the grace of God, etc. . . . Know that I have granted to my citizens of Lincoln all their liberties and customs and laws which they had in the time of Edward [King Edward the Confessor] and William and Henry, kings of England. And I have granted them their gild-merchant, comprising men of the city and other merchants of the shire, as well and freely as they had it in the time of our aforesaid predecessors. . . . And all the men who live within the four divisions of the city and attend the market, shall stand in relation to gelds [taxes] and customs and the assizes [ordinances or laws] of the city as well as ever they stood in the time of Edward, William and Henry, kings of England. I also confirm to them that if anyone has lived in Lincoln for a year and a day without dispute from any claimant, and has paid the customs, and if the citizens can show by the laws and customs of the city that the claimant has remained in England during that period and has made no claim, then let the defendant remain in peace in my city of Lincoln as my citizen, without [having to defend his] right.[18]

Kings and lords were reluctant to grant towns self-government, fearing loss of authority and revenue if they gave the merchant guilds full independence. But the lords discovered that towns attracted increasing numbers of people to an area—people whom the lords could tax. Moreover, when burghers bargained for a town's political independence, they offered sizable amounts of ready cash. Consequently, feudal lords ultimately agreed to self-government.

Town Life

Protective walls surrounded almost all medieval towns and cities. The valuable goods inside a town were too much of a temptation to marauding bands for the town to be without the security of bricks and mortar. Gates pierced the walls, and visitors waited at the gates to gain entrance to the town. When the gates were opened early in the morning, guards inspected the quantity and quality of the goods brought in and collected the customary taxes. Part of the taxes went to the lord on whose land the town stood, part to the town council for civic purposes. Constant repair of the walls was usually the town's greatest expense.

Peasants coming from the countryside and merchants traveling from afar set up their carts as stalls just inside the gates. The result was that the road nearest the gate was the widest thoroughfare. It was the ideal place for a market, because everyone coming in or going out used it. Most streets in a medieval town were marketplaces as much as passages for transit.

Medieval cities served, above all else, as markets. In some respects the entire city was a marketplace. The place where a product was made and sold was also typically the merchant's residence. Usually the ground floor was the scene of production. A window or door opened from the main workroom directly onto the street. The window displayed the finished product, and passersby could look in and see the goods being produced. The merchant's family lived above the business on the second or third floor. As the business and the family expanded, the merchant built additional stories on top of the house.

Because space within the town walls was limited, expansion occurred upward. Second and third stories were built jutting out over the ground floor and thus over the street. Neighbors on the opposite side did the same. Since the streets were narrow to begin with, houses lacked fresh air and light. Initially, houses were made of wood and thatched with straw. Fire represented a constant danger, and because houses were built so close together, fires spread rapidly. Municipal governments consequently urged construction in stone or brick.

Most medieval cities developed haphazardly. There was little town planning. As the population increased, space became more and more limited. Air and water pollution presented serious problems. Many families raised pigs for household consumption in sties next to the house. Horses and oxen, the chief means of transportation and power, dropped tons of dung on the streets every year. It was universal practice in the early towns to dump household waste, both animal and human, into the road in front of one's house. The stench must have been abominable. In 1298 the burgesses of the town of Boutham in Yorkshire, England, received the following order (one long, vivid sentence):

To the bailiffs of the abbot of St. Mary's York, at Boutham. Whereas it is sufficiently evident that the pavement of the said town of Boutham is so very greatly broken up . . . , and in addition the air is so corrupted and infected by the pigsties situated in the king's highways and in the lanes of that town and by the swine feeding and frequently wander-

ing about . . . and by dung and dunghills and many other foul things placed in the streets and lanes, that great repugnance overtakes the king's ministers staying in that town and also others there dwelling and passing through, the advantage of more wholesome air is impeded, the state of men is grievously injured, and other unbearable inconveniences . . . , to the nuisance of the king's ministers aforesaid and of others there dwelling and passing through, and to the peril of their lives . . . : the king, being unwilling longer to tolerate such great and unbearable defects there, orders the bailiffs to cause the pavement to be suitably repaired within their liberty before All Saints next, and to cause the pigsties, aforesaid streets and lanes to be cleansed from all dung . . . and to cause them to be kept thus cleansed hereafter.[19]

A great deal of traffic passed through Boutham in 1298 because of the movement of English troops to battlefronts in Scotland. Conditions there were probably not typical. Still, this document suggests that space, air pollution, and sanitation problems bedeviled urban people in medieval times, as they do today.

People wanted to get into medieval cities because they represented a means of economic advancement, social mobility, and improvement in legal status. For the adventurous, the ambitious, and the shrewd, cities offered tremendous opportunities. (See the feature "Listening to the Past: London in the Late Twelfth Century" on pages 374–375.)

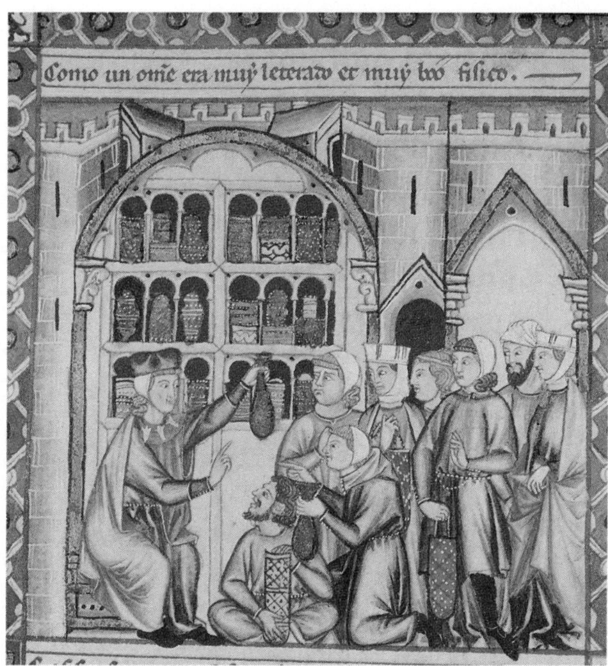

Spanish Apothecary Town life meant variety—of peoples and products. Within the town walls, a Spanish pharmacist, seated outside his shop, describes the merits of his goods to a crowd of Christians and Muslims. *(From the* Cantigas *of Alfonso X, ca 1283. El Escorial/Laurie Platt Winfrey, Inc.)*

The Revival of Long-Distance Trade

The eleventh century witnessed a remarkable revival of trade, as artisans and craftsmen manufactured goods for local and foreign consumption (Map 11.5). Most trade centered in towns and was controlled by professional traders. Because long-distance trade was risky and required large investments of capital, it could be practiced only by professionals. The transportation of goods involved serious risks. Shipwrecks were common. Pirates infested the sea lanes, and robbers and thieves roamed virtually all of the land routes. Since the risks were so great, merchants preferred to share them. A group of people would thus pool some of their capital to finance an expedition to a distant place. When the ship or caravan returned and the goods brought back were sold, the investors would share the profits. If disaster struck the caravan, an investor's loss was limited to the amount of that individual's investment.

What goods were exchanged? What towns took the lead in medieval "international" trade? In the late eleventh century, the Italian cities, especially Venice, led the West in trade in general and completely dominated the oriental market. Ships carried salt from the Venetian lagoon, pepper and other spices from North Africa, and silks and purple textiles from the East to northern and western Europe. In the thirteenth century, Venetian caravans brought slaves from the Crimea and Chinese silks from Mongolia to the West. Lombard and Tuscan merchants exchanged those goods at the town markets and regional fairs of France, Flanders, and England. (Fairs were periodic gatherings that attracted buyers, sellers, and goods from all over Europe.) Flanders controlled the cloth industry. The towns of Bruges, Ghent, and Ypres built up a vast industry in the manufacture of cloth. Italian merchants exchanged their products for Flemish tapestries, fine broadcloth, and various other textiles.

Two circumstances help to explain the lead Venice and the Flemish towns gained in long-distance trade. Both enjoyed a high degree of peace and political stability. Geographical factors were equally, if not more, important. Venice was ideally located at the northwestern end of the Adriatic Sea, with easy access to the transalpine land routes as well as the Adriatic and Mediterranean sea lanes. The markets of North Africa,

Textile and manufacturing areas
Northern sea routes
Venetian sea routes
Genoese sea routes
Overland routes
0 200 400 Km.
0 200 400 Mi
ATLANTIC OCEAN
North Sea
Baltic Sea
Black Sea
Sea of Azov
Adriatic Sea
Aegean Sea
Mediterranean Sea
Bay of Biscay
Ireland
Gotland
Corsica
Sardinia
Balearic Is.
Sicily
Crete
Rhodes
Cyprus
Edinburgh
Carlisle
Durham
York
Chester
Bristol
London
Southampton
Calais
Bruges
Brussels
Rouen
Paris
Rennes
Nantes
Tours
Orléans
Limoges
Clermont
Bordeaux
Bayonne
Toulouse
Lyons
Avignon
Marseilles
Geneva
Basel
Strasbourg
Cologne
Amsterdam
Bremen
Hamburg
Lübeck
Magdeburg
Leipzig
Frankfurt
Nuremberg
Augsburg
Prague
Breslau
Vienna
Milan
Genoa
Pisa
Florence
Bologna
Venice
Rome
Naples
Taranto
Messina
Palermo
Syracuse
Tunis
Tripoli
Algiers
Ceuta
Lisbon
Seville
Cordoba
Granada
Almeira
Cartagena
Valencia
Barcelona
Toledo
Leon
Santiago
Bergen
Oslo
Stockholm
Copenhagen
Danzig
Königsberg
Riga
Reval
Novgorod
Warsaw
Cracow
Kiev
Buda
Pest
Belgrade
Ragusa
Constantinople
Smyrna
Ankara
Sinope
Trebizond
Sivas
Caffa
Rostov
Antioch
Tripoli
Damascus
Beirut
Sidon
Tyre
Jerusalem
Cairo
Alexandria
Fish
Pitch
Grain
Copper
Flax
Hemp
Wax
Furs
Honey
Slave market
Wool
Iron
Lead
Tin
Salt
Wine
Wheat
Paper
Silver
Tar
Mfd. wares
Glass
Artwares
Timber
Skins + hides
Horses
Olives
Raisins
Currants
Opium
Cotton
Carpets + rugs
Fruits+foodstuffs
Glassware
Precious woods
Silk
Indigo
Dates
Metalwares
Leather
Cork

Byzantium, and Russia and the great fairs of Ghent in Flanders and Champagne in France provided commercial opportunities that Venice quickly seized. (See the feature "Individuals in Society: Enrico Dandolo.") The geographical situation of Flanders also offered unusual possibilities. Just across the Channel from England, Flanders had easy access to English wool. Indeed, Flanders and England developed a very close economic relationship.

Sheep had been raised for their wool in England since Roman times. The rocky soil and damp climate of Yorkshire and Lincolnshire, though poorly suited for agriculture, were excellent for sheep farming. Beginning in the early twelfth century, but especially after the arrival of Cistercian monks around 1130, the size of the English flocks doubled and then tripled. Scholars have estimated that, by the end of the twelfth century, roughly six million sheep grazed on the English moors and downs. They produced fifty thousand sacks of wool a year.[20] Originally, a "sack" of wool was the burden one packhorse could carry, an amount eventually fixed at 364 pounds; fifty thousand sacks, then, represented huge production.

Wool was the cornerstone of the English medieval economy. Population growth in the twelfth century and the success of the Flemish and Italian textile industries created foreign demand for English wool. The production of English wool stimulated Flemish manufacturing, and the expansion of the Flemish cloth industry in turn spurred the production of English wool. The availability of raw wool also encouraged the development of domestic cloth manufacture within England. The towns of Lincoln, York, Leicester, Northampton, Winchester, and Exeter became important cloth-producing towns. The port cities of London, Hull, Boston, and Bristol thrived on the wool trade. In the thirteenth century, commercial families in these towns grew fabulously rich.

The Commercial Revolution

A steadily expanding volume of international trade from the late eleventh through the thirteenth centuries was a sign of the great economic surge, but it was not the only one. Beginning in the 1160s, the opening of new silver mines in Germany, Bohemia, northern Italy, northern France, and western England led to the minting and circulation of vast quantities of silver coins. The widespread use of cash brought about an enormous quantitative change in the volume of international trade. Demand for sugar (to replace honey), pepper, cloves, and Asian spices to season a bland diet; for fine wines from the Rhineland, Burgundy, and Bordeaux; for luxury woolens from Flanders and Tuscany; for furs from Ireland and Russia; for brocades and tapestries from Flanders and silks from Constantinople and even China; for household furnishings such as silver plate—not to mention the desire for products associated with a military aristocracy such as swords and armor—surged phenomenally.

Business procedures changed radically. The individual traveling merchant who alone handled virtually all aspects of exchange evolved into an operation involving three separate types of merchants: the sedentary merchant who ran the "home office" financing and organizing the firm's entire export-import trade; the carriers who transported goods by land and sea; and the company agents resident in cities abroad who, on the advice of the home office, looked after sales and procurements. Commercial correspondence, unnecessary when one businessperson oversaw everything and made direct bargains with buyers and sellers, proliferated. Regular courier service among commercial cities began. Commercial accounting became more complex when firms had to deal with shareholders, manufacturers, customers, branch offices, employees, and competing firms. Tolls on roads became high enough to finance what has been called a "road revolution," involving new surfaces, bridges, new passes through the Alps, and new inns and hospices for travelers. The growth of mutual confidence among merchants facilitated the growth of sales on credit and led to the development of the bill of exchange, which in turn made the long, slow, and very dangerous shipment of coins unnecessary. Begun in the late twelfth century, the bill of exchange was by the early fourteenth century the normal method of making commercial payments among the cities of western Europe. In central Europe, only Prague in Bohemia, with its mining revenues and large population, attracted a resident foreign business community. In all these transformations, merchants of the Italian cities led the way.[21]

The ventures of the German Hanseatic League also illustrate these impulses. The Hanseatic League was a mercantile association of towns. Though scholars trace the league's origin to the foundation of the city of Lübeck in 1159, the mutual protection treaty later

MAP 11.5 Trade and Manufacturing in Medieval Europe Note the number of cities and the sources of silver, iron, copper, lead, paper, wool, carpets and rugs, and slaves.

Individuals in Society

Enrico Dandolo (1107?–1205)

In the first week of Lent,[1] 1201, six French barons—the diplomatic envoys of a contingent of northern French and Flemish barons who had taken the cross—appeared in Venice. They wanted Venetian help in transporting them to the Holy Land. The lords had selected Venice, at the northwestern edge of the Adriatic Sea, as the port of departure because of the city's vast maritime facilities, which no French or other Italian shipyard (at Genoa or Pisa) could match. The ambassadors were formally received by the head of state, Doge Enrico Dandolo, with great pomp and splendor.

Dandolo was ninety-four years old. Partially blind, and doge since 1192, he had already reformed the Venetian currency, revised the penal code, and published the republic's first collection of civil statutes. A skilled diplomat and strategist and an eloquent speaker, he was above all a passionate patriot.

The Crusaders requested transportation for 33,500 men and 4,500 horses. For a fee of 85,000 marks the Venetians agreed to transport them to Palestine and to provision horses and men for one year; the expedition was to sail in April 1202, its first object Egypt.

From this treaty would stem momentous consequences and ultimately great wealth for Venice. Immediately after the treaty, the city built five hundred ships to carry men and horses. When it became apparent that the Crusaders could produce neither the manpower promised nor about a third of the fee, Doge Enrico Dandolo proposed that the crusading army conquer Zara (modern Zadar in Croatia on the Adriatic coast), a fueling station for Venetian ships and the port through which oak, essential for Venetian shipbuilding, passed; Zara had recently been seized by the king of Hungary. Some Crusaders objected to an attack on a Christian city, but the majority acceded to the doge's request. Zara was assaulted and fell. Then Alexius, son of the deposed Byzantine emperor, arrived at Zara and promised financial support for the crusade and the reunion of the Greek and Latin churches, if the Crusaders would help him regain the Byzantine throne; sharp divisions again arose among Crusaders. Doge Dandolo, who had recently seen Venetian trading rights in Constantinople rescinded and given to Genoa, eloquently urged support for an attack on Constantinople; the restoration of Alexius would offer a perfect opportunity for the recovery of Venetian privileges. Moreover, he reminded the army, Venice controlled the fleet. Although a thousand Crusaders defected and went home, Venice and the remaining Crusaders signed the Treaty of Zara, agreeing to assault the Byzantine capital and to restore Alexius. The fleet sailed and, after a long siege, Constantinople was conquered and mercilessly sacked on April 13–15, 1204.

Enrico Dandolo. *(Biblioteca Nazionale Marciana, Venice)*

In the division of the Byzantine Empire, Venice got the lion's share: three-eighths of Constantinople, including the harbor area crucial to Venice's commercial interests, plus several strategic islands in the eastern Mediterranean. The conquest of Constantinople, a contradiction of the entire religious enterprise, laid the foundation for Venetian commercial power for the next three centuries.

Doge Enrico Dandolo, in spite of his age and handicap, represents the values of the modern, not the medieval, world. Whereas the Crusaders' interests were religious and chivalric, Dandolo's were secular and bourgeois. He displayed great vitality and a willingness to seize opportunities when they arose. Whereas the Crusaders appeared indecisive and lacked effective leadership, Dandolo's policy was consistent and calculating. He used every crisis in this sorry expedition to advance the commercial interests of Venice.

Questions for Analysis

1. How did commercial, financial, and political issues determine the course of the Fourth Crusade?
2. What is meant by "secular values"? How did Enrico Dandolo display them?

1. In Christian medieval Europe, people dated events by the church year—Advent, Lent, Pentecost, or saints' feast days. Everyone would have known that the first week of Lent came between mid-February and early March.

Source: D. E. Queller, *The Fourth Crusade: The Conquest of Constantinople, 1201–1204* (Philadelphia: University of Pennsylvania Press, 1977).

signed by Lübeck and Hamburg marks the league's actual expansion. Lübeck and Hamburg wanted mutual security, exclusive trading rights, and, where possible, a monopoly. During the next century, perhaps two hundred cities from Holland to Poland, including Cologne, Brunswick, Dortmund, Danzig, and Riga, joined the league, but Lübeck always remained the dominant member. From the thirteenth to the sixteenth century, the Hanseatic League controlled trade over an axis of Novgorod-Reval-Lübeck-Hamburg-Bruges-London, that is, the trade of northern Europe (see Map 11.5). In the fourteenth century, the Hanseatics branched out into southern Germany and Italy by land and into French, Spanish, and Portuguese ports by sea.

Across regular, well-defined trade routes along the Baltic and North Seas, the ships of league cities carried furs, wax, copper, fish, grain, timber, and wine. These goods were exchanged for finished products, mainly cloth and salt, from western cities. At cities such as Bruges and London, Hanseatic merchants secured special trading concessions exempting them from all tolls and allowing them to trade at local fairs. Hanseatic merchants established foreign trading centers, called "factories," the most famous of which was the London Steelyard, a walled community with warehouses, offices, a church, and residential quarters for company representatives.[22]

By the late thirteenth century, Hanseatic merchants had developed an important business technique, the business register. Merchants publicly recorded their debts and contracts and received a league guarantee for them. This device proved a decisive factor in the later development of credit and commerce in northern Europe.[23] These activities required capital, risk taking, and aggressive pursuit of opportunities—the essential ingredients of capitalism. They also yielded fat profits.

These developments added up to what one modern scholar has called "a commercial revolution, . . . probably the greatest turning point in the history of our civilization."[24] This is not a wildly extravagant statement. In the long run, the commercial revolution of the High Middle Ages brought about radical change in European society. One remarkable aspect of this change is that the commercial classes constituted a small part of the total population—never more than 10 percent. They exercised an influence far in excess of their numbers.

The commercial revolution created a great deal of new wealth. Wealth meant a higher standard of living.

Wismar, founded in 1229 in Mecklenburg on the Baltic Sea, won full rights of self-government in 1236 from the dukes of Mecklenburg-Pomerania, who resided there. A fishing and shipbuilding center, Wismar became one of the most powerful members of the Hanseatic League. Warehouses lined the shore, while the town's many church steeples dominated the skyline. *(From Ernst Hering,* Die Deutsche Hanse *[Leipzig: Wilhelm Goldmann Verlag]. Courtesy, Harvard University Library.)*

Contact with Eastern civilizations introduced Europeans to eating utensils, and table manners improved. Nobles learned to eat with forks and knives, instead of tearing the meat from a roast with their hands. They began to use napkins, instead of wiping their greasy fingers on the dogs lying under the table.

The existence of wealth did not escape the attention of kings and other rulers. Wealth could be taxed, and through taxation kings could create strong and centralized states. In the years to come, alliances with the middle classes were to enable kings to defeat feudal powers and aristocratic interests and to build the states that came to be called "modern."

The commercial revolution also provided the opportunity for thousands of serfs to improve their social position. The slow but steady transformation of European society from almost completely rural and isolated to relatively more sophisticated constituted the greatest effect of the commercial revolution that began in the eleventh century.

Even so, merchants and business people did not run medieval communities, except in central and northern Italy and in the county of Flanders. Most towns remained small. The castle, the manorial village, and the monastery dominated the landscape. The feudal nobility and churchmen determined the preponderant social attitudes, values, and patterns of thought and behavior. The commercial changes of the eleventh through thirteenth centuries did, however, lay the economic foundations for the development of urban life and culture.

Medieval Universities

Just as the first strong secular states emerged in the thirteenth century, so did the first universities. This was no coincidence. The new bureaucratic states and the church needed educated administrators, and universities were a response to this need. The word *university* derives from the Latin *universitas,* meaning "corporation" or "guild." Medieval universities were educational guilds that produced educated and trained individuals. They were also an expression of the tremendous vitality and creativity of the High Middle Ages. Their organization, methods of instruction, and goals continue to influence institutionalized learning in the Western world.

Origins

In the early Middle Ages, outside of the aristocratic court or the monastery, anyone who received education got it from a priest. Priests instructed the clever boys on the manor in the Latin words of the Mass and taught them the rudiments of reading and writing. Few boys acquired elementary literacy, however, and peasant girls did not obtain even that. The peasant who wished to send his son to school had to secure the permission of his lord, because the result of formal schooling tended to be a career in the church or some trade. If a young man were to pursue either, he would have to leave the manor and gain free status. Because the lord stood to lose the services of educated peasants, he limited the number of serfs sent to school.

Few schools were available anyway. Society was organized for war and defense and gave slight support to education. By the late eleventh century, however, social conditions had markedly improved. There was greater political stability, and favorable economic conditions had advanced many people beyond the level of bare subsistence. The curious and able felt the lack of schools and teachers.

Since the time of the Carolingian Empire, monasteries and cathedral schools had offered the only formal instruction. The monasteries were geared to religious concerns, and the monastic curriculum consisted of studying the Scriptures and the writings of the church fathers. Monasteries wished to maintain an atmosphere of seclusion and silence and were unwilling to accept large numbers of noisy lay students. In contrast, schools attached to cathedrals and run by the bishop and his clergy were frequently situated in bustling cities, and in the eleventh century in Italian cities like Bologna, wealthy businessmen had established municipal schools. Cities inhabited by peoples of many backgrounds and "nationalities" stimulated the growth and exchange of ideas. In the course of the twelfth century, cathedral schools in France and municipal schools in Italy developed into universities (Map 11.6). "The term *studium generale* ('general centre of study'), eventually the most common medieval designation of a university, probably indicated the capacity of certain centres to attract students from beyond their immediate area." Members of the *studium generale* (university) formed professional associations for the protection of their members, the most typical examples being the students university at Bologna and the masters university at Paris.[25]

The school at Chartres in France became famous for its studies of the Latin classics and for the broad literary interests it fostered in its students. The most famous graduate of Chartres was the Englishman John of Salisbury (d. 1180), who wrote *The Statesman's Book,* an important treatise on the corrupting effects of political power. But Chartres, situated in the center of rich farmland, remote from the currents of commercial traffic and intellectual ideas, did not develop into a university. The first European universities appeared in Italy, at Bologna and Salerno.

The growth of the University of Bologna coincided with a revival of interest in Roman law during the investiture controversy. The study of Roman law as embodied in the Justinian *Code* had never completely died out in the West, but this sudden burst of interest seems to have been inspired by Irnerius (d. 1125), a great teacher at Bologna. His fame attracted students from all over Europe. Irnerius not only explained the Roman law of the Justinian *Code,* he applied it to difficult practical situations. An important school of civil law was founded at Montpellier in France, but Bologna remained the greatest law school throughout the Middle Ages.

At Salerno interest in medicine had persisted for centuries. Greek and Muslim physicians there had studied the use of herbs as cures and experimented with surgery. The twelfth century ushered in a new interest in Greek medical texts and in the work of Arab and Greek doctors. Students of medicine poured into Salerno and soon attracted royal attention. In 1140, when King Roger II of Sicily took the practice of medicine under royal control, his ordinance stated:

Who, from now on, wishes to practice medicine, has to present himself before our officials and examiners, in order to pass their judgment. Should he be bold enough to disregard this, he will be punished by imprisonment and confiscation of his entire property. In this way we are taking care that our subjects are not endangered by the inexperience of the physicians.[26]

In the first decades of the twelfth century, students converged on Paris. They crowded into the cathedral school of Notre Dame and spilled over into the area later called the "Latin Quarter"—whose name probably reflects the Italian origin of many of the students attracted to Paris by the surge of interest in the classics, logic, and theology. The cathedral school's international reputation had already drawn to Paris scholars from all over Europe, one of whom was Peter Abelard.

The son of a minor Breton knight, Peter Abelard (1079–1142) studied in Paris, quickly absorbed a large amount of material, and set himself up as a teacher. Abelard was fascinated by logic, which he believed could be used to solve most problems. He had a brilliant mind and, though orthodox in his philosophical teaching, appeared to challenge ecclesiastical authorities. His book *Sic et Non* (Yes and No) was a list of apparently contradictory propositions drawn from the Bible and the writings of the church fathers. One such proposition, for example, stated that sin is pleasing to God and is not pleasing to God. Abelard used a method of systematic doubting in his writing and teaching. As he put it in the preface to *Sic et Non,* "By doubting we come to questioning, and by questioning we perceive the truth." While other scholars merely asserted theological principles, Abelard discussed and analyzed them. Through reasoning he even tried to describe the attributes of the three persons of the Trinity, the central mystery of the Christian faith. Abelard was severely censured by a church council, but his cleverness, boldness, and imagination made him a highly popular figure among students.

The influx of students eager for learning, together with dedicated and imaginative teachers, created the atmosphere in which universities grew. In northern Europe—at Paris and later at Oxford and Cambridge in England—associations or guilds of professors organized universities. They established the curriculum, set the length of time for study, and determined the form and content of examinations.

Instruction and Curriculum

University faculties grouped themselves according to academic disciplines—law, medicine, arts, and theology. The professors (a term first used in the fourteenth century) were known as "schoolmen" or "Scholastics"; they developed a method of thinking, reasoning, and writing in which questions were raised and authorities cited on both sides of the question. The goal of the Scholastic method was to arrive at definitive answers and to provide a rational explanation for what was believed on faith. Schoolmen held that reason and faith constituted two harmonious realms whose truths complemented each other.

The Scholastic approach rested on the recovery of classical philosophical texts. Ancient Greek and Arabic texts had entered Europe in the early twelfth century. Knowledge of Aristotle and other Greek philosophers came to Paris and Oxford by way of Islamic intellectual centers at Baghdad, Córdoba, and Toledo. But these Aristotelian texts, forming the basis of Western philosophical and theological speculation, were not the only Islamic gifts. The major contribution of Arabic culture to the new currents of Western thought rested in the stimulus Arabic philosophers and commentators gave to Europeans' reflection on the Greek texts. For example, in Islam a strong tension exists between faith and reason. Western scholars' understanding of Aristotle's philosophy was closely tied to their discovery of Arabic

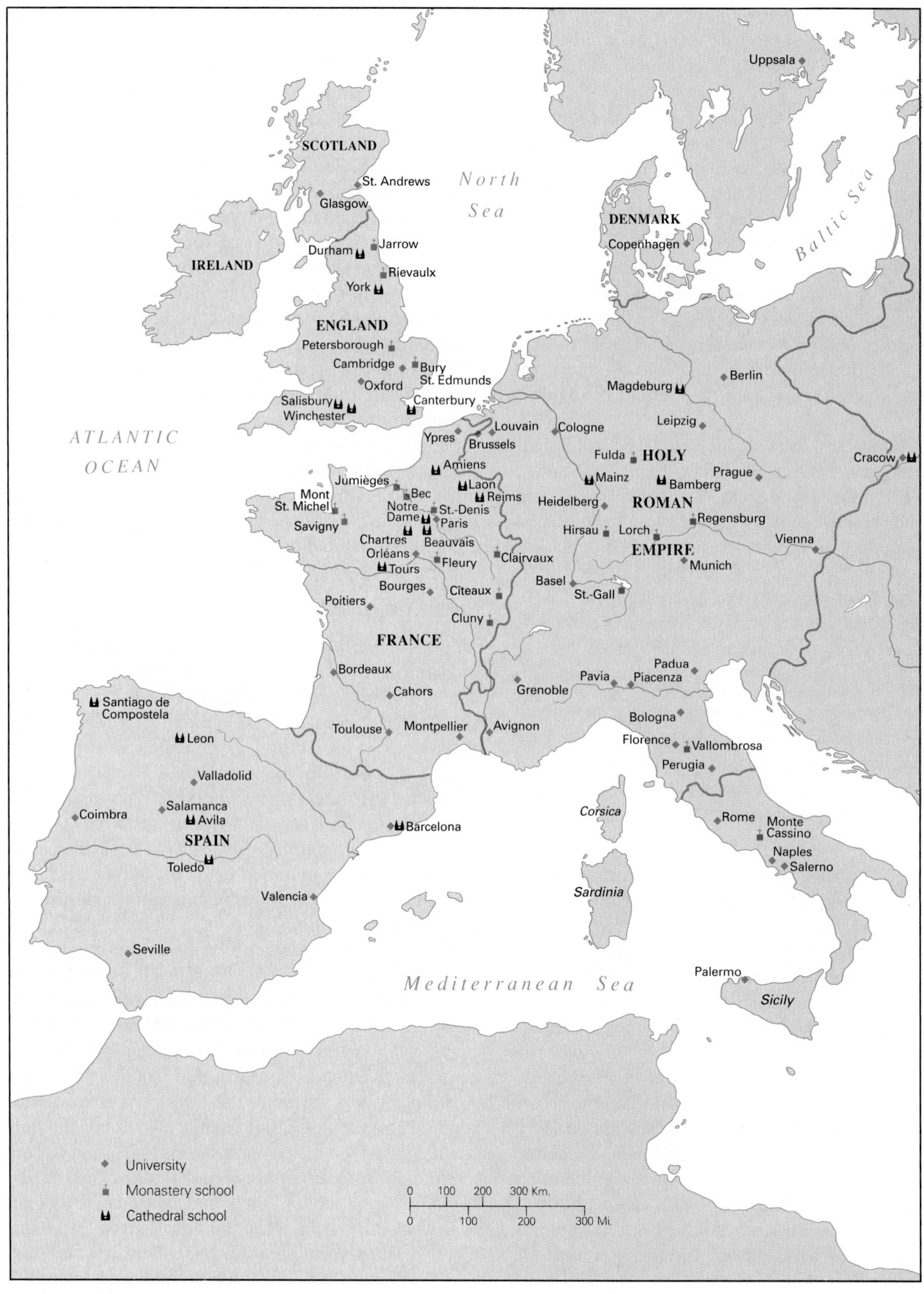

Uppsala
SCOTLAND
St. Andrews
Glasgow
North Sea
DENMARK
Copenhagen
Baltic Sea
IRELAND
Durham
Jarrow
Rievaulx
York
ENGLAND
Petersborough
Cambridge
Bury St. Edmunds
Oxford
Salisbury
Winchester
Canterbury
Magdeburg
Berlin
ATLANTIC OCEAN
Ypres
Louvain
Brussels
Cologne
Leipzig
Fulda
HOLY ROMAN EMPIRE
Cracow
Amiens
Prague
Jumièges
Bec
Laon
Reims
Mainz
Bamberg
Mont St. Michel
Savigny
Notre Dame
St.-Denis
Paris
Heidelberg
Regensburg
Hirsau
Lorch
Vienna
Chartres
Beauvais
Orléans
Fleury
Clairvaux
Munich
Tours
Bourges
Basel
St.-Gall
Poitiers
Cîteaux
Cluny
FRANCE
Bordeaux
Padua
Pavia
Piacenza
Grenoble
Cahors
Santiago de Compostela
Bologna
Toulouse
Montpellier
Avignon
Leon
Florence
Vallombrosa
Perugia
Valladolid
Coimbra
Salamanca
Avila
Corsica
Rome
Monte Cassino
Barcelona
SPAIN
Toledo
Naples
Salerno
Valencia
Sardinia
Seville
Palermo
Mediterranean Sea
Sicily
University
Monastery school
Cathedral school
0 100 200 300 Km.
0 100 200 300 Mi.

thought. The tension between reason and faith became a fundamental theme in Christian thought.[27]

Aristotle had stressed the importance of the direct observance of nature, as well as the principles that theory must follow fact and that knowledge of a thing requires an explanation of its causes. The schoolmen reinterpreted Aristotelian texts in a Christian sense. But in their exploration of the natural world, they did not precisely follow Aristotle's axioms. Medieval scientists argued from authority, such as the Bible, the Justinian *Code,* or an ancient scientific treatise, rather than from direct observation and experimentation, as modern scientists do. Thus the conclusions of medieval scientists were often wrong. Nevertheless, natural science gradually emerged as a discipline distinct from philosophy. Scholastics made important contributions to the advancement of knowledge. They preserved the Greek and Arabic texts that contained the body of ancient scientific knowledge, which would otherwise have been lost. And by inquiring about nature and the universe, Scholastics laid the foundations for later scientific work.

Many of the problems that Scholastic philosophers raised dealt with theological issues. For example, they addressed the question that interested all Christians, educated and uneducated: how is a person saved? Saint Augustine's thesis—that, as a result of Adam's fall, human beings have a propensity to sin—had become a central feature of medieval church doctrine. The church taught that it possessed the means to forgive the sinful: grace conveyed through the sacraments. However, although grace provided a predisposition to salvation, the Scholastics held that one must also *decide* to use the grace received. In other words, a person must use his or her reason to advance to God.

Thirteenth-century Scholastics devoted an enormous amount of time to collecting and organizing knowledge on all topics. These collections were published as *summa,* or reference books. There were summa on law, philosophy, vegetation, animal life, and theology. Saint Thomas Aquinas (1225–1274), a professor at Paris, produced the most famous collection, the *Summa Theologica,* which deals with a vast number of theological questions.

Aquinas drew an important distinction between faith and reason. He maintained that, although reason can demonstrate many basic Christian principles such as the existence of God, other fundamental teachings such as the Trinity and original sin cannot be proved by logic. That reason cannot establish them does not, however, mean they are contrary to reason. Rather, people understand such doctrines through revelation embodied in Scripture. Scripture cannot contradict reason, nor reason Scripture:

The light of faith that is freely infused into us does not destroy the light of natural knowledge [reason] implanted in us naturally. For although the natural light of the human mind is insufficient to show us these things made manifest by faith, it is nevertheless impossible that these things which the divine principle gives us by faith are contrary to these implanted in us by nature [reason]. Indeed, were that the case, one or the other would have to be false, and, since both are given to us by God, God would have to be the author of untruth, which is impossible. . . . [I]t is impossible that those things which are of philosophy can be contrary to those things which are of faith.[28]

Aquinas also investigated the branch of philosophy called *epistemology,* which is concerned with how a person knows something. Aquinas stated that one knows, first, through sensory perception of the physical world—seeing, hearing, touching, and so on. He maintained that there can be nothing in the mind that is not first in the senses. Second, knowledge comes through reason, the mind exercising its natural abilities. Aquinas stressed the power of human reason to know, even to know God. Proofs of the existence of God exemplify the Scholastic method of knowing.

Aquinas began with the things of the natural world—earth, air, trees, water, birds. Then he inquired about their original source or cause: the mover, creator, planner who started it all. Everything, Aquinas maintained, has an ultimate and essential explanation, a reason for existing. Here he was following Aristotle. Aquinas went further and identified the reason for existing, or first mover, with God. Aquinas and all medieval intellectuals held that the end of faith and reason was the knowledge of, and union with, God. His work later became the fundamental text of Roman Catholic doctrine.

At all universities, the standard method of teaching was the *lecture*—that is, a reading. The professor read a passage from the Bible, the Justinian *Code,* or one of Aristotle's treatises. He then explained and interpreted the passage; his interpretation was called a *gloss.* Students wrote down everything. Texts and glosses were sometimes collected and reproduced as textbooks. For example, the Italian Peter Lombard (d. 1160), a professor at Paris, wrote what became the standard textbook

MAP 11.6 Intellectual Centers of Medieval Europe
Universities obviously provided more sophisticated instruction than did monastery and cathedral schools. What other factors distinguish the three kinds of intellectual centers?

in theology, *Sententiae* (The Sentences), a compilation of basic theological principles.

Because books had to be copied by hand, they were extremely expensive, and few students could afford them. Students therefore depended for study on their own or friends' notes accumulated over a period of years. The choice of subjects was narrow. The syllabus at all universities consisted of a core of ancient texts that all students studied and, if they wanted to get ahead, mastered.

There were no examinations at the end of a series of lectures. Examinations were given after three, four, or five years of study, when the student applied for a degree. The professors determined the amount of material students had to know for each degree, and students frequently insisted that the professors specify precisely what that material was. When the candidate for a degree believed himself prepared, he presented himself to a committee of professors for examination.

Examinations were oral and very difficult. If the candidate passed, he was awarded the first, or bachelor's, degree. Further study, about as long, arduous, and expensive as it is today, enabled the graduate to try for the master's and doctor's degrees. All degrees certified competence in a given subject, and degrees were technically licenses to teach. Most students, however, did not become teachers. They staffed the expanding royal and papal administrations.

Gothic Art

Medieval churches stand as the most spectacular manifestations of medieval vitality and creativity. It is difficult for twentieth-century people to appreciate the extraordinary amounts of energy, imagination, and money involved in building them. Between 1180 and 1270 in France alone, eighty cathedrals, about five hundred abbey churches, and tens of thousands of parish churches were constructed. This construction represents a remarkable investment for a country of scarcely 18 million people. More stone was quarried for churches in medieval France than had been mined in ancient Egypt, where the Great Pyramid alone consumed 40.5 million cubic feet of stone. All these churches displayed a new architectural style. Fifteenth-century critics called the new style "Gothic" because they mistakenly believed the fifth-century Goths had invented it. It actually developed partly in reaction to the earlier "Romanesque" style, which resembled ancient Roman architecture.

Gothic cathedrals were built in towns and reflect both bourgeois wealth and enormous civic pride. The manner in which a society spends its wealth expresses its values. Cathedrals, abbeys, and village churches testify to the deep religious faith and piety of medieval people. If the dominant aspect of medieval culture had not been the Christian faith, the builder's imagination and the merchant's money would have been used in other ways.

From Romanesque Gloom to "Uninterrupted Light"

The relative political stability and increase of ecclesiastical wealth in the eleventh century encouraged the arts of peace. In the ninth and tenth centuries, the Vikings and Magyars had burned hundreds of wooden churches. In the eleventh century, the abbots wanted to rebuild in a more permanent fashion, and after the year 1000, church building increased on a wide scale. Because fireproofing was essential, ceilings had to be made of stone. Therefore, builders replaced wooden roofs with arched stone ceilings called "vaults." The stone ceilings were heavy; only thick walls could support them. Because the walls were so thick, the windows were small, allowing little light into the interior of the church. The basic features of such Romanesque architecture are stone vaults in the ceiling, a rounded arch over the nave (the central part of the church), and thick, heavy walls. In northern Europe, twin bell towers often crowned Romanesque churches, giving them a powerful, fortresslike appearance. Built primarily by monasteries, Romanesque churches reflect the quasi-military, aristocratic, and pre-urban society that built them.

The inspiration for the Gothic style originated in the brain of one monk, Suger, abbot of Saint-Denis (1122–1151). When Suger became abbot, he decided to reconstruct the old Carolingian abbey church at Saint-Denis. Work began in 1137. On June 11, 1144, King Louis VII and a large crowd of bishops, dignitaries, and common people witnessed the solemn consecration of the first Gothic church in France.

The basic features of Gothic architecture—the pointed arch, the ribbed vault, and the flying buttress—were not unknown before 1137. What was without precedent was the interior lightness they made possible. Since the ceiling of a Gothic church weighed less than that of a Romanesque church, the walls could be thinner. Stained-glass windows were cut into the stone, flooding the church with light. The bright interior was astounding. Suger, describing his achievement, exulted:

bines. But Gregory did not foresee the consequences of this order. Laypersons assumed they could remove immoral priests. Critics and heretics could accuse clergymen of immorality and thus weaken their influence. Moreover, by forbidding sinful priests to administer the sacraments, Gregory unwittingly revived the old Donatist heresy, which held that sacraments given by an immoral priest were useless; thus Donatist beliefs spread. The clergy's inability to provide adequate instruction weakened its position.

In northern Italian towns, Arnold of Brescia, a vigorous advocate of strict clerical poverty, denounced clerical wealth. In France Peter Waldo, a rich merchant of Lyons, gave his money to the poor and preached that only prayers, not sacraments, were needed for salvation. The "Waldensians"—as Peter's followers were called—bitterly attacked the sacraments and church hierarchy, and they carried these ideas across Europe. Another group, known either as the Cathars (from the Greek *katharos,* meaning "pure") or as the Albigensians (from the town of Albi in southern France), rejected not only the hierarchical organization and the sacraments of the church, but the Roman church itself. The Cathars' primary tenet was the dualist belief that God had created spiritual things and the Devil had created material things; thus the soul was good and the body evil. Forces of good and evil battled constantly, and leading a perfect life meant being stripped of all physical and material things. Thus sexual intercourse was evil because it led to the creation of more physical bodies. To free oneself from the power of evil, a person had to lead a life of extreme asceticism, avoiding all material things. Albigensians were divided into the "perfect," who followed the principles of Catharism, and the "believers," who led ordinary lives until their deaths, when they repented and were saved.

The Albigensian heresy won many adherents in southern France. Townspeople admired the virtuous lives of the "perfect," which contrasted very favorably with the luxurious living of the Roman clergy. Women were attracted because the Albigensians treated them as men's equals, and nobles were drawn because they coveted the wealth of the clergy. Faced with widespread defection in southern France, Pope Innocent III in 1208 proclaimed a crusade against the Albigensian heretics. When the papal legate was murdered by a follower of Count Raymond of Toulouse, the greatest lord in southern France and a suspected heretic, the crusade took on a political character; heretical beliefs became fused with feudal rebellion against the French crown. Northern French lords joined the crusade and inflicted severe defeats on the towns of the province of Languedoc. The Albigensian crusade, however, was a political rather than a religious success, and the heresy went underground.

In its continuing struggle against heresy, the church gained the support of two remarkable men, Saint Dominic and Saint Francis, and of the orders they founded. Born in Castile, the province of Spain famous for its zealous Christianity and militant opposition to Islam, Domingo de Gúzman (1170?–1221) received a sound education and was ordained a priest. In 1206 he accompanied his bishop on a mission to preach to the Albigensian heretics in Languedoc. Although the austere simplicity in which they traveled contrasted favorably with the pomp and display of the papal legate in the area, Dominic's efforts had little practical success. Determined to win the heretics back with ardent preaching, Dominic subsequently returned to France with a few followers. In 1216 the group—known as the "Preaching Friars"—won papal recognition as a new religious order. Their name indicates their goal; they were to preach, and in order to preach effectively, they had to study. Dominic sent his recruits to the universities for training in theology.

Francesco di Bernardone (1181–1226), son of a wealthy cloth merchant from the northern Italian town of Assisi, was an extravagant wastrel until he had a sudden conversion. Then he determined to devote himself entirely to living the Gospel. Directed by a vision to rebuild the dilapidated chapel of Saint Damiano in Assisi, Francis sold some of his father's cloth to finance the reconstruction. His enraged father insisted that he return the money and enlisted the support of the bishop. When the bishop told Francis to obey his father, Francis took off all his clothes and returned them to his father. Thereafter he promised to obey only his Father in heaven. Francis was particularly inspired by two biblical texts: "If you seek perfection, go, sell your possessions, and give to the poor. You will have treasure in heaven. Afterward, come back and follow me" (Matthew 19:21); and Jesus' advice to his disciples as they went out to preach, "Take nothing for the journey, neither walking staff nor travelling bag, nor bread, nor money" (Luke 9:3). Over the centuries, these words have stimulated countless young people. With Francis, however, there was a radical difference: he intended to observe them literally and without compromise. He set out to live and preach the Gospel in absolute poverty.

The simplicity, humility, and joyful devotion with which Francis carried out his mission soon attracted companions. Although he resisted pressure to establish an order, his followers became so numerous that he was obliged to develop some formal structure. In 1221 the

Saint Dominic and the Inquisition The fifteenth-century court painter to the Spanish rulers Ferdinand and Isabella, Pedro Berruguete here portrays an event from the life of Saint Dominic: Dominic presides at the trial of Count Raymond of Toulouse who had supported the Albigensian heretics. Raymond, helmeted and on horseback, repented and was pardoned; his companions, who would not repent, were burned. Smoke from the fire has put one of the judges to sleep, and other officials, impervious to the human tragedy, chat among themselves. *(Museo del Prado, Madrid)*

papacy approved the "Rule of the Little Brothers of Saint Francis," as the Franciscans were known.

The new Dominican and Franciscan orders differed significantly from older monastic orders such as the Benedictines and the Cistercians. (So also did the Beguines, laywomen who wished to live a religious life without becoming cloistered nuns; they lived in or near cities in northwestern Europe, led prayerful lives, and supported themselves through manual labor, teaching, or writing.) First, the Dominicans and Franciscans were friars, not monks. Their lives and work centered on the cities and university towns, the busy centers of commercial and intellectual life, not the secluded and cloistered world of monks. Second, the friars stressed apostolic poverty, a life based on the Gospel's teachings, in which they would own no property and depend on Christian people for their material needs. Hence they were called *mendicants*, begging friars. Benedictine and Cistercian abbeys, on the other hand, held land—not infrequently great tracts of land. Finally, the friars usually drew their members largely from the burgher class, from small property owners and shopkeepers. The monastic orders, by contrast, gathered their members (at least until the thirteenth century) overwhelmingly from the nobility.[38]

The friars represented a response to the spiritual and intellectual needs of the thirteenth century. Research on the German friars has shown that, while the Franciscans initially accepted uneducated men, the Dominicans always showed a marked preference for university graduates.[39] A more urban and sophisticated society required a highly educated clergy. The Dominicans soon held professorial chairs at leading universities, and they count Thomas Aquinas, probably the greatest medieval philosopher in Europe, as their most famous member. But the Franciscans followed suit at the universities and also produced intellectual leaders. The Franciscans' mission to the towns and the poor, their ideal of poverty, and their compassion for the human condition made them vastly popular. The friars interpreted Christian doctrine for the new urban classes. By living Christianity as well as by preaching it, they won the respect of the medieval bourgeoisie.

Dominic started his order to combat heresy. Francis's followers were motivated by the ideal of absolute poverty. Beginning in 1233, the papacy used the friars to staff a new ecclesiastical court, the Inquisition. Popes selected the friars to direct the Inquisition because bishops proved unreliable and because special theological training was needed. *Inquisition* means "investigation," and the Franciscans and Dominicans developed expert methods of rooting out unorthodox thought. Modern Americans consider the procedures of the Inquisition exceedingly unjust, and there was substantial criticism of it in the Middle Ages. The accused did not learn the evidence against them or see their accusers; they were subjected to lengthy interrogations often designed to trap them; and torture could be used to extract confessions. Medieval people, however, believed that heretics destroyed the souls of their neighbors. By attacking religion, it was also thought, heretics destroyed the very bonds of society. By the mid-thirteenth century secular governments steadily pressed for social conformity, and they had the resources to search out and to punish heretics. So successful was the Inquisition as a tool of royal power that within a century heresy had been virtually extinguished.

A Challenge to Religious Authority

Societies, like individuals, cannot maintain a high level of energy indefinitely. In the later years of the thirteenth century, Europeans seemed to run out of steam. The crusading movement gradually fizzled out. Few new cathedrals were constructed, and if a cathedral had not been completed by 1300, the chances were high that it never would be. The strong rulers of England and France, building on the foundations of their predecessors, increased their authority and gained the loyalty of all their subjects. The vigor of those kings, however, did not pass to their immediate descendants. Meanwhile, the church, which for two centuries had guided Christian society, began to face grave difficulties. A violent dispute between the papacy and the kings of England and France badly damaged the prestige of the pope.

In 1294 King Edward I of England and Philip the Fair of France declared war on each other. To finance this war, both kings laid taxes on the clergy. Kings had been taxing the church for decades. Pope Boniface VIII (1294–1303), arguing from precedent, insisted that kings gain papal consent for taxation of the clergy and forbade churchmen to pay the taxes. But Edward and Philip refused to accept this decree, partly because it hurt royal finances and partly because the papal order threatened royal authority within their countries. Edward immediately denied the clergy the protection of the law, an action that meant its members could be attacked with impunity. Philip halted the shipment of all ecclesiastical revenue to Rome. Boniface had to back down.

Philip the Fair and his ministers continued their attack on all powers in France outside royal authority. Philip arrested a French bishop who was also the papal legate. When Boniface defended the ecclesiastical status and diplomatic immunity of the bishop, Philip replied with the trumped-up charge that the pope was a heretic. The papacy and the French monarchy waged a bitter war of propaganda. Finally, in 1302, in a letter titled *Unam Sanctam* (because its opening sentence spoke of one holy Catholic church), Boniface insisted that all Christians were subject to the pope. Although the letter made no specific reference to Philip, it held that kings should submit to papal authority. Philip's university-trained advisers responded with an argument drawn from Roman law. They maintained that the king of France was completely sovereign in his kingdom and responsible to God alone. French mercenary troops went to Italy and assaulted and arrested the aged pope at Anagni. Although Boniface was soon freed, he died shortly afterward. The confrontation at Anagni foreshadowed serious difficulties within the Christian church, but religious struggle was only one of the crises that would face Western society in the fourteenth century.

Summary

The High Middle Ages represent one of the most creative periods in the history of Western society. Advances were made in the evolution of strong government and urban life, economic development, architectural design, and education. Through the instruments of justice and finance, the kings of England and France attacked feudal rights and provincial practices, built centralized bureaucracies, and gradually came in contact with all their subjects. In so doing these rulers laid the foundations for modern nation states. The German emperors, who were preoccupied with Italian affairs and with a quest for the imperial crown, supported feudal and local interests.

Medieval cities—whether beginning around the sites of cathedrals, fortifications, or market towns—recruited people from the countryside and brought into being a new social class, the middle class. Cities provided economic opportunity, which, together with the revival of long-distance trade and a new capitalistic spirit, led to greater wealth, a higher standard of living, and upward social mobility. The soaring Gothic cathedrals that medieval towns erected demonstrate civic pride, deep religious faith, and economic vitality. Universities, institutions of higher learning unique to the West, emerged from cathedral and municipal schools and provided trained officials for the new government bureaucracies. While the church exercised leadership of Christian society in the High Middle Ages, the clash between the papacy and the kings of France and England at the end of the thirteenth century seriously challenged papal power.

Notes

1. S. Reynolds, *Fiefs and Vassals: The Medieval Evidence Reconsidered* (Oxford: Clarendon Press, 1996), p. 27.
2. C. W. Hollister, "Normandy, France and the Anglo-Norman Regnum," in *Monarchy, Magnates and Institutions in the Anglo-Norman World* (London: Hambledon Press, 1986), p. 20.
3. D. C. Douglas and G. E. Greenaway, eds., *English Historical Documents,* vol. 2 (London: Eyre & Spottiswoode, 1961), p. 853.
4. W. L. Warren, *Henry II* (Berkeley: University of California Press, 1973), pp. 229–230.
5. See G. E. Spiegel, "The Cult of Saint Denis and Capetian Kingship," *Journal of Medieval History* 1 (April 1975): 43–65, esp. pp. 56–64.
6. B. Arnold, *Princes and Territories in Medieval Germany* (New York: Cambridge University Press, 1991), pp. 65–72.
7. Ibid., pp. 45–52, 73, passim.
8. R. Bartlett, *Trial by Fire and Water: The Medieval Judicial Ordeal* (Oxford: Clarendon Press, 1986), pp. 25–27 and chap. 3.
9. Arnold, *Princes and Territories,* pp. 186–200.
10. J. Boswell, *Christianity, Social Tolerance, and Homosexuality: Gay People in Western Europe from the Beginning of the Christian Era to the Fourteenth Century* (Chicago: University of Chicago Press, 1980), pp. 270–293; the quotation is from p. 293. For alternative interpretations, see K. Thomas, "Rescuing Homosexual History," *New York Review of Books,* December 4, 1980, 26ff.; and J. DuQ. Adams, *Speculum* 56 (April 1981): 350ff. For the French monarchy's persecution of the Jews, see J. W. Baldwin, *The Government of Philip Augustus: Foundations of French Royal Power in the Middle Ages* (Berkeley: University of California Press, 1986), pp. 51–52; and W. C. Jordan, *The French Monarchy and the Jews* (Philadelphia: University of Pennsylvania Press, 1989).
11. J. C. Russell, *Medieval Regions and Their Cities* (Bloomington: University of Indiana Press, 1972), p. 91.
12. Ibid., pp. 113–117.
13. Quoted in R. S. Lopez, "Of Towns and Trade," in *Life and Thought in the Early Middle Ages,* ed. R. S. Hoyt (Minneapolis: University of Minnesota Press, 1967), p. 33.
14. H. Pirenne, *Economic and Social History of Medieval Europe* (New York: Harcourt Brace, 1956), p. 53.
15. See D. Herlihy, *Medieval and Renaissance Pistoia: The Social History of an Italian Town, 1200–1430* (New Haven, Conn.: Yale University Press, 1967), p. 257.
16. Quoted in J. O'Faolain and L. Martines, eds., *Not in God's Image: Women in History from the Greeks to the Victorians* (New York: Harper & Row, 1973), pp. 155–156.
17. W. C. Jordan, *Women and Credit in Pre-Industrial and Developing Societies* (Philadelphia: University of Pennsylvania Press, 1993), pp. 20 et seq.
18. Douglas and Greenaway, *English Historical Documents,* vol. 2, pp. 969–970.
19. H. Rothwell, ed., *English Historical Documents,* vol. 3 (London: Eyre & Spottiswoode, 1975), p. 854.
20. M. M. Postan, *The Medieval Economy and Society: An Economic History of Britain in the Middle Ages* (Baltimore: Penguin Books, 1975), pp. 213–214.
21. See P. Spufford, *Money and Its Use in Medieval Europe* (Cambridge: Cambridge University Press, 1988), pp. 250–255.
22. See P. Dollinger, *The German Hansa,* trans. and ed. D. S. Ault and S. H. Steinberg (Stanford, Calif.: Stanford University Press, 1970).
23. C. M. Cipolla, *Before the Industrial Revolution: European Society and Economy, 1000–1700,* 2d ed. (New York: W. W. Norton, 1980), p. 197.
24. R. S. Lopez, "The Trade of Medieval Europe: The South," in *The Cambridge Economic History of Europe,* vol. 2, ed. M. M. Postan and E. E. Rich (Cambridge: Cambridge University Press, 1952), p. 289.
25. M. Haren, *Medieval Thought: The Western Intellectual Tradition from Antiquity to the Thirteenth Century,* 2d ed. (Toronto: University of Toronto Press, 1992), pp. 137–138.
26. Quoted in H. E. Sigerist, *Civilization and Disease* (Chicago: University of Chicago Press, 1943), p. 102.
27. See Haren, *Medieval Thought,* pp. 117–119.
28. Quoted in J. H. Mundy, *Europe in the High Middle Ages, 1150–1309* (New York: Basic Books, 1973), pp. 474–475.
29. E. Panofsky, trans. and ed., *Abbot Suger on the Abbey Church of St. Denis and Its Art Treasures* (Princeton, N.J.: Princeton University Press, 1946), p. 101.
30. See C. M. Radding and W. W. Clark, *Medieval Architecture, Medieval Learning: Builders and Masters in the Age of Romanesque and Gothic* (New Haven, Conn.: Yale University Press, 1992), pp. 34–36.
31. See J. Gimpel, *The Cathedral Builders* (New York: Grove Press, 1961), pp. 42–49.
32. Quoted in J. J. Wilhelm, ed., *Lyrics of the Middle Ages: An Anthology* (New York: Garland Publishers, 1993), pp. 83–84.
33. Quoted in R. Boase, *The Origin and Meaning of Courtly Love* (Manchester, 1977), pp. 129–130.
34. I have leaned on the very persuasive interpretation of M. R. Menocal, *The Arabic Role in Medieval Literary History* (Philadelphia: University of Pennsylvania Press, 1990), pp. ix–xv and 27–33.
35. J. B. Freed, *The Friars and German Society in the Thirteenth Century* (Cambridge, Mass.: Medieval Academy of America, 1977), p. 8.
36. Ibid., p. 9.
37. See F. Oakley, *The Western Church in the Later Middle Ages* (Ithaca, N.Y.: Cornell University Press, 1979), p. 175.
38. See Freed, *The Friars and German Society,* pp. 119–128.
39. Ibid., esp. p. 125.

SUGGESTED READING

For Anglo-Saxon, Norman, Angevin, and Plantagenet England see, in addition to the excellent studies by Hollister and Warren cited in the Notes, R. P. Abels, *Lordship and Military Obligation in Anglo-Saxon England* (1988), which is based on a wide variety of sources and explores the fundamental relationship between lordship and military obligation; J. Hudson, *Land, Law, and Lordship in Anglo-Norman England* (1994), which studies the importance of land tenure; C. A. Newman, *The Anglo-Norman Nobility in the Reign of Henry I: The Second Generation* (1988), which focuses on the familial, economic, religious, and political network of relationships used as means of noble advancement; R. V. Turner, *Men Raised from the Dust: Administrative Service and Upward Mobility in Angevin England* (1988), which gives the biographies of six men who rose to high office through service to the Crown. Students interested in virtually any aspect of English warfare will find M. Prestwich, *Armies and Warfare in the Middle Ages: The English Experience* (1996), exciting and readable. S. Morillo, *Warfare Under the Anglo-Norman Kings, 1066–1135* (1994), is also useful.

Several older studies contain helpful perspectives: R. A. Brown, *The Normans* (1983), revitalizes the old thesis that the conquerors of England and Sicily were an exceptionally creative force in the eleventh and twelfth centuries. D. Howarth, *1066: The Year of the Conquest* (1981), is a lively and cleverly written account of the Norman Conquest of England from Norman, Scandinavian, and Anglo-Saxon perspectives. G. O. Sayles, *The Medieval Foundations of England* (1961), traces political and social developments to the end of the twelfth century, while H. G. Richardson and G. O. Sayles, *The Governance of Medieval England from the Conquest to Magna Carta* (1963), focuses on administrative change. For the Celtic fringe, S. Duffy, *Ireland in the Middle Ages* (1997), incorporates the latest research; M. Richter, *Medieval Ireland: The Enduring Tradition* (1996), concentrates on Irish society; and B. Webster, *Medieval Scotland* (1997), stresses the evolution of a distinctly Scottish identity.

Students interested in crime, society, and legal developments will find the following works useful and sound: J. S. Cockburn and T. A. Green, *Twelve Good Men and True: The Criminal Trial Jury in England, 1200–1800* (1988); J. B. Given, *Society and Homicide in Thirteenth-Century England* (1977); R. C. Palmer, *The County Courts of Medieval England, 1150–1350* (1982). E. M. Hallam, *Domesday Book Through Nine Centuries* (1986), is an excellent appreciation of that important document, while J. R. Strayer, *On the Medieval Origins of the Modern State* (1970), is a good synthesis of political, legal, and administrative developments. The standard study of Magna Carta is J. C. Holt, *Magna Carta,* 2d ed. (1992).

For the Becket controversy, see F. Barlow, *Thomas Becket* (1986), the best recent study; D. Knowles, *Thomas Becket* (1970); and B. Smalley, *The Becket Controversy and the Schools: A Study of Intellectuals in Politics in the Twelfth Century* (1973).

For France, both E. Hallam, *The Capetian Kings of France, 987–1328* (1980), and R. Fawtier, *The Capetian Kings of France* (1962), are readable introductions. Advanced students of medieval French administrative history should see J. Baldwin, *The Government of Philip Augustus: Foundations of French Royal Power in the Middle Ages* (1986); W. C. Jordan, *Louis IX and the Crusade* (1979); and J. R. Strayer, *The Reign of Philip the Fair* (1980).

For important revisionist interpretations of medieval Germany, see, in addition to the title by Arnold cited in the Notes, B. Arnold, *Count and Bishop in Medieval Germany* (1992), which is essential for understanding regional power and diversity; and J. B. Freed, *Noble Bondsmen: Ministerial Marriages in the Archdiocese of Salzburg, 1100–1343* (1995), a fine exploration of the disparity between the social status of the nobility and their legal status in southeastern Germany. P. Gorecki, *Economy, Society and Lordship in Poland, 1100–1250* (1992), contains helpful material on Germany as well as Poland. A. Haverkamp, *Medieval Germany 1056–1273,* trans. H. Braun and R. Mortimer (1992), gives a comprehensive picture. H. Furhman, *Germany in the High Middle Ages,* trans. T. Reuther (1986), and G. Barraclough, *The Origins of Modern Germany* (1963), are still helpful. M. Pacaut, *Frederick Barbarossa,* trans. A. J. Pomerans (1980), is perhaps the best one-volume treatment of that important ruler, but P. Munz, *Frederick Barbarossa* (1979), is also useful. D. Abulafia, *Frederick II: A Medieval Emperor* (1992), is a beautifully written revisionist study, but T. Van Cleve, *The Emperor Frederick II of Hohenstaufen* (1972), remains fundamental.

For the economic revival of Europe, see, in addition to the titles by Dollinger, Herlihy, Postan, Russell, and Spufford given in the Notes, D. Nicholas, *Medieval Flanders* (1992), and T. H. Lloyd, *England and the German Hanse, 1157–1611: A Study in Their Trade and Commercial Diplomacy* (1992). The effect of climate on population and economic growth is discussed in E. L. Ladurie, *Times of Feast, Times of Famine: A History of Climate Since the Year 1000,* trans. B. Bray (1971). A masterful account of agricultural changes and their sociological implications is to be found in G. Duby, *The Early Growth of the European Economy: Warriors and Peasants from the Seventh to the Twelfth Century* (1978).

For women, see C. Klapisch-Zuber, ed., *A History of Women.* Vol. 2: *Silences of the Middle Ages* (1992), which contains useful essays on many aspects of women's lives and status; and S. Shahar, *The Fourth Estate: Women in the Middle Ages* (1983), a provocative work. J. M. Bennett, *Women in the Medieval English Countryside: Gender and Household in Brigstock Before the Plague* (1987), is a fascinating case study, while E. Amt, ed., *Women's Lives in Medieval Europe: A Sourcebook* (1993), has fresh primary material on many aspects of women's lives. P. J. P. Gold

(continued on page 376)

LISTENING TO THE PAST

London in the Late Twelfth Century

As a background to his Life of Thomas Becket *(ca 1175), the chronicler William fitz-Stephen provided a lengthy description of London, which is excerpted here. The author clearly knew London well, and his account represents a superb example of civic pride and patriotism.*

Among the noble and celebrated cities of the world that of London, the capital of the kingdom of the English, is one which extends its glory farther than all the others and sends its wealth and merchandise more widely into distant lands. . . . It is happy in the healthiness of its air; in its observance of Christian practice; in the strength of its fortifications; in its natural situation; in the honour of its citizens; and in the modesty of its matrons. It is cheerful in its sports, and the fruitful mother of noble men. . . . The citizens of London are regarded as conspicuous above all others for their polished manners, for their dress and for the good tables, which they keep. . . .

In London the three principal churches have famous schools by special privilege and by virtue of their ancient dignity. But through the favour of some magnate, or through the presence of teachers who are notable or famous in philosophy, there are also other schools. On feast-days the masters hold meetings for their pupils in the church whose festival it is. The scholars dispute, some with oratory and some with argument. . . .

Those engaged in business of various kinds, sellers of merchandise, hirers of labour, are distributed every morning into their several localities according to their trade. Besides, there is in London on the river bank among the wines for sale in ships and in the cellars of the vintners a public cook-shop. There daily you may find food according to the season, dishes of meat, roast, fried and boiled, large and small fish, coarser meats for the poor and more delicate for the rich, such as venison and big and small birds. If any of the citizens should unexpectedly receive visitors, weary from their journey, who would fain not wait until fresh food is bought and cooked, or until the servants have brought bread or water for washing, they hasten to the river bank and there find all they need. . . .

Immediately outside one of the gates there is a field [Smithfield] which is smooth both in fact and in name. On every sixth day of the week, unless it be a major feast-day, there takes place there a famous exhibition of fine horses for sale. Earls, barons and knights, who are in the town, and many citizens come out to see or to buy. It is pleasant to see the high-stepping palfreys with their gleaming coats, as they go through their paces, putting down their feet alternately on one side together. . . .

By themselves in another part of the field stand the goods and animals of the country-folk: implements of husbandry, swine with long flanks, cows with full udders, oxen of immense size, and woolly sheep. There also stand the mares fit for plough, some big with foal, and others with brisk young colts closely following them.

To this city from every nation under heaven merchants delight to bring their trade by sea. The Arabian sends gold; the Sabaean spice and incense. The Scythian brings arms, and from the rich, fat lands of Babylon comes oil of palms. The Nile sends precious stones; the men of Norway and Russia, furs and sables; nor is China absent with pure silk. The Gauls come with their wines.

I do not think there is a city with a better record for church-going, doing honour to God's ordinances, keeping feast-days, giving alms and hospitality to strangers, confirming betrothals, contracting marriages, celebrating weddings, providing feasts, entertaining guests, and also, it may be added, in care for funerals and for the burial of the dead. The only plagues of London are the immoderate drinking of fools and the frequency of fires.

Instead of shows in the theatre and stage-plays, London provides plays of a more sacred character, wherein are presented the miracles worked by saintly confessors or the sufferings which made illustrious the constancy of martyrs. Furthermore, every year on the day called Carnival—to begin with the sports of boys (for we were all boys once)—scholars from the different schools bring fighting-cocks to their masters, and the whole morning is set apart to watch their cocks do battle in the schools, for the boys are given a holiday that day. After dinner all the young men of the town go out into the fields in the suburbs to play ball. The scholars of the various schools have their own ball, and almost all the followers of each occupation have theirs also. The seniors and the fathers and the wealthy magnates of the city come on horseback to watch the contests of the younger generation, and in their turn recover their lost youth. . . .

Every Sunday in Lent after dinner a fresh swarm of young men goes forth into the fields on warhorses, steeds foremost in the contest, each of which is skilled and schooled to run in circles. . . . They make a pretence at war, carry out field-exercises and indulge in mimic combats. Thither too come many courtiers, when the king is in town, and from the households of bishops, earls and barons come youths and adolescents, not yet girt with the belt of knighthood, for the pleasure of engaging in combat with one another. Each is inflamed with the hope of victory.

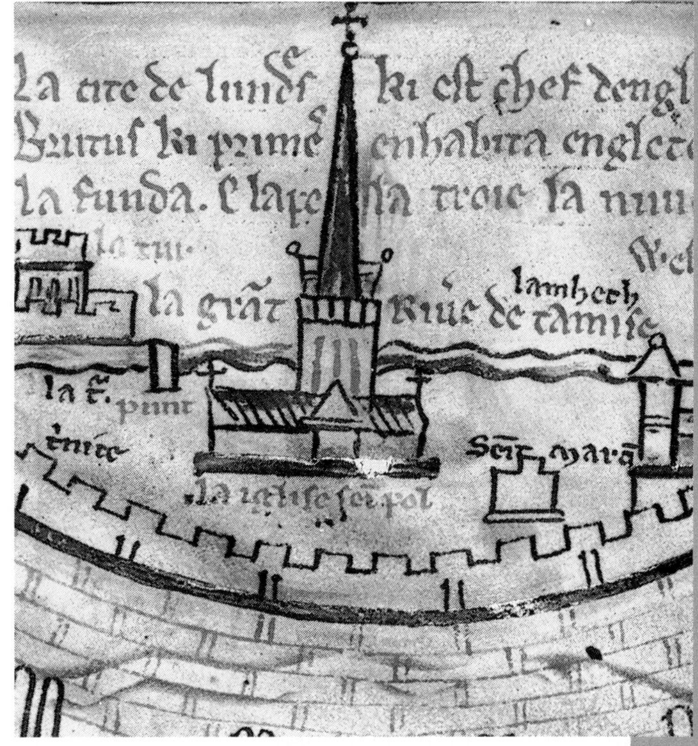

✣ The first-known view of London, from a road map, 1252. *(British Library)*

Questions for Analysis

1. What educational, commercial, religious, and recreational opportunities did late-twelfth-century London offer? Which of these did the author consider most important? Why?
2. According to fitz-Stephen, what were London's disadvantages?
3. A modern scholar would welcome more contemporary information about London's government and business activity. Why, in your judgment, did fitz-Stephen fail to give more detail on these topics?

Source: "Life of Thomas Beckett" by William fitz-Stephen from *English Historical Documents II,* by D. C. Douglas and G. E. Greenaway, eds.

berg, ed., *Women in England, 1275–1525* (1996), is also a useful collection of sources. For royal women, P. Stafford, *Queen Emma and Queen Edith: Queenship and Women's Power in Eleventh-Century England* (1997), describes the integral role of queens in royal government; and J. C. Parsons, *Eleanor of Castile* (1995), is an important study of Edward I's wife and her public image.

Students interested in the origins of medieval towns and cities will learn how historians use the evidence of coins, archaeology, tax records, geography, and laws in J. F. Benton, ed., *Town Origins: The Evidence of Medieval England* (1968). S. Reynolds, *An Introduction to the History of English Medieval Towns* (1982), explores the social structure, political organization, and economic livelihood of English towns, while R. H. Hilton, *English and French Towns in Feudal Society* (1992), is an exciting comparative study. R. Muir, *The English Village* (1980), offers a survey of many aspects of ordinary people's daily lives. C. Tilly and W. P. Blockmans, eds., *Cities and the Rise of States in Europe, A.D. 1000–1800* (1994), contains valuable articles on cities in Italy, Spain, the German Empire, Scandinavia, and the Low Countries.

For the new currents of thought in the High Middle Ages, see, in addition to the title by Haren cited in the Notes, D. W. Robertson, Jr., *Abélard and Héloise* (1972), which is highly readable and commonsensical; M. T. Clanchy, *Abelard: A Medieval Life* (1997), which incorporates the most recent international research; C. H. Haskins, *The Renaissance of the Twelfth Century* (1971), a classic; and C. W. Hollister, ed., *The Twelfth-Century Renaissance* (1969), a well-constructed anthology with source materials on many aspects of twelfth-century culture. N. Orme, *Education and Society in Medieval and Renaissance England* (1989), focuses on early education, schools, and literacy in English medieval society, while J. Leclercq, *The Love of Learning and the Desire of God* (1974), discusses monastic literary culture. For the development of literacy among laypeople and the formation of a literate mentality, the advanced student should see M. T. Clanchy, *From Memory to Written Record: England, 1066–1307*, 2d ed. (1992). Written by outstanding scholars in a variety of fields, R. L. Benson and G. Constable with C. D. Lanham, eds., *Renaissance and Renewal in the Twelfth Century* (1982), contains an invaluable collection of articles.

On the medieval universities, H. De Ridder-Symoens, ed., *A History of the University in Europe.* Vol. 1: *Universities in the Middle Ages* (1991), offers up-to-date interpretations by leading scholars, while H. Rashdall, *The Universities of Europe in the Middle Ages* (1936), is the standard scholarly work. G. Leff, *Paris and Oxford Universities in the Thirteenth and Fourteenth Centuries* (1968), gives a fascinating sketch and includes a useful bibliography. For the beginnings of Scholasticism and humanism, see the essential R. W. Southern, *Scholastic Humanism and the Unification of Western Europe,* vol. 1 (1994).

F. and J. Gies, *Cathedral, Forge, and Waterwheel* (1993), provides an exciting and illustrated survey of medieval technological achievements. The following studies are all valuable for the evolution and development of the Gothic style: J. Harvey, *The Gothic World* (1969) and *The Master Builders* (1971); P. Frankl, *The Gothic* (1960); and J. Bony, *French Gothic Architecture of the Twelfth and Thirteenth Centuries* (1983). D. Grivot and G. Zarnecki, *Gislebertus, Sculptor of Autun* (1961), is the finest appreciation of Romanesque architecture written in English. For the actual work of building, see D. Macaulay, *Cathedral: The Story of Its Construction* (1961), which explores the engineering problems involved in cathedral building and places the subject within its social context. Advanced students will enjoy E. Male, *The Gothic Image: Religious Art in France in the Thirteenth Century* (1958), which contains a wealth of fascinating and useful detail. For the most important cathedrals in France, architecturally and politically, see A. Temko, *Notre Dame of Paris: The Biography of a Cathedral* (1968); G. Henderson, *Chartres* (1968); and A. Katzenellengoben, *The Sculptural Programs of Chartres Cathedral* (1959). E. Panofsky, *Abbot Suger on the Abbey Church of St.-Denis and Its Art Treasures* (1946), provides a contemporary background account of the first Gothic building, while C. A. Bruzelius, *The Thirteenth-Century Church at St. Denis* (1985), traces later reconstruction. J. Gimpel, *The Medieval Machine: The Industrial Revolution of the Middle Ages* (1977), an extremely useful book, discusses the mechanical and scientific problems involved in early industrialization and shows how construction affected the medieval environment.

On troubadour poetry, see, in addition to the titles by Boase and Wilhelm cited in the Notes, M. Bogin, *The Women Troubadours* (1980).

The following works are helpful for an understanding of medieval heresy: M. Lambert, *Medieval Heresy: Popular Movements from the Gregorian Reform to the Reformation,* rev. ed. (1992); E. Peters, *Heresy and Authority in Medieval Europe* (1980), *Inquisition* (1989), and *Torture* (1985); and R. Kieckhefer, *Magic in the Middle Ages* (1990).

The conflict between Pope Boniface VIII and the kings of France and England is well treated in J. R. Strayer, *The Reign of Philip the Fair* (1980), and M. Prestwich, *Edward I* (1988), both sound and important biographies.

CHAPTER

12 The Crisis of the Later Middle Ages

Dante's Inferno: frontispiece from an early manuscript of the *Divine Comedy.* Dante, wearing a red robe, is guided by Virgil, in blue, through the agonies of hell. *(Bibliothèque Nationale, Paris)*

During the later Middle Ages, the last book of the New Testament, the Book of Revelation, inspired thousands of sermons and hundreds of religious tracts. The Book of Revelation deals with visions of the end of the world, with disease, war, famine, and death. It is no wonder this part of the Bible was so popular. Between 1300 and 1450, Europeans experienced a frightful series of shocks: economic dislocation, plague, war, social upheaval, and increased crime and violence. Death and preoccupation with death make the fourteenth century one of the most wrenching periods of Western civilization. Yet, in spite of the pessimism and crises, important institutions and ideas, such as representative assemblies and national literatures, emerged.

The miseries and disasters of the later Middle Ages bring to mind a number of questions.

- What economic difficulties did Europe experience?
- What were the social and psychological effects of repeated attacks of plague and disease?
- Some scholars maintain that war is often the catalyst for political, economic, and social change. Does this theory have validity for the fourteenth century?
- What provoked schism in the church, and what impact did it have on the lives of ordinary people?
- How did new national literatures reflect political and social developments?
- How and why did the laws of settlers in frontier regions reveal a strong racial or ethnic discrimination?

This chapter will focus on these questions.

Prelude to Disaster

Economic difficulties began to emerge in the later thirteenth century; by the start of the fourteenth century, they were widespread. In the first decade, the countries of northern Europe experienced a considerable price inflation. The cost of grain, livestock, and dairy products rose sharply. Severe weather, which historical geographers label the "Little Ice Age," made a serious situation frightful. An unusual number of storms brought torrential rains, ruining the wheat, oat, and hay crops on which people and animals almost everywhere depended. Since long-distance transportation of food was expensive and difficult, most urban areas depended for bread and meat on areas no more than a day's journey away. Poor harvests—and one in four was likely to be poor—led to scarcity and starvation. Almost all of northern Europe suffered a terrible famine in the years 1315–1322, which contemporaries interpreted as a recurrence of the biblical "seven lean years" (Genesis 42).

Reduced caloric intake meant increased susceptibility to disease, especially for infants, children, and the elderly. Workingmen and workingwomen on a reduced diet had less energy, which in turn meant lower productivity, lower output, and higher grain prices. The great famine proved a demographic disaster in France; in Burgundy perhaps one-third of the population died. The many religious houses of Flanders experienced a high loss of monks, nuns, and priests.

Hardly had western Europe begun to recover from this disaster when another struck. An epidemic of typhoid fever carried away thousands. In 1316, 10 percent of the population of the city of Ypres may have died between May and October alone. Then in 1318 disease hit cattle and sheep, drastically reducing the herds and flocks. Another bad harvest in 1321 brought famine and death.

The province of Languedoc in France presents a classic example of agrarian crisis. For over 150 years, Languedoc had enjoyed continual land reclamation, steady agricultural expansion, and enormous population growth. Then the fourteenth century opened with four years of bad harvests. Torrential rains in 1310 ruined the harvest and brought on terrible famine. Harvests failed again in 1322 and 1329. In 1332 desperate peasants survived the winter on raw herbs. In the half century from 1302 to 1348, poor harvests occurred twenty times. The undernourished population was ripe for the Grim Reaper, who appeared in 1348 in the form of the Black Death.

These catastrophes had grave social consequences. Poor harvests and famine led to the abandonment of homesteads. In parts of the Low Countries and in the Scottish-English borderlands, entire villages were abandoned. This meant a great increase in the number of vagabonds, what we call "homeless people." In Flanders and East Anglia (eastern England), where aspects of the famine have been carefully analyzed, some rustics were forced to mortgage, sublease, or sell their holdings to get money to buy food. Rich farmers bought out their poorer neighbors. When conditions improved, debtors tried to get their lands back, leading to a very volatile land market. To reduce the labor supply and the mouths to feed in the countryside, young males sought work in the towns.[1] Poor harvests probably meant that marriage had to be postponed. Later marriages and the deaths caused by famine and disease meant a reduction in population. Meanwhile, the international character of trade and commerce meant that a disaster in one country had serious implications elsewhere. For example, the infection that attacked English sheep in 1318 caused a sharp decline in wool exports in the following years. Without wool, Flemish weavers could not work, and thousands were laid off. Without woolen cloth, the businesses of Flemish, Hanseatic, and Italian merchants suffered. Unemployment encouraged people to turn to crime.

To none of these problems did governments have effective solutions. The three sons of Philip the Fair who sat on the French throne between 1314 and 1328 condemned speculators, who held stocks of grain back until conditions were desperate and prices high, forbade the sale of grain abroad, and published legislation prohibiting fishing with traps that took large catches. These measures had few positive results. As the subsistence crisis deepened, popular discontent and paranoia increased. Starving people focused their anger on the rich, speculators, and the Jews, who were targeted as creditors fleecing the poor through pawnbroking. (Expelled from France in 1306, Jews were readmitted in 1315 and granted the privilege of lending at high interest rates.) Rumors spread of a plot by Jews and their agents, the lepers, to kill Christians by poisoning the wells. With "evidence" collected by torture, many lepers and Jews were killed, beaten, or hit with heavy fines.

In England Edward I's incompetent son, Edward II (r. 1307–1327), used Parliament to set price controls, first on the sale of livestock after disease and poor lambing had driven prices up, and then on ale, which was made from barley (the severe rains of 1315 had contributed to molds and mildews, sharply reducing the crop). Baronial conflicts and wars with the Scots dominated Edward II's reign. Fearing food riots and violence, Edward condemned speculators, which proved easier than enforcing price controls. He did try to buy grain abroad, but yields in the Baltic were low; the French crown, as we have seen, forbade exports; and the grain shipped from Castile in northern Spain was grabbed by Scottish, English, and rogue Hanseatic pirates on the high seas. Such grain as reached southern English ports was stolen by looters and sold on the black market. The Crown's efforts at famine relief failed.

In Scandinavia and the Baltic countries, low cereal harvests, declines in meat and dairy production, economic recessions, and the lack of salt, used for preserving herring, resulted in terrible food shortages. One scholar describes conditions there as "catastrophic."[2] Economic and social problems were aggravated by the appearance of a frightful disease.

The Black Death

In 1291 Genoese sailors had opened the Strait of Gibraltar to Italian shipping by defeating the Moroccans. Then, shortly after 1300, important advances were made in the design of Italian merchant ships. A square rig was added to the mainmast, and ships began to carry three masts instead of just one. Additional sails better utilized wind power to propel the ship. The improved design permitted year-round shipping for the first time, and Venetian and Genoese merchant ships could sail the dangerous Atlantic coast even in the winter months. With ships continually at sea, their rats too were constantly on the move, and thus any rat-transmitted disease could spread rapidly.

Scholars dispute the origins of the bubonic plague, often known as the Black Death. One legend holds that the plague broke out in the Tatar (or Tartar) army under Khan Djani-Beg that was besieging the city of Caffa (modern Feodosiya) in the Crimea, in southern Russia. The Khan ordered the heads of Tatar victims hurled into Caffa to infect the defenders.[3] Some scholars hold that the plague broke out in China or central Asia around 1331, and during the next fifteen years merchants and soldiers carried it over the caravan routes until in 1346 it reached the Crimea. Other scholars believe the plague was endemic in southern Russia. In either case, from the Crimea the plague had easy access to Mediterranean lands and western Europe.

In October 1347, Genoese ships brought the plague to Messina, from which it spread across Sicily. Venice and Genoa were hit in January 1348, and from the port of Pisa the disease spread south to Rome and east to Florence and all Tuscany. By late spring, southern Germany was attacked. Frightened French authorities chased a galley bearing the disease from the port of Marseilles, but not before plague had infected the city, from which it spread to Languedoc and Spain. In June 1348, two ships entered the Bristol Channel and intro-

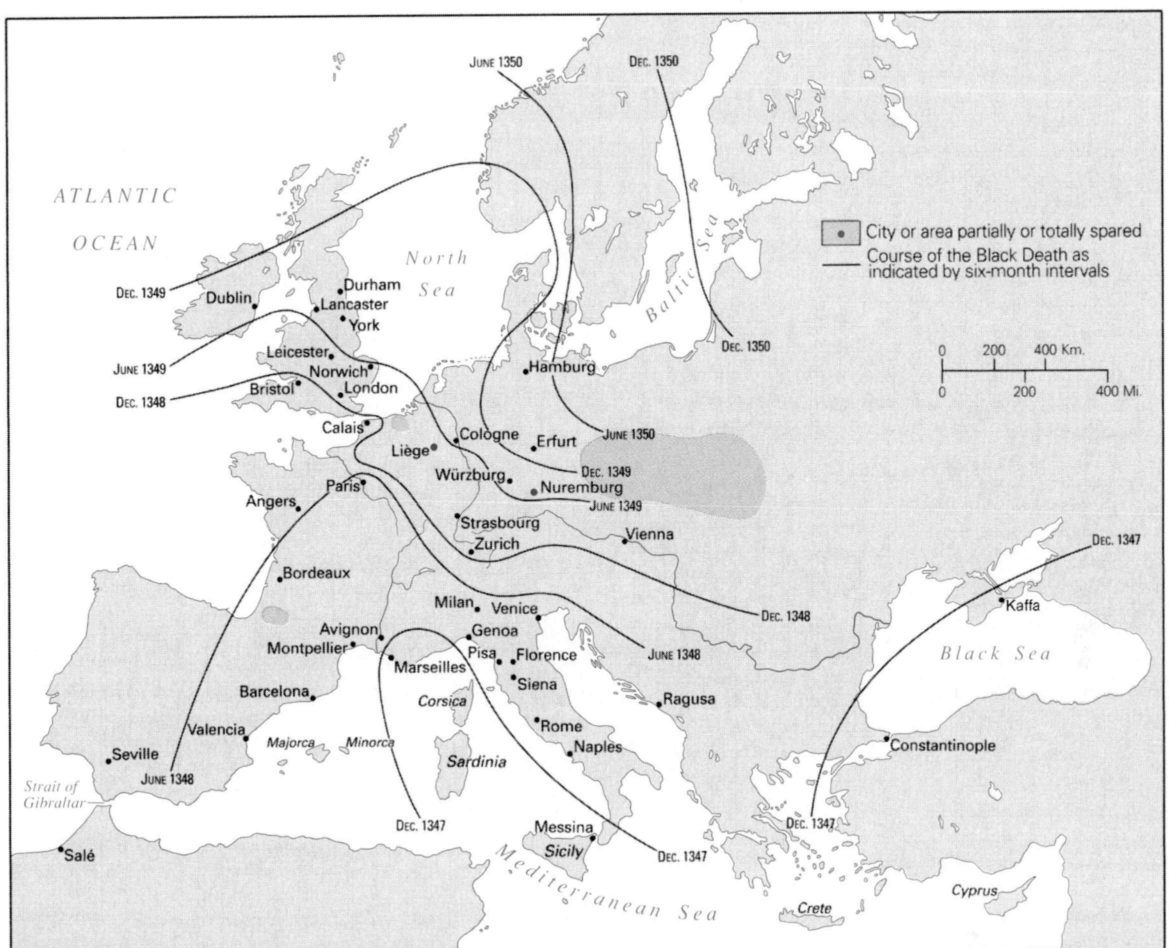

MAP 12.1 The Course of the Black Death in Fourteenth-Century Europe Note the routes that the bubonic plague took across Europe. How do you account for the fact that several regions were spared the "dreadful death"?

duced it into England. All Europe felt the scourge of this horrible disease (Map 12.1).

Pathology and Care

Modern understanding of the bubonic plague rests on the research of two bacteriologists, one French and one Japanese, who in 1894 independently identified the bacillus that causes the plague, *Pasteurella pestis* (so labeled after the French scientist's teacher, Louis Pasteur). The bacillus liked to live in the bloodstream of an animal or, ideally, in the stomach of a flea. The flea in turn resided in the hair of a rodent, sometimes a squirrel but preferably the hardy, nimble, and vagabond black rat. Why the host black rat moved so much, scientists still do not know, but it often traveled by ship. There the black rat could feast for months on a cargo of grain or live snugly among bales of cloth. Fleas bearing the bacillus also had no trouble nesting in saddlebags.[4] Comfortable, well-fed, and often having greatly multiplied, the black rats ended their ocean voyage and descended on the great cities of Europe.

The plague took two forms—bubonic and pneumonic. In the bubonic form, the flea was the vector, or transmitter, of the disease. In the pneumonic form, the plague was communicated directly from one person to another.

Although by the fourteenth century urban authorities from London to Paris to Rome had begun to try to achieve a primitive level of sanitation, urban conditions

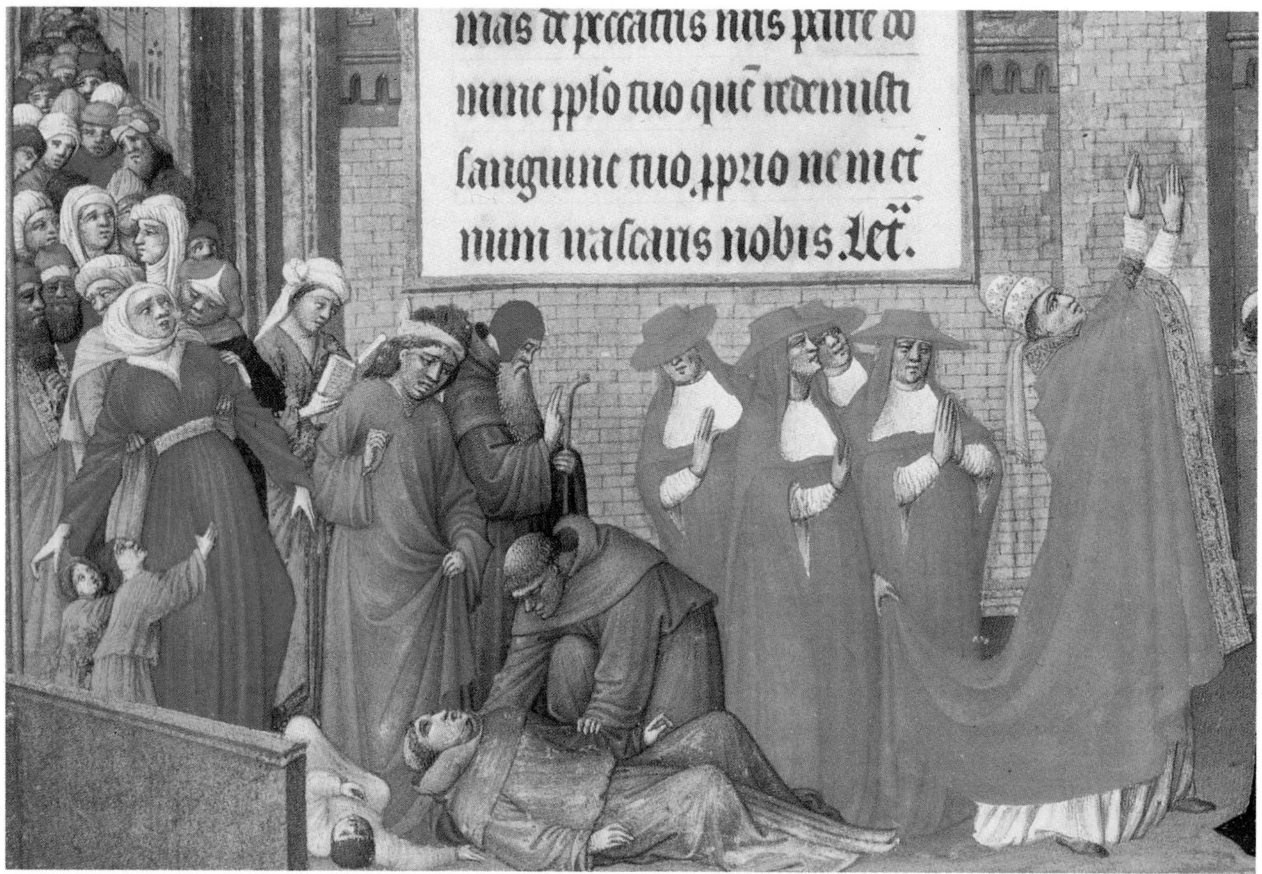

Procession of Saint Gregory According to the *Golden Legend,* a thirteenth-century collection of saints' lives, the bubonic plague ravaged Rome when Gregory I was elected pope (590–604). He immediately ordered special prayers and processions around the city. Here, as people circle the walls, new victims fall (below left). The architecture, the cardinals, and the friars all indicate that this painting dates from the fourteenth, not the sixth, century. *(Musée Condé, Chantilly/Art Resource, NY)*

remained ideal for the spread of disease. Narrow streets filled with mud, refuse, and human excrement were as much cesspools as thoroughfares. Dead animals and sore-covered beggars greeted the traveler. Houses whose upper stories projected over the lower ones eliminated light and air. And extreme overcrowding was commonplace. When all members of an aristocratic family lived and slept in one room, it should not be surprising that six or eight persons in a middle-class or poor household slept in one bed—if they had one. Closeness, after all, provided warmth. Houses were beginning to be constructed of brick, but many remained of wood, clay, and mud. A determined rat had little trouble entering such a house.

Standards of personal hygiene remained frightfully low. True, most large cities had public bathhouses, but we have no way of knowing how frequently ordinary people used them. Lack of personal cleanliness, combined with any number of temporary ailments such as diarrhea and the common cold, weakened the body's resistance to serious disease. Fleas and body lice were universal afflictions: everyone from peasants to archbishops had them. One more bite did not cause much alarm. But if that nibble came from a bacillus-bearing flea, an entire household or area was doomed.

The symptoms of the bubonic plague started with a growth the size of a nut or an apple in the armpit, in the groin, or on the neck. This was the boil, or *buba,* that gave the disease its name and caused agonizing pain. If the buba was lanced and the pus thoroughly drained, the victim had a chance of recovery. The secondary stage was the appearance of black spots or blotches caused by bleeding under the skin. (This syndrome did not give the disease its common name; contemporaries did not call the plague the Black Death. Sometime in the fifteenth century, the Latin phrase *atra mors,* meaning "dreadful death," was translated "black death," and the phrase stuck.) Finally, the victim began to cough violently and spit blood. This stage, indicating the presence of millions of bacilli in the bloodstream, signaled the end, and death followed in two or three days. Rather than evoking compassion for the victim, a French scientist has written, everything about the bubonic plague provoked horror and disgust: "All the matter which exuded from their bodies let off an unbearable stench; sweat, excrement, spittle, breath, so fetid as to be overpowering; urine turbid, thick, black or red."[5]

Medieval people had no rational explanation for the disease or any effective medical treatment for it. Fourteenth-century medical literature indicates that physicians could sometimes ease the pain, but they had no cure. Most people—lay, scholarly, and medical—believed that the Black Death was caused by some "vicious property in the air" that carried the disease from place to place. When ignorance was joined to fear and ancient bigotry, savage cruelty sometimes resulted. Many people believed that the Jews had poisoned the wells of Christian communities and thereby infected the drinking water. This charge led to the murder of thousands of Jews across Europe. According to one chronicler, sixteen thousand were killed at the imperial city of Strasbourg alone in 1349. Though sixteen thousand is probably a typical medieval numerical exaggeration, the horror of the massacre is not lessened. Scholars have yet to explain the economic impact that the loss of such a productive people had on Strasbourg and other cities.

The Italian writer Giovanni Boccaccio (1313–1375), describing the course of the disease in Florence in the preface to his book of tales *The Decameron,* pinpointed the cause of the spread:

> *Moreover, the virulence of the pest was the greater by reason that intercourse was apt to convey it from the sick to the whole, just as fire devours things dry or greasy when they are brought close to it. Nay, the evil went yet further, for not merely by speech or association with the sick was the malady communicated to the healthy with consequent peril of common death, but any that touched the clothes of the sick or aught else that had been touched or used by them, seemed thereby to contract the disease.*[6]

The highly infectious nature of the plague, especially in areas of high population density, was recognized by a few sophisticated Muslims. When the disease struck the town of Salé in Morocco, Ibu Abu Madyan shut in his household with sufficient food and water and allowed no one to enter or leave until the plague had passed. Abu Madyan was entirely successful. The rat that carried the disease-bearing flea avoided travel outside the cities. Thus the countryside was relatively safe. City dwellers who could afford to move fled to the country.

If fourteenth- and fifteenth-century medical science had no effective treatment for the disease, how could victims' suffering be eased? Perhaps in hospitals. What was the geographical distribution of hospitals, and, although our estimates of medieval populations remain rough, what was the hospital-to-population ratio? How many patients could a hospital serve? Whereas earlier the feudal lord had made philanthropic foundations, beginning in the thirteenth century individual merchants—out of compassion, generosity, and the custom of giving to parish collections, and in the belief that the sick would be prayerful intercessors with God for the donors' sins—endowed hospitals. Business people established hospitals in the towns and cities of northern France and Flanders; Milan, Genoa, and Venice were well served, and the 30 hospitals in Florence provided 1,000 beds in 1339. Sixty hospitals served the French capital city of Paris in 1328—but probably not enough for its population of 200,000. The many hospitals in the Iberian Peninsula continued the Muslim tradition of care for the poor and ill. Merchants in the larger towns of the German Empire, in Poland, and in Hungary also founded hospitals in the fourteenth century, generally later than those in western Europe. Sailors, long viewed as potential carriers of disease, benefited from hospitals reserved for them; in 1300 the Venetian government appointed and paid a surgeon to care for sick sailors. At the time the plague erupted, therefore, most towns and cities had hospital facilities.

When trying to determine the number of people a hospital could accommodate, the modern researcher considers the number of beds, the size of the staff, and the building's physical layout. Since each medieval hospital bed might serve two or more patients, we cannot calculate the number of patients on the basis of the beds alone. We do know that rural hospices usually had twelve to fifteen beds, and city hospitals, as at Lisbon, Narbonne, and Genoa, had on average twenty-five to thirty beds, but these figures do not tell us how many patients were accommodated. Only the very rare document listing the number of wrapping sheets and coffins for the dead purchased in a given period provides the modern scholar with precise information on the number of patients a hospital had.

Hospitals actually provided shelter for the sick, homeless, and poor more than medical care. Financially limited hospitals could hardly afford the rich foods recommended by the University of Paris medical faculty to avoid the plague. Hospitals could offer only shelter, compassion, and care for the dying.[7]

Mortality rates cannot be specified, because population figures for the period before the arrival of the plague do not exist for most countries and cities. The largest amount of material survives for England, but it is difficult to use; after enormous scholarly controversy, only educated guesses can be made. Of a total English population of perhaps 4.2 million, probably 1.4 million died of the Black Death in its several visits.[8] Densely populated Italian cities endured incredible losses. Florence lost between one-half and two-thirds of its 1347 population of 85,000 when the plague visited in 1348.

Nor did central and eastern Europe escape the ravages of the disease. Moving northward from the Balkans, eastward from France, and southward from the Baltic, the plague swept through the German Empire. In the Rhineland in 1349, Cologne and Mainz endured heavy losses. In 1348 it swept through Bavaria, entered the Moselle Valley, and pushed into northern Germany. One chronicler records that in the summer and autumn of 1349, between five hundred and six hundred died every day in Vienna. Styria, in what today is central Austria, was very hard hit, with cattle straying unattended in the fields.

As the Black Death took its toll on the German Empire, waves of emigrants fled to Poland, Bohemia, and Hungary. The situation there was better, though not completely absent of disease. The plague seems to have entered Poland through the Baltic seaports and spread from there. Still, population losses were lower than elsewhere in Europe. In Hungary, at least, that may have been due to blood type. Historians of medicine have postulated that people with type O blood, which predominated in that area, are immune to the bubonic plague. The plague spread from Poland to Russia, reaching Pskov, Novgorod, and Moscow, where it felled Grand Duke Simeon.[9] No estimates have been made of population losses there or in the Balkans. In Serbia, though, the plague left vast tracts of land unattended, which prompted an increase in Albanian immigration to meet the labor shortage.

Across Europe the Black Death recurred intermittently in the 1360s and 1370s. It reappeared many times with reduced virulence, making its last appearance in the French port city of Marseilles in 1721. Survivors became more prudent. Because periods of famine had caused malnutrition, making people vulnerable to disease, the Europeans controlled population growth so that population did not outstrip food supply. Western Europeans improved navigation techniques and increased long-distance trade, which permitted the importation of grain from sparsely populated Baltic regions (see page 380). They strictly enforced quarantine measures.[10] They worked on the development of vaccines. But it was only in 1947, six hundred years after the arrival of the plague in the West, that the American microbiologist Selman Waksman discovered an effective vaccine, streptomycin.

Social and Cultural Consequences

Economic historians and demographers sharply dispute the impact of the plague on the economy in the late fourteenth century. The traditional view that the plague had a disastrous effect has been greatly modified. The clearest evidence comes from England, where the agrarian economy showed remarkable resilience. While the severity of the disease varied from region to region, it appears that by about 1375 most landlords enjoyed revenues near those of the pre-plague years. By the early fifteenth century, seigneurial prosperity reached a medieval peak. Why? The answer appears to lie in the fact that England and many parts of Europe suffered from overpopulation in the early fourteenth century. Population losses caused by the Black Death "led to increased productivity by restoring a more efficient balance between labour, land, and capital."[11] Population decline meant a sharp increase in per capita wealth. Increased demand for labor meant greater mobility among peasant and working classes. Wages rose, providing better distribution of income. The shortage of labor and steady requests for higher wages put landlords on the defensive. They retaliated with such measures as the English Statute of Laborers (1351), which attempted to freeze salaries and wages at pre-1347 levels. The statute could not be enforced and therefore was largely unsuccessful. Some places, such as Florence, experienced economic prosperity as a long-term consequence of the plague.

Labor shortages caused by the Black Death throughout the Mediterranean region, from Constantinople to Spain, presented aggressive businessmen with a golden opportunity. The price of slaves rose sharply. Venetian slavers from their colony at Tana on the Sea of Azov in the Crimea took advantage of the boom in demand as prices soared between 1350 and 1410. "By about 1408, no less than 78 per cent of Tana's export earnings came from slaves. Out of their misery, and out of the profits born of the Black Death, one palace after another was raised along the (Venetian) Rialto."[12]

Patients in a Hospital Ward, Fifteenth Century In many cities hospitals could not cope with the large numbers of plague victims. The practice of putting two or more adults in the same bed, as shown here, contributed to the spread of the disease. At the Hôtel-Dieu, in Paris, nurses complained of being forced to put eight to ten children in a single bed in which a patient had recently died. *(Musée de l'Assistance Publique, Paris/Giraudon/Art Resource, NY)*

Even more significant than the social effects were the psychological consequences. The knowledge that the disease meant almost certain death provoked the most profound pessimism. Imagine an entire society in the grip of the belief that it was at the mercy of a frightful affliction about which nothing could be done, a disgusting disease from which family and friends would flee, leaving one to die alone and in agony. It is not surprising that some sought release in orgies and gross sensuality, while others turned to the severest forms of asceticism and frenzied religious fervor. Some extremists joined groups of *flagellants,* who whipped and scourged themselves as penance for their and society's sins, in the belief that the Black Death was God's punishment for humanity's wickedness.

Plague ripped apart the social fabric, dividing the healthy and the sick, those in the mainstream and those on the margins—beggars, lepers, strangers, the Jews, cultural leaders such as rulers and priests, and the masses. In the thirteenth century, funerals, traditionally occasions for the mutual consolation of the living as much as memorial services for the dead, grew increasingly elaborate, with large corteges and many mourners. In the fourteenth century, public horror at the suffering of the afflicted and at the dead reduced the size of mourning processions and eventually resulted in failure even to perform the customary death rites. Fear of infection led to the dead being buried hastily, sometimes in mass graves.

Fear also drove people out of urban centers. These people often used pilgrimages to holy places as justification for their flight. Suspected of being carriers of plague, travelers, pilgrims, and the homeless aroused deep hostility. While professional medicine had no theory of infection, those who witnessed the disease certainly did. Thus, all European port cities followed the example of Ragusa (modern Dubrovnik in southwestern Croatia on the Dalmatian coast) and quarantined arriving ships, crews, passengers, and cargoes to determine whether they brought the plague. Deriving from a Venetian word, the English term *quarantine* originally meant forty days' isolation.

Popular endowments of educational institutions multiplied. The years of the Black Death witnessed the foundation of new colleges at old universities, such as Corpus Christi and Clare Colleges at Cambridge and New College at Oxford, and of entirely new universities. The beginnings of Charles University in Prague (1348) and the Universities of Florence (1350), Vienna (1364), Cracow (1364), and Heidelberg (1385) were all associated with the plague: their foundation charters specifically mention the shortage of priests and the decay of learning. Whereas universities such as those at Bologna and Paris had an international student body, new institutions established in the wake of the Black Death had more national or local constituencies. Thus the international character of medieval culture greatly weakened. The decline of cultural cohesion paved the way for schism in the Catholic church even before the Reformation.[13]

The literature and art of the fourteenth century reveal a terribly morbid concern with death. One highly popular artistic motif, the Dance of Death, depicted a dancing skeleton leading away a living person. No wonder survivors experienced a sort of shell shock and a terrible crisis of faith. Lack of confidence in the leaders of society, lack of hope for the future, defeatism, and malaise wreaked enormous anguish and contributed to the decline of the Middle Ages. A long international war added further misery to the frightful disasters of the plague.

The Hundred Years' War (ca 1337–1453)

In January 1327, Queen Isabella of England, her lover Mortimer, and a group of barons, having deposed and murdered Isabella's incompetent husband, King Edward II, proclaimed his fifteen-year-old son king as Edward III. Isabella and Mortimer, however, held real power until 1330, when Edward seized the reins of government. In 1328 Charles IV of France, the last surviving son of the French king Philip the Fair, died childless. With him ended the Capetian dynasty. An assembly of French barons, meaning to exclude Isabella—who was Charles's sister and the daughter of Philip the Fair—and her son Edward III from the French throne, proclaimed that "no woman nor her son could succeed to the [French] monarchy." The French barons rested their position on the Salic Law, a Germanic law code that forbade females or those descended in the female line to succeed to offices. The barons passed the crown to Philip VI of Valois (r. 1328–1350), a nephew of Philip the Fair. In these actions lie the origins of another phase of the centuries-old struggle between the English and French monarchies, one that was fought intermittently from 1337 to 1453.

Causes

The Hundred Years' War had both distant and immediate causes. In 1259 France and England signed the Treaty of Paris, in which the English king agreed to become—for himself and his successors—vassal of the French crown for the duchy of Aquitaine. The English claimed Aquitaine as an ancient inheritance. French policy, however, was strongly expansionist, and the French kings resolved to absorb the duchy into the kingdom of France. In 1329 Edward III paid homage to Philip VI for Aquitaine. In 1337 Philip, determined to exercise full jurisdiction there, confiscated the duchy. This action was the immediate cause of the war. Edward III maintained that the only way he could exercise his rightful sovereignty over Aquitaine was by assuming the title of king of France.[14] As the eldest surviving male descendant of Philip the Fair, he believed he could rightfully make this claim. Moreover, the dynastic argument upset the feudal order in France: in order to increase their independent power, French vassals of Philip VI used the excuse that they had to transfer their loyalty to a more legitimate overlord, Edward III. One reason the war lasted so long was that it became a French civil war, with some French barons supporting English monarchs in order to thwart the centralizing goals of the French crown.

Economic factors involving the wool trade and the control of Flemish towns had served as justifications for war between France and England for centuries. The wool trade between England and Flanders served as the cornerstone of both countries' economies; they were closely interdependent. Flanders was a fief of the French crown, and the Flemish aristocracy was highly sympathetic to the monarchy in Paris. But the wealth of Flemish merchants and cloth manufacturers depended on English wool, and Flemish burghers strongly supported the claims of Edward III. The disruption of commerce with England threatened their prosperity.

The Popular Response

The governments of both England and France manipulated public opinion to support the war. Whatever significance modern scholars ascribe to the economic factor, public opinion in fourteenth-century England held that the war was waged for one reason: to secure for King Edward the French crown he had been denied.[15] Edward III issued letters to the sheriffs describing in graphic terms the evil deeds of the French and listing royal needs. Kings in both countries instructed the clergy to deliver sermons filled with patriotic sentiment. The royal courts sensationalized the wickedness of the other side and stressed the great fortunes to be made from the war. Philip VI sent agents to warn communities about the dangers of invasion and to stress the French crown's revenue needs to meet the attack.

The royal campaign to rally public opinion was highly successful, at least in the early stage of the war. Edward III gained widespread support in the 1340s and 1350s. The English developed a deep hatred of the French and feared that King Philip intended "to have seized and slaughtered the entire realm of England." As England was successful in the field, pride in the country's military proficiency increased.

Most important of all, the Hundred Years' War was popular because it presented unusual opportunities for wealth and advancement. Poor knights and knights who were unemployed were promised regular wages. Criminals who enlisted were granted pardons. The great nobles expected to be rewarded with estates. Royal exhortations to the troops before battles repeatedly stressed that, if victorious, the men might keep whatever they seized. The French chronicler Jean Froissart wrote that, at the time of Edward III's expedition of 1359, men of all ranks flocked to the English king's banner. Some came to acquire honor, but many came in order "to loot and pillage the fair and plenteous land of France."[16]

The Indian Summer of Medieval Chivalry

The period of the Hundred Years' War witnessed the final flowering of the aristocratic code of medieval chivalry. Indeed, the enthusiastic participation of the nobility in both France and England was in response primarily to the opportunity the war provided to display chivalric behavior. What better place to display chivalric qualities than on the field of battle?

War was considered an ennobling experience; there was something elevating, manly, fine, and beautiful about it. When Shakespeare in the sixteenth century wrote of "the pomp and circumstance of glorious war," he was echoing the fourteenth- and fifteenth-century chroniclers who had glorified the trappings of war. Describing the French army before the Battle of Poitiers (1356), a contemporary said: "Then you might see banners and pennons unfurled to the wind, whereon fine gold and azure shone, purple, gules and ermine. Trumpets, horns and clarions—you might hear sounding through the camp; the Dauphin's [title borne by the eldest son of the king of France] great battle made the earth ring."[17]

This romantic view of war holds little appeal for modern men and women, who are more conscious of the slaughter, brutality, dirt, and blood that war inevitably involves. Also, modern thinkers are usually conscious of the broad mass of people, while the chivalric code applied only to the aristocratic military elite. Chivalry had no reference to those outside the knightly class.

The knight was supposed to show courtesy, graciousness, and generosity to his social equals, but certainly not to his social inferiors. When English knights fought French ones, they were social equals fighting according to a mutually accepted code of behavior. The infantry troops were looked on as inferior beings. When a French peasant force at Longueil destroyed a contingent of English knights, their comrades mourned them because "it was too much that so many good fighters had been killed by mere peasants."[18]

The Course of the War to 1419

The war was fought almost entirely in France and the Low Countries (Map 12.2). It consisted mainly of a series of random sieges and cavalry raids. In 1335 the French began supporting Scottish incursions into northern England, ravaging the countryside in Aquitaine, and sacking and burning English coastal towns, such as Southampton. Naturally such tactics lent weight to Edward III's propaganda campaign. In fact, royal propaganda on both sides fostered a kind of early nationalism.

During the war's early stages, England was highly successful. At Crécy in northern France in 1346, English longbowmen scored a great victory over French knights and crossbowmen. Although the aim of the longbow was not very accurate, it allowed for rapid reloading, and English archers could send off three arrows to the French crossbowmen's one. The result was a blinding shower of arrows that unhorsed the French knights and caused mass confusion. The firing of cannon—probably the first use of artillery in the West—

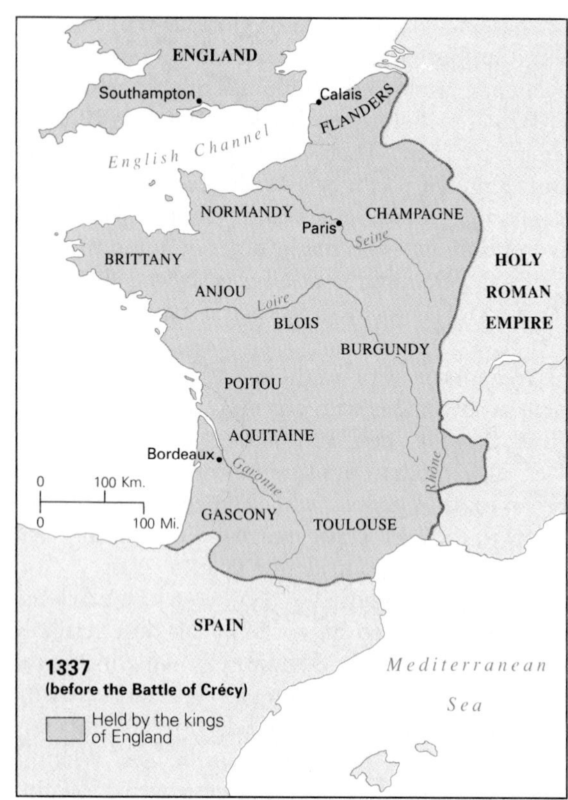
ENGLAND
Southampton
Calais
FLANDERS
English Channel
NORMANDY
Paris
Seine
CHAMPAGNE
BRITTANY
ANJOU
Loire
BLOIS
BURGUNDY
HOLY ROMAN EMPIRE
POITOU
AQUITAINE
Bordeaux
Garonne
Rhône
GASCONY
TOULOUSE
0 100 Km.
0 100 Mi.
SPAIN
Mediterranean Sea
1337
(before the Battle of Crécy)
Held by the kings of England

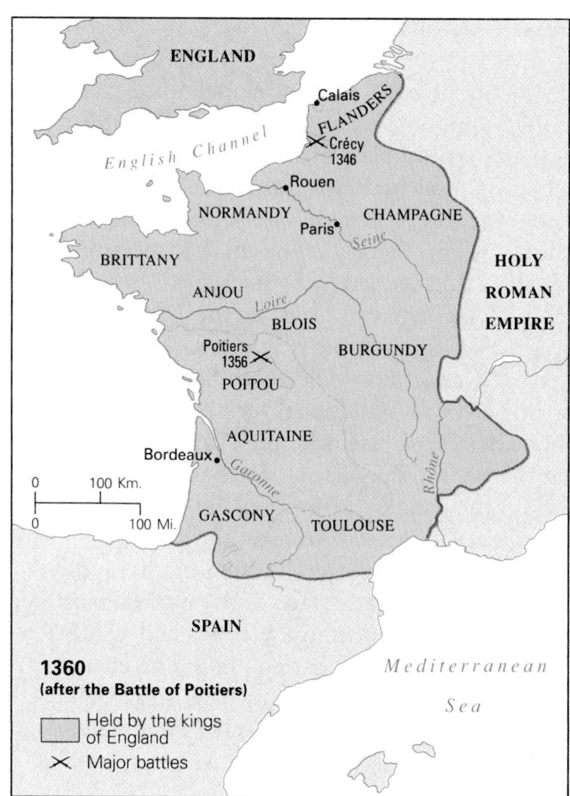
ENGLAND
Calais
FLANDERS
Crécy 1346
English Channel
Rouen
NORMANDY
Paris
Seine
CHAMPAGNE
BRITTANY
ANJOU
Loire
BLOIS
Poitiers 1356
BURGUNDY
HOLY ROMAN EMPIRE
POITOU
AQUITAINE
Bordeaux
Garonne
Rhône
GASCONY
TOULOUSE
0 100 Km.
0 100 Mi.
SPAIN
Mediterranean Sea
1360
(after the Battle of Poitiers)
Held by the kings of England
Major battles

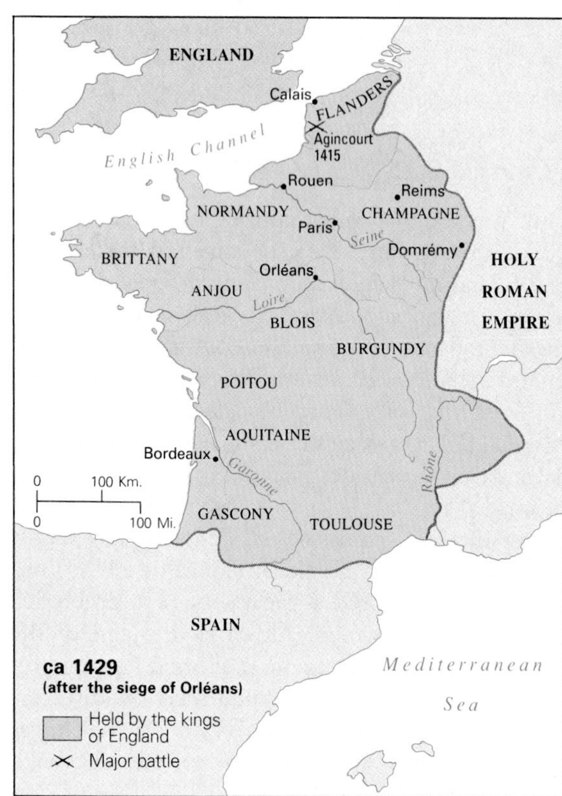
ENGLAND
Calais
FLANDERS
Agincourt 1415
English Channel
Rouen
Reims
NORMANDY
Paris
Seine
CHAMPAGNE
Domrémy
BRITTANY
Orléans
ANJOU
Loire
BLOIS
BURGUNDY
HOLY ROMAN EMPIRE
POITOU
AQUITAINE
Bordeaux
Garonne
Rhône
GASCONY
TOULOUSE
0 100 Km.
0 100 Mi.
SPAIN
Mediterranean Sea
ca 1429
(after the siege of Orléans)
Held by the kings of England
Major battle

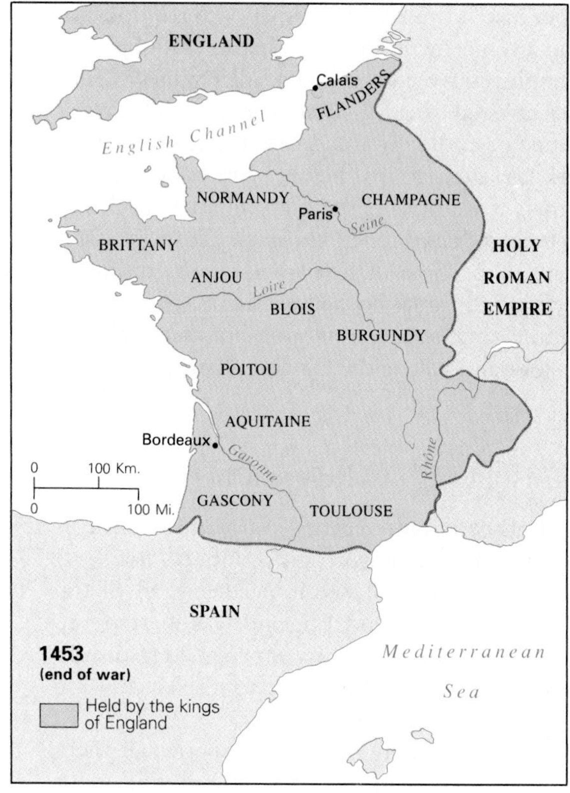
ENGLAND
Calais
FLANDERS
English Channel
NORMANDY
Paris
Seine
CHAMPAGNE
BRITTANY
ANJOU
Loire
BLOIS
BURGUNDY
HOLY ROMAN EMPIRE
POITOU
AQUITAINE
Bordeaux
Garonne
Rhône
GASCONY
TOULOUSE
0 100 Km.
0 100 Mi.
SPAIN
Mediterranean Sea
1453
(end of war)
Held by the kings of England

The Battle of Crécy, 1346
Pitched battles were unusual in the Hundred Years' War. At Crécy, the English (on the right with lions on their royal standard) scored a spectacular victory. The longbow proved a more effective weapon over the French crossbow, but characteristically the artist concentrated on the aristocratic knights. *(Bibliothèque Nationale, Paris)*

created further panic. Thereupon the English horsemen charged and butchered the French.

This was not war according to the chivalric rules that Edward III would have preferred. Nevertheless, his son Edward the Black Prince used the same tactics ten years later to smash the French at Poitiers, where he captured the French king and held him for ransom. Again, at Agincourt near Arras in 1415, the chivalric English soldier-king Henry V (r. 1413–1422) gained the field over vastly superior numbers. Henry followed up his triumph at Agincourt with the reconquest of Normandy. By 1419 the English had advanced to the walls of Paris (see Map 12.2). But the French cause was not lost. Though England had scored the initial victories, France won the war.

MAP 12.2 English Holdings in France During the Hundred Years' War The year 1429 marked the greatest extent of English holdings in France. Why was it unlikely that England could have held these territories permanently?

Joan of Arc and France's Victory

The ultimate French success rests heavily on the actions of an obscure French peasant girl, Joan of Arc, whose vision and work revived French fortunes and led to victory. A great deal of pious and popular legend surrounds Joan the Maid, because of her peculiar appearance on the scene, her astonishing success, her martyrdom, and her canonization by the Catholic church. The historical fact is that she saved the French monarchy, which was the embodiment of France.

Born in 1412 to well-to-do peasants in the village of Domrémy in Champagne, Joan of Arc grew up in a religious household. During adolescence she began to hear voices, which she later said belonged to Saint Michael, Saint Catherine, and Saint Margaret. In 1428 these voices spoke to her with great urgency, telling her that the dauphin (the uncrowned King Charles VII) had to be crowned and the English expelled from France. Joan went to the French court, persuaded the king to reject the rumor that he was illegitimate, and secured his support for her relief of the besieged city of Orléans.

The astonishing thing is not that Joan the Maid overcame serious obstacles to see the dauphin, not even that Charles and his advisers listened to her. What is amazing is the swiftness with which they were convinced. French fortunes had been so low for so long that the court believed only a miracle could save the country. Because Joan cut her hair short and dressed like a man, she scandalized the court. But hoping she would provide the miracle, Charles allowed her to accompany the army that was preparing to raise the English siege of Orléans.

In the meantime Joan, herself illiterate, dictated this letter calling on the English to withdraw:

Jhesus Maria
King of England, and you Duke of Bedford, calling yourself regent of France, you William Pole, Count of Suffolk . . . , do right in the King of Heaven's sight. Surrender to The Maid *sent hither by God the King of Heaven, the keys of all the good towns you have taken and laid waste in France. She comes in God's name to establish the Blood Royal, ready to make peace if you agree to abandon France and repay what you have taken. And you, archers, comrades in arms, gentles and others, who are before the town of Orléans, retire in God's name to your own country.*[19]

Joan arrived before Orléans on April 28, 1429. Seventeen years old, she knew little of warfare and believed that if she could keep the French troops from swearing and frequenting brothels, victory would be theirs. On May 8 the English, weakened by disease and lack of supplies, withdrew from Orléans. Ten days later, Charles VII was crowned king at Reims. These two events marked the turning point in the war.

Joan's presence at Orléans, her strong belief in her mission, and the fact that she was wounded in the breast enhanced her reputation and strengthened the morale of the army. It went on to win a victory at Patay in the Loire Valley. In 1430 England's allies, the Burgundians, captured Joan and sold her to the English. When the English handed her over to the ecclesiastical authorities for trial, the French court did not intervene. While the English wanted Joan eliminated for obvious political reasons, sorcery (witchcraft) was the ostensible charge at her trial. Witch persecution was increasing in the fifteenth century, and Joan's wearing of men's clothes appeared not only aberrant but indicative of contact with the devil. In 1431 the court condemned her as a heretic—her claim of direct inspiration from God, thereby denying the authority of church officials, constituted heresy—and burned her at the stake in the marketplace at Rouen. A new trial in 1456 rehabilitated her name. In 1920 she was canonized and declared a holy maiden, and today she is revered as the second patron saint of France. The nineteenth-century French historian Jules Michelet extolled Joan of Arc as a symbol of the vitality and strength of the French peasant classes.

The relief of Orléans stimulated French pride and rallied French resources. As the war dragged on, loss of life mounted, and money appeared to be flowing into a bottomless pit, demands for an end increased in England. The clergy and intellectuals pressed for peace. Parliamentary opposition to additional war grants stiffened. Slowly the French reconquered Normandy and, finally, ejected the English from Aquitaine. At the war's end in 1453, only the town of Calais remained in English hands.

Costs and Consequences

For both France and England, the war proved a disaster. In France the English had slaughtered thousands of soldiers and civilians. In the years after the sweep of the Black Death, this additional killing meant a grave loss of population. The English had laid waste to hundreds of thousands of acres of rich farmland, leaving the rural economy of many parts of France a shambles. The war had disrupted trade and the great fairs, resulting in the drastic reduction of French participation in international commerce. Defeat in battle and heavy taxation contributed to widespread dissatisfaction and aggravated peasant grievances.

In England only the southern coastal ports experienced much destruction, and the demographic effects of the Black Death actually worked to restore the land-labor balance (see page 384). The costs of the war, however, were tremendous. England spent over £5 million on the war effort, a huge sum in the fourteenth and fifteenth centuries. Manpower losses had greater social consequences. The knights who ordinarily handled the work of local government as sheriffs, coroners, jurymen, and justices of the peace were abroad, and their absence contributed to the breakdown of order at the local level. The English government attempted to finance the war effort by raising taxes on the wool crop. Because of steadily increasing costs, the Flemish and Italian buyers could not afford English wool. Consequently, raw wool exports slumped drastically between 1350 and 1450.

Many men of all social classes had volunteered for service in France in the hope of acquiring booty and becoming rich. The chronicler Walsingham, describing the period of Crécy, tells of the tremendous prosperity and abundance resulting from the spoils of war: "For the woman was of no account who did not possess something from the spoils of . . . cities overseas in clothing, furs, quilts, and utensils . . . tablecloths and jewels, bowls of murra [semiprecious stone] and silver, linen and linen cloths."[20] Walsingham is referring to 1348, in the first generation of war. As time went on, most fortunes seem to have been squandered as fast as they were made.

If English troops returned with cash, they did not invest it in land. In the fifteenth century, returning soldiers were commonly described as beggars and vagabonds, roaming about making mischief. Even the large sums of money received from the ransom of the great—such as the £250,000 paid to Edward III for the freedom of King John of France—and the money paid as indemnities by captured towns and castles did not begin to equal the more than £5 million spent. England suffered a serious net loss.[21]

The long war also had a profound impact on the political and cultural lives of the two countries. Most notably, it stimulated the development of the English Parliament. Between 1250 and 1450, representative assemblies from several classes of society flourished in many European countries. In the English Parliament, French Estates, German diets, and Spanish cortes, deliberative practices developed that laid the foundations for the representative institutions of modern liberal-democratic nations. While representative assemblies declined in most countries after the fifteenth century, the English Parliament endured. Edward III's constant need for money to pay for the war compelled him to summon not only the great barons and bishops, but knights of the shires and burgesses from the towns as well. Between the outbreak of the war in 1337 and the king's death in 1377, parliamentary assemblies met twenty-seven times. Parliament met in thirty-seven of the fifty years of Edward's reign.[22]

The frequency of the meetings is significant. Representative assemblies were becoming a habit. Knights and burgesses—or the "Commons," as they came to be called—recognized their mutual interests and began to meet apart from the great lords. The Commons gradually realized that they held the country's purse strings, and a parliamentary statute of 1341 required that all nonfeudal levies have parliamentary approval. When Edward III signed the law, he acknowledged that the king of England could not tax without Parliament's consent. Increasingly, during the course of the war, money grants were tied to royal redress of grievances: if the government was to raise money, it had to correct the wrongs its subjects protested.

Joan of Arc This is how the court scribe who made this sketch in 1429, the year Joan raised the siege of Orléans, imagined her. He had never seen her. *(Archives Nationales, Paris)*

In England theoretical consent to taxation and legislation was given in one assembly for the entire country. France had no such single assembly; instead, there were many regional or provincial assemblies. Why did a national representative assembly fail to develop in France? The initiative for convening assemblies rested with the king, who needed revenue almost as much as the English ruler. But the French monarchy found the idea of representative assemblies thoroughly distasteful. Large gatherings of the nobility potentially or actually threatened the king's power. The advice of a counselor to King Charles VI (r. 1380–1422), "above all things be sure that no great assemblies of nobles or of *communes* take place in your kingdom," was accepted.[23] Charles

VII (r. 1422–1461) even threatened to punish those proposing a national assembly.

No one in France wanted a national assembly. Linguistic, geographical, economic, legal, and political differences were very strong. People tended to think of themselves as Breton, Norman, Burgundian, or whatever, rather than French. Through much of the fourteenth and early fifteenth centuries, weak monarchs lacked the power to call a national assembly. Provincial assemblies, highly jealous of their independence, did not want a national assembly. The costs of sending delegates to it would be high, and the result was likely to be increased taxation. Finally, the Hundred Years' War itself hindered the growth of a representative body of government. Possible violence on dangerous roads discouraged people from travel.

In both countries, however, the war did promote the growth of *nationalism*—the feeling of unity and identity that binds together a people who speak the same language, have a common ancestry and customs, and live in the same area. After victories, each country experienced a surge of pride in its military strength. Just as English patriotism ran strong after Crécy and Poitiers, so French national confidence rose after Orléans. French national feeling demanded the expulsion of the enemy not merely from Normandy and Aquitaine but from French soil. Perhaps no one expressed this national consciousness better than Joan of Arc, when she exulted that the enemy had been "driven out of *France*."

The Decline of the Church's Prestige

In times of crisis or disaster, people of all faiths have sought the consolation of religion. In the fourteenth century, however, the official Christian church offered very little solace. In fact, the leaders of the church added to the sorrow and misery of the times.

The Babylonian Captivity

From 1309 to 1376, the popes lived in Avignon in southeastern France. In order to control the church and its policies, Philip the Fair of France pressured Pope Clement V to settle in Avignon (see Map 11.6 on page 362). Clement, critically ill with cancer, lacked the will to resist Philip. This period in church history is often called the Babylonian Captivity (referring to the seventy years the ancient Hebrews were held captive in Mesopotamian Babylon).

The Babylonian Captivity badly damaged papal prestige. The Avignon papacy reformed its financial administration and centralized its government. But the seven popes at Avignon concentrated on bureaucratic matters to the exclusion of spiritual objectives. Though some of the popes led austere lives there, the general atmosphere was one of luxury and extravagance. The leadership of the church was cut off from its historic roots and the source of its ancient authority, the city of Rome. In the absence of the papacy, the Papal States in Italy lacked stability and good government. The economy of Rome had long been based on the presence of the papal court and the rich tourist trade the papacy attracted. The Babylonian Captivity left Rome poverty-stricken.

Many devout Christians urged the popes to return to Rome. The Dominican mystic Catherine of Siena (1347–1380), for example, made a special trip to Avignon to plead with the pope to return. Public opinion credited her influence as decisive. Her 350 letters and compositions describing her mystical experiences, dictated because she could not write, survive. Catherine was canonized by the Sienese pope Pius II and is revered as one of the patron saints of Italy.

In 1377 Pope Gregory XI brought the papal court back to Rome. Unfortunately, he died shortly after the return. At Gregory's death, Roman citizens demanded an Italian pope who would remain in Rome. Determined to influence the papal conclave (the assembly of cardinals who chose the new pope) to elect an Italian, a Roman mob surrounded Saint Peter's Basilica, blocked the roads leading out of the city, and seized all boats on the Tiber River. Between the time of Gregory's death and the opening of the conclave, great pressure was put on the cardinals to elect an Italian. At the time, none of them protested this pressure.

Sixteen cardinals—eleven Frenchmen, four Italians, and one Spaniard—entered the conclave on April 7, 1378. After two ballots, they unanimously chose a distinguished administrator, the archbishop of Bari, Bartolomeo Prignano, who took the name Urban VI. Each of the cardinals swore that Urban had been elected "sincerely, freely, genuinely, and canonically."

Urban VI (1378–1389) had excellent intentions for church reform. He wanted to abolish simony, *pluralism* (holding several church offices at the same time), absenteeism, clerical extravagance, and ostentation. These were the very abuses being increasingly criticized by Christian people across Europe. Unfortunately, Pope Urban went about the work of reform in a tactless, arrogant, and bullheaded manner. The day after his coronation, he delivered a blistering attack on cardinals who lived in Rome while drawing their income from benefices elsewhere. His criticism was well-founded but ill-timed and provoked opposition among the hierarchy before Urban had consolidated his authority.

In the weeks that followed, Urban stepped up attacks on clerical luxury, denouncing individual cardinals by name. He threatened to strike the cardinal archbishop of Amiens. Urban even threatened to excommunicate certain cardinals, and when he was advised that such excommunications would not be lawful unless the guilty had been warned three times, he shouted, "I can do anything, if it be my will and judgment."[24] Urban's quick temper and irrational behavior have led scholars to question his sanity. Whether he was medically insane or just drunk with power is a moot point. In any case, Urban's actions brought on disaster.

In groups of two and three, the cardinals slipped away from Rome and met at Anagni. They declared Urban's election invalid because it had come about under threats from the Roman mob, and they asserted that Urban himself was excommunicated. The cardinals then proceeded to the city of Fondi between Rome and Naples and elected Cardinal Robert of Geneva, the cousin of King Charles V of France, as pope. Cardinal Robert took the name Clement VII. There were thus two popes—Urban at Rome and the antipope Clement VII (1378–1394), who set himself up at Avignon in opposition to the legally elected Urban. So began the Great Schism, which divided Western Christendom until 1417.

The Great Schism

The powers of Europe aligned themselves with Urban or Clement along strictly political lines. France naturally recognized the French antipope, Clement. England, France's historic enemy, recognized Pope Urban. Scotland, whose attacks on England were subsidized by France, followed the French and supported Clement. Aragon, Castile, and Portugal hesitated before deciding for Clement at Avignon. The emperor, who bore ancient hostility to France, recognized Urban VI. At first the Italian city-states recognized Urban; when he alienated them, they opted for Clement.

John of Spoleto, a professor at the law school at Bologna, eloquently summed up intellectual opinion of the schism: "The longer this schism lasts, the more it appears to be costing, and the more harm it does; scandal, massacres, ruination, agitations, troubles and disturbances."[25] The scandal "rent the seamless garment of Christ," as the church was called, and provoked horror and vigorous cries for reform. The common people, wracked by inflation, wars, and plague, were thoroughly confused about which pope was legitimate. The schism weakened the religious faith of many Christians and gave rise to instability and religious excesses. It brought the church leadership into serious disrepute. At a time when ordinary Christians needed the consolation of religion and confidence in religious leaders, church officials were fighting among themselves for power. The schism also brought to the fore conciliar ideas about church government.

The Conciliar Movement

Theories about the nature of the Christian church and its government originated in the very early church, but the years of the Great Schism witnessed their maturity. Conciliarists believed that reform of the church could best be achieved through periodic assemblies, or general councils, representing all the Christian people. While acknowledging that the pope was head of the church, conciliarists, such as the French theologian Pierre d'Ailly and the German Conrad of Gelnhausen, held that the pope derived his authority from the entire Christian community, whose well-being he existed to promote. Thus the pope was not an absolute authority incapable of doctrinal error. Conciliarists favored a balanced or constitutional form of church government, with papal authority shared with a general council, in contrast to the monarchial one that prevailed.

A half century before the Great Schism, in 1324, Marsiglio of Padua, then rector of the University of Paris, had published *Defensor Pacis* (The Defender of the Peace). Dealing as it did with the authority of state and church, *Defensor Pacis* proved to be one of the most controversial works written in the Middle Ages.

Marsiglio argued that the state was the great unifying power in society and that the church was subordinate to the state. He put forth the revolutionary ideas that the church had no inherent jurisdiction and should own no property. Authority in the Christian church, according to Marsiglio, should rest in a general council, made up of laymen as well as priests and superior to the pope. These ideas directly contradicted the medieval notion of a society governed by the church and the state, with the church supreme. *Defensor Pacis* was condemned by the pope, and Marsiglio was excommunicated.

Even more earthshaking than the theories of Marsiglio of Padua were the ideas of the English scholar and theologian John Wyclif (ca 1330–1384). Wyclif wrote that papal claims of temporal power had no foundation in the Scriptures and that the Scriptures alone should be the standard of Christian belief and practice. He urged the abolition of such practices as the veneration of saints,

The Holy Roman Emperor Sigismund (1410–1437), persuaded to take the initiative in summoning the Council of Constance, is here shown in procession at the council. When the Bohemian reformer John Hus declared that sin vitiates a clerical or civil office, Hus lost the emperor's support and was tried, condemned, and burned at the stake. Sigismund thereby kindled Bohemian nationalism, which led to the Hussite wars. *(Rosgarten Museum, Konstanz)*

pilgrimages, pluralism, and absenteeism. Sincere Christians, according to Wyclif, should read the Bible for themselves. In response to that idea, the first English translation of the Bible was produced and circulated. Wyclif's views had broad social and economic significance. He urged that the church be stripped of its property. His idea that every Christian free of mortal sin possessed lordship was seized on by peasants in England during a revolt in 1381 and used to justify their goals.

In advancing these views, Wyclif struck at the roots of medieval church structure and religious practices. Consequently, he has been hailed as the precursor of the Reformation of the sixteenth century. Although Wyclif's ideas were vigorously condemned by ecclesiastical authorities, they were widely disseminated by humble clerics and enjoyed great popularity in the early fifteenth century. Wyclif's followers were called "Lollards." The term, which means "mumblers of prayers and psalms," refers to what they criticized. Lollard teaching allowed women to preach and to consecrate the Eucharist. Women, some well educated, played a significant role in the movement. After Anne, sister of Wenceslaus, king of Germany and Bohemia, married Richard II of England, members of her household carried Lollard principles back to Bohemia.

In response to continued calls throughout Europe for a council, the two colleges of cardinals—one at Rome, the other at Avignon—summoned a council at Pisa in 1409. A distinguished gathering of prelates and theologians deposed both popes and selected another. Neither the Avignon pope nor the Roman pope would resign, however, and the appalling result was the creation of a threefold schism.

Finally, because of the pressure of the German emperor Sigismund, a great council met at the imperial city of Constance (1414–1418). It had three objectives: to end the schism, to reform the church "in head and members" (from top to bottom), and to wipe out heresy. The council condemned the Czech reformer Jan Hus (see the feature "Individuals in Society: Jan Hus"), and he was burned at the stake. The council eventually deposed both the Roman pope and the successor of the pope chosen at Pisa, and it isolated the Avignon antipope. A conclave elected a new leader, the Roman cardinal Colonna, who took the name Martin V (1417–1431).

Martin proceeded to dissolve the council. Nothing was done about reform. The schism was over, and though councils subsequently met at Basel and at Ferrara-Florence, in 1450 the papacy held a jubilee, celebrating its triumph over the conciliar movement. In the later fifteenth century, the papacy concentrated on Italian problems to the exclusion of universal Christian interests. But the schism and the conciliar movement had exposed the crying need for ecclesiastical reform,

Individuals in Society

Jan Hus (ca 1369–1415)

The execution of Jan Hus. *(University Library, Prague)*

In May 1990, the Czech Republic's parliament declared July 6, the date of Jan Hus's execution in 1415, a Czech national holiday. The son of free farmers, Hus was born in Husinec in southern Bohemia, an area of heavy German settlement, and grew up conscious of the ethnic differences between Czechs and Germans. Most of his professors at Charles University in Prague were Germans. In 1396 he received a master's degree, and just before his ordination as priest in 1400, he wrote that he would not "be a clerical careerist," implying that ambition for church offices motivated many of his peers.

The young priest lectured at the university and preached at the private Bethlehem Chapel. During his twelve years there, Hus preached only in Czech. He denounced superstition, the sale of indulgences, and other abuses, but his remarks were thoroughly orthodox. He attracted attention among artisans, the small Czech middle class, but not Germans. His austere life and lack of ambition enhanced his reputation.

Around 1400, Czech students returning from study at Oxford introduced into Bohemia the reforming ideas of the English theologian John Wyclif. When German professors condemned Wyclif's ideas as heretical, Hus and the Czechs argued "academic freedom," the right to read and teach Wyclif's works regardless of their particular merits. When popular demonstrations against ecclesiastical abuses and German influence at the university erupted, King Vaclav IV (1378–1419) placed control of the university in Czech hands. Hus was elected rector, the top administrative official.

The people of Prague, with perhaps the largest urban population in central Europe, 40 percent of it living below the poverty line and entirely dependent on casual labor, found Hus's denunciations of an overendowed church appealing. Hus considered the issues theological; his listeners saw them as socioeconomic.

Hus went into exile, where he wrote *On the Church.* He disputed papal authority, denounced abuses, and approved *utraquism,* the reception of the Eucharist under both species, bread and wine. Hus also defended transubstantiation (see page 459); insisted that church authority rested on Scripture, conscience, and tradition (in contrast to sixteenth-century Protestant reformers, who placed authority in Scripture alone); and made it clear that he had no intention of leaving the church or inciting a popular movement.

In 1413 the emperor Sigismund urged the calling of a general council to end the schism. Hus was invited, and, given the emperor's safe conduct (protection from attack or arrest), agreed to go. What he found was an atmosphere of inquisition. The safe conduct was disregarded, and Hus was arrested. Under questioning about his acceptance of Wyclif's ideas, Hus repeatedly replied, "I have not held; I do not hold." Council members were more interested in proving Hus a Wyclifite than in his responses. They took away his priesthood, banned his teachings, burned his books, and burned Hus himself at the stake. He then belonged to the ages.

The ages have made good use of him. His death aggravated the divisions between the bishops at Constance and the Czech clerics and people. In September 1415, 452 nobles from all parts of Bohemia signed a letter saying that Hus had been unjustly executed and rejecting council rulings. This event marks the first time that an ecclesiastical decision was publicly defied. Revolution swept through Bohemia, with Hussites—Czech nobles and people—insisting on clerical poverty and Communion under both species, and German citizens remaining loyal to the Roman church. In the sixteenth century, reformers hailed Hus as the forerunner of Protestantism. In the eighteenth century, Enlightenment philosophes evoked Hus as a defender of freedom of expression. In the nineteenth century, central European nationalists used Hus's name to defend national sentiment against Habsburg rule. And in the twentieth century, Hus's name was used against German fascist and Russian communist tyranny.

Questions for Analysis

1. Since Jan Hus lived and died insisting that his religious teaching was thoroughly orthodox, why has he been hailed as a reformer?
2. What political and cultural interests did the martyred Hus serve?

thus laying the foundations for the great reform efforts of the sixteenth century.

The Life of the People

In the fourteenth century, economic and political difficulties, disease, and war profoundly affected the lives of European peoples. Decades of slaughter and destruction, punctuated by the decimating visits of the Black Death, made a grave economic situation virtually disastrous. In many parts of France and the Low Countries, fields lay in ruin or untilled for lack of labor power. In England, as taxes increased, criticisms of government policy and mismanagement multiplied. Crime, aggravated economic troubles, and throughout Europe the frustrations of the common people erupted into widespread revolts. But for most people, marriage and the local parish church continued to be the center of their lives.

Marriage

Marriage and the family provided such peace and satisfaction as most people attained. What do we know about peasant marriages in the later Middle Ages? Scholars long believed that because peasants were illiterate and left very few statements about their marriages, generalizations could not be made about them. Recent research in English manorial, ecclesiastical, and coroners' records, however, has uncovered fascinating material. Evidence abounds of teenage flirtations, and many young people had sexual contacts—some leading to conception. Premarital pregnancy may have been deliberate: because children were economically important, the couple wanted to be sure of fertility before entering marriage.

"Whether rich or poor, male or female, the most important rite de passage for peasant youth was marriage."[26] Did they select their own spouses? or accept parents' choices? Church law stressed that for a marriage to be valid, both parents must freely consent to it. The evidence overwhelmingly shows, above all where land or property accompanied the union, that parents took the lead in arranging their children's marriages; if the parents were dead, the responsibility fell to the inheriting son. Marriage determined not only the life partner and the economic circumstances in which the couple would live, but also the son-in-law who might take over the family land or the daughter-in-law who might care for her elderly in-laws. These kinds of interests required careful planning.

Most marriages were between men and women of the same village; where the name and residence of a husband is known, perhaps 41 percent were outsiders. Once the prospective bride or groom had been decided on, parents paid the *merchet* (fine to the lord for a woman's marriage—since he stood to lose a worker). Parents saw that the parish priest published on three successive Sundays the *banns,* public announcements that the couple planned to marry, to allow for objections to the union. And parents made the financial settlement. The couple then proceeded to the church door, where they made the vows, rings were blessed and exchanged, and the ceremony concluded with some kind of festivity. The church strongly discouraged the solemnization of marriage during the holy seasons of Lent and Advent and on the Rogation Days (prescribed days of fasting and prayer for the harvest). Therefore, most marriages took place in the summer months, during the harvest season (October, November), or in January.[27]

Although most peasants were illiterate, the gentry could write. The letters exchanged between Margaret and John Paston, who lived in Norfolk, England, in the fifteenth century provide important evidence for the experience of one couple. John and Margaret Paston were married about 1439, after an arrangement concluded entirely by their parents. John spent most of his time in London fighting through the law courts to increase his family properties and business interests; Margaret remained in Norfolk to supervise the family lands. Her enormous responsibilities involved managing the Paston estates, hiring workers, collecting rents, ordering supplies for the large household, hearing complaints and settling disputes among tenants, and marketing her crops. In these duties, she proved herself a remarkably shrewd businessperson. Moreover, when an army of over a thousand men led by the aristocratic thug Lord Moleyns attacked her house, she successfully withstood the siege. When the Black Death entered her area, Margaret moved her family to safety.

Margaret Paston did all this on top of raising eight children (there were probably other children who did not survive childhood). Her husband died before she was forty-three, and she later conducted the negotiations for the children's marriages. Her children's futures, like her estate management, were planned with an eye toward economic and social advancement. When one daughter secretly married the estate bailiff, an alliance considered beneath her, the girl was cut off from the family as if she were dead.[28]

The many letters surviving between Margaret and John reveal slight tenderness toward their children. They seem to have reserved their love for each other, and during many of his frequent absences they wrote to express mutual affection and devotion. How typical the Paston relationship was modern historians cannot say, but the marriage of John and Margaret, although completely arranged by their parents, was based on respect, responsibility, and love.[29]

At what age did people usually marry? The largest amount of evidence on age at first marriage survives from Italy, and a comparable pattern probably existed in northern Europe. For girls population surveys at Prato place the age at 16.3 years in 1372 and 21.1 in 1470. Chaucer's Wife of Bath says that she married first in her twelfth year. Among the German nobility, recent research has indicated that in the Hohenzollern family in the late Middle Ages, "five brides were between 12 and 13; five about 14, and five about 15."

Men were older. An Italian chronicler writing about 1354 says that men did not marry before the age of 30. At Prato in 1371, the average age of men at first marriage was 24 years, very young for Italian men, but these data may represent an attempt to regain population losses due to the recent attack of the plague. In England Chaucer's Wife of Bath describes her first three husbands as "goode men, and rich, and old." Among seventeen males in the noble Hohenzollern family, eleven were over 20 years when married, five between 18 and 19, one 16. The general pattern in late medieval Europe was marriage between men in their middle or late 20s and women under 20.[30] Poor peasants and wage laborers did not marry until their mid- or late 20s.

With marriage for men postponed, was there any socially accepted sexual outlet? Recent research on the southern French province of Languedoc in the fourteenth and fifteenth centuries has revealed the establishment of legal houses of prostitution. Prostitution involves "a socially definable group of women [who] earn their living primarily or exclusively from the [sexual] commerce of their bodies."[31] Municipal authorities in Toulouse, Montpellier, Albi, and other towns set up houses or red-light districts either outside the city walls or away from respectable neighborhoods. For example, authorities in Montpellier set aside Hot Street for prostitution, required public women to live there, and forbade anyone to molest them. Prostitution thus passed from being a private concern to a social matter requiring public supervision.[32] Publicly owned brothels were more easily policed and supervised than privately run ones. Prostitution was an urban phenomenon, because only populous towns had large numbers of unmarried young men, communities of transient merchants, and a culture accustomed to a cash exchange. Although the risk of disease limited the number of years a woman could practice this profession, many women prospered. Some acquired sizable incomes. In 1361 Françoise of Florence, a prostitute working in a brothel in Marseilles, made a will in which she made legacies to various charities and left a large sum as a dowry for a poor girl to marry. Archives in several cities show expensive properties bought by women who named their occupation as prostitution.

The towns of Languedoc were not unique. Public authorities in Amiens, Dijon, Paris, Venice, Genoa, London, Florence, Rome, most of the larger German towns, and in the English port of Sandwich set up brothels. Legalized prostitution suggests that public officials believed the prostitute could make a positive contribution to the society; it does not mean the prostitute was respected. Rather, she was scorned and distrusted. Legalized brothels also reflect a greater tolerance for male than for female sexuality.[33]

In the later Middle Ages, as earlier—indeed, until the late nineteenth century—economic factors, rather than

Prostitute Invites a Traveling Merchant Poverty and male violence drove women into prostitution, which, though denounced by moralists, was accepted as a normal part of the medieval social fabric. In the cities and larger towns where prostitution flourished, public officials passed laws requiring prostitutes to wear a special mark on their clothing, regulated hours of business, forbade women to drag men into their houses, and denied business to women with the "burning sickness," gonorrhea. *(The Bodleian Library, Oxford)*

romantic love or physical attraction, determined whom and when a person married. The young agricultural laborer on the manor had to wait until he had sufficient land. Thus most men had to wait until their fathers died or yielded the holding. The age of marriage was late, and this in turn affected the number of children a couple had. The journeyman craftsman in the urban guild faced the same material difficulties. Once a couple married, the union ended only with the death of one partner.

Deep emotional bonds knit members of medieval families. Most parents delighted in their children, and the church encouraged a cult of paternal care. The church stressed its right to govern and sanctify marriage, and it emphasized monogamy. Tighter moral and emotional unity within marriages resulted.

Divorce did not exist in the Middle Ages. The church held that a marriage validly entered into could not be dissolved. A valid marriage consisted of the mutual oral consent or promise of two parties. Church theologians of the day urged that the couple's union be celebrated and witnessed in a church ceremony and blessed by a priest.

A great number of couples did not observe the church's regulations. Some treated marriage as a private act—they made the promise and spoke the words of marriage to each other without witnesses and then proceeded to enjoy the sexual pleasures of marriage. This practice led to a great number of disputes, because one of the two parties could later deny having made a marriage agreement. The records of the ecclesiastical courts reveal many cases arising from privately made contracts. Evidence survives of marriages contracted in a garden, in a blacksmith's shop, at a tavern, and, predictably, in a bed. The records of church courts that relate to marriage reveal that, rather than suing for divorce, the great majority of petitions asked the court to enforce the marriage contract that one of the parties believed she or he had validly made. Annulments were granted in extraordinary circumstances, such as male impotence, on the grounds that a lawful marriage had never existed.[34]

Life in the Parish

In the later Middle Ages, the land and the parish remained the focus of life for the European peasantry. Work on the land continued to be performed collectively. Both men and women cooperated in the annual tasks of planting and harvesting. The close association of the cycle of agriculture and the liturgy of the Christian calendar endured. The parish priest blessed the fields before the annual planting, offering prayers on behalf of the people for a good crop. If the harvest was rich, the priest led the processions and celebrations of thanksgiving.

How did the common people feel about their work? Since the vast majority were illiterate and inarticulate, it is difficult to say. It is known that the peasants hated the ancient services and obligations on the lords' lands and tried to get them commuted for money rents. When lords attempted to reimpose service duties, the peasants revolted.

In the thirteenth century, the craft guilds provided the small minority of men and women living in towns and cities with the psychological satisfaction of involvement in the manufacture of a superior product. The guild member also had economic security. The craft guilds set high standards for their merchandise. The guilds looked after the sick, the poor, the widowed, and the orphaned. Masters and employees worked side by side.

In the fourteenth century, those ideal conditions began to change. The fundamental objective of the craft guild was to maintain a monopoly on its product, and to do so recruitment and promotion were carefully restricted. Some guilds required a high entrance fee for apprentices; others admitted only relatives of members. Apprenticeship increasingly lasted a long time, seven years. Even after a young man had satisfied all the tests for full membership in the guild and had attained the rank of master, other hurdles had to be passed, such as finding the funds to open his own business or special connections just to get into a guild. Restrictions limited the number of apprentices and journeymen to match the anticipated openings for masters. In a time of labor shortage after the Black Death, how were guilds able to be restrictive? Even with drastically reduced populations, towns and cities still had some available workers, either survivors or immigrants from elsewhere. Second, guild masters passed regulations setting familial, gender, and ethnic qualifications that allowed them to limit numbers and perpetuate control.

Women experienced the same exclusion. A careful study of the records of forty-two craft guilds in Cologne shows that in the fifteenth century all but six had become male preserves, either greatly restricting women's participation or allowing so few female members that they cannot be considered mixed guilds.[35] Popular and educated culture, supporting a patriarchal system that held women to be biologically and intellectually inferior, consigned them to low-status and low-paying jobs.

The larger a particular business was, the greater was the likelihood that the master did not know his em-

rebellions. Violence took different forms in different places. The townspeople of Cambridge expressed their hostility toward the university by sacking one of the colleges and building a bonfire of academic property. In towns containing skilled Flemish craftsmen, fear of competition led to their being attacked and murdered. Urban discontent merged with rural violence. Apprentices and journeymen, frustrated because the highest positions in the guilds were closed to them, rioted.

The boy-king Richard II (r. 1377–1399) met the leaders of the revolt, agreed to charters ensuring peasants' freedom, tricked them with false promises, and then proceeded to crush the uprising with terrible ferocity. Although the nobility tried to restore ancient duties of serfdom, virtually a century of freedom had elapsed, and the commutation of manorial services continued. Rural serfdom had disappeared in England by 1550.

Conditions in England and France were not unique. In Florence in 1378, the *ciompi,* the poor propertyless workers, revolted. Serious social trouble occurred in Lübeck, Brunswick, and other German cities. In Spain in 1391, aristocratic attempts to impose new forms of serfdom, combined with demands for tax relief, led to massive working-class and peasant uprisings in Seville and Barcelona. These took the form of vicious attacks on Jewish communities. Rebellions and uprisings everywhere reveal deep peasant and working-class frustration and the general socioeconomic crisis of the time.

Race and Ethnicity on the Frontiers

As we saw in Chapter 9, large numbers of people in the twelfth and thirteenth centuries migrated from one part of Europe to another: the English into Scotland and Ireland; Germans, French, and Flemings into Poland, Bohemia, and Hungary; the French into Spain. In the fourteenth century, many Germans moved into eastern Europe, fleeing the Black Death. The colonization of frontier regions meant that peoples of different ethnic or racial backgrounds lived side by side. Race relations became a basic factor in the lives of peoples living in those frontier areas.

Racial categories rest on socially constructed beliefs and customs, not on any biological or anthropological classification. When late medieval chroniclers used the language of race—words such as *gens* (race or clan) and *natio* (species, stock, or kind)—they meant cultural differences. Medieval scholars held that peoples differed according to descent, language, customs, and laws. Descent or blood, basic to the color racism of the United States, played an insignificant part in eleventh- and twelfth-century ideas about race and ethnicity. Rather, the chief marks of an ethnic group were language (which could be learned), customs (for example, dietary practices, dance, marriage and death rituals, clothing, and hairstyles, all of which could be adopted), and laws (which could be changed or modified). How did the law reflect attitudes and race relations in the Middle Ages? Did greater harmony exist in regions such as Ireland, where native peoples and settlers were of the same religious faith, than in countries such as Spain, where colonists and natives held different faiths? What role did race and ethnicity play in relations between the two groups in the later Middle Ages?

In the early periods of conquest and colonization, and in all frontier regions, a legal dualism existed: native peoples remained subject to their traditional laws; newcomers brought and were subject to the laws of the countries from which they came. On the Prussian and Polish frontier, for example, the law was that "men who come there . . . should be judged on account of any crime or contract engaged in there according to Polish custom if they are Poles and according to German custom if they are Germans."[42] Likewise, in Spain Mudéjars, Muslim subjects of Christian kings, received guarantees of separate but equal judicial rights. King Alfonso I of Aragon's charter to the Muslims of Toledo states, "They shall be in lawsuits and pleas under their (Muslim) qadi (judges) . . . as it was in the times of the Moors."[43] Thus conquered peoples, whether Muslims in Spain, or minority immigrant groups, such as Germans in eastern Europe, had legal protection and lived in their own juridical enclaves. Subject peoples experienced some disabilities, but the broad trend was toward a legal pluralism.

The great exception to this broad pattern was Ireland. From the start, the English practiced an extreme form of racial discrimination toward the native Irish. The English distinguished between the free and the unfree, and the entire Irish population, simply by the fact of Irish birth, was unfree. In 1210 King John declared that "English law and custom be established there (in Ireland)." Accordingly, a legal structure modeled on that of England, with county courts, itinerant justices, and the common law (see pages 345–348), was set up. But the Irish had no access to the common-law courts. In civil (property) disputes, an English defendant need not respond to his Irish plaintiff; no Irish person could make a will; and an Irish widow could not claim her dower rights (enjoyment of part of the estate during her lifetime). In criminal procedures, the murder of an Irishman was not considered a felony. In 1317–1318, Irish princes sent a Remonstrance to the pope complaining that "any non-Irishman is allowed to bring legal action against an Irishman, but an Irishman . . . except any prelate (bishop or abbot) is barred from every action by that fact alone." An English defendant in the criminal matter would claim "that he is not held to answer . . . since he [the plaintiff] is Irish and not of free blood."[44] This emphasis on blood descent naturally provoked bitterness, but only in the Tudor period (see Chapter 14) was the English common law opened to the subject Irish population.

The later Middle Ages witnessed a movement away from legal pluralism or dualism and toward a legal homogeneity and an emphasis on blood descent. Competition for ecclesiastical offices and the cultural divisions between town and country people became arenas for ethnic tension and racial conflict. Since bishoprics and abbacies carried religious authority, spiritual charisma, and often rights of appointment to subordinate positions, they were natural objects of ambition. When prelates of a language or "nationality" different from those of the local people gained church positions, the latter felt a loss of influence. Bishops were supposed to be pastors. Their pastoral work involved preaching, teaching, and comforting, duties that could be performed effectively only when the bishop (or priest) could communicate with the people. Ideally in a pluralistic society, he should be bilingual; often he was not.

In the late thirteenth century, as waves of Germans migrated into Danzig on the Baltic, into Silesia, and into the Polish countryside and towns, they encountered Jakub Swinka, archbishop of Gniezno (1283–1314), whose jurisdiction included these areas of settlement. The bishop hated Germans and referred to them as "dog heads." His German contemporary, Bishop John of Cracow, detested the Poles, wanted to expel all Polish people, and refused to appoint Poles to any church office. In Ireland, English colonists and the native Irish competed for ecclesiastical offices until 1217, when the English government in London decreed:

Since the election of Irishmen in our land of Ireland has often disturbed the peace of that land, we command you . . . that henceforth you allow no Irishman to be elected . . . or preferred in any cathedral . . . (and) you should seek by all means to procure election and promotion to vacant bishoprics of . . . honest Englishmen.[45]

Although criticized by the pope and not totally enforceable, this law remained in effect in many dioceses for centuries.

Likewise, the arrival of Cistercians and mendicants (Franciscans and Dominicans) from France and Germany in Baltic and Slavic lands provoked racial and "national" hostilities. In the fourteenth and fifteenth centuries, in contrast to earlier centuries, racial or ethnic prejudices became conspicuous. Slavic prelates and princes saw the German mendicants as "instruments of cultural colonization," and Slavs were strongly discouraged from becoming members. In 1333, when John of Drazic, bishop of Prague, founded a friary at Roudnice (Raudnitz), he specified that "we shall admit no one to this convent or monastery of any nation except a Bohemian [Czech], born of two Czech-speaking parents."[46]

Everywhere in Europe, towns recruited people from the countryside (see pages 349–351). In frontier regions, townspeople were usually long-distance immigrants and, in eastern Europe, Ireland, and Scotland, ethnically different from the surrounding rural population. In eastern Europe, German was the language of the towns; in Ireland, French, the tongue of noble Norman or English settlers, predominated. In fourteenth-century Prague, between 63 percent and 80 percent of new burgesses bore identifiable German names, as did almost all city council members. Towns in eastern Europe "had the character of German islands in Slav, Baltic, Estonian, or Magyar seas."[47] Although native peoples commonly held humbler positions, both immigrant and native townspeople prospered during the expanding economy of the thirteenth century. When economic recession hit during the fourteenth century, ethnic tensions multiplied.

Just as the social and legal status of the Jews in western Europe worsened in the wake of the great famine and the Black Death (see pages 380 and 383), on the frontiers of Latin Europe discrimination, ghettoization, and racism—now based on blood descent—characterized the attitudes of colonists toward native peoples. But the latter also could express racial savagery. In the *Dalimil Chronicle,* a survey of Bohemian history pervaded with Czech hostility toward Germans, one anti-German prince offered 100 marks of silver "to anyone who brought him one hundred noses cut off from the Germans."[48] Regulations drawn up by various guilds were explicitly racist, with protectionist bars for some groups and exclusionist laws for others. The Deutschtum paragraph of the *Chronicle,* applicable to parts of eastern Europe, required that applicants for guild membership be of German descent, and sometimes prove it. Cobblers in fourteenth-century Beeskow, a town close to the large Slavic population of Lausitz in Silesia, required that "an apprentice who comes to learn his craft should be brought before the master and guild mem-

Castleroche in County Louth Fortified castles served several functions: they were places of defense and protection against foreign invaders; places where food, water, and munitions were stored (against time of attack); and headquarters for control of the local population. As few as a dozen knights could hold off besiegers for months. Castleroche marked the border between Anglo-Irish resisters of English rule. *(Dúchas, The Heritage Service)*

bers. . . . We forbid the sons of barbers, linen workers, shepherds, Slavs." The bakers of the same town decreed:

Whoever wishes to be a member must bring proof to the councillors and guildsmen that he is born of legitimate, upright, German folk. . . . No one of Wendish (Slavic) race may be in the guild. In Limerick and Dublin in Ireland, guild masters agreed to accept "noo apprentice but that he be of English berthe."[49]

Intermarriage was forbidden in many places, such as Riga on the Baltic (now the capital of Latvia), where legislation for the bakers guild stipulated that "whoever wishes to have the privilege of membership in our company shall not take as a wife any woman who is ill-famed . . . or non-German; if he does marry such a woman, he must leave the company and office." Not only the guilds but eligibility for public office depended on racial purity, as at the German burgher settlement of Pest in Hungary, where a town judge had to have four German grandparents. The most extensive attempt to prevent intermarriage and protect racial purity is embodied in Ireland's Statute of Kilkenny (1366), which states that "there were to be no marriages between those of immigrant and native stock; that the English inhabitants of Ireland must employ the English language and bear English names; that they must ride in the English way (i.e., with saddles) and have English apparel; that no Irishmen were to be granted ecclesiastical benefices or admitted to monasteries in the English parts of Ireland; and that the Irish game of hurling and the maintenance of Irish minstrels were forbidden to English settlers."[50] Rulers of the Christian kingdoms of Spain drew up comparable legislation discriminating against the Mudéjars.

All these laws had an economic basis: to protect the financial interests of the privileged German, English, or Spanish colonial minorities. The laws also reflect a racism that not only pervaded the lives of frontier peoples at the end of the Middle Ages but sowed the seeds of difficulties still unresolved at the end of the twentieth century.

Vernacular Literature

Few developments expressed the development of national consciousness more vividly than the emergence of national literatures. Across Europe people spoke the language and dialect of their particular locality and class. In England, for example, the common people spoke regional English dialects, while the upper classes conversed in French. Official documents and works of literature were written in Latin or French. Beginning in the fourteenth century, however, national languages—the vernacular—came into widespread use not only in verbal communication but in literature as well. Three masterpieces of European culture, Dante's *Divine Comedy* (1310–1320), Chaucer's *Canterbury Tales* (1387–1400), and Villon's *Grand Testament* (1461), brilliantly manifest this new national pride.

Dante Alighieri (1265–1321) descended from an aristocratic family in Florence, where he held several positions in the city government. Dante called his work a "comedy" because he wrote it in Italian and in a different style from the "tragic" Latin; a later generation added the adjective *divine,* referring both to its sacred subject and to Dante's artistry. The *Divine Comedy* is an allegorical trilogy of one hundred cantos (verses) whose three equal parts (1 + 33 + 33 + 33) each describe one of the realms of the next world: Hell, Purgatory, and Paradise. Dante recounts his imaginary journey through these regions toward God. The Roman poet Virgil, representing reason, leads Dante through Hell, where he observes the torments of the damned and denounces the disorders of his own time, especially ecclesiastical ambition and corruption. Passing up into Purgatory, Virgil shows the poet how souls are purified of their disordered inclinations. From Purgatory, Beatrice, a woman Dante once loved and the symbol of divine revelation in the poem, leads him to Paradise. In Paradise, home of the angels and saints, Saint Bernard—representing mystic contemplation—leads Dante to the Virgin Mary. Through her intercession, he at last attains a vision of God.

The *Divine Comedy* portrays contemporary and historical figures, comments on secular and ecclesiastical affairs, and draws on Scholastic philosophy. Within the framework of a symbolic pilgrimage to the City of God, the *Divine Comedy* embodies the psychological tensions of the age. A profoundly Christian poem, it also contains bitter criticism of some church authorities. In its symmetrical structure and use of figures from the ancient world, such as Virgil, the poem perpetuates the classical tradition, but as the first major work of literature in the Italian vernacular, it is distinctly modern.

Geoffrey Chaucer (1340–1400), the son of a London wine merchant, was an official in the administrations of the English kings Edward III and Richard II and wrote poetry as an avocation. Chaucer's *Canterbury Tales* is a collection of stories in lengthy, rhymed narrative. On a pilgrimage to the shrine of Saint Thomas Becket at Canterbury (see page 346), thirty people of various social backgrounds each tell a tale. The Prologue sets the scene and describes the pilgrims, whose characters are further revealed in the story each one tells. For example, the gentle Christian Knight relates a chivalric romance; the gross Miller tells a vulgar story about a deceived husband; the earthy Wife of Bath, who has buried five husbands, sketches a fable about the selection of a spouse; and the elegant Prioress, who violates her vows by wearing jewelry, delivers a homily on the Virgin. In depicting the interests and behavior of all types of people, Chaucer presents a rich panorama of English social life in the fourteenth century. Like the *Divine Comedy, Canterbury Tales* reflects the cultural tensions of the times. Ostensibly Christian, many of the pilgrims are also materialistic, sensual, and worldly, suggesting the ambivalence of the broader society's concern for the next world and frank enjoyment of this one.

Our knowledge of François Villon (1431–1463), probably the greatest poet of late medieval France, derives from Paris police records and his own poetry. Born to poor parents in the year of Joan of Arc's execution, Villon was sent by his guardian to the University of Paris, where he earned the master of arts degree. A rowdy and free-spirited student, he disliked the stuffiness of academic life. In 1455 Villon killed a man in a street brawl; banished from Paris, he joined one of the bands of wandering thieves that harassed the countryside after the Hundred Years' War. For his fellow bandits, he composed ballads in thieves' jargon.

Villon's *Lais* (1456), a pun on the word *legs* ("legacy"), is a series of farcical bequests to friends and enemies. "Ballade des Pendus" (Ballad of the Hanged) was written while contemplating that fate in prison. (His execution was commuted.) Villon's greatest and most self-revealing work, the *Grand Testament,* contains another string of bequests, including a legacy to a prostitute, and describes his unshakable faith in the beauty of life on earth. The *Grand Testament* possesses elements of social rebellion, bawdy humor, and rare emotional depth. While the themes of Dante's and Chaucer's poetry are distinctly medieval, Villon's celebration of the human condition brands him as definitely modern. Although he used medieval forms of versification, Villon's language was the despised vernacular of the poor and the criminal.

Perhaps the most versatile and prolific French writer of the later Middle Ages was Christine de Pisan (1363?–1434?). The daughter of a professor of astrology at Bologna whose international reputation won him a post at the French royal court, where she received her excellent education, Christine had a broad knowledge of Greek, Latin, French, and Italian literature. The deaths of her father and husband left her with three small children and her mother to support, and she resolved to earn her living with her pen. In addition to poems and books on love, religion, and morality, Christine produced the *Livre de la mutacion de fortune,* a major historical work; a biography of King Charles V; the *Ditié,* celebrating Joan of Arc's victory; and many letters. *The City of Ladies* lists the great women of history and their contributions to society, and *The Book of Three Virtues* provides prudent and practical advice on household management for women of all social classes and at all stages of life. Christine de Pisan's wisdom and wit are illustrated in her autobiographical *Avison-Christine.* She records that a man told her an educated woman is unattractive, since there are so few, to which she responded that an ignorant man was even less attractive, since there are so many. (See the feature "Listening to the Past: Christine de Pisan" on pages 412–413.)

Schoolmaster and His Wife Teaching Ambrosius Holbein, elder brother of the more famous Hans Holbein, produced this signboard for the Swiss educator Myconius; it is an excellent example of what we would call commercial art—art used to advertise, in this case Myconius's profession. The German script above promised that all who enrolled would learn to read and write. By modern standards the classroom seems bleak: the windows have glass panes but they don't admit much light, and the schoolmaster is prepared to use the sticks if the boy makes a mistake. *(Öffentliche Kunstsammlung Basel/Martin Bühler, photographer)*

In the fourteenth century, a vernacular literature also emerged in eastern Europe, often as a reaction to other cultures. In Bohemia, for example, the immigration of large numbers of Germans elicited increasing Czech self-consciousness, leading to an interest among the Czechs in their own language. Translations of knightly sagas from German into Czech multiplied. So did translations of religious writings—Psalters, prayers, a life of Christ—from Latin into Czech. Vernacular literature in eastern Europe especially represents an ethnic and patriotic response to foreigners.

From the fifth through the thirteenth century, the overwhelming majority of people who could read and write were priests, monks, and nuns. Beginning in the fourteenth century, a variety of evidence attests to the increasing literacy of laypeople. Wills and inventories reveal that many people, not just nobles, possessed books, mainly devotional, but also romances, manuals on manners and etiquette, histories, and sometimes legal and philosophical texts. In England, as one scholar has recently shown, the number of schools in the diocese of York quadrupled between 1350 and 1500. Information from Flemish and German towns is similar: children were sent to schools and received the fundamentals of reading, writing, and arithmetic. Laymen increasingly served as managers or stewards of estates and as clerks to guilds and town governments; such positions obviously required that they be able to keep administrative and financial records.

The penetration of laymen into the higher positions of governmental administration, long the preserve of clerics, also illustrates rising lay literacy. For example, in 1400 beneficed clerics held most of the posts in the English Exchequer; by 1430 clerics were the exception. With growing frequency, the upper classes sent their daughters to convent schools, where, in addition to instruction in singing, religion, needlework, deportment, and household management, girls gained the rudiments of reading and sometimes writing. Reading and writing represent two kinds of literacy. Scholars estimate that many more people, especially women, possessed the first literacy, but not the second. The spread of literacy represents a response to the needs of an increasingly complex society. Trade, commerce, and expanding governmental bureaucracies required more and more literate people. Late medieval culture remained an oral culture in which most people received information by word of mouth. But by the mid-fifteenth century, even before the printing press was turning out large quantities of reading materials, the evolution toward a literary culture was already perceptible.[51]

SUMMARY

Late medieval preachers likened the crises of their times to the Four Horsemen of the Apocalypse in the Book of Revelation, who brought famine, war, disease, and death. The crises of the fourteenth and fifteenth centuries were acids that burned deeply into the fabric of traditional medieval European society. Bad weather brought poor harvests, which contributed to the international economic depression. Disease, over which people also had little control, fostered widespread depression and dissatisfaction. Population losses caused by the Black Death and the Hundred Years' War encouraged the working classes to try to profit from the labor shortage by selling their services higher: they wanted to move up the economic ladder. The theological ideas of thinkers like John Wyclif, John Hus, and John Ball fanned the flames of social discontent. When peasant frustrations exploded in uprisings, the frightened nobility and upper middle class joined to crush the revolts and condemn heretical preachers as agitators of social rebellion. But the war had heightened social consciousness among the poor.

The Hundred Years' War served as a catalyst for the development of representative government in England. In France, on the other hand, the war stiffened opposition to national assemblies.

The war also stimulated technological experimentation, especially with artillery. Cannon revolutionized warfare, because the stone castle was no longer impregnable. Because only central governments, and not private nobles, could afford cannon, they strengthened the military power of national states.

The migration of peoples from the European heartland to the frontier regions of Ireland, the Baltic, eastern Europe, and Spain led to ethnic frictions between native peoples and new settlers. Economic difficulties heightened ethnic consciousness and spawned a vicious racism.

Religion held society together. European culture was a Christian culture. But the Great Schism weakened the prestige of the church and people's faith in papal authority. The conciliar movement, by denying the church's universal sovereignty, strengthened the claims of secular government to jurisdiction over all their peoples. The later Middle Ages witnessed a steady shift of basic loyalty from the church to the emerging national states.

The increasing number of schools leading to the growth of lay literacy represents another positive achievement of the later Middle Ages. So also does the development of national literatures. The first sign of a literary culture appeared.

NOTES

1. W. C. Jordan, *The Great Famine: Northern Europe in the Early Fourteenth Century* (Princeton, N.J.: Princeton University Press, 1996), pp. 97–102.
2. Ibid., pp. 167–179.
3. N. Ascherson, *Black Sea* (New York: Hill & Wang, 1996), pp. 95–96.
4. W. H. McNeill, *Plagues and Peoples* (New York: Doubleday, 1976), pp. 151–168.
5. Quoted in P. Ziegler, *The Black Death* (Harmondsworth, England: Pelican Books, 1969), p. 20.
6. J. M. Rigg, trans., *The Decameron of Giovanni Boccaccio* (London: J. M. Dent & Sons, 1903), p. 6.
7. M. Mollatt, *The Poor in the Middle Ages: An Essay in Social History,* trans. A. Goldhammer (New Haven, Conn.: Yale University Press, 1986), pp. 146–153, 193–197.
8. Ziegler, *The Black Death,* pp. 232–239.
9. Ibid., p. 84.
10. G. Huppert, *After the Black Death: A Social History of Early Modern Europe* (Bloomington, Ind.: Indiana University Press, 1986), p. ix.
11. J. Hatcher, *Plague, Population and the English Economy, 1348–1530* (London: Macmillan Education, 1986), p. 33.
12. Ascherson, *Black Sea,* p. 96.
13. See D. Herlihy, *The Black Death and the Transformation of the West* (Cambridge, Mass.: Harvard University Press, 1997), pp. 59–81.
14. See P. Cuttino, "Historical Revision: The Causes of the Hundred Years' War," *Speculum* 31 (July 1956): 463–472.
15. J. Barnie, *War in Medieval English Society: Social Values and the Hundred Years' War* (Ithaca, N.Y.: Cornell University Press, 1974), p. 6.
16. Quoted ibid., p. 34.
17. Quoted ibid., p. 73.
18. Quoted ibid., pp. 72–73.
19. W. P. Barrett, trans., *The Trial of Jeanne d'Arc* (London: George Routledge, 1931), pp. 165–166.
20. Quoted in Barnie, *War in Medieval English Society,* pp. 36–37.
21. M. M. Postan, "The Costs of the Hundred Years' War," *Past and Present* 27 (April 1964): 34–53.
22. See G. O. Sayles, *The King's Parliament of England* (New York: W. W. Norton, 1974), app., pp. 137–141.
23. Quoted in P. S. Lewis, "The Failure of the Medieval French Estates," *Past and Present* 23 (November 1962): 6.
24. Quoted in J. H. Smith, *The Great Schism 1378: The Disintegration of the Medieval Papacy* (New York: Weybright & Talley, 1970), p. 141.
25. Ibid., p. 15.
26. B. A. Hanawalt, *The Ties That Bound: Peasant Families in Medieval England* (New York: Oxford University Press, 1986), p. 197. This section leans heavily on Hanawalt's work.
27. Quoted ibid., pp. 194–204.
28. A. S. Haskell, "The Paston Women on Marriage in Fifteenth Century England," *Viator* 4 (1973): 459–469.
29. Ibid., p. 471.
30. See D. Herlihy, *Medieval Households* (Cambridge, Mass.: Harvard University Press, 1985), pp. 103–111.
31. L. L. Otis, *Prostitution in Medieval Society: The History of an Urban Institution in Languedoc* (Chicago: University of Chicago Press, 1987), p. 2.
32. Ibid., pp. 25–27, 64–66, 100–106.
33. Ibid., pp. 118–130.
34. See R. H. Helmholz, *Marriage Litigation in Medieval England* (Cambridge: Cambridge University Press, 1974), pp. 28–29, et passim.
35. See M. C. Howell, *Women, Production, and Patriarchy in Late Medieval Cities* (Chicago: University of Chicago Press, 1986), pp. 134–135.
36. A. F. Scott, ed., *Everyone a Witness: The Plantagenet Age* (New York: Thomas Y. Crowell, 1976), p. 263.
37. See E. Mason, "The Role of the English Parishioner, 1000–1500," *Journal of Ecclesiastical History* 27 (January 1976): 17–29.
38. B. A. Hanawalt, "Fur Collar Crime: The Pattern of Crime Among the Fourteenth-Century English Nobility," *Journal of Social History* 8 (Spring 1975): 1–14.
39. Quoted ibid., p. 7.
40. Quoted in M. Bloch, *French Rural History,* trans. J. Sondeimer (Berkeley: University of California Press, 1966), p. 169.
41. C. Stephenson and G. Marcham, eds., *Sources of English Constitutional History,* rev. ed. (New York: Harper & Row, 1972), p. 225.
42. Quoted in R. Bartlett, *The Making of Europe: Conquest, Colonization and Cultural Change, 950–1350* (Princeton, N.J.: Princeton University Press, 1993), p. 205. For an alternative, if abstract, discussion of medieval racism, see I. Hannaford, *Race: The History of an Idea in the West* (Baltimore: Johns Hopkins University Press, 1995), pp. 87–146.
43. Quoted in Bartlett, *The Making of Europe,* p. 208.
44. Quoted ibid., p. 215.
45. Quoted ibid., p. 224.
46. Quoted ibid., p. 228.
47. Quoted ibid., p. 233.
48. Quoted ibid., p. 236.
49. Quoted ibid., p. 238.
50. Quoted ibid., p. 239.

51. See M. Keen, *English Society in the Later Middle Ages, 1348–1500* (New York: Penguin Books, 1990), pp. 219–239.

Suggested Reading

The best starting point for study of the great epidemic that swept the European continent is D. Herlihy, *The Black Death and the Transformation of the West* (1997), a fine treatment of the causes and cultural consequences of the disease. P. Binski, *Medieval Death: Ritual and Representation* (1995), discusses the impact of the Black Death on medieval art and literature. For the social implications of the Black Death, see L. Poos, *A Rural Society After the Black Death: Essex, 1350–1525* (1991); G. Huppert, *After the Black Death: A Social History of Early Modern Europe* (1986); and W. H. McNeill, *Plagues and Peoples* (1976). For the economic effects of the plague, see J. Hatcher, *Plague, Population, and the English Economy, ca. 1300–1450* (1977). The older study of P. Ziegler, *The Black Death* (1969), remains important.

For the background and early part of the long military conflicts of the fourteenth and fifteenth centuries, see the provocative M. M. Vale, *The Origins of the Hundred Years War: The Angevin Legacy, 1250–1340* (1996). The standard study of this subject is still E. Perroy, *The Hundred Years War* (1959), but see also C. Allmand, *The Hundred Years War: England and France at War, ca 1300–1450* (1988). The broad survey of J. Keegan, *A History of Warfare* (1993), contains a useful summary of significant changes in military technology during the war. The main ruler of the age has found his biographer in W. M. Ormrod, *The Reign of Edward III: Crown and Political Society in England, 1327–1377* (1990). J. Henneman, *Royal Taxation in Fourteenth Century France: The Development of War Financing, 1322–1356* (1971), is an important technical work by a distinguished historian. J. Keegan, *The Face of Battle* (1977), chap. 2, "Agincourt," describes what war meant to the ordinary soldier. B. Tuchman, *A Distant Mirror: The Calamitous Fourteenth Century* (1980), gives a vivid picture of many facets of fourteenth-century life, while concentrating on the war. For strategy, tactics, armaments, and costumes of war, see H. W. Koch, *Medieval Warfare* (1978), a beautifully illustrated book. R. Barber, *The Knight and Chivalry* (1982), and M. Keen, *Chivalry* (1984), give fresh interpretations of the cultural importance of chivalry.

For political and social conditions in the fourteenth and fifteenth centuries, see the works by Lewis, Sayles, Bloch, and especially Hanawalt and Helmholz cited in the Notes. C. Dyer, *Standards of Living in the Later Middle Ages* (1989), contains much valuable social history. The papers in R. H. Hilton and T. H. Aston, eds., *The English Rising of 1381* (1984), stress the importance of urban, as well as rural, participation in the movement, but see also R. Hilton, *Bond Men Made Free: Medieval Peasant Movements and the English Rising of 1381* (1973), a comparative study; and M. Keen, *The Outlaws of Medieval Legend* (1961). T. F. Glick, *From Muslim Fortress to Christian Castle: Social and Cultural Change in Medieval Spain* (1995), which is based in part on rare archaeological information, explores the reorganization of Spanish society after the reconquest, bringing considerable cultural change. J. S. Gerber, *The Jews of Spain: A History of the Sephardic Experience* (1992), treats growing anti-Jewish sentiment in the wake of the Black Death. P. C. Maddern, *Violence and Social Order: East Anglia, 1422–1442* (1991), deals with social disorder in eastern England. I. M. W. Harvey, *Jack Cade's Rebellion of 1450* (1991), is an important work in local history. Students are especially encouraged to consult the brilliant work of E. L. Ladurie, *The Peasants of Languedoc*, trans. J. Day (1976). J. C. Holt, *Robin Hood* (1982), is a soundly researched and highly readable study of the famous outlaw. For the Pastons, see R. Barber, ed., *The Pastons: Letters of a Family in the Wars of the Roses* (1984).

D. Herlihy, *Women, Family and Society in Medieval Europe: Historical Essays, 1978–1991* (1995), contains several valuable articles dealing with the later Middle Ages, while the exciting study by B. Gottlieb, *The Family in the Western World from the Black Death to the Industrial Age* (1993), explores the family's political, emotional, and cultural roles. For prostitution, see, in addition to the title by Otis cited in the Notes, J. Rossiaud, *Medieval Prostitution* (1995), a very good treatment of prostitution's social and cultural significance.

For women's economic status in the late medieval period, see the titles by Howell and Hanawalt cited in the Notes. J. S. Bennett, *Ale, Beer, and Brewsters in England: Women's Work in a Changing World, 1300–1600* (1996), uses the experience of women in the brewing industry to stress the persistence of patriarchal attitudes. D. Nicholas, *The Domestic Life of a Medieval City: Women, Children, and the Family in Fourteenth-Century Ghent* (1985), focuses on an urban society. P. J. P. Goldberg, *Women, Work, and Life Cycle in a Medieval Economy: Women in York and Yorkshire, c 1300–1520* (1992), explores the relationship between economic opportunity and marriage.

The poetry of Dante, Chaucer, and Villon may be read in the following editions: D. Sayers, trans., *Dante: The Divine Comedy*, 3 vols. (1963); N. Coghill, trans., *Chaucer's Canterbury Tales* (1977); P. Dale, trans., *The Poems of Villon* (1973). The social setting of *Canterbury Tales* is brilliantly evoked in D. W. Robertson, Jr., *Chaucer's London* (1968). Students interested in further study of Christine de Pisan should consult A. J. Kennedy, *Christine de Pisan: A Bibliographical Guide* (1984); and C. C. Willard, *Christine de Pisan: Her Life and Works* (1984).

For religion and lay piety, A. D. Brown, *Popular Piety in Late Medieval England: The Diocese of Salisbury, 1250–1550*

(1995), is a good case study showing the importance of guilds, charity, and heresy and how they affected parish life. F. Oakley, *The Western Church in the Later Middle Ages* (1979), is an excellent broad survey, while R. N. Swanson, *Church and Society in Late Medieval England* (1989), provides a good synthesis of English conditions. S. Ozment, *The Age of Reform, 1250–1550* (1980), discusses the Great Schism and the conciliar movement in the intellectual context of the ecclesiopolitical tradition of the Middle Ages. For great detail, consult H. Beck et al., *From the High Middle Ages to the Eve of the Reformation,* trans. A. Biggs, vol. 14 in the History of the Church series edited by H. Jedin and J. Dolan (1980). J. Bossy, "The Mass as a Social Institution, 1200–1700," *Past and Present* 100 (August 1983): 29–61, provides a technical study of the central public ritual of the Latin church. The important achievement of A. Vauchez, *The Laity in the Middle Ages: Religious Beliefs and Devotional Practices,* ed. D. E. Bornstein and trans. M. J. Schneider (1993), explores many aspects of popular piety and contains considerable material on women.

LISTENING TO THE PAST

Christine de Pisan

The passage below is taken from The Book of the City of Ladies, *one of the many writings of Christine de Pisan (1363?–1434?). Christine was a highly educated woman who wrote prolifically in French, her native tongue. Her patron was the queen of France. Christine wrote amid the chaos of the Hundred Years' War about a wide range of topics. The excerpt below is not reflective of all French women. Rather, it focuses on the behavior of courtly women only. And it expresses Christine's and her patron's views about women's role in the creation and stabilization of an elite court culture during a time of political and social upheaval.*

Just as the good shepherd takes care that his lambs are maintained in health, and if any of them becomes mangy, separates it from the flock for fear that it may infect the others, so the princess will take upon herself the responsibility for the care of her women servants and companions, who she will ensure are all good and chaste, for she will not want to have any other sort of person around her. Since it is the established custom that knights and squires and all men (especially certain men) who associate with women have a habit of pleading for love tokens from them and trying to seduce them, the wise princess will so enforce her regulations that there will be no visitor to her court so foolhardy as to dare to whisper privately with any of her women or give the appearance of seduction. If he does it or if he is noticed giving any sign of it, immediately she should take such an attitude towards him that he will not dare to importune them any more. The lady who is chaste will want all her women to be so too, on pain of being banished from her company.

She will want them to amuse themselves with decent games, such that men cannot mock, as they do the games of some women, though at the time the men laugh and join in. The women should restrain themselves with seemly conduct among knights and squires and all men. They should speak demurely and sweetly and, whether in dances or other amusements, divert and enjoy themselves decorously and without wantonness. They must not be frolicsome, forward, or boisterous in speech, expression, bearing or laughter. They must not go about with their heads raised like wild deer. This kind of behaviour would be very unseemly and greatly derisory in a woman of the court, in whom there should be more modesty, good manners and courteous behaviour than in any others, for where there is most honour there ought to be the most perfect manners and behaviour. Women of the court in any country would be deceiving themselves very much if they imagined that it was more appropriate for them to be frolicsome and saucy than for other women. For this reason we hope that in time to come our doctrine in this book may be carried into many kingdoms, so that it may be valuable in all places where there might be any shortcoming.

We say generally to all women of all countries that it is the duty of every lady and maiden of the court, whether she be young or old, to be more prudent, more decorous, and better schooled in all things than other women. The ladies of the court ought to be models of all good things and all honour to other women, and if they do otherwise they will do no honour to their mistress nor to themselves. In addition, so that everything may be consistent in modesty, the wise princess will wish that the clothing and the ornaments of her women, though they be appropriately beautiful and rich, be of a modest fashion, well fitting and seemly, neat and properly cared for. There should be no deviation from this modesty nor any immodesty in the matter of plunging necklines or other excesses.

In all things the wise princess will keep her women in order just as the good and prudent abbess does her convent, so that bad reports about it may not circulate in the town, in distant regions or anywhere else. This princess will be so feared and respected because of the wise management that she will be seen to practise that no man or woman will be so foolhardy as to disobey her commands in any respect or to question her will, for there is no doubt that a lady is more feared and respected and held in greater reverence when she is seen to be wise and chaste and of firm behaviour. But there is nothing wrong or inconsistent in her being kind and gentle, for the mere look of the wise lady and her subdued reception is enough of a sign to correct those men and women who err and to inspire them with fear.

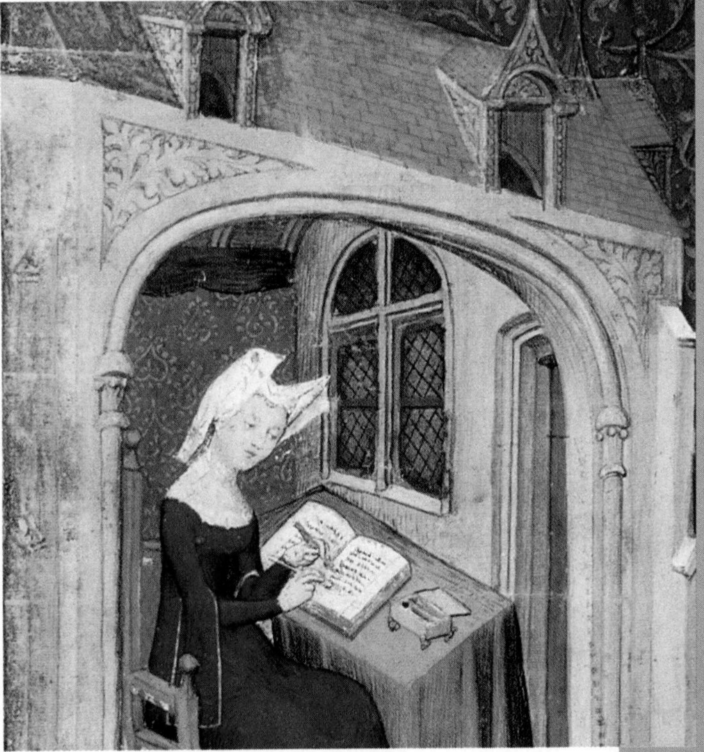

✣ Christine de Pisan, shown here producing her *Collected Works,* was devoted to scholarship. *(British Library)*

Questions for Analysis

1. How did Christine think courtly women should behave around men?
2. How did women fit into the larger picture of court culture? What was their role at court?

Source: Christine de Pisan, "The Book of the City of Ladies," in *Treasures of the City of Ladies,* trans. Sarah Lawson (Penguin, 1985), pp. 74–76.

CHAPTER

13 European Society in the Age of the Renaissance

Michelangelo painted the entire Sistine Chapel ceiling by himself, in 1508–1512. *(Vatican Museum)*

While the Four Horsemen of the Apocalypse seemed to be carrying war, plague, famine, and death across the continent, a new culture was emerging in southern Europe. The fourteenth century witnessed the beginnings of remarkable changes in many aspects of Italian society. In the fifteenth century, these phenomena spread beyond Italy and gradually influenced society in northern Europe. These cultural changes have been collectively labeled the "Renaissance."

- What does the term *Renaissance* mean?
- How was the Renaissance manifested in politics, government, and social organization?
- What were the intellectual and artistic hallmarks of the Renaissance?
- Did the Renaissance involve shifts in religious attitudes?
- What developments occurred in the evolution of the nation-state?

This chapter will concentrate on these questions.

The Evolution of the Italian Renaissance

Economic growth laid the material basis for the Italian Renaissance. The period extending roughly from 1050 to 1300 witnessed phenomenal commercial and financial development, the growing political power of self-governing cities, and great population expansion. Then the period from the late thirteenth to the late sixteenth century was characterized by an incredible efflorescence of artistic energies.[1] Scholars commonly use the term *Renaissance* to describe the cultural achievements of the fourteenth through sixteenth centuries; those achievements rest on the economic and political developments of earlier centuries.

In the great commercial revival of the eleventh century, northern Italian cities led the way. By the middle of the twelfth century, Venice, supported by a huge merchant marine, had grown enormously rich through overseas trade. It profited tremendously from the diversion of the Fourth Crusade to Constantinople (see page 358). Genoa and Milan also enjoyed the benefits of a large volume of trade with the Middle East and northern Europe. These cities fully exploited their geographical positions as natural crossroads for mercantile exchange between the East and West. Furthermore, in the early fourteenth century, Genoa and Venice made important strides in shipbuilding that allowed their ships for the first time to sail all year long. Advances in ship construction greatly increased the volume of goods that could be transported; improvements in the mechanics of sailing accelerated speed. Most goods were purchased directly from the producers and sold a good distance away. For example, Italian merchants bought fine English wool directly from the Cistercian abbeys of Yorkshire in northern England. The wool was transported to the bazaars of North Africa either overland or by ship through the Strait of Gibraltar. The risks in such an operation were great, but the profits were enormous. These profits were continually reinvested to earn more.

Scholars tend to agree that the first artistic and literary manifestations of the Italian Renaissance appeared in Florence, which possessed enormous wealth despite geographical constraints: it was an inland city without easy access to sea transportation. But toward the end of the thirteenth century, Florentine merchants and bankers acquired control of papal banking. From their position as tax collectors for the papacy, Florentine mercantile families began to dominate European banking on both sides of the Alps. These families had offices in Paris, London, Bruges, Barcelona, Marseilles, Tunis and other North African ports, and, of course, Naples and Rome. The profits from loans, investments, and money exchanges that poured back to Florence were pumped into urban industries. Such profits contributed to the city's economic vitality.

The Florentine wool industry, however, was the major factor in the city's financial expansion and population increase. Florence purchased the best-quality wool from England and Spain, developed remarkable techniques for its manufacture into cloth, and employed thousands of workers in the manufacturing process. Florentine weavers produced immense quantities of superb woolen cloth, which brought the highest prices in the fairs, markets, and bazaars of Europe, Asia, and Africa.

By the first quarter of the fourteenth century, the economic foundations of Florence were so strong that even severe crises could not destroy the city. In 1344 King Edward III of England repudiated his huge debts to Florentine bankers and forced some of them into bankruptcy. Florence suffered frightfully from the Black

A Bank Scene, Florence Originally a "bank" was just a counter; if covered with a carpet like this Ottoman geometric rug with a kufic border, it became a bank of distinction. Money-changers who sat behind the counter became "bankers," exchanging different currencies and holding deposits for merchants and business people. *(Prato, San Francesco/Scala/Art Resource, NY)*

Death, losing at least half of its population. Serious labor unrest, such as the *ciompi* revolts of 1378 (see page 403), shook the political establishment. Nevertheless, the basic Florentine economic structure remained stable. Driving enterprise, technical know-how, and competitive spirit saw Florence through the difficult economic period of the late fourteenth century.

Communes and Republics

The northern Italian cities were *communes,* sworn associations of free men seeking complete political and economic independence from local nobles. The merchant guilds that formed the communes built and maintained the city walls, regulated trade, raised taxes, and kept civil order. In the course of the twelfth century, communes at Milan, Florence, Genoa, Siena, and Pisa fought for and won their independence from surrounding feudal nobles. The nobles, attracted by the opportunities of long-distance and maritime trade, the rising value of urban real estate, the new public offices available in the expanding communes, and the chances for advantageous marriages into rich commercial families, frequently settled within the cities. Marriage vows often sealed business contracts between the rural nobility and the mercantile aristocracy. This merger of the northern Italian feudal nobility and the commercial aristocracy constituted the formation of a new social class, an urban nobility. Within this nobility, groups tied by blood, economic interests, and social connections formed tightly knit alliances to defend and expand their rights.

This new class made citizenship in the communes dependent on a property qualification, years of residence within the city, and social connections. Only a tiny percentage of the male population possessed these qualifications and thus could hold office in the commune's political councils. A new force, called the *popolo,* disenfranchised and heavily taxed, bitterly resented their exclusion from power. The popolo wanted places in the communal government and equality of taxation. Throughout most of the thirteenth century, in city after city, the popolo used armed force and violence to take over the city governments. Republican governments—in which political power theoretically resides in the people and is exercised by its chosen representatives—were established in Bologna, Siena, Parma, Florence, Genoa, and other cities. The victory of the popolo, however, proved temporary. Because they practiced the same sort of political exclusivity as had the noble communes—denying influence to the classes below them, whether the poor, the unskilled, or new immigrants—the popolo never won the support of other groups. Moreover, the popolo could not establish civil order within their cities. Consequently, these movements for republican government failed. By 1300 *signori* (despots, or one-man rulers) or *oligarchies* (the rule of merchant aristocracies) had triumphed everywhere in Italy.[2]

For the next two centuries, the Italian city-states were ruled by signori or by constitutional oligarchies. In signorial governments, despots pretended to observe the law while actually manipulating it to conceal their basic illegality. Oligarchic regimes possessed constitutions, but through a variety of schemes a small, restricted class of wealthy merchants exercised the judicial, executive, and legislative functions of government. Thus in 1422 Venice had a population of eighty-four thousand, but two hundred men held all the power; Florence had about forty thousand people, but six hundred men ruled. Oligarchic regimes maintained only a façade of republican government. The Renaissance nostalgia for the Roman form of government, combined with calculating shrewdness, prompted the leaders of Venice, Milan, and Florence to use the old forms.

In the fifteenth century, political power and elite culture centered on the princely courts of despots and oligarchs. "A court was the space and personnel around a prince as he made laws, received ambassadors, made appointments, took his meals, and proceeded through the streets."[3] The princely court afforded the despot or oligarch the opportunity to display and assert his wealth and power. He flaunted his patronage of learning and the arts by munificent gifts to writers, philosophers, and artists. He used ceremonies connected with family births, baptisms, marriages, funerals, or triumphant entrances into the city as occasions for magnificent pageantry and elaborate ritual.

The Balance of Power Among the Italian City-States

Renaissance Italians had a passionate attachment to their individual city-states: political loyalty and feeling centered on the local city. This intensity of local feeling perpetuated the dozens of small states and hindered the development of one unified state. Italy, consequently, was completely disunited.

In the fifteenth century, five powers dominated the Italian peninsula: Venice, Milan, Florence, the Papal States, and the kingdom of Naples (Map 13.1). The rulers of the city-states—whether despots in Milan, patrician elitists in Florence, or oligarchs in Venice—governed as monarchs. They crushed urban revolts, levied taxes, killed their enemies, and used massive building programs to employ, and the arts to overawe, the masses.

Venice, with its enormous trade and vast colonial empire, ranked as an international power. Though Venice had a sophisticated constitution and was a republic in name, an oligarchy of merchant aristocrats actually ran the city. Milan was also called a republic, but despots of the Sforza family ruled harshly and dominated the smaller cities of the north. Likewise in Florence the form of government was republican, with authority vested in several councils of state. In reality, between 1434 and 1494, power in Florence was held by the great Medici banking family. Though not public officers, Cosimo (1434–1464) and Lorenzo (1469–1492) ruled from behind the scenes.

Central Italy consisted mainly of the Papal States, which during the Babylonian Captivity had come under the sway of important Roman families. Pope Alexander VI (1492–1503), aided militarily and politically by his son Cesare Borgia, reasserted papal authority in the papal lands. Cesare Borgia became the hero of Machiavelli's *The Prince* (see page 429) because he began the work of uniting the peninsula by ruthlessly conquering and exacting total obedience from the principalities making up the Papal States.

South of the Papal States was the kingdom of Naples, consisting of virtually all of southern Italy and, at times, Sicily. The kingdom of Naples had long been disputed by the Aragonese and by the French. In 1435 it passed to Aragon.

The major Italian city-states controlled the smaller ones, such as Siena, Mantua, Ferrara, and Modena, and competed furiously among themselves for territory. The large cities used diplomacy, spies, paid informers, and any other available means to get information that could be used to advance their ambitions. While the states of northern Europe were moving toward centralization and consolidation, the world of Italian politics resembled a jungle where the powerful dominated the weak.

In one significant respect, however, the Italian city-states anticipated future relations among competing European states after 1500. Whenever one Italian state appeared to gain a predominant position within the

MAP 13.1 The Italian City-States, ca 1494 In the fifteenth century, the Italian city-states represented great wealth and cultural sophistication. The political divisions of the peninsula invited foreign intervention.

peninsula, other states combined to establish a balance of power against the major threat. In 1450, for example, Venice went to war against Milan in protest against Francesco Sforza's acquisition of the title of duke of Milan. Cosimo de' Medici of Florence, a long-time supporter of a Florentine-Venetian alliance, switched his position and aided Milan. Florence and Naples combined with Milan against powerful Venice and the papacy. In the peace treaty signed at Lodi in 1454, Venice received territories in return for recognizing Sforza's right to the duchy. This pattern of shifting alliances continued until 1494. In the formation of these alliances, Renaissance Italians invented the machinery of modern diplomacy: permanent embassies with resident ambassadors in capitals where political relations and commercial ties needed continual monitoring. The resident ambassador was one of the great achievements of the Italian Renaissance.

At the end of the fifteenth century, Venice, Florence, Milan, and the papacy possessed great wealth and represented high cultural achievement. However, their imperialistic ambitions at one another's expense and their resulting inability to form a common alliance against potential foreign enemies made Italy an inviting target for invasion. When Florence and Naples entered into an agreement to acquire Milanese territories, Milan called on France for support.

At Florence the French invasion had been predicted by Dominican friar Girolamo Savonarola (1452–1498). In a number of fiery sermons between 1491 and 1494, Savonarola attacked what he considered the paganism and moral vice of the city, the undemocratic government of Lorenzo de' Medici, and the corruption of Pope Alexander VI. For a time, Savonarola enjoyed popular support among the ordinary people; he became the religious leader of Florence and as such contributed to the fall of the Medici dynasty. Eventually, however, people tired of his moral denunciations, and he was excommunicated by the pope and executed. Savonarola stands as proof that the common people did not share the worldly outlook of the commercial and intellectual elite. His career also illustrates the internal instability of Italian cities such as Florence, an instability that invited foreign invasion.

The invasion of Italy in 1494 by the French king Charles VIII (r. 1483–1498) inaugurated a new period in Italian and European power politics. Italy became the focus of international ambitions and the battleground of foreign armies. Charles swept down the peninsula with little opposition, and Florence, Rome, and Naples soon bowed before him. When Piero de' Medici, Lorenzo's son, went to the French camp seeking peace, the Florentines exiled the Medicis and restored republican government.

Charles's success simply whetted French appetites. In 1508 his cousin and heir, Louis XII, formed the League of Cambrai with the pope and the German emperor Maximilian for the purpose of stripping rich Venice of its mainland possessions. Pope Leo X (1513–1521) soon found France a dangerous friend and in a new alliance called on the Spanish and Germans to expel the French from Italy. This anti-French combination was temporarily successful. In 1519 Charles V succeeded his grandfather Maximilian (1493–1519) as Holy Roman emperor. When the French returned to Italy in 1522, a series of conflicts called the Habsburg-Valois Wars (named for the German and French dynasties) began. The battlefield was often Italy.

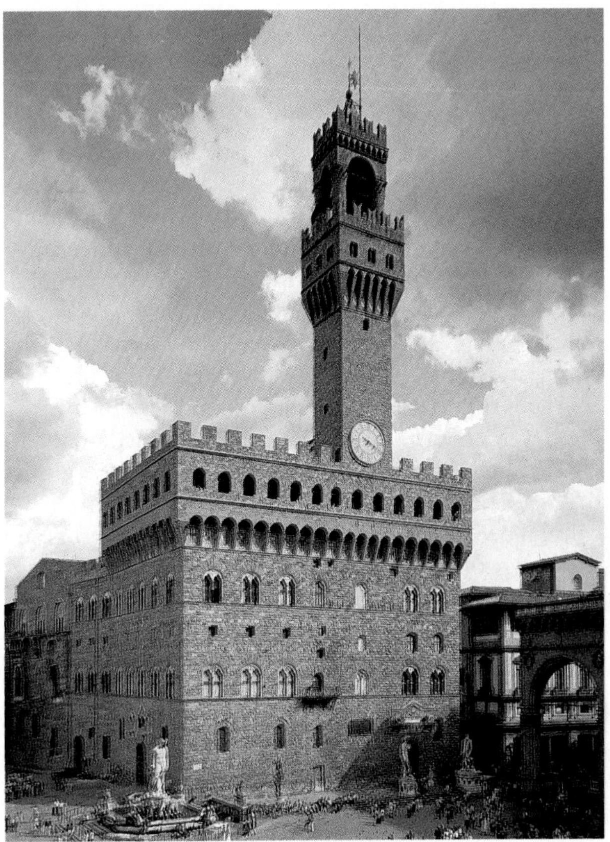

Palazzo Vecchio, Florence Built during the late thirteenth and early fourteenth centuries as a fortress of defense against both popular uprising and foreign attack, the building housed the *podesta,* the city's highest magistrate, and all the offices of the government. *(Scala/Art Resource, NY)*

In the sixteenth century, the political and social life of Italy was upset by the relentless competition for dominance between France and the empire. The Italian cities suffered severely from continual warfare, especially in the frightful sack of Rome in 1527 by imperial forces under Charles V. Thus the failure of the city-states to form some federal system, consolidate, or at least establish a common foreign policy led to the continuation of the centuries-old subjection of the peninsula by outside invaders. Italy was not to achieve unification until 1870.

Intellectual Hallmarks of the Renaissance

The Renaissance was characterized by self-conscious awareness among fourteenth- and fifteenth-century Italians that they were living in a new era. The realization that something new and unique was happening first came to men of letters in the fourteenth century, especially to the poet and humanist Francesco Petrarch (1304–1374). Petrarch thought that he was living at the start of a new age, a period of light following a long night of Gothic gloom. He considered the first two centuries of the Roman Empire to represent the peak in the development of human civilization. Medieval people had believed that they were continuing the glories that had been ancient Rome and had recognized no cultural division between the world of the emperors and their own times. But for Petrarch, the Germanic invasions had caused a sharp cultural break with the glories of Rome and inaugurated what he called the "Dark Ages." He believed, with many of his contemporaries, that the thousand-year period between the fourth and the fourteenth centuries constituted a barbarian, Gothic, or "middle" age. The sculptors, painters, and writers of the Renaissance spoke contemptuously of their medieval predecessors and identified themselves with the thinkers and artists of Greco-Roman civilization. Petrarch believed that he was witnessing a new golden age of intellectual achievement—a rebirth or, to use the French word that came into English, a renaissance. The division of historical time into periods is often arbitrary and done for the convenience of historians. In terms of the way most people lived and thought, no sharp division exists between the Middle Ages and the Renaissance. Some important poets, writers, and artists, however, believed they were living in a new golden age.

The Renaissance also manifested itself in a new attitude toward men, women, and the world—an attitude that may be described as individualism. A humanism characterized by a deep interest in the Latin classics and a deliberate attempt to revive antique lifestyles emerged, as did a bold new secular spirit.

Individualism

Though the Middle Ages had seen the appearance of remarkable individuals, recognition of such persons was limited. The examples of Saint Augustine in the fifth century and Peter Abelard and Guibert of Nogent in the twelfth—men who perceived themselves as unique and produced autobiographical statements—stand out for that very reason: Christian humility discouraged self-absorption. In the fourteenth and fifteenth centuries, moreover, such characteristically medieval and corporate attachments as the guild and the parish continued to provide strong support for the individual and to exercise great social influence. Yet in the Renaissance intellectuals, unlike their counterparts in the Middle Ages, developed a new sense of historical distance from earlier periods. A large literature specifically concerned with the nature of individuality emerged. This literature represented the flowering of a distinctly Renaissance individualism.

The Renaissance witnessed the emergence of many distinctive personalities who gloried in their uniqueness. Italians of unusual abilities were self-consciously aware of their singularity and unafraid to be unlike their neighbors; they had enormous confidence in their ability to achieve great things. Leon Battista Alberti (1404–1474), a writer, architect, and mathematician, remarked, "Men can do all things if they will."[4] Florentine goldsmith and sculptor Benvenuto Cellini (1500–1574) prefaced his *Autobiography* with a declaration:

My cruel fate hath warr'd with me in vain:
Life, glory, worth, and all unmeasur'd skill,
Beauty and grace, themselves in me fulfill
That many I surpass, and to the best attain.[5]

Cellini, certain of his genius, wrote so that the whole world might appreciate it.

Individualism stressed personality, uniqueness, genius, and full development of one's capabilities and talents. Artist, athlete, painter, scholar, sculptor, whatever—a person's abilities should be stretched until fully realized. Thirst for fame, a driving ambition, and a burning desire for success drove such people to the complete achievement of their potential. The quest for glory was a central component of Renaissance individualism.

Humanism

In the cities of Italy, especially Rome, civic leaders and the wealthy populace showed phenomenal archaeological zeal for the recovery of manuscripts, statues, and monuments. Pope Nicholas V (1447–1455), a distinguished scholar, planned the Vatican Library for the nine thousand manuscripts he had collected. Pope Sixtus IV (1471–1484) built that library, which remains one of the richest repositories of ancient and medieval documents.

The revival of antiquity also took the form of profound interest in and study of the Latin classics. This feature of the Renaissance became known as the "new learning," or simply *humanism,* the term of Florentine rhetorician and historian Leonardo Bruni (1370–1444). The words *humanism* and *humanist* derive ultimately from the Latin *humanitas,* which Cicero used to mean the literary culture needed by anyone who would be considered educated and civilized. Humanists studied the Latin classics to learn what they reveal about human nature. Humanism emphasized human beings, their achievements, interests, and capabilities. Although churchmen supported the new learning, by the later fifteenth century Italian humanism was increasingly a lay phenomenon.

Appreciation for the literary culture of the Romans had never died in the West. Bede and John of Salisbury, for example, had studied and imitated the writings of the ancients. Medieval writers, however, had studied the ancients in order to come to know God. Medieval scholars had interpreted the classics in a Christian sense and had invested the ancients' poems and histories with Christian meaning.

Renaissance humanists, although deeply Christian, approached the classics differently. Whereas medieval writers accepted pagan and classical authors uncritically, Renaissance humanists were skeptical of their authority, conscious of the historical distance separating themselves from the ancients, and fully aware that classical writers often disagreed among themselves. Whereas medieval writers looked to the classics to reveal God, Renaissance humanists studied the classics to understand human nature, and while they fully grasped the moral thought of pagan antiquity, Renaissance humanists viewed humanity from a strongly Christian perspective: men and women were made in the image and likeness of God. For example, in a remarkable essay, *On the Dignity of Man,* the Florentine writer Pico della Mirandola stressed that man possesses great dignity because he was made as Adam in the image of God before the Fall and as Christ after the Resurrection. According to Pico, man's place in the universe is somewhere between the beasts and the angels, but because of the divine image planted in him, there are no limits to what he can accomplish. Humanists rejected classical ideas that were opposed to Christianity. Or they sought through reinterpretation an underlying harmony between the pagan and secular and the Christian faith. The fundamental difference between Renaissance humanists and medieval ones is that the former were more self-conscious about what they were doing, and they stressed the realization of human potential.[6]

The fourteenth- and fifteenth-century humanists loved the language of the classics and considered it superior to the corrupt Latin of the medieval schoolmen. Renaissance writers were very excited by the purity of ancient Latin. They eventually became concerned more about form than about content, more about the way an idea was expressed than about the significance and validity of the idea. Literary humanists of the fourteenth century wrote each other highly stylized letters imitating ancient authors, and they held witty philosophical dialogues in conscious imitation of the Platonic Academy of the fourth century B.C. Renaissance humanists heaped scorn on the "barbaric" Latin style of the medievalists. The leading humanists of the early Renaissance were rhetoricians, seeking effective and eloquent communication, both oral and written.

Secular Spirit

Secularism involves a basic concern with the material world instead of with the eternal world of spirit. A sec-

Jan Massys (1509–1575): The Usurers At a desk heaped with coins, pawned goods, jewelry, and a sandbox (for sprinkling sand on an inky page to dry it), one man records the day's receipts in his ledger (his wealth indicated by his ring, fur collar, and pearl brooch on his hat), while his partner casts a sneering, grasping eye on the viewer, no doubt calculating his worth. *(Staatliche Museen zu Berlin/Bildarchiv Preussischer Kulturbesitz)*

ular way of thinking tends to find the ultimate explanation of everything and the final end of human beings within the limits of what the senses can discover. Even though medieval business people ruthlessly pursued profits and medieval monks fought fiercely over property, the dominant ideals focused on the otherworldly, on life after death. Renaissance people often held strong and deep spiritual interests, but in their increasingly secular society, attention was concentrated on the here and now, often on the acquisition of material things. The fourteenth and fifteenth centuries witnessed the slow but steady growth of such secularism in Italy.

The economic changes and rising prosperity of the Italian cities in the thirteenth century worked a fundamental change in social and intellectual attitudes and values. Worries about shifting rates of interest, shipping routes, personnel costs, and employee relations did not leave much time for thoughts about penance and purgatory. The busy bankers and merchants of the Italian cities calculated ways of making and increasing their money. Such wealth allowed greater material pleasures, a more comfortable life, the leisure time to appreciate and patronize the arts. Money could buy many sensual gratifications, and the rich, social-climbing patricians of Venice, Florence, Genoa, and Rome came to see life more as an opportunity to be enjoyed than as a painful pilgrimage to the City of God.

In *On Pleasure,* humanist Lorenzo Valla (1406–1457) defends the pleasures of the senses as the highest good. Scholars praise Valla as a father of modern historical criticism. His study *On the False Donation of Constantine* (1444) demonstrates by careful textual examination that an anonymous eighth-century document supposedly giving the papacy jurisdiction over vast territories in western Europe was a forgery. Medieval people had accepted the Donation of Constantine as a reality, and the proof that it was an invention weakened the foundations of papal claims to temporal authority. Lorenzo Valla's work exemplifies the application of critical scholarship to old and almost-sacred writings as well as the new secular spirit of the Renaissance.

The tales in *The Decameron* by the Florentine Giovanni Boccaccio (1313–1375), which describe ambitious merchants, lecherous friars, and cuckolded husbands, portray a frankly acquisitive, sensual, and worldly society. Although Boccaccio's figures were stock literary characters, *The Decameron* contains none of the "contempt of the world" theme so pervasive in medieval literature. Renaissance writers justified the accumulation and enjoyment of wealth with references to ancient authors.

Nor did church leaders do much to combat the new secular spirit. In the fifteenth and early sixteenth centuries, the papal court and the households of the cardinals were just as worldly as those of great urban patricians. Of course, most of the popes and higher church officials had come from the bourgeois aristocracy. Renaissance popes beautified the city of Rome, patronized artists and men of letters, and expended enormous enthusiasm and huge sums of money. A new papal chancellery, begun in 1483 and finished in 1511, stands as one of the architectural masterpieces of the High Renaissance. Pope Julius II (1503–1513) tore down the old Saint Peter's Basilica and began work on the present structure in 1506. Michelangelo's dome for Saint Peter's is still considered his greatest work. Papal interests, which were far removed from spiritual concerns, fostered, rather than discouraged, the new worldly attitude.

The broad mass of the people and the intellectuals and leaders of society remained faithful to the Christian church. Few people questioned the basic tenets of the Christian religion. Italian humanists and their aristocratic patrons were anti-ascetic, anti-Scholastic, and ambivalent, but they were not agnostics or skeptics. The thousands of pious paintings, sculptures, processions, and pilgrimages of the Renaissance period prove that strong religious feeling persisted.

ART AND THE ARTIST

No feature of the Renaissance evokes greater admiration than its artistic masterpieces. The 1400s *(quattrocento)* and 1500s *(cinquecento)* bore witness to a dazzling creativity in painting, architecture, and sculpture. In all the arts, the city of Florence led the way. According to Renaissance art historian Giorgio Vasari (1511–1574), the painter Perugino once asked why it was in Florence and not elsewhere that men achieved perfection in the arts. The first answer he received was, "There were so many good critics there, for the air of the city makes men quick and perceptive and impatient of mediocrity."[7] But Florence was not the only artistic center. In the period art historians describe as the "High Renaissance" (1500–1527), Rome took the lead. The main characteristics of High Renaissance art—classical balance, harmony, and restraint—are revealed in the masterpieces of Leonardo da Vinci (1452–1519), Raphael (1483–1520), and Michelangelo (1475–1564), all of whom worked in Rome.

Andrea Mantegna: Adoration of the Magi (ca 1495–1505). Applying his study of ancient Roman relief sculpture, and elaborating on a famous Scriptural text (Matthew 2:1), Mantegna painted for the private devotion of the Gonzaga family of Mantua this scene of the Three Kings coming to recognize the divinity of Christ. The Three Kings represent the entire world—that is, the three continents known to medieval Europeans: Europe, Asia, and Africa. They also symbolize the three stages of life: youth, maturity, and old age. Here Melchior, the oldest, his large cranium symbolizing wisdom, personifies Europe. He offers gold in a Chinese porcelain cup from the Ming Dynasty. Balthazar, with an olive complexion and dark beard, stands for Asia and maturity. He presents frankincense in a stunning vessel of Turkish tombac ware. Caspar, representing Africa and youth, gives myrrh in an urn of striped marble. The child responds with a blessing. The black background brings out the rich colors. (*The J. Paul Getty Museum, Los Angeles. Mantegna, Andrea,* Adoration of the Magi, *ca 1495–1505, distemper on linen, 54.6 × 70.7 cm [85.PA.417]*)

Art and Power

In early Renaissance Italy, art manifested corporate power. Powerful urban groups such as guilds or religious confraternities commissioned works of art. The Florentine cloth merchants, for example, delegated Filippo Brunelleschi to build the magnificent dome on the cathedral of Florence and selected Lorenzo Ghiberti to design the bronze doors of the Baptistry. These works represented the merchants' dominant influence in the community. Corporate patronage was also reflected in the Florentine government's decision to hire Michelangelo to create the sculpture of David, the great Hebrew hero and king. The subject matter of art through the early fifteenth century, as in the Middle Ages, remained overwhelmingly religious. Religious themes appeared in all media—woodcarvings, painted frescoes, stone sculptures, paintings. As in the Middle Ages, art served an educational purpose. A religious picture or statue was intended to spread a particular doctrine, act as a profession of faith, or recall sinners to a moral way of living.

Increasingly in the later fifteenth century, individuals and oligarchs, rather than corporate groups, sponsored works of art. Patrician merchants and bankers, popes and princes, supported the arts as a means of glorifying themselves and their families. Vast sums were spent on family chapels, frescoes, religious panels, and tombs.

Gentile Bellini: Procession in the Piazza San Marco Gentile's masterpiece celebrates Venice's annual festival on the Feast of Saint Mark (April 25). In the center of the piazza, a vast section of a cosmopolitan society appears: patricians and ordinary citizens, German merchants, priests, Greeks in black hats, Turks, a black man. The picture shows the artist's superb understanding of perspective, eye for detail (women witness the scene from the arched openings), insight into individual personalities (contemporaries could have identified many persons), and rich appreciation of color. Under the red canopy is a golden monstrance holding a relic of the True Cross. A fine example of Renaissance narrative painting. *(Scala/Art Resource, NY)*

Writing about 1470, Florentine oligarch Lorenzo de' Medici declared that over the previous thirty-five years his family had spent the astronomical sum of 663,755 gold florins for artistic and architectural commissions. Yet "I think it casts a brilliant light on our estate [public reputation] and it seems to me that the monies were well spent and I am very pleased with this." Powerful men wanted to exalt themselves, their families, and their offices. A magnificent style of living, enriched by works of art, served to prove the greatness and the power of the despot or oligarch.[8]

In addition to power, art reveals changing patterns of consumption in Renaissance Italy. Wealthy people spent their money on art and architectural works, and the purchase of artworks became both a worthy economic activity and a significant cultural phenomenon. ". . . Consumer habits introduced into economic life a creative and dynamic process for growth and change that was fundamental to the development of the West."[9] If modern consumerism has its roots in the eighteenth century, the latter period's consumer practices can be traced to the Italian Renaissance.

In the rural world of the Middle Ages, society had been organized for war. Men of wealth spent their money on military gear—swords, armor, horses, crenelated castles, towers, family compounds—all of which represent offensive or defensive warfare. As Italian nobles settled in towns (see page 416), they adjusted to an urban culture. Rather than employing knights for warfare, cities hired mercenaries. Expenditure on military hardware declined. For the rich merchant or the noble recently arrived from the countryside, the urban palace represented the greatest outlay of cash. It was his chief luxury, and although a private dwelling, the palace implied grandeur.[10] Within the palace, the merchant-prince's chamber, or bedroom, where he slept and received his intimate guests, was the most important room. In the fourteenth and fifteenth centuries, a large, intricately carved wooden bed, a chest, and perhaps a bench served as its sole decorations. The chest held the master's most precious goods—silver, tapestries, jewelry, clothing. Other rooms, even in palaces of fifteen to twenty rooms, were very sparsely furnished. As the fifteenth century advanced and wealth increased, other rooms were gradually furnished with carved chests, tables, benches, chairs, tapestries for the walls, paintings (an innovation), and sculptural decorations, and a private chapel was added. By the late sixteenth century, the Strozzi banking family of Florence spent more on household goods than on anything else except food; the value of those furnishings was three times that of their silver and jewelry.[11]

After the palace itself, the private chapel within the palace symbolized the largest expenditure. Equipped with the ecclesiastical furniture—tabernacles, chalices, thuribles, and other liturgical utensils—and decorated with religious scenes, the chapel served as the center of the household's religious life and its cult of remembrance of the dead. In fifteenth-century Florence, only the Medici had a private chapel. It became a catalyst for a great building boom, and by the late sixteenth century, most wealthy Florentine families had private chapels. Since the merchant banker or prince appointed the chaplain, usually a younger son of the family, religious power passed into private hands.[12]

As the fifteenth century advanced, the subject matter of art became steadily more secular. The study of classical texts brought deeper understanding of ancient ideas. Classical themes and motifs, such as the lives and loves of pagan gods and goddesses, figured increasingly in painting and sculpture. Religious topics, such as the Annunciation of the Virgin and the Nativity, remained popular among both patrons and artists, but frequently the patron had himself and his family portrayed. People were conscious of their physical uniqueness and wanted their individuality immortalized. Paintings were also means of displaying wealth.

The content and style of Renaissance art were decidedly different from those of the Middle Ages. The individual portrait emerged as a distinct artistic genre. In the fifteenth century, members of the newly rich middle class often had themselves painted in a scene of romantic chivalry or courtly society. Rather than reflecting a spiritual ideal, as medieval painting and sculpture tended to do, Renaissance portraits mirrored reality. The Florentine painter Giotto (1276–1337) led the way in the use of realism; his treatment of the human body and face replaced the formal stiffness and artificiality that had for so long characterized representation of the human body. The sculptor Donatello (1386–1466) probably exerted the greatest influence of any Florentine artist before Michelangelo. His many statues express an appreciation of the incredible variety of human nature. Whereas medieval artists had depicted the nude human body only in a spiritualized and moralizing context, Donatello revived the classical figure, with its balance and self-awareness. The short-lived Florentine Masaccio (1401–1428), sometimes called the father of modern painting, inspired a new style characterized by great realism, narrative power, and remarkably effective use of light and dark. As important as realism was the new "international style," so called because of the wandering careers of influential artists, the close communications and rivalry of princely courts, and the increased trade in works of art. Rich color, decorative detail, curvilinear rhythms, and swaying forms characterized the international style. As the term *international* implies, this style was European, not merely Italian.

Narrative artists depicted the body in a more scientific and natural manner. The female figure is voluptuous and sensual. The male body, as in Michelangelo's *David* and *The Last Judgment*, is strong and heroic. Renaissance glorification of the human body revealed the secular spirit of the age. Filippo Brunelleschi (1377–1446) and Piero della Francesca (1420–1492) seem to have pioneered *perspective* in painting, the linear representation of distance and space on a flat surface. *The Last Supper* by Leonardo da Vinci, with its stress on the tension between Christ and the disciples, is an incredibly subtle psychological interpretation.

The Status of the Artist

In the Renaissance, the social status of the artist improved. Whereas the lower-middle-class medieval master mason had been viewed in the same light as a mechanic, the Renaissance artist was considered a free intellectual worker. Artists did not produce unsolicited pictures or statues for the general public; that could mean loss of status. They usually worked on commission from a powerful prince. The artist's reputation depended on the support of powerful patrons, and through them some artists and architects achieved not only economic security but also very great wealth. (See the feature "Individuals in Society: Gentile Bellini.")

Lorenzo Ghiberti's salary of 200 florins a year compared very favorably with that of the head of the city government, who earned 500 florins. Moreover, at a time when a person could live in a princely fashion on 300 ducats a year, Leonardo da Vinci was making 2,000 annually. Michelangelo was paid 3,000 ducats for painting the ceiling of the Sistine Chapel. When he agreed to

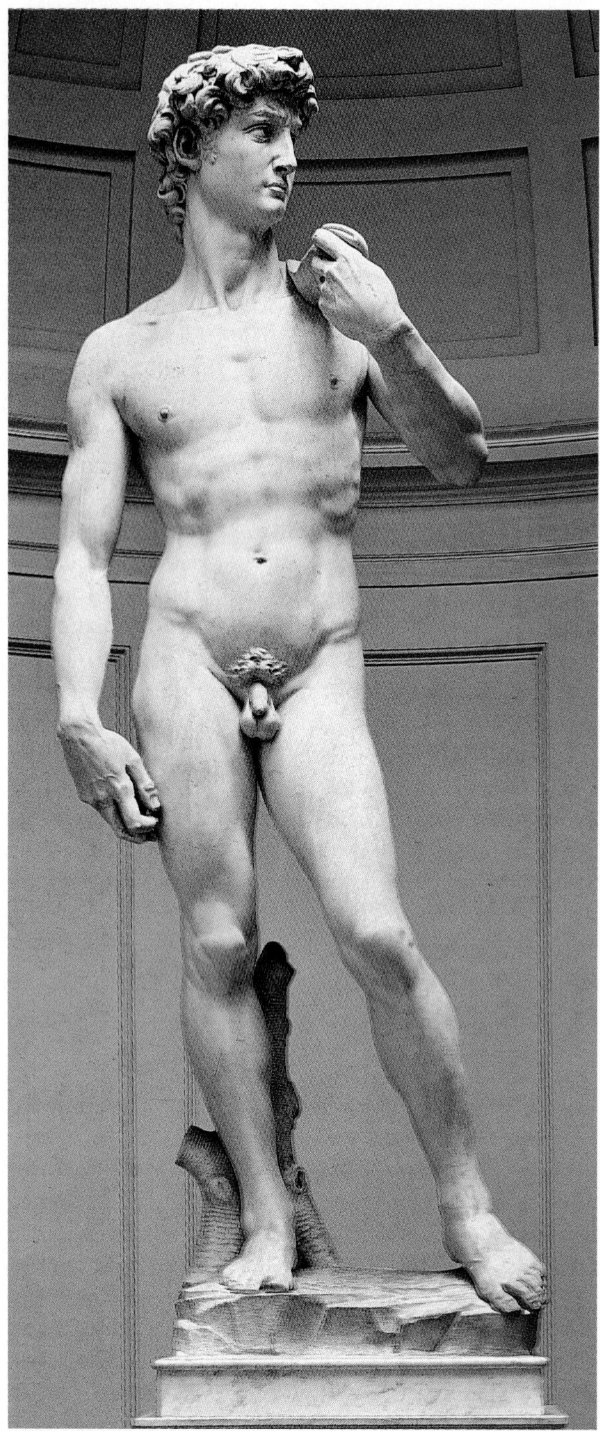

Michelangelo: David In 1501 the new republican government of Florence commissioned the twenty-six-year-old Michelangelo to carve David as a symbol of civic independence and resistance to oligarchial tyranny. Tensed in anticipation of action but certain of victory over his unseen enemy Goliath (1 Samuel 17), this male nude represents the ideal of youthful physical perfection. *(Scala/Art Resource, NY)*

work on Saint Peter's Basilica, he refused a salary; he was already a wealthy man.[13]

Renaissance society respected and rewarded the distinguished artist. In 1537 the prolific letter writer, humanist, and satirizer of princes Pietro Aretino (1492–1556) wrote to Michelangelo while he was painting the Sistine Chapel:

> *To the Divine Michelangelo:*
> *Sir, just as it is disgraceful and sinful to be unmindful of God so it is reprehensible and dishonourable for any man of discerning judgment not to honour you as a brilliant and venerable artist whom the very stars use as a target at which to shoot the rival arrows of their favour. You are so accomplished, therefore, that hidden in your hands lives the idea of a new king of creation. . . . It is surely my duty to honour you with this salutation, since the world has many kings but only one Michelangelo.*[14]

When Holy Roman emperor Charles V (r. 1519–1556) visited the workshop of the great Titian (1477–1576) and stooped to pick up the artist's dropped paintbrush, the emperor was demonstrating that the patron himself was honored in the act of honoring the artist. The social status of the artist of genius was immortally secured.

Renaissance artists were not only aware of their creative power; they also boasted about it. Describing his victory over five others, including Brunelleschi, in the competition to design the bronze doors of Florence's Baptistry, Ghiberti exulted, "The palm of victory was conceded to me by all the experts and by all my fellow-competitors. By universal consent and without a single exception the glory was conceded to me."[15] Some medieval painters and sculptors had signed their works; Renaissance artists almost universally did so, and many of them incorporated self-portraits, usually as bystanders, in their paintings.

The Renaissance, in fact, witnessed the birth of the concept of the artist as genius. In the Middle Ages, people believed that only God created, albeit through individuals; the medieval conception recognized no particular value in artistic originality. Renaissance artists and humanists came to think that a work of art was the deliberate creation of a unique personality, of an individual who transcended traditions, rules, and theories. A genius had a peculiar gift, which ordinary laws should not inhibit. Cosimo de' Medici described a painter, because of his genius, as "divine," implying that the artist shared in the powers of God. The word *divine* was widely applied to Michelangelo.

But students must guard against interpreting Italian Renaissance culture in twentieth-century democratic

Individuals in Society

Gentile Bellini (ca 1431–1507)

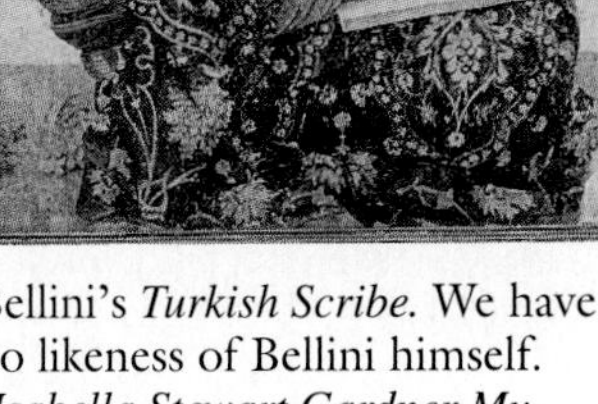

Bellini's *Turkish Scribe.* We have no likeness of Bellini himself. *(Isabella Stewart Gardner Museum, Boston)*

In 1474 the Venetian Senate, the city's governing body, voted to accept the offer of "Maistro Gentile Bellini, eminent painter and excellent master," to restore the paintings in the Great Council Hall, "which is one of the principal ornaments of our city."[1] The son, brother, and brother-in-law of distinguished artists, named for Gentile da Fabriano (ca 1370–1427), the exponent of the international Gothic style, Gentile Bellini was formed in a rich artistic milieu. His father, Jacopo, taught his sons the elements of design; father and sons worked together in the family workshop. By 1469 Gentile's reputation was so strong that the Holy Roman emperor Frederick III on a visit to Venice rewarded him with the title palatine knight, possibly for a portrait of Frederick. The sixteenth-century biographer Giorgio Vasari combined Jacopo and his sons Giovanni and Gentile in one sketch of their lives and works, but Gentile stands out from them as a narrative painter, a representative of civil humanism, and a diplomat to Constantinople.

Venetian commercial ties with Constantinople stretching back to the eleventh century and vastly expanded by the Fourth Crusade (see page 284) were jeopardized by the Ottoman conquest of Constantinople. An agreement signed at Venice in 1479 provided the opportunity for the sultan's ambassador to see Gentile Bellini's paintings in the Great Council Hall. Four months later, "a Jewish orator[2] from the Lord Turk arrived with letters. He wished the Senate to send him a good painter. . . . The Senate responded . . . and sent Gentile Bellini."[3] He went both as an artist and as a sort of "extraordinary ambassador," or informant, charged with reporting conditions in the Ottoman capital.

Bellini spent about a year in Constantinople. He did a splendid portrait on canvas of Mehmet II, another portrait in bronze, various genre paintings of the city, and *cosi di lussuria,* usually translated as "erotic pictures" but recently described as scenes of festive occasions at the Ottoman court. The sultan was so pleased that he made him a Golden Knight of the Ottoman Empire and showered him with gifts, including a heavy gold chain. He was welcomed home with fanfare, but the contents of his political report have not survived.

Perhaps the most famous of Bellini's extant paintings is the *Procession in the Piazza San Marco,* executed between 1494 and 1505 for a local confraternity. Confraternities provided social and financial support for their members. Venetian confraternities, in contrast to those in other Italian cities, also performed a civic function: they used artworks and festive occasions to glorify the Republic of Saint Mark. In a long procession, members of the confraternity hold center stage. To the left, other confraternities have completed marching and wait in formal ranks. To the right, officials and dignitaries bring up the rear of the procession. Dominating the scene is the great basilica of Saint Mark, the republic's political and religious center, with its Byzantine architectural style.

Someone once wrote, "There are more valid facts and details in works of art than there are in history books." This reflects a mistaken notion of what history is all about. Art is a history book. Gentile Bellini has left us a richly appealing slice of Renaissance life.

Questions for Analysis

1. How did Gentile Bellini follow the pattern of other humanists, such as Petrarch and Machiavelli?
2. What does the *Procession in the Piazza San Marco* tell us about Venetian society? (See page 424.)

1. Quoted in Patricia Fortini Brown, *Venetian Narrative Painting in the Age of Carpaccio* (New Haven, Conn.: Yale University Press, 1989), p. 51.
2. Just as Jews sometimes served in the papal bureaucracy, so they served in Muslim governments. Because Muslims found Europeans hostile, they often employed Jews on commercial and diplomatic missions.
3. Quoted in Brown, *Venetian Narrative Painting,* p. 54.

Benozzo Gozzoli: Journey of the Magi Few Renaissance paintings better illustrate art in the service of the princely court, in this case the Medici. Commissioned by Piero de' Medici to adorn his palace chapel, everything in this fresco—the large crowd, the feathers and diamonds adorning many of the personages, the black servant in front—serve to flaunt the power and wealth of the House of Medici. There is nothing especially religious about it; the painting could more appropriately be called "Journey of the Medici." The artist has discreetly placed himself in the crowd, the name Benozzo embroidered on his cap. *(Scala/Art Resource, NY)*

terms. The culture of the Renaissance was that of a small mercantile elite, a business patriciate with aristocratic pretensions. Renaissance culture did not directly affect the broad middle classes, let alone the vast urban proletariat. A small, highly educated minority of literary humanists and artists created the culture of and for an exclusive elite. They cared little for ordinary people. The Renaissance maintained a gulf between the learned minority and the uneducated multitude that has survived for many centuries.

Social Change

The Renaissance changed many aspects of Italian, and subsequently European, society. New developments brought real breaks with the medieval past. Renaissance ideals permeated educational theory and practice and political thought. The era's most stunning technological invention, printing, affected many forms of social life. Renaissance culture witnessed a shift in the status and experience of women. Numbers of black Africans also played a role in Renaissance society.

Education and Political Thought

One of the central preoccupations of the humanists was education and moral behavior. Humanists poured out treatises, often in the form of letters, on the structure and goals of education and the training of rulers. In one of the earliest systematic programs for the young, Peter Paul Vergerio (1370–1444) wrote Ubertinus, the ruler of Carrara:

For the education of children is a matter of more than private interest; it concerns the State, which indeed regards the right training of the young as, in certain aspects, within its proper sphere. . . . Tutors and comrades alike should be chosen from amongst those likely to bring out the best qualities, to attract by good example, and to repress the first signs of evil. . . . Above all, respect for Divine ordinances is of the deepest importance; it should be incul-

cated from the earliest years. Reverence towards elders and parents is an obligation closely akin.

We call those studies liberal which are worthy of a free man; those studies by which we attain and practice virtue and wisdom.[16]

Part of Vergerio's treatise specifies subjects for the instruction of young men in public life: history teaches virtue by examples from the past, ethics focuses on virtue itself, and rhetoric or public speaking trains for eloquence.

No book on education had broader influence than Baldassare Castiglione's *The Courtier* (1528). This treatise sought to train, discipline, and fashion the young man into the courtly ideal, the gentleman. According to Castiglione, the educated man of the upper class should have a broad background in many academic subjects, and his spiritual and physical as well as intellectual capabilities should be trained. The courtier should have easy familiarity with dance, music, and the arts. Castiglione envisioned a man who could compose a sonnet, wrestle, sing a song and accompany himself on an instrument, ride expertly, solve difficult mathematical problems, and, above all, speak and write eloquently. (See the feature "Listening to the Past: A Universal Man" on pages 448–449.)

In the sixteenth and seventeenth centuries, *The Courtier* was widely read. It influenced the social mores and patterns of conduct of elite groups in Renaissance and early modern Europe. The courtier became the model of the European gentleman.

No Renaissance book on any topic, however, has been more widely read and studied in all the centuries since its publication (1513) than the short political treatise *The Prince,* by Niccolò Machiavelli (1469–1527). The subject of *The Prince* is political power: how the ruler should gain, maintain, and increase it. Machiavelli implicitly addresses the question of the citizen's relationship to the state. As a good humanist, he explores the problems of human nature and concludes that human beings are selfish and out to advance their own interests. This pessimistic view of humanity led him to maintain that the prince may have to manipulate the people in any way he finds necessary:

For a man who, in all respects, will carry out only his professions of good, will be apt to be ruined amongst so many who are evil. A prince therefore who desires to maintain himself must learn to be not always good, but to be so or not as necessity may require.[17]

The prince should combine the cunning of a fox with the ferocity of a lion to achieve his goals. Asking rhetorically whether it is better for a ruler to be loved or feared, Machiavelli writes: "It will naturally be answered that it would be desirable to be both the one and the other; but as it is difficult to be both at the same time, it is much more safe to be feared than to be loved, when you have to choose between the two."[18]

Medieval political theory had derived ultimately from Saint Augustine's view that the state arose as a consequence of Adam's fall and people's propensity to sin. The test of good government was whether it provided justice, law, and order. Political theorists and theologians from Alcuin to Marsiglio of Padua had stressed the way government *ought* to be; they had set high moral and Christian standards for the ruler's conduct.

Machiavelli maintained that the ruler should be concerned not with the way things ought to be but with the way things actually are. The sole test of a "good" government is whether it is effective, whether the ruler increases his power. Machiavelli did not advocate amoral behavior, but he believed that political action cannot be restricted by moral considerations. While amoral action might be the most effective approach in a given situation, he did not argue for generally amoral, rather than moral, behavior. Nevertheless, on the basis of a crude interpretation of *The Prince,* the word *Machiavellian* entered the language as a synonym for the politically devious, corrupt, and crafty, indicating actions in which the end justifies the means. The ultimate significance of Machiavelli rests on two ideas: first, that one permanent social order reflecting God's will cannot be established, and second, that politics has its own laws and ought to be a science.[19]

The Printed Word

Sometime in the thirteenth century, paper money and playing cards from China reached the West. They were *block-printed*—that is, Chinese characters or pictures were carved into a wooden block, the block was inked, and the words or illustrations were transferred to paper. Since each word, phrase, or picture was on a separate block, this method of reproduction was extraordinarily expensive and time-consuming.

Around 1455, probably through the combined efforts of three men—Johann Gutenberg, Johann Fust, and Peter Schöffer, all experimenting at Mainz—movable type came into being. The mirror image of each letter (rather than entire words or phrases) was carved in relief on a small block. Individual letters, easily movable, were put together to form words; words separated by blank spaces formed lines of type; and lines of type were brought together to make up a page. Since letters could be arranged into any format, an infinite variety of texts could be printed by reusing and rearranging pieces of type.

By the middle of the fifteenth century, paper was no problem. The knowledge of paper manufacture had originated in China, and the Arabs introduced it to the West in the twelfth century. Europeans quickly learned that durable paper was far less expensive than the vellum (calfskin) and parchment (sheepskin) on which medieval scribes had relied for centuries.

The effects of the invention of movable-type printing were not felt overnight. Nevertheless, within a half century of the publication of Gutenberg's Bible of 1456, movable type had brought about radical changes. Printing transformed both the private and the public lives of Europeans (Map 13.2). Governments that "had employed the cumbersome methods of manuscripts to communicate with their subjects switched quickly to print to announce declarations of war, publish battle accounts, promulgate treaties or argue disputed points in pamphlet form. Theirs was an effort 'to win the psychological war.'" Printing made propaganda possible, emphasizing differences between opposing groups, such as Crown and nobility, church and state. These differences laid the basis for the formation of distinct political parties. Printed materials reached an invisible public, allowing silent individuals to join causes and groups of individuals widely separated by geography to form a common identity; this new group consciousness could compete with older, localized loyalties.[20]

Printing also stimulated the literacy of laypeople and eventually came to have a deep effect on their private lives. Although most of the earliest books and pamphlets dealt with religious subjects, students, housewives, businessmen, and upper- and middle-class people sought books on all subjects. Printers responded with moralizing, medical, practical, and travel manuals. Pornography as well as piety assumed new forms. For example, satirist Pietro Aretino (1492–1556) used the shock of sex in pornography as a vehicle to criticize: his *Sonnetti Lussuriosi* (1527) and *Ragionamenti* (1534–1536), sonnets accompanying sixteen engravings of as many sexual positions, attacked princely court life, humanist education, and false clerical piety.[21] Broadsides and flysheets allowed great public festivals, religious ceremonies, and political events to be experienced vicariously by the stay-at-home. Since books and other printed materials were read aloud to illiterate listeners, print bridged the gap between written and oral cultures.

Clocks

The English word *quantification* was first used in 1840, but five centuries earlier, before the invention of movable type, Europeans learned how to quantify, or measure, time with the mechanical clock. Who invented the clock remains a subject of scientific debate. Between A.D. 700 and 1000, Arabs relied on the sundial, using their knowledge of astronomy to correct for the varying motion of the sun during the course of the year. The Arabs knew that the length of daylight, caused by the changing distance between the earth and the sun as the earth moves in elliptical orbit, varies with the seasons.

The Print Shop Sixteenth-century printing involved a division of labor. Two persons (left) at separate benches set the pieces of type. Another (center, rear) inks the chase (or locked plate containing the set type). Another (right) operates the press, which prints the sheets. The boy removes the printed pages and sets them to dry. Meanwhile, a man carries in fresh paper on his head. *(Corbis-Bettmann)*

MAP 13.2 The Growth of Printing in Europe Although many commercial and academic centers developed printing technology, the press at Venice, employing between four hundred and five hundred people and producing one-eighth of all printed books, was by far the largest in Europe.

By the tenth century, the Chinese had a huge mechanical clock, knowledge of which may have allowed Gerbert, later Pope Sylvester II (999–1003), to build the first mechanical clock in the West.

The English word *clock* resembles the French *cloche* and the German *Glocke*, all meaning "bells." In monastic houses, bells determined the times for the recitation of the Hours, the Work of God. Bells also paced the life of the rural world nearby, but country people needed only approximate times—dawn, noon, sunset—for their work. The measurement of time played a much more urgent role for city people.

Buying and selling goods had initiated city people into the practice of quantification: they needed precise measurement of the day's hours. City people's time was what the American polymath Benjamin Franklin later called it: money. In the Italian cities, clocks must have been widespread, since the poet Dante, writing about 1320, took them for granted. Mechanical clocks, usually installed on the cathedral or town church, were in general use in Germany by the 1330s, in England by the 1370s, and in France by the 1380s.[22]

Clocks contributed to the development of a mentality that conceived of the universe in visual and quantita-

Mechanical Clock Slowly falling weights provide the force that pushes the figures' arms to strike the bells on the quarter hour in this sixteenth-century German clock. The short hand indicates the quarter-hour; the long hand shows the hour. The sound of a machine now marked time. *(Biblíothèque royale Albert 1er, Brussels)*

tive terms. Measuring the world brought not only understanding of it but the urge to control it. The mechanical clock enabled Europeans to divide time into equal hours, allowing the working day to be fixed in both winter and summer. Although other peoples in the world, such as the Maya in Central America and the Chinese, had theoretical knowledge of time, Europeans put that knowledge to practical use. Along with cannon and printing, clocks gave Europeans technological advantages over other peoples.[23]

Women

Did women have a Renaissance? Did women participate in the intellectual and artistic changes of the period? How did the status of women in the fourteenth to sixteenth centuries compare with that of the eleventh to thirteenth centuries?

During the Renaissance, the status of upper-class women declined. In terms of the kind of work they performed, their access to property and political power, and their role in shaping the outlook of their society, women in the Renaissance ruling classes generally had less power than comparable women in the feudal age.

In the cities of Renaissance Italy, well-to-do girls received an education similar to boys'. Young ladies learned their letters and studied the classics. Many read Greek as well as Latin, knew the poetry of Ovid and Virgil, and could speak one or two "modern" languages, such as French or Spanish. In this respect, Renaissance humanism represented a real educational advance for women. Some women, though a small minority among humanists, acquired great learning and fame. In the later sixteenth century, at least twenty-five women published books in Italy, Sofonisba Anguissola (1530–1625) and Artemisia Gentileschi (1593–1653) achieved international renown for their paintings, and Isabella Andreini (1562–1604) enjoyed a reputation as the greatest actress of her day.

Laura Cereta (1469–1499) illustrates the successes and failures of educated Renaissance women. Educated by her father, who was a member of the governing elite of Brescia in Lombardy, she learned languages, philosophy, theology, and mathematics. She also gained self-confidence and a healthy respect for her own potential. By the age of fifteen, when she married, her literary career was already launched, as her letters to several cardinals attest. For Laura Cereta, however, as for all educated women of the period, the question of marriage forced the issue: she could choose a husband, family, and full participation in social life or else study and withdrawal from the world. Marriage brought domestic responsibilities and usually prevented women from fulfilling their scholarly potential. Although Cereta chose marriage, she was widowed at eighteen, and she spent the remaining twelve years of her life in study. But she had to bear the envy of other women and the hostility of men who felt threatened. In response, Cereta condemned "empty women, who strive for no good but exist to adorn themselves. . . . These women of majestic pride, fantastic coiffures, outlandish ornament, and necks bound with gold or pearls bear the glittering symbols of their captivity to men." For Laura Cereta, women's inferiority was derived not from the divine order of things but from women themselves: "For knowledge is not given as a gift, but through study. . . . The free mind, not afraid of labor, presses on to attain the good."[24] Despite Cereta's faith in women's potential, men frequently believed that in becoming learned, a woman violated nature and thus ceased to be a woman.

Spain and in the Hispanic territories in America. This power enabled the "Catholic Kings of Spain," a title granted Ferdinand and Isabella by the papacy, to establish, in effect, a national church.[43]

Revenues from ecclesiastical estates provided the means to raise an army to continue the reconquista. The victorious entry of Ferdinand and Isabella into Granada on January 6, 1492, signaled the culmination of eight centuries of Spanish struggle against the Arabs in southern Spain and the conclusion of the reconquista (see Map 9.3 on page 292). Granada in the south was incorporated into the Spanish kingdom, and in 1512 Ferdinand conquered Navarre in the north.

There still remained a sizable and, in the view of the majority of the Spanish people, potentially dangerous minority, the Jews. During the long centuries of the reconquista, Christian kings had renewed Jewish rights and privileges; in fact, Jewish industry, intelligence, and money had supported royal power. While Christians of all classes borrowed from Jewish moneylenders, and while all who could afford them sought Jewish physicians, a strong undercurrent of resentment of Jewish influence and wealth festered. When the kings of France and England had expelled the Jews from their kingdoms (see pages 348–349), many had sought refuge in Spain. In the fourteenth century, Jews formed an integral and indispensable part of Spanish life. With vast numbers of Muslims, Jews, and Moorish Christians, medieval Spain represented the most diverse and cosmopolitan country in Europe. Diversity and cosmopolitanism, however, were not medieval social ideals.

Since ancient times, governments had seldom tolerated religious pluralism; religious faiths that differed from the official state religion were considered politically dangerous. But in the fourteenth century, anti-Semitism in Spain rose more from popular sentiment than from royal policies. Aggravated by fiery anti-Jewish preaching, by economic dislocation, and by the search for a scapegoat during the Black Death, the fourteenth century witnessed rising anti-Semitic feeling. In

Felipe Bigarny: Ferdinand the Catholic and Isabella the Catholic All governments try to cultivate a popular image. For Ferdinand and Isabella, it was the appearance of piety. Contemporaries, such as the Burgundian sculptor Bigarny, portrayed them as paragons of Christian piety, as shown in these polychrome wooden statues. If Isabella's piety was perhaps more genuine, she used it—together with rich ceremony, elaborate dress, and a fierce determination—to assert royal authority. *(Capilla Real, Granada/Laurie Platt Winfrey, Inc.)*

1331 a mob attacked the Jewish community of Gerona in Catalonia. In 1355 royal troops massacred Jews in Toledo. On June 4, 1391, inflamed by "religious" preaching, mobs sacked and burned the Jewish community in Seville and compelled such Jews as survived to accept baptism. From Seville anti-Semitic pogroms swept the towns of Valencia, Majorca, Barcelona, Burgos, Madrid, Segovia, and Cuenca. One scholar estimates that 40 percent of the Jewish population of Spain was killed or forced to convert.[44] Those converted were called *conversos, Marranos,* or *New Christians,* the three terms here used interchangeably.

King Ferdinand was not a religious fanatic. He was a Renaissance prince who wanted to *appear* as a moral and devout Christian, respectful of public opinion. He deeply feared urban rioting and disorder, but he knew that the vast majority of the Spanish people hated the conversos. If the Crown protected them, it would lose popular support. Ferdinand resolved the dilemma by seeking papal permission to set up the Inquisition in Spain; if the actions of the Inquisition provoked public criticism, the papacy could be blamed. Pope Sixtus IV's bull authorizing the Inquisition reached Spain in November 1478, and on September 28, 1480, Ferdinand and Isabella ordered the establishment of tribunals to judge "heretical depravity, . . . to search out and punish converts from Judaism who had transgressed against Christianity by secretly adhering to Jewish beliefs and performing rites of the Jews."[45]

What do we know of these "New Christians"? Why did they inspire such hostility? How did they view their religious position? In the administration of Castile, "New Christians" held the royal secretaryship, controlled the royal treasury, and composed a third of the royal council. In the church, they held high positions as archbishops, bishops, and abbots. In the administration of the towns, conversos often held the highest public offices; in Toledo they controlled the collection of royal revenues. They included some of the leading merchants and business people. They also served great magnates, and by intermarrying with the nobility, they gained great political leverage. In the liberal professions of medicine and law, "New Christians" held the most prominent positions. Numbering perhaps 200,000 in a total Spanish population of about 7.5 million, "New Christians" and Jews exercised influence quite disproportionate to their numbers. Aristocratic grandees resented their financial dependence, the poor hated the conversos tax collectors, and churchmen doubted the sincerity of their conversions.

Recent scholarship has carefully analyzed documents written by "New Christians" for their reactions to the rising anti-Semitism. They identified themselves as Christians. In the 1480s, they unanimously insisted that they were happy to be Christians and failed to see why they should be labeled "New" Christians: many came from families that had received baptism generations before. They argued that just as Christ had never abandoned the ancient (Hebrew) Law and prophets, so they had not abandoned them; in fact, they had a better and clearer understanding of the Christian faith. For the "New Christians," the issue was not that they had relinquished the faith of the Jews (and secretly reconverted); rather, in accepting Christianity, they had become real Jews and, in following Jesus, real Christians.[46]

This argument satisfied neither the Jews nor the conversos' enemies. The Jewish reaction to persecution of the conversos was, bluntly put, "Well, we told you so; it's just what you get."[47] Searching for a viable principle to use against both "New Christians" and Jews, their detractors hit not on what conversos believed, not on what they did, but on what they *were* as human beings. Hence arose the following racial theory: "Since race, they maintained, formed man's qualities and indeed his entire mental constitution, the Marranos, who were all offspring of Jews, retained the racial makeup of their forebears. . . . [E]thnically they were what they (or their ancestors) had been before their conversion to Christianity; in other words, they were Jews."[48] This absurd racist theory, which violated Scriptural teaching, maintained that all conversos were malicious, immoral, and criminally inclined by their nature, and thus they could not be truly converted to Christianity.

Fifteenth-century Spanish anti-Semitism emerged at the very time a Spanish national feeling was emerging, a national sentiment that looked to the building of a single nation. Whereas earlier anti-Semitism, such as that during the time of the Black Death, alleged Jewish schemes to kill off entire Christian populations—by poisoning the wells, for example, from which Jews derived no profit—fifteenth-century theories held that Jews or "New Christians" planned to take over all public offices in Spain. Jews, therefore, represented a grave threat to national unity.[49]

Although the Inquisition was a religious institution established to ensure the Catholic faith, it was controlled by the Crown and served primarily as a politically unifying force in Spain. Because the Spanish Inquisition commonly applied torture to extract confessions, first from lapsed conversos, then from Muslims, and later from Protestants, it gained a notorious reputation. Thus the word *inquisition,* meaning "any judicial inquiry conducted with ruthless severity," came into the English language. The methods of the Spanish

Inquisition were cruel, though not as cruel as the investigative methods of some twentieth-century governments. Shortly after the reduction of the Moorish stronghold at Granada in 1492, Isabella and Ferdinand issued an edict expelling all practicing Jews from Spain. Of the community of perhaps 200,000 Jews, 150,000 fled. (Efforts were made, through last-minute conversions, to retain good Jewish physicians.) Absolute religious orthodoxy and purity of blood (untainted by Jews or Muslims) served as the theoretical foundation of the Spanish national state.

The diplomacy of the Catholic rulers of Spain achieved a success they never anticipated. Partly out of hatred for the French and partly out of a desire to gain international recognition for their new dynasty, Ferdinand and Isabella in 1496 married their second daughter, Joanna, heiress to Castile, to the archduke Philip, heir through his mother to the Burgundian Netherlands and through his father to the Holy Roman Empire. Philip and Joanna's son, Charles V (r. 1519–1556), thus succeeded to a vast patrimony. When Charles's son Philip II joined Portugal to the Spanish crown in 1580, the Iberian Peninsula was at last politically united. The various kingdoms, however, were administered separately.

SUMMARY

The Italian Renaissance rested on the phenomenal economic growth of the High Middle Ages. In the period from about 1050 to 1300, a new economy emerged based on Venetian and Genoese shipping and long-distance trade and on Florentine banking and cloth manufacture. These commercial activities, combined with the struggle of urban communes for political independence from surrounding feudal lords, led to the appearance of a new aristocratic class. The centuries extending roughly from 1300 to 1600 witnessed a remarkable intellectual flowering. Based on a strong interest in the ancient world, the Renaissance had a classicizing influence on many facets of culture: law, literature, government, education, religion, and art. In the city-states of fifteenth- and sixteenth-century Italy, oligarchic or despotic powers governed; Renaissance culture was manipulated to enhance the power of those rulers.

Expanding outside Italy, the intellectual features of this movement affected the culture of all Europe. The intellectual characteristics of the Renaissance were a secular attitude toward life, a belief in individual potential, and a serious interest in the Latin classics. The printing press revolutionized communication. Meanwhile, the status of women in society declined, and black people entered Europe in sizable numbers for the first time since the collapse of the Roman Empire. Male culture in Italian cities had a strongly homoerotic character, reflecting a significant contrast between Renaissance attitudes toward male sexuality and attitudes today. In northern Europe, city merchants and rural gentry allied with rising monarchies. With taxes provided by business people, kings established greater peace and order, both essential for trade. Northern humanism had a more pietistic strain than did the Italian. In Spain, France, and England, rulers also emphasized royal dignity and authority, and they utilized Machiavellian ideas to ensure the preservation and continuation of their governments. Feudal monarchies gradually evolved in the direction of nation-states.

NOTES

1. See L. Martines, *Power and Imagination: City-States in Renaissance Italy* (New York: Vintage Books, 1980), esp. pp. 332–333.
2. Ibid., pp. 22–61.
3. Ibid., p. 221.
4. Quoted in J. Burckhardt, *The Civilization of the Renaissance in Italy* (London: Phaidon Books, 1951), p. 89.
5. *Memoirs of Benvenuto Cellini; A Florentine Artist; Written by Himself* (London: J. M. Dent & Sons, 1927), p. 2.
6. See C. Trinkaus, *In Our Image and Likeness: Humanity and Divinity in Italian Humanist Thought,* vol. 2 (London: Constable, 1970), pp. 505–529.
7. B. Burroughs, ed., *Vasari's Lives of the Artists* (New York: Simon & Schuster, 1946), pp. 164–165.
8. See Martines, *Power and Imagination,* chap. 13, esp. pp. 241, 243.
9. R. A. Goldthwaite, *Wealth and the Demand for Art in Italy, 1300–1600* (Baltimore: Johns Hopkins University Press, 1993), p. 5.
10. Ibid., p. 213.
11. Ibid., pp. 224–229.
12. Ibid., pp. 121–129.
13. See A. Hauser, *The Social History of Art,* vol. 2 (New York: Vintage Books, 1959), chap. 3, esp. pp. 60, 68.
14. G. Bull, trans., *Aretino: Selected Letters* (Baltimore: Penguin Books, 1976), p. 109.
15. Quoted in P. and L. Murray, *A Dictionary of Art and Artists* (Baltimore: Penguin Books, 1963), p. 125.
16. Quoted in W. H. Woodward, *Vittorino da Feltre and Other Humanist Educators* (Cambridge: Cambridge University Press, 1897), pp. 96–97.
17. C. E. Detmold, trans., *The Historical, Political and Diplomatic Writings of Niccolò Machiavelli* (Boston: J. R. Osgood, 1882), pp. 51–52.

18. Ibid., pp. 54–55.
19. See F. Gilbert, *Machiavelli and Guicciardini: Politics and History in Sixteenth Century Florence* (New York: W. W. Norton, 1984), pp. 197–200.
20. E. L. Eisenstein, *The Printing Press as an Agent of Change: Communications and Cultural Transformations in Early Modern Europe,* vol. 1 (New York: Cambridge University Press, 1979), p. 135. For an overall discussion, see pp. 126–159.
21. See L. Hunt, *The Invention of Pornography: Obscenity and the Origins of Modernity, 1500–1800* (New York: Zone Books, 1993), pp. 10, 93–95.
22. See A. W. Crosby, *The Measure of Reality: Quantification and Western Society* (New York: Cambridge University Press, 1997), pp. 76–78.
23. Ibid., pp. 49–74.
24. M. L. King, "Book-Lined Cells: Women and Humanism in the Early Italian Renaissance," in *Beyond Their Sex: Learned Women of the European Past,* ed. P. H. Labalme (New York: New York University Press, 1980), pp. 66–81, esp. p. 73.
25. This account rests on J. Kelly-Gadol, "Did Women Have a Renaissance?" in *Becoming Visible: Women in European History,* ed. R. Bridenthal and C. Koontz (Boston: Houghton Mifflin, 1977), pp. 137–161, esp. p. 161.
26. See Peter Burke, "What Is the History of Popular Culture?" in *What Is History Today?,* ed. J. Gardiner (Atlantic Highlands, N.J.: Humanities Press, 1989), pp. 121–123.
27. G. Ruggerio, "Sexual Criminality in Early Renaissance Venice, 1338–1358," *Journal of Social History* 8 (Spring 1975): 18–31.
28. For these and a variety of other remarkable court cases, see S. K. Cohn, Jr., *Women in the Streets: Essays on Sex and Power in Renaissance Italy* (Baltimore: Johns Hopkins University Press, 1996), pp. 103–121.
29. Ibid., pp. 30–35, 105–115.
30. M. Rocke, *Forbidden Friendships: Homosexuality and Male Culture in Renaissance Florence* (New York: Oxford University Press, 1996), pp. 10–11.
31. Ibid.
32. Ibid., p. 45.
33. See Ibid., chap. 3, "Age and Gender in the Social Organization of Sodomy," and chap. 4, "Social Profiles."
34. Ibid., p. 148.
35. Ibid., pp. 190–191.
36. Quoted in J. Devisse and M. Mollat, *The Image of the Black in Western Art,* trans. W. G. Ryan, vol. 2 (New York: William Morrow, 1979), pt. 2, pp. 187–188.
37. See A. C. DE. C. M. Saunders, *A Social History of Black Slaves and Freedmen in Portugal, 1441–1555* (New York: Cambridge University Press, 1982), pp. 59, 62–88, 176–179.
38. Ibid., pp. 190–194.
39. Ibid., pp. 255–258.
40. See I. Hannaford, *Race: The History of an Idea in the West* (Washington, D.C.: Woodrow Wilson Center Press, 1996), pp. 3–182 passim; pp. 182–187.
41. Quoted in E. H. Harbison, *The Christian Scholar and His Calling in the Age of the Reformation* (New York: Charles Scribner's Sons, 1956), p. 109.
42. Quoted in F. Seebohm, *The Oxford Reformers* (London: J. M. Dent & Sons, 1867), p. 256.
43. See J. H. Elliott, *Imperial Spain, 1469–1716* (New York: Mentor Books, 1963), esp. pp. 75, 97–108.
44. See B. F. Reilly, *The Medieval Spains* (New York: Cambridge University Press, 1993), pp. 198–203.
45. B. Netanyahu, *The Origins of the Inquisition in Fifteenth Century Spain* (New York: Random House, 1995), p. 921.
46. Ibid., pp. 934–935.
47. Ibid., p. 930.
48. Ibid., p. 982.
49. Ibid., pp. 996–1005.

Suggested Reading

There are scores of exciting studies available on virtually all aspects of the Renaissance. The curious student might begin with M. Mallett, "Politics and Society in Italy, 1250–1600," a lucid sketch of political change in the various cities, and G. Holmes, "Renaissance Culture," a fine appreciation of the conflict of secular and religious values in art and literature. These articles appear in G. Holmes, ed., *The Oxford History of Italy* (1997). G. Chittolini, "Cities, 'City-States,' and Regional States in North-Central Italy," in *Cities and the Rise of States in Europe, A.D. 1000 to 1800,* ed. C. Tilly and W. P. Blockmans (1994), provides a good explanation of why Italy lagged in developing a national state, while P. Burke, *The Italian Renaissance: Culture and Society in Italy* (1986), offers an important sociological interpretation. J. H. Plumb, *The Italian Renaissance* (1965), is a superbly written book. P. Burke, *The Historical Anthropology of Early Modern Italy* (1987), contains many useful essays on Italian cultural history in a comparative European framework, while G. Holmes, ed., *Art and Politics in Renaissance Italy* (1993), treats the art of Florence and Rome against the political background. J. R. Hale, *Renaissance Europe: The Individual and Society, 1480–1520* (1978), is an excellent treatment of individualism by an authority. For Renaissance humanism and education, see P. F. Grendler, *Schooling in Renaissance Italy: Literacy and Learning, 1300–1600* (1989); J. H. Moran, *The Growth of English Schooling, 1340–1548: Learning, Literacy, and Laicization in Pre-Reformation York Diocese* (1985); and J. F. D'Amico, *Renaissance Humanism in Papal Rome: Humanists and Churchmen on the Eve of the Reformation* (1983), all highly readable works of outstanding scholarship. Learned, provocative, beautifully written, and the work on which this chapter leans, the book by Martines listed in the Notes is probably the best broad appreciation of the period produced in several decades. For the Renaissance court, see the splendid achievement of G. Lubkin, *A Renaissance Court: Milan Under Galeazzo Maria Sforza* (1994).

J. R. Hale, *Machiavelli and Renaissance Italy* (1966), is a sound short biography, but advanced students may want to consult the sophisticated intellectual biography S. de Grazia, *Machiavelli in Hell* (1989), which is based on Machiavelli's literary as well as political writing. C. Singleton, trans., *The Courtier* (1959), presents an excellent picture of Renaissance court life.

The best introduction to the Renaissance in northern Europe and a book that has greatly influenced twentieth-century scholarship is J. Huizinga, *The Waning of the Middle Ages: A Study of the Forms of Life, Thought, and Art in France and the Netherlands in the Dawn of the Renaissance* (1954): it challenges the whole idea of the Renaissance. R. J. Knecht, *Renaissance Warrior and Patron: The Reign of Francis I* (1994), is the standard study of that important French ruler. L. Febvre, *Life in Renaissance France* (1977), is a brilliant evocation of French Renaissance civilization. W. Blockmans and W. Prevenier, *The Burgundian Netherlands* (1986), is essential for the culture of Burgundy. The leading northern humanist is sensitively treated in M. M. Phillips, *Erasmus and the Northern Renaissance* (1956), and J. Huizinga, *Erasmus of Rotterdam* (1952). R. Marius, *Thomas More: A Biography* (1984), is an original study of the English humanist and statesman, but students may also want to consult E. E. Reynolds, *Thomas More* (1962). J. Leclercq, trans., *The Complete Works of Rabelais* (1963), is easily available.

The following titles should prove useful for various aspects of Renaissance social history: E. L. Eisenstein, *The Printing Press as an Agent of Change: Communications and Cultural Transformations in Early Modern Europe*, 2 vols. (1979), a fundamental work; G. Ruggerio, *Violence in Early Renaissance Venice* (1980), a pioneering study of crime and punishment in a stable society; D. Weinstein and R. M. Bell, *Saints and Society: The Two Worlds of Christendom, 1000–1700* (1982), an essential book for understanding the perception of holiness and of the social origins of saints in early modern Europe. For the role and status of women, see C. Klapisch-Zuper, ed., *A History of Women*, vol. 3 (1994); R. Chartier, ed., *A History of Private Life*. Vol. 3: *Passions of the Renaissance* (1990); and I. Maclean, *The Renaissance Notion of Women* (1980). For adolescents and young people, G. Levy and J.-C. Schmitt, eds., *A History of Young People in the West: Ancient and Medieval Rites of Passage*, vol. 1 (1997), contains a provocative collection of articles but must be used with caution. For issues of gender and culture, see, in addition to the titles by Rocke and Cohn cited in the Notes, J. C. Brown, *The Life of a Lesbian Nun in Renaissance Italy* (1985), and J. M. Saslow, *Ganymede in the Renaissance* (1986), which uses images of Ganymede as a metaphor for relations between men and youth.

Students interested in issues related to health and medical care should see J. Arrizabalaga, J. Henderson, and R. French, *The Great Pox: The French Disease in Renaissance Europe* (1997), which focuses on the plague later called syphilis, and the appropriate sections of N. Orme and M. Webster, *The English Hospital, 1070–1570* (1995), a useful illustrated study.

Renaissance art has understandably inspired vast research. In addition to Burroughs's edited version of Vasari's volume of biographical sketches on the masters referred to in the Notes, see, for Vasari's aims and methods of interpretation, P. L. Rubin, *Giorgio Vasari: Art and History* (1995). For Venice, see P. F. Brown, *Venice and Antiquity: The Venetian Sense of the Past* (1997), which treats the ways Venice invented its past to celebrate the city and its people; P. F. Brown, *Venetian Narrative Painting in the Age of Carpaccio* (1989); P. Humfrey, *Painting in Renaissance Venice* (1995), a useful survey for the beginning student; and P. Humfrey, *Lorenzo Lotto* (1997), a fine study of a distinctive Venetian painter. For artist families, see P. Burke, *The Italian Renaissance: Culture and Society in Italy* (1986). For the city of Milan, see E. S. Welch, *Art and Authority in Milan* (1996); and for Rome, see C. Hibbert, *Rome: The Biography of a City* (1985), an elegantly illustrated work, and P. Partner, *Renaissance Rome, 1500–1559: A Portrait of a Society* (1979). For Florence, D. C. Ahl, *Benozzo Gozzoli* (1996), places Gozzoli's art in its social context. All of the following older studies have important material on Florentine art: E. Panofsky, *Meaning in the Visual Arts* (1955), written by one of the great art historians of this century; B. Berenson, *Italian Painters of the Renaissance* (1957), the classic work of a famous American expatriate; and M. Baxandall, *Painting and Experience in Fifteenth Century Italy* (1988). The magisterial achievement of J. Pope-Hennessy, *Cellini* (1985), is a superb evocation of that artist's life and work, while R. Jones and N. Penny, *Raphael* (1983), celebrates the work of that master. Da Vinci's scientific and naturalistic ideas and drawings are available in I. A. Richter, ed., *The Notebooks of Leonardo da Vinci* (1985). The best introduction to the art of northern Europe is C. Harbison, *The Mirror of the Artist: Northern Renaissance Art in Its Historical Context* (1995).

The following studies should be helpful to students interested in issues relating to the political and religious history of Spain: N. Rubin, *Isabella of Castile: The First Renaissance Queen* (1991); P. Lis, *Isabel the Queen: Life and Times* (1992); J. S. Gerber, *The Jews of Spain: A History of the Sephardic Experience* (1992); H. Kamen, *Inquisition and Society in Spain in the Sixteenth and Seventeenth Centuries* (1985); J. H. Elliott, *Imperial Spain: 1469–1716* (1966); P. F. Albaladejo, "Cities and the State in Spain," in *Cities and the Rise of States in Europe, A.D. 1000 to 1800*, eds. C. Tilly and W. M. Blockmans (1994); and B. Netanyahu, *The Origins of the Inquisition in Fifteenth Century Spain* (1995).

LISTENING TO THE PAST

A Universal Man

Some people of the Renaissance believed in the ideal of universality, the achievement of distinction in many different skills and branches of knowledge. As one humanist put it, "A man is able to learn many things and make himself universal in many excellent arts." (Not everyone thought this: while Michelangelo was painting the Sistine Chapel, he complained to his father that "painting is not my profession.") Leon Battista Alberti (1404–1474), the illegitimate son of a family exiled from Florence, strongly believed he could be a universal man. A scholar-humanist, mathematician, and musician, he wrote treatises on domestic morality, the physical remains of antiquity, painting, and architecture. Here is a section of Alberti's autobiography.

And finally he embraced with zeal and forethought everything which pertained to fame. To omit the rest, he strove so hard to attain a name in modelling and painting that he wished to neglect nothing by which he might gain the approbation of good men. His genius was so versatile that you might almost judge all the fine arts to be his. . . .

He played ball, hurled the javelin, ran, leaped, wrestled, and above all delighted in the steep ascent of mountains; he applied himself to all these things for the sake of health rather than sport or pleasure. As a youth he excelled in warlike games. With his feet together, he could leap over the shoulders of men standing by; he had almost no equal among those hurling the lance. An arrow shot by his hand from his chest could pierce the strongest iron breastplate. . . . On horseback, holding in his hand one end of a long wand, while the other was firmly fixed to his foot, he could ride his horse violently in all directions for hours at a time as he wished, and the wand would remain completely immobile. Strange and marvellous! that the most spirited horses and those most impatient of riders would, when he first mounted them, tremble violently and shudder as if in great fear. He learned music without teachers, and his compositions were approved by learned musicians. He sang throughout his whole life, but in private, or alone. . . . He delighted in the organ and was considered an expert among the leading musicians.

When he had begun to mature in years, neglecting everything else, he devoted himself entirely to the study of letters, and spent some years of labour on canon and civil law. Finally after so many nightly vigils and such great constancy, he fell gravely ill from the exertion of his studies. Since his relatives were neither kind nor humane to him in his illness, by way of consoling himself between his convalescence and cure he wrote the play *Philodoxeos*, putting aside his legal studies—this when he was only twenty years old. And as soon as his health permitted, he resumed his studies, intending to complete the law, but again he was seized by a grave illness. . . .

At length, on the orders of his doctors, he desisted from those studies which were most fatiguing to the memory, just when they were about to flourish. But in truth, because he could not live without letters, at the age of twenty-four he turned to physics and the mathematical arts. . . .

Although he was affable, gentle, and harmful to no one, nevertheless he felt the animosity of many evil men, and hidden enmities, both annoying and very burdensome; in particular the harsh injuries and intolerable insults from his own relatives. He lived among the envious and malevolent with such modesty and equanimity that none of his detractors or rivals, although very hostile towards him, dared to utter a word about him in the presence of good and worthy men unless it was full of praise and admiration. . . .

When he heard that a learned man of any kind had arrived, he would at once work his way into a position of familiarity with him and thus from any source whatsoever he began to learn what he was ignorant of. From craftsmen, architects, shipbuilders, and even from cobblers he sought information to see if by chance they preserved anything rare or unusual or special in their arts; and he would then communicate such things to those citizens who wished to know them. He pretended to be ignorant in many things so that he might observe the talents and habits and skill of others. And so he was a zealous observer of whatsoever pertained to inborn talent or the arts.

He wholly despised the pursuit of material gain. He gave his money and goods to his friends to take care of and to enjoy. Among those by whom he believed himself loved, he was not only outgoing about his affairs and his habits but even about his secrets. He never betrayed the secrets of another but remained silent forever. . . .

He was by nature prone to wrath and bitter in spirit, but he could repress his rising indignation immediately by taking thought. Sometimes he deliberately fled from the verbose and the headstrong because with them he could not subdue his wrath. At other times he voluntarily submitted to the bold, in order to grow in patience. . . .

He wrote some books entitled *On Painting,* and in this very art of painting he created works unheard of and unbelievable to those who saw them. . . .

He had within himself a ray by which he could sense the good or evil intentions of men towards himself. Simply by looking at them, he could discover most of the defects of anyone in his presence. He used all kinds of reasoning and great effort, but in vain, to make more gentle towards himself those whom he had learned at one glance would be inimical. . . .

He could endure pain and cold and heat. When, not yet fifteen, he received a serious wound in the foot, and the physician, according to his custom and skill, drew together the broken parts of the foot and sewed them through the skin with a needle, he scarcely uttered a sound of pain. With his own hands, though in such great pain, he even aided the ministering doctor and treated his own wound though he was burning with fever. . . . By some defect in his nature he loathed garlic and also honey, and the mere sight of them, if by chance they were offered to him, brought on vomiting. But he conquered himself by force of looking at and handling the disagreeable objects, so that they came to offend him less, thus showing by example that men can do anything with themselves if they will.

He took extraordinary and peculiar pleasure in looking at things in which there was any mark of beauty or adornment. He never ceased to wonder at old men who were endowed with dignity of countenance, and unimpaired and vigorous, and he proclaimed that he honoured them as "delights of nature." He declared that quadrupeds, birds, and other living things of outstanding beauty were worthy of benevolence because by the very distinction of their nature they deserved favour. When his favourite dog died he wrote a funeral oration for him.

✣ Bronze medallion of Leon Battista Alberti, by Matteo di Andrea de' Pasti. *(Alinari/Art Resource, NY)*

Questions for Analysis

1. What distinctively Renaissance traits did Alberti show?
2. According to his assessment, what personal or human qualities did Alberti possess?
3. Did Alberti appear to have any psychological complexes or difficulties? How would you explain them?

CHAPTER

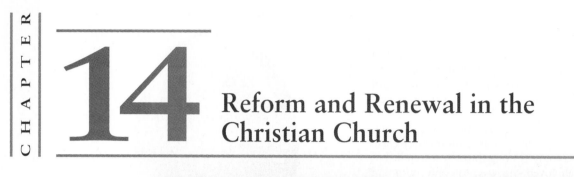

14 Reform and Renewal in the Christian Church

Women praying in church, from a 15th-century painting by Friedrich Herlin. *(Photo Services, Gruppo Editoriale Fabbri, Milan)*

The idea of reform is as old as Christianity itself. In his letter to the Christians at Rome, Saint Paul exhorted, "Do not model yourselves on the behavior of the world around you, but let your behavior change, reformed by your new mind. That is the only way to discover the will of God." In the early fifth century, Saint Augustine of Hippo, describing the final stage of world history, wrote, "In the sixth age of the world our reformation becomes manifest, in newness of mind, according to the image of Him who created us." In the middle of the twelfth century, Saint Bernard of Clairvaux complained about the church of his day: "There is as much difference between us and the men of the primitive Church as there is between muck and gold." The Christian humanists of the late fifteenth and early sixteenth centuries—More, Erasmus, and Colet—urged reform of the church on the pattern of the early church, primarily through educational and social change.

The need for reform of the individual Christian and of the institutional church is central to the Christian faith. Men and women of every period believed the early Christian church represented a golden age, and critics in every period called for reform. Thus sixteenth-century cries for reformation were hardly new. What was new, however, were the criticisms of educated laypeople whose religious needs were not being met. Many scholars interpret the sixteenth-century Reformation against the background of reforming trends begun in the fourteenth century. Unlike any other period, the sixteenth century experienced religious changes that had profound social, political, and cultural consequences.

- What late medieval religious developments paved the way for the adoption and spread of Protestant thought?
- What role did political and social factors play in the several reformations?
- What were the consequences of religious division?
- Why did the theological ideas of Martin Luther trigger political, social, and economic reactions?
- What response did the Catholic church make to the movements for reform?

These are some of the questions that this chapter will explore.

THE CONDITION OF THE CHURCH (CA 1400–1517)

The papal conflict with the German emperor Frederick II in the thirteenth century, followed by the Babylonian Captivity and then the Great Schism, badly damaged the prestige of church leaders. In the fourteenth and fifteenth centuries, leaders of the conciliar movement reflected educated public opinion when they called for the reform of the church "in head and members." The humanists of Italy and the Christian humanists of the north denounced corruption in the church. As Machiavelli put it, "We Italians are irreligious and corrupt above others, because the Church and her representatives set us the worst example."[1] In *The Praise of Folly,* Erasmus condemned the absurd superstitions of the parish clergy and the excessive rituals of the monks. The records of episcopal visitations of parishes, civil court records, and even such literary masterpieces as Chaucer's *Canterbury Tales* and Boccaccio's *Decameron* tended to confirm the sarcasm of the humanists.

Signs of Disorder

The religious life of most people in early-sixteenth-century Europe took place at the village or local level. At this parish level, priests were peasants, and they were poor. All too frequently, the spiritual quality of their lives was not much better than that of the people to whom they ministered. The clergy identified religion with life; that is, they injected religious symbols and practices into everyday living. Some historians have therefore accused the clergy of vulgarizing religion. But even if the level of belief and practice was vulgarized, the lives of rural, isolated, and semipagan people were still spiritualized.

In the early sixteenth century, critics of the church concentrated their attacks on three disorders: clerical immorality, clerical ignorance, and clerical pluralism, with the related problem of absenteeism. There was little pressure for doctrinal change; the emphasis was on moral and administrative reform.

Since the fourth century, church law had required that candidates for the priesthood accept absolute celibacy. That requirement had always been difficult to enforce. Many priests, especially those ministering to country people, had concubines, and reports of neglect of the rule of celibacy were common. Immorality, of course, included more than sexual transgressions. Clerical drunkenness, gambling, and indulgence in fancy dress were frequent charges. There is no way of knowing how many priests were guilty of such behavior. But because such conduct was so much at odds with the church's rules and moral standards, it scandalized the educated faithful.

The bishops only casually enforced regulations regarding the education of priests. As a result, standards for ordination were shockingly low. When Saint Antonio, archbishop of Florence, conducted a visitation of his metropolitan see in the late fifteenth century, he found churches and service books in a deplorable state and many priests barely able to read and write. The evidence points consistently to the low quality of the Italian clergy, although in northern Europe—in England, for example—recent research shows an improvement in clerical educational standards in the early sixteenth century. Nevertheless, parish priests throughout Europe were not as educated as the educated laity. Predictably, Christian humanists, with their concern for learning, condemned the ignorance or low educational level of the clergy. Many priests could barely read and write, and critics laughed at the illiterate priest mumbling Latin words of the Mass that he could not understand.

In regard to absenteeism and pluralism, many clerics, especially higher ecclesiastics, held several *benefices* (or offices) simultaneously but seldom visited their benefices, let alone performed the spiritual responsibilities those offices entailed. Instead, they collected revenues from all of them and hired a poor priest, paying him just a fraction of the income to fulfill the spiritual duties of a particular local church. King Henry VIII's chancellor Thomas Wolsey was archbishop of York for fifteen years before he set foot in his diocese. The French king Louis XII's famous diplomat Antoine du Prat was perhaps the most notorious example of absenteeism: as archbishop of Sens, the first time he entered his cathedral was in his own funeral procession.

Many Italian officials in the papal curia held benefices in England, Spain, and Germany. Revenues from those countries paid the Italian priests' salaries, provoking not only charges of absenteeism but also nationalistic resentment. Critics condemned pluralism, absenteeism, and the way money seemed to change hands when a bishop entered into his office.

Although royal governments strengthened their positions and consolidated their territories in the fifteenth and sixteenth centuries, rulers lacked sufficient revenues to pay and reward able civil servants. The Christian church, with its dioceses and abbeys, possessed a large proportion of the wealth of the countries of Europe. What better way to reward government officials, who were usually clerics in any case, than with high church offices? After all, the practice was sanctioned by centuries of tradition. Thus in Spain, France, England, and the Holy Roman Empire—in fact, all over Europe—because church officials served their monarchs, those officials were allowed to govern the church. Churchmen served as royal councilors, diplomats, treasury officials, chancellors, viceroys, and judges. These positions had nothing whatsoever to do with spiritual matters. Bishops worked for their respective states as well as for the church, and they were paid by the church for their services to the state. It is astonishing that so many conscientiously tried to carry out their religious duties on top of their public burdens.

In most countries except England, members of the nobility occupied the highest church positions. The sixteenth century was definitely not a democratic age. The spectacle of proud, aristocratic prelates living in magnificent splendor contrasted very unfavorably with the simple fishermen who had been Christ's disciples.

Nor did the popes of the period 1450 to 1550 set much of an example. They lived like secular Renaissance princes. Pius II (1458–1464), although deeply learned and a tireless worker, enjoyed a reputation as a clever writer of love stories and Latin poetry. Sixtus IV (1471–1484) beautified the city of Rome, built the famous Sistine Chapel, and generously supported several artists. Innocent VIII (1484–1492) made the papal court a model of luxury and scandal. All three popes used papal power and wealth to advance the material interests of their own families. The court of the Spanish pope Alexander VI (Rodrigo Borgia) (1492–1503), who publicly acknowledged his mistress and children, reached new heights of impropriety. Because of the prevalence of intrigue, sexual promiscuity, and supposed poisonings, the name *Borgia* became a synonym for moral corruption. Julius II (1503–1513), the nephew of Sixtus IV, donned military armor and personally led papal troops against the French invaders of Italy in 1506. After him, Giovanni de' Medici, the son of Lorenzo de' Medici, carried on as Pope Leo X (1513–1521) the Medicean tradition of being a great patron of the arts.

Signs of Vitality

Calls for reform testify to the spiritual vitality of the church as well as to its numerous problems. In the late fifteenth and early sixteenth centuries, both individuals and groups within the church were working actively for reform. In Spain, for example, Cardinal Francisco

Jiménez (1436–1517) visited religious houses, encouraged the monks and friars to uphold their rules and constitutions, and set high standards for the training of the diocesan clergy.

In Holland beginning in the late fourteenth century, a group of pious laypeople called the "Brethren of the Common Life" lived in stark simplicity while daily carrying out the Gospel teaching of feeding the hungry, clothing the naked, and visiting the sick. The Brethren also taught in local schools with the goal of preparing devout candidates for the priesthood and the monastic life. Through prayer, meditation, and careful study of the Scriptures, the Brethren sought to make religion a personal, inner experience. The spirituality of the Brethren of the Common Life found its finest expression in the classic *The Imitation of Christ* by Thomas à Kempis. Though written in Latin for monks and nuns, *The Imitation* gained wide appeal among laypeople. It urges Christians to take Christ as their model and seek perfection in a simple way of life. Like the Protestants who came later, the Brethren stressed the centrality of the Scriptures in spiritual life.[2] In the mid-fifteenth century, the movement had founded houses in the Netherlands, in central Germany, and in the Rhineland; it was a true religious revival.

If external religious observances are a measure of depth of heartfelt conviction, Europeans in the early sixteenth century remained deeply pious and loyal to the Roman Catholic church. Villagers participated in processions honoring the local saints. Middle-class people made pilgrimages to the great shrines, such as Saint Peter's in Rome. The upper classes continued to remember the church in their wills. In England, for example, between 1480 and 1490 almost 30,000 pounds, a prodigious sum in those days, was bequeathed to religious foundations. People of all social classes devoted an enormous amount of their time and income to religious causes and foundations.

The papacy also expressed concern for reform. Pope Julius II summoned an ecumenical (universal) council, which met in the church of Saint John Lateran in Rome from 1512 to 1517. Since most of the bishops were Italian and did not represent a broad cross section of international opinion, the term *ecumenical* is not really appropriate to describe their meetings. Nevertheless, the bishops and theologians present strove earnestly to reform the church. The council recommended higher standards for education of the clergy and instruction of the common people. The bishops placed the responsibility for eliminating bureaucratic corruption squarely on the papacy and suggested significant doctrinal reforms. But many obstacles stood in the way of ecclesiastical change. Meantime, difficulties were brewing in Germany.

Arm Reliquary of Saint Babylas Silver, glass paste, stones, rock crystals, and an amethyst were attached to an oak base to create this arm reliquary for a third-century martyred bishop of Antioch. Containers for relics were designed in forms related to the objects they held; here the bishop's hand is raised in blessing. Shrines possessing saints' relics drew pilgrims, who represented a demand for food, shelter, and souvenirs. *(Germany, Brunswick, 1467. Philadelphia Museum of Art, purchased with Museum funds. 1951-12-1)*

Martin Luther and the Birth of Protestantism

As the result of a personal religious struggle, a German Augustinian friar, Martin Luther (1483–1546), launched the Protestant Reformation of the sixteenth century. Luther was not a typical person of his time; miners' sons who become professors of theology are never typical. But Luther was representative of his time in the sense that he articulated the widespread desire for reform of the Christian church and a deep yearning for salvation. In the sense that concern for salvation was an important motivating force for Luther and other reformers, the sixteenth-century Reformation was in part a continuation of the medieval religious search.

Lucas Cranach the Younger: Luther and the Wittenberg Reformers The massive figure of John Frederick, Elector of Saxony, who protected and supported Luther, dominates this group portrait. Luther is on the far left, his associate Philipp Melanchthon in the front row on the right. Luther's face shows a quiet determination. *(The Toledo Museum of Art, Toledo, Ohio; Gift of Edward Drummond Libbey)*

Luther's Early Years

Martin Luther was born at Eisleben in Saxony, the second son of a copper miner and, later, mine owner. At considerable sacrifice, his father sent him to school and then to the University of Erfurt, where he earned a master's degree with distinction at the young age of twenty-one. Hans Luther intended his son to proceed to the study of law and a legal career, which for centuries had been the steppingstone to public office and material success. Badly frightened during a thunderstorm, however, Martin Luther vowed to become a friar. Without consulting his father, he entered the monastery of the Augustinian friars at Erfurt in 1505. Luther was ordained a priest in 1507 and after additional study earned a doctorate of theology. From 1512 until his death in 1546, he served as professor of the Scriptures at the new University of Wittenberg. Luther was deadly serious when he said, years later, "I would not take all the world's goods for my doctorate." His doctorate led to his professorship, and his professorship conferred on him the *authority* to teach: throughout his life, he frequently cited his professorship as justification for his reforming work.

Martin Luther was a very conscientious friar. His scrupulous observance of the religious routine, frequent confessions, and fasting, however, gave him only temporary relief from anxieties about sin and his ability to meet God's demands. These apprehensions in turn led him to doubt the value of the monastic life itself. Since the medieval church had long held that the monastic life was a sure and certain road to salvation, Luther's confusion and anxieties increased.

Luther's wise and kindly confessor, John Staupitz, directed him to the study of Saint Paul's letters. Gradually, Luther arrived at a new understanding of the Pauline letters and of all Christian doctrine. He came to believe that salvation comes not through external observances and penance but through a simple faith in Christ. Faith is the means by which God sends humanity his grace, and faith is a free gift that cannot be earned. Thus Martin Luther discovered himself, God's work for him, and the centrality of faith in the Christian life.

The Ninety-five Theses

An incident illustrative of the condition of the church in the early sixteenth century propelled Martin Luther onto the stage of history and brought about the Reformation. The University of Wittenberg lay within the ecclesiastical jurisdiction of the archdiocese of Magde-

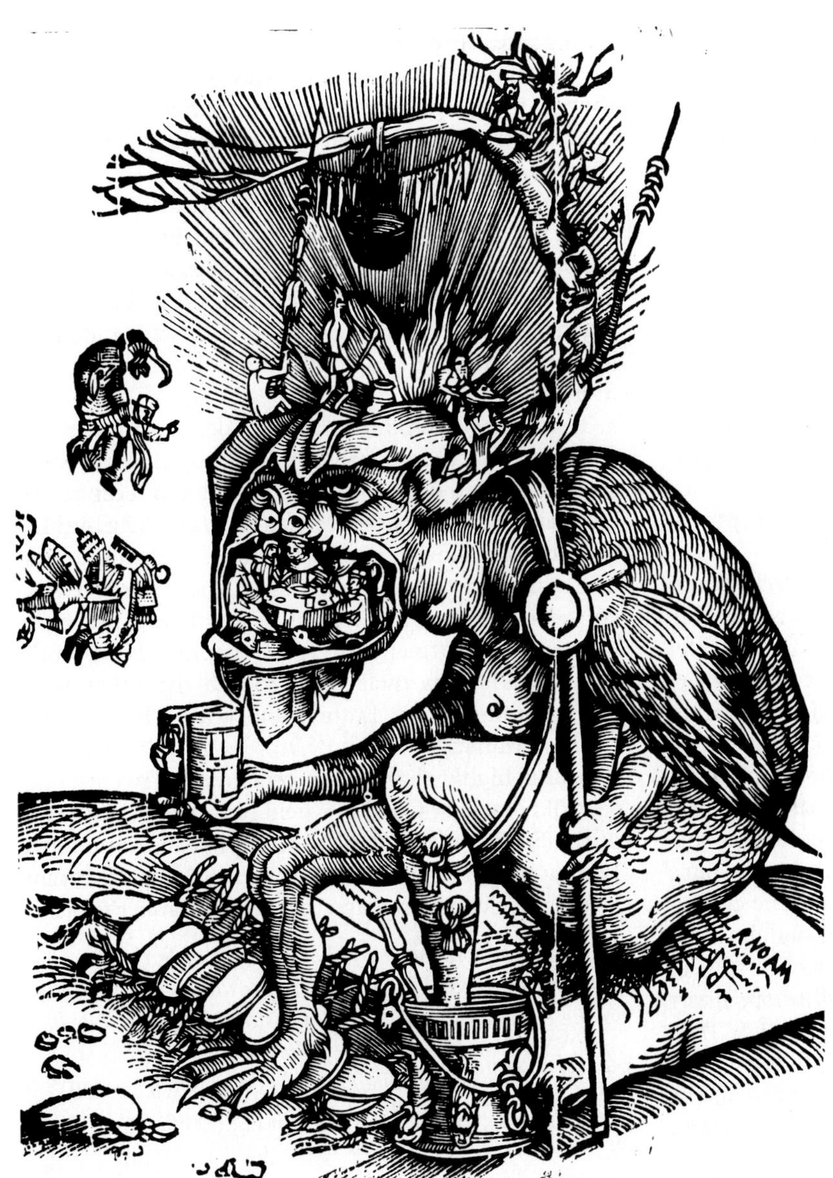

The Folly of Indulgences In this woodcut the church's sale of indulgences is viciously satirized. With one claw in the holy water symbolizing the rite of purification (Psalm 50), and the other claw resting on the coins paid for indulgences, the church, in the form of a rapacious eagle with its right hand stretched out for offerings, writes out an indulgence with excrement—which represents its worth. Fools, in a false security, sit in the animal's gaping mouth, representing hell, to which a devil delivers the pope in a three-tiered crown and holding the keys to heaven originally given to Saint Peter. *(Kunstsammlungen der Veste Coburg)*

burg. The twenty-seven-year-old archbishop of Magdeburg, Albert, was also administrator of the see of Halberstadt and had been appointed archbishop of Mainz. To hold all three offices simultaneously—blatant pluralism—required papal dispensation. At that moment, Pope Leo X was eager to continue the construction of Saint Peter's Basilica but was hard-pressed for funds. Archbishop Albert borrowed money from the Fuggers, a wealthy banking family of Augsburg, to pay for the papal dispensation allowing him to hold the several episcopal benefices. Only a few powerful financiers and churchmen knew the details of the arrangement, but Leo X authorized Archbishop Albert to sell indulgences in Germany to repay the Fuggers.

Wittenberg was in the political jurisdiction of Frederick of Saxony, one of the seven electors of the Holy Roman Empire. When Frederick forbade the preaching and sale of indulgences within his duchy, the people of Wittenberg, including some of Professor Luther's students, streamed across the border from Saxony into Jütenborg in Thuringia to buy indulgences.

What exactly was an *indulgence?* According to Catholic theology, individuals who sin alienate themselves from God and his love. In order to be reconciled to God, the sinner must confess his or her sins to a priest and do the penance assigned. For example, a person who steals must first return the stolen goods and then perform the penance given by the priest, usually certain prayers or good works. This is known as the temporal (or earthly) penance since no one knows what penance God will ultimately require.

The doctrine of indulgence rested on three principles. First, God is merciful, but he is also just. Second, Christ and the saints, through their infinite virtue, established a "treasury of merits" on which the church, through its special relationship with Christ and the saints, can draw. Third, the church has the authority to grant sinners the spiritual benefits of those merits. Originally an indulgence was a remission of the temporal (priest-imposed) penalties for sin. Beginning in the twelfth century, the papacy and bishops had given Crusaders such indulgences. By the later Middle Ages, people widely believed that an indulgence secured total remission of penalties for sin—on earth or in purgatory—and ensured swift entry into heaven.

Archbishop Albert hired Dominican friar John Tetzel to sell the indulgences. Tetzel mounted an advertising blitz. One of his slogans—"As soon as coin in coffer rings, the soul from purgatory springs"—brought phenomenal success. Men and women could buy indulgences not only for themselves but also for deceased parents, relatives, or friends. Tetzel even drew up a chart with specific prices for the forgiveness of particular sins.

Luther was severely troubled that ignorant people believed they had no further need for repentance once they had purchased an indulgence. Because the church at the time had no official doctrine on indulgences, Luther thought he was entitled to discuss the subject critically. Thus he wrote a letter to Archbishop Albert on the subject and enclosed in Latin "Ninety-five Theses on the Power of Indulgences." His argument was that indulgences undermined the seriousness of the sacrament of penance, competed with the preaching of the Gospel, and downplayed the importance of charity in Christian life. After Luther's death, his disciple Philipp Melanchthon reported that the theses were also posted on the door of the church at Wittenberg Castle on October 31, 1517. Some modern scholars believe that event never happened, meaning all the subsequent dramatic and artistic renderings of it rest on myth.

In any case, Luther intended the theses for academic debate. By December 1517, they had been translated into German and were read throughout the empire.

Luther firmly rejected the notion that salvation could be achieved by good works, such as indulgences. Some of his theses challenged the pope's power to grant indulgences, and others criticized papal wealth. Immediately, broad theological issues were raised. When questioned, Luther rested his fundamental argument on the principle that there was no biblical basis for indulgences. But, replied Luther's opponents, to deny the legality of indulgences was to deny the authority of the pope who had authorized them. The issue was drawn: where did authority lie in the Christian church?

Through 1518 and 1519, Luther studied the history of the papacy. In 1519 in a large public disputation with Catholic debater John Eck at Leipzig, Luther denied both the authority of the pope and the infallibility of a general council. The Council of Constance, he said, had erred when it had condemned Jan Hus (see page 395).

The papacy responded with a letter condemning some of Luther's propositions, ordering that his books be burned, and giving him two months to recant or be excommunicated. Luther retaliated by publicly burning the letter. By January 3, 1521, when the excommunication was supposed to become final, the controversy involved more than theological issues. The papal legate wrote, "All Germany is in revolution. Nine-tenths shout 'Luther' as their war cry; and the other tenth cares nothing about Luther, and cries 'Death to the court of Rome.'"[3]

In this highly charged atmosphere, the twenty-one-year-old emperor Charles V held his first diet (assembly of the Estates of the empire) at Worms and summoned Luther to appear before it. When ordered to recant, Luther replied in language that rang all over Europe:

> *Unless I am convinced by the evidence of Scripture or by plain reason—for I do not accept the authority of the Pope or the councils alone, since it is established that they have often erred and contradicted themselves—I am bound by the Scriptures I have cited and my conscience is captive to the Word of God. I cannot and will not recant anything, for it is neither safe nor right to go against conscience. God help me. Amen.*[4]

When Charles V declared Luther an outlaw, meaning he was denied legal protection, Duke Frederick of Saxony protected him.

Meanwhile, the Swiss humanist and admirer of Erasmus, Ulrich Zwingli (1484–1531), introduced the reformation in Switzerland. Elected People's Priest at the New Minster in Zurich, Zwingli first mounted the pulpit on January 1, 1519, and announced that he would preach not from the church's prescribed readings but, relying on Erasmus's New Testament, go right through the New Testament "from A to Z," that is, from Matthew to Revelations. Zwingli was convinced that Christian life rested on the Scriptures, which were the pure words of God and the sole basis of religious truth. He went on to attack indulgences, the Mass, the institution of monasticism, and clerical celibacy. In his gradual reform of the church in Zurich, where he remained the rest of his life, he had the strong support of the town's civil authorities. He disagreed, however, with Luther on various theological issues, notably the nature of the Eucharist. The Colloquy of Marburg, summoned in 1529 to unite Protestant opinion, failed to resolve those differences.

Protestant Thought

Between 1520 and 1530, Luther worked out the basic theological tenets that became the articles of faith for his new church and subsequently for all Protestant groups. The word *Protestant* derives from the protest drawn up by a small group of reforming German princes at the Diet of Speyer in 1529. The princes "protested" the decisions of the Catholic majority. At first Protestant meant "Lutheran," but with the appearance of many protesting sects, it became a general term applied to all non-Catholic Christians. Lutheran Protestant thought was officially formulated in the Confession of Augsburg in 1530.

Ernst Troeltsch, a German student of the sociology of religion, has defined Protestantism as a "modification of Catholicism, in which the Catholic formulation

Jerome Bosch: Christ before Pilate. Pilate (right) grasps the pitcher of water as he prepares to wash his hands. The peasant faces around Christ are vicious, grotesque, even bestial, perhaps signifying humanity's stupidity and blindness. Notice the duncecap on one man, Christ's embroidered undergarment, the nose and lip rings on some faces. *(The Art Museum, Princeton University. Gift of Allan Marquand)*

of questions was retained, while a different answer was given to them." Luther provided new answers to four old, basic theological issues.

First, how is a person to be saved? Traditional Catholic teaching held that salvation is achieved by both faith and good works. Luther held that salvation comes by faith alone. Women and men are saved, said Luther, by the arbitrary decision of God, irrespective of good works or the sacraments. God, not people, initiates salvation.

Second, where does religious authority reside? Christian doctrine had long maintained that authority rests both in the Bible and in the traditional teaching of the church. Luther maintained that authority rests in the Word of God as revealed in the Bible alone and as interpreted by an individual's conscience. (Luther, of course, did not have the advantage of modern biblical research, which has demonstrated that tradition *preceded* the writing of the New Testament—that is, the New Testament is not exactly contemporaneous with

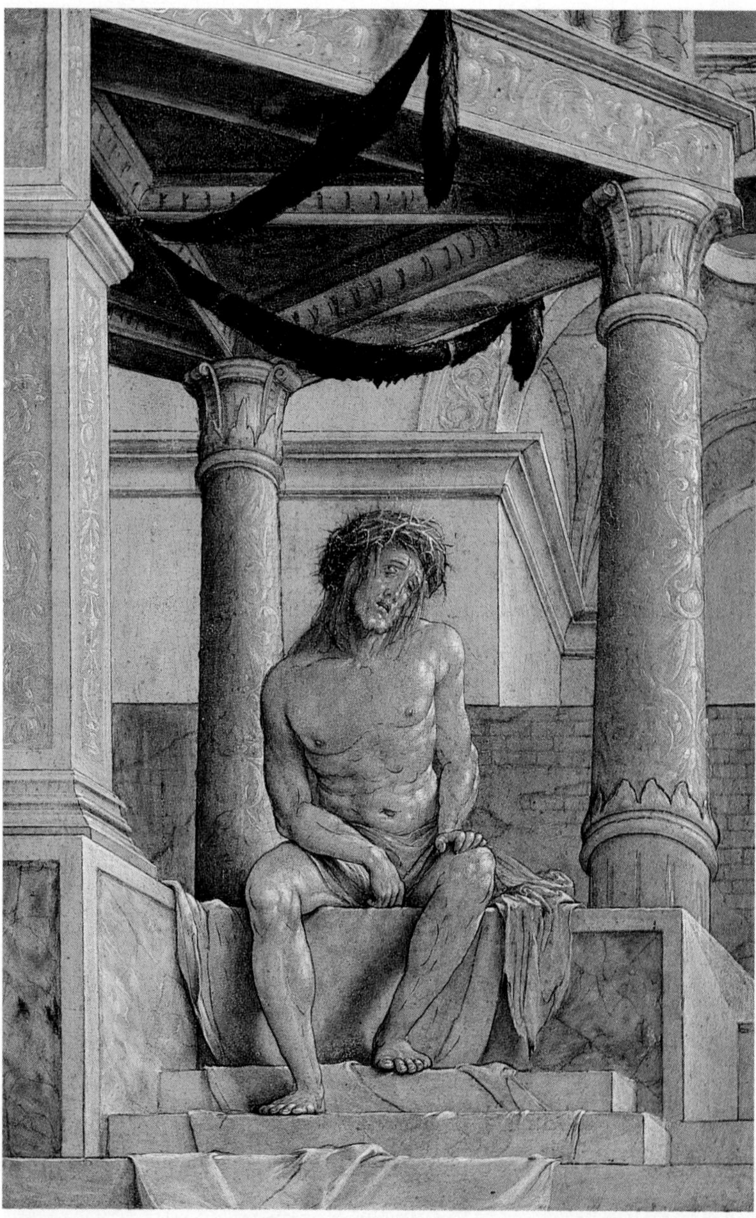

Hans Holbein the Younger: Christ as the Man of Sorrows The scriptural foundation for this concept rests on Isaiah 53:3–5: "He was pierced for our offenses, crushed by our sins. Upon him was the chastisement that makes us whole, by his stripes we were healed." Using a theme characteristic of early-sixteenth-century German piety, and placing the subject within a Renaissance architectural structure, Holbein produced this devotional painting in 1520 for the private use of the donor. (*Öffentliche Kunstsammlung Basel)*

Jesus but is based on the traditional understanding of his life and teachings current in first-century Christian communities.) He urged that each person read and reflect on the Scriptures.

Third, what is the church? Luther re-emphasized the Catholic teaching that the church consists of the entire community of Christian believers. Medieval churchmen, however, had tended to identify the church with the clergy.

Fourth, what is the highest form of Christian life? The medieval church had stressed the superiority of the monastic and religious life over the secular. Luther argued that all vocations have equal merit, whether ecclesiastical or secular, and that every person should serve God in his or her individual calling.[5]

As Protestant thought developed, it differed from Roman Catholic teaching on several other fundamental issues. Luther's idea of the church as a spiritual *priesthood of all believers,* an invisible fellowship not fixed in any place or person, differed markedly from the Roman Catholic practice of a clerical, hierarchical institution headed by the pope in Rome. Because faith required no institutional structure, Luther stressed the invisibility of the church. Whereas Catholic doctrine holds that there are seven sacraments (see Chapter 10), Luther believed that the Scriptures support only three sacraments—baptism, penance, and the Eucharist, or Lord's Supper. Protestant sects, as they emerged, developed a theology of the Eucharist, because it is an important source of grace. Catholics hold the dogma of *transubstantiation:* by the consecrating words of the priest during the Mass, the bread and wine become the actual body and blood of Christ, who is then fully present in the bread and wine. In opposition, Luther defined *consubstantiation,* the belief that after consecration the bread and wine undergo a spiritual change whereby Christ is really present (the Real Presence) but the bread and wine are not transformed. Swiss reformer Ulrich Zwingli affirmed that the Lord's Supper is a *memorial* of the Last Supper and that no change whatever occurs in the elements. John Calvin believed that the body and blood of Christ are spiritually but not physically present in the bread and wine, and they are consumed spiritually. Catholics and Protestants agreed that the sacrament must be received worthily and that it is a source of grace.

The Social Impact of Luther's Beliefs

As early as 1521, Luther had a vast following. Every encounter he had with ecclesiastical or political authorities attracted attention. Pulpits and printing presses spread his message all over Germany. By the time of his death, people of all social classes had become Lutheran. What was the immense appeal of Luther's religious ideas?

Recent historical research on the German towns has shown that two significant late medieval developments prepared the way for Luther's ideas. First, since the fifteenth century, city governments had expressed resentment of clerical privileges and immunities. Priests, monks, and nuns paid no taxes and were exempt from civic responsibilities, such as defending the city. Yet religious orders frequently held large amounts of urban property. At Zurich in 1467, for example, religious orders held one-third of the city's taxable property. City governments were determined to integrate the clergy into civic life by reducing their privileges and giving them public responsibilities. Accordingly, the Zurich magistracy subjected the religious to taxes, inspected wills so that legacies to the church and legacies left by churchmen could be controlled, and placed priests and monks under the jurisdiction of the civil courts.

Second, critics of the late medieval church, especially informed and intelligent townspeople, condemned the irregularity and poor quality of sermons. As a result, prosperous burghers in many towns established preacherships. Preachers were men of superior education who were required to deliver about a hundred sermons a year, each lasting about forty-five minutes. Endowed preacherships had important consequences after 1517. Luther's ideas attracted many preachers, and in such towns as Stuttgart, Reutlingen, Eisenach, and Jena, preachers became Protestant leaders. Preacherships also encouraged the Protestant form of worship, in which the sermon, not the Eucharist, was the central part of the service.[6]

In the countryside, the attraction of the German peasants to Lutheran beliefs was predictable. Luther himself came from a peasant background, and he admired the peasants' ceaseless toil. For their part, peasants respected Luther's defiance of church authority. Moreover, they thrilled to the words Luther used in his treatise *On Christian Liberty* (1520): "A Christian man is the most free lord of all and subject to none." Taken by themselves, these words easily contributed to social unrest.

Fifteenth-century Germany had witnessed several peasant revolts. In the early sixteenth century, the economic condition of the peasantry varied from place to place but was generally worse than it had been in the fifteenth century and was deteriorating. Crop failures in 1523 and 1524 aggravated an explosive situation. In

German Burgher Domestic Scene With what Jesus called the greatest commandment ("You shall love the Lord your God with all your heart and all your soul and your neighbor as yourself" [Deut. 6, Matt. 22]) inscribed on tablets over the room, a German family begins a meal. The father listens as his son says the grace, mother passes bread, older daughters seem to have begun eating, and a small child biting a chicken drumstick seems dangerously close to the fire. The little dog begs for food; the cat laps milk. *(Mary Evans Picture Library)*

1525 representatives of the Swabian peasants met at the city of Memmingen and drew up the Twelve Articles, which expressed their grievances. The Twelve Articles condemned lay and ecclesiastical lords and summarized the agrarian crisis of the early sixteenth century. The articles complained that nobles had seized village common lands, which traditionally had been used by all; that they had imposed new rents on manorial properties and new services on the peasants working those properties; and that they had forced the poor to pay unjust death duties in the form of the peasants' best horses or cows. Wealthy, socially mobile peasants especially resented these burdens, which they emphasized as new.[7] The peasants believed their demands conformed to the Scriptures and cited Luther as a theologian who could prove that they did.

Luther wanted to prevent rebellion. Initially he sided with the peasants, and in his tract *An Admonition to Peace* (1525) he blasted the lords:

We have no one on earth to thank for this mischievous rebellion, except you lords and princes, especially you blind bishops and mad priests and monks. . . . In your government you do nothing but flay and rob your subjects in order that you may lead a life of splendor and pride, until the poor common folk can bear it no longer.[8]

But, he warned, nothing justified the use of armed force: "The fact that rulers are unjust and wicked does not excuse tumult and rebellion; to punish wickedness does not belong to everybody, but to the worldly rulers who bear the sword." As for biblical support for the peasants' demands, he maintained that Scripture had nothing to do with earthly justice or material gain.[9]

Massive revolts first broke out near the Swiss frontier and then swept through Swabia, Thuringia, the Rhineland, and Saxony. The crowds' slogans came directly from Luther's writings. "God's righteousness" and the "Word of God" were invoked in an effort to secure social and economic justice. The peasants who expected Luther's support were soon disillusioned. He had written of the "freedom" of the Christian, but he had meant the freedom to obey the Word of God, for in sin men and women lose their freedom and break their relationship with God. Freedom for Luther meant independence from the authority of the Roman church; it did *not* mean opposition to legally established secular powers. Firmly convinced that rebellion hastened the end of civilized society, he wrote the tract *Against the Murderous, Thieving Hordes of the Peasants:* "Let everyone who can smite, slay, and stab [the peasants], secretly and openly, remembering that nothing can be more poisonous, hurtful or devilish than a rebel."[10] The nobility ferociously crushed the revolt. Historians estimate that over seventy-five thousand peasants were killed in 1525.

Luther took literally these words of Saint Paul's Letter to the Romans: "Let every soul be subject to the higher powers. For there is no power but of God: the powers that be are established by God. Whosoever resists the power, resists the ordinance of God: and they that resist shall receive to themselves damnation."[11] As Lutheran theology developed, it exalted the state, subordinated the church to the state, and everywhere championed "the powers that be." The consequences for German society were profound and have redounded into the twentieth century. The revolt of 1525 greatly strengthened the authority of lay rulers. Peasant economic conditions, however, moderately improved. For example, in many parts of Germany, enclosed fields, meadows, and forests were returned to common use.

Scholars in many disciplines have attributed Luther's fame and success to the invention of the printing press, which rapidly reproduced and made known his ideas. Equally important was Luther's incredible skill with language. Some thinkers have lavished praise on the Wittenberg reformer; others have bitterly condemned him. But in the words of psychologist Erik Erikson:

> *The one matter on which professor and priest, psychiatrist and sociologist, agree is Luther's immense gift for language: his receptivity for the written word; his memory for the significant phrase; and his range of verbal expression (lyrical, biblical, satirical, and vulgar) which in English is paralleled only by Shakespeare.*[12]

Language proved to be the weapon with which this peasant's son changed the world.

Like the peasants, educated people and humanists were much attracted by Luther's words. He advocated a simpler, personal religion based on faith, a return to the spirit of the early church, the centrality of the Scriptures in the liturgy and in Christian life, and the abolition of elaborate ceremonies—precisely the reforms the northern humanists had been calling for. Nobleman Ulrich von Hutten (1488–1523), who had published several humanistic tracts, in 1519 dedicated his life to the advancement of Luther's Reformation. And Frenchman John Calvin (1509–1564), often called the organizer of Protestantism, owed a great deal to Luther's thought.

Luther's linguistic skill, together with his translation of the New Testament into German in 1523, led to the acceptance of his dialect of German as the standard version of German. His insistence that everyone should read and reflect on the Scriptures attracted the literate and thoughtful middle classes partly because Luther appealed to their intelligence. Moreover, the business classes, preoccupied with making money, envied the church's wealth, disapproved of the luxurious lifestyle of some churchmen, and resented tithes and ecclesiastical taxation. Luther's doctrines of salvation by faith and the priesthood of all believers not only raised the religious status of the commercial classes but also protected their pocketbooks.

Hymns, psalms, and Luther's two catechisms (1529), compendiums of basic religious knowledge, also show the power of language in spreading the ideals of the Reformation. The reformers knew "that rhyme, meter, and melodies could forcefully impress minds and affect sensibilities." Such hymns as the famous "A Mighty Fortress Is Our God" expressed deep human feelings, were easily remembered, and imprinted on the mind central points of doctrine. Luther's *Larger Catechism* contained brief sermons on the main articles of faith, whereas the *Shorter Catechism* gave concise explanations of doctrine in question-and-answer form. Both catechisms stressed the importance of the Ten Commandments, the Lord's Prayer, the Apostle's Creed, and the sacraments for the believing Christian. Although originally intended for the instruction of pastors, these catechisms became powerful techniques for the indoctrination of men and women of all ages, especially the young.[13]

What appeal did Luther's message have for women? Luther's argument that all vocations have equal merit in the sight of God gave dignity to those who performed ordinary, routine, domestic tasks. The abolition of monasticism in Protestant territories led to the exaltation of the home, which Luther and other reformers stressed as the special domain of the wife. The Christian home, in contrast to the place of business, became the place for the exercise of the gentler virtues—love, tenderness, reconciliation, the carrying of one another's burdens. The Protestant abolition of private confession to a priest freed women from embarrassing explorations of their sexual lives and activities. Protestants established schools where girls as well as boys became literate in the catechism and the Bible. Finally, the reformers stressed marriage as the cure for clerical concupiscence. Protestantism thus proved attractive to the many women who had been priests' concubines and mistresses: now they became legal and honorable wives.[14]

For his time, Luther held enlightened views on matters of sexuality and marriage. He wrote a letter to a young man, "Dear lad, be not ashamed that you desire a girl, nor you my maid, the boy. Just let it lead you into matrimony and not into promiscuity, and it is no more cause for shame than eating and drinking."[15] Luther was confident that God took delight in the sexual act and denied that original sin affected the goodness of creation. He believed, however, that marriage was a woman's career. A student recorded Luther as saying early in his public ministry, "Let them bear children until they are dead of it; that is what they are for." A happy marriage to ex-nun Katharine von Bora mellowed him, and another student later quoted him as saying, "Next to God's Word there is no more precious treasure than holy matrimony. God's highest gift on earth is a pious, cheerful, God-fearing, home-keeping wife, with whom you may live peacefully, to whom you may entrust your goods, and body and life."[16] Though Luther deeply loved his "dear Katie," he believed that women's concerns revolved exclusively around the children, the kitchen, and the church. A happy woman was a patient wife, an efficient manager, and a good mother. Kate was an excellent financial manager (which Luther—much inclined to give money and goods away—was not). Himself a stern, if often indulgent, father, Luther held that the father should rule the household, while the wife controlled its economy. With many relatives and constant visitors, Luther's home was a large and happy household, certainly a model for Protestants, if an abomination for Catholics. The wives of other reformers, though they exercised no leadership role in the reform, shared their husbands' work and concerns.

Germany and the Protestant Reformation

The history of the Holy Roman Empire in the late Middle Ages is a story of dissension, disintegration, and debility. Unlike Spain, France, and England, the empire lacked a strong central power. The Golden Bull of 1356 legalized what had long existed—government by an aristocratic federation. Each of seven electors—the archbishops of Mainz, Trier, and Cologne, the margrave of Brandenburg, the duke of Saxony, the count palatine of the Rhine, and the king of Bohemia—gained virtual sovereignty in his own territory. The agreement ended disputed elections in the empire; it also reduced the central authority of the emperor. Germany was characterized by weak borders, localism, and chronic disorder. The nobility strengthened its hold on its territories, while imperial power declined.

Against this background of decentralization and strong local power, Martin Luther had launched a movement to reform the church. Two years after Luther published the Ninety-five Theses, the electors chose as emperor a nineteen-year-old Habsburg prince who ruled as Charles V. Luther's interests and motives were primarily religious, but many people responded to his teachings for political, social, or economic reasons. How did the goals and interests of the emperor influence the course of the Reformation in Germany? What impact did the upheaval in the Christian church have on the political condition in Germany?

The Rise of the Habsburg Dynasty

The marriage in 1477 of Maximilian I of the house of Habsburg and Mary of Burgundy was a decisive event in early modern European history. Burgundy consisted of two parts: the French duchy, with its capital at Dijon, and the Burgundian Netherlands, with its capital at Brussels. Through this union with the rich and powerful duchy of Burgundy, the Austrian house of Habsburg, already the strongest ruling family in the empire, became an international power.

In the fifteenth and sixteenth centuries, as in the Middle Ages, relations among states continued to be

THE HERITAGE OF CHARLES V

Maximilian I of Habsburg (r. 1493–1519) — Mary of Burgundy
Ferdinand of Aragon — Isabella of Castile
Philip of Burgundy — Joanna of Castile
Catherine of Aragon — Henry VIII King of England
Charles V (r. 1519–1556)
Philip II (r. 1556–1598) — Mary Tudor

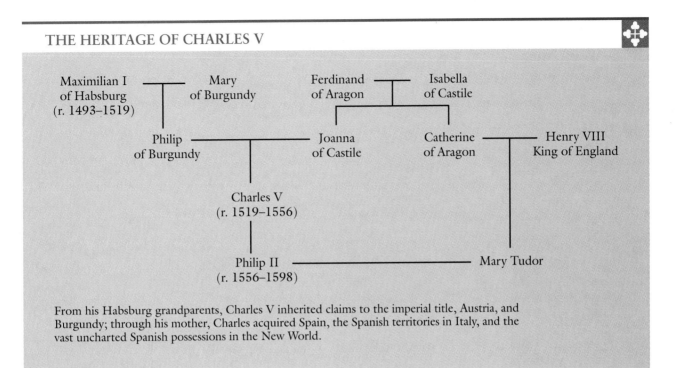

From his Habsburg grandparents, Charles V inherited claims to the imperial title, Austria, and Burgundy; through his mother, Charles acquired Spain, the Spanish territories in Italy, and the vast uncharted Spanish possessions in the New World.

greatly affected by the connections of royal families. Marriage often determined the diplomatic status of states. The Habsburg-Burgundian marriage angered the French, who considered Burgundy part of French territory and had lusted after the Burgundian Netherlands (Flanders) for centuries. Louis XI of France repeatedly ravaged parts of the Burgundian Netherlands until he was able to force Maximilian to accept French terms: the Treaty of Arras (1482) declared French Burgundy a part of the kingdom of France. The Habsburgs, however, never really renounced their claim to Burgundy, and intermittent warfare over it continued between France and Maximilian. But Louis could not conquer it. It remained outside French control (see Chapters 15 and 16). Within the empire, German principalities that resented Austria's pre-eminence began to see that they shared interests with France. The marriage of Maximilian and Mary inaugurated centuries of conflict between the Austrian house of Habsburg and the kings of France. And Germany was to be the chief arena of the struggle.

"Other nations wage war; you, Austria, marry." Historians dispute the origins of this adage, but no one questions its accuracy. The heir of Mary and Maximilian, Philip of Burgundy, married Joanna of Castile, daughter of Ferdinand and Isabella of Spain. Philip and Joanna's son Charles V (1500–1558) fell heir to a vast conglomeration of territories. Through a series of accidents and unexpected deaths, Charles inherited Spain from his mother, together with her possessions in the New World and the Spanish dominions in Italy, Sicily, Sardinia, and Naples. From his father he inherited the Habsburg lands in Austria, southern Germany, the Low Countries, and Franche-Comté in east-central France.

Charles's inheritance was an incredibly diverse collection of states and peoples, each governed in a different manner and held together only by the person of the emperor (Map 14.1). Charles's Italian adviser, the grand chancellor Gattinara, told the young ruler, "God has set you on the path toward world monarchy." Charles not only believed this, but also was convinced that it was his duty to maintain the political and religious unity of Western Christendom. In this respect, Charles V was the last medieval emperor.

Charles needed and in 1519 secured the imperial title. Forward-thinking Germans proposed governmental reforms. They urged placing the administration in the hands of an imperial council whose president, the emperor's appointee, would have ultimate executive power. Reforms of the imperial finances, the army, and the judiciary were also recommended. Such ideas did not interest the young emperor at all. When he finally

MAP 14.1 The European Empire of Charles V Charles V exercised theoretical jurisdiction over more territory than anyone since Charlemagne. This map does not show his Latin American possessions.

arrived in Germany from Spain and opened his first diet at Worms in January 1521, he naively announced that "the empire from of old has had not many masters, but one, and it is our intention to be that one." Charles went on to say that he was to be treated as of greater account than his predecessors because he was more powerful than they had been. In view of the long history of aristocratic power, Charles's notions were pure fantasy. He continued the Burgundian policy of his grandfather Maximilian. That is, German revenues and German troops were subordinated to the needs of other parts of the empire, first Burgundy and then Spain. Habsburg international interests came before the need for reform in Germany.

The Political Impact of Luther's Beliefs

In the sixteenth century, the practice of religion remained a public matter. Everyone participated in the religious life of the community, just as almost everyone shared in the local agricultural work. Whatever spiritual convictions individuals held in the privacy of their consciences, the emperor, king, prince, magistrate, or other civil authority determined the official form of religious practice within his jurisdiction. Almost everyone believed that the presence of a faith different from that of the majority represented a political threat to the security of the state. Only a tiny minority, and certainly none of the princes, believed in religious liberty.

Against this background, the religious storm launched by Martin Luther swept across Germany. Several elements in his religious reformation stirred patriotic feelings. Anti-Roman sentiment ran high. Humanists lent eloquent intellectual support. And Luther's translation of the New Testament evoked national pride.

For decades devout laypeople and churchmen had called on the German princes to reform the church. In 1520 Luther took up the cry in his *Appeal to the Christian Nobility of the German Nation.* Unless the princes destroyed papal power in Germany, Luther argued, reform was impossible. He urged the princes to confiscate ecclesiastical wealth and to abolish indulgences, dispensations, pardons, and clerical celibacy. He told them that it was their public duty to bring about the moral reform of the church. Luther based his argument in part on the papacy's financial exploitation of Germany:

How comes it that we Germans must put up with such robbery and such extortion of our property at the hands of the pope? If the Kingdom of France has prevented it, why do we Germans let them make such fools and apes of us? It would all be more bearable if in this way they only stole our property; but they lay waste the churches and rob Christ's sheep of their pious shepherds, and destroy the worship and the Word of God. As it is they do nothing for the good of Christendom; they only wrangle about the incomes of bishoprics and prelacies, and that any robber could do.[17]

These words fell on welcome ears and itchy fingers. Luther's appeal to German patriotism gained him strong support, and national feeling influenced many princes otherwise confused by or indifferent to the complexities of the religious issues.

The church in Germany possessed great wealth. And unlike other countries, Germany had no strong central government to check the flow of gold to Rome. Rejection of Roman Catholicism and adoption of Protestantism would mean the legal confiscation of lush farmlands, rich monasteries, and wealthy shrines. Some German princes, such as the prince-archbishop of Cologne, Hermann von Wied, were sincerely attracted to Lutheranism, but many civil authorities realized that they had a great deal to gain by embracing the new faith. A steady stream of duchies, margraviates, free cities, and bishoprics secularized church property, accepted Lutheran theological doctrines, and adopted simpler services conducted in German. The decision reached at Worms in 1521 to condemn Luther and his teaching was not enforced because the German princes did not want to enforce it.

Charles V was a vigorous defender of Catholicism, and contemporary social and political theory denied the possibility of two religions coexisting peacefully in one territory. Thus many princes used the religious issue to extend their financial and political independence. When doctrinal differences became linked to political ambitions and financial receipts, the results were unfortunate for the improvement of German government. The Protestant movement ultimately proved a political disaster for Germany.

Charles V must share blame with the German princes for the disintegration of imperial authority in the empire. He neither understood nor took an interest in the constitutional problems of Germany, and he lacked the material resources to oppose Protestantism effectively there. Throughout his reign, he was preoccupied with his Flemish, Spanish, Italian, and American territories. Moreover, the Turkish threat prevented him from acting effectively against the Protestants; Charles's brother, Ferdinand, needed Protestant support against the Turks who besieged Vienna in 1529.

Fresco of Pope Clement VII and the Emperor Charles V by Giorgio Vasari. Since Vasari's *Lives of the Most Eminent Italian Painters, Architects, Painters, and Sculptors* (rev. ed. 1568), still the basic historical source for Renaissance art and culture, held that "art is the imitation of nature," we may assume that these are faithful likenesses of the Medici pope and the Holy Roman Emperor. *(Alinari/Art Resource, NY)*

Five times between 1521 and 1555, Charles V went to war with the Valois kings of France. The issue each time was the Habsburg lands acquired by the marriage of Maximilian and Mary of Burgundy. Much of the fighting occurred in Germany. The cornerstone of French foreign policy in the sixteenth and seventeenth centuries was the desire to keep the German states divided. Thus Europe witnessed the paradox of the Catholic king of France supporting the Lutheran princes in their challenge to his fellow Catholic, Charles V. French foreign policy contributed to the continuing division of Germany. The long dynastic struggle commonly called the Habsburg-Valois Wars advanced the cause of Protestantism and promoted the political fragmentation of the German Empire.

Finally, in 1555 Charles agreed to the Peace of Augsburg, which, in accepting the status quo, officially recognized Lutheranism. Each prince was permitted to determine his territory's religion. Most of northern and central Germany became Lutheran, while the south remained Roman Catholic. There was no freedom of religion, however. Princes or town councils established state churches to which all subjects of the area had to belong. Dissidents, whether Lutheran or Catholic, had to convert or leave. The political difficulties Germany inherited from the Middle Ages had been compounded by the religious crisis of the sixteenth century.

The Growth of the Protestant Reformation

By 1555 much of northern Europe had broken with the Roman Catholic church. All of Scandinavia, England (except under Mary Tudor), Scotland, and such self-governing cities as Geneva and Zurich in Switzerland and Strasbourg in Germany had rejected the religious authority of Rome and adopted new faiths. Because a common religious faith had been the one element uniting all of Europe for almost a thousand years, the fragmentation of belief led to profound changes in European life and society. The most significant new form of Protestantism was Calvinism, of which the Peace of Augsburg had made no mention at all.

Calvinism

In 1509 while Luther was studying for a doctorate at Wittenberg, John Calvin (1509–1564) was born in Noyon in northwestern France. Luther inadvertently launched the Protestant Reformation. Calvin, however, had the greater impact on future generations. His theological writings profoundly influenced the social thought and attitudes of Europeans and English-speaking peoples all over the world, especially in Canada and the United States. Although he had originally intended to have an ecclesiastical career, Calvin studied law, which had a decisive impact on his mind and later thought. In 1533 he experienced a religious crisis, as a result of which he converted to Protestantism.

Convinced that God selects certain people to do his work, Calvin believed that God had specifically called him to reform the church. Accordingly, he accepted an invitation to assist in the reformation of the city of Geneva. There, beginning in 1541, Calvin worked assiduously to establish a Christian society ruled by God through civil magistrates and reformed ministers. Geneva, "a city that was a Church," became the model of a Christian community for sixteenth-century Protestant reformers.

To understand Calvin's Geneva, it is necessary to understand Calvin's ideas. These he embodied in *The Institutes of the Christian Religion,* first published in 1536 and definitively issued in 1559. The cornerstone of Calvin's theology was his belief in the absolute sovereignty and omnipotence of God and the total weakness of humanity. Before the infinite power of God, he asserted, men and women are as insignificant as grains of sand.

Calvin did not ascribe free will to human beings because that would detract from the sovereignty of God. Men and women cannot actively work to achieve salvation; rather, God in his infinite wisdom decided at the beginning of time who would be saved and who damned. This viewpoint constitutes the theological principle called *predestination:*

Predestination we call the eternal decree of God, by which he has determined in himself, what he would have become of every individual. . . . For they are not all created with a similar destiny; but eternal life is foreordained for some, and eternal damnation for others. . . . In conformity, therefore, to the clear doctrine of the Scripture, we assert, that by an eternal and immutable counsel, God has once for all determined, both whom he would admit to salvation, and whom he would condemn to destruction. We affirm that this counsel, as far as concerns the elect, is founded on his gratuitous mercy, totally irrespective of human merit; but that to those whom he devotes to condemnation, the gate of life is closed by a just and irreprehensible, but incomprehensible, judgment. How exceedingly presumptuous it is only to inquire into the causes of the Divine will; which is in fact, and is justly entitled to be, the cause of everything that exists. . . . For the will of God is the highest justice; so that what he wills must be considered just, for this very reason, because he wills it.[18]

Many people have found the doctrine of predestination, which dates back to Saint Augustine and Saint Paul, a pessimistic view of the nature of God, who, they feel, revealed himself in the Old and New Testaments as merciful as well as just. But "this terrible decree," as

John Calvin The lean, ascetic face with the strong jaw reflects the iron will and determination of the organizer of Protestantism. The fur collar represents his training in law. *(Bibliothèque Nationale/Snark/Art Resource, NY)*

Calvinist Worship A converted house in Lyons, France, serves as a church for the simple Calvinist service. Although Calvin's followers believed in equality and elected officials administered the church, here men and women are segregated, and some people sit on hard benches while others sit in upholstered pews. Beside the pulpit an hourglass hangs to time the preacher's sermon. (Could the dog sit still for that long?) *(Bibliothèque publique et universitaire, Geneva)*

even Calvin called it, did not lead to pessimism or fatalism. Rather, the Calvinist believed in the redemptive work of Christ and was confident that God had elected (saved) him or her. Predestination served as an energizing dynamic, forcing a person to undergo hardships in the constant struggle against evil.

Calvin aroused Genevans to a high standard of morality. He had two remarkable assets: complete mastery of the Scriptures and exceptional eloquence. Through his sermons and a program of religious education, God's laws and man's were enforced in Geneva. Calvin's powerful sermons delivered the Word of God and thereby monopolized the strongest contemporary means of communication: preaching. Through his *Genevan Catechism,* published in 1541, children and adults memorized set questions and answers and acquired a summary of their faith and a guide for daily living. Calvin's sermons and his *Catechism* gave a whole generation of Genevans thorough instruction in the reformed religion.[19]

In the reformation of the city, the Genevan Consistory also exercised a powerful role. This body consisted of twelve laymen plus the Company of Pastors, of which Calvin was the permanent moderator (presider). The duties of the Consistory were "to keep watch over every man's life [and] to admonish amiably those whom they see leading a disorderly life." Even though Calvin emphasized that the Consistory's activities should be thorough and "its eyes may be everywhere," corrections were considered only "medicine to turn sinners to the Lord."[20] (See the feature "Listening to the Past: Calvin's Vision for Christian Renewal" on pages 484–485.)

Although all municipal governments in early modern Europe regulated citizens' conduct, none did so with the severity of Geneva's Consistory under Calvin's leadership. Nor did it make any distinction between what we would consider crimes against society and simple un-Christian conduct. Absence from sermons, criticism of ministers, dancing, card playing, family quarrels, and heavy drinking were all investigated and punished by the Consistory. Serious crimes and heresy were handled by the civil authorities, which, with the Consistory's approval, sometimes used torture to extract confessions. Between 1542 and 1546 alone, seventy-six persons were banished from Geneva and fifty-eight executed for heresy, adultery, blasphemy, and witchcraft.

Calvin reserved his harshest condemnation for religious dissenters, declaring them "dogs and swine":

God makes plain that the false prophet is to be stoned without mercy. We are to crush beneath our heel all affections of nature when His honor is concerned. The father should not spare his child, . . . nor husband his own wife or the friend who is dearer to him than life. No human relationship is more than animal unless it be grounded in God.[21]

In the 1550s, Spanish humanist Michael Servetus had gained international notoriety for his publications denying the Christian dogma of the Trinity. Servetus had been arrested by the Inquisition but escaped to Geneva, where he was promptly rearrested. At his trial, he not only held to his belief that there is no Scriptural basis for the Trinity but also rejected child baptism and insisted that a person under twenty cannot commit a mortal sin. The city fathers considered this last idea dangerous to public morality, "especially in these days when the young are so corrupted." Though Servetus begged that he be punished by banishment, Calvin and the town council maintained that the denial of child baptism and the Trinity amounted to a threat to all society. Servetus was burned at the stake.

To many sixteenth-century Europeans, Calvin's Geneva seemed "the most perfect school of Christ since the days of the Apostles." Religious refugees from France, England, Spain, Scotland, and Italy visited the city. Subsequently, the Reformed church of Calvin served as the model for the Presbyterian church in Scotland, the Huguenot church in France, and the Puritan churches in England and New England. For women, the Calvinist provision for congregational participation and vernacular liturgy helped satisfy their desire to belong to and participate in a meaningful church organization.

On women the views of reformers such as Calvin did not differ much from those of medieval Scholastic theologians. Protestants exalted marriage, stressing the husband's authority over his family and the wife's duty of obedience to her husband. Marriage provided the outlet for women's sexual urges, which reformers believed were stronger than men's. The reformers looked with considerable suspicion on unmarried women, because they were fighting their natural sexual desires and because they were upsetting the natural order. Calvin and other reformers did not distinguish between noblewomen and commoners, but they recognized that noblewomen had influence and power. Thus Calvin maintained a large correspondence with them and worked hard to persuade Marguerite d'Angoulême and her daughter Jeanne of Navarre to support the Calvinist cause. Most women expressed their religious feelings in a domestic setting—praying, reciting the catechism, and reading the Bible with their children and servants. As public welfare, long the responsibility of local Catholic institutions, became secularized, well-to-do Protestant women aided the poor on a case-by-case basis; some wealthy women founded and endowed schools, orphanages, and dowries for girls and provided funds for poor widows. Women's charitable interests focused specifically on other women.[22]

Calvinism became the compelling force in international Protestantism. The Calvinist ethic of the "calling" dignified all work with a religious aspect. Hard work, well done, was pleasing to God. This doctrine encouraged an aggressive, vigorous activism. In *The Institutes,* Calvin provided a systematic theology for Protestantism. The Reformed church of Calvin had a strong and well-organized machinery of government. These factors, together with the social and economic applications of Calvin's theology, made Calvinism the most dynamic force in sixteenth- and seventeenth-century Protestantism.

The Anabaptists

The name *Anabaptist* derives from a Greek word meaning "to baptize again." The Anabaptists, sometimes described as the "left wing of the Reformation," believed that only adults could make a free choice about religious faith, baptism, and entry into the Christian community. Thus they considered the practice of baptizing infants and children preposterous and claimed there was no Scriptural basis for it. They wanted to rebaptize believers who had been baptized as children. Anabaptists took the Gospel and, at first, Luther's teachings absolutely literally and favored a return to the kind of church that they thought had existed among the earliest Christians—a voluntary association of believers who had experienced an inner light.

Anabaptists maintained that only a few people would receive the inner light. This position meant that the Christian community and the Christian state were not identical. In other words, Anabaptists believed in religious toleration. They almost never tried to force their values on others. In an age that believed in the necessity of state-established churches, Anabaptist views on religious liberty were thought to undermine that concept.

Each Anabaptist community or church was entirely independent; it selected its own ministers and ran its own affairs. In 1534 the community at Münster in Germany, for example, established a legal code that decreed the death penalty for insubordinate wives. Moreover, the Münster community also practiced polygamy and forced all women under a certain age to marry or face expulsion or execution. Münster, however, was not typical of Anabaptism.

Anabaptists admitted women to the ministry. They shared goods as the early Christians had done, refused all public offices, and would not serve in the armed forces. In fact, they laid great stress on pacifism. A favorite Anabaptist Scriptural quotation was "By their fruits you shall know them," suggesting that if Christianity was a religion of peace, then the Christian should not fight. Good deeds were the sign of Christian faith, and to be a Christian meant to imitate the meekness and mercy of Christ. With such beliefs Anabaptists were inevitably a minority. Anabaptism later attracted the poor, the unemployed, and the uneducated. Geographically, Anabaptists drew their members from depressed urban areas—from among the followers of Zwingli in Zurich and from Basel, Augsburg, and Nuremberg.

Ideas such as absolute pacifism and the distinction between the Christian community and the state brought down on these unfortunate people fanatical hatred and bitter persecution. Zwingli, Luther, Calvin, and Catholics all saw—quite correctly—the separation of church and state as leading ultimately to the complete secularization of society. The powerful rulers of Swiss and German society immediately saw the connection between religious heresy and economic dislocation. Civil authorities feared that the combination of religious differences and economic grievances would lead to civil disturbances. In Saxony, in Strasbourg, and in the Swiss cities, Anabaptists were either banished or cruelly executed by burning, beating, or drowning. Their community spirit and the edifying example of their lives, however, contributed to the survival of Anabaptist ideas. Later, the Quakers, with their gentle pacifism; the Baptists, with their emphasis on an inner spiritual light; the Congregationalists, with their democratic church organization; and, in 1787, the authors of the U.S. Constitution, with their opposition to the "establishment of religion" (state churches), would all trace their origins, in part, to the Anabaptists of the sixteenth century.

The English Reformation

As on the continent, the Reformation in England had economic causes as well as religious ones. As elsewhere, too, Christian humanists had for decades been calling for the purification of the church. When the personal matter of the divorce of King Henry VIII (r. 1509–1547) became enmeshed with political issues, a complete break with Rome resulted.

Demands for ecclesiastical reform dated back at least to the fourteenth century. The Lollards (see page 394) had been driven underground in the fifteenth century but survived in parts of southern England and the Midlands. Working-class people, especially cloth workers, were attracted to their ideas. The Lollards stressed the individual's reading and interpretation of the Bible, which they considered the only standard of Christian faith and holiness. Consequently, they put no stock in the value of the sacraments and were vigorously anticlerical. Lollards opposed ecclesiastical wealth, the veneration of the saints, prayers for the dead, and all war. Although they had no notion of justification by faith, like Luther they insisted on the individual soul's direct responsibility to God.

The work of English humanist William Tyndale (1494?–1536) stimulated cries for reform. Tyndale visited Luther at Wittenberg in 1524 and a year later at Antwerp began printing an English translation of the New Testament. From Antwerp, merchants carried the New Testament into England, where it was distributed by Lollards. Fortified with copies of Tyndale's English Bible and some of Luther's ideas, the Lollards represented the ideal of "a personal, scriptural, nonsacramental, and lay-dominated religion."[23] In this manner, doctrines that would later be called Protestant flourished underground in England before any official or state-approved changes. The Lollards, however, represented a very small group.

Recent scholarship indicates that the English church was in a very healthy condition in the early sixteenth century. Traditional Catholicism exerted an enormously strong and vigorous hold over the imagination and loyalty of the people. The teachings of Christianity were graphically represented in the liturgy, reiterated in sermons, enacted in plays, carved and printed on walls, screens, and the windows of churches. A zealous clergy, increasingly better educated, engaged in a "massive catechetical enterprise." No substantial gulf existed between the religion of the clergy and educated elite and the broad mass of the English people.[24] The Reformation in England was an act of state initiated by the king's emotional life.

In 1527, having fallen in love with Anne Boleyn, Henry wanted his marriage to Catherine of Aragon annulled. When Henry had married Catherine, he had secured a dispensation from Pope Julius II eliminating all legal technicalities about Catherine's previous union with Henry's late brother, Arthur (see page 441). Henry claimed that a disputed succession and the anarchy of the Wars of the Roses would be repeated if a woman, the princess Mary, sole surviving child of his marriage to Catherine, inherited the throne. Accordingly, Henry petitioned Pope Clement VII for an annulment, stating that a valid marriage to Catherine had never existed. The pope was an indecisive man whose attention at the time was focused on the Lutheran revolt in Germany and the Habsburg-Valois struggle for control of Italy. But there is a stronger reason Clement could not grant Henry's petition. Henry argued that Pope Julius's dispensation had contradicted the law of God—that a man may not marry his brother's widow. The English king's request reached Rome at the very time that Luther was widely publishing tracts condemning the papacy as the core of wickedness. Had Clement granted Henry's annulment and thereby admitted that his recent predecessor, Julius II, had erred, Clement would have given support to the Lutheran assertion that popes substituted their own evil judgments for the law of God. This Clement could not do, so he delayed acting on Henry's request.[25] The capture and sack of Rome in 1527 by the emperor Charles V (see page 419), Queen Catherine's nephew, thoroughly tied the pope's hands.

Since Rome appeared to be thwarting Henry's matrimonial plans, he decided to remove the English church from papal jurisdiction. Henry used Parliament to legalize the Reformation in England. The Act in Restraint of Appeals (1533) declared the king to be the supreme sovereign in England and forbade judicial appeals to the papacy, thus establishing the Crown as the highest legal authority in the land. The Act for the Submission of the Clergy (1534) required churchmen to submit to the king and forbade the publication of ecclesiastical laws without royal permission. The Supremacy Act (1534) declared the king the supreme head of the Church of England. Both the Act in Restraint of Appeals and the Supremacy Act led to heated debate in the House of Commons. An authority on the Reformation Parliament has written that probably only a small number of those who voted for the Restraint of Appeals actually knew they were voting for a permanent break with Rome.[26] Some opposed the king. John Fisher, the bishop of Rochester, a distinguished scholar and a humanist, lashed the clergy with scorn for its cowardice in abjectly bending to the king's will. Another humanist, Thomas More, resigned the chancellorship: he could not take the oath required by the Supremacy Act because it rejected papal authority and made the king head of the English church. Fisher, More, and other dissenters were beheaded.

When Anne Boleyn failed twice to produce a male child, Henry VIII charged her with adulterous incest and in 1536 had her beheaded. Parliament promptly proclaimed Anne's daughter, the princess Elizabeth, illegitimate and, with the royal succession thoroughly confused, left the throne to whomever Henry chose. His third wife, Jane Seymour, gave Henry the desired son, Edward, but died in childbirth. Henry went on to three more wives. Before he passed to his reward in 1547, he got Parliament to reverse the decision of 1536, relegitimating Mary and Elizabeth and fixing the succession first in his son and then in his daughters.

Between 1535 and 1539, under the influence of his chief minister, Thomas Cromwell, Henry decided to dissolve the English monasteries because he wanted their wealth. The king ended nine hundred years of English monastic life, dispersed the monks and nuns, and confiscated their lands. Hundreds of properties were sold to the middle and upper classes and the proceeds spent on war. The dissolution of the monasteries did not achieve a more equitable distribution of land and wealth. Rather, the "bare ruined choirs where late the sweet birds sang"—as Shakespeare described in Sonnet 73 the desolate religious houses—testified to the loss of a valuable cultural force in English life. The redistribution of land strengthened the upper classes and tied them to the Tudor dynasty.

Did the religious changes accompanying this political upheaval have broad popular support?. The surviving evidence does not allow us to gauge the degree of opposition to (or support for) Henry's break with Rome. Certainly, many laypeople wrote to the king begging him to spare the monasteries. "Most laypeople acquiesced in the Reformation because they hardly knew what was going on, were understandably reluctant to jeopardise life or limb, a career or the family's good name."[27] But all did not quietly acquiesce. In 1536 popular opposition in the north to the religious changes led to the Pilgrimage of Grace, a massive multiclass re-

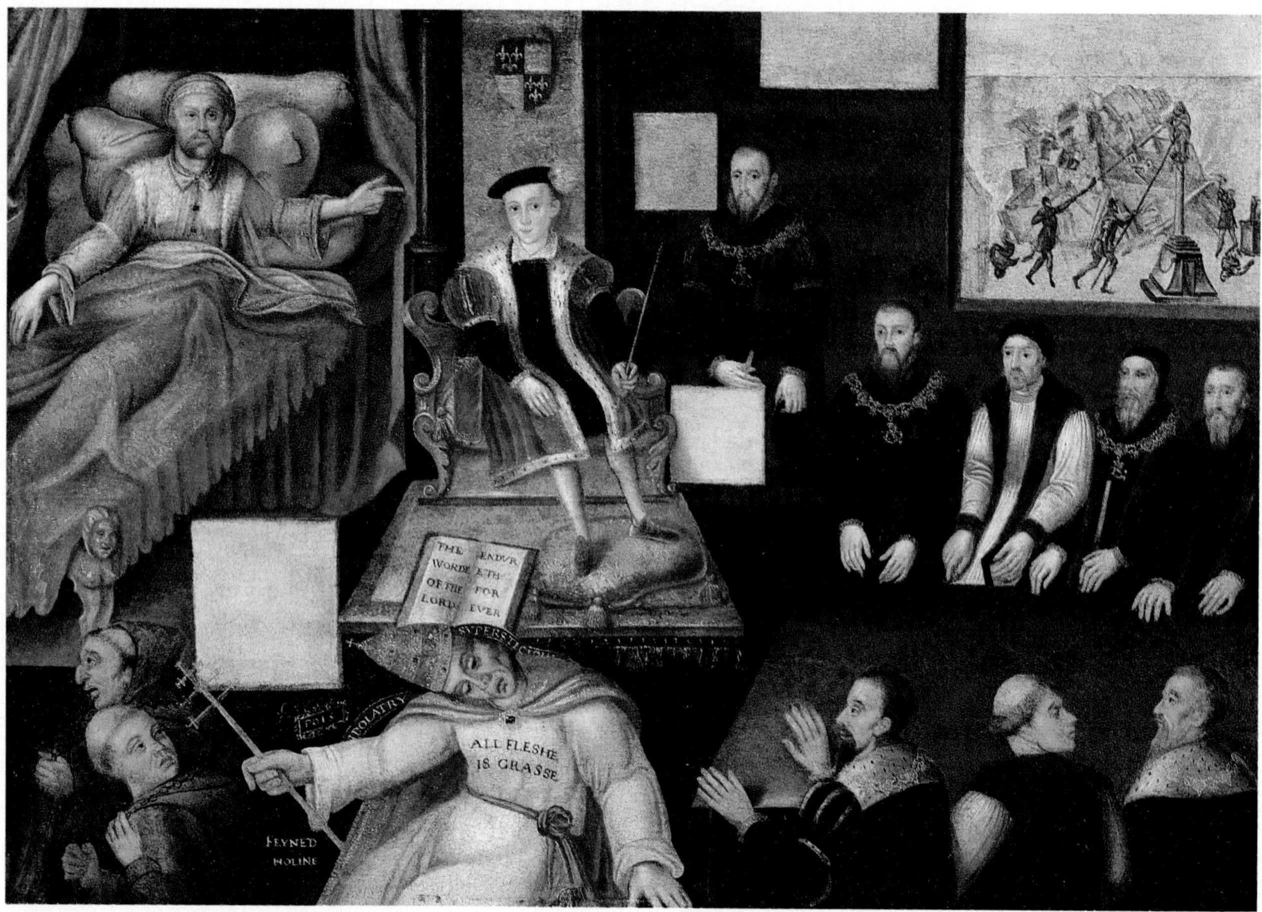

Allegorical Painting, ca 1548 Henry VIII on his deathbed points to his heir Edward, surrounded by Protestant worthies, as the wave of the future. The pope collapses, monks flee, through the window iconoclasts knock down statues, symbolizing error and superstition; stressing Protestantism's focus on Scripture, the Bible is open to 1 Peter 1:24: "The word of the Lord endures forever." Since the new order lacked broad popular support, propagandistic paintings like this and the printing press had to be mobilized to sway public opinion. *(Reproduced by courtesy of the Trustees, National Portrait Gallery, London)*

bellion that proved the largest in English history. The "pilgrims" accepted a truce, and their leaders were arrested, tried, and executed. In 1546 serious rebellions in East Anglia and in the west, despite possessing economic and Protestant components, reflected considerable public opposition to the state-ordered religious changes.[28]

Henry's motives combined personal, political, social, and economic elements. Theologically he retained such traditional Catholic practices and doctrines as auricular confession, clerical celibacy, and transubstantiation. Meanwhile, Protestant literature circulated, and Henry approved the selection of men of Protestant sympathies as tutors for his son.

The nationalization of the church and the dissolution of the monasteries led to important changes in government administration. Vast tracts of formerly monastic land came temporarily under the Crown's jurisdiction, and new bureaucratic machinery had to be developed to manage those properties. Cromwell reformed and centralized the king's household, the council, the secretariats, and the Exchequer. New departments of state were also set up. Surplus funds from all of the departments went into a liquid fund to be applied to areas where there were deficits. This balancing resulted in greater efficiency and economy. Henry VIII's reign saw the growth of the modern centralized bureaucratic state.

After Henry's death, the English church shifted left and right. In the short reign of Henry's sickly son, Edward VI (r. 1547–1553), strongly Protestant ideas exerted a significant influence on the religious life of the country. Archbishop Thomas Cranmer simplified the liturgy, invited Protestant theologians to England, and prepared the first *Book of Common Prayer* (1549). In stately and dignified English, the *Book of Common Prayer* included, together with the Psalter, the order for all services of the Church of England.

The equally brief reign of Mary Tudor (r. 1553–1558) witnessed a sharp move back to Catholicism. The devoutly Catholic daughter of Catherine of Aragon, Mary rescinded the Reformation legislation of her father's reign and fully restored Roman Catholicism. Mary's marriage to her cousin Philip of Spain, son of the emperor Charles V, proved highly unpopular in England, and her persecution and execution of several hundred Protestants further alienated her subjects. During her reign, many Protestants fled to the continent. Mary's death raised to the throne her sister, Elizabeth (r. 1558–1603), and inaugurated the beginnings of religious stability.

Elizabeth had been raised a Protestant, but at the start of her reign sharp differences existed in England. On the one hand, Catholics wanted a Roman Catholic ruler. On the other hand, a vocal number of returning exiles wanted all Catholic elements in the Church of England eliminated. The latter, because they wanted to "purify" the church, were called "Puritans." Probably one of the shrewdest politicians in English history, Elizabeth chose a middle course between Catholic and Puritan extremes. She insisted on dignity in church services and political order in the land. She did not care what people believed as long as they kept quiet about it. Avoiding precise doctrinal definitions, Elizabeth had herself styled "Supreme Governor of the Church of England, Etc.," and left it to her subjects to decide what the "Etc." meant.

The parliamentary legislation of the early years of Elizabeth's reign—laws sometimes labeled the "Elizabethan Settlement"—required outward conformity to the Church of England and uniformity in all ceremonies. Everyone had to attend Church of England services; those who refused were fined. In 1563 a convocation of bishops approved the Thirty-nine Articles, a summary in thirty-nine short statements of the basic tenets of the Church of England. During Elizabeth's reign, the Anglican church (from the Latin *Ecclesia Anglicana*), as the Church of England was called, moved in a moderately Protestant direction. Services were conducted in English, monasteries were not re-established, and clergymen were allowed to marry. But the episcopate was not abolished and the bishops remained as church officials; apart from language, the services were quite traditional.

The Establishment of the Church of Scotland

Reform of the church in Scotland did not follow the English model. In the early sixteenth century, the church in Scotland presented an extreme case of clerical abuse and corruption, and Lutheranism initially attracted sympathetic support. In Scotland as elsewhere, political authority was the decisive influence in reform. The monarchy was weak, and factions of virtually independent nobles competed for power. King James V and his daughter, Mary, Queen of Scots (r. 1560–1567), staunch Catholics and close allies of Catholic France, opposed reform. The Scottish nobles supported it. One man, John Knox (1505?–1572), dominated the movement for reform in Scotland.

In 1559 Knox, a dour, single-minded, and fearless man with a reputation as a passionate preacher, set to work reforming the church. He had studied and worked with Calvin in Geneva and was determined to structure the Scottish church after the model of Calvin's Geneva. In 1560 Knox persuaded the Scottish parliament, which was dominated by reform-minded barons, to enact legislation ending papal authority. The Mass was abolished and attendance at it forbidden under penalty of death. Knox then established the Presbyterian Church of Scotland, so named because *presbyters,* or ministers, not bishops, governed it. The Church of Scotland was strictly Calvinist in doctrine, adopted a simple and dignified service of worship, and laid great emphasis on preaching. Knox's *Book of Common Order* (1564) became the liturgical directory for the church. The Presbyterian Church of Scotland was a national, or state, church, and many of its members maintained close relations with English Puritans.

Protestantism in Ireland

To the ancient Irish hatred of English political and commercial exploitation, the Reformation added the bitter antagonism of religion. Henry VIII wanted to "reduce that realm to the knowledge of God and obedience to us." English rulers in the sixteenth century regarded the Irish as barbarians, and a policy of complete extermination was rejected only because "to enterprise [attempt] the whole extirpation and total destruction of

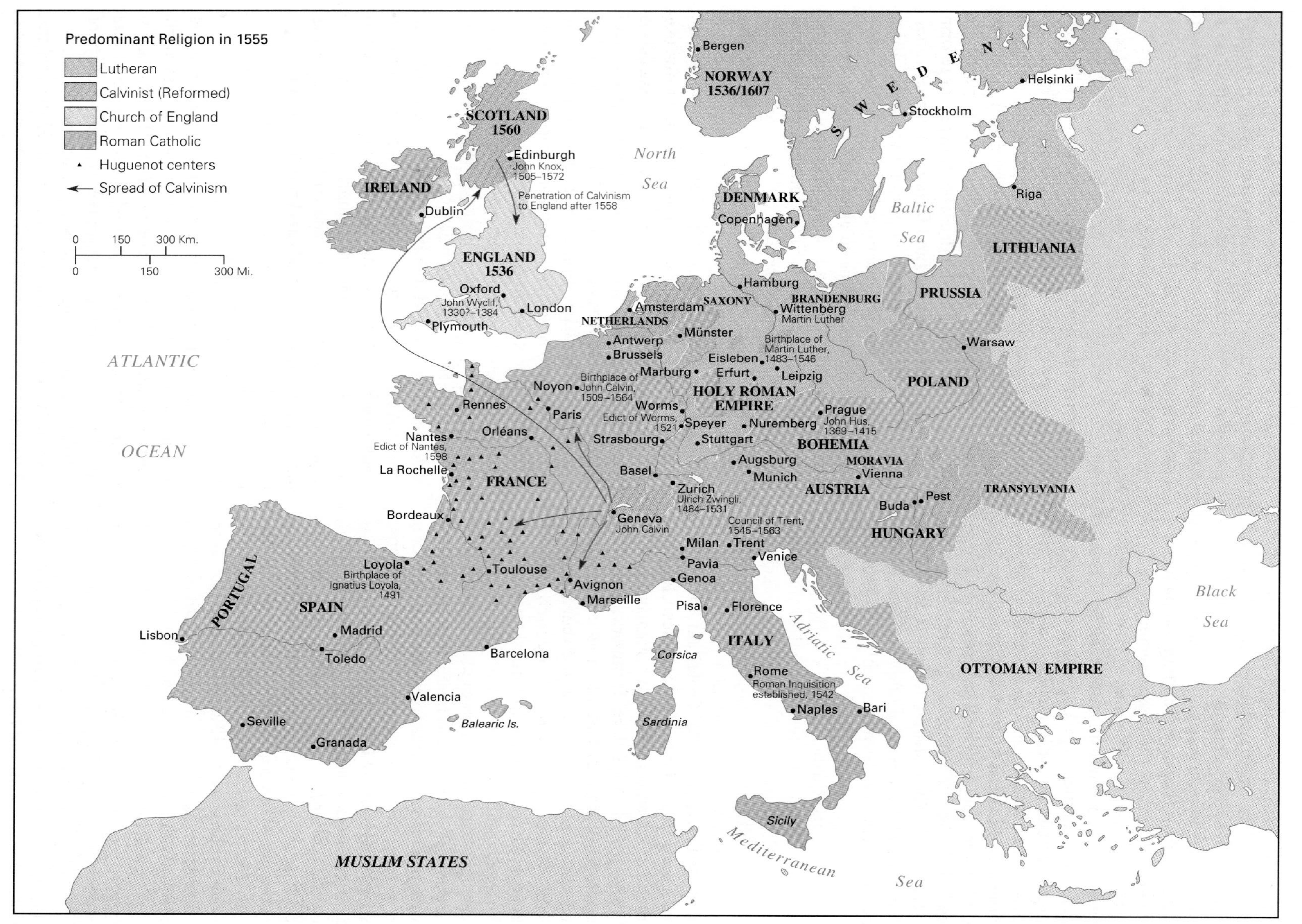
Predominant Religion in 1555
Lutheran
Calvinist (Reformed)
Church of England
Roman Catholic
Huguenot centers
Spread of Calvinism
0 150 300 Km.
0 150 300 Mi.
ATLANTIC
OCEAN
North
Sea
Baltic
Sea
Black
Sea
Adriatic
Sea
Mediterranean
Sea
SWEDEN
Helsinki
Stockholm
Riga
NORWAY
1536/1607
Bergen
DENMARK
Copenhagen
SCOTLAND
1560
Edinburgh
John Knox,
1505–1572
Penetration of Calvinism
to England after 1558
IRELAND
Dublin
ENGLAND
1536
Oxford
John Wyclif,
1330?–1384
London
Plymouth
LITHUANIA
PRUSSIA
POLAND
Warsaw
Hamburg
SAXONY
BRANDENBURG
Wittenberg
Martin Luther
Amsterdam
NETHERLANDS
Münster
Antwerp
Brussels
Birthplace of
Martin Luther,
1483–1546
Eisleben
Erfurt
Leipzig
Marburg
Birthplace of
John Calvin,
1509–1564
Noyon
HOLY ROMAN
EMPIRE
Worms
Edict of Worms,
1521
Speyer
Nuremberg
Prague
John Hus,
1369–1415
Paris
Strasbourg
Stuttgart
BOHEMIA
Augsburg
Munich
MORAVIA
Vienna
Basel
Zurich
Ulrich Zwingli,
1484–1531
AUSTRIA
Pest
Buda
TRANSYLVANIA
HUNGARY
Geneva
John Calvin
Council of Trent,
1545–1563
Milan
Trent
Venice
Pavia
Genoa
Pisa
Florence
ITALY
Rome
Roman Inquisition
established, 1542
Naples
Bari
Corsica
Sardinia
Sicily
OTTOMAN EMPIRE
Rennes
Nantes
Edict of Nantes,
1598
Orléans
La Rochelle
FRANCE
Bordeaux
Toulouse
Avignon
Marseille
Loyola
Birthplace of
Ignatius Loyola,
1491
PORTUGAL
SPAIN
Lisbon
Madrid
Toledo
Barcelona
Valencia
Balearic Is.
Seville
Granada
MUSLIM STATES

all the Irishmen in the land would be a marvelous sumptious charge and great difficulty."[29] In other words, it would have cost too much.

In 1536 on orders from London, the Irish parliament, which represented only the English landlords and the people of the Pale (the area around Dublin), approved the English laws severing the church from Rome and making the English king sovereign over ecclesiastical organization and practice. The Church of Ireland was established on the English pattern, and the (English) ruling class adopted the new reformed faith. Most of the Irish, probably for political reasons, defiantly remained Roman Catholic. Monasteries were secularized. Catholic property was confiscated and sold and the profits were shipped to England. With the Roman church driven underground, Catholic churchmen acted as national as well as religious leaders.

Lutheranism in Sweden, Norway, and Denmark

In Sweden, Norway, and Denmark, the monarchy took the initiative in the religious Reformation. The resulting institutions were Lutheran state churches. Since the late fourteenth century, the Danish kings had ruled Sweden and Norway as well as Denmark. In 1520 Swedish nobleman Gustavus Vasa (r. 1523–1560) led a successful revolt against Denmark, and Sweden became independent. As king, Gustavus Vasa seized church lands and required the bishops' loyalty to the Swedish crown. Wittenberg-educated Swedish reformer Olaus Petri (1493–1552) translated the New Testament into Swedish and, with the full support of Gustavus Vasa, organized the church along strict Lutheran lines. This consolidation of the Swedish monarchy in the sixteenth century was to profoundly affect the development of Germany in the seventeenth century.

Christian III, king of Denmark (r. 1503–1559) and of Norway (r. 1534–1559), secularized church property and set up a Lutheran church. Norway, which was governed by Denmark until 1814, adopted Lutheranism as its state religion under Danish influence.

MAP 14.2 The Protestant and the Catholic Reformations The Reformations shattered the religious unity of Western Christendom. What common cultural traits predominated in regions where a particular branch of the Christian faith was maintained or took root?

THE CATHOLIC REFORMATION AND THE COUNTER-REFORMATION

Between 1517 and 1547, the reformed versions of Christianity known as Protestantism made remarkable advances. All of England and Scandinavia, much of Scotland and Germany, and sizable parts of France and Switzerland adopted the creeds of Luther, Calvin, and other reformers. Nevertheless, the Roman Catholic church made a significant comeback. After about 1540, no new large areas of Europe, except for the Netherlands, accepted Protestant beliefs (Map 14.2).

Historians distinguish between two types of reform within the Catholic church in the sixteenth and seventeenth centuries. The Catholic Reformation began before 1517 and sought renewal basically through the stimulation of a new spiritual fervor. The Counter-Reformation started in the 1540s as a reaction to the rise and spread of Protestantism. The Counter-Reformation involved Catholic efforts to convince or coerce dissidents or heretics to return to the church lest they corrupt the entire community of Catholic believers. Fear of the "infection" of all Christian society by the religious dissident was a standard sixteenth-century attitude. If the heretic could not be persuaded to reconvert, counter-reformers believed it necessary to call on temporal authorities to defend Christian society by expelling or eliminating the dissident. The Catholic Reformation and the Counter-Reformation were not mutually exclusive; in fact, after about 1540 they progressed simultaneously.

The Slowness of Institutional Reform

The Renaissance princes who sat on the throne of Saint Peter were not blind to the evils that existed. Modest reform efforts had begun with the Lateran Council called in 1512 by Pope Julius II. The Dutch pope Adrian VI (1522–1523) instructed his legate in Germany to "say that we frankly confess that God permits this [Lutheran] persecution of his church on account of the sins of men, especially those of the priests and prelates. . . . We know that in this Holy See now for some years there have been many abominations."[30] Adrian VI tried desperately to reform the church and to check the spread of Protestantism. His reign lasted only thirteen months, however, and the austerity of his life and his Dutch nationality provoked the hostility of pleasure-loving Italian curial bureaucrats.

Overall, why did the popes, spiritual leaders of the Western church, move so slowly? The answers lie in the personalities of the popes themselves, their preoccupation with political affairs in Italy, and the awesome difficulty of reforming so complicated a bureaucracy as the Roman curia.

Clement VII (r. 1523–1534), a true Medici, was far more interested in elegant tapestries and Michelangelo's painting of the Last Judgment than in theological disputes in barbaric Germany. Indecisive and vacillating, Pope Clement must bear much of the responsibility for the great spread of Protestantism. While Emperor Charles V and the French king Francis I competed for the domination of divided Italy, the papacy worried about the security of the Papal States. Clement tried to follow a middle course, backing first the emperor and then the French ruler. At the Battle of Pavia in 1525, Francis I suffered a severe defeat and was captured. In a reshuffling of diplomatic alliances, the pope switched from Charles and the Spanish to Francis I. In retaliation for Clement's diplomatic shift, and to pay his near mutinous soldiers, Charles allowed his German and Spanish troops to sack Rome (May 1527) and to capture the pope. With the city destroyed, its art treasures stolen, and its population decimated, a contemporary reported that "hell itself must have been a prettier sight." Erasmus called the sack a catastrophe for civilization, and the event marked the end of the High Renaissance in Rome.

The idea of reform was closely linked to the idea of a general council representing the entire church. A strong contingent of countries beyond the Alps—Spain, Germany, and France—wanted to reform the vast bureaucracy of Latin officials, reducing offices, men, and revenues. Popes from Julius II to Clement VII, remembering fifteenth-century conciliar attempts to limit papal authority, resisted calls for a council. The papal bureaucrats who were the popes' intimates warned the popes against a council, fearing loss of power, revenue, and prestige. Five centuries before, Saint Bernard of Clairvaux had anticipated the situation: "The most grievous danger of any Pope lies in the fact that, encompassed as he is by flatterers, he never hears the truth about his own person and ends by not wishing to hear it."

The Council of Trent

In the papal conclave that followed the death of Clement VII, Cardinal Alexander Farnese promised two German cardinals that if he was elected pope, he would summon a council. He won the election and ruled as Pope Paul III (1534–1549). This Roman aristocrat, humanist, and astrologer, who immediately made his teenage grandsons cardinals, seemed an unlikely person to undertake serious reform. Yet Paul III appointed as cardinals several learned and reform-minded men, such as Gian Pietro Caraffa (later Pope Paul IV); established the Inquisition in the Papal States; and—true to his word—called a council, which finally met at Trent, an imperial city close to Italy.

The Council of Trent met intermittently from 1545 to 1563. It was called not only to reform the church but also to secure reconciliation with the Protestants. Lutherans and Calvinists were invited to participate, but their insistence that the Scriptures be the sole basis for discussion made reconciliation impossible. International politics repeatedly cast a shadow over the theological debates. Charles V opposed discussions on any matter that might further alienate his Lutheran subjects, fearing the loss of additional imperial territory to Lutheran princes. Meanwhile, the French kings worked against the reconciliation of Roman Catholicism and Lutheranism. As long as religious issues divided the German states, the empire would be weakened, and a weak and divided empire meant a stronger France. Portugal, Poland, Hungary, and Ireland sent representatives, but very few German bishops attended.

Another problem was the persistence of the conciliar theory of church government (see page 393). Some bishops wanted a concrete statement asserting the supremacy of a church council over the papacy. The adoption of the conciliar principle could have led to a divided church. The bishops had a provincial and national outlook; only the papacy possessed an international religious perspective. The centralizing tenet was established that all acts of the council required papal approval.

In spite of the obstacles, the achievements of the Council of Trent were impressive. It dealt with both doctrinal and disciplinary matters. The council gave equal validity to the Scriptures and to tradition as sources of religious truth and authority. It reaffirmed the seven sacraments and the traditional Catholic teaching on transubstantiation. Thus it rejected Lutheran and Calvinist positions.

The council tackled the problems arising from ancient abuses by strengthening ecclesiastical discipline. Tridentine (from *Tridentum,* the Latin word for Trent) decrees required bishops to reside in their own dioceses, suppressed pluralism and simony, and forbade the sale of indulgences. Clerics who kept concubines were to give them up. The jurisdiction of bishops over all the clergy of their dioceses was made almost absolute, and bishops were ordered to visit every religious house within the diocese at least once every two years. In a highly original canon, the council required every dio-

School of Titian: The Council of Trent Since the early sessions were sparsely attended, this well-attended meeting seems to be a later session. Few bishops from northern Europe, however, ever attended. The Swiss guards (forefront) of the Vatican were founded by Pope Julius II in 1505 to defend the papacy. *(Louvre © R.M.N.—Jean Schormans)*

cese to establish a seminary for the education and training of the clergy; the council even prescribed the curriculum and insisted that preference for admission be given to sons of the poor. Seminary professors were to determine if candidates for ordination had *vocations,* genuine callings as determined by purity of life, detachment from the broader secular culture, and a steady inclination toward the priesthood. This was a novel idea since from the time of the early church, parents had determined their sons' (and daughters') religious careers (see page 322). Finally, great emphasis was laid on preaching and instructing the laity, especially the uneducated.

One decision had especially important social consequences for laypeople. Since the time of the Roman Empire, many couples had treated marriage as a completely personal matter, exchanged vows privately without witnesses, and thus formed what were called clandestine (secret) unions. This widespread practice frequently led later to denials by one party, conflicts over property, and disputes in the ecclesiastical courts that had jurisdiction over marriage once it became a sacrament (which occurred in the twelfth century). The Tridentine decree Tametsi (November 1563) stipulated that for a marriage to be valid, consent (the essence of marriage) as given in the vows had to be made publicly before witnesses, one of whom had to be the parish priest. Trent thereby ended secret marriages in Catholic countries. (They remained a problem for civil and church courts in England until the Hardwicke Act of 1753 abolished them.)

The Council of Trent did not meet everyone's expectations. Reconciliation with Protestantism was not achieved, nor was reform brought about immediately. Nevertheless, the Tridentine decrees laid a solid basis for the spiritual renewal of the church and for the enforcement of correction. For four centuries, the doctrinal and disciplinary legislation of Trent served as the basis for Roman Catholic faith, organization, and practice.

New Religious Orders

The establishment of new religious orders within the church reveals a central feature of the Catholic Reformation. Most of these new orders developed in response to one crying need: to raise the moral and intellectual level of the clergy and people. (See the feature "Individuals in Society: Teresa of Ávila.") Education was a major goal of the two most famous orders.

The Ursuline order of nuns, founded by Angela Merici (1474–1540), attained enormous prestige for the education of women. The daughter of a country gentleman, Angela Merici worked for many years among the poor, sick, and uneducated around her native Brescia in northern Italy. In 1535 she established the Ursuline order to combat heresy through Christian education. The first women's religious order concentrating exclusively on teaching young girls, the Ursulines sought to re-Christianize society by training future wives and mothers. Because the Council of Trent placed great stress on the *claustration* (strict enclosure) of religious women and called for the end of all active ministries for women, Angela had great difficulty gaining papal approval. Official recognition finally came in 1565, and the Ursulines rapidly grew and spread to France and the New World. Their schools in North America, stretching from Quebec to New Orleans, provided superior education for young women and inculcated the spiritual ideals of the Catholic Reformation.

The Society of Jesus, founded by Ignatius Loyola (1491–1556), a former Spanish soldier, played a powerful international role in resisting the spread of Protestantism, converting Asians and Latin American Indians to Catholicism, and spreading Christian education all over Europe. While recuperating from a severe battle wound in his legs, Loyola studied a life of Christ and other religious books and decided to give up his military career and become a soldier of Christ. During a year spent in seclusion, prayer, and personal mortification, he gained the religious insights that went into his great classic, *Spiritual Exercises* (1548). This work, intended for study during a four-week period of retreat, directed the individual imagination and will to the reform of life and a new spiritual piety.

Loyola was apparently a man of considerable personal magnetism. After study at universities in Salamanca and Paris, he gathered a group of six companions and in 1540 secured papal approval of the new Society of Jesus, whose members were called "Jesuits." The first Jesuits, recruited primarily from the wealthy merchant and professional classes, saw the Reformation as a pastoral problem, its causes and cures related not to doctrinal issues but to people's spiritual condition. Reform of the church, as Luther and Calvin understood that term, played no role in the future the Jesuits planned for themselves. Their goal was "to help souls." Loyola also possessed a gift for leadership that consisted in spotting talent and in seeing "how at a given juncture change is more consistent with one's scope than staying the course."[31]

The Society of Jesus developed into a highly centralized, tightly knit organization. Candidates underwent a two-year novitiate, in contrast to the usual one-year probation. In addition to the traditional vows of poverty, chastity, and obedience, professed members vowed "special obedience to the sovereign pontiff regarding missions."[32] Thus as stability—the promise to live his life in the monastery—was what made a monk, so mobility—the commitment to go anywhere for the help of souls—was the defining characteristic of a Jesuit. Flexibility and the willingness to respond to the needs of time and circumstance formed the Jesuit tradition. In this respect, Jesuits were very modern, and they attracted many recruits.

They achieved phenomenal success for the papacy and the reformed Catholic church. Jesuit schools adopted the modern humanist curricula and methods, and even though they first concentrated on the children of the poor, they were soon educating the sons of the nobility. As confessors and spiritual directors to kings, Jesuits exerted great political influence. Operating on the principle that the end sometimes justifies the means, they were not above spying. Indifferent to physical comfort and personal safety, they carried Christianity to India and Japan before 1550, to Brazil, North America, and the Congo in the seventeenth century. Within Europe the Jesuits brought southern Germany and much of eastern Europe back to Catholicism.

The Congregation of the Holy Office

In 1542 Pope Paul III established the Sacred Congregation of the Holy Office, with jurisdiction over the Roman Inquisition, a powerful instrument of the Counter-Reformation. The Inquisition was a committee of six cardinals with judicial authority over all Catholics and the power to arrest, imprison, and execute. Under the fanatical Cardinal Caraffa, it vigorously attacked heresy.

Individuals in Society

Teresa of Ávila (1515–1582)

Seventeenth-century cloisonné enamel work illustrating Teresa of Ávila's famous vision. *(By gracious permission of Catherine Hamilton Kappauf)*

Her family derived from Toledo, center of the Moorish, Jewish, and Christian cultures in medieval Spain. Her grandfather, Juan Sanchez, made a fortune in the cloth trade. A "New Christian," he was accused of secretly practicing Judaism. Although he endured the humiliation of a public repentance, he moved his family south to Ávila. Beginning again, he recouped his wealth and, aspiring to the prestige of an "Old Christian," bought noble status. Juan's son Alzonzo Sanchez de Cepeda married a woman of thoroughly Christian background, giving his family an aura of impeccable orthodoxy. The third of their nine children, Teresa, became a saint and the first woman declared a Doctor of the Church—a theologian of outstanding merit and saintliness (1970).

At age twenty, inspired more by the fear of hell than the love of God, Teresa entered the Carmelite Convent of the Incarnation in Ávila. The 140 nuns there were supported by rents from their lands; they did not practice poverty. Nor did they observe enclosure, as guests were frequently entertained. The nuns, privileged daughters of Ávila's leading citizens, were obsessed with status and social prestige.

For twenty years Teresa remained in this worldly atmosphere that contradicted the convent's religious ideals. Francesco de Osuna's book *The Third Spiritual Alphabet* introduced Teresa to a more meaningful spiritual life, and she began to devour devotional literature. In her late thirties, she had profound mystical experiences—visions and voices in which Christ chastised her for her frivolous life and friends. She described one such experience in 1560:

> *It pleased the Lord that I should see an angel. . . . Short, and very beautiful, his face was so aflame that he appeared to be one of the highest types of angels. . . . In his hands I saw a long golden spear and at the end of an iron tip I seemed to see a point of fire. With this he seemed to pierce my heart several times so that it penetrated to my entrails. When he drew it out . . . he left me completely afire with the great love of God.*[1]

Teresa responded with a new sense of purpose: although she encountered stiff opposition, she resolved to found a reformed house. Four basic principles were to guide the new convent. First, poverty was to be fully observed, symbolized by the nuns being barefoot, hence *discalced*. Ending a long-established monastic practice, Teresa rejected rents: charity and the nuns' own work must support the community. Second, the convent must keep strict enclosure; the visits of powerful benefactors with material demands were forbidden. Third, Teresa intended an egalitarian atmosphere where class distinctions were forbidden. She had always rejected the emphasis on "purity of blood," a distinctive and racist feature of Spanish society especially out of place in the cloister. All sisters, including those of aristocratic background, must share the manual chores. Finally, like Ignatius Loyola and the Jesuits, Teresa placed great emphasis on obedience, especially to one's confessor.

Between 1562 and Teresa's death in 1582, she founded or reformed fourteen other houses of nuns, no small feat for a woman in a very sexist society. She was the first spiritual author to provide a scientific description of the life of prayer from simple meditation to mystical union with God. Her books, along with her five hundred extant letters, show her as capable of great discernment of individual character. But for all her mystical experiences, Teresa was a motherly, practical, and down-to-earth woman with a strong sense of humor. From her brother who had obtained wealth in the Spanish colonies, Teresa learned about conditions in Peru and instructed her nuns "to pray unceasingly for the missionaries working among the heathens." In this way, they shared in evangelization.

Teresa of Ávila responded to change not with doubt, but with deeper belief.

Questions for Analysis

1. How did sixteenth-century convent life reflect the values of Spanish society?
2. How does Teresa of Ávila represent the spirit of the Catholic Reformation?

1. *The Autobiography of St. Teresa of Ávila,* trans. and ed. E. A. Peers (New York: Doubleday, 1960), pp. 273–274.

Juan de Valdes Leal: Pope Paul III Approves the Jesuit Constitutions Although Paul III devoted considerable energy to advancing the interests of his (Farnese) family, he also tried to meet the challenge of Protestantism—through the Council of Trent and new religious orders. When the Jesuit constitutions were read to him, Paul III supposedly murmured, "There is the finger of God." The portrait of Ignatius Loyola is a reasonable likeness, that of the pope an idealization: in 1540 he was a very old man. *(Institut Amatller d'Art Hispanic, Barcelona)*

The Roman Inquisition operated under the principles of Roman law. It accepted hearsay evidence, was not obliged to inform the accused of charges against them, and sometimes applied torture. Echoing one of Calvin's remarks about heresy, Cardinal Caraffa wrote, "No man is to lower himself by showing toleration towards any sort of heretic, least of all a Calvinist."[33] The Holy Office published the *Index of Prohibited Books,* a catalogue of forbidden reading.

Within the Papal States, the Inquisition effectively destroyed heresy (and some heretics). Outside the papal territories, however, its influence was slight. Governments had their own judicial systems for the suppression of treasonable activities, as religious heresy was then considered. The republic of Venice is a good case in point.

In the sixteenth century, Venice was one of the great publishing centers of Europe. The Inquisition and the *Index* could have badly damaged the Venetian book trade, but authorities there cooperated with the Holy Office only when heresy became a great threat to the security of the republic. The *Index* had no influence on scholarly research in nonreligious areas such as law, classical literature, and mathematics. As a result of the Inquisition, Venetians and Italians were *not* cut off from the main currents of European learning.

Summary

Demands for reform of the Christian church is a continuing theme in European history. In the fifteenth and early sixteenth centuries, movements such as the Brethren of the Common Life, Lollardy, the Oratories of Divine Love, and the efforts of the Roman papacy itself paved the way for institutional reform. Martin Luther's strictly religious call for reform, rapidly spread by preaching, hymns, and the printing press, soon became enmeshed in social, economic, and political issues. The German peasants interpreted Luther's ideas in an economic sense: Christian liberty for them meant the end of harsh manorial burdens. Princes used the cloak of the new religious ideas both to acquire the material wealth of the church and to thwart the centralizing goals of the emperor. In England the political issue of the royal succession triggered that country's break with Rome, and in Switzerland and France the political and social ethos of Calvinism attracted many people. The Protestant doctrine that all callings have equal merit in God's sight and its stress on the home as the special domain of women drew women to Protestantism. The reformulation of Roman Catholic doctrine at the Council of Trent and the new religious orders such as the Jesuits and the Ursulines represented the Catholic response to the demands for reform.

The age of the Reformation presents very real paradoxes. The break with Rome and the rise of Lutheran, Anglican, Calvinist, and other faiths destroyed the unity of Europe as an organic Christian society. Saint Paul's exhortation, "There should be no schism in the body [of the church]. . . . You are all one in Christ,"[34] was widely ignored. Yet religious belief remained tremendously strong. In fact, the strength of religious convictions caused political fragmentation. In the later sixteenth century and through most of the seventeenth, religion and religious issues continued to play a major role in the lives of individuals and in the policies and actions of governments. Religion, whether Protestant or Catholic, decisively influenced the growth of national states.

Scholars have maintained that the sixteenth century witnessed the beginnings of the modern world. They are both right and wrong. Although most of the church reformers rejected the idea of religious toleration, they helped pave the way for it. They also paved the way for the eighteenth-century revolt against the Christian God, one of the strongest supports of life in Western culture. In this respect, the Reformation marked the beginning of the modern world, with its secularism and rootlessness. At the same time, it can equally be argued that the sixteenth century represented the culmination of the Middle Ages. Martin Luther's anxieties about salvation showed him to be very much a medieval man. His concerns had deeply troubled serious individuals since the time of Saint Augustine. In modern times, such concerns have tended to take different forms.

NOTES

1. Quoted in J. Burckhardt, *The Civilization of the Renaissance in Italy* (London: Phaidon Books, 1951), p. 262.
2. See R. R. Post, *The Modern Devotion: Confrontation with Reformation and Humanism* (Leiden: E. J. Brill, 1968), esp. pp. 237–238, 255, 323–348.
3. Quoted in O. Chadwick, *The Reformation* (Baltimore: Penguin Books, 1976), p. 55.
4. Quoted in E. H. Harbison, *The Age of Reformation* (Ithaca, N.Y.: Cornell University Press, 1963), p. 52.
5. This passage leans on ibid., pp. 52–55.
6. See S. E. Ozment, *The Reformation in the Cities: The Appeal of Protestantism to Sixteenth-Century Germany and Switzerland* (New Haven: Yale University Press, 1975), pp. 32–45.
7. See S. E. Ozment, *The Age of Reform, 1250–1550: An Intellectual and Religious History of Late Medieval and Reformation Europe* (New Haven, Conn.: Yale University Press, 1980), pp. 273–279.
8. Quoted ibid., p. 280.
9. Ibid., p. 281.
10. Quoted ibid., p. 284.
11. Romans 13:1–2.
12. E. Erikson, *Young Man Luther: A Study in Psychoanalysis and History* (New York: W. W. Norton, 1962), p. 47.
13. G. Strauss, *Luther's House of Learning: Indoctrination of the Young in the German Reformation* (Baltimore: Johns Hopkins University Press, 1978), esp. pp. 159–162, 231–233.
14. See R. H. Bainton, *Women of the Reformation in Germany and Italy* (Minneapolis: Augsburg, 1971), pp. 9–10; and Ozment, *The Reformation in the Cities,* pp. 53–54, 171–172.
15. Quoted in H. G. Haile, *Luther: An Experiment in Biography* (Garden City, N.Y.: Doubleday, 1980), p. 272.
16. Quoted in J. Atkinson, *Martin Luther and the Birth of Protestantism* (Baltimore: Penguin Books, 1968), pp. 247–248.
17. *Martin Luther: Three Treatises* (Philadelphia: Muhlenberg Press, 1947), pp. 28–31.
18. J. Allen, trans., *John Calvin: The Institutes of the Christian Religion* (Philadelphia: Westminster Press, 1930), bk. 3, chap. 21, paras. 5, 7.
19. E. W. Monter, *Calvin's Geneva* (New York: John Wiley & Sons, 1967), pp. 98–108.
20. Ibid., p. 137.
21. Quoted in Bainton, *Women of the Reformation,* pp. 69–70.
22. See M. E. Wiesner-Hanks, "Women," in *The Oxford Encyclopedia of the Reformation,* ed. H. J. Hillerbrand, vol.

4 (New York: Oxford University Press, 1996), pp. 290–298.

23. A. G. Dickens, *The English Reformation* (New York: Schocken Books, 1964), p. 36.
24. E. Duffy, *The Stripping of the Altars: Traditional Religion in England, 1400–1580* (New Haven, Conn.: Yale University Press, 1992), pp. 2–6.
25. See R. Marius, *Thomas More: A Biography* (New York: Alfred A. Knopf, 1984), pp. 215–216.
26. See S. E. Lehmberg, *The Reformation Parliament, 1529–1536* (Cambridge: Cambridge University Press, 1970), pp. 174–176, 204–205.
27. J. J. Scarisbrick, *The Reformation and the English People* (Oxford: Basil Blackwell, 1984), p. 81.
28. Ibid.
29. Quoted in P. Smith, *The Age of the Reformation,* rev. ed. (New York: Henry Holt, 1951), p. 346.
30. Quoted ibid., p. 84.
31. See J. W. O'Malley, *The First Jesuits* (Cambridge, Mass.: Harvard University Press, 1993), p. 376.
32. Ibid., p. 298.
33. Quoted in Chadwick, *The Reformation,* p. 270.
34. 1 Corinthians 1:25, 27.

SUGGESTED READING

There are many easily accessible and lucidly written general studies of the reformations of the sixteenth century. P. Chaunu, ed., *The Reformation* (1989), is a lavishly illustrated anthology of articles by an international team of scholars—a fine appreciation of both theological and historical developments. The best reference work is H. J. Hillerbrand, ed., *The Oxford Encyclopedia of the Reformation,* 4 vols. (New York: Oxford University Press, 1996), which contains an up-to-date bibliography. E. Cameron, *The European Reformation* (1991), provides a comprehensive survey based on recent research; A. Pettegree, ed., *The Early Reformation in Europe* (1992), explores the reformation as an international movement and compares developments in different parts of Europe, and the books by Chadwick and Harbison listed in the Notes are good general introductions. L. W. Spitz, *The Protestant Reformation, 1517–1559* (1985), provides a comprehensive survey that incorporates sound scholarly research. For the trend in scholarship interpreting the Reformation against the background of fifteenth-century reforming developments, see the excellent study of J. F. D'Amico, *Renaissance Humanism in Papal Rome: Humanists and Churchmen on the Eve of the Reformation* (1983); and J. H. Overfield, *Humanism and Scholasticism in Late Medieval Germany* (1984), which portrays the intellectual life of the German universities, the milieu from which the Protestant Reformation emerged. Older studies include G. Strauss, ed., *Manifestations of Discontent in Germany on the Eve of the Reformation* (1971), a useful and exciting collection of documents; and S. Ozment, *The Age of Reform, 1250–1550: An Intellectual and Religious History of Late Medieval and Reformation Europe* (1980), which combines intellectual and social history. For the condition of the church in the late fifteenth and early sixteenth centuries, see D. Hay, *The Church in Italy in the Fifteenth Century* (1977); P. Heath, *The English Parish Clergy on the Eve of the Reformation* (1969); and J. Moran, *The Growth of English Schooling, 1340–1548* (1985).

For the central figure of the early Reformation, Martin Luther, students should see the works by Atkinson, Erikson, and Haile mentioned in the Notes; G. Brendler, *Martin Luther: Theology and Revolution* (1991), a response to the Marxist interpretation of Luther as a tool of the aristocracy who sold out the peasantry; and H. Boehmer, *Martin Luther: Road to Reformation* (1960), a well-balanced work treating Luther's formative years. Students may expect thorough and sound treatments of Luther's theology in the following distinguished works: H. Bornkamm, *Luther in Mid-Career, 1521–1530* (1983); A. E. McGrath, *Luther's Theology of the Cross: Martin Luther on Justification* (1985); M. Brecht, *Martin Luther: His Road to Reformation* (1985), which includes an exploration of Luther's background and youth; and J. Pelikan, *Reformation of Church and Dogma, 1300–1700* (1986).

The best study of John Calvin is W. J. Bouwsma, *John Calvin: A Sixteenth-Century Portrait* (1988), an authoritative study that situates Calvin within Renaissance culture. D. C. Steinmetz, *Calvin in Context* (1995), treats Calvin as an interpreter of the Bible. See also F. Wendel, *Calvin: The Origins and Development of His Thought* (1963). W. E. Monter, *Calvin's Geneva* (1967), shows the effect of Calvin's reforms on the social life of that Swiss city. R. T. Kendall, *Calvinism and English Calvinism to 1649* (1981), presents English conditions, whereas R. M. Mitchell, *Calvin and the Puritan's View of the Protestant Ethic* (1979), interprets the socioeconomic implications of Calvin's thought. Students interested in the left wing of the Reformation should see the profound, though difficult, work of G. H. Williams, *The Radical Reformers* (1962). For reform in other parts of Switzerland, see T. Brady, *Turning Swiss* (1985); and L. P. Wendel, *Always Among Us: Images of the Poor in Zwingli's Zurich* (1990). W. P. Stephens, *Zwingli: An Introduction to His Thought* (1992), emphasizes the major themes in Zwingli's theology.

For various aspects of the social history of the period, see, in addition to the titles by Bainton and Ozment cited in the Notes, S. Ozment, *Magdalena and Balthasar* (1987), which reveals many features of social life through the letters of a Nuremberg couple; and K. von Greyerz, ed., *Religion and Society in Early Modern Europe, 1500–1800* (1984), which contains interesting essays on religion, society, and popular culture. For women, see M. E. Wiesner, *Women and Gender in Early Modern Europe* (1993); L. Roper, *The Holy Household: Women and Morals in Reformation Augsburg* (1991), an important study in local religious history as well as the history of gender; M. Wiesner, *Women in the Sixteenth Century: A Bibliography* (1983), a useful reference tool; and S. M. Wyntjes, "Women in the Reformation Era," in R. Bridenthal and C. Koonz, eds., *Becoming Visible: Women in European History* (1977), an interesting general survey. The best recent treatment of marriage and the family is S. Ozment, *When Fathers Ruled: Family Life in Reformation Europe* (1983). Ozment's edition of *Reformation Europe: A Guide to Research* (1982), contains not only helpful references but also valuable articles such as "The German Peasants," "The Anabaptists," and "The Confessional Age: The Late Reformation in Germany." For Servetus, see R. H. Bainton, *Hunted Heretic: The Life and Death of Michael Servetus* (1953), which remains valuable.

For England, in addition to the fundamental works by Duffy and Dickens cited in the Notes, K. Thomas, *Religion and the Decline of Magic* (1971), provides a useful treatment of pre-Reformation popular religion, as does Scarisbrick, also mentioned in the Notes, and S. T. Bindoff, *Tudor England* (1959), a good short synthesis. S. J. Gunn and P. G. Lindley, eds., *Cardinal Wolsey: Church, State and Art* (1991), is a useful study of that important prelate. The marital trials of Henry VIII are treated in both the sympathetic study by G. Mattingly, *Catherine of Aragon* (1949), and A. Fraser, *The Wives of Henry VIII* (1992). The legal implications of Henry VIII's divorces have been thoroughly analyzed in J. J. Scarisbrick, *Henry VIII* (1968), an almost definitive biography. On the dissolution of the English monasteries, see D. Knowles, *The Religious Orders in England,* vol. 3 (1959), one of the finest examples of historical prose in English written in the twentieth century. D. Knowles, *Bare Ruined Choirs* (1976), is an attractively illustrated abridgment of *The Religious Orders.* G. R. Elton, *The Tudor Revolution in Government* (1959), discusses the modernization of English government under Thomas Cromwell, whereas the same author's *Reform and Reformation: England, 1509–1558* (1977), combines political and social history in a broad study. Many aspects of English social history are discussed in J. Youings, *Sixteenth Century England* (1984), a beautifully written work, which is highly recommended. The biography of Thomas More by Marius, listed in the Notes, provides a perceptive study of the great humanist, lord chancellor, and saint.

P. Janelle, *The Catholic Reformation* (1951), is a comprehensive treatment of the Catholic Reformation from a Catholic point of view, and A. G. Dickens, *The Counter Reformation* (1969), gives the Protestant standpoint in a beautifully illustrated book. The definitive study of the Council of Trent was written by H. Jedin, *A History of the Council of Trent,* 3 vols. (1957–1961). For the Jesuits, see W. W. Meissner, *Ignatius of Loyola: The Psychology of a Saint* (1993), and J. W. O'Malley, *The First Jesuits* (1993). These books are basic not only for the beginnings of the society but also for the refutation of many myths. Perhaps the best recent work on the Spanish Inquisition is W. Monter, *Frontiers of Heresy: The Spanish Inquisition from the Basque Lands to Sicily* (1990). For the impact of the Counter-Reformation on ordinary Spanish people, see H. Kamen, *The Phoenix and the Flame: Catalonia and the Counter Reformation* (New Haven, Conn.: Yale University Press, 1993).

LISTENING TO THE PAST

Calvin's Vision for Christian Renewal

John Calvin (1509–1564) was one of the many reformers who challenged the tradition and doctrine of the Christian church in the sixteenth century. As part of his reform efforts, Calvin established a community in Geneva, Switzerland. The members of his community were to live according to his social and moral ideas. The first excerpt below derives from his writings on this community and, in particular, on its posture toward its members who erred.

In the second excerpt, Calvin tries to clarify one version of his teachings for Geneva's youth. This piece concerns the Eucharist. Like other reformers, Calvin departed from Catholics on their interpretation of the Eucharist, for he rejected the notion of transubstantiation, that is, the idea that the bread and wine of the Last Supper become the body and blood of Christ during the church service.

Our Lord established excommunication as a means of correction and discipline, by which those who led a disordered life unworthy of a Christian, and who despised to mend their ways and return to the strait way after they had been admonished, should be expelled from the body of the church and cut off as rotten members until they come to themselves and acknowledge their fault. . . . We have an example given by St. Paul (1 Tim. i and 1 Cor. v), in a solemn warning that we should not keep company with one who is called a Christian but who is, none the less, a fornicator, covetous, an idolater, a railer, a drunkard, or an extortioner. So if there be in us any fear of God, this ordinance should be enforced in our Church.

To accomplish this we have determined to petition you [i.e., the town council] to establish and choose, according to your good pleasure, certain persons [namely, the elders] of upright life and good repute among all the faithful, likewise constant and not easy to corrupt, who shall be assigned and distributed in all parts of the town and have an eye on the life and conduct of every individual. If one of these see any obvious vice which is to be reprehended, he shall bring this to the attention of some one of the ministers, who shall admonish whoever it may be who is at fault and exhort him in a brotherly way to correct his ways. If it is apparent that such remonstrances do no good, he shall be warned that his obstinacy will be reported to the church. Then if he repents, there is in that alone excellent fruit of this form of discipline. If he will not listen to warnings, it shall be time for the minister, being informed by those who have the matter in charge, to declare publicly to the congregation the efforts which have been made to bring the sinner to amend, and how all has been in vain.

Should it appear that he proposes to persevere in his hardness of heart, it shall be time to excommunicate him; that is to say, that the offender shall be regarded as cast out from the companionship of Christians and left in the power of the devil for his temporal confusion, until he shall give good proofs of penitence and amendment. In sign of his casting out he shall be excluded from the communion, and the faithful shall be forbidden to hold familiar converse with him. Nevertheless he shall not omit to attend the sermons in order to receive instruction, so that it may be seen whether it shall please the Lord to turn his heart to the right way.

The offenses to be corrected in this manner are those named by St. Paul above, and others like them. When others than the said deputies—for example, neighbors or relatives—shall first have knowledge of such offenses, they may make the necessary remonstrances themselves. If they accomplish nothing, then they shall notify the deputies to do their duty.

This then is the manner in which it would seem expedient to us to introduce excommunication into our Church and maintain it in its full force; for beyond this form of correction the Church does not go. But should there be insolent persons, . . . who only laugh when they are excommunicated and do not mind living and dying in that condition of rejection, it shall be your affair to determine whether you should long suffer such contempt and mocking of God to pass unpunished. . . .

If those who agree with us in faith should be punished by excommunication for their offenses, how much more should the Church refuse to tolerate those who oppose us in religion? The remedy that we have thought of is to petition you to require all the inhabitants of your city to make a confession and give an account of their faith, so that you may know who agree with the gospel and who, on the contrary, would prefer the kingdom of the pope to the kingdom of Jesus Christ.

In the passage on the Eucharist that follows, Calvin adopts a different tone. He imagines a conversation between a minister and a child who responds to his minister's questions. But what follows not only illuminates Calvin's position on a key doctrinal issue; it also reveals his belief that social reform is an integral part of spiritual renewal. Here he goes beyond the prescription in the previous passage to teach children, who represent the future of the community, the fundamental principles of his religion.

Concerning the Lord's Supper.

The minister. Have we in the supper simply a signification of the things above mentioned, or are they given to us in reality?

The child. Since Jesus Christ is truth itself there can be no doubt that the promises he has made regarding the supper are accomplished, and that what is figured there is verified there also. Wherefore according as he promises and represents I have no doubt that he makes us partakers of his own substance, in order that he may unite us with him in one life.

The minister. But how may this be, when the body of Jesus Christ is in heaven, and we are on this earthly pilgrimage?

The child. It comes about through the incomprehensible power of his spirit, which may indeed unite things widely separated in space.

The minister. You do not understand then that the body is enclosed in the bread, or the blood in the cup?

The child. No. On the contrary, in order that the reality of the sacrament be achieved our hearts must be raised to heaven, where Jesus Christ dwells in the glory of the Father, whence we await him for our redemption; and we are not to seek him in these corruptible elements.

The minister. You understand then that there are two things in this sacrament: the natural bread and wine, which we see with the eye, touch with the hand and perceive with the taste; and Jesus Christ, through whom our souls are inwardly nourished?

The child. I do. In such a way moreover that we have there the very witness and so say a pledge of the resurrection of our bodies; since they are made partakers in the symbol of life.

✣ In this Limoges enamel, Swiss reformer Pierre Viret (1511–1571) preaches before Calvin and others on the fourth petition of the Lord's Prayer, "Give us this day our daily bread." *(Louvre © Photo R.M.N.)*

Questions for Analysis

1. What happened in Calvin's community if one of its members sinned?
2. Does it seem fair to you that the state—in this case, the leaders of Calvin's community—legislate morality?
3. How does this picture of community differ from that of Martin Luther? How does it differ from the community envisioned by the post-Reform Catholic church?
4. Why did Calvin consider the topic of the Eucharist so critical?
5. Do you think the passage on the Eucharist would have effectively persuaded young Protestants to espouse Calvin's position?

Sources: "John Calvin's Proposal to Geneva Town Council," in *Readings in European History,* ed. James Harvey Robinson (Boston: Ginn, 1904), 2:124–126; John Calvin, *The Genevan Catechism,* in *Translations and Reprints from the Original Sources of European History* (Philadelphia: University of Pennsylvania Press, 1898), 3/2:8–9.

CHAPTER

15 The Age of Religious Wars and European Expansion

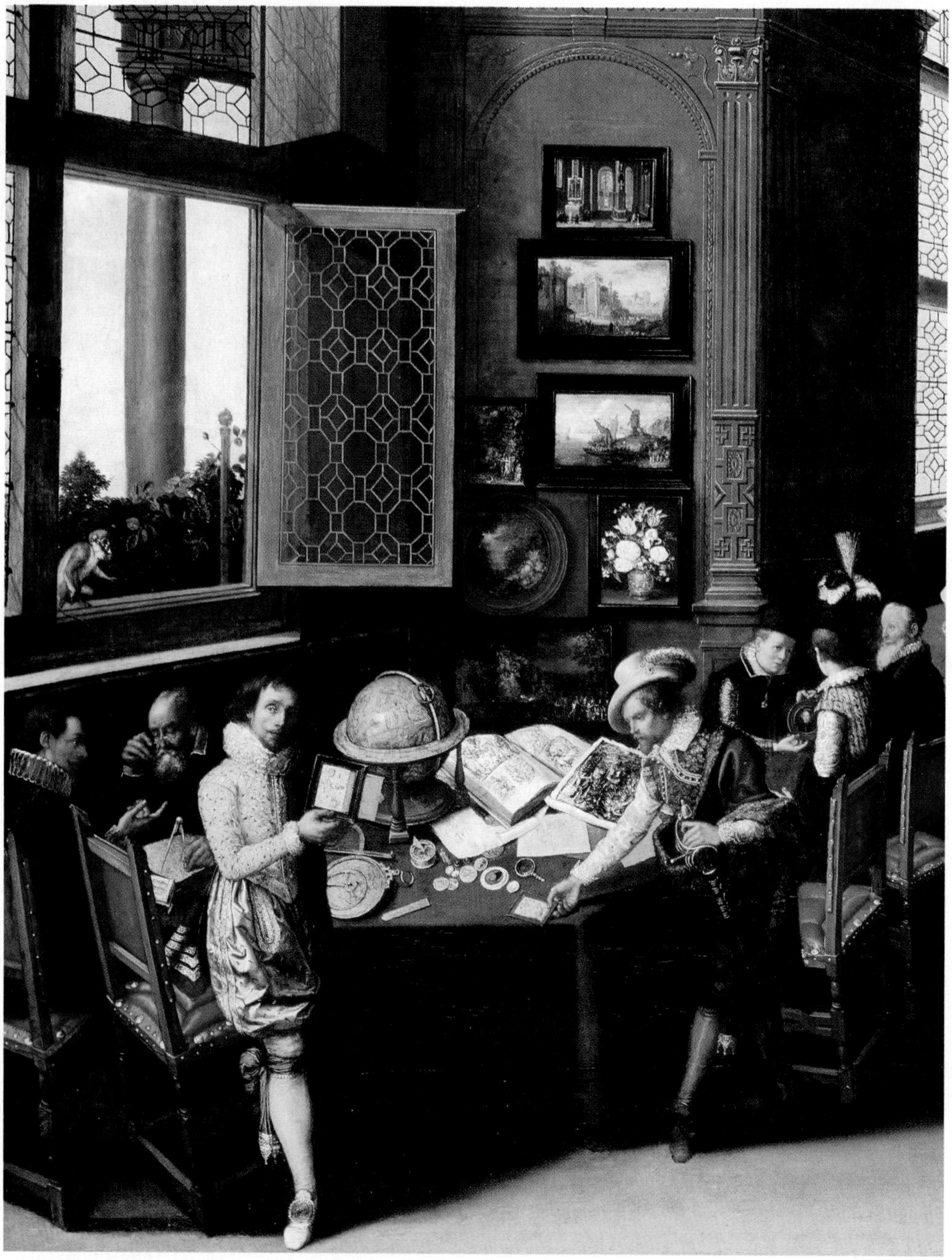

A detail from an early-seventeenth-century Flemish painting depicting maps, illustrated travel books, a globe, a compass, and an astrolabe. *(Reproduced by courtesy of the Trustees, The National Gallery, London)*

Between 1560 and 1648, two developments dramatically altered the world in which Europeans lived: the Reformations of the Christian churches and overseas expansion. The Renaissance and the Reformations drastically changed cultural, political, religious, and social life in Europe and inspired magnificent literary, artistic, and musical achievements. Overseas expansion broadened the geographical horizons of Europeans and brought them into confrontation with ancient civilizations in Africa, Asia, and the Americas. These confrontations led first to conquest, then to exploitation, and finally to profound social changes in both Europe and the conquered territories. War and religious issues dominated politics and were intertwined: religion was commonly used to rationalize wars, which were often fought for power and territorial expansion. Meanwhile, Europeans carried their political, religious, and social attitudes to their newly acquired territories.

- What were the causes and consequences of the religious wars in France, the Netherlands, and Germany?
- How and why, in the sixteenth and seventeenth centuries, did a relatively small group living on the edge of the Eurasian landmass gain control of the major sea-lanes of the world and establish political and economic hegemony on distant continents?
- What immediate effect did overseas expansion have on Europe and on the conquered societies?
- How and why did slave labor become the dominant form of labor organization in the New World?
- How did the religious crises of this period affect religious faith, literary and artistic developments, and the status of women?

This chapter will address these questions.

Politics, Religion, and War

In 1559 France and Spain signed the Treaty of Cateau-Cambrésis, which ended the long conflict known as the Habsburg-Valois Wars. Spain was the victor. France, exhausted by the struggle, had to acknowledge Spanish dominance in Italy, where much of the wars had been fought. Spanish governors ruled in Sicily, Naples, and Milan, and Spanish influence was strong in the Papal States and Tuscany.

Emperor Charles V had divided his attention between the Holy Roman Empire and Spain. Under his son Philip II (r. 1556–1598), however, the center of the Habsburg empire and the political center of gravity for all of Europe shifted westward to Spain. This event marked a watershed in early modern European history. Before 1559 Spain and France had fought bitterly for control of Italy; after 1559 the two Catholic powers aimed their guns at Protestantism. The Treaty of Cateau-Cambrésis ended an era of strictly dynastic wars and initiated a period of conflicts in which politics and religion played the dominant roles.

Because a variety of issues were stewing, it is not easy to generalize about the wars of the late sixteenth century. Some were continuations of struggles between the centralizing goals of monarchies and the feudal reactions of nobilities. Some were crusading battles between Catholics and Protestants. Some were struggles for national independence or for international expansion.

These wars differed considerably from earlier wars. Sixteenth- and seventeenth-century armies were bigger than medieval ones; some forces numbered as many as fifty thousand men. Because large armies were expensive, governments had to reorganize their administrations to finance these armies. The use of gunpowder altered both the nature of war and popular attitudes toward it. Guns and cannon killed and wounded from a distance, indiscriminately. Writers scorned gunpowder as a coward's weapon that allowed a common soldier to kill a gentleman. Italian poet Ariosto lamented:

Through thee is martial glory lost, through
Thee the trade of arms becomes a worthless art:
And at such ebb are worth and chivalry that
The base often plays the better part.[1]

Gunpowder weakened the notion, common during the Hundred Years' War, that warfare was an ennobling experience. At the same time, governments utilized propaganda, pulpits, and the printing press to arouse public opinion to support war.[2]

Late-sixteenth-century conflicts fundamentally tested the medieval ideal of a unified Christian society governed by one political ruler, the emperor, to whom all rulers were theoretically subordinate, and one church, to which all people belonged. The Protestant Reformation had killed this ideal, but few people recognized it as dead. Catholics continued to believe that Calvinists

François Clouet: Francis I Having succeeded his father as official painter at the French court, Clouet (1520?–1572) executed this royal portrait. The rich gold doublet has been embroidered with black velvet designs, satin, and more gold. His left hand rests on his golden sword hilt. *(© Photo R.M.N.—Herve Lewandowski)*

and Lutherans could be reconverted; Protestants persisted in thinking that the Roman church should be destroyed. Most people believed that a state could survive only if its members shared the same faith. Catholics and Protestants alike feared people of the other faith living in their midst. The settlement finally achieved in 1648, known as the Peace of Westphalia, signaled the end of the medieval ideal.

The Origins of Difficulties in France (1515–1559)

In the first half of the sixteenth century, France continued the recovery begun under Louis XI (see page 441). The population losses caused by the plague and the disorders accompanying the Hundred Years' War had created such a labor shortage that serfdom virtually disappeared. Cash rents replaced feudal rents and servile obligations. This development clearly benefited the peasantry. Meanwhile, the declining buying power of money hurt the nobility. The increase in France's population in the late fifteenth and sixteenth centuries brought new lands under cultivation, but the division of property among sons meant that most peasant holdings were very small. Domestic and foreign trade picked up, mercantile centers such as Rouen and Lyons expanded, and in 1517 a new port city was founded at Le Havre.

The charming and cultivated Francis I (r. 1515–1547) and his athletic, emotional son Henry II (r. 1547–1559) governed through a small, efficient council. Great nobles held titular authority in the provinces as governors, but Paris-appointed baillis and seneschals continued to exercise actual fiscal and judicial responsibility (see page 338). In 1539 Francis issued an ordinance that placed the whole of France under the jurisdiction of the royal law courts and made French the language of those courts. This act had a powerful centralizing impact. The taille, a tax on land, provided what strength the monarchy had and supported a strong standing army. Unfortunately, the tax base was too narrow for Francis's extravagant promotion of the arts and ambitious foreign policy.

Deliberately imitating the Italian Renaissance princes, the Valois monarchs lavished money on a magnificent court, a vast building program, and Italian artists. Francis I commissioned Paris architect Pierre Lescot to rebuild the palace of the Louvre. Francis secured the services of Michelangelo's star pupil, Il Rosso, who decorated the wing of the Fontainebleau chateau, subsequently called the Gallery Francis I, with rich scenes from classical and mythological literature. After acquiring Leonardo da Vinci's *Mona Lisa,* Francis brought Leonardo himself to France. Henry II built a castle at Dreux for his mistress, Diane de Poitiers, and a palace in Paris, the Tuileries, for his wife, Catherine de' Medici. Art historians credit Francis I and Henry II with importing Italian Renaissance art and architecture to France. But whatever praise these monarchs deserve for their cultural achievement, they spent far more than they could afford.

The Habsburg-Valois Wars, waged intermittently through the first half of the sixteenth century, also cost more than the government could afford. Financing the wars posed problems. In addition to the time-honored practices of increasing taxes and engaging in heavy borrowing, Francis I tried two new devices to raise revenue: the sale of public offices and a treaty with the papacy. The former proved to be only a temporary

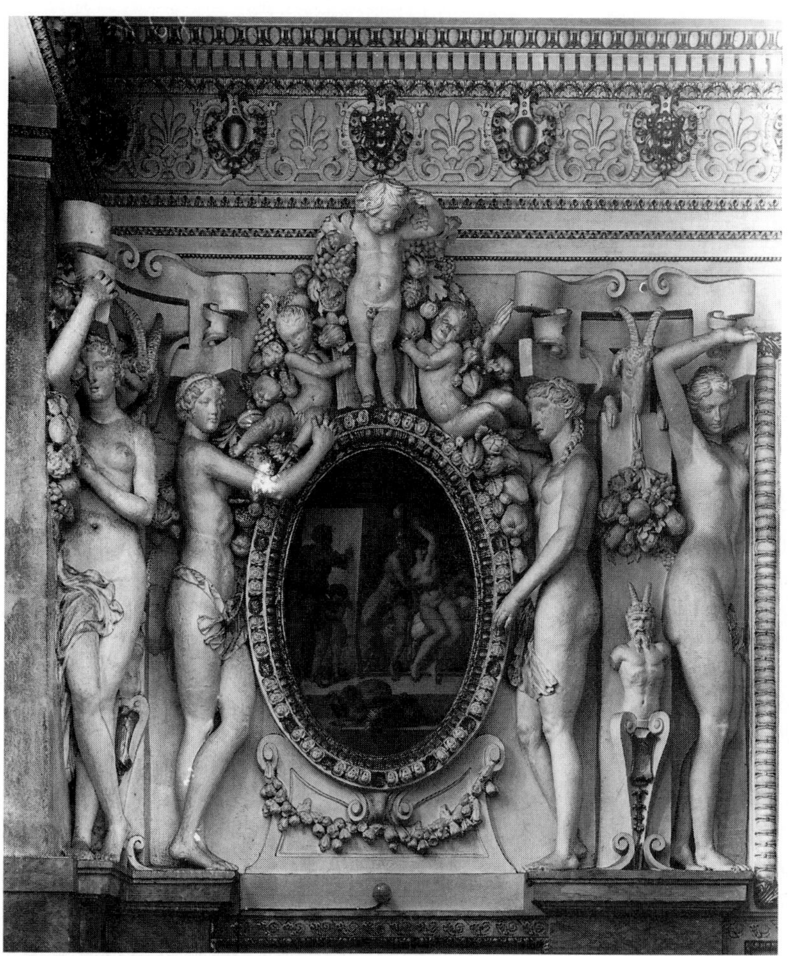

Primaticcio: Duchess of Etampes's Chamber In spite of the enormous financial burdens that continuous war placed on his resources, Francis I lavished money on architecture and the arts. To "modernize" the royal residence at Fontainebleau, he summoned the Italian architect and designer Francesco Primaticcio (1504/5–1570), who spent decades on the bedchamber of the king's mistress, Diana, ornamenting it with garlands, woodworking, mythological figures, fresco paintings, and, according to Vasari, the first stucco works in France. Primaticcio inaugurated what was called the School of Fontainebleau. *(Foto Marburg/Art Resource, NY)*

source of money. The offices sold tended to become hereditary within a family, and once a man bought an office, he and his heirs were tax-exempt. The sale of public offices thus created a tax-exempt class called the "nobility of the robe," which held positions beyond the jurisdiction of the Crown.

The treaty with the papacy was the Concordat of Bologna (see page 441), in which Francis agreed to recognize the supremacy of the papacy over a universal council. In return, the French crown gained the right to appoint all French bishops and abbots. This understanding gave the monarchy a rich supplement of money and offices and a power over the church that lasted until the Revolution of 1789. The Concordat of Bologna helps explain why France did not later become Protestant: in effect, it established Catholicism as the state religion. Because French rulers possessed control over appointments and had a vested financial interest in Catholicism, they had no need to revolt against Rome.

However, the Concordat of Bologna perpetuated disorders within the French church. Ecclesiastical offices were used primarily to pay and reward civil servants. Churchmen in France, as elsewhere, were promoted to the hierarchy not because they possessed any special spiritual qualifications but because they had rendered services to the state. Such bishops were unlikely to work to elevate the intellectual and moral standards of the parish clergy. Few of the many priests in France devoted scrupulous attention to the needs of their parishioners. Thus the teachings of Luther and Calvin, as the presses disseminated them, found a receptive audience.

Luther's tracts first appeared in France in 1518, and his ideas attracted some attention. After the publication of Calvin's *Institutes* in 1536, sizable numbers of French people were attracted to the "reformed religion," as Calvinism was called. Because Calvin wrote in French rather than Latin, his ideas gained wide circulation.

Initially, Calvinism drew converts from among reform-minded members of the Catholic clergy, the industrious middle classes, and artisan groups. Most Calvinists lived in major cities, such as Paris, Lyons, Meaux, and Grenoble.

In spite of condemnation by the universities, government bans, and massive burnings at the stake, the numbers of Protestants grew steadily. When Henry II died in 1559, there were 40 well-organized Calvinist churches and 2,150 mission stations in France. Perhaps one-tenth of the population had become Calvinist.

Religious Riots and Civil War in France (1559–1598)

For forty years, from 1559 to 1598, violence and civil war divided and shattered France. The feebleness of the monarchy was the seed from which the weeds of civil violence sprang. The three weak sons of Henry II who occupied the throne could not provide the necessary leadership. Francis II (r. 1559–1560) died after seventeen months. Charles IX (r. 1560–1574) succeeded at the age of ten and was thoroughly dominated by his opportunistic mother, Catherine de' Medici, who would support any party or position to maintain her influence. The intelligent and cultivated Henry III (r. 1574–1589) divided his attention between debaucheries with his male lovers and frantic acts of repentance.

The French nobility took advantage of this monarchial weakness. In the second half of the sixteenth century, between two-fifths and one-half of the nobility at one time or another became Calvinist. Just as German princes in the Holy Roman Empire had adopted Lutheranism as a means of opposition to Emperor Charles V, so French nobles frequently adopted the reformed religion as a religious cloak for their independence. No one believed that peoples of different faiths could coexist peacefully within the same territory. The Reformation thus led to a resurgence of feudal disorder. Armed clashes between Catholic royalist lords and Calvinist antimonarchial lords occurred in many parts of France.

Among the upper classes, the Catholic-Calvinist conflict was the surface issue, but the fundamental object of the struggle was power. At lower social levels, however, religious concerns were paramount. Working-class crowds composed of skilled craftsmen and the poor wreaked terrible violence on other people and property. Both Calvinists and Catholics believed that the others' books, services, and ministers polluted the community. Preachers incited violence, and ceremonies such as baptisms, marriages, and funerals triggered it. Protestant pastors encouraged their followers to destroy statues and liturgical objects in Catholic churches. Catholic priests urged their flocks to shed the blood of the Calvinist heretics.

In 1561 in the Paris church of Saint-Médard, a Protestant crowd cornered a baker guarding a box containing the consecrated Eucharistic bread. Taunting "Does your God of paste protect you now from the pains of death?" the mob proceeded to kill the poor man.[3] Calvinists believed that the Catholic emphasis on symbols in religious ritual desecrated what was truly sacred and promoted the worship of images. In scores of attacks on Catholic churches, religious statues were knocked down, stained-glass windows were smashed, and sacred vestments, vessels, and Eucharistic elements were defiled. In 1561 a Catholic crowd charged a group of just-released Protestant prisoners, killed them, and burned their bodies in the street. Hundreds of Huguenots, as French Calvinists were called, were tortured, had their tongues cut out or throats slit, or were maimed or murdered.

In the fourteenth and fifteenth centuries, crowd action—attacks on great nobles and rich prelates—had expressed economic grievances. In contrast, religious rioters of the sixteenth century believed that they could assume the power of public magistrates and rid the community of corruption. Municipal officials criticized the crowds' actions, but the participation of pastors and priests in these riots lent them some legitimacy.[4]

A savage Catholic attack on Calvinists in Paris on August 24, 1572 (Saint Bartholomew's Day), followed the usual pattern. The occasion was a religious ceremony, the marriage of the king's sister Margaret of Valois to the Protestant Henry of Navarre, which was intended to help reconcile Catholics and Huguenots. Among the many Calvinists present for the wedding festivities was Admiral Gaspard de Coligny, head of one of the great noble families of France and leader of the Huguenot party. Coligny had recently replaced Catherine de' Medici in influence over the young king Charles IX. When, the night before the wedding, the leader of the Catholic aristocracy, Henry of Guise, had Coligny attacked, rioting and slaughter followed. The Huguenot gentry in Paris was massacred, and religious violence spread to the provinces. Between August 25 and October 3, perhaps twelve thousand Huguenots perished at Meaux, Lyons, Orléans, and Paris. The contradictory orders of Charles IX worsened the situation.

The Saint Bartholomew's Day massacre led to fighting that launched the War of the Three Henrys, a civil conflict among factions led by the Catholic Henry of Guise, the Protestant Henry of Navarre, and King Henry III, who succeeded the tubercular Charles IX. Though King Henry remained Catholic, he realized that the Catholic Guise group represented his greatest danger. The Guises wanted, through an alliance of Catholic nobles called the "Holy League," not only to destroy Calvinism but also to replace Henry III with a member of the Guise family. France suffered fifteen more years of religious rioting and domestic anarchy. Agriculture in many areas was destroyed, commercial life declined severely, and starvation and death haunted the land.

What ultimately saved France was a small group of moderates of both faiths called *politiques* who believed that only the restoration of strong monarchy could reverse the trend toward collapse. No religious creed was worth the incessant disorder and destruction. Therefore, the politiques favored accepting the Huguenots as an officially recognized and organized pressure group. (But religious toleration, the full acceptance of peoples of different religious persuasions within a pluralistic society, with minorities having the same civil liberties as the majority, developed only in the eighteenth century.) The death of Catherine de' Medici, followed by the assassinations of Henry of Guise and King Henry III, paved the way for the accession of Henry of Navarre, a politique who became Henry IV (r. 1589–1610).

This glamorous prince, "who knew how to fight, to make love, and to drink," as a contemporary remarked, wanted above all a strong and united France. He knew, too, that the majority of the French were Roman Catholics. Declaring "Paris is worth a Mass," Henry knelt before the archbishop of Bourges and was received into the Roman Catholic church. Henry's willingness to sacrifice religious principles to political necessity saved France. The Edict of Nantes, which Henry published in 1598, granted to Huguenots liberty of conscience and liberty of public worship in 150 fortified towns, such as La Rochelle. The reign of Henry IV and the Edict of Nantes prepared the way for French absolutism in the seventeenth century by helping restore internal peace in France.

The Netherlands Under Charles V

In the last quarter of the sixteenth century, the political stability of England, the international prestige of Spain, and the moral influence of the Roman papacy all became mixed up with the religious crisis in the Low Countries. The Netherlands was the pivot around which European money, diplomacy, and war revolved. What began as a movement for the reformation of the church developed into a struggle for Dutch independence.

Emperor Charles V (r. 1519–1556) had inherited the seventeen provinces that compose present-day Belgium and Holland (see page 463). Since the time of the great medieval fairs, cities of the Low Countries (so called because much of the land lies below sea level) had been important sites for the exchange of products from the Baltic and Italy. Antwerp, ideally situated on the Scheldt River at the intersection of many trading routes, steadily expanded as the chief intermediary for international commerce and finance. English woolens; Baltic wheat, fur, and timber; Portuguese spices; German iron and copper; Spanish fruit; French wines and dyestuffs; Italian silks, marble, and mirrors; and vast amounts of cash—all were exchanged at Antwerp. The city's harbor could dock twenty-five hundred vessels at once, and five thousand merchants from many nations gathered daily in the *bourse* (or exchange). Other great towns—Bruges, Ghent, Brussels, Arras, and Amsterdam—made their living by trade and industry as well. The French-speaking southern towns produced fine linens and woolens, while the wealth of the Dutch-speaking northern cities rested on fishing, shipping, and international banking. In these cities, trade and commerce had produced a vibrant atmosphere, as personified in the urbane Erasmus of Rotterdam (see pages 437–439).

Each of the seventeen provinces of the Netherlands possessed historical liberties: each was self-governing and enjoyed the right to make its own laws and collect its own taxes. In addition to important economic connections, only the recognition of a common ruler in the person of Emperor Charles V united the provinces. Delegates from the various provinces met together in the States General, but important decisions had to be referred back to each province for approval. In the middle of the sixteenth century, the provinces of the Netherlands had a limited sense of federation.

In the Low Countries as elsewhere, corruption in the Roman church and the critical spirit of the Renaissance provoked pressure for reform. Lutheran tracts and Dutch translations of the Bible flooded the seventeen provinces in the 1520s and 1530s, attracting many people to Protestantism. Charles V's government responded with condemnation and mild repression. This policy was not particularly effective, however, because ideas circulated freely in the cosmopolitan atmosphere of the commercial centers. But Charles's loyalty to the Flemings checked the spread of Lutheranism. Charles had been born in Ghent and raised in the Netherlands;

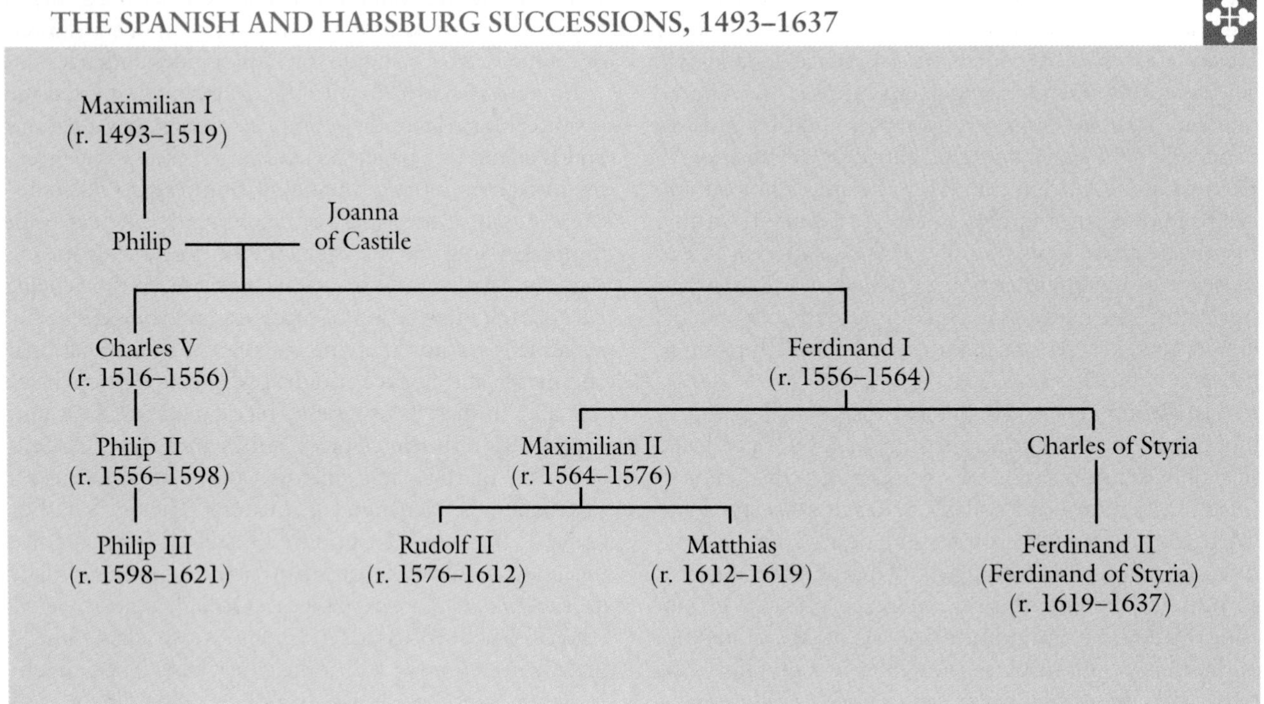

he was Flemish in language and culture. He identified with the Flemish and they with him.

In 1556, however, Charles V abdicated, dividing his territories between his brother Ferdinand, who received Austria and the Holy Roman Empire, and his son Philip, who inherited Spain, the Low Countries, Milan and the kingdom of Sicily, and the Spanish possessions in the Americas. Charles delivered his abdication speech before the States General at Brussels. The emperor was then fifty-five years old, white-haired, and so crippled in the legs that he had to lean for support on the young Prince William of Orange. According to one contemporary account of the emperor's appearance:

His under lip, a Burgundian inheritance, as faithfully transmitted as the duchy and county, was heavy and hanging, the lower jaw protruding so far beyond the upper that it was impossible for him to bring together the few fragments of teeth which still remained, or to speak a whole sentence in an intelligible voice.[5]

Charles spoke in Flemish. Philip responded in Spanish; he could speak neither French nor Flemish. Netherlanders had always felt that Charles was one of their own. They were never to forget that Philip was Spanish.

The Revolt of the Netherlands (1566–1587)

Lutheranism had posed no serious threat to Spanish rule; it was the spread of Calvinism that upset the apple cart. By the 1560s, there was a strong, militant minority of Calvinists in most of the cities of the Netherlands. The seventeen provinces possessed a large middle-class population, and the reformed religion, as a contemporary remarked, had a powerful appeal "to those who had grown rich by trade and were therefore ready for revolution."[6] Calvinism appealed to the middle classes because of its intellectual seriousness, moral gravity, and emphasis on any form of labor well done. It took deep root among the merchants and financiers in Amsterdam and the northern provinces. Working-class people were also converted, partly because their employers would hire only other Calvinists. Well organized and backed by rich merchants, Calvinists quickly gained a wide following. Whereas Lutherans taught respect for the powers that be, Calvinist reformed religion in the 1570s tended to encourage opposition to "illegal" civil authorities.

In 1559 Philip II appointed his half-sister Margaret as regent of the Netherlands (r. 1559–1567). A proud, energetic, and strong-willed woman who once had Ignatius Loyola as her confessor, Margaret pushed Philip's orders to wipe out Protestantism. She introduced the Inquisition. Her more immediate problem, however, was revenue to finance the government of the provinces. Charles V had steadily increased taxes in the Low Countries. When Margaret appealed to the States General, it claimed that the Low Countries were more heavily taxed than Spain. Nevertheless, Margaret raised taxes and succeeded in uniting the opposition to the government's fiscal policy with the opposition to official repression of Calvinism.

In August 1566, a year of very high grain prices, fanatical Calvinists, primarily of the poorest classes, embarked on a rampage of frightful destruction. As in France, Calvinist destruction in the Low Countries was incited by popular preaching, and attacks were aimed at religious images as symbols of false doctrines, not at people. The cathedral of Notre Dame at Antwerp was the first target.

Begun in 1124 and finished only in 1518, this church stood as a monument to the commercial prosperity of Flanders, the piety of the business classes, and the artistic genius of centuries. On six successive summer evenings, crowds swept through the nave. While the town harlots held tapers to the greatest concentration of artworks in northern Europe, people armed with axes and sledgehammers smashed altars, paintings, books, tombs, ecclesiastical vestments, missals, manuscripts, ornaments, stained-glass windows, and sculptures. Before the havoc was over, thirty more churches had been sacked and irreplaceable libraries burned. From Antwerp the destruction spread to Brussels and Ghent and north to the provinces of Holland and Zeeland.

To Purify the Church The destruction of pictures and statues representing biblical events, Christian doctrine, or sacred figures was a central feature of the Protestant Reformation. Here Dutch Protestant soldiers destroy what they consider idols in the belief that they are purifying the church. *(Fotomas Index)*

MAP 15.1 The Netherlands, 1578–1609 Though small in geographical size, the Netherlands held a strategic position in the religious struggles of the sixteenth century. Why?

From Madrid Philip II sent twenty thousand Spanish troops under the duke of Alva to pacify the Low Countries. Alva interpreted "pacification" to mean the ruthless extermination of religious and political dissidents. On top of the Inquisition, he opened his own tribunal, soon called the "Council of Blood." On March 3, 1568, fifteen hundred men were executed. Even Margaret was sickened and resigned her regency. Alva resolved the financial crisis by levying a 10 percent sales tax on every transaction, which in a commercial society caused widespread hardship and confusion.

For ten years, between 1568 and 1578, civil war raged in the Netherlands between Catholics and Protestants and between the seventeen provinces and Spain. A series of Spanish generals could not halt the fighting. In 1576 the seventeen provinces united under the leadership of Prince William of Orange, called "the Silent" because of his remarkable discretion. In 1578 Philip II sent his nephew Alexander Farnese, duke of Parma, to crush the revolt once and for all. A general with a superb sense of timing, an excellent knowledge of the geography of the Low Countries, and a perfect plan, Farnese arrived with an army of German mercenaries. Avoiding pitched battles, he fought by patient sieges. One by one, the cities of the south fell—Maastricht, Tournai, Bruges, Ghent, and, finally, the financial capital of northern Europe, Antwerp. Calvinism was forbidden in these territories, and Protestants were compelled to convert or leave. The collapse of Antwerp marked the farthest extent of Spanish jurisdiction and ultimately the religious division of the Netherlands.

The ten southern provinces, the Spanish Netherlands (the future Belgium), remained under the control of the Spanish Habsburgs. The seven northern provinces, led by Holland, formed the Union of Utrecht and in 1581 declared their independence from Spain. Thus was born the United Provinces of the Netherlands (Map 15.1). One of the key players in the early history of the United Provinces was Johan van Oldenbarnevelt. (See the feature "Individuals in Society: Johan van Oldenbarnevelt.")

Geography and sociopolitical structure differentiated the two countries. The northern provinces were ribboned with sluices and canals and therefore were highly defensible. Several times the Dutch had broken the dikes and flooded the countryside to halt the advancing Farnese. In the southern provinces, the Ardennes mountains interrupted the otherwise flat terrain. In the north, the commercial aristocracy possessed the predominant power; in the south, the landed nobility had the greater influence. The north was Protestant; the south remained Catholic.

Philip II and Alexander Farnese did not accept this geographical division, and the struggle continued after 1581. The United Provinces repeatedly asked the Protestant queen of England, Elizabeth, for assistance.

The crown on the head of Elizabeth I (see page 473) did not rest easily. She had steered a moderately Protestant course between the Puritans, who sought the total elimination of Roman Catholic elements in the English church, and the Roman Catholics, who wanted full restoration of the old religion. Elizabeth survived a massive uprising by the Catholic north in 1569 to 1570. She survived two serious plots against her life. In the 1570s, the presence in England of Mary, Queen of Scots, a Roman Catholic and the legal heir to the English throne, produced a very embarrassing situation. Mary was the rallying point of all opposition to Elizabeth, yet the English sovereign hesitated to order Mary executed, fearing the terrible example of regicide.

Individuals in Society

Johan van Oldenbarnevelt (1547–1619)

Johan van Oldenbarnevelt was the second founder (after William the Silent) of the United Provinces of the Netherlands, or the Dutch republic. Lawyer, statesman, diplomat, administrator, and financier of great vision, Oldenbarnevelt built the foundations of Dutch political independence and commercial prosperity in seventeenth-century Europe. His career illustrates the fragile union of strong provinces in the weak confederation that became the Netherlands.

Oldenbarnevelt came from a lower-gentry family in Utrecht. Trained as a lawyer, he joined the independence movement that began in 1572, when the provinces of Holland and Zeeland shook off Spanish rule. When Alexander Farnese's forces threatened reconquest, Oldenbarnevelt helped negotiate the Union of Utrecht (1579). Two years later, the seven northern provinces declared independence from Spain, and the United Provinces of the Netherlands was born. When William the Silent was murdered in 1584, Oldenbarnevelt began to direct meetings of the States General. He mobilized the nation for war and, on a diplomatic mission to England in 1585, won the military and financial help of Elizabeth I for independence.

Commercial matters also preoccupied him. In the later sixteenth century, small groups of Dutch businessmen competed for the lucrative Indian Ocean spice trade. Oldenbarnevelt persuaded these separate entrepreneurs to combine and in 1602 launched the Dutch East India Company; its purpose was to protect Dutch trade in the East and to damage the enemy, Spain, on the seas. The Dutch government granted the DEIC a monopoly of all trade in eastern waters and the sovereign right to govern territories that came under the company's control. After 1602 one policy, not many, controlled Dutch affairs in Asia.

In 1596 France and England recognized the seven provinces as an independent state. War with Spain erupted again in 1600, but trade and war booty enriched the Dutch republic. The Twelve Years' Truce (1609) with Spain is considered Oldenbarnevelt's greatest achievement: Spain's recognition of the United Provinces (if temporary) gave it the opportunity to consolidate its government and to strengthen its position on the seas.

Vast Amsterdam warehouses of the Dutch East India Company. *(Rijksmuseum-Stichting Amsterdam)*

From 1609 to 1621, two grave issues emerged. First, were the wars with Spain religious or political? Oldenbarnevelt believed that the Dutch had fought for freedom from Spain. He had accepted membership in the Dutch Reformed church, which he understood to be open to all sects. (He favored religious toleration.) Calvinist ministers, however, argued that the Dutch revolt against Spain had been entirely about doctrinal issues; they favored the establishment of a Genevan-type church independent of civil authorities, whose fitness to govern would be judged by churchmen.

Second, to whom did Oldenbarnevelt owe basic loyalty—to Holland, to which he was pledged by oath, or to the United Provinces? Since the ministers insisted that the Reformed church as they defined it was the "cement" that held the United Provinces together, the issue of federalism was itself connected with religion.

Decision rested with Maurice of Nassau, son of William the Silent. In 1617 Oldenbarnevelt and the regents of Holland, as was their constitutional right, urged the towns to recruit their own militias, troops not subject to Maurice's control. Maurice considered this treasonous, a violation of United Provinces law, and arrested Oldenbarnevelt. After a year of imprisonment, Oldenbarnevelt was condemned to death not for treason, but for "subversion" of the United Provinces' religion. At The Hague in May 1619, the 72-year-old Oldenbarnevelt was beheaded.

Questions for Analysis

1. Consider Oldenbarnevelt's contribution to the rise of Dutch commercial power.
2. How were religious and political issues tied up in the United Provinces of the Netherlands?

Sources: J. den Tex, *Oldenbarnevelt,* 2 vols. (New York: Cambridge University Press, 1973); "Muurits van Nassau," "Oldenbarnevelt," and "Revolt of the Netherlands," in *The Oxford Encyclopedia of the Reformation,* ed. H. J. Hillerbrand (New York: Oxford University Press, 1996).

Elizabeth faced a grave dilemma. If she responded favorably to Dutch pleas for military support against the Spanish, she would antagonize Philip II. The Spanish king had the steady flow of silver from the Americas at his disposal, and Elizabeth, lacking such treasure, wanted to avoid war. But if she did not help the Protestant Netherlands and it was crushed by Farnese, the likelihood was that the Spanish would invade England.

Three developments forced Elizabeth's hand. First, the wars in the Low Countries—the chief market for English woolens—badly hurt the English economy. When wool was not exported, the Crown lost valuable customs revenues. Second, the murder of William the Silent in July 1584 eliminated not only a great Protestant leader but also the chief military check on the Farnese advance. Third, the collapse of Antwerp appeared to signal a Catholic sweep through the Netherlands. The next step, the English feared, would be a Spanish invasion of their island. For these reasons, Elizabeth pumped 250,000 pounds and two thousand troops into the Protestant cause in the Low Countries between 1585 and 1587.

Philip II and the Spanish Armada

Philip pondered the Dutch and English developments at the Escorial, northwest of Madrid. Begun in 1563 and completed under the king's personal supervision in 1584, the monastery of Saint Lawrence of the Escorial served as a residence for Jeromite monks, a tomb for the king's Habsburg ancestors, and a royal palace for Philip and his family. The vast buildings resemble a gridiron, the instrument on which Saint Lawrence (d. 258) had supposedly been roasted alive. The royal apartments were in the center of the Italian Renaissance building complex. King Philip's tiny bedchamber possessed a concealed sliding window that opened directly onto the high altar of the monastery church so that he could watch the services and pray along with the monks. In this somber atmosphere, surrounded by a community of monks and close to the bones of his ancestors, the Catholic ruler of Spain and much of the globe passed his days.

In 1587 Philip turned sixty, by the standards of his day an old man. Traditional scholarship, shaped largely by his Protestant enemies, has depicted Philip as morose and melancholic, a fanatical religious bigot determined to reimpose Roman Catholicism on northern Europe. Recent research portrays him as a more complicated, even paradoxical, figure. In his youth, "he had visited northern Italy, the Alps, southern Germany, the Rhineland, the Netherlands, parts of France, and southern England." He had walked the streets of Antwerp, Augsburg, Brussels, Cologne, London, and Trent. With the exception of his father, Charles V, no other European ruler of the time had traveled or seen so much, or accumulated so much political experience in international relations. Philip impressed ambassadors as formal, tight-lipped, and forbidding, perhaps because he spoke only his native Castilian (and Latin) and thus was limited in his ability to communicate with others. He was deeply pious: attendance at daily Mass was always part of his routine, and every year he retired to a monastery during Holy Week. On the other hand, in his younger days, he was much given to pleasure, and a critical contemporary wrote, "He is dissipated with women, likes to go in disguise at night, and enjoys all types of gaming (gambling)." He also enjoyed jokes and had a good sense of humor.[7]

After Philip buried his fourth wife (enough to make any man "melancholic"), Anna of Austria, to whom he had been deeply devoted, contemporaries noticed a more marked devotion to religion. He relied more and more on God for political help. He did not believe the state could impose morality on private citizens, and when told that homosexuality was rampant in Madrid, he ordered his officials to drop the matter—the charges were too vague. On the issues of the Inquisition and religious toleration, however, Philip was completely inflexible. He identified toleration with the growth of heresy, civil disorder, violence, and bloodshed: "Had there been no inquisition (in Spain) there would have been more heretics, and the country would be in a lamentable state like others (the Netherlands) where there is no inquisition as we have in Spain."[8] In this respect, Philip II differed little from the Protestant reformers Luther and Calvin, who initially called for individual liberty of conscience and then insisted on the right of church and civil powers to extirpate heresy within their jurisdictions. Philip was a man of his times, and the times did not favor religious toleration. And just as the Protestant princes of northern Europe governed religious life within their states, so Philip II controlled ecclesiastical appointments and revenues in Spain.

In 1586, Mary, Queen of Scots, cousin and heir of Elizabeth of England, became implicated in a plot to assassinate Elizabeth. Philip, hoping to reunite England with Catholic Europe through Mary, gave the conspiracy his full backing. Mary was discovered and beheaded on February 18, 1587. News of her execution reached Philip in mid-April. When Pope Sixtus V (1585–1590) learned of Mary's death on March 24 (the dates suggest

NOT LONGE TIME SINCE I SAWE A COWE.
DID FLAVNDERS REPRESENTE
VPON WHOSE BACKE KINGE PHILLIP RODE
AS BEING MALECONTNT.
THE QVEENE OF ENGLAND GIVING HAY
WHEARE ON THE COW DID FEEDE
AS ONE THAT WAS HER GREATEST HELPE.
IN HER DISTRESSE AND NEEDE.
THE PRINCE OF ORANGE MILKT THE
AND MADE HIS PVRSE THE PAYLE.
THE COW DID SHYT IN MONSIEVRS
WHILE HE DID HOLD HER TAYLE.

The Milch Cow In this late-sixteenth-century allegorical cartoon, the cow is Flanders: Queen Elizabeth feeds it hay, King Philip rides and beats it, William of Orange milks it, and the duke of Anjou (of France) pulls its tail. The artist apparently thought all these rulers were exploiting the Low Countries. *(Rijkmuseum-Stichting Amsterdam)*

the slowness of communication in the late sixteenth century), the pope promised to pay Philip 1 million gold ducats the moment Spanish troops landed in England. Alexander Farnese had repeatedly warned that to subdue the Dutch, he would have to conquer England and cut off the source of Dutch support. Philip also worried that the vast amounts of South American silver he was pouring into the conquest of the Netherlands seemed to be going down a bottomless pit. Two plans for an expedition were considered. Philip's naval adviser recommended that a fleet of 150 ships sail from Lisbon, attack the English navy in the Channel, and invade England. Another proposal was to assemble a collection of barges and troops in Flanders to stage a cross-Channel assault. With the expected support of English Catholics, Spain would achieve a great victory. Farnese opposed this plan as militarily unsound.

As plans for an armada proceeded in 1587, two serious difficulties burdened the king. First, he suffered very poor health, so badly crippled by gout: in his hands that he could not sign documents, in his feet that he could walk, painfully, only with a cane. Second, official reports indicated that the Ottoman Turks might seize the moment of preoccupation with the Netherlands and England to attack Spain from the Mediterranean. With premonitions of disaster, Philip compromised between the two plans given him. He prepared a vast fleet to sail from Lisbon to Flanders, fight off Elizabeth's navy if it attacked, rendezvous with Farnese, and escort his barges across the English Channel. The expedition's purpose was to transport the Flemish army.

On May 9, 1588, *la felícissima armada*—"the most fortunate fleet," as it was ironically called in official documents—sailed from Lisbon harbor. The Spanish fleet of 130 vessels carried 123,790 cannonballs and perhaps 30,000 men, every one of whom had confessed his sins and received the Eucharist. An English fleet of about 150 ships met the Spanish in the Channel. The English fleet was composed of smaller, faster, more maneuverable ships, many of which had greater firing power than their Spanish counterparts. A combination of storms and squalls, spoiled food and rank water, inadequate Spanish ammunition, and, to a lesser extent, English fire ships that caused the Spanish to scatter gave England the victory. Many Spanish ships went down on the journey home around Ireland; perhaps 65 managed to reach home ports.

The battle in the Channel has frequently been described as one of the decisive battles in the history of the world. In fact, it had mixed consequences. Spain soon rebuilt its navy, and after 1588 the quality of the Spanish fleet improved. The destruction of the Spanish Armada did not halt the flow of silver from the New World. More silver reached Spain between 1588 and 1603 than in any other fifteen-year period. The war between England and Spain dragged on for years.

The defeat of the Spanish Armada was decisive, however, in the sense that it prevented Philip II from reimposing unity on western Europe by force. He did not conquer England, and Elizabeth continued her financial and military support of the Dutch. In the Netherlands, neither side gained significant territory. The borders of 1581 tended to become permanent. In 1609 Philip III of Spain (r. 1598–1621) agreed to a truce, in effect recognizing the independence of the United Provinces. In seventeenth-century Spain, memory of the defeat of the Spanish Armada contributed to a spirit of defeatism. In England the victory contributed to a David and Goliath legend that enhanced English national sentiment.

The Thirty Years' War (1618–1648)

While Philip II dreamed of building a second armada and Henry IV began the reconstruction of France, the political-religious situation in central Europe deteriorated. An uneasy truce had prevailed in the Holy Roman Empire since the Peace of Augsburg of 1555 (see page 466). The Augsburg settlement, in recognizing the independent power of the German princes, further undermined any authority of the central government. The Habsburg ruler in Vienna enjoyed the title of "emperor" but had no imperial power.

According to the Augsburg settlement, the faith of the prince determined the religion of his subjects. Later in the century, however, Catholics grew alarmed because Lutherans, in violation of the Peace of Augsburg, were steadily acquiring German bishoprics. The spread of Calvinism further confused the issue. The Augsburg settlement had pertained only to Lutheranism and Catholicism, so Calvinists ignored it and converted several princes. Lutherans feared that the Augsburg principles would be totally undermined by Catholic and Calvinist gains. Also, the militantly active Jesuits had reconverted several Lutheran princes to Catholicism. In an increasingly tense situation, Lutheran princes formed the Protestant Union (1608), and Catholics retaliated with the Catholic League (1609). Each alliance was determined that the other should make no religious (that is, territorial) advance. The empire was composed of two armed camps.

Dynastic interests were also involved in the German situation. When Charles V abdicated in 1556, he had divided his possessions between his son Philip II and his brother Ferdinand I. This partition began the Austrian and Spanish branches of the Habsburg family. Ferdinand inherited the imperial title and the Habsburg lands in central Europe, including Austria. Ferdinand's grandson Matthias had no direct heirs and promoted the candidacy of his fiercely Catholic cousin Ferdinand of Styria. The Spanish Habsburgs strongly supported the goals of their Austrian relatives: the unity of the empire and the preservation of Catholicism within it.

In 1617 Ferdinand of Styria secured election as king of Bohemia, a title that gave him jurisdiction over Silesia and Moravia as well as Bohemia. The Bohemians were Czech and German in nationality and Lutheran, Calvinist, Catholic, and Hussite in religion; all these faiths enjoyed a fair degree of religious freedom. When Ferdinand proceeded to close some Protestant churches, the heavily Protestant Estates of Bohemia protested. On May 23, 1618, Protestants hurled two of Ferdinand's officials from a castle window in Prague. They fell seventy feet but survived: Catholics claimed that angels had caught them; Protestants said that the officials had fallen on a heap of soft horse manure. Called the "defenestration of Prague," this event marked the beginning of the Thirty Years' War (1618–1648).

Historians traditionally divide the war into four phases. The first, or Bohemian, phase (1618–1625) was characterized by civil war in Bohemia between the Catholic League, led by Ferdinand, and the Protestant

Union, headed by Prince Frederick of the Palatinate. The Bohemians fought for religious liberty and independence from Habsburg rule. In 1618 the Bohemian Estates deposed Ferdinand and gave the crown of Bohemia to Frederick, thus uniting the interests of German Protestants with those of the international enemies of the Habsburgs. Frederick wore his crown only a few months. In 1620 he was defeated by Catholic forces at the Battle of the White Mountain. Ferdinand, who had recently been elected Holy Roman emperor as Ferdinand II, followed up his victories by wiping out Protestantism in Bohemia through forcible conversions and the activities of militant Jesuit missionaries. Within ten years, Bohemia was completely Catholic.

The second, or Danish, phase of the war (1625–1629)—so called because of the participation of King Christian IV of Denmark (r. 1588–1648), the ineffective leader of the Protestant cause—witnessed additional Catholic victories. The Catholic imperial army led by Albert of Wallenstein scored smashing victories. It swept through Silesia, north through Schleswig and Jutland to the Baltic, and east into Pomerania. Wallenstein, who had made himself indispensable to the emperor Ferdinand, was an unscrupulous opportunist who used his vast riches to build an army loyal only to himself. The general seemed interested more in carving out an empire for himself than in aiding the Catholic cause. He quarreled with the Catholic League, and soon the Catholic forces were divided. Religion was eclipsed as a basic issue of the war.

The year 1629 marked the peak of Habsburg power. The Jesuits persuaded the emperor to issue the Edict of Restitution, whereby all Catholic properties lost to Protestantism since 1552 were to be restored and only Catholics and Lutherans (not Calvinists, Hussites, or other sects) were to be allowed to practice their faiths. Ferdinand appeared to be embarked on a policy to unify the empire. When Wallenstein began ruthless enforcement of the edict, Protestants throughout Europe feared collapse of the balance of power in north-central Europe.

The third, or Swedish, phase of the war (1630–1635) began with the arrival in Germany of the Swedish king Gustavus Adolphus (r. 1594–1632). The ablest administrator of his day and a devout Lutheran, Gustavus Adolphus intervened to support the oppressed Protestants within the empire and to assist his relatives, the exiled dukes of Mecklenburg. Cardinal Richelieu, the chief minister of King Louis XIII of France (r. 1610–1643), subsidized the Swedes, hoping to weaken Habsburg power in Europe. In 1631, with a small but well-disciplined army equipped with superior muskets and warm uniforms, Gustavus Adolphus won a brilliant victory at Breitenfeld. Again in 1632 he was victorious at Lützen, though he was fatally wounded in the battle.

The participation of the Swedes in the Thirty Years' War proved decisive for the future of Protestantism and later German history. When Gustavus Adolphus landed on German soil, he had already brought Denmark, Poland, Finland, and the smaller Baltic states under Swedish influence. The Swedish victories ended the Habsburg ambition of uniting all the German states under imperial authority.

The death of Gustavus Adolphus in 1632, followed by the defeat of the Swedes at the Battle of Nördlingen in 1634, prompted the French to enter the war on the side of the Protestants. Thus began the French, or international, phase of the Thirty Years' War (1635–1648). For almost a century, French foreign policy had been based on opposition to the Habsburgs because a weak empire divided into scores of independent principalities enhanced France's international stature. In 1622, when the Dutch had resumed the war against Spain, the French had supported Holland. Now in 1635 Cardinal Richelieu declared war on Spain and again sent financial and military assistance to the Swedes and the German Protestant princes. The war dragged on. French, Dutch, and Swedes, supported by Scots, Finns, and German mercenaries, burned, looted, and destroyed German agriculture and commerce. The Thirty Years' War lasted so long because neither side had the resources to win a quick, decisive victory. Finally, in October 1648, peace was achieved.

The treaties signed at Münster and Osnabrück, commonly called the "Peace of Westphalia," marked a turning point in European political, religious, and social history. The treaties recognized the sovereign, independent authority of the German princes. Each ruler could govern his particular territory and make war and peace as well. With power in the hands of more than three hundred princes, with no central government, courts, or means of controlling unruly rulers, the Holy Roman Empire as a real state was effectively destroyed (Map 15.2).

The independence of the United Provinces of the Netherlands was acknowledged. The international stature of France and Sweden was also greatly improved. The political divisions within the empire, the weak German frontiers, and the acquisition of the province of Alsace increased France's size and prestige.

Austrian Habsburg lands
Spanish Habsburg lands
Prussian lands
German states
Swedish lands
Boundary of Holy Roman Empire
Major battles
0 150 300 Km.
0 150 300 Mi.
NORWAY
SWEDEN
FINLAND
RUSSIA
ESTONIA
LIVONIA
SCOTLAND
Edinburgh
North Sea
IRELAND
Dublin
DENMARK
JUTLAND
Copenhagen
Baltic Sea
SCHLESWIG
PRUSSIA
Vilna
ENGLAND
Lübeck
Hamburg
POMERANIA
Danzig
MECKLENBURG
Bremen
UNITED NETHERLANDS
London
Amsterdam
BRANDENBURG
Berlin
POLAND
Vistula
Warsaw
Osnabrück
Münster
Magdeburg
Essen
Breitenfeld
1631
Antwerp
SPANISH NETHERLANDS
Cologne
Lützen 1632
SAXONY
Elbe
Rhine
SILESIA
Dnieper
White Mountain 1620
Prague
Paris
BOHEMIA
Metz
MORAVIA
Dniester
ATLANTIC OCEAN
Nantes
Nördlingen 1634
BAVARIA
Augsburg
Vienna
MOLDAVIA
Loire
FRANCHE-COMTÉ
ALSACE
Danube
Pest
FRANCE
Zurich
STYRIA
Buda
TRANSYLVANIA
CRIMEA
Geneva
SWITZERLAND
SAVOY
CARNIOLA
PIEDMONT
MILAN
REPUBLIC OF VENICE
WALLACHIA
GENOA
Belgrade
Black Sea
Ebro
FLORENCE
PAPAL STATES
PORTUGAL
SPAIN
Madrid
Tagus
CORSICA (To Genoa)
OTTOMAN EMPIRE
Lisbon
Rome
Constantinople
NAPLES
Naples
SARDINIA
BALEARIC IS.
Mediterranean Sea
Palermo
Athens
SICILY
CRETE (To Rep. of Venice)

Thus he had witnessed the Spanish reconquest of Granada and shared fully in the religious and nationalistic fervor surrounding that event. Just seven months separated Isabella and Ferdinand's entry into Granada on January 2 and Columbus's departure westward on August 3, 1492. In his mind, the two events were clearly linked. Long after Europeans knew something of Columbus's discoveries in the Caribbean, they nevertheless considered the restoration of Muslim Granada to Christian hands as Ferdinand and Isabella's greatest achievement; for the reconquest the Spanish pope Alexander VI rewarded them in 1494 with the title "Most Catholic Kings." Like the Spanish rulers and most Europeans of his age, Columbus understood Christianity as a missionary religion that should be carried to places and peoples where it did not exist. Although Columbus certainly had material and secular goals, first and foremost, as he wrote in 1498, he believed he was a divine agent: "God made me the messenger of the new heaven and the new earth of which he spoke in the Apocalypse of St. John after having spoken of it through the mouth of the prophet Isaiah; and he showed me the post where to find it."[19]

Columbus was also very knowledgeable about the sea. He was familiar with such fifteenth-century Portuguese navigational developments as *portolans*—written descriptions of the courses along which ships sailed, showing bays, coves, capes, ports, and the distances between these places—and the use of the magnetic needle as a nautical instrument. Columbus had spent years consulting geographers, mapmakers, and navigators. And, as he implied in his *Journal,* he had acquired not only theoretical but also practical experience: "I have spent twenty-three years at sea and have not left it for any length of time worth mentioning, and I have seen everything from east to west [meaning he had been to England] and I have been to Guinea [north and west Africa]."[20] Although some of Columbus's geographical theories, such as his measurement of the distance from Portugal to Japan at 2,760 miles, when it is actually 12,000, proved inaccurate, his successful thirty-three-day voyage to the Caribbean owed a great deal to his seamanship and his knowledge of the accurate use of instruments.

What was the object of this first voyage? What did Columbus set out to do? He gave the answer in the very title of the expedition, "The Enterprise of the Indies." He wanted to find a direct ocean route to Asia that would provide the opportunity for a greatly expanded trade in which the European economy, and especially Spain, would participate. Two recent scholars have written, "If Columbus had not sailed westward in search of Asia, someone else would have done so. The time was right for such a bold undertaking." Someone else might have done so, but the fact remains that Columbus, displaying a characteristic Renaissance curiosity and restless drive, actually did it.

How did Columbus interpret what he had found, and in his mind did he achieve what he had set out to do? His mind had been formed by the Bible and the geographical writings of classical authors, as had the minds of most educated people of his times. Thus as people have often done in every age, Columbus ignored the evidence of his eyes and described what he saw in the Caribbean as an idyllic paradise, a peaceful garden of Eden. (See the feature "Listening to the Past: Columbus Describes His First Voyage" on pages 526–527.) When accounts of his travels were published, Europeans' immediate fascination with this image of the New World meant that Columbus's propaganda created an instant myth. But having sensed that he had not found the spice markets and bazaars of Asia, his goal shifted from establishing trade with the (East) Indians and Chinese to establishing the kind of trade the Portuguese then conducted with Africa and with the Atlantic islands. That meant setting up some form of government in the islands, and Columbus had little interest in or capacity for governing. In 1496 he had forcibly subjugated the island of Hispaniola, enslaved the Indians, and laid the basis for a system of land grants tied to the Indians' labor service. Borrowing practices and institutions from reconquest Spain and the Canary Islands, Columbus laid the foundation for Spanish imperial administration. In all of this, Columbus was very much a man of his times. He never understood, however, that the scale of his discoveries created problems of trade, settlers, governmental bureaucracy, and, from a late-twentieth-century perspective, the rights of native peoples.[21]

LATER EXPLORERS

News of Columbus's first voyage rapidly spread across Europe. On April 1, 1493, a printer in Barcelona published in Spanish Columbus's letter describing what he believed he had found. By the end of that month, the letter had been translated into Latin and published in Rome as *De Insulis Inventis* (On the Discoveries of the Islands). Within a year, printers in Paris, Basel, Antwerp, and Venice had brought out six more Latin editions, which were soon followed by translations in German and Tuscan, the dialect of the Florentines. In a 1503 letter, Florentine navigator Amerigo Vespucci (1454–1512), in whose honor America was named, wrote, "Those new regions which we found and explored with the fleet . . . we may rightly call a New World." This letter, titled *Mundus Novus* (The New World), was the first document to describe America as a continent separate from Asia. Some scholars today try to avoid the terms *discovery* and *New World,* lest they be considered Eurocentric, but the use of those words rests on a tradition begun by the early explorers themselves.

The Caribbean islands—the West Indies—represented to zealous Spanish missionaries millions of Indian natives for conversion to Christianity. Hispaniola, Cuba, and Puerto Rico also offered gold. Forced labor and starvation in the Spaniards' gold mines rapidly killed off the Indians. Even more, diseases brought by Europeans, against which the long-isolated Indians had no immunity, had a devastating effect on the native people. When Columbus arrived in 1492, the population of Hispaniola stood at approximately 100,000; in 1570, 300 people survived. Indian slaves from the Bahamas and black Africans from Guinea were then imported to do the mining.

The search for precious metals determined the direction of Spanish exploration and expansion into South America. When it became apparent that placer mining (in which ore is separated from soil by panning) in the Caribbean islands was slow and the rewards were slim, new routes to the East and new sources of gold and silver were sought.

In 1519 Spanish ruler Charles V commissioned Ferdinand Magellan (1480–1521) to find a direct route to the spices of the Moluccas Islands off the southeast coast of Asia. Magellan sailed southwest across the Atlantic to Brazil and proceeded south around Cape Horn into the Pacific Ocean (see Map 15.3). He crossed the Pacific, sailing west, to the Malay Archipelago, which he called the "Western Isles." (Some of these islands were conquered in the 1560s and named the "Philippines" for Philip II of Spain.)

Though Magellan was killed, the expedition continued, returning to Spain in 1522 from the east by way of the Indian Ocean, the Cape of Good Hope, and the Atlantic. Terrible storms, mutiny, starvation, and disease haunted this voyage. Nevertheless, it verified the theory that the earth was round and brought information about the vastness of the Pacific. Magellan also proved that the earth was much larger than Columbus had estimated.

In the West Indies, the slow recovery of gold, the shortage of a healthy labor force, and sheer restlessness speeded up Spain's search for wealth. In 1519, the year Magellan departed on his worldwide expedition, a brash and determined Spanish adventurer named Hernando Cortés (1485–1547) crossed from Hispaniola to mainland Mexico with six hundred men, seventeen horses, and ten cannon. Within three years, Cortés had taken captive the Aztec emperor Montezuma, conquered the fabulously rich Aztec Empire, and founded Mexico City as the capital of New Spain. The subjugation of northern Mexico took longer, but between 1531 and 1550 the Spanish gained control of Zacatecas and Guanajuato, where rich silver veins were soon tapped.

Another Spanish conquistador, Francisco Pizarro (1470–1541), repeated Cortés's feat in Peru. Between 1531 and 1536, with even fewer resources, Pizarro crushed the Inca Empire in western South America and established the Spanish viceroyalty of Peru, with its center at Lima. In 1545 the Spanish opened at Potosí in the Peruvian highlands what became the richest silver mines in the New World.

Between 1525 and 1575, the riches of the Americas poured into the Spanish port of Seville and the Portuguese capital of Lisbon. For all their new wealth, however, Lisbon and Seville did not become important trading centers. It was the Flemish city of Antwerp, controlled by the Spanish Habsburgs, that developed into the great entrepôt for overseas bullion and Portuguese spices and served as the commercial and financial capital of the entire European world.

By the end of the sixteenth century, Amsterdam had overtaken Antwerp as the financial capital of Europe. The Dutch had also embarked on foreign exploration and conquest. The Dutch East India Company, founded in 1602, became the major organ of Dutch imperialism and within a few decades expelled the Portuguese from Ceylon and other East Indian islands. By 1650 the Dutch West India Company had successfully intruded on the Spanish possessions in the Americas, in the process gaining control of much of the African and American trade.

English and French explorations lacked the immediate, sensational results of those of the Spanish and Portuguese. In 1497 John Cabot, a Genoese merchant living in London, sailed for Brazil but discovered Newfoundland. The next year he returned and explored the New England coast and perhaps as far south as Delaware. Since these expeditions found no spices or gold, King Henry VII lost interest in exploration. Between 1534 and 1541, Frenchman Jacques Cartier

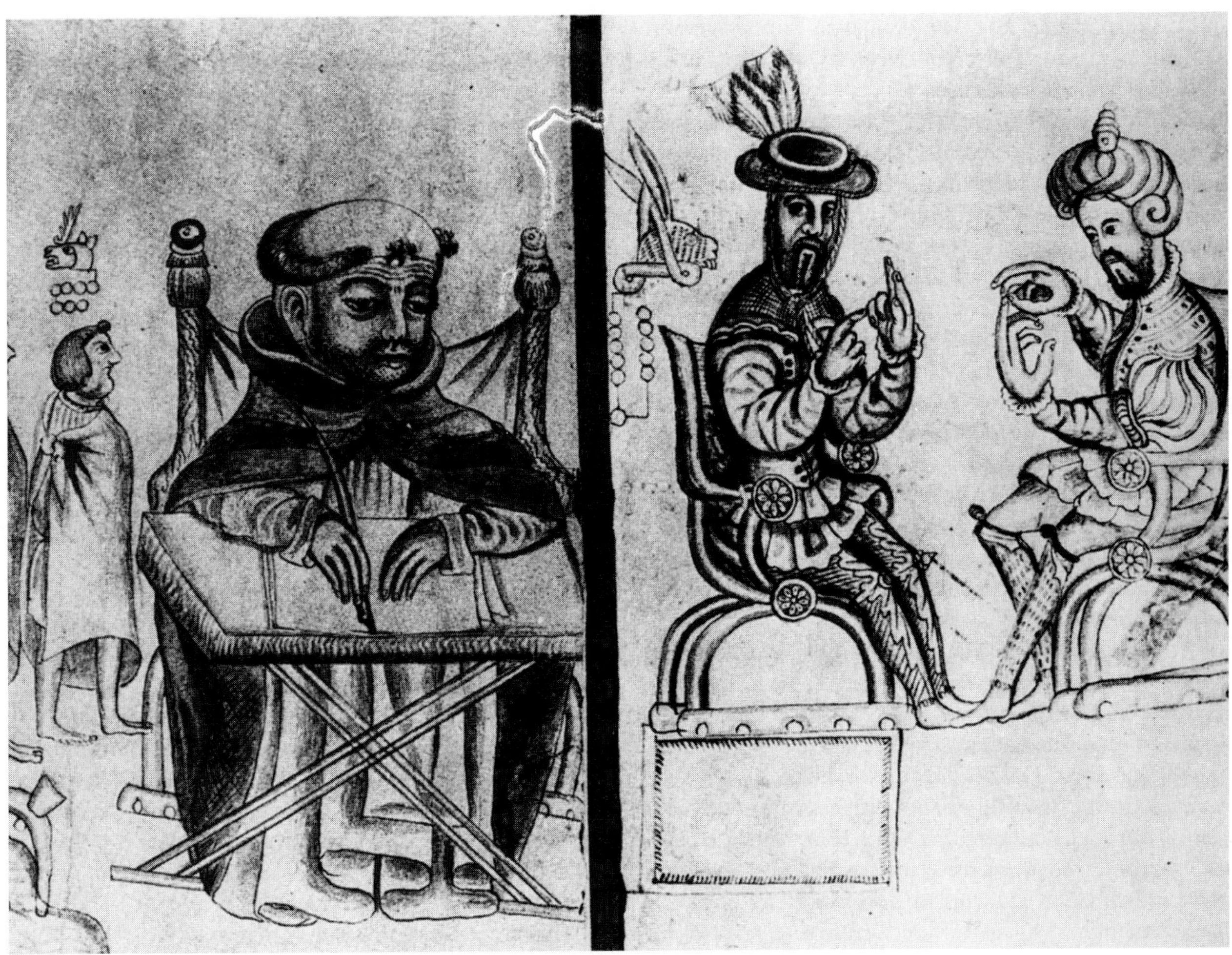

Yanhuitlan Codex The Mixtec people in southern Mexico, having assimilated and reinterpreted European forms, possessed an advanced and sophisticated culture. About 1550, Mesoamerican scholars of the Mixtec produced this codex (manuscript), which shows those they considered leaders of colonial society: from left, Indian *caciques* (leaders, chiefs); a Dominican friar of the order charged with converting the region; and Spanish administrators. *(Academia de Bella Artes, Puebla. Courtesy, Library of Congress)*

made several voyages and explored the St. Lawrence region of Canada, but the first permanent French settlement, at Quebec, was not founded until 1608.

The Economic Effects of Spain's Discoveries in the New World

The sixteenth century has often been called the "Golden Century" of Spain. The influence of Spanish armies, Spanish Catholicism, and Spanish wealth was felt all over Europe. This greatness rested largely on the influx of precious metals from the New World. The mines at Zacatecas and Guanajuato in Mexico and Potosí in Peru poured out huge quantities of precious metals. To protect this treasure from French and English pirates, armed convoys transported it each year to Spain. Between 1503 and 1650, 16 million kilograms of silver and 185,000 kilograms of gold entered the port of Seville.

Meanwhile, Spain was experiencing a steady population increase, creating a sharp rise in the demand for food and goods. Spanish colonies in the Americas also represented a demand for products. Because Spain had expelled some of its best farmers and business people, the Jews in 1492 and the Muslims in the sixteenth and seventeenth centuries, the Spanish economy suffered and could not meet the new demands. Prices rose and with them the costs of manufacturing cloth and other goods. As a result, Spanish products could not compete in the international market with cheaper products made elsewhere. The textile industry was badly hurt. Prices spiraled upward faster than the government could levy taxes to dampen the economy. (Higher taxes would have cut the public's buying power; with fewer goods sold, prices would have come down.)

Did the flood of American silver bullion cause the inflation? Scholars have long debated this question. Prices rose most steeply before 1565, but bullion imports reached their peak between 1580 and 1620. Thus there is no direct correlation between silver imports and the inflation rate. Did the substantial population growth accelerate the inflation rate? Perhaps: when the population pressure declined after 1600, prices gradually stabilized. One fact is certain: the price revolution severely strained government budgets. Several times between 1557 and 1647, Philip II and his successors were forced to repudiate the state debt, which in turn undermined confidence in the government. By the seventeenth century, the economy was a shambles, and Spanish predominance was over.

As Philip II paid his armies and foreign debts with silver bullion, the Spanish inflation was transmitted to the rest of Europe. Between 1560 and 1600, much of Europe experienced large price increases. Prices doubled and in some cases quadrupled, and wages did not keep pace with prices. Spain suffered most severely, but all European countries were affected. People who lived on fixed incomes, such as the continental nobles, were badly hurt because their money bought less. Those who owed fixed sums of money, such as the middle class, prospered: in a time of rising prices, debts had less value each year. Food costs rose most sharply, and the poor fared worst of all.

Colonial Administration

Columbus, Cortés, and Pizarro claimed the lands they had "discovered" for the Crown of Spain. How were these lands to be governed? According to the Spanish theory of absolutism, the Crown was entitled to exercise full authority over all imperial lands. In the sixteenth century, the Crown divided its New World territories into four viceroyalties, or administrative divisions: New Spain, which consisted of Mexico, Central America, and present-day California, Arizona, New Mexico, and Texas, with the capital at Mexico City; Peru, originally all the lands in continental South America, later reduced to the territory of modern Peru, Chile, Bolivia, and Ecuador, with the viceregal seat at Lima; New Granada, including present-day Venezuela, Colombia, Panama, and, after 1739, Ecuador, with Bogotá as its administrative center; and La Plata, consisting of Argentina, Uruguay, and Paraguay, with Buenos Aires as the capital. Within each territory, the viceroy, or imperial governor, exercised broad military and civil authority as the direct representative of the sovereign in Madrid. The viceroy presided over the *audiencia,* a board of twelve to fifteen judges that served as his advisory council and the highest judicial body. The enlightened Spanish king Charles III (r. 1759–1788) introduced the system of *intendants.* These royal officials possessed broad military, administrative, and financial authority within their intendancy and were responsible not to the viceroy but to the monarchy in Madrid.

From the early sixteenth century to the beginning of the nineteenth, the Spanish monarchy acted on the mercantilist principle that the colonies existed for the financial benefit of the home country. The mining of gold and silver was always the most important industry in the colonies. The Crown claimed the *quinto,* one-fifth of all precious metals mined in South America. Gold and silver yielded the Spanish monarchy 25 percent of its total income. In return, it shipped manufactured goods to the Americas and discouraged the development of native industries.

The Portuguese governed their colony of Brazil in a similar manner. After the union of the Crowns of Portugal and Spain in 1580, Spanish administrative forms were introduced. Local officials called *corregidores* held judicial and military powers. Mercantilist policies placed severe restrictions on Brazilian industries that might compete with those of Portugal. In the seventeenth century, the use of black slave labor made possible the cultivation of coffee and cotton, and in the eighteenth century Brazil led the world in the production of sugar. The unique feature of colonial Brazil's culture and society was its thoroughgoing intermixture of Indians, whites, and blacks.

CHANGING ATTITUDES

What were the cultural consequences of the religious wars and of the worldwide discoveries? What impact did the discoveries and wars have on Europeans' attitudes? The clash of traditional religious and geographical beliefs with the new knowledge provided by explorers—combined with decades of devastation and disorder within Europe—bred confusion, uncertainty, and insecurity. Geographical evidence based on verifiably scientific proofs contradicted the evidence of the Scriptures and of the classical authors.

The age of religious wars was one of extreme and violent contrasts. It was a deeply religious period in which people fought passionately for their beliefs; 70 percent of the books printed dealt with religious subjects. Yet the times saw the beginnings of religious skepticism. Europeans explored new continents, partly with the missionary aim of Christianizing the peoples they encountered. Yet the Spanish, Portuguese, Dutch, and English proceeded to dominate and enslave the Indians and blacks they found. While Europeans indulged in gross sensuality, the social status of women declined. The exploration of new continents reflected deep curiosity and broad intelligence, yet Europeans believed in witches and burned thousands at the stake. Sexism, racism, and skepticism had all originated in ancient times. But late in the sixteenth century, they began to take on their familiar modern forms.

The Status of Women

Did new ideas about women appear in this period? Theological and popular literature on marriage in Reformation Europe helps answer this question (see pages 462, 469). These manuals emphasized the qualities expected of each partner. A husband was obliged to provide for the material welfare of his wife and children. He was directed to protect his family while remaining steady and self-controlled. Especially was a husband and father to rule his household firmly but justly. But he was not to behave as a tyrant, a guideline counselors repeated frequently. A wife should be a mature person, a good household manager, and a subservient and faithful spouse. The husband also owed fidelity, and both Protestant and Catholic moralists rejected the double standard of sexual morality as a threat to family unity. Counselors believed that marriage should be based on mutual respect and trust. While they discouraged impersonal unions arranged by parents, they did not think romantic attachments—based on physical attraction and emotional love—a sound basis for an enduring relationship.

Moralists held that the household was a woman's first priority. She might assist in her own or her husband's business and do charitable work. Involvement in social or public activities, however, was inappropriate because it distracted the wife from her primary responsibility, her household. If women suffered under their husbands' yokes, writers explained that submission was the punishment they had inherited from Eve, penance for man's fall, like the pain of childbearing. Moreover, they said, a woman's lot was no worse than a man's: he had to earn the family's bread by the sweat of his brow.[22]

Catholics viewed marriage as a sacramental union, which, validly entered into, could not be dissolved. Protestants saw marriage as a contract, whereby each partner promised the other support, companionship, and the sharing of mutual goods. Protestants recognized a mutual right to divorce and remarriage for various reasons, including adultery and irreparable breakdown.[23] Society in the early modern period was patriarchal. While women neither lost their identity nor lacked meaningful work, the pervasive assumption was that men ruled. Leading students of the Lutherans, Catholics, French Calvinists, and English Puritans tend to concur that there was no amelioration in women's definitely subordinate status.

There were some remarkable success stories, however. Elizabeth Hardwick, the orphaned daughter of an obscure English country squire, made four careful marriages, each of which brought her more property and carried her higher up the social ladder. She managed her estates, amounting to more than 100,000 acres, with a degree of business sense rare in any age. The two great mansions she built, Chatsworth and Hardwick, stand today as monuments to her acumen. Having established several aristocratic dynasties, she died in 1608, past her eightieth year, one of the richest people in England.[24]

Artists' drawings of plump, voluptuous women and massive, muscular men revealed the contemporary standards of physical beauty. It was a sensual age that gloried in the delights of the flesh. Some people, such as humanist poet Aretino, found sexual satisfaction with both sexes. Reformers and public officials simultaneously condemned and condoned sexual "sins." The oldest profession had many practitioners, and when in 1566 Pope Pius IV expelled all the prostitutes from Rome, so many people left and the city suffered such a loss of revenue that in less than a month the pope was forced to rescind the order. Scholars debated Saint Augustine's notion that whores served a useful social function by preventing worse sins. Prostitution was common because poverty forced women and young men into it. Since the later Middle Ages, licensed houses of prostitution had been common in urban centers (see page 397). The general public took the matter for granted. Consequently, civil authorities in both Catholic and Protestant countries licensed houses of public prostitution. These establishments were intended, however, for the convenience of single men, and some Protestant cities, such as Geneva and Zurich, installed officials in the brothels with the express purpose of preventing married men from patronizing them.

Moralists naturally railed against prostitution. For example, Melchior Ambach, the Lutheran editor of many tracts against adultery and whoring, wrote in 1543 that if "houses of women" for single and married men were allowed, why not provide a "house of boys" for women who lacked husbands to service them? "Would whoring be any worse for the poor, needy female sex?"[25] Ambach, of course, was not being serious: by treating infidelity from the perspective of female, rather than male, customers, he was still insisting that prostitution destroyed the family and society.

Single women of the middle and working classes in the sixteenth and seventeenth centuries worked in many occupations and professions—as butchers, shopkeepers, nurses, goldsmiths, midwives, and workers in the weaving and printing industries. Women who were married normally assisted in their husbands' businesses. And what became of the thousands of women who left convents and nunneries during the Reformation? This question concerns primarily women of the upper classes, who formed the dominant social group in the religious houses of late medieval Europe.

Luther and the Protestant reformers believed that celibacy had no Scriptural basis, that young girls were forced by their parents into convents, and that once there they were bullied by men into staying. Therefore, reformers favored the suppression of women's religious houses and encouraged ex-nuns to marry. Marriage, the reformers maintained, not only gave women emotional and sexual satisfaction, it also freed them from clerical domination, cultural deprivation, and sexual repression.[26] Consequently, these women apparently passed from clerical domination to subservience to husbands.

If some nuns in the Middle Ages lacked a genuine religious vocation and if some religious houses witnessed financial mismanagement and moral laxness, convents nevertheless provided women of the upper classes with scope for their literary, artistic, medical, or administrative talents if they could not or would not marry. With the closing of convents, marriage became virtually the only occupation for upper-class Protestant women. This helps explain why Anglicans, Calvinists, and Lutherans established communities of religious women, such as the Lutheran one at Kaiserwerth in the Rhineland, in the eighteenth and nineteenth centuries.[27]

The Great European Witch-hunt

The great European witch scare reveals something about contemporary attitudes toward women. The period of the religious wars witnessed a startling increase in the phenomenon of witch-hunting, whose prior history was long but sporadic. "A witch," according to Chief Justice Coke of England, "was a person who hath conference with the Devil to consult with him or to do some act." This definition by the highest legal authority in England demonstrates that educated as well as ignorant people believed in witches. Witches were thought to be individuals who could mysteriously injure other people or animals—by causing a person to become blind or impotent, for instance, or by preventing a cow from giving milk. Belief in witches predated Christianity. For centuries, tales had circulated about old women who made nocturnal travels on greased broomsticks to *sabbats,* or assemblies of witches, where they participated in sexual orgies and feasted on the flesh of infants. In the popular imagination, witches had definite characteristics. The vast majority were married women or widows between fifty and seventy years old, crippled or bent with age, with pockmarked skin. They often practiced midwifery or folk medicine, and most had sharp tongues and were quick to scold.

Religious reformers' extreme notions of the devil's powers and the insecurity created by the religious wars contributed to the growth of belief in witches. The idea developed that witches made pacts with the Devil in return for the power to work mischief on their enemies. Since pacts with the devil meant the renunciation of God, witchcraft was considered heresy. Persecution for witchcraft had actually begun in the later fourteenth century, when witchcraft was declared heresy. The century between 1560 and 1660, when mainstream Protestantism and Tridentine Catholicism had begun to settle into definite confessional blocs, saw witch-hunting on an unprecedented and virulent scale, touching every part of Europe from Iceland to Russia.

Fear of witches took a terrible toll on innocent lives in parts of Europe. In southwestern Germany, 3,229 witches were executed between 1561 and 1670, most by burning. The communities of the Swiss Confederation tried 8,888 persons between 1470 and 1700 and executed 5,417 of them as witches. In all the centuries before 1500, witches in England had been suspected of causing perhaps "three deaths, a broken leg, several de-

Hans Baldung Grien (1484/5–1545): Witches' Sabbat (1510) Trained by the great German graphic artist and painter Albrecht Dürer at Nuremberg, Baldung (as he was known) in this woodcut combines learned and stereotypical beliefs about witches: They traveled at night on broomsticks, met at sabbats or assemblies, feasted on infants (in dish held high), concocted strange potions, and possessed an aged and debauched sensuality. *(Germanisches Nationalmuseum Nürnberg)*

structive storms and some bewitched genitals." Yet between 1559 and 1736, witches were thought to have caused thousands of deaths, and in that period almost 1,000 witches were executed in England.[28]

Historians and anthropologists have offered a variety of explanations for the great European witch-hunt. Some scholars maintain that charges of witchcraft were a means of accounting for inexplicable misfortunes. Just as the English in the fifteenth century had blamed their military failures in France on Joan of Arc's witchcraft, so in the seventeenth century the English Royal College of Physicians attributed undiagnosable illnesses to witchcraft. Some scholars hold that in small communities, which typically insisted on strict social conformity, charges of witchcraft were a means of attacking and eliminating the nonconformist; witches, in other words, served the collective need for scapegoats. The evidence of witches' trials, some writers suggest, shows that women were not accused because they harmed or threatened their neighbors; rather, their communities believed such women worshiped the Devil, engaged in wild sexual activities with him, and ate infants. Other scholars argue the exact opposite: that people were tried and executed as witches because their neighbors feared their evil powers. Finally, there is the theory that the unbridled sexuality attributed to witches was a psychological projection on the part of their accusers resulting from Christianity's repression of sexuality.

Though these different hypotheses exist, scholars still cannot fully understand the phenomenon. The exact reasons for the persecution of women as witches probably varied from place to place. Nevertheless, given the broad strand of misogyny (hatred of women) in Western religion, the long-held belief in the susceptibility of women (so-called weaker vessels) to the Devil's allurements, and the pervasive seventeenth-century belief about women's multiple and demanding orgasms and thus their sexual insatiability, it is not difficult to understand why women were accused of all sorts of mischief and witchcraft. Charges of witchcraft provided a legal basis for the execution of tens of thousands of women. As the most important capital crime for women in early modern times, witchcraft has considerable significance for the history and status of women.[29] Witch-hunting declined only in the late eighteenth century, as fear of the Devil and his powers of malevolent sorcery waned among the educated ruling classes.

African Slave and Indian Woman A black slave approaches an Indian prostitute. Unable to explain what he wants, he points with his finger; she eagerly grasps for the coin. The Spanish caption above moralizes on the black man using stolen money—yet the Spaniards ruthlessly expropriated all South American mineral wealth. *(New York Public Library)*

European Slavery and the Origins of American Racism

Almost all peoples in the world have engaged in the enslavement of other human beings at some time in their histories. Since ancient times, victors in battle have enslaved conquered peoples. In the later Middle Ages, slavery was deeply entrenched in southern Italy, Sicily, Crete, and Mediterranean Spain. The bubonic plague, famines, and other epidemics created a severe shortage of agricultural and domestic workers throughout Europe, encouraging Italian merchants to buy slaves from the Balkans, Thrace, southern Russia, and central Anatolia for sale in the West. In 1364 the Florentine government allowed the unlimited importation of slaves so long as they were not Christians. Between 1414 and 1423, at least ten thousand slaves were sold in Venice alone. The slave trade represented one aspect of Italian business enterprise during the Renaissance: where profits were lucrative, papal threats of excommunication completely failed to stop Genoese slave traders. The Genoese set up colonial stations in the Crimea and along the Black Sea, and according to an international authority on slavery, these outposts were "virtual laboratories" for the development of slave plantation agriculture in the New World.[30] This form of slavery had nothing to do with race; almost all slaves were white. How, then, did black African slavery enter the European picture and take root in the New World?

In 1453 the Ottoman capture of Constantinople halted the flow of white slaves from the Black Sea region and the Balkans. Mediterranean Europe, cut off from its traditional source of slaves, had no alternative source for slave labor but sub-Saharan Africa. The centuries-old trans-Saharan trade was greatly stimulated by the existence of a ready market in the vineyards and sugar plantations of Sicily and Majorca. By the later fifteenth century, the Mediterranean had developed an "American" form of slavery before the discovery of America.

Meanwhile, the Genoese and other Italians had colonized the Canary Islands in the eastern Atlantic. Prince Henry the Navigator's sailors (see page 503) discovered

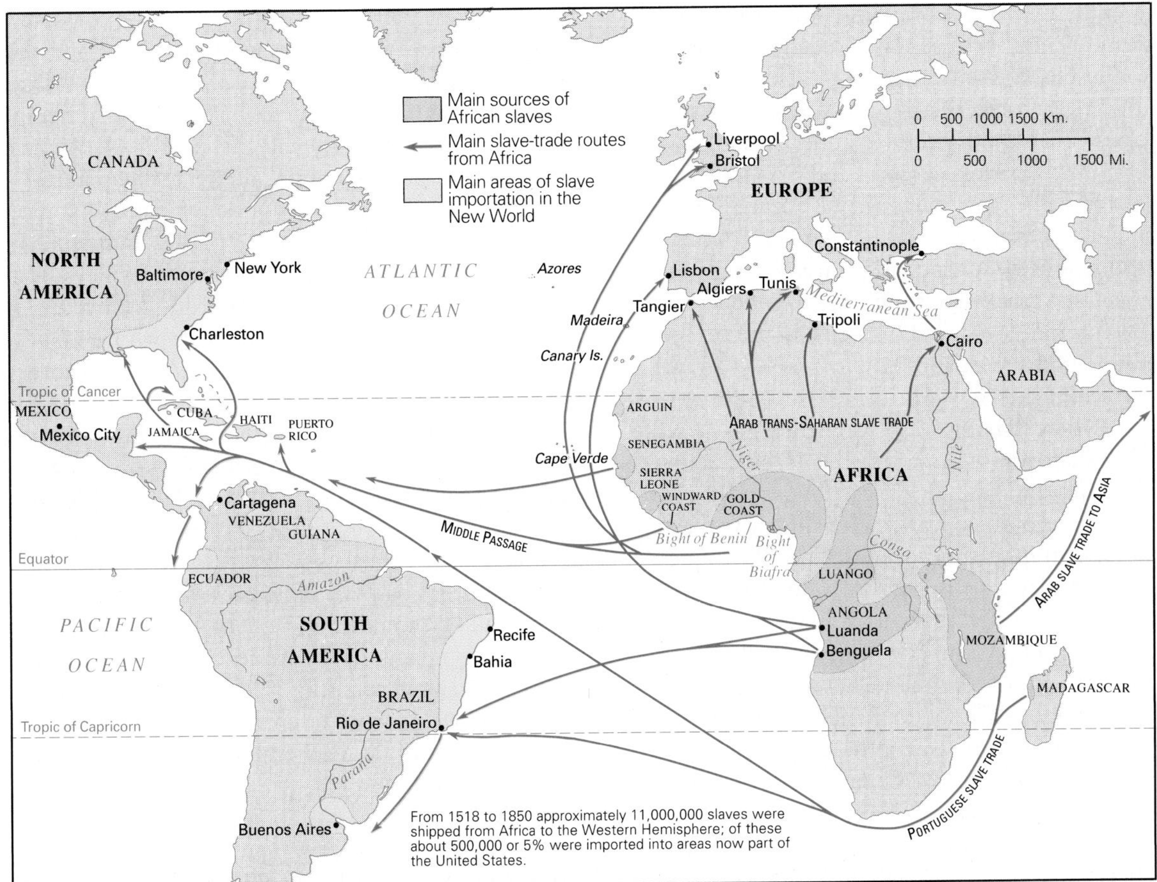

MAP 15.4 The African Slave Trade Decades before the discovery of America, Greek, Russian, Bulgarian, Armenian, and then black slaves worked the plantation economies of southern Italy, Sicily, Portugal, and Mediterranean Spain—thereby serving as models for the American form of slavery.

the Madeira Islands and made settlements there. In this stage of European expansion, "the history of slavery became inextricably tied up with the history of sugar." Though it was an expensive luxury that only the affluent could afford, population increases and monetary expansion in the fifteenth century led to an increasing demand for sugar. Resourceful Italians provided the capital, cane, and technology for sugar cultivation on plantations in southern Portugal, Madeira, and the Canary Islands. Meanwhile, in the period 1490 to 1530, the port of Lisbon saw between three hundred and two thousand black slaves arrive annually (Map 15.4). From Lisbon, where African slaves performed most of the manual labor and constituted 10 percent of the city's population, slaves were transported to the sugar plantations of Madeira, the Azores, the Cape Verde Islands, and then to Brazil. Sugar and the small Atlantic islands gave New World slavery its distinctive shape. Columbus himself, who spent a decade in Madeira, brought sugar plants on his voyages to "the Indies." [31]

As already discussed, European expansion across the Atlantic led to the economic exploitation of the Americas. In the New World, the major problem settlers faced was a shortage of labor. As early as 1495, the Spanish solved the problem by enslaving the native Indians. In the next two centuries, the Portuguese, Dutch, and English followed suit.

Unaccustomed to any form of forced labor, certainly not to panning gold for more than twelve hours a day in the broiling sun, the Indians died "like fish in a bucket," as one Spanish settler reported.[32] In 1515 a Spanish missionary, Bartolomé de las Casas (1474–1566), who had seen the evils of Indian slavery, urged the future emperor Charles V to end Indian slavery in his American dominions. Las Casas recommended the importation of blacks from Africa, both because church law did not strictly forbid black slavery and because he thought blacks could better survive under South American conditions. Charles agreed, and in 1518 the African slave trade began. (When the blacks arrived, Las Casas immediately regretted his suggestion.) Columbus's introduction of sugar plants, moreover, stimulated the need for black slaves; and the experience and model of plantation slavery in Portugal and the Atlantic islands encouraged the establishment of a similar agricultural pattern in the New World.

In Africa, where slavery was entrenched (as it was in pre-Columbian South America, the Islamic world, southern Europe, and China), African kings and dealers sold black slaves to European merchants who participated in the transatlantic trade. The Portuguese brought the first slaves to Brazil; by 1600, 4,000 were being imported annually. After its founding in 1621, the Dutch West India Company, with the full support of the government of the United Provinces, transported thousands of Africans to Brazil and the Caribbean. Only in the late seventeenth century, with the chartering of the Royal African Company, did the English get involved. Thereafter, large numbers of African blacks poured into the West Indies and North America. In 1790 there were 757,181 blacks in a total U.S. population of 3,929,625. When the first census was taken in Brazil in 1798, blacks numbered about 2 million in a total population of 3.25 million.

Settlers brought to the Americas the racial attitudes they had absorbed in Europe. Settlers' beliefs and attitudes toward blacks derived from two basic sources: Christian theological speculation (see page 436) and Arab ideas. In the sixteenth and seventeenth centuries, the English, for example, were extremely curious about Africans' lives and customs, and slavers' accounts were extraordinarily popular. Travel literature depicted Africans as savages because of their eating habits, morals, clothing, and social customs; as barbarians because of their language and methods of war; and as heathens because they were not Christian (virtually the identical language with which the English described the Irish—see page 404). Africans were believed to possess a potent sexuality. One seventeenth-century observer considered Africans "very lustful and impudent, . . . (for a Negroes hiding his members, their extraordinary greatness) is a token of their lust." African women were considered sexually aggressive, with a "temper hot and lascivious."[33]

"At the time when Columbus sailed to the New World, Islam was the largest world religion, and the only world religion that showed itself capable of expanding rapidly in areas as far apart and as different from each other as Senegal [in northwest Africa], Bosnia [in the Balkans], Java, and the Philippines."[34] Medieval Arabic literature emphasized blacks' physical repulsiveness, mental inferiority, and primitivism. In contrast to civilized peoples from the Mediterranean to China, some Arab writers absurdly claimed, sub-Saharan blacks were the only peoples who had produced no sciences or stable states. Fourteenth-century Arab historian ibn-Khaldun wrote that "the only people who accept slavery are the Negroes, owing to their low degree of humanity and their proximity to the animal stage." Though black kings, Khaldun alleged, sold their subjects without even a pretext of crime or war, the victims bore no resentment because they gave no thought to the future and had "by nature few cares and worries; dancing and rhythm are for them inborn."[35] It is easy to see how such ridiculous myths developed into the classic stereotypes used to justify black slavery in South and North America in the seventeenth, eighteenth, and nineteenth centuries. Medieval Christians and Arabs had similar notions of blacks as inferior and primitive people ideally suited to enslavement. Perhaps centuries of commercial contacts between Middle Eastern and Mediterranean peoples had familiarized the latter with Arab racial attitudes. The racial beliefs that the Portuguese, Spanish, Dutch, and English brought to the New World, however, derived primarily from Christian theological speculation.

Literature and Art

The age of religious wars and overseas expansion also witnessed an extraordinary degree of intellectual and artistic ferment. This effervescence can be seen in the development of the essay as a distinct literary genre; in other prose, poetry, and drama; in art; and in music. In many ways, literature, the visual arts, music, and the drama of the period mirrored the social and cultural conditions that gave rise to them.

The Essay: Michel de Montaigne

Decades of religious fanaticism, bringing famine, civil anarchy, and death, led both Catholics and Protestants to doubt that any one faith contained absolute truth.

The late sixteenth and seventeenth centuries witnessed the beginning of modern skepticism. Skepticism is a school of thought founded on doubt that total certainty or definitive knowledge is ever attainable. The skeptic is cautious and critical and suspends judgment. Perhaps the finest representative of early modern skepticism is Frenchman Michel de Montaigne (1533–1592).

Montaigne descended from a bourgeois family that had made a fortune selling salted herring and wine and in 1477 had purchased the title and property of Montaigne in Gascony; his mother came from a Jewish family that had been forced to flee Spain. Montaigne received a classical education before studying law and securing a judicial appointment in 1554. Though a member of the nobility, in embarking on a judicial career, he identified with the new nobility of the robe. He condemned the ancient nobility of the sword for being more concerned with war and sports than with the cultivation of the mind.

At the age of thirty-eight, Montaigne resigned his judicial post, retired to his estate, and devoted the rest of his life to study, contemplation, and an effort to understand himself. His wealth provided him with the leisure time to do so. A humanist, he believed that the object of life was to "know thyself," for self-knowledge teaches men and women how to live in accordance with nature and God. Montaigne developed a new literary genre, the essay—from the French *essayer,* meaning "to test or try"—to express his thoughts and ideas.

Montaigne's *Essays* provide insight into the mind of a remarkably humane, tolerant, and civilized man. From the ancient authors, especially the Roman Stoic Seneca, Montaigne acquired a sense of calm, inner peace, and patience. The ancient authors also inculcated in him tolerance and broad-mindedness. Montaigne had grown up during the French civil wars, perhaps the worst kind of war. Religious ideology had set family against family, even brother against brother. He wrote:

In this controversy . . . France is at present agitated by civil wars, the best and soundest side is undoubtedly that which maintains both the old religion and the old government of the country. However, among the good men who follow that side . . . we see many whom passion drives outside the bounds of reason, and makes them sometimes adopt unjust, violent, and even reckless courses.[36]

Though he remained a Catholic, Montaigne possessed a detachment, an independence, an openness of mind, and a willingness to look at all sides of a question. As he wrote, "I listen with attention to the judgment of all men; but so far as I can remember, I have followed none but my own. Though I set little value upon my own opinion, I set no more on the opinions of others."

In a violent and cruel age, Montaigne was a gentle and sensitive man. In his famous essay "On Cruelty," he stated:

Among other vices I cruelly hate cruelty, both by nature and by judgment, as the extreme of all vices. . . .

I live in a time when we abound in incredible examples of this vice, through the license of our civil wars; and we see in the ancient histories nothing more extreme than what we experience of this every day. But that has not reconciled me to it at all.[37]

In the book-lined tower where Montaigne passed his days, he became a deeply learned man. Yet he was not ignorant of worldly affairs, and he criticized scholars and bookworms who ignored life around them. Montaigne's essay "On Cannibals" reflects the impact of overseas discoveries on Europeans' consciousness. His tolerant mind rejected the notion that one culture is superior to another:

I long had a man in my house that lived ten or twelve years in the New World, discovered in these latter days, and in that part of it where Villegaignon landed [Brazil]. . . .

I find that there is nothing barbarous and savage in [that] nation, by anything that I can gather, excepting, that every one gives the title of barbarism to everything that is not in use in his own country. As, indeed, we have no other level of truth and reason, than the example and idea of the opinions and customs of the place wherein we live.[38]

In his belief in the nobility of human beings in the state of nature, uncorrupted by organized society, and in his cosmopolitan attitude toward different civilizations, Montaigne anticipated many eighteenth-century thinkers.

The thought of Michel de Montaigne marked a sharp break with the past. Faith and religious certainty had characterized the intellectual attitudes of Western society for a millennium. Montaigne's rejection of any kind of dogmatism, his secularism, and his skepticism thus represented a basic change. In his own time and throughout the seventeenth century, few would have agreed with him. The publication of his ideas, however, anticipated a basic shift in attitudes. Montaigne inaugurated an era of doubt. "Wonder," he said, "is the foundation of all philosophy, research is the means of all learning, and ignorance is the end."[39]

Elizabethan and Jacobean Literature

In addition to the essay as a literary genre, the period fostered remarkable creativity in other branches of literature. England, especially in the latter part of Elizabeth's reign and in the first years of her successor, James I (r. 1603–1625), witnessed remarkable literary expression. The terms *Elizabethan* and *Jacobean* (referring to the reign of James) are used to designate the English music, poetry, prose, and drama of this period. The poetry of Sir Philip Sidney (1554–1586), such as *Astrophel* and *Stella,* strongly influenced later poetic writing. The *Faerie Queene* of Edmund Spenser (1552–1599) endures as one of the greatest moral epics in any language. The rare poetic beauty of the plays of Christopher Marlowe (1564–1593), such as *Tamburlaine* and *The Jew of Malta,* paved the way for the work of Shakespeare. Above all, the immortal dramas of William Shakespeare (1564–1616) and the stately prose of the Authorized, or King James, Bible marked the Elizabethan and Jacobean periods as the golden age of English literature.

William Shakespeare, the son of a successful glove manufacturer who rose to the highest municipal office in the Warwickshire town of Stratford-on-Avon, chose a career on the London stage. By 1592 he had gained recognition as an actor and playwright. Between 1599 and 1603, Shakespeare performed in the Lord Chamberlain's Company and became co-owner of the Globe Theatre, which after 1603 presented his plays.

Shakespeare's genius lay in the originality of his characterizations, the diversity of his plots, his understanding of human psychology, and his unexcelled gift for language. Shakespeare was a Renaissance man in his deep appreciation for classical culture, individualism, and humanism. Such plays as *Julius Caesar, Pericles,* and *Antony and Cleopatra* deal with classical subjects and figures. Several of his comedies have Italian Renaissance settings. The nine history plays, including *Richard II, Richard III,* and *Henry IV,* enjoyed the greatest popularity among Shakespeare's contemporaries. Written during the decade after the defeat of the Spanish Armada, the history plays express English national consciousness. Lines such as these from *Richard II* reflect this sense of national greatness with unparalleled eloquence:

This royal Throne of Kings, this sceptre'd Isle,
This earth of Majesty, this seat of Mars,
This other Eden, demi-paradise,
This fortress built by Nature for herself,
Against infection and the hand of war:
This happy breed of men, this little world,
This precious stone, set in the silver sea,
Which serves it in the office of a wall,
Or as a moat defensive to a house,
Against the envy of less happier Lands,
This blessed plot, this earth, this Realm, this England.

Shakespeare's later plays, above all the tragedies *Hamlet, Othello,* and *Macbeth,* explore an enormous range of human problems and are open to an almost infinite variety of interpretations. *Othello,* which nineteenth-century historian Thomas Macaulay called "perhaps the greatest work in the world," portrays an honorable man destroyed by a flaw in his own character and the satanic evil of his supposed friend Iago. *Macbeth*'s central theme is exorbitant ambition. Shakespeare analyzes the psychology of sin in the figures of Macbeth and Lady Macbeth, whose mutual love under the pressure of ambition leads to their destruction. The central figure in *Hamlet,* a play suffused with individuality, wrestles with moral problems connected with revenge and with the human being's relationship to life and death. The soliloquy in which Hamlet debates suicide is perhaps the most widely quoted passage in English literature:

To be, or not to be: that is the question:
Whether 'tis nobler in the mind to suffer
The slings and arrows of outrageous fortune,
Or to take arms against a sea of troubles,
And by opposing end them?

Hamlet's sad cry "There is nothing either good or bad but thinking makes it so" expresses the anguish and uncertainty of modern life. *Hamlet* has always enjoyed great popularity because in the title character's many-faceted personality people have seen an aspect of themselves.

Shakespeare's dynamic language bespeaks his extreme sensitivity to the sounds and meanings of words. Perhaps no phrase better summarizes the reason for his immortality than this line from *Antony and Cleopatra:* "Age cannot wither [him], nor custom stale/ [his] infinite variety."

Another great masterpiece of the Jacobean period was the Authorized Bible. At a theological conference in 1604, a group of Puritans urged James I to support a new translation of the Bible. The king in turn assigned the task to a committee of scholars, who published their efforts in 1611. Divided into chapters and verses, the Authorized Version is actually a revision of earlier Bibles

Titus Andronicus With classical allusions, fifteen murders and executions, a Gothic queen who takes a black lover, and incredible violence, this early Shakespearean tragedy (1594) was a melodramatic thriller that enjoyed enormous popularity with the London audience. Modern critics believe that it foreshadowed King Lear with its emphasis on suffering and madness. *(The Folger Shakespeare Library)*

more than an original work. Yet it provides a superb expression of the mature English vernacular in the early seventeenth century. Consider Psalm 37:

Fret not thy selfe because of evill doers, neither bee thou envious against the workers of iniquitie.
For they shall soone be cut downe like the grasse; and wither as the greene herbe.
Trust in the Lord, and do good, so shalt thou dwell in the land, and verely thou shalt be fed.
Delight thy selfe also in the Lord; and he shall give thee the desires of thine heart.
Commit thy way unto the Lord: trust also in him, and he shall bring it to passe.
And he shall bring forth thy righteousness as the light, and thy judgement as the noone day.

The Authorized Version, so called because it was produced under royal sponsorship—it had no official ecclesiastical endorsement—represented the Anglican and Puritan desire to encourage laypeople to read the Scriptures. It quickly achieved great popularity and displaced all earlier versions. British settlers carried this Bible to the North American colonies, where it became known as the King James Bible. For centuries the King James Bible has had a profound influence on the language and lives of English-speaking peoples.

Baroque Art and Music

Throughout European history, the cultural tastes of one age have often seemed quite unsatisfactory to the next. So it was with the baroque. The term *baroque* itself may have come from the Portuguese word for an "odd-shaped, imperfect pearl" and was commonly used by late-eighteenth-century art critics as an expression of scorn for what they considered an overblown, unbalanced style. The hostility of these critics, who also scorned the Gothic style of medieval cathedrals in favor of a classicism inspired by antiquity and the Renaissance, has long since passed. Specialists now agree that the triumphs of the baroque marked one of the high points in the history of Western culture.

The early development of the baroque is complex, but most scholars stress the influence of Rome and the revitalized Catholic church of the later sixteenth century. The papacy and the Jesuits encouraged the growth of an intensely emotional, exuberant art. These patrons wanted artists to go beyond the Renaissance focus on pleasing a small, wealthy, cultural elite. They wanted artists to appeal to the senses and thereby touch the souls and kindle the faith of ordinary churchgoers while proclaiming the power and confidence of the reformed Catholic church. In addition to this underlying religious emotionalism, the baroque drew its sense of drama, motion, and ceaseless striving from the Catholic Reformation. The interior of the famous Jesuit Church of Jesus in Rome—the Gesù—combined all these characteristics in its lavish, shimmering, wildly active decorations and frescoes.

Taking definite shape in Italy after 1600, the baroque style in the visual arts developed with exceptional vigor in Catholic countries—in Spain and Latin America, Austria, southern Germany, and Poland. Yet baroque art was more than just "Catholic art" in the seventeenth century and the first half of the eighteenth. True, neither Protestant England nor the Netherlands ever came fully under the spell of the baroque, but neither did Catholic France. And Protestants accounted for some of the finest examples of baroque style, especially in music. The baroque style spread partly because its tension and bombast spoke to an agitated age, which was experiencing great violence and controversy in politics and religion.

In painting, the baroque reached maturity early with Peter Paul Rubens (1577–1640), the most outstanding and representative of baroque painters. Studying in

Veronese: Feast in the House of Levi Using the story in Mark 2:15, which says that many tax collectors and sinners joined Jesus at dinner, the Venetian painter celebrated patrician wealth and luxury in Venice's golden age. The black servants, dwarfs, and colonnades all contribute to the sumptuous setting. *(Cameraphoto Venezia/Art Resource, NY)*

his native Flanders and in Italy, where he was influenced by masters of the High Renaissance such as Michelangelo, Rubens developed his own rich, sensuous, colorful style, which was characterized by animated figures, melodramatic contrasts, and monumental size. Although Rubens excelled in glorifying monarchs such as Queen Mother Marie de' Medici of France, he was also a devout Catholic. Nearly half of his pictures treat Christian subjects. Yet one of Rubens's trademarks was fleshy, sensual nudes, who populate his canvases as Roman goddesses, water nymphs, and remarkably voluptuous saints and angels.

Rubens was enormously successful. To meet the demand for his work, he established a large studio and hired many assistants to execute his rough sketches and gigantic murals. Sometimes the master artist added only the finishing touches. Rubens's wealth and position—on occasion he was given special diplomatic assignments by the Habsburgs—affirmed that distinguished artists continued to enjoy the high social status they had won in the Renaissance.

In music, the baroque style reached its culmination almost a century later in the dynamic, soaring lines of the endlessly inventive Johann Sebastian Bach (1685–1750), one of the greatest composers the Western world has ever produced. Organist and choirmaster of several Lutheran churches across Germany, Bach was equally at home writing secular concertos and sublime religious cantatas. Bach's organ music, the greatest ever written, combined the baroque spirit of invention, tension, and emotion in an unforgettable striving toward the infinite. Unlike Rubens, Bach was not fully appreciated in his lifetime, but since the early nineteenth century his reputation has grown steadily.

Velázquez: Juan de Pareja This portrait (1650) of the Spanish painter Velázquez's one-time assistant, a black man of obvious intellectual and sensual power and himself a renowned religious painter, suggests the integration of some blacks in seventeenth-century society. The elegant lace collar attests to his middle-class status. *(The Metropolitan Museum of Art, Fletcher Fund, Rogers Fund, and Bequest of Miss Adelaide Milton de Groot (1876–1967), by exchange, supplemented by gifts from friends of the Museum, 1971. [1971.86]. Photograph © 1986 The Metropolitan Museum of Art)*

SUMMARY

European expansion and colonization took place against a background of religious conflict and rising national consciousness. The seventeenth century was by no means a secular period. Though the medieval religious framework had broken down, people still thought largely in religious terms. Europeans explained what they did politically and economically in terms of religious doctrine. Religious ideology served as a justification for a variety of goals, such as the French nobles' opposition to the Crown and the Dutch struggle for political and economic independence from Spain. In Germany, religious hatred and foreign ambition led to the Thirty Years' War. After 1648 the divisions between Protestant and Catholic tended to become permanent. Religious skepticism and racial attitudes were harbingers of developments to come. The essays of Montaigne, the plays of Marlowe and Shakespeare, the King James Bible, and the splendors of baroque art remain classic achievements of the Western cultural heritage.

In the sixteenth and seventeenth centuries, Europeans for the first time gained access to large parts of the globe. European peoples had the intellectual curiosity, driving ambition, and scientific technology to attempt feats that were as difficult and expensive then as going to the moon is today. Exploration and exploitation contributed to a more sophisticated standard of living, in the form of spices and Asian luxury goods, and to a terrible international inflation resulting from the influx of South American silver and gold. Governments, the upper classes, and the peasantry were badly hurt by the resulting inflation. Meanwhile, the middle class of bankers, shippers, financiers, and manufacturers prospered for much of the seventeenth century.

NOTES

1. Quoted in J. Hale, "War and Public Opinion in the Fifteenth and Sixteenth Centuries," *Past and Present* 22 (July 1962): 29.
2. See ibid., pp. 18–32.
3. N. Z. Davis, "The Rites of Violence: Religious Riot in Sixteenth Century France," *Past and Present* 59 (May 1973): 59.
4. See ibid., pp. 51–91.
5. Quoted in J. L. Motley, *The Rise of the Dutch Republic* (Philadelphia: David McKay, 1898), 1.109.
6. Quoted in P. Smith, *The Age of the Reformation* (New York: Henry Holt, 1951), p. 248.
7. H. Kamen, *Philip of Spain* (New Haven, Conn.: Yale University Press, 1997), pp. 76–78. The quotations are on pp. 77 and 76, respectively.
8. Quoted ibid., p. 235.
9. H. Kamen, "The Economic and Social Consequences of the Thirty Years' War," *Past and Present* 39 (April 1968): 44–61.
10. Quoted in C. M. Cipolla, *Guns, Sails, and Empires: Technological Innovation and the Early Phases of European Expansion, 1400–1700* (New York: Minerva Press, 1965), pp. 115–116.
11. J. H. Parry, *The Age of Reconnaissance* (New York: Mentor Books, 1963), chaps. 3 and 5.
12. See C. R. Phillips, *Ciudad Real, 1500–1750: Growth, Crisis, and Readjustment in the Spanish Economy* (Cambridge, Mass.: Harvard University Press, 1979), pp. 103–104, 115.
13. Quoted in Cipolla, *Guns, Sails, and Empires,* p. 132.
14. Quoted in F. H. Littell, *The Macmillan Atlas: History of Christianity* (New York: Macmillan, 1976), p. 75.
15. Quoted in Cipolla, *Guns, Sails, and Empires,* p. 133.
16. S. E. Morison, *Admiral of the Ocean Sea: A Life of Christopher Columbus* (Boston: Little, Brown, 1942), p. 339.
17. T. K. Rabb, "Columbus: Villain or Hero," *The Princeton Alumni Weekly,* October 14, 1992, p. 13.
18. J. M. Cohen, ed. and trans., *The Four Voyages of Christopher Columbus* (New York: Penguin Books, 1969), p. 37.
19. Quoted in R. L. Kagan, "The Spain of Ferdinand and Isabella," in *Circa 1492: Art in the Age of Exploration,* ed. J. A. Levenson (Washington, D.C.: National Gallery of Art, 1991), p. 60.
20. Quoted in F. Maddison, "Tradition and Innovation: Columbus' First Voyage and Portuguese Navigation in the Fifteenth Century," in *Circa 1492: Art in the Age of Exploration,* ed. J. A. Levinson (Washington, D.C.: National Gallery of Art, 1991), p. 69.
21. See W. D. Phillips and C. R. Phillips, *The Worlds of Christopher Columbus* (Cambridge: Cambridge University Press, 1992), p. 273.
22. This passage is based heavily on S. Ozment, *When Fathers Ruled: Family Life in Reformation Europe* (Cambridge, Mass.: Harvard University Press, 1983), pp. 50–99.
23. Ibid., pp. 85–92.
24. See D. Durant, *Bess of Hardwick: Portrait of an Elizabethan Dynasty* (London: Weidenfeld & Nicolson, 1977).
25. Quoted in Ozment, *When Fathers Ruled,* p. 56.
26. Ibid., pp. 9–14.
27. See F. Biot, *The Rise of Protestant Monasticism* (Baltimore: Helicon Press, 1968), pp. 74–78.
28. N. Cohn, *Europe's Inner Demons: An Enquiry Inspired by the Great Witch-hunt* (New York: Basic Books, 1975), pp. 253–254; and K. Thomas, *Religion and the Decline of Magic* (New York: Charles Scribner's Sons, 1971), pp. 450–455.
29. See E. W. Monter, "The Pedestal and the Stake: Courtly Love and Witchcraft," in *Becoming Visible: Women in European History,* ed. R. Bridenthal and C. Koonz (Boston: Houghton Mifflin, 1977), pp. 132–135; and A. Fraser, *The Weaker Vessel* (New York: Random House, 1985), pp. 100–103.
30. C. Verlinden, *The Beginnings of Modern Colonization*, trans. Y. Freccero (Ithaca, N.Y.: Cornell University Press, 1970), pp. 5–6, 80–97.
31. This section leans heavily on D. B. Davis, *Slavery and Human Progress* (New York: Oxford University Press, 1984), pp. 54–62; the quotation is on p. 58.
32. Quoted in D. P. Mannix, with M. Cowley, *Black Cargoes: A History of the Atlantic Slave Trade* (New York: Viking Press, 1968), p. 5.
33. Quoted ibid., p. 19.
34. See P. Brown, "Understanding Islam," *New York Review of Books,* February 22, 1979, pp. 30–33.
35. Quoted in Davis, *Slavery and Human Progress,* pp. 43–44.
36. D. M. Frame, trans., *The Complete Works of Montaigne* (Stanford, Calif.: Stanford University Press, 1958), pp. 175–176.
37. Ibid., p. 306.
38. C. Cotton, trans., *The Essays of Michel de Montaigne* (New York: A. L. Burt, 1893), pp. 207, 210.
39. Ibid., p. 523.

SUGGESTED READING

For the religious wars, in addition to the references in the Suggested Reading for Chapter 14 and the Notes to this chapter, see H. Kamen, *The Iron Century: Social Change in Europe, 1550–1660* (1971), a fundamental work; and G.

Huppert, *After the Black Death: A Social History of Early Modern Europe* (1986), a lucidly written and highly recommended work for students. P. Roberts, *A City in Conflict: Troyes During the French Wars of Religion* (1996), provides a fascinating account of the bitter divisions the religious conflicts created among neighbors in one important French city. J. H. M. Salmon, *Society in Crisis: France in the Sixteenth Century* (1975), traces the fate of French institutions during the civil wars. A. N. Galpern, *The Religions of the People in Sixteenth-Century Champagne* (1976), is a useful case study in religious anthropology, and W. A. Christian, Jr., *Local Religion in Sixteenth-Century Spain* (1981), traces the attitudes and practices of ordinary Spanish people.

A cleverly illustrated introduction to the Low Countries is K. H. D. Kaley, *The Dutch in the Seventeenth Century* (1972). For Spanish military operations in the Low Countries, see G. Parker, *The Army of Flanders and the Spanish Road, 1567–1659: The Logistics of Spanish Victory and Defeat in the Low Countries' Wars* (1972); and the more recent R. A. Stradling, *The Armada of Flanders: Spanish Maritime Policy and European War, 1568–1668* (1992). G. Parker, *Spain and the Netherlands, 1559–1659: Ten Studies* (1979), contains useful essays, of which students may especially want to consult "Why Did the Dutch Revolt Last So Long?" For the later phases of the Dutch-Spanish conflict, see J. I. Israel, *The Dutch Republic and the Hispanic World, 1606–1661* (1982), which treats the struggle in global perspective.

The starting point for the study of England's great ruler is W. MacCaffrey, *Elizabeth I* (1993). N. Jones, *The Birth of the Elizabethan Age* (1993), brings to life the concerns of the English people. S. Frye, *Elizabeth I: The Competition for Representation* (1996), uses feminist analysis to describe the way Elizabeth built her public image and used her authority. W. MacCaffrey, *Queen Elizabeth and the Making of Policy* (1981), focuses on the political and religious problems of Elizabeth's reign and her solutions to them. C. Erickson, *The First Elizabeth* (1983), gives a psychologically resonant portrait, and C. Haight, *Elizabeth I* (1988), J. E. Neale, *Queen Elizabeth I* (1957), and L. B. Smith, *Elizabeth Tudor: Portrait of a Queen* (1980), remain helpful.

Nineteenth- and early-twentieth-century historians described the defeat of the Spanish Armada as a great victory for Protestantism, democracy, and capitalism, which those scholars tended to link together. Recent historians have treated the event in terms of its contemporary significance. H. Kamen, *Philip of Spain* (1971), offers a fine revisionist portrait of the ruler at the center of late-sixteenth-century international affairs. A. W. Lovett, *Early Habsburg Spain, 1517–1598* (1986), discusses many facets of Spanish culture as well as giving a provocative portrait of Philip II. D. Howarth, *The Voyage of the Armada* (1982), discusses the expedition largely in terms of the individuals involved, whereas G. Mattingly, *The Armada* (1959), gives the diplomatic and political background; both Howarth and Mattingly tell very exciting tales. The best recent account of the Spanish Armada is G. Parker and C. Martin, *The Spanish Armada* (1988). Significant aspects of Portuguese culture are treated in A. Hower and R. Preto-Rodas, eds., *Empire in Transition: The Portuguese World in the Time of Camões* (1985).

C. V. Wedgwood, *The Thirty Years' War* (1961), must be qualified in light of recent research on the social and economic effects of the war. R. G. Asch, *The Thirty Years War: The Holy Roman Empire and Europe* (1997), is an important revisionist study with valuable material on the role of war finance in domestic and international aspects of the conflict. G. Parker, *The Thirty Years' War* (1984), is an important but densely written work. A variety of opinions on the causes and results of the war are given in T. K. Rabb's anthology, *The Thirty Years' War* (1981). Several articles in the scholarly journal *Past and Present* provide some of the latest important findings. Two of these articles, by Kamen and Hale, are mentioned in the Notes; the others are J. V. Polisensky, "The Thirty Years' War and the Crises and Revolutions of Sixteenth Century Europe," *Past and Present* 39 (1968); and M. Roberts, "Queen Christina and the General Crisis of the Seventeenth Century," *Past and Present* 22 (1962), which treats the overall significance of Swedish participation. As background to the intellectual changes instigated by the Reformation, D. C. Wilcox, *In Search of God and Self: Renaissance and Reformation Thought* (1975), contains a perceptive analysis, and T. Ashton, ed., *Crisis in Europe, 1560–1660* (1967), is fundamental.

Perhaps the best starting point for the study of European society in the age of exploration is J. A. Levenson's anthology *Circa 1492: Art in the Age of Exploration* (1991), which treats geographical, nautical, political, and humanistic developments in a worldwide context. Parry, cited in the Notes, which addresses the causes and consequences of the voyage of discovery, and J. H. Parry, *The Discovery of South America* (1979), which examines Europeans' reactions to the maritime discoveries and the whole concept of discovery, are still valuable. The urbane studies of C. M. Cipolla, including the one cited in the Notes, *Clocks and Culture, 1300–1700* (1967), *Cristofano and the Plague: A Study in the History of Public Health in the Age of Galileo* (1973), and *Public Health and the Medical Profession in the Renaissance* (1976), present fascinating material on technological and sociological developments in a lucid style. Morison's work cited in the Notes is the standard biography of Columbus, but the recent work of W. D. Phillips and C. R. Phillips, also cited in the Notes, is strongly recommended. The advanced student should consult F. Braudel, *Civilization and Capitalism, 15th–18th Century.* Vol. 1: *The Structures of Everyday Life* (1981); Vol. 2: *The Wheels of Commerce* (1982); and Vol. 3: *The Perspective of the World* (1984). These three fat volumes combine vast erudition, a global perspective, and remarkable illustrations.

(continued on page 528)

LISTENING TO THE PAST

Columbus Describes His First Voyage

On his return voyage to Spain in January 1493, Christopher Columbus composed a letter intended for wide circulation and had copies of it sent ahead to Isabella and Ferdinand and others when the ship docked at Lisbon. Because the letter sums up Columbus's understanding of his achievements, it is considered the most important document of his first voyage. Remember that his knowledge of Asia rested heavily on Marco Polo's Travels, *published around 1298.*

Since I know that you will be pleased at the great success with which the Lord has crowned my voyage, I write to inform you how in thirty-three days I crossed from the Canary Islands to the Indies, with the fleet which our most illustrious sovereigns gave me. I found very many islands with large populations and took possession of them all for their Highnesses; this I did by proclamation and unfurled the royal standard. No opposition was offered.

I named the first island that I found "San Salvador," in honour of our Lord and Saviour who has granted me this miracle. . . . When I reached Cuba, I followed its north coast westwards, and found it so extensive that I thought this must be the mainland, the province of Cathay.[1] . . . From there I saw another island eighteen leagues eastwards which I then named "Hispaniola."[2] . . .

Hispaniola is a wonder. The mountains and hills, the plains and meadow lands are both fertile and beautiful. They are most suitable for planting crops and for raising cattle of all kinds, and there are good sites for building towns and villages. The harbours are incredibly fine and there are many great rivers with broad channels and the majority contain gold.[3] The trees, fruits and plants are very different from those of Cuba. In Hispaniola there are many spices and large mines of gold and other metals. . . .[4]

The inhabitants of this island, and all the rest that I discovered or heard of, go naked, as their mothers bore them, men and women alike. A few of the women, however, cover a single place with a leaf of a plant or piece of cotton which they weave for the purpose. They have no iron or steel or arms and are not capable of using them, not because they are not strong and well built but because they are amazingly timid. All the weapons they have are canes cut at seeding time, at the end of which they fix a sharpened stick, but they have not the courage to make use of these, for very often when I have sent two or three men to a village to have conversation with them a great number of them have come out. But as soon as they saw my men all fled immediately, a father not even waiting for his son. And this is not because we have harmed any of them; on the contrary, wherever I have gone and been able to have conversation with them, I have given them some of the various things I had, a cloth and other articles, and received nothing in exchange. But they have still remained incurably timid. True, when they have been reassured and lost their fear, they are so ingenuous and so liberal with all their possessions that no one who has not seen them would believe it. If one asks for anything they have they never say no. On the contrary, they offer a share to anyone with demonstrations of heartfelt affection, and they are immediately content with any small thing, valuable or valueless, that is given them. I forbade the men to give them bits of broken crockery, fragments of glass or tags of laces, though if they could get them they fancied them the finest jewels in the world.

I hoped to win them to the love and service of their Highnesses and of the whole Spanish nation and to persuade them to collect and give us of the things which they possessed in abundance and which we needed. They have no religion and are not idolaters; but all believe that power and goodness dwell in the sky and they are firmly convinced that I have come from the sky with these ships and people. In this belief they gave me a good reception everywhere, once they had overcome their fear; and this is not because they are stupid—far from it, they are men of great intelligence, for they navigate all those seas, and give a marvellously good account of everything—but because they have never before seen men clothed or ships like these. . . .

In all these islands the men are seemingly content with one woman, but their chief or king is allowed more than twenty. The women appear to work more than the men and I have not been able to find out if they have private property. As far as I could see whatever a man had was shared among all the rest and this particularly applies to food. . . . In another island, which I am told is larger than Hispaniola, the people have no hair. Here there is a vast quantity of gold, and from here and the other islands I bring Indians as evidence.

In conclusion, to speak only of the results of this very hasty voyage, their Highnesses can see that I will give them as much gold as they require, if they will render me some very slight assistance; also I will give them all the spices and cotton they want. . . . I will also bring them as much aloes as they ask and as many slaves, who will be taken from the idolaters. I believe also that I have found rhubarb and cinnamon and there will be countless other things in addition. . . .

So all Christendom will be delighted that our Redeemer has given victory to our most illustrious King and Queen and their renowned kingdoms, in this great matter. They should hold great celebrations and render solemn thanks to the Holy Trinity with many solemn prayers, for the great triumph which they will have, by the conversion of so many peoples to our holy faith and for the temporal benefits which will follow, for not only Spain, but all Christendom will receive encouragement and profit.

This is a brief account of the facts.

Written in the caravel off the Canary Islands.[5]

15 February 1493

At your orders
THE ADMIRAL

✣ German woodcut depicting Columbus's landing of San Salvador. *(New York Public Library)*

Questions for Analysis

1. How did Columbus explain the success of his voyage?
2. What was Columbus's view of the native Americans he met?
3. Evaluate his statements that the Caribbean islands possessed gold, cotton, and spices.
4. Why did Columbus cling to the idea that he had reached Asia?

1. Cathay is the old name for China. In the log-book and later in this letter Columbus accepts the native story that Cuba is an island which they can circumnavigate in something more than twenty-one days, yet he insists here and later, during the second voyage, that it is in fact part of the Asiatic mainland.
2. Hispaniola is the second-largest island of the West Indies; Haiti occupies the western third of the island, the Dominican Republic the rest.
3. This did not prove to be true.
4. These statements are also inaccurate.
5. Actually, Columbus was off Santa Maria in the Azores.

Source: J. M. Cohen, ed. and trans., *The Four Voyages of Christopher Columbus* (Penguin Classics, 1969), pp. 115–123.

On witches and witchcraft, see, in addition to the titles by Cohn and Thomas cited in the Notes, J. B. Russell, *Witchcraft in the Middle Ages* (1976), and *Lucifer: The Devil in the Middle Ages* (1984); R. Kieckhefer, *European Witch Trials: Their Foundations in Popular and Learned Culture, 1300–1500* (1976), which places the subject within the social context; H. C. E. Midelfort, *Witch Hunting in Southwestern Germany: The Social and Intellectual Foundations* (1972), a sensitive and informed work; E. W. Monter, *Witchcraft in France and Switzerland* (1976), which discusses the subject with wit and wisdom; C. Ginzburg, *The Night Battle: Witchcraft and Agrarian Cults in the Sixteenth and Seventeenth Centuries* (1983), for small Italian communities; J. C. Baroja, *The World of Witches* (1964), for Spain; and G. R. Quaife, *Godly Zeal and Furious Rage: The Witch in Early Modern Europe* (1987), an excellent and lucidly written synthesis.

For women, marriage, and the family, see L. Stone, *The Family, Sex, and Marriage in England, 1500–1800* (1977), a controversial work; D. Underdown, "The Taming of the Scold," and S. Amussen, "Gender, Family, and the Social Order," in *Order and Disorder in Early Modern England,* ed. A. Fletcher and J. Stevenson (1985); A. Macfarlane, *Marriage and Love in England: Modes of Reproduction, 1300–1848* (1986); C. R. Boxer, *Women in Iberian Expansion Overseas, 1415–1815* (1975), an invaluable study of women's role in overseas migration; S. M. Wyntjes, "Women in the Reformation Era," in *Becoming Visible: Women in European History,* ed. R. Bridenthal and C. Koonz (1977), a quick survey of conditions in different countries; A. Clark, *The Working Life of Women in the Seventeenth Century* (1968); K. M. Wilson, ed., *Women Writers of the Renaissance and Reformation* (1987); M. J. M. Ezell, *The Patriarch's Wife: Literary Evidence and the History of the Family* (1987); L. Pollock, *A Lasting Relationship: Parents and Children over Three Centuries* (1987); and L. Schwoerer, *Lady Russel: One of the Best Women* (1988). Ozment's work listed in the Notes is a seminal study concentrating on Germany and Switzerland.

As background to slavery and racism in North and South America, students should see J. L. Watson, ed., *Asian and African Systems of Slavery* (1980), a valuable collection of essays, as well as the works by Davis and by Mannix and Cowley mentioned in the Notes: Davis shows how slavery was viewed as a progressive force in the expansion of the Western world, and Mannix and Cowley provide a hideously fascinating account of the slave trade. For North American conditions, interested students should consult W. D. Jordan, *The White Man's Burden: Historical Origins of Racism in the United States* (1974). The excellent essays in G. M. Frederickson, *The Arrogance of Race: Historical Perspectives on Slavery, Racism, and Social Inequality* (1988), stress the social and economic circumstances associated with the rise of plantation slavery. For Caribbean and South American developments, see F. P. Bowser, *The African Slave in Colonial Peru* (1974); J. S. Handler and F. W. Lange, *Plantation Slavery in Barbados: An Archeological and Historical Investigation* (1978); and R. E. Conrad, *Children of God's Fire: A Documentary History of Black Slavery in Brazil* (1983).

The leading authority on Montaigne is D. M. Frame; see his *Montaigne's Discovery of Man* (1955) and his translation listed in the Notes. For baroque art, see V. L. Tapié, *The Age of Grandeur: Baroque Art and Architecture* (1961), a standard work; and J. Montagu, *Roman Baroque Sculpture: The Industry of Art* (1985), an original and entertaining recent study.

CHAPTER

16 Absolutism and Constitutionalism in Western Europe (ca 1589–1715)

The Queen's staircase is among the grandest of the surviving parts of Louis XIV's Versailles. *(© Photo R.M.N.—Mercator)*

The seventeenth century was a period of revolutionary transformation. That century witnessed agricultural and manufacturing crises that had profound political consequences. A colder and wetter climate throughout most of the period meant a shorter farming season. Grain yields declined. In an age when cereals constituted the bulk of the diet for most people everywhere, smaller harvests led to food shortages and starvation. Food shortages in turn meant population decline or stagnation. Industry also suffered. While the evidence does not permit broad generalizations, it appears that the output of woolen textiles, one of the most important manufactures, declined sharply in the first half of the century. This economic crisis was not universal: it struck various sections of Europe at different times and to different degrees. In the middle decades of the century, Spain, France, Germany, and England all experienced great economic difficulties; but these years saw the golden age of the Netherlands.

Meanwhile, governments increased their spending, primarily for state armies; in the seventeenth century, armies grew larger than they had been since the time of the Roman Empire. To pay for these armies, governments taxed. The greatly increased burden of taxation, falling on a population already existing at a subsistence level, triggered revolts. Peasant revolts were extremely common;[1] in France, urban disorders were so frequent an aspect of the social and political landscape as to be "a distinctive feature of life."[2]

Princes struggled to free themselves from the restrictions of custom, powerful social groups, or competing institutions. Spanish and French monarchs gained control of the major institution in their domains, the Roman Catholic church. Rulers of England and some of the German principalities, who could not completely regulate the Catholic church, set up national churches. In the German Empire, the Treaty of Westphalia placed territorial sovereignty in the princes' hands. The kings of France, England, and Spain claimed the basic loyalty of their subjects. Monarchs made laws, to which everyone within their borders was subject. These powers added up to something close to sovereignty.

A state may be termed *sovereign* when it possesses a monopoly over the instruments of justice and the use of force within clearly defined boundaries. In a sovereign state, no system of courts, such as ecclesiastical tribunals, competes with state courts in the dispensation of justice; and private armies, such as those of feudal lords, present no threat to royal authority because the state's army is stronger. Royal law touches all persons within the country.

Sovereignty had been evolving during the late sixteenth century. Most seventeenth-century governments now needed to address the problem of *which* authority within the state would possess sovereignty—the Crown or privileged groups. In the period between roughly 1589 and 1715, two basic patterns of government emerged in Europe: absolute monarchy and the constitutional state. Almost all subsequent European governments have been modeled on one of these patterns.

- How did these forms of government differ from the feudal and dynastic monarchies of earlier centuries?
- In what sense were these forms "modern"?
- What social and economic factors limited absolute monarchs?
- Which Western countries most clearly illustrate the new patterns of political organization?
- Why is the seventeenth century considered the "golden age of the Netherlands"?

This chapter will explore these questions.

ABSOLUTISM

In the *absolutist* state, sovereignty is embodied in the person of the ruler. Absolute kings claimed to rule by divine right, meaning they were responsible to God alone. (Medieval kings governed "by the grace of God," but invariably they acknowledged that they had to respect and obey the law.) Absolute monarchs in the seventeenth and eighteenth centuries had to respect the fundamental laws of the land, though they claimed to rule by divine right.

Absolute rulers tried to control competing jurisdictions, institutions, or interest groups in their territories. They regulated religious sects. They abolished the liberties long held by certain areas, groups, or provinces. Absolute kings also secured the cooperation of the one class that historically had posed the greatest threat to monarchy, the nobility. Medieval governments, restrained by the church, the feudal nobility, and their own financial limitations, had been able to exert none of these controls.

In some respects, the key to the power and success of absolute monarchs lay in how they solved their financial problems. Medieval kings frequently had found temporary financial support through bargains with the nobility: the nobility agreed to an ad hoc grant of money in return for freedom from future taxation. In contrast, the absolutist solution was the creation of new state bureaucracies that directed the economic life of the country in the interests of the king, either forcing taxes ever higher or devising alternative methods of raising revenue.

Bureaucracies were composed of career officials appointed by and solely accountable to the king. The backgrounds of these civil servants varied. Absolute monarchs sometimes drew on the middle class, as in France, or utilized members of the nobility, as in Spain and eastern Europe. Where there was no middle class or an insignificant one, as in Austria, Prussia, Spain, and Russia, the government of the absolutist state consisted of an interlocking elite of monarchy, aristocracy, and bureaucracy.

Royal agents in medieval and Renaissance kingdoms had used their public offices and positions to benefit themselves and their families. In England, for example, Crown servants from Thomas Becket to Thomas Wolsey had treated their high offices as their private property and reaped considerable profit from them. The most striking difference between seventeenth-century bureaucracies and their predecessors was that seventeenth-century civil servants served the state as represented by the king. Bureaucrats recognized that the offices they held were public, or state, positions. The state paid them salaries to handle revenues that belonged to the Crown, and they were not supposed to use their positions for private gain. Bureaucrats gradually came to distinguish between public duties and private property.

Absolute monarchs also maintained permanent standing armies. Medieval armies had been raised by feudal lords for particular wars or campaigns, after which the troops were disbanded. In the seventeenth century, monarchs alone recruited and maintained armies—in peacetime as well as wartime. Kings deployed their troops both inside and outside the country in the interests of the monarchy. Armies became basic features of absolutist, and modern, states. Absolute rulers also invented new methods of compulsion. They concerned themselves with the private lives of potentially troublesome subjects, often through the use of secret police.

The word *absolutism* was coined only in 1830, two centuries after the developments it attempts to classify occurred. Some scholars today deny that absolute monarchy was a stage in the evolution of the modern state between medieval feudal monarchies and the constitutional governments of recent centuries. As one student of early modern France writes, "I believe the prevailing historiographical concept of 'absolute monarchy' is a myth promulgated by the royal government and legitimized by historians."[3] Such historians prefer the term *administrative monarchy,* by which they mean that the French state in the seventeenth century became stronger in that it could achieve more of its goals, it was centralized from Paris, and its administrative bureaucracy greatly expanded. Although the administrative monarchy interfered in many aspects of the private individual's daily life, it did not have the consent of the governed, and it especially lacked the idea of the rule of law—law made by a representative body—the administrative monarchy was actually limited, or checked, in ways that traditional interpretations of absolute monarchy did not consider.[4]

The rule of absolute monarchs was not all-embracing because they lacked the financial and military resources and the technology to make it so. Thus the absolutist state was not the same as a totalitarian state. *Totalitarianism* is a twentieth-century phenomenon; it seeks to direct all facets of a state's culture—art, education, religion, the economy, and politics—in the interests of the state. By definition, totalitarian rule is *total* regulation. By twentieth-century standards, the ambitions of absolute monarchs were quite limited: each sought the exaltation of himself or herself as the embodiment of the state. Whether or not Louis XIV of France actually said, "*L'état, c'est moi!*" (I am the state!), the remark expresses his belief that he personified the French nation. Yet the absolutist state did foreshadow recent totalitarian regimes in two fundamental respects: in the glorification of the state over all other aspects of the culture and in the use of war and an expansionist foreign policy to divert attention from domestic ills. All of this is best illustrated by the experience of France, aptly known as the model of absolute monarchy.

The Foundations of French Absolutism: Henry IV, Sully, and Richelieu

In 1589 Henry IV (see page 491) inherited an enormous mess. Civil wars had wracked France since 1561. Catastrophically poor harvests meant that all across France peasants lived on the verge of starvation, fighting off wolves and bands of demobilized soldiers. Some provinces, such as Burgundy, suffered almost complete depopulation. Commercial activity had fallen to one-third its 1580 level. Nobles, officials, merchants, and peasants wanted peace, order, and stability. "Henri le

Procession of the Catholic League In response to what many French Catholics considered the monarchy's laxness in crushing heresy, nobles, burghers, and friars formed groups or leagues to fight Protestantism at the local level. The resulting chaos, with armed private citizens indiscriminately firing guns, is illustrated in this scene, probably in Paris. *(Musée de Beaux-Arts, Valenciennes/Giraudon/Art Resource, NY)*

Grand" (Henry the Great), as the king was called, promised "a chicken in every pot" and inaugurated a remarkable recovery. Henry may have been the first French ruler since Louis IX, in the thirteenth century, genuinely to care about his people, and he was the only king whose statue the Paris crowd did not tear down in the Revolution of 1789.

Henry converted to Catholicism and sought better relations with the pope. He tried to gain Protestant confidence by issuing the Edict of Nantes in 1598 (see pages 491 and 553) and by appointing the devout Protestant Maximilien de Béthune, duke of Sully, as his chief minister. Aside from a short, successful war with Savoy in 1601, Henry kept France at peace. Maintaining that "if we are without compassion for the people, they must succumb and we all perish with them," Henry sharply lowered taxes on the overburdened peasants. In compensation for the lost revenues, in 1602–1604 he introduced the *paulette,* an annual fee paid by royal officials to guarantee heredity in their offices.

Sully proved to be an effective administrator. He combined the indirect taxes on salt, sales, and transit and leased their collection to financiers. Although the number of taxes declined, revenues increased because of the revival of trade.[5] One of the first French officials to appreciate the possibilities of overseas trade, Sully subsidized the Company for Trade with the Indies.

He started a country-wide highway system and even dreamed of an international organization for the maintenance of peace.

In only twelve years, Henry IV and Sully restored public order in France and laid the foundations for economic prosperity. By the standards of the time, Henry IV's government was progressive and promising. His murder in 1610 by a crazed fanatic led to a severe crisis.

After the death of Henry IV, the queen-regent Marie de' Medici headed the government for the child-king Louis XIII (r. 1610–1643), but in fact feudal nobles and princes of the blood dominated the political scene. In 1624 Marie de' Medici secured the appointment of Armand Jean du Plessis—Cardinal Richelieu (1585–1642)—to the council of ministers. It was a remarkable appointment. The next year, Richelieu became president of the council, and after 1628 he was first minister of the French crown. Richelieu used his strong influence over King Louis XIII to exalt the French monarchy as the embodiment of the French state. One of the greatest servants of that state, Richelieu set in place the cornerstone of French absolutism, and his work served as the basis for France's cultural hegemony of Europe in the later seventeenth century.

Richelieu's policy was the total subordination of all groups and institutions to the French monarchy. The French nobility, with its selfish and independent interests, had long constituted the foremost threat to the centralizing goals of the Crown and to a strong national state. Therefore, Richelieu sought to curb the power of the nobility. In 1624 he succeeded in reshuffling the royal council, eliminating such potential power brokers as the prince of Condé. Thereafter Richelieu dominated the council in an unprecedented way. He leveled castles, long the symbol of feudal independence, and crushed aristocratic conspiracies with quick executions. For example, when the duke of Montmorency, the first peer of France and godson of Henry IV, became involved in a revolt, he was summarily beheaded.

The constructive genius of Cardinal Richelieu is best reflected in the administrative system he established. He extended the use of the royal commissioners called intendants. France was divided into thirty-two *généralités* (districts), in each of which after 1634 a royal intendant held a commission to perform specific tasks, often financial but also judicial and policing. Intendants transmitted information from local communities to Paris and delivered royal orders from the capital to their généralités. Almost always recruited from the newer judicial nobility, the *noblesse de robe,* intendants were appointed directly by the monarch, to whom they were solely responsible. They could not be natives of the districts where they held authority; thus they had no vested interest in their localities. The intendants recruited men for the army, supervised the collection of taxes, presided over the administration of local law, checked up on the local nobility, and regulated economic activities—commerce, trade, the guilds, marketplaces—in their districts. They were to use their power for two related purposes: to enforce royal orders in the généralités of their jurisdiction and to weaken the power and influence of the regional nobility. As the intendants' power increased under Richelieu, so did the power of the centralized French state.

In 1598 Henry IV's lawyers had drawn up the "Law of Concord." It had been published as the Edict of Nantes to create a temporary and provisional situation of religious toleration in order to secure not the permanent coexistence of two religions (the Calvinist, Reformed, or Huguenot faith and Roman Catholicism), but "religious and civil concord"—that is the confessional reunification of all French people under the king's religion, Roman Catholicism. The Edict of Nantes named 150 towns throughout France; the king granted Protestants the right to practice their faith in those towns, and he gave the towns 180,000 écus to support the maintenance of their military garrisons. Huguenots numbered perhaps 10 percent of the total French population, most of them concentrated in the southwest. In 1627 Louis XIII, with the unanimous consent of the royal council, decided to end Protestant military and political independence, because, he said, it constituted "a state within a state." According to Louis, Huguenots demanded freedom of conscience, but they did not allow Catholics to worship in their cities, which he interpreted as *political* disobedience.[6]

Attention focused on La Rochelle, fourth largest of the French Atlantic ports and a major commercial center with strong ties to the northern Protestant states of Holland and England. Louis intended to cut off English aid, and he personally supervised the siege of La Rochelle. The city fell in October 1628. Its municipal government was suppressed, and its walled fortifications were destroyed. Although Protestants retained the right of public worship, the king reinstated the Catholic liturgy, and Cardinal Richelieu himself celebrated the first Mass. The military fall of La Rochelle weakened the influence of aristocratic adherents of Calvinism and was one step in the evolution of a unified French state.

Louis XIII, Richelieu, and later Louis XIV also faced serious urban protests. Real or feared unemployment, high food prices, grain shortages, new taxes, and what ordinary townspeople perceived as oppressive taxation all triggered domestic violence. Major insurrections occurred at Dijon in 1630 and 1668, at Bordeaux in 1635 and 1675, at Montpellier in 1645, in Lyons in 1667–1668 and 1692, and in Amiens in 1685, 1695, 1704, and 1711. Sometimes rumor and misinformation sparked these riots. In any case, they were all characterized by deep popular anger, a vocabulary of violence, and what a recent historian calls "the culture of retribution"—that is, the punishment of royal "outsiders," officials who attempted to announce or to collect taxes. These officials often were seized, beaten, and hacked to death. For example, in 1673 Louis XIV's imposition of new taxes on legal transactions, tobacco, and pewterware provoked a major uprising in Bordeaux.

Municipal and royal authorities responded feebly. They lacked the means of strong action. They feared that stern repressive measures, such as sending in troops to fire on crowds, would create martyrs and further inflame the situation, while forcible full-scale military occupation of a city would be very expensive. Thus authorities allowed the crowds to "burn themselves out," as long as they did not do too much damage. Royal edicts were suspended, prisoners were released, and discussions were initiated. By the end of the century, municipal governments were better integrated into the national structure, and local authorities had the prompt military support of the Paris government. Those who publicly opposed government policies and taxes received swift and severe punishment.[7]

French foreign policy under Richelieu was aimed at the destruction of the fence of Habsburg territories that surrounded France. Consequently, Richelieu supported the Habsburgs' enemies. In 1631 he signed a treaty with the Lutheran king Gustavus Adolphus promising French support against the Catholic Habsburgs in what has been called the Swedish phase of the Thirty Years' War (see page 499). French influence became an important factor in the political future of the German Empire. Richelieu acquired for France extensive rights in Alsace in the east and Arras in the north.

Richelieu's efforts at centralization extended even to literature. In 1635 he gave official recognition to a group of philologists who were interested in grammar and rhetoric. Thus was born the French Academy. With Richelieu's encouragement, the French Academy began the preparation of a dictionary to standardize the French language; it was completed in 1694. The French Academy survives as a prestigious society, and its membership now includes people outside the field of literature.

All of these new policies, especially war, cost money. In his *Political Testament,* Richelieu wrote, "I have always said that finances are the sinews of the state." He fully realized that revenues determine a government's ability to inaugurate and enforce policies and programs. A state secures its revenues through taxation. But the political and economic structure of France greatly limited the government's ability to tax. Seventeenth-century France remained "a collection of local economies and local societies dominated by local elites." The rights of some assemblies in some provinces, such as Brittany, to vote their own taxes; the hereditary exemption from taxation of many wealthy members of the nobility and the middle class; and the royal pension system drastically limited the government's power to tax.

Philippe de Champaigne: Cardinal Richelieu This portrait, with its penetrating eyes, expression of haughty and imperturbable cynicism, and dramatic sweep of red robes, suggests the authority, grandeur, and power that Richelieu wished to convey as first minister of France. *(Reproduced by courtesy of the Trustees, The National Gallery, London)*

Richelieu and, later, Louis XIV temporarily solved their financial problems by securing the cooperation of local elites. The central government shared the proceeds of tax revenue with local powers. It never gained all the income it needed. Because the French monarchy could not tax at will, it never completely controlled the financial system. In practice, therefore, French absolutism was limited.[8]

In building the French state, Richelieu believed he had to resort to drastic measures against persons and groups within France and to conduct a tough anti-Habsburg foreign policy. He knew also that his approach sometimes seemed to contradict traditional Christian teaching. As a priest and bishop, how did he justify his policies? He developed his own *raison d'état* (reason of state): "Where the interests of the state are concerned, God absolves actions which, if privately committed, would be a crime."[9]

Richelieu persuaded Louis XIII to appoint protégé Jules Mazarin (1602–1661) as his successor. An Italian diplomat of great charm, Mazarin had served on the council of state under Richelieu, acquiring considerable political experience. He became a cardinal in 1641 and a French citizen in 1643. When Louis XIII followed Richelieu to the grave in 1643 and a regency headed by Queen Anne of Austria governed for the child-king Louis XIV, Mazarin became the dominant power in the government. He continued Richelieu's centralizing policies, but his attempts to increase royal revenues led to the civil wars of 1648–1653 known as the "Fronde."

The word *fronde* means "slingshot" or "catapult," and a *frondeur* was originally a street urchin who threw mud at the passing carriages of the rich. But the Fronde originated in the provinces, not Paris, and the term *frondeur* came to be applied to anyone who opposed the policies of the government. Many individuals and groups did so. Influential segments of the nobility resented the increased power of the monarchy under Louis XIII and what they perceived as their diminished role in government. Mazarin could not control them as Richelieu had done. Royal bureaucrats, judges in the parlements, and intendants who considered their positions the means to social and economic advancement felt that they were being manipulated by the Crown and their interests ignored.[10] The state's financial situation steadily weakened because entire regions of France refused to pay taxes. The French defeat of Spanish armies at Rocroi in 1643 marked the final collapse of Spanish military power in Europe; the victory also led the French people to believe that because peace was at hand, taxes were unnecessary. When a desperate government devised new taxes, the Parlement of Paris rejected them. Popular rebellions led by aristocratic factions broke out in the provinces and spread to Paris.[11] As rebellion continued, civil order broke down completely. A vast increase in the state bureaucracy, representing an expansion of royal power, and new means of extracting money from working people incurred the bitter opposition of peasants and urban artisans. Violence continued intermittently for the next twelve years.

The conflicts of the Fronde had three significant results for the future. First, it became apparent that the government would have to compromise with the bureaucrats and social elites that controlled local institutions and constituted the state bureaucracy. These groups were already largely exempt from taxation, and Louis XIV confirmed their privileged social status. Second, the French economy was badly disrupted and would take years to rebuild. Third, the Fronde had a traumatic effect on the young Louis XIV. The king and his mother were frequently threatened and sometimes treated as prisoners by aristocratic factions. On one occasion, a mob broke into the royal bedchamber to make sure the king was actually there; it succeeded in giving him a bad fright. Louis never forgot such humiliations. The period of the Fronde formed the cornerstone of his political education and of his conviction that the sole alternative to anarchy was absolute monarchy. The personal rule of Louis XIV represented the culmination of the process of centralization, but it also witnessed the institutionalization of procedures that would ultimately undermine the absolute monarchy.

The Absolute Monarchy of Louis XIV

According to the court theologian Bossuet, the clergy at the coronation of Louis XIV in Reims Cathedral asked God to cause the splendors of the French court to fill all who beheld it with awe. God subsequently granted that prayer. In the reign of Louis XIV (r. 1643–1715), the longest in European history, the French monarchy reached the peak of absolutist development. In the magnificence of his court, in his absolute power, in the brilliance of the culture that he presided over and that permeated all of Europe, and in his remarkably long life, the "Sun King" dominated his age. No wonder scholars have characterized the second half of the seventeenth century as the "Grand Century," the "Age of Magnificence," and, echoing the eighteenth-century philosopher Voltaire, the "Age of Louis XIV."

In old age, Louis claimed that he had grown up learning very little, but recent historians think he was being modest. True, he knew little Latin and only the rudiments of arithmetic and thus by Renaissance standards was not well educated. Nevertheless, he learned to speak Italian and Spanish fluently, he spoke and wrote elegant French, and he knew some French history and more European geography than the ambassadors accredited to his court. He imbibed the devout Catholicism of his mother, Anne of Austria, and throughout his long life scrupulously performed his religious duties. (Beginning in 1661, Louis attended Mass daily, but rather than paying attention to the liturgy, he said his rosary—to the scorn of his courtiers, who considered this practice "rustic.") Religion, Anne, and Mazarin all taught Louis that God had established kings as his rulers on earth. The royal coronation consecrated Louis to God's service, and he was certain—to use Shakespeare's phrase—that there was a divinity that doth hedge a king. Though kings were a race apart, they could not do as they pleased: they had to obey God's laws and rule for the good of the people.

Louis's education was more practical than formal. Under Mazarin's instruction, he studied state papers as they arrived, and he attended council meetings and sessions at which French ambassadors were dispatched abroad and foreign ambassadors received. He learned by direct experience and gained professional training in the work of government. Above all, the misery he suffered during the Fronde gave him an eternal distrust of the nobility and a profound sense of his own isolation. Accordingly, silence, caution, and secrecy became political tools for the achievement of his goals. His characteristic answer to requests of all kinds became the enigmatic "*Je verrai*" (I shall see).

Louis grew up with an absolute sense of his royal dignity. Contemporaries considered him tall (he was actually five feet five inches) and distinguished in appearance but inclined to heaviness because of the gargantuan meals in which he indulged. A highly sensual man easily aroused by an attractive female face and figure, Louis nonetheless ruled without the political influence of either his wife, Queen Maria Theresa, whom he married as a result of a diplomatic agreement with Spain, or his mistresses. Louis XIV was a consummate actor, and his "terrifying majesty" awed all who saw him. He worked extremely hard and succeeded in being "every moment and every inch a king." Because he so relished the role of monarch, historians have had difficulty distinguishing the man from the monarch.

Historians have often said that Louis XIV introduced significant government innovations, the greatest of which was "the complete domestication of the nobility." By this phrase scholars mean that he exercised complete control over the powerful social class that historically had opposed the centralizing goals of the French monarchy. Recent research has demonstrated, however, that notions of "domestication" represent an exaggeration. What Louis XIV actually achieved was the cooperation or collaboration of the nobility. Throughout France the nobility agreed to participate in projects that both exalted the monarchy and reinforced the aristocrats' ancient prestige. Thus the relationship between the Crown and the nobility constituted collaboration rather than absolute control.

In the province of Languedoc, for example, Louis and his agents persuaded the notables to support the construction of the Canal des Deux Mers, a waterway linking the Mediterranean Sea and the Atlantic Ocean.

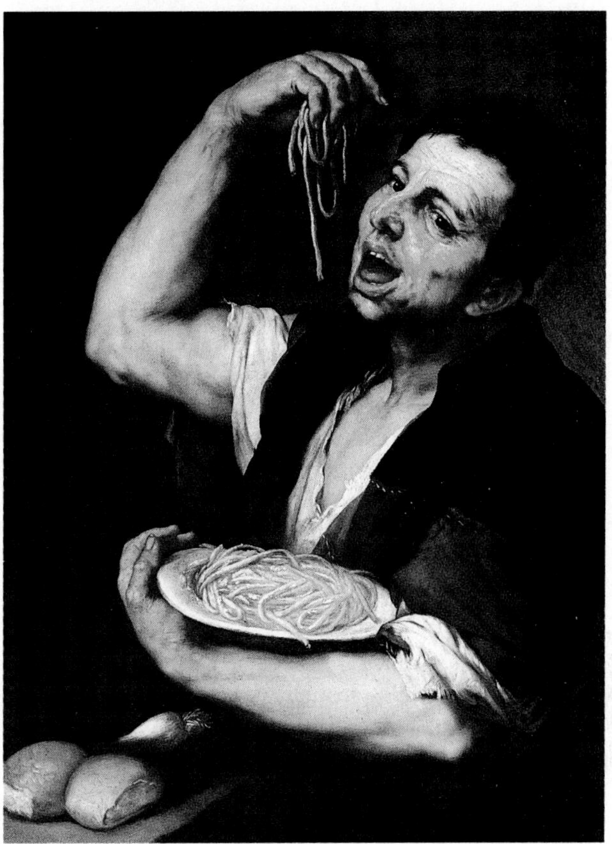

Luca Giordano: The Pasta Eater In the seventeenth century, rich people carried a fork when they dined out, but its use spread very slowly from Italy and came into common use only about 1750. A German preacher damned the fork as a diabolical luxury: "God would not have given us fingers if he wanted us to use forks." So, if King Louis XIV could eat chicken stew with his fingers without spilling it, how can we fault this Neapolitan workingman for enjoying his spaghetti without a fork? *(The Art Museum, Princeton University Museum purchase, John Maclean Magie and Gertrude Magie Fund. Photo: Bruce White)*

Royal encouragement for the manufacture of luxury draperies in Languedocian towns likewise tied provincial business people to national goals, although French cloths subsequently proved unable to compete with cheaper Dutch ones. Above all, in the campaign for the repression of the Huguenots, the interests of the monarchy and nobility coincided (see page 541). Through mutual collaboration, the nobility and the king achieved goals that neither could have won without the other. For his part, Louis won increased military taxation from the Estates of Languedoc. In return, Louis graciously granted the nobility and dignitaries privileged social status and increased access to his person, which meant access to the enormous patronage the king had to dispense. French government rested on the social and political structure of seventeenth-century France, a structure in which the nobility historically exercised great influence. In this respect, therefore, French absolutism was not so much modern as the last phase of a historical feudal society.[12]

Louis XIV installed his royal court at Versailles, a small town ten miles from Paris. He required all the great nobility of France, at the peril of social, political, and sometimes economic disaster, to come live at Versailles for at least part of the year. Today Versailles stands as the best surviving museum of a vanished society on earth. In the seventeenth century, it became a model of rational order, the center of France, and the perfect symbol of the king's power. (See the feature "Listening to the Past: The Court at Versailles" on pages 562–563.)

Louis XIII had begun Versailles as a hunting lodge, a retreat from a queen he did not like. His son's architects, Le Nôtre and Le Vau, turned what the duke of Saint-Simon called "the most dismal and thankless of sights" into a veritable paradise. Wings were added to the original building to make the palace U-shaped. Everywhere at Versailles the viewer had a sense of grandeur, vastness, and elegance. Enormous staterooms became display galleries for inlaid tables, Italian marble statuary, Gobelin tapestries woven at the state factory in Paris, silver ewers, and beautiful (if uncomfortable) furniture. If genius means attention to detail, Louis XIV and his designers had it: the decor was perfected down to the last doorknob and keyhole. In the gigantic Hall of Mirrors, later to reflect so much of German as well as French history, hundreds of candles illuminated the domed ceiling, where allegorical paintings celebrated the king's victories.

The art and architecture of Versailles served as fundamental tools of state policy under Louis XIV. The king used architecture to overawe his subjects and foreign visitors. Versailles was seen as a reflection of French genius. Thus the Russian tsar Peter the Great imitated Versailles in the construction of his palace, Peterhof, as did the Prussian emperor Frederick the Great in his palace at Potsdam outside Berlin.

As in architecture, so too in language. Beginning in the reign of Louis XIV, French became the language of polite society and the vehicle of diplomatic exchange. French also gradually replaced Latin as the language of international scholarship and learning. The wish of other kings to ape the courtly style of Louis XIV and the imitation of French intellectuals and artists spread the language all over Europe. The royal courts of Sweden, Russia, Poland, and Germany all spoke French. In the eighteenth century, the great Russian aristocrats were more fluent in French than in Russian. In England the first Hanoverian king, George I, spoke fluent French and only halting English. France inspired a cosmopolitan European culture in the late seventeenth century, and that culture was inspired by the king. The French today revere Louis XIV as one of their greatest national heroes because of the culture that he inspired and symbolized.

Against this background of magnificent splendor, Saint-Simon writes, Louis XIV

> *reduced everyone to subjection, and brought to his court those very persons he cared least about. Whoever was old enough to serve did not dare demur. It was still another device to ruin the nobles by accustoming them to equality and forcing them to mingle with everyone indiscriminately. . . .*
>
> *Louis XIV took great pains to inform himself on what was happening everywhere, in public places, private homes, and even on the international scene. . . . Spies and informers of all kinds were numberless. . . .*
>
> *But the King's most vicious method of securing information was opening letters.*[13]

Though this passage was written by one of Louis's severest critics, all agree that the king used court ceremonials to undermine the power of the great nobility. By excluding the highest nobles from his councils, he weakened their ancient right to advise the king and to participate in government; they became mere instruments of royal policy. Operas, fetes, balls, gossip, and trivia occupied the nobles' time and attention. Through painstaking attention to detail and precisely calculated showmanship, Louis XIV reduced the major threat to his power. He separated power from status and grandeur: he secured the nobles' cooperation, and the nobles enjoyed the status and grandeur in which they lived.

Constitutionalism is the limitation of government by law. Constitutionalism also implies a balance between the authority and power of the government, on the one hand, and the rights and liberties of the subjects, on the other. The balance is often very delicate.

A nation's constitution may be written or unwritten. It may be embodied in one basic document, occasionally revised by amendment or judicial decision, like the Constitution of the United States. Or it may be partly written and partly unwritten and include parliamentary statutes, judicial decisions, and a body of traditional procedures and practices, like the English, Canadian, and Dutch constitutions. Whether written or unwritten, a constitution gets its binding force from the government's acknowledgment that it must respect that constitution—that is, that the state must govern according to the laws. Likewise, in a constitutional state, the people look on the laws and the constitution as the protectors of their rights, liberties, and property.

Modern constitutional governments may take either a republican or a monarchial form. In a constitutional republic, the sovereign power resides in the electorate and is exercised by the electorate's representatives. In a constitutional monarchy, a king or queen serves as the head of state and possesses some residual political authority, but again the ultimate, or sovereign, power rests in the electorate.

A constitutional government is not, however, quite the same as a democratic government. In a complete democracy, *all* the people have the right to participate either directly or indirectly (through their elected representatives) in the government of the state. Democratic government, therefore, is intimately tied up with the *franchise* (the vote). Most men could not vote until the late nineteenth century. Even then, women—probably the majority in Western societies—lacked the franchise; they gained the right to vote only in the twentieth century. Consequently, although constitutionalism developed in the seventeenth century, full democracy was achieved only in very recent times.

The Decline of Royal Absolutism in England (1603–1649)

In 1588 Queen Elizabeth I of England exercised very great personal power; by 1689 the English monarchy was severely circumscribed. Change in England was anything but orderly. Seventeenth-century England displayed little political stability. It executed one king, experienced a bloody civil war; experimented with military dictatorship, then restored the son of the murdered king; and finally, after a bloodless revolution, established constitutional monarchy. Political stability came only in the 1690s. How do we account for the fact that after such a violent and tumultuous century, England laid the foundations for constitutional monarchy? What combination of political, socioeconomic, and religious factors brought on a civil war in 1642 to 1649 and then the constitutional settlement of 1688 to 1689?

The extraordinary success of Elizabeth I had rested on her political shrewdness and flexibility, her careful management of finances, her wise selection of ministers, her clever manipulation of Parliament, and her sense of royal dignity and devotion to hard work. The aging queen had always refused to discuss the succession. After her Scottish cousin James Stuart succeeded her as James I (r. 1603–1625), Elizabeth's strengths seemed even greater than they actually had been.

King James was well educated, learned, and, with thirty-five years' experience as king of Scotland, politically shrewd. But he was not as interested in displaying the majesty and mystique of monarchy as Elizabeth had been. He also lacked the common touch. Urged to wave at the crowds who waited to greet their new ruler, James complained that he was tired and threatened to drop his breeches "so they can cheer at my arse." The new king failed to live up to the role expected of him in England. Moreover, James, in contrast to Elizabeth, was a poor judge of character, and in a society already hostile to the Scots and concerned about proper spoken English, James's Scottish accent was a disadvantage.[26]

James was devoted to the theory of the divine right of kings. He expressed his ideas about divine right in his essay "The Trew Law of Free Monarchy." According to James I, a monarch has a divine (or God-given) right to his authority and is responsible only to God. Rebellion is the worst of political crimes. If a king orders something evil, the subject should respond with passive disobedience but should be prepared to accept any penalty for noncompliance.

He went so far as to lecture the House of Commons: "There are no privileges and immunities which can stand against a divinely appointed King." This notion, implying total royal jurisdiction over the liberties, persons, and properties of English men and women, formed the basis of the Stuart concept of absolutism. Such a view ran directly counter to the long-standing English idea that a person's property could not be taken away without due process of law. James's expression of such views before the English House of Commons constituted a grave political mistake.

The House of Commons guarded the state's pocketbook, and James and later Stuart kings badly needed to open that pocketbook. Elizabeth had bequeathed to

James a sizable royal debt. Through prudent management, the debt could have been gradually reduced, but James I looked on all revenues as a happy windfall to be squandered on a lavish court and favorite courtiers. In reality, the extravagance displayed in James's court as well as the public flaunting of his male lovers weakened respect for the monarchy.

Elizabeth had also left to her Stuart successors a House of Commons that appreciated its own financial strength and intended to use that strength to acquire a greater say in the government of the state. The knights and burgesses who sat at Westminster in the late sixteenth and early seventeenth centuries wanted a voice in royal expenditures, religious reform, and foreign affairs. Essentially, the Commons wanted sovereignty.

Profound social changes had occurred since the sixteenth century. The English House of Commons during the reigns of James I and his son Charles I (r. 1625–1649) was very different from the assembly Henry VIII had manipulated into passing his Reformation legislation. A social revolution had brought about the change. The dissolution of the monasteries and the sale of monastic land had enriched many people. Agricultural techniques such as the draining of wasteland and the application of fertilizers had improved the land and its yield. In the seventeenth century, old manorial common land was enclosed and turned into sheep runs, breeding was carefully supervised, and the size of the flocks increased. In these activities, as well as in the renting and leasing of parcels of land, precise accounts were kept.

Many people invested in commercial ventures at home, such as the expanding cloth industry, and through partnerships and joint stock companies engaged in foreign enterprises. Many also made prudent marriages. All these developments led to a great deal of social mobility. Both in commerce and in agriculture, the English in the late sixteenth and early seventeenth centuries were capitalists, investing their profits to make more money. Though the international inflation of the period hit everywhere, in England commercial and agricultural income rose faster than prices. Wealthy country gentry, rich city merchants, and financiers invested abroad.

The typical pattern was for the commercially successful to set themselves up as country gentry, thus creating an elite group that possessed a far greater proportion of land and of the national wealth in 1640 than had been the case in 1540. Small wonder that in 1640 someone could declare in the House of Commons, probably accurately, "We could buy the House of Lords three times over." Increased wealth had also produced a better-educated and more articulate House of Commons. Many members had acquired at least a smattering of legal knowledge, which they used to search for medieval precedents from which to argue against the king. The class that dominated the Commons wanted political power corresponding to its economic strength.

In England, unlike France, there was no social stigma attached to paying taxes. Members of the House of Commons were willing to tax themselves provided they had some say in the expenditure of those taxes and in the formulation of state policies. The Stuart kings, however, considered such ambitions intolerable presumption and a threat to their divine-right prerogative. Consequently, at every Parliament between 1603 and 1640, bitter squabbles erupted between the Crown and the wealthy, articulate, and legally minded Commons. Charles I's attempt to govern without Parliament (1629–1640) and to finance his government by arbitrary non-parliamentary levies, brought the country to a crisis.

An issue graver than royal extravagance and Parliament's desire to make law also disturbed the English and embittered relations between the king and the House of Commons. That problem was religion. In the early seventeenth century, increasing numbers of English people felt dissatisfied with the Church of England established by Henry VIII and reformed by Elizabeth. Many Puritans (see page 473) believed that the Reformation had not gone far enough. They wanted to "purify" the Anglican church of Roman Catholic elements—elaborate vestments and ceremonials, the position of the altar in the church, even the giving and wearing of wedding rings.

It is very difficult to establish what proportion of the English population was Puritan. According to the present scholarly consensus, the dominant religious groups in the early seventeenth century were Calvinist; their more zealous members were Puritans. It also seems clear that many English men and women were attracted by the socioeconomic implications of John Calvin's theology. Calvinism emphasized hard work, sobriety, thrift, competition, and postponement of pleasure, and it tended to link sin and poverty with weakness and moral corruption. These attitudes fit in precisely with the economic approaches and practices of many (successful) business people and farmers. These values have frequently been called the "Protestant ethic," "middle-class ethic," or "capitalist ethic." While it is hazardous to identify capitalism with Protestantism—there were many successful Catholic capitalists, for example—the "Protestant virtues" represented the prevailing values of members of the House of Commons.

Puritans wanted to abolish bishops in the Church of England, and when James I said, "No bishop, no king,"

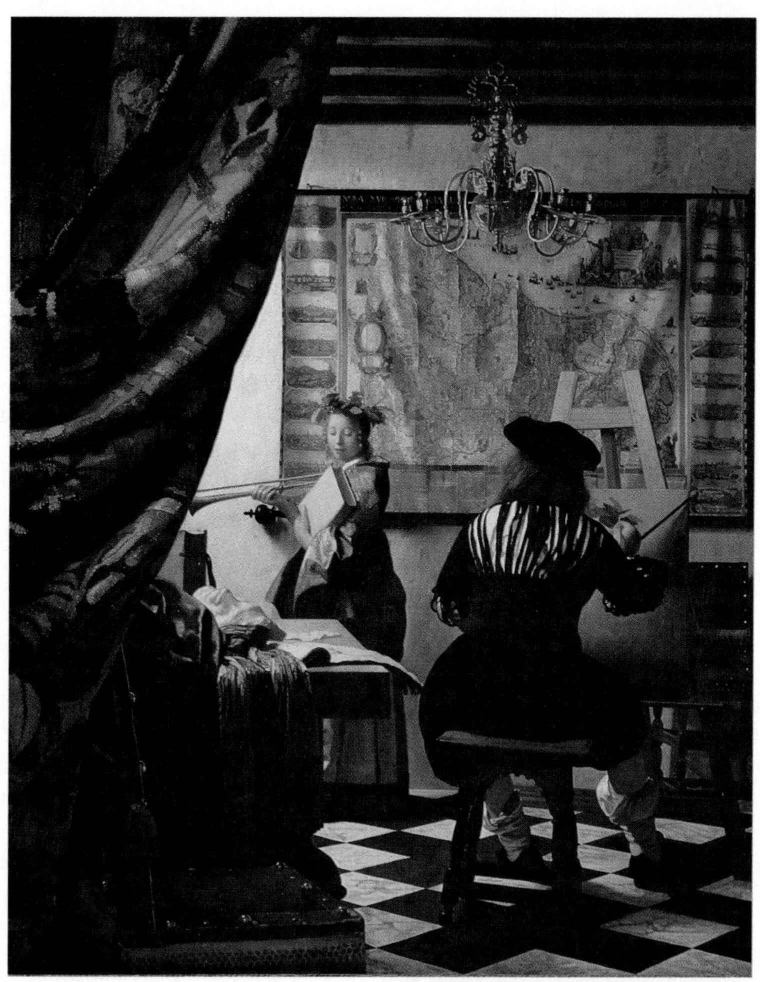

Jan Vermeer: The Art of Painting or The Artist's Studio In a typically Dutch interior—black and white marble floor, brass chandelier, map of Holland on the wall—an artist paints an allegory of Clio, the Muse of History (often shown holding a book and a trumpet); the muses, nine goddesses of Greek mythology, were thought to inspire the arts. Considered the second-greatest Dutch painter (after Rembrandt), Vermeer (1632–1675) was a master of scenes of everyday life, but he probably meant his work to be understood on more than one level. *(Kunsthistorisches Museum, Vienna/Art Resource, NY)*

independence from Spain as the Republic of United Provinces of the Netherlands—an independence that was confirmed by the Peace of Westphalia ending the Thirty Years' War in 1648 (see pages 499–500). The seventeenth century witnessed an unparalleled flowering of Dutch scientific, artistic, and literary achievement. In this period, often called the "golden age of the Netherlands," Dutch ideas and attitudes played a profound role in shaping a new and modern world-view. At the same time, the United Provinces was another model of the development of the modern constitutional state.

Within each province, an oligarchy of wealthy merchants called "regents" handled domestic affairs in the local Estates. The provincial Estates held virtually all the power. A federal assembly, or States General, handled matters of foreign affairs, such as war. But the States General did not possess sovereign authority since all issues had to be referred back to the local Estates for approval. The States General appointed a representative, the *stadholder,* in each province. As the highest executive there, the stadholder carried out ceremonial functions and was responsible for defense and good order. The sons of William the Silent, Maurice and William Louis, held the office of stadholder in all seven provinces. As members of the House of Orange, they were closely identified with Dutch patriotism. The regents in each province jealously guarded local independence and resisted efforts at centralization. Nevertheless, Holland, which had the largest navy and the most wealth, dominated the republic and the States General. Significantly, the Estates assembled at Holland's capital, The Hague.

The government of the United Provinces fit none of the standard categories of seventeenth-century political organization. The Dutch were not monarchial but fiercely republican. The government was controlled by wealthy merchants and financiers. Though rich, their values were not aristocratic but strongly middle-class, emphasizing thrift, hard work, and simplicity in living. The Dutch republic was not a strong federation but a confederation—that is, a weak union of strong provinces. The provinces were a temptation to powerful neighbors, yet the Dutch resisted the long Spanish effort at reconquest and withstood both French and English attacks in the second half of the century.

The political success of the Dutch rested on the phenomenal commercial prosperity of the Netherlands. The moral and ethical bases of that commercial wealth were thrift, frugality, and religious toleration. John Calvin had written, "From where do the merchant's profits come except from his own diligence and industry?" This attitude undoubtedly encouraged a sturdy people who had waged a centuries-old struggle against the sea.

Alone of all European peoples in the seventeenth century, the Dutch practiced religious toleration. Peoples of all faiths were welcome within their borders. Although there is scattered evidence of anti-Semitism, Jews enjoyed a level of acceptance and absorption in Dutch business and general culture unique in early modern Europe. (See the feature "Individuals in Society: Glückel of Hameln.") It is a testimony to the urbanity of Dutch society that in a century when patriotism was closely identified with religious uniformity, the Calvinist province of Holland under its highest official, Johan van Oldenbarnevelt, allowed Catholics to practice their faith. As long as business people conducted their religion in private, the government did not interfere with them.

Toleration also paid off: it attracted a great deal of foreign capital and investment. Deposits at the Bank of Amsterdam were guaranteed by the city council, and in the middle years of the century, the bank became Europe's best source of cheap credit and commercial intelligence and the main clearing-house for bills of exchange. People of all races and creeds traded in Amsterdam, at whose docks on the Amstel River five thousand ships were berthed. Joost van den Vondel, the poet of Dutch imperialism, exulted:

God, God, the Lord of Amstel cried, hold every conscience free;
And Liberty ride, on Holland's tide, with billowing sails to sea,
And run our Amstel out and in; let freedom gird the bold,
And merchant in his counting house stand elbow deep in gold.[28]

The fishing industry was the cornerstone of the Dutch economy. For half the year, from June to December, fishing fleets combed the dangerous English coast and the North Sea and raked in tiny herring. Profits from herring stimulated shipbuilding, and even before 1600 the Dutch were offering the lowest shipping rates in Europe. The Dutch merchant marine was the largest in Europe. In 1650 contemporaries estimated that the Dutch had sixteen thousand merchant ships,

Room from Het Scheepje (The Little Ship) A retired sea captain who became a successful brewer in Haarlem owned the house (adjacent to his brewery) that included this room. The brass chandelier, plates, tiles, Turkish rug on the table (probably from Transylvania in the then Ottoman Empire), oak mantelpiece, and paneling make this superb example of a Dutch domestic interior during the Golden Age. A bed, built into the wall paneling, was warmed at night by coals in the pan hanging by the fireplace. *(Room from Het Scheepje, Haarlem, The Netherlands, early 17th century. Philadelphia Museum of Art, Gift of Edward W. Bok. 1928-66-1)*

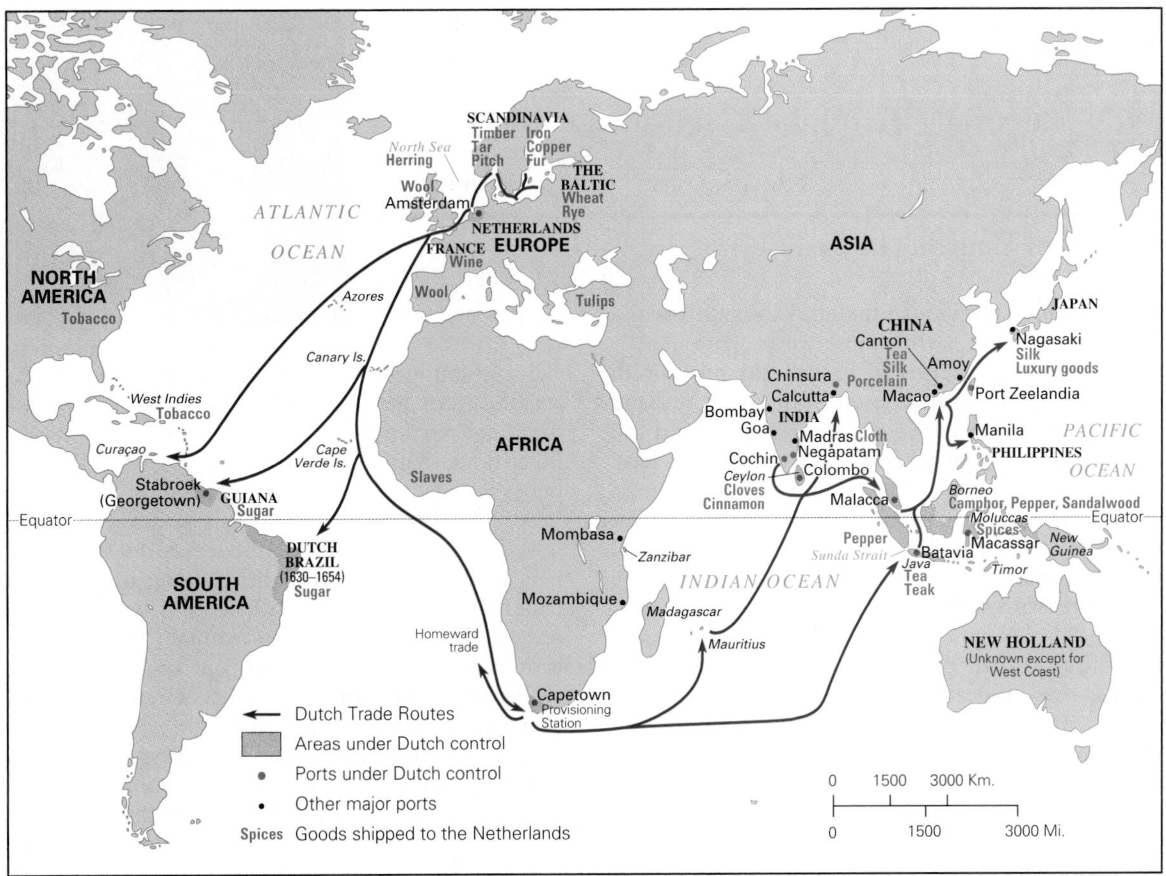

MAP 16.3 Seventeenth-Century Dutch Commerce Dutch wealth rested on commerce, and commerce depended on the huge Dutch merchant marine, manned by perhaps forty-eight thousand sailors. The fleet carried goods from all parts of the globe to the port of Amsterdam.

half the European total. All the wood for these ships had to be imported: the Dutch bought whole forests from Norway. They also bought entire vineyards from French growers before the grapes were harvested. They controlled the Baltic grain trade, buying entire wheat and rye crops in Poland, east Prussia, and Swedish Pomerania. Because the Dutch dealt in bulk, nobody could undersell them. Foreign merchants coming to Amsterdam could buy anything from precision lenses for the microscope (recently invented by Dutchman Anton van Leeuwenhoek) to muskets for an army of five thousand. Although Dutch cities became famous for their exports—diamonds and linens from Haarlem, pottery from Delft—Dutch wealth depended less on exports than on transport.

In 1602 a group of the regents of Holland formed the Dutch East India Company, a joint stock company. The investors each received a percentage of the profits proportional to the amount of money they had put in. Within half a century, the Dutch East India Company had cut heavily into Portuguese trading in East Asia. The Dutch seized the Cape of Good Hope, Ceylon, and Malacca and established trading posts in each place. In the 1630s, the Dutch East India Company was paying its investors about a 35 percent annual return on their investments. (See the feature "Individuals in Society: Johan van Oldenbarnevelt" on page 495.) The Dutch West India Company, founded in 1621, traded extensively with Latin America and Africa (Map 16.3).

Trade and commerce brought the Dutch prodigious wealth. In the seventeenth century, the Dutch enjoyed the highest standard of living in Europe, perhaps in the world. Amsterdam and Rotterdam built massive granaries where the surplus of one year could be stored against possible shortages the next. Thus, excepting the 1650s, when bad harvests reduced supplies, food

Individuals in Society

Glückel of Hameln (1646–1724)

Gentleness and deep mutual devotion seem to pervade Rembrandt's *The Jewish Bride. (Rijksmuseum-Stichting Amsterdam)*

In 1690 a Jewish widow in the small German town of Hameln[1] in Lower Saxony sat down to write her autobiography. She wanted to distract her mind from the terrible grief she felt over the death of her husband and to provide her twelve children with a record "so you will know from what sort of people you have sprung, lest today or tomorrow your beloved children or grand-children came and know naught of their family." Out of her pain and heightened consciousness, Glückel produced an invaluable source for scholars.

She was born in Hamburg two years before the end of the Thirty Years' War. In 1649 the merchants of Hamburg expelled the Jews, who moved to nearby Altona, then under Danish rule. When the Swedes overran Altona in 1657–1658, the Jews returned to Hamburg "purely at the mercy of the Town Council." Glückel's narrative proceeds against a background of the constant difficulties (harassment) to which Jews were subjected—special papers, permits, bribes—and in Hamburg she wrote, "And so it has been to this day and, I fear, will continue in like fashion."

When Glückel was "barely twelve," her father betrothed her to Chayim Hameln. She married at age fourteen. She describes him as "the perfect pattern of the pious Jew," a man who stopped his work every day for study and prayer, fasted, and was scrupulously honest in his business dealings. Only a few years older than Glückel, Chayim earned his living dealing in precious metals and in making small loans on pledges (articles held on security). This work required his constant travel to larger cities, markets, and fairs, often in bad weather, always over dangerous roads. Chayim consulted his wife about all his business dealings. As he lay dying, a friend asked if he had any last wishes. "None," he replied. "My wife knows everything. She shall do as she has always done." For thirty years, Glückel had been his friend, full business partner, and wife. They had thirteen children, twelve of whom survived their father, eight then unmarried. As Chayim had foretold, Glückel succeeded in launching the boys in careers and in providing dowries for the girls.

Glückel's world was her family, the Jewish community of Hameln, and the Jewish communities into which her children married. Social and business activities took her to Amsterdam, Baiersdorf, Bamberg, Berlin, Cleves, Danzig, Metz, and Vienna, so her world was not a narrow or provincial one. She took great pride that Prince Frederick of Cleves, later king of Prussia, danced at the wedding of her eldest daughter. The rising prosperity of Chayim's businesses allowed the couple to maintain up to six servants. Jews, however, lived on the margins of Christian society, and traditional sociological categories cannot be applied to them.

Glückel was deeply religious, and her culture was steeped in Jewish literature, legends, and mystical and secular works. Above all, she relied on the Bible. Her language, heavily sprinkled with Scriptural references, testifies to a rare familiarity with the basic book of Western civilization. The Scriptures were her consolation, the source of her great strength in a hostile world.

Students who would learn about business practices, the importance of the dowry in marriage, childbirth, the ceremony of bris, birthrates, family celebrations, even the meaning of life can gain a good deal from the memoirs of this extraordinary woman, who was, in the words of one of her descendants, the poet Heinrich Heine, "the gift of a world to me."

Questions for Analysis

1. Consider the ways in which Glückel of Hameln was an ordinary woman of her times.
2. How was Glückel's life affected by the broad events and issues of the seventeenth century?

1. Town immortalized by the Brothers Grimm. In 1284 the town contracted with the Pied Piper to rid it of rats and mice; he lured them away by playing his flute. When the citizens refused to pay, he charmed away their children in revenge.

Source: The Memoirs of Glückel of Hameln, trans. M. Lowenthal (New York: Schocken Books, 1977).

prices fluctuated very little. By the standards of Cologne, Paris, or London, salaries were high for all workers—except women, and even women's wages were high when compared with those of women in other parts of Europe. All classes of society, including unskilled laborers, ate well. The low price of bread meant that, compared to other places in Europe, a higher percentage of the worker's income could be spent on fish, cheese, butter, vegetables, even meat. A scholar has described the Netherlands as "an island of plenty in a sea of want." Consequently, the Netherlands experienced very few of the food riots that characterized the rest of Europe.[29]

Although the initial purpose of the Dutch East and West India Companies was commercial—the import of spices and silks to Europe—the Dutch found themselves involved in the imperialist exploitation of parts of East Asia and Latin America, with great success. In 1652 the Dutch founded Cape Town on the southern tip of Africa as a fueling station for ships planning to cross the Pacific. But war with France and England in the 1670s hurt the United Provinces. The long War of the Spanish Succession—in which the Dutch prince William of Orange utilized, as King William III of England, English wealth in the Dutch fight against Louis XIV—was a costly drain on Dutch labor and financial resources. The peace signed in 1713 to end the war marked the beginning of Dutch economic decline.

SUMMARY

According to Thomas Hobbes, the central drive in every human is "a perpetual and restless desire of Power, after Power, that ceaseth only in Death." The seventeenth century solved the problem of sovereign power in two fundamental ways: absolutism and constitutionalism. The France of Louis XIV witnessed the emergence of the fully absolutist state. The king commanded all the powers of the state: judicial, military, political, and, to a great extent, ecclesiastical. France developed a centralized bureaucracy, a professional army, and a state-directed economy, all of which Louis personally supervised. For the first time in history, all the institutions and powers of the national state were effectively controlled by a single person. The king saw himself as the representative of God on earth, and it has been said that "to the seventeenth century imagination God was a sort of image of Louis XIV."[30]

As Louis XIV personifies absolutism, so Stuart England exemplifies the evolution of the first modern constitutional state. The conflicts between Parliament and the first two Stuart rulers, James I and Charles I, tested where sovereign power would rest in the state. The resulting civil war did not solve the problem. The Instrument of Government, the document produced in 1653 by the victorious parliamentary army, provided for a balance of government authority and recognition of popular rights; as such, the Instrument has been called the first modern constitution. Unfortunately, it lacked public support. James II's absolutist tendencies brought on the Glorious Revolution of 1688 to 1689, and the people who made that revolution settled three basic issues. Sovereign power was divided between king and Parliament, with Parliament enjoying the greater share. Government was to be based on the rule of law. And the liberties of English people were made explicit in written form in the Bill of Rights. The framers of the English constitution left to later generations the task of making constitutional government work.

The models of governmental power established by seventeenth-century England and France strongly influenced other states then and ever since. As American novelist William Faulkner wrote, "The past isn't dead; it's not even past."

NOTES

1. G. Parker and L. M. Smith, "Introduction," and N. Steensgaard, "The Seventeenth Century Crisis," in *The General Crisis of the Seventeenth Century,* ed. G. Parker and L. M. Smith (London: Routledge & Kegan Paul, 1985), pp. 1–53, esp. p. 12.
2. See W. Beik, *Urban Protest in Seventeenth-Century France: The Culture of Retribution* (New York: Cambridge University Press, 1997), p. 1.
3. J. B. Collins, *The State in Early Modern France* (Cambridge, England: Cambridge University Press, 1995), p. 1.
4. Ibid., p. 3.
5. Ibid., pp. 22–26.
6. See M. Turchetti, "The Edict of Nantes," in *The Oxford Encyclopedia of the Reformation,* ed. H. J. Hillerbrand, vol. 3 (New York: Oxford University Press, 1996), pp. 126–128.
7. See W. Beik, *Urban Protest,* chaps. 1, 2, 3, and 11.
8. J. B. Collins, *Fiscal Limits of Absolutism: Direct Taxation in Early Seventeenth-Century France* (Berkeley and Los Angeles: University of California Press, 1988), pp. 1, 3–4, 215–222.
9. Quoted in J. H. Elliott, *Richelieu and Olivares* (Cambridge: Cambridge University Press, 1984), p. 135; and in W. F. Church, *Richelieu and Reason of State* (Princeton, N.J.: Princeton University Press, 1972), p. 507.
10. D. Parker, *The Making of French Absolutism* (New York: St. Martin's Press, 1983), pp. 146–148.

11. J. B. Collins, *The State in Early Modern France,* pp. 65–78.
12. See W. Beik, *Absolutism and Society in Seventeenth-Century France: State Power and Provincial Aristocracy in Languedoc* (Cambridge: Cambridge University Press, 1985), pp. 279–302.
13. S. de Gramont, ed., *The Age of Magnificence: Memoirs of the Court of Louis XIV by the Duc de Saint Simon* (New York: Capricorn Books, 1964), pp. 141–145.
14. Quoted in J. Wolf, *Louis XIV* (New York: W. W. Norton, 1968), p. 146.
15. Quoted in A. Trout, *Jean-Baptiste Colbert* (Boston: Twayne, 1978), p. 128.
16. Quoted in Wolf, *Louis XIV,* p. 394.
17. Ibid.
18. See W. C. Scoville, *The Persecution of the Huguenots and French Economic Development: 1680–1720* (Berkeley and Los Angeles: University of California Press, 1960).
19. F. Bluche, *Louis XIV,* trans. M. Greengrass (Oxford: Basil Blackwell, 1990), p. 607.
20. Ibid., p. 458.
21. Quoted in Bluche, *Louis XIV,* p. 519.
22. W. F. Church, *Louis XIV in Historical Thought: From Voltaire to the Annales School* (New York: W. W. Norton, 1976), p. 92.
23. Quoted in Gramont, *The Age of Magnificence,* p. 183.
24. J. H. Elliott, *Imperial Spain, 1469–1716* (New York: Mentor Books, 1963), pp. 306–308.
25. B. Bennassar, *The Spanish Character: Attitudes and Mentalities from the Sixteenth to the Nineteenth Century,* trans. B. Keen (Berkeley and Los Angeles: University of California Press, 1979), p. 125.
26. For a revisionist interpretation, see J. Wormald, "James VI and I: Two Kings or One?" *History* 62 (June 1983): 187–209.
27. C. Stephenson and G. F. Marcham, *Sources of English Constitutional History* (New York: Harper & Row, 1937), p. 601.
28. Quoted in D. Maland, *Europe in the Seventeenth Century* (New York: Macmillan, 1967), pp. 198–199.
29. S. Schama, *The Embarrassment of Riches: An Interpretation of Dutch Culture in the Golden Age* (New York: Alfred A. Knopf, 1987), pp. 165–170; quotation is on p. 167.
30. C. J. Friedrich and C. Blitzer, *The Age of Power* (Ithaca, N.Y.: Cornell University Press, 1957), p. 112.

Suggested Reading

Students who wish to explore the problems presented in this chapter in greater depth will easily find a rich and exciting literature. The following surveys all provide good background material: H. Kamen, *The Iron Century: Social Change in Europe, 1550–1660* (1971); G. Parker, *Europe in Crisis, 1598–1618* (1980), a sound introduction to the social, economic, and religious tensions of the period; R. S. Dunn, *The Age of Religious Wars, 1559–1715* (1979), which examines the period from the perspective of the confessional strife between Protestants and Catholics but contains material on absolutism and constitutionalism; and P. Anderson, *Lineages of the Absolutist State* (1974), a Marxist interpretation of absolutism in western and eastern Europe. The classic treatment of constitutionalism remains C. H. McIlwain, *Constitutionalism: Ancient and Modern* (1940), written by a great scholar during the rise of German fascism.

For the period of Louis XIII, Richelieu, and the Fronde, see L. Moote, *Louis XIII: The Just* (1989), an important biography; J. Bergin, *Richelieu: Power and the Pursuit of Wealth* (1989), a detailed study of how Richelieu used his various offices to acquire great wealth for himself and his family; and O. Ranum, *The Fronde* (1994), probably the best work in English on the Fronde. Two important studies of French local administration are J. B. Collins, *Classes, Estates, and Order in Early Modern Brittany* (1994); and R. Schneider, *Public Life in Toulouse, 1463–1789* (1989). Students interested in medical history should find L. Brockless, *The Medical World of Early Modern France* (1997), useful, while G. Calvi, *Histories of a Plague Year: The Social and the Imaginary in Baroque Florence* (1989), offers comparable information on Italian conditions. Those with facility in French might tackle P. Goubert, *Mazarin* (1991), for his administration. K. Norberg, *Rich and Poor in Grenoble, 1600–1815* (1985), provides an interesting case study of the wretched conditions of the poor, while W. Beik, *Urban Protest in Seventeenth-Century France* (1997), explores the cultural significance of the widespread incidence of urban violence.

Louis XIV and his age have predictably attracted the attention of many scholars. Bluche, although hagiographical, is an almost definitive study, and Wolf remains valuable; both are cited in the Notes. The excellent work of P. Burke, *The Fabrication of Louis XIV* (1992), explores the images or representations of the king in stone, bronze, paint, plays, operas, and rituals. Two works of W. H. Lewis, *The Splendid Century* (1957) and *The Sunset of the Splendid Century* (1963), make delightful light reading, especially for the beginning student. For the court of Louis XIV, see also K. A. Hoffmann, *Society of Pleasures: Interdisciplinary Readings in Pleasure and Power During the Reign of Louis XIV* (1997), a sophisticated study of the uses of pleasure as a political tool; R. Chartier, *The Cultural Origins of the French Revolution* (1991); and J.-F. Solnon, *La Cour de France* (1987). The advanced student will want to consult the excellent historiographical analysis by Church mentioned in the Notes. Perhaps the best works of the Annales school on the period are P. Goubert, *Louis XIV and Twenty Million Frenchmen* (1972), and his heavily detailed *The Ancien Régime: French Society, 1600–1750,* 2 vols. (1969–1973), which contains invaluable material on the lives and work of ordinary people. For the French economy and financial conditions, the old study C. W. Cole, *Colbert and a Century of French Mercantilism,* 2 vols.

(1939), is still valuable but should be supplemented by R. Bonney, *The King's Debts: Finance and Politics in France, 1589–1661* (1981), and by the works of Trout and Scoville listed in the Notes. Scoville's book is a significant contribution to revisionist history. For Louis XIV's foreign policy and wars, see P. Sonnino, *Louis XIV and the Origins of the Dutch Wars* (1988); H. Kamen, *The War of Succession in Spain, 1700–1715* (1969); and R. Hatton, ed., *Louis XIV and Europe* (1976), an important collection of essays. R. Hatton, *Europe in the Age of Louis XIV* (1979), is a splendidly illustrated survey of many aspects of seventeenth-century European culture. O. Ranum, *Paris in the Age of Absolutism* (1968), describes the geographical, political, economic, and architectural significance of the cultural capital of Europe, whereas V. L. Tapie, *The Age of Grandeur: Baroque Art and Architecture* (1960), emphasizes the relationship between art and politics and has excellent illustrations.

For Spain and Portugal, in addition to the works in the Notes, see H. Kamen, *Spain in the Later Seventeenth Century, 1665–1700* (1980); M. Defourneaux, *Daily Life in Spain in the Golden Age* (1976), highly useful for an understanding of ordinary people and of Spanish society; and C. R. Phillips, *Ciudad Real, 1500–1750: Growth, Crisis, and Readjustment in the Spanish Economy* (1979), a significant case study. A. Pagden, *Spanish Imperialism and the Political Imagination* (1990), explores Spanish ideas of empire, primarily in Italy and the Americas, and shows that the failure to revise ideas to meet changing circumstances led to the empire's decline.

The following works all offer solid material on English political and social issues of the seventeenth century: M. Ashley, *England in the Seventeenth Century* (1980), and *The House of Stuart: Its Rise and Fall* (1980); J. P. Kenyon, *Stuart England* (1978); and K. Wrightson, *English Society, 1580–1680* (1982). Perhaps the most comprehensive treatments of Parliament are C. Russell, *Crisis of Parliaments, 1509–1660* (1971), and *Parliaments and English Politics, 1621–1629* (1979). On the background of the English civil war, L. Stone, *The Crisis of the Aristocracy* (1965), and *The Causes of the English Revolution* (1972), are standard works; both B. Manning, *The English People and the English Revolution* (1976), and D. Underdown, *Revel, Riot, and Rebellion* (1985), discuss the extent of popular involvement; Underdown's is the more sophisticated treatment. For English intellectual currents, see J. O. Appleby, *Economic Thought and Ideology in Seventeenth-Century England* (1978); and C. Hill, *Intellectual Origins of the English Revolution* (1966). M. J. Braddick, *The Nerves of State: Taxation and the Financing of the English State, 1558–1714* (1996), surveys the evolution of parliamentary taxation as the means of financing state expenses, especially military ones. S. Porter, ed., *London and the Civil War* (1996), treats the city's choice of allegiance and contribution to the war effort.

C. Durston and J. Eales, eds., *The Culture of English Puritanism, 1560–1700* (1996), provides a revisionist definition of the term *Puritan* and explores topics such as Sabbatarianism and iconoclasm. For the several shades of Protestant sentiment in the early seventeenth century, see P. Collinson, *The Religion of Protestants* (1982). C. M. Hibbard, *Charles I and the Popish Plot* (1983), is an important reference work for several religious issues.

For women, see R. Thompson, *Women in Stuart England and America* (1974); and A. Fraser, *The Weaker Vessel* (1985). For Cromwell and the Interregnum, C. Firth, *Oliver Cromwell and the Rule of the Puritans in England* (1956), C. Hill, *God's Englishman* (1972), and A. Fraser, *Cromwell, the Lord Protector* (1973), are all valuable. J. Morrill, *The Revolt of the Provinces* (1980), is the best study of religious neutralism, whereas C. Hill, *The World Turned Upside Down* (1972), discusses radical thought during the period.

For the Restoration and the Glorious Revolution, see R. Hutton, *Charles II: King of England, Scotland and Ireland* (1989), and A. Fraser, *Royal Charles: Charles II and the Restoration* (1979), two highly readable biographies; R. Ollard, *The Image of the King: Charles I and Charles II* (1980), which examines the nature of monarchy; J. Miller, *James II: A Study in Kingship* (1977); J. Childs, *The Army, James II, and the Glorious Revolution* (1980); J. R. Jones, *The Revolution of 1688 in England* (1972); and L. G. Schwoerer, *The Declaration of Rights, 1689* (1981), a fine assessment of that fundamental document. For the continuation of an older system during the rise of the Whigs and Tories, see B. Hill, *The Early Parties and Politics in Britain, 1688–1832* (1996). Other helpful books on the beginning of political parties are J. P. Kenyon, *Revolution Principles: The Politics of Party, 1689–1720* (1977), which also analyzes the ideas of John Locke; and R. Hatton, *The Restoration, 1658–1667* (1985), a thorough but difficult narrative.

On Holland, the starting point for serious study is Schama, mentioned in the Notes, a brilliant and beautifully illustrated achievement. J. L. Price, *Culture and Society in the Dutch Republic During the Seventeenth Century* (1974), is a sound scholarly work. R. Boxer, *The Dutch Seaborne Empire* (1980), and the appropriate chapters of the Maland work cited in the Notes are useful for Dutch overseas expansion and the reasons for Dutch prosperity. The following works focus on the economic and cultural life of the leading Dutch city: V. Barbour, *Capitalism in Amsterdam in the Seventeenth Century* (1950); and D. Regin, *Traders, Artists, Burghers: A Cultural History of Amsterdam in the Seventeenth Century* (1977). J. M. Montias, *Artists and Artisans in Delft: A Socio-economic Study of the Seventeenth Century* (1982), examines another major city. The leading statesmen of the period may be studied in these biographies: H. H. Rowen, *John de Witt, Grand Pensionary of Holland, 1625–1672* (1978); S. B. Baxter, *William the III and the Defense of European Liberty, 1650–1702* (1966); and J. den Tex, *Oldenbarnevelt,* 2 vols. (1973).

Many facets of the lives of ordinary French, Spanish, English, and Dutch people are discussed in P. Burke, *Popular Culture in Early Modern Europe* (1978), an important and provocative study.

LISTENING TO THE PAST

The Court at Versailles

Although the Duc de Saint-Simon (1675–1755) was a soldier, courtier, and diplomat, his enduring reputation rests on his Memoirs *(1788), an eyewitness account of the personality and court of Louis XIV. A nobleman of ancient lineage, Saint-Simon resented Louis's "domestication" of the nobility and his promotion of the bourgeoisie.* The Memoirs, *excerpted here, remains a monument of French literature and an indispensable historical source, partly for its portrait of the court at Versailles.*

Very early in the reign of Louis XIV the Court was removed from Paris, never to return. The troubles of the minority had given him a dislike to that city; his enforced and surreptitious flight from it still rankled in his memory; he did not consider himself safe there, and thought cabals would be more easily detected if the Court was in the country, where the movements and temporary absences of any of its members would be more easily noticed. . . . No doubt that he was also influenced by the feeling that he would be regarded with greater awe and veneration when no longer exposed every day to the gaze of the multitude.

His love-affair with Mademoiselle de la Vallière, which at first was covered as far as possible with a veil of mystery, was the cause of frequent excursions to Versailles. . . . The visits of Louis XIV becoming more frequent, he enlarged the *château* by degrees till its immense buildings afforded better accommodation for the Court than was to be found at St. Germain, where most of the courtiers had to put up with uncomfortable lodgings in the town. The Court was therefore removed to Versailles in 1682, not long before the Queen's death. The new building contained an infinite number of rooms for courtiers, and the King liked the grant of these rooms to be regarded as a coveted privilege.

He availed himself of the frequent festivities at Versailles, and his excursions to other places, as a means of making the courtiers assiduous in their attendance and anxious to please him; for he nominated beforehand those who were to take part in them, and could thus gratify some and inflict a snub on others. He was conscious that the substantial favours he had to bestow were not nearly sufficient to produce a continual effect; he had therefore to invent imaginary ones, and no one was so clever in devising petty distinctions and preferences which aroused jealousy and emulation. The visits to Marly later on were very useful to him in this way; also those to Trianon [Marly and Trianon were small country houses], where certain ladies, chosen beforehand, were admitted to his table. It was another distinction to hold his candlestick at his *coucher;* as soon as he had finished his prayers he used to name the courtier to whom it was to be handed, always choosing one of the highest rank among those present. . . .

Not only did he expect all persons of distinction to be in continual attendance at Court, but he was quick to notice the absence of those of inferior degree; at his *lever* [formal rising from bed in the morning], his *coucher* [preparations for going to bed], his meals, in the gardens of Versailles (the only place where the courtiers in general were allowed to follow him), he used to cast his eyes to right and left; nothing escaped him, he saw everybody. If any one habitually living at Court absented himself he insisted on knowing the reason; those who came there only for flying visits had also to give a satisfactory explanation; any one who seldom or never appeared there was certain to incur his displeasure. If asked to bestow a favour on such persons he would reply haughtily: "I do not know him"; of such as rarely presented themselves he would say, "He is a man I never see"; and from these judgements there was no appeal.

He always took great pains to find out what was going on in public places, in society, in private houses, even family secrets, and maintained an immense number of spies and tale-bearers. These

Punishing Serfs This seventeenth-century illustration from Olearius's famous *Travels to Moscovy* suggests what eastern serfdom really meant. The scene is set in eastern Poland. There, according to Olearius, a common command of the lord was, "Beat him till the skin falls from the flesh." Selections from Olearius's graphic account are found in this chapter's Listening to the Past. *(University of Illinois Library, Champaign)*

The re-emergence of serfdom in eastern Europe in the early modern period was clearly a momentous human development, and historians have advanced a variety of explanations for it. Some scholars have stressed the economic interpretation. Agricultural depression and population decline in the fourteenth and fifteenth centuries led to a severe labor shortage, they have argued, and thus eastern landlords naturally tied their precious peasants to the land. With the return of prosperity and the development of export markets in the sixteenth century, the landlords finished the job, grabbing the peasants' land and making them work as unpaid serfs on the resulting enlarged estates. This argument by itself is not very convincing, for almost identical economic developments "caused" the opposite result in the west. Indeed, some historians have maintained that labor shortage and economic expansion were key factors in the virtual disappearance of western serfdom.

It seems fairly clear, therefore, that political, rather than economic, factors were crucial in the simultaneous rise of serfdom in the east and decline of serfdom in the west. Specifically, eastern lords enjoyed much greater political power than their western counterparts. In the late Middle Ages, when much of eastern Europe experienced innumerable wars and general political chaos, the noble landlord class greatly increased its political power at the expense of the ruling monarchs. There were, for example, many disputed royal successions, so that weak kings were forced to grant political favors to win the support of the nobility. Thus while strong monarchs were rising in Spain, France, and England and providing effective central government, kings were generally losing power in the east. Such kings could not resist the demands of lords regarding peasants.

Moreover, most eastern monarchs did not want to resist even if they could. The typical king was only first among equals in the noble class. He, too, thought mainly in private, rather than public, terms. He, too, wanted to squeeze as much as he could out of his peasants and enlarge his estates. The western concept and reality of sovereignty, as embodied in a king who protected the interests of all his people, was not well developed in eastern Europe before 1650.

The political power of the peasants was also weaker in eastern Europe and declined steadily after about 1400. Although there were occasional bloody peasant uprisings against the oppression of the landlords, they never succeeded. Nor did eastern peasants effectively resist day-by-day infringements on their liberties by their landlords. Part of the reason was that the lords, rather than the kings, ran the courts—one of the important concessions nobles extorted from weak monarchs. It has also been suggested that peasant solidarity was weaker in the east, possibly reflecting the lack of long-established village communities on the eastern frontier.

Finally, with the approval of weak kings, the landlords systematically undermined the medieval privileges of the towns and the power of the urban classes. Instead of selling products to local merchants in the towns, as required in the Middle Ages, the landlords sold directly to big foreign capitalists. For example, Dutch ships sailed up the rivers of Poland and eastern Germany to the loading docks of the great estates, completely short-circuiting the local towns. Moreover, "town air" no longer "made people free," for the eastern towns had lost their medieval right of refuge and were now compelled to return runaways to their lords. The population of the towns and the importance of the urban middle classes declined greatly. These developments both reflected and promoted the supremacy of noble landlords in most of eastern Europe in the sixteenth century.

The Rise of Austria and Prussia

Despite the strength of the nobility and the weakness of many monarchs before 1600, strong kings did begin to emerge in many lands in the course of the seventeenth century. War and the threat of war aided rulers greatly in their attempts to build absolute monarchies. There was also an endless struggle for power, as eastern rulers not only fought each other but also battled with armies of Asiatic invaders. In this atmosphere of continual wartime emergency, monarchs reduced the political power of the landlord nobility. Cautiously leaving the nobles the unchallenged masters of their peasants, the would-be absolutist monarchs of eastern Europe gradually gained and monopolized political power in three key areas. First, they imposed and collected permanent taxes without consent. Second, they maintained permanent standing armies, which policed the country in addition to fighting abroad. Third, they conducted relations with other states as they pleased.

As with all general historical developments, there were important variations on the absolutist theme in eastern Europe. The royal absolutism created in Prussia was stronger and more effective than that established in Austria. This advantage gave Prussia a thin edge over Austria in the struggle for power in east-central Europe in the eighteenth century. That edge had enormous long-term political significance, for it was a rising Prussia that unified the German people in the nineteenth century and imposed on them a fateful Prussian stamp.

Austria and the Ottoman Turks

Like all the other peoples and rulers of central Europe, the Habsburgs of Austria emerged from the brutal Thirty Years' War, which lasted from 1618 to 1648, impoverished and exhausted. Their efforts to root out Protestantism in the German lands and to turn the weak Holy Roman Empire into a real state had failed utterly. The Habsburgs did remain the hereditary emperors of the ancient Holy Roman Empire, which was inhabited mainly by German-speakers and was more accurately called the German Empire. But the authority of the empire and its Habsburg emperors had declined almost to the vanishing point. Real power in the German Empire lay in the hands of a bewildering variety of three hundred separate political jurisdictions, which included independent cities, small principalities, medium-size states such as Bavaria and Saxony, and some (but not all) of the territories of Prussia and the Habsburgs.

Defeat in central Europe opened new vistas for the Habsburgs. They were forced to turn inward and eastward in an attempt to fuse their diverse holdings into a strong unified state. An important step in this direction had actually been taken in Bohemia during the Thirty Years' War. Protestantism had been strong among the Czechs, a Slavic people concentrated in Bohemia. Indeed, the lesser Czech nobility was largely Protestant in 1600 and had considerable political power because it dominated the Bohemian Estates—the representative body of the different legal orders in Bohemia. In 1618 the Bohemian Estates had risen up in defense of Protestant rights. This revolt was crushed in 1620 at the Battle of the White Mountain, a momentous turning point in Czech history. The victorious Habsburg king, Ferdinand II (r. 1619–1637), drastically reduced the power of the Bohemian Estates. Ferdinand also confiscated the landholdings of many Protestant nobles and gave them to a few great Catholic nobles who had remained loyal and to a motley band of aristocratic soldiers of fortune who had nothing in common with the Czech-speaking peasants. After 1650 a large portion of the Bohemian

The struggle between the Great Elector and the provincial Estates was long, complicated, and intense. After the Thirty Years' War, representatives of the nobility zealously reasserted the right of the Estates to vote taxes, a right the Swedish armies of occupation had simply ignored. Yet first in Brandenburg in 1653 and then in Prussia between 1661 and 1663, the Great Elector eventually had his way.

To pay for the permanent standing army he first established in 1660, Frederick William forced the Estates to accept the introduction of permanent taxation without consent. Moreover, the soldiers doubled as tax collectors and policemen, becoming the core of the rapidly expanding state bureaucracy. The power of the Estates declined rapidly thereafter, for the Great Elector had both financial independence and superior force. He turned the screws of taxation: the state's total revenue tripled during his reign. The size of the army leaped about tenfold. In 1688 a population of one million was supporting a peacetime standing army of thirty thousand. Many of the soldiers were French Huguenot immigrants, whom the Great Elector welcomed as the talented, hard-working subjects they were.

In accounting for the Great Elector's fateful triumph, two factors appear central. First, as in the formation of every absolutist state, war was a decisive factor. The ongoing struggle between Sweden and Poland for control of the Baltic after 1648 and the wars of Louis XIV in western Europe created an atmosphere of permanent crisis. The wild Tartars of the Crimea in southern Russia swept through Prussia in the winter of 1656 to 1657, killing and carrying off as slaves more than fifty

Molding the Prussian Spirit Discipline was strict and punishment brutal in the Prussian army. This scene, from an eighteenth-century book used to teach schoolchildren in Prussia, shows one soldier being flogged while another is being beaten with canes as he walks between rows of troops. The officer on horseback proudly commands. *(University of Illinois Library, Champaign)*

thousand people, according to an old estimate. This invasion softened up the Estates and strengthened the urgency of the elector's demands for more money for more soldiers.

Second, the nobility had long dominated the government through the Estates, but only for its own narrow self-interest. When the crunch came, Prussian nobles proved unwilling to join the representatives of the towns in a consistent common front against royal pretensions. The nobility was all too concerned with its own rights and privileges, especially its freedom from taxation and its unlimited control over the peasants. When, therefore, the Great Elector reconfirmed these privileges in 1653 and after, even while reducing the political power of the Estates, the nobility growled but did not bite. It accepted a compromise whereby the bulk of the new taxes fell on towns and royal authority stopped at the landlords' gates. The elector could and did use naked force to break the liberties of the towns. The main leader of the urban opposition in the key city of Königsberg, for example, was simply arrested and imprisoned for life without trial.

The Consolidation of Prussian Absolutism

By the time of his death in 1688, the Great Elector had created a single state out of scattered principalities. But his new creation was still small and fragile. All the leading states of Europe had many more people—France with 20 million was fully twenty times as populous—and strong monarchy was still a novelty. Moreover, the Great Elector's successor, Elector Frederick III, "the Ostentatious" (r. 1688–1713), was weak of body and mind, and he focused on imitating the style of Louis XIV, building an expensive palace and cultivating the arts. His main political accomplishment was winning a prestigious royal title and being crowned King Frederick I in 1701 as a reward for aiding the Holy Roman emperor in the War of the Spanish Succession.

This tendency toward luxury-loving, petty tyranny was completely reversed by Frederick William I, "the Soldiers' King" (r. 1713–1740). A crude, dangerous psychoneurotic, Frederick William I was nevertheless the most talented reformer ever produced by the Hohenzollern family. It was he who truly established Prussian absolutism and gave it a unique character. It was he who created the best army in Europe, for its size, and it was he who infused strict military values into a whole society. In the words of an outstanding historian of Prussia:

> *For a whole generation, the Hohenzollern subjects were victimized by a royal bully, imbued with an obsessive bent for military organization and military scales of value. This left a deep mark upon the institutions of Prussiandom and upon the molding of the "Prussian spirit."*[3]

Frederick William's attachment to the army and military life was intensely emotional. He had, for example, a bizarre, almost pathological love for tall soldiers, whom he credited with superior strength and endurance. Austere and always faithful to his wife, he nevertheless confided to the French ambassador, "The most beautiful girl or woman in the world would be a matter of indifference to me, but tall soldiers—they are my weakness." Like some fanatical modern-day basketball coach in search of a championship team, he sent his agents throughout Prussia and all of Europe to trick, buy, and kidnap top recruits. Neighboring princes sent him their giants as gifts to win his gratitude. Prussian mothers told their sons, "Stop growing or the recruiting agents will get you."[4]

Profoundly military in temperament, Frederick William always wore an army uniform, and he lived the highly disciplined life of the professional soldier. He began his work by five or six in the morning; at ten he almost always went to the parade ground to drill or inspect his troops. A man of violent temper, Frederick William personally punished the most minor infractions on the spot: a missing button off a soldier's coat quickly provoked a savage beating with a heavy walking stick.

Frederick William's love of the army was also based on a hardheaded conception of the struggle for power and a dog-eat-dog view of international politics. Even before ascending the throne, he bitterly criticized his father's ministers: "They say that they will obtain land and power for the king with the pen; but I say it can be done only with the sword." Years later he summed up his life's philosophy in his instructions to his son: "A formidable army and a war chest large enough to make this army mobile in times of need can create great respect for you in the world, so that you can speak a word like the other powers."[5] This unshakable belief that the welfare of king and state depended on the army above all else reinforced Frederick William's passion for the soldier's life.

The cult of military power provided the rationale for a great expansion of royal absolutism. As the ruthless king himself put it: "I must be served with life and limb, with house and wealth, with honour and conscience, everything must be committed except eternal salvation—that belongs to God, but all else is mine."[6] To make good these extraordinary demands, Frederick William created a strong centralized bureaucracy. More commoners probably rose to top positions in the civil government than at any other time in Prussia's history. Meanwhile the last traces of the parliamentary Estates and local self-government vanished.

The king's grab for power brought him into considerable conflict with the noble landowners, the Junkers. In his early years, he even threatened to destroy them; yet, in the end, the Prussian nobility was not destroyed but enlisted—into the army. Responding to a combination of threats and opportunities, the Junkers became the officer caste. By 1739 all but 5 of 245 officers with the rank of major or above were aristocrats, and most of them were native Prussians. A new compromise had been worked out whereby the proud nobility imperiously commanded the peasantry in the army as well as on the estates.

Coarse and crude, penny-pinching and hard-working, Frederick William achieved results. Above all, he built a first-rate army, although he had only third-rate resources. The standing army increased from thirty-eight thousand to eighty-three thousand during his reign. Prussia, twelfth in Europe in population, had the fourth largest army by 1740. Only the much more populous states of France, Russia, and Austria had larger forces, and even France's army was only twice as large as Prussia's. Moreover, soldier for soldier, the Prussian army became the best in Europe, astonishing foreign observers with its precision, skill, and discipline. For the next two hundred years, Prussia and then Prussianized Germany would usually win the crucial military battles.

Frederick William and his ministers also built an exceptionally honest and conscientious bureaucracy, which not only administered the country but also tried with some success to develop the country economically. Finally, like the miser he was known to be, living very frugally off the income of his own landholdings, the king loved his "blue boys" so much that he hated to "spend" them. This most militaristic of kings was, paradoxically, almost always at peace.

Nevertheless, the Prussian people paid a heavy and lasting price for the obsessions of their royal drillmaster. Civil society became rigid and highly disciplined. Prussia became the "Sparta of the North"; unquestioning obedience was the highest virtue. As a Prussian minister later summed up, "To keep quiet is the first civic duty."[7] Thus the policies of Frederick William I combined with harsh peasant bondage and Junker tyranny to lay the foundations for probably the most militaristic country of modern times.

A Prussian Giant Grenadier Frederick William I wanted tall, handsome soldiers. He dressed them in tight bright uniforms to distinguish them from the peasant population from which most soldiers came. He also ordered several portraits of his favorites from his court painter, J. C. Merk. Grenadiers wore the miter cap instead of an ordinary hat so that they could hurl their heavy grenades unimpeded by a broad brim. *(The Royal Collection © Her Majesty Queen Elizabeth II)*

 THE DEVELOPMENT OF RUSSIA

One of the favorite parlor games of nineteenth-century Russian (and non-Russian) intellectuals was debating whether Russia was a Western, European or a non-Western, Asiatic society. This question was particularly fascinating because it was unanswerable. To this day Russia differs fundamentally from the West in some basic ways, though Russian history has paralleled that of the West in other aspects.

Certainly Russian developments in the early medieval period had important parallels with those in the West. Both the conversion of the eastern Slavs to Christianity (of the Eastern Orthodox variety) and the loose but real political unification of the eastern Slavic territories under a single prince and a single dynasty in the eleventh century were in the mainstream of European medieval civilization. So, too, was the typical feudal division of the land-based society into a boyard nobility and a commoner peasantry. After the death of Great Prince Iaroslav the Wise (r. 1019–1054), the powerful Kievan principality in present-day Ukraine disintegrated into competing political units. But similar fragmentations of central authority occurred in many European kingdoms at various points in the Middle Ages, and a strong native ruler might have emerged in Russia eventually to resume the centralizing work of earlier Kievan monarchs.

Such was not the case, however. Brutally conquered and subjugated by a foreign invader, Russia created a system of rule that was virtually unknown in the West. Thus the differences between Russia and the West became striking and profound in the long period from about 1250 until 1700. And when absolute monarchy triumphed under the rough guidance of Peter the Great in the early eighteenth century, it was a quite different type of absolute monarchy from that of France or even Prussia.

The Mongol Yoke and the Rise of Moscow

Like the Germans and the Italians, the eastern Slavs might have emerged from the Middle Ages weak and politically divided had it not been for the Mongol conquest of the Kievan. Nomadic tribes from present-day Mongolia, the Mongols were temporarily unified in the thirteenth century by Jenghiz Khan (1162–1227), one of history's greatest conquerors. In five years his armies subdued all of China. His successors then turned westward, smashing everything in their path and reaching the plains of Hungary victorious before they pulled back in 1242. The Mongol army—the Golden Horde—was savage in the extreme, often slaughtering entire populations of cities before burning them to the ground. En route to Mongolia in 1245, Archbishop John of Plano Carpini, the papal ambassador to Mongolia, passed through Kiev, which the Mongols had sacked in 1242, and wrote an unforgettable eyewitness account:

> *The Mongols went against Russia and enacted a great massacre in the Russian land. They destroyed towns and fortresses and killed people. They besieged Kiev, which had been the capital of Russia, and after a long siege they took it and killed the inhabitants of the city. For this reason, when we passed through that land, we found lying in the field countless heads and bones of dead people; for this city had been extremely large and very populous, whereas now it has been reduced to nothing: barely two hundred houses stand there, and those people are held in the harshest slavery.*[8]

Having devastated and conquered, the Mongols ruled the eastern Slavs for more than two hundred years. They built their capital of Saray on the lower Volga (Map 17.3). They forced all the bickering Slavic princes to submit to their rule and to give them tribute and slaves. If the conquered peoples rebelled, the Mongols were quick to punish with death and destruction. Thus the Mongols unified the eastern Slavs, for the Mongol khan was acknowledged by all as the supreme ruler.

The Mongol unification completely changed the internal political situation. Although the Mongols conquered, they were quite willing to use local princes as obedient servants and tax collectors. Therefore, they did not abolish the title of "great prince," bestowing it instead on the prince who served them best and paid them most handsomely.

Beginning with Alexander Nevsky in 1252, the previously insignificant princes of Moscow became particularly adept at serving the Mongols. They loyally put down popular uprisings and collected the khan's harsh taxes. By way of reward, the princes of Moscow emerged as hereditary great princes. Eventually the

MAP 17.3 The Expansion of Russia to 1725 After the disintegration of the Kievan state and the Mongol conquest, the princes of Moscow and their descendants gradually extended their rule over an enormous territory. Ivan the Terrible acquired more territory than Peter the Great.

Palm Sunday in Moscow Noble boyars celebrate in Red Square outside the walled Kremlin; St. Basil's Cathedral stands on the left, with its onion-shaped domes reflecting strong Byzantine influences. The boyars wear their traditional beards and long gowns, which Peter the Great would ban in his efforts to establish Western practices in Russia. Note the absence of women. *(British Museum/Fotomas Index)*

the Cossack rebellion at the gates of Moscow. In 1613 the nobles elected Ivan the Terrible's sixteen-year-old grandnephew, Michael Romanov, the new hereditary tsar. Then they rallied around him in the face of common internal and external threats. Michael's election was a real restoration, and his reign saw the gradual reestablishment of tsarist autocracy. (See the feature "Listening to the Past: A Foreign Traveler in Russia" on pages 590–591.) Michael was understandably more kindly disposed toward the supportive nobility than toward the sullen peasants. Thus while peasants were completely enserfed in 1649, Ivan's heavy military obligations on the nobility were relaxed considerably. In the long reign of Michael's successor, the pious Alexis (r. 1645–1676), this asymmetry of obligations was accentuated. The nobility gained more exemptions from military service, while the peasants were further ground down.

The result was a second round of mass upheaval and protest. In the later seventeenth century, the unity of the Russian Orthodox church was torn apart by a great split. The initiating event was the religious reforms introduced in 1652 by the patriarch Nikon, a dogmatic purist who wished to bring "corrupted" Russian practices of worship into line with the Greek Orthodox model. The self-serving church hierarchy quickly went along, but the intensely religious common people resisted. They saw Nikon as the Antichrist, who was stripping them of the only thing they had—the true religion of "holy Russia."

Great numbers left the church and formed illegal communities of "Old Believers," who were hunted down and persecuted. As many as twenty thousand people burned themselves alive, singing the "hallelujah" in their chants three times rather than twice, as Nikon had demanded, and crossing themselves in the old style, with two rather than three fingers, as they went down in flames. After the great split, the Russian masses were alienated from the established church, which became dependent on the state for its authority.

Again the Cossacks revolted against the state, which was doggedly trying to catch up with them on the frontiers and reduce them to serfdom. Under Stenka Razin they moved up the Volga River in 1670 and 1671, attracting a great army of urban poor and peasants, killing landlords and government officials, and proclaiming freedom from oppression. This rebellion to overthrow the established order was finally defeated by the government. (See the feature "Individuals in Society: Stenka Razin, Russian Rebel.") In response, the thoroughly scared upper classes tightened the screws of serfdom even further. Holding down the peasants, and thereby maintaining the tsar, became almost the principal obligation of the nobility until 1689.

The Reforms of Peter the Great

It is now possible to understand the reforms of Peter the Great (r. 1682–1725) and his kind of monarchial absolutism. Contrary to some historians' assertions, Peter was interested primarily in military power, not in some grandiose westernization plan. A giant for his time, at six feet seven inches, and possessing enormous energy and willpower, Peter was determined to redress the defeats the tsar's armies had occasionally suffered in their wars with Poland and Sweden since the time of Ivan the Terrible.

Peter was equally determined to continue the tsarist tradition of territorial expansion. After a long war, Russia had gained a large mass of Ukraine from weak and decentralized Poland in 1667 (see Map 17.3). And tsarist forces had completed the conquest of the primitive tribes of all Siberia in the seventeenth century. After the seventeen-year-old Peter overturned the regency in 1689, the thirty-six years of his personal rule knew only one year of peace.

When Peter took control in 1689, the heart of his army still consisted of cavalry made up of boyars and service nobility. Foot soldiers played a secondary role, and the whole army served on a part-time basis. The Russian army was lagging behind the professional standing armies being formed in Europe in the seventeenth century. The core of such armies was a highly disciplined infantry that fired and refired rifles as it fearlessly advanced, until it charged with bayonets fixed. Such a large, permanent army was enormously expensive and could be created only with time and at the cost of great sacrifice. Thus Peter's military moves were cautious in the 1690s.

Maintaining an existing Russian alliance with Austria and Poland against the Ottoman Empire, Peter campaigned first against Turkish forts and Tartar vassals on the Black Sea. Learning from early mistakes, he conquered Azov in 1696. Fascinated by weapons and foreign technology, the confident tsar then led a group of 250 Russian officials and young nobles on an eighteen-month tour of western European capitals. Traveling unofficially as an ordinary Russian to avoid formal ceremonies, Peter worked with his hands at various crafts and met with foreign kings and experts. He was particularly impressed with the growing power of the Dutch and the English and considered how Russia could profit from their example.

Returning to Russia, Peter made a fateful decision that would shape his reign and bring massive reforms. He entered into a secret alliance with Denmark and the elector of Saxony, who was also the elected king of Poland, to wage a sudden war of aggression against Sweden. Sweden was then a leading power in northern Europe. Despite the country's small population and limited agricultural resources, Swedish rulers in the seventeenth century had developed a strong absolutist state and built an excellent standing army. Expanding beyond Sweden, they held substantial territory in northern Germany, Finland, and Estonia. Yet these possessions were scattered and appeared vulnerable. Above all, Peter and his allies believed that their combined forces could win easy victories because Sweden was in the hands of a new and inexperienced king. They were mistaken.

Eighteen-year-old Charles XII (1697–1718) surprised Peter when he showed daring military genius. Defeating Denmark quickly in 1700 and forcing it to make peace, Charles turned on Russia. In a blinding snowstorm, his well-trained professional army attacked and routed unsuspecting Russians besieging the Swedish fortress of Navra on the Baltic coast. Peter and the survivors fled in panic to Moscow. It was, for the Russians, a grim beginning to the long and brutal Great Northern War, which lasted from 1700 to 1721.

focused on the ruler. More typically, the monarch's architects added new urban areas alongside the old city; these areas then became the real heart of the expanding capital.

The distinctive features of these new additions were their broad avenues, their imposing government buildings, and their rigorous mathematical layout. Along these major thoroughfares nobles built elaborate baroque townhouses; stables and servants' quarters were built on the alleys behind. Wide avenues also facilitated the rapid movement of soldiers through the city to quell any disturbance (the king's planners had the needs of the military constantly in mind). Under the arcades along the avenues appeared smart and very expensive shops, the first department stores, with plate-glass windows and fancy displays.

The new avenues brought reckless speed to European cities all across the continent. Whereas everyone had walked through the narrow, twisting streets of the medieval town, the high and mighty now raced down the broad boulevards in their elegant carriages. A social gap opened between the wealthy riders and the gaping, dodging pedestrians. "Mind the carriages!" wrote one eighteenth-century observer in Paris:

Here comes the black-coated physician in his chariot, the dancing master in his coach, the fencing master in his surrey—and the Prince behind six horses at the gallop as if he were in the open country. . . . The threatening wheels of the overbearing rich drive as rapidly as ever over stones stained with the blood of their unhappy victims.[13]

Speeding carriages on broad avenues, an endless parade of power and position: here were the symbols and substance of the baroque city.

The Growth of St. Petersburg

No city illustrated better than St. Petersburg the close ties among politics, architecture, and urban development in this period. In 1700, when the Great Northern War between Russia and Sweden began, the city did not exist. There was only a small Swedish fortress on one of the waterlogged islands at the mouth of the Neva River, where it flows into the Baltic Sea. In 1702 Peter the Great's armies seized this desolate outpost. Within a year the reforming tsar had decided to build a new city there and to make it, rather than ancient Moscow, his capital.

Since the first step was to secure the Baltic coast, military construction was the main concern for the next eight years. A mighty fortress was built on Peter Island, and a port and shipyards were built across the river on the mainland as a Russian navy came into being. The land was swampy and uninhabited, the climate damp and unpleasant. But Peter cared not at all: for him the inhospitable northern marshland was a future metropolis, gloriously bearing his name.

After the decisive Russian victory at Poltava in 1709 greatly reduced the threat of Swedish armies, Peter moved into high gear. In one imperious decree after another, he ordered his people to build a city that would equal any in the world. Such a city had to be Western and baroque, just as Peter's army had to be Western and permanent. From such a new city, his "window on Europe," Peter also believed it would be easier to reform the country militarily and administratively.

These general political goals matched Peter's architectural ideas, which had been influenced by his travels in western Europe. First, Peter wanted a comfortable, "modern" city. Modernity meant broad, straight, stone-paved avenues; houses built in a uniform line and not haphazardly set back from the street; large parks; canals for drainage; stone bridges; and street lighting. Second, all building had to conform strictly to detailed architectural regulations set down by the government. Finally, each social group—the nobility, the merchants, the artisans, and so on—was to live in a certain section of town. In short, the city and its population were to conform to a carefully defined urban plan of the baroque type.

Peter used the traditional but reinforced methods of Russian autocracy to build his modern capital. The creation of St. Petersburg was just one of the heavy obligations he dictatorially imposed on all social groups in Russia. The peasants bore the heaviest burdens. Just as the government drafted peasants for the army, it also drafted twenty-five thousand to forty thousand men each summer to labor in St. Petersburg for three months without pay. Every ten to fifteen peasant households had to furnish one such worker each summer and then pay a special tax in order to feed that worker in St. Petersburg.

Peasants hated this forced labor in the capital, and each year one-fourth to one-third of those sent risked brutal punishment and ran away. Many peasant construction workers died each summer from hunger, sickness, and accidents. Many also died because peasant villages tended to elect old men or young boys to labor in St. Petersburg since strong and able-bodied men were desperately needed on the farm in the busy summer months. Thus beautiful St. Petersburg was built on the shoveling, carting, and paving of a mass of conscripted serfs.

St. Petersburg, ca 1760 Rastrelli's remodeled Winter Palace, which housed the royal family until the Russian Revolution of 1917, stands on the left along the Neva River. The Navy Office with its famous golden spire and other government office buildings are nearby and across the river. Russia became a naval power and St. Petersburg a great port. *(Michael Holford)*

Peter also drafted more privileged groups to his city, but on a permanent basis. Nobles were summarily ordered to build costly stone houses and palaces in St. Petersburg and to live in them most of the year. The more serfs a noble possessed, the bigger his dwelling had to be. Merchants and artisans were also commanded to settle and build in St. Petersburg. These nobles and merchants were then required to pay for the city's avenues, parks, canals, embankments, pilings, and bridges, all of which were very costly in terms of both money and lives because they were built on a swamp. The building of St. Petersburg was, in truth, an enormous direct tax levied on the wealthy, which in turn forced the peasantry to do most of the work. The only immediate beneficiaries were the foreign architects and urban planners. No wonder so many Russians hated Peter's new city.

Yet the tsar had his way. By the time of his death in 1725, there were at least six thousand houses and numerous impressive government buildings in St. Petersburg. Under the remarkable women who ruled Russia throughout most of the eighteenth century, St. Petersburg blossomed fully as a majestic and well-organized city, at least in its wealthy showpiece sections. Peter's youngest daughter, the quick-witted Elizabeth (r. 1741–1762), named as her chief architect Bartolomeo Rastrelli, who had come to Russia from Italy as a boy of fifteen in 1715. Combining Italian and Russian traditions into a unique, wildly colorful St. Petersburg style, Rastrelli built many palaces for the nobility and all the larger government buildings erected during Elizabeth's reign. He also rebuilt the Winter Palace as an enormous, aqua-colored royal residence, now the Hermitage Museum. There Elizabeth established a flashy, luxury-loving, and slightly crude court, which Catherine the Great in turn made truly imperial. All the while St. Petersburg grew rapidly, and its almost 300,000 inhabitants in 1782 made it one of the world's largest cities. Peter and his successors had created out of nothing a magnificent and harmonious royal city, which unmistakably proclaimed the power of Russia's rulers and the creative potential of the absolutist state.

Summary

From about 1400 to 1650, social and economic developments in eastern Europe increasingly diverged from those in western Europe. In the east, peasants and townspeople lost precious freedoms, while the nobility increased its power and prestige. It was within this framework of resurgent serfdom and entrenched nobility that Austrian and Prussian monarchs fashioned absolutist states in the seventeenth and early eighteenth centuries. These monarchs won absolutist control over standing armies, permanent taxes, and legislative bodies. But they did not question underlying social and economic relationships. Indeed, they enhanced the privileges of the nobility, which furnished the leading servitors for enlarged armies and growing state bureaucracies.

In Russia the social and economic trends were similar, but the timing of political absolutism was different. Mongol conquest and rule were a crucial experience, and a harsh, indigenous tsarist autocracy was firmly in place by the reign of Ivan the Terrible in the sixteenth century. More than a century later, Peter the Great succeeded in tightening up Russia's traditional absolutism and modernizing it by reforming the army, the bureaucracy, and the defense industry. In Russia and throughout eastern Europe, war and the needs of the state in time of war weighed heavily in the triumph of absolutism.

Triumphant absolutism interacted spectacularly with the arts. Baroque art, which had grown out of the Catholic Reformation's desire to move the faithful and exalt the true faith, admirably suited the secular aspirations of eastern European rulers. They built grandiose baroque palaces, monumental public squares, and even whole cities to glorify their power and majesty. Thus baroque art attained magnificent heights in eastern Europe, symbolizing the ideal and harmonizing with the reality of imperious royal absolutism.

Notes

1. Quoted in F. L. Carsten, *The Origins of Prussia* (Oxford: Clarendon Press, 1954), p. 152.
2. Ibid., p. 175.
3. H. Rosenberg, *Bureaucracy, Aristocracy, and Autocracy: The Prussian Experience, 1660–1815* (Boston: Beacon Press, 1966), p. 38.
4. Quoted in R. Ergang, *The Potsdam Fuhrer: Frederick William I, Father of Prussian Militarism* (New York: Octagon Books, 1972), pp. 85, 87.
5. Ibid., pp. 6–7, 43.
6. Quoted in R. A. Dorwart, *The Administrative Reforms of Frederick William I of Prussia* (Cambridge, Mass.: Harvard University Press, 1953), p. 226.
7. Quoted in Rosenberg, *Bureaucracy, Aristocracy, and Autocracy,* p. 40.
8. Quoted in N. V. Riasanovsky, *A History of Russia* (New York: Oxford University Press, 1963), p. 79.
9. Quoted in I. Grey, *Ivan III and the Unification of Russia* (New York: Collier Books, 1967), p. 42.
10. Both quoted in R. Pipes, *Russia Under the Old Regime* (New York: Charles Scribner's Sons, 1974), pp. 65, 85.
11. Quoted in Ergang, *The Potsdam Fuhrer,* p. 13.
12. Quoted in J. Summerson, in *The Eighteenth Century: Europe in the Age of Enlightenment,* ed. A. Cobban (New York: McGraw-Hill, 1969), p. 80.
13. Quoted in L. Mumford, *The Culture of Cities* (New York: Harcourt Brace Jovanovich, 1938), p. 97.

Suggested Reading

All of the books cited in the Notes are recommended. Carsten's is the best study on early Prussian history, and Rosenberg's is a masterful analysis of the social context of Prussian absolutism. In addition to Ergang's work, an exciting and critical biography of ramrod Frederick William I, there is G. Ritter, *Frederick the Great* (1968), a more sympathetic study of the talented son by one of Germany's most famous conservative historians. G. Craig, *The Politics of the Prussian Army, 1640–1945* (1964), expertly traces the great influence of the military on the Prussian state over three hundred years. A good general account is provided in D. McKay and H. Scott, *The Rise of the Great Powers, 1648–1815* (1983). J. Gagliardo, *Germany Under the Old Regime, 1600–1790* (1991), is an impressive survey of developments in all the German states and provides an excellent bibliography. M. Hughes, *Early Modern Germany, 1477–1802* (1992), is also recommended. R. J. Evans, *The Making of the Habsburg Empire, 1550–1700* (1979), is an impressive achievement. C. Ingrao, *The Habsburg Monarchy, 1618–1815* (1994), is a superior synthesis with an up-to-date bibliography. J. Stoye, *The Siege of Vienna* (1964), is a fascinating account of the last great Ottoman offensive, which is also treated in the interesting study by P. Coles, *The Ottoman Impact on Europe, 1350–1699* (1968).

The Austro-Ottoman conflict is a theme of L. S. Stavrianos, *The Balkans Since 1453* (1977), and D. McKay's fine biography, *Prince Eugene of Savoy* (1978). On the Balkans,

(continued on page 592)

LISTENING TO THE PAST

A Foreign Traveler in Russia

Russia in the seventeenth century remained a remote and mysterious land for western and even central Europeans, who had few direct contacts with the tsar's dominion. Knowledge of Russia came mainly from occasional travelers who had visited Muscovy and sometimes wrote accounts of what they had seen.

The most famous of these accounts was by the German Adam Olearius (ca 1599–1671), who was sent to Moscow by the duke of Holstein on three diplomatic missions in the 1630s. These missions ultimately proved unsuccessful, but they provided Olearius with a rich store of information for his Travels in Moscovy, *from which the following excerpts are taken. Published in German in 1647 and soon translated into several languages (but not Russian), Olearius's unflattering but well-informed study played a major role in shaping European ideas about Russia.*

The government of the Russians is what political theorists call a "dominating and despotic monarchy," where the sovereign, that is, the tsar or the grand prince who has obtained the crown by right of succession, rules the entire land alone, and all the people are his subjects, and where the nobles and princes no less than the common folk—townspeople and peasants—are his serfs and slaves, whom he rules and treats as a master treats his servants. . . .

If the Russians be considered in respect to their character, customs, and way of life, they are justly to be counted among the barbarians. . . . The vice of drunkenness is so common in this nation, among people of every station, clergy and laity, high and low, men and women, old and young, that when they are seen now and then lying about in the streets, wallowing in the mud, no attention is paid to it, as something habitual. If a cart driver comes upon such a drunken pig whom he happens to know, he shoves him onto his cart and drives him home, where he is paid his fare. No one ever refuses an opportunity to drink and to get drunk, at any time and in any place, and usually it is done with vodka. . . .

The Russians being naturally tough and born, as it were, for slavery, they must be kept under a harsh and strict yoke and must be driven to do their work with clubs and whips, which they suffer without impatience, because such is their station, and they are accustomed to it. Young and half-grown fellows sometimes come together on certain days and train themselves in fisticuffs, to accustom themselves to receiving blows, and, since habit is second nature, this makes blows given as punishment easier to bear. Each and all, they are slaves and serfs. . . .

Because of slavery and their rough and hard life, the Russians accept war readily and are well suited to it. On certain occasions, if need be, they reveal themselves as courageous and daring soldiers. . . .

Although the Russians, especially the common populace, living as slaves under a harsh yoke, can bear and endure a great deal out of love for their masters, yet if the pressure is beyond measure, then it can be said of them: "Patience, often wounded, finally turned into fury." A dangerous indignation results, turned not so much against their sovereign as against the lower authorities, especially if the people have been much oppressed by them and by their supporters and have not been protected by the higher authorities. And once they are aroused and enraged, it is not easy to appease them. Then, disregarding all dangers that may ensue, they resort to every kind of violence and behave like madmen. . . . They own little; most of them have no feather beds; they lie on cushions, straw, mats, or their clothes; they sleep on benches and, in winter, like the non-Germans [i.e., natives] in Livonia, upon the oven, which serves them for cooking and is flat on the top; here husband, wife, children, servants, and maids huddle together. In some houses in the countryside we saw chickens and pigs under the benches and the ovens. . . .

Russians are not used to delicate food and dainties; their daily food consists of porridge, turnips, cabbage, and cucumbers, fresh and pickled, and in Moscow mostly of big salt fish which stink badly, because of the thrifty use of salt, yet are eaten with relish. . . .

The Russians can endure extreme heat. In the bathhouse they stretch out on benches and let themselves be beaten and rubbed with bunches of birch twigs and wisps of bast (which I could not stand); and when they are hot and red all over and so exhausted that they can bear it no longer in the bathhouse, men and women rush outdoors naked and pour cold water over their bodies; in winter they even wallow in the snow and rub their skin with it as if it were soap; then they go back into the hot bathhouse. And since bathhouses are usually near rivers and brooks, they can throw themselves straight from the hot into the cold bath. . . .

Generally noble families, even the small nobility, rear their daughters in secluded chambers, keeping them hidden from outsiders; and a bridegroom is not allowed to have a look at his bride until he receives her in the bridal chamber. Therefore some happen to be deceived, being given a misshapen and sickly one instead of a fair one, and sometimes a kinswoman or even a maidservant instead of a daughter; of which there have been examples even among the highborn. No wonder therefore that often they live together like cats and dogs and that wife-beating is so common among Russians. . . .

In the Kremlin and in the city there are a great many churches, chapels, and monasteries, both within and without the city walls, over two thousand in all. This is so because every nobleman who has some fortune has a chapel built for himself, and most of them are of stone. The stone churches are round and vaulted inside. . . . They allow neither organs nor any other musical instruments in their churches, saying: Instruments that have neither souls nor life cannot praise God. . . .

In their churches there hang many bells, sometimes five or six, the largest not over two hundredweights. They ring these bells to summon people to church, and also when the priest during mass raises the chalice. In Moscow, because of the multitude of churches and chapels, there are several thousand bells, which during the divine service create such a clang and din that one unaccustomed to it listens in amazement.

✣ A school in Moscow: A seventeenth-century illustration from a children's reader shows the fruits of rebellion and obedience. *(Novosti/Sovfoto)*

Questions for Analysis

1. In what ways were all social groups in Russia similar, according to Olearius?
2. How did Olearius characterize the Russians in general? What supporting evidence did he offer for his judgment?
3. Does Olearius's account help explain Stenka Razin's rebellion? In what ways?
4. On the basis of these representative passages, why do you think Olearius's book was so popular and influential in central and western Europe?

Source: G. Vernadsky and R. T. Fisher, Jr., eds., *A Source Book for Russian History.* Copyright © 1972 by Yale University Press. Reprinted by permission.

also see T. Stoianovich, *Balkan Worlds: The First and Last Europe* (1994); and the innovative study M. Todorova, *Imaging the Balkans* (1997). M. Pinson, ed., *The Muslims of Bosnia-Herzegovina: Their Historic Development from the Middle Ages to the Dissolution of Yugoslavia* (1993), is a good introduction.

On eastern European peasants and serfdom, D. Chirot, ed., *The Origins of Backwardness in Eastern Europe: Economics and Politics from the Middle Ages Until the Twentieth Century* (1989), is a wide-ranging introduction, which may be compared with J. Blum, "The Rise of Serfdom in Eastern Europe," *American Historical Review* 62 (July 1957): 807–836. E. Levin, *Sex and Society in the World of the Orthodox Slavs, 900–1700* (1989), carries family history to eastern Europe. R. Mousnier, *Peasant Uprisings in Seventeenth-Century France, Russia, and China* (1970), is a fine comparative study. Another valuable comparative study, analyzing the political struggle between rulers and nobles in Poland, Hungary, Latvia, Moldavia, and Ukraine, is O. Subtelny, *Domination in Eastern Europe* (1986). Also see L. and M. Frey, *Societies in Upheaval: Insurrections in France, Hungary and Spain in the Early Eighteenth Century* (1989). J. Blum, *Lord and Peasant in Russia from the Ninth to the Nineteenth Century* (1961), provides a good look at conditions in rural Russia, and P. Avrich, *Russian Rebels, 1600–1800* (1972), treats some of the violent peasant upheavals those conditions produced. R. Hellie, *Enserfment and Military Change in Muscovy* (1971), is outstanding, as is A. Yanov's provocative *Origins of Autocracy: Ivan the Terrible in Russian History* (1981). In addition to the fine surveys by Pipes and Riasanovsky cited in the Notes, J. Billington, *The Icon and the Axe* (1970), is a stimulating history of early Russian intellectual and cultural developments, such as the great split in the church. M. Raeff, *Origins of the Russian Intelligentsia* (1966), skillfully probes the mind of the Russian nobility in the eighteenth century. James Cracraft, ed., *Peter the Great Transforms Russia,* 3d ed. (1991), groups interpretive essays by leading scholars, and B. H. Sumner, *Peter the Great and the Emergence of Russia* (1962), is a fine brief introduction. These works may be compared with the brilliant biography by Russia's greatest prerevolutionary historian, V. Klyuchevsky, *Peter the Great* (English trans., 1958), and with N. Riasanovsky, *The Image of Peter the Great in Russian History and Thought* (1985). G. Vernadsky and R. Fisher, eds., *A Source Book of Russian History from Early Times to 1917,* 3 vols. (1972), is an invaluable, highly recommended collection of documents and contemporary writings. S. Baron, ed., *The Travels of Olearius in Seventeenth-Century Russia* (1967), is also highly recommended.

Three good books on art and architecture are E. Hempel, *Baroque Art and Architecture in Central Europe* (1965); G. Hamilton, *The Art and Architecture of Russia* (1954); and N. Pevsner, *An Outline of European Architecture,* 6th ed. (1960).

CHAPTER

18 Toward a New World-view

Painting by Jean-Honoré Fragonard of Denis Diderot, one of the editors of the *Encyclopedia,* the greatest intellectual achievement of the Age of Enlightenment. *(Louvre © Photo R.M.N.)*

Most people are not philosophers, but they nevertheless have a basic outlook on life, a more or less coherent world-view. At the risk of oversimplification, one may say that the world-view of medieval and early modern Europe was primarily religious and theological. Not only did Christian or Jewish teachings form the core of people's spiritual and philosophical beliefs, but religious teachings also permeated all the rest of human thought and activity. Political theory relied on the divine right of kings, for example, and activities ranging from marriage and divorce to business and eating habits were regulated by churches and religious doctrines.

In the course of the eighteenth century, this religious and theological world-view underwent a fundamental transformation among the European upper and comfortable classes. Economically secure and increasingly well educated, these privileged groups of preindustrial Europe interacted with talented writers and as a result often came to see the world primarily in secular and scientific terms. And while few individuals abandoned religious beliefs altogether, the role of churches and religious thinking in earthly affairs and in the pursuit of knowledge was substantially reduced. Among many in the aristocracy and solid middle classes, a new critical, scientific, and very "modern" world-view took shape.

- Why did this momentous change occur?
- How did this new world-view affect the way people thought about society and human relations?
- What impact did this new way of thinking have on political developments and monarchial absolutism?

This chapter will focus on these questions.

 THE SCIENTIFIC REVOLUTION

The foremost cause of the change in world-view was the scientific revolution. Modern science—precise knowledge of the physical world based on the union of experimental observations with sophisticated mathematics—crystallized in the seventeenth century. Whereas science had been secondary and subordinate in medieval intellectual life, it became independent and even primary for many educated people in the eighteenth century.

The emergence of modern science was a development of tremendous long-term significance. A noted historian has even said that the scientific revolution of the late sixteenth and seventeenth centuries "outshines everything since the rise of Christianity and reduces the Renaissance and Reformation to the rank of mere episodes, mere internal displacements, within the system of medieval Christendom." The scientific revolution was "the real origin both of the modern world and the modern mentality."[1] This statement is an exaggeration, but not much of one. Of all the great civilizations, only that of the West developed modern science. With the scientific revolution Western society began to acquire its most distinctive traits.

Though historians agree that the scientific revolution was enormously important, they approach it in quite different ways. Some scholars believe that the history of scientific achievement in this period had its own basic "internal" logic and that "nonscientific" factors had quite limited significance. These scholars write brilliant, often highly technical, intellectual studies, but they neglect the broader historical context. Other historians stress "external" economic, social, and religious factors, brushing over the scientific developments themselves. Historians of science now realize that these two approaches need to be brought together. Therefore, let us examine the milestones on the fateful march toward modern science first and then search for the nonscientific influences along the route.

Scientific Thought in 1500

Since developments in astronomy and physics were at the heart of the scientific revolution, one must begin with the traditional European conception of the universe and movement within it. In the early 1500s, traditional European ideas about the universe were still based primarily on the ideas of Aristotle, the great Greek philosopher of the fourth century B.C. These ideas had gradually been recovered during the Middle Ages and then brought into harmony with Christian doctrines by medieval theologians. According to this revised Aristotelian view, a motionless earth was fixed at the center of the universe. Around it moved ten separate transparent crystal spheres. In the first eight spheres were embedded, in turn, the moon, the sun, the five known planets, and the fixed stars. Then followed two spheres added during the Middle Ages to account for slight changes in the positions of the stars over the centuries. Beyond the tenth sphere was heaven, with the throne of God and the souls of the saved. Angels kept the spheres moving in perfect circles.

Aristotle's views, suitably revised by medieval philosophers, also dominated thinking about physics and motion on earth. Aristotle had distinguished sharply between the world of the celestial spheres and that of the earth—the sublunar world. The spheres consisted of a perfect, incorruptible "quintessence," or fifth essence. The sublunar world, however, was made up of four imperfect, changeable elements. The "light" elements (air and fire) naturally moved upward, while the "heavy" elements (water and earth) naturally moved downward. These natural directions of motion did not always prevail, however, for elements were often mixed together and could be affected by an outside force such as a human being. Aristotle and his followers also believed that a uniform force moved an object at a constant speed and that the object would stop as soon as that force was removed.

Aristotle's ideas about astronomy and physics were accepted with minor revisions for two thousand years, and with good reason. First, they offered an understandable, commonsense explanation for what the eye actually saw. Second, Aristotle's science as interpreted by Christian theologians fit neatly with Christian doctrines. It established a home for God and a place for Christian souls. It put human beings at the center of the universe and made them the critical link in a "great chain of being" that stretched from the throne of God to the most lowly insect on earth. Thus science was primarily a branch of theology, and it reinforced religious thought. At the same time, medieval "scientists" were already providing closely reasoned explanations of the universe, explanations they felt were worthy of God's perfect creation.

The Copernican Hypothesis

The desire to explain and thereby glorify God's handiwork led to the first great departure from the medieval system. This departure was the work of the Polish clergyman and astronomer Nicolaus Copernicus (1473–1543). As a young man, Copernicus studied church law and astronomy in various European universities. He saw how professional astronomers still depended for their most accurate calculations on the work of Ptolemy, the last great ancient astronomer, who had lived in Alexandria in the second century A.D. Ptolemy's achievement had been to work out complicated rules to explain the minor irregularities in the movement of the planets. These rules enabled stargazers and astrologers to track the planets with greater precision. Many people then (and now) believed that the changing relationships between planets and stars influenced and even determined the future.

The young Copernicus was uninterested in astrology and felt that Ptolemy's cumbersome and occasionally inaccurate rules detracted from the majesty of a perfect Creator. He preferred an old Greek idea being discussed in Renaissance Italy: that the sun, rather than the earth, was at the center of the universe. Finishing his university studies and returning to a church position in east Prussia, Copernicus worked on his hypothesis from 1506 to 1530. Never questioning the Aristotelian belief in crystal spheres or the idea that circular motion was most perfect and divine, Copernicus theorized that the stars and planets, including the earth, revolved around a fixed sun. Yet Copernicus was a cautious man. Fearing the ridicule of other astronomers, he did not publish his *On the Revolutions of the Heavenly Spheres* until 1543, the year of his death.

Copernicus's theory had enormous scientific and religious implications, many of which the conservative Copernicus did not anticipate. First, it put the stars at rest, their apparent nightly movement simply a result of the earth's rotation. Thus it destroyed the main reason for believing in crystal spheres capable of moving the stars around the earth. Second, Copernicus's theory suggested a universe of staggering size. If in the course of a year the earth moved around the sun and yet the stars appeared to remain in the same place, then the universe was unthinkably large or even infinite. Finally, by characterizing the earth as just another planet, Copernicus destroyed the basic idea of Aristotelian physics—that the earthly world was quite different from the heavenly one. Where, then, was the realm of perfection? Where were heaven and the throne of God?

The Copernican theory quickly brought sharp attacks from religious leaders, especially Protestants. Hearing of Copernicus's work even before it was published, Martin Luther spoke of him as the "new astrologer who wants to prove that the earth moves and goes round. . . . The fool wants to turn the whole art of astronomy upside down." Luther noted that "as the Holy Scripture tells us, so did Joshua bid the sun stand still and not the earth." John Calvin also condemned Copernicus, citing as evidence the first verse of Psalm 93: "The world also is established that it cannot be moved." "Who," asked Calvin, "will venture to place the authority of Copernicus above that of the Holy Spirit?"[2] Catholic reaction was milder at first. The Catholic church had never been hypnotized by literal interpretations of the Bible, and not until 1616 did it officially declare the Copernican theory false.

The Geometry Room at Cracow The young Copernicus sat in this classroom at the University of Cracow, where he first studied astronomy and mathematics and began to ponder the universe. Diagrams illustrating principles of Euclidean geometry were permanently painted on the walls. *(Erich Lessing/Art Resource, NY)*

This slow reaction also reflected the slow progress of Copernicus's theory for many years. Other events were almost as influential in creating doubts about traditional astronomical ideas. In 1572 a new star appeared and shone very brightly for almost two years. The new star, which was actually a distant exploding star, made an enormous impression on people. It seemed to contradict the idea that the heavenly spheres were unchanging and therefore perfect. In 1577 a new comet suddenly moved through the sky, cutting a straight path across the supposedly impenetrable crystal spheres. It was time, as a typical scientific writer put it, for "the radical renovation of astronomy."[3]

From Brahe to Galileo

One astronomer who agreed was Tycho Brahe (1546–1601). Born into a leading Danish noble family and earmarked for a career in government, Brahe was at an early age tremendously impressed when a partial eclipse of the sun occurred exactly as expected. It seemed to him "something divine that men could know the motions of the stars so accurately that they were able a long time beforehand to predict their places and relative positions."[4] Completing his studies abroad and returning to Denmark, Brahe established himself as Europe's leading astronomer with his detailed observations of the new star of 1572. Aided by generous grants from the king of Denmark, Brahe built the most sophisticated observatory of his day. For twenty years he meticulously observed the stars and planets with the naked eye. An imposing man who had lost a piece of his nose in a duel and replaced it with a special bridge of gold and silver alloy, a noble who exploited his peasants arrogantly and approached the heavens humbly, Brahe's great contribution was his mass of data. His limited understanding of mathematics prevented him, however, from making much sense out of his data. Part Ptolemaic, part Copernican, he believed that all the planets revolved around the sun and that the entire group of sun and planets revolved in turn around the earth-moon system.

It was left to Brahe's brilliant young assistant, Johannes Kepler (1571–1630), to go much further. Kepler was a medieval figure in many ways. Coming from a minor German noble family and trained for the Lutheran ministry, he long believed that the universe was built on mystical mathematical relationships and a musical harmony of the heavenly bodies. Working and reworking Brahe's mountain of observations in a staggering sustained effort after the Dane's death, this brilliant mathematician eventually went beyond mystical intuitions.

Kepler formulated three famous laws of planetary motion. First, building on Copernican theory, he demonstrated in 1609 that the orbits of the planets around the sun are elliptical rather than circular. Second, he demonstrated that the planets do not move at a uniform speed in their orbits. Third, in 1619 he showed that the time a planet takes to make its complete orbit is precisely related to its distance from the sun. Kepler's contribution was monumental. Whereas Copernicus had speculated, Kepler proved mathematically the precise relations of a sun-centered (solar) system. His work demolished the old system of Aristotle and Ptolemy, and in his third law he came close to formulating the idea of universal gravitation.

While Kepler was unraveling planetary motion, a young Florentine named Galileo Galilei (1564–1642) was challenging all the old ideas about motion. Like so many early scientists, Galileo was a poor nobleman first marked for a religious career. However, he soon became fascinated by mathematics. A brilliant student, Galileo became a professor of mathematics in 1589 at age twenty-five. He proceeded to examine motion and mechanics in a new way. Indeed, his great achievement was the elaboration and consolidation of the modern experimental method. That is, rather than speculate about what might or should happen, Galileo conducted controlled experiments to find out what actually *did* happen.

In his famous acceleration experiment, he showed that a uniform force—in this case, gravity—produced a uniform acceleration. Here is how Galileo described his pathbreaking method and conclusion in his *Two New Sciences:*

A piece of wooden moulding . . . was taken; on its edge was cut a channel a little more than one finger in breadth. Having made this groove very straight, smooth and polished, and having lined it with parchment, also as smooth and polished as possible, we rolled along it a hard, smooth and very round bronze ball. . . . Noting . . . the time required to make the descent . . . we now rolled the ball only one-quarter the length of the channel; and having measured the time of its descent, we found it precisely one-half of the former. . . . In such experiments [over many distances], repeated a full hundred times, we always found that the spaces traversed were to each other as the squares of the times, and that this was true for all inclinations of the plane.[5]

With this and other experiments, Galileo also formulated the law of inertia. Rest was not the natural state of objects. Rather, an object continues in motion forever unless stopped by some external force. Aristotelian physics was in a shambles.

In the tradition of Brahe, Galileo also applied the experimental method to astronomy. His astronomical discoveries had a great impact on scientific development. On hearing details about the invention of the telescope in Holland, Galileo made one for himself and trained it on the heavens. He quickly discovered the first four moons of Jupiter, which clearly suggested that Jupiter could not possibly be embedded in any impenetrable crystal sphere. This discovery provided new evidence for the Copernican theory, in which Galileo already believed.

Galileo then pointed his telescope at the moon. He wrote in 1610 in *Siderus Nuncius:*

I feel sure that the moon is not perfectly smooth, free from inequalities, and exactly spherical, as a large school of philosophers considers with regard to the moon and the other heavenly bodies. On the contrary, it is full of inequalities, uneven, full of hollows and protuberances, just like the surface of the earth itself, which is varied. . . . The next object which I have observed is the essence or substance of the Milky Way. By the aid of a telescope anyone may behold this in a manner which so distinctly appeals to the senses that all the disputes which have tormented philosophers through so many ages are exploded by the irrefutable evidence of our eyes, and we are freed from wordy disputes upon the subject. For the galaxy is nothing else but a mass of innumerable stars planted together in clusters.[6]

Reading these famous lines, one feels a crucial corner in Western civilization being turned. The traditional religious and theological world-view, which rested on determining and accepting the proper established authority, was beginning to give way in certain fields to a critical, scientific method. This new method of learning and investigating was the greatest accomplishment of the entire scientific revolution, for it proved capable of great extension. A historian investigating documents of the past, for example, is not so different from a Galileo studying stars and rolling balls.

Galileo was employed in Florence by the Medici grand dukes of Tuscany, and his work eventually aroused the ire of some theologians. The issue was presented in 1624 to Pope Urban VIII, who permitted Galileo to write about different possible systems of the world as long as he did not presume to judge which one actually existed. After the publication in Italian of his widely read *Dialogue on the Two Chief Systems of the World* in 1632, which openly lampooned the traditional views of Aristotle and Ptolemy and defended those of Copernicus, Galileo was tried for heresy by the papal Inquisition. Imprisoned and threatened with torture, the aging Galileo recanted, "renouncing and cursing" his Copernican errors. Of minor importance in the development of science, Galileo's trial later became for some writers the perfect symbol of the inherent conflict between religious belief and scientific knowledge.

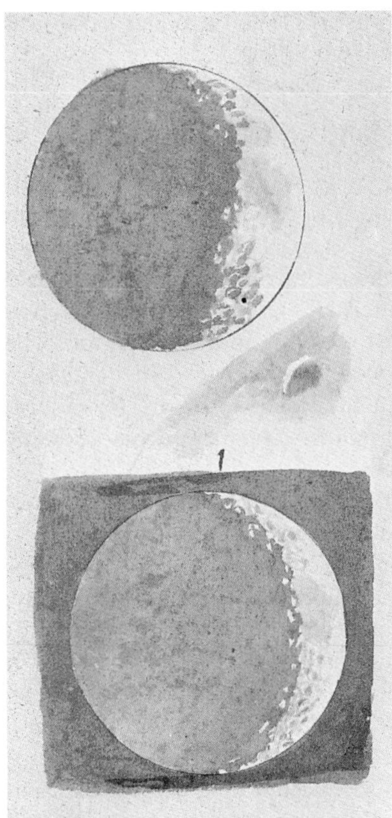

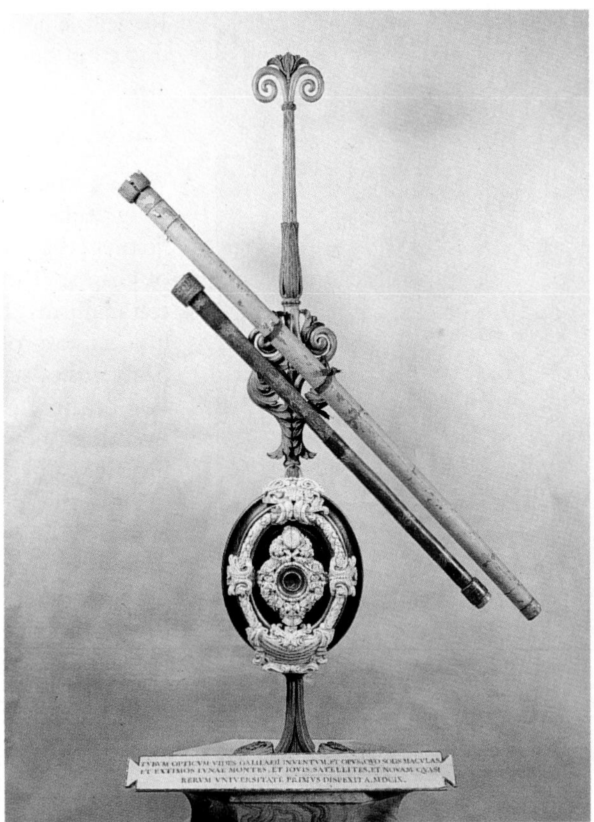

Galileo's Paintings of the Moon When Galileo published the results of his telescopic observations of the moon, he added these paintings to illustrate the marvels he had seen. Galileo made two telescopes, which are shown here. The larger one magnifies 14 times, the smaller 20 times. *(Biblioteca Nazionale Centrale, Florence; Museum of Science, Florence/Scala/Art Resource, NY)*

Newton's Synthesis

The accomplishments of Kepler, Galileo, and other scientists had taken effect by about 1640. The old astronomy and physics were in ruins, and several fundamental breakthroughs had been made. The new findings had not, however, been fused together in a new synthesis, a single explanatory system that would comprehend motion both on earth and in the skies. That synthesis, which prevailed until the twentieth century, was the work of Isaac Newton (1642–1727).

Newton was born into lower English gentry and attended Cambridge University. A genius who spectacularly united the experimental and theoretical-mathematical sides of modern science, Newton was also fascinated by alchemy. He sought the elixir of life and a way to change base metals into gold and silver. Not without reason did the twentieth-century economist John Maynard Keynes call Newton the "last of the magicians." Newton was also intensely religious. He was far from being the perfect rationalist so endlessly eulogized by writers in the eighteenth and nineteenth centuries.

Of his intellectual genius and incredible powers of concentration there can be no doubt, however. Arriving at some of his most basic ideas about physics in 1666 at age twenty-four, but unable to prove these theories mathematically, he attained a professorship and studied optics for many years. In 1684 Newton returned to physics for eighteen extraordinarily intensive months. For weeks on end he seldom left his room except to read his lectures. His meals were sent up, but he usually forgot to eat them, his mind fastened like a vise on the laws of the universe. He opened the third book of his immortal *Mathematical Principles of Natural Philosophy,* published in Latin in 1687 and generally known as the *Principia,* with these lines:

In the preceding books I have laid down the principles of philosophy [that is, science]. . . . These principles are the

Isaac Newton This portrait suggests the depth and complexity of the great genius. Is the powerful mind behind those piercing eyes thinking of science or of religion, or perhaps of both? *(Scala/Art Resource, NY)*

laws of certain motions, and powers or forces, which chiefly have respect to philosophy. . . . It remains that from the same principles I now demonstrate the frame of the System of the World.

Newton made good his grandiose claim. His towering accomplishment was to integrate in a single explanatory system the astronomy of Copernicus, as corrected by Kepler's laws, with the physics of Galileo and his predecessors. Newton did this by means of a set of mathematical laws that explain motion and mechanics. These laws of dynamics are complex, and it took scientists and engineers two hundred years to work out all their implications. Nevertheless, the key feature of the Newtonian synthesis was the law of universal gravitation. According to this law, every body in the universe attracts every other body in the universe in a precise mathematical relationship, whereby the force of attraction is proportional to the quantity of matter of the objects and inversely proportional to the square of the distance between them. The whole universe—from Kepler's elliptical orbits to Galileo's rolling balls—was unified in one majestic system.

Causes of the Scientific Revolution

With a charming combination of modesty and self-congratulation, Newton once wrote, "If I have seen further [than others], it is by standing on the shoulders of Giants."[7] Surely the path from Copernicus to Newton confirms the "internal" view of the scientific revolution as a product of towering individual genius. The problems of science were inherently exciting, and solution of those problems was its own reward for inquisitive, high-powered minds. Yet there were certainly broader causes as well.

First, the long-term contribution of medieval intellectual life and medieval universities to the scientific revolution was much more considerable than historians unsympathetic to the Middle Ages once believed. By the thirteenth century, permanent universities with professors and large student bodies had been established in western Europe. These universities were supported by society because they trained the lawyers, doctors, and church leaders that society required. By 1300 philosophy had taken its place alongside law, medicine, and theology. Medieval philosophers developed a limited but real independence from theologians and a sense of free inquiry. They nobly pursued a body of knowledge and tried to arrange it meaningfully by means of abstract theories.

Within this framework, science was able to emerge as a minor but distinct branch of philosophy. In the fourteenth and fifteenth centuries, first in Italy and then elsewhere in Europe, leading universities established new professorships of mathematics, astronomy, and physics (natural philosophy) within their faculties of philosophy. Although the prestige of the new fields was low among both professors and students, the pattern of academic science, which grew out of the medieval commitment to philosophy and did not change substantially until the late eighteenth century, undoubtedly promoted scientific development. Rational, critical thinking was applied to scientific problems by a permanent community of scholars. And an outlet existed for the talents of a Galileo or a Newton: all the great pathfinders either studied or taught at universities.

Second, the Renaissance also stimulated scientific progress. One of the great deficiencies of medieval science was its rather rudimentary mathematics. The recovery of the finest works of Greek mathematics—a byproduct of Renaissance humanism's ceaseless search for the knowledge of antiquity—greatly improved European mathematics well into the early seventeenth century. The recovery of more texts also showed that classical mathematicians had their differences; Europeans were thus forced to resolve, if possible, these ancient controversies by means of their own efforts. Finally, the Renaissance pattern of patronage, especially in Italy, was often scientific as well as artistic and humanistic. Various rulers and wealthy business people supported scientific investigations, as the Medicis of Florence supported those of Galileo.

The navigational problems of long sea voyages in the age of overseas expansion were a third factor in the scientific revolution. Ship captains on distant shores needed to be able to chart their positions as accurately as possible so that reliable maps could be drawn and the risks of international trade reduced. As early as 1484, the king of Portugal appointed a commission of mathematicians to perfect tables to help seamen find their latitude. This resulted in the first European navigation manual.

The problem of fixing longitude was much more difficult. In England the government and the great capitalistic trading companies turned to science and scientific education in an attempt to solve this pressing practical problem. When the famous Elizabethan financier Sir Thomas Gresham left a large amount of money to establish Gresham College in London, he stipulated that three of the college's seven professors had to concern themselves exclusively with scientific subjects. The professor of astronomy was directed to teach courses on the science of navigation. A seventeenth-century popular ballad took note of the new college's calling:

This college will the whole world measure
Which most impossible conclude,
And navigation make a pleasure
By finding out the longitude.[8]

At Gresham College scientists had, for the first time in history, an important, honored role in society. They enjoyed close ties with top officials of the Royal Navy and with leading merchants and shipbuilders. Gresham College became the main center of scientific activity in England in the first half of the seventeenth century. The close tie between practical men and scientists also led to the establishment in 1662 of the Royal Society of London, which published scientific papers and sponsored scientific meetings.

Navigational problems were also critical in the development of many new scientific instruments, such as the telescope, barometer, thermometer, pendulum clock, microscope, and air pump. Better instruments, which permitted more accurate observations, often led to

The Observatory at Nuremberg The quest for scientific knowledge in the seventeenth century was already an expensive undertaking that required teamwork and government support, as this encyclopedic illustration suggests. Nuremberg was a historic center of commerce and culture in southern Germany, and its observatory played a pioneering role in early astronomical advance. *(Kunstsammlungen der Veste Coburg)*

important new knowledge. Galileo with his telescope was by no means unique.

Better instruments were part of a fourth factor in the scientific revolution, the development of better ways of obtaining knowledge about the world. Two important thinkers, Francis Bacon (1561–1626) and René Descartes (1596–1650), represented key aspects of this improvement in scientific methodology.

The English politician and writer Francis Bacon was the greatest early propagandist for the new experimental method, as Galileo was its greatest early practitioner. Rejecting the Aristotelian and medieval method of using speculative reasoning to build general theories, Bacon argued that new knowledge had to be pursued through empirical, experimental research. That is, the researcher who wants to learn more about leaves or rocks should not speculate about the subject but rather collect a multitude of specimens and then compare and analyze them. Thus freed from sterile medieval speculation, the facts will speak for themselves, and important general principles will then emerge. Knowledge will increase. Bacon's contribution was to formalize the empirical method, which had already been used by Brahe and Galileo, into the general theory of inductive reasoning known as *empiricism.*

Bacon claimed that the empirical method would result not only in more knowledge but also in highly practical, useful knowledge. According to Bacon, scientific discoveries like those so avidly sought at Gresham College would bring about much greater control over the physical environment and make people rich and nations powerful. Thus Bacon helped provide a radically new and effective justification for private and public support of scientific inquiry.

The French philosopher René Descartes was a true genius who made his first great discovery in mathematics. As a twenty-three-year-old soldier serving in the Thirty Years' War, he experienced on a single night in 1619 a life-changing intellectual vision. Descartes saw that there was a perfect correspondence between geometry and algebra and that geometrical, spatial figures could be expressed as algebraic equations and vice versa. A major step forward in the history of mathematics, Descartes's discovery of analytic geometry provided scientists with an important new tool. Spending much of his adult life in the Netherlands, Descartes also made contributions to the science of optics. But his greatest achievement was to develop his initial vision into a whole philosophy of knowledge and science.

Like Bacon, Descartes scorned traditional science and had great faith in the powers of the human mind. Yet Descartes was much more systematic and mathematical than Bacon. He decided it was necessary to doubt everything that could reasonably be doubted and then, as in geometry, to use deductive reasoning from self-evident principles to ascertain scientific laws. Descartes's reasoning ultimately reduced all substances to "matter" and "mind"—that is, to the physical and the spiritual. His view of the world as consisting of two fundamental entities is known as *Cartesian dualism.* Descartes was a profoundly original and extremely influential thinker.

Bacon's inductive experimentalism and Descartes's deductive, mathematical rationalism are combined in the modern scientific method, which began to crystallize in the late seventeenth century. Neither man's extreme approach was sufficient by itself. Bacon's inability to appreciate the importance of mathematics and his obsession with practical results clearly showed the limitations of antitheoretical empiricism. Likewise, some of Descartes's positions—he believed, for example, that it was possible to deduce the whole science of medicine from first principles—aptly demonstrated the inadequacy of rigid, dogmatic rationalism. Thus the modern scientific method has joined precise observations and experimentalism with the search for general laws that may be expressed in rigorously logical, mathematical language.

Finally, there is the question of the role of religion in the development of science. Just as some historians have argued that Protestantism led to the rise of capitalism, others have concluded that Protestantism was a fundamental factor in the rise of modern science. Protestantism, particularly in its Calvinist varieties, supposedly made scientific inquiry a question of individual conscience and not of religious doctrine. The Catholic church, in contrast, supposedly suppressed scientific theories that conflicted with its teachings and thus discouraged scientific progress.

The truth of the matter is more complicated. *All* religious authorities—Catholic, Protestant, and Jewish—opposed the Copernican system to a greater or lesser extent until about 1630, by which time the scientific revolution was definitely in progress. The Catholic church was initially less hostile than Protestant and Jewish religious leaders. This early Catholic toleration and the scientific interests of Renaissance Italy helped account for the undeniable fact that Italian scientists played a crucial role in scientific progress right up to the trial of Galileo in 1633. Thereafter, the Counter-Reformation church became more hostile to science, a change that helped account for the decline of science in

The Philosophes and the Public

By the time Louis XIV died in 1715, many of the ideas that would soon coalesce into the new world-view had been assembled. Yet Christian Europe was still strongly attached to its traditional beliefs, as witnessed by the powerful revival of religious orthodoxy in the first half of the eighteenth century (see pages 681–683). By the outbreak of the American Revolution in 1775, however, a large portion of western Europe's educated elite had embraced many of the new ideas. This acceptance was the work of one of history's most influential groups of intellectuals, the *philosophes.* It was the philosophes who proudly and effectively proclaimed that they, at long last, were bringing the light of knowledge to their ignorant fellow creatures in an Age of Enlightenment.

Philosophe is the French word for "philosopher," and it was in France that the Enlightenment reached its highest development. There were at least three reasons for this. First, French was the international language of the educated classes in the eighteenth century, and the education of the rich and the powerful across Europe often lay in the hands of French tutors espousing Enlightenment ideas. France's cultural leadership was reinforced by the fact that it was still the wealthiest and most populous country in Europe.

Second, after the death of Louis XIV, French absolutism and religious orthodoxy remained strong, but not too strong. Critical books were often banned by the censors, and their authors were sometimes jailed or exiled—but not tortured or burned. Intellectual radicals battled against powerful opposition in France, but they did not face the overwhelming restraints generally found in eastern and east-central Europe. French thinkers were not, however, fighting for widely accepted liberties, as was the case in the Netherlands and in England (to a lesser extent).

Third, the French philosophes were indeed philosophers, asking fundamental philosophical questions about the meaning of life, God, human nature, good and evil, and cause and effect. But in the tradition of Bayle and Fontenelle, they were not content with abstract arguments or ivory-tower speculations. They were determined to reach and influence all the French (and European) economic and social elites, many of which were joined together in the eighteenth-century concept of the educated or enlightened public, or simply the "public."

As a wealth of recent scholarship has shown, the public was quite different from the great majority of the population, which was known as the common people, or simply the "people." French philosophe Jean le Rond d'Alembert (1717–1783) characteristically made a sharp distinction between "the truly enlightened public" and "the blind and noisy multitude."[10] A leading scholar has even concluded that the differences between the upper and comfortable middling groups that made up the French public were "insignificant" in comparison with the great gulf between the public and the common people.[11] Above all, the philosophes believed that the great majority of the common people were doomed to superstition and confusion because they lacked the money and leisure to look beyond their bitter struggle with grinding poverty (see pages 629–631).

Suspicious of the people but intensely committed to reason, reform, and slow, difficult progress, the great philosophes and their imitators were not free to write as they wished, since it was illegal in France to criticize openly either church or state. Their most radical works had to circulate in manuscript form. Knowing that direct attacks would probably be banned or burned, the philosophes wrote novels and plays, histories and philosophies, dictionaries and encyclopedias, all filled with satire and double meanings to spread their message to the public.

One of the greatest philosophes, the baron de Montesquieu (1689–1755), brilliantly pioneered this approach in *The Persian Letters,* an extremely influential social satire published in 1721. Montesquieu's work consisted of amusing letters supposedly written by Persian travelers, who see European customs in unique ways and thereby cleverly criticize existing practices and beliefs.

Having gained fame by using wit as a weapon against cruelty and superstition, Montesquieu settled down on his family estate to study history and politics. His interest was partly personal, for, like many members of the high French nobility, he was dismayed that royal absolutism had triumphed in France under Louis XIV. But Montesquieu was also inspired by the example of the physical sciences, and he set out to apply the critical method to the problem of government in *The Spirit of Laws* (1748). The result was a complex comparative study of republics, monarchies, and despotisms—a great pioneering inquiry in the emerging social sciences.

Showing that forms of government were shaped by history, geography, and customs, Montesquieu focused on the conditions that would promote liberty and prevent tyranny. He argued that despotism could be avoided if political power was divided and shared by a variety of classes and legal orders holding unequal rights and privileges. A strong, independent upper class was especially important, according to Montesquieu, because in order to prevent the abuse of power, "it is necessary that by the arrangement of things, power checks power." Admiring greatly the English balance of power among the king, the houses of Parliament, and the independent courts, Montesquieu believed that in France the thirteen high courts—the *parlements*—were front-line defenders of liberty against royal despotism. Apprehensive about the uneducated poor, Montesquieu was clearly no democrat, but his theory of separation of powers had a great impact on France's wealthy, well-educated elite. The constitutions of the young United States in 1789 and of France in 1791 were based in large part on this theory.

The most famous and in many ways most representative philosophe was François Marie Arouet, who was known by the pen name Voltaire (1694–1778). In his long career, this son of a comfortable middle-class family wrote more than seventy witty volumes, hobnobbed with kings and queens, and died a millionaire because of shrewd business speculations. His early career, however, was turbulent. In 1717 Voltaire was imprisoned for eleven months in the Bastille in Paris for insulting the regent of France. In 1726 a barb from his sharp tongue led a great French nobleman to have him beaten and arrested. This experience made a deep impression on Voltaire. All his life he struggled against legal injustice and unequal treatment before the law. Released from prison after promising to leave the country, Voltaire lived in England for three years and came to share Montesquieu's enthusiasm for English institutions.

Madame du Châtelet was fascinated by the new world system of Isaac Newton. She helped to spread Newton's ideas in France by translating his *Principia* and by influencing Voltaire, her companion for fifteen years until her death. *(Private Collection/Bulloz)*

Returning to France and soon threatened again with prison in Paris, Voltaire had the great fortune of meeting Gabrielle-Emilie Le Tonnelier de Breteuil, marquise du Châtelet (1706–1749), an intellectually gifted woman from the high aristocracy with a passion for science. Inviting Voltaire to live in her country house at Cirey in Lorraine and becoming his long-time companion (under the eyes of her tolerant husband), Madame du Châtelet studied physics and mathematics and published scientific articles and translations.

Perhaps the finest representative of a small number of elite Frenchwomen and their scientific accomplishments during the Enlightenment, Madame du Châtelet suffered nonetheless because of her gender. Excluded on principle from the Royal Academy of Sciences and from stimulating interchange with other scientists because she was a woman, she depended on private tutors for instruction and became uncertain of her ability to make important scientific discoveries. Madame du Châtelet therefore concentrated on spreading the ideas of others, and her translation with an accompanying commentary of Newton's *Principia* into French for the first (and only) time was her greatest work. But she, who had patiently explained Newton's complex mathematical proofs to Europe's foremost philosophe, had no doubt that women's limited scientific contributions in the past were due to limited and unequal education. She once wrote that if she were a ruler, "I would reform an abuse which cuts off, so to speak, half the human race. I would make women participate in all the rights of humankind, and above all in those of the intellect."[12]

While living at Cirey, Voltaire wrote various works praising England and popularizing English scientific progress. Newton, he wrote, was history's greatest man, for he had used his genius for the benefit of humanity. "It is," wrote Voltaire, "the man who sways our minds by the prevalence of reason and the native force of truth, not they who reduce mankind to a state of slavery by force and downright violence . . . that claims our reverence and admiration."[13] In the true style of the Enlightenment, Voltaire mixed the glorification of science and reason with an appeal for better individuals and institutions.

Yet like almost all of the philosophes, Voltaire was a reformer, not a revolutionary, in social and political matters. He was eventually appointed royal historian in 1743, and his *Age of Louis XIV* portrayed Louis as the dignified leader of his age. Voltaire also began a long correspondence with Frederick the Great and, after the death of his beloved Emilie, accepted Frederick's invitation to come brighten up the Prussian court in Berlin. The two men later quarreled, but Voltaire always admired Frederick as a free thinker and an enlightened monarch.

Unlike Montesquieu, Voltaire pessimistically concluded that the best one could hope for in the way of government was a good monarch, since human beings "are very rarely worthy to govern themselves." Nor did he believe in social and economic equality in human affairs. The idea of making servants equal to their masters was "absurd and impossible." The only realizable equality, Voltaire thought, was that "by which the citizen only depends on the laws which protect the freedom of the feeble against the ambitions of the strong."[14]

Voltaire's philosophical and religious positions were much more radical. In the tradition of Bayle, Voltaire's voluminous writings challenged, often indirectly, the Catholic church and Christian theology at almost every point. Though he was considered by many devout Christians to be a shallow blasphemer, Voltaire's religious views were influential and quite typical of the mature Enlightenment. Voltaire clearly believed in a God, but his was a distant, deistic God, a great Clockmaker who built an orderly universe and then stepped aside and let it run. Above all, Voltaire and most of the philosophes hated all forms of religious intolerance, which they believed often led to fanaticism and savage, inhuman action. Simple piety and human kindness—as embodied in Christ's great commandments to "love God and your neighbor as yourself"—were religion enough, even Christianity enough, as may be seen in Voltaire's famous essay on religion. (See the feature "Listening to the Past: Voltaire on Religion" on pages 626–627.)

The ultimate strength of the French philosophes lay in their number, dedication, and organization. The philosophes felt keenly that they were engaged in a common undertaking that transcended individuals. Their greatest and most representative intellectual achievement was, quite fittingly, a group effort—the seventeen-volume *Encyclopedia: The Rational Dictionary of the Sciences, the Arts, and the Crafts,* edited by Denis Diderot (1713–1784) and Jean le Rond d'Alembert. Diderot and d'Alembert made a curious pair. Diderot began his career as a hack writer, first attracting attention with a skeptical tract on religion that was quickly burned by the judges of Paris. D'Alembert was one of Europe's leading scientists and mathematicians, the orphaned and illegitimate son of celebrated aristocrats. From different circles and with different interests, the two men set out to find coauthors who would examine the rapidly expanding whole of human knowledge. Even more fundamentally, they set out to teach people how to think critically and objectively about all matters. As Diderot said, he wanted the *Encyclopedia* to "change the general way of thinking."[15]

The editors of the *Encyclopedia* had to conquer innumerable obstacles. After the appearance in 1751 of the first volume, which dealt with such controversial subjects as atheism, the soul, and blind people (all words beginning with *a* in French), the government temporarily banned publication. The pope later placed the work on the Catholic church's index of forbidden works and pronounced excommunication on all who read or bought it. The timid publisher watered down some of the articles in the last ten volumes without the editors' consent in an attempt to appease the authorities. Yet Diderot's unwavering belief in the importance of his mission held the encyclopedists together for fifteen years, and the enormous work was completed in 1765. Hundreds of thousands of articles by leading scientists, famous writers, skilled workers, and progressive priests treated every aspect of life and knowledge.

Not every article was daring or original, but the overall effect was little short of revolutionary. Science and the industrial arts were exalted, religion and immortality questioned. Intolerance, legal injustice, and out-of-date social institutions were openly criticized. More generally, the writers of the *Encyclopedia* showed that human beings could use the process of reasoning to expand human knowledge. The encyclopedists were convinced that greater knowledge would result in greater human happiness, for knowledge was useful and made possible economic, social, and political progress. The *Encyclopedia* was widely read, especially in less expensive reprint editions published in Switzerland, and it was extremely influential in France and throughout

Voltaire leans forward at left to exchange ideas with King Frederick the Great in the center of the picture, as Prussian officials look on. As this painting suggests, Voltaire's radicalism was mainly intellectual and philosophical, not social or political. The men and women of the Enlightenment prized witty, spirited conversation. *(Bildarchiv Preussischer Kulturbesitz)*

western Europe as well. It summed up the new world-view of the Enlightenment.

The Later Enlightenment

After about 1770, the harmonious unity of the philosophes and their thought began to break down. As the new world-view became increasingly accepted by the educated public, some thinkers sought originality by exaggerating certain Enlightenment ideas to the exclusion of others. These latter-day philosophes often built rigid, dogmatic systems.

In his *System of Nature* (1770) and other works, the wealthy German-born but French-educated Baron Paul d'Holbach (1723–1789) argued that human beings were machines completely determined by outside forces. Free will, God, and immortality of the soul were foolish myths. D'Holbach's aggressive atheism and determinism, which were coupled with deep hostility toward Christianity and all other religions, dealt the unity of the Enlightenment movement a severe blow. Deists such as Voltaire, who believed in God but not in established churches, were repelled by the inflexible atheism they found in the *System of Nature.* They saw in it the same dogmatic intolerance they had been fighting all their lives.

D'Holbach published his philosophically radical works anonymously in the Netherlands to avoid possi-

Prussia, Russia, and Austria, and they deserve primary attention.

Frederick the Great of Prussia Frederick II (r. 1740–1786), commonly known as Frederick the Great, built masterfully on the work of his father, Frederick William I (see pages 478–479). This was somewhat surprising, for, like many children with tyrannical parents, he rebelled against his family's wishes in his early years. Rejecting the crude life of the barracks, Frederick embraced culture and literature, even writing poetry and fine prose in French, a language his father detested. He threw off his father's dour Calvinism and dabbled with atheism. After trying unsuccessfully to run away in 1730 at age eighteen, he was virtually imprisoned and even compelled to watch his companion in flight beheaded at his father's command. Yet like many other rebellious youths, Frederick eventually reached a reconciliation with his father, and by the time he came to the throne ten years later, Frederick was determined to use the splendid army that his father had left him.

Therefore, when the ruler of Austria, Charles VI, also died in 1740 and his young and charismatic daughter, Maria Theresa, inherited the Habsburg dominions, Frederick suddenly and without warning invaded her rich, mainly German province of Silesia. This action defied solemn Prussian promises to respect the Pragmatic Sanction, which guaranteed Maria Theresa's succession—but no matter. For Frederick it was the opportunity of a lifetime to expand the size and power of Prussia. Although Maria Theresa succeeded in dramatically rallying the normally quarrelsome Hungarian nobility, her ethnically diverse army was no match for Prussian precision. In 1742, as other greedy powers were falling on her lands in the general European War of the Austrian Succession (1740–1748), which also expanded into a world war for empire between France and Britain, she was forced to cede almost all of Silesia to Prussia (see Map 17.2 on page 571). In one stroke Prussia doubled its population to six million people. Now Prussia unquestionably towered above all the other German states and stood as a European Great Power.

Though successful in 1742, Frederick had to spend much of his reign fighting against great odds to save Prussia from total destruction. Maria Theresa was determined to regain Silesia, and when the ongoing competition between Britain and France for colonial empire brought another great conflict in 1756 (see page 647), her able chief minister, Count Wenzel Anton Kaunitz (1711–1794), fashioned an aggressive alliance with France and Russia. During the Seven Years' War (1756–1763), the aim of the alliance was to conquer Prussia and divide up its territory, just as Frederick II and other monarchs had so recently sought to partition the Austrian Empire. Frederick led his army brilliantly, striking repeatedly at vastly superior forces invading from all sides. At times he believed all was lost, but he fought on with stoic courage. In the end, he was miraculously saved: Peter III came to the Russian throne in 1762 and called off the attack against Frederick, whom he greatly admired.

In the early years of his reign, Frederick II had kept his enthusiasm for Enlightenment culture strictly separated from a brutal concept of international politics. He wrote:

Of all States, from the smallest to the biggest, one can safely say that the fundamental rule of government is the principle of extending their territories. . . . The passions of rulers have no other curb but the limits of their power. Those are the fixed laws of European politics to which every politician submits.[18]

But the terrible struggle of the Seven Years' War tempered Frederick and brought him to consider how more humane policies for his subjects might also strengthen the state.

Thus Frederick went beyond a superficial commitment to Enlightenment culture for himself and his circle. He tolerantly allowed his subjects to believe as they wished in religious and philosophical matters. He promoted the advancement of knowledge, improving his country's schools and permitting scholars to publish their findings. Moreover, Frederick tried to improve the lives of his subjects more directly. As he wrote his friend Voltaire, "I must enlighten my people, cultivate their manners and morals, and make them as happy as human beings can be, or as happy as the means at my disposal permit." The legal system and the bureaucracy were Frederick's primary tools. Prussia's laws were simplified, torture of prisoners was abolished, and judges decided cases quickly and impartially. Prussian officials became famous for their hard work and honesty. After the Seven Years' War ended in 1763, Frederick's government also energetically promoted the reconstruction of agriculture and industry in his war-torn country. In all this Frederick set a good example. He worked hard and lived modestly, claiming that he was "only the first servant of the state." Thus Frederick justified monarchy in terms of practical results and said nothing of the divine right of kings.

Frederick's dedication to high-minded government went only so far, however. He never tried to change Prussia's existing social structure. True, he condemned serfdom in the abstract, but he accepted it in practice and did not even free the serfs on his own estates. He accepted and extended the privileges of the nobility, which he saw as his primary ally in the defense and extension of his realm. It became practically impossible for a middle-class person to gain a top position in the government. The Junker nobility remained the backbone of the army and the entire Prussian state.

Nor did Frederick listen to thinkers like Moses Mendelssohn (1729–1786), who urged that Jews be given freedom and civil rights. (See the feature "Individuals in Society: Moses Mendelssohn and the Jewish Enlightenment.") As in other German states, Jews in Prussia remained an oppressed group. The vast majority were confined to tiny, overcrowded ghettos, were excluded by law from most business and professional activities, and could be ordered out of the kingdom at a moment's notice. A very few Jews in Prussia did manage to succeed and obtain the right of permanent settlement, usually by performing some special service for the state. But they were the exception, and Frederick firmly opposed any general emancipation for the Jews, as he did for the serfs.

Catherine the Great of Russia Catherine the Great of Russia (r. 1762–1796) was one of the most remarkable rulers who ever lived, and the French philosophes adored her. Catherine was a German princess from Anhalt-Zerbst, a totally insignificant principality sandwiched between Prussia and Saxony. Her father commanded a regiment of the Prussian army, but her mother was related to the Romanovs of Russia, and that proved to be Catherine's chance.

Peter the Great had abolished the hereditary succession of tsars so that he could name his successor and thus preserve his policies. This move opened a period of palace intrigue and a rapid turnover of rulers until Peter's youngest daughter, Elizabeth, came to the Russian throne in 1741. A shrewd but crude woman—one of her official lovers was an illiterate shepherd boy—Elizabeth named her nephew Peter heir to the throne and chose Catherine to be his wife in 1744. It was a mismatch from the beginning. The fifteen-year-old Catherine was intelligent and attractive; her husband was stupid and ugly, his face badly scarred by smallpox. Ignored by her childish husband, Catherine carefully studied Russian, endlessly read writers such as Bayle and Voltaire, and made friends at court. Soon she knew what she wanted. "I did not care about Peter," she wrote in her *Memoirs,* "but I did care about the crown."[19]

As the old empress Elizabeth approached death, Catherine plotted against her unpopular husband. She selected as her new lover a tall, dashing young officer named Gregory Orlov, who with his four officer brothers commanded considerable support among the soldiers stationed in St. Petersburg. When Peter came to the throne in 1762, his decision to withdraw Russian troops from the coalition against Prussia alienated the army. Nor did Peter III's attempt to gain support from the Russian nobility by freeing it from compulsory state service succeed. At the end of six months, Catherine and her military conspirators deposed Peter III in a palace revolution. Then the Orlov brothers murdered him. The German princess became empress of Russia.

Catherine had drunk deeply at the Enlightenment well. Never questioning the common assumption that absolute monarchy was the best form of government, she set out to rule in an enlightened manner. She had three main goals. First, she worked hard to bring the sophisticated culture of western Europe to backward Russia. To do so, she imported Western architects, sculptors, musicians, and intellectuals. She bought masterpieces of Western art in wholesale lots and patronized the philosophes. An enthusiastic letter writer, she corresponded extensively with Voltaire and praised him as the "champion of the human race." When the French government banned the *Encyclopedia,* she offered to publish it in St. Petersburg. She sent money to Diderot when he needed it. With these and countless similar actions, Catherine won good press in the West for herself and for her country. Moreover, this intellectual ruler, who wrote plays and loved good talk, set the tone for the entire Russian nobility. Peter the Great westernized Russian armies, but it was Catherine who westernized the thinking of the Russian nobility.

Catherine's second goal was domestic reform, and she began her reign with sincere and ambitious projects. Better laws were a major concern. In 1767 she drew up enlightened instructions for the special legislative commission she had appointed to prepare a new law code. No new unified code was ever produced, but Catherine did restrict the practice of torture and allowed limited religious toleration. She also tried to improve education and strengthen local government. The philosophes applauded these measures and hoped more would follow.

Such was not the case. In 1773 a common Cossack soldier named Emelian Pugachev sparked a gigantic uprising of serfs, very much as Stenka Razin had done a century earlier (see page 583). Proclaiming himself the true tsar, Pugachev issued "decrees" abolishing serfdom, taxes, and army service. Thousands joined his cause, slaughtering landlords and officials over a vast area of southwestern Russia. Pugachev's untrained hordes eventually proved no match for Catherine's noble-led regular army. Betrayed by his own company, Pugachev was captured and savagely executed.

Pugachev's rebellion was a decisive turning point in Catherine's domestic policy. On coming to the throne, she had condemned serfdom in theory, but she had been smart enough to realize that any changes would have to be very gradual, or else she would quickly follow her departed husband. Pugachev's rebellion put an end to any illusions she might have had about reforming serfdom. The peasants were clearly dangerous, and her empire rested on the support of the nobility. After 1775 Catherine gave the nobles absolute control of their serfs. She extended serfdom into new areas, such as Ukraine. In 1785 she formalized the nobility's privileged position, freeing nobles forever from taxes and state service. She also confiscated the lands of the Russian Orthodox church and gave them to favorite officials. Under Catherine the Russian nobility attained its most exalted position, and serfdom entered its most oppressive phase.

Catherine's third goal was territorial expansion, and in this respect she was extremely successful. Her armies subjugated the last descendants of the Mongols, the Crimean Tartars, and began the conquest of the Caucasus. Her greatest coup by far was the partitioning of

Pugachev and Catherine This haunting portrait of Pugachev has been painted over an existing portrait of empress Catherine the Great, who seems to be peeking over the rebel leader's head. Painting from life in 1773, the artist may have wanted to represent Pugachev's legitimacy as Catherine's rightful successor. *(From* Pamiatniki Kul'tury, *No. 32, 1961)*

Individuals in Society

Moses Mendelssohn and the Jewish Enlightenment

In 1743 a small, humpbacked Jewish boy with a stammer left his poor parents in Dessau in central Germany and walked eighty miles to Berlin, the capital of Frederick the Great's Prussia. According to one story, when the boy reached the Rosenthaler Gate, the only one through which Jews could pass, he told the inquiring watchman that his name was Moses, and that he had come to Berlin "to learn." The watchman laughed and waved him through. "Go Moses, the sea has opened before you."[1] Embracing the Enlightenment and seeking a revitalization of Jewish religious thought, Moses Mendelssohn did point his people in a new and uncharted direction.

Turning in Berlin to a learned rabbi he had previously known in Dessau, the young Mendelssohn studied Jewish law and eked out a living copying Hebrew manuscripts in a beautiful hand. But he was soon fascinated by an intellectual world that had been closed to him in the Dessau ghetto. There, like most Jews throughout central Europe, he had spoken Yiddish—a mixture of German, Polish, and Hebrew. Now, working mainly on his own, he mastered German; learned Latin, Greek, French, and English; and studied mathematics and Enlightenment philosophy. Word of his exceptional abilities spread in Berlin's Jewish community, (1,500 of the city's 100,000 inhabitants). He began tutoring the children of a wealthy Jewish silk merchant, and he soon became the merchant's clerk and later his partner. But his great passion remained the life of the mind and the spirit, which he avidly pursued in his off hours.

Gentle and unassuming in his personal life, Mendelssohn was a bold thinker. Reading eagerly in Western philosophy since antiquity, he was, as a pious Jew, soon convinced that Enlightenment teachings need not be opposed to Jewish thought and religion. Indeed, he concluded that reason could complement and strengthen religion, although each would retain its integrity as a separate sphere.[2] Developing his idea in his first great work, "On the Immortality of the Soul" (1767), Mendelssohn used the neutral setting of a philosophical dialogue between Socrates and his followers in ancient Greece to argue that the human soul lived forever. In refusing to bring religion and critical thinking into conflict, he was strongly influenced by contemporary German philosophers who argued similarly on behalf of Christianity. He reflected the way the German Enlightenment generally supported established religion, while the French Enlightenment attacked it. This was the most important difference in Enlightenment thinking between the two countries.

Lavater (on the right) attempts to convert Mendelssohn, in a painting by Moritz Oppenheim of an imaginary encounter. *(Collection of the Judah L. Magnes Museum, Berkeley)*

Mendelssohn's treatise on the human soul captivated the educated German public, which marveled that a Jew could have written a philosophical masterpiece. In the excitement, a Christian zealot named Lavater challenged Mendelssohn in a pamphlet to accept Christianity or to demonstrate how the Christian faith was not "reasonable." Replying politely but passionately, the Jewish philosopher affirmed that all his studies had only strengthened him in the faith of his fathers, although he certainly did not seek to convert anyone not born into Judaism. Rather, he urged toleration in religious matters. He spoke up courageously for his fellow Jews and decried the oppression they endured, and he continued to do so for the rest of his life.

Orthodox Jew and German philosophe, Moses Mendelssohn serenely combined two very different worlds. He built a bridge from the ghetto to the dominant culture over which many Jews would pass, including his novelist daughter Dorothea and his famous grandson, the composer Felix Mendelssohn.

Questions for Analysis

1. How did Mendelssohn seek to influence Jewish religious thought in his time?
2. How do Mendelssohn's ideas compare with those of the French Enlightenment?

1. H. Kupferberg, *The Mendelssohns: Three Generations of Genius* (New York: Charles Scribner's Sons, 1972), p. 3.
2. D. Sorkin, *Moses Mendelssohn and the Religious Enlightenment* (Berkeley: University of California Press, 1996), pp. 8ff.

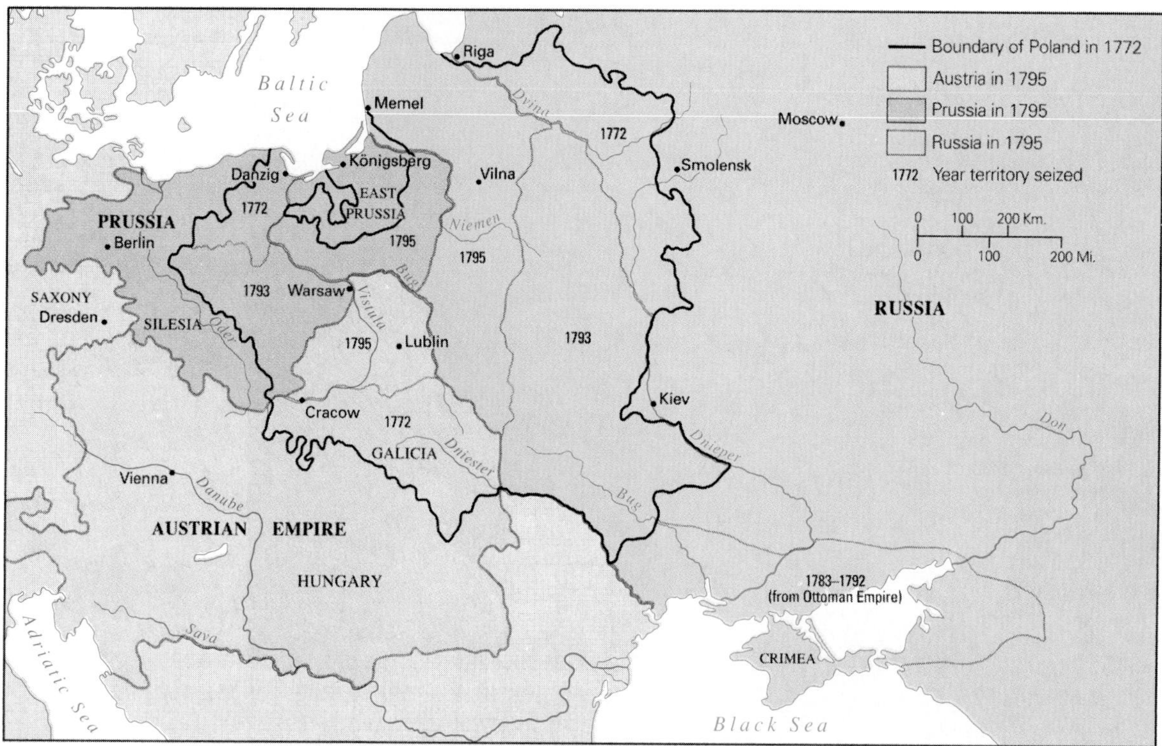

MAP 18.1 The Partition of Poland and Russia's Expansion, 1772–1795 Though all three of the great eastern absolutist states profited from the division of large but weak Poland, Catherine's Russia gained the most. Russia's European border moved far to the west, and the Russian empire became a leading actor in European politics.

Poland (Map 18.1). By 1700 Poland had become a weak and decentralized republic with an elected king (page 572), and Poland's fate in the late eighteenth century demonstrated the dangers of failing to build a strong absolutist state. All important decisions continued to require the unanimous agreement of all nobles elected to the Polish diet, which meant that nothing could ever be done to strengthen the state. When, between 1768 and 1772, Catherine's armies scored unprecedented victories against the Turks and thereby threatened to disturb the balance of power between Russia and Austria in eastern Europe, Frederick of Prussia obligingly came forward with a deal. He proposed that Turkey be let off easily and that Prussia, Austria, and Russia each compensate itself by taking a gigantic slice of Polish territory. Catherine jumped at the chance. The first partition of Poland took place in 1772. Two more partitions, in 1793 and 1795, gave all three powers more Polish territory, and the ancient republic of Poland simply vanished from the map.

Expansion helped Catherine keep the nobility happy, for it provided her with vast new lands to give to her faithful servants and her many lovers. On all the official royal favorites she lavished large estates with many serfs, as if to make sure there were no hard feelings when her interest cooled. Until the end this remarkable woman—who always believed that, in spite of her domestic setbacks, she was slowly civilizing Russia—kept her zest for life. Fascinated by a new twenty-two-year-old flame when she was a roly-poly grandmother in her sixties, she happily reported her good fortune to a favorite former lover: "I have come back to life like a frozen fly; I am gay and well."[20]

The Austrian Habsburgs In Austria two talented rulers did manage to introduce major reforms, although traditional power politics was more important than Enlightenment teachings. One was Joseph II (r. 1780–1790), a fascinating individual. For an earlier generation of historians, he was the "revolutionary

Maria Theresa and her husband pose with eleven of their sixteen children at Schönbrunn palace in this family portrait by court painter Martin Meytens (1695–1770). Joseph, the heir to the throne, stands at the center of the star pattern. Wealthy women often had very large families, in part because they seldom nursed their babies as poor women usually did. *(Kunsthistorisches Museum, Vienna)*

emperor," a tragic hero whose lofty reforms were undone by the landowning nobility he dared to challenge. More recent scholarship has revised this romantic interpretation and stressed how Joseph II continued the state-building work of his mother, the empress Maria Theresa, a remarkable but old-fashioned absolutist.

Maria Theresa's long reign (1740–1780) began with her neighbors, led by Frederick II of Prussia, invading her lands and trying to dismember them. Emerging from the long War of the Austrian Succession in 1748 with only the serious loss of Silesia, Maria Theresa and her closest ministers were determined to introduce reforms that would make the state stronger and more efficient. Three aspects of these reforms were most important. First, Maria Theresa introduced measures to bring relations between church and state under government control. Like some medieval rulers, the most devout and very Catholic Maria Theresa aimed at limiting the papacy's political influence in her realm. Second, a whole series of administrative reforms strengthened the central bureaucracy, smoothed out some provincial differences, and revamped the tax system, taxing even the lands of nobles without special exemptions. Third, the government sought to improve the lot of the agricultural population, cautiously reducing the power of lords over their hereditary serfs and their partially free peasant tenants.

Coregent with his mother from 1765 onward and a strong supporter of change, Joseph II moved forward rapidly when he came to the throne in 1780. He controlled the established Catholic church even more closely in an attempt to ensure that it produced better citizens. He granted religious toleration and civic rights to Protestants and Jews—a radical innovation that impressed his contemporaries. In even more spectacular peasant reforms, Joseph abolished serfdom in 1781, and in 1789 he decreed that all peasant labor obligations be converted into cash payments. This ill-conceived measure was violently rejected not only by the nobility but also by the peasants it was intended to help since their primitive barter economy was woefully lacking in money. When a disillusioned Joseph died prematurely at forty-nine, the entire Habsburg empire was in turmoil. His brother Leopold II (r. 1790–1792) was forced to cancel Joseph's radical edicts in order to reestablish order. Peasants lost most of their recent gains, and once again they were required to do forced labor for their lords, as in the 1770s under Maria Theresa.

Absolutism in France

The Enlightenment's influence on political developments in France was complex. The monarchy maintained its absolutist claims, and some philosophes, such as Voltaire, believed that the king was still the best source of needed reform. At the same time, discontented nobles and learned judges drew on thinkers such as Montesquieu for liberal arguments. They sought with some success to limit the king's power, as France diverged from the absolutist states just considered.

In building French absolutism, Louis XIV had successfully drawn on the middle class to curb the political power of the nobility. As long as the Grand Monarch lived, the nobility could only grumble and, like the duke of Saint-Simon in his *Memoirs,* scornfully lament the rise of "the vile bourgeoisie." But when Louis XIV finally died in 1715, to be succeeded by his five-year-old great-grandson, Louis XV (r. 1715–1774), the Sun King's elaborate system of absolutist rule was challenged in a general reaction. Favored by the duke of Orléans (1674–1723), a licentious rake and nephew of Louis XIV who governed as regent until 1723, the nobility made a strong comeback.

Most important, in 1715 the duke, in return for recognition of his desire to become the sole regent, restored to the high courts of France—the parlements—the ancient right to evaluate royal decrees publicly in writing before they were registered and given the force of law. The restoration of this right to evaluate, or "remonstrate," which had been suspended under Louis XIV, was a fateful step. The high court judges, of which those at the Parlement of Paris were the most important and influential, had originally come from the middle class, and their high position reflected the way that Louis XIV (and earlier French monarchs) had chosen to use that class to build the royal bureaucracy so necessary for an absolutist state. By the eighteenth century, however, these middle-class judges had risen to become hereditary nobles. Moreover, although Louis XIV had curbed the political power of the nobility, he had never challenged its enormous social prestige. Thus high position in the government continued to bestow the noble status that middle-class officials wanted, either right away or after three generations of continual service. The judges of Paris and the provincial high courts, like many high-ranking officials, actually owned their government jobs and freely passed them on as private property from father to son. By allowing this well-entrenched and increasingly aristocratic group to evaluate the king's decrees before they became law, the duke of Orléans sanctioned a counterweight to absolute power.

These implications became clear when the heavy expenses of the War of the Austrian Succession plunged France into financial crisis. In 1748 Louis XV appointed a finance minister who decreed a 5 percent income tax on every individual regardless of social status. Exemption from most taxation had long been a hallowed privilege of the nobility, and other important groups—the clergy, the large towns, and some wealthy bourgeoisie—had also gained special tax advantages over time. The result was a vigorous protest from many sides. Leading the attack, the Parlement of Paris denounced the proposed tax law and rallied public opinion against it. The monarchy retreated; the new tax was dropped.

Following the disastrously expensive Seven Years' War, the conflict re-emerged. The government tried to maintain emergency taxes after the war ended. The Parlement of Paris protested and even challenged the basis of royal authority, claiming that the king's power had to be limited to protect liberty. Once again the government caved in and withdrew the wartime taxes in 1764. Emboldened by this striking victory and widespread support from France's educated elite, the judicial opposition in Paris and the provinces pressed its demands. In a barrage of pamphlets and legal briefs, it asserted that the king could not levy taxes without the consent of the Parlement of Paris acting as the representative of the entire nation.

Indolent and sensual by nature, more interested in his many mistresses than in affairs of state, Louis XV finally roused himself for a determined defense of his absolutist inheritance. "The magistrates," he angrily told the Parlement of Paris in a famous face-to-face confrontation, "are my officers. . . . In my person only does the sovereign power rest."[21] In 1768 Louis appointed a tough career official named René de Maupeou as chancellor and ordered him to crush the judicial opposition.

Maupeou abolished the existing parlements and exiled the vociferous members of the Parlement of Paris to isolated backwaters in the provinces. He created a new and docile parlement of royal officials, and he began once again to tax the privileged groups. A few philosophes applauded these measures: the sovereign was using his power to introduce badly needed reforms that had been blocked by a self-serving aristocratic elite. Most philosophes and educated public opinion as a whole sided with the old parlements, however, and there was widespread criticism of "royal despotism." The illegal stream of scandalmongering, pornographic attacks on the king and his court, became a torrent, and some scholars now believe these lurid denunciations ate away at the foundations of royal authority, especially among the common people in turbulent Paris. The king was being stripped of the sacred aura of God's anointed on earth and was being reinvented in the popular imagination as a loathsome degenerate. Yet the monarchy's power was still great enough for Maupeou simply to ride over the opposition, and Louis XV would probably have prevailed—if he had lived to a very ripe old age.

But Louis XV died in 1774. The new king, Louis XVI (r. 1774–1792), was a shy twenty-year-old with good intentions. Taking the throne, he is reported to have said, "What I should like most is to be loved."[22] The eager-to-please monarch decided to yield in the face of such strong criticism from so much of France's educated elite. He dismissed Maupeou and repudiated the strong-willed minister's work. All the old parlements were reinstated, as enlightened public opinion cheered and anticipated moves toward more representative government. But such moves were not forthcoming. Instead, a weakened but unreformed monarchy faced a judicial opposition that claimed to speak for the entire French nation. Increasingly locked in stalemate, the country was drifting toward renewed financial crisis and political upheaval.

The Overall Influence of the Enlightenment

Having examined the evolution of monarchial absolutism in four leading states, we can begin to look for meaningful generalizations and evaluate the overall influence of Enlightenment thought on politics. That thought was clustered in two distinct schools: the liberal critique of unregulated monarchy promoted by Montesquieu and the defenders of royal absolutism led by Voltaire.

France clearly diverged from its eastern neighbors in its political development in the eighteenth century. Although neither the French monarchy nor the eastern rulers abandoned the absolutist claims and institutions they had inherited, the monarch's capacity to govern in a truly absolutist manner declined substantially in France. This was not the case in eastern Europe. The immediate cause of this divergence was the political resurgence of the French nobility after 1715 and the growth of judicial opposition, led by the Parlement of Paris. More fundamentally, however, the judicial and aristocratic opposition in France achieved its still rather modest successes because it received major support from educated public opinion, which increasingly made the liberal critique of unregulated royal authority its own. In France, then, the proponents of absolute monarchy were increasingly on the defensive, as was the French monarchy.

The situation in eastern and east-central Europe was different. The liberal critique of absolute monarchy remained an intellectual curiosity, and proponents of reform from above held sway. Moreover, despite differences, the leading eastern European monarchs of the later eighteenth century all claimed that they were acting on the principles of the Enlightenment. The philosophes generally agreed with this assessment and cheered them on. Beginning in the mid-nineteenth century, historians developed the idea of a common "enlightened despotism" or "enlightened absolutism," and they canonized Frederick, Catherine, and Joseph as its most outstanding examples. More recent research has raised doubts about this old interpretation and has led to a fundamental revaluation.

There is general agreement that these absolutists, especially Catherine and Frederick, did encourage and spread the cultural values of the Enlightenment. Perhaps this was their greatest achievement. Skeptical in religion and intensely secular in basic orientation, they unabashedly accepted the here and now and sought their happiness in the enjoyment of it. At the same time, they were proud of their intellectual accomplishments and good taste, and they supported knowledge, education, and the arts. No wonder the philosophes felt these monarchs were kindred spirits.

Historians also agree that the absolutists believed in change from above and tried to enact needed reforms. Yet the results of these efforts brought only very modest improvements, and the life of the peasantry remained very hard in the eighteenth century. Thus some historians have concluded that these monarchs were not really sincere in their reform efforts. Others disagree, arguing that powerful nobilities blocked the absolutists' genuine commitment to reform. (The old interpretation of Joseph II as the tragic revolutionary emperor forms part of this argument.)

The emerging answer to this controversy is that the later eastern absolutists were indeed committed to reform but that humanitarian objectives were of quite secondary importance. Above all, the absolutists wanted reforms that would strengthen the state and allow them to compete militarily with their neighbors. Modern scholarship has therefore stressed how Catherine, Frederick, and Joseph were in many ways simply continuing the state building of their predecessors, reorganizing armies and expanding bureaucracies to raise more taxes and troops. The reason for this continuation was simple. The international political struggle was brutal, and the stakes were high. First Austria under Maria Theresa and then Prussia under Frederick the Great had to engage in bitter fighting to escape dismemberment, while decentralized Poland was coldly divided and eventually liquidated.

Yet in this drive for more state power, the later absolutists were also innovators, and the idea of an era of enlightened absolutism retains a certain validity. Sharing the Enlightenment faith in critical thinking and believing that knowledge meant power, these absolutists really were more enlightened than their predecessors because they put state-building reforms in a new, broader perspective. Above all, the later absolutists considered how more humane laws and practices could help their populations become more productive and satisfied and thus able to contribute more substantially to the welfare of the state. It was from this perspective that they introduced many of their most progressive reforms, tolerating religious minorities, simplifying legal codes, and promoting practical education.

The primacy of state over individual interests also helps explain some puzzling variations in social policies. For example, Catherine the Great took measures that worsened the peasants' condition because she looked increasingly to the nobility as her natural ally and sought to strengthen it. Frederick the Great basically favored the status quo, limiting only the counterproductive excesses of his trusted nobility against its peasants. Joseph II believed that greater freedom for peasants was the means to strengthen his realm, and he acted accordingly. Each enlightened absolutist sought greater state power, but each believed a different policy would attain it.

The eastern European absolutists of the later eighteenth century combined old-fashioned state building with the culture and critical thinking of the Enlightenment. In doing so, they succeeded in expanding the role of the state in the life of society. Unlike the successors of Louis XIV, they perfected bureaucratic machines that were to prove surprisingly adaptive and capable of enduring into the twentieth century.

SUMMARY

This chapter has focused on the complex development of a new world-view in Western civilization. This new view was essentially critical and secular, drawing its inspiration from the scientific revolution and crystallizing in the Enlightenment.

Decisive breakthroughs in astronomy and physics in the seventeenth century, which demolished the imposing medieval synthesis of Aristotelian philosophy and Christian theology, had only limited practical consequences despite the expectations of scientific enthusiasts. Yet the impact of new scientific knowledge on intellectual life became great. Interpreting scientific findings and Newtonian laws in an antitraditional, antireligious manner, the French philosophes of the Enlightenment extolled the superiority of rational, critical thinking. This new method, they believed, promised not just increased knowledge but even the discovery of the fundamental laws of human society. Although they reached different conclusions when they turned to social and political realities, they did stimulate absolute monarchs to apply reason to statecraft and the search for useful reforms. Above all, the philosophes succeeded in shaping an emerging public opinion and spreading their radically new world-view. These were momentous accomplishments.

NOTES

1. H. Butterfield, *The Origins of Modern Science* (New York: Macmillan, 1951), p. viii.
2. Quoted in A. G. R. Smith, *Science and Society in the Sixteenth and Seventeenth Centuries* (New York: Harcourt Brace Jovanovich, 1972), p. 97.
3. Quoted in Butterfield, *The Origins of Modern Science,* p. 47.
4. Quoted in Smith, *Science and Society,* p. 100.
5. Ibid., pp. 115–116.
6. Ibid., p. 120.
7. A. R. Hall, *From Galileo to Newton, 1630–1720* (New York: Harper & Row, 1963), p. 290.
8. Quoted in R. K. Merton, *Science, Technology and Society in Seventeenth-Century England,* rev. ed. (New York: Harper & Row, 1970), p. 164.
9. Quoted in P. Hazard, *The European Mind, 1680–1715* (Cleveland: Meridian Books, 1963), pp. 304–305.
10. Quoted in R. Chartier, *The Cultural Origins of the French Revolution* (Durham, N.C.: Duke University Press, 1991), p. 27.
11. J. Bosher, *The French Revolution* (New York: W. W. Norton, 1988), p. 31.
12. L. Schiebinger, *The Mind Has No Sex? Women in the Origins of Modern Science* (Cambridge, Mass.: Harvard University Press, 1989), p. 64.
13. Quoted in L. M. Marsak, ed., *The Enlightenment* (New York: John Wiley & Sons, 1972), p. 56.
14. Quoted in G. L. Mosse et al., eds., *Europe in Review* (Chicago: Rand McNally, 1964), p. 156.
15. Quoted in P. Gay, "The Unity of the Enlightenment," *History* 3 (1960): 25.
16. See E. Fox-Genovese, "Women in the Enlightenment," in *Becoming Visible: Women in European History,* 2d ed., ed. R. Bridenthal, C. Koonz, and S. Stuard (Boston: Houghton Mifflin, 1987), esp. pp. 252–259, 263–265.
17. Quoted in G. P. Gooch, *Catherine the Great and Other Studies* (Hamden, Conn.: Archon Books, 1966), p. 149.
18. Quoted in L. Krieger, *Kings and Philosophers, 1689–1789* (New York: W. W. Norton, 1970), p. 257.
19. Quoted in Gooch, *Catherine the Great,* p. 15.
20. Ibid., p. 53.
21. Quoted in R. R. Palmer, *The Age of Democratic Revolution,* vol. 1 (Princeton, N.J.: Princeton University Press, 1959), pp. 95–96.
22. Quoted in G. Wright, *France in Modern Times,* 4th ed. (New York: W. W. Norton, 1987), p. 34.

SUGGESTED READING

The first three authors cited in the Notes—Butterfield, Smith, and Hall—have written excellent general interpretations of the scientific revolution. These may be compared with an outstanding work by M. Jacob, *The Cultural Meaning of the Scientific Revolution* (1988), which has a useful bibliography. The older study of England by Merton, mentioned in the Notes, also analyzes ties between science and the larger community. Schiebinger, cited in the Notes, provides a brilliant analysis of how the new science gradually excluded women interested in science, a question completely neglected in older studies. A. Debus, *Man and Nature in the Renaissance* (1978), is good on the Copernican revolution. M. Boas, *The Scientific Renaissance, 1450–1630* (1966), is especially insightful about the influence of magic on science. S. Drake, *Galileo* (1980), is a good short biography. T. Kuhn, *The Structure of Scientific Revolutions* (1962), is a challenging, much-discussed attempt to understand major breakthroughs in scientific thought over time. E. Andrade, *Sir Isaac Newton* (1958), is a good brief biography, which may be compared with R. Westfall, *Never at Rest: A Biography of Isaac Newton* (1993); and F. Manuel, *The Religion of Isaac Newton* (1974).

Hazard, listed in the Notes, is a classic study of the formative years of Enlightenment thought, and his *European Thought in the Eighteenth Century* (1954) is also recommended. Important recent studies from the cultural perspective include D. Goodman, *The Republic of Letters: A Cultural History of the Enlightenment* (1994); and A. Farge, *Subversive Worlds: Public Opinion in Eighteenth Century France* (1994). P. Gay has written several major studies on the Enlightenment: *Voltaire's Politics* (1959) and *The Party of Humanity* (1971) are two of the best. J. Sklar, *Montesquieu* (1987), is an engaging biography. I. Wade, *The Structure and Form of the French Enlightenment* (1977), is a major synthesis. F. Baumer, *Religion and the Rise of Skepticism* (1969); H. Payne, *The Philosophes and the People* (1976); and H. Chisick, *The Limits of Reform in the Enlightenment: Attitudes Toward the Education of the Lower Classes in Eighteenth-Century France* (1981), are interesting studies of important aspects of Enlightenment thought. D. Van Kley, *The Religious Origins of the French Revolution* (1996), is a stimulating reinterpretation. The changing attitudes of the educated public are imaginatively analyzed by R. Chartier, *The Cultural Origins of the French Revolution* (1991) and *French Historical Studies* (Fall 1992). R. Danton, *The Literary Underground of the Old Regime* (1982), provides a fascinating glimpse of low-life publishing. On women, see the stimulating study by Fox-Genovese cited in the Notes, as well as E. Goldsmith and

D. Goodman, eds., *Going Public: Women and Publishing in Early Modern France* (1995); S. Spencer, ed., *French Women and the Age of Enlightenment* (1984); and K. Rogers, *Feminism in Eighteenth-Century England* (1982). J. Landes, *Women and the Public Sphere in the Age of the French Revolution* (1988), is a fascinating and controversial study of women and politics. L. Wolff, *Inventing Eastern Europe: The Map of Civilization on the Mind of the Enlightenment* (1994), argues that the philosophes were the first to divide Europe into a backward east and an advanced west. Above all, one should read some of the philosophes and let them speak for themselves. Two good anthologies are C. Brinton, ed., *The Portable Age of Reason* (1956); and F. Manuel, ed., *The Enlightenment* (1951). Voltaire's most famous and very amusing novel, *Candide,* is highly recommended, as is S. Gendzier, ed., *Denis Diderot: The Encyclopedia: Selections* (1967). A. Wilson's biography, *Diderot* (1972), is long but rewarding.

In addition to the works mentioned in the Suggested Reading for Chapters 16 and 17, the monarchies of Europe are carefully analyzed in H. Scott, *Enlightened Absolutism* (1990); C. Tilly, ed., *The Formation of National States in Western Europe* (1975); and J. Gagliardo, *Enlightened Despotism* (1967), all of which have useful bibliographies. M. Anderson, *Historians and Eighteenth-Century Europe* (1979), is a valuable introduction to modern scholarship, and C. Behrens, *Society, Government, and the Enlightenment: The Experience of Eighteenth-Century France and Prussia* (1985), is a stimulating comparative study. E. Le Roy Ladurie, *The Ancien Régime* (1996), is an impressive synthesis by a leading French historian. J. Lynch, *Bourbon Spain, 1700–1808* (1989); and R. Herr, *The Eighteenth-Century Revolution in Spain* (1958), skillfully analyze the impact of Enlightenment thought in Spain. Important works on Austria include C. Macartney, *Maria Theresa and the House of Austria* (1970); D. Beales, *Joseph II* (1987); and T. Blanning, *Joseph II and Enlightened Absolutism* (1970). There are several fine works on Russia. J. Alexander, *Catherine the Great: Life and Legend* (1989), is the best biography of the famous ruler, which may be compared with the empress's own story, *The Memoirs of Catherine the Great,* ed. D. Maroger (1961). I. de Madariaga, *Russia in the Age of Catherine the Great* (1981); and P. Dukes, *The Making of Russian Absolutism, 1613–1801* (1982), are strongly recommended. The ambitious reader should also look at A. N. Radishchev, *A Journey from St. Petersburg to Moscow* (English trans., 1958), a famous 1790 attack on Russian serfdom and an appeal to Catherine the Great to free the serfs, for which Radishchev was exiled to Siberia. Two excellent works on Moses Mendelssohn are the brilliant study by D. Sorkin, *Moses Mendelssohn and the Religious Enlightenment* (1996), and the popular biography of the family by H. Kupferberg, *The Mendelssohns: Three Generations of Genius* (1972).

The musical and artistic culture of the time may be approached through A. Cobban, ed., *The Eighteenth Century* (1969), a richly illustrated work with excellent essays; and C. B. Behrens, *The Ancien Régime* (1967). T. Crow, *Painters and Public Life in Eighteenth-Century Paris* (1985), examines artists and cultural politics. C. Rosen, *The Classical Style: Haydn, Mozart, Beethoven* (1972), brilliantly synthesizes music and society, as did Mozart himself in his great opera *The Marriage of Figaro,* where the count is the buffoon and his servant the hero.

LISTENING TO THE PAST

Voltaire on Religion

Voltaire was the most renowned and probably the most influential of the French philosophes. His biting, satirical novel Candide *(1759) is still widely assigned in college courses, and his witty yet serious* Philosophical Dictionary *remains a source of pleasure and stimulation. The* Dictionary *consists of a series of essays on topics ranging from Adam to Zoroaster, from certainty to circumcision. The following passage is taken from the essay on religion.*

Voltaire began writing the Philosophical Dictionary *in 1752, at the age of fifty-eight, after arriving at the Prussian court in Berlin. Frederick the Great applauded Voltaire's efforts, but Voltaire put the project aside after leaving Berlin, and the first of several revised editions was published anonymously in 1764. It was an immediate, controversial success. Snapped up by an "enlightened" public, it was denounced by religious leaders as a threat to the Christian community and was burned in Geneva and Paris.*

I meditated last night; I was absorbed in the contemplation of nature; I admired the immensity, the course, the harmony of those infinite globes which the vulgar do not know how to admire.

I admired still more the intelligence which directs these vast forces. I said to myself: "One must be blind not to be dazzled by this spectacle; one must be stupid not to recognize its author; one must be mad not to worship the Supreme Being. What tribute of worship should I render Him? Should not this tribute be the same in the whole of space, since it is the same Supreme Power which reigns equally in all space?

"Should not a thinking being who dwells on a star in the Milky Way offer Him the same homage as a thinking being on this little globe of ours? Light is the same for the star Sirius as for us; moral philosophy must also be the same. If a feeling, thinking animal on Sirius is born of a tender father and mother who have been occupied with his happiness, he owes them as much love and care as we owe to our parents. If someone in the Milky Way sees a needy cripple, and if he can aid him and does not do so, then he is guilty toward all the globes.

"Everywhere the heart has the same duties: on the steps of the throne of God, if He has a throne; and in the depths of the abyss, if there is an abyss."

I was deep in these ideas when one of those genii who fill the spaces between the worlds came down to me. I recognized the same aerial creature who had appeared to me on another occasion to teach me that the judgments of God are different from our own, and how a good action is preferable to a controversy.

The genie transported me into a desert all covered with piles of bones. . . . He began with the first pile. "These," he said, "are the twenty-three thousand Jews who danced before a calf, together with the twenty-four thousand who were killed while fornicating with Midianitish women. The number of those massacred for such errors and offences amounts to nearly three hundred thousand.

"In the other piles are the bones of the Christians slaughtered by each other because of metaphysical disputes. They are divided into several heaps of four centuries each. One heap would have mounted right to the sky; they had to be divided."

"What!" I cried, "brothers have treated their brothers like this, and I have the misfortune to be of this brotherhood!"

"Here," said the spirit, "are the twelve million native Americans killed in their own land because they had not been baptized."

"My God! . . . Why assemble here all these abominable monuments to barbarism and fanaticism?"

"To instruct you. . . . Follow me now." [The genie takes Voltaire to the "heroes of humanity, who tried to banish violence and plunder from the world," and tells Voltaire to question them.]

[At last] I saw a man with a gentle, simple face, who seemed to me to be about thirty-five years old. From afar he looked with compassion upon those piles of whitened bones, through which I had been led to reach the sage's dwelling place. I was astonished to find his feet swollen and bleeding, his hands likewise, his side pierced, and his ribs laid bare by the cut of the lash. "Good God!" I said to him, "is it possible for a just man, a sage, to be in this state? I have just seen one who was treated in a very hateful way, but there is no comparison between his torture and yours. Wicked priests and wicked judges poisoned him; is it by priests and judges that you were so cruelly assassinated?"

With great courtesy he answered, "Yes."

"And who were these monsters?"

"They were hypocrites."

"Ah! that says everything; I understand by that one word that they would have condemned you to the cruelest punishment. Had you then proved to them, as Socrates did, that the Moon was not a goddess, and that Mercury was not a god?"

"No, it was not a question of planets. My countrymen did not even know what a planet was; they were all arrant ignoramuses. Their superstitions were quite different from those of the Greeks."

"Then you wanted to teach them a new religion?"

"Not at all; I told them simply: 'Love God with all your heart and your neighbor as yourself, for that is the whole of mankind's duty.' Judge yourself if this precept is not as old as the universe; judge yourself if I brought them a new religion." . . .

"But did you say nothing, do nothing that could serve them as a pretext?"

"To the wicked everything serves as pretext."

"Did you not say once that you were come not to bring peace, but a sword?"

"It was a scribe's error; I told them that I brought peace and not a sword. I never wrote anything; what I said can have been changed without evil intention."

"You did not then contribute in any way by your teaching, either badly reported or badly interpreted, to those frightful piles of bones which I saw on my way to consult with you?"

"I have only looked with horror upon those who have made themselves guilty of all these murders."

. . . [Finally] I asked him to tell me in what true religion consisted.

"Have I not already told you? Love God and your neighbor as yourself."

"Is it necessary for me to take sides either for the Greek Orthodox Church or the Roman Catholic?"

"When I was in the world I never made any difference between the Jew and the Samaritan."

"Well, if that is so, I take you for my only master." Then he made a sign with his head that filled me with peace. The vision disappeared, and I was left with a clear conscience.

✣ An impish Voltaire, by the French sculptor Houdon. *(Courtesy of Board of Trustees of the Victoria & Albert Museum)*

Questions for Analysis

1. Why did Voltaire believe in a Supreme Being? Does this passage reflect the influence of Isaac Newton's scientific system?
2. Was Voltaire trying to entertain or teach or both? Was he effective? Why or why not?
3. If Voltaire was trying to convey serious ideas about religion and morality, what were those ideas? What was he attacking?
4. If a person today thought and wrote like Voltaire, would that person be called a defender or a destroyer of Christianity? Why?

Source: F. M. Arouet de Voltaire, *Oeuvres completes,* vol. 8, trans. J. McKay (Paris: Firmin-Didot, 1875), pp. 188–190.

CHAPTER 19

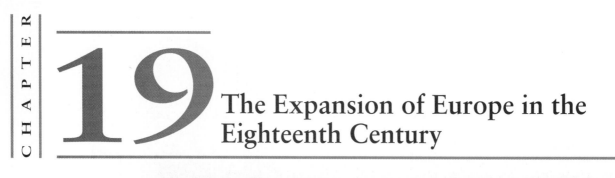

The Expansion of Europe in the Eighteenth Century

Port of Dieppe (detail), by Joseph Vernet. *(Musée de la Marine, Paris/Bridgeman Art Library, London/New York)*

The world of absolutism and aristocracy, a combination of raw power and elegant refinement, was a world apart from that of the common people. For the overwhelming majority of the population in the eighteenth century, life remained a struggle with poverty and uncertainty, with the landlord and the tax collector. In 1700 peasants on the land and artisans in their shops lived little better than had their ancestors in the Middle Ages. Only in science and thought, and there only among a few intellectual elites and their followers, had Western society succeeded in going beyond the great achievements of the High Middle Ages, achievements that in turn owed so much to Greece and Rome.

Everyday life was a struggle because European societies, despite their best efforts, still could not produce very much by modern standards. Ordinary men and women might work like their beasts in the fields, and they often did, but there was seldom enough good food, warm clothing, and decent housing. Life went on; history went on. The wars of religion ravaged Germany in the seventeenth century; Russia rose to become a Great Power; the state of Poland simply disappeared; monarchs and nobles continually jockeyed for power and wealth. In 1700 or even 1750, the idea of progress, of substantial improvement in the lives of great numbers of people, was still only the dream of a small elite in fashionable salons.

Yet the economic basis of European life was beginning to change. In the course of the eighteenth century, the European economy emerged from the long crisis of the seventeenth century, responded to challenges, and began to expand once again. Population resumed its growth, while colonial empires developed and colonial elites prospered. Some areas were more fortunate than others. The rising Atlantic powers—Holland, France, and, above all, England—and their colonies led the way. The expansion of agriculture and industry, trade and population, marked the beginning of a surge comparable to that of the eleventh- and twelfth-century springtime of European civilization. But this time, broadly based expansion was not cut short. This time the response to new challenges led toward one of the most influential developments in human history, the Industrial Revolution, considered in Chapter 22.

- What were the causes of this renewed surge?
- Why were the fundamental economic underpinnings of European society beginning to change and what were the dimensions of these changes?
- How did these changes affect people and their work?

These are the questions this chapter will address.

Agriculture and the Land

At the end of the seventeenth century, the economy of Europe was agrarian, as it had been for several hundred years. With the possible exception of Holland, at least 80 percent of the people of all western European countries drew their livelihoods from agriculture. In eastern Europe the percentage was considerably higher.

Men and women lavished their attention on the land, plowing fields and sowing seed, reaping harvests and storing grain. The land repaid these efforts, year after year yielding up the food and most of the raw materials for industry that made life possible. Yet the land was stingy. Even in a rich agricultural region such as the Po Valley in northern Italy, every bushel of wheat sown yielded on average only five or six bushels of grain at harvest during the seventeenth century. The average French yield in the same period was somewhat less. Such yields were barely more than those attained in fertile, well-watered areas in the thirteenth century or in ancient Greece. By modern standards, output was distressingly low. (For each bushel of wheat seed sown today on fertile land with good rainfall, an American or French farmer can expect roughly forty bushels of produce.) In 1700 European agriculture was much more ancient and medieval than it was modern.

If the land was stingy, it was also capricious. In most regions of Europe in the sixteenth and seventeenth centuries, harvests were poor, or even failed completely, every eight or nine years. The vast majority of the population, which lived off the land, might survive a single bad harvest by eating less and drawing on their reserves of grain. But when the land's caprices combined with persistent bad weather—too much rain rotting the seed or drought withering the young stalks—the result was catastrophic. Meager grain reserves were soon exhausted, and the price of grain soared. Provisions from other areas with better harvests were hard to obtain.

In such crisis years, which periodically stalked Europe in the seventeenth and even into the early eighteenth century, a terrible tightening knot in the belly forced people to use substitutes—the "famine foods" of a desperate population. People gathered chestnuts and stripped bark in the forests, they cut dandelions and grass, and they ate these substitutes to escape starvation. In one community in Norway in the early 1700s, people were forced to wash dung from the straw in old manure piles in order to bake a pathetic substitute for bread. Even cannibalism occurred in the seventeenth century.

Such unbalanced and inadequate food in famine years made people weak and extremely susceptible to illness and epidemics. Eating material unfit for human consumption, such as bark or grass, resulted in dysentery and intestinal ailments of many kinds. Influenza and smallpox preyed with particular savagery on populations weakened by famine. In famine years the number of deaths soared far above normal. A third of a village's population might disappear in a year or two. Indeed, the 1690s were as dismal as many of the worst periods of earlier times. One county in Finland, probably typical of the entire country, lost fully 28 percent of its inhabitants in 1696 and 1697. Certain well-studied villages in the Beauvais region of northern France suffered a similar fate. In preindustrial Europe the harvest was the real king, and the king was seldom generous and often cruel.

To understand why Europeans produced barely enough food in good years and occasionally agonized through years of famine throughout the later seventeenth century, one must follow the plowman, his wife, and his children into the fields to observe their battle for food and life. There the ingenious pattern of farming that Europe had developed in the Middle Ages, a pattern that allowed fairly large numbers of people to survive but could never produce material abundance, was still dominant.

The Open-Field System

The greatest accomplishment of medieval agriculture was the open-field system of village farming developed by European peasants. That system divided the land to be cultivated by the peasants of a given village into several large fields, which were in turn cut up into long, narrow strips. The fields were open, and the strips were not enclosed into small plots by fences or hedges. An individual peasant family—if it was fortunate—held a

Farming the Land Agricultural methods in Europe changed very slowly from the Middle Ages to the early eighteenth century. This realistic picture from Diderot's *Encyclopedia* has striking similarities with agricultural scenes found in medieval manuscripts. *(University of Illinois Library, Champaign)*

number of strips scattered throughout the various large fields. The land of those who owned but did not till, primarily the nobility, the clergy, and wealthy townspeople, was also in scattered strips. Peasants farmed each large field as a community, with each family following the same pattern of plowing, sowing, and harvesting in accordance with tradition and the village leaders.

The ever-present problem was exhaustion of the soil. When the community planted wheat year after year in a field, the nitrogen in the soil was soon depleted, and crop failure was certain. Since the supply of manure for fertilizer was limited, the only way for the land to recover its life-giving fertility was for a field to lie fallow for a period of time. In the early Middle Ages, a year of fallow was alternated with a year of cropping, so that half the land stood idle in a given year. With time, three-year rotations were introduced, especially on more fertile lands. This system permitted a year of wheat or rye to be followed by a year of oats or beans and only then by a year of fallow. Even so, only awareness of the tragic consequences of continuous cropping forced undernourished populations to let a third (or half) of their cropland lie idle, especially when the fallow still had to be plowed two or three times a year to keep down the weeds.

Traditional village rights reinforced the traditional pattern of farming. In addition to rotating field crops in a uniform way, villages maintained open meadows for hay and natural pasture. These lands were "common" lands, set aside primarily for the draft horses and oxen so necessary in the fields, but open to the cows and pigs of the village community as well. After the harvest, the men and women of the village also pastured their animals on the wheat or rye stubble. In many places such pasturing followed a brief period, also established by tradition, for the gleaning of grain. Poor women would go through the fields picking up the few single grains that had fallen to the ground in the course of the harvest. The subject of a great nineteenth-century painting, *The Gleaners* by Jean François Millet (page 632), this backbreaking work by hard-working but impoverished women meant quite literally the slender margin of survival for some people in the winter months.

In the age of absolutism and nobility, state and landlord continued to levy heavy taxes and high rents as a matter of course. In so doing, they stripped the peasants of much of their meager earnings. The level of exploitation varied.

Generally speaking, the peasants of eastern Europe were worst off. As we saw in Chapter 17, they were serfs bound to their lords in hereditary service. Though serfdom in eastern Europe in the eighteenth century had much in common with medieval serfdom in central and western Europe, it was, if anything, harsher and more oppressive. In much of eastern Europe, there were few limitations on the amount of forced labor the lord could require, and five or six days of unpaid work per week on the lord's land were not uncommon. Well into the nineteenth century, individual Russian serfs and serf families were regularly sold with and without land.

Social conditions were better in western Europe. Peasants were generally free from serfdom. In France, western Germany, and the Low Countries, they owned land and could pass it on to their children. Yet life in the village was unquestionably hard, and poverty was the great reality for most people. For the Beauvais region of France at the beginning of the eighteenth century, it has been carefully estimated that in good years and bad only a tenth of the peasants could live satisfactorily off the fruits of their landholdings. Owning considerably less than half of the land, the peasants of this region had to pay heavy royal taxes, the church's tithe, and dues to the lord, as well as set aside seed for the next season. Left with only half of their crop for their own use, these peasants had to toil and till for others and seek work for wages in a variety of jobs. It was a constant scramble for a meager living. And this was in a rich agricultural region in a country where peasants were comparatively well-off. The privileges of Europe's ruling elites weighed heavily on the people of the land.

Agricultural Revolution

One possible way for European peasants to improve their difficult position was to take land from those who owned but did not labor. Yet the social and political conditions that enabled the ruling elites to squeeze the peasants were ancient and deeply rooted, and powerful forces stood ready to crush any protest. Only with the coming of the French Revolution were European peasants, mainly in France, able to improve their position by means of radical mass action.

Technological progress offered another possibility. The great need was for new farming methods that would enable Europeans to produce more and eat more. Uncultivated fields were the heart of the matter. If peasants (and their noble landlords) could replace the idle fallow with crops, they could increase the land under cultivation by 50 percent. So remarkable were the possibilities and the results that historians have often spoken of the progressive elimination of the fallow, which occurred slowly throughout Europe from the mid-seventeenth century on, as an agricultural revolution.

Millet: The Gleaners Poor French peasant women search for grains and stalks that the harvesters (in the background) have missed. The open-field system seen here could still be found in parts of Europe in 1857, when this picture was painted. Millet is known for his great paintings expressing social themes. *(Louvre © Photo R.M.N.)*

This agricultural revolution, which took longer than historians used to believe, was a great milestone in human development. The famous French scholar Marc Bloch, who gave his life in the resistance to the Nazis in World War II, summed it up well: "The history of the conquest of the fallow by new crops, a fresh triumph of man over the earth that is just as moving as the great land clearing of the Middle Ages, [is] one of the noblest stories that can be told."[1]

Because grain crops exhaust the soil and make fallowing necessary, the secret to eliminating the fallow lies in alternating grain with certain nitrogen-storing crops. Such crops not only rejuvenate the soil even better than fallowing but also give more produce. The most important of these land-reviving crops are peas and beans, root crops such as turnips and potatoes, and clovers and grasses. In the eighteenth century, peas and beans were old standbys; turnips, potatoes, and clover were newcomers to the fields. As the eighteenth century went on, the number of crops that were systematically rotated grew. New patterns of organization allowed some farmers to develop increasingly sophisticated patterns of rotation to suit different kinds of soils. For example, farmers in French Flanders near Lille in the late eighteenth century used a ten-year rotation, alternating a number of grain, root, and hay crops in a given field on a ten-year schedule. Continual experimentation led to more scientific farming.

Improvements in farming had multiple effects. The new crops made ideal feed for animals. Because peasants and larger farmers had more fodder, hay, and root crops for the winter months, they could build up their small herds of cattle and sheep. More animals meant more meat and better diets for the people. More animals also meant more manure for fertilizer and therefore more grain for bread and porridge. The vicious cycle in which few animals meant inadequate manure, which meant little grain and less fodder, which led to fewer animals, and so on, could certainly be broken.

Advocates of the new rotations, who included an emerging group of experimental scientists, some government officials, and a few big landowners, believed that new methods were scarcely possible within the traditional framework of open fields and common rights. A farmer who wanted to experiment with new methods would have to get all the landholders in a village to agree to the plan, and advocates of improvement maintained that this would be difficult, if not impossible, given peasant caution and the force of tradition. Therefore, they argued that innovating agriculturalists needed to enclose and consolidate their scattered holdings into compact, fenced-in fields in order to farm more effectively. In doing so, the innovators also needed to enclose their individual shares of the natural pasture, the common. According to this view, a revolution in village life and organization was the necessary price of technical progress.

That price seemed too high to many rural people. Above all, the village poor believed that they were being asked to pay an unfair and disproportionate share of the bill. With land distributed very unequally all across Europe by 1700, large groups of village poor held small, inadequate holdings or very little land at all. Common rights were precious to these poor peasants. The rights to glean and to graze a cow on the common, to gather firewood in the lord's forest and pick berries in the marsh, were vital because they helped poor peasants retain a modicum of independence and status and avoid falling into the growing group of landless, "proletarian" wage workers. Thus when the small landholders and the village poor could effectively oppose the enclosure of the open fields and the common pasture, they did so. Moreover, in many countries they usually found allies among the larger, predominately noble landowners, who were also wary of enclosure because it required large investments and posed risks for them as well. Only powerful social and political pressures could overcome such combined opposition.

The old system of unenclosed open fields and the new system of continuous rotation coexisted in Europe for a very long time. In large parts of central Russia, for example, the old system did not disappear until after the Bolshevik Revolution in 1917. It could also be found in much of France and Germany in the early years of the nineteenth century because peasants there had successfully opposed efforts to introduce the new techniques in the late eighteenth century. Indeed, until the end of the eighteenth century, the promise of the new system was extensively realized only in the Low Countries and in England.

The Leadership of the Low Countries and England

The new methods of the agricultural revolution originated in the Low Countries. The vibrant, dynamic, middle-class society of seventeenth-century republican Holland was the most advanced in Europe in many areas of human endeavor (pages 554–559). In shipbuilding and navigation, in commerce and banking, in drainage and agriculture, the people of the Low Countries, especially the Dutch, provided models the jealous English and French sought to copy or to cripple.

By the middle of the seventeenth century, intensive farming was well established throughout much of the Low Countries. Enclosed fields, continuous rotation, heavy manuring, and a wide variety of crops—all these innovations were present. Agriculture was highly specialized and commercialized. The same skills that grew turnips produced flax to be spun into linen for clothes and tulip bulbs to lighten the heart with their beauty. The fat cattle of Holland, so beloved by Dutch painters, gave the most milk in Europe. Dutch cheeses were already world renowned.

The reasons for early Dutch leadership in farming were basically twofold. In the first place, since the end of the Middle Ages the Low Countries had been one of the most densely populated areas in Europe. Thus in order to feed themselves and provide employment, the Dutch were forced at an early date to seek maximum yields from their land and to increase the cultivated area through the steady draining of marshes and swamps. Even so, they had to import wheat from Poland and eastern Germany.

The pressure of population was connected with the second cause, the growth of towns and cities in the Low Countries. Stimulated by commerce and overseas trade, Amsterdam grew from 30,000 inhabitants to 200,000 in its golden seventeenth century. The growth of urban population provided Dutch peasants with good markets for all they could produce and allowed each region to specialize in what it did best. Thus the Dutch could

Hendrick Sorgh: Vegetable Market, 1662 The wealth and well-being of the industrious, capitalistic Dutch shine forth in this winsome market scene. The market woman's baskets are filled with delicious fresh produce that ordinary citizens can afford—eloquent testimony to the responsive, enterprising character of Dutch agriculture. *(Historisch Museum, Rotterdam)*

develop their potential, and the Low Countries became "the Mecca of foreign agricultural experts who came . . . to see Flemish agriculture with their own eyes, to write about it and to propagate its methods in their home lands."[2]

The English were the best students. Drainage and water control were one subject in which they received instruction. Large parts of seventeenth-century Holland had once been sea and sea marsh, and the efforts of centuries had made the Dutch the world's leaders in the skills of drainage. In the first half of the seventeenth century, Dutch experts made a great contribution to draining the extensive marshes, or fens, of wet and rainy England.

The most famous of these Dutch engineers, Cornelius Vermuyden, directed one large drainage project in Yorkshire and another in Cambridgeshire. In the Cambridge fens, Vermuyden and his Dutch workers eventually reclaimed forty thousand acres, which were then farmed intensively in the Dutch manner. Although all these efforts were disrupted in the turbulent 1640s by the English civil war, Vermuyden and his countrymen largely succeeded. Swampy wilderness was converted into thousands of acres of some of the best land in England. On such new land, where traditions and common rights were not yet firmly established, farmers introduced new crops and new rotations fairly easily.

Dutch experience was also important to Viscount Charles Townsend (1674–1738), one of the pioneers of English agricultural improvement. This lord from the upper reaches of the English aristocracy learned about turnips and clover while serving as English ambassador to Holland. In the 1710s, he was using these crops in the sandy soil of his large estates in Norfolk in eastern England, already one of the most innovative agricultural areas in the country. When Lord Charles retired from politics in 1730 and returned to Norfolk, it was said that he spoke of turnips, turnips, and nothing but turnips. This led some wit to nickname his lordship "Turnip" Townsend. But Townsend had the last laugh. Draining extensively, manuring heavily, and sowing crops in regular rotation without fallowing, the farmers

There was also an unusual degree of economic equality by European standards. Few people were extremely rich, and few were extremely poor. Remarkably, on the eve of the American Revolution, white men and women in the mainland British colonies probably had the highest average income and standard of living in the world.[9] Thus it is clear just how much the colonists benefited from hard work and the mercantile system created by the Navigation Acts.

The Growth of Foreign Trade

Britain and especially England, its most important part, also profited greatly from the mercantile system, as contemporary observers like novelist Daniel Defoe (1659–1731) proudly proclaimed. Above all, the rapidly growing and increasingly wealthy agricultural populations of the mainland colonies provided an expanding market for English manufactured goods. This situation was extremely fortunate, for England in the eighteenth century was gradually losing, or only slowly expanding, its sales to many of its traditional European markets. However, rising demand for manufactured goods in North America as well as in the West Indies, Africa, and Latin America allowed English cottage industry to continue growing and diversifying. Merchant capitalists and manufacturers found new and exciting opportunities for profit and wealth.

Since the late Middle Ages, England had relied very heavily on the sale of woolen cloth in foreign markets. Indeed, as late as 1700, woolen cloth was the only important manufactured good exported from England, and fully 90 percent of it was sold to Europeans. In the course of the eighteenth century, the states of continental Europe were trying to develop their own cottage textile industries in an effort to deal with rural poverty and overpopulation. Like England earlier, these states adopted protectionist, mercantilist policies. They tried by means of tariffs and other measures to exclude competing goods from abroad, whether English woolens or the cheap but beautiful cotton calicoes that the English East India Company brought from India and sold in Europe.

France had already closed its markets to the English in the seventeenth century. In the eighteenth century, German states purchased much less woolen cloth from

A Sugar Mill in Brazil, 1640 European settlers first brought African slaves to the Americas to grow sugar, because Europe's sweet tooth promised quick wealth to planters who succeeded. The slaves' work was extremely demanding and disagreeable, long days under a brutal sun, with dangerous round-the-clock pressing and boiling when the crop came in. *(Musées Royaux des Beaux-Arts de Belgique)*

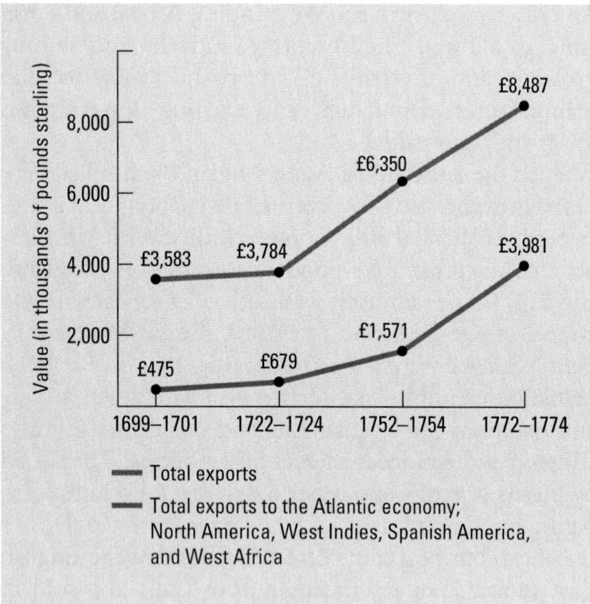

FIGURE 19.3 Exports of English Manufactured Goods, 1700–1774 While trade between England and Europe stagnated after 1700, English exports to Africa and the Americas boomed and greatly stimulated English economic development. *(Source: R. Davis, "English Foreign Trade, 1700–1774,"* Economic History Review, *2d ser., 15 (1962): 302–303.)*

England and encouraged cottage production of coarse, cheap linens, which became a feared competitor in all of central and southern Europe. By 1773 England was selling only about two-thirds as much woolen cloth to northern and western Europe as it had in 1700. Stagnation or decline in many markets on the continent meant that the English economy badly needed new markets and new products in order to develop and prosper.

Protected colonial markets came to the rescue, more than offsetting stagnating trade with Europe. The markets of the Atlantic economy led the way (Figure 19.3). English exports of manufactured goods to continental Europe increased very modestly, from roughly £2.9 million in 1700 to only £3.3 million in 1773. Meanwhile, sales of manufactured products to the Atlantic economy—primarily the mainland colonies of North America and the West Indian sugar islands, with an important assist from West Africa and Latin America—soared from £500,000 to £4.0 million. Sales to other colonies—Ireland and India—also rose substantially in the eighteenth century.

English exports became much more balanced and diversified. To America and Africa went large quantities of metal items—axes to frontier settlers, firearms, chains to slaveowners. There were also clocks and coaches, buttons and saddles, china and furniture, musical instruments and scientific equipment, and a host of other things. By 1750 half the nails made in England were going to the colonies. Foreign trade became the bread and butter of some industries.

Thus the mercantilist system formed in the seventeenth century to attack the Dutch and to win power and profit for England achieved remarkable success in the eighteenth century. The English concentrated in their hands much of the trade flowing through the growing Atlantic economy. Of great importance, the pressure of demand from three continents on the cottage industry of one medium-size country heightened the efforts of English merchant capitalists to find new and improved ways to produce more goods. By the 1770s England stood on the threshold of the epoch-making industrial changes that will be described in Chapter 22.

Revival in Colonial Latin America

When the last Spanish Habsburg, the feeble-minded Charles II, died in 1700 (see page 545), Spain's vast empire lay ready for dismemberment. Yet in one of those striking reversals with which history is replete, Spain revived. The empire held together and even prospered, while a European-oriented landowning aristocracy enhanced its position in colonial society.

Spain recovered in part because of better leadership. Louis XIV's grandson, who took the throne as Philip V (r. 1700–1746), brought new men and fresh ideas with him from France and rallied the Spanish people to his Bourbon dynasty in the long War of the Spanish Succession. When peace was restored, a series of reforming ministers reasserted royal authority, overhauling state finances and strengthening defense.

Revitalization in Madrid had positive results in the colonies. They succeeded in defending themselves from numerous British attacks and even increased in size. Spain received Louisiana from France in 1763, and missionaries and ranchers extended Spanish influence all the way to northern California.

Political success was matched by economic improvement. After declining markedly in the seventeenth century, silver mining recovered greatly, and in 1800 Spanish America accounted for half of world silver production. Silver mining also encouraged food production for large mining camps and gave the *Creoles*—people of Spanish blood born in America—the means to purchase more and more European luxuries and manufactured goods. A class of wealthy Creole mer-

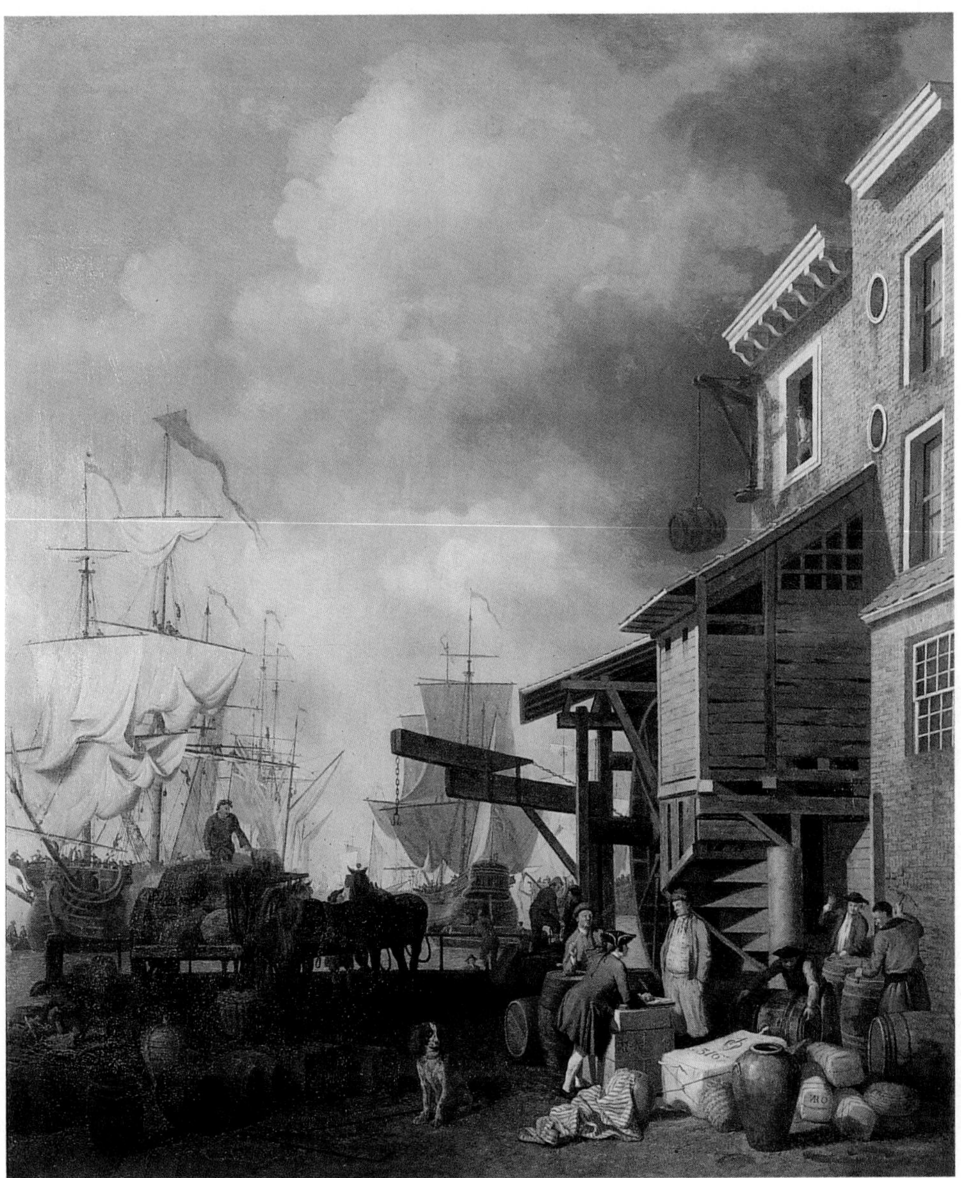

The East India Dock, London This painting by Samuel Scott captures the spirit and excitement of British maritime expansion. Great sailing ships line the quay, bringing profit and romance from far-off India. London grew in population from 350,000 in 1650 to 900,000 in 1800, when it was twice as big as Paris, its nearest rival. *(Courtesy of Board of Trustees of the Victoria & Albert Museum)*

chants arose to handle this flourishing trade, which often relied on smuggled goods from Great Britain.

The Creole elite came to rival the top government officials dispatched from Spain to govern the colonies. Creole estate owners controlled much of the land, and they strove to become a genuine European aristocracy. Estate owners believed that work in the fields was the proper occupation of an impoverished peasantry. The defenseless Indians suited their needs. As the indigenous population recovered in numbers, slavery and periodic forced labor gave way to widespread debt peonage from 1600 on. Under this system, a planter or rancher would keep the estate's Christianized, increasingly Hispanicized Indians in perpetual debt bondage by periodically advancing food, shelter, and a little money. Debt peonage was a form of serfdom.

The large middle group in Spanish colonies consisted of racially mixed *mestizos,* the offspring of Spanish men and Indian women. The most talented mestizos realistically aspired to join the Creoles, for enough wealth and power could make one considered white. Thus by the end of the colonial era, roughly 20 percent of the population was classified as white and about 30 percent as mestizo. Pure-blooded Indians accounted for most of the remainder, but some black slaves were found in every part of Spanish America. Great numbers of blacks went in chains to work the enormous sugar plantations of Portuguese Brazil, and about half the Brazilian population in the early nineteenth century was of African origin. The people of Brazil intermingled sexually and culturally, and the population grew to include every color in the racial rainbow. Thus in the eighteenth century, Spanish and Portuguese colonies developed a growing commerce in silver, sugar, and slaves as well as in manufactured goods for a Europeanized elite. South America occupied an important place in the expanding Atlantic economy.

Adam Smith and Economic Liberalism

Although mercantilist policies strengthened both the Spanish and British colonial empires in the eighteenth

Forming the Mexican People This painting by an unknown eighteenth-century artist presents a naive but sympathetic view of interracial unions and marriages in colonial Mexico. On the left, the union of a Spanish man and a native American woman has produced a racially mixed mestizo. The handsome group on the right features a mestizo woman and a Spaniard with their little daughter. *(Private Collection/Banco Nacional de Mexico)*

century, a strong reaction against mercantilism ultimately set in. Creole merchants chafed at regulations imposed from Madrid. Small English merchants complained loudly about the injustice of handing over exclusive trading rights to great trading combines such as the East India Company. Wanting a bigger position in overseas commerce, independent merchants in many countries began campaigning against "monopolies" and calling for "free trade."

The general idea of freedom of enterprise in foreign trade was persuasively developed by Scottish professor of philosophy Adam Smith (1723–1790). Smith, whose *Inquiry into the Nature and Causes of the Wealth of Nations* (1776) established the basis for modern economics, was highly critical of eighteenth-century mercantilism. Mercantilism, he said, meant a combination of stifling government regulations and unfair privileges for state-approved monopolies and government favorites. Far preferable was free competition, which would best protect consumers from price gouging and give all citizens a fair and equal right to do what they did best. In keeping with the "system of natural liberty" that he advocated, Smith argued that government should limit itself to "only three duties." It should provide a defense against foreign invasion, maintain civil order with courts and police protection, and sponsor certain indispensable public works and institutions that could never adequately profit private investors.

Often lampooned in the nineteenth and twentieth centuries as a mouthpiece for business interests, Smith was one of the Enlightenment's most original and characteristic thinkers. He relied on the power of reason to unlock the secrets of the secular world, and he believed that he spoke for truth, not for special interests. Thus unlike many disgruntled merchant capitalists, Smith applauded the modest rise in real wages of British workers in the eighteenth century and went on to say, "No society can surely be flourishing and happy, of which the far greater part of the members are poor and miserable." Discussing bargaining between employers and workers over wages, Smith was brutally realistic:

We rarely hear, it has been said, of the combinations of masters; though frequently of those of workmen. But whoever imagines, upon this account, that masters rarely combine, is as ignorant of the world as of the subject. Masters are always and everywhere in a sort of tacit, but constant and uniform combination, not to raise the wages of labour above their actual rate. . . . Masters too sometimes enter into particular combinations to sink the wages even below this rate. These are always conducted with the utmost silence and secrecy, till the moment of execution.[10]

Adam Smith Appointed professor at Glasgow University at age twenty-seven, Smith established an international reputation with his first book. He then became the well-paid tutor of a rich young lord and traveled widely before publishing *The Wealth of Nations,* the point of departure for modern economics. *(Special Collections/Glasgow University Library)*

Believing, then, that employers as well as workers and consumers were motivated primarily by narrow self-interest, Smith did not call for more laws and more police power to force people to behave properly toward each other in economic affairs. Instead, he made the pursuit of self-interest in a competitive market the source of an underlying and previously unrecognized harmony, a harmony that would result in gradual progress.

According to Smith:

[Every individual generally] neither intends to promote the public interest, nor knows how much he is promoting it. . . .

He is in this case, as in many cases, led by an invisible hand to promote an end which was no part of his intention. Nor is it always the worse for society that it was not part of it. I have never known much good done by those who affected to trade for the public good.[11]

The "invisible hand" of free competition for one and for all disciplined the greed of selfish individuals and provided the most effective means of increasing the wealth of both rich and poor.

Smith's provocative work had a great international impact. Going through eight editions in English and translated into several languages within twenty years, it quickly emerged as the classic argument for economic liberalism and unregulated capitalism.

SUMMARY

While some European intellectual elites and parts of the educated public were developing a new view of the world in the eighteenth century, Europe as a whole was experiencing a gradual but far-reaching expansion. As agriculture began showing signs of modest improvement across the continent, first the Low Countries and then England launched changes that gradually revolutionized agriculture. Plague disappeared, and the populations of all countries grew significantly, thereby encouraging the growth of wage labor, cottage industry, and merchant capitalism.

Europeans also continued their overseas expansion, fighting for empire and profit and, in particular, consolidating their hold on the Americas. A revived Spain and its Latin American colonies participated fully in this expansion. As in agriculture and cottage industry, however, England and its empire proved most successful. The English concentrated much of the growing Atlantic trade in their hands, a development that challenged and enriched English industry and intensified interest in new methods of production and in an emerging economic liberalism. Thus by the 1770s, England was approaching an economic breakthrough fully as significant as the great political upheaval destined to develop shortly in neighboring France.

NOTES

1. M. Bloch, *Les caractères originaux de l'histoire rurale française,* vol. 1 (Paris: Librarie Armand Colin, 1960), pp. 244–245.
2. B. H. Slicher van Bath, *The Agrarian History of Western Europe, A.D. 500–1850* (New York: St. Martin's Press, 1963), p. 240.
3. E. P. Thompson, *The Making of the English Working Class* (New York: Vintage Books, 1966), p. 218.
4. Quoted in E. E. Rich and C. H. Wilson, eds., *The Cambridge Economic History of Europe,* vol. 4 (Cambridge: Cambridge University Press, 1967), p. 85.
5. Quoted in I. Pinchbeck, *Women Workers and the Industrial Revolution, 1750–1850* (New York: F. S. Crofts, 1930), p. 113.
6. Quoted in S. Chapman, *The Lancashire Cotton Industry* (Manchester, England: Manchester University Press, 1903), p. 13.
7. Quoted in P. Mantoux, *The Industrial Revolution in the Eighteenth Century* (New York: Harper & Row, 1961), p. 75.
8. Quoted in C. Wilson, *England's Apprenticeship, 1603–1763* (London: Longmans, Green, 1965), p. 169.
9. G. Taylor, "America's Growth Before 1840," *Journal of Economic History* 24 (December 1970): 427–444.
10. R. Heilbroner, ed., *The Essential Adam Smith* (New York: W. W. Norton, 1986), p. 196.
11. Ibid., p. 265.

SUGGESTED READING

The works by Slicher van Bath and Bloch listed in the Notes are wide-ranging general introductions to the gradual transformation of European agriculture. Bloch's classic has been translated as *French Rural History* (1966). J. Blum, *The End of the Old Order in Rural Europe* (1978), is an impressive comparative study. J. de Vries, *The Dutch Rural Economy in the Golden Age, 1500–1700* (1974), skillfully examines the causes of early Dutch leadership in farming. M. Overton, *Agricultural Revolution in England* (1996), and A. Kussmaul, *A General View of the Rural Economy of England, 1538–1840* (1989), chart the path of agricultural progress in England. J. Neeson, *Commoners: Common Right, Enclosure and Social Change, 1700–1820* (1993), stresses popular resistance to enclosure and the losses it brought for the common people. J. Gargliardo, *From Pariah to Patriot: The Changing Image of the German Peasant, 1770–1840* (1969), examines the development of reforms designed to improve the lot of the peasantry in Germany. R. Forster, *The Nobility of Toulouse in the Eighteenth Century* (1960), and A. Goodwin, ed., *The European Nobility in the Eighteenth Century* (1967), are excellent studies on aristocrats in different countries. E. Le Roy Ladurie, *The Peasants of Languedoc* (1976), a brilliant and challenging study of rural life in southern France for several centuries, complements J. Goody et al., eds., *Family and Inheritance: Rural Society in Western Europe, 1200–1800*

(1976). J. Brewer and R. Porter, eds., *Consumption and the World of Goods* (1993), is a fascinating collection of studies and reflects the growing historical interest in consumption as well as production. O. Hufton deals vividly and sympathetically with rural migration, work, women, and much more in *The Poor in Eighteenth-Century France* (1974).

S. Ogilvie and M. Cerman, eds., *European Proto-industrialization* (1996), is a stimulating, up-to-date survey of several countries by leading scholars. An ambitious re-examination with extensive bibliographical references, M. Gutman, *Toward the Modern Economy: Early Modern Industry in Europe, 1500–1800* (1988), highlights the creativity of rural industry, as does J. Goodman and K. Honeyman, *Gainful Pursuits: The Making of Industrial Europe, 1600–1914* (1988). D. Landes, *The Unbound Prometheus* (1969), places more emphasis on the growing limitations of cottage production. G. Gullickson, *Spinners and Weavers of Auffay: Rural Industry and the Sexual Division of Labor in a French Village, 1750–1850* (1986), and M. Sonenscher, *The Hatters of Eighteenth-Century France* (1987), are valuable studies.

Two excellent multivolume series, one edited by Rich and Wilson and mentioned in the Notes, and the other edited by C. Cipolla, *The Fontana Economic History of Europe,* cover the sweep of economic developments from the Middle Ages to the present and have extensive bibliographies. So does R. Cameron, *A Concise Economic History of the World* (1989), which deals mainly with Europe. F. Braudel, *Civilization and Capitalism, Fifteenth–Eighteenth Centuries* (1981, 1984), is a monumental and highly recommended three-volume synthesis. In the area of trade and colonial competition, V. Barbour, *Capitalism in Amsterdam* (1963), and C. R. Boxer, *The Dutch Seaborne Empire* (1970), are very interesting on Holland. R. Herr, *The Eighteenth-Century Revolution in Spain* (1958), studies economic policy and colonial revival. J. Brewer, *The Sinews of Power: War, Money, and the English State, 1688–1783* (1989), looks at English victories, whereas G. Parker, *The Military Revolution: Military Technology in the Rise of the West* (1988), a masterful, beautifully illustrated work, explores the roots of European power and conquest. J. Black, *Cambridge Illustrated Atlas of Warfare: Renaissance to Revolution, 1492–1792* (1996), surveys war in a global perspective with dramatic pictures and outstanding maps. D. K. Fieldhouse, *The Colonial Empires* (1971), and R. Davies, *The Rise of Atlantic Economies* (1973), are all valuable works on the struggle for empire. W. J. Eccles, *France in America,* rev. ed. (1990), is outstanding and supersedes F. Parkman, *France and England in North America,* a multivolume classic and a famous example of nineteenth-century romantic history.

LISTENING TO THE PAST

An Insight into Slavery

Born in Benin, West Africa, Olaudah Equiano (1745?–1797) was captured when he was about eleven and sold into slavery. He soon found himself on a slave ship bound for the West Indies. He went on to learn English and served a lieutenant in the British navy and a Quaker merchant. Granted his freedom in his twenties, he became a clerk in Britain's growing oceanic trade. Equiano adopted Christianity. His own experiences of slavery combined with his religious beliefs to propel him into the British abolitionist movement. He traveled the British Isles lecturing against slavery and wrote his remarkable memoir, The Interesting Narrative of Olaudah Equiano. *First published in 1789, the book saw eight editions. This selection details Equiano's capture and experiences in the brutal Middle Passage.*

Generally when the grown people in the neighborhood were gone far in the fields to labor, the children assembled together in some of the neighbors' premises to play, and commonly some of us used to get up a tree to look out for any assailant or kidnapper that might come upon us, for they sometimes took those opportunities of our parents' absence to attack and carry off as many as they could seize. . . . One day, when all our people were gone out to their work as usual and only I and my dear sister were left to mind the house, two men and a woman got over our walls, and in a moment seized us both, and without giving us time to cry out or make resistance they stopped our mouths and ran off with us into the nearest wood. . . .

For a long time we had kept to the woods, but at last we came into a road which I believed I knew. I had now some hopes of being delivered, for we had advanced but a little way before I discovered some people at a distance, on which I began to cry out for their assistance: but my cries had no other effect than to make them tie me faster and stop my mouth, and then they put me into a large sack. They also stopped my sister's mouth and tied her hands, and in this manner we proceeded till we were out of the sight of these people. . . . The next day proved a day of greater sorrow than I had yet experienced, for my sister and I were then separated while we lay clasped in each other's arms. It was in vain that we besought them not to part us; she was torn from me and immediately carried away, while I was left in a state of distraction not to be described. I cried and grieved continually, and for several days I did not eat anything but what they forced into my mouth. At length, after many days' traveling, during which I had often changed masters, I got into the hands of a chieftain in a very pleasant country. This man had two wives and some children, and they all used me extremely well and did all they could to comfort me, particularly the first wife, who was something like my mother. . . .

I did not long remain after my sister [departed]. I was again sold and carried through a number of places till, after traveling a considerable time, I came to a town called Tinmah in the most beautiful country I had yet seen in Africa. . . . I was sold here . . . by a merchant who lived and brought me there. I had been about two or three days at his house when a wealthy widow, a neighbor of his, came there one evening, and brought with her an only son, a young gentleman about my own age and size. Here they saw me; and, having taken a fancy to me, I was bought of the merchant, and went home with them. . . . The next day I was washed and perfumed, and when meal-time came I was led into the presence of my mistress, and ate and drank before her with her son. This filled me with astonishment; and I could scarce help expressing my surprise that the young gentleman should suffer me, who was bound, to eat with him who was free; and not only so, but that he would not at any time either eat or drink till I had taken first, because I was the eldest, which was agreeable to our custom. Indeed everything here, and all their treatment of me, made me forget that I was a slave. . . . In this resemblance to my former happy state I passed about two months; and I now began to think I was to be adopted into the family, and was beginning to be reconciled to my situation, and to forget by degrees my misfortunes, when all at once the delusion vanished; for without the least previous knowledge, one morning early, while my dear master and companion was still asleep, I was wakened out of my reverie to fresh sorrow, and hurried away. . . .

Thus I continued to travel, sometimes by land, sometimes by water, through different countries and various nations, till at the end of six or seven months after I had been kidnapped I arrived at the sea coast.

The first object which saluted my eyes when I arrived on the coast was the sea, and a slave ship which was then riding at anchor and waiting for its cargo. These filled me with astonishment, which was soon converted into terror when I was carried on board. . . .

I was soon put down under the decks, and there I received such a salutation in my nostrils as I had never experienced in my life: so that with the loathsomeness of the stench and crying together, I became so sick and low that I was not able to eat, nor had I the least desire to taste anything. I now wished for the last friend, death, to relieve me; but soon, to my grief, two of the white men offered me eatables, and on my refusing to eat, one of them held me fast by the hands and laid me across I think the windlass, and tied my feet while the other flogged me severely. . . . The white people looked and acted, as I thought, in so savage a manner; for I had never seen among my people such instances of brutal cruelty, and this not only shown towards us blacks but also to some of the whites themselves. . . .

One day, when we had a smooth sea and moderate wind, two of my wearied countrymen who were chained together (I was near them at the time), preferring death to such a life of misery, somehow made through the nettings and jumped into the sea: immediately another quite dejected fellow, who on account of his illness was suffered to be out of irons, also followed their example; and I believe many more would very soon have done the same if they had not been prevented by the ship's crew. . . .

At last we came in sight of the island of Barbados, at which the whites on board gave a great shout and made many signs of joy to us. We did not know what to think of this, but as the vessel drew nearer we plainly saw the harbor and other ships of different kinds and sizes, and we soon anchored amongst them off Bridgetown. . . .

We were not many days in the merchant's custody before we were sold after their usual manner, which is this: On a signal given, (as the beat of a drum) the buyers rush at once into the yard where the slaves are confined, and make choice of that parcel they like best. . . . In this manner, without scruple, are relations and friends separated, most of them never to see each other again. I remember in the vessel in which I was brought over, in the men's apartment there were several brothers who, in the sale, were sold in different lots; and it was very moving on this occasion to see and hear their cries at parting. O, ye nominal Christians! might not an African ask you, learned you this from your God who says unto you, Do unto all men as you would men should do unto you?

✣ Olaudah Equiano, in an engraving from his autobiography, *The Interesting Narrative of . . . Olaudah Equiano* (London, 1789). *(National Portrait Gallery, Smithsonian Institution)*

Questions for Analysis

1. How did Equiano view the Africans who captured people for slavery and the whites who bought and sold them?
2. How did Equiano and others respond to their enslavement?
3. How do Equiano's religious beliefs show through in the passages reprinted here?

Source: Paul Edwards, ed. and trans., *Equiano's Travels* (Oxford: Heinemann Educational Books, 1967), pp. 25–42.

CHAPTER

20 The Changing Life of the People

Market in Piazza San Carlo, Turin (detail), by Michele Graneri (1736–1778). *(Museo Civico, Turin/Madeline Grimaldi)*

The discussion of agriculture and industry in the last chapter showed the common people at work, straining to make ends meet within the larger context of population growth, gradual economic expansion, and ferocious political competition. Yet the world of work was only part of life. That life was embedded in a rich complex of family organization, community practices, everyday experiences, and collective attitudes.

In recent years, historians have intensively studied all these aspects of popular life. The challenge has been formidable because regional variations abounded and the common people left few written records. Yet despite many ongoing debates among specialists, imaginative research has resulted in major findings and much greater knowledge. It is now possible to follow the common people beyond the world of work and ask, "What about the rest of the human experience?"

- What changes occurred in marriage and the family in the course of the eighteenth century?
- What was life like for children, and how did attitudes toward children evolve?
- What did people eat, and how did changes in diet and medical care affect people's lives?
- What were the patterns of popular religion and culture? How did these patterns come into contact—and conflict—with the critical world-view of the educated public and thereby widen the cultural divide between rich and poor in the era of the Enlightenment?

Such questions help us better understand how the peasant masses and urban poor really lived in western Europe before the age of revolution opened at the end of the eighteenth century. These questions will be the focus of this chapter.

Marriage and the Family

The basic unit of social organization is the family. It is within the structure of the family that human beings love, mate, and reproduce themselves. It is primarily the family that teaches the child, imparting values and customs that condition an individual's behavior for a lifetime. The family is also an institution woven into the web of history. It evolves and changes, assuming different forms in different times and places.

Extended and Nuclear Families

In many traditional Asian and African societies, the typical family has often been an extended family. A newly married couple, instead of establishing a home, will go to live with either the bride's or the groom's family. The wife and husband raise their children while living under the same roof with their own brothers and sisters, who may also be married. The family is a big, three- or four-generation clan, headed by a patriarch or perhaps a matriarch, and encompassing everyone from the youngest infant to the oldest grandparent.

Extended families, it is often said, provide security for adults and children in traditional agrarian peasant economies. Everyone has a place within the extended family, from cradle to grave. Sociologists frequently assume that the extended family gives way to the conjugal, or nuclear, family with the advent of industrialization and urbanization. In a society characterized by nuclear families, couples establish their own households when they marry, and they raise their children apart from their parents. A similar process has indeed been occurring in much of Asia and Africa today. And since Europe was once agrarian and preindustrial, it has often been believed that the extended family must also have prevailed in Europe before being destroyed by the Industrial Revolution.

In recent years, innovative historians, analyzing previously neglected parish registers of births, deaths, and marriages, have greatly increased knowledge about the details of family life for the great majority of people before the nineteenth century. It seems clear that the extended, three-generation family was a great rarity in western and central Europe by 1700. Indeed, the extended family may never have been common in Europe, although it is hard to know about the early Middle Ages because fewer records survive. When young European couples married, they normally established their own households and lived apart from their parents. When a three-generation household came into existence, it was usually a parent who moved in with a married child rather than a newly married couple moving in with either set of parents.

Most people did not marry young in the seventeenth and early eighteenth centuries. The average person, who was neither rich nor aristocratic, married surprisingly late, many years after reaching adulthood and many more after beginning to work. In one well-studied, apparently typical English village, both men and women married for the first time at an average age of twenty-seven or older in the seventeenth and eighteenth centuries. A similar pattern existed in early-eighteenth-century France. Moreover, a substantial portion of men and women never married at all.

The custom of late marriage combined with a nuclear-family household was a distinctive characteristic of European society. It seems likely that the aggressive dynamism and creativity that have characterized European society were due in large part to the pattern of marriage and family. This pattern fostered and required self-reliance and independence. In preindustrial western Europe in the sixteenth through eighteenth centuries, marriage normally joined a mature man and a mature woman—two adults who had already experienced a great deal of life and could transmit self-reliance and real skills to the next generation.

Chardin: The Kitchen Maid Lost in thought as she pauses in her work, perhaps this young servant is thinking about her village and loved ones there. Chardin was one of eighteenth-century France's greatest painters, and his scenes from everyday life provide valuable evidence for the historian. *(National Gallery of Art, Washington, D.C. Samuel H. Kress Collection)*

Why was marriage delayed? The main reason was that couples normally could not marry until they could support themselves economically. The land was still the main source of income. The peasant son often needed to wait until his father's death to inherit the family farm and marry his sweetheart. Similarly, the peasant daughter and her family needed to accumulate a small dowry to help her fiancé buy land or build a house.

There were also laws and community controls to temper impetuous love and physical attraction. In some areas, couples needed the legal permission or tacit approval of the local lord or landowner in order to marry. In Austria and Germany, there were legal restrictions on marriage, and well into the nineteenth century poor couples had particular difficulty securing the approval of local officials. These officials believed that freedom to marry for the lower classes would mean more landless paupers, more abandoned children, and more money for welfare. Village elders often agreed. Thus prudence, law, and custom combined to postpone the march to the altar. This pattern helped society maintain some kind of balance between the number of people and the available economic resources.

Work Away from Home

Many young people worked within their families until they could start their own households. Boys plowed and wove; girls spun and tended the cows. Many others left home temporarily to work elsewhere. In the towns, a lad might be apprenticed to a craftsman for seven or fourteen years to learn a trade. During that time, he would not be permitted to marry. In most trades, he earned little and worked hard, but if he was lucky, he might eventually be admitted to a guild and establish his economic independence. More often, the young man would drift from one tough job to another: hired hand for a small farmer, wage laborer on a new road, carrier of water in a nearby town. He was always subject to economic fluctuations, and unemployment was a constant threat.

Girls also temporarily left their families to work, at an early age and in large numbers. The range of opportunities open to them was more limited, however. Service in another family's household was by far the most common job, and even middle-class families often sent their daughters into service. Thus a few years away from home as a servant were often a normal part of growing up.

The legions of young servant girls worked hard but had little real independence. Sometimes the employer paid the girl's wages directly to her parents. Constantly under the eye of her mistress, the servant girl found her tasks were many—cleaning, shopping, cooking, caring for the baby. Often the work was endless, for there were no laws to limit exploitation. Rarely were girls so brutalized that they snapped under the strain of such treatment like Varka—the Russian servant girl in Chekhov's chilling story "Sleepy"—who, driven beyond exhaustion, finally quieted her mistress's screaming child by strangling it in its cradle. But court records are full of complaints by servant girls of physical mistreatment by their mistresses. There were many others like the fifteen-year-old English girl in the early eighteenth century who told the judge that her mistress had not only called her "very opprobrious names, as Bitch, Whore and the like," but also "beat her without provocation and beyond measure."[1]

There was also the pressure of seducers and sexual attack. In theory, domestic service offered protection and security within a new family for a young girl leaving home. But in practice, she was often the easy prey of a lecherous master or his sons or friends. Indeed, "the evidence suggests that in all European countries, from Britain to Russia, the upper classes felt perfectly free to exploit sexually girls who were at their mercy."[2] If the girl became pregnant, she was quickly fired and thrown out in disgrace to make her own way. Prostitution and petty thievery were often the harsh consequences of unwanted pregnancy. "What are we?" exclaimed a bitter Parisian prostitute. "Most of us are unfortunate women, without origins, without education, servants and maids for the most part."[3]

Premarital Sex and Community Controls

Did the plight of some former servant girls mean that late marriage in preindustrial Europe went hand in hand with premarital sex and many illegitimate children? For most of western and central Europe until at least 1750, the answer seems to have been no. English parish registers seldom listed more than one bastard out of every twenty children baptized. Some French parishes in the seventeenth century had extraordinarily low rates of illegitimacy, with less than 1 percent of the babies born out of wedlock. Illegitimate babies were apparently a rarity, at least as far as the official church records are concerned.

At the same time, premarital sex was clearly commonplace. In one well-studied English village, 33 percent of all first children were conceived before the couple was married, and many were born within three months of the marriage ceremony. In the mid-eighteenth century, 20 percent of the women in the French village of Auffay, in Normandy, were pregnant when they got married, although only 2 percent of all babies in the village were born to unwed mothers. No doubt many of these French and English couples were already betrothed, or at least "going steady," before they entered into an intimate relationship, and pregnancy simply set the marriage date once and for all.

But the combination of very low rates of illegitimate birth with large numbers of pregnant brides also reflected the powerful social controls of the traditional village, particularly the open-field village, with its pattern of cooperation and common action. That spirit of common action was rapidly mobilized by the prospect of an unwed (and therefore poor) mother with an illegitimate child, a condition inevitably viewed as a grave threat to the economic, social, and moral stability of the closely knit community. Irate parents and anxious village elders, indignant priests and authoritative landlords, all combined to pressure any young people who wavered about marriage in the face of unexpected pregnancy. These controls meant in the countryside that premarital sex was not entered into lightly and that it was generally limited to those contemplating marriage.

The concerns of the village and the family weighed heavily on most aspects of a couple's life, both before and after marriage. One leading authority describes the traditional French peasant household in these terms:

> *The individuality of the couple, or rather, its tendency towards individuality, was crushed by the family institutions, and also by the social pressures exercised by the village community as a whole, and by the neighborhood in particular. Anything that might endanger the [couple's] household might also prejudice the village community, and the community reacted, occasionally violently, to punish those who contravened the rules. The intrusion of the community into every aspect of family life was very noticeable.*[4]

Whereas uninvolved individuals today are inclined to ignore the domestic disputes and marital scandals of others, the people in peasant communities gave such affairs the loudest and most unfavorable publicity, either at the time of the event or during the Carnival season (see page 683). Relying on degrading public rituals, the young men of the village would typically gang up on the person they wanted to punish and force him or her to sit astride a donkey facing backward and holding up the donkey's tail. They would parade the overly brutal spouse-beating husband (or wife), or the couple whose adultery had been discovered, all around the village, loudly proclaiming the offender's misdeeds with scorn and ridicule. The donkey ride and similar colorful humiliations ranging from rotten vegetables splattered on the doorstep to obscene and insulting midnight serenades were common punishments throughout much of Europe. They epitomized the community's far-reaching effort to police personal behavior and maintain community standards.

Community controls did not extend to family planning, however. Once a couple married, it generally had several children. Birth control within marriage was not unknown in western and central Europe before the nineteenth century, but it was primitive and quite undependable. The most common method was *coitus interruptus*—withdrawal by the male before ejaculation. The French, who were apparently early leaders in contraception, were using this method extensively to limit family size by the end of the eighteenth century.

Mechanical and other means of contraception were also used in the eighteenth century, but mainly by certain sectors of the urban population. The "fast set" of London used the "sheath" regularly, although primarily to protect against venereal disease, not pregnancy. Prostitutes used various contraceptive techniques to prevent pregnancy, and such information was available in large towns if a person really sought it.

New Patterns of Marriage and Illegitimacy

In the second half of the eighteenth century, the pattern of late marriage and few births out of wedlock began to change and break down. The number of illegitimate births soared between about 1750 and 1850 as much of Europe experienced an "illegitimacy explosion." In Frankfurt, Germany, for example, illegitimate births rose steadily from about 2 percent of all births in the early 1700s to a peak of about 25 percent around 1850. In Bordeaux, France, 36 percent of all babies were being born out of wedlock by 1840. Small towns and villages experienced less startling climbs, but increases from a range of 1 to 3 percent initially to 10 to 20 percent between 1750 and 1850 were commonplace. Fewer young women were abstaining from premarital intercourse, and, more important, fewer young men were marrying the women they got pregnant. Thus a profound sexual and cultural transformation took place.

Historians are still debating the meaning of this transformation, but two interrelated ideas dominate most interpretations. First, the growth of cottage industry created new opportunities for earning a living, opportunities not tied to the land. Cottage industry tended to develop in areas where the land was poor in quality and divided into small, inadequate holdings. As cottage industry took hold in such areas, population grew rapidly because young people attained greater independence and did not have to wait to inherit a farm in order to get married and have children. A scrap of ground for a garden and a cottage for the loom and spinning wheel could be quite enough for a modest living. A contemporary observer of an area of rapidly growing cottage industry in Switzerland at the end of the eighteenth century described these changes:

The increased and sure income offered by the combination of cottage manufacture with farming hastened and multiplied marriages and encouraged the division of landholdings, while enhancing their value; it also promoted the expansion and embellishment of houses and villages.[5]

Cottage workers married not only at an earlier age but also for different reasons. Nothing could be so businesslike, so calculating, as a peasant marriage that was often dictated by the needs of the couple's families. After 1750, however, courtship became more extensive and freer as cottage industry grew. It was easier to yield to the attraction of the opposite sex and fall in love. Members of the older generation were often highly critical of the lack of responsibility they saw in the early marriages of the poor, the union of "people with only two spinning wheels and not even a bed." But such scolding did not stop cottage workers from marrying for love rather than for economic considerations as they blazed a path that factory workers would follow in the nineteenth century.

Second, the needs of a growing population sent many young villagers to towns and cities in search of temporary or permanent employment. Mobility in turn encouraged new sexual and marital relationships, which were less subject to village tradition and resulted in more illegitimate births. Yet most young women in urban areas found work only as servants or textile workers. Poorly paid, insecure, and with little possibility of truly independent, "liberated" lives, they looked mainly to marriage and family life as an escape from hard work and as the foundation of a satisfying life.

Promises of marriage from a man of the working girl's own class led naturally enough to sex, which was widely viewed as part of serious courtship. In one medium-size French city in 1787 to 1788, the great majority of unwed mothers stated that sexual intimacy had followed promises of marriage. Their sisters in rural Normandy reported again and again that they had been "seduced in anticipation of marriage."[6] Many soldiers, day laborers, and male servants were no doubt sincere in their proposals. But their lives were also insecure, and many hesitated to take on the heavy economic burdens of wife and child.

David Allan: The Penny Wedding (1795) The spirited merry-making of a peasant wedding was a popular theme of European artists. In rural Scotland "penny weddings" like this one were common: guests paid a fee for the food and fun; the money left over went to the newlyweds to help them get started. Music, dancing, feasting, and drinking characterized these community parties, which led the Presbyterian church to oppose them and hasten their decline. *(National Galleries of Scotland)*

Thus it became increasingly difficult for a woman to convert pregnancy into marriage, and in a growing number of cases the intended marriage did not take place. The romantic, yet practical dreams and aspirations of many young workingmen and workingwomen in towns and villages were frustrated by low wages, inequality, and changing economic and social conditions. Old patterns of marriage and family were breaking down among the common people. Only in the late nineteenth century would more stable patterns reappear.

 CHILDREN AND EDUCATION

In the traditional framework of agrarian Europe, women married late but then began bearing children rapidly. If a woman married before she was thirty, and if both she and her husband lived to forty-five, the chances were roughly one in two that she would give birth to six or more children. The newborn child entered a dangerous world. Infant mortality was high. One in five was sure to die, and one in three was quite likely to in the poorer areas. Newborn children were very likely to catch mysterious infectious diseases of the chest and stomach, and many babies died of dehydration brought about by a bad bout of ordinary diarrhea. Even in rich families, little could be done for an ailing child. Childhood itself was dangerous because of adult indifference, neglect, and even abuse.

Schools and formal education played only a modest role in the lives of ordinary children, and many boys and many more girls never learned to read. Nevertheless, basic literacy was growing among the popular classes, whose reading habits have been intensively studied in recent years. Attempting to peer into the collective attitudes of the common people and compare them with those of the book-hungry cultivated public, historians have produced some fascinating insights.

Child Care and Nursing

Women of the lower classes generally breast-fed their infants and for a much longer period than is customary today. Breast-feeding decreases the likelihood of pregnancy for the average woman by delaying the resumption of ovulation. By nursing their babies, women limited their fertility and spaced their children—from two to three years apart. If a newborn baby died, nursing stopped and a new life could be created. Nursing also saved lives: the breast-fed infant received precious immunity-producing substances with its mother's milk and was more likely to survive than when it was given any artificial food. In many areas of Russia, where the common practice was to give a new child a sweetened (and germ-laden) rag to suck on for its subsistence, half the babies did not survive the first year.

In contrast to the laboring poor, the women of the aristocracy and upper middle class seldom nursed their own children. The upper-class woman felt that breast-feeding was crude, common, and undignified. Instead, she hired a wet nurse to suckle her child. The urban mother of more modest means—the wife of a shop-keeper or an artisan—also commonly used a wet nurse in order to facilitate full-time work in the shop.

Wet-nursing was a very widespread and flourishing business in the eighteenth century, a dismal business within the framework of the putting-out system. The traffic was in babies rather than in wool and cloth, and two or three years often passed before the wet-nurse worker finished her task. The great French historian Jules Michelet described with compassion the plight of the wet nurse, who was still going to the homes of the rich in early-nineteenth-century France:

People do not know how much these poor women are exploited and abused, first by the vehicles which transport them (often barely out of their confinement), and afterward by the employment offices which place them. Taken as nurses on the spot, they must send their own child away, and consequently it often dies. They have no contact with the family that hires them, and they may be dismissed at the first caprice of the mother or doctor. If the change of air and place should dry up their milk, they are discharged without any compensation. If they stay here [in the city] they pick up the habits of the easy life, and they suffer enormously when they are forced to return to their life of [rural] poverty. A good number become servants in order to stay in the town. They never rejoin their husbands, and the family is broken.[7]

Other observers noted the flaws of wet-nursing. It was a common belief that with her milk a nurse passed her bad traits to a baby. When the child turned out poorly, it was assumed that "the nurse had changed it." Many observers charged that nurses were often negligent and greedy. They claimed that there were large numbers of "killing nurses" with whom no child ever survived. The nurse let the child die quickly so that she could take another child and another fee.

Foundlings and Infanticide

In the ancient world it was not uncommon to allow or force newborn babies, particularly girl babies, to die when there were too many mouths to feed. To its great and eternal credit, the early medieval church, strongly influenced by Jewish law, denounced infanticide as a pagan practice and insisted that every human life was sacred. The willful destruction of newborn children became a crime punishable by death. And yet, as the previous reference to killing nurses suggests, direct and indirect methods of eliminating unwanted babies did not disappear. There were, for example, many cases of "overlaying"—parents rolling over and suffocating the child placed between them in their bed. Such parents claimed they had been drunk and had acted unintentionally. In Austria in 1784, suspicious authorities made it illegal for parents to take children under five into bed with them. Severe poverty, on the one hand, and increasing illegitimacy, on the other, conspired to force the very poor to thin their own ranks.

The young girl—very likely a servant—who could not provide for her child had few choices. If she would not have an abortion or employ the services of a killing nurse, she could bundle up her baby and leave it on the doorstep of a church. In the late seventeenth century, Saint Vincent de Paul was so distressed by the number of babies brought to the steps of Notre Dame in Paris that he established a home for foundlings. Others followed his example. In England the government acted on a petition calling for a foundling hospital "to prevent the frequent murders of poor, miserable infants at birth" and "to suppress the inhuman custom of exposing newborn children to perish in the streets."

In much of Europe in the eighteenth century, foundling homes emerged as a favorite charity of the rich and powerful. Great sums were spent on them. The foundling home in St. Petersburg, perhaps the most elaborate and lavish of its kind, occupied the former palaces of two members of the high nobility. In the early nineteenth century it had twenty-five thousand children in its care and was receiving five thousand new babies a year. At their best, foundling homes in the eighteenth century were a good example of Christian charity and social concern in an age of great poverty and inequality.

Yet the foundling home was no panacea. By the 1770s, one-third of all babies born in Paris were being immediately abandoned to the foundling home by their mothers. Fully one-third of all those foundlings were abandoned by married couples, a powerful commentary on the standard of living among the working poor, for whom an additional mouth to feed often meant tragedy.

Furthermore, great numbers of babies entered the foundling homes, but few left. Even in the best of these homes, 50 percent of the babies normally died within a year. In the worst, fully 90 percent did not survive. They succumbed to long journeys over rough roads, the intentional and unintentional neglect of their wet nurses, and the customary childhood illnesses. So great was the carnage that some contemporaries called the foundling hospitals "legalized infanticide."

Attitudes Toward Children

What were the more typical circumstances of children's lives? Did the treatment of foundlings reflect the attitudes of normal parents? Although some scholars argue otherwise, it seems that the young child was often of minor concern to its parents and to society in the eighteenth century. This indifference toward children was found in all classes; rich children were by no means exempt. The practice of using wet nurses, who were casually selected and often negligent, is one example of how even the rich and the prosperous put the child out of sight and out of mind. One French moralist, writing in 1756 about how to improve humanity, observed that "one blushes to think of loving one's children." It has been said that the English gentleman of the period "had more interest in the diseases of his horses than of his children."[8]

Feelings toward children were greatly influenced by the terrible frequency of death among children of all classes. Doctors and clergymen urged parents not to become too emotionally involved with their children, who were so unlikely to survive. Mothers especially did not always heed such warnings, but the risk of emotional devastation was very real for them. The great eighteenth-century English historian Edward Gibbon (1737–1794) wrote that "the death of a new born child before that of its parents may seem unnatural but it is a strictly probable event, since of any given number the greater part are extinguished before the ninth year, before they possess the faculties of the mind and the body." Gibbon's father named all his boys Edward after himself, hoping that at least one of them would survive to carry his name. His prudence was not misplaced. Edward the future historian and eldest survived. Five brothers and sisters who followed him all died in infancy.

The medical establishment was seldom interested in the care of children. One contemporary observer quoted a famous doctor as saying that "he never wished to be called to a young child because he was really at a loss to know what to offer for it." There were "physicians of note who make no scruple to assert that there is nothing to be done for children when they are ill." The best hope for children was often treatment by women healers and midwives, who helped many women deliver their babies and provided advice on child care. Nevertheless, children were still caught in a vicious circle: they were neglected because they were very likely to die, and they were likely to die because they were neglected.

Abandoned Children At this French foundlings' home a desperate, secretive mother could give up her baby without any questions, day or night. She placed her child on the revolving table and the nun on duty took it in. Similar practices existed in many countries. *(Jean-Loup Charmet)*

Emotional detachment from children often shaded off into abuse. When parents and other adults did turn toward children, it was normally to discipline and control them. The novelist Daniel Defoe (1659–1731), always delighted when he saw very young children working hard in cottage industry, coined the axiom "Spare the rod and spoil the child." He meant it. So did Susannah Wesley (1669–1742), mother of John Wesley, the founder of Methodism. According to her, the first task of a parent toward her children was "to conquer the will, and bring them to an obedient temper." She reported that her babies were "taught to fear the rod, and to cry softly; by which means they escaped the abundance of correction they might otherwise have had, and that most odious noise of the crying of children was rarely heard in the house."[9]

It was hardly surprising that when English parish officials dumped their paupers into the first factories late in the eighteenth century, the children were beaten and brutalized (see pages 744–745). That was part of the child-rearing pattern—considerable indifference, on the one hand, and strict physical discipline, on the other—that prevailed throughout most of the eighteenth century.

From the middle of the century, this pattern came under increasing attack and began to change. Critics, led by Jean-Jacques Rousseau in his famous treatise *Emile* (see the feature "Listening to the Past: A New Way to Educate Children" on pages 686–687), called for greater love, tenderness, and understanding toward children. In addition to supporting foundling homes to discourage infanticide and urging wealthy women to nurse their own babies, these new voices ridiculed the practice of swaddling: wrapping youngsters in tight-fitting clothes and blankets was generally believed to form babies properly by "straightening them out." By the end of the eighteenth century, small children were often being dressed in simpler, more comfortable clothing, allowing much greater freedom of movement. More parents expressed a delight in the love and intimacy of the child and found real pleasure in raising their offspring. These changes were part of the general growth of humanitarianism and cautious optimism about human potential that characterized the eighteenth-century Enlightenment.

Schools and Popular Literature

The role of schools and formal education outside the home was also growing more important. The aristocracy and the rich had led the way in the sixteenth century with special colleges, often run by Jesuits. But schools charged specifically with elementary education of the children of the common people usually did not appear until the seventeenth century. Unlike medieval schools, which mingled all age groups, these elementary schools specialized in boys and girls from seven to twelve, who were taught basic literacy and religion.

Scholars generally agree that the religious struggle unleashed by the Protestant and Catholic Reformations served as the catalyst in promoting popular literacy between 1500 and 1800. Both Protestant and Catholic reformers pushed reading as a means of instilling their

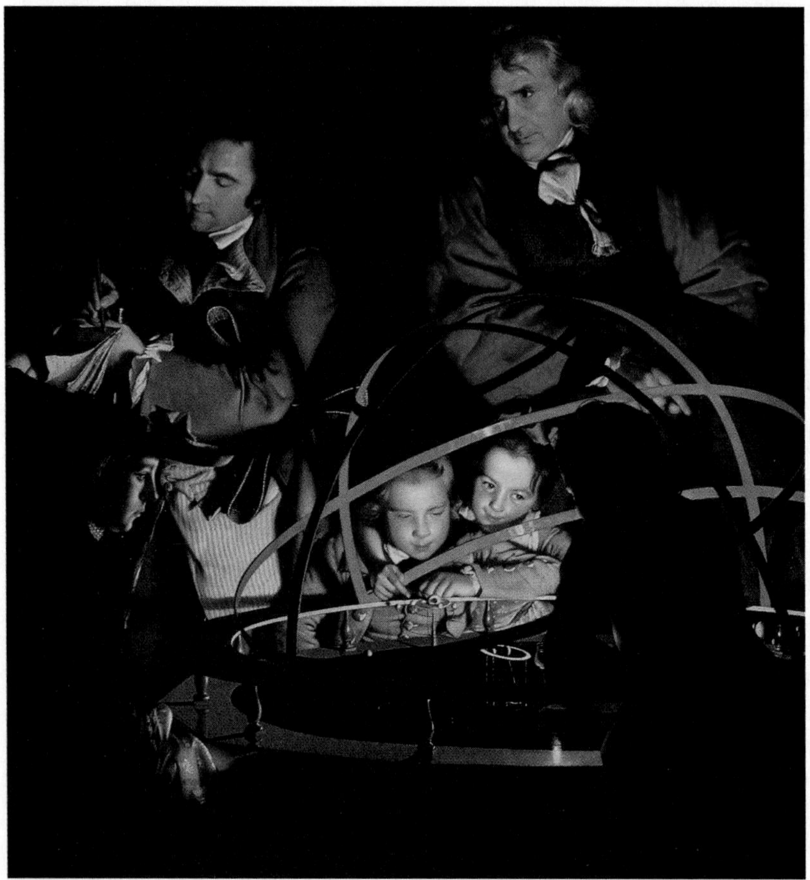

Cultivating the Joy of Discovery This English painting by Joseph Wright of Derby (1734–1797) reflects new attitudes toward child development and education, which advocated greater freedom and direct experience. The children rapturously watch a planetarium, which illustrates the movements and positions of the planets in the solar system. Wise teachers stand by, letting the children learn at their own pace. *(Derby Museum & Art Gallery/Bridgeman Art Library, London/New York)*

teachings more effectively. Thus literacy was often highest in border areas, such as eastern France, which were open to outside influences and to competition for believers from different churches. The growth of popular education quickened in the eighteenth century, but there was no revolutionary acceleration, and many common people received no formal education.

Prussia led the way in the development of universal education, inspired by the old Protestant idea that every believer should be able to read and study the Bible in the quest for personal salvation and by the new idea of a population capable of effectively serving the state. As early as 1717, Prussia made attendance at elementary schools compulsory, and more Protestant German states, such as Saxony and Württemberg, followed in the eighteenth century. Religious motives were also extremely important elsewhere. From the middle of the seventeenth century, Presbyterian Scotland was convinced that the path to salvation lay in careful study of the Scriptures, and it established an effective network of parish schools for rich and poor alike. The Church of England and the dissenting congregations established "charity schools" to instruct the children of the poor, and in 1682 France began setting up Christian schools to teach the catechism and prayers as well as reading and writing. France did less well than the Habsburg state, the only Catholic land to promote elementary education enthusiastically in the eighteenth century. In 1774 Maria Theresa established a general system of elementary education that called for compulsory education and a school in every community. Some elementary education was becoming a reality for European peoples, and schools were of growing significance in the life of the child.

The result of these efforts was a remarkable growth in basic literacy between 1600 and 1800. Whereas in 1600 only one male in six was barely literate in France and Scotland, and one in four in England, by 1800 almost nine out of ten Scottish males, two out of three French males (Map 20.1), and more than half of English males were literate. In all three countries, the bulk of the jump occurred in the eighteenth century. Women were also increasingly literate, although they lagged behind men in most countries.

The growth in literacy promoted a growth in reading, and historians have carefully examined what the common people read in an attempt to discern what they were thinking. One thing seems certain: the major philosophical works of the Enlightenment had little impact on peasants and workers, who could neither afford nor understand those favorites of the book-hungry educated public.

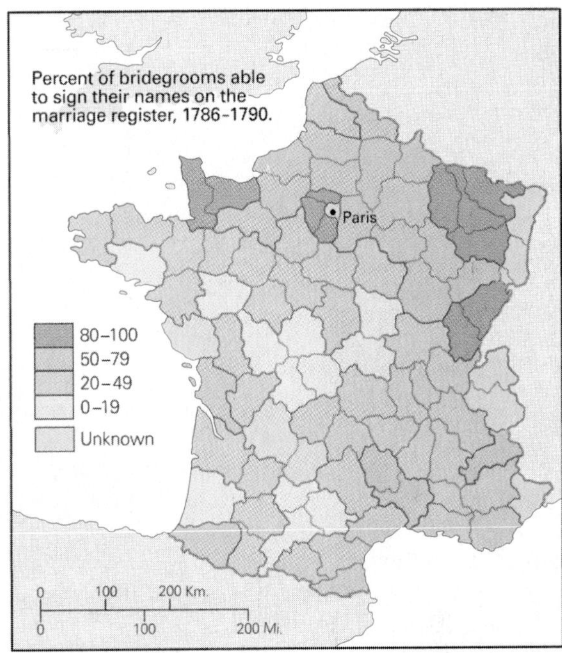

MAP 20.1 Literacy in France on the Eve of the French Revolution Literacy rates increased but still varied widely between and within states in eighteenth-century Europe. Northern France was clearly ahead of southern France.

Although the Bible remained the overwhelming favorite, especially in Protestant countries, the staple of popular literature was short pamphlets known as chapbooks. Printed on the cheapest paper available, many chapbooks dealt with religious subjects. They featured Bible stories, prayers, devotions, and the lives of saints and exemplary Christians. Promising happiness after death, devotional literature was also intensely practical. It gave the believer moral teachings and a confidence in God that helped in daily living.

Entertaining, often humorous stories formed a second element of popular literature. Fairy tales, medieval romances, fictionalized history, and fantastic adventures—these were some of the delights that filled the peddler's pack as he approached a village. Both heroes and villains possessed superhuman powers in this make-believe world, a world of danger and magic, of fairy godmothers and evil trolls. But the good fairies always triumphed over the evil ones in the story's marvelous resolution.

The significance of these entertaining stories for the peasant reader is debated. Many scholars see them reflecting a desire for pure escapism and a temporary

A Peasant Family Reading the Bible Praised by the philosophe Diderot for its moralistic message, this engraving of a painting by Jean-Baptiste Greuze (1725–1805) does capture the power of sacred texts and the spoken word. The peasant patriarch reads aloud from the massive family Bible and the close-knit circle of absorbed listeners concentrates on every word. Only the baby is distracted. *(Bibliothèque Nationale/Giraudon/Art Resource, NY)*

flight from harsh everyday reality. Others see these tales reflecting ancient folk wisdom and counseling prudence in a world full of danger and evil, where wolves dress up like grandmothers and eat Little Red Riding Hoods.

Finally, some popular literature was highly practical, dealing with rural crafts, household repairs, useful plants, and similar matters. Much of such lore was stored in almanacs. With calendars listing secular, religious, and astrological events mixed in with agricultural schedules, bizarre bits of information, and jokes, the almanac was universal, noncontroversial, and highly appreciated, even by many in the comfortable classes. "Anyone who could would read an almanac."[10]

In general, however, the reading of the common people had few similarities with that of educated elites. Popular literature was simple and practical, both as devotional self-help and as how-to instruction. It was also highly escapist, not unlike the mass of inexpensive paperbacks sold in drugstores today. Neither the practical nor the escapist elements challenged the established order. Rather, the common people were apparently content with works that reinforced traditional values and did not foster social or religious criticism. These results fit well with the modest educational objectives of rulers and educated elites. They believed that carefully limited instruction stressing religion and morals was useful to the masses but that too much study would only disorient them and foster discontent.

 FOOD AND MEDICAL PRACTICE

As we saw in Chapter 19, the European population increased rapidly in the eighteenth century. Plague and starvation gradually disappeared, and Europeans lived longer. What were the characteristics of diets and nutrition in this era of improving health and longevity? Although medical practice played only a small part, what was it like in the eighteenth century? What does a comparison of rich and poor reveal?

Diets and Nutrition

At the beginning of the eighteenth century, ordinary men and women depended on grain as fully as they had in the past. Bread was quite literally the staff of life. Peasants in the Beauvais region of France ate two pounds of bread a day, washing it down with water, green wine, beer, or a little skim milk. Their dark bread was made from a mixture of roughly ground wheat and rye—the standard flour of the common people. The poor also ate grains in soup and gruel. In rocky northern Scotland, for example, people depended on oatmeal, which they often ate half-cooked so that it would swell in their stomachs and make them feel full.

Little wonder, then, that an adequate supply of grain and an affordable price of bread loomed large in the popular imagination. Even peasants normally needed to buy some grain for food, and, in full accord with landless laborers and urban workers, they believed in the old medieval idea of the "just price." That is, they believed that prices should be "fair," protecting both consumers and producers and imposed by government decree if necessary.

In the later eighteenth century, this traditional, moral view of prices and the economy clashed repeatedly with the emerging free-market philosophy of unregulated supply and demand, which was increasingly favored by government officials, large landowners, and economists led by Adam Smith (see page 654). In years of poor harvests and soaring prices, this clash often resulted in food riots and popular disturbances. Peasants and workers would try to stop wagons loaded with grain from leaving their region, or they would seize grain held by speculators and big merchants accused of hoarding and rigging the market. (Usually the tumultuous crowd paid what it considered to be a fair price for what it took.) Governments were keenly aware of the problem of adequate grain supplies, and they would sometimes try to control prices to prevent unrest in crisis years.

Although breadstuffs were all important for the rural and urban poor, they also ate a fair quantity of vegetables. Indeed, vegetables were considered "poor people's food." Peas and beans were probably the most common; grown as field crops in much of Europe since the Middle Ages, they were eaten fresh in late spring and summer. Dried, they became the basic ingredients in the soups and stews of the long winter months. In most regions, other vegetables appeared in season on the tables of the poor, primarily cabbages, carrots, and wild greens. Fruit was uncommon and limited to the summer months.

The common people of Europe loved meat and eggs, but they seldom ate their fill. Indeed, the poor ate less meat in 1700 than in 1500 because their general standard of living had declined as the population surged in the sixteenth century (see page 637) and meat became more expensive. In the eighteenth century, the beginnings of agricultural transformation (see pages 631–

Le Nain: Peasant Family A little wine and a great deal of dark bread: the traditional food of the poor French peasantry accentuates the poetic dignity of this masterpiece, painted about 1640 by Louis Le Nain. *(Louvre © Photo R.M.N.—G. Blot/J. Schor)*

633) increased per capita meat consumption only in Britain and the Low Countries. Moreover, in most European countries harsh game laws deprived the poor of the right to hunt and eat game such as rabbits, deer, and partridges. Only nobles and large landowners could legally kill game. Few laws were more bitterly resented—or more frequently broken—by ordinary people than those governing hunting. When the poor did eat meat—on a religious holiday or at a wedding or other festive occasion—it was most likely lamb or mutton. Sheep could survive on rocky soils and did not compete directly with humans for the slender resources of grain.

Milk was rarely drunk. Perhaps because some individuals do suffer seriously from dairy allergies, it was widely believed that milk caused sore eyes, headaches, and a variety of ills, except among the very young and very old. Milk was used primarily to make cheese and butter, which did not spoil as milk did and which the poor liked but could afford only occasionally. Medical and popular opinion considered whey, the watery liquid left after milk was churned, "an excellent temperate drink."

The diet of the rich—aristocrats, officials, and the comfortable bourgeoisie—was traditionally quite different from that of the poor. The men and women of the upper classes were rapacious carnivores. A truly elegant dinner among the great and powerful consisted of one rich meat after another: a chicken pie, a leg of lamb, a grilled steak, for example. Three separate meat courses might be followed by three fish courses laced with piquant sauces and complemented with sweets, cheeses, and nuts of all kinds. Fruits and vegetables were not often found on the tables of the rich.

There was also an enormous amount of overdrinking among the rich. The English squire, for example, who loved to hunt with his hounds, loved to drink with a similar passion. He became famous as the "four-bottle man." With his dinner he drank red wine from France or white wine from the Rhineland, and with his dessert he took sweet but strong port or Madeira from Portugal. Sometimes he ended the evening under the table in a drunken stupor, but very often he did not. The wine and the meat were consumed together in long hours of sustained excess, permitting the gentleman and his guests to drink enormous quantities without getting stupefyingly drunk.

The diet of small traders, master craftsmen, minor bureaucrats—the people of the towns and cities—was generally less monotonous than that of the peasantry. The markets, stocked by market gardens on the outskirts, provided a substantial variety of meats, vegetables, and fruits, although bread and beans still formed the bulk of such families' diets.

There were also regional dietary differences in 1700. Generally speaking, northern, Atlantic Europe ate better than southern, Mediterranean Europe. The poor of England probably ate best of all. Contemporaries on both sides of the Channel often contrasted the English citizen's consumption of meat with the French peasants' greater dependence on bread and vegetables. The Dutch were also considerably better fed than the average European, in large part because of their advanced agriculture and diversified gardens.

The Impact of Diet on Health

How were the poor and the rich served by their quite different diets? At first glance, the diet of the laboring poor, relying as it did on grains and vegetables, might seem low in protein. However, the whole-grain wheat or rye flour used in eighteenth-century bread retained most of the bran—the ground-up husk—and the all-important wheat germ, which contains higher proportions of some minerals, vitamins, and good-quality proteins than does the rest of the grain. In addition, the field peas and beans eaten by poor people since the early Middle Ages contained protein that complemented the proteins in whole-grain bread. The proteins in whey, cheese, and eggs, which the poor ate at least occasionally, also supplemented the bread and vegetables.

The basic bread-and-vegetables diet of the poor *in normal times* was adequate. But a key dietary problem in some seasons, particularly in the late winter and early spring, was probably getting enough green vegetables (or milk) to ensure adequate supplies of vitamins A and C. A severe deficiency of vitamin C produces scurvy, a disease that leads to rotting gums, swelling of the limbs, and great weakness. Before the season's first vegetables, many people experienced shortages of vitamin C and suffered from mild cases of scurvy. (Scurvy was an acute problem for sailors on long voyages and by the end of the sixteenth century was being controlled on ships by a daily ration of lime juice.)

The practice of gorging on meat, sweets, and spirits caused the rich their own nutritional problems. Because of their great disdain for fresh vegetables, they, too, were very often deficient in vitamins A and C. Gout was a common affliction of the overfed and underexercised rich. No wonder they were often caricatured as dragging their flabby limbs and bulging bellies to the table to stuff their swollen cheeks and poison their livers. People of moderate means, who could afford some

Royal Interest in the Potato Frederick the Great of Prussia, shown here supervising cultivation of the potato, used his influence and position to promote the new food on his estates and throughout Prussia. Peasants could grow potatoes with the simplest hand tools, but it was backbreaking labor, as this painting by R. Warthmüller suggests. *(Private Collection, Hamburg/AKG London)*

meat and dairy products with fair regularity but who had not abandoned the bread and vegetables of the poor, were best off from a nutritional standpoint.

Patterns of food consumption changed rather markedly as the century progressed. More varied diets associated with new methods of farming were confined largely to the Low Countries and England, but a new food—the potato—came to the aid of the poor everywhere. Introduced into Europe from the Americas—along with corn, squash, tomatoes, and many other useful plants—the humble potato is actually an excellent food. Containing a good supply of carbohydrates, calories, and vitamins A and C (especially if it is not overcooked and the skin is eaten), the potato offset the lack of vitamins from green vegetables in the poor person's winter and early-spring diet, and it provided a much higher caloric yield than grain for a given piece of land.

For some desperately poor peasants who needed to get every possible calorie from a tiny plot of land, the potato replaced grain as the primary food in the eighteenth century. This happened first in Ireland, where English (Protestant) repression and exploitation forced large numbers of poor (Catholic) peasants to live off tiny scraps of rented ground. Elsewhere in Europe, potatoes took hold more slowly because many people did not like them. Thus, potatoes were first fed to pigs and livestock, and there was even debate over whether they were fit for humans. In Germany the severe famines caused by the Seven Years' War settled the matter: potatoes were edible and not just "famine food." By the end of the century, the potato had become an important dietary supplement in much of Europe.

There was also a general growth of market gardening, and a greater variety of vegetables appeared in towns and cities. In the course of the eighteenth century, the large towns and cities of maritime Europe began to receive semitropical fruits, such as oranges and lemons, from Portugal and the West Indies, although they were not cheap.

Not all changes in the eighteenth century were for the better, however. Bread began to change, most noticeably for the English and for the comfortable groups on the European continent. Rising incomes and new tastes led to a shift from whole-grain black or brown bread to "bread as white as snow" and started a decline in bread's nutritional value. The high-roughage bran and some of the dark but high-vitamin germ were increasingly sifted out by millers. This foretold further "improvements" in the nineteenth century, which would leave bread perfectly white and greatly reduced in nutritional value.

Another sign of nutritional decline was the growing consumption of sugar. Initially a luxury, sugar dropped rapidly in price as slave-based production increased in the Americas and the sweetener was much more widely used in the eighteenth century. This development probably led to an increase in cavities and to other ailments as well, although the greater or lesser poverty of the laboring poor still protected most of them from the sugar-tooth virus of the rich and well-to-do.

Medical Practitioners

Although sickness, pain, and disease—intractable challenges built into the human condition—permeated the European experience in the eighteenth century, medical science played a very small part in improving the health of most people. Yet the Enlightenment's growing focus on discovering the laws of nature and on human problems did give rise to a great deal of research and experimentation. The century also saw a remarkable rise in the number of medical practitioners. Therefore, when significant breakthroughs in knowledge came in the middle and late nineteenth century, they could be rapidly evaluated and diffused.

Care of the sick in the eighteenth century was the domain of several competing groups: faith healers, apothecaries (or pharmacists), physicians, surgeons, and midwives. Both men and women were prominent in the healing arts, as had been the case since the Middle Ages. But by 1700 the range of medical activities open to women was severely restricted, because women were generally denied admission to medical colleges and lacked the diplomas necessary for practice as physicians and surgeons. In the course of the eighteenth century, women encountered growing criticism and discrimination from competing male practitioners and the medical schools they dominated. The position of women as midwives and healers further eroded, pointing toward the virtual exclusion of women from "scientific medicine" in the early nineteenth century.

Faith healers, one of the most important kinds of healers in medieval Europe, remained active. They and their patients believed that demons and evil spirits caused disease by lodging in people and that the proper treatment was to exorcise, or drive out, the offending devil. This demonic view of disease was strongest in the countryside, where popular belief placed great faith in the healing power of religious relics, prayer, and the laying on of hands. Faith healing was particularly effective in the treatment of mental disorders such as hysteria and depression, where the link between attitude and illness is most direct.

In the larger towns and cities, apothecaries sold a vast number of herbs, drugs, and patent medicines for every conceivable "temperament and distemper." Their prescriptions were incredibly complex—a hundred or more drugs might be included in a single prescription—and often very expensive. Some of the drugs and herbs undoubtedly worked. For example, strong laxatives were given to the rich for their constipated bowels. Indeed, the medical profession continued to believe that regular "purging" of the bowels was essential for good health and the treatment of illness. Much purging was harmful, however, and only bloodletting for the treatment of disease was more effective in speeding patients to their graves. In the countryside, people often turned to midwives and women healers for herbs and folk remedies.

Physicians, who were invariably men, were apprenticed in their teens to a practicing physician for several years of on-the-job training. This training was then rounded out with hospital work or some university courses. Because such prolonged training was expensive, physicians continued to come mainly from prosperous families, and they usually concentrated on urban patients from similar social backgrounds. They had little contact with urban workers and less with peasants.

To their credit, physicians in the eighteenth century were increasingly willing to experiment with new methods, but time-honored practices lay heavily on them. Physicians, like apothecaries, laid great stress on purging. And bloodletting was still considered a medical cure-all. It was the way "bad blood," the cause of illness, was removed and the balance of humors necessary for good health was restored. According to a physician practicing medicine in Philadelphia in 1799, bleeding was proper at the onset of all inflammatory fevers, in all inflammations, and for "asthma, sciatic pains, coughs, head-aches, rheumatisms, the apoplexy, epilepsy, and bloody fluxes."[11] It was also necessary after all falls, blows, and bruises.

Surgeons, in contrast to physicians, made considerable medical and social progress in the eighteenth century. Long considered as ordinary male artisans comparable to butchers and barbers, surgeons began studying anatomy seriously and improved their art. With endless opportunities to practice, army surgeons on gory battlefields led the way. They learned that a soldier with an extensive wound, such as a shattered leg or arm, could perhaps be saved if the surgeon could obtain above the wound a flat surface that could be cauterized with fire. Thus if a soldier (or a civilian) had a broken limb and the bone stuck out, the surgeon amputated so that the remaining stump could be cauterized and the likelihood of death reduced.

The eighteenth-century surgeon (and patient) labored in the face of incredible difficulties. Almost all operations were performed without any painkiller, for the anesthesias of the day were hard to control and were believed too dangerous for general use. The terrible screams of people whose limbs were being sawed off echoed across battlefields and through hospitals. Many patients died from the agony and shock of such operations. Surgery was also performed in the midst of filth and dirt, for there simply was no knowledge of bacteriology and the nature of infection. The simplest wound treated by a surgeon could fester and lead to death.

Midwives, who were a special object of suspicion and persecution in the witch-hunt craze of the sixteenth and seventeenth centuries, continued to deliver the overwhelming majority of babies throughout the eighteenth century. The typical midwife was an older, often widowed woman of modest social origins and long professional experience. Trained initially by another woman practitioner, the midwife primarily assisted in labor and delivering babies. But the midwife also treated female problems, such as irregular menstrual cycles, breast-feeding difficulties, sterility, and venereal disease, and she ministered to small children. (See the feature "Individuals in Society: Martha Ballard, American Midwife.")

The midwife orchestrated labor and birth in a woman's world, where friends and relatives offered the pregnant woman assistance and encouragement in the familiar surroundings of her own home. Excluded by tradition and modesty, the male surgeon (and the husband) rarely entered this world, because most births, then as now, were normal and spontaneous. In seventeenth-century England, for example, a surgeon was called only if the child died without having been born and instruments were needed to deliver the dead baby. Following the invention of the forceps, which might help in an exceptionally difficult birth, surgeon-physicians used their monopoly over this and other instruments to seek lucrative new business. Attacking midwives as ignorant and dangerous, they persuaded growing numbers of wealthy women of the superiority of their services and sought to undermine faith in midwives.

Recent research suggests that women practitioners successfully defended much but not all of their practice in the eighteenth century. In France one enterprising Parisian midwife, Madame du Coudray, skillfully secured royal financing to teach better techniques, which she claimed would lower infant deaths. She then traveled all over France to promote her widely used midwifery textbook and to give hands-on instruction with life-size mannequins and doll-babies to roughly ten thousand women. In northern Italy, state and church

Teaching Midwives This plate from Madame du Coudray's manual for midwives, *The Art of Childbirth,* illustrates "another incorrect method of delivery." The caption tells the midwife that she should have rotated the baby within the womb to face the mother's back, so that the chin does not catch on the pubis bone and dislocate the jaw. *(Rare Books Division, Countway [Francis A.] Library of Medicine)*

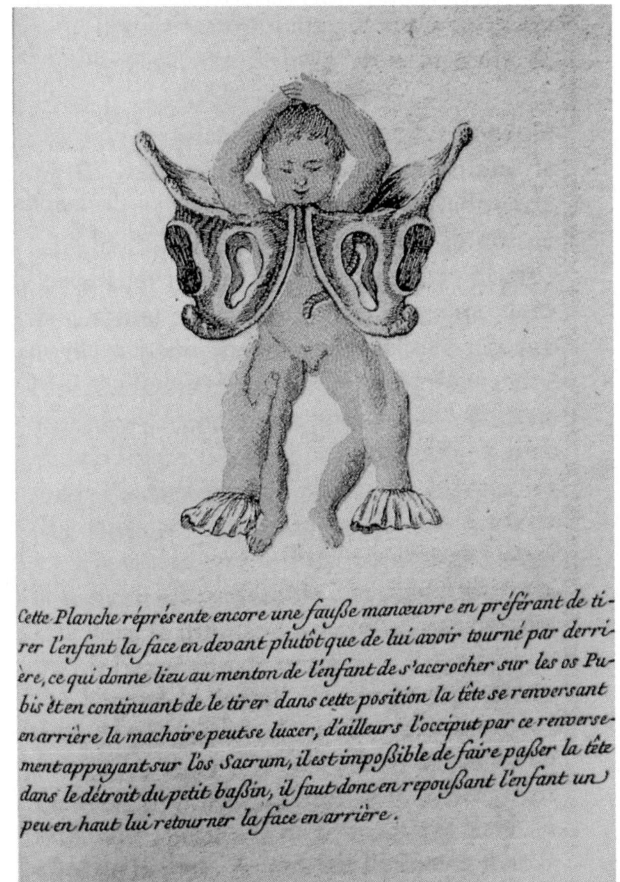
Cette Planche répresente encore une fauße manœuvre en préférant de ti-
rer l'enfant la face en devant plutôt que de lui avoir tourné par derri-
ère, ce qui donne lieu au menton de l'enfant de s'accrocher sur les os Pubis èt en continuant de le tirer dans cette position la tête se renversant
en arrière la machoire peut se luxer, d'ailleurs l'occiput par ce renverse-
ment appuyant sur l'os Sacrum, il est impoßible de faire paßer la tête
dans le détroit du petit baßin, il faut donc en repoußant l'enfant un
peu en haut lui retourner la face en arrière.

Individuals in Society

Martha Ballard, American Midwife

The journal of Martha Ballard. *(Maine State Archives)*

In the cold spring of 1789, Martha Ballard delivered fourteen babies in two months of high drama and unsung heroism. An American midwife in a small town on the Kennebec River in central Maine, Ballard attended women on both sides of the icy flooding river, paddling back and forth and braving the harsh and erratic weather. On her way to one patient, she and her terrified horse were caught in a violent rainstorm and almost struck by a falling tree. She recorded the outcome in her diary, which she kept for twenty-seven years: "Assisted by the same allmighty power I got safe thru and arrived unhurt. Mrs Hewins safe delivered at ten hours evening of a daughter."[1] Ballard had persevered and triumphed.

Exceptional in her meticulous record keeping, Ballard embodied many characteristics of the midwife in the eighteenth-century Western world. A mature woman of fifty when her diary opened in 1785, she had learned her trade on the job, assisting other midwives delivering the babies of friends and relatives. She had also learned birthing practices and compassion from her own experience, for she gave birth to nine children between 1756 and 1779. Ballard worked as she was trained, assisted by other women in each patient's own home. She received payment for services in money or in goods, such as food and cloth. In the 1790s, the arrival of a young and inexperienced male doctor brought some competition, but the midwife continued to preside over the vast majority of births in the town.

The great adventures in Ballard's diary were her journeys to expectant mothers and her struggles with the elements. The deliveries themselves were described simply, in matter-of-fact terms. Ballard's women were "unwell," and their "illness" only increased as they passed into labor. Complications were rarely noted, and then only briefly in nontechnical language. Indeed, birthing tragedies hardly appeared in her everyday record. How, the modern reader may ask, can this be?

Part of the answer lies in Ballard's strength of constitution and character, her accepting nature, and her faith in God. Perhaps more lies in her skill, justifiable self-confidence, and enviable record of success. She attended more than eight hundred deliveries and lost not a single mother in birthing, although five died in the recovery period. Moreover, only nineteen babies died stillborn or within an hour or two of birth. These levels of maternal and infant death were not surpassed until 1930 in the United States. Ballard's success shows that if a woman had adequate nutrition (as in New England) and the care of an experienced midwife, childbirth at home was a natural physical process that normally ended well.

Tough and tender, Ballard also practiced as a nurse, physician, mortician, and pharmacist, relying on herbal medicines. For example, she administered mandrake and pinkroot as powerful laxatives and emetics to cause the expulsion of children's intestinal worms, which were contracted by playing in soil infected by human feces and which could grow up to fourteen inches in length.

A large portion of Ballard's time was occupied with laborious housecleaning, gardening, sewing, and bearing, nursing, raising, and teaching her children. Nursing for pay and simply helping her neighbors overlapped. In later life, she endured the disasters of an alcoholic son and her husband's indifference to her fatigue and stomach pain. Unlike the women she delivered, she found relief from these trials only with death at age seventy-seven in 1812.

Questions for Analysis

1. Describe Martha Ballard. What kind of a person was she?
2. What challenges did Ballard face as a midwife? How successfully did she meet them?

1. L. Ulrich, *A Midwife's Tale: The Life of Martha Ballard, Based on Her Diary, 1785–1812* (New York: Alfred A. Knopf, 1990), p. 6. This section draws on Ulrich's pioneering study, a masterpiece of the biographer's art. Abbreviations have been spelled out.

Hospital Life Patients crowded into hospitals like this one in Hamburg in 1746 had little chance of recovery. A priest by the window administers last rites, while in the center a surgeon coolly saws off the leg of a man who has received no anesthesia. *(Germanisches Nationalmuseum, Nuremberg)*

pressures led to major changes in midwife training and certification, but women remained dominant in the birthing trade. It appears that midwives generally lost no more babies than male doctors, who were still summoned to treat nonelite women only when a life-threatening situation required surgery.

While ordinary physicians were bleeding, apothecaries purging, surgeons sawing, faith healers praying, and midwives assisting, the leading medical thinkers were attempting to pull together and assimilate all the information and misinformation they had been accumulating. The attempt was ambitious: to systematize medicine around simple, basic principles, as Newton had done in physics. But the schools of thought resulting from such speculation and theorizing did little to improve medical care.

Hospitals and Medical Experiments

Hospitals were terrible places throughout most of the eighteenth century. There was no isolation of patients. Operations were performed in a patient's bed. Nurses were old, ignorant, greedy, and often drunk women. Fresh air was considered harmful, and infections of every kind were rampant. Diderot's article in the *Encyclopedia* on the Hôtel-Dieu in Paris, the "richest and most terrifying of all French hospitals," vividly describes normal conditions of the 1770s:

Imagine a long series of communicating wards filled with sufferers of every kind of disease who are sometimes packed three, four, five or even six into a bed, the living alongside the dead and dying, the air polluted by this mass of unhealthy bodies, passing pestilential germs of their afflictions from one to the other, and the spectacle of suffering and agony on every hand. That is the Hôtel-Dieu.

The result is that many of these poor wretches come out with diseases they did not have when they went in, and often pass them on to the people they go back to live with. Others are half-cured and spend the rest of their days in an invalidism as hard to bear as the illness itself; and the rest perish, except for the fortunate few whose strong constitutions enable them to survive.[12]

No wonder the poor of Paris hated hospitals and often saw confinement there as a plot to kill paupers.

In the last years of the century, the humanitarian concern already reflected in Diderot's description of the Hôtel-Dieu led to a movement for hospital reform throughout western Europe. Efforts were made to improve ventilation and eliminate filth on the grounds that bad air caused disease. The theory was wrong, but the results were beneficial, since the spread of infection was somewhat reduced.

Mental hospitals, too, were incredibly savage institutions. The customary treatment for mental illness was bleeding and cold water, administered more to maintain discipline than to effect a cure. Violent persons were chained to the wall and forgotten. A breakthrough of sorts occurred in the 1790s when William Tuke founded the first humane sanatorium in England. In Paris an innovative warden, Philippe Pinel, took the chains off the mentally disturbed in 1793 and tried to treat them as patients rather than as prisoners.

In the eighteenth century, all sorts of wildly erroneous ideas about mental illness circulated. One was that moonlight caused madness, a belief reflected in the word *lunatic*—someone harmed by lunar light. Another mid-eighteenth-century theory, which lasted until at least 1914, was that masturbation caused madness, not to mention acne, epilepsy, and premature ejaculation. Thus parents, religious institutions, and schools waged relentless war on masturbation by males, although they were curiously uninterested in female masturbation.

In the second half of the eighteenth century, medicine in general turned in a more practical and experimental direction. Some of the experimentation was creative quackery involving the recently discovered phenomenon of electricity. One magnificent quack in London promoted sleep on a cure-all Celestial Bed, which was lavishly decorated with magnets and electrical devices. A single night on the bed cost a small fortune. The rich could buy expensive treatments, but the prevalence of quacks and the general lack of knowledge meant they often got little for their money. Because so many treatments were harmful, the common people were probably much less deprived by their reliance on faith healers and folk medicine than one might think.

Experimentation and the intensified search for solutions to human problems led to some real advances in medicine after 1750, however. The eighteenth century's greatest medical triumph was the conquest of smallpox. With the progressive decline of bubonic plague, smallpox became the most terrible of the infectious diseases. In the words of historian Thomas Macaulay, "Smallpox was always present, filling the churchyard with corpses, tormenting with constant fears all whom it had not stricken." In the seventeenth century, 25 percent of the deaths in the British Isles were due to smallpox, and it is estimated that 60 million Europeans died of it in the eighteenth century. Fully 80 percent of the population was stricken at some point in life, and 25 percent of the total population was left permanently scarred. If ever a human problem cried out for a solution, it was smallpox.

The first step in the conquest of this killer came in the early eighteenth century. An English aristocrat whose great beauty had been marred by the pox, Lady Mary Wortley Montagu, learned about the practice of inoculation in the Ottoman Empire while her husband was serving as British ambassador there. She had her own son successfully inoculated in Constantinople and was instrumental in spreading the practice in England after her return in 1722.

Inoculation against smallpox had long been practiced in the Muslim lands of western Asia. The skin was deliberately broken, and a small amount of matter taken from the pustule of a smallpox victim was applied. The person thus contracted a mild case of smallpox that gave lasting protection against further attack. Inoculation was risky, however, and about one person in fifty died from it. In addition, people who had been inoculated were infectious and often spread the disease, leading to widespread condemnation of inoculation against smallpox in the 1730s.

Success in reducing the risks of inoculation in British colonies and a successful search for cheaper methods led to something approaching mass inoculation in England in the 1760s. Both the danger and the cost had been reduced, and deadly smallpox struck all classes less frequently. On the continent, the well-to-do were also inoculated, beginning with royal families such as those of Maria Theresa and Catherine the Great. The practice then spread to the middle classes. By the later years of the century, smallpox inoculation was playing some part in the decline of the death rate and the general increase in European population.

The final breakthrough against smallpox came at the end of the century. Edward Jenner (1749–1823), a talented country doctor, noted that in the English countryside there was a long-standing belief that dairy maids who had contracted cowpox did not get smallpox. Cowpox produces sores on the cow's udder and on the hands of the milker. The sores resemble those of smallpox, but the disease is mild and not contagious.

For eighteen years Jenner practiced a kind of Baconian science, carefully collecting data on protection against smallpox by cowpox. Finally, in 1796 he performed his first vaccination on a young boy using matter taken from a milkmaid with cowpox. In the next two years, he performed twenty-three successful vaccinations, and in 1798 Jenner published his findings. After Austrian medical authorities replicated Jenner's results, the new method of treatment spread rapidly. Smallpox soon declined to the point of disappearance in Europe and then throughout the world. Jenner eventually received prizes totaling £30,000 from the British government for his great discovery, a fitting recompense for a man who gave an enormous gift to humanity and helped lay the foundation for the science of immunology in the nineteenth century.

 RELIGION AND POPULAR CULTURE

Though the critical spirit of the Enlightenment spread among the educated elite in the eighteenth century, the majority of ordinary men and women remained firmly committed to the Christian religion, especially in rural areas. Religious faith promised salvation and eternal life, and it gave comfort and courage in the face of sorrow and death. Religion also remained strong because it was usually embedded in local traditions, everyday social experience, and popular culture.

Yet the popular religion of village Europe was everywhere enmeshed in a larger world of church hierarchies and state power. These powerful outside forces sought to regulate religious life at the local level. Their efforts created tensions that helped set the scene for a vigorous religious revival in Germany and England. Similar tensions arose in Catholic countries, where powerful elites criticized and attacked popular religious practices that their increasingly rationalistic minds deemed foolish and superstitious.

The Institutional Church

As in the Middle Ages, the local parish church remained the basic religious unit all across Europe. Still largely coinciding with the agricultural village, the parish fulfilled many needs. The parish church was the focal point of religious devotion, which went far beyond sermons and Holy Communion. The parish church organized colorful processions and pilgrimages to local shrines. Even in Protestant countries, where such activities were severely restricted, congregations gossiped and swapped stories after services, and neighbors came together in church for baptisms, marriages, funerals, and

A Religious Festival in Urban France This vibrant painting suggests how religious life interacted with powerful institutions in Catholic Europe. Moving past crowds and through the city, this procession is celebrating the Blessed Sacrament on the Feast of Corpus Christi (the Body of Christ). Church dignitaries are grouped in the center; the colorful nobility is on the left; and the middle orders, with their sober black suits, are on the right. Both participation and hierarchical inequality are the rule. *(Bibliothèque des Arts Décoratifs/Jean-Loup Charmet)*

special events. Thus the parish church was woven into the very fabric of community life.

Moreover, the local church had important administrative tasks. Priests and parsons were truly the bookkeepers of agrarian Europe, and it is because parish registers were so complete that historians have learned so much about population and family life. Parishes also normally distributed charity to the destitute, looked after orphans, and provided whatever primary education was available for the common people.

The many tasks of the local church were usually the responsibility of a resident priest or pastor, a full-time professional working with assistants and lay volunteers. All clerics—whether Roman Catholic, Protestant, Greek Orthodox, or Russian Orthodox—also shared the fate of middlemen in a complicated institutional system. Charged most often with ministering to poor peasants, the priest or parson was the last link in a powerful church-state hierarchy that was everywhere determined to control religion down to the grassroots. However, the regulatory framework of belief, which went back at least to the fourth century when Christianity became the official religion of the Roman Empire, had undergone important changes since 1500.

The Protestant Reformation had burst forth as a culmination of medieval religiosity and a desire to purify Christian belief. Martin Luther, the most influential of the early reformers, preached that all men and women were saved from their sins and God's damnation only by personal faith in Jesus Christ. The individual could reach God directly, without need of priestly intermediaries. This was the revolutionary meaning of Luther's "priesthood of all believers," which broke forever the monopoly of the priestly class over medieval Europe's most priceless treasure—eternal salvation.

As the Reformation gathered force, with peasant upheaval and doctrinal competition, German princes and monarchs in northern Europe put themselves at the head of official churches in their territories. Protestant authorities, with generous assistance from state-certified theologians like Luther, then proceeded to regulate their "territorial churches" strictly, selecting personnel and imposing detailed rules. They joined with Catholics to crush the Anabaptists, who, with their belief in freedom of conscience and separation of church and state, had become the real revolutionaries. Thus the Reformation, initially so radical in its rejection of Rome and its stress on individual religious experience, eventually resulted in a bureaucratization of the church and local religious life in Protestant Europe.

The Reformation era also increased the practical power of Catholic rulers over "their" churches, but it was only in the eighteenth century that some Catholic monarchs began to impose striking reforms. These reforms, which had their counterparts in Orthodox Russia, had a very "Protestant" aspect. They increased state control over the Catholic church, making it less subject to papal influence.

Spain provides a graphic illustration of changing church-state relations in Catholic lands. A deeply Catholic country with devout rulers, Spain nevertheless took firm control of ecclesiastical appointments. Papal proclamations could not even be read in Spanish churches without prior approval from the government. Spain also asserted state control over the Spanish Inquisition, which had been ruthlessly pursuing heresy as an independent agency under Rome's direction for two hundred years. Spain went far toward creating a "national" Catholic church, as France had done earlier.

A more striking indication of state power and papal weakness was the fate of the Society of Jesus. As the most successful of the Catholic Reformation's new religious orders, the well-educated Jesuits were extraordinary teachers, missionaries, and agents of the papacy. In many Catholic countries, the Jesuits exercised tremendous political influence, since individual members held high government positions and Jesuit colleges formed the minds of Europe's Catholic nobility. Yet by playing politics so effectively, the Jesuits eventually elicited a broad coalition of enemies. Especially bitter controversies over the Jesuits rocked the entire Catholic hierarchy in France. Following the earlier example of Portugal, the French king ordered the Jesuits out of France in 1763 and confiscated their property. France and Spain then pressured Rome to dissolve the Jesuits completely. In 1773 a reluctant pope caved in, although the order was revived after the French Revolution.

Some Catholic rulers also turned their reforming efforts on monasteries and convents, believing that the large monastic clergy should make a more practical contribution to social and religious life. Austria, a leader in controlling the church (see page 620) and promoting primary education, showed how far the process could go. Whereas Maria Theresa sharply restricted entry into "unproductive" orders, Joseph II recalled the radical initiatives of the Protestant Reformation. In his Edict on Idle Institutions, Joseph abolished contemplative orders, henceforth permitting only orders that were engaged in teaching, nursing, or other practical work. The number of monks plunged from sixty-five thousand to twenty-seven thousand. The state also expropriated the dissolved monasteries and used their great wealth for charitable purposes and higher salaries for ordinary priests.

Protestant Revival

In their attempt to recapture the vital core of the Christian religion, the Protestant reformers had rigorously suppressed all the medieval practices that they considered nonessential or erroneous. For example, they had taken very seriously the commandment "Thou shalt not make any graven image" (Exodus 20:4), and their radical reforms had reordered church interiors. Relics and crucifixes had been permanently removed from crypt and altar, while stained-glass windows had been smashed and walls and murals covered with whitewash. Processions and pilgrimages, saints and shrines—all such practices had been eliminated because they were not founded on Scripture. Such revolutionary changes had often troubled ordinary churchgoers, but by the late seventeenth century the vast reforms of the Reformation had been completed and thoroughly routinized in most Protestant churches.

Indeed, official Protestant churches had generally settled into a smug complacency. In the Reformation heartland, one concerned German minister wrote that the Lutheran church "had become paralyzed in forms of dead doctrinal conformity" and badly needed a return to its original inspiration.[13] This voice was one of many that would prepare and then guide a powerful Protestant revival, which was largely successful because it answered the intense but increasingly unsatisfied needs of common people.

The Protestant revival began in Germany. It was known as "Pietism," and three aspects helped explain its powerful appeal. First, Pietism called for a warm, emotional religion that everyone could experience. Enthusiasm—in prayer, in worship, in preaching, in life itself—was the key concept. "Just as a drunkard becomes full of wine, so must the congregation become filled with spirit," declared one exuberant writer. Another said simply, "The heart must burn."[14]

Second, Pietism reasserted the earlier radical stress on the priesthood of all believers, thereby reducing the large gulf between the official clergy and the Lutheran laity. Bible reading and study were enthusiastically extended to all classes, and this provided a powerful spur for popular education as well as individual religious development (see page 669). Finally, Pietists believed in the practical power of Christian rebirth in everyday affairs. Reborn Christians were expected to lead good, moral lives and come from all social classes.

Pietism had a major impact on John Wesley (1703–1791), who served as the catalyst for popular religious revival in England. Wesley came from a long line of ministers, and when he went to Oxford University to prepare for the clergy, he mapped a fanatically earnest "scheme of religion." Like some students during final-

A Midsummer Afternoon with a Methodist Preacher This detail from a painting by de Loutherbourg suggests in a humorous manner how Wesley and his followers took their optimistic Christianity to the people of England. Methodist ministers championed open-air preaching and week-long revivals. *(National Gallery of Canada, Ottawa)*

exam period, he organized every waking moment. After becoming a teaching fellow at Oxford, he organized a Holy Club for similarly minded students, who were soon known contemptuously as "Methodists" because they were so methodical in their devotion. Yet like the young Luther, Wesley remained intensely troubled about his own salvation, even after his ordination as an Anglican priest in 1728.

Wesley's anxieties related to grave problems of the faith in England. The Church of England was shamelessly used by the government to provide favorites with high-paying jobs and sinecures. Building of churches practically stopped while the population grew, and in many parishes there was a grave shortage of pews. Services and sermons had settled into an uninspiring routine. That the properly purified religion had been separated from local customs and social life was symbolized by church doors that were customarily locked on weekdays. Moreover, the skepticism of the Enlightenment was making inroads among the educated classes, and deism was becoming popular. Some bishops and church leaders acted as if they believed that doctrines such as the Virgin Birth or the Ascension were little more than particularly elegant superstitions.

Spiritual counseling from a sympathetic Pietist minister from Germany prepared Wesley for a mystical, emotional "conversion" in 1738. He described this critical turning point in his *Journal:*

In the evening I went to a [Christian] society in Aldersgate Street where one was reading Luther's preface to the Epistle to the Romans. About a quarter before nine, while he was describing the change which God works in the heart through faith in Christ, I felt my heart strangely warmed. I felt I did trust in Christ, Christ alone for salvation; and an assurance was given me that he had taken away my sins, even mine, and saved me from the law of sin and death.[15]

Wesley's emotional experience resolved his intellectual doubts. Moreover, he was convinced that any person, no matter how poor or uneducated, might have a similarly heartfelt conversion and gain the same blessed assurance.

Wesley took the good news to the people, traveling some 225,000 miles by horseback and preaching more than forty thousand sermons in fifty years. Since existing churches were often overcrowded and the church-state establishment was hostile, Wesley preached in open fields. People came in large numbers. Of critical importance was Wesley's rejection of Calvinist predestination—the doctrine of salvation granted only to a select few. Expanding on earlier Dutch theologians' views, he preached that *all* men and women who earnestly sought salvation might be saved. It was a message of hope and joy, of free will and universal salvation.

Wesley's ministry won converts, formed Methodist cells, and eventually resulted in a new denomination. And as Wesley had been inspired by Pietist revival in Germany, so evangelicals in the Church of England and the old dissenting groups now followed Wesley's example, giving impetus to an even broader awakening among the lower classes. In Protestant countries, religion remained a vital force in the lives of the people.

Catholic Piety

Religion also flourished in Catholic Europe around 1700, but there were important differences with Protestant practice. First of all, the visual contrast was striking; baroque art had lavished rich and emotionally exhilarating figures and images on Catholic churches, just as Protestants had removed theirs. From almost every indication, people in Catholic Europe remained intensely religious. More than 95 percent of the population probably attended church for Easter Communion, the climax of the Catholic church year.

The tremendous popular strength of religion in Catholic countries reflected religion's integral role in community life and popular culture. Thus although Catholics reluctantly confessed their sins to priests, they enthusiastically joined together in religious festivals to celebrate the passage of the liturgical year. In addition to the great processional days—such as Palm Sunday, the joyful re-enactment of Jesus' triumphal entry into Jerusalem, or the chanted supplications and penances for three Rogation days before the bodily ascent of Jesus into heaven on Ascension Day—each parish had its own saints' days, processions, and pilgrimages. Led by its priest, a congregation might march around the village or across the countryside to a local shrine or chapel. Before each procession or feast day, the priest explained its religious significance to kindle group piety. But processions were also folklore and tradition, an escape from work, and a form of recreation. A holiday atmosphere sometimes reigned on longer processions, with drinking and dancing and couples disappearing into the woods.

Indeed, devout Catholics held many religious beliefs that were marginal to the Christian faith, often of obscure or even pagan origin. On the Feast of Saint Anthony, for example, priests were expected to bless salt and bread for farm animals to protect them from disease. One saint's relics could help cure a child of fear, and there were healing springs for many ailments. The ordinary person combined a strong Christian faith with a wealth of time-honored superstitions.

Inspired initially by the fervor of the Catholic Counter-Reformation and then to some extent by the critical rationalism of the Enlightenment, parish priests and Catholic hierarchies sought increasingly to "purify" popular religious practice and to detach that purified religion from everyday life in the eighteenth century. Thus one parish priest in France lashed out at his parishioners, claiming that they were "more superstitious than devout . . . and sometimes appear as baptized idolators."[16] Another priest tried to abolish pilgrimages to a local sacred spring of Our Lady reputed to revive dead babies long enough for a proper baptism. French priests particularly denounced the "various remnants of paganism" found in popular bonfire ceremonies during Lent, in which young men, "yelling and screaming like madmen," tried to jump over the bonfires in order to help the crops grow and protect themselves from illness. One priest saw rational Christians regressing into pagan animals—"the triumph of Hell and the shame of Christianity."[17]

In contrast with Protestant reformers, who had already used the power of the territorial state to crush such practices, many Catholic priests and hierarchies preferred a compromise between theological purity and the people's piety, perhaps realizing that the line between divine truth and mere superstition is not easily drawn. Thus the severity of the attack on popular Catholicism varied widely by country and region. Where authorities pursued purification vigorously, as in Austria under Joseph II, pious peasants saw only an incomprehensible attack on the true faith and drew back in anger. Their reaction dramatized the growing tension between the attitudes of educated elites and the common people.

Leisure and Recreation

The combination of religious celebration and popular recreation seen in festivals and processions was most strikingly displayed at Carnival, a time of reveling and excess in Catholic and Mediterranean Europe. Carnival preceded Lent—the forty days of fasting and penitence before Easter—and for a few exceptional days in January or February, a wild release of drinking, masquerading, and dancing reigned. Moreover, a combination of plays, processions, and rowdy spectacles turned the established order upside down. Peasants became nobles, fools turned into philosophers, and the rich were humbled. These once-a-year rituals gave people a much-appreciated chance to release their pent-up frustrations and aggressions before life returned to the usual pattern of leisure and recreation.

That pattern featured socializing in groups, for despite the spread of literacy, the culture of the common people was largely oral rather than written. In the cold, dark winter months, families gathered around the fireplace to talk, sing, tell stories, do craftwork, and keep warm. In some parts of Europe, women would gather together in groups in someone's cottage to chat, sew, spin, and laugh. Sometimes a few young men would be invited so that the daughters (and mothers) could size up potential suitors in a supervised atmosphere. A favorite recreation of men was drinking and talking with buddies in public places, and it was a sorry village that had no tavern. In addition to old favorites such as beer and wine, the common people turned with gusto toward cheap and potent hard liquor, which fell in price because of improved techniques for distilling grain in the eighteenth century.

Towns and cities offered a wide range of amusements. Many of these had to be paid for because the eighteenth century saw a sharp increase in the commercialization of leisure-time activities—a trend that continues to this day. Urban fairs featured prepared foods, acrobats, freak shows, open-air performances, optical illusions, and the like. Such entertainments attracted a variety of social classes. So did the growing number of commercial, profit-oriented spectator sports. These ranged from traveling circuses and horse races to boxing matches and bullfights. Modern sports heroes, such as brain-bashing heavyweight champions and haughty matadors, made their appearance on the historical scene.

"Blood sports," such as bullbaiting and cockfighting, remained popular with the masses. In bullbaiting the bull, usually staked on a chain in the courtyard of an inn, was attacked by ferocious dogs for the amusement of the innkeeper's clients. Eventually the maimed and tortured animal was slaughtered by a butcher and sold as meat. In cockfighting two roosters, carefully trained by their owners and armed with razor-sharp steel spurs, slashed and clawed each other in a small ring until the victor won—and the loser died. An added attraction of cockfighting was that the screaming spectators could bet on the lightning-fast combat and its uncertain outcome.

In trying to place the vibrant popular culture of the common people in broad perspective, historians have stressed the growing criticism levied against it by the educated elites in the second half of the eighteenth century. These elites, which had previously shared the popular enthusiasm for religious festivals, Carnival, drinking in taverns, blood sports, and the like, now

Cockfighting in England This engraving by William Hogarth (1697–1764) satirizes the popular taste for blood sports, which Hogarth despised and lampooned in his famous *Four Stages of Cruelty.* The central figure in the wildly excited gathering is a blind nobleman, who actually existed and seldom missed a fight. Note the steel spurs on the birds' legs. *(Courtesy of Trustees of the British Museum)*

tended to see only superstition, sin, disorder, and vulgarity.[18] The resulting attack on popular culture, which had its more distant origins in the Protestant clergy's efforts to eliminate frivolity and superstition, was intensified as educated elites embraced the critical world-view of the Enlightenment. This shift in cultural attitudes drove a wedge between the common people and the educated public. The mutual hostility that this separation engendered played an important role in the emergence of sharp class conflict in the era of the French and the Industrial Revolutions.

Summary

In recent years, imaginative research has greatly increased the specialist's understanding of ordinary life and social patterns in the past. The human experience as recounted by historians has become richer and more meaningful, and many mistaken ideas have fallen by the wayside. This has been particularly true of eighteenth-century, predominately agrarian Europe, which combined a fascinating mixture of continuity and change.

To summarize, the life of the people remained primarily rural and oriented toward the local community. Tradition, routine, and well-established codes of behavior framed much of the everyday experience of the typical villager. Thus just as the three-field agricultural cycle and its pattern of communal rights had determined traditional patterns of grain production, so did community values in the countryside strongly encourage a late age of marriage, a low rate of illegitimate births, and a strict attitude toward children. Patterns of recreation and leisure, from churchgoing and religious festivals to sewing and drinking in groups within an oral culture, also reflected and reinforced community ties and values. Many long-standing ideas and beliefs, ranging from obscure religious customs to support for fair prices, remained strong forces and sustained continuity in popular life.

Yet powerful forces also worked for change. Many of these came from outside and above, from the aggressive capitalists, educated elites, and government officials discussed in the last two chapters. Closely knit villages began to lose control over families and marital practices, as could be seen in the earlier, more romantic marriages of cottage workers and in the beginning of the explosion in illegitimate births. Although the new, less rigorous attitudes toward children that were emerging in elite culture did not reach the people, the elite belief in the usefulness of some education did result in growing popular literacy. The grain-based diet became more varied with the grudging acceptance of the potato, and the benefits of the spectacular conquest of smallpox began to reach the common people in the late eighteenth century. Finally, the common people found that their beliefs and customs were being increasingly attacked by educated elites, who thought they knew better. The popular reaction to these attacks generally remained muted in the eighteenth century, but the common people and their advocates would offer vigorous responses and counterattacks in the revolutionary era.

NOTES

1. Quoted in J. M. Beattie, "The Criminality of Women in Eighteenth-Century England," *Journal of Social History* 8 (Summer 1975): 86.
2. W. L. Langer, "Infanticide: A Historical Survey," *History of Childhood Quarterly* 1 (Winter 1974): 357.
3. Quoted in R. Cobb, *The Police and the People: French Popular Protest, 1789–1820* (Oxford: Clarendon Press, 1970), p. 238.
4. M. Segalen, *Love and Power in the Peasant Family: Rural France in the Nineteenth Century* (New York: Basil Blackwell, 1983), p. 41. The passage as cited here has been edited to the past tense.
5. Quoted in D. S. Landes, ed., *The Rise of Capitalism* (New York: Macmillan, 1966), pp. 56–57.
6. G. Gullickson, *Spinners and Weavers of Auffay: Rural Industry and the Sexual Division of Labor in a French Village, 1750–1850* (Cambridge: Cambridge University Press, 1986), p. 186. See also L. A. Tilly, J. W. Scott, and M. Cohen, "Women's Work and European Fertility Patterns," *Journal of Interdisciplinary History* 6 (Winter 1976): 447–476.
7. J. Michelet, *The People,* trans. with an introduction by J. P. McKay (Urbana: University of Illinois Press, 1973; original publication, 1846), pp. 38–39.
8. Quoted in B. W. Lorence, "Parents and Children in Eighteenth-Century Europe," *History of Childhood Quarterly* 2 (Summer 1974): 1–2.
9. Ibid., pp. 13, 16.
10. E. Kennedy, *A Cultural History of the French Revolution* (New Haven, Conn.: Yale University Press, 1989), p. 47.
11. Quoted in L. S. King, *The Medical World of the Eighteenth Century* (Chicago: University of Chicago Press, 1958), p. 320.
12. Quoted in R. Sand, *The Advance to Social Medicine* (London: Staples Press, 1952), pp. 86–87.
13. Quoted in K. Pinson, *Pietism as a Factor in the Rise of German Nationalism* (New York: Columbia University Press, 1934), p. 13.
14. Ibid., pp. 43–44.
15. Quoted in S. Andrews, *Methodism and Society* (London: Longmans, Green, 1970), p. 327.
16. Quoted in I. Woloch, *Eighteenth-Century Europe: Tradition and Progress, 1715–1789* (New York: W. W. Norton, 1982), p. 292.
17. Quoted in T. Tackett, *Priest and Parish in Eighteenth-Century France* (Princeton, N.J.: Princeton University Press, 1977), p. 214.
18. Woloch, *Eighteenth-Century Europe,* pp. 220–221; see also pp. 214–220 for this section.

SUGGESTED READING

Social topics of the kind considered in this chapter have come into their own in recent years, and the reader is strongly advised to take time to look through recent volumes of some leading journals: *Journal of Social History, Past and Present,* and *Journal of Interdisciplinary History.* In addition, the number of book-length studies continues to expand rapidly. Several of these studies are mentioned in the Notes.

Among general introductions to the history of the family, women, and children, J. Casey, *The History of the Family* (1989), is recommended. A. Imhof, *Lost Worlds: How Our European Ancestors Coped with Everyday Life and Why Life Is So Hard Today* (1996), sheds new light on family ties and attitudes toward death, which may be compared with P. Laslett, *The World We Have Lost* (1965), a pioneering investigation of England before the Industrial Revolution. L. Stone, *The Family, Sex and Marriage in England, 1500–1800* (1977), is a provocative general interpretation, and L. Tilly and J. Scott, *Women, Work and Family* (1978), remains an excellent introduction. Two valuable works on women, both with good bibliographies, are M. Boxer and J. Quataert, eds., *Connecting Spheres: Women in the Western*

(continued on page 688)

LISTENING TO THE PAST

A New Way to Educate Children

Emile, by Jean-Jacques Rousseau, is one of history's most original books. Sometimes called a declaration of rights for children, Emile *challenged existing patterns of child rearing and pleaded for humane treatment of children.*

Rousseau's work also had a powerful impact on theories of education. As the following passage suggests, Emile *argued that education must shield the unspoiled child from the corrupting influences of civilization and allow the child to develop naturally and spontaneously. It is eloquent testimony to Rousseau's troubled life that he neglected his own children and placed all five of them in orphanages.*

Rousseau believed that the sexes were by nature intended for different occupations. Thus Emile *might eventually tackle difficult academic subjects, but Sophie, his future wife in the book, needed to learn only how to manage the home and be a good mother and an obedient wife. The idea that girls and boys should be educated to operate in "separate spheres" was to gain wide acceptance in the nineteenth century.*

A man must know many things which seem useless to a child, but need the child learn, or can he indeed learn, all that the man must know? Try to teach the child what is of use to a child and you will find that it takes all his time. Why urge him to the studies of an age he may never reach, to the neglect of those studies which meet his present needs? "But," you ask, "will it not be too late to learn what he ought to know when the time comes to use it?" I cannot tell; but this I do know, it is impossible to teach it sooner, for our real teachers are experience and emotion, and man will never learn what befits a man except under its own conditions. A child knows he must become a man; all the ideas he may have as to man's place in life are so many opportunities for his instruction, but he should remain in complete ignorance of those ideas which are beyond his grasp. My whole book is one continued argument in support of this fundamental principle of education.

As soon as we have contrived to give our pupil [Emile] an idea of the word "useful," we have got an additional means of controlling him, for this word makes a great impression on him, provided that its meaning for him is a meaning relative to his own age, and provided he clearly sees its relation to his own well-being. . . . "What is the use of that?" In the future this is the sacred formula, the formula by which he and I test every action of our lives. . . .

I do not like verbal explanations. Young people pay little heed to them, nor do they remember them. Things! Things! I cannot repeat it too often. We lay too much stress upon words; we teachers babble, and our students follow our example.

Suppose we are studying the course of the sun and the way to find our bearings, when all at once Emile interrupts me with the question, "What is the use of that?" What a fine lecture I might give [going on and on]! . . . When I have finished I shall have shown myself a regular pedant, I shall have made a great display of learning, and not one single idea has he understood. . . .

But Emile is educated in a simpler fashion. We take so much pains to teach him a difficult idea that he will have heard nothing of all this. At the first word he does not understand, he will run away, he will prance about the room, and leave me to speechify by myself. Let us seek a more commonplace explanation; my scientific learning is of no use to him.

We were observing the position of the forest to the north of Montmorency when he interrupted me with the usual question, "What is the use of that?" "You are right," I said. "Let us take time to think it over, and if we find it is no use we will drop it, for we only want useful games." We find something else to do and geography is put aside for the day.

Next morning I suggest a walk; there is nothing he would like better; children are always ready to run about, and he is a good walker. We climb up to the forest, we wander through its clearings and lose ourselves. . . . At last we [are exhausted and] sit down to rest and to consider our position. I assume that Emile has been educated like an ordinary child. He does not think, he begins to cry; he has no idea we are close to Montmorency, which is hidden from our view by a mere thicket. . . .

Jean-Jacques. "My dear Emile, what shall we do to get out?"

Emile. "I am sure I do not know. I am tired, I am hungry, I am thirsty, I cannot go any further."

Jean-Jacques. "Do you suppose I am any better off? I would cry too if I could make my lunch off tears. Crying is no use, we must look about us. What time is it?"

Emile. "It is noon and I am so hungry!"

Jean-Jacques. "I am so hungry too. . . . Unluckily my dinner won't come to find me. It is twelve o'clock. This time yesterday we were observing the position of the forest from Montmorency. If only we could see the position of Montmorency from the forest—"

Emile. "But yesterday we could see the forest, and here we cannot see the town."

Jean-Jacques. "That is just it. If we could only find it without seeing it. . . . Did not we say the forest was—"

Emile. "North of Montmorency."

Jean-Jacques. "Then Montmorency must lie—"

Emile. "South of the forest."

Jean-Jacques. "We know how to find the north at midday."

Emile. "Yes, by the direction of the shadows."

Jean-Jacques. "But the south?"

Emile. "What shall we do?"

Jean-Jacques. "The south is opposite the north."

Emile. "That is true; we need only find the opposite of the shadows. That is the south! That is the south! Montmorency must be over there! Let us look for it there!"

Jean-Jacques. "Perhaps you are right; let us follow this path through the wood."

Emile. (Clapping his hands.) "Oh, I can see Montmorency! there it is, quite plain, just in front of us! Come to lunch, come to dinner, make haste! Astronomy is some use after all."

Be sure that he thinks this if he does not say it; no matter which, provided I do not say it myself. He will certainly never forget this day's lesson as long as he lives, while if I had only led him to think of all this at home, my lecture would have been forgotten the next day. Teach by doing whenever you can, and only fall back upon words when doing is out of the question.

✣ Jean-Jacques Rousseau (1712–1778), portrayed as a gentle teacher and a pensive philosopher in this contemporary illustration. *(The Granger Collection, New York)*

Questions for Analysis

1. What criticism did Rousseau direct at the social and educational practices of his time?
2. How did Rousseau propose to educate his pupil?
3. Do you think Rousseau's plan appealed to peasants and urban workers in the eighteenth century? Why or why not?
4. In what ways did Rousseau's plan of education and his assumptions on human nature reflect some major ideas of the Enlightenment?

Source: Slightly adapted from J.-J. Rousseau, *Emile, or Education,* trans. B. Foxley (New York: E. P. Dutton, 1911), pp. 141–144.

World, 1500 to the Present (1987); and R. Bridenthal, C. Koonz, and S. Stuard, eds., *Becoming Visible: Women in European History,* 2d ed. (1987). P. Aries, *Centuries of Childhood: A Social History of Family Life* (1962), is another stimulating study. E. Shorter, *The Making of the Modern Family* (1975), is a lively, controversial interpretation, which should be compared with the excellent study by M. Segalen, *Love and Power in the Peasant Family: Rural France in the Nineteenth Century* (1983). A. MacFarlane, *The Family Life of Ralph Josselin* (1970), is a brilliant re-creation of the intimate family circle of a seventeenth-century English clergyman who kept a detailed diary; MacFarlane's *Origins of English Individualism: The Family, Property and Social Transition* (1978) is a major work. L. Pollack, *Forgotten Children: Parent-Child Relations from 1500 to 1900* (1983), is a general introduction. B. Lorence-Kot, *Child-Rearing and Reform: A Study of Nobility in Eighteenth-Century Poland* (1985), stresses the harshness of parental discipline. Various aspects of sexual relationships are treated imaginatively by M. Foucault, *The History of Sexuality* (1981), and R. Wheaton and T. Hareven, eds., *Family and Sexuality in French History* (1980).

L. Moch, *Moving Europeans: Migration in Western Europe Since 1650* (1992), offers a rich, human, and highly recommended account of the movements of millions of ordinary people. J. Burnett, *A History of the Cost of Living* (1969), has a great deal of interesting information about what people spent their money on in the past. J. C. Drummond and A. Wilbraham, *The Englishman's Food: A History of Five Centuries of English Diet,* 2d ed. (1958), remains a valuable and fascinating introduction. J. Knyveton, *Diary of a Surgeon in the Year 1751–1752* (1937), gives a contemporary's unforgettable picture of both eighteenth-century medicine and social customs, as does M. Romsey, *Professional and Popular Medicine in France, 1770–1830: The Social World of Medical Practice* (1988). Good introductions to the evolution of medical practices are B. Ingles, *History of Medicine* (1965); Roy Porter, ed., *The Cambridge Illustrated History of Medicine* (1996); and A. Digby, *Making a Medical Living: Doctors and Patients in the English Market for Medicine, 1720–1991* (1994). M. Lindemann, *Health and Healing in Eighteenth-Century Germany* (1996), is a wide-ranging synthesis. H. Marland, ed., *The Art of Midwifery: Early Modern Midwives in Europe* (1993), discusses developments in several countries and complements L. Ulrich, *A Midwife's Tale: The Life of Martha Ballard, Based on Her Diary, 1785–1812* (1990), a superb reconstruction. W. Boyd, *History of Western Education* (1966), is a standard survey, whereas R. Houston, *Literacy in Early Modern Europe: Culture and Education, 1500–1800* (1988), is brief and engaging.

The study of popular culture is expanding. Among older studies, M. George, *London Life in the Eighteenth Century* (1965), is a delight, whereas D. Roche, *The People of Paris: An Essay in Popular Culture in the Eighteenth Century* (1987), presents an unforgettable portrait of the Paris poor. I. Woloch, *Eighteenth-Century Europe: Tradition and Progress, 1715–1789* (1982), includes a survey of popular culture and a good bibliography; E. Kennedy, *A Cultural History of the French Revolution* (1989), beautifully captures rural and urban attitudes in France before and during the French Revolution. R. Malcolmson, *Popular Recreation in English Society, 1700–1850* (1973), provides a colorful account of boxers, bettors, bullbaiting, and more. L. Hunt, *The New Cultural History* (1989), provides an engaging discussion of conceptual issues. G. Rude, *The Crowd in History, 1730–1848* (1964), is an influential effort to see politics and popular protest from below. An important series edited by R. Forster and O. Ranuum considers neglected social questions such as diet, abandoned children, and deviants, as does P. Burke's excellent study, *Popular Culture in Early Modern Europe* (1978). J. Gillis, *For Better, for Worse: Marriage in Britain Since 1500* (1985), and R. Philips, *Untying the Knot: A Short History of Divorce* (1991), are good introductions to institutional changes.

Good works on religious life include J. Delumeau, *Catholicism Between Luther and Voltaire: A New View of the Counter-Reformation* (1977); B. Semmel, *The Methodist Revolution* (1973); and J. Bettey, *Church and Community: The Parish Church in English Life* (1979).

CHAPTER 21 The Revolution in Politics, 1775–1815

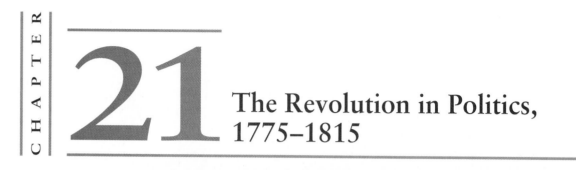

The Planting of a Liberty Tree, by Pierre Antoine Leseur. *(Giraudon/Art Resource, NY)*

The last years of the eighteenth century were a time of great upheaval. A series of revolutions and revolutionary wars challenged the old order of monarchs and aristocrats. The ideas of freedom and equality, ideas that have not stopped shaping the world since that era, flourished and spread. The revolutionary era began in North America in 1775. Then in 1789 France, the most influential country in Europe, became the leading revolutionary nation. It established first a constitutional monarchy, then a radical republic, and finally a new empire under Napoleon. The armies of France also joined forces with patriots and radicals abroad in an effort to establish new governments based on new principles throughout much of Europe. The world of modern domestic and international politics was born.

- What caused this era of revolution?
- What were the ideas and objectives of the men and women who rose up violently to undo the established system?
- What were the gains and losses for privileged groups and for ordinary people in a generation of war and upheaval?

These are the questions underlying this chapter's examination of the revolutionary era.

Liberty and Equality

Two ideas fueled the revolutionary period in both America and Europe: liberty and equality. What did eighteenth-century politicians and other people mean by liberty and equality, and why were those ideas so radical and revolutionary in their day?

The call for liberty was first of all a call for individual human rights. Even the most enlightened monarchs customarily claimed that it was their duty to regulate what people wrote and believed. Liberals of the revolutionary era protested such controls from on high. They demanded freedom to worship according to the dictates of their consciences, an end to censorship, and freedom from arbitrary laws and from judges who simply obeyed orders from the government. The Declaration of the Rights of Man, issued at the beginning of the French Revolution, proclaimed, "Liberty consists in being able to do anything that does not harm another person." In theory, therefore, a citizen's rights had "no limits except those which assure to the other members of society the enjoyment of these same rights." In the context of the monarchial and absolutist forms of government then dominating Europe, this was a truly radical idea.

The call for liberty was also a call for a new kind of government. Revolutionary liberals believed that the people were sovereign—that is, that the people alone had the authority to make laws limiting an individual's freedom of action. In practice, this system of government meant choosing legislators who represented the people and were accountable to them.

Equality was a more ambiguous idea. Eighteenth-century liberals argued that, in theory, all citizens should have identical rights and civil liberties and that the nobility had no right to special privileges based on the accident of birth. However, liberals accepted some well-established distinctions.

First, most eighteenth-century liberals were *men* of their times, and they generally shared with other men the belief that equality between men and women was neither practical nor desirable. Women played an important political role in the French Revolution at several points, but the men of the French Revolution limited formal political rights—the right to vote, to run for office, to participate in government—to men.

Second, liberals never believed that everyone should be equal economically. Quite the contrary. As Thomas Jefferson wrote in an early draft of the American Declaration of Independence (before he changed "property" to the more noble-sounding "happiness"), everyone was equal in "the pursuit of property." Jefferson and other liberals certainly did not expect equal success in that pursuit. Great differences in wealth and income between rich and poor were perfectly acceptable to liberals. The essential point was that everyone should legally have an equal chance.

In eighteenth-century Europe, however, such equality of opportunity was a truly revolutionary idea. Society was still legally divided into groups with special privileges, such as the nobility and the clergy, and groups with special burdens, such as the peasantry. And in most countries, various middle-class groups—professionals, business people, townspeople, and craftsmen—enjoyed privileges that allowed them to monopolize all sorts of economic activity. Liberals criticized not economic inequality itself but this kind of economic inequality based on artificial legal distinctions.

The ideas of liberty and equality—the central ideas of classical liberalism—had deep roots in Western history. The classical Greeks and the Judeo-Christian traditions had affirmed for hundreds of years the sanctity and value of the individual human being, as well as personal responsibility on the part of both common folk and exalted rulers. The hounded and persecuted Protestant radicals of the later sixteenth century had died for the revolutionary idea that individuals were entitled to their own religious beliefs.

Although the liberal creed was rooted in the Western tradition, classical liberalism first crystallized at the end of the seventeenth century and during the Enlightenment of the eighteenth century. Liberal ideas reflected the Enlightenment's stress on human dignity and human happiness on earth and its faith in science, rationality, and progress. Almost all the writers of the Enlightenment were passionately committed to greater personal liberty and equal treatment before the law.

Certain English and French thinkers were mainly responsible for joining the Enlightenment's concern for personal freedom and legal equality to a theoretical justification of liberal self-government. The two most important were John Locke and the baron de Montesquieu. Locke maintained that England's long political tradition rested on "the rights of Englishmen" and on representative government through Parliament. He admired especially the great Whig nobles who had deposed James II and made the bloodless revolution of 1688–1689, and he argued that if a government oversteps its proper function of protecting the natural rights of life, liberty, and private property, it becomes a tyranny. Montesquieu was also inspired by English constitutional history. He, too, believed that powerful "intermediary groups"—such as the judicial nobility of which he was a proud member—offered the best defense of liberty against despotism.

The belief that representative institutions could defend their liberty and interests appealed powerfully to well-educated, prosperous groups, which historians have traditionally labeled as the bourgeoisie. Yet liberal ideas about individual rights and political freedom also appealed to much of the hereditary nobility, at least in western Europe and as formulated by Montesquieu. Representative government did not mean democracy, which liberal thinkers tended to equate with mob rule. Rather, they envisioned voting for representatives as being restricted to those who owned property—those with "a stake in society." England had shown the way. After 1688 it had combined a parliamentary system and considerable individual liberty with a restricted franchise and unquestionable aristocratic pre-eminence. In the course of the eighteenth century, many leading French nobles, led by high-ranking noble judges, who were inspired by the doctrines of Montesquieu, were increasingly eager to follow the English example. Thus eighteenth-century liberalism found broad support among the prosperous, well-educated elites in western Europe.

What liberalism lacked from the beginning was strong popular support. At least two reasons account for the people's wary attitude. First, for common people, the great questions were theoretical and political but immediate and economic; getting enough to eat was a crucial challenge. Second, some of the traditional practices and institutions that liberals wanted to abolish were dear to peasants and urban workers. Comfortable elites had already come into conflict with the people in the eighteenth century over the enclosure of common lands and the regulation of food prices. This conflict would sharpen in the revolutionary era as differences in outlook and well-being led to many misunderstandings and disappointments for both groups.

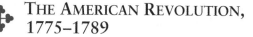

The American Revolution, 1775–1789

The era of liberal political revolution began in the New World. The thirteen mainland colonies of British North America revolted against their home country and then succeeded in establishing a new unified government.

Americans have long debated the meaning of their revolution. Some have even questioned whether it was a real revolution, as opposed to a war for independence. According to some scholars, the Revolution was conservative and defensive in that its demands were for the traditional liberties of English citizens; Americans were united against the British, but otherwise they were a satisfied people, not torn by internal conflict. Other scholars have argued that, on the contrary, the American Revolution was quite radical. It split families between patriots and Loyalists and divided the country. It achieved goals that were fully as advanced as those obtained by the French in their great revolution a few years later.

How does one reconcile these positions? Both contain large elements of truth. The American revolutionaries did believe that they were demanding only the traditional rights of English men and women. But those traditional rights were liberal rights, and in the American context they had very strong democratic and popular overtones. Thus the American Revolution was fought in the name of established ideals that were still quite radical in the context of the times. And in founding a government firmly based on liberal principles, the Americans set an example that had a forceful impact on Europe and sped up political development there.

The Origins of the Revolution

The American Revolution had its immediate origins in a squabble over increased taxes. The British government had fought and decisively won the Seven Years' War (see page 647) on the strength of its professional army and navy. The American colonists had furnished little real aid. The high cost of the war to the British, however, had led to a doubling of the British national debt. Anticipating further expense defending its recently conquered western lands from native American uprisings, the British government in London set about reorganizing the empire with a series of bold, largely unprecedented measures. Breaking with tradition, the British decided to maintain a large army in North America after peace was restored in 1763. Moreover, they sought to exercise strict control over their newly conquered western lands and to tax the colonies directly. In 1765 the government pushed through Parliament the Stamp Act, which levied taxes on a long list of commercial and legal documents, diplomas, pamphlets, newspapers, almanacs, dice, and playing cards. A stamp glued to each article indicated the tax had been paid.

This effort to increase taxes as part of a tightening up of the empire seemed perfectly reasonable to the British. Heavier stamp taxes had been collected in Great Britain for two generations, and Americans were being asked only to pay a share of their own defense costs. Moreover, Americans had been paying only very low local taxes. The Stamp Act would have doubled taxes to about 2 shillings per person per year. No other people in the European or colonial world (except the Poles) paid so little. Meanwhile, the British paid the highest taxes in the Western world—26 shillings per person. It is not surprising that taxes per person in the newly independent American nation were much higher in 1785 than in 1765, when the British no longer subsidized American defense. The colonists protested the Stamp Act vigorously and violently, however, and after their rioting and boycotts against British goods, Parliament reluctantly repealed the new tax.

As the fury over the Stamp Act revealed, much more was involved than taxes. The key questions were political. To what extent could the home government refashion the empire and reassert its power while limiting the authority of colonial legislatures and their elected representatives? Accordingly, who should represent the colonies, and who had the right to make laws for Americans? While a troubled majority of Americans searched hard for a compromise, some radicals began to proclaim that "taxation without representation is tyranny." The British government replied that Americans were represented in Parliament, albeit indirectly (like most English people themselves), and that the absolute supremacy of Parliament throughout the empire could not be questioned. Many Americans felt otherwise. As John Adams put it, "A Parliament of Great Britain can have no more rights to tax the colonies than a Parliament of Paris." Thus imperial reorganization and parliamentary supremacy came to appear as grave threats to Americans' existing liberties and time-honored institutions.

Americans had long exercised a great deal of independence and gone their own way. In British North America, unlike England and Europe, no powerful established church existed, and personal freedom in questions of religion was taken for granted. The colonial assemblies made the important laws, which were seldom overturned by the home government. The right to vote was much more widespread than in England. In many parts of colonial Massachusetts, for example, as many as 95 percent of the adult males could vote.

Moreover, greater political equality was matched by greater social and economic equality. Neither a hereditary nobility nor a hereditary serf population existed, although the slavery of the Americas consigned blacks to a legally oppressed caste. Independent farmers were the largest group in the country and set much of its tone. In short, the colonial experience had slowly formed a people who felt themselves separate and distinct from the home country. The controversies over taxation intensified those feelings of distinctiveness and separation and brought them to the fore.

In 1773 the dispute over taxes and representation flared up again. The British government had permitted the financially hard-pressed East India Company to ship its tea from China directly to its agents in the colonies rather than through London middlemen who sold to independent merchants in the colonies. Thus the company secured a vital monopoly on the tea trade, and colonial merchants were suddenly excluded from a lucrative business. The colonists were quick to protest.

In Boston men disguised as Indians had a rowdy "tea party" and threw the company's tea into the harbor. This led to extreme measures. The so-called Coercive Acts closed the port of Boston, curtailed local elections and town meetings, and greatly expanded the royal governor's power. County conventions in Massachusetts protested vehemently and urged that the acts be

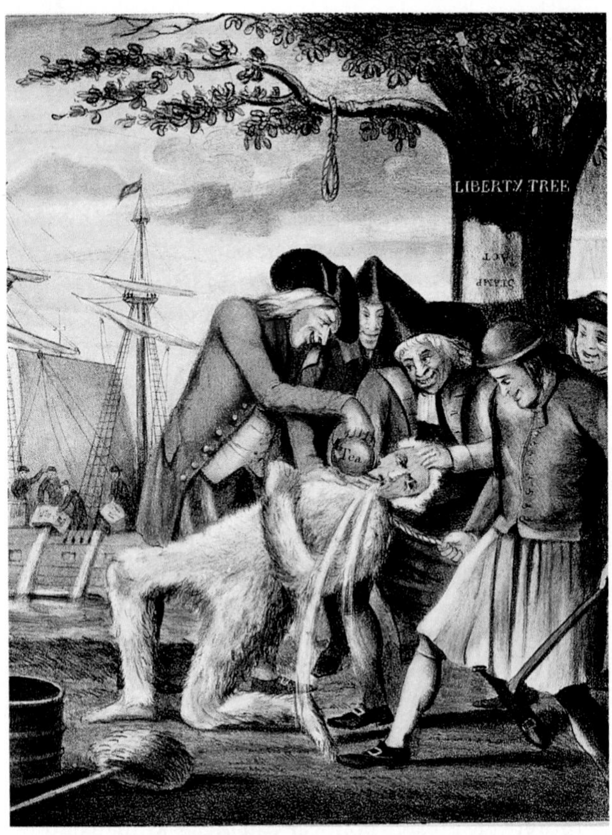

Toward Revolution in Boston The Boston Tea Party was only one of many angry confrontations between British officials and Boston patriots. On January 27, 1774, an angry crowd seized a British customs collector and then tarred and feathered him. This French engraving of 1784 commemorates the defiant and provocative action. *(The Granger Collection, New York)*

"rejected as the attempts of a wicked administration to enslave America." Other colonial assemblies joined in the denunciations. In September 1774, the First Continental Congress met in Philadelphia, where the more radical members argued successfully against concessions to the Crown. Compromise was also rejected by the British Parliament, and in April 1775 fighting began at Lexington and Concord.

Independence

The fighting spread, and the colonists moved slowly but inevitably toward open rebellion and a declaration of independence. The uncompromising attitude of the British government and its use of German mercenaries went a long way toward dissolving long-standing loyalties to the home country and rivalries among the separate colonies. *Common Sense* (1775), a brilliant attack by the recently arrived English radical Thomas Paine (1737–1809), also mobilized public opinion in favor of independence. A runaway bestseller with sales of 120,000 copies in a few months, Paine's tract ridiculed the idea of a small island ruling a great continent. In his call for freedom and republican government, Paine expressed Americans' growing sense of separateness and moral superiority.

On July 4, 1776, the Second Continental Congress adopted the Declaration of Independence. Written by Thomas Jefferson, the Declaration of Independence boldly listed the tyrannical acts committed by George III (r. 1760–1820) and confidently proclaimed the natural rights of mankind and the sovereignty of the American states. Sometimes called the world's greatest political editorial, the Declaration of Independence in effect universalized the traditional rights of English people and made them the rights of all mankind. It stated that "all men are created equal. . . . They are endowed by their Creator with certain unalienable rights. . . . Among these are life, liberty, and the pursuit of happiness." No other American political document has ever caused such excitement, either at home or abroad.

Many American families remained loyal to Britain; many others divided bitterly. After the Declaration of Independence, the conflict often took the form of a civil war pitting patriot against Loyalist. The Loyalists tended to be wealthy and politically moderate. Many patriots, too, were wealthy—individuals such as John Hancock and George Washington—but willingly allied themselves with farmers and artisans in a broad coalition. This coalition harassed the Loyalists and confiscated their property to help pay for the American war effort. The broad social base of the revolutionaries tended to make the liberal revolution democratic. State governments extended the right to vote to many more men (but not to any women) in the course of the war and re-established themselves as republics.

On the international scene, the French sympathized with the rebels from the beginning. They wanted revenge for the humiliating defeats of the Seven Years' War. Officially neutral until 1778, they supplied the great bulk of guns and gunpowder used by the American revolutionaries, very much as foreign great powers have supplied weapons for "wars of national liberation" in our time. By 1777 French volunteers were arriving in Virginia, and a dashing young nobleman, the marquis de Lafayette (1757–1834), quickly became one of Washington's most trusted generals. In 1778 the French government offered a formal alliance to the

American ambassador in Paris, Benjamin Franklin, and in 1779 and 1780 the Spanish and Dutch declared war on Britain. Catherine the Great of Russia helped organize the League of Armed Neutrality in order to protect neutral shipping rights, which Britain refused to recognize.

Thus by 1780 Great Britain was engaged in an imperial war against most of Europe as well as the thirteen colonies. In these circumstances, and in the face of severe reverses in India, the West Indies, and at Yorktown in Virginia, a new British government decided to cut its losses. American negotiators in Paris were receptive. They feared that France wanted a treaty that would bottle up the new United States east of the Allegheny Mountains and give British holdings west of the Alleghenies to France's ally, Spain. Thus the American negotiators deserted their French allies and accepted the extraordinarily favorable terms Britain offered.

By the Treaty of Paris of 1783, Britain recognized the independence of the thirteen colonies and ceded all its territory between the Allegheny Mountains and the Mississippi River to the Americans. Out of the bitter rivalries of the Old World, the Americans snatched dominion over a vast territory.

Framing the Constitution

The liberal program of the American Revolution was consolidated by the federal Constitution, the Bill of Rights, and the creation of a national republic. Assembling in Philadelphia in the summer of 1787, the delegates to the Constitutional Convention were determined to end the period of economic depression, social uncertainty, and very weak central government that had followed independence. The delegates thus decided to grant the federal, or central, government important powers: regulation of domestic and foreign trade, the right to tax, and the means to enforce its laws.

Strong rule would be placed squarely in the context of representative self-government. Senators and congressmen would be the lawmaking delegates of the voters, and the president of the republic would be an elected official. The central government would operate in Montesquieu's framework of checks and balances.

The Signing of the Declaration of Independence, July 4, 1776 John Trumbull's famous painting shows the dignity and determination of America's revolutionary leaders. An extraordinarily talented group, they succeeded in rallying popular support without losing power to more radical forces in the process. *(Yale University Art Gallery)*

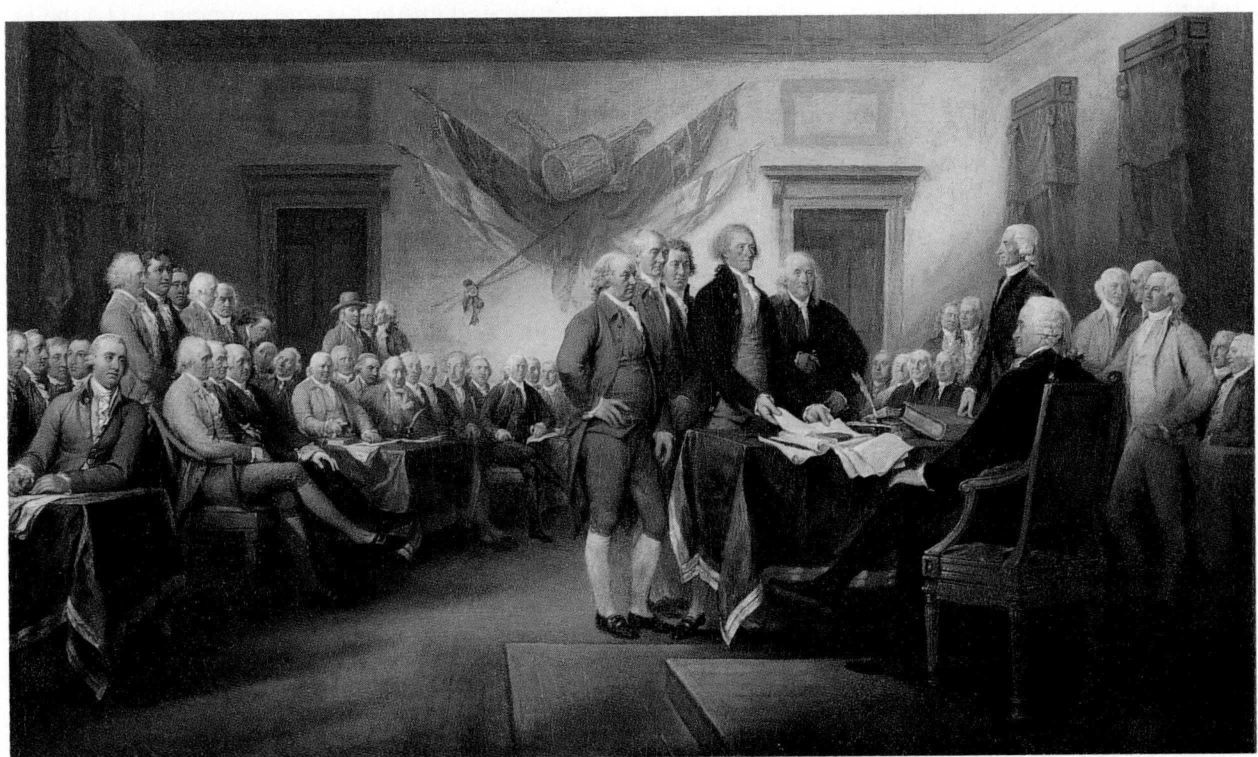

The executive, legislative, and judicial branches would systematically balance one another. The power of the federal government would in turn be checked by the powers of the individual states.

When the results of the secret deliberations of the Constitutional Convention were presented to the states for ratification, a great public debate began. The opponents of the proposed constitution—the Antifederalists—charged that the framers of the new document had taken too much power from the individual states and made the federal government too strong. Moreover, many Antifederalists feared for the personal liberties and individual freedoms for which they had just fought. In order to overcome these objections, the Federalists solemnly promised to spell out these basic freedoms as soon as the new constitution was adopted. The result was the first ten amendments to the Constitution, which the first Congress passed shortly after it met in New York in March 1789. These amendments formed an effective bill of rights to safeguard the individual. Most of them—trial by jury, due process of law, right to assemble, freedom from unreasonable search—had their origins in English law and the English Bill of Rights of 1689. Others—the freedoms of speech, the press, and religion—reflected natural-law theory and the American experience.

The American Constitution and the Bill of Rights exemplified the great strengths and the limits of what came to be called "classical liberalism." Liberty meant individual freedoms and political safeguards. Liberty also meant representative government but did not necessarily mean democracy, with its principle of one person, one vote.

Equality—slaves excepted—meant equality before the law, not equality of political participation or wealth. Indeed, economic inequality was resolutely defended by the elite that framed the Constitution. The right to own property was guaranteed by the Fifth Amendment, and if the government took private property, the owner was to receive "just compensation." The radicalism of liberal revolution in America was primarily legal and political, *not* economic or social.

The Revolution's Impact on Europe

Hundreds of books, pamphlets, and articles analyzed and romanticized the American upheaval. Thoughtful Europeans noted, first of all, its enormous long-term implications for international politics. A secret report by the Venetian ambassador to Paris in 1783 stated what many felt: "If only the union of the Provinces is preserved, it is reasonable to expect that, with the favorable effects of time, and of European arts and sciences, it will become the most formidable power in the world."[1] More generally, American independence fired the imaginations of those aristocrats who were uneasy with their hereditary privileges and those commoners who yearned for equality. Many Europeans believed that the world was advancing and that America was leading the way. As one French writer put it in 1789, "This vast continent which the seas surround will soon change Europe and the universe."

Europeans who dreamed of a new era were fascinated by the political lessons of the American Revolution. The Americans had begun with a revolutionary defense against tyrannical oppression, and they had been victorious. They had then shown how rational beings could assemble together to exercise sovereignty and write a permanent constitution—a new social contract. All this gave greater reality to the concepts of individual liberty and representative government and reinforced one of the primary ideas of the Enlightenment: that a better world was possible.

The French Revolution, 1789–1791

No country felt the consequences of the American Revolution more directly than France. Hundreds of French officers served in America and were inspired by the experience. The most famous of these, the young and impressionable marquis de Lafayette, left home as a great aristocrat determined only to fight France's traditional foe, England. He returned with a love of liberty and firm republican convictions. French intellectuals and publicists engaged in passionate analysis of the federal Constitution as well as the constitutions of the various states of the new United States. The American Revolution undeniably hastened upheaval in France.

Yet the French Revolution did not mirror the American example. It was more radical and more complex, more influential and more controversial, more loved and more hated. For Europeans and most of the rest of the world, it was the great revolution of the eighteenth century, *the* revolution that opened the modern era in politics.

The Breakdown of the Old Order

Like the American Revolution, the French Revolution had its immediate origins in the financial difficulties of the government. The efforts of Louis XV's ministers to raise taxes had been thwarted by the high courts, led by

The Extravagance of the French Court This painting idealizes a party given at the intimate playtime retreat that Queen Marie-Antoinette had built at Versailles. Torches softly light the summer evening as guests talk and enter the artificial caves on the left. Widespread criticism of royal excess undermined support for the monarchy, although Louis XVI was a modest spender compared to Louis XIV. *(Versailles/Photo Bulloz)*

the Parlement of Paris, which was strengthened in its opposition by widespread popular support (see pages 621–622). When renewed efforts to reform the tax system met a similar fate in 1776, the government was forced to finance all of its enormous expenditures during the American war with borrowed money. As a result, the national debt and the annual budget deficit soared. By the 1780s, fully 50 percent of France's annual budget went for ever-increasing interest payments on the ever-increasing debt. Another 25 percent went to maintain the military, while 6 percent was absorbed by the costly and extravagant king and his court at Versailles. Less than 20 percent of the entire national budget was available for the productive functions of the state, such as transportation and general administration. This was an impossible financial situation.

One way out would have been for the government to declare partial bankruptcy, forcing its creditors to accept greatly reduced payments on the debt. The powerful Spanish monarchy had regularly repudiated large portions of its debt in earlier times, and France had done likewise after an attempt to establish a French national bank had ended in financial disaster in 1720. Yet by the 1780s, the French debt was being held by an army of aristocratic and bourgeois creditors, and the French monarchy, though absolute in theory, had become too weak for such a drastic and unpopular action.

Nor could the king and his ministers, unlike modern governments, print money and create inflation to cover their deficits. Unlike England and Holland, which had far larger national debts relative to their populations, France had no central bank, no paper currency, and no means of creating credit. French money was good gold coin. Therefore, when a depressed economy and a lack of public confidence made it increasingly difficult for the government to obtain new gold loans in 1786, it had no alternative but to try increasing taxes. And since France's tax system was unfair and out-of-date, increased revenues were possible only through fundamental reforms. Such reforms, which would affect all groups in France's complex and fragmented society, opened a Pandora's box of social and political demands. Thus historians have usually looked to social forces and social relationships in their efforts to understand the Revolution, as we shall now see.

Legal Orders and Social Realities

As in the Middle Ages, France's 25 million inhabitants were still legally divided into three orders, or "estates"—the clergy, the nobility, and everyone else. As the nation's first estate, the clergy numbered about 100,000 and had important privileges. It owned about 10 percent of the land and paid only a "voluntary gift," rather than regular taxes, to the government every five years. Moreover, the church levied a tax (the tithe) on landowners, which averaged somewhat less than 10 percent. Much of the church's income was actually drained away from local parishes by political appointees and worldly aristocrats at the top of the church hierarchy—to the intense dissatisfaction of the poor parish priests.

The Three Estates In this political cartoon from 1789 a woman of the third estate struggles under the burden of a nun and an aristocrat. The third estate is being represented in a new way as the true nation, oppressed by the parasitic clergy and nobility. *(Musée Carnavalet/Photo Bulloz)*

The second legally defined estate consisted of some 400,000 noblemen and noblewomen—the descendants of "those who had fought" in the Middle Ages. The nobles owned outright about 25 percent of the land in France, and they, too, were taxed very lightly. Moreover, nobles continued to enjoy certain manorial rights, or privileges of lordship, that dated back to medieval times and allowed them to tax the peasantry for their own profit. This was done by means of exclusive rights to hunt and fish, village monopolies on baking bread and pressing grapes for wine, fees for justice, and a host of other "useful privileges." In addition, nobles had "honorific privileges," such as the right to precedence on public occasions and the right to wear a sword. These rights conspicuously proclaimed the nobility's legal superiority and exalted social position.

Everyone else was a commoner, legally a member of the third estate. A few commoners—prosperous merchants or lawyers and officials—were well educated and rich, and might even buy up manorial rights as profitable investments. Many more commoners were urban artisans and unskilled day laborers. The vast majority of the third estate consisted of the peasants and agricultural workers in the countryside. Thus the third estate was a conglomeration of vastly different social groups united only by their shared legal status as distinct from the nobility and clergy.

In discussing the long-term origins of the French Revolution, historians have long focused on growing tensions between the nobility and the comfortable members of the third estate, usually known as the *bourgeoisie,* or middle class. A dominant historical interpretation, which has held sway for at least two generations, maintains that the bourgeoisie was basically united by economic position and class interest. Aided by the general economic expansion discussed in Chapter 19, the middle class grew rapidly in the eighteenth century, tripling to about 2.3 million persons, or about 8 percent of France's population. Increasing in size, wealth, culture, and self-confidence, this rising bourgeoisie became progressively exasperated by archaic "feudal" laws restraining the economy and by the growing pretensions of a reactionary nobility, which was closing ranks against middle-class needs and aspirations. As a result, the French bourgeoisie eventually rose up to lead the entire third estate in a great social revolution, a revolution that destroyed feudal privileges and established a capitalist order based on individualism and a market economy.

In recent years, a flood of new research has challenged these accepted views, and once again the French Revolution is a subject of heated scholarly debate. Above all, revisionist historians have questioned the existence of a growing social conflict between a progressive capitalistic bourgeoisie and a reactionary feudal nobility in eighteenth-century France. Instead, these historians see both bourgeoisie and nobility as highly fragmented, riddled with internal rivalries. The great nobility, for example, was profoundly separated from the lesser nobility by differences in wealth, education, and world-view. Differences within the bourgeoisie—between wealthy financiers and local lawyers, for example—were no less profound. Rather than standing as unified blocs against each other, nobility and bourgeoisie formed two parallel social ladders increasingly linked together at the top by wealth, marriage, and Enlightenment culture.

Revisionist historians stress three developments in particular. First, the nobility remained a fluid and relatively open order. Throughout the eighteenth century, substantial numbers of successful commoners continued to seek and obtain noble status through government service and purchase of expensive positions conferring nobility. Thus the nobility of the robe continued to attract the wealthiest members of the middle class and to permit social mobility. Second, key sections of the nobility and the prosperous bourgeoisie formed together the core of the book-hungry Enlightenment public discussed in Chapter 18. Both groups saw themselves as forming part of the educated elite and standing well above the common people—the peasants and the urban poor. Both groups were also equally liberal until revolution actually began, and they generally supported the judicial opposition to the government led by the Parlement of Paris. Third, the nobility and the bourgeoisie were not really at odds in the economic sphere. Both looked to investment in land and government service as their preferred activities, and the ideal of the merchant capitalist was to gain enough wealth to retire from trade, purchase estates, and live nobly as a large landowner. At the same time, wealthy nobles often acted as aggressive capitalists, investing especially in mining, metallurgy, and foreign trade.

The revisionists have clearly shaken the belief that the bourgeoisie and the nobility were inevitably locked in growing conflict before the Revolution. But in stressing the similarities between the two groups, especially at the top, revisionists have also reinforced the view, long maintained by historians, that the Old Regime had ceased to correspond with social reality by the 1780s. Legally, society was still based on rigid orders inherited from the Middle Ages. In reality, France had already moved far toward being a society based on wealth and education, where an emerging elite that included both aristocratic and bourgeois notables was frustrated by a bureaucratic monarchy that continued to claim the right to absolute power.

The Formation of the National Assembly

The Revolution was under way by 1787, though no one could have realized what was to follow. Spurred by a depressed economy and falling tax receipts, Louis XVI's minister of finance revived old proposals to impose a general tax on all landed property as well as to form provincial assemblies to help administer the tax, and he convinced the king to call an assembly of notables to gain support for the idea. The assembled notables, who were mainly important noblemen and high-ranking clergy, were not in favor of it. In return for their support, they demanded that control over all government spending be given to the provincial assemblies. When the government refused, the notables responded that such sweeping tax changes required the approval of the Estates General, the representative body of all three estates, which had not met since 1614.

Facing imminent bankruptcy, the king tried to reassert his authority. He dismissed the notables and established new taxes by decree. In stirring language, the judges of the Parlement of Paris promptly declared the royal initiative null and void. The Parlement went so far as to specify some of the "fundamental laws" against which no king could transgress, such as national consent to taxation and freedom from arbitrary arrest and imprisonment. When the king tried to exile the judges, a tremendous wave of protest swept the country. Frightened investors also refused to advance more loans to the state. Finally in July 1788, a beaten Louis XVI bowed to public opinion and held a spring session of the Estates General. Absolute monarchy was collapsing.

What would replace it? Throughout the unprecedented election campaign of 1788 and 1789, that question excited France. All across the country, clergy, nobles, and commoners came together in their respective orders to draft petitions for change and to elect their respective delegates to the Estates General. The local assemblies of the clergy showed considerable dissatisfaction with the church hierarchy, and two-thirds of the delegates were chosen from among the poorer parish priests, who were commoners by birth. The nobles, already badly split by wealth and education, remained politically divided. A conservative majority was drawn from the poorer and more numerous provincial nobility, but fully one-third of the nobility's representatives were liberals committed to major changes.

As for the third estate, there was great popular participation in the elections. Almost all male commoners twenty-five years of age or older had the right to vote. However, voting required two stages, which meant that most of the representatives finally selected by the third estate were well-educated, prosperous members of the middle class. Most of them were not businessmen but lawyers and government officials. Social status and prestige were matters of particular concern to this economic elite. There were no delegates elected from the great mass of laboring poor, an exclusion that would encourage the peasants and especially the urban artisans to intervene directly and dramatically at numerous points in the Revolution, as we shall see.

The petitions for change coming from the three estates showed a surprising degree of consensus on most issues, as recent research has clearly revealed. There was general agreement that royal absolutism should give way to constitutional monarchy, in which laws and taxes would require the consent of the Estates General meeting regularly. All agreed that in the future individual liberties would have to be guaranteed by law and that the economic position of the parish clergy would have to be improved. It was generally acknowledged that economic development required reforms, such as the abolition of internal trade barriers. The striking similarities in the grievance petitions of the clergy, nobility, and third estate reflected the broad commitment of France's educated elite to liberalism.

Yet an increasingly bitter quarrel undermined this consensus during the intense electoral campaign: *how* would the Estates General vote, and precisely *who* would lead in the political reorganization that was generally desired? The Estates General of 1614 had sat as three separate houses. Any action had required the agreement of at least two branches, a requirement that had virtually guaranteed control by the nobility and the clergy. Immediately after the victory over the king, the aristocratic Parlement of Paris, mainly out of respect for tradition but partly out of a desire to enhance the nobility's political position, ruled that the Estates General should once again sit separately. The ruling was quickly denounced by certain middle-class intellectuals and some liberal nobles. They demanded instead a single assembly dominated by representatives of the third estate to ensure fundamental reforms. Reflecting increased political competition and a growing hostility toward aristocratic aspirations, the abbé Emmanuel Joseph Sieyès argued in 1789 in his famous pamphlet *What Is the Third Estate?* that the nobility was a tiny, overprivileged minority and that the neglected third estate constituted the true strength of the French nation. When the government agreed that the third estate should have as many delegates as the clergy and the nobility combined, but then rendered this act meaningless by upholding voting by separate order, middle-class leaders saw fresh evidence of an aristocratic conspiracy.

In May 1789, the twelve hundred delegates of the three estates paraded in medieval pageantry through the streets of Versailles to an opening session resplendent with feudal magnificence. The estates were almost immediately deadlocked. Delegates of the third estate refused to transact any business until the king ordered the clergy and nobility to sit with them in a single body. Finally, after a six-week war of nerves, a few parish priests began to go over to the third estate, which on June 17 voted to call itself the "National Assembly." On June 20, the delegates of the third estate, excluded from their hall because of "repairs," moved to a large indoor tennis court. There they swore the famous Oath of the Tennis Court, pledging not to disband until they had written a new constitution.

The king's actions were then somewhat contradictory. On June 23, he made a conciliatory speech urging reforms to a joint session, and four days later he ordered the three estates to meet together. At the same time, the vacillating and indecisive monarch apparently followed the advice of relatives and court nobles, who urged him to dissolve the Estates General by force. The king called an army of eighteen thousand troops toward Versailles, and on July 11 he dismissed his finance minister and his other more liberal ministers. Faced with growing opposition since 1787, Louis XVI had resigned himself to bankruptcy. Now he belatedly sought to reassert his historic "divine right" to rule. The middle-class delegates and their allies from the liberal nobility had done their best, but they were resigned to being disbanded at bayonet point. One third-estate delegate reassured a worried colleague, "You won't hang—you'll only have to go back home."[2]

The Revolt of the Poor and the Oppressed

While the educated delegates of the third estate pressed for symbolic equality with the nobility and clergy in a single legislative body at Versailles, economic hardship gripped the common people of France in a tightening vise. Grain was the basis of the diet of ordinary people in the eighteenth century, and in 1788 the harvest had been extremely poor. The price of bread, which had

The Oath of the Tennis Court This painting, based on an unfinished work by Jacques-Louis David (1748–1825), enthusiastically celebrates the revolutionary rupture of June 20, 1789. Locked out of their assembly hall at Versailles and joined by some sympathetic priests, the delegates of the third estate have moved to an indoor tennis court and are swearing never to disband until they have written a new constitution and put France on a firm foundation. *(Musée Carnavalet/Photo Bulloz)*

been rising gradually since 1785, began to soar. By July 1789, it had climbed as high as 8 sous per pound in the provinces. In Paris, where bread was regularly subsidized by the government in an attempt to prevent popular unrest, the price rose to 4 sous. The poor could scarcely afford to pay 2 sous per pound, for even at that price a laborer with a wife and three children had to spend half of his wages to buy the family's bread.

Harvest failure and high bread prices unleashed a classic economic depression of the preindustrial age. With food so expensive and with so much uncertainty, the demand for manufactured goods collapsed. Thousands of artisans and small traders were thrown out of work. By the end of 1789, almost half of the French people would be in need of relief. One person in eight was a pauper living in extreme want. In Paris the situation was so desperate in July 1789 that perhaps 150,000 of the city's 600,000 people were without work.

Against this background of dire poverty and excitement generated by the political crisis, the people of Paris entered decisively onto the revolutionary stage. They believed in a general, though ill-defined, way that the economic distress had human causes. They believed that they should have steady work and enough bread at fair prices to survive. Specifically, they feared that the dismissal of the king's moderate finance minister would put them at the mercy of aristocratic landowners and grain speculators. Stories like that quoting the wealthy financier Joseph François Foulon as saying that the poor "should eat grass, like my horses" and rumors that the king's troops would sack the city began to fill the air. Angry crowds formed, and passionate voices urged action. On July 13, the people began to seize arms for

Storming the Bastille This representation by an untrained contemporary artist shows civilians and members of the Paris militia—the "conquerors of the Bastille"—on the attack. This successful action had enormous practical and symbolic significance, and July 14 has long been France's most important national holiday. *(Musée Carnavalet/Photo Hubert Josse)*

the defense of the city as the king's armies moved toward Paris, and on July 14 several hundred of the most determined people marched to the Bastille to search for weapons and gunpowder.

A medieval fortress with walls ten feet thick and eight great towers each one hundred feet high, the Bastille had long been used as a prison. It was guarded by eighty retired soldiers and thirty Swiss mercenaries. The governor of the fortress-prison refused to hand over the powder, panicked, and ordered his men to fire, killing ninety-eight people attempting to enter. Cannon were brought to batter the main gate, and fighting continued until the prison surrendered. The governor of the prison was later hacked to death, and his head and that of the mayor of Paris, who had been slow to give the crowd arms, were stuck on pikes and paraded through the streets. The next day a committee of citizens appointed the marquis de Lafayette commander of the city's armed forces. Paris was lost to the king, who was forced to recall the finance minister and disperse his troops. The popular uprising had broken the power monopoly of the royal army and thereby saved the National Assembly.

As the delegates resumed their long-winded and inconclusive debates at Versailles, the countryside sent them a radical and unmistakable message. Throughout France, peasants began to rise in spontaneous, violent, and effective insurrection against their lords, ransacking manor houses and burning feudal documents that recorded the peasants' obligations. Neither middle-class landowners, who often owned manors and village monopolies, nor the larger, more prosperous farmers were spared. In some areas, peasants reinstated traditional village practices, undoing recent enclosures and reoccupying old common lands. Peasants seized forests, and taxes went unpaid. Fear of vagabonds and outlaws—called the Great Fear by contemporaries—seized the countryside and fanned the flames of rebellion. The long-suffering peasants were doing their best to free themselves from manorial rights and exploitation.

Faced with chaos, yet afraid to call on the king to restore order, some liberal nobles and middle-class delegates at Versailles responded to peasant demands with a surprise maneuver on the night of August 4, 1789. The duke of Aiguillon, also notably one of France's greatest noble landowners, declared that

in several provinces the whole people forms a kind of league for the destruction of the manor houses, the ravaging of the lands, and especially for the seizure of the archives where the title deeds to feudal properties are kept. It seeks to throw off at last a yoke that has for many centuries weighted it down.[3]

He urged equality in taxation and the elimination of feudal dues. In the end, all the old exactions imposed on the peasants—serfdom where it still existed, exclusive hunting rights for nobles, fees for justice, village monopolies, the right to make peasants work on the roads, and a host of other dues—were abolished, generally without compensation. Though a clarifying law passed a week later was less generous, the peasants ignored the "fine print." They never paid feudal dues again. Thus the French peasantry, which already owned about 30 percent of all the land, achieved a great and unprecedented victory in the early days of revolutionary upheaval. Henceforth, the French peasants would seek mainly to protect and consolidate their revolutionary triumph. As the Great Fear subsided in the countryside, they became a force for order and stability.

A Limited Monarchy

The National Assembly moved forward. On August 27, 1789, it issued the Declaration of the Rights of Man, which stated, "Men are born and remain free and equal in rights." The declaration also maintained that mankind's natural rights are "liberty, property, security, and resistance to oppression" and that "every man is presumed innocent until he is proven guilty." As for law, "it is an expression of the general will; all citizens have the right to concur personally or through their representatives in its formation. . . . Free expression of thoughts and opinions is one of the most precious rights of mankind: every citizen may therefore speak, write, and publish freely." In short, this clarion call of the liberal revolutionary ideal guaranteed equality before the law, representative government for a sovereign people, and individual freedom. This revolutionary credo, only two pages long, was propagandized throughout France and Europe and around the world.

Moving beyond general principles to draft a constitution proved difficult. The questions of how much power the king should retain and whether he could permanently veto legislation led to another deadlock. Once again the decisive answer came from the poor—in this instance, the poor women of Paris.

Women customarily bought the food and managed the poor family's slender resources. In Paris great numbers of women also worked for wages, often within the putting-out system, making garments and beautiful luxury items destined for an aristocratic and international clientele. Immediately after the fall of the Bastille, many of France's great court nobles began to leave Versailles for foreign lands so that a plummeting demand for luxuries intensified the general economic crisis; international markets also declined. The church was no longer able to give its traditional grants of food and money to the poor. Increasing unemployment and hunger put tremendous pressure on household managers, and the result was another popular explosion.

On October 5 some seven thousand desperate women marched the twelve miles from Paris to Versailles to demand action. A middle-class deputy looking out from the Assembly saw "multitudes arriving from Paris including fishwives and bullies from the market, and these people wanted nothing but bread." This great crowd invaded the Assembly, "armed with scythes, sticks and pikes." One tough old woman directing a large group of younger women defiantly shouted into the debate, "Who's that talking down there? Make the chatterbox shut up. That's not the point: the point is that we want bread."[4] Hers was the genuine voice of the people, essential to any understanding of the French Revolution.

The women invaded the royal apartments, slaughtered some of the royal bodyguards, and furiously searched for the queen, Marie Antoinette, who was widely despised for her frivolous and supposedly immoral behavior. "We are going to cut off her head, tear out her heart, fry her liver, and that won't be the end of it," they shouted, surging through the palace in a frenzy. It seems likely that only the intervention of Lafayette and the National Guard saved the royal family. But the only way to calm the disorder was for the king to go and live in Paris, as the crowd demanded.

The next day, the king, the queen, and their son left for Paris in the midst of a strange procession. The heads of two aristocrats, stuck on pikes, led the way. They were followed by the remaining members of the royal bodyguard, unarmed and surrounded and mocked by fierce men holding sabers and pikes. A mixed and victorious multitude surrounded the carriage of the captured royal family, hurling crude insults at the queen. There was drinking and eating among the women, who had clearly emerged as a major and enduring element in the Parisian revolutionary crowd.[5]

The National Assembly followed the king to Paris, and the next two years, until September 1791, saw the consolidation of the liberal revolution. Under middle-class leadership, the National Assembly abolished the French nobility as a legal order and pushed forward with the creation of a constitutional monarchy, which Louis XVI reluctantly agreed to accept in July 1790. In the final constitution, the king remained the head of state, but all lawmaking power was placed in the hands of the National Assembly, elected by the economic upper half of French males.

New laws broadened women's rights to seek divorce, to inherit property, and to obtain financial support from fathers for illegitimate children. But women were not allowed to vote or hold political office for at least two reasons. First, the great majority of comfortable, well-educated males in the National Assembly believed that women should be limited to child rearing and domestic duties and should leave politics and most public activities to men. This was, of course, a hoary idea, but it had been dressed up and re-energized by Rousseau in his influential *Emile* (see page 668). Second, the delegates to the National Assembly were convinced that political life in absolutist France had been profoundly corrupt and that a prime example of this corruption was the way that some talented but immoral aristocratic women had used their sexual charms to manipulate weak rulers and their ministers. Delegates therefore believed that excluding women from politics would help create the civic virtue that had been missing: the political system would be freed from the harmful effects of sexual favors; and pure, home-focused wives would raise the high-minded sons needed to govern the nation.

The National Assembly replaced the complicated patchwork of historic provinces with eighty-three departments of approximately equal size. The jumble of weights and measures that varied from province to province was reformed, leading to the introduction of the simple, rational metric system in 1793. The National Assembly promoted the liberal concept of economic freedom. Monopolies, guilds, and workers combinations were prohibited, and barriers to trade within France were abolished in the name of economic liberty. Thus the National Assembly applied the critical spirit of the Enlightenment to reform France's laws and institutions completely.

The Assembly also imposed a radical reorganization on the country's religious life. It granted religious freedom to the tiny minority of French Jews and Protestants. Of greater impact, it then nationalized the Catholic church's property and abolished monasteries as useless relics of a distant past. The government used all former church property as collateral to guarantee a new paper currency, the *assignats,* and then sold these properties in an attempt to put the state's finances on a solid footing. Although the church's land was sold in large blocks, a procedure that favored nimble speculators and the rich, peasants eventually purchased much of this land when it was subdivided. These purchases strengthened their attachment to the new revolutionary order in the countryside.

The most unfortunate aspect of the religious reorganization of France was that it brought the new government into conflict with the Catholic church and many sincere Christians, especially in the countryside. Many delegates to the National Assembly, imbued with the rationalism and skepticism of the eighteenth-century philosophes, harbored a deep distrust of popular piety and "superstitious religion." They were interested in the church only to the extent that they could seize its land and use the church to strengthen the new state. Thus they established a national church, with priests chosen by voters. In the face of widespread resistance, the National Assembly then required the clergy to take a loyalty oath to the new government. The Catholic clergy became just so many more employees of the state. The pope formally condemned this attempt to subjugate the church, and only half the priests of France took the oath of allegiance. The result was a deep division within both the country and the clergy on the religious question; confusion and hostility among French Catholics were pervasive. The attempt to remake the Catholic church, like the Assembly's abolition of guilds and workers combinations, sharpened the conflict between the educated classes and the common people that had been emerging in the eighteenth century. This policy toward the church was the revolutionary government's first important failure.

World War and Republican France, 1791–1799

When Louis XVI accepted the final version of the completed constitution in September 1791, a young and still obscure provincial lawyer and member of the National Assembly named Maximilien Robespierre (1758–1794) evaluated the work of two years and concluded, "The Revolution is over." Robespierre was both right and wrong. He was right in the sense that the most constructive and lasting reforms were in place. Nothing substantial in the way of liberty and useful reform would be gained in the next generation. He was wrong in the sense that a much more radical stage lay ahead. New heroes and new ideologies were to emerge in revolutionary wars and international conflict.

Foreign Reactions and the Beginning of War

The outbreak and progress of revolution in France produced great excitement and a sharp division of opinion in Europe and the United States. Liberals and radicals saw a mighty triumph of liberty over despotism. In Great Britain especially, they hoped that the French example would lead to a fundamental reordering of the political system. That system, which had been consolidated in the revolution of 1688 to 1689, placed Parliament in the hands of the aristocracy and a few wealthy merchants; the great majority of people had very little say in the government. After the French Revolution began, conservative leaders such as Edmund Burke (1729–1797) were deeply troubled by the aroused spirit of reform. In 1790 Burke published *Reflections on the Revolution in France,* one of the great intellectual defenses of European conservatism. He defended inherited privileges in general and those of the English monarchy and aristocracy. He glorified the unrepresentative Parliament and predicted that thoroughgoing reform like that occurring in France would lead only to chaos and tyranny. Burke's work sparked much debate.

Mary Wollstonecraft Painted by an unknown artist when Mary Wollstonecraft was thirty-two and writing her revolutionary *Vindication of the Rights of Woman,* this portrait highlights the remarkable strength of character that energized Wollstonecraft's brilliant intellect. *(The Board of Trustees of the National Museums and Galleries on Merseyside, Walker Art Gallery)*

One passionate rebuttal came from a young writer in London, Mary Wollstonecraft (1759–1797). Born into the middle class, Wollstonecraft was schooled in adversity by a mean-spirited father who beat his wife and squandered his inherited fortune. Determined to be independent in a society that generally expected women of her class to become homebodies and obedient wives, she struggled for years to earn her living as a governess and teacher—practically the only acceptable careers for single, educated women—before attaining success as a translator and author. Interested in politics and believing that "a desperate disease requires a powerful remedy" in Great Britain as well as France, Wollstonecraft was incensed by Burke's book. She immediately wrote a blistering, widely read attack, *A Vindication of the Rights of Man* (1790).

Then, fired up on controversy and commitment, she made a daring intellectual leap. She developed for the first time the logical implications of natural-law philosophy in her masterpiece, *A Vindication of the Rights of Woman* (1792). To fulfill the still-unrealized potential of the French Revolution and to eliminate the sexual inequality she had felt so keenly, she demanded that

> *the Rights of Women be respected . . . [and] JUSTICE for one-half of the human race. . . . It is time to effect a revolution in female manners, time to restore to them their lost dignity, and make them, as part of the human species, labor, by reforming themselves, to reform the world.*

Setting high standards for women—"I wish to persuade women to endeavor to acquire strength, both of mind and body"—Wollstonecraft broke with those who had a low opinion of women's intellectual potential. She advocated rigorous coeducation, which would make women better wives and mothers, good citizens, and even economically independent people. Women could manage businesses and enter politics if only men would give them the chance. Men themselves would benefit from women's rights, for Wollstonecraft believed that "the two sexes mutually corrupt and improve each other."[6] Wollstonecraft's analysis testified to the power of the Revolution to excite and inspire outside of France. Paralleling ideas put forth independently in France by Olympe de Gouges (1748–1793), a self-taught writer and woman of the people (see the feature "Listening to the Past: Revolution and Women's Rights" on pages 722–723), Wollstonecraft's work marked the birth of the modern women's movement for equal rights, and it was ultimately very influential.

The kings and nobles of continental Europe, who had at first welcomed the revolution in France as weakening a competing power, began to feel no less threatened than Burke and his supporters. At their courts, they listened to the diatribes of great court nobles who had fled France and were urging intervention in France's affairs. When Louis XVI and Marie Antoinette were arrested and returned to Paris after trying unsuccessfully to slip out of France in June 1791, the monarchs of Austria and Prussia issued the Declaration of Pillnitz. This carefully worded statement declared their willingness to intervene in France in certain circumstances and was expected to have a sobering effect on revolutionary France without causing war.

But the crowned heads of Europe misjudged the revolutionary spirit in France. When the National Assembly disbanded, it sought popular support by decreeing that none of its members would be eligible for election to the new Legislative Assembly. This meant that when the new representative body convened in October 1791, it had a different character. The great majority of the legislators were still prosperous, well-educated, middle-class men, but they were younger and less cautious than their predecessors. Many of the deputies were loosely allied and called "Jacobins," after the name of their political club.

The new representatives to the Assembly were passionately committed to liberal revolution and distrustful of monarchy after Louis's attempted flight. They increasingly lumped "useless aristocrats" and "despotic monarchs" together, and they easily whipped themselves into a patriotic fury with bombastic oratory. If the courts of Europe were attempting to incite a war of kings against France, then "we will incite a war of people against kings. . . . Ten million Frenchmen, kindled by the fire of liberty, armed with the sword, with reason, with eloquence would be able to change the face of the world and make the tyrants tremble on their thrones."[7] Only Robespierre and a very few others argued that people would not welcome liberation at the point of a gun. Such warnings were brushed aside. France would "rise to the full height of her mission," as one deputy urged. In April 1792, France declared war on Francis II, the Habsburg monarch.

France's crusade against tyranny went poorly at first. Prussia joined Austria in the Austrian Netherlands (present-day Belgium), and French forces broke and fled at their first encounter with armies of this First Coalition. The road to Paris lay open, and it is possible that only conflict between the eastern monarchs over the division of Poland saved France from defeat.

Military reversals and Austro-Prussian threats caused a wave of patriotic fervor to sweep France. The Legislative Assembly declared the country in danger. Volunteer armies from the provinces streamed through Paris, fraternizing with the people and singing patriotic songs like the stirring "Marseillaise," later the French national anthem.

In this supercharged wartime atmosphere, rumors of treason by the king and queen spread in Paris. Once again, as in the storming of the Bastille, the common people of Paris acted decisively. On August 10, 1792, a revolutionary crowd attacked the royal palace at the Tuileries, capturing it after heavy fighting with the Swiss Guards. The king and his family fled for their lives to the nearby Legislative Assembly, which suspended the king from all his functions, imprisoned him, and called for a new National Convention to be elected by universal male suffrage. Monarchy in France was on its deathbed, mortally wounded by war and popular upheaval.

The Second Revolution

The fall of the monarchy marked a rapid radicalization of the Revolution, a phase that historians often call the "second revolution." Louis's imprisonment was followed by the September Massacres. Wild stories seized the city that imprisoned counter-revolutionary aristocrats and priests were plotting with the allied invaders. As a result, angry crowds invaded the prisons of Paris and summarily slaughtered half the men and women they found. In late September 1792, the new, popularly elected National Convention proclaimed France a republic.

The republic sought to create a new popular culture to ensure its future and fashioned compelling symbols that broke with the past and glorified the new order. It adopted a brand-new revolutionary calendar, which eliminated saints' days and renamed the days and the months after the seasons of the year. Citizens were expected to address each other with the friendly "thou" of the people rather than with the formal "you" of the rich and powerful. The republic energetically promoted broad, open-air, democratic festivals. These spectacles brought the entire population together and sought to redirect the people's traditional enthusiasm for Catholic religious celebrations to secular holidays instilling republican virtue and a love of nation. These spectacles were less successful in villages than in cities, where popular interest in politics was greater and Catholicism was weaker.

All of the members of the National Convention were republicans, and at the beginning almost all belonged to the Jacobin club of Paris. The great majority also continued to come from the well-educated middle class. But control of the Convention was increasingly contested by two bitterly competitive groups—the Girondists, named after a department in southwestern France, and the Mountain, led by Robespierre and another young lawyer, Georges Jacques Danton. The Mountain was so called because its members sat on the uppermost left-hand benches of the assembly hall. A majority of the indecisive Convention members, seated in the "Plain" below, floated back and forth between the rival factions.

This division was clearly apparent after the National Convention overwhelmingly convicted Louis XVI of treason. By a narrow majority, the Convention then sentenced him to death in January 1793. Louis died with tranquil dignity on the newly invented guillotine. One of his last statements was "I am innocent and shall die without fear. I would that my death might bring happiness to the French, and ward off the dangers which I foresee."[8]

Both the Girondists and the Mountain were determined to continue the "war against tyranny." The Prussians had been stopped at the Battle of Valmy on September 20, 1792, one day before the republic was proclaimed. Saving the nascent republic with their victory, the armies of revolutionary France then successfully invaded Savoy and captured Nice. A second army corps invaded the German Rhineland and took the city of Frankfurt. To the north, the revolutionary armies won their first major battle at Jemappes and by November 1792 were occupying the entire Austrian Netherlands. Everywhere they went, French armies of occupation chased the princes, "abolished feudalism," and found support among some peasants and middle-class people.

But the French armies also lived off the land, requisitioning food and supplies and plundering local treasures. The liberators looked increasingly like foreign invaders. International tensions mounted. In February 1793, the National Convention, at war with Austria and Prussia, declared war on Britain, Holland, and Spain as well. Republican France was now at war with almost all of Europe, a great war that would last almost without interruption until 1815.

As the forces of the First Coalition drove the French from the Austrian Netherlands, peasants in western France revolted against being drafted into the army. They were supported and encouraged in their resistance by devout Catholics, royalists, and foreign agents.

In Paris the quarrelsome National Convention found itself locked in a life-and-death political struggle between the Girondists and the Mountain. The two groups were in general agreement on questions of policy. Sincere republicans, they hated privilege and wanted to temper economic liberalism with social concern. Yet personal hatreds ran deep. The Girondists feared a bloody dictatorship by the Mountain, and the Mountain was no less convinced that the more moderate Girondists would turn to conservatives and even royalists in order to retain power. With the middle-class delegates so bitterly divided, the laboring poor of Paris emerged as the decisive political factor.

The laboring men and women of Paris always constituted—along with the peasantry in the summer of 1789—the elemental force that drove the Revolution

The End of Louis XVI (detail) The executioner holds up the severed head of the dead king for the soldiers and the crowd to see in the large, central square of Paris, which is now known as the Place de la Concorde. The execution of the king was a victory for the radicals in Paris, but it horrified Europe's monarchs and conservatives and strengthened their opposition to the French Revolution. *(Musée Carnavalet/Laurie Platt Winfrey, Inc.)*

forward. It was the artisans, day laborers, market women, and garment workers who had stormed the Bastille, marched on Versailles, driven the king from the Tuileries, and carried out the September Massacres. The petty traders and laboring poor were often known as the *sans-culottes,* "without breeches," because sans-culottes men wore trousers instead of the knee breeches of the aristocracy and the solid middle class. The immediate interests of the sans-culottes were mainly economic, and in the spring of 1793 the economic situation was as bad as the military situation. Rapid inflation, unemployment, and food shortages were again weighing heavily on poor families.

Moreover, by the spring of 1793, the sans-culottes had become keenly interested in politics. Encouraged by the so-called angry men, such as the passionate young ex-priest and journalist Jacques Roux, sans-culottes men and women were demanding radical political action to guarantee them their daily bread. At first the Mountain joined the Girondists in violently rejecting these demands. But in the face of military defeat, peasant revolt, and hatred of the Girondists, the Mountain and especially Robespierre became more sympathetic. The Mountain joined with sans-culottes activists in the city government to engineer a popular uprising, which forced the Convention to arrest thirty-one Girondist deputies for treason on June 2. All power passed to the Mountain.

Robespierre and others from the Mountain joined the recently formed Committee of Public Safety, to which the Convention had given dictatorial power to deal with the national emergency. These developments in Paris triggered revolt in leading provincial cities, such as Lyons and Marseilles, where moderates denounced Paris and demanded a decentralized government. The peasant revolt spread, and the republic's armies were driven back on all fronts. By July 1793, only the areas around Paris and on the eastern frontier were firmly held by the central government. Defeat seemed imminent.

Total War and the Terror

A year later, in July 1794, the Austrian Netherlands and the Rhineland were once again in the hands of conquering French armies, and the First Coalition was falling apart. This remarkable change of fortune was due to the revolutionary government's success in harnessing, for perhaps the first time in history, the explosive forces of a planned economy, revolutionary terror, and modern nationalism in a total war effort.

Robespierre and the Committee of Public Safety advanced with implacable resolution on several fronts in 1793 and 1794. First, in an effort to save revolutionary France, they collaborated with the fiercely patriotic and democratic sans-culottes, who retained the common people's traditional faith in fair prices and a moral economic order and who distrusted most wealthy capitalists and all aristocrats. Thus Robespierre and his coworkers established, as best they could, a planned economy with egalitarian social overtones. Rather than let supply and demand determine prices, the government decreed the maximum allowable prices for a host of key products. Though the state was too weak to enforce all its price regulations, it did fix the price of bread in Paris at levels the poor could afford. Rationing was introduced, and quality was also controlled. Bakers were permitted to make only the "bread of equality"—a brown bread made of a mixture of all available flours. White bread and pastries were outlawed as luxuries. The poor of Paris may not have eaten well, but at least they ate.

They also worked, mainly to produce arms and munitions for the war effort. Craftsmen and small manufacturers were told what to produce and when to deliver. The government nationalized many small workshops and requisitioned raw materials and grain from the peasants. Sometimes planning and control did not go beyond orders to meet the latest emergency: "Ten thousand soldiers lack shoes. You will take the shoes of all the aristocrats in Strasbourg and deliver them ready for transport to headquarters at 10 A.M. tomorrow." Failures to control and coordinate were failures of means and not of desire: seldom if ever before had a government attempted to manage an economy so thoroughly. The second revolution and the ascendancy of the sans-culottes had produced an embryonic emergency socialism, which thoroughly frightened Europe's propertied classes and had great influence on the subsequent development of socialist ideology.

Second, while radical economic measures supplied the poor with bread and the armies with weapons, the Reign of Terror (1793–1794) was solidifying the home front. Special revolutionary courts responsible only to Robespierre's Committee of Public Safety tried rebels and "enemies of the nation" for political crimes. Drawing on popular, sans-culottes support centered in the local Jacobin clubs, these local courts ignored normal legal procedures and judged severely. Some 40,000 French men and women were executed or died in prison. Another 300,000 suspects crowded the prisons and often brushed close to death in a revolutionary court.

Robespierre's Reign of Terror was one of the most controversial phases of the French Revolution. Most historians now believe that the Reign of Terror was not

Goya: The Third of May, 1808 This great painting screams in outrage at the horrors of war, which Goya witnessed in Spain. Spanish rebels, focused around the Christ-like figure at the center, are gunned down by anonymous French soldiers, grim forerunners of modern death squads and their atrocities. *(Museo del Prado, Madrid)*

France and in the satellites (Map 21.1), Napoleon introduced many French laws, abolishing feudal dues and serfdom where French revolutionary armies had not already done so. Some of the peasants and middle class benefited from these reforms. Yet while he extended progressive measures to his cosmopolitan empire, Napoleon had to put the prosperity and special interests of France first in order to safeguard his power base. Levying heavy taxes in money and men for his armies, Napoleon came to be regarded more as a conquering tyrant than as an enlightened liberator.

MAP 21.1 Napoleonic Europe in 1810 Only Great Britain remained at war with Napoleon at the height of the Grand Empire. Many British goods were smuggled through Helgoland, a tiny but strategic British possession off the German coast.

The first great revolt occurred in Spain. In 1808 a coalition of Catholics, monarchists, and patriots rebelled against Napoleon's attempts to make Spain a French satellite with a Bonaparte as its king. French armies occupied Madrid, but the foes of Napoleon fled to the hills and waged uncompromising guerrilla warfare. Spain was a clear warning: resistance to French imperialism was growing.

Yet Napoleon pushed on, determined to hold his complex and far-flung empire together. In 1810, when the Grand Empire was at its height, Britain still remained at war with France, helping the guerrillas in Spain and Portugal. The continental system, organized to exclude British goods from the continent and force that "nation of shopkeepers" to its knees, was a failure. Instead, it was France that suffered from Britain's counter-blockade, which created hard times for French artisans and the middle class. Perhaps looking for a scapegoat, Napoleon turned on Alexander I of Russia, who in 1811 openly repudiated Napoleon's war of prohibitions against British goods.

Napoleon's invasion of Russia began in June 1812 with a force that eventually numbered 600,000, probably the largest force yet assembled in a single army. Only one-third of this Great Army was French, however; nationals of all the satellites and allies were drafted into the operation. (See the feature "Individuals in Society: Jakob Walter, German Draftee with Napoleon.") Originally planning to winter in the Russian city of Smolensk if Alexander did not sue for peace, Napoleon reached Smolensk and recklessly pressed on toward Moscow. The great Battle of Borodino that followed was a draw, and the Russians retreated in good order. Alexander ordered the evacuation of Moscow, which then burned in part, and he refused to negotiate. Finally, after five weeks in the abandoned city, Napoleon ordered a retreat. That retreat was one of the great military disasters in history. The Russian army, the Russian winter, and starvation cut Napoleon's army to pieces. When the frozen remnants staggered into Poland and Prussia in December, 370,000 men had died and another 200,000 had been taken prisoner.[12]

Leaving his troops to their fate, Napoleon raced to Paris to raise yet another army. Possibly he might still have saved his throne if he had been willing to accept a France reduced to its historical size—the proposal offered by Austria's foreign minister, Prince Klemens von Metternich. But Napoleon refused. Austria and Prussia deserted Napoleon and joined Russia and Great Britain in the Fourth Coalition. All across Europe, patriots called for a "war of liberation" against Napoleon's oppression, and the well-disciplined regular armies of Napoleon's enemies closed in for the kill. This time the coalition held together, cemented by the Treaty of Chaumont, which created a Quadruple Alliance intended to last for twenty years. Less than a month later, on April 4, 1814, a defeated, abandoned Napoleon abdicated his throne. After this unconditional abdication, the victorious allies granted Napoleon the island of Elba off the coast of Italy as his own tiny state. Napoleon was even allowed to keep his imperial title, and France was required to pay him a yearly income of 2 million francs.

The allies also agreed to the restoration of the Bourbon dynasty, in part because demonstrations led by a few dedicated French monarchists indicated some support among the French people for that course of action. The new monarch, Louis XVIII (r. 1814–1824), tried to consolidate that support by issuing the Constitutional Charter, which accepted many of France's revolutionary changes and guaranteed civil liberties. Indeed, the Charter gave France a constitutional monarchy roughly similar to that established in 1791, although far fewer people had the right to vote for representatives to the resurrected Chamber of Deputies. Moreover, in an attempt to strengthen popular support for Louis XVIII's new government, France was treated leniently by the allies, which agreed to meet in Vienna to work out a general peace settlement.

Yet Louis XVIII—old, ugly, and crippled by gout—totally lacked the glory and magic of Napoleon. Hearing of political unrest in France and diplomatic tensions in Vienna, Napoleon staged a daring escape from Elba in February 1815. Landing in France, he issued appeals for support and marched on Paris with a small band of followers. French officers and soldiers who had fought so long for their emperor responded to the call. Louis XVIII fled, and once more Napoleon took command. But Napoleon's gamble was a desperate long shot, for the allies were united against him. At the end of a frantic period known as the Hundred Days, they crushed his forces at Waterloo on June 18, 1815, and imprisoned him on the rocky island of St. Helena, far off the western coast of Africa. Old Louis XVIII returned again—this time "in the baggage of the allies," as his detractors scornfully put it—and recommenced his reign. The allies now dealt more harshly with the apparently incorrigible French. And Napoleon, doomed to suffer crude insults at the hands of English jailers on distant St. Helena, could take revenge only by writing his memoirs, skillfully nurturing the myth that he had been Europe's revolutionary liberator, a romantic hero whose lofty work had been undone by oppressive reactionaries. An era had ended.

SUMMARY

The French Revolution left a compelling and many-sided political legacy. This legacy included, most notably, liberalism, assertive nationalism, radical democratic republicanism, embryonic socialism, and self-conscious conservatism. It also left a rich and turbulent history of electoral competition, legislative assemblies, and even mass politics. Thus the French Revolution and conflict-

Individuals in Society

Jakob Walter, German Draftee with Napoleon

The retreat from Moscow; detail of engraving by G. Küstler. Soldiers strip the sick of their blankets and boots, leaving them to die in the cold. *(New York Public Library, Slavonic Division)*

In January 1812, a young German named Jakob Walter (1788–1864) was recalled to active duty in the army of Württemberg, a Napoleonic satellite in the Confederation of the Rhine. Stonemason and common draftee, Walter later wrote a rare enlisted man's account of the Russian campaign, a personal history that testified to the terrible price paid by the common people for a generation of war.

Napoleon's invasion of Russia was a desperate gamble from the beginning. French armies were accustomed to living off well-developed local economies, but this strategy did not work well in poor, sparsely populated eastern Europe. Scrounging for food dominated Walter's recollection of earlier fighting in Poland, and now, in 1812, the food situation was much worse. Crossing into Russia, Walter and his buddies found the nearby villages half-burned and stripped of food. Running down an occasional hog, they greedily tore it to pieces and ate it raw. Strangled by dust and thirst and then pelted for days by cold rain, the Great Army raced to catch the retreating Russians and force them into battle. When the famished troops stopped, the desperate search for food began.

In mid-August Walter's company helped storm the city of Smolensk in heavy fighting. From there onward, the road was littered with men, horses, and wagons, and all the towns and villages had been burned by the Russians to deprive the enemy of supplies. Surrounded by all these horrors, Walter almost lost his nerve, but he drew on his Catholic faith and found the courage "to go on trustingly to meet my fate."[1] Fighting at the great Battle of Borodino, "where the death cries and the shattering gunfire seemed a hell," he and the allied troops entered a deserted and fire-damaged Moscow in mid-September. But food, liquor, and fancy silks were there for the taking, and the weather was warm.

On October 18, the reprieve was over, and the retreating allied infantrymen re-entered hell. Yet Walter, "still alert and spirited," was asked by an officer to be his attendant and received for his services a horse to ride. The horse proved a lifesaver. It allowed Walter to forage for food farther off the highway, to flee from approaching Cossacks, and to conserve his strength as vicious freezing winter weather set in. Yet food found at great peril could be quickly lost. Once Walter fought off some French soldiers with the help of some nearby Germans, who then robbed him of his bread. But what, he reflected later, could one expect? The starving men had simply lost their humanity. "I myself could look cold-bloodedly into the lamenting faces of the wounded, the freezing, and the burned," he wrote. When his horse was stolen as he slept, he silently stole someone else's. Struggling on in this brutal every-man-for-himself environment, Walter reached Poland in late December and hobbled home, a rare survivor. He went on to recover, marry, and have ten children.

Why did Jakob Walter survive? Pure chance surely played a large part. So did his robust constitution and street smarts. His faith in God also provided strength to meet each day's challenges. The beautiful vision of returning home and seeing his family offered equal encouragement. Finally, he lacked hatred and animosity, whether toward the Russians, the French, or whomever. He accepted the things he could not change and concentrated on those he could.

Questions for Analysis

1. Why was obtaining food such a problem for Jakob Walter and his fellow soldiers?
2. What impresses you most about Walter's account of the Russian campaign?

1. Jakob Walter, *The Diary of a Napoleonic Foot Soldier,* ed. with an introduction by M. Raeff (New York: Penguin Books, 1993), p. 53. Also pp. 54, 66.

ing interpretations of its significance presented a whole range of political options and alternative visions of the future. For this reason, it was truly the revolution in modern European politics.

The revolution that began in America and spread to France was a liberal revolution. Revolutionaries on both sides of the Atlantic wanted to establish civil liberties and equality before the law within the framework of representative government, and they succeeded. In France liberal nobles and an increasingly class-conscious middle class overwhelmed declining monarchial absolutism and feudal privilege, thanks to the intervention of the common people—the sans-culottes and the peasants. Featuring electoral competition and civil equality, the government established by the Declaration of the Rights of Man and the French constitution of 1791 was remarkably similar to that created in America by the federal Constitution and the Bill of Rights. France's new political system reflected a social structure based increasingly on wealth and achievement rather than on tradition and legal privileges.

After the establishment of the republic, the radical phase of the Revolution during the Terror, and the fall of Robespierre, the educated elites and the solid middle class reasserted themselves under the Directory. And though Napoleon sharply curtailed representative institutions and individual rights, he effectively promoted the reconciliation of old and new, of centralized bureaucracy and careers open to talent, of noble and bourgeois in a restructured property-owning elite. Louis XVIII had to accept the commanding position of this restructured elite, and in granting representative government and civil liberties to facilitate his restoration to the throne in 1814, he submitted to the rest of the liberal triumph of 1789 to 1791. The liberal core of the French Revolution had successfully survived a generation of war and dictatorship.

Revolution in France, as opposed to in the United States, also left a multiplicity of legacies that extended well beyond the triumphant liberalism of 1789. Indeed, the lived experience of the French Revolution and the wars that went with it exercised a pervasive influence on politics and the political imagination in the nineteenth century, not only in France but throughout Europe and even the rest of the world. First, there was the radical legacy of the embattled republic of 1793 and 1794, with its sans-culottes democratic republicanism and its egalitarian ideology and embryonic socialism. This legacy would inspire republicans, democrats, and early socialists. Second, there was the legacy of a powerful and continuing reaction to the French Revolution and to aggressive French nationalism. Monarchists and traditionalists now believed that 1789 had been a tragic mistake. They concluded that democratic republicanism and sans-culottes activism led only to war, class conflict, and savage dictatorship. And even though revolutionary upheaval encouraged generations of radicals to believe that political revolution might remake society and even create a new humanity, conservatives and many comfortable moderates were profoundly disillusioned by the revolutionary era. They looked with nostalgia toward the supposedly ordered world of benevolent monarchy, firm government, and respectful common people.

NOTES

1. Quoted in R. R. Palmer, *The Age of the Democratic Revolution,* vol. 1 (Princeton, N.J.: Princeton University Press, 1959), p. 239.
2. G. Lefebvre, *The Coming of the French Revolution* (New York: Vintage Books, 1947), p. 81.
3. P. H. Beik, ed., *The French Revolution* (New York: Walker, 1970), p. 89.
4. G. Pernoud and S. Flaisser, eds., *The French Revolution* (Greenwich, Conn.: Fawcett, 1960), p. 61.
5. O. Hufton, *Women and the Limits of Citizenship in the French Revolution* (Toronto: University of Toronto Press, 1992), pp. 3–22.
6. Quotations from Wollstonecraft are drawn from E. W. Sunstein, *A Different Face: The Life of Mary Wollstonecraft* (New York: Harper & Row, 1975), pp. 208, 211; and H. R. James, *Mary Wollstonecraft: A Sketch* (London: Oxford University Press, 1932), pp. 60, 62, 69.
7. Quoted in L. Gershoy, *The Era of the French Revolution, 1789–1799* (New York: Van Nostrand, 1957), p. 150.
8. Pernoud and Flaisser, *The French Revolution,* pp. 193–194.
9. T. Blanning, *The French Revolutionary Wars, 1787–1802* (London: Arnold, 1996), pp. 116–128.
10. Quoted ibid., p. 123.
11. Hufton, *Women and the Limits of Citizenship,* p. 130.
12. D. Sutherland, *France, 1789–1815: Revolution and Counterrevolution* (New York: Oxford University Press, 1986), p. 420.

SUGGESTED READING

For fascinating eyewitness reports on the French Revolution, see the edited works by Beik and by Pernoud and Flaisser mentioned in the Notes. In addition, A. Young, *Travels in France During the Years 1787, 1788 and 1789*

(1969), offers an engrossing contemporary description of France and Paris on the eve of revolution. E. Burke, *Reflections on the Revolution in France,* first published in 1790, is the classic conservative indictment. The intense passions the French Revolution has generated may be seen in nineteenth-century French historians, notably the enthusiastic J. Michelet, *History of the French Revolution;* the hostile H. Taine; and the judicious A. de Tocqueville, whose masterpiece, *The Old Regime and the French Revolution,* was first published in 1856. Important general studies on the entire period include the work by Palmer, cited in the Notes, which paints a comparative international picture; E. J. Hobsbawm, *The Age of Revolution, 1789–1848* (1962); and O. Connelly, *French Revolution—Napoleonic Era* (1979). P. Schroeder, *The Transformation of European Politics, 1763–1848* (1994), is a masterful synthesis and reinterpretation, which may be compared with L. Dehio, *The Precarious Balance: Four Centuries of the European Power Struggle* (1962).

Revisionist scholarship has created a wealth of new scholarship and interpretation. A. Cobban, *The Social Interpretation of the French Revolution* (1964), and F. Furet, *Interpreting the French Revolution* (1981), are major reassessments of long-dominant ideas, which are admirably presented in N. Hampson, *A Social History of the French Revolution* (1963), and in the volume by Lefebvre listed in the Notes. E. Kennedy, *A Cultural History of the French Revolution* (1989), beautifully written and handsomely illustrated, and W. Doyle, *Origins of the French Revolution,* 3d ed. (1988), are excellent on long-term developments. Among valuable studies, which generally are often quite critical of revolutionary developments, several are noteworthy: J. Bosher, *The French Revolution* (1988); S. Schama, *Citizens: A Chronicle of the French Revolution* (1989); W. Doyle, *The Oxford History of the French Revolution* (1989); and D. Sutherland, *France, 1789–1815: Revolution and Counterrevolution* (1986).

Two excellent anthologies concisely presenting a range of interpretations are F. Kafker and J. Laux, eds., *The French Revolutions: Conflicting Interpretations,* 4th ed. (1989); and G. Best, ed., *The Permanent Revolution: The French Revolution and Its Legacy, 1789–1989* (1988). G. Rudé makes the men and women of the great days of upheaval come alive in his *The Crowd in the French Revolution* (1959), whereas R. R. Palmer studies sympathetically the leaders of the Terror in *Twelve Who Ruled* (1941). Four other particularly interesting, detailed works are B. Shapiro, *Revolutionary Justice in Paris, 1789–1790* (1993); D. Jordan, *The Revolutionary Career of Maximilien Robespierre* (1985); J. P. Bertaud, *The Army of the French Revolution: From Citizen-Soldier to Instrument of Power* (1988); and C. L. R. James, *The Black Jacobins* (1938, 1980), on black slave revolt in Haiti. Other significant studies on aspects of revolutionary France include P. Jones's pathbreaking *The Peasantry in the French Revolution* (1988); W. Sewell, Jr.'s imaginative *Work and Revolution in France: The Language of Labor from the Old Regime to 1848* (1980); and L. Hunt's innovative *The Family Romance of the French Revolution* (1992). Two major studies on the era's continuous wars are Blanning, cited in the Notes, and O. Connelly, *Blundering to Glory: Napoleon's Military Campaigns* (1987).

An ongoing explosion of studies on women in the French Revolution is increasing knowledge and also raising conflicting interpretations. This may be seen by comparing two particularly important works: J. Landes, *Women and the Public Sphere in the Age of the French Revolution* (1988); and Hufton, listed in the Notes. D. Outram, *The Body and the French Revolution: Sex, Class and Political Culture* (1989), and L. Hunt, *The Family Romance of the French Revolution* (1992), provide innovative analyses of the gender-related aspects of revolutionary politics and are highly recommended. H. Applewhite and D. Levy, eds., *Women and Politics in the Age of Democratic Revolution* (1990), compares developments in leading countries. Mary Wollstonecraft's dramatic life is the subject of several good biographies, including those by Sunstein and James, cited in the Notes.

Two important works placing political developments in a comparative perspective are P. Higonnet, *Sister Republics: The Origins of French and American Republicanism* (1988); and E. Morgan, *Inventing the People: The Rise of Popular Sovereignty in England and America* (1988). B. Bailyn, *The Ideological Origins of the American Revolution* (1967), is also noteworthy.

The best synthesis on Napoleonic France is L. Bergeron, *France Under Napoleon* (1981). E. Arnold, Jr., ed., *A Documentary Survey of Napoleonic France* (1994), includes political and cultural selections. K. Kafker and J. Laux, eds., *Napoleon and His Times: Selected Interpretations* (1989), is an interesting collection of articles, which may be compared with R. Jones, *Napoleon: Man and Myth* (1977). Good biographies are J. Thompson, *Napoleon Bonaparte: His Rise and Fall* (1952); F. Markham, *Napoleon* (1964); and V. Cronin, *Napoleon Bonaparte* (1972). Wonderful novels inspired by the period include Raphael Sabatini's *Scaramouche,* a swashbuckler of revolutionary intrigue with accurate historical details; Charles Dickens's fanciful *A Tale of Two Cities;* and Leo Tolstoy's monumental saga of Napoleon's invasion of Russia (and much more), *War and Peace.*

LISTENING TO THE

PAST

Revolution and Women's Rights

The 1789 Declaration of the Rights of Man was a revolutionary call for legal equality, representative government, and individual freedom. But the new rights were strictly limited to men; Napoleon tightened further the subordination of French women.

Among those who saw the contradiction in granting supposedly universal rights to only half the population was Marie Gouze (1748–1793), known to history as Olympe de Gouges. The daughter of a provincial butcher and peddler, she pursued a literary career in Paris after the death of her husband. Between 1790 and 1793, she wrote more than two dozen political pamphlets under her new name. De Gouges's great work was her "Declaration of the Rights of Woman" (1791). Excerpted here, de Gouges's manifesto went beyond the 1789 Rights of Man. It called on males to end their oppression of women and give women equal rights. A radical on women's issues, de Gouges sympathized with the monarchy and criticized Robespierre in print. Convicted of sedition, she was guillotined in November 1793.

. . . Man, are you capable of being just? . . . Tell me, what gives you sovereign empire to oppress my sex? Your strength? Your talents? Observe the Creator in his wisdom . . . and give me, if you dare, an example of this tyrannical empire. Go back to animals, consult the elements, study plants . . . and distinguish, if you can, the sexes in the administration of nature. Everywhere you will find them mingled; everywhere they cooperate in harmonious togetherness in this immortal masterpiece.

Man alone has raised his exceptional circumstances to a principle. . . . [H]e wants to command as a despot a sex which is in full possession of its intellectual faculties; he pretends to enjoy the Revolution and to claim his rights to equality in order to say nothing more about it.

DECLARATION OF THE RIGHTS OF WOMAN AND THE FEMALE CITIZEN

For the National Assembly to decree in its last sessions, or in those of the next legislature:

Preamble

Mothers, daughters, sisters and representatives of the nation demand to be constituted into a national assembly. Believing that ignorance, omission, or scorn for the rights of woman are the only causes of public misfortunes and of the corruption of governments, [the women] have resolved to set forth in a solemn declaration the natural, inalienable, and sacred rights of woman. . . .

. . . the sex that is as superior in beauty as it is in courage during the sufferings of maternity recognizes and declares in the presence and under the auspices of the Supreme Being, the following Rights of Woman and of Female Citizens:

I. Woman is born free and lives equal to man in her rights. Social distinctions can be based only on the common utility.

II. The purpose of any political association is the conservation of the natural and imprescriptible rights of woman and man; these rights are liberty, property, security, and especially resistance to oppression.

III. The principle of all sovereignty rests essentially with the nation, which is nothing but the union of woman and man. . . .

IV. Liberty and justice consist of restoring all that belongs to others; thus, the only limits on the exercise of the natural rights of woman are perpetual male tyranny; these limits are to be reformed by the laws of nature and reason.

V. Laws of nature and reason proscribe all acts harmful to society. . . .

VI. The law must be the expression of the general will; all female and male citizens must contribute either personally or through their representatives to its formation; it must be the same for all: male and female citizens, being equal in the eyes of the law, must be equally admitted to all honors, positions, and public employment according to their capacity and without other distinctions besides those of their virtues and talents.

VII. No woman is an exception; she is accused, arrested, and detained in cases determined by law. Women, like men, obey this rigorous law.

VIII. The law must establish only those penalties that are strictly and obviously necessary. . . .

IX. Once any woman is declared guilty, complete rigor is [to be] exercised by the law.

X. No one is to be disquieted for his very basic opinions; woman has the right to mount the scaffold; she must equally have the right to mount the rostrum, provided that her demonstrations do not disturb the legally established public order.

XI. The free communication of thoughts and opinions is one of the most precious rights of woman, since that liberty assures the recognition of children by their fathers. Any female citizen thus may say freely, I am the mother of a child which belongs to you, without being forced by a barbarous prejudice to hide the truth. . . .

XIII. For the support of the public force and the expenses of administration, the contributions of woman and man are equal; she shares all the duties . . . and all the painful tasks; therefore, she must have the same share in the distribution of positions, employment, offices, honors, and jobs. . . .

XIV. Female and male citizens have the right to verify, either by themselves or through their representatives, the necessity of the public contribution. This can only apply to women if they are granted an equal share, not only of wealth, but also of public administration. . . .

XV. The collectivity of women, joined for tax purposes to the aggregate of men, has the right to demand an accounting of his administration from any public agent.

XVI. No society has a constitution without the guarantee of rights and the separation of powers; the constitution is null if the majority of individuals comprising the nation have not cooperated in drafting it.

XVII. Property belongs to both sexes whether united or separate; for each it is an inviolable and sacred right. . . .

Postscript

Women, wake up. . . . Discover your rights. . . . Oh, women, women! When will you cease to be blind? What advantage have you received from the Revolution? A more pronounced scorn, a more marked disdain. . . . [If men persist in contradicting their revolutionary principles,] courageously oppose the force of reason to the empty pretensions of superiority . . . and you will soon see these haughty men, not groveling at your feet as servile adorers, but proud to share with you the treasure of the Supreme Being. Regardless of what barriers confront you; it is in your power to free yourselves; you have only to want to. . . .

✣ The late-eighteenth-century French painting *La Liberté. (Bibliothèque Nationale/Giraudon/Art Resource, NY)*

Questions for Analysis

1. On what basis did de Gouges argue for gender equality? Did she believe in natural law?
2. What consequences did "scorn for the rights of woman" have for France, according to de Gouges?
3. Did de Gouges stress political rights at the expense of social and economic rights? If so, why?

Source: Olympe de Gouges, "Declaration of the Rights of Woman," in Darline G. Levy, Harriet B. Applewhite, and Mary D. Johnson, eds., *Women in Revolutionary Paris, 1789–1795* (Urbana: University of Illinois Press, 1979), pp. 87–96.

CHAPTER

22 The Revolution in Energy and Industry

A colored engraving by J. C. Bourne of the Great Western Railway emerging from a tunnel. *(Science & Society Picture Library, London)*

The shortage of energy had become particularly severe in Britain by the eighteenth century. Because of the growth of population, most of the great forests of medieval Britain had long ago been replaced by fields of grain and hay. Wood was in ever-shorter supply, yet it remained tremendously important. It served as the primary source of heat for all homes and industries and as a basic raw material. Processed wood (charcoal) was the fuel that was mixed with iron ore in the blast furnace to produce pig iron. The iron industry's appetite for wood was enormous, and by 1740 the British iron industry was stagnating. Vast forests enabled Russia to become the world's leading producer of iron, much of which was exported to Britain. But Russia's potential for growth was limited, too, and in a few decades Russia would reach the barrier of inadequate energy that was already holding England back.

The Steam Engine Breakthrough

As this early energy crisis grew worse, Britain looked toward its abundant and widely scattered reserves of coal as an alternative to its vanishing wood. Coal was first used in Britain in the late Middle Ages as a source of heat. By 1640 most homes in London were heated with it, and it also provided heat for making beer, glass, soap, and other products. Coal was not used, however, to produce mechanical energy or to power machinery. It was there that coal's potential was enormous, as a simple example shows.

One pound of good bituminous coal contains about 3,500 calories of heat energy. A hard-working miner can dig out 500 pounds of coal a day using hand tools. Even an extremely inefficient converter, which transforms only 1 percent of the heat energy in coal into mechanical energy, will produce 27 horsepower-hours of work from the 500 pounds of coal the miner cut out of the earth. The miner, by contrast, produces only about 1 horsepower-hour in the course of a day.

Early steam engines were just such inefficient converters. As more coal was produced, mines were dug deeper and deeper and were constantly filling with water. Mechanical pumps, usually powered by animals walking in circles at the surface, had to be installed. At one mine, fully five hundred horses were used in pumping. Such power was expensive and bothersome. In an attempt to overcome these disadvantages, Thomas Savery in 1698 and Thomas Newcomen in 1705 invented the first primitive steam engines.

Both engines were extremely inefficient. Both burned coal to produce steam, which was then injected into a cylinder or reservoir. In Newcomen's engine, the steam in the cylinder was cooled, creating a partial vacuum in the cylinder. This vacuum allowed the pressure of the earth's atmosphere to push the piston in the cylinder down and operate a pump. By the early 1770s, many of the Savery engines and hundreds of the Newcomen engines were operating successfully, though inefficiently, in English and Scottish mines.

In the early 1760s, a gifted young Scot named James Watt (1736–1819) was drawn to a critical study of the steam engine. Watt was employed at the time by the University of Glasgow as a skilled craftsman making scientific instruments. The Scottish universities were pioneers in practical technical education, and in 1763 Watt was called on to repair a Newcomen engine being used in a physics course. After a series of observations, Watt

Watt's First Steam Engine, 1774 Watt's early engines, like those of Newcomen, were used mainly to pump water from coal mines, as this nineteenth-century photograph suggests. The development of industrial archaeology has led to many open-air reconstructions and industrial museums. *(Hulton-Getty/Tony Stone Images)*

saw why the Newcomen engine wasted so much energy: the cylinder was being heated and cooled for every single stroke of the piston. To remedy this problem, Watt added a separate condenser where the steam could be condensed without cooling the cylinder. This splendid invention greatly increased the efficiency of the steam engine.

To invent something in a laboratory is one thing; to make it a practical success is quite another. Watt needed skilled workers, precision parts, and capital, and the relatively advanced nature of the British economy proved essential. A partnership with a wealthy English toymaker provided risk capital and a manufacturing plant. In the craft tradition of locksmiths, tinsmiths, and millwrights, Watt found skilled mechanics who could install, regulate, and repair his sophisticated engines. From ingenious manufacturers such as the cannonmaker John Wilkinson, who learned to bore cylinders with a fair degree of accuracy, Watt was gradually able to purchase precision parts. This support allowed him to create an effective vacuum and regulate a complex engine. In more than twenty years of constant effort, Watt made many further improvements. By the late 1780s, the steam engine had become a practical and commercial success in Britain.

The steam engine of Watt and his followers was the Industrial Revolution's most fundamental advance in technology. For the first time in history, humanity had, at least for a few generations, almost unlimited power at its disposal. For the first time, inventors and engineers could devise and implement all kinds of power equipment to aid people in their work. For the first time, abundance was at least a possibility for ordinary men and women.

The steam engine was quickly put to use in several industries in Britain. It drained mines and made possible

James Nasmyth's Mighty Steam Hammer Nasmyth's invention was the forerunner of the modern pile driver, and its successful introduction in 1832 epitomized the rapid development of steam power technology in Britain. In this painting by the inventor himself, workers manipulate a massive iron shaft being hammered into shape at Nasmyth's foundry near Manchester. *(Science & Society Picture Library, London)*

the production of ever more coal to feed steam engines elsewhere. The steam-power plant began to replace waterpower in the cotton-spinning mills during the 1780s, contributing greatly to that industry's phenomenal rise. Steam also took the place of waterpower in flour mills, in the malt mills used in breweries, in the flint mills supplying the china industry, and in the mills exported by Britain to the West Indies to crush sugar cane.

Steam power promoted important breakthroughs in other industries. The British iron industry was radically transformed. The use of powerful, steam-driven bellows in blast furnaces helped ironmakers switch over rapidly from limited charcoal to unlimited coke (which is made from coal) in the smelting of pig iron after 1770. In the 1780s, Henry Cort developed the puddling furnace, which allowed pig iron to be refined in turn with coke. Strong, skilled ironworkers—the puddlers—"cooked" molten pig iron in a great vat, raking off globs of refined iron for further processing. Cort also developed heavy-duty, steam-powered rolling mills, which were capable of spewing out finished iron in every shape and form.

The economic consequence of these technical innovations was a great boom in the British iron industry. In 1740 annual British iron production was only 17,000 tons. With the spread of coke smelting and the first impact of Cort's inventions, production reached 68,000 tons in 1788, 125,000 tons in 1796, and 260,000 tons in 1806. In 1844 Britain produced 3 million tons of iron. This was a truly amazing expansion. Once scarce and expensive, iron became the cheap, basic, indispensable building block of the economy.

The Coming of the Railroads

The second half of the eighteenth century saw extensive construction of hard and relatively smooth roads, particularly in France before the Revolution. Yet it was passenger traffic that benefited most from this construction. Overland shipment of freight, relying solely on horsepower, was still quite limited and frightfully expensive; shippers used rivers and canals for heavy freight whenever possible. It was logical, therefore, that inventors would try to use steam power.

As early as 1800, an American ran a "steamer on wheels" through city streets. Other experiments followed. In the 1820s, English engineers created steam cars capable of carrying fourteen passengers at ten miles an hour—as fast as the mail coach. But the noisy, heavy steam automobiles frightened passing horses and damaged themselves as well as the roads with their vibrations. For the rest of the century, horses continued to reign on highways and city streets.

The coal industry had long been using plank roads and rails to move coal wagons within mines and at the surface. Rails reduced friction and allowed a horse or a human being to pull a heavier load. Thus once a rail capable of supporting a heavy locomotive was developed in 1816, all sorts of experiments with steam engines on rails went forward. In 1825 after ten years of work, George Stephenson built an effective locomotive. In 1830 his *Rocket* sped down the track of the just-completed Liverpool and Manchester Railway at sixteen miles per hour. This was the world's first important railroad, fittingly steaming in the heart of industrial England.

The line from Liverpool to Manchester was a financial as well as a technical success, and many private companies were quickly organized to build more rail lines. These companies had to get permission for their projects from Parliament and pay for the rights of way they needed; otherwise, their freedom was great. Within twenty years, they had completed the main trunk lines of Great Britain. Other countries were quick to follow.

The significance of the railroad was tremendous. The railroad dramatically reduced the cost and uncertainty of shipping freight overland. This advance had many economic consequences. Previously, markets had tended to be small and local; as the barrier of high transportation costs was lowered, markets became larger and even nationwide. Larger markets encouraged larger factories with more sophisticated machinery in a growing number of industries. Such factories could make goods more cheaply and gradually subjected most cottage workers and many urban artisans to severe competitive pressures.

In all countries, the construction of railroads contributed to the growth of a class of urban workers. Cottage workers, farm laborers, and small peasants did not generally leave their jobs and homes to go directly to work in factories. However, the building of railroads created a strong demand for labor, especially unskilled labor, throughout a country. Hard work on construction gangs was done in the open air with animals and hand tools. Many landless farm laborers and poor peasants, long accustomed to leaving their villages for temporary employment, went to build railroads. By the time the work was finished, life back home in the village often seemed dull and unappealing, and many men drifted to towns in search of work—with the railroad companies, in construction, in factories. By the time they sent for their wives and sweethearts to join them, they had become urban workers.

Railroad Construction presented innumerable challenges, such as the building of bridges to span rivers and gorges. Civil engineers responded with impressive feats and their profession bounded ahead. This painting captures the inauguration of I. K. Brunel's Saltash Bridge, which crosses the Tamar River into Cornwall in southwest England. The high spans allow large ships to pass underneath. *(Elton Collection, Ironbridge Gorge Museum Trust)*

The railroad changed the outlook and values of the entire society. The last and culminating invention of the Industrial Revolution, the railroad dramatically revealed the power and increased the speed of the new age. Racing down a track at sixteen miles per hour or, by 1850, at a phenomenal fifty miles per hour was a new and awesome experience. As a French economist put it after a ride on the Liverpool and Manchester in 1833, "There are certain impressions that one cannot put into words!"

Some great painters, notably Joseph M. W. Turner (1775–1851) and Claude Monet (1840–1926), succeeded in expressing this sense of power and awe. So did the massive new train stations, the cathedrals of the industrial age. Leading railway engineers such as Isambard Kingdom Brunel and Thomas Brassey, whose tunnels pierced mountains and whose bridges spanned valleys, became public idols—the astronauts of their day. Everyday speech absorbed the images of railroading. After you got up a "full head of steam," you "highballed" along. And if you didn't "go off the track," you might "toot your own whistle." The railroad fired the imagination.

Industry and Population

In 1851 London was the site of a famous industrial fair. This Great Exposition was held in the newly built Crystal Palace, an architectural masterpiece made entirely of glass and iron, both of which were now cheap and abundant. For the millions who visited, one fact stood out: the little island of Britain was the "workshop of the world." It alone produced two-thirds of the world's coal and more than one-half of its iron and cotton cloth. More generally, it has been carefully estimated that in 1860 Britain produced a truly remarkable 20 percent of the entire world's output of industrial goods, whereas it had produced only about 2 percent of the world total in 1750.[2] Experiencing revolutionary industrial change, Britain became the first industrial nation (Map 22.2).

As the British economy significantly increased its production of manufactured goods, the gross national product (GNP) rose roughly fourfold at constant prices between 1780 and 1851. In other words, the British people as a whole increased their wealth and their national income dramatically. At the same time, the population of Britain boomed, growing from about 9 million in 1780 to almost 21 million in 1851. Thus growing numbers consumed much of the increase in total production. According to one important study, average consumption per person increased by only 75 percent between 1780 and 1851, as the growth in the total population ate up a large part of the fourfold increase in GNP in those years.[3]

Although the question is still debated, many economic historians now believe that rapid population growth in Great Britain was not harmful because it facilitated industrial expansion. More people meant a more mobile labor force, with a wealth of young workers in need of employment and ready to go where the jobs were. Contemporaries were much less optimistic. In his famous and influential *Essay on the Principle of Population* (1798), Thomas Malthus (1766–1834) argued that population would always tend to grow faster than the food supply. In Malthus's opinion, the only hope of warding off such "positive checks" to population growth as war, famine, and disease was "prudential restraint." That is, young men and women had to limit the growth of population by the old tried-and-true means of marrying late in life. But Malthus was not optimistic about this possibility. The powerful attraction of the sexes would cause most people to marry early and have many children.

Wealthy English stockbroker and leading economist David Ricardo (1772–1823) coldly spelled out the pessimistic implications of Malthus's thought. Ricardo's depressing "iron law of wages" posited that because of the pressure of population growth, wages would always

The Crystal Palace The Great Exhibition of 1851 attracted more than six million visitors, many of whom journeyed to London on the newly built railroads. Companies and countries displayed their products and juries awarded prizes in the strikingly modern Crystal Palace. Are today's malls really different? *(Courtesy of the Trustees of the British Museum)*

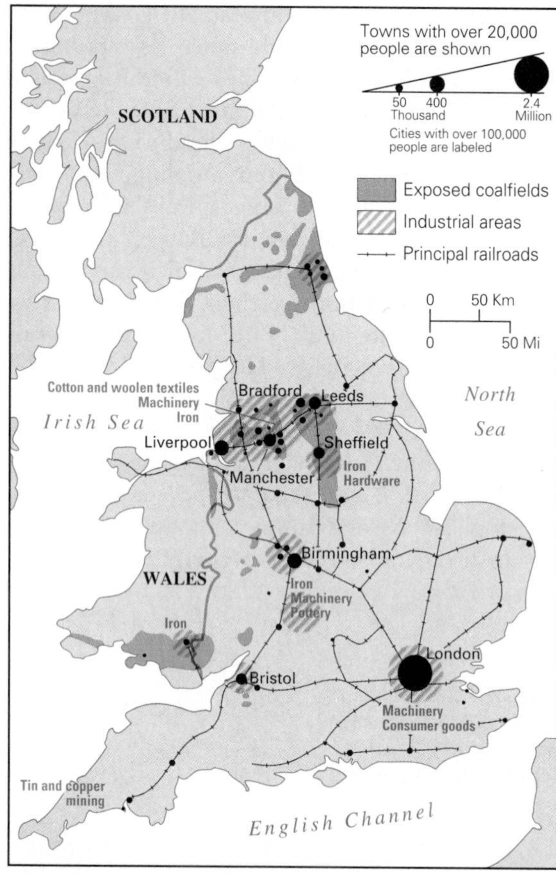

MAP 22.2 The Industrial Revolution in England, ca 1850 Industry concentrated in the rapidly growing cities of the north and the Midlands, where rich coal and iron deposits were in close proximity.

sink to subsistence level. That is, wages would be just high enough to keep workers from starving. With Malthus and Ricardo setting the tone, economics was soon dubbed "the dismal science."

Malthus, Ricardo, and their many followers were proved wrong—in the long run. However, as the great economist John Maynard Keynes quipped during the Great Depression of the 1930s, "we are all dead in the long run." Those who lived through the Industrial Revolution could not see the long run in advance. As modern quantitative studies show, until the 1820s, or even the 1840s, contemporary observers might reasonably have concluded that the economy and the total population were racing neck and neck, with the outcome very much in doubt. The closeness of the race added to the difficulties inherent in the unprecedented journey toward industrial civilization.

There was another problem as well. Perhaps workers, farmers, and ordinary people did not get their rightful share of the new wealth. Perhaps only the rich got richer, while the poor got poorer or made no progress. We will turn to this great issue after looking at the process of industrialization in continental countries in the nineteenth century.

Industrialization in Continental Europe

The new technologies developed in the British Industrial Revolution were adopted rather slowly by businesses in continental Europe. Yet by the end of the nineteenth century, several European countries as well as the United States had also industrialized their economies to a considerable but variable degree. This meant that the process of Western industrialization proceeded gradually, with uneven jerks and national (and regional) variations.

Scholars are still struggling to explain these variations, especially since good answers may offer valuable lessons in our own time for poor countries seeking to improve their material condition through industrialization and economic development. The latest findings on the Western experience are encouraging. They suggest that there were alternative paths to the industrial world in the nineteenth century and that, today as then, there was no need to follow a rigid, predetermined British model.

National Variations

European industrialization, like most economic developments, requires some statistical analysis as part of the effort to understand it. Comparative data on industrial production in different countries over time help give us an overview of what happened. One set of data, the work of a Swiss scholar, compares the level of industrialization on a per capita basis in several countries from 1750 to 1913. These data are far from perfect because there are gaps in the underlying records. But they reflect basic trends and are presented in Table 22.1 for closer study.

As the heading of Table 22.1 makes clear, this is a per capita comparison of levels of industrialization—a comparison of how much industrial product was available, on average, to each person in a given country in a given year. Therefore, all the numbers in Table 22.1 are expressed in terms of a single index number of 100, which

TABLE 22.1 PER CAPITA LEVELS OF INDUSTRIALIZATION, 1750–1913

	1750	1800	1830	1860	1880	1900	1913
Great Britain	10	16	25	64	87	100	115
Belgium	9	10	14	28	43	56	88
United States	4	9	14	21	38	69	126
France	9	9	12	20	28	39	59
Germany	8	8	9	15	25	52	85
Austria-Hungary	7	7	8	11	15	23	32
Italy	8	8	8	10	12	17	26
Russia	6	6	7	8	10	15	20
China	8	6	6	4	4	3	3
India	7	6	6	3	2	1	2

Note: All entries are based on an index value of 100, equal to the per capita level of industrialization in Great Britain in 1900.

Source: P. Bairoch, "International Industrialization Levels from 1750 to 1980," *Journal of European Economic History* 11 (Fall 1982): 294. Data for Great Britain are actually for the United Kingdom, thereby including Ireland with England, Wales, and Scotland. Reprinted with permission.

equals the per capita level of industrial goods in Great Britain (and Ireland) in 1900. Every number is thus a percentage of the 1900 level in Britain and is directly comparable. The countries are listed in roughly the order that they began to use large-scale, power-driven technology.

What does this overview of European industrialization tell us? First, and very significantly, one sees that in 1750 all countries were fairly close together and that Britain was only slightly ahead of its archenemy, France. Second, Britain had opened up a noticeable lead over all continental countries by 1800, and that gap progressively widened as the British Industrial Revolution accelerated to 1830 and reached full maturity by 1860. The British level of per capita industrialization was twice the French level in 1830, for example, and more than three times the French level in 1860. All other large countries (except the United States) had fallen even further behind Britain than France had at both dates. Sophisticated quantitative history confirms the primacy and relative rapidity of Britain's Industrial Revolution.

Third, variations in the timing and in the extent of industrialization in the continental powers and the United States are also apparent. Belgium, independent in 1831 and rich in iron and coal, led in adopting Britain's new technology. France developed factory production more gradually, and most historians now detect no burst in French mechanization and no acceleration in the growth of overall industrial output that may accurately be called revolutionary. They stress instead France's relatively good pattern of early industrial growth, which was unjustly tarnished by the spectacular rise of Germany and the United States after 1860. By 1913 Germany was rapidly closing in on Britain, while the United States had already passed the first industrial nation in per capita production.

Finally, all European states (as well as the United States, Canada, and Japan) managed to raise per capita industrial levels in the nineteenth century. These continent-wide increases stood in stark contrast to the large and tragic decreases that occurred at the same time in most non-Western countries, most notably in China and India. European countries industrialized to a greater or lesser extent even as most of the non-Western world *de*-industrialized. Thus differential rates of wealth- and power-creating industrial development, which heightened disparities within Europe, also greatly magnified existing inequalities between Europe and the rest of the world. We shall return to this momentous change in Chapter 26.

The Challenge of Industrialization

The different patterns of industrial development suggest that the process of industrialization was far from automatic. Indeed, building modern industry was an awesome challenge. To be sure, throughout Europe the eighteenth century was an era of agricultural improvement, population increase, expanding foreign trade, and growing cottage industry. Great Britain led in these developments, but other countries participated in the general trend. Thus when the pace of British industry began to accelerate in the 1780s, continental businesses began to adopt the new methods as they proved their profitability. British industry enjoyed clear superiority, but at first the continent was close behind.

By 1815, however, the situation was quite different. In spite of wartime difficulties, British industry maintained the momentum of the 1780s and continued to grow and improve between 1789 and 1815. On the continent, the unending political and economic upheavals that began with the French Revolution had another effect: they disrupted trade, created runaway inflation, and fostered social anxiety. War severed normal communications between Britain and the continent, severely handicapping continental efforts to use new British machinery and technology. Moreover, the years from 1789 to 1815 were, even for the privileged French economy receiving special favors from Napoleon, a time of "national catastrophe"—in the graphic words of a leading French scholar.[4] Thus whatever the French Revolution and the Napoleonic era meant politically, economically and industrially they meant that France and the rest of Europe were further behind Britain in 1815 than in 1789.

This widening gap made it more difficult, if not impossible, for other countries to follow the British pattern in energy and industry after peace was restored in 1815. Above all, in the newly mechanized industries, British goods were being produced very economically, and these goods had come to dominate world markets completely while the continental states were absorbed in war between 1792 and 1815. Continental firms had little hope of competing with mass-produced British goods in foreign markets for a long time. In addition, British technology had become so advanced and complicated that very few engineers or skilled technicians outside England understood it. Moreover, the technology of steam power had grown much more expensive. It involved large investments in the iron and coal industries and, after 1830, required the existence of railroads, which were very costly. Continental business people had great difficulty finding the large sums of money the new methods demanded, and there was a shortage of laborers accustomed to working in factories. Landowners and government officials were often so suspicious of the new form of industry and the changes it brought that they did little at first to encourage it. All these disadvantages slowed the spread of modern industry (Map 22.3).

After 1815, however, when continental countries began to face up to the British challenge, they had at least three important advantages. First, most continental countries had a rich tradition of putting-out enterprise, merchant capitalists, and skilled urban artisans. Such a tradition gave continental firms the ability to adapt and survive in the face of new market conditions. Second, continental capitalists did not need to develop, ever so slowly and expensively, their own advanced technology. Instead, they could simply "borrow" the new methods developed in Great Britain as well as engineers and some of the financial resources these countries lacked. European countries such as France and Russia also had a third asset that many non-Western areas lacked in the nineteenth century. They had strong independent governments, which did not fall under foreign political control. These governments could fashion economic policies to serve their own interests, as they proceeded to do. They would eventually use the power of the state to promote industry and catch up with Britain.

Agents of Industrialization

The British realized the great value of their technical discoveries and tried to keep their secrets to themselves. Until 1825 it was illegal for artisans and skilled mechanics to leave Britain; until 1843 the export of textile machinery and other equipment was forbidden. Many talented, ambitious workers, however, slipped out of the country illegally and introduced the new methods abroad.

One such man was William Cockerill, a Lancashire carpenter. He and his sons began building cotton-

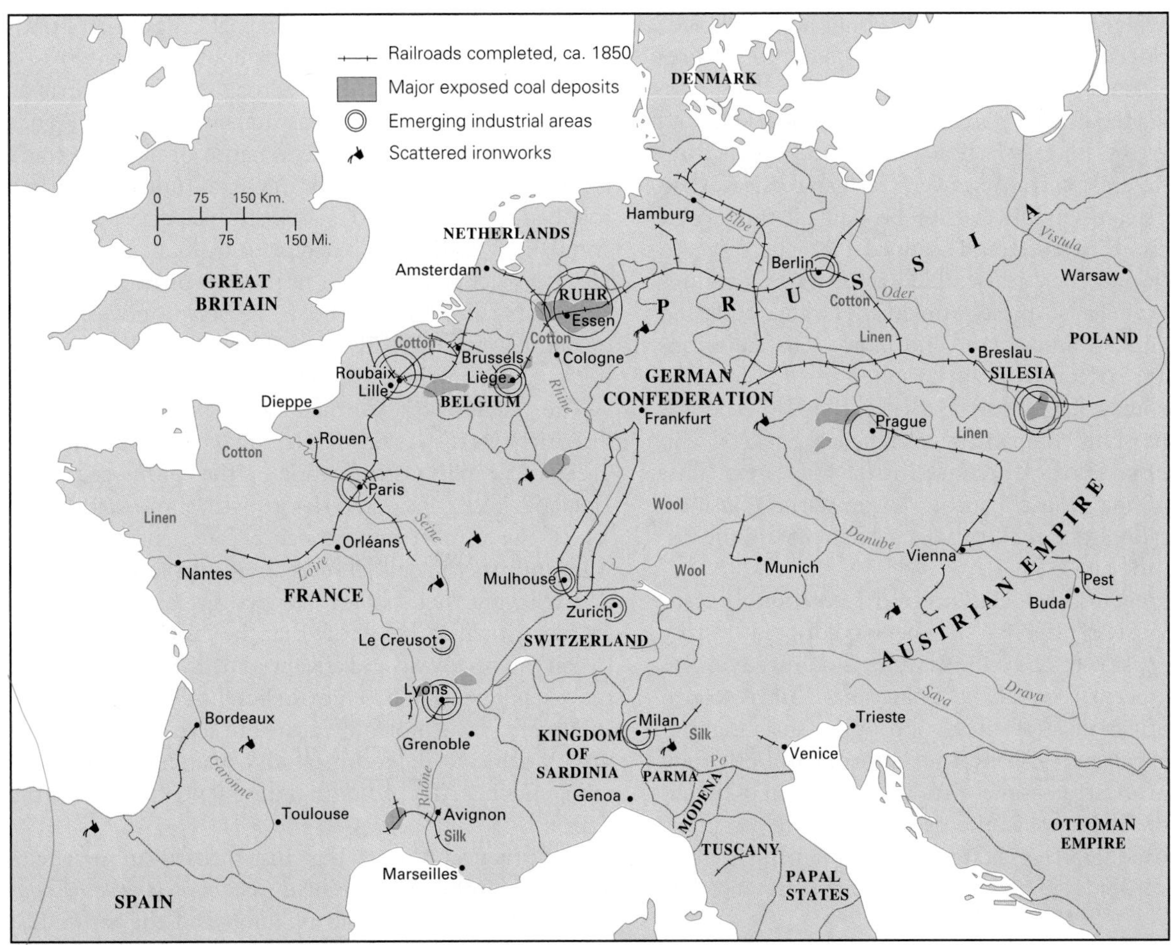

MAP 22.3 Continental Industrialization, ca 1850 Although continental countries were beginning to make progress by 1850, they still lagged far behind Britain. For example, continental railroad building was still in an early stage, whereas the British rail system was essentially complete.

spinning equipment in French-occupied Belgium in 1799. In 1817 the most famous son, John Cockerill, purchased the old summer palace of the deposed bishops of Liège in southern Belgium. Cockerill converted the palace into a large industrial enterprise, which produced machinery, steam engines, and then railway locomotives. He also established modern ironworks and coal mines.

Cockerill's plants in the Liège area became an industrial nerve center, continually gathering new information and transmitting it across Europe. Many skilled British workers came illegally to work for Cockerill, and some went on to found their own companies throughout Europe. Newcomers brought the latest plans and secrets, so Cockerill could boast that ten days after an industrial advance occurred in Britain, he knew all about it in Belgium. Thus British technicians and skilled workers were a powerful force in the spread of early industrialization.

A second agent of industrialization were talented entrepreneurs such as Fritz Harkort, a business pioneer in the German machinery industry. Serving in England as a Prussian army officer during the Napoleonic wars, Harkort was impressed and enchanted with what he saw. He concluded that Germany had to match all these English achievements as quickly as possible. Setting up shop in an abandoned castle in the still-tranquil Ruhr Valley, Harkort felt an almost religious calling to build steam engines and become the "Watt of Germany."

Harkort's basic idea was simple, but it was enormously difficult to carry out. Lacking skilled laborers to do the job, Harkort turned to England for experienced, though expensive, mechanics. He could not be choosy, and he longed for the day when he could afford to replace the haughty foreigners with his fellow Germans. Getting materials also posed a great problem. He had to import the thick iron boilers that he needed from England at great cost. Moreover, German roads were so bad that steam engines had to be built at the works, completely dismantled and shipped piece by piece to the buyer, and then reassembled by Harkort's technicians. In spite of all these problems, Harkort built and sold engines, winning fame and praise. His ambitious efforts over sixteen years also resulted in large financial losses for himself and his partners, and in 1832 he was forced out of his company by his financial backers, who cut back operations to reduce losses. His career illustrates both the great efforts of a few important business leaders to duplicate the British achievement and the difficulty of the task.

Entrepreneurs like Harkort were obviously exceptional. Most continental businesses adopted factory technology slowly, and handicraft methods lived on. Indeed, as recent research on France has shown, continental industrialization usually brought substantial but uneven expansion of handicraft industry in both rural and urban areas for a time. Artisan production of luxury items grew in France as the rising income of the international middle class created foreign demand for silk scarfs, embroidered needlework, perfumes, and fine wines.

A third force for industrialization was government, which often helped business people in continental countries to overcome some of their difficulties. Tariff protection was one such support. For example, after Napoleon's wars ended in 1815, France was suddenly flooded with cheaper and better British goods. The French government responded by laying high tariffs on many British imports in order to protect the French economy. After 1815 continental governments bore the cost of building roads and canals to improve transportation.

They also bore to a significant extent the cost of building railroads. Belgium led the way in the 1830s and 1840s. In an effort to tie the newly independent nation together, the Belgian government decided to construct a state-owned system. Built rapidly as a unified network, Belgium's state-owned railroads stimulated the development of heavy industry and made the country an early industrial leader. Several of the smaller German states also built state systems.

The Prussian government provided another kind of invaluable support. It guaranteed that the state treasury would pay the interest and principal on railroad bonds if the closely regulated private companies in Prussia were unable to do so. Thus railroad investors in Prussia ran little risk, and capital was quickly raised. In France the state shouldered all the expense of acquiring and laying roadbed, including bridges and tunnels. Finished roadbed was leased to a carefully supervised private company, which usually benefited from a state guarantee of its debts and which needed to provide only the rails, cars, and management. In short, governments helped pay for railroads, the all-important leading sector in continental industrialization.

The career of German journalist and thinker Friedrich List (1789–1846) reflects government's greater role in industrialization on the continent than in England. List considered the growth of modern industry of the utmost importance because manufacturing was a primary means of increasing people's well-being and relieving their poverty. Moreover, List was a dedicated nationalist. He wrote that the "wider the gap between the backward and advanced nations becomes, the more dangerous it is to remain behind." For an agricultural nation was not only poor but also weak, increasingly unable to defend itself and maintain its political independence. To promote industry was to defend the nation.

The practical policies that List focused on in articles and in his influential *National System of Political Economy* (1841) were railroad building and the tariff. List supported the formation of a customs union, or *Zollverein,* among the separate German states. Such a tariff union came into being in 1834. Building on the successful elimination of all internal tariffs in Prussia in 1818, the new customs union allowed goods to move between the German member states without tariffs, and a single uniform tariff was erected against all other nations. List wanted a high protective tariff, which would encourage infant industries, allowing them to develop and eventually hold their own against their more advanced British counterparts. List denounced the British doctrine of free trade as little more than Britain's attempt "to make the rest of the world, like the Hindus, its serfs in all industrial and commercial relations." By the 1840s List's economic nationalism had become increasingly popular in Germany and elsewhere.

Finally, banks, like governments, also played a larger and more creative role on the continent than in England. Previously, almost all banks in Europe had been private, organized as secretive partnerships. All the active partners were liable for all the debts of the firm, which meant that in the event of a disastrous bank-

A German Ironworks, 1850 This big business enterprise has mastered the new British method of smelting iron with coke. Germany, and especially the state of Prussia, was well endowed with both iron and coal, and the rapid exploitation of these resources after 1840 transformed a poor agricultural country into an industrial powerhouse. *(Deutsches Museum Munich)*

ruptcy, each partner could lose all of his or her personal wealth in addition to all the money invested in the partnership. Because of the possibility of unlimited financial loss, the partners of private banks tended to be quite conservative and were content to deal with a few rich clients and a few big merchants. They generally avoided industrial investment as being too risky.

In the 1830s, two important Belgian banks pioneered in a new direction. They received permission from the growth-oriented government to establish themselves as corporations enjoying limited liability. That is, a stockholder could lose only his or her original investment in the bank's common stock and could not be assessed for any additional losses. Publicizing the risk-reducing advantage of limited liability, these Belgian banks were able to attract many shareholders, large and small. They mobilized impressive resources for investment in big industrial companies, became industrial banks, and successfully promoted industrial development.

Similar corporate banks became important in France and Germany in the 1850s and 1860s. Usually working in collaboration with governments, they established and developed many railroads and many companies working in heavy industry, which were increasingly organized as limited liability corporations. The most famous such bank was the Crédit Mobilier of Paris, founded by Isaac and Emile Pereire, two young Jewish journalists from Bordeaux. The Crédit Mobilier advertised extensively. It used the savings of thousands of small investors as well as the resources of big ones. The activities of the bank were far-reaching; it built railroads all over France and Europe. As Emile Pereire had said in 1835, "It is not enough to outline gigantic programs on paper. I must write my ideas on the earth."

The combined efforts of skilled workers, entrepreneurs, governments, and industrial banks meshed successfully between 1850 and the financial crash of 1873. This was a period of unprecedentedly rapid economic growth on the continent. In Belgium, Germany, and

France, key indicators of modern industrial development—such as railway mileage, iron and coal production, and steam-engine capacity—increased at average annual rates of 5 to 10 percent compounded. As a result, rail networks were completed in western and much of central Europe, and the leading continental countries mastered the industrial technologies that had first been developed in Great Britain. In the early 1870s, Britain was still Europe's most industrial nation, but a select handful of countries were closing the gap that had been opened up by the Industrial Revolution.

Capital and Labor

Industrial development brought new social relations and intensified long-standing problems between capital and labor in both urban workshops and cottage industry (see pages 640–644). A new group of factory owners and industrial capitalists arose. These men and women and their families strengthened the wealth and size of the middle class, which had previously been made up mainly of merchants and professional people. The nineteenth century became the golden age of the middle class. Modern industry also created a much larger group, the factory workers. For the first time, large numbers of men, women, and children came together under one roof to work with complicated machinery for a single owner or a few partners in large companies.

The growth of new occupational groups in industry stimulated new thinking about social relations. Often combined with reflections on the French Revolution, this thinking led to the development of a new overarching interpretation—a new paradigm—regarding social relationships (see Chapter 23). Briefly, this paradigm argued, with considerable success, that individuals were members of economically determined classes, which had conflicting interests. Accordingly, the comfortable, well-educated "public" of the eighteenth century came increasingly to see itself as the backbone of the middle class (or the middle classes), and the "people" gradually transformed themselves into the modern working class (or working classes). And if the new class interpretation was more of a deceptive simplification than a fundamental truth for some critics, it appealed to many because it seemed to explain what was happening. Therefore, conflicting classes existed, in part, because many individuals came to believe they existed and developed an appropriate sense of class feeling—what Marxists call "class consciousness."

What, then, was the relationship between capital and labor in the early Industrial Revolution? Did the new industrial middle class ruthlessly exploit the workers, as Karl Marx and others have charged?

The New Class of Factory Owners

Early industrialists operated in a highly competitive economic system. As the careers of Watt and Harkort illustrate, there were countless production problems, and success and large profits were by no means certain. Manufacturers therefore waged a constant battle to cut their production costs and stay afloat. Much of the profit had to go back into the business for new and better machinery. "Dragged on by the frenzy of this terrible life," according to one of the dismayed critics, the struggling manufacturer had "no time for niceties. He must conquer or die, make a fortune or drown himself."[5]

Most early industrialists drew upon their families and friends for labor and capital, but they came from a variety of backgrounds. Many, such as Harkort, were from well-established merchant families, which provided a rich network of contacts and support. Others, such as Watt and Cockerill, were of modest means, especially in the early days. Artisans and skilled workers of exceptional ability had unparalleled opportunities. Members of ethnic and religious groups who had been discriminated against in the traditional occupations controlled by the landed aristocracy jumped at the new chances and often helped each other. Scots, Quakers, and other Protestant dissenters were tremendously important in Britain; Protestants and Jews dominated banking in Catholic France. Many of the industrialists were newly rich, and, not surprisingly, they were very proud and self-satisfied.

As factories and firms grew larger, opportunities declined, at least in well-developed industries. It became considerably harder for a gifted but poor young mechanic to start a small enterprise and end up as a wealthy manufacturer. Formal education (for sons and males) became more important as a means of success and advancement, and formal education at the advanced level was expensive. In Britain by 1830 and in France and Germany by 1860, leading industrialists were more likely to have inherited their well-established enterprises, and they were financially much more secure than their struggling fathers and mothers had been. They also had a greater sense of class consciousness, fully aware that ongoing industrial development had widened the gap between themselves and their workers.

The Third-Class Carriage The French artist Honoré Daumier was fascinated by the railroad and its human significance. This great painting focuses on the peasant grandmother, absorbed in memories. The nursing mother represents love and creativity, the sleeping boy innocence. *(The Metropolitan Museum of Art. Bequest of Mrs. H. O. Havemeyer, 1929. The H. O. Havemeyer Collection [29.100.129])*

The wives and daughters of successful businessmen also found fewer opportunities for active participation in Europe's increasingly complex business world. Rather than contributing as vital partners in a family-owned enterprise, as so many middle-class women such as Elizabeth Strutt had done (see the feature "Individuals in Society: The Strutts: Family Enterprise in Action"), these women were increasingly valued for their ladylike gentility. By 1850 some influential women writers and most businessmen assumed that middle-class wives and daughters should steer clear of undignified work in offices and factories. Rather, a middle-class lady should protect and enhance her femininity. She should concentrate on her proper role as wife and mother, preferably in an elegant residential area far removed from ruthless commerce and the volatile working class.

The New Factory Workers

The social consequences of the Industrial Revolution have long been hotly debated. The condition of British workers during the transformation has always generated the most controversy among historians because Britain was the first country to industrialize and because the social consequences seemed harshest there. Before 1850 other countries had not proceeded very far with industrialization, and almost everyone agrees that the eco-

Individuals in Society

The Strutts: Family Enterprise in Action

For centuries economic life in Europe revolved around hundreds of thousands of small family enterprises. These family enterprises worked farms, crafted products, and traded goods. They built and operated the firms and factories of the early industrialization era, with the notable exceptions of the capital-hungry railroads and a few big banks. Indeed, until late in the nineteenth century, close-knit family groups continued to control most successful businesses, including those organized as corporations.

One successful and fairly well-documented family enterprise began with the marriage of Jedediah Strutt (1726–1797) and Elizabeth Woollat (1729–1774) in Derbyshire in northern England in 1755. The son of a farmer, Jedediah fell in love with Elizabeth when he was apprenticed away from home as a wheelwright and lodged with her parents. Both young people grew up in the close-knit dissenting Protestant community, which did not accept the doctrines of the state-sponsored Church of England, and the well-educated Elizabeth worked in a local school for dissenters and then for a dissenter minister in London. Indecisive and self-absorbed, Jedediah inherited in 1754 a small stock of animals from an uncle and finally married Elizabeth the following year.

Aided by Elizabeth, who was "obviously a very capable woman" and who supplied some of the drive her husband had previously lacked, Jedediah embarked on a new career.[1] He invented a machine to make handsome, neat-fitting ribbed silk stockings, which had previously been made by hand. He secured a patent, despite strong opposition from competitors, and went into production. Elizabeth helped constantly in the enterprise, which was nothing less than an informal partnership between husband and wife.[2]

In 1757, for example, when Jedediah was fighting to uphold his patent in the local court, Elizabeth left her son of nine months and journeyed to London to seek a badly needed loan from her former employer. She also canvassed her London relatives and dissenter friends for orders for stockings and looked for sales agents and sources of capital. Elizabeth's letters reveal a detailed knowledge of ribbed stockings and the prices and quality of different kinds of thread. The family biographers, old-line economic historians writing without a trace of feminist concerns, conclude that her husband "owed much of his success to her energy and counsel." Elizabeth was always "active in the business—a partner in herself."[3] Historians have often overlooked such invaluable contributions from wives like Elizabeth, partly because the legal rights and consequences of partnership were denied to married women in Britain and Europe in the eighteenth and nineteenth centuries.

Jedediah Strutt; painting ca 1790 by Joseph Wright of Derby. *(Derby Museum & Art Gallery/The Bridgeman Art Library, London/New York)*

The Strutt enterprise grew and gradually prospered, but it always retained its family character. The firm built a large silk mill and then went into cotton spinning in partnership with Richard Arkwright, the inventor of the water frame (see page 727). The brothers of both Jedediah and Elizabeth worked for the firm, and their eldest daughter worked long hours in the warehouse. Bearing three sons, Elizabeth fulfilled yet another vital task because the typical family firm looked to its own members for managers and continued success. All three sons entered the business and became cotton textile magnates. Elizabeth never saw these triumphs. The loyal and talented wife in the family partnership died suddenly at age forty-five while in London with Jedediah on a business trip.

Questions for Analysis

1. How and why did the Strutts succeed?
2. What does Elizabeth's life tell us about the role of British women in the early Industrial Revolution?

1. R. Fitton and A. Wadsworth, *The Strutts and the Arkwrights, 1758–1830: A Study of the Early Factory System* (Manchester, England: Manchester University Press, 1958), p. 23.
2. See the excellent discussion by C. Hall, "Strains in the 'Firm of Wife, Children and Friends'? Middle-Class Women and Employment in Early Nineteenth-Century England," in P. Hudson and W. Lee, eds., *Women's Work and the Family Economy in Historical Perspective* (Manchester, England: Manchester University Press, 1990), pp. 106–132.
3. Fitton and Wadsworth, *The Strutts,* pp. 110–111.

nomic conditions of European workers improved after 1850. The countries that followed Britain were able to benefit from British experience in social as well as technical matters. Thus the experience of British workers to about 1850 deserves special attention. (Industrial growth also promoted rapid urbanization, with its own awesome problems, as will be shown in Chapter 24.)

From the beginning, the Industrial Revolution in Britain had its critics. Among the first were the romantic poets. William Blake (1757–1827) called the early factories "satanic mills" and protested against the hard life of the London poor. William Wordsworth (1770–1850) lamented the destruction of the rural way of life and the pollution of the land and water. Some handicraft workers—notably the Luddites, who attacked whole factories in northern England in 1812 and after—smashed the new machines, which they believed were putting them out of work. Doctors and reformers wrote eloquently of problems in the factories and new towns, while Malthus and Ricardo concluded that workers would earn only enough to stay alive.

This pessimistic view was accepted and reinforced by Friedrich Engels (1820–1895), the future revolutionary and colleague of Karl Marx. After studying conditions in northern England, this young middle-class German published in 1844 *The Condition of the Working Class in England,* a blistering indictment of the middle classes. "At the bar of world opinion," he wrote, "I charge the English middle classes with mass murder, wholesale robbery, and all the other crimes in the calendar."[6] The new poverty of industrial workers was worse than the old poverty of cottage workers and agricultural laborers, according to Engels. The culprit was industrial capitalism, with its relentless competition and constant technical change. Engels's extremely influential charge of middle-class exploitation and increasing worker poverty was embellished by Marx and later socialists.

Meanwhile, other observers believed that conditions were improving for the working people. Andrew Ure wrote in 1835 in his study of the cotton industry that conditions in most factories were not harsh and were even quite good. Edwin Chadwick, a great and conscientious government official well acquainted with the problems of the working population, concluded that the "whole mass of the laboring community" was increasingly able "to buy more of the necessities and minor luxuries of life."[7] Nevertheless, if all the contemporary assessments had been counted up, those who thought conditions were getting worse for working people would probably have been the majority.

In an attempt to go beyond the contradictory judgments of contemporaries, some historians have looked at different kinds of sources. Statistical evidence is one such source. If working people suffered a great economic decline, as Engels and later socialists asserted, then they must have bought less and less food, clothing, and other necessities as time went on. The purchasing power of the working person's wages must have declined drastically.

Scholarly statistical studies, which continue to multiply rapidly in an age of easy calculations with computer technology, have weakened the idea that the condition of the working class got much worse with industrialization. But the most recent studies also confirm the view that the early years of the Industrial Revolution were hard ones for British workers. There was little or no increase in the purchasing power of the average British worker from about 1780 to about 1820. The years from 1792 to 1815, a period of almost constant warfare with France, were particularly difficult. Food prices rose faster than wages, and the living conditions of the laboring poor declined. Only after 1820, and especially after 1840, did real wages rise substantially, so that the average worker earned and consumed roughly 50 percent more in real terms in 1850 than in 1770.[8] In short, there was considerable economic improvement for workers throughout Great Britain by 1850, but that improvement was hard won and slow in coming.

This important conclusion must be qualified, however. Increased purchasing power meant more goods, but not necessarily greater happiness. More goods may have provided meager compensation for work that was dangerous and monotonous, for example. Also, statistical studies do not say anything about how the level of unemployment may have risen for the simple reason that there are no good unemployment statistics from this period. Furthermore, the hours in the average workweek increased; to an unknown extent, workers earned more simply because they worked more. Finally, the wartime decline was of great importance. The war years were formative years for the new factory labor force. They were also some of the hardest yet experienced. They colored the early experience of modern industrial life in somber tones.

Another way to consider the workers' standard of living is to look at the goods that they purchased. Again the evidence is somewhat contradictory. Speaking generally, workers ate somewhat more food of higher nutritional quality as the Industrial Revolution progressed, except during wartime. Diets became more varied; people ate more potatoes, dairy products, fruits, and vegetables. Clothing improved, but housing for working people probably deteriorated somewhat. In short, per capita use of specific goods supports the position that the standard of living of the working classes rose, at least moderately, after the long wars with France.

Conditions of Work

What about working conditions? Did workers eventually earn more only at the cost of working longer and harder? Were workers exploited harshly by the new factory owners?

The first factories were cotton mills, which began functioning along rivers and streams in the 1770s. Cottage workers, accustomed to the putting-out system, were reluctant to work in factories even when they received relatively good wages because factory work was different from what they were used to and was unappealing. In the factory, workers had to keep up with the machine and follow its tempo. They had to show up every day and work long, monotonous hours. Factory workers had to adjust their daily lives to the shrill call of the factory whistle.

Cottage workers were not used to that kind of life and discipline. All members of the family worked hard and long, but in spurts, setting their own pace. They could interrupt their work when they wanted to. Women and children could break up their long hours of spinning with other tasks. On Saturday afternoon the head of the family delivered the week's work to the merchant manufacturer and got paid. Saturday night was a time of relaxation and drinking, especially for the men. Recovering from his hangover on Tuesday, the weaver bent to his task on Wednesday and then worked frantically to meet his deadline on Saturday. Like some students today, he might "pull an all-nighter" on Thursday or Friday in order to get his work in.

Also, early factories resembled English poorhouses, where totally destitute people went to live on welfare. Some poorhouses were industrial prisons, where the inmates had to work in order to receive their food and lodging. The similarity between large brick factories and large stone poorhouses increased the cottage workers' fear of factories and their hatred of factory discipline.

It was cottage workers' reluctance to work in factories that prompted the early cotton mill owners to turn to abandoned and pauper children for their labor. As we have seen, these owners contracted with local officials to employ large numbers of these children, who had no say in the matter. Pauper children were often badly treated and terribly overworked in the mills, as they were when they were apprenticed as chimney sweeps, market girls, shoemakers, and so forth. In the eighteenth century, semiforced child labor seemed necessary and was socially accepted. From our modern point of view, it was cruel exploitation and a blot on the record of the new industrial system.

By 1790 the early pattern was rapidly changing. The use of pauper apprentices was in decline, and in 1802 it was forbidden by Parliament. Many more factories were being built, mainly in urban areas, where they could use steam power rather than waterpower and attract a workforce more easily than in the countryside. The need for workers was great. Indeed, people came from near and far to work in the cities, both as factory workers and as laborers, builders, and domestic servants. Yet as they took these new jobs, working people did not simply give in to a system of labor that had formerly repelled them. Rather, they helped modify the system by carrying over old, familiar working traditions.

For one thing, they often came to the mills and the mines as family units. This was how they had worked on farms and in the putting-out system. The mill or mine owner bargained with the head of the family and paid him or her for the work of the whole family. In the cotton mills, children worked for their mothers or fathers, collecting wastes and "piecing" broken threads together. In the mines, children sorted coal and worked the ventilation equipment. Their mothers hauled coal in the tunnels below the surface, while their fathers hewed with pick and shovel at the face of the seam.

The preservation of the family as an economic unit in the factories from the 1790s on made the new surroundings more tolerable, both in Great Britain and in other countries, during the early stages of industrialization. Parents disciplined their children, making firm measures socially acceptable, and directed their upbringing. The presence of the whole family meant that children and adults worked the same long hours (twelve-hour shifts were normal in cotton mills in 1800). In the early years, some very young children were employed solely to keep the family together. Jedediah Strutt, for example, believed children should be at least ten years old to work in his mills, but he reluctantly employed seven-year-olds to satisfy their parents. Adult workers were not particularly interested in limiting the minimum working age or hours of their children as long as family members worked side by side. Only when technical changes threatened to place control and discipline in the hands of impersonal managers and foremen did adult workers protest against inhuman conditions in the name of their children.

Some enlightened employers and social reformers in Parliament definitely felt otherwise. They argued that more humane standards were necessary, and they used widely circulated parliamentary reports to influence

Cotton Mill Workers Family members often worked side by side in early British factories, and the child on the left is quite possibly the daughter of the woman nearby. They are combing raw cotton and drawing it into loose strands called rovings, which will be spun into fine thread on the machines to the right. *(Mary Evans Picture Library)*

public opinion. (See the feature "Listening to the Past: The Testimony of Young Mining Workers" on pages 752–753) For example, Robert Owen (1771–1858), a very successful manufacturer in Scotland, testified in 1816 before an investigating committee on the basis of his experience. He stated that "very strong facts" demonstrated that employing children under ten years of age as factory workers was "injurious to the children, and not beneficial to the proprietors." The parliamentary committee asked him to explain, and the testimony proceeded as follows:

"Seventeen years ago, a number of individuals, with myself, purchased the New Lanark establishment from the late Mr Dale, of Glasgow. At that period I find that there were 500 children, who had been taken from poor-houses, chiefly in Edinburgh. . . . The hours of work at that time were thirteen, inclusive of meal times, and an hour and a half was allowed for meals. I very soon discovered that although those children were very well fed, well clothed, well lodged, and very great care taken of them when out of the mills, their growth and their minds were materially injured by being employed at those ages within the cotton mills for eleven and a half hours per day. . . . Their limbs were generally deformed, their growth was stunted, and although one of the best school-masters upon the old plan was engaged to instruct those children every night, in general they made but a very slow progress, even in learning the common alphabet. . . ."

"Do you think the age of ten the best period for the admission of children into full and constant employment for ten or eleven hours per day, within woollen, cotton, and other mills or manufactories?"

"I do not."

"What other period would you recommend for their full admission to full work?"

"Twelve years."[9]

Owen's testimony rang true because he had already raised the age of employment in his mills and was promoting education for young children. Workers also provided graphic testimony at such hearings as the reformers pressed Parliament to pass corrective laws. They scored some important successes.

Their most significant early accomplishment was the Factory Act of 1833. It limited the factory workday for children between nine and thirteen to eight hours and that of adolescents between fourteen and eighteen to twelve hours, although the act made no effort to regulate the hours of work for children at home or in small businesses. The law also prohibited the factory employment of children under nine; they were to be enrolled in the elementary schools that factory owners were required to establish. The employment of children declined rapidly. Thus the Factory Act broke the pattern of whole families working together in the factory because efficiency required standardized shifts for all workers.

Ties of blood and kinship were important in other ways in Great Britain in the formative years between about 1790 and 1840. Many manufacturers and builders hired workers through subcontractors. They paid the subcontractors on the basis of what the subcontractors and their crews produced—for smelting so many tons of pig iron or moving so much dirt or gravel for a canal or roadbed. Subcontractors in turn hired and fired their own workers, many of whom were friends and relations. The subcontractor might be as harsh as the greediest capitalist, but the relationship between subcontractor and work crew was close and personal. This kind of personal relationship had traditionally existed in cottage industry and in urban crafts, and it was more acceptable to many workers than impersonal factory discipline. This system also provided people with an easy way to find a job. Even today, a friend or relative who is a supervisor is frequently worth a hundred formal application forms.

Ties of kinship were particularly important for newcomers, who often traveled great distances to find work. Many urban workers in Great Britain were from Ireland. Forced out of rural Ireland by population growth and deteriorating economic conditions from 1817 on, Irish in search of jobs could not be choosy; they took what they could get. As early as 1824, most of the workers in the Glasgow cotton mills were Irish; in 1851 one-sixth of the population of Liverpool was Irish. Even when Irish workers were not related directly by blood, they were held together by ethnic and religious ties. Like other immigrant groups elsewhere, they worked together, formed their own neighborhoods, and not only survived but also thrived.

The Sexual Division of Labor

The era of the Industrial Revolution witnessed major changes in the sexual division of labor. In preindustrial Europe most people generally worked in family units. By tradition, certain jobs were defined by sex—women and girls for milking and spinning, men and boys for plowing and weaving. But many tasks might go to either sex because particular circumstances dictated a family's response in its battle for economic survival. This pattern of family employment carried over into early factories and subcontracting, but it collapsed as child labor was restricted and new attitudes emerged. A different sexual division of labor gradually arose to take its place. The man emerged as the family's primary wage earner, while the woman found only limited job opportunities. Generally denied good jobs at good wages in the growing urban economy, women were expected to concentrate on unpaid housework, child care, and craftwork at home.

This new pattern of "separate spheres" had several aspects. First, all studies agree that married women from the working classes were much less likely to work full-time for wages outside the house after the first child arrived, although they often earned small amounts doing putting-out handicrafts at home and taking in boarders. Second, when married women did work for wages outside the house, they usually came from the poorest, most desperate families, where the husbands were poorly paid, sick, unemployed, or missing. Third, these poor married (or widowed) women were joined by legions of young unmarried women, who worked full-time but only in certain jobs. Fourth, all women were generally confined to low-paying, dead-end jobs. Virtually no occupation open to women paid a wage sufficient for a person to live independently. Men predominated in the better-paying, more promising employments. Evolving gradually as family labor declined, but largely in place in the urban sector of the British economy by 1850, the new sexual division of labor constituted a major development in the history of women and of the family.

If the reorganization of paid work along gender lines is widely recognized, there is as yet no agreement on its causes. One school of scholars sees little connection with industrialization and finds the answer in the deeply ingrained sexist attitudes of a "patriarchal tradition," which predated the economic transformation. These scholars stress the role of male-dominated craft unions in denying workingwomen access to good jobs and in reducing them to unpaid maids dependent on their husbands. Other scholars, believing that the gender roles of women and men can vary enormously with time and culture, look more to a combination of economic and biological factors in order to explain why the mass of women were either unwilling or unable to halt the emergence of a sex-segregated division of labor.

Three ideas stand out in this more recent interpretation. First, the new and unfamiliar discipline of the clock and the machine was especially hard on married women of the laboring classes. Above all, relentless factory discipline conflicted with child care in a way that labor on the farm or in the cottage had not. A woman operating earsplitting spinning machinery could mind a child of seven or eight working beside her (until such work was outlawed), but she could no longer pace herself through pregnancy, even though overwork during pregnancy heightened the already high risks of childbirth. Nor could a woman breast-feed her baby on the job, although breast-feeding extended the life span of the child. Thus a working-class woman had strong incentives to concentrate on child care within her home if her family could afford it.

Second, running a household in conditions of primitive urban poverty was an extremely demanding job in its own right. There were no supermarkets or discount department stores, no running water or public transportation. Everything had to be done on foot. As in the poor sections of many inner cities today, shopping and feeding the family constituted a never-ending challenge. The woman marched from one tiny shop to another, dragging her tired children (for who was to watch them?) and struggling valiantly with heavy sacks, tricky shopkeepers, and walkup apartments. Yet another brutal job outside the house—a "second shift"—had limited appeal for the average married woman. Thus women might well have accepted the emerging division of labor as the best available strategy for family survival in the industrializing society.[10]

Third, why were the women who did work for wages outside the home segregated and confined to certain "women's jobs"? No doubt the desire of males to monopolize the best opportunities and hold women down provides part of the answer. Yet as some feminist scholars have argued, sex-segregated employment was also a collective response to the new industrial system. Previously, at least in theory, young people worked under a watchful parental eye. The growth of factories and mines brought unheard-of opportunities for girls and boys to mix on the job, free of familial supervision. Continuing to mix after work, they were "more likely to form liaisons, initiate courtships, and respond to advances."[11] Such intimacy also led to more unplanned pregnancies and fueled the illegitimacy explosion that had begun in the late eighteenth century and that gathered force until at least 1850 (see pages 664–665). Thus segregation of jobs by gender was partly an effort by older people to help control the sexuality of working-class youths.

Investigations into the British coal industry before 1842 provide a graphic example of this concern. (See the feature "Listening to the Past: The Testimony of Young Mining Workers" on pages 752–753.) The middle-class men leading the inquiry, who expected their daughters and wives to pursue ladylike activities, often failed to appreciate the physical effort of the girls and women who dragged with belt and chain the unwheeled carts of coal along narrow underground passages. But they professed horror at the sight of girls and women working without shirts, which was a common practice because of the heat, and they quickly assumed the prevalence of licentious sex with the male miners, who also wore very little clothing. In fact, most girls and married women worked for related males in a family unit that provided considerable protection and restraint. Yet many witnesses from the working class believed that "blackguardism and debauchery" were common and that "they are best out of the pits, the lasses." Some miners stressed particularly the sexual danger of letting girls work past puberty. As one explained:

I consider it a scandal for girls to work in the pits. Till they are 12 or 14 they may work very well but after that it's an abomination. . . . The work of the pit does not hurt them, it is the effect on their morals that I complain of, and after 14 they should not be allowed to go. . . . After that age it is dreadful for them.[12]

The Mines Act of 1842 prohibited underground work for all women as well as for boys under ten.

Some women who had to support themselves protested against being excluded from coal mining, which paid higher wages than most other jobs open to working-class women. But provided they were part of families that could manage economically, the girls and the women who had worked underground were generally pleased with the law. In explaining her satisfaction in 1844, one mother of four provided a real insight into why many women accepted the emerging sexual division of labor:

While working in the pit I was worth to my [miner] husband seven shillings a week, out of which we had to pay 2 1/2 shillings to a woman for looking after the younger children. I used to take them to her house at 4 o'clock in the morning, out of their own beds, to put them into hers. Then there was one shilling a week for washing; besides, there was mending to pay for, and other things. The house was not guided. The other children broke things; they did not go to school when they were sent; they would be playing about, and get ill-used by other children, and their clothes torn. Then when I came home in the evening, everything was to do after the day's labor, and I was so tired I had no heart for it; no fire lit, nothing cooked, no water fetched, the house dirty, and nothing comfortable for my husband. It is all far better now, and I wouldn't go down again.[13]

The Early Labor Movement in Britain

Many kinds of employment changed slowly during and after the Industrial Revolution in Great Britain. In 1850 more British people still worked on farms than in any other occupation. The second-largest occupation was domestic service, with more than one million household servants, 90 percent of whom were women. Thus many old, familiar jobs outside industry lived on and provided alternatives for individual workers. This helped ease the transition to industrial civilization.

Within industry itself, the pattern of small-scale production with handicraft skills remained unchanged in many trades, even as some others were revolutionized by technological change. For example, as in the case of cotton and coal, the British iron industry was completely dominated by large-scale capitalist firms by 1850. One iron magnate in Wales employed six thousand workers in his plant, and many large ironworks had more than one thousand people on their payrolls. Yet the firms that fashioned iron into small metal goods, such as tools, tableware, and toys, employed on average fewer than ten wage workers, who used time-honored handicraft skills. Only gradually after 1850 did some owners find ways to reorganize some handicraft industries with new machines and new patterns of work. The survival of small workshops gave many workers an alternative to factory employment.

Working-class solidarity and class-consciousness developed in small workshops as well as in large factories, however. In the northern factory districts, where thousands of "hired hands" looked across at a tiny minority of managers and owners, anticapitalist sentiments were frequent by the 1820s. Commenting in 1825 on a strike in the woollen center of Bradford and the support it had gathered from other regions, one paper claimed with pride that "it is all the workers of England against a few masters of Bradford."[14] Modern technology had created a few versus a many.

The transformation of some traditional trades by organizational changes, rather than technological innova-

Girl Dragging Coal Wagons Published by reformers in Parliament as part of a multivolume investigation into child labor in coal mines (see pages 752–753), this picture was one of several that shocked public opinion and contributed to the Mines Act of 1842. Stripped to the waist and harnessed to the wagon with belt and chain, this underground worker is "hurrying" coal from the face of the seam to the mine shaft. *(The British Library)*

tions, could also create ill will and class feeling. The liberal concept of economic freedom, which by 1760 in Great Britain had already broken down many old guild restrictions on wages and cottage industry, gathered strength in the late eighteenth and early nineteenth centuries. As in France during the French Revolution, the British government attacked monopolies, guilds, and workers combinations in the name of individual liberty. In 1799 Parliament passed the Combination Acts, which outlawed unions and strikes. In 1813 to 1814, Parliament repealed the old and often disregarded law of 1563 regulating the wages of artisans and the conditions of apprenticeship. As a result of these and other measures, certain skilled artisan workers, such as bootmakers and high-quality tailors, found aggressive capitalists ignoring traditional work rules and flooding their trades with unorganized women workers and children to beat down wages.

The liberal capitalist attack on artisan guilds and work rules was bitterly resented by many craftworkers, who subsequently played an important part in Great Britain and in other countries in gradually building a modern labor movement to improve working conditions and to serve worker needs. The Combination Acts were widely disregarded by workers. Printers, papermakers, carpenters, tailors, and other such craftsmen continued to take collective action, and societies of skilled factory workers also organized unions. Unions sought to control the number of skilled workers, limit apprenticeship to members' own children, and bargain with owners over wages. They were not afraid to strike; there was, for example, a general strike of adult cotton spinners in Manchester in 1810. In the face of widespread union activity, Parliament repealed the Combination Acts in 1824, and unions were tolerated, though not fully accepted, after 1825.

The next stage in the development of the British trade-union movement was the attempt to create a single large national union. This effort was led not so much by working people as by social reformers such as Robert Owen. Owen, a self-made cotton manufacturer (see page 745), had pioneered in industrial relations by combining firm discipline with concern for the health, safety, and hours of his workers. After 1815 he experimented with cooperative and socialist communities, including one at New Harmony, Indiana. Then in 1834 Owen organized one of the largest and most visionary of the early national unions, the Grand National Consolidated Trades Union. When this and other grandiose schemes collapsed, the British labor movement moved once again after 1851 in the direction of craft unions (see Chapter 23). The most famous of these "new model unions" was the Amalgamated Society of Engineers. These unions won real benefits for members by fairly conservative means and thus became an accepted part of the industrial scene.

British workers also engaged in direct political activity in defense of their own interests. After the collapse of Owen's national trade union, a great deal of the energy of working people went into the Chartist movement, whose goal was political democracy. The key Chartist demand—that all men be given the right to vote—became the great hope of millions of aroused people. Workers were also active in campaigns to limit the workday in factories to ten hours and to permit duty-free importation of wheat into Great Britain to secure cheap bread. Thus working people developed a sense of their own identity and played an active role in shaping the new industrial system. Clearly, they were neither helpless victims nor passive beneficiaries.

SUMMARY

Western society's industrial breakthrough grew out of a long process of economic and social change in which the rise of capitalism, overseas expansion, and the growth of rural industry stood out as critical preparatory developments. Eventually taking the lead in all of these developments, and also profiting from stable government, abundant natural resources, and a flexible labor force, Britain experienced between the 1780s and the 1850s an epoch-making transformation, one that is still aptly termed the Industrial Revolution.

Building on technical breakthroughs, power-driven equipment, and large-scale enterprise, the Industrial Revolution in England greatly increased output in certain radically altered industries, stimulated the large handicraft and commercial sectors, and speeded up overall economic growth. Rugged Scotland industrialized at least as fast as England, and Great Britain became the first industrial nation. By 1850 the level of British per capita industrial production was surpassing continental levels by a growing margin, and Britain savored a near monopoly in world markets for mass-produced goods.

Continental countries inevitably took rather different paths to the urban industrial society. They relied more on handicraft production in both towns and villages. Only in the 1840s did railroad construction begin to create the strong demand for iron, coal, and railway equipment that speeded up the process of industrialization in the 1850s and 1860s.

The rise of modern industry had a profound impact on people and their lives. In the early stages, Britain again led the way, experiencing in a striking manner the long-term social changes accompanying the economic transformation. Factory discipline and Britain's stern capitalist economy weighed heavily on working people, who, however, actively fashioned their destinies, refusing to be passive victims. Improvements in the standard of living came slowly, although they were substantial by 1850. The era of industrialization fostered new attitudes toward child labor, encouraged protective factory legislation, and called forth a new sense of class feeling and an assertive labor movement. It also promoted a more rigid division of roles and responsibilities within the family that was detrimental to women, another gradual but profound change of revolutionary proportions.

NOTES

1. N. F. R. Crafts, *British Economic Growth During the Industrial Revolution* (Oxford: Oxford University Press, 1985), p. 32.
2. P. Bairoch, "International Industrialization Levels from 1750 to 1980," *Journal of European Economic History* 11 (Spring 1982): 269–333.
3. Crafts, *British Economic Growth,* pp. 45, 95–102.
4. M. Lévy-Leboyer, *Les banques européennes et l'industrialisation dans la première moitié du XIXe siècle* (Paris: Presses Universitaires de France, 1964), p. 29.
5. J. Michelet, *The People,* trans. with an introduction by J. P. McKay (Urbana: University of Illinois Press, 1973; original publication, 1846), p. 64.
6. F. Engels, *The Condition of the Working Class in England,* trans. and ed. W. O. Henderson and W. H. Chaloner (Stanford, Calif.: Stanford University Press, 1968), p. xxiii.
7. Quoted in W. A. Hayek, ed., *Capitalism and the Historians* (Chicago: University of Chicago Press, 1954), p. 126.
8. Crafts, *British Economic Growth,* p. 95.
9. Quoted in E. R. Pike, *"Hard Times": Human Documents of the Industrial Revolution* (New York: Praeger, 1966), p. 109.
10. See especially J. Brenner and M. Rama, "Rethinking Women's Oppression," *New Left Review* 144 (March–-April 1984): 33–71, and sources cited there.
11. J. Humphries, ". . . 'The Most Free from Objection' . . . : The Sexual Division of Labor and Women's Work in Nineteenth-Century England," *Journal of Economic History* 47 (December 1987): 948.
12. Ibid., p. 941; Pike, *"Hard Times,"* p. 266.
13. Pike, *"Hard Times,"* p. 208.
14. Quoted in D. Geary, ed., *Labour and Socialist Movements in Europe Before 1914* (Oxford: Berg, 1989), p. 29.

SUGGESTED READING

There is a vast and exciting literature on the Industrial Revolution. R. Cameron, *A Concise Economic History of the World* (1989), provides an introduction to the issues and has a carefully annotated bibliography. J. Goodman and K. Honeyman, *Gainful Pursuits: The Making of Industrial Europe, 1600–1914* (1988), D. S. Landes, *The Unbound Prometheus: Technological Change and Industrial Development in Western Europe from 1750 to the Present* (1969), and S. Pollard, *Peaceful Conquest: The Industrialization of Europe* (1981), are excellent general treatments of European industrial growth. These studies also suggest the range of issues and interpretations. R. Sylla and G. Toniolo, eds., *Patterns of European Industrialization* (1991), is an important collection by specialists. T. Kemp, *Industrialization in Europe,* 2d ed. (1985), is also useful. P. Hudson, *The Industrial Revolution* (1992), M. Berg, *The Age of Manufactures: Industry, Innovation and Work in Britain, 1700–1820* (1985), and P. Mathias, *The First Industrial Nation: An Economic History of Britain, 1700–1914* (1969), admirably discuss the various aspects of the British breakthrough and offer good bibliographies, as does the work by Crafts mentioned in the Notes. W. Rostow, *The Stages of Economic Growth: A Non-Communist Manifesto* (1960), has been a popular, provocative study.

W. Walton, *France and the Crystal Palace: Bourgeois Taste and Artisan Manufacture in the 19th Century* (1992), and H. Kirsh, *From Domestic Manufacturing to Industrial Revolution: The Case of the Rhineland Textile Districts* (1989), examine the gradual transformation of handicraft techniques and their persistent importance in the international economy. R. Cameron, *France and the Economic Development of Europe, 1800–1914* (1961), traces the spread of railroads and industry across Europe. A. S. Milward and S. B. Saul, *The Economic Development of Continental Europe, 1780–1870* (1973) and *The Development of the Economies of Continental Europe, 1850–1914* (1977), may be compared with J. Clapham's old-fashioned classic, *Economic Development of France and Germany* (1963). P. O'Brien, "Path Dependency, or Why Britain Became an Industrialized and Urbanized National Economy Long Before France," *Economic History Review* 49 (May 1966): 213–249, is a stimulating comparative essay, and C. Heywood, *The Economic Development of France, 1750–1914* (1992), introduces the main issues and provides an up-to-date bibliography. Other important works on industrial developments are C. Tilly and E. Shorter, *Strikes in France, 1830–1848* (1974); D. Ringrose, *Transportation and Economic Stagnation in Spain, 1750–1850* (1970); L. Schofer, *The Formation of a Modern Labor Force* (1975), which focuses on the Silesian part of Germany; and W. Blackwell, *The Industrialization of Russia,* 2d ed. (1982). L. Moch, *Paths to the City: Regional Migration in Nineteenth-Century France* (1983), and W. Schivelbusch, *Disenchanted Night: The Industrialization of Light in the Nineteenth Century* (1983), imaginatively analyze quite different aspects of industrialization's many consequences.

The debate between "optimists" and "pessimists" about the consequences of industrialization in Britain goes on. Two excellent studies with a gender perspective revitalize the debate: D. Valenze, *The First Industrial Woman* (1995); and P. Hudson and W. Lee, eds., *Women's Work and the Family Economy in Historical Perspective* (1990). P. Taylor, ed., *The Industrial Revolution: Triumph or Disaster?* (1970), is a useful introduction to older studies. Hayek's collection of essays, cited in the Notes, stresses positive aspects. It is also fascinating to compare Engels's classic condemnation, cited in the Notes, with Andrew Ure's optimistic defense, *The Philosophy of Manufactures,* first published in 1835 and reprinted recently. J. Rule, *The Labouring Classes in Early Industrial England, 1750–1850* (1987), is a recommended synthesis. E. P. Thompson continues and enriches the Engels tradition in *The Making of the English Working Class* (1963), an exciting book rich in detail and early working-class lore. Pike's documentary collection, cited in the Notes, provides fascinating insights into the lives of working people. An unorthodox but moving account of a doomed group is D. Bythell, *The Handloom Weavers* (1969). L. Davidoff and C. Hall, *Family Fortunes: Men and Women of the English Middle Class, 1750–1850* (1987), examines both economic activities and cultural beliefs with great skill. F. Klingender, *Art and the Industrial Revolution,* rev. ed. (1968), is justly famous, and M. Ignatieff, *A Just Measure of Pain* (1980), is an engrossing study of prisons during British industrialization. D. S. Landes, *Revolution in Time: Clocks and the Making of the Modern World* (1983), is a brilliant integration of industrial and cultural history.

Among general studies, G. S. R. Kitson Clark, *The Making of Victorian England* (1967), is particularly imaginative. A. Briggs, *Victorian People* (1955), provides an engrossing series of brief biographies. H. Ausubel discusses a major reformer in *John Bright* (1966), and B. Harrison skillfully illuminates the problem of heavy drinking in *Drink and the Victorians* (1971). The most famous contemporary novel dealing with the new industrial society is Charles Dickens's *Hard Times,* an entertaining but exaggerated story. *Mary Barton* and *North and South* by Elizabeth Gaskell are more realistic portrayals, and both are highly recommended.

LISTENING TO THE PAST

The Testimony of Young Mining Workers

The use of child labor in British industrialization quickly attracted the attention of humanitarians and social reformers. This interest led to investigations by parliamentary commissions, which resulted in laws limiting the hours and the ages of children working in large factories. Designed to build a case for remedial legislation, parliamentary inquiries gave large numbers of workers a rare chance to speak directly to contemporaries and to historians.

The moving passages that follow are taken from testimony gathered in 1841 and 1842 by the Ashley Mines Commission. Interviewing employers and many male and female workers, the commissioners focused on the physical condition of the youth and on the sexual behavior of workers far underground. The subsequent Mines Act of 1842 sought to reduce immoral behavior and sexual bullying by prohibiting underground work for all women (and for boys younger than ten).

Mr. Payne, coal master:

That children are employed generally at nine years old in the coal pits and sometimes at eight. In fact, the smaller the vein of coal is in height, the younger and smaller are the children required; the work occupies from six to seven hours per day in the pits; they are not ill-used or worked beyond their strength; a good deal of depravity exists but they are certainly not worse in morals than in other branches of the Sheffield trade, but upon the whole superior; the morals of this district are materially improving; Mr. Bruce, the clergyman, has been zealous and active in endeavoring to ameliorate their moral and religious education. . . .

Ann Eggley, hurrier, 18 years old:

I'm sure I don't know how to spell my name. We go at four in the morning, and sometimes at half-past four. We begin to work as soon as we get down. We get out after four, sometimes at five, in the evening. We work the whole time except an hour for dinner, and sometimes we haven't time to eat. I hurry [move coal wagons underground] by myself, and have done so for long. I know the corves [small coal wagons] are very heavy, they are the biggest corves anywhere about. The work is far too hard for me; the sweat runs off me all over sometimes. I am very tired at night. Sometimes when we get home at night we have not power to wash us, and then we go to bed. Sometimes we fall asleep in the chair. Father said last night it was both a shame and a disgrace for girls to work as we do, but there was naught else for us to do. I began to hurry when I was seven and I have been hurrying ever since. I have been 11 years in the pits. The girls are always tired. I was poorly twice this winter; it was with headache. I hurry for Robert Wiggins; he is not akin to me. . . . We don't always get enough to eat and drink, but we get a good supper. I have known my father go at two in the morning to work . . . and he didn't come out till four. I am quite sure that we work constantly 12 hours except on Saturdays. We wear trousers and our shifts in the pit and great big shoes clinkered and nailed. The girls never work naked to the waist in our pit. The men don't insult us in the pit. The conduct of the girls in the pit is good enough sometimes and sometimes bad enough. I never went to a day-school. I went a little to a Sunday-school, but I soon gave it over. I thought it too bad to be confined both Sundays and week-days. I walk about and get the fresh air on Sundays. I have not learnt to read. I don't know my letters. I never learnt naught. I never go to church or chapel; there is no church or chapel at Gawber, there is none nearer than a mile. . . . I have never heard that a good man came into the world who was God's son to save sinners. I never heard of Christ at all. Nobody has ever told me about him, nor have my father and mother ever taught me to pray. I know no prayer; I never pray.

Patience Kershaw, aged 17:

My father has been dead about a year; my mother is living and has ten children, five lads and five lasses; the oldest is about thirty, the youngest is four; three lasses go to mill; all the lads are colliers, two getters and three hurriers; one lives at home and does nothing; mother does nought but look after home.

All my sisters have been hurriers, but three went to the mill. Alice went because her legs swelled from hurrying in cold water when she was hot. I never went to day-school; I go to Sunday-school, but I cannot read or write; I go to pit at five o'clock in the morning and come out at five in the evening; I get my breakfast of porridge and milk first; I take my dinner with me, a cake, and eat it as I go; I do not stop or rest any time for the purpose; I get nothing else until I get home, and then have potatoes and meat, not every day meat. I hurry in the clothes I have now got on, trousers and ragged jacket; the bald place upon my head is made by thrusting the corves; my legs have never swelled, but sisters' did when they went to mill; I hurry the corves a mile and more under ground and back; they weigh 300; I hurry 11 a day; I wear a belt and chain at the workings to get the corves out; the putters [miners] that I work for are *naked* except their caps; they pull off all their clothes; I see them at work when I go up; sometimes they beat me, if I am not quick enough, with their hands; they strike me upon my back; the boys take liberties with me, sometimes, they pull me about; I am the only girl in the pit; there are about 20 boys and 15 men; all the men are naked; I would rather work in mill than in coal-pit.

✣ Female mine worker, from a parliamentary report, 1842. *(Mary Evans Picture Library)*

Isabel Wilson, 38 years old, coal putter:

When women have children thick [fast] they are compelled to take them down early. I have been married 19 years and have had 10 bairns [children]; seven are in life. When on Sir John's work was a carrier of coals, which caused me to miscarry five times from the strains, and was gai [very] ill after each. Putting is no so oppressive; last child was born on Saturday morning, and I was at work on the Friday night.

Once met with an accident; a coal brake my cheek-bone, which kept me idle some weeks.

I have wrought below 30 years, and so has the guid man; he is getting touched in the breath now.

None of the children read, as the work is no regular. I did read once, but no able to attend to it now; when I go below lassie 10 years of age keeps house and makes the broth or stir-about.

Questions for Analysis

1. To what extent are the testimonies of Ann Eggley and Patience Kershaw in harmony with that of Payne?
2. Describe the work of Eggley and Kershaw. What do you think of their work? Why?
3. What strikes you most about the lives of these workers?
4. The witnesses were responding to questions from middle-class commissioners. What did the commissioners seem interested in? Why?

Source: J. Bowditch and C. Ramsland, eds., *Voices of the Industrial Revolution.*

CHAPTER

23 Ideologies and Upheavals, 1815–1850

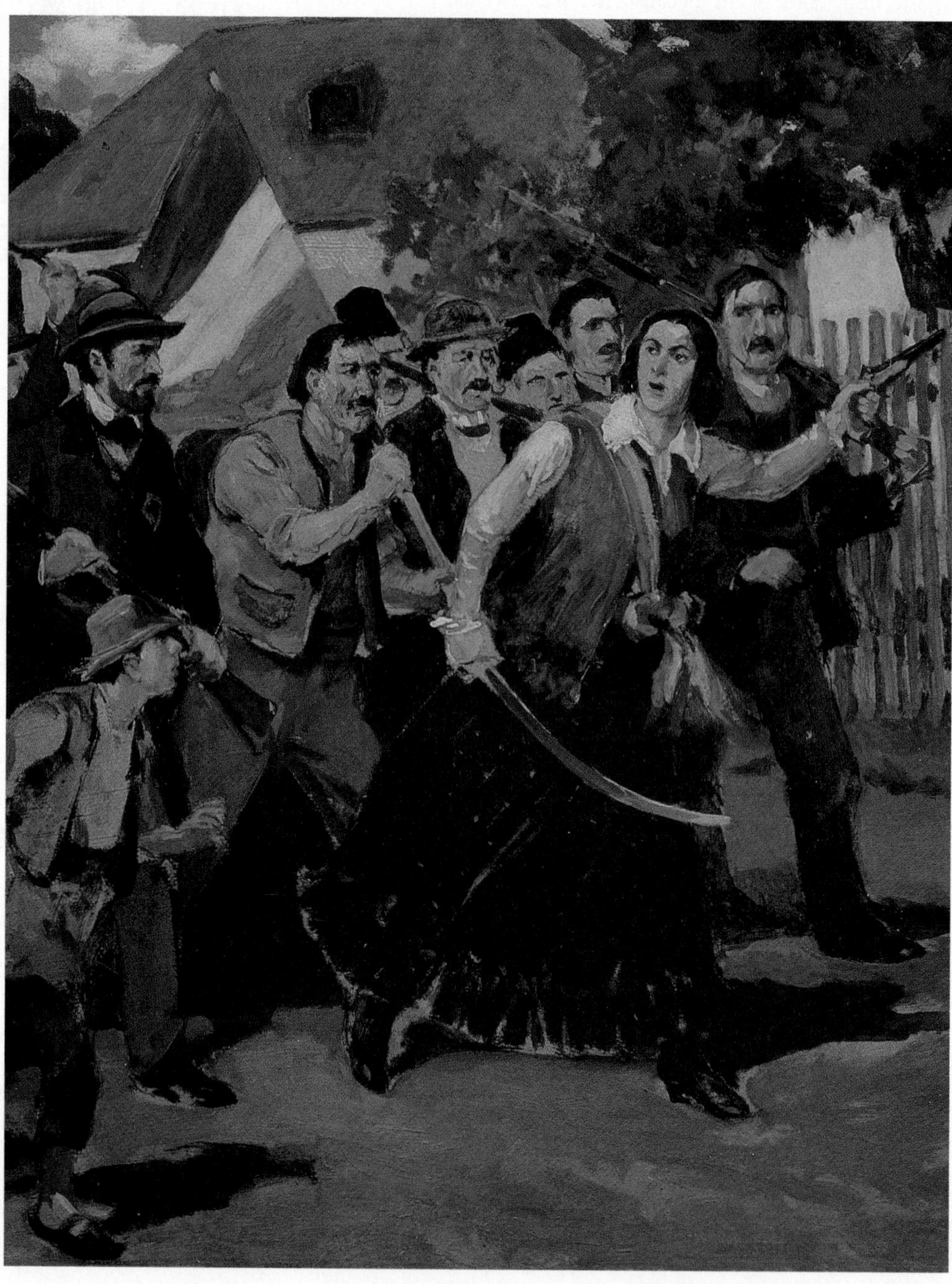

Revolutionaries in Transylvania. Ana Ipatescu, of the first group of revolutionaries in Transylvania against Russia, 1848. *(National Historical Museum, Bucharest/E.T. Archive)*

1859) was an internationally oriented aristocrat who made a brilliant diplomatic career in Austria. Austrian foreign minister from 1809 to 1848, the cosmopolitan Metternich always remained loyal to his class and jealously defended its rights and privileges to the day he died. Like most other conservatives of his time, he did so with a clear conscience. The nobility was one of Europe's most ancient institutions, and conservatives regarded tradition as the basic source of human institutions. In their view, the proper state and society remained those of pre-1789 Europe, which rested on a judicious blend of monarchy, bureaucracy, aristocracy, and respectful commoners.

Metternich firmly believed that liberalism, as embodied in revolutionary America and France, had been responsible for a generation of war with untold bloodshed and suffering. Liberal demands for representative government and civil liberties had unfortunately captured the imaginations of some middle-class lawyers, business people, and intellectuals, who were engaged in a vast conspiracy to impose their beliefs on society and destroy the existing order. Like many other conservatives then and since, Metternich blamed liberal revolutionaries for stirring up the lower classes, which he believed desired nothing more than peace and quiet.

The threat of liberalism appeared doubly dangerous to Metternich because it generally went with national aspirations. Liberals believed that each people, each national group, had a right to establish its own independent government and seek to fulfill its own destiny. The idea of national self-determination was repellent to Metternich. It not only threatened the existence of the aristocracy but also threatened to destroy the Austrian Empire and revolutionize central Europe.

The vast Austrian Empire of the Habsburgs was a great dynastic state. Formed over centuries by war, marriage, and luck, it was made up of many peoples (Map 23.2). The Germans had long dominated the empire, yet they accounted for only one-fourth of the population. The Magyars (Hungarians), a substantially smaller group, dominated the kingdom of Hungary, though they did not account for a majority of the population in that part of the Austrian Empire.

The Czechs, the third major group, were concentrated in Bohemia and Moravia. There were also large numbers of Italians, Poles, and Ukrainians as well as smaller groups of Slovenes, Croats, Serbs, Ruthenians, and Romanians. The various Slavic peoples, together with the Italians and the Romanians, represented a widely scattered and completely divided majority in an empire dominated by Germans and Hungarians. Different ethnic groups often lived in the same provinces and even in the same villages. Thus the different parts and provinces of the empire differed in languages, customs, and institutions.

Metternich This portrait by Sir Thomas Lawrence reveals much about Metternich the man. Handsome, refined, and intelligent, Metternich was a great aristocrat who was passionately devoted to the defense of his class and its interests. *(The Royal Collection © Her Majesty Queen Elizabeth II)*

The multinational state Metternich served was both strong and weak. It was strong because of its large population and vast territories; it was weak because of its many and potentially dissatisfied nationalities. In these circumstances, Metternich virtually had to oppose liberalism and nationalism, for Austria was simply unable to accommodate these ideologies, which had gathered strength in the French Revolution and were part of its enduring legacy. Other conservatives supported Austria because they could imagine no better fate for the jumble of small nationalities wedged precariously between masses of Germans and hordes of Russians in east-central Europe. Metternich's repressive conservatism had understandable roots in the dilemma of rising nationalism.

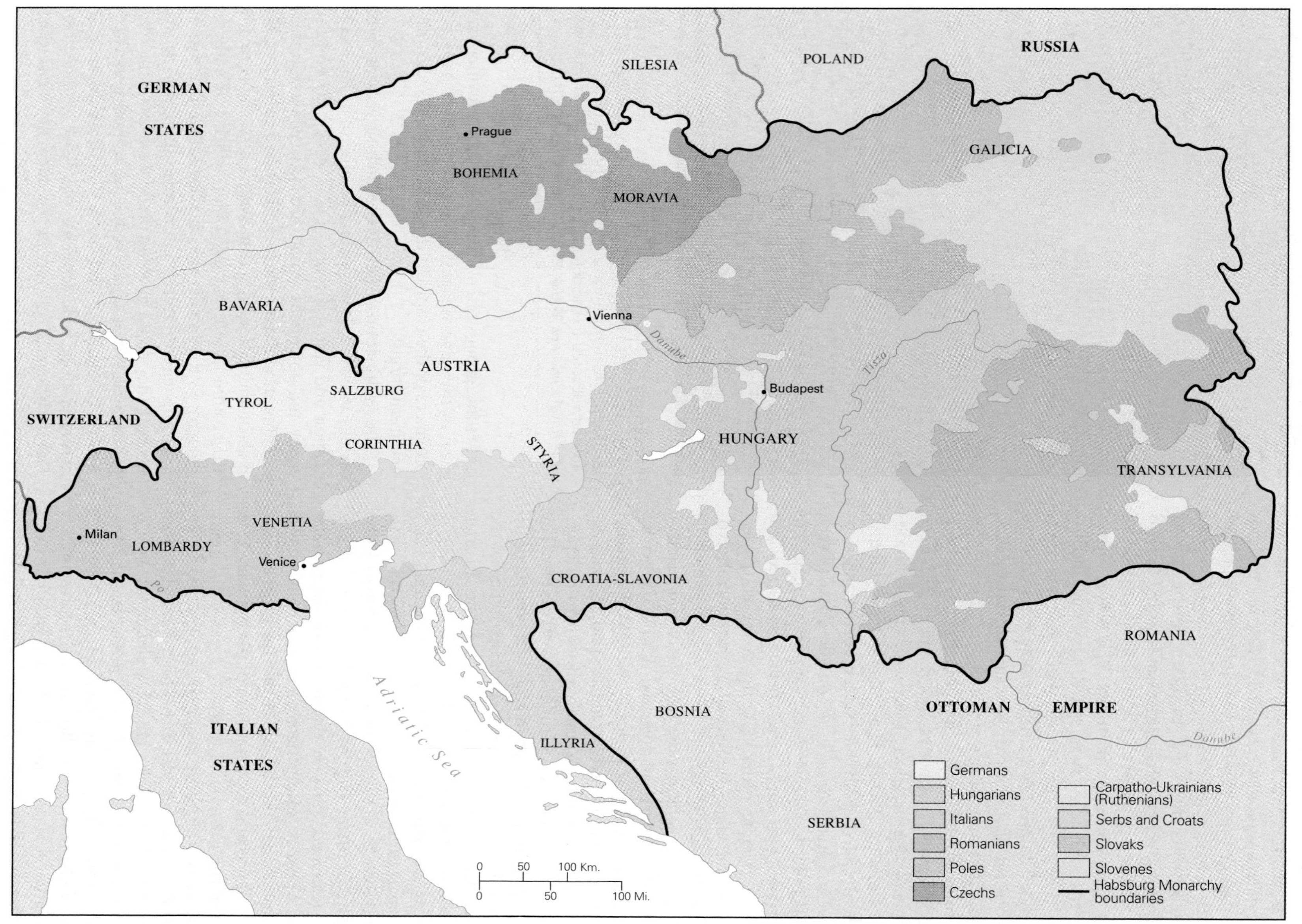
GERMAN
STATES
SILESIA
POLAND
RUSSIA
Prague
BOHEMIA
MORAVIA
GALICIA
BAVARIA
Vienna
Danube
AUSTRIA
SALZBURG
TYROL
SWITZERLAND
Budapest
Tisza
HUNGARY
CORINTHIA
STYRIA
TRANSYLVANIA
Milan
LOMBARDY
VENETIA
Venice
Po
CROATIA-SLAVONIA
ROMANIA
Adriatic Sea
BOSNIA
OTTOMAN
EMPIRE
Danube
ITALIAN
STATES
ILLYRIA
SERBIA
Germans
Hungarians
Italians
Romanians
Poles
Czechs
Carpatho-Ukrainians (Ruthenians)
Serbs and Croats
Slovaks
Slovenes
Habsburg Monarchy boundaries
0 50 100 Km.
0 50 100 Mi.

Radical Ideas and Early Socialism

The years following the peace settlement of 1815 were years of profound intellectual activity. Intellectuals and social observers were seeking to understand the revolutionary changes that had occurred and were still taking place. These efforts led to ideas that still motivate the world.

Almost all of these basic ideas were radical. In one way or another, they opposed the old, deeply felt conservatism that Metternich exemplified so well. Revived conservatism, with its stress on tradition, a hereditary monarchy, a strong and privileged landowning aristocracy, and an official church, was rejected by radicals. Instead, they developed and refined alternative visions—alternative ideologies—and tried to convince society to act on them. With time, they were very successful.

Liberalism

The principal ideas of liberalism—liberty and equality—were by no means defeated in 1815. First realized successfully in the American Revolution and then achieved in part in the French Revolution, this political and social philosophy continued to pose a radical challenge to revived conservatism. Liberalism demanded representative government as opposed to autocratic monarchy, equality before the law as opposed to legally separate classes. The idea of liberty also continued to mean specific individual freedoms: freedom of the press, freedom of speech, freedom of assembly, and freedom from arbitrary arrest. In Europe only France with Louis XVIII's Constitutional Charter and Great Britain with its Parliament and historic rights of English men and women had realized much of the liberal program in 1815. Even in those countries, liberalism had not fully succeeded; elsewhere, liberal demands were a call for freedom and revolutionary change.

Although liberalism retained its cutting edge, it was seen by many as being a somewhat duller tool than it had been. The reasons for this were that liberalism faced more radical ideological competitors in the early nineteenth century and that liberalism resolutely opposed government intervention in social and economic affairs, even if the need for action seemed great to social critics and reformers. This form of liberalism is often called "classical" liberalism in the United States in order to distinguish it sharply from modern American liberalism, which usually favors more government programs to meet social needs and to regulate the economy. Opponents of classical liberalism especially criticized its economic principles, which called for unrestricted private enterprise and no government interference in the economy. This philosophy was popularly known as the doctrine of laissez faire.

The idea of a free economy had first been persuasively formulated by Scottish philosophy professor Adam Smith, whose *Inquiry into the Nature and Causes of the Wealth of Nations* (1776) founded modern economics. Smith was highly critical of eighteenth-century mercantilism and its attempt to regulate trade and economic activity. Far preferable were free competition and the "invisible hand" of the self-regulating market, which would give all citizens a fair and equal opportunity to do what they did best. Smith argued effectively that freely competitive private enterprise would result in greater income for everyone, not just the rich. He was a spokesman for general economic development, not narrow business interests.

In the early nineteenth century, the British economy was progressively liberalized as old restrictions on trade and industry were relaxed or eliminated. This liberalization promoted continued economic growth in the Industrial Revolution. At the same time, however, economic liberalism and laissez-faire economic thought were embraced most enthusiastically by business groups and became a doctrine associated with business interests. Businessmen used the doctrine to defend their right to do exactly as they wished in their factories. Labor unions were outlawed because they supposedly restricted free competition and the individual's "right to work."

The teachings of Thomas Malthus and David Ricardo especially helped make economic liberalism an ideology of business interests in many people's minds. As we have seen (page 733), Malthus argued that population would always tend to grow faster than the supply of food. This led Ricardo to formulate his iron law of wages, which said that because of the pressure of population growth, wages would be just high enough to keep workers from starving. Malthus and Ricardo thought of themselves as objective social scientists. Yet their teachings were often used by industrial and middle-class interests in England, the continent, and the United States to justify opposing any kind of

MAP 23.2 Peoples of the Habsburg Monarchy, 1815
The old dynastic state was a patchwork of nationalities. Note the widely scattered pockets of Germans and Hungarians.

government action to protect or improve the lot of workers: if workers were poor, it was their own fault, the result of their breeding like rabbits.

In the early nineteenth century, liberal political ideals also became more closely associated with narrow class interests. Early-nineteenth-century liberals favored representative government, but they generally wanted property qualifications attached to the right to vote. In practice, this meant limiting the vote to well-to-do aristocratic landowners, substantial businessmen, and successful members of the professions. Workers and peasants as well as the lower middle class of shopkeepers, clerks, and artisans did not own the necessary property and thus could not vote.

As liberalism became increasingly identified with the middle class after 1815, some intellectuals and foes of conservatism felt that liberalism did not go nearly far enough. Inspired by memories of the French Revolution and the contemporary example of exuberant Jacksonian democracy in the young American republic, they called for an end to property ownership as a qualification for voting, at least for males. Giving all men the vote, they felt, would allow the masses to join in government and would lead to democracy.

Many people who believed in democracy also believed in the republican form of government. They detested the power of the monarchy, the privileges of the aristocracy, and the great wealth of the upper middle class. These democrats and republicans were more radical than the liberals. Taking for granted much of the liberal program, they sought to go beyond it. Democrats and republicans were also more willing than most liberals to endorse violent upheaval to achieve goals. All of this meant that liberals and radical, democratic republicans could join forces against conservatives only up to a point.

Nationalism

Nationalism was a second radical idea in the years after 1815, an idea destined to have an enormous influence in the modern world. In this complex ideology, three points stand out. First, nationalism has normally evolved from a real or imagined *cultural* unity, manifesting itself especially in a common language, history, and territory. Second, nationalists have usually sought to turn this cultural unity into *political* reality so that the territory of each people coincides with its state boundaries. It was this goal that made nationalism so potentially explosive in central and eastern Europe after 1815, when there were either too few states (Austria, Russia, and the Ottoman Empire) or too many (the Italian peninsula and the German Confederation) and when different peoples overlapped and intermingled. Third, modern nationalism had its immediate origins in the French Revolution and the Napoleonic wars. Nationalism was effectively harnessed by the French republic during the Reign of Terror to help repel foreign foes, and all across Europe patriots tried to kindle nationalist flames in the war against Napoleon. Thus by 1815 there were already hints of nationalism's remarkable ability to spread and develop.

Between 1815 and 1850, most people who believed in nationalism also believed in either liberalism or radical, democratic republicanism. In more recent times, however, many governments have been very nationalistic without favoring liberty and democracy. Why, then, was love of liberty almost synonymous with love of nation in the early nineteenth century?

A common faith in the creativity and nobility of the people was perhaps the single most important reason for the linking of these two concepts. Liberals and especially democrats saw the people as the ultimate source of all government. The people (or some of them) elected their officials and governed themselves within a framework of personal liberty. Yet such self-government would be possible only if the people were united by common traditions and common loyalties. In practice, common loyalties rested above all on a common language. Thus liberals and nationalists agreed that a shared language forged the basic unity of a people, a unity that transcended local or provincial interests and even class differences.

Early nationalists usually believed that every nation, like every citizen, had the right to exist in freedom and to develop its character and spirit. They were confident that the independence and freedom of other nations, as in the case of other citizens within a nation, would not lessen the freedom of their own country. Rather, the symphony of nations would promote the harmony and ultimate unity of all peoples. As French historian Jules Michelet put it in *The People* in 1846, each citizen "learns to recognize his country . . . as a note in the grand concert; through it he himself participates and loves the world." Similarly, the great Italian patriot Giuseppe Mazzini believed that "in laboring according to the true principles of our country we are laboring for Humanity." (See the feature "Listening to the Past: Faith in Democratic Nationalism" on pages 786–787.) Thus the liberty of the individual and the love of a free nation overlapped greatly in the early nineteenth century.

Nationalism also had a negative side. Even as early nationalists talked of serving the cause of humanity,

Carbonari Going to Jail, 1821
Emerging out of a guild of charcoal burners, the Carbonari became a secret society opposed to Napoleonic rule. After 1815, the Carbonari pressed for an Italian republic and led unsuccessful uprisings against the Austrian occupiers. National ideals appealed especially to the middle class, as these prisoners with their top hats suggest. *(© Fabbri/Artephot)*

they stressed the differences among peoples. German pastor and philosopher Johann Herder (1744–1803) had argued that every people has its own particular spirit and genius, which it expresses through culture and language. Yet Herder (and others after him) could not define the uniqueness of the French, German, and Slavic peoples without comparing and contrasting one people with another. Thus even early nationalism developed a strong sense of "we" and "they."

"They" were often the enemy. The leader of the Czech cultural revival, the passionate democrat and nationalist historian Francis Palacký, is a good example of this tendency. In his histories, he lauded the Czech people's achievements, which he characterized as a long struggle against brutal German domination. To this "we-they" outlook, it was all too easy for nationalists to add two other highly volatile ingredients: a sense of national mission and a sense of national superiority. As Mazzini characteristically wrote, "Peoples never stop before they have achieved the ultimate aim of their existence, before having fulfilled their mission." Even Michelet, so alive to the aspirations of other peoples, could not help speaking in 1846 of the "superiority of France"; the principles espoused in the French Revolution had made France the "salvation of mankind."

German and Spanish nationalists had a very different opinion of France. To them, the French often seemed as oppressive as the Germans seemed to the Czechs, as hateful as the Russians seemed to the Poles. The despised enemy's mission might seem as oppressive as the American national mission seemed to the Mexicans after the U.S. annexation of Texas. In 1845 American journalist and strident nationalist John Louis O'Sullivan wrote that taking land from an "imbecile and distracted Mexico" was a laudable step in the "fulfillment of our manifest destiny to overspread the continent allotted by Providence for the free development of our yearly multiplying millions."[1]

Early nationalism was thus ambiguous. Its main thrust was liberal and democratic. But below the surface lurked ideas of national superiority and national mission, which could lead to aggressive crusades and counter-crusades, as had happened in the French Revolution and in the "wars of liberation" against Napoleon.

French Utopian Socialism

Socialism was the new radical doctrine after 1815, and to understand it one must begin with France. Despite the fact that France lagged far behind Great Britain in developing modern industry, almost all the early socialists were French. Although they differed on many specific points, these French thinkers were acutely aware that the political revolution in France and the rise of modern industry in England had begun a transformation of society. Yet they were disturbed by what they saw. Liberal practices in politics, such as competition for votes, and in economics, such as free markets and the end of guild regulation, appeared to be fomenting selfish individualism and splitting the community into isolated fragments. There was, they believed, an urgent need for a further reorganization of society to establish cooperation and a new sense of community. Starting from this shared outlook, individual French thinkers went in many different directions. They searched the past, analyzed existing conditions, and fashioned luxurious utopias. Yet certain ideas tied their critiques and visions together.

Early French socialists believed in economic planning. Inspired by the emergency measures of 1793 and 1794 in France, they argued that the government should rationally organize the economy and not depend on destructive competition to do the job. Early socialists also shared an intense desire to help the poor and protect them from the rich. With passionate moral fervor, they preached that the rich and the poor should be more nearly equal economically. Finally, socialists believed that private property should be strictly regulated by the government or that it should be abolished and replaced by state or community ownership. Planning, greater economic equality, and state regulation of property—these were the key ideas of early French socialism and of all socialism since.

One of the most influential early socialist thinkers was a nobleman, Count Henri de Saint-Simon (1760–1825). A curious combination of radical thinker and successful land speculator, Saint-Simon optimistically proclaimed the tremendous possibilities of industrial development: "The age of gold is before us!" The key to progress was proper social organization. Such an arrangement of society required the "parasites"—the court, the aristocracy, lawyers, churchmen—to give way, once and for all, to the "doers"—the leading scientists, engineers, and industrialists. The doers would carefully plan the economy and guide it forward by undertaking vast public works projects and establishing investment banks. Saint-Simon also stressed in highly moralistic terms that every social institution ought to have as its main goal improved conditions for the poor. Saint-Simon's stress on industry and science inspired middle-class industrialists and bankers such as the Pereire brothers, founders of the Crédit Mobilier (see page 739).

After 1830 the socialist critique of capitalism became sharper. Charles Fourier (1772–1837), a lonely, saintly man with a tenuous hold on reality, described a socialist utopia in lavish mathematical detail. Hating the urban wage system, Fourier envisaged self-sufficient communities of 1,620 people living communally on 5,000 acres devoted to a combination of agriculture and industry. Although Fourier waited in vain each day at noon in his apartment for a wealthy philanthropist to endow his visionary schemes, he was very influential. Several utopian communities were founded along the lines he prescribed. The majority were founded in the United States.

Fourier was also an early proponent of the total emancipation of women. Extremely critical of middle-class family life, Fourier believed that most marriages were only another kind of prostitution. According to Fourier, young single women were shamelessly "sold" to their future husbands for dowries and other financial considerations. Therefore, Fourier called for the abolition of marriage, free unions based only on love, and sexual freedom. Many middle-class men and women found these ideas, which were shared and even practiced by some followers of Saint-Simon, shocking and immoral. The socialist program for the liberation of women as well as workers appeared to them as doubly dangerous and revolutionary.

Louis Blanc (1811–1882), a sharp-eyed, intelligent journalist, was much more practical. In his *Organization of Work* (1839), he urged workers to agitate for universal voting rights and to take control of the state peacefully. Blanc believed that the full power of the state should be directed at setting up government-backed workshops and factories to guarantee full employment. The right to work had to become as sacred as any other right.

Finally, there was Pierre Joseph Proudhon (1809–1865), a self-educated printer who wrote a pamphlet in 1840 titled *What Is Property?* His answer was that it was nothing but theft. Property was profit that was stolen from the worker, who was the source of all wealth. Unlike most socialists, Proudhon feared the power of the state and was often considered an anarchist.

Of great importance, the message of French utopian socialists interacted with the experiences of French urban workers, as recent research stresses. In Paris especially, workers cherished the memory of the radical phase of the French Revolution and its efforts to regulate economic life and protect the poor. Skilled artisans, with a long tradition of guilds, apprenticeship, and control of quality and wage rates, became violently opposed to laissez-faire laws that denied workers the right to organize and promoted brutal, unrestrained competition instead. Trying to maintain some control of their trades and conditions of work and developing a sense of class in the process, workers favored collective action and government intervention in economic life. Thus the aspirations of workers and utopian theorists reinforced each other, and a genuine socialist movement emerged in Paris in the 1830s and 1840s.

French utopian ideas had some influence outside France. But the economic arguments of the French utopians were weak, and their specific programs often seemed too fanciful to be taken seriously. To Karl Marx was left the task of establishing firm foundations for modern socialism.

The Birth of Marxian Socialism

In 1848 the thirty-year-old Karl Marx (1818–1883) and the twenty-eight-year-old Friedrich Engels (1820–1895) published *The Communist Manifesto,* which became the bible of socialism. The son of a Jewish lawyer who had converted to Christianity, the atheistic young Marx had studied philosophy at the University of Berlin before turning to journalism and economics. He read widely in French socialist thought and was influenced by it. He shared Fourier's view of middle-class marriage as legalized prostitution, and he, too, looked forward to the emancipation of women and the abolition of the family. But by the time Marx was twenty-five, he was developing his own socialist ideas.

Early French socialists often appealed to the middle class and the state to help the poor. Marx ridiculed such appeals as naive. He argued that the interests of the middle class and those of the industrial working class were inevitably opposed to each other. Indeed, according to the *Manifesto,* the "history of all previously existing society is the history of class struggles." In Marx's view, one class had always exploited the other, and with the advent of modern industry, society was split more clearly than ever before: between the middle class (the bourgeoisie) and the modern working class (the proletariat). The bourgeoisie had reduced everything to a matter of money and "naked self-interest." "In a word, for exploitation, veiled by religious and political illusions, the bourgeoisie had substituted naked, shameless, direct brutal exploitation."

Just as the bourgeoisie had triumphed over the feudal aristocracy, Marx predicted, the proletariat would conquer the bourgeoisie in a violent revolution. While a tiny minority owned the means of production and grew richer, the ever-poorer proletariat was constantly growing in size and in class-consciousness. In this process, the proletariat was aided, according to Marx, by a portion of the bourgeoisie who had gone over to the proletariat and who (like Marx and Engels) "had raised themselves to the level of comprehending theoretically the historical moment." And the critical moment was very near. "Let the ruling classes tremble at a Communist revolution. The proletarians have nothing to lose but their chains. They have a world to win. WORKING MEN OF ALL COUNTRIES, UNITE!" So ends *The Communist Manifesto.*

Karl Marx Active in the revolution of 1848, Marx fled from Germany in 1849 and settled in London. There he wrote *Capital,* the weighty exposition of his socialist theories, and worked to organize the working class. Marx earned a modest living as a journalist, supplemented by financial support from his coauthor, Friedrich Engels. *(Istar-Tass/Sovfoto)*

In brief outline, Marx's ideas may seem to differ only slightly from the wild and improbable ideas of the utopians of his day. Yet Marx must be taken seriously because his ideas—practically unknown in 1848—became very influential in the later nineteenth century. He appeared to unite sociology, economics, and all human history in a vast and imposing edifice. In doing so, he synthesized in his socialism not only French utopian schemes but also English classical economics and German philosophy—the major intellectual currents of his day. Moreover, after the young Marx fled to England as a penniless political refugee following the revolutions of 1848, he continued to show a rare flair for combining complex theorization with both lively popular writing and practical organizational ability. This combination of theoretical and practical skills contributed greatly to the subsequent diffusion of Marx's socialist synthesis after 1860, as will be shown in Chapter 25.

Marx's debt to England was great. He was the last of the classical economists. Following David Ricardo, who had taught that labor was the source of all value, Marx went on to argue that profits were really wages stolen from the workers. Moreover, Marx incorporated Engels's charges of terrible oppression of the new class of factory workers in England; thus Marx's doctrines seemed to be based on hard facts.

Marx's theory of historical evolution was built on the philosophy of the German Georg Hegel (1770–1831). Hegel believed that history is "ideas in motion": each age is characterized by a dominant set of ideas, which produces opposing ideas and eventually a new synthesis. The idea of being had been dominant initially, for example, and it had produced its antithesis, the idea of nonbeing. This idea in turn had resulted in the synthesis of becoming. Thus history has pattern and purpose.

Marx retained Hegel's view of history as a dialectic process of change but made economic relationships between classes the driving force. This dialectic explained the decline of agrarian feudalism and the rise of industrial capitalism. And Marx stressed again and again that the "bourgeoisie, historically, has played a most revolutionary part. . . . During its rule of scarcely one hundred years the bourgeoisie has created more massive and more colossal productive forces than have all preceding generations together." Here was a convincing explanation for people trying to make sense of the dual revolution. Marx's next idea, that it was now the bourgeoisie's turn to give way to the socialism of revolutionary workers, appeared to many the irrefutable capstone of a brilliant interpretation of humanity's long development. Thus Marx pulled together powerful ideas and insights to create one of the great secular religions out of the intellectual ferment of the early nineteenth century.

The Romantic Movement

Radical concepts of politics and society were accompanied by comparable changes in literature and other arts during the dual revolution. The early nineteenth century marked the acme of the romantic movement, which profoundly influenced the arts and enriched European culture immeasurably.

The romantic movement was in part a revolt against classicism and the Enlightenment. Classicism was essentially a set of artistic rules and standards that went hand in glove with the Enlightenment's belief in rationality, order, and restraint. The classicists believed that the ancient Greeks and Romans had discovered eternally valid aesthetic rules and that playwrights and painters should continue to follow them. Classicists could enforce these rules in the eighteenth century because they dominated the courts and academies for which artists worked.

Forerunners of the romantic movement appeared from about 1750 on. Of these, Rousseau (see page 611)—the passionate advocate of feeling, freedom, and natural goodness—was the most influential. Romanticism then crystallized fully in the 1790s, primarily in England and Germany. The French Revolution kindled the belief that radical reconstruction was also possible in cultural and artistic life (even though many early English and German romantics became disillusioned with events in France and turned from liberalism to conservatism in politics). Romanticism gained strength until the 1840s.

Romanticism's Tenets

Romanticism was characterized by a belief in emotional exuberance, unrestrained imagination, and spontaneity in both art and personal life. In Germany early romantics of the 1770s and 1780s called themselves the "Storm and Stress" (*Sturm und Drang*) group, and many romantic artists of the early nineteenth century lived lives of tremendous emotional intensity. Suicide, duels to the death, madness, and strange illnesses were not uncommon among leading romantics. Romantic artists typically led bohemian lives, wearing their hair long and uncombed in preference to powdered wigs and living in cold garrets rather than frequenting stiff drawing rooms. They rejected materialism and sought to escape to lofty spiritual heights through their art. Great individualists, the romantics believed the full development of one's

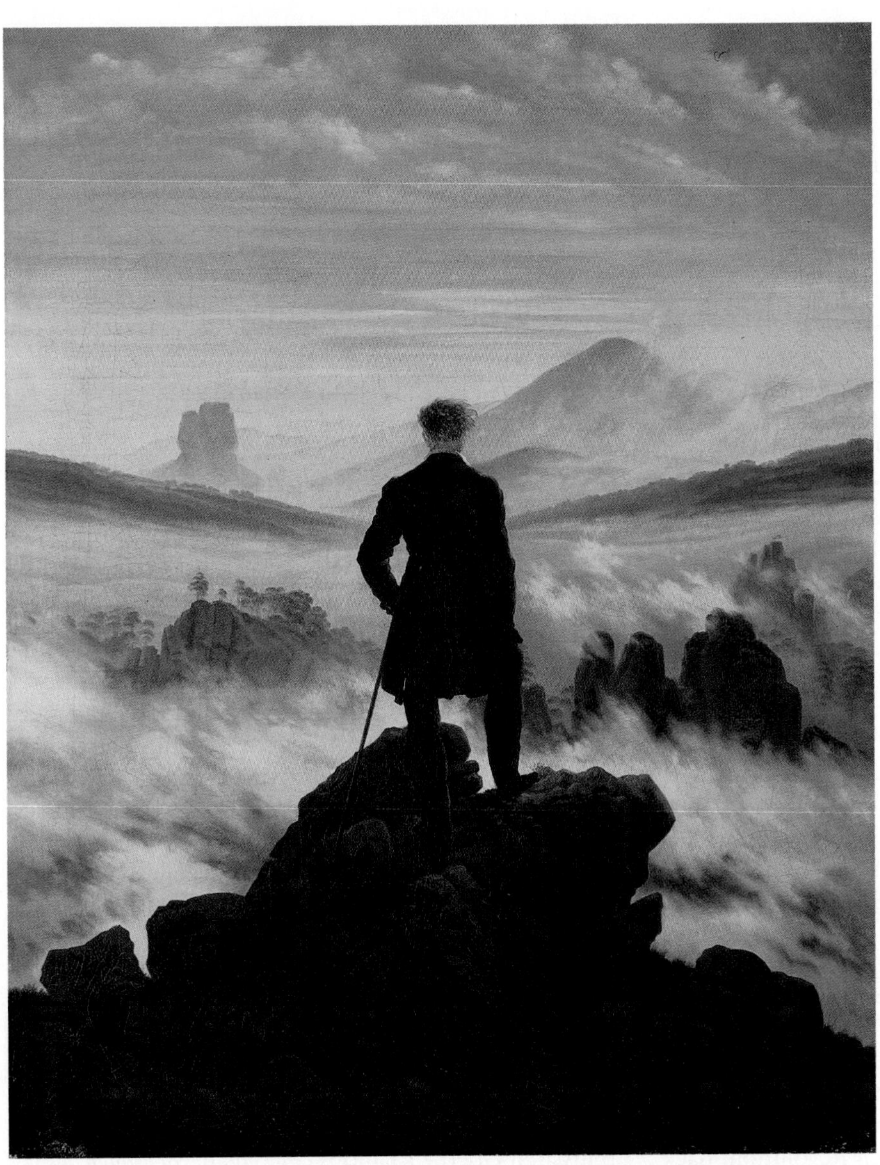

Nature and the Meaning of Life Caspar David Friedrich (1774–1840) was Germany's greatest romantic painter, and his *Traveler Looking over a Sea of Fog* (1815) is a representative masterpiece. Friedrich's paintings often focus on dark silhouetted figures, silently contemplating an eerie landscape. Friedrich came to believe that humans were only an insignificant part of an all-embracing higher unity. *(Hamburger Kunsthalle)*

unique human potential to be the supreme purpose in life. The romantics were driven by a sense of an unlimited universe and by a yearning for the unattained, the unknown, the unknowable.

Nowhere was the break with classicism more apparent than in romanticism's general conception of nature. Classicism was not particularly interested in nature. In the words of eighteenth-century English author Samuel Johnson, "A blade of grass is always a blade of grass; men and women are my subjects of inquiry." Nature was portrayed by classicists as beautiful and chaste, like an eighteenth-century formal garden. The romantics, in contrast, were enchanted by nature. Sometimes they found it awesome and tempestuous, as in Théodore Géricault's painting *The Raft of the Medusa,* which shows the survivors of a shipwreck adrift in a turbulent sea. Others saw nature as a source of spiritual inspiration. As the great English landscape artist John Constable declared, "Nature is Spirit visible."

Most romantics saw the growth of modern industry as an ugly, brutal attack on their beloved nature and on the human personality. They sought escape—in the unspoiled Lake District of northern England, in exotic North Africa, in an idealized Middle Ages. Yet some romantics found a vast, awesome, terribly moving power in the new industrial landscape. In ironworks and cotton mills, they saw the flames of hell and the evil genius of Satan himself.

Fascinated by color and diversity, the romantic imagination turned toward the study and writing of history with a passion. For romantics, history was not a minor branch of philosophy from which philosophers picked suitable examples to illustrate their teachings. History was beautiful, exciting, and important in its own right. It was the art of change over time—the key to a universe that was now perceived to be organic and dynamic. It was no longer perceived to be mechanical and static, as it had to the philosophes of the eighteenth-century Enlightenment.

Historical studies supported the development of national aspirations and encouraged entire peoples to seek in the past their special destinies. This trend was especially strong in Germany and other eastern European countries. As the famous English historian Lord Acton put it, the growth of historical thinking associated with the romantic movement was a most fateful step in the story of European thought.

Literature

Britain was the first country where romanticism flowered fully in poetry and prose, and the British romantic writers were among the most prominent in Europe. Wordsworth, Coleridge, and Scott were all active by 1800, to be followed shortly by Byron, Shelley, and Keats. All were poets: romanticism found its distinctive voice in poetry, as the Enlightenment had in prose.

A towering leader of English romanticism, William Wordsworth (1770–1850) traveled in France after his graduation from Cambridge. There he fell passionately in love with a Frenchwoman, who bore him a daughter. He was deeply influenced by the philosophy of Rousseau and the spirit of the early French Revolution. Back in England, prevented by war and the Terror from returning to France, Wordsworth settled in the countryside with his sister, Dorothy, and Samuel Taylor Coleridge (1772–1834).

In 1798 the two poets published their *Lyrical Ballads,* one of the most influential literary works in the history of the English language. In defiance of classical rules, Wordsworth and Coleridge abandoned flowery poetic conventions for the language of ordinary speech, simultaneously endowing simple subjects with the loftiest majesty. This twofold rejection of classical practice was at first ignored and then harshly criticized, but by 1830 Wordsworth had triumphed.

One of the best examples of Wordsworth's romantic credo and genius is "Daffodils":

I wandered lonely as a cloud
That floats on high o'er vales and hills,
When all at once I saw a crowd,
A host, of golden daffodils;
Beside the lake, beneath the trees,
Fluttering and dancing in the breeze.

. . . .

The waves beside them danced, but they
Out-did the sparkling waves in glee:
A poet could not but be gay,
In such a jocund company:
I gazed—and gazed—but little thought
What wealth the show to me had brought:

For oft, when on my couch I lie
In vacant or in pensive mood,
They flash upon that inward eye
Which is the bliss of solitude;
And then my heart with pleasure fills,
And dances with the daffodils.

Here indeed are simplicity and love of nature in commonplace forms, which could be appreciated, very democratically, by everyone and not just by an intellectual elite. Here, too, is Wordsworth's romantic conviction that nature has the power to elevate and instruct. Wordsworth's conception of poetry as the "spontaneous overflow of powerful feeling recollected in tranquility" is well illustrated by the last stanza.

Born in Edinburgh, Walter Scott (1771–1832) personified the romantic movement's fascination with history. Raised on his grandfather's farm, Scott fell under the spell of the old ballads and tales of the Scottish border. He was also deeply influenced by German romanticism, particularly by the immortal poet and dramatist Johann Wolfgang von Goethe (1749–1832). Scott translated Goethe's famous *Gotz von Berlichingen,* a play about a sixteenth-century knight who revolted against centralized authority and championed individual freedom—at least in Goethe's romantic drama. A natural storyteller, Scott then composed long narrative poems and a series of historical novels. Scott excelled in faithfully re-creating the spirit of bygone ages and great historical events, especially those of Scotland.

Classicism remained strong in France under Napoleon and inhibited the growth of romanticism there. In 1813 Germaine de Staël (1766–1817), a Franco-Swiss writer living in exile, urged the French to throw away their worn-out classical models. Her study *On Germany* (1810) extolled the spontaneity and enthusiasm of German writers and thinkers, and it had a powerful impact on the post-1815 generation in France. (See the feature

"Individuals in Society: Germaine de Staël, Romantic Genius.") Between 1820 and 1850, the romantic impulse broke through in the poetry and prose of Lamartine, de Vigny, Hugo, Dumas, and Sand. Of these, Victor Hugo (1802–1885) was the greatest in both poetry and prose.

Son of a Napoleonic general, Hugo achieved an amazing range of rhythm, language, and image in his lyric poetry. His powerful novels exemplified the romantic fascination with fantastic characters, strange settings, and human emotions. The hero of Hugo's famous *Hunchback of Notre Dame* (1831) is the great cathedral's deformed bellringer, a "human gargoyle" overlooking the teeming life of fifteenth-century Paris. A great admirer of William Shakespeare, whom classical critics had derided as undisciplined and excessive, Hugo also championed romanticism in drama. His play *Hernani* (1830) consciously broke all the old rules, as Hugo renounced his early conservatism and equated freedom in literature with liberty in politics and society. Hugo's political evolution was thus exactly the opposite of Wordsworth's, in whom youthful radicalism gave way to middle-aged caution. As the contrast between the two artists suggests, romanticism was a cultural movement compatible with many political beliefs.

Amandine Aurore Lucie Dupin (1804–1876), a strong-willed and gifted woman generally known by her pen name, George Sand, defied the narrow conventions of her time in an unending search for self-fulfillment. After eight years of unhappy marriage in the provinces, she abandoned her dullard of a husband and took her two children to Paris to pursue a career as a writer. There Sand soon achieved fame and wealth, eventually writing over eighty novels on a variety of romantic and social themes. All were shot through with a typically romantic love of nature and moral idealism. George Sand's striking individualism went far beyond her flamboyant preference for men's clothing and cigars and her notorious affairs with poet Alfred de Musset and composer Frédéric Chopin, among others. Her semi-autobiographical novel *Lélia* was shockingly modern, delving deeply into her tortuous quest for sexual and personal freedom.

In central and eastern Europe, literary romanticism and early nationalism often reinforced each other. Seeking a unique greatness in every people, well-educated romantics plumbed their own histories and cultures. Like modern anthropologists, they turned their attention to peasant life and transcribed the folksongs, tales, and proverbs that the cosmopolitan Enlightenment had disdained. The brothers Jacob and Wilhelm Grimm were particularly successful at rescuing German fairy tales from oblivion. In the Slavic lands, romantics played a decisive role in converting spoken peasant languages into modern written languages. The greatest of all Russian poets, Aleksander Pushkin (1799–1837), rejecting eighteenth-century attempts to force Russian poetry into a classical straitjacket, used his lyric genius to mold the modern literary language.

Art and Music

The greatest and most moving romantic painter in France was Eugène Delacroix (1798–1863), probably the illegitimate son of French foreign minister Talleyrand. Delacroix was a master of dramatic, colorful scenes that stirred the emotions. He was fascinated with remote and exotic subjects, whether lion hunts in Morocco or the languishing, sensuous women of a sultan's harem. Yet he was also a passionate spokesman for freedom. His masterpiece, *Liberty Leading the People,* celebrated the nobility of popular revolution in general and revolution in France in particular.

In England the most notable romantic painters were Joseph M. W. Turner (1775–1851) and John Constable (1776–1837). Both were fascinated by nature, but their interpretations of it contrasted sharply, aptly symbolizing the tremendous emotional range of the romantic movement. Turner depicted nature's power and terror; wild storms and sinking ships were favorite subjects. Constable painted gentle Wordsworthian landscapes in which human beings were at one with their environment, the comforting countryside of unspoiled rural England.

It was in music that romanticism realized most fully and permanently its goals of free expression and emotional intensity. Whereas the composers of the eighteenth century had remained true to well-defined structures, such as the classical symphony, the great romantics used a great range of forms to create a thousand musical landscapes and evoke a host of powerful emotions. Romantic composers also transformed the small classical orchestra, tripling its size by adding wind instruments, percussion, and more brass and strings. The crashing chords evoking the surge of the masses in Chopin's Revolutionary Etude, the bottomless despair of the funeral march in Beethoven's Third Symphony, the solemn majesty of a great religious event in Schumann's Rhenish Symphony—such were the modern orchestra's musical paintings that plumbed the depths of human feeling.

Individuals in Society

Germaine de Staël, Romantic Genius

Germaine de Staël, by J.-B. Isabey. *(© Photo R.M.N.–J. G. Berizzi)*

Rich, intellectual, passionate, and assertive, Germaine Necker de Staël (1766–1817) astonished contemporaries and still fascinates historians. She was strongly influenced by her parents, poor Swiss Protestants who soared to the top of prerevolutionary Parisian society. Her brilliant but rigid mother filled Germaine's head with knowledge, and each week the precocious child listened, wide-eyed and attentive, to illustrious writers and philosophers performing at her mother's salon. At age twelve, she suffered a physical and mental breakdown. Only then was she allowed to have a playmate and romp and run on the family estate. Her adoring father was Jacques Necker, a banker who made an enormous fortune and became France's reform-minded minister of finance before the Revolution. Worshiping her father in adolescence, Germaine also came to love politics.

Accepting at nineteen an arranged marriage with Baron de Staël-Holstein, a womanizing Swedish diplomat bewitched by her dowry, Germaine began her life's work. She opened an intellectual salon and began to write and publish. Her wit and exuberance attracted foreigners and liberal French aristocrats, one of whom became the first of many lovers as her marriage soured and she searched unsuccessfully for the happiness of her parents' union. Fleeing Paris in 1792 and returning after the Thermidorian reaction, she subsequently angered Napoleon by criticizing his dictatorial rule. In 1803 he permanently banished her from Paris.

Retiring again to her isolated estate in Switzerland and skillfully managing her inherited wealth, Staël fought insomnia with opium and boredom with parties that attracted luminaries from all over Europe. Always seeking stimulation for her restless mind, she traveled widely in Italy and Germany and drew upon these experiences in her novel *Corinne* (1807) and her study *On Germany* (1810). Both works summed up her romantic faith and enjoyed enormous success.

Staël urged creative individuals to abandon traditional rules and classical models. She encouraged them to embrace experimentation, emotion, and enthusiasm. Enthusiasm, which she had in abundance, was the key, the royal road to creativity, personal fulfillment, and human improvement. Thrilling to music, for example, she felt that only an enthusiastic person could really appreciate this gift of God, this wordless message that "unifies our dual nature and blends senses and spirit in a common rapture."[1]

Yet a profound sadness runs through her writing. This sadness, so characteristic of the romantic temperament, grew in part out of disappointments in love and prolonged exile. But it also grew out of the insoluble predicament of being an enormously gifted woman in an age of intense male chauvinism. Little wonder that uneasy male competitors and literary critics took delight in ridiculing and defaming her as a neurotic and masculine woman, a mediocre and unnatural talent who had foolishly dared to enter the male world of serious thought and action. Even her supporters could not accept her for what she was. The admiring poet Lord Byron recognized her genius and called her "the most eminent woman author of this, or perhaps of any century." But he quickly added that "she should have been born a man."[2]

Buffeted and saddened by scorn and condescension because of her gender, Staël advocated equal rights for women throughout her life. Only with equal rights and duties—in education and careers, in love and marital relations—could an exceptional woman like herself, or indeed any woman, ever hope to realize her intellectual and emotional potential. Practicing what she preached as best she could, Germaine de Staël was a trailblazer in the struggle for women's rights.

Questions for Analysis

1. In what ways did Germaine de Staël's life and thought reflect basic elements of the romantic movement?
2. Why did male critics often attack Staël? What do these criticisms tell us about gender relations in the early nineteenth century?

1. Quoted in G. R. Besser, *Germaine de Staël Revisited* (New York: Twayne Publishers, 1994), p. 106. Enhanced by a feminist perspective, this is the best recent study.
2. Quoted ibid., p. 139.

Heroes of Romanticism Observed by a portrait of Byron and bust of Beethoven, Liszt plays for friends in this painting by Josef Danhauser. From left to right sit Alexander Dumas, George Sand (characteristically wearing men's garb), and Marie d'Agoult, Liszt's mistress. Standing are Victor Hugo, Paganini, and Rossini. In fact, this gathering of geniuses was imaginary, part of an advertising campaign by a German piano manufacturer to sell pianos to the comfortable middle class. *(Bildarchiv Preussischer Kulturbesitz)*

This range and intensity gave music and musicians much greater prestige than in the past. Music no longer simply complemented a church service or helped a nobleman digest his dinner. Music became a sublime end in itself. It became for many the greatest of the arts, precisely because it achieved the most ecstatic effect and most perfectly realized the endless yearning of the soul. It was worthy of great concert halls and the most dedicated sacrifice. The unbelievable one-in-a-million performer—the great virtuoso who could transport the listener to ecstasy and hysteria—became a cultural hero. The composer Franz Liszt (1811–1886) vowed to do for the piano what Nicolo Paganini (1784–1840) had done for the violin, and he was lionized as the greatest pianist of his age. People swooned for Liszt as they scream for rock stars today.

Though romanticism dominated music until late in the nineteenth century, no composer ever surpassed its first great master, Ludwig van Beethoven (1770–1827). Extending and breaking open classical forms, Beethoven used contrasting themes and tones to produce dramatic conflict and inspiring resolutions. As the contemporary German novelist Ernst Hoffmann (1776–1822) wrote, "Beethoven's music sets in motion the lever of fear, of awe, of horror, of suffering, and awakens just that infinite longing which is the essence of Romanticism." Beethoven's range was tremendous; his output included symphonies, chamber music, sonatas for violin and piano, Masses, an opera, and a great many songs.

At the peak of his fame, in constant demand as a composer and recognized as the leading concert pianist of his day, Beethoven began to lose his hearing. He considered suicide but eventually overcame despair: "I will take fate by the throat; it will not bend me completely to its will."[2] Beethoven continued to pour out immortal music. Among other achievements, he fully exploited for the first time the richness and beauty of the piano. Beethoven never heard much of his later work, including the unforgettable choral finale to the Ninth Symphony, for his last years were silent, spent in total deafness.

Reforms and Revolutions

While the romantic movement was developing, liberal, national, and socialist forces battered against the conservatism of 1815. In some countries, change occurred gradually and peacefully. Elsewhere, pressure built up like steam in a pressure cooker without a safety valve and eventually caused an explosion in 1848. Three important countries—Greece, Great Britain, and France—experienced variations on this basic theme.

National Liberation in Greece

National, liberal revolution, frustrated in Italy and Spain by conservative statesmen, succeeded first after 1815 in Greece. Since the fifteenth century, the Greeks had been living under the domination of the Ottoman Turks. In spite of centuries of foreign rule, the Greeks had survived as a people, united by their language and the Greek Orthodox religion. It was perfectly natural that the general growth of national aspirations and a desire for independence would inspire some Greeks in the early nineteenth century. This rising national movement led to the formation of secret societies and then to revolt in 1821, led by Alexander Ypsilanti, a Greek patriot and a general in the Russian army.

The Great Powers, particularly Metternich, were opposed to all revolution, even revolution against the Islamic Turks. They refused to back Ypsilanti and supported the Ottoman Empire. Yet for many Europeans, the Greek cause became a holy one. Educated Americans and Europeans were in love with the culture of classical Greece; Russians were stirred by the piety of their Orthodox brethren. Writers and artists, moved by the romantic impulse, responded enthusiastically to the Greek struggle.

The Greeks, though often quarreling among themselves, battled on against the Turks and hoped for the eventual support of European governments. In 1827 Great Britain, France, and Russia responded to popular demands at home and directed Turkey to accept an armistice. When the Turks refused, the navies of these three powers trapped the Turkish fleet at Navarino and destroyed it. Russia then declared another of its periodic wars of expansion against the Turks. This led to the establishment of a Russian protectorate over much of present-day Romania, which had also been under Turkish rule. Great Britain, France, and Russia finally declared Greece independent in 1830 and installed a German prince as king of the new country in 1832. In the end, the Greeks had won: a small nation had gained its independence in a heroic war against a foreign empire.

Liberal Reform in Great Britain

Eighteenth-century British society had been both flexible and remarkably stable. It was dominated by the landowning aristocracy, but that class was neither closed nor rigidly defined. Successful business and professional people could buy land and become gentlefolk, while the common people had more than the usual opportunities of the preindustrial world. Basic civil rights for all were balanced by a tradition of deference to one's social superiors. Parliament was manipulated by the king and was thoroughly undemocratic. Only about 8 percent of the population could vote for representatives to Parliament, and by the 1780s there was growing interest in some kind of political reform.

But the French Revolution threw the British aristocracy into a panic for a generation, making it extremely hostile to any attempts to change the status quo. The Tory party, completely controlled by the landed aristocracy, was particularly fearful of radical movements at home and abroad. Castlereagh initially worked closely with Metternich to restrain France and restore a conservative balance in central Europe. This same intense conservatism motivated the Tory government at home. After 1815 the aristocracy defended its ruling position by repressing every kind of popular protest.

The first step in this direction began with revision of the Corn Laws in 1815. Corn Laws to regulate the foreign grain trade had long existed, but they were not needed during a generation of war with France because the British had been unable to import cheap grain from eastern Europe. As shortages occurred and agricultural prices skyrocketed, a great deal of marginal land had been brought under cultivation. This development had been a bonanza for the landed aristocracy, whose fat rent rolls became even fatter. Peace meant that grain could be imported again and that the price of wheat and bread would go down. To almost everyone except the aristocracy, lower prices seemed highly desirable. The aristocracy, however, rammed far-reaching changes in the Corn Laws through Parliament. The new regulation prohibited the importation of foreign grain unless the price at home rose above 80 shillings per quarter ton—a level reached only in time of harvest disaster before 1790. Seldom has a class legislated more selfishly for its own narrow economic advantage or done more to promote a class-based view of political action.

Delacroix: Massacre at Chios The Greek struggle for freedom and independence won the enthusiastic support of liberals, nationalists, and romantics. The Ottoman Turks were portrayed as cruel oppressors who were holding back the course of history, as in this moving masterpiece by Delacroix. *(Louvre © Photo R.M.N.)*

THE PRELUDE TO 1848

March 1814	Russia, Prussia, Austria, and Britain form the Quadruple Alliance to defeat France.
April 1814	Napoleon abdicates.
May–June 1814	Bourbon monarchy is restored; Louis XVIII issues the Constitutional Charter providing for civil liberties and representative government. First Peace of Paris: allies combine leniency with a defensive posture toward France.
October 1814–June 1815	Congress of Vienna peace settlement establishes balance-of-power principle and creates the German Confederation.
February 1815	Napoleon escapes from Elba and marches on Paris.
June 1815	Battle of Waterloo is fought.
September 1815	Austria, Prussia, and Russia form the Holy Alliance to repress liberal and revolutionary movements.
November 1815	Second Peace of Paris and renewal of Quadruple Alliance punish France and establish the European "congress system."
1819	In Carlsbad Decrees, Metternich imposes harsh measures throughout the German Confederation.
1820	Revolution occurs in Spain and the kingdom of the Two Sicilies. At the Congress of Troppau, Metternich and Alexander I of Russia proclaim the principle of intervention to maintain autocratic regimes.
1821	Austria crushes a liberal revolution in Naples and restores the Sicilian autocracy. Greeks revolt against the Ottoman Turks.
1823	French armies restore the Spanish regime. United States proclaims the Monroe Doctrine.
1824	Reactionary Charles X succeeds Louis XVIII in France.
1830	Charles X repudiates the Constitutional Charter; insurrection and collapse of the government follow. Louis Philippe succeeds to the throne and maintains a narrowly liberal regime until 1848. Greece wins independence from the Ottoman Empire.
1832	Reform Bill expands British electorate and encourages the middle class.
1839	Louis Blanc publishes *Organization of Work.*
1840	Pierre Joseph Proudhon publishes *What Is Property?*
1846	Jules Michelet publishes *The People.*
1848	Karl Marx and Friedrich Engels publish *The Communist Manifesto.*

Hayter: The House of Commons, 1833 This collective portrait of the first parliament elected after the Reform Bill of 1832 was painted over several years. The arrangement of the members reflects Britain's historic two-party system, with the majority on one side and the "loyal opposition" on the other. Most European countries developed multiparty systems and coalition politics, with competing groups seated in a large half circle. *(Trustees of the National Portrait Gallery, London)*

The change in the Corn Laws, coming as it did at a time of widespread unemployment and postwar economic distress, resulted in protests and demonstrations by urban laborers. The laborers were supported by radical intellectuals, who campaigned for a reformed House of Commons that would serve the nation and not just the aristocracy. In 1817 the Tory government responded by temporarily suspending the traditional rights of peaceable assembly and habeas corpus. Two years later, Parliament passed the infamous Six Acts, which, among other things, placed controls on a heavily taxed press and practically eliminated all mass meetings. These acts followed an enormous but orderly protest, at Saint Peter's Fields in Manchester, that had been savagely broken up by armed cavalry. Nicknamed the "Battle of Peterloo," in scornful reference to the British victory at Waterloo, this incident demonstrated the government's determination to repress and stand fast.

Ongoing industrial development was not only creating urban and social problems but also strengthening the upper middle classes. The new manufacturing and commercial groups insisted on a place for their new wealth alongside the landed wealth of the aristocracy in the framework of political power and social prestige. They called for many kinds of liberal reform: reform of town government, organization of a new police force, more rights for Catholics and dissenters, and reform of the Poor Laws that provided aid to some low-paid workers. In the 1820s, a less frightened Tory government moved in the direction of better urban administration, greater economic liberalism, and civil equality for Catholics. The prohibition on imports of foreign grain was replaced by a heavy tariff. These actions encouraged the middle classes to press on for reform of Parliament so they could have a larger say in government and perhaps repeal the latest revision of the Corn Laws, that symbol of aristocratic domination.

The Whig party, though led like the Tories by great aristocrats, had by tradition been more responsive to commercial and manufacturing interests. In 1830 a Whig ministry introduced "an act to amend the representation of the people of England and Wales." Defeated, then passed by the House of Commons, this reform bill was rejected by the House of Lords. But when in 1832 the Whigs got the king to promise to create enough new peers to pass the law, the House of Lords reluctantly gave in rather than see its snug little club ruined by upstart manufacturers and plutocrats. A mighty surge of popular protest had helped the king and lords make up their minds.

The Reform Bill of 1832 had profound significance. The House of Commons had emerged as the all-important legislative body. In the future, an obstructionist House of Lords could always be brought into line by the threat of creating new peers. The new industrial areas of the country gained representation in the Commons, and many old "rotten boroughs"—electoral districts that had very few voters and that the landed aristocracy had bought and sold—were eliminated.

The redistribution of seats reflected the shift in population to the northern manufacturing counties and the gradual emergence of an urban society. As a result of the Reform Bill of 1832, the number of voters increased by about 50 percent, giving about 12 percent of the total population the right to vote. Comfortable middle-class groups in the urban population, as well as some substantial farmers who leased their land, received the vote. Thus the pressures building in Great Britain were successfully—though only temporarily—released. A major reform had been achieved peacefully, without revolution or civil war. More radical reforms within the system appeared difficult but not impossible. Legislation could solve problems and improve social conditions.

The principal radical program was embodied in the "People's Charter" of 1838 and the Chartist movement (see page 749). Partly inspired by the economic distress of the working class in the 1830s and 1840s, the Chartists' core demand was universal male (but not female) suffrage. They saw complete political democracy and rule by the common people as the means to a good and just society. Hundreds of thousands of people signed gigantic petitions calling on Parliament to grant all men the right to vote, first and most seriously in 1839, again in 1842, and yet again in 1848. Parliament rejected all three petitions. In the short run, the working poor failed with their Chartist demands, but they learned a valuable lesson in mass politics.

While calling for universal male suffrage, many working-class people joined with middle-class manufacturers in the Anti–Corn Law League, founded in Manchester in 1839. Mass participation made possible a popular crusade against the tariff on imported grain and against the landed aristocracy. People were fired up by dramatic popular orators such as John Bright and Richard Cobden. These fighting liberals argued that lower food prices and more jobs in industry depended on repeal of the Corn Laws. Much of the working class agreed. The climax of the movement came in 1845. In that year, Ireland's potato crop failed, and rapidly rising food prices marked the beginning of the Irish famine. Famine prices for food and even famine itself also seemed likely in England. To avert the impending catastrophe, Tory prime minister Robert Peel joined with the Whigs and a minority of his own party to repeal the Corn Laws in 1846 and allow free imports of grain. England escaped famine. Thereafter, the liberal doctrine of free trade became almost sacred dogma in Great Britain.

The following year, the Tories passed a bill designed to help the working classes, but in a different way. This was the Ten Hours Act of 1847, which limited the workday for women and young people in factories to ten hours. Tory aristocrats continued to champion legislation regulating factory conditions. They were competing vigorously with the middle class for the support of the working class. This healthy competition between a still-vigorous aristocracy and a strong middle class was a crucial factor in Great Britain's peaceful evolution. The working classes could make temporary alliances with either competitor to better their own conditions.

The people of Ireland did not benefit from this political competition. Long ruled as a conquered people, the great mass of the population (outside the northern counties of Ulster, which were partly Presbyterian) were Irish Catholic peasants who rented their land from a tiny minority of Church of England Protestants, many of whom lived in England (see Chapter 20). Ruthlessly exploited and growing rapidly in numbers, Irish peasants had come to depend on the potato crop, the size of which varied substantially from year to year. Potato failures could not be detected in time to plant other crops, nor could potatoes be stored for more than a year. Moreover, Ireland's precarious potato economy was a subsistence economy, which therefore lacked a well-developed network of roads and trade capable of distributing other foods in time of disaster. When the crop failed in 1845, the Irish were very vulnerable.

In 1846, 1848, and 1851, the potato crop failed again in Ireland and throughout much of Europe. The

Evictions of Irish Peasants who could not pay their rent continued for decades after the Great Famine. Surrounded by a few meager possessions, this family has been turned out of its cottage in the 1880s. The door is nailed shut to prevent their return. *(Lawrence Collection, National Library of Ireland, Dublin)*

general result was high food prices, widespread suffering, and, frequently, social upheaval. In Ireland the result was unmitigated disaster—the Great Famine. Blight attacked the young plants, and the tubers rotted. Widespread starvation and mass fever epidemics followed. Total losses of population were staggering. Fully 1 million emigrants fled the famine between 1845 and 1851, going primarily to the United States and Great Britain, and at least 1.5 million people died or were not born because of the disaster. The British government's efforts at famine relief were too little, too late. Moreover, the government energetically supported heartless landowner demands with armed force. Tenants who could not pay their rents were evicted and their homes broken up or burned. Famine or no, Ireland remained a conquered province, a poor agricultural land that had gained little from the liberal reforms and the industrial developments that were transforming Britain.

The Revolution of 1830 in France

Louis XVIII's Constitutional Charter of 1814—theoretically a gift from the king but actually a response to political pressures—was basically a liberal constitution (see page 720). The economic and social gains made by sections of the middle class and the peasantry in the French Revolution were fully protected, great intellectual and artistic freedom was permitted, and a real parliament with upper and lower houses was created. Immediately after Napoleon's abortive Hundred Days, the moderate, worldly king refused to bow to the wishes of die-hard aristocrats such as his brother Charles, who wished to sweep away all the revolutionary changes and return to a bygone age of royal absolutism and aristocratic pretension. Instead, Louis appointed as his ministers moderate royalists, who sought and obtained the support of a majority of the representatives elected to the lower Chamber of Deputies between 1816 and Louis's death in 1824.

Louis XVIII's charter was anything but democratic. Only about 100,000 of the wealthiest people out of a total population of 30 million had the right to vote for the deputies who, with the king and his ministers, made the laws of the nation. Nonetheless, the "notable people" who did vote came from very different backgrounds. There were wealthy businessmen, war profiteers, successful professionals, ex-revolutionaries, large landowners from the old aristocracy and the middle class, Bourbons, and Bonapartists.

The old aristocracy, with its pre-1789 mentality, was a minority within the voting population. It was this situation that Louis's successor, Charles X (r. 1824–1830), could not abide. Crowned in a lavish, utterly medieval, five-hour ceremony in the cathedral of Reims in 1824, Charles was a true reactionary. He wanted to re-establish the old order in France. Increasingly blocked by the opposition of the deputies, Charles finally repudiated the Constitutional Charter in an attempted coup in July 1830. He issued decrees stripping much of the wealthy middle class of its voting rights, and he censored the press. The immediate reaction, encouraged by journalists and lawyers, was an insurrection in the capital by printers, other artisans, and small traders. In "three glorious days," the government collapsed. Paris boiled with revolutionary excitement, and Charles fled. Then the upper middle class, which had fomented the revolt, skillfully seated Charles's cousin, Louis Philippe, duke of Orléans, on the vacant throne.

Louis Philippe (r. 1830–1848) accepted the Constitutional Charter of 1814; adopted the red, white, and blue flag of the French Revolution; and admitted that he was merely the "king of the French people." In spite of such symbolic actions, the situation in France remained fundamentally unchanged. Casimir Périer, a wealthy banker and Louis Philippe's new chief minister, bluntly told a deputy who complained when the vote was extended only from 100,000 to 170,000 citizens, "The trouble with this country is that there are too many people like you who imagine that there has been a revolution in France."[3] The wealthy notable elite actually tightened its control as the old aristocracy retreated to the provinces to sulk harmlessly. For the upper middle class, there had been a change in dynasty in order to protect the status quo and the narrowly liberal institutions of 1815. Republicans, democrats, social reformers, and the poor of Paris were bitterly disappointed. They had made a revolution, but it seemed for naught.

 THE REVOLUTIONS OF 1848

In 1848 revolutionary political and social ideologies combined with severe economic crisis and the romantic impulse to produce a vast upheaval across Europe. Only the most advanced and the most backward major countries—reforming Great Britain and immobile Russia—escaped untouched. Governments toppled; monarchs and ministers bowed or fled. National independence, liberal-democratic constitutions, and social reform: the lofty aspirations of a generation seemed at hand. Yet in the end, the revolutions failed. Why was this so?

A Democratic Republic in France

The late 1840s in Europe were hard economically and tense politically. The potato famine in Ireland in 1845 and in 1846 had echoes on the continent. Bad harvests jacked up food prices and caused misery and unemployment in the cities. "Prerevolutionary" outbreaks occurred all across Europe: an abortive Polish revolution in the northern part of Austria in 1846, a civil war between radicals and conservatives in Switzerland in 1847, and an armed uprising in Naples, Italy, in January 1848. Revolution was almost universally expected, but it took revolution in Paris—once again—to turn expectations into realities.

Louis Philippe's "bourgeois monarchy" had been characterized by stubborn inaction and complacency. There was a glaring lack of social legislation, and politics was dominated by corruption and selfish special interests. With only the rich voting for deputies, many of the deputies were docile government bureaucrats.

The government's stubborn refusal to consider electoral reform heightened a sense of class injustice among middle-class shopkeepers, skilled artisans, and unskilled working people, and it eventually touched off a popular revolt in Paris. Barricades went up on the night of February 22, 1848, and by February 24 Louis Philippe had abdicated in favor of his grandson. But the common people in arms would tolerate no more monarchy. This refusal led to the proclamation of a provisional republic, headed by a ten-man executive committee and certified by cries of approval from the revolutionary crowd.

A generation of historians and journalists had praised the First French Republic, and their work had borne fruit: the revolutionaries were firmly committed to a republic (as opposed to any form of constitutional monarchy), and they immediately set about drafting a constitution for France's Second Republic. Moreover, they wanted a truly popular and democratic republic so that the healthy, life-giving forces of the common people—the peasants, the artisans, and the unskilled workers—could reform society with wise legislation. In practice, building such a republic meant giving the right to vote to every adult male, and this was quickly done. Revolutionary compassion and sympathy for freedom were expressed in the freeing of all slaves in French colonies, the abolition of the death penalty, and the establishment of a ten-hour workday for Paris.

Yet there were profound differences within the revolutionary coalition in Paris. On the one hand, there were the moderate, liberal republicans of the middle class. They viewed universal male suffrage as the ultimate concession to be made to popular forces, and they strongly opposed any further radical social measures. On the other hand, there were radical republicans and hard-pressed artisans. Influenced by a generation of utopian socialists, and appalled by the poverty and misery of the urban poor, the radical republicans were

Delacroix: Liberty Leading the People This famous romantic painting glorifies the July Revolution in Paris in 1830. Raising high the revolutionary tricolor, Liberty unites the worker, bourgeois, and street child in a righteous crusade against privilege and oppression. The revolution of 1848 began as a similar crusade, but class warfare in Paris soon shattered the hope of rich and poor joined together for freedom. *(Louvre © Photo R.M.N)*

THE REVOLUTIONS OF 1848

February	Revolt against Louis Philippe's "bourgeois monarchy" takes place in Paris; Louis Philippe abdicates; a provisional republic is proclaimed.
February–June	Establishment and rapid growth of government-sponsored workshops occur in France.
March 3	Hungarians under Kossuth demand autonomy from the Austrian Empire.
March 13	Uprising of students and workers occurs in Vienna; Metternich flees to London.
March 19–21	Frederick William IV of Prussia is forced to salute the bodies of slain revolutionaries in Berlin and agrees to a liberal constitution and merger into a new German state.
March 20	Ferdinand I of Austria abolishes serfdom and promises reforms.
March 26	Workers in Berlin issue a series of socialist demands.
April 22	French voters favor moderate republicans over radicals 5 to 1.
May 15	Parisian socialist workers invade the Constitutional Assembly and unsuccessfully proclaim a new revolutionary state.
May 18	Frankfurt Assembly begins writing a new German constitution.
June 17	Austrian army crushes a working-class revolt in Prague.
June 22–26	French government abolishes the national workshops, provoking an uprising. June Days: republican army defeats the rebellious Parisian working class.
October	Austrian army besieges and retakes Vienna from students and working-class radicals.
December	Conservatives force Ferdinand I of Austria to abdicate in favor of young Francis Joseph. Frederick William IV disbands the Prussian Constituent Assembly and grants Prussia a conservative constitution. Louis Napoleon wins a landslide victory in the French presidential elections.
March 1849	Frankfurt Assembly elects Frederick William IV of Prussia emperor of the new German state; Frederick William refuses and reasserts his royal authority in Prussia.
June–August 1849	Habsburg and Russian forces defeat the Hungarian independence movement.

committed to some kind of socialism. So were many artisans, who hated the unrestrained competition of cutthroat capitalism and who advocated a combination of strong craft unions and worker-owned businesses.

Worsening depression and rising unemployment brought these conflicting goals to the fore in 1848. Louis Blanc, who along with a worker named Albert represented the republican socialists in the provisional government, pressed for recognition of a socialist right to work. Blanc asserted that permanent government-sponsored cooperative workshops should be established for workers. Such workshops would be an alternative to capitalist employment and a decisive step toward a new, noncompetitive social order.

The moderate republicans wanted no such thing. They were willing to provide only temporary relief. The resulting compromise set up national workshops—soon to become little more than a vast program of pick-and-shovel public works—and established a special commission under Blanc to "study the question." This satisfied no one. The national workshops were, however, better than nothing. An army of desperate poor from the French provinces and even from foreign countries streamed into Paris to sign up. As the economic crisis worsened, the number enrolled in the workshops soared from 10,000 in March to 120,000 by June, and another 80,000 were trying unsuccessfully to join.

While the workshops in Paris grew, the French masses went to the election polls in late April. Voting in most cases for the first time, the people of France elected to the new Constituent Assembly about five hundred moderate republicans, three hundred monarchists, and one hundred radicals who professed various brands of socialism. One of the moderate republicans was the author of *Democracy in America,* Alexis de Tocqueville (1805–1859), who had predicted the overthrow of Louis Philippe's government. To this brilliant observer, socialism was the most characteristic aspect of the revolution in Paris.

This socialist revolution was evoking a violent reaction not only among the frightened middle and upper classes but also among the bulk of the population—the peasants. The French peasants owned land, and according to Tocqueville, "private property had become with all those who owned it a sort of bond of fraternity."[4] The countryside, Tocqueville wrote, had been seized with a universal hatred of radical Paris. Returning from Normandy to take his seat in the new Constituent Assembly, Tocqueville saw that a majority of the members were firmly committed to the republic and strongly opposed to the socialists and their artisan allies, and he shared their sentiments.

This clash of ideologies—of liberal capitalism and socialism—became a clash of classes and arms after the elections. The new government's executive committee dropped Blanc and thereafter included no representative of the Parisian working class. Fearing that their socialist hopes were about to be dashed, artisans and unskilled workers invaded the Constituent Assembly on May 15 and tried to proclaim a new revolutionary state. But the government was ready and used the middle-class National Guard to squelch this uprising. As the workshops continued to fill and grow more radical, the fearful but powerful propertied classes in the Assembly took the offensive. On June 22, the government dissolved the national workshops in Paris, giving the workers the choice of joining the army or going to workshops in the provinces.

The result was a spontaneous and violent uprising. Frustrated in attempts to create a socialist society, masses of desperate people were now losing even their life-sustaining relief. As a voice from the crowd cried out when the famous astronomer François Arago counseled patience, "Ah, Monsieur Arago, you have never been hungry!"[5] Barricades sprang up in the narrow streets of Paris, and a terrible class war began. Working people fought with the courage of utter desperation, but the government had the army and the support of peasant France. After three terrible "June Days" and the death or injury of more than ten thousand people, the republican army under General Louis Cavaignac stood triumphant in a sea of working-class blood and hatred.

The revolution in France thus ended in spectacular failure. The February coalition of the middle and working classes had in four short months become locked in mortal combat. In place of a generous democratic republic, the Constituent Assembly completed a constitution featuring a strong executive. This allowed Louis Napoleon, nephew of Napoleon Bonaparte, to win a landslide victory in the election of December 1848. The appeal of his great name as well as the desire of the propertied classes for order at any cost had produced a semi-authoritarian regime.

The Austrian Empire in 1848

Throughout central Europe, the first news of the upheaval in France evoked feverish excitement and eventually revolution. Liberals demanded written constitutions, representative government, and greater civil liberties from authoritarian regimes. When governments hesitated, popular revolts followed. Urban workers and students served as the shock troops, but they were allied with middle-class liberals and peasants. In the face of this united front, monarchs collapsed and granted almost everything. The popular revolutionary coalition, having secured great and easy victories, then broke down as it had in France. The traditional forces—the monarchy, the aristocracy, and the regular army—recovered their nerve, reasserted their authority, and took back many, though not all, of the concessions. Reaction was everywhere victorious.

The revolution in the Austrian Empire began in Hungary, where nationalistic Hungarians demanded national autonomy, full civil liberties, and universal suffrage. When the monarchy in Vienna hesitated, Viennese students and workers took to the streets, and peasant disorders broke out in parts of the empire. The Habsburg emperor Ferdinand I (r. 1835–1848) capitulated and promised reforms and a liberal constitution. Metternich fled in disguise toward London. The old absolutist order seemed to be collapsing with unbelievable rapidity.

The coalition of revolutionaries was not stable, however. The Austrian Empire was overwhelmingly agricultural, and serfdom still existed. On March 20, as part of its capitulation before upheaval, the monarchy abolished serfdom, with its degrading forced labor and feudal services. Feeling they had won a victory reminiscent of that in France in 1789, newly free men and women of the land then lost interest in the political and social questions agitating the cities. Meanwhile, the coalition of urban revolutionaries also broke down. When artisan workers and the urban poor rose in arms and presented their own demands for socialist workshops and universal voting rights for men, the prosperous middle classes recoiled in alarm.

The coalition of March was also weakened, and ultimately destroyed, by conflicting national aspirations. In March the Hungarian revolutionary leaders pushed through an extremely liberal, almost democratic, constitution. But the Hungarian revolutionaries also sought to transform the mosaic of provinces and peoples that was the kingdom of Hungary into a unified, centralized, Hungarian nation. To the minority groups that formed half of the population—the Croats, Serbs, and Romanians—such unification was completely unacceptable. Each felt entitled to political autonomy and cultural independence. The Habsburg monarchy in Vienna exploited the fears of the minority groups, and they were soon locked in armed combat with the new Hungarian government. In a somewhat similar way, Czech nationalists based in Bohemia and the city of Prague came into conflict with German nationalists. Thus the national aspirations within the Austrian Empire enabled the monarchy to play off one group against the other.

Finally, the conservative aristocratic forces gathered around Emperor Ferdinand I regained their nerve and reasserted their great strength. The archduchess Sophia, a conservative but intelligent and courageous Bavarian princess married to the emperor's brother, provided a rallying point. Deeply ashamed of the emperor's collapse before a "mess of students," she insisted that Ferdinand, who had no heir, abdicate in favor of her son, Francis Joseph.[6] Powerful nobles who held high positions in the government, the army, and the church agreed completely. They organized around Sophia in a secret conspiracy to reverse and crush the revolution.

Their first breakthrough came when the army bombarded Prague and savagely crushed a working-class revolt there on June 17. Other Austrian officials and nobles began to lead the minority nationalities of Hungary against the revolutionary government proclaimed by the Hungarian patriots. At the end of October, the well-equipped, predominantly peasant troops of the regular Austrian army attacked the student and working-class radicals in Vienna and retook the city at the cost of more than four thousand casualties. Thus the determination of the Austrian aristocracy and the loyalty of its army were the final ingredients in the triumph of reaction and the defeat of revolution.

When Francis Joseph (r. 1848–1916) was crowned emperor of Austria immediately after his eighteenth birthday in December 1848, only Hungary had yet to be brought under control. But another determined conservative, Nicholas I of Russia (r. 1825–1855), obligingly lent his iron hand. On June 6, 1849, 130,000 Russian troops poured into Hungary and subdued the country after bitter fighting. For a number of years, the Habsburgs ruled Hungary as a conquered territory.

Prussia and the Frankfurt Assembly

After Austria, Prussia was the largest and most influential German kingdom. Prior to 1848, the goal of middle-class Prussian liberals had been to transform absolutist Prussia into a liberal constitutional monarchy, which would lead the thirty-eight states of the German Confederation into the liberal, unified nation desired by liberals throughout the German states. The agitation following the fall of Louis Philippe encouraged Prussian liberals to press their demands. When the artisans and factory workers in Berlin exploded in March and joined temporarily with the middle-class liberals in the struggle against the monarchy, the autocratic yet paternalistic Frederick William IV (r. 1840–1861) vacillated and finally caved in. On March 21, he promised to grant Prussia a liberal constitution and to merge Prussia into a new national German state that was to be created. But urban workers wanted much more and the Prussian aristocracy wanted much less than the moderate constitutional liberalism the king conceded. The workers issued a series of democratic and vaguely socialist demands that troubled their middle-class allies, and the conservative clique gathered around the king to urge counter-revolution.

As an elected Prussian Constituent Assembly met in Berlin to write a constitution for the Prussian state, a self-appointed committee of liberals from various German states successfully called for a national assembly to manity; our Country is the fulcrum of the lever which we have to wield for the common good. If we give up this fulcrum we run the risk of becoming useless to our Country and to Humanity. . . .

There is no true Country without a uniform law. There is no true Country where the uniformity of that law is violated by the existence of caste, privilege, and inequality, where the powers and faculties of a large number of individuals are suppressed or dormant, where there is no common principle accepted, recognized, and developed by all. In such a state of things there can be no Nation, no People, but only a multitude, a fortuitous agglomeration of men whom circumstances have brought together and different circumstances will separate. In the name of your love for your Country you must combat without truce the existence of every privilege, every inequality, upon the soil which has given you birth. . . .

Your Country should be your Temple. God at the summit, a People of equals at the base. Do not accept any other formula, any other moral law, if you do not want to dishonour your Country and yourselves. Let the secondary laws for the gradual regulation of your existence be the progressive application of this supreme law.

And in order that they should be so, it is necessary that *all* should contribute to the making of them. The laws made by one fraction of the citizens only can never by the nature of things and men do otherwise than reflect the thoughts and aspirations and desires of that fraction; they represent, not the whole country, but a third, a fourth part, a class, a zone of the country. The law must express the general aspiration, promote the good of all, respond to a beat of the nation's heart. The whole nation therefore should be, directly or indirectly, the legislator. By yielding this mission to a few men, you put the egoism of one class in the place of the Country, which is the union of *all* the classes.

A Country is not a mere territory; the particular territory is only its foundation. The Country is the idea which rises upon that foundation; it is the sentiment of love, the sense of fellowship which binds together all the sons of that territory.

So long as a single one of your brothers is not represented by his own vote in the development of the national life—so long as a single one vegetates uneducated among the educated—so long as a single one able and willing to work languishes in poverty for want of work—you have not got a Country such as it ought to be, the Country of all and for all.

Votes, education, work are the three main pillars of the nation; do not rest until your hands have solidly erected them.

✣ Portrait of Giuseppe Mazzini, from the Museo del Risorgimento, Milan. *(Museo del Risorgimento/Scala/Art Resource, NY)*

Questions for Analysis

1. What did Mazzini mean by "evil governments"? Why are they evil?
2. What are the characteristics of the "true Country"?
3. What form of government is best? Why?
4. Why, according to Mazzini, should poor workingmen have been interested in the political unification of Italy?
5. How might a woman today criticize Mazzini's program? Debate how Mazzini might respond to such criticism.

Source: Slightly adapted from J. Mazzini, *The Duties of Man and Other Essays* (London: J. M. Dent and Sons, 1907), pp. 51–57.

CHAPTER

24 Life in the Emerging Urban Society

A painting by Gustav Klimt of the old Burgtheater in Vienna. *(Museen der Stadt Wien)*

found that fermentation depended on the growth of living organisms and that the activity of these organisms could be suppressed by heating the beverage—by "pasteurizing" it. The breathtaking implication was that specific diseases were caused by specific living organisms—germs—and that those organisms could be controlled in people as well as in beer, wine, and milk.

By 1870 the work of Pasteur and others had demonstrated the general connection between germs and disease. When, in the middle of the 1870s, German country doctor Robert Koch and his coworkers developed pure cultures of harmful bacteria and described their life cycles, the dam broke. Over the next twenty years, researchers—mainly Germans—identified the organisms responsible for disease after disease. These discoveries led to the development of a number of effective vaccines.

Acceptance of the germ theory brought about dramatic improvements in the deadly environment of hospitals and surgery. In 1865, when Pasteur showed that the air was full of bacteria, English surgeon Joseph Lister (1827–1912) immediately grasped the connection between aerial bacteria and the problem of wound infection. He reasoned that a chemical disinfectant applied to a wound dressing would "destroy the life of the floating particles." Lister's "antiseptic principle" worked wonders. In the 1880s, German surgeons developed the more sophisticated practice of sterilizing not only the wound but also everything—hands, instruments, clothing—that entered the operating room.

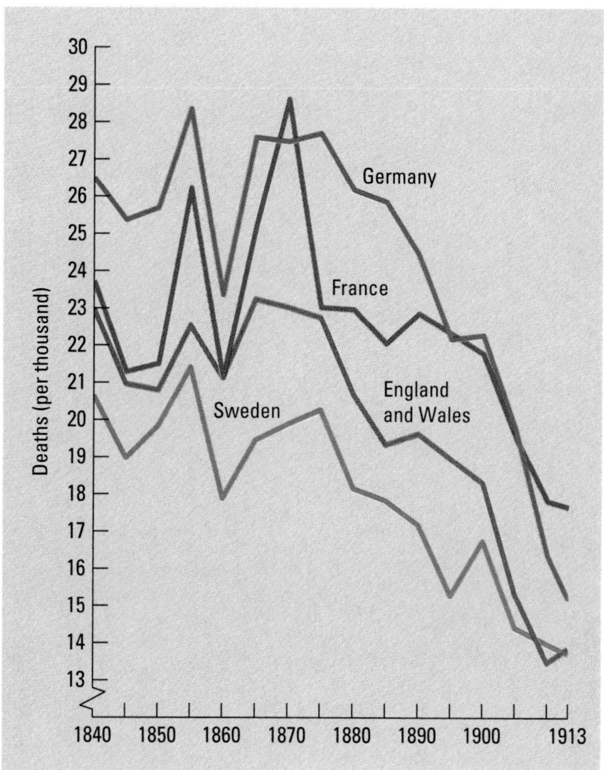

FIGURE 24.1 The Decline of Death Rates in England and Wales, Germany, France, and Sweden, 1840–1913 A rising standard of living, improvements in public health, and better medical knowledge all contributed to the dramatic decline of death rates in the nineteenth century.

The achievements of the bacterial revolution coupled with the ever more sophisticated public health movement saved millions of lives, particularly after about 1880. Mortality rates began to decline dramatically in European countries (Figure 24.1) as the awful death sentences of the past—diphtheria, typhoid, typhus, cholera, yellow fever—became vanishing diseases. City dwellers benefited especially from these developments. By 1910 a great silent revolution had occurred: the death rates for people of all ages in urban areas were generally no greater than those for people in rural areas, and sometimes they were less.

Urban Planning and Public Transportation

If public health was greatly improved in the course of the nineteenth century, that was only part of the urban challenge. Overcrowding, bad housing, and lack of transportation could not be solved by sewers and better medicine; yet in these areas, too, important transformations significantly improved the quality of urban life after midcentury.

More effective urban planning was one of the keys to improvement. Urban planning was in decline by the early nineteenth century, but after 1850 its practice was revived and extended. France took the lead during the rule of Napoleon III (r. 1848–1870), who sought to stand above class conflict and promote the welfare of all his subjects through government action. He believed that rebuilding much of Paris would provide employment, improve living conditions, and testify to the power and glory of his empire. In the baron Georges Haussmann (1809–1884), an aggressive, impatient Alsatian whom he placed in charge of Paris, Napoleon III found an authoritarian planner capable of bulldozing both buildings and opposition. In twenty years, Paris was transformed (Map 24.2).

The Paris of 1850 was a labyrinth of narrow, dark streets, the results of desperate overcrowding. In a central city not twice the size of New York's Central Park lived more than one-third of the city's 1 million inhabitants. Terrible slum conditions and extremely

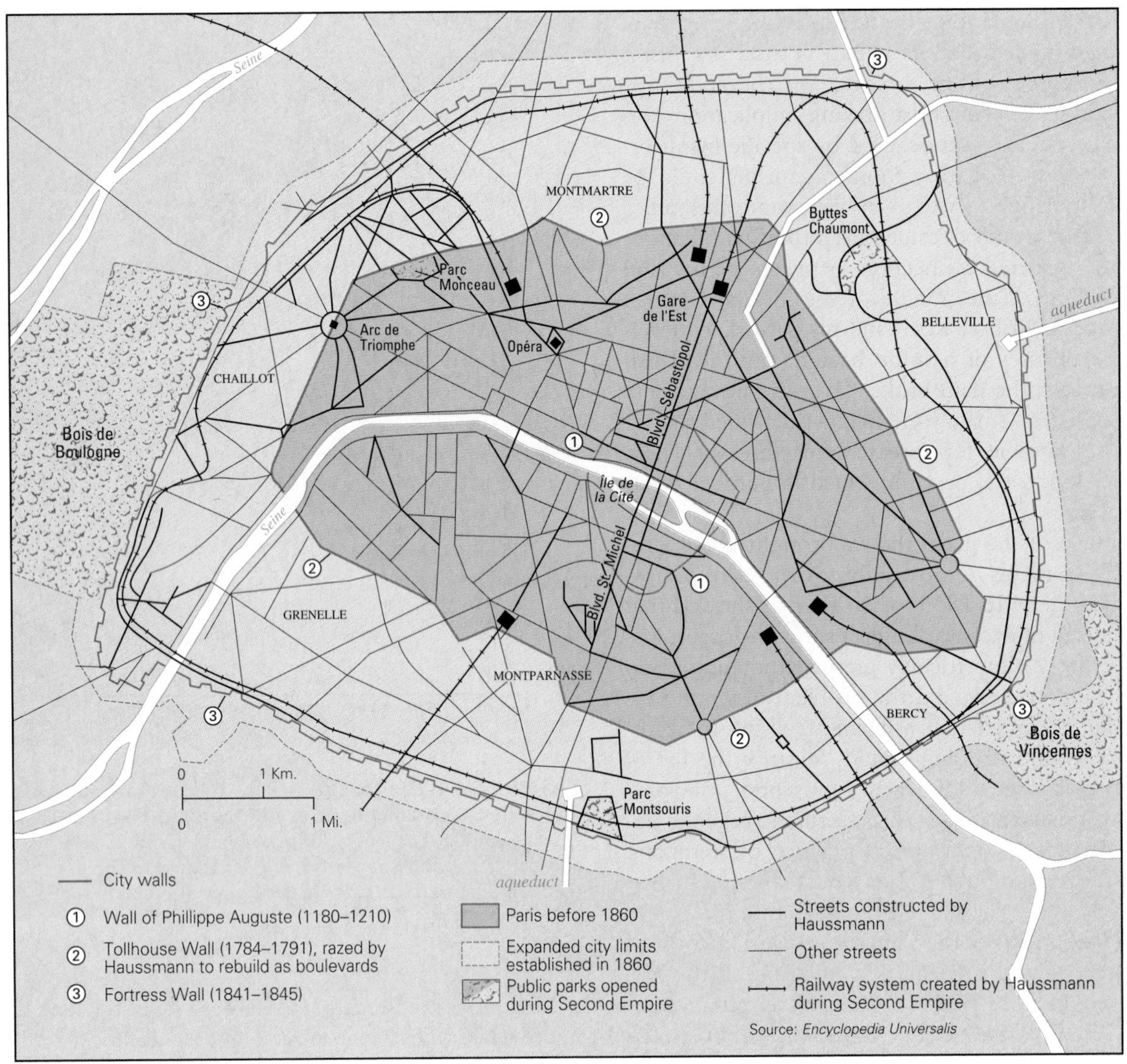

MAP 24.2 The Modernization of Paris, ca 1850–1870 Broad boulevards, large parks, and grandiose train stations transformed Paris. The cutting of the new north-south axis—known as the Boulevard Saint-Michel—was one of Haussmann's most controversial projects. It razed much of Paris's medieval core and filled the Île de la Cité with massive government buildings.

high death rates were facts of life. There were few open spaces and only two public parks for the entire metropolis. Public transportation played a very small role in this enormous walking city.

Haussmann and his fellow planners proceeded on many interrelated fronts. With a bold energy that often shocked their contemporaries, they razed old buildings in order to cut broad, straight, tree-lined boulevards through the center of the city as well as in new quarters on the outskirts. These boulevards, designed in part to prevent the easy construction and defense of barricades by revolutionary crowds, permitted traffic to flow freely. Their creation also demolished some of the worst slums. New streets stimulated the construction of better housing, especially for the middle classes. Small neighborhood parks and open spaces were created throughout the city, and two very large parks suitable for all kinds of holiday activities were developed—one on the wealthy west side and one on the poor east side of the city. The city also improved its sewers, and a system of aqueducts more than doubled the city's supply of good fresh water.

Apartment Living in Paris This drawing shows how different social classes lived close together in European cities about 1850. Passing the middle-class family on the first (American second) floor, the economic condition of the tenants declined until one reached abject poverty in the garret. *(Bibliothèque Nationale, Paris)*

Haussmann and Napoleon III tried to make Paris a more beautiful city, and to a large extent they succeeded. The broad, straight boulevards, such as those radiating out like the spokes of a wheel from the Arch of Triumph and those centering on the new Opera House, afforded impressive vistas. If for most people Paris remains one of the world's most beautiful and enchanting cities, it is in part because of the transformations of Napoleon III's Second Empire.

Rebuilding Paris provided a new model for urban planning and stimulated modern urbanism throughout Europe, particularly after 1870. In city after city, public authorities mounted a coordinated attack on many of the interrelated problems of the urban environment. As in Paris, improvements in public health through better water supply and waste disposal often went hand in hand with new boulevard construction. Cities such as Vienna and Cologne followed the Parisian example of tearing

The Urban Landscape: Madrid in 1900 This wistful painting of a Spanish square on a rainy day, by Enrique Martinez Cubells y Ruiz (1874–1917), includes a revealing commentary on public transportation. Coachmen wait atop their expensive hackney cabs for a wealthy clientele, while modern electric streetcars that carry the masses converge on the square from all directions. *(Museo Municipal, Madrid/The Bridgeman Art Library, London/New York)*

Part of the reason for this change was that the construction of churches failed to keep up with the rapid growth of urban population, especially in new working-class neighborhoods. Thus the vibrant, materialistic urban environment undermined popular religious impulses, which were poorly served in the cities. Equally important, however, was the fact that throughout the nineteenth century both Catholic and Protestant churches were normally seen as they saw themselves—as conservative institutions defending social order and custom. Therefore, as the European working classes became more politically conscious, they tended to see the established (or quasi-established) "territorial church" as defending what they wished to change and as allied with their political opponents. Especially the men of the urban working classes developed vaguely antichurch attitudes, even though they remained neutral or positive toward religion. They tended to regard regular church attendance as "not our kind of thing"—not part of urban working-class culture.

The pattern was different in the United States. There, most churches also preached social conservatism in the nineteenth century. But because church and state had always been separate and because there was always a host of competing denominations and even different religions, working people identified churches much less with the political and social status quo. Instead, individual churches in the United States were often closely identified with an ethnic group rather than with a social class; and churches thrived, in part, as a means of asserting ethnic identity. This same process did occur in Europe if the church or synagogue had never been linked to the state and served as a focus for ethnic cohesion. Irish Catholic churches in Protestant Britain and Jewish synagogues in Russia were outstanding examples.

THE CHANGING FAMILY

Urban life wrought many fundamental changes in the family. Although much is still unknown, it seems clear that in the second half of the nineteenth century the family had stabilized considerably after the disruption of the late eighteenth and early nineteenth centuries. The home became more important for both men and women. The role of women and attitudes toward children underwent substantial change, and adolescence emerged as a distinct stage of life. These are but a few of the transformations that affected all social classes in varying degrees.

Premarital Sex and Marriage

By 1850 the preindustrial pattern of lengthy courtship and mercenary marriage was pretty well dead among the working classes. In its place, the ideal of romantic love had triumphed. Couples were ever more likely to come from different, even distant, towns and to be more nearly the same age, further indicating that romantic sentiment was replacing tradition and financial considerations.

Economic considerations in marriage remained more important to the middle classes than to the working classes after 1850. In France dowries and elaborate legal marriage contracts were common practice among the middle classes in the later nineteenth century, and marriage was for many families one of life's most crucial financial transactions. A popular author advised young Frenchmen that "marriage is in general a means of increasing one's credit and one's fortune and of insuring one's success in the world."[11] This preoccupation with money led many middle-class men in France and elsewhere to marry late, after they had been established economically, and to choose women considerably younger and less sexually experienced than themselves. These differences between husband and wife became a source of tension in many middle-class marriages.

A young woman of the middle class found her romantic life carefully supervised by her well-meaning mother, who schemed for a proper marriage and guarded her daughter's virginity like the family's credit. (See the feature "Listening to the Past: Middle-Class Youth and Sexuality" on pages 820–821.) After marriage, middle-class morality sternly demanded fidelity.

Middle-class boys were watched, too, but not as vigilantly. By the time they reached late adolescence, they had usually attained considerable sexual experience with maids or prostitutes. With marriage a distant, uncertain possibility, it was all too easy for the young man of the middle classes to turn to the urban underworld of prostitution and sexual exploitation to satisfy his desires.

In the early nineteenth century, sexual experimentation before marriage also triumphed, as did illegitimacy. There was an "illegitimacy explosion" between 1750 and 1850 (see page 664). By the 1840s, as many as one birth in three was occurring outside of wedlock in many large cities. Although poverty and economic uncertainty undoubtedly prevented many lovers from marrying, there were also many among the poor and propertyless who saw little wrong with having illegitimate offspring. One young Bavarian woman answered happily when asked why she kept having illegitimate children, "It's O.K. to make babies. . . . The king has o.k.'d it!"[12] Thus the pattern of romantic ideals, premarital sexual activity, and widespread illegitimacy was firmly established by midcentury among the urban working classes.

It is hard to know how European couples managed sex, pregnancy, and marriage after 1850 because such questions were considered improper both in polite conversation and in public opinion polls. Yet there are many telltale clues. In the second half of the century, the rising rate of illegitimacy was reversed: more babies were born to married mothers. Some observers have argued that this shift reflected the growth of puritanism and a lessening of sexual permissiveness among the unmarried. This explanation, however, is unconvincing.

The percentage of brides who were pregnant continued to be high and showed little or no tendency to decline after 1850. In many parts of urban Europe around 1900, as many as one woman in three was going to the altar an expectant mother. Moreover, unmarried people almost certainly used the cheap condoms and diaphragms the industrial age had made available to prevent pregnancy, at least in predominately Protestant countries.

Thus unmarried young people were probably engaging in just as much sexual activity as their parents and grandparents who had created the illegitimacy explosion of 1750 to 1850. But in the later nineteenth century, pregnancy for a young single woman led increasingly to marriage and the establishment of a two-parent household. This important development reflected the growing respectability of the working classes as well as their gradual economic improvement. Skipping out was less acceptable, and marriage was less of an economic challenge. Thus the urban working-class couple became more stable, and that stability strengthened the family as an institution.

Prostitution

In Paris alone, 155,000 women were registered as prostitutes between 1871 and 1903, and 750,000 others were suspected of prostitution in the same years. Men of all classes visited prostitutes, but the middle and upper classes supplied much of the motivating cash. Thus, though many middle-class men abided by the publicly professed code of stern puritanical morality, others indulged their appetites for prostitutes and sexual promiscuity.

My Secret Life, the anonymous eleven-volume autobiography of an English sexual adventurer from the servant-keeping classes, provides a remarkable picture of such a man. Beginning at an early age with a maid, the author becomes progressively obsessed with sex and devotes his life to living his sexual fantasies. In almost every one of his innumerable encounters all across Europe, this man of wealth simply buys his pleasure. Usually meetings are arranged in a businesslike manner: regular and part-time prostitutes quote their prices; working-class girls are corrupted by hot meals and baths.

At one point, he offers a young girl a sixpence for a kiss and gets it. Learning that the pretty, unskilled working girl earns nine pence a day, he offers her the equivalent of a week's salary for a few moments of fondling. When she finally agrees, he savagely exults that "*her* want was my opportunity." Later he offers more money for more gratification, and when she refuses, he tries unsuccessfully to rape her in a hackney cab. On another occasion he takes a farm worker by force: "Her tears ran down. If I had not committed a rape, it looked uncommonly like one." He then forces his victim to take money to prevent a threatened lawsuit, while the foreman advises the girl to keep quiet and realize that "you be in luck if he likes you."[13]

Obviously atypical in its excesses, *My Secret Life,* in its encyclopedic thoroughness, does reveal the dark side of sex and class in urban society. Frequently thinking of their wives largely in terms of money, family, and social position, the men of the comfortable classes often purchased sex and even affection from poor girls both before and after marriage. Moreover, the great continuing differences between rich and poor made for every kind of debauchery and sexual exploitation, including the brisk trade in poor virgins that the author of *My Secret Life* particularly relishes. Brutal sexist behavior was part of life—a part the sternly moral women (and men) of the upper working class detested and tried to shield their daughters from. For many poor young women, prostitution, like domestic service, was a stage of life and not a permanent employment. Having chosen it for two or three years in their twenties, they went on to marry (or live with) men of their own class and establish homes and families.

Kinship Ties

Within working-class homes, ties to relatives after marriage—kinship ties—were in general much stronger than many social observers have recognized. Most newlyweds tried to live near their parents, though not in the same house. Indeed, for many married couples in later-nineteenth-century cities, ties to mothers and fathers, uncles and aunts, were more important than ties to nonrelated acquaintances.

Toulouse-Lautrec: A la Mie Wealthy nobleman by birth and tragically disabled by accident, Henri de Toulouse-Lautrec (1864–1901) was irresistibly drawn to the bizarre individuals who made Paris night life the scandal of Europe. This painting portrays an aging prostitute and her reptile-like companion, a powerful study in degradation. *(S. A. Denio Collection and General Income. Courtesy of Museum of Fine Arts, Boston)*

People turned to their families for help in coping with sickness, unemployment, death, and old age. Although governments were generally providing more welfare services by 1900, the average couple and its children inevitably faced crises. Funerals, for example, brought sudden demands, requiring a large outlay for special clothes, carriages, and burial services. Unexpected death or desertion could leave the bereaved or abandoned, especially widows and orphans, in need of financial aid or perhaps a foster home. Relatives responded hastily to such cries, knowing full well that their own time of need and repayment would undoubtedly come.

Relatives were also valuable at less tragic moments. If a couple was very poor, an aged relation often moved in to cook and mind the children so that the wife could earn badly needed income outside the home. Sunday dinners were often shared, as were outgrown clothing and useful information. Often the members of a large family group all lived in the same neighborhood.

Gender Roles and Family Life

Industrialization and the growth of modern cities brought great changes to the lives of European women. These changes were particularly consequential for married women, and most women did marry in the nineteenth century.

After 1850 the work of most wives became increasingly distinct and separate from that of their husbands. Husbands became wage earners in factories and offices, while wives tended to stay home and manage households and care for children. The preindustrial pattern among both peasants and cottage workers, in which husbands and wives worked together and divided up household duties and child rearing, declined. Only in a few occupations, such as retail trade, did married couples live where they worked and struggle together to make their mom-and-pop operations a success. Factory employment for married women also declined as the early practice of hiring entire families in the factory disappeared.

As economic conditions improved, most men expected married women to work outside the home only in poor families. One old English worker recalled that "the boy wanted to get into a position that would enable him to keep a wife and family, as it was considered a thoroughly unsatisfactory state of affairs if the wife had to work to help maintain the home."[14] The ideal became a strict division of labor by gender: the wife as mother and homemaker, the husband as wage earner.

This rigid gender division of labor meant that married women faced great injustice when they needed—or wanted—to move into the man's world of employment outside the home. Husbands were unsympathetic or hostile. Well-paying jobs were off-limits to women, and a woman's wage was almost always less than a man's, even for the same work.

Moreover, married women were subordinated to their husbands by law and lacked many basic legal rights. In England the situation in the early nineteenth century was summed up in a famous line from jurist William Blackstone: "In law husband and wife are one person, and the husband is that person." Thus a wife in England had no legal identity and hence no right to own property in her own name. Even the wages she might earn belonged to her husband. In France the Napoleonic Code (see pages 712–713) also enshrined the principle of female subordination and gave the wife few legal rights regarding property, divorce, and custody of the children. Legal inferiority for women permeated Western society.

With all women facing discrimination in education and employment and with middle-class women suffering especially from a lack of legal rights, there is little wonder that some women rebelled and began the long-continuing fight for equality of the sexes and the rights of women. Their struggle proceeded on two main fronts. First, following in the steps of women such as Mary Wollstonecraft (see page 705), organizations founded by middle-class feminists campaigned for equal legal rights for women as well as access to higher education and professional employment. These middle-class feminists argued that unmarried women and middle-class widows with inadequate incomes simply had to have more opportunities to support themselves. Middle-class feminists also recognized that paid (as opposed to unpaid) work could relieve the monotony that some women found in their sheltered middle-class existence and put greater meaning into their lives.

In the later nineteenth century, these organizations scored some significant victories, such as the 1882 law giving English married women full property rights. But progress was always slow and hard won. For example, in Germany before 1900, women were not admitted as fully registered students at a single university, and it was virtually impossible for a woman to receive certification and practice as a lawyer or doctor. (See the feature "Individuals in Society: Franziska Tiburtius, Pioneering Professional.") In the years before 1914, middle-class feminists increasingly shifted their attention to political action and fought for the right to vote for women.

Women inspired by utopian and especially Marxian socialism blazed a second path. Often scorning the programs of middle-class feminists, socialist women leaders argued that the liberation of (working-class) women would come only with the liberation of the entire working class through revolution. In the meantime, they championed the cause of workingwomen and won some practical improvements, especially in Germany, where the socialist movement was most effectively organized. In a general way, these different approaches to women's issues reflected the diversity of classes in urban society.

If the ideology and practice of rigidly separate roles undoubtedly narrowed women's horizons and caused some women to rebel, there was a brighter side to the same coin. As home and children became the typical wife's main concerns in the late nineteenth century, her control and influence there apparently became increasingly strong throughout Europe. Among the English working classes, it was the wife who generally determined how the family's money was spent. In many families, the husband gave all his earnings to his wife to manage, whatever the law might read. She returned to him only a small allowance for carfare, beer, tobacco, and union dues. All the major domestic decisions, from the children's schooling and religious instruction to the

Individuals in Society

Franziska Tiburtius, pioneering woman physician in Berlin. *(Ullstein Bilderdienst)*

Franziska Tiburtius, Pioneering Professional

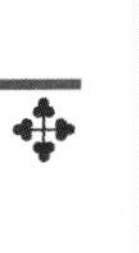

Why did a small number of women in the late nineteenth century brave great odds and embark on a professional career? And how did a few of those manage to reach their objectives? The career and personal reflections of Franziska Tiburtius, a pioneer in German medicine, suggests that talent, determination, and economic necessity were critical ingredients.[1]

Like many women of her time who would study and pursue a professional career, Franziska Tiburtius (1843–1927) was born into a property-owning family of modest means. The youngest of nine children on a small estate in northeastern Germany, the sensitive child wilted with a harsh governess but flowered with a caring teacher and became an excellent student.

Graduating at sixteen and needing to support herself, Tiburtius had few opportunities. A young woman from a "proper" background could work as a governess or a teacher without losing her respectability and spoiling her matrimonial prospects, but that was about it. She tried both avenues. Working for six years as a governess in a noble family and no doubt learning that poverty was often one's fate in this genteel profession, she then turned to teaching. Called home from her studies in Britain in 1871 to care for her brother, who had contracted typhus as a field doctor in the Franco-Prussian War, she found her calling. She decided to become a medical doctor.

Supported by her family, Tiburtius's decision was truly audacious. In all Europe, only the University of Zurich in republican Switzerland accepted female students. Moreover, if it became known that she had studied medicine and failed, she would never get a job as a teacher. No parent would entrust a daughter to an "emancipated" radical who had carved up dead bodies!

Although the male students at the university sometimes harassed the women with crude pranks, Tiburtius thrived. The revolution of the microscope and the discovery of microorganisms was rocking Zurich, and she was fascinated by her studies. She became close friends with a fellow female medical student from Germany, Emilie Lehmus, with whom she would form a lifelong partnership in medicine. She did her internship with families of cottage workers around Zurich and loved her work.

Graduating at age thirty-three in 1876, Tiburtius went to stay with her brother the doctor in Berlin. Well qualified to practice, she ran into pervasive discrimination. She was not even permitted to take the state medical exams and could practice only as an unregulated (and unprofessional) "natural healer." But after persistent fighting with the bureaucrats, she was able to display her diploma and practice as "Franziska Tiburtius, M.D. University of Zurich." She and Lehmus were in business.

Soon the two women realized their dream and opened a clinic, subsidized by a wealthy industrialist, for women factory workers. The clinic filled a great need and was soon treating many patients. A room with beds for extremely sick women was later expanded into a second clinic.

Tiburtius and Lehmus became famous. For fifteen years, they were the only women doctors in all Berlin. An inspiration for a new generation of women, they added the wealthy to their thriving practice. But Tiburtius's clinics always concentrated on the poor, providing them with subsidized and up-to-date treatment. Talented, determined, and working with her partner, Tiburtius experienced the joys of personal achievement and useful service, joys that women and men share in equal measure.

Questions for Analysis

1. How does Franziska Tiburtius's life reflect both the challenges and the changing roles of middle-class women in the later nineteenth century?
2. In what ways was Tiburtius's career related to improvements in health in urban society and to the expansion of the professions?

1. This portrait draws on Conradine Lück, *Frauen: Neun Lebensschicksale* (Reutlingen: Ensslin & Laiblin, n.d.), pp. 153–185.

selection of new furniture or a new apartment, were hers. In France women had even greater power in their assigned domain. One English feminist noted in 1908 that "though legally women occupy a much inferior status than men [in France], in practice they constitute the superior sex. They are the power behind the throne."[15]

Women ruled at home partly because running the urban household was a complicated, demanding, and valuable task. Twice-a-day food shopping, penny-pinching, economizing, and the growing crusade against dirt—not to mention child rearing—were a full-time occupation. Nor were there any laborsaving appliances to help, and even when servants were present, they had to be carefully watched and supervised. Working yet another job for wages outside the home had limited appeal for most married women unless such earnings were essential for family survival. Many married women in the working classes did make a monetary contribution to family income by taking in boarders or doing piecework at home in the sweated industries (see page 802).

The wife also guided the home because a good deal of her effort was directed toward pampering her husband as he expected. In countless humble households, she saw that he had meat while she ate bread, that he relaxed by the fire while she did the dishes.

The woman's guidance of the household went hand in hand with the increased emotional importance of home and family. The home she ran was idealized as a warm shelter in a hard and impersonal urban world. For a child of the English slums in the early 1900s,

home, however poor, was the focus of all love and interests, a sure fortress against a hostile world. Songs about its beauties were ever on people's lips. "Home, sweet home," first heard in the 1870s, had become "almost a second national anthem." Few walls in lower-working-class houses lacked "mottoes"—colored strips of paper, about nine inches wide and eighteen inches in length, attesting to domestic joys: EAST, WEST, HOME'S BEST; BLESS OUR HOME; GOD IS MASTER OF THIS HOUSE; HOME IS THE NEST WHERE ALL IS BEST.[16]

By 1900 home and family were what life was all about for millions of people of all classes.

Married couples also developed stronger emotional ties to each other. Even in the comfortable classes, marriages in the late nineteenth century were based more on sentiment and sexual attraction than they had been earlier in the century, as money and financial calculation declined in importance. Affection and eroticism became more central to the couple after marriage. Gustave Droz, whose bestseller *Mr., Mrs., and Baby* went through 121 editions between 1866 and 1884, saw love within marriage as the key to human happiness. He condemned men who made marriage sound dull and practical, men who were exhausted by prostitutes and rheumatism and who wanted their young wives to be little angels. He urged women to follow their hearts and marry a man more nearly their own age:

A husband who is stately and a little bald is all right, but a young husband who loves you and who drinks out of your glass without ceremony, is better. Let him, if he ruffles your dress a little and places a kiss on your neck as he passes. Let him, if he undresses you after the ball, laughing like a fool. You have fine spiritual qualities, it is true, but your little body is not bad either and when one loves, one loves completely. Behind these follies lies happiness.[17]

Many French marriage manuals of the late 1800s stressed that women had legitimate sexual needs, such as the "right to orgasm." Perhaps the French were a bit more enlightened in these matters than other nationalities. But the rise of public socializing by couples in cafés and music halls as well as franker affection within the family suggests a more erotic, pleasurable intimate life for women throughout Western society. This, too, helped make the woman's role as mother and homemaker acceptable and even satisfying.

Child Rearing

One striking sign of deepening emotional ties within the family was the growing love and concern that mothers gave their tiny infants. Because so many babies died so early in life, mothers in preindustrial Western society often avoided making a strong emotional commitment to a newborn in order to shield themselves from recurrent heartbreak. Early emotional bonding and a willingness to make real sacrifices for the welfare of the infant were beginning to spread among the comfortable classes by the end of the eighteenth century, but the ordinary mother of modest means adopted new attitudes only as the nineteenth century progressed. The baby became more important, and women became better mothers.

Mothers increasingly breast-fed their infants, for example, rather than paying wet nurses to do so. Breast-feeding involved sacrifice—a temporary loss of freedom, if nothing else. Yet in an age when there was no good alternative to mother's milk, it saved lives. This surge of maternal feeling also gave rise to a wave of specialized books on child rearing and infant hygiene, such as Droz's phenomenally successful book. Droz urged fathers to get into the act and pitied those "who do not know how to roll around on the carpet, play at being a horse and a great wolf, and undress their baby."[18] Another sign, from France, of increased affection is that fewer illegitimate babies were abandoned as foundlings after about 1850. Moreover, the practice of swaddling disappeared completely. Instead, ordinary mothers allowed their babies freedom of movement and delighted in their spontaneity.

The loving care lavished on infants was matched by greater concern for older children and adolescents. They, too, were wrapped in the strong emotional ties of a more intimate and protective family. For one thing, European women began to limit the number of children they bore in order to care adequately for those they had. It was evident by the end of the nineteenth century that the birthrate was declining across Europe, as Figure 24.4 shows, and it continued to do so until after World War II. The Englishwoman who married in the 1860s, for example, had an average of about six children; her daughter marrying in the 1890s had only four; and her granddaughter marrying in the 1920s had only two or possibly three.

The most important reason for this revolutionary reduction in family size, in which the comfortable and well-educated classes took the lead, was parents' desire to improve their economic and social position and that of their children. Children were no longer an economic asset in the later nineteenth century. By having fewer youngsters, parents could give those they had valuable advantages, from music lessons and summer vacations to long, expensive university educations and suitable dowries. A young German skilled worker with only one child spoke for many in his class when he said, "We want to get ahead, and our daughter should have things better than my wife and sisters did."[19] Thus the growing tendency of couples in the late nineteenth century to use a variety of contraceptive methods—rhythm method, withdrawal method, and mechanical devices—certainly reflected increased concern for children.

Indeed, many parents, especially in the middle classes, probably became *too* concerned about their children, unwittingly subjecting them to an emotional pressure cooker of almost unbearable intensity. The result was that many children and especially adolescents came to feel trapped and in need of greater independence.

Prevailing biological and medical theories led parents to believe in the possibility that their own emotional characteristics were passed on to their offspring and that they were thus directly responsible for any abnormality in a child. The moment the child was conceived was thought to be of enormous importance. "Never run the risk of conception when you are sick or overtired or unhappy," wrote one influential American woman. "For the bodily condition of the child, its vigor and magnetic qualities, are much affected by conditions ruling this great moment."[20] So might the youthful "sexual excess" of the father curse future generations. Although this was true in the case of syphilis, which could be transmitted to unborn children, the rigid determinism of such views left little scope for the child's individual development.

Another area of excessive parental concern was the sexual behavior of the child. Masturbation was viewed with horror, for it represented an act of independence and even defiance. Diet, clothing, games, and sleeping were carefully regulated. Girls were discouraged from riding horses and bicycling because rhythmic friction simulated masturbation. Boys were dressed in trousers with shallow and widely separated pockets. Between 1850 and 1880, there were surgical operations for children who persisted in masturbating. Thereafter until about 1905, various restraining apparatuses were more often used.

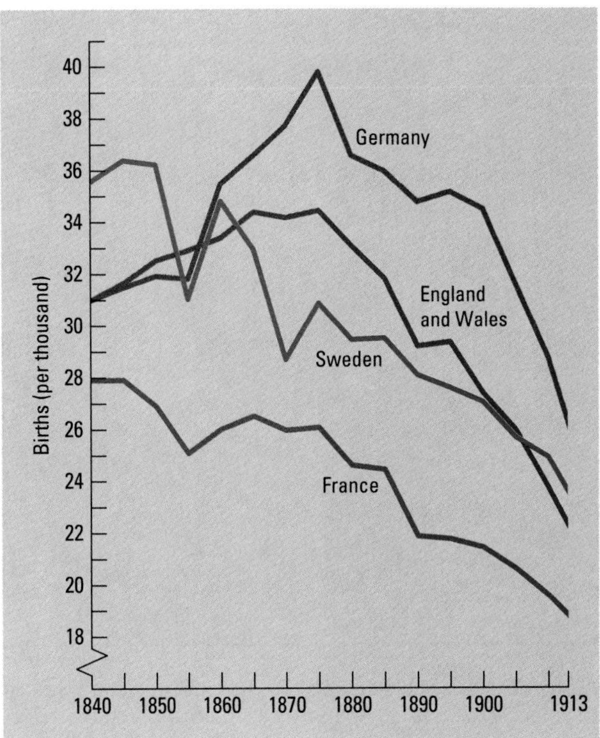

FIGURE 24.4 The Decline of Birthrates in England and Wales, France, Germany, and Sweden, 1840–1913 Women had fewer babies for a variety of reasons, including the fact that their children were increasingly less likely to die before reaching adulthood. Compare with Figure 24.1 on page 793.

A Working-Class Home, 1875 Emotional ties within ordinary families grew stronger in the nineteenth century. Parents gave their children more love and better care. *(Illustrated London News, LXVI, 1875. Photo courtesy of Boston Public Library)*

These and less blatant attempts to repress the child's sexuality were a source of unhealthy tension, often made worse by the rigid division of gender roles within the family. It was widely believed that mother and child loved each other easily but that relations between father and child were necessarily difficult and often tragic. The father was a stranger; his world of business was far removed from the maternal world of spontaneous affection. Moreover, the father was demanding, often expecting the child to succeed where he himself had failed and making his love conditional on achievement. Little wonder that the imaginative literature of the late nineteenth century came to deal with the emotional and destructive elements of father-son relationships. In the Russian Feodor Dostoevski's great novel *The Brothers Karamazov* (1880–1881), for example, four sons work knowingly or unknowingly to destroy their father. Later at the murder trial, one of the brothers claims to speak for all mankind and screams out, "Who doesn't wish his father dead?"

Sigmund Freud (1856–1939), the Viennese founder of psychoanalysis, formulated the most striking analysis of the explosive dynamics of the family, particularly the middle-class family in the late nineteenth century. A physician by training, Freud began his career treating mentally ill patients. He noted that the hysteria of his patients appeared to originate in bitter early-childhood experiences wherein the child had been obliged to repress strong feelings. When these painful experiences were recalled and reproduced under hypnosis or through the patient's free association of ideas, the patient could be brought to understand his or her unhappiness and eventually deal with it.

One of Freud's most influential ideas concerned the Oedipal tensions resulting from the son's instinctive competition with the father for the mother's love and affection. More generally, Freud postulated that much of human behavior is motivated by unconscious emotional needs whose nature and origins are kept from conscious awareness by various mental devices he called "defense mechanisms." Freud concluded that much unconscious psychological energy is sexual energy, which is repressed and precariously controlled by rational thinking and moral rules. If Freud exaggerated the sexual and familial roots of adult behavior, that exaggeration was itself a reflection of the tremendous emotional intensity of family life in the late nineteenth century.

The working classes probably had more avenues of escape from such tensions than did the middle classes. Unlike their middle-class counterparts, who remained economically dependent on their families until a long education was finished or a proper marriage secured, working-class boys and girls went to work when they reached adolescence. Earning wages on their own, they could bargain with their parents for greater independence within the household by the time they were sixteen or seventeen. If they were unsuccessful, they could and did leave home to live cheaply as paying lodgers in other working-class homes. Thus the young person from the working classes broke away from the family more easily when emotional ties became oppressive. In the twentieth century, middle-class youths would follow this lead.

SCIENCE AND THOUGHT

Major changes in Western science and thought accompanied the emergence of urban society. Two aspects of these complex intellectual developments stand out as especially significant. First, scientific knowledge expanded rapidly, influencing the Western world-view even more profoundly than ever before and spurring the creation of new products and whole industries. Second, between about the 1840s and the 1890s, European literature underwent a shift from soaring romanticism to tough-minded realism.

The Triumph of Science

As the pace of scientific advance quickened and as theoretical advances resulted in great practical benefits, science exercised growing influence on human thought. The intellectual achievements of the scientific revolution had resulted in few such benefits, and theoretical knowledge had also played a relatively small role in the Industrial Revolution in England. But breakthroughs in industrial technology enormously stimulated basic scientific inquiry, as researchers sought to explain theoretically how such things as steam engines and blast furnaces actually worked. The result was an explosive growth of fundamental scientific discoveries from the 1830s onward. And in contrast to earlier periods, these theoretical discoveries were increasingly transformed into material improvements for the general population.

A perfect example of the translation of better scientific knowledge into practical human benefits was the work of Louis Pasteur and his followers in biology and the medical sciences. Another was the development of the branch of physics known as *thermodynamics*. Building on Isaac Newton's laws of mechanics and on studies of steam engines, thermodynamics investigated the relationship between heat and mechanical energy. By midcentury, physicists had formulated the fundamental laws of thermodynamics, which were then applied to mechanical engineering, chemical processes, and many other fields. The *law of conservation of energy* held that different forms of energy—such as heat, electricity, and magnetism—could be converted but neither created nor destroyed. Nineteenth-century thermodynamics demonstrated that the physical world was governed by firm, unchanging laws.

Chemistry and electricity were two other fields characterized by extremely rapid scientific progress. And in both fields, "science was put in the service of industry," as the influential economist Alfred Marshall (1842–1924) argued at the time.

Chemists devised ways of measuring the atomic weight of different elements, and in 1869 the Russian chemist Dmitri Mendeleev (1834–1907) codified the rules of chemistry in the periodic law and the periodic table. Chemistry was subdivided into many specialized branches, such as *organic chemistry*—the study of the compounds of carbon. Applying theoretical insights gleaned from this new field, researchers in large German chemical companies discovered ways of transforming the dirty, useless coal tar that accumulated in coke ovens into beautiful, expensive synthetic dyes for the world of fashion. The basic discoveries of Michael Faraday (1791–1867) on electromagnetism in the 1830s and 1840s resulted in the first dynamo (generator) and opened the way for the subsequent development of the telegraph, electric motors, electric lights, and electric streetcars. The successful application of scientific research in the fast-growing electrical and organic chemical industries promoted solid economic growth between 1880 and 1913 and provided a model for other industries. Systematic "R & D"—research and development—was born in the late nineteenth century.

The triumph of science and technology had at least three more significant consequences. First, though ordinary citizens continued to lack detailed scientific knowledge, everyday experience and innumerable popularizers impressed the importance of science on the popular mind.

Second, as science became more prominent in popular thinking, the philosophical implications of science formulated in the Enlightenment spread to broad sections of the population. Natural processes appeared to be determined by rigid laws, leaving little room for either divine intervention or human will. Yet scientific and technical advances had also fed the Enlightenment's optimistic faith in human progress, which now appeared endless and automatic to many middle-class minds.

Third, the methods of science acquired unrivaled prestige after 1850. For many, the union of careful experiment and abstract theory was the only reliable route to truth and objective reality. The "unscientific" intuitions of poets and the revelations of saints seemed hopelessly inferior.

Social Science and Evolution

From the 1830s onward, many thinkers tried to apply the objective methods of science to the study of society. In some ways, these efforts simply perpetuated the critical thinking of the philosophes. Yet there were important differences. The new "social scientists" had access to the massive sets of numerical data that governments had begun to collect on everything from children to crime, from population to prostitution. In response, social scientists developed new statistical methods to analyze these facts "scientifically" and supposedly to test their theories. And the systems of the leading nineteenth-century social scientists were more unified, all-encompassing, and dogmatic than those of the philosophes. Marx was a prime example (see pages 765–766).

Another extremely influential system builder was French philosopher Auguste Comte (1798–1857). Initially a disciple of the utopian socialist Saint-Simon (see pages 764–765), Comte wrote the six-volume *System of Positive Philosophy* (1830–1842), which was largely overlooked during the romantic era. But when the political failures of 1848 completed the swing to realism, Comte's philosophy came into its own. Its influence has remained great to this day.

Comte postulated that all intellectual activity progresses through predictable stages:

> *The great fundamental law . . . is this:—that each of our leading conceptions—each branch of our knowledge—passes successively through three different theoretical conditions: the Theological, or fictitious; the Metaphysical, or abstract; and the Scientific, or positive. . . . The first is the necessary point of departure of human understanding, and the third is the fixed and definitive state. The second is merely a transition.*[21]

By way of example, Comte noted that the prevailing explanation of cosmic patterns had shifted, as knowledge of astronomy developed, from the will of God (the theological) to the will of an orderly nature (the metaphysical) to the rule of unchanging laws (the scientific). Later, this same intellectual progression took place in increasingly complex fields—physics, chemistry, and, finally, the study of society. By applying the scientific, or *positivist,* method, Comte believed, his new discipline of sociology would soon discover the eternal laws of human relations. This colossal achievement would in turn enable expert social scientists to impose a disciplined harmony and well-being on less enlightened citizens. Dismissing the "fictions" of traditional religions, Comte became the chief priest of the religion of science and rule by experts.

Comte's stages of knowledge exemplify the nineteenth-century fascination with the idea of evolution and dynamic development. Thinkers in many fields, such as the romantic historians and "scientific" Marxists, shared and applied this basic concept. In geology, Charles Lyell (1797–1875) effectively discredited the long-standing view that the earth's surface had been formed by short-lived cataclysms, such as biblical floods and earthquakes. Instead, according to Lyell's principle of uniformitarianism, the same geological processes that are at work today slowly formed the earth's surface over an immensely long time. The evolutionary view of biological development, first proposed by the Greek Anaximander in the sixth century B.C., re-emerged in a more modern form in the work of Jean Baptiste Lamarck (1744–1829). Lamarck asserted that all forms of life had arisen through a long process of continuous adjustment to the environment.

Lamarck's work was flawed—he believed that the characteristics parents acquired in the course of their lives could be inherited by their children—and was not accepted, but it helped prepare the way for Charles Darwin (1809–1882), the most influential of all nineteenth-century evolutionary thinkers. As the official naturalist on a five-year scientific cruise to Latin America and the South Pacific beginning in 1831, Darwin carefully collected specimens of the different animal species he encountered on the voyage. Back in England, convinced by fossil evidence and by his friend Lyell that the earth and life on it were immensely ancient, Darwin came to doubt the general belief in a special divine creation of each species of animal. Instead, he concluded, all life had gradually evolved from a common ancestral origin in an unending "struggle for survival." After long hesitation, Darwin published his research, which immediately attracted wide attention.

Darwin's great originality lay in suggesting precisely *how* biological evolution might have occurred. His theory is summarized in the title of his work *On the Origin of Species by the Means of Natural Selection* (1859). Decisively influenced by Thomas Malthus's gloomy theory that populations naturally grow faster than their food supplies (see page 733), Darwin argued that chance differences among the members of a given species help some survive while others die. Thus the variations that prove useful in the struggle for survival are selected naturally and gradually spread to the entire species through reproduction. Darwin did not explain why such variations occurred in the first place, and not until the early twentieth century did the study of genetics and the concept of mutation provide some answers.

As the capstone of already-widespread evolutionary thinking, Darwin's theory had a powerful and many-sided influence on European thought and the European middle classes. Darwin was hailed as the great scientist par excellence, the "Newton of biology," who had revealed once again the powers of objective science. Darwin's findings also reinforced the teachings of secularists such as Comte and Marx, who scornfully dismissed religious belief in favor of agnostic or atheistic materialism. In the great cities especially, religion was on the defensive. Finally, many writers applied the theory of biological evolution to human affairs. Herbert Spencer (1820–1903), an English disciple of Auguste Comte, saw the human race as driven forward to ever-greater specialization and progress by the brutal economic struggle. According to Spencer, this unending struggle efficiently determined the "survival of the fittest." The poor were the ill-fated weak; the prosperous were the chosen strong. Understandably, Spencer and other Social Darwinists were especially popular with the upper middle class.

Attracting Females was an integral part of the struggle for survival, according to Darwin. He theorized that those males who were most attractive to females would have the most offspring, like this type of monkey that had developed ornamental hair, giving him devastating sex appeal. Darwin used this illustration in *The Descent of Man* (1871). *(Library of Congress)*

Realism in Literature

In 1868 Emile Zola (1840–1902), the giant of the realist movement in literature, defended his violently criticized first novel against charges of pornography and corruption of morals. Such accusations were meaningless, Zola claimed: he was only a purely objective scientist using

> *the modern method, the universal instrument of inquiry of which this age makes such ardent use to open up the future. . . . I chose characters completely dominated by their nerves and their blood, deprived of free-will, pushed to each action of their lives by the fatality of their flesh. . . . I have simply done on living bodies the work of analysis which surgeons perform on corpses.*[22]

Zola's literary manifesto articulated the key themes of realism, which had emerged in the 1840s and continued to dominate Western culture and style until the 1890s. Realist writers believed that literature should depict life exactly as it was. Forsaking poetry for prose and the personal, emotional viewpoint of the romantics for strict, scientific objectivity, the realists simply observed and recorded—content to let the facts speak for themselves.

The major realist writers focused their extraordinary powers of observation on contemporary everyday life. Emphatically rejecting the romantic search for the exotic and the sublime, they energetically pursued the typical and the commonplace. Beginning with a dissection of the middle classes, from which most of them sprang, many realists eventually focused on the working classes, especially the urban working classes, which had been neglected in imaginative literature before this time. The realists put a microscope to many unexplored

"Life Is Everywhere" The simple but profound joys of everyday life infuse this outstanding example of Russia's powerful realist tradition. Painted in 1888 by N. A. Yaroshenko, this representation of the mother and child and adoring men also draws on the classic theme of the infant Jesus and the holy family. *(Sovfoto)*

and taboo subjects—sex, strikes, violence, alcoholism—and hastened to report that slums and factories teemed with savage behavior. Many shocked middle-class critics denounced realism as ugly sensationalism wrapped provocatively in pseudoscientific declarations and crude language.

The realists' claims of objectivity did not prevent the elaboration of a definite world-view. Unlike the romantics, who had gloried in individual freedom and an unlimited universe, realists such as Zola were strict determinists. Human beings, like atoms, were components of the physical world, and all human actions were caused by unalterable natural laws. Heredity and environment determined human behavior; good and evil were merely social conventions.

The realist movement began in France, where romanticism had never been completely dominant, and three of its greatest practitioners—Balzac, Flaubert, and Zola—were French. Honoré de Balzac (1799–1850) spent thirty years writing a vastly ambitious panorama of postrevolutionary French life. Known collectively as *The Human Comedy,* this series of nearly one hundred books vividly portrays more than two thousand characters from virtually all sectors of French society. Balzac pictures urban society as grasping, amoral, and brutal, characterized by a Darwinian struggle for wealth and power. In *Le Père Goriot* (1835), the hero, a poor student from the provinces, eventually surrenders his idealistic integrity to feverish ambition and society's pervasive greed.

Madame Bovary (1857), the masterpiece of Gustave Flaubert (1821–1880), is far narrower in scope than Balzac's work but unparalleled in its depth and accuracy of psychological insight. Unsuccessfully prosecuted as an outrage against public morality and religion, Flaubert's carefully crafted novel tells the ordinary, even banal, story of a frustrated middle-class housewife who has an adulterous love affair and is betrayed by her lover. Without moralizing, Flaubert portrays the provincial middle class as petty, smug, and hypocritical.

Zola was most famous for his seamy, animalistic view of working-class life. But he also wrote gripping, carefully researched stories featuring the stock exchange, the big department store, and the army, as well as urban slums and bloody coal strikes. Like many later realists, Zola sympathized with socialism, a sympathy evident in his overpowering *Germinal* (1885).

Realism quickly spread beyond France. In England, Mary Ann Evans (1819–1880), who wrote under the pen name George Eliot, brilliantly achieved a more deeply felt, less sensational kind of realism. "It is the habit of my imagination," George Eliot wrote, "to strive after as full a vision of the medium in which a character moves as one of the character itself." Her great novel *Middlemarch: A Study of Provincial Life* (1871–1872) examines masterfully the ways in which people are shaped by their social medium as well as their own inner strivings, conflicts, and moral choices. Thomas Hardy (1840–1928) was more in the Zola tradition. His novels, such as *Tess of the D'Urbervilles* (1891) and *The Return of the Native* (1878), depict men and women frustrated and crushed by fate and bad luck.

The greatest Russian realist, Count Leo Tolstoy (1828–1910), combined realism in description and character development with an atypical moralizing, which came to dominate his later work. Tolstoy's greatest work is *War and Peace* (1864–1869), a monumental novel set against the historical background of Napoleon's invasion of Russia in 1812. Tolstoy probed deeply into the lives of a multitude of unforgettable characters, such as the ill-fated Prince Andrei; the shy, fumbling Pierre; and the enchanting, level-headed Natasha. Tolstoy went to great pains to develop his fatalistic theory of history, which regards free will as an illusion and the achievements of even the greatest leaders as only the channeling of historical necessity. Yet Tolstoy's central message is one that most of the people discussed in this chapter would have readily accepted: human love, trust, and everyday family ties are life's enduring values.

Thoroughgoing realism (or "naturalism," as it was often called) arrived late in the United States, most arrestingly in the work of Theodore Dreiser (1871–1945). His first novel, *Sister Carrie* (1900), a story of an ordinary farm girl who does well going wrong in Chicago, so outraged conventional morality that the publisher withdrew the book. The United States subsequently became a bastion of literary realism in the twentieth century after the movement had faded away in Europe.

SUMMARY

The revolution in industry had a decisive influence on the urban environment. The populations of towns and cities grew rapidly because it was economically advantageous to locate factories and offices in urban areas. This rapid growth worsened long-standing overcrowding and unhealthy living conditions and posed a frightening challenge for society. Eventually government leaders, city planners, reformers, scientists, and ordinary citizens responded. They took effective action in public health and provided themselves with other badly needed urban services. Gradually they tamed the ferocious savagery of the traditional city.

As urban civilization emerged, there were major changes in family life. Especially among the working classes, family life became more stable, more loving, and less mercenary. These improvements had a price, however. Gender roles for men and women became sharply defined and rigidly separate. Women especially tended to be locked into a subordinate and stereotypical role. Nonetheless, on balance, the quality of family life improved for all family members. Better, more stable family relations reinforced the benefits for the masses of higher real wages, increased social security, political participation, and education.

While the quality of urban and family life improved, the class structure became more complex and diversified than before. Urban society featured many distinct social groups, which existed in a state of constant flux and competition. The gap between rich and poor remained enormous and really quite traditional in mature urban society, although there were countless gradations between the extremes. Large numbers of poor women in particular continued to labor as workers in sweated industries, as domestic servants, and as prostitutes in order to satisfy the demands of their masters in the servant-keeping classes. Urban society in the late nineteenth century represented a long step forward for humanity, but it remained very unequal.

Inequality was a favorite theme of realist novelists such as Balzac and Zola. More generally, literary realism reflected Western society's growing faith in science, material progress, and evolutionary thinking. The emergence of urban, industrial civilization accelerated the secularization of the Western world-view.

NOTES

1. A. Weber, *The Growth of Cities in the Nineteenth Century* (New York: Columbia University Press, 1899), p. 1.
2. Quoted in W. Ashworth, *The Genesis of Modern British Town Planning* (London: Routledge & Kegan Paul, 1954), p. 17.
3. S. Marcus, "Reading the Illegible," in *The Victorian City: Images and Realities,* ed. H. J. Dyos and Michael Wolff, vol. 1 (London: Routledge & Kegan Paul, 1973), p. 266.
4. E. Gauldie, *Cruel Habitations: A History of Working-Class Housing, 1780–1918* (London: George Allen & Unwin, 1974), p. 21.

5. Quoted in E. Chadwick, *Report on the Sanitary Condition of the Labouring Population of Great Britain,* ed. M. W. Flinn (Edinburgh: University of Edinburgh Press, 1965; original publication, 1842), pp. 315–316.
6. J. P. McKay, *Tramways and Trolleys: The Rise of Urban Mass Transport in Europe* (Princeton, N.J.: Princeton University Press, 1976), p. 81.
7. Quoted in R. P. Neuman, "The Sexual Question and Social Democracy in Imperial Germany," *Journal of Social History* 7 (Winter 1974): 276.
8. Quoted in B. Harrison, "Underneath the Victorians," *Victorian Studies* 10 (March 1967): 260.
9. Quoted in J. A. Banks, "The Contagion of Numbers," in *The Victorian City: Images and Realities,* ed. H. J. Dyos and Michael Wolff, vol. 1 (London: Routledge & Kegan Paul, 1973), p. 112.
10. Quoted in R. Roberts, *The Classic Slum: Salford Life in the First Quarter of the Century* (Manchester, England: University of Manchester Press, 1971), p. 95.
11. Quoted in T. Zeldin, *France, 1848–1945,* vol. 1 (Oxford: Clarendon Press, 1973), p. 288.
12. Quoted in J. M. Phayer, "Lower-Class Morality: The Case of Bavaria," *Journal of Social History* 8 (Fall 1974): 89.
13. Quoted in S. Marcus, *The Other Victorians: A Study of Sexuality and Pornography in Mid-Nineteenth-Century England* (New York: Basic Books, 1966), p. 142.
14. Quoted in G. S. Jones, "Working-Class Culture and Working-Class Politics in London, 1870–1900: Notes on the Remaking of a Working Class," *Journal of Social History* 7 (Summer 1974): 486.
15. Quoted in Zeldin, *France,* p. 346.
16. Roberts, *The Classic Slum,* p. 35.
17. Quoted in Zeldin, *France,* p. 295.
18. Quoted ibid., p. 328.
19. Quoted in Neuman, "The Sexual Question," p. 281.
20. Quoted in S. Kern, "Explosive Intimacy: Psychodynamics of the Victorian Family," *History of Childhood Quarterly* 1 (Winter 1974): 439.
21. A. Comte, *The Positive Philosophy of Auguste Comte,* trans. H. Martineau, vol. 1 (London: J. Chapman, 1853), pp. 1–2.
22. Quoted in G. J. Becker, ed., *Documents of Modern Literary Realism* (Princeton, N.J.: Princeton University Press, 1963), p. 159.

SUGGESTED READING

All of the books and articles cited in the Notes are highly recommended. T. Zeldin, *France, 1848–1945,* 2 vols. (1973, 1977), is a pioneering social history that opens many doors, as is the ambitious synthesis by T. Hamerow, *The Birth of a New Europe: State and Society in the Nineteenth Century* (1983). F. Thompson, *The Rise of Respectable Society: A Social History of Victorian Britain, 1830–1900* (1986), is a laudable survey.

On the European city, D. Harvey, *Consciousness and the Urban Experience* (1985), is provocative. D. Silverman, *Art Nouveau in Fin-de-Siècle France: Politics, Psychology, and Style* (1989), and D. Pickney, *Napoleon III and the Rebuilding of Paris* (1972), are major studies. Also recommended are P. Fritzsche, *Reading Berlin in 1900* (1996), an imaginative cultural investigation; O. Olsen, *The City as a Work of Art: London, Paris, and Vienna* (1986), an architectural feast; and M. Hamm, ed., *The City in Russian History* (1976), which still has no equal. D. Grew, *Town in the Ruhr: A Social History of Bochum, 1860–1914* (1979), is an influential study. T. Clark, *The Painting of Modern Life: Paris in the Age of Manet and His Followers* (1985), and J. Merriman, *Margins of City Life: Explorations on the French Urban Frontier* (1991), are important works on France. The outstanding study by J. Schmiechen, *Sweated Industries and Sweated Labor: The London Clothing Trades* (1984), complements H. Mayhew's wonderful contemporary study, *London Labour and the Labouring Poor* (1861), reprinted recently. Michael Crichton's realistic historical novel on organized crime, *The Great Train Robbery* (1976), is excellent. E. Johnson, *Urbanization and Crime: Germany, 1871–1914* (1995), presents a portrait of a police state zealously defending property rights. J. P. Goubert, *The Conquest of Water: The Advent of Health in the Industrial Age* (1989), and A. Corbin, *The Foul and the Fragrant: Odor and the French Social Imagination of Public Health* (1986), are excellent introductions to sanitary developments and attitudes toward smells. For society as a whole, J. Burnett, *History of the Cost of Living* (1969), cleverly shows how different classes spent their money, and B. Tuchman, *The Proud Tower* (1966), draws an unforgettable portrait of people and classes before 1914. B. Gottlieb, *The Family in the Western World* (1993), is a wide-ranging recent synthesis. L. Pollock, *Forgotten Children: Parent-Child Relations from 1500 to 1900* (1983), explores long-term changes and patterns. J. Laver's handsomely illustrated *Manners and Morals in the Age of Optimism, 1848–1914* (1966) investigates the urban underworld and relations between the sexes. Sexual attitudes are also examined in J. Walkowitz, *Prostitution and Victorian Society: Women, Class and State* (1980); and L. Engelstein, *The Key to Happiness: Sex and the Search for Modernity in Fin-de-Siècle Russia* (1992). G. Alter, *Family and Female Life Course: The Women of Verviers, Belgium, 1849–1880* (1988), and A. McLaren, *Sexuality and Social Order: Birth Control in Nineteenth-Century France* (1982), explore attitudes toward family planning.

Studies on women continue to expand rapidly. In addition to the general works by Shorter, Wrigley, Stone, and Tilly and Scott cited in Chapter 20, recommended recent surveys include U. Frevert, *Women in German History: From Bourgeois Emancipation to Sexual Liberation* (1990); and M. Perrot, ed., *A History of Private Life* (1990), a fascinating book. Eye-opening specialized investigations include L. Davidoff, *The Best Circles* (1973), and P. Jalland, *Women, Marriage and Politics, 1860–1914* (1986), on upper-class society types; B. Engel, *Between the Fields and the City: Women, Work and Family in Russia, 1861–1914* (1994); and P. Smith, *Feminism in the Third Republic* (1996). M. J. Peterson, *Love and Work in the Lives of Victorian Gentlewomen* (1989), J. Coffin, *The Politics of Women's Work: The Paris Garment Trades, 1750–1914* (1996), and M. Vicinus, *Independent Women: Work and Community for Single Women, 1850–1920* (1985), examine women at work. M. Vicinus, ed., *Suffer and Be Still* (1972) and *A Widening Sphere* (1981), are far-ranging collections of essays on women's history, as is R. Bridenthal, C. Koonz, and S. Stuard, eds., *Becoming Visible: Women in European History,* 2d ed. (1987). Feminism is treated perceptively in R. Evans, *The Feminists: Women's Emancipation in Europe, America, and Australia* (1979), and C. Moses, *French Feminism in the Nineteenth Century* (1984). L. Tickner, *The Spectacle of Women: Imagery of the Suffrage Campaign, 1907–1914* (1988), perceptively discusses Britain. J. Gillis, *Youth and History* (1974), is a good introduction. J. Donzelot, *The Policing of Families* (1979), stresses the loss of family control of all aspects of life to government agencies.

Among studies on the working classes, M. Maynes, *Taking the Hard Road: Life Course in French and German Workers' Biographies in the Era of Industrialization* (1995), provides fascinating stories and shows how workers saw themselves. Everyday life in a great city comes wonderfully alive in W. S. Haine, *The World of the Paris Café: Sociability Among the French Working Class, 1789–1914* (1996). J. Wegs, *Growing Up Working Class: Continuity and Change Among Viennese Youth, 1890–1938* (1989), is recommended.

Two recommended studies on the middle classes are P. Pillbeam, *The Middle Classes in Europe, 1789–1914: France, Germany, Italy, and Russia* (1990), a stimulating introduction, and J. Kocka and A. Mitchell, eds., *Bourgeois Society in the Nineteenth Society* (1993), an up-to-date collection by leading specialists. Two fine recent studies on the professions are A. Digby, *Making a Medical Living: Doctors and Patients in the English Market for Medicine, 1720–1922* (1994); and A. Quartaro, *Women Teachers and Popular Education in Nineteenth-Century France* (1995). Servants and their employers receive excellent treatment in T. McBride, *The Domestic Revolution: The Modernization of Household Service in England and France, 1820–1912* (1976); and B. Smith, *Ladies of the Leisure Class: The Bourgeoises of Northern France in the Nineteenth Century* (1981), which may be compared with the innovative study by M. Miller, *The Bon Marché: Bourgeois Culture and the Department Store, 1869–1920* (1981).

On Darwin, M. Ruse, *The Darwinian Revolution* (1979), is a good starting point, as are P. Bowler, *Evolution: The History of an Idea,* rev. ed. (1989); and G. Himmelfarb, *Darwin and the Darwinian Revolution* (1968). O. Chadwick, *The Secularization of the European Mind in the Nineteenth Century* (1976), analyzes the impact of science (and other factors) on religious belief. M. Teich and R. Porter, eds., *Fin de Siècle and Its Legacy* (1990), is a fascinating collection of essays, ranging widely from industry and cars to sports and painting. The masterpieces of the great realist social novelists remain among the best and most memorable introductions to nineteenth-century culture and thought. In addition to the novels discussed in this chapter and those cited in the Suggested Reading for Chapters 22 and 23, Ivan Turgenev's *Fathers and Sons* and Emile Zola's *The Dram-Shop* are especially recommended.

LISTENING TO THE PAST

Middle-Class Youth and Sexuality

Growing up in Vienna in a prosperous Jewish family, Stephan Zweig (1881–1942) became an influential voice calling for humanitarian values and international culture in early-twentieth-century Europe. Passionately opposed to the First World War, Zweig wrote poetry, plays, and novels. But he was most famous for many outstanding biographies, which featured shrewd psychological portraits of intriguing historical figures such as Magellan and Marie Antoinette. After Hitler came to power in Germany in 1933, Zweig lived in exile until his death in 1942.

Zweig's last work was The World of Yesterday *(1943), one of the truly fascinating autobiographies of the twentieth century. In the following passage taken from that work, Zweig recalls and also interprets the romantic experiences and the sexual frustrations of middle-class youth before the First World War.*

During the eight years of our higher schooling [beyond grade school], something had occurred which was of great importance to each one of us: we ten-year-olds had grown into virile young men of sixteen, seventeen, and eighteen, and Nature began to assert its rights. . . . It did not take us long to discover that those authorities in whom we had previously confided—school, family, and public morals—manifested an astonishing insincerity in this matter of sex. But what is more, they also demanded secrecy and reserve from us in this connection. . . .

This "social morality," which on the one hand privately presupposed the existence of sexuality and its natural course, but on the other would not recognize it openly at any price, was doubly deceitful. While it winked one eye at a young man and even encouraged him with the other "to sow his wild oats," as the kindly language of the home put it, in the case of a woman it studiously shut both eyes and acted as if it were blind. That a man could experience desires, and was permitted to experience them, was silently admitted by custom. But to admit frankly that a woman could be subject to similar desires, or that creation for its eternal purposes also required a female polarity, would have transgressed the conception of the "sanctity of womanhood." In the pre-Freudian era, therefore, the axiom was agreed upon that a female person could have no physical desires as long as they had not been awakened by man, and that, obviously, was officially permitted only in marriage. But even in those moral times, in Vienna in particular, the air was full of dangerous erotic infection, and a girl of good family had to live in a completely sterilized atmosphere, from the day of her birth until the day when she left the altar on her husband's arm. In order to protect young girls, they were not left alone for a single moment. . . . They had to practise the piano, learn singing and drawing, foreign languages, and the history of literature and art. They were educated and overeducated. But while the aim was to make them as educated and as socially correct as possible, at the same time society anxiously took great pains that they should remain innocent of all natural things to a degree unthinkable today. . . .

What possibilities actually existed for a young man of the middle-class world? In all the others, in the so-called lower classes, the problem was no problem at all. . . . In most of our Alpine villages the number of natural children greatly exceeded the legitimate ones. Among the proletariat, the worker, before he could get married, lived with another worker in free love. . . . It was only in our middle-class society that such a remedy as an early marriage was scorned. . . . And so there was an artificial interval of six, eight, or ten years between actual manhood and manhood as society accepted it; and in this interval the young man had to take care of his own "affairs" or adventures.

Those days did not give him too many opportunities. Only a very few particularly rich young men could afford the luxury of keeping a mistress, that

The revolutions of 1848 closed one era and opened another. Urban industrial society began to take a strong hold on the continent and in the young United States, as it already had in Great Britain. Internationally, the repressive peace and diplomatic stability of Metternich's time were replaced by a period of war and rapid change. In thought and culture, exuberant romanticism gave way to hardheaded realism. In the Atlantic economy, the hard years of the 1840s were followed by good times and prosperity throughout most of the 1850s and 1860s. Perhaps most important of all, Western society progressively found, for better or worse, a new and effective organizing principle capable of coping with the many-sided challenge of the dual revolution and the emerging urban civilization. That principle was nationalism—dedication to an identification with the nation-state.

The triumph of nationalism is an enormously significant historical development that was by no means completely predictable. After all, nationalism had been a powerful force since at least 1789. Yet it had repeatedly failed to realize its goals, most spectacularly so in 1848.

- Why, then, did nationalism become in one way or another an almost universal faith in Europe and in the United States between 1850 and 1914?
- More specifically, how did nationalism evolve so that it appealed not only to predominately middle-class liberals but also to the broad masses of society?

These are the questions this chapter will seek to answer.

 NAPOLEON III IN FRANCE

Early nationalism was generally liberal and idealistic and often democratic and radical as well. The ideas of nationhood and popular sovereignty posed a fearful revolutionary threat to conservatives like Metternich. Yet from the vantage point of the twentieth century, it is clear that nationalism wears many masks: it may be narrowly liberal or democratic and radical, as it was for Mazzini and Michelet, but it can also flourish in dictatorial states, which may be conservative, fascist, or communist. Napoleon I's France had already combined national devotion with authoritarian rule. Significantly, it was Napoleon's nephew, Louis Napoleon, who revived and extended this merger. He showed how governments could reconcile popular and conservative forces in an authoritarian nationalism. In doing so, he provided a model for political leaders elsewhere.

The Second Republic and Louis Napoleon

Although Louis Napoleon Bonaparte had played no part in French politics before 1848, universal male suffrage gave him three times as many votes as the four other presidential candidates combined in the French presidential election of December 1848. This outcome occurred for several reasons. First, Louis Napoleon had the great name of his uncle, whom romantics had transformed from a dictator into a demigod as they created a Napoleonic legend after 1820. Second, as Karl Marx stressed at the time, middle-class and peasant property owners feared the socialist challenge of urban workers, and they wanted a tough ruler to provide protection. Third, in late 1848 Louis Napoleon had a positive "program" for France, which was to guide him through most of his long reign. This program had been elaborated earlier in two pamphlets, *Napoleonic Ideas* and *The Elimination of Poverty,* which he had written while imprisoned for an attempt to overthrow Louis Philippe's government. Prior to the presidential election, these pamphlets had been widely circulated.

Above all, Louis Napoleon believed that the government should represent the people and that it should try hard to help them economically. But how were these tasks to be done? Parliaments and political parties were not the answer, according to Louis Napoleon. French politicians represented special-interest groups, particularly middle-class ones. When they ran a parliamentary government, they stirred up class hatred because they were not interested in helping the poor. The answer was a strong, even authoritarian, national leader, like the first Napoleon, who would serve all the people, rich and poor. This leader would be linked to the people by direct democracy, his sovereignty uncorrupted by politicians and legislative bodies. These political ideas went hand in hand with Louis Napoleon's vision of national unity and social progress. Rather than doing nothing or providing only temporary relief for the awful poverty of the poor, the state and its leader had a sacred duty to provide jobs and stimulate the economy. All classes would benefit by such action.

Louis Napoleon's political and social ideas were at least vaguely understood by large numbers of French

Rebuilding Paris Cutting new boulevards through Paris was like smashing superhighways through inner cities after World War II. Expensive and time-consuming, it brought massive demolitions, protests that the old city was being ruined, and big new buildings, such as the lavish opera house seen in the distance. Napoleon believed that boulevards would be harder for revolutionaries to barricade than narrow streets. *(Photo Bulloz)*

peasants and workers in December 1848. To many common people, he appeared to be a strong man *and* a forward-looking champion of their interests, and that is why they voted for him.

Elected to a four-year term, President Louis Napoleon had to share power with a conservative National Assembly. With some misgivings, he signed a bill to increase greatly the role of the Catholic church in primary and secondary education. In France, as elsewhere in Europe after 1848, the anxious well-to-do saw religion as a bulwark against radicalism. As one leader of the church in France put it, "There is only one recipe for making those who own nothing believe in property-rights: that is to make them believe in God, who dictated the Ten Commandments and who promises eternal punishment to those who steal."[1] Very reluctantly, Louis Napoleon also signed another law depriving many poor people of the right to vote. He took these conservative measures for two main reasons: he wanted the Assembly to vote funds to pay his personal debts, and he wanted it to change the constitution so he could run for a second term.

The Assembly did neither. Thus in 1851 Louis Napoleon began to conspire with key army officers. On December 2, 1851, he illegally dismissed the Assembly and seized power in a *coup d'état.* There was some armed resistance in Paris and widespread insurrection in the countryside in southern France, but these protests were crushed by the army. Restoring universal male suffrage, Louis Napoleon called on the French people, as his uncle had done, to legalize his actions. They did: 92 percent voted to make him president for ten years. A year later, 97 percent in a plebiscite made him hereditary emperor; for the third time, and by the greatest margin yet, the authoritarian Louis Napoleon was overwhelmingly elected to lead the French nation.

Napoleon III's Second Empire

Louis Napoleon—now proclaimed Emperor Napoleon III—experienced both success and failure between 1852 and 1870. His greatest success was with the economy, particularly in the 1850s. His government encouraged the new investment banks and massive railroad construction that were at the heart of the Industrial Revolution on the continent. The government also fostered general economic expansion through an ambitious program of public works, which included the rebuilding of Paris to improve the urban environment (see pages 793–797). The profits of business people soared with prosperity, and the working classes did not fare poorly either. Their wages more than kept up with inflation, and jobs were much easier to find.

Louis Napoleon always hoped that economic progress would reduce social and political tensions. This hope was at least partially realized. Until the mid-1860s, there was little active opposition and there was even considerable support for his government from France's most dissatisfied group, the urban workers. Napoleon III's regulation of pawnshops and his support of credit unions and better housing for the working classes were evidence of positive concern in the 1850s. In the 1860s, he granted workers the right to form unions and the right to strike—important economic rights denied by earlier governments.

At first, political power remained in the hands of the emperor. He alone chose his ministers, and they had great freedom of action. At the same time, Napoleon III restricted but did not abolish the Assembly. Members were elected by universal male suffrage every six years, and Louis Napoleon and his government took the parliamentary elections very seriously. They tried to entice notable people, even those who had opposed the regime, to stand as government candidates in order to expand the base of support. Moreover, the government used its officials and appointed mayors to spread the word that the election of the government's candidates—and the defeat of the opposition—was the key to roads, tax rebates, and a thousand other local concerns.

In 1857 and again in 1863, Louis Napoleon's system worked brilliantly and produced overwhelming electoral victories. Yet in the 1860s, Napoleon III's electoral system gradually disintegrated. A sincere nationalist, Napoleon had wanted to reorganize Europe on the principle of nationality and gain influence and territory for France and himself in the process. Instead, problems in Italy and the rising power of Prussia led to increasing criticism at home from his Catholic and nationalist supporters. With increasing effectiveness, the middle-class liberals who had always wanted a less authoritarian regime continued to denounce his rule.

Napoleon was always sensitive to the public mood. Public opinion, he once said, always wins the last victory. Thus in the 1860s, he progressively liberalized his empire. He gave the Assembly greater powers and the opposition candidates greater freedom, which they used to good advantage. In 1869 the opposition, consisting of republicans, monarchists, and liberals, polled almost 45 percent of the vote.

The next year, a sick and weary Louis Napoleon again granted France a new constitution, which combined a basically parliamentary regime with a hereditary emperor as chief of state. In a final great plebiscite on the eve of the disastrous war with Prussia, 7.5 million Frenchmen voted in favor of the new constitution, and only 1.5 million opposed it. Napoleon III's attempt to reconcile a strong national state with universal male suffrage was still evolving and was doing so in a democratic direction.

NATION BUILDING IN ITALY AND GERMANY

Louis Napoleon's triumph in 1848 and his authoritarian rule in the 1850s provided the old ruling classes of Europe with a new model in politics. To what extent might the expanding urban middle classes and even portions of the growing working classes rally to a strong and essentially conservative national state? This was one of the great political questions in the 1850s and 1860s. In central Europe, a resounding answer came with the national unification of Italy and Germany.

Italy to 1850

Italy had never been united prior to 1850. Part of Rome's great empire in ancient times, the Italian peninsula was divided in the Middle Ages into competing city-states, which led the commercial and cultural revival of the West with amazing creativity. A battleground for great powers after 1494, Italy was reorganized in 1815 at the Congress of Vienna. The rich northern provinces of Lombardy and Venetia were taken by Metternich's Austria. Sardinia and Piedmont were under the rule of an Italian monarch, and Tuscany, with its famous capital Florence, shared north-central Italy with several smaller states. Central Italy and Rome were ruled by the papacy, which had always considered an independent political existence necessary to fulfill its spiritual mission. Naples and Sicily were ruled, as they had been for almost a hundred years, by a branch of the Bourbons. Metternich was not wrong in dismissing Italy as "a geographical expression" (Map 25.1).

Between 1815 and 1848, the goal of a unified Italian nation captured the imaginations of many Italians. There were three basic approaches. The first was the radical program of the idealistic patriot Giuseppe Mazzini, who preached a centralized democratic republic based on universal male suffrage and the will of the people (see page 762). The second was that of Vincenzo Gioberti, a Catholic priest who called for a federation of existing states under the presidency of a progressive pope. The third was the program of those who looked for leadership to the autocratic kingdom of Sardinia-Piedmont, much as many Germans looked to Prussia.

The third alternative was strengthened by the failures of 1848, when Austria smashed Mazzini's republicanism. Almost by accident, Sardinia's monarch, Victor Emmanuel, retained the liberal constitution granted under duress in March 1848. This constitution provided for a fair degree of civil liberties and real parliamentary government, with deputies elected on the basis of a narrow franchise limited to the nobility and the comfortable middle class. To the Italian middle classes, Sardinia appeared to be a liberal, progressive state ideally suited to achieve the goal of national unification. By contrast, the middle-class elite and its allies in the liberal aristocracy distrusted Mazzini's vision of democratic republicanism. They feared it might lead to renewed upheaval, social revolution, and intervention by France or Austria. Nationalists in the lower middle class and on the left usually continued to support a republican Italy.

As for the papacy, the initial cautious support by Pius IX (r. 1846–1878) for unification had given way to fear and hostility after he was temporarily driven from Rome during the upheavals of 1848. For a long generation, the papacy would stand resolutely opposed not only to national unification but also to most modern trends. In 1864 in the *Syllabus of Errors,* Pius IX strongly denounced rationalism, socialism, separation of church and state, and religious liberty, denying that "the Roman pontiff can and ought to reconcile and align himself with progress, liberalism, and modern civilization."

Cavour and Garibaldi in Italy

Sardinia had the good fortune of being led by a brilliant statesman, Count Camillo Benso di Cavour, the dominant figure in the Sardinian government from 1850 until his death in 1861. Indicative of the coming tacit alliance between the aristocracy and the solid middle class under the banner of the strong nation-state, Cavour came from a noble family and embraced the economic doctrines and business activities associated with the prosperous middle class. Before entering politics, he made a substantial fortune in sugar mills, steamships, banks, and railroads. Cavour's national goals were limited and realistic. Until 1859 he sought unity only for the states of northern and perhaps central Italy in a greatly expanded kingdom of Sardinia. He did not seek to incorporate the Papal States or the kingdom of the Two Sicilies, with their very different cultures and governments, into an Italy of all the Italians.

In the 1850s, Cavour worked to consolidate Sardinia as a liberal constitutional state capable of leading northern Italy. His program of highways and railroads, of civil liberties and opposition to clerical privilege, increased support for Sardinia throughout northern Italy. Yet Cavour realized that Sardinia could not drive Austria out of Lombardy and Venetia and unify northern Italy under Victor Emmanuel without the help of a powerful ally. He sought that ally in the person of Napoleon III, who believed in national consolidation, especially if it could be combined with modest expansion for France.

In a complicated series of diplomatic maneuvers, Cavour worked for a secret diplomatic alliance with Napoleon III against Austria. Finally, in July 1858 he succeeded and goaded Austria into attacking Sardinia in 1859. Napoleon III came to Sardinia's defense. Then after the victory of the combined Franco-Sardinian forces, Napoleon III did a sudden about-face. Deciding it was not in his interest to have too strong a state on his southern border and criticized by French Catholics for supporting the pope's declared enemy, Napoleon III abandoned Cavour. He made a compromise peace with the Austrians at Villafranca in July 1859. Sardinia would receive only Lombardy, the area around Milan. The rest of the map of Italy would remain essentially unchanged. Cavour resigned in a rage.

Yet Cavour's plans were salvaged by the skillful maneuvers of his allies in the moderate nationalist movement. While the war against Austria had raged in the north, pro-Sardinian nationalists in central Italy had fanned revolts and driven out their easily toppled princes. Large crowds demonstrated, singing "Foreigners, get out of Italy!" and passionately chanting, "Italy and Victor Emmanuel!" Using and controlling the popular enthusiasm, the middle-class nationalist leaders in central Italy ignored the compromise peace of Villafranca and called for fusion with Sardinia.

This was not at all what France and the other Great Powers wanted, but the nationalists held firm. Cavour

MAP 25.1 The Unification of Italy, 1859–1870 The leadership of Sardinia-Piedmont and nationalist fervor were decisive factors in the unification of Italy.

returned to power in early 1860 to work out a deal with Napoleon III. Sardinia had to cede Savoy and Nice to France, but for this price Napoleon III dropped his objections. The people of central Italy then voted overwhelmingly to join a greatly enlarged kingdom of Sardinia. Cavour had achieved his original goal of a northern Italian state (see Map 25.1).

For superpatriots such as Giuseppe Garibaldi (1807–1882), the job of unification was still only half done. The son of a poor sailor, Garibaldi had long personified the romantic, revolutionary nationalism of Mazzini and 1848. (See the feature "Individuals in Society: Garibaldi, Hero of the People.") All his life, he had fought and plotted wars of national liberation. In the early

Individuals in Society

Garibaldi, Hero of the People

Giuseppe Garibaldi, the charismatic leader, shown in an 1856 engraving based on a photograph. *(Corbis-Bettmann)*

When Giuseppe Garibaldi (1807–1882) visited England in 1864, he received the most triumphant welcome ever given to any foreigner. Honored and feted by politicians and high society, he also captivated the masses. An unprecedented crowd of a half million people cheered his carriage through the streets of London. These ovations were no fluke. In his time, Garibaldi was probably the most famous and most beloved figure in the world.[1] How could this be?

A rare combination of wild adventure and extraordinary achievement partly accounted for his demigod status. Born in Nice, Garibaldi went to sea at fifteen and sailed the Mediterranean for twelve years. At seventeen his travels took him to Rome, and he was converted in an almost religious experience to the "New Italy, the Italy of all the Italians." As he later wrote in his best-selling *Autobiography,* "The Rome that I beheld with the eyes of youthful imagination was the Rome of the future—the dominant thought of my whole life."

Sentenced to death in 1834 for his part in a revolutionary uprising in Genoa, Garibaldi barely escaped to South America. For twelve years, he led a guerrilla band in Uruguay's struggle for independence from Argentina. "Shipwrecked, ambushed, shot through the neck," he found in a tough young woman, Anna da Silva, a mate and companion in arms. Their first children nearly starved in the jungle while Garibaldi, clad in his long red shirt, fashioned a legend as a fearless freedom fighter.

Returning to Italy in 1848, the campaigns of his patriotic volunteers against the Austrians in 1848 and 1859 mobilized democratic nationalists. The stage was set for his volunteer army to liberate Sicily against enormous odds, astonishing the world and creating a large Italian state. Garibaldi's achievement matched his legend.

A brilliant fighter, the handsome and inspiring leader was an uncompromising idealist of absolute integrity. He never drew any personal profit from his exploits, continuing to milk his goats and rarely possessing more than one change of clothing. When Victor Emmanuel offered him lands and titles after his great victory in 1861, even as the left-leaning volunteers were disbanded and humiliated, Garibaldi declined, saying he could not be bought off. Returning to his farm on a tiny rocky island, he denounced the government without hesitation when he concluded that it was betraying the dream of unification with its ruthless rule in the south. Yet even after a duplicitous Italian government caused two later attacks on Rome to fail, his faith in the generative power of national unity never wavered. Garibaldi showed that ideas and ideals count in history.

Above all, millions of ordinary men and women identified with Garibaldi because they believed that he was fighting for them. They recognized him as one of their own and saw that he remained true to them in spite of his triumphs, thereby ennobling their own lives and aspirations. Welcoming runaway slaves as equals in Latin America, advocating the emancipation of women, introducing social reforms in the south, and pressing for free education and a broader suffrage in the new Italy, Garibaldi the national hero fought for freedom and human dignity. The common people understood, and loved him for it.

Questions for Analysis

1. Why was Garibaldi so famous and popular?
2. Nationalism evolved and developed in the nineteenth century. How did Garibaldi fit into this evolution? What kind of a nationalist was he?

1. Denis Mack Smith, *Garibaldi: A Great Life in Brief* (New York: Alfred A. Knopf, 1956), pp. 136–147; and Denis Mack Smith, "Giuseppe Garibaldi," *History Today,* August 1991, pp. 20–26.

1860s Garibaldi, ever a radical man of action, devised a bold plan to use a private army of patriotic volunteers to "liberate" the kingdom of the Two Sicilies. Cavour opposed the invasion, but he dared not stop it because of Garibaldi's enormous popular appeal. Slipping out of Genoa and landing on the shores of Sicily in May 1860, Garibaldi's guerrilla band of a thousand "Red Shirts" captured the imagination of the Sicilian peasantry. Outwitting the twenty-thousand-man royal army, the guerrilla leader won battles, gained volunteers, and took Palermo. Then he and his men crossed to the mainland, marched triumphantly toward Naples, and prepared to attack Rome and the pope.

Expecting and probably hoping at first that Garibaldi would fail, the wily Cavour now moved quickly to profit from his victories. He sent Sardinian forces to occupy most of the Papal States (but not Rome) and to intercept Garibaldi. Knowing that an attack on Rome might bring about war with France, Cavour feared Garibaldi's radicalism above all. As temporary ruler of Sicily and Naples, Garibaldi had already introduced free education and tentative social reforms and had disbanded the Jesuits and nationalized their property. Therefore, Cavour immediately organized a plebiscite in the conquered territories. Despite the urging of some more radical supporters, the patriotic Garibaldi did not oppose Cavour, and the people of the south voted to join Sardinia. When Garibaldi and Victor Emmanuel rode through Naples to cheering crowds, they symbolically sealed the union of north and south, of monarch and nation-state.

Garibaldi and Victor Emmanuel The historic meeting in Naples between the leader of Italy's revolutionary nationalists and the king of Sardinia sealed the unification of northern and southern Italy in a unitary state. With only the sleeve of his red shirt showing, Garibaldi offers his hand—and his conquests—to the uniformed king and his moderate monarchical government. *(Fabio Lensini/Madeline Grimoldi)*

Cavour had succeeded. He had controlled Garibaldi and had turned popular nationalism in a conservative direction. The new kingdom of Italy, which expanded to include Venice in 1866 and Rome in 1870, mainly because of Prussian victories over Austria and then France in those years, was neither radical nor democratic. Italy was a parliamentary monarchy under Victor Emmanuel, but in accordance with the liberal Sardinian constitution of 1848, only a small minority of Italian males had the right to vote. The propertied classes and the common people were divided.

Moreover, a great gap separated the progressive, industrializing north from the stagnant, agrarian south. This gap would actually increase in the new Italian state. Harsh administrators from Sardinia immediately canceled Garibaldi's wartime reforms, and they often ruled Sicily and Naples like a conquered territory, dashing the hopes "liberation" had raised and leading to disillusionment and widespread banditry. The peasant industries of the south also declined precipitously, increasing the weight of existing poverty and sending millions abroad in search of a better life. The new Italy was united on paper, but profound divisions remained.

Germany Before Bismarck

In the aftermath of 1848, while Louis Napoleon consolidated his rule and Cavour schemed, the German states were locked in a political stalemate. With Russian diplomatic support, Austria had blocked the halfhearted attempt of Frederick William IV of Prussia (r. 1840–1861) to unify Germany "from above." This action contributed to a growing tension between Austria and Prussia as each power sought to block the other within the reorganized German Confederation, made up of thirty-eight sovereign states after 1815 (see pages 758 and 782–784). Stalemate also prevailed in the domestic politics of the individual states as Austria, Prussia, and the smaller German kingdoms entered a period of reaction and immobility in the 1850s.

At the same time, powerful economic forces were undermining the political status quo. As we have seen, modern industry grew rapidly in Europe throughout the 1850s. Nowhere was this growth more rapid than within the German customs union (Zollverein). Developing gradually under Prussian leadership after 1818 and founded officially in 1834 to stimulate trade and increase the revenues of member states, the Zollverein had not included Austria. After 1848 this exclusion became a crucial factor in the Austro-Prussian rivalry.

The Zollverein's tariff duties were substantially reduced so that Austria's highly protected industry could not bear to join. In retaliation, Austria tried to destroy the Zollverein by inducing the south German states to leave it, but without success. Indeed, by the end of 1853 all the German states except Austria had joined the customs union. A new Germany excluding Austria was becoming an economic reality. Middle-class and business groups in the Zollverein were enriching themselves and finding solid economic reasons to bolster their idealistic support of national unification. The growing economic integration of the states within the Zollverein gave Prussia a valuable advantage in its struggle against Austria's supremacy in German political affairs.

The national uprising in Italy in 1859 made a profound impression in the German states. In Prussia great political change and war—perhaps with Austria, perhaps with France—seemed quite possible. Along with his top military advisers, the tough-minded William I of Prussia (r. 1861–1888), who had replaced the unstable Frederick William IV as regent in 1858 and become king himself in 1861, was convinced of the need for major army reforms. William I wanted to double the size of the highly disciplined regular army. He also wanted to reduce the importance of the reserve militia, a semipopular force created during the Napoleonic wars. Army reforms meant a bigger defense budget and higher taxes.

Prussia had emerged from 1848 with a parliament of sorts, which was in the hands of the liberal middle class by 1859. The wealthy middle class, like the landed aristocracy, was greatly overrepresented by the Prussian electoral system, and it wanted society to be less, not more, militaristic. Above all, middle-class representatives wanted to establish once and for all that the parliament, not the king, had the ultimate political power. They also wanted to ensure that the army was responsible to Prussia's elected representatives and was not a "state within a state." These demands were popular. The parliament rejected the military budget in 1862, and the liberals triumphed completely in new elections. King William then called on Count Otto von Bismarck to head a new ministry and defy the parliament. This was a momentous choice.

Bismarck Takes Command

The most important figure in German history between Luther and Hitler, Otto von Bismarck (1815–1898) has been the object of enormous interest and debate. A great hero to some, a great villain to others, Bismarck was above all a master of politics. Born into the Prussian landowning aristocracy, the young Bismarck was a wild and tempestuous student given to duels and drinking. Proud of his Junker heritage and always devoted to

Freeing the Peasants in 1861 A noble landowner reads the emancipation decree to his serfs, dutifully assembled in front of his mansion on Prozorov estate. As this photograph suggests, the gap between the peasants and their former owners would remain enormous after 1861, in part because the government feared that complete freedom would lead to anarchy and upheaval. *(Novosti)*

mightily to the spread of Marxian thought and the transformation of the Russian revolutionary movement after 1890.

In 1881 Alexander II was assassinated by a small group of terrorists. The era of reform came to an abrupt end, for the new tsar, Alexander III (r. 1881–1894), was a determined reactionary. Russia, and indeed all of Europe, experienced hard times economically in the 1880s. Political modernization remained frozen until 1905, but economic modernization sped forward in the massive industrial surge of the 1890s. Nationalism played a decisive role, as it had after the Crimean War. The key leader was Sergei Witte, the tough, competent minister of finance from 1892 to 1903. Early in his career, Witte found in the writings of Friedrich List (see page 738) an analysis and a program for action. List had stressed the peril for Germany of remaining behind England in the 1830s and 1840s. Witte saw the same threat of industrial backwardness threatening Russia's power and greatness.

Witte moved forward on several fronts. A railroad manager by training, he believed that railroads were "a very powerful weapon . . . for the direction of the economic development of the country."[4] Therefore, the government built state-owned railroads rapidly, doubling the network to thirty-five thousand miles by the end of the century. The gigantic trans-Siberian line connecting Moscow with Vladivostok on the Pacific Ocean five thousand miles away was Witte's pride, and it was largely completed during his term of office. Following List's advice, Witte established high protective tariffs to build Russian industry, and he put the country on the gold standard of the "civilized world" in order to strengthen Russian finances.

Witte's greatest innovation, however, was to use the West to catch up with the West. He aggressively encouraged foreigners to use their abundant capital and advanced technology to build great factories in backward Russia. As he told the tsar, "The inflow of foreign capital is . . . the only way by which our industry will be able to supply our country quickly with abundant and cheap products."[5] This policy was brilliantly successful, especially in southern Russia. There, in eastern Ukraine, foreign capitalists and their engineers built an enormous and very modern steel and coal industry almost from scratch in little more than a decade. By 1900 only the United States, Germany, and Great Britain were producing more steel than Russia. The Russian petroleum industry had even pulled up alongside that of the United States and was producing and refining half the world's oil.

Witte knew how to keep foreigners in line. Once a leading foreign businessman came to him and angrily demanded that the Russian government fulfill a contract it had signed and pay certain debts immediately. Witte asked to see the contract. He read it and then carefully tore it to pieces and threw it in the wastepaper basket without a word of explanation. It was just such a fiercely autocratic and independent Russia that was catching up with the advanced nations of the West.

Bloody Sunday This print from a contemporary French newspaper shows the tragic conclusion of the effort to present a petition to the tsar on January 22, 1905. Soldiers on the left fire directly into the crowd of unarmed workers led by Father Gapon, who holds the petition and an upraised cross. A Cossack brigade charges another group of peaceful demonstrators on the bridge. *(Jean-Loup Charmet)*

The Revolution of 1905

Catching up partly meant vigorous territorial expansion, for this was the age of Western imperialism. By 1903 Russia had established a sphere of influence in Chinese Manchuria and was casting greedy eyes on northern Korea. When the diplomatic protests of equally imperialistic Japan were ignored, the Japanese launched a surprise attack in February 1904. To the amazement of self-confident Europeans, Asian Japan scored repeated victories, and Russia was forced in September 1905 to accept a humiliating defeat.

As is often the case, military disaster abroad brought political upheaval at home. The business and professional classes had long wanted to match economic with political modernization. Their minimal goal was to turn the last of Europe's absolutist monarchies into a liberal, representative regime. Factory workers, strategically concentrated in the large cities, had all the grievances of early industrialization and were organized in a radical and still illegal labor movement. Peasants had gained little from the era of reforms and were suffering from poverty and overpopulation. At the same time, nationalist sentiment was emerging among the empire's minorities. The politically and culturally dominant ethnic Russians were only about 45 percent of the population, and by 1900 some intellectuals among the subject nationalities were calling for self-rule and autonomy. Separatist nationalism was strongest among the Poles and Ukrainians. With the army pinned down in Manchuria, all these currents of discontent converged in the revolution of 1905.

The beginning of the revolution pointed up the incompetence of the government. On a Sunday in January 1905, a massive crowd of workers and their families converged peacefully on the Winter Palace in St. Petersburg to present a petition to the tsar. The workers were led by a trade-unionist priest named Father Gapon, who had been secretly supported by the police as a preferable alternative to more radical unions. Carrying icons and respectfully singing "God save the tsar," the workers did not know Nicholas II had fled the city. Suddenly troops opened fire, killing and wounding hundreds. The "Bloody Sunday" massacre turned ordinary workers against the tsar and produced a wave of general indignation.

Outlawed political parties came out into the open, and by the summer of 1905 strikes, peasant uprisings, revolts among minority nationalities, and troop mutinies were sweeping the country. The revolutionary surge culminated in October 1905 in a great paralyzing general strike, which forced the government to capitulate. The tsar issued the October Manifesto, which granted full civil rights and promised a popularly elected duma (parliament) with real legislative power. The manifesto split the opposition. It satisfied most moderate and liberal demands, but the Social Democrats rejected it and led a bloody workers' uprising in Moscow in December 1905. Frightened middle-class leaders helped the government repress the uprising and survive as a constitutional monarchy.

On the eve of the opening of the first Duma in May 1906, the government issued the new constitution, the Fundamental Laws. The tsar retained great powers. The Duma, elected indirectly by universal male suffrage, and a largely appointive upper house could debate and pass laws, but the tsar had an absolute veto. As in Bismarck's Germany, the emperor appointed his ministers, who did not need to command a majority in the Duma.

The disappointed, predominately middle-class liberals, the largest group in the newly elected Duma, saw the Fundamental Laws as a step backward. Efforts to cooperate with the tsar's ministers soon broke down. The tsar then dismissed the Duma, only to find that a more hostile and radical opposition was elected in 1907. After three months of deadlock, the tsar dismissed the second Duma. Thereupon he and his reactionary advisers unilaterally rewrote the electoral law so as to increase greatly the weight of the propertied classes at the expense of workers, peasants, and national minorities.

The new law did have the intended effect. With landowners assured half the seats in the Duma, the government secured a loyal majority in 1907 and again in 1912. Thus armed, the tough, energetic chief minister, Peter Stolypin, pushed through important agrarian reforms that were designed to break down collective village ownership of land and to encourage the more enterprising peasants—a strategy known as the "wager on the strong." On the eve of the First World War, Russia was partially modernized, a conservative constitutional monarchy with a peasant-based but industrializing economy.

THE RESPONSIVE NATIONAL STATE, 1871–1914

For central and western Europe, the unification of Italy and Germany by "blood and iron" marked the end of a dramatic period of nation building. After 1871 the heartland of Europe was organized into strong national states. Only on the borders of Europe—in Ireland and Russia, in Austria-Hungary and the Balkans—did subject peoples still strive for political unity and independence. Despite national differences, European domestic politics after 1871 had a common framework, the firmly established national state. The common themes within that framework were the emergence of mass politics and growing mass loyalty toward the national state.

For good reason, ordinary people—the masses of an industrializing, urbanizing society—felt increasing loyalty to their governments. More people could vote. By 1914 universal male suffrage had become the rule rather than the exception. This development had as much psychological as political significance. Ordinary men were no longer denied the right to vote because they lacked wealth or education. They felt that they counted; they could influence the government to some extent. They were becoming "part of the system."

Women also began to demand the right to vote. The women's suffrage movement achieved its first success in the western United States, and by 1913 women could vote in twelve states. Europe, too, moved slowly in this direction. In 1914 Norway gave the vote to most women. Elsewhere, women such as the English Emmeline Pankhurst were very militant in their demands. They heckled politicians and held public demonstrations. These efforts generally failed before 1914, but they prepared the way for the triumph of the women's suffrage movement immediately after World War I.

As the right to vote spread, politicians and parties in national parliaments represented the people more responsively. The multiparty system prevailing in most countries meant that parliamentary majorities were built on shifting coalitions of different parties, and this gave individual parties leverage to obtain benefits for their supporters. Governments also passed laws to alleviate general problems, thereby acquiring greater legitimacy and appearing more worthy of support.

There was a less positive side to building support for strong nation-states after 1871. Governments, often led by conservatives inspired by the examples of Cavour and Bismarck, found that they could manipulate national feeling to create a sense of unity and to divert attention away from underlying class conflicts. For example, conservative and moderate leaders who despised socialism found that workers who voted socialist would still rally around the flag in a diplomatic crisis or that they would cheer enthusiastically when distant territory of doubtful value was seized in Africa or Asia (see Chapter 26). Therefore, governing elites frequently channeled national sentiment in an antiliberal and militaristic direction after 1871. This policy helped manage domestic conflicts, but only at the expense of increasing the international tensions that erupted in 1914 in cataclysmic war and revolution (see Chapter 27).

The German Empire

Politics in Germany after 1871 reflected many of the general developments. The new German Empire was a federal union of Prussia and twenty-four smaller states. Much of the everyday business of government was conducted by the separate states, but there was a strong national government with a chancellor—until 1890, Bismarck—and a popularly elected lower house, called the *Reichstag.* Although Bismarck refused to be bound by a parliamentary majority, he tried nonetheless to maintain one. This situation gave the political parties opportunities. Until 1878 Bismarck relied mainly on the National Liberals, who had rallied to him after 1866. They supported legislation useful for further economic and legal unification of the country.

Less wisely, they backed Bismarck's attack on the Catholic church, the so-called *Kulturkampf,* or "struggle for civilization." Like Bismarck, the middle-class National Liberals were particularly alarmed by Pius IX's declaration of papal infallibility in 1870. That dogma seemed to ask German Catholics to put loyalty to their church above loyalty to their nation. Only in Protestant Prussia did the Kulturkampf have even limited success. Catholics throughout the country generally voted for the Catholic Center party, which blocked passage of national laws hostile to the church. Finally, in 1878 Bismarck abandoned his attack. Indeed, he and the Catholic Center party entered into an uneasy but mutually advantageous alliance. Their reasons for doing so were largely economic.

After a worldwide financial bust in 1873, European agriculture was in an increasingly difficult position. Wheat prices plummeted as cheap grain poured in from the United States, Canada, and Russia. New lands were opening up in North America and Russia, and the combination of railroads and technical improvements in shipping cut freight rates for grain drastically. European peasants, with their smaller, less efficient farms, could not compete in cereal production, especially in western and southern Germany. The peasantry there was largely Catholic, and the Catholic Center party was thus converted to higher tariffs to protect the economic interests of its supporters.

The same competitive pressures caused the Protestant Junkers, who owned large estates in eastern Germany, to embrace the cause of higher tariffs. These noble landowners were joined by some of the iron and steel magnates of the Prussian Rhineland and Westphalia who had previously favored free trade. With three such influential groups lobbying energetically, Bismarck was happy to go along with a new protective tariff in 1879. In doing so, he won new supporters in the Reichstag—the Center party of the Catholics and the Conservative party of the Prussian landowners—and he held on to most of the National Liberals.

Bismarck had been looking for a way to increase taxes and raise more money for the government. The solution he chose was higher tariffs. Many other governments acted similarly. The 1880s and 1890s saw a widespread return to protectionism. France, in particular, established very high tariffs to protect agriculture and industry, peasants and manufacturers, from foreign competition. Thus the German government and other governments responded effectively to a major economic problem and won greater loyalty. The general rise of protectionism in the late nineteenth century was also an outstanding example of the dangers of self-centered nationalism: high tariffs led to international name-calling and nasty trade wars.

As for socialism, Bismarck tried to stop its growth in Germany because he genuinely feared its revolutionary language and allegiance to a movement transcending the nation-state. In 1878, after two attempts on the life of William I by radicals (though not socialists), Bismarck used a carefully orchestrated national outcry to ram through the Reichstag a law that strictly controlled socialist meetings and publications and outlawed the Social Democratic party, which was thereby driven underground. However, German socialists displayed a discipline and organization worthy of the Prussian army itself. Bismarck decided to try another tack.

Thus Bismarck's essentially conservative nation-state pioneered with social measures designed to win the support of working-class people. In 1883 he pushed through the Reichstag the first of several modern social security laws to help wage earners. The laws of 1883 and 1884 established national sickness and accident insurance; the law of 1889 established old-age pensions and retirement benefits. Henceforth sick, injured, and retired workers could look forward to some regular benefits from the state. This national social security system, paid for through compulsory contributions by wage earners and employers as well as grants from the state, was the first of its kind anywhere. (The United States would not take similar measures for fifty years.) Bismarck's social security system did not wean workers from voting socialist, but it did give them a small stake in the system and protect them from some of the uncertainties of the complex urban industrial world. This enormously significant development was a product of political competition and government efforts to win popular support.

Increasingly, the great issues in German domestic politics were socialism and the Marxian Social Democratic party. In 1890 the new emperor, the young, idealistic, and unstable William II (r. 1888–1918), opposed Bismarck's attempt to renew the law outlawing the Social Democratic party. Eager to rule in his own right and to earn the support of the workers, William II forced Bismarck to resign. After the "dropping of the pilot," German foreign policy changed profoundly and mostly for the worse, but the government did pass new laws to aid workers and to legalize socialist political activity.

Yet William II was no more successful than Bismarck in getting workers to renounce socialism. Indeed, socialist ideas spread rapidly, and more and more Social

The Need for Social Security This dramatic painting of busy workers in an iron-rolling mill in Berlin highlights the many dangers of the industrial workplace. Industrial accidents that killed or maimed were a fact of life, as were work-related illnesses and periodic unemployment. Germany's pioneering social security laws were an influential response to these challenges. *(Alte Nationalgalerie, Berlin/AKG London)*

Democrats were elected to the Reichstag in the 1890s. After opposing a colonial war in German Southwest Africa in 1906 that led to important losses in the general elections of 1907, the German Social Democratic party broadened its base and adopted a more patriotic tone. In the elections of 1912, the party scored a great victory, becoming the largest single party in the Reichstag. This victory shocked aristocrats and their wealthy conservative middle-class allies, heightening the fears of an impending socialist upheaval in both groups. Yet the "revolutionary" socialists were actually becoming less and less revolutionary in Germany. In the years before World War I, the strength of socialist opposition to greater military spending and imperialist expansion declined substantially, for example. German socialists identified increasingly with the German state, and they concentrated on gradual social and political reform.

Republican France

Although Napoleon III's reign made some progress in reducing antagonisms between classes, the war with Prussia undid these efforts, and in 1871 France seemed hopelessly divided once again. The patriotic republicans who proclaimed the Third Republic in Paris after the military disaster at Sedan refused to admit defeat. They defended Paris with great heroism for weeks, living off rats and zoo animals until they were starved into submission by German armies in January 1871. When national elections then sent a large majority of conservatives and monarchists to the National Assembly and France's new leaders decided they had no choice but to surrender Alsace and Lorraine to Germany, the traumatized Parisians exploded in patriotic frustration and proclaimed the Paris Commune in March 1871. Vaguely radical, the leaders of the Commune wanted to govern Paris without interference from the conservative French countryside. The National Assembly, led by aging politician Adolphe Thiers, would hear none of it. The Assembly ordered the French army into Paris and brutally crushed the Commune. Twenty thousand people died in the fighting. As in June 1848, it was Paris against the provinces, French against French.

Out of this tragedy, France slowly formed a new national unity, achieving considerable stability before 1914. How is one to account for this? Luck played a part. Until 1875 the monarchists in the "republican" National Assembly had a majority but could not agree who should be king. The compromise Bourbon candidate refused to rule except under the white flag of his ancestors—a completely unacceptable condition. In the meantime, Thiers's destruction of the radical Commune and his other firm measures showed the fearful provinces and the middle class that the Third Republic might be moderate and socially conservative, escaping the excesses that many still associated with the republican government of Robespierre and the Terror (see pages 704–706). France therefore retained the republic, though reluctantly. As President Thiers cautiously said, this was "the government which divides us least."

Another stabilizing factor was the skill and determination of the moderate republican leaders in the early years. The most famous of these was Léon Gambetta, the son of an Italian grocer, a warm, easygoing, unsuccessful lawyer who had turned professional politician. A master of emerging mass politics, Gambetta combined eloquence with the personal touch as he preached a republic of truly equal opportunity. Gambetta was also instrumental in establishing absolute parliamentary supremacy between 1877 and 1879, when the deputies challenged Marshall MacMahon and forced the somewhat autocratic president of the republic to resign. By 1879 the great majority of members of both the upper and the lower houses of the National Assembly were republicans. Although these republicans were split among many parliamentary groups and later among several parties—a situation that led to constant coalition politics and the rapid turnover of ministers—the Third Republic had firm foundations after almost a decade.

The moderate republicans sought to preserve their creation by winning the hearts and minds of the next generation. Trade unions were fully legalized, and France acquired a colonial empire. More important, under the leadership of Jules Ferry, the moderate republicans of small towns and villages passed a series of laws between 1879 and 1886 establishing free compulsory elementary education for both girls and boys. At the same time, they greatly expanded the state system of public tax-supported schools. Thus France shared fully in the general expansion of public education, which served as a critical nation-building tool throughout the Western world in the late nineteenth century.

In France most elementary and much secondary education had traditionally been in the parochial schools of the Catholic church, which had long been hostile to republics and to much of secular life. Free compulsory elementary education in France became secular republican education. The pledge of allegiance and the national anthem replaced the catechism and the "Ave Maria." Militant young male and female teachers carried the ideology of patriotic republicanism into every corner of France. In their classes, these women and men

Captain Alfred Dreyfus Leaving an 1899 reconsideration of his original court martial, Dreyfus receives an insulting "guard of dishonor" from soldiers whose backs are turned. Top army leaders were determined to brand Dreyfus as a traitor. *(Bibliothèque Nationale, Paris)*

sought to win the loyalty of the young citizens to the republic so that France would never again vote en masse for dictators like the two Napoleons.

Unlike most Western countries (including the United States), which insisted on the total "purity" of their female elementary teachers and would not hire married women, the Third Republic actively encouraged young teachers to marry and guaranteed that both partners would teach in the same location. There were three main reasons for this unusual policy. First, married female (and male) teachers with their own children provided a vivid contrast to celibate nuns (and priests), who had for generations stood for most primary education in the popular mind. Second, the republican leaders believed that married women (and men) would better cope with the potential loneliness and social isolation of unfamiliar towns and villages, especially where the local Catholic school was strong. Third, French politicians and opinion leaders worried continually about France's very low birthrate after 1870, and they believed that women combining teaching careers and motherhood would provide the country with a good example. Hiring married schoolteachers was part of an effort to create a whole new culture of universal, secular, and republican education. This illustrates a larger truth—that truly lasting political change must usually be supported by changes in the underlying culture.

Although the educational reforms of the 1880s disturbed French Catholics, many of them rallied to the republic in the 1890s. The limited acceptance of the modern world by the more liberal Pope Leo XIII (1878–1903) eased tensions between church and state. Unfortunately, the Dreyfus affair changed all that.

Alfred Dreyfus, a Jewish captain in the French army, was falsely accused and convicted of treason. His family never doubted his innocence and fought to reopen the case, enlisting the support of prominent republicans and intellectuals such as novelist Emile Zola. In 1898 and 1899, the case split France apart. On one side was the army, which had manufactured evidence against Dreyfus, joined by anti-Semites and most of the Catholic establishment. On the other side stood the civil libertarians and most of the more radical republicans.

This battle, which eventually led to Dreyfus's being declared innocent, revived republican feeling against the church. Between 1901 and 1905, the government severed all ties between the state and the Catholic church after centuries of close relations. The salaries of priests and bishops were no longer paid by the government, and all churches were given to local committees of lay Catholics. Catholic schools were put completely on their own financially, and in a short time they lost a third of their students. The state school system's power of indoctrination was greatly strengthened. In France only the growing socialist movement, with its very different and thoroughly secular ideology, stood in opposition to patriotic, republican nationalism.

Great Britain and Ireland

Britain in the late nineteenth century has often been seen as a shining example of peaceful and successful political evolution. Germany was stuck with a manipulated parliament that gave an irresponsible emperor too much power; France had a quarrelsome parliament that gave its presidents too little power. Great Britain, in contrast, seemed to enjoy an effective two-party parliament that skillfully guided the country from classical liberalism to full-fledged democracy with hardly a misstep.

This view of Great Britain is not so much wrong as it is incomplete. After the right to vote was granted to males of the solid middle class in 1832, opinion leaders and politicians wrestled with the uncertainties of a further expansion of the franchise. In his famous essay *On Liberty,* published in 1859, philosopher John Stuart Mill (1806–1873), the leading heir to the Benthamite tradition (see page 792), probed the problem of how to protect the rights of individuals and minorities in the emerging age of mass electoral participation. Mill pleaded eloquently for the practical and moral value inherent in safeguarding individual differences and unpopular opinions. In 1867 Benjamin Disraeli and the Conservatives extended the vote to all middle-class males and the best-paid workers. The son of a Jewish stockbroker and himself a novelist and urban dandy, the ever-fascinating Disraeli (1804–1881) was willing to risk this "leap in the dark" in order to gain new supporters. The Conservative party, he believed, needed to broaden its traditional base of aristocratic and landed support if it was to survive. After 1867 English political parties and electoral campaigns became more modern, and the "lower orders" appeared to vote as responsibly as their "betters." Hence the Third Reform Bill of 1884 gave the vote to almost every adult male.

While the House of Commons was drifting toward democracy, the House of Lords was content to slumber nobly. Between 1901 and 1910, however, that bastion of aristocratic conservatism tried to reassert itself. Acting as supreme court of the land, it ruled against labor unions in two important decisions. And after the Liberal party came to power in 1906, the Lords vetoed several measures passed by the Commons, including the so-called People's Budget. The Lords finally capitulated, as they had done in 1832, when the king threatened to create enough new peers to pass the bill.

Aristocratic conservatism yielded to popular democracy once and for all. The result was that extensive social welfare measures, slow to come to Great Britain, were passed in a spectacular rush between 1906 and 1914. During those years, the Liberal party, inspired by the fiery Welshman David Lloyd George (1863–1945), substantially raised taxes on the rich as part of the People's Budget. This income helped the government pay for national health insurance, unemployment benefits, old-age pensions, and a host of other social measures. The state was integrating the urban masses socially as well as politically.

This record of accomplishment was only part of the story, however. On the eve of World War I, the ever-emotional, ever-unanswered question of Ireland brought Great Britain to the brink of civil war. In the 1840s, Ireland had been decimated by famine, which fueled an Irish revolutionary movement. Thereafter, the English slowly granted concessions, such as the abolition of the privileges of the Anglican church and rights for Irish peasants. Liberal prime minister William Gladstone (1809–1898), who had proclaimed twenty years earlier that "my mission is to pacify Ireland," introduced bills to give Ireland self-government in 1886 and in 1893. They failed to pass. After two decades of relative quiet, Irish nationalists in the British Parliament saw their chance. They supported the Liberals in their battle for the People's Budget and received a home-rule bill for Ireland in return.

Thus Ireland, the emerald isle, was on the brink of achieving self-government. Yet Ireland was (and is) composed of two peoples. As much as the Irish Catholic majority in the southern counties wanted home rule, precisely that much did the Irish Protestants of the northern counties of Ulster come to oppose it. Motivated by the accumulated fears and hostilities of generations, the Protestants of Ulster refused to submerge themselves in a Catholic Ireland, just as Irish Catholics had refused to submit to a Protestant Britain.

The Ulsterites vowed to resist home rule in northern Ireland. By December 1913 they had raised 100,000 armed volunteers, and they were supported by much of English public opinion. Thus in 1914 the Liberals in the House of Lords introduced a compromise home-rule bill that did not apply to the northern counties. This bill, which openly betrayed promises made to Irish nationalists, was rejected, and in September the original home-rule bill was passed but simultaneously suspended for the duration of the hostilities—the momentous Irish question had been overtaken by an earth-shattering world war in August 1914.

Irish developments illustrated once again the power of national feeling and national movements in the nineteenth century. Moreover, they were proof that governments could not elicit greater loyalty unless they could capture and control that elemental current of national feeling. Though Great Britain had much going for it—power, Parliament, prosperity—none of these availed in the face of the conflicting nationalisms espoused by Catholics and Protestants in northern Ireland. Similarly, progressive Sweden was powerless to stop the growth of the Norwegian national movement, which culminated in Norway's breaking away from Sweden and becoming a fully independent nation in 1905. In this light, one can also see how hopeless was the case of the Ottoman Empire in Europe in the later nineteenth century. It was only a matter of time before the Serbs, Bulgarians, and Romanians would break away, and they did.

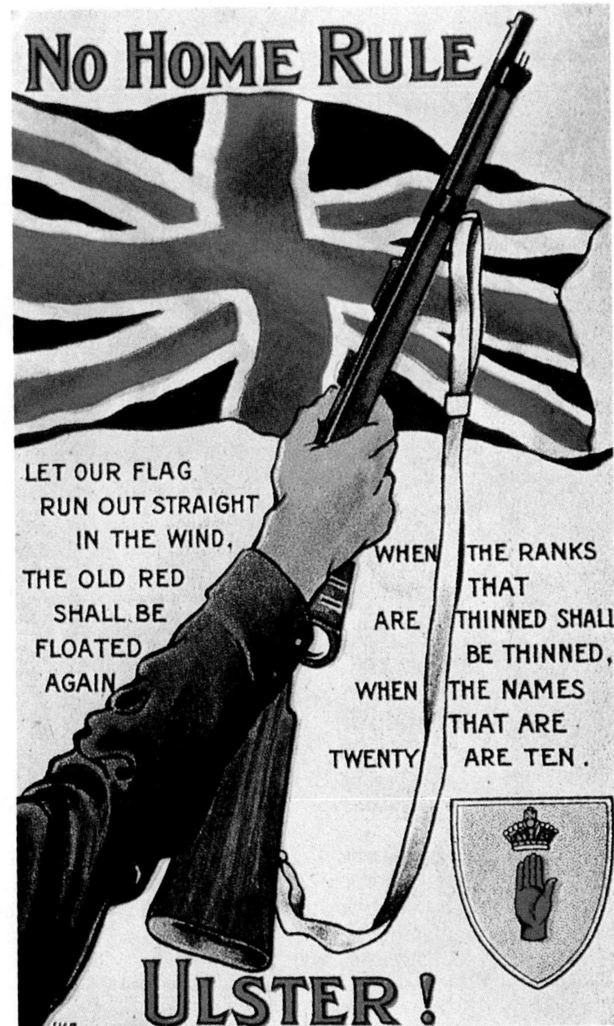

"No Home Rule" Posters like this one helped to foment pro-British, anti-Catholic sentiment in the northern Irish counties of Ulster before the First World War. The rifle raised defiantly and the accompanying rhyme are a thinly veiled threat of armed rebellion and civil war. *(Courtesy, Ulster Museum, Belfast)*

The Austro-Hungarian Empire

The dilemma of conflicting nationalisms in Ireland also helps one appreciate how desperate the situation in the Austro-Hungarian Empire had become by the early twentieth century. In 1849 Magyar nationalism had driven Hungarian patriots to declare an independent Hungarian republic, which was savagely crushed by Russian and Austrian armies (see pages 781–782). Throughout the 1850s, Hungary was ruled as a conquered territory, and Emperor Francis Joseph and his bureaucracy tried hard to centralize the state and Germanize the language and culture of the different nationalities.

Then in the wake of defeat by Prussia in 1866, a weakened Austria was forced to strike a compromise and establish the so-called dual monarchy. The empire was divided in two, and the nationalistic Magyars gained virtual independence for Hungary. Henceforth each half of the empire agreed to deal with its own "barbarians"—its own minorities—as it saw fit. The two states were joined only by a shared monarch and common ministries for finance, defense, and foreign affairs. The popular mayor of Vienna from 1897 to 1910, Dr. Karl Lueger, combined anti-Semitic rhetoric with calls for "Christian socialism" and municipal ownership of basic services. Lueger appealed especially to the

The Language Ordinances of 1897, which were intended to satisfy the Czechs by establishing equality between German and the local language in non-German districts of Austria, produced a powerful backlash among Germans. This wood engraving shows troops dispersing German protesters of the new law before the parliament building. *(Österreichische Nationalbibliothek)*

German lower middle class—and to an unsuccessful young artist named Adolf Hitler.

In Hungary the Magyar nobility in 1867 restored the constitution of 1848 and used it to dominate both the Magyar peasantry and the minority populations until 1914. Only the wealthiest one-fourth of adult males had the right to vote, making the parliament the creature of the Magyar elite. Laws promoting the use of the Magyar (Hungarian) language in schools and government were rammed through and bitterly resented, especially by the Croatians and Romanians. While Magyar extremists campaigned loudly for total separation from Austria, the radical leaders of the subject nationalities dreamed in turn of independence from Hungary. Unlike most major countries, which harnessed nationalism to strengthen the state after 1871, the Austro-Hungarian Empire was progressively weakened and destroyed by it.

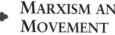

Marxism and the Socialist Movement

Nationalism served, for better or worse, as a new unifying principle. But what about socialism? Did the rapid growth of socialist parties, which were generally Marxian parties dedicated to an international proletarian revolution, mean that national states had failed to gain the support of workers? Certainly, many prosperous and conservative citizens were greatly troubled by the socialist movement. And numerous historians have portrayed the years before 1914 as a time of increasing conflict between revolutionary socialism, on the one hand, and a nationalist alliance of the conservative aristocracy and the prosperous middle class, on the other. This question requires close examination.

The Socialist International

Socialism appealed to large numbers of workingmen and workingwomen in the late nineteenth century, and the growth of socialist parties after 1871 was phenomenal. (See the feature "Listening to the Past: The Making of a Socialist" on pages 854–855.) Neither Bismarck's antisocialist laws nor his extensive social security system checked the growth of the German Social Democratic party, which espoused the Marxian ideology. By 1912 it had millions of followers and was the largest party in the Reichstag. Socialist parties also grew in other countries, though nowhere else with such success. In 1883 Russian exiles in Switzerland founded the Russian Social Democratic party, which grew rapidly after 1890 despite internal disputes. In France various socialist parties re-emerged in the 1880s after the carnage of the Paris Commune. They were finally unified in 1905 in an increasingly powerful Marxian party called the French Section of the Workers International. Belgium and Austria-Hungary also had strong socialist parties.

As the name of the French party suggests, Marxian socialist parties were eventually linked together in an international organization. As early as 1848, Marx had laid out his intellectual system in *The Communist Manifesto* (see pages 765–766). He had declared that "the working men have no country," and he had urged proletarians of all nations to unite against their governments. Joining the flood of radicals and republicans who fled continental Europe for England and America after the unsuccessful revolutions of 1848, Marx settled in London. Poor and depressed, he lived on his meager earnings as a journalist and on the gifts of his friend Friedrich Engels. Marx never stopped thinking of revolution. Digging deeply into economics and history, he concluded that revolution follows economic crisis and tried to prove this position in *Critique of Political Economy* (1859) and in his greatest theoretical work, *Capital* (1867).

The bookish Marx also excelled as a practical organizer. In 1864 he played an important role in founding the First International of socialists—the International Working Men's Association. In the following years, he battled successfully to control the organization and used its annual meetings as a means of spreading his realistic, "scientific" doctrines of inevitable socialist revolution. Then Marx enthusiastically embraced the passionate, vaguely radical patriotism of the Paris Commune and its terrible conflict with the French National Assembly as a giant step toward socialist revolution. This impetuous action frightened many of his early supporters, especially the more moderate British labor leaders. The First International collapsed.

Yet international proletarian solidarity remained an important objective for Marxists. In 1889, as the individual parties in different countries grew stronger, socialist leaders came together to form the Second International, which lasted until 1914. The International was only a federation of national socialist parties, but it had a great psychological impact. Every three years, delegates from the different parties met to interpret Marxian doctrines and plan coordinated action. May 1 (May Day) was declared an annual international one-day strike, a day of marches and demonstrations. A permanent executive for the International was established. Many feared and many others rejoiced in the growing power of socialism and the Second International.

Unions and Revisionism

Was socialism really radical and revolutionary in these years? On the whole, it was not. Indeed, as socialist parties grew and attracted large numbers of members, they looked more and more toward gradual change and steady improvement for the working class and less and less toward revolution. The mainstream of European socialism became militantly moderate; that is, socialists increasingly combined radical rhetoric with sober action.

Workers themselves were progressively less inclined to follow radical programs. There were several reasons for this. As workers gained the right to vote and to participate politically in the nation-state, they focused their attention more on elections than on revolutions. And as workers won real, tangible benefits, this furthered the process. Workers were also not immune to patriotic education and indoctrination during military service, and many responded positively to drum-beating parades and aggressive foreign policy as they loyally voted for socialists. Nor were workers a unified social group.

Perhaps most important of all, workers' standard of living rose gradually but substantially after 1850 as the promise of the Industrial Revolution was at least

"Greetings from the May Day Festival" Workers participated enthusiastically in the annual one-day strike on May 1 to honor internationalist socialist solidarity, as this postcard from a happy woman visitor to her cousin suggests. Speeches, picnics, and parades were the order of the day, and workers celebrated their respectability and independent culture. Picture postcards developed with railroads and mass travel. *(AKG London)*

partially realized. In Great Britain, for example, workers could buy almost twice as much with their wages in 1906 as in 1850, and most of the increase came after 1870. Workers experienced similar gradual increases in most continental countries after 1850, though much less strikingly in late-developing Russia. Improvement in the standard of living was much more than merely a matter of higher wages. The quality of life improved dramatically in urban areas. For all these reasons, workers tended more and more to become militantly moderate: they demanded gains, but they were less likely to take to the barricades in pursuit of them.

The growth of labor unions reinforced this trend toward moderation. In the early stages of industrialization, modern unions were generally prohibited by law. A famous law of the French Revolution had declared all guilds and unions illegal in the name of "liberty" in 1791. In Great Britain, attempts by workers to unite were considered criminal conspiracies after 1799. Other countries had similar laws, and these obviously hampered union development. In France, for example, about two hundred workers were imprisoned each year between 1825 and 1847 for taking part in illegal combinations. Unions were considered subversive bodies, only to be hounded and crushed.

From this sad position workers struggled to escape. Great Britain led the way in 1824 and 1825 when unions won the right to exist but (generally) not the right to strike. After the collapse of Robert Owen's attempt to form one big union in the 1830s (see page 749), new and more practical kinds of unions appeared. Limited primarily to highly skilled workers such as machinists and carpenters, the "new model unions" avoided both radical politics and costly strikes. Instead, their sober, respectable leaders concentrated on winning better wages and hours for their members through were ascribed to the Anarchists, and the police made use of them to oppress the rising workmen's movement. . . . I followed the trial of the Anarchists with passionate sympathy. I read all the speeches, and because, as always happens, Social Democrats, whom the authorities really wanted to attack, were among the accused, I learned their views. I became full of enthusiasm. Every single Social Democrat . . . seemed to me a hero. . . .

There was unrest among the workers . . . and demonstrations of protest followed. When these were repeated the military entered the "threatened" streets. . . . In the evenings I rushed in the greatest excitement from the factory to the scene of the disturbance. The military did not frighten me; I only left the place when it was "cleared."

Later on my mother and I lived with one of my brothers who had married. Friends came to him, among them some intelligent workmen. One of these workmen was particularly intelligent, and . . . could talk on many subjects. He was the first Social Democrat I knew. He brought me many books, and explained to me the difference between Anarchism and Socialism. I heard from him, also for the first time, what a republic was, and in spite of my former enthusiasm for royal dynasties, I also declared myself in favour of a republican form of government. I saw everything so near and so clearly, that I actually counted the weeks which must still elapse before the revolution of state and society would take place.

From this workman I received the first Social Democratic party organ. . . . I first learned from it to understand and judge of my own lot. I learned to see that all I had suffered was the result not of a divine ordinance, but of an unjust organization of society. . . .

In the factory I became another woman. . . . I told my [female] comrades all that I had read of the workers' movement. Formerly I had often told stories when they had begged me for them. But instead of narrating . . . the fate of some queen, I now held forth on oppression and exploitation. I told of accumulated wealth in the hands of a few, and introduced as a contrast the shoemakers who had no shoes and the tailors who had no clothes. On breaks I read aloud the articles in the Social Democratic paper and explained what Socialism was as far as I understood it. . . . [While I was reading] it often happened that one of the clerks passing by shook his head and said to another clerk: "The girl speaks like a man."

✣ 1890 engraving of a meeting of workers in Berlin. *(Bildarchiv Preussischer Kulturbesitz)*

Questions for Analysis

1. How did Popp describe and interpret work in the factory?
2. To what extent did her socialist interpretation of factory life fit the facts she described?
3. What were Popp's political interests before she became a socialist?
4. How and why did she become a Social Democrat?
5. Was this account likely to lead other working-women to socialism? Why or why not?

Source: Slightly adapted from A. Popp, *The Autobiography of a Working Woman,* trans. E. C. Harvey (Chicago: F. G. Browne, 1913), pp. 29, 34–35, 39, 66–69, 71, 74, 82–90.

CHAPTER

26 The West and the World

The Emigrant Ship by the British painter Charles J. Staniland, 1898. *(Bradford Art Galleries and Museums/Bridgeman Art Library, London/New York)*

he promoted caused cotton production and exports to Europe to boom. Ismail also borrowed large sums to install modern communications, and with his support the Suez Canal was completed by a French company in 1869. The Arabic of the masses, rather than the Turkish of the conquerors, became the official language, and young Egyptians educated in Europe helped spread new skills and new ideas in the bureaucracy. Cairo acquired modern boulevards, Western hotels, and an opera house. As Ismail proudly declared, "My country is no longer in Africa, we now form part of Europe."[4]

Yet Ismail was too impatient and too reckless. His projects were enormously expensive, and the sale of his stock in the Suez Canal to the British government did not relieve the situation. By 1876 Egypt owed foreign bondholders a colossal $450 million and could not pay the interest on its debt. Rather than let Egypt go bankrupt and repudiate its loans, as had some Latin American countries and U.S. state governments in the early nineteenth century, the governments of France and Great Britain intervened politically to protect the European bankers who held the Egyptian bonds. They forced Ismail to appoint French and British commissioners to oversee Egyptian finances so that the Egyptian debt would be paid in full. This was a momentous decision. It implied direct European political control and was a sharp break with the previous pattern of trade and investment. Throughout most of the nineteenth century, Europeans had used naked military might and political force primarily to make sure that non-Western lands would accept European trade and investment. Now Europeans were going to determine the state budget and effectively rule Egypt.

Foreign financial control evoked a violent nationalistic reaction among Egyptian religious leaders, young intellectuals, and army officers. In 1879, under the leadership of Colonel Ahmed Arabi, they formed the Egyptian Nationalist party. Continuing diplomatic pressure, which forced Ismail to abdicate in favor of his weak son, Tewfiq (r. 1879–1892), resulted in bloody anti-European riots in Alexandria in 1882. A number of Europeans were killed, and Tewfiq and his court had to flee to British ships for safety. When the British fleet bombarded Alexandria, more riots swept the country, and Colonel Arabi declared that "an irreconcilable war existed between the Egyptians and the English." But a British expeditionary force decimated Arabi's forces and as a result occupied all of Egypt.

The British said their occupation was temporary, but British armies remained in Egypt until 1956. They maintained the façade of the khedive's government as an autonomous province of the Ottoman Empire, but the khedive was a mere puppet. The able British consul, General Evelyn Baring, later Lord Cromer, ruled the country after 1883. Once a vocal opponent of involvement in Egypt, Baring was a paternalistic reformer who had come to believe that "without European interference and initiative reform is impossible here." Baring's rule did result in tax reforms and better conditions for peasants, while foreign bondholders tranquilly collected the interest on their investments and Egyptian nationalists nursed their injured pride.

In Egypt Baring and the British reluctantly but spectacularly provided a new model for European expansion in densely populated lands. Such expansion was based on military force, political domination, and a self-justifying ideology of beneficial reform. This model was to predominate until 1914. Thus did Europe's Industrial Revolution lead to tremendous political as well as economic expansion throughout the world.

The Great Migration

A poignant human drama was interwoven with economic expansion: millions of people pulled up stakes and left their ancestral lands in the course of history's greatest migration. To millions of ordinary people, for whom the opening of China and the interest on the Egyptian debt had not the slightest significance, this great movement was the central experience in the saga of Western expansion. It was, in part, because of this great migration that the West's impact on the world in the nineteenth century was so powerful and many-sided.

The Pressure of Population

In the early eighteenth century, the growth of European population entered its third and decisive stage, which continued unabated until the twentieth century (see Chapter 19). Birthrates eventually declined in the nineteenth century, but so did death rates, mainly because of the rising standard of living and secondarily because of the medical revolution. Thus the population of Europe (including Asiatic Russia) more than doubled, from approximately 188 million in 1800 to roughly 432 million in 1900.

These figures actually understate Europe's population explosion, for between 1815 and 1932 more than

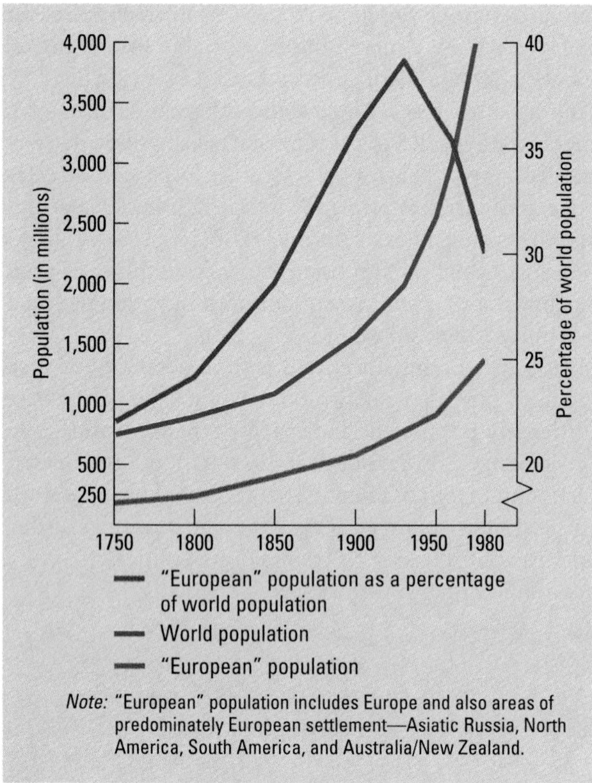

FIGURE 26.2 The Increase of European and World Populations, 1750–1980 *(Sources: W. Woodruff,* Impact of Western Man: A Study of Europe's Role in the World Economy. *St. Martin's Press, New York, 1967, p. 103; United Nations,* Statistical Yearbook, 1982, *1985, pp. 2–3.)*

60 million people left Europe. These migrants went primarily to the "areas of European settlement"—North and South America, Australia, New Zealand, and Siberia—where they contributed to a rapid growth in numbers. The population of North America (the United States and Canada) alone grew from 6 million to 81 million between 1800 and 1900 because of continual immigration and high fertility rates. Since population grew more slowly in Africa and Asia than in Europe, as Figure 26.2 shows, Europeans and people of European origin jumped from about 22 percent of the world's total to about 38 percent on the eve of World War I.

The growing number of Europeans provided further impetus for Western expansion. It was a driving force behind emigration. As in the eighteenth century, the rapid increase in numbers put pressure on the land and led to land hunger and relative overpopulation in area after area. In most countries, migration increased twenty years after a rapid growth in population, as many children of the baby boom grew up, saw little available land and few opportunities, and migrated. This pattern was especially prevalent when rapid population increase predated extensive industrial development, which offered the best long-term hope of creating jobs within the country and reducing poverty. Thus millions of country folk went abroad as well as to nearby cities in search of work and economic opportunity. The case of the Irish, who left in large numbers for Britain during the Industrial Revolution and for the United States after the potato famine, was extreme but not unique.

Before looking at the people who migrated, let us consider three facts. First, the number of men and women who left Europe increased rapidly before World War I. As Figure 26.3 shows, more than 11 million left in the first decade of the twentieth century, over five times the number departing in the 1850s. The outflow of migrants was clearly an enduring characteristic of European society for the entire period.

Second, different countries had very different patterns of movement. As Figure 26.3 also shows, people left Britain and Ireland (which are not distinguished in the British figures) in large numbers from the 1840s on. This emigration reflected not only rural poverty but also the movement of skilled, industrial technicians and the preferences shown to British migrants in the British Empire. Ultimately, about one-third of all European migrants between 1840 and 1920 came from the British Isles. German migration was quite different. It grew irregularly after about 1830, reaching a first peak in the early 1850s and another in the early 1880s. Thereafter it declined rapidly, for Germany's rapid industrialization was providing adequate jobs at home. This pattern contrasted sharply with that of Italy. More and more Italians left the country right up to 1914, reflecting severe problems in Italian villages and relatively slow industrial growth. Thus, migration patterns mirrored social and economic conditions in the various European countries and provinces.

Third, although the United States absorbed the largest number of European migrants, less than half of all migrants went to the United States. Asiatic Russia, Canada, Argentina, Brazil, Australia, and New Zealand also attracted large numbers, as Figure 26.4 shows. Moreover, migrants accounted for a larger proportion of the total population in Argentina, Brazil, and Canada than in the United States. Between 1900 and 1910,

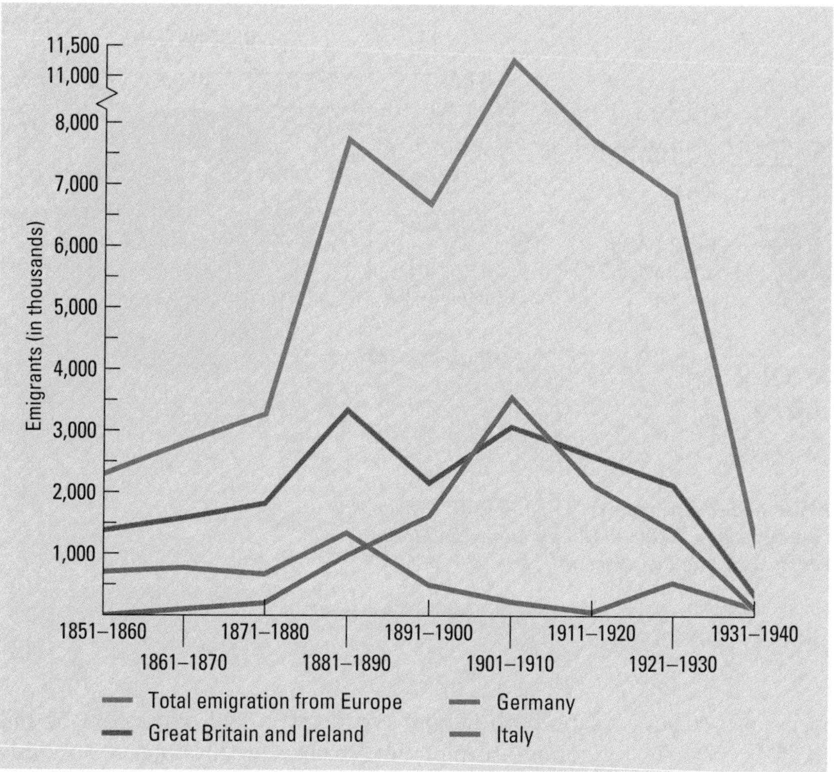

FIGURE 26.3 Emigration from Europe by Decades, 1851–1940 *(Source: W. Woodruff, ed.,* Impact of Western Man: A Study of Europe's Role in the World Economy. *Copyright © 1967 by W. Woodruff. Reprinted by permission of St. Martin's Press, Inc.)*

for example, new arrivals represented 3 percent of Argentina's population each year, as opposed to only 1 percent for the United States. The common American assumption that European migration meant migration to the United States is quite inaccurate.

European Migrants

What kind of people left Europe, and what were their reasons for doing so? Most were poor people from rural areas, though seldom from the poorest classes. Indeed, the European migrant was most often a small peasant landowner or a village craftsman whose traditional way of life was threatened by too little land, estate agriculture, and cheap, factory-made goods. German peasants who left the Rhineland and southwestern Germany between 1830 and 1854, for example, felt trapped by what Friedrich List called the "dwarf economy," with its tiny landholdings and declining craft industries. Selling out and moving to buy much cheaper land in the American Midwest became a common response. Contrary to what is often said, the European migrant was generally not a desperately impoverished landless peasant or urban proletarian, but an energetic small farmer or skilled artisan trying hard to stay ahead of poverty.

Determined to maintain or improve their status, migrants were a great asset to the countries that received them. This was doubly so because the vast majority were young and very often unmarried. Fully 67 percent of those admitted to the United States were under thirty-one years of age, and 90 percent were under forty. They came in the prime of life and were ready to work hard in the new land, at least for a time. Many Europeans moved but remained within Europe, settling temporarily or permanently in another European country. Jews from eastern Europe and peasants from Ireland migrated to Great Britain, Russians and Poles

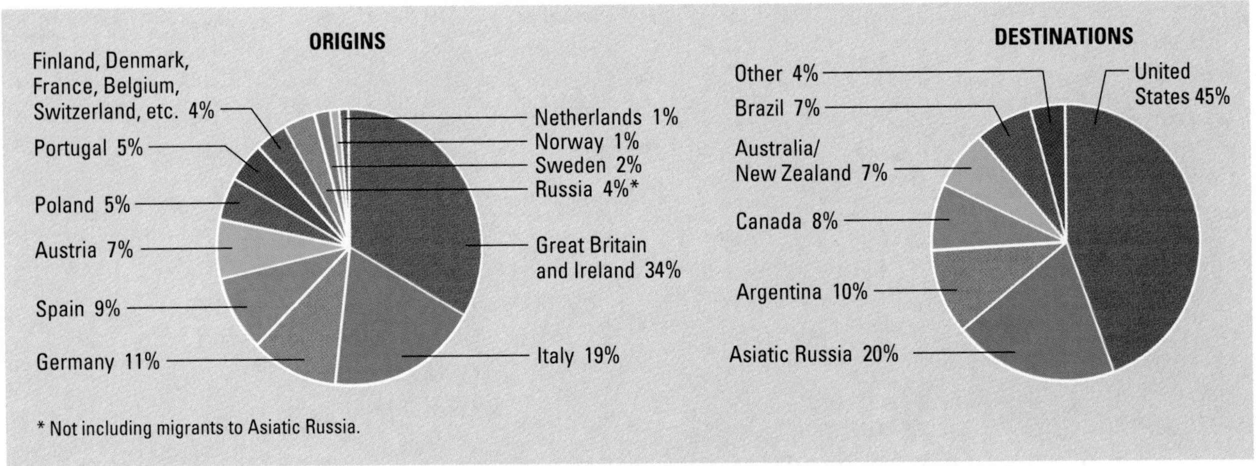

FIGURE 26.4 Origin and Destination of European Emigrants, 1851–1960 *(Source: W. Woodruff,* Impact of Western Man: A Study of Europe's Role in the World Economy. *St. Martin's Press, New York, 1967, pp. 108–109 and references cited therein. Reprinted with permission of St. Martin's Press, Inc.)*

sought work in Germany, and Latin peoples from Spain, Portugal, and Italy entered France.

Even in the New World, many Europeans, especially by the end of the nineteenth century, were truly migrants as opposed to immigrants—that is, they returned home after some time abroad. One in two migrants to Argentina and probably one in three to the United States eventually returned to their native land. The likelihood of repatriation varied greatly by nationality. Seven out of eight people who migrated from the Balkans to the United States in the late nineteenth century returned to their countries. At the other extreme, only one person in ten from Ireland and only one in twenty among eastern European Jews returned to their country of origin.

Once again, the possibility of buying land in the old country was of central importance. Land in Ireland (as well as in England and Scotland) was tightly held by large, often absentee landowners, and little land was available for purchase. In Russia Jews were left in relative peace until the assassination of Alexander II by non-Jewish terrorists in 1881 brought a new tsar and an official policy of pogroms and savage discrimination. Russia's 5 million Jews were already confined to the market towns and small cities of the so-called Pale of Settlement, where they worked as artisans and petty traders. Most land was held by non-Jews. Therefore, when Russian Jewish artisans began in the 1880s to escape both factory competition and oppression by migrating—a migration that eventually totaled 2 million people—this was basically a once-and-for-all departure. Non-Jewish migrants from Russia, who constituted a majority of those leaving the tsar's empire after 1905, had access to land and thus returned much more frequently to their peasant villages in central Russia, Poland, and Ukraine.

The mass movement of Italians illustrates many of the characteristics of European migration. As late as the 1880s, which was for Italians, as for Russian Jews, the first decade of substantial exodus, three in every four Italians depended on agriculture. With the influx of cheap North American wheat, the long-standing problems of the Italian village became more acute. And since industry was not advancing fast enough to provide jobs for the rapidly growing population, many Italians began to leave their country for economic reasons. Most Italian migrants were not landless laborers from areas dominated by large estates; such people tended to stay in Italy and turned increasingly toward radical politics. Instead, most migrants were small landowning peasants whose standard of living was falling because of rural overpopulation and agricultural depression. Migration provided them with an escape valve and possible income to buy more land.

Many Italians went to the United States, but before 1900 more went to Argentina and Brazil; indeed, two out of three migrants to both countries came from Italy. In Brazil the large coffee planters, faced with the collapse of black slavery, attracted Italians to their plantations with subsidized travel and promises of relatively high wages.

Many Italians had no intention of settling abroad permanently. Some called themselves "swallows": after harvesting their own wheat and flax in Italy, they "flew" to Argentina to harvest wheat between December and April. Returning to Italy for the spring planting, they repeated this exhausting process. This was a very hard life, but a frugal worker could save $250 to $300 in the course of a season. A one-way passage from Latin America to Italy usually cost only $25 to $30 and sometimes as little as $8. Italian migrants also dominated the building trades and the architectural profession in Latin America and succeeded in giving a thoroughly Italian character to many Latin American cities.

Other Italians migrated to other European countries. France was a favorite destination. In 1911 the Italian-born population of France was roughly a third as large as that in the United States.

Ties of family and friendship played a crucial role in the movement of peoples. Many people from a given province or village settled together in rural enclaves or tightly knit urban neighborhoods thousands of miles away. Very often a strong individual—a businessman, a religious leader—would blaze the way and others would follow, in a pattern called "chain migration."

Many landless young European men and women were spurred to leave by a spirit of revolt and independence. In Sweden and in Norway, in Jewish Russia and

The Jewish Market on New York's Lower East Side was a bustling center of economic and social life in 1900. Jewish immigrants could usually find work with Jewish employers, and New York's Jewish population soared from 73,000 in 1880 to 1.1 million in 1910. *(The Granger Collection, New York)*

in Italy, these young people felt frustrated by the small privileged classes, which often controlled both church and government and resisted demands for change and greater opportunity. Many a young Norwegian seconded the passionate cry of Norway's national poet, Martinius Bjørnson: "Forth will I! Forth! I will be crushed and consumed if I stay."[5]

Many young Jews wholeheartedly agreed with a spokesman of Kiev's Jewish community in 1882, who declared, "Our human dignity is being trampled upon, our wives and daughters are being dishonored, we are looted and pillaged: either we get decent human rights or else let us go wherever our eyes may lead us."[6] Thus for many, migration was a radical way to "get out from under." Migration slowed down when the people won basic political and social reforms, such as the right to vote and social security.

Asian Migrants

Not all migration was from Europe. A substantial number of Chinese, Japanese, Indians, and Filipinos—to name only four key groups—responded to rural hardship with temporary or permanent migration. At least 3 million Asians (as opposed to more than 60 million Europeans) moved abroad before 1920. Most went as indentured laborers to work under incredibly difficult conditions on the plantations or in the gold mines of Latin America, southern Asia, Africa, California, Hawaii, and Australia. White estate owners very often used Asians to replace or supplement blacks after the suppression of the slave trade.

In the 1840s, for example, there was a strong demand for field hands in Cuba, and the Spanish government actively recruited Chinese laborers. They came

Chinese Laborers Arriving in South Africa In the early twentieth century many black Africans refused to work in the harsh conditions that prevailed in South Africa's rapidly expanding gold mines. Thus capitalists turned to Chinese migrants on strict three-year contracts for additional labor power. The Chinese were limited to unskilled jobs and could not settle or own property in South Africa. *(Courtesy, Dr. Oscar Norwich)*

under eight-year contracts, were paid about 25 cents a day, and were fed potatoes and salted beef. Between 1853 and 1873, when such migration was stopped, more than 130,000 Chinese laborers went to Cuba. The majority spent their lives as virtual slaves. The great landlords of Peru also brought in more than 100,000 workers from China in the nineteenth century, and there were similar movements of Asians elsewhere.

Such migration from Asia would undoubtedly have grown to much greater proportions if planters and mine owners in search of cheap labor had been able to hire as many Asian workers as they wished. But they could not. Asians fled the plantations and gold mines as soon as possible, seeking greater opportunities in trade and towns. There they came into conflict with local populations, whether in Malaya, East Africa, or areas settled by Europeans.

These European settlers demanded a halt to Asian migration. One Australian brutally summed up the typical view: "The Chinaman knows nothing about Caucasian civilization. . . . It would be less objectionable to drive a flock of sheep to the poll than to allow Chinamen to vote. The sheep at all events would be harmless."[7] By the 1880s, Americans and Australians were building "great white walls"—discriminatory laws designed to keep Asians out. Thus a final, crucial factor in the migrations before 1914 was the general policy of "whites only" in the open lands of possible permanent settlement. This, too, was part of Western dominance in the increasingly lopsided world. Largely successful in monopolizing the best overseas opportunities, Europeans and people of European ancestry reaped the main benefits from the great migration. By 1913 people in Australia, Canada, and the United States all had higher average incomes than people in Great Britain, still Europe's wealthiest nation.

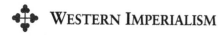

WESTERN IMPERIALISM

The expansion of Western society reached its apex between about 1880 and 1914. In those years, the leading European nations not only continued to send massive streams of migrants, money, and manufactured goods around the world, but also rushed to create or enlarge vast *political* empires abroad. This political empire building contrasted sharply with the economic penetration of non-Western territories between 1816 and 1880, which had left a China or a Japan "opened" but politically independent. By contrast, the empires of the late nineteenth century recalled the old European colonial empires of the seventeenth and eighteenth centuries and led contemporaries to speak of the new imperialism.

Characterized by a frantic rush to plant the flag over as many people and as much territory as possible, the new imperialism had momentous consequences. It resulted in new tensions among competing European states, and it led to wars and rumors of war with non-European powers. The new imperialism was aimed primarily at Africa and Asia. It put millions of black, brown, and yellow peoples directly under the rule of whites. How and why did whites come to rule these peoples?

The Scramble for Africa

The most spectacular manifestation of the new imperialism was the seizure of Africa, which broke sharply with previous patterns and fascinated contemporary Europeans and Americans. As late as 1880, European nations controlled only 10 percent of the African continent, and their possessions were hardly increasing. The French had begun conquering Algeria in 1830, and within fifty years substantial numbers of French, Italian, and Spanish colonists had settled among the overwhelming Arab majority.

At the other end of the continent, in South Africa, the British had taken possession of the Dutch settlements at Cape Town during the wars with Napoleon I. This takeover had led disgruntled Dutch cattle ranchers and farmers in 1835 to make their so-called Great Trek into the interior, where they fought the Zulu and Xhosa peoples for land. After 1853, while British colonies such as Canada and Australia were beginning to evolve toward self-government, the Boers, or Afrikaners (as the descendants of the Dutch in the Cape Colony were beginning to call themselves), proclaimed their political independence and defended it against British armies. By 1880 Afrikaner and British settlers, who detested each other, had wrested control of much of South Africa from the Zulu, Xhosa, and other African peoples.

European trading posts and forts dating back to the Age of Discovery and the slave trade dotted the coast of West Africa. The Portuguese proudly but ineffectively held their old possessions in Angola and Mozambique. Elsewhere over the great mass of the continent, Europeans did not rule.

Between 1880 and 1900, the situation changed drastically. Britain, France, Germany, and Italy scrambled for African possessions as if their national livelihoods depended on it. By 1900 nearly the whole continent

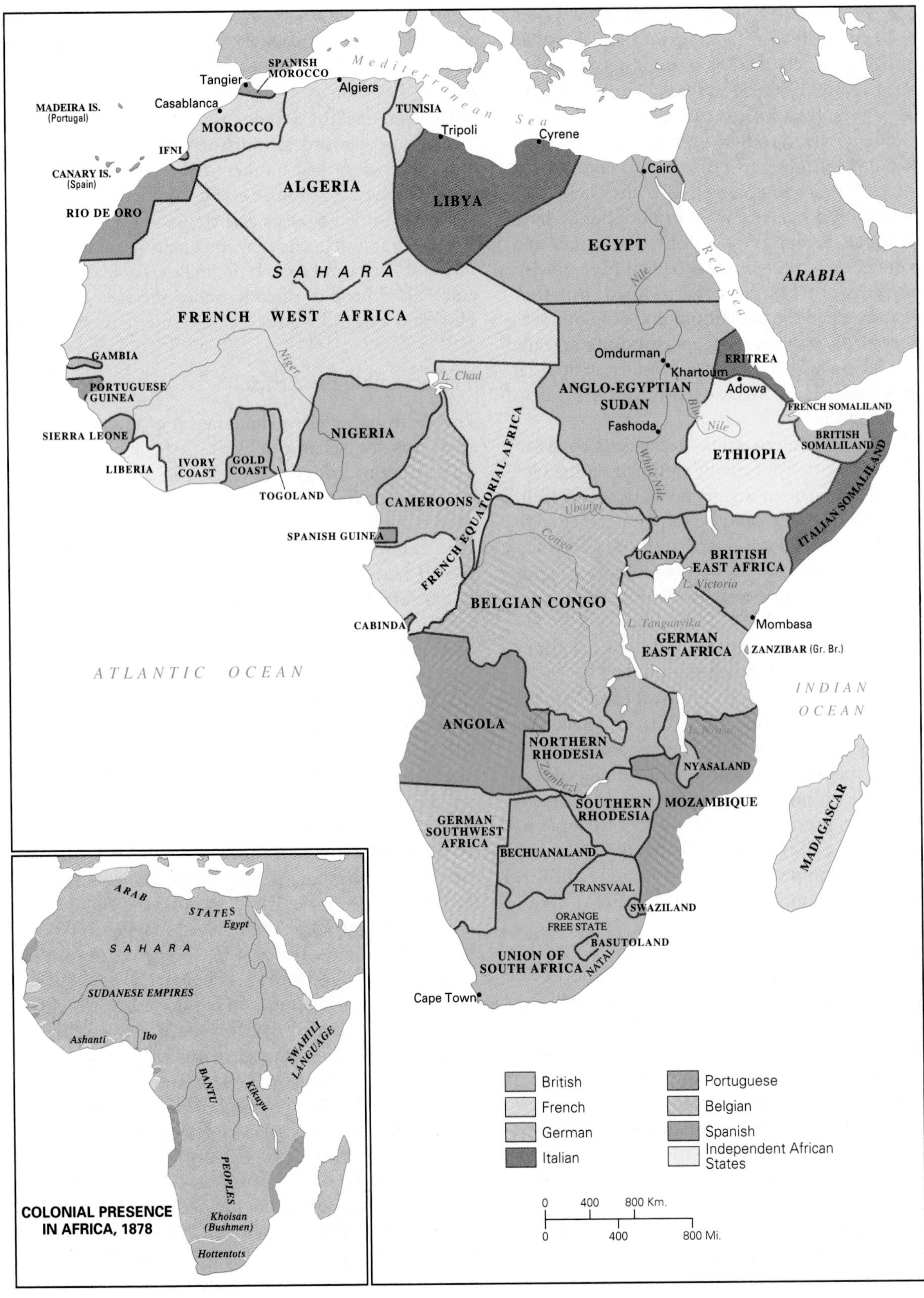

Mediterranean Sea
SPANISH MOROCCO
Tangier
Algiers
Casablanca
MADEIRA IS. (Portugal)
MOROCCO
TUNISIA
Tripoli
Cyrene
IFNI
CANARY IS. (Spain)
ALGERIA
LIBYA
Cairo
RIO DE ORO
EGYPT
Red Sea
ARABIA
SAHARA
FRENCH WEST AFRICA
Nile
Niger
GAMBIA
PORTUGUESE GUINEA
Omdurman
Khartoum
ERITREA
Adowa
L. Chad
ANGLO-EGYPTIAN SUDAN
FRENCH SOMALILAND
Blue Nile
SIERRA LEONE
NIGERIA
Fashoda
BRITISH SOMALILAND
LIBERIA
IVORY COAST
GOLD COAST
FRENCH EQUATORIAL AFRICA
White Nile
ETHIOPIA
TOGOLAND
CAMEROONS
Ubangi
ITALIAN SOMALILAND
SPANISH GUINEA
Congo
UGANDA
BRITISH EAST AFRICA
L. Victoria
BELGIAN CONGO
CABINDA
L. Tanganyika
Mombasa
GERMAN EAST AFRICA
ZANZIBAR (Gr. Br.)
ATLANTIC OCEAN
INDIAN OCEAN
ANGOLA
NORTHERN RHODESIA
L. Nyasa
NYASALAND
Zambezi
SOUTHERN RHODESIA
MOZAMBIQUE
GERMAN SOUTHWEST AFRICA
MADAGASCAR
BECHUANALAND
TRANSVAAL
SWAZILAND
ORANGE FREE STATE
BASUTOLAND
UNION OF SOUTH AFRICA
NATAL
Cape Town
ARAB STATES
Egypt
SAHARA
SUDANESE EMPIRES
Ashanti
Ibo
SWAHILI LANGUAGE
BANTU
Kikuyu
PEOPLES
Khoisan (Bushmen)
Hottentots
COLONIAL PRESENCE IN AFRICA, 1878
British
French
German
Italian
Portuguese
Belgian
Spanish
Independent African States
0 400 800 Km.
0 400 800 Mi.

had been carved up and placed under European rule: only Ethiopia in northeast Africa, which repulsed Italian invaders, and Liberia on the West African coast remained independent. In the years before 1914, the European powers tightened their control and established colonial governments to rule their gigantic empires (Map 26.2).

The Dutch settler republics also succumbed to imperialism, but the final outcome was quite different. The British, led by Cecil Rhodes in the Cape Colony, leapfrogged over the Afrikaner states in the early 1890s and established protectorates over Bechuanaland (now Botswana) and Rhodesia (now Zimbabwe and Zambia), named in honor of its freelance imperial founder. Trying unsuccessfully to undermine the stubborn Afrikaners in the Transvaal, where English-speaking capitalists like Rhodes were developing fabulously rich gold mines, the British conquered their white rivals in the bloody Boer War (1899–1902). In 1910 their territories were united with the old Cape Colony and the eastern province of Natal in a new Union of South Africa, established—unlike any other territory in Africa—as a largely "self-governing" colony. This enabled the defeated Afrikaners to use their numerical superiority over the British settlers to gradually take political power, as even the most educated nonwhites lost the right to vote outside the Cape Colony. (See the feature "Individuals in Society: Cecil Rhodes: Empire Building in Southern Africa.")

In the complexity of the European seizure of Africa, certain events and individuals stand out. Of enormous importance was the British occupation of Egypt, which established the new model of formal political control. There was also the role of Leopold II of Belgium (r. 1865–1909), an energetic, strong-willed monarch with a lust for distant territory. "The sea bathes our coast, the world lies before us," he had exclaimed in 1861. "Steam and electricity have annihilated distance, and all the non-appropriated lands on the surface of the globe can become the field of our operations and of our success."[8] By 1876 Leopold was focusing on central Africa. Subsequently, he formed a financial syndicate under his personal control to send Henry M. Stanley, a sensation-seeking journalist and part-time explorer, to the Congo basin. Stanley was able to establish trading stations, sign "treaties" with African chiefs, and plant Leopold's flag. Leopold's actions alarmed the French, who quickly sent out an expedition under Pierre de Brazza. In 1880 de Brazza signed a treaty of protection with the chief of the large Teke tribe and began to establish a French protectorate on the north bank of the Congo River.

Leopold's buccaneering intrusion into the Congo area raised the question of the political fate of Africa. By 1882, when the British successfully invaded and occupied Egypt, the richest and most developed land in Africa, Europe had caught "African fever." There was a gold rush mentality, and the race for territory was on.

To lay down some basic rules for this new and dangerous game of imperialist competition in sub-Saharan Africa, Jules Ferry of France and Otto von Bismarck of Germany arranged an international conference on Africa in Berlin in 1884 and 1885. The conference established the principle that European claims to African territory had to rest on "effective occupation" in order to be recognized by other states. This principle was very important. It meant that Europeans would push relentlessly into interior regions from all sides and that no single European power would be able to claim the entire continent. The conference recognized Leopold's personal rule over a neutral Congo free state and declared all of the Congo basin a free-trade zone. The conference also agreed to work to stop slavery and the slave trade in Africa.

The Berlin conference coincided with Germany's sudden emergence as an imperial power. Prior to about 1880, Bismarck, like many other European leaders at the time, had seen little value in colonies. Colonies reminded him, he said, of a poor but proud nobleman who wore a fur coat when he could not afford a shirt underneath. Then in 1884 and 1885, as political agitation for expansion increased, Bismarck did an abrupt about-face, and Germany established protectorates over a number of small African kingdoms and tribes in Togo, Cameroons, southwest Africa, and, later, East Africa. In acquiring colonies, Bismarck cooperated against the British with France's Ferry, who was as ardent for empire as he was for education. With Bismarck's tacit approval, the French pressed vigorously southward from Algeria, eastward from their old forts on the Senegal coast, and northward from de Brazza's newly formed protectorate on the Congo River. The object of these three thrusts was Lake Chad, a malaria-infested swamp on the edge of the Sahara Desert.

Meanwhile, the British began enlarging their West African enclaves and impatiently pushing northward from the Cape Colony and westward from Zanzibar.

MAP 26.2 The Partition of Africa European nations carved up Africa after 1880 and built vast political empires. What African states remained independent?

Individuals in Society

Cecil Rhodes: Empire Building in Southern Africa

Cecil Rhodes, after crushing the last African revolt in Rhodesia in 1896. *(Brown Brothers)*

Cecil Rhodes (1853–1902) epitomized the dynamism and the ruthlessness of the new imperialism. He built a corporate monopoly, claimed vast tracts in Africa, and established the famous Rhodes scholarships to develop colonial (and American) leaders who would love and strengthen the British Empire. But to Africans, he left a bitter legacy.

Rhodes came from a large middle-class family and at seventeen went to southern Africa to seek his fortune. He soon turned to diamonds, newly discovered at Kimberley, picked good partners, and was wealthy by 1876. But Rhodes, often called a dreamer, wanted more. He entered Oxford University, while returning periodically to Africa, and his musings crystallized in a belief in progress through racial competition and territorial expansion. "I contend," he wrote, "that we [English] are the finest race in the world and the more of the world we inhabit the better it is for the human race."[1]

Rhodes's belief in British expansion never wavered. In 1880 he formed the De Beers Mining Company, and by 1888 his firm monopolized southern Africa's diamond production and earned fabulous profits. Rhodes also entered the Cape Colony's legislature and became the all-powerful prime minister from 1890 to 1896. His main objective was to dominate the Afrikaner republics and to impose British rule on as much land as possible beyond their northern borders. Working through a state-approved private company financed in part by De Beers, Rhodes's agents forced and cajoled African kings to accept British "protection," then put down rebellions with Maxim machine guns. Britain thus obtained a great swath of empire on the cheap.

But Rhodes, like many high achievers obsessed with power and personal aggrandizement, went too far. He backed, and then in 1896 failed to call back, a failed invasion of the Transvaal, which was designed to topple the Dutch-speaking republic. Repudiated by top British leaders who had encouraged his plan, Rhodes had to resign as prime minister. In declining health, he continued to agitate against the Afrikaner republics. He died at age forty-nine as the Boer War (1899–1902) ended.

In accounting for Rhodes's remarkable but flawed achievements, both sympathetic and critical biographers stress his imposing size, enormous energy, and powerful personality. His ideas were commonplace, but he believed in them passionately, and he could persuade and inspire others to follow his lead. Rhodes the idealist was nonetheless a born negotiator, a crafty dealmaker who believed that everyone could be had for a price. According to his best biographer, Rhodes's homosexuality—discreet, partially repressed, and undeniable—was also "a major component of his magnetism and his success."[2] Never comfortable with women, he loved male companionship. He drew together a "band of brothers," both gay and straight, to share in the pursuit of power.

Rhodes cared nothing for the rights of blacks. Ever a combination of visionary and opportunist, he looked forward to an eventual reconciliation of Afrikaners and British in a united white front. Therefore, as prime minister of the Cape Colony, he broke with the colony's liberal tradition and supported Afrikaner demands to reduce drastically the number of black voters and limit black freedoms. This helped lay the foundation for the Union of South Africa's brutal policy of racial segregation known as *apartheid* after 1948.

Questions for Analysis

1. How did Rhodes relate to Afrikaners and to black Africans? How do you account for the differences and the similarities?
2. In what ways does Rhodes's career throw additional light on the debate over the causes of the new imperialism?

1. Robert Rotberg, *The Founder: Cecil Rhodes and the Pursuit of Power* (New York: Oxford University Press, 1988), p. 150.
2. Ibid., p. 408.

Omdurman, 1898 European machine guns cut down the charging Muslim tribesmen again and again. "It was not a battle but an execution," said one witness. Thus the Sudan was conquered and one million square miles were added to the British Empire. *(E.T. Archive)*

Their thrust southward from Egypt was blocked in the Sudan by fiercely independent Muslims, who massacred a British force at Khartoum in 1885.

A decade later, another British force, under General Horatio H. Kitchener, moved cautiously and more successfully up the Nile River, building a railroad to supply arms and reinforcements as it went. Finally, in 1898 these British troops met their foe at Omdurman (see Map 26.2), where Muslim tribesmen armed with spears charged time and time again only to be cut down by the recently invented machine gun. For one smug participant, the young British officer Winston Churchill, it was "like a pantomime scene" in a play. "These extraordinary foreign figures . . . march up one by one from the darkness of Barbarism to the footlights of civilization . . . and their conquerors, taking their possessions, forget even their names. Nor will history record such trash." For another, more somber English observer, "It was not a battle but an execution. The bodies were not in heaps . . . but they spread evenly over acres and acres."[9] In the end, eleven thousand brave but poorly armed Muslim tribesmen lay dead, while only twenty-eight Britons had been killed.

Continuing up the Nile after the Battle of Omdurman, Kitchener's armies found that a small French force had already occupied the village of Fashoda. Locked in imperial competition with Britain ever since the British occupation of Egypt, France had tried to beat the British to one of Africa's last unclaimed areas—the upper reaches of the Nile. The result was a serious diplomatic crisis and even the threat of war. Eventually, wracked by the Dreyfus affair (see page 845) and unwilling to fight, France backed down and withdrew its forces, allowing the British to take over.

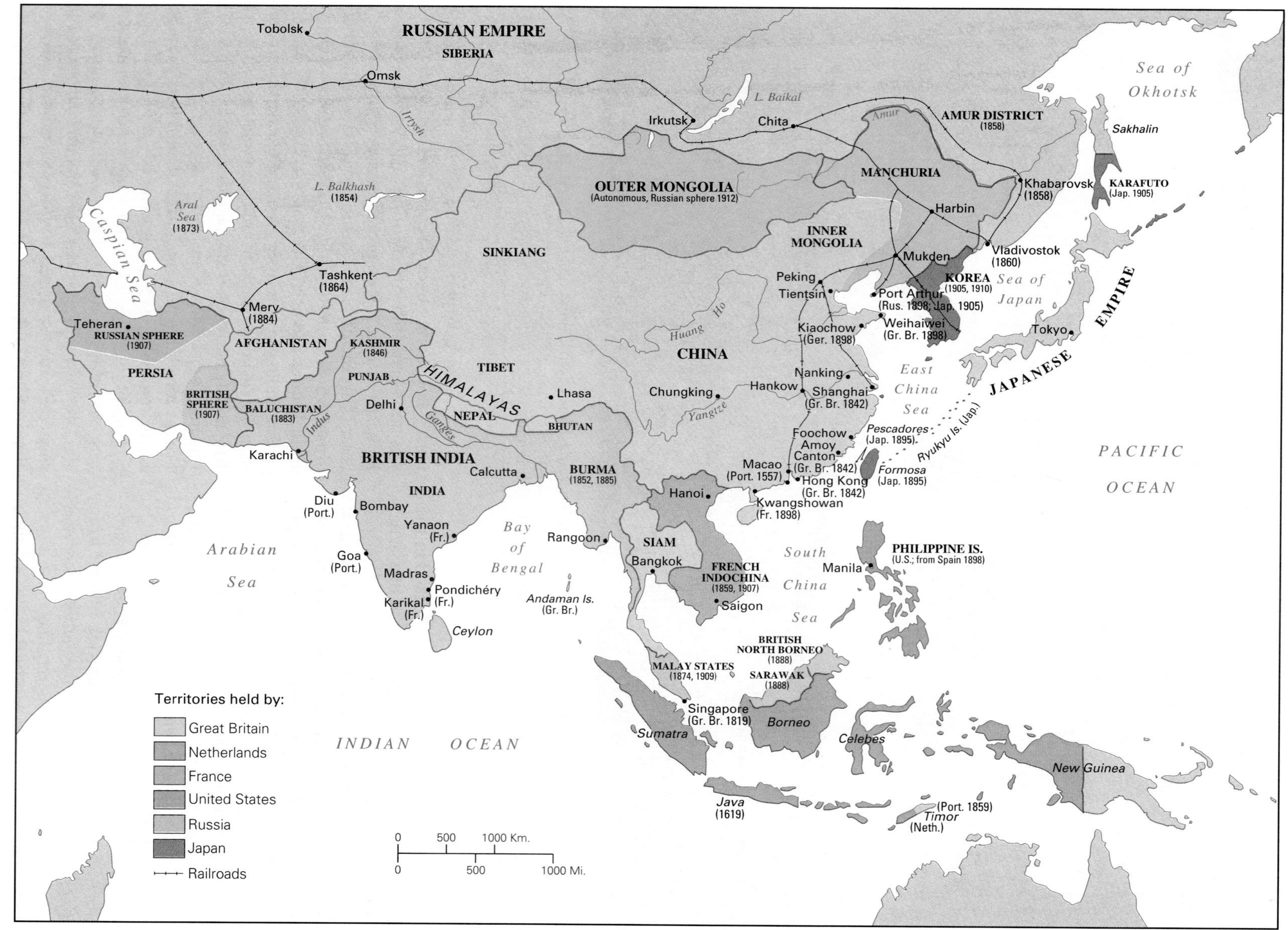

RUSSIAN EMPIRE
SIBERIA
Tobolsk
Omsk
Irtysh
Irkutsk
L. Baikal
Chita
Amur
AMUR DISTRICT (1858)
Sea of Okhotsk
Sakhalin
KARAFUTO (Jap. 1905)
Khabarovsk (1858)
MANCHURIA
Harbin
Vladivostok (1860)
OUTER MONGOLIA (Autonomous, Russian sphere 1912)
L. Balkhash (1854)
Aral Sea (1873)
Caspian Sea
Tashkent (1864)
Merv (1884)
SINKIANG
INNER MONGOLIA
Mukden
KOREA (1905, 1910)
Sea of Japan
Peking
Tientsin
Port Arthur (Rus. 1898; Jap. 1905)
Weihaiwei (Gr. Br. 1898)
Tokyo
JAPANESE EMPIRE
Teheran
RUSSIAN SPHERE (1907)
PERSIA
AFGHANISTAN
KASHMIR (1846)
PUNJAB
TIBET
HIMALAYAS
Huang Ho
CHINA
Kiaochow (Ger. 1898)
Nanking
Hankow
Shanghai (Gr. Br. 1842)
East China Sea
Chungking
Yangtze
Lhasa
BRITISH SPHERE (1907)
BALUCHISTAN (1883)
Indus
Delhi
Ganges
NEPAL
BHUTAN
Foochow
Amoy
Canton
Pescadores (Jap. 1895)
Ryukyu Is. (Jap.)
Karachi
BRITISH INDIA
Calcutta
BURMA (1852, 1885)
Macao (Port. 1557)
(Gr. Br. 1842)
Hong Kong (Gr. Br. 1842)
Formosa (Jap. 1895)
PACIFIC OCEAN
INDIA
Diu (Port.)
Bombay
Hanoi
Kwangshowan (Fr. 1898)
Yanaon (Fr.)
Bay of Bengal
Rangoon
SIAM
Arabian Sea
Goa (Port.)
Madras
Bangkok
FRENCH INDOCHINA (1859, 1907)
South China Sea
Manila
PHILIPPINE IS. (U.S.; from Spain 1898)
Pondichéry (Fr.)
Karikal (Fr.)
Andaman Is. (Gr. Br.)
Saigon
Ceylon
BRITISH NORTH BORNEO (1888)
MALAY STATES (1874, 1909)
SARAWAK (1888)
Territories held by:
Great Britain
Netherlands
France
United States
Russia
Japan
Railroads
Singapore (Gr. Br. 1819)
Sumatra
Borneo
Celebes
INDIAN OCEAN
New Guinea
Java (1619)
(Port. 1859) Timor (Neth.)
0 500 1000 Km.
0 500 1000 Mi.

The British conquest of the Sudan exemplifies the general process of empire building in Africa. The fate of the Muslim force at Omdurman was eventually inflicted on all native peoples who resisted European rule: they were blown away by vastly superior military force. But however much the European powers squabbled for territory and privilege around the world, they always had the sense to stop short of actually fighting each other. Imperial ambitions were not worth a great European war.

Imperialism in Asia

Although the sudden division of Africa was more spectacular, Europeans also extended their political control in Asia. In 1815 the Dutch ruled little more than the island of Java in the East Indies. Thereafter they gradually brought almost all of the three-thousand-mile archipelago under their political authority, though—in good imperialist fashion—they had to share some of the spoils with Britain and Germany. In the critical decade of the 1880s, the French under the leadership of Ferry took Indochina. India, Japan, and China also experienced a profound imperialist impact (Map 26.3).

Two other great imperialist powers, Russia and the United States, also acquired rich territories in Asia. Russia, whose history since the later Middle Ages had been marked by almost continual expansion, moved steadily forward on two fronts throughout the nineteenth century. Russians conquered Muslim areas to the south in the Caucasus and in central Asia and also proceeded to nibble greedily on China's outlying provinces in the Far East, especially in the 1890s.

The United States' great conquest was the Philippines, taken from Spain in 1898 after the Spanish-American War. When it quickly became clear that the United States had no intention of granting independence, Philippine patriots rose in revolt and were suppressed only after long, bitter fighting. (Not until 1934 was a timetable for independence established.) Some Americans protested the taking of the Philippines, but to no avail. Thus another great Western power joined the imperialist ranks in Asia.

MAP 26.3 Asia in 1914 India remained under British rule, while China precariously preserved its political independence. The Dutch empire in modern-day Indonesia was old, but French control of Indochina was a product of the new imperialism.

Causes of the New Imperialism

Many factors contributed to the late-nineteenth-century rush for territory and empire, which was in turn one aspect of Western society's generalized expansion in the age of industry and nationalism. It is little wonder that controversies have raged over interpretation of the new imperialism, especially since authors of every persuasion have often exaggerated particular aspects in an attempt to prove their own theories. Yet despite complexity and controversy, basic causes are clearly identifiable.

Economic motives played an important role in the extension of political empires, especially the British Empire. By the late 1870s, France, Germany, and the United States were industrializing rapidly behind rising tariff barriers. Great Britain was losing its early lead and facing increasingly tough competition in foreign markets. In this new economic situation, Britain came to value old possessions, such as India and Canada, more highly. The days when a leading free-trader such as Richard Cobden could denounce the "bloodstained fetish of Empire" and statesman Benjamin Disraeli could call colonies a "millstone round our necks" came to an abrupt end. When continental powers began to grab any and all unclaimed territory in the 1880s, the British followed suit immediately. They feared that France and Germany would seal off their empires with high tariffs and restrictions and that future economic opportunities would be lost forever.

Actually, the overall economic gains of the new imperialism proved quite limited before 1914. The new colonies were simply too poor to buy much, and they offered few immediately profitable investments. Nonetheless, even the poorest, most barren desert was jealously prized, and no territory was ever abandoned. Colonies became important for political and diplomatic reasons. Each leading country saw colonies as crucial to national security, military power, and international prestige. For instance, safeguarding the Suez Canal played a key role in the British occupation of Egypt, and protecting Egypt in turn led to the bloody conquest of the Sudan. National security was a major factor in the U.S. decision to establish firm control over the Panama Canal Zone in 1903. Far-flung possessions guaranteed ever-growing navies the safe havens and the dependable coaling stations they needed in time of crisis or war.

Many people were convinced that colonies were essential to great nations. "There has never been a great power without great colonies," wrote one French publicist in 1877. "Every virile people has established colonial power," echoed the famous nationalist historian of Germany, Heinrich von Treitschke. "All great nations in the fullness of their strength have desired to set their mark upon barbarian lands and those who fail to participate in this great rivalry will play a pitiable role in time to come."[10]

Treitschke's harsh statement reflects not only the increasing aggressiveness of European nationalism after Bismarck's wars of German unification but also Social Darwinian theories of brutal competition among races. As one prominent English economist argued, the "strongest nation has always been conquering the weaker . . . and the strongest tend to be best." Thus European nations, which were seen as racially distinct parts of the dominant white race, had to seize colonies to show they were strong and virile. Moreover, since racial struggle was nature's inescapable law, the conquest of inferior peoples was just. "The path of progress is strewn with the wreck . . . of inferior races," wrote one professor in 1900. "Yet these dead peoples are, in very truth, the stepping stones on which mankind has risen to the higher intellectual and deeper emotional life of today."[11] Social Darwinism and harsh racial doctrines fostered imperialist expansion.

So did the industrial world's unprecedented technological and military superiority. Three aspects were crucial. First, the rapidly firing machine gun, so lethal at Omdurman in the Sudan, was an ultimate weapon in many another unequal battle. Second, newly discovered quinine proved no less effective in controlling attacks of malaria, which had previously decimated whites in the tropics whenever they left breezy coastal enclaves and dared to venture into mosquito-infested interiors. Third, the combination of the steamship and the international telegraph permitted Western powers to quickly concentrate their firepower in a given area when it was needed. Never before—and never again after 1914—would the technological gap between the West and non-Western regions of the world be so great.

Social tensions and domestic political conflicts also contributed mightily to overseas expansion, according to a prominent interpretation of recent years. Certainly in Germany, in Russia, and in other countries to a lesser extent, contemporary critics of imperialism charged conservative political leaders with manipulating colonial issues in order to divert popular attention from the class struggle at home and to create a false sense of national unity. Therefore, imperial propagandists relentlessly stressed that colonies benefited workers as well as capitalists, providing jobs and cheap raw materials that raised workers' standard of living. Government leaders and their allies in the tabloid press successfully encouraged the masses to savor foreign triumphs and glory in the supposed increase in national prestige. In short, conservative leaders defined imperialist development as a national necessity, and then they used the realization of that necessity to justify the status quo and their continued hold on power.

Finally, certain special-interest groups in each country were powerful agents of expansion. Shipping companies wanted lucrative subsidies. White settlers on dangerous, turbulent frontiers constantly demanded more land and greater protection. Missionaries and humanitarians wanted to spread religion and stop the slave trade. Explorers and adventurers sought knowledge and excitement. Military men and colonial officials, whose role has often been overlooked by those who write on imperialism, foresaw rapid advancement and high-paid positions in growing empires. The actions of such groups and the determined individuals who led them thrust the course of empire forward.

Western society did not rest the case for empire solely on naked conquest and a Darwinian racial struggle or on power politics and the need for naval bases on every ocean. Imperialists developed additional arguments in order to satisfy their consciences and answer their critics.

A favorite idea was that Europeans could and should "civilize" more primitive, nonwhite peoples. According to this view, nonwhites would eventually receive the benefits of modern economies, cities, advanced medicine, and higher standards of living. In time, they might be ready for self-government and Western democracy. Thus the French spoke of their sacred "civilizing mission." Rudyard Kipling (1865–1936), who wrote masterfully of Anglo-Indian life and was perhaps the most influential British writer of the 1890s, exhorted Europeans (and Americans in the United States) to unselfish service in distant lands:

Take up the White Man's Burden—
Send forth the best ye breed—
Go bind your sons to exile
To serve your captives' need,
To wait in heavy harness,
On fluttered folk and wild—
Your new-caught, sullen peoples
Half-devil and half-child.[12]

Many Americans accepted the ideology of the white man's burden. It was an important factor in the decision to rule, rather than liberate, the Philippines after the Spanish-American War. Like their European coun-

every man will become a soldier, and not a single region in the country will be without defense. Thus our defense will become complete.

The second concern of the Ministry is coastal defense. This includes building of warships and constructing coastal batteries. Actually, battleships are movable batteries. Our country has thousands of miles of coastline, and any mobile corner of our country can become the advance post of our enemy. . . .

The third concern of the Military is to create resources for the navy and the army. There are three items under consideration, namely military academies, a bureau of military supplies, and a bureau of munitions depots. It is not difficult to have one million soldiers in a short time, but it is difficult to gain one good officer during the same span of time. Military academies are intended to train officers for these two services. If we pay little attention to this need today, we shall not be able to have the services of capable officers for another day. Therefore, without delay military academies must be created and be allowed to prosper. . . . The bureau of military supplies shall be in charge of procuring military provisions and manufacturing weapons of war for the two services. The bureau of munitions depots shall store such provisions and munitions. If we lack military provisions and weapons and our munitions depots are empty, what good will the million soldiers in the army or thousands of warships do? . . .

Some people may argue that while they are aware of the urgency in the need for the Ministry of Military Affairs, they cannot permit the entire national resources to be committed to the need of one ministry alone. They further aver that from the larger perspective of the imperial government, there are so many other projects covering a wide range of things which require governmental attention. . . . This argument fails to discern the fundamental issues. The recommendations herein presented by the Ministry of Military Affairs in no way asks for the stoppage of all governmental activities or for the monopolization of all government revenues. But in a national emergency, a new set of priorities must be established. Those of us who are given the task of governing must learn from the past, discern the present, and weigh all matters carefully. . . .

Those of us who govern must first of all discern the conditions prevailing in the world, set up priorities and take appropriate measures. In our opinion Russia has been acting very arrogantly. Previously, contrary to the provisions of the Treaty of Sevastopol, she placed her warships in the Black Sea. Southward, she has shown her aggressive intent toward Muslim countries and toward India. Westward, she has crossed the borders of Manchuria and has been navigating the Amur River. Her intents being thus, it is inevitable that she will move eastward sooner or later by sending troops to Hokkaido, and then taking advantage of the seasonal wind move to the warmer areas.

✣ The new Japanese army, with Western uniforms, ca 1870. *(Tsuneo Tamba Collection, Yokohama, Japan/Laurie Platt Winfrey, Inc.)*

At a time like this it is very clear where the priority of this country must lie. We must now have a well-trained standing army supplemented by a large number of reservists. We must build warships and construct batteries. We must train officers and soldiers. We must manufacture and store weapons and ammunitions. The nation may consider that it cannot bear the expenses. However, even if we wish to ignore it, this important matter cannot disappear from us. Even if we prefer to enter into this type of defense undertaking, we cannot do without our defense for a single day.

Questions for Analysis

1. What aspects of military modernization are highlighted here? What goals was Aritomo trying to achieve with each proposal?
2. How does Aritomo use the examples of European countries to reach conclusions?
3. How does Aritomo anticipate criticism and explain the need for prompt action?

Source: David John Lu, *Japan: A Documentary History* (Armonk, N.Y.: M. E. Sharpe, 1997), pp. 315–318. Excerpted with permission.

CHAPTER

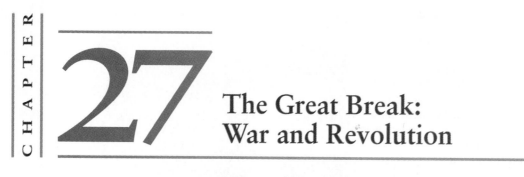

27 The Great Break: War and Revolution

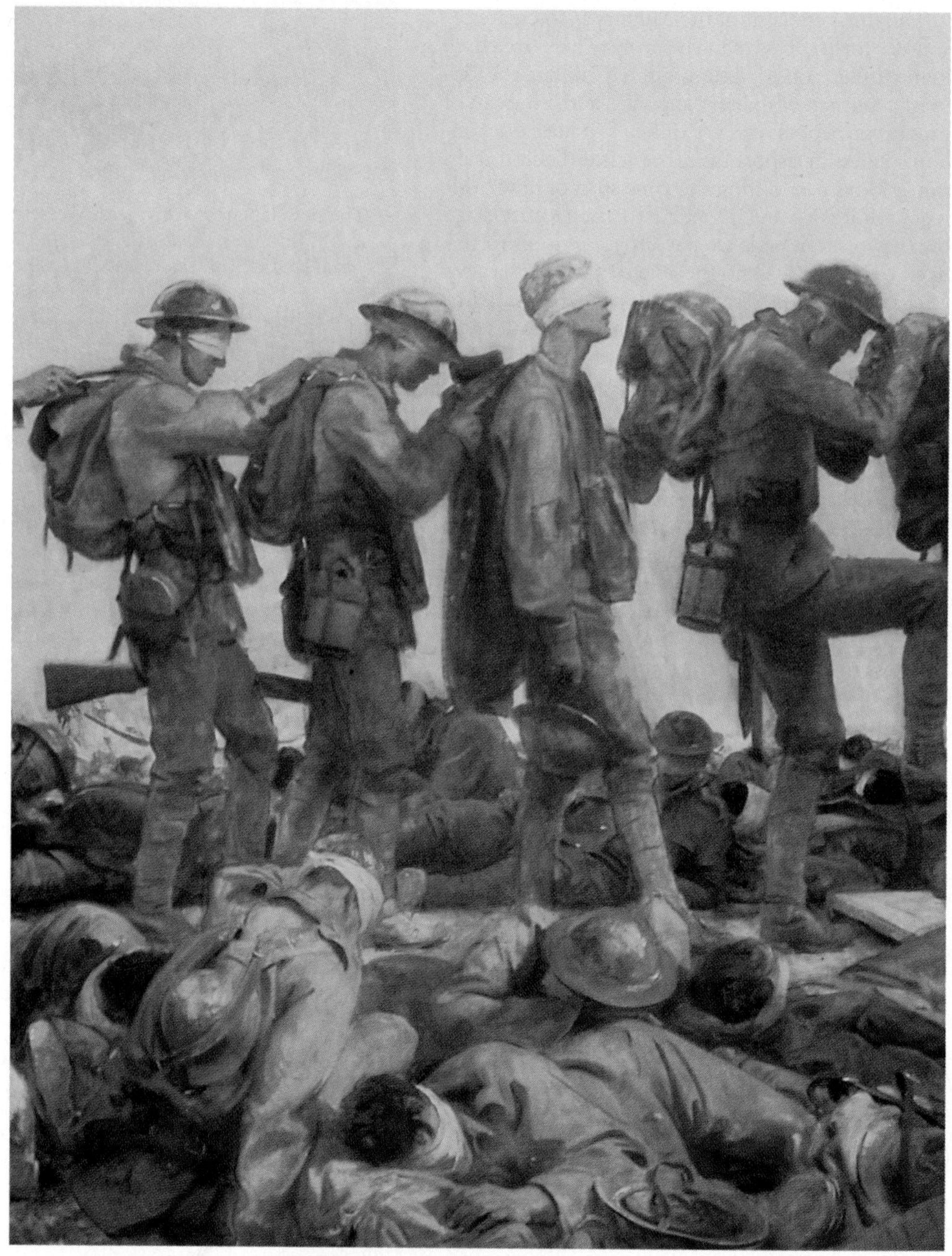

John Singer Sargent's World War I painting *Gassed.* *(By courtesy of the Trustees of the Imperial War Museum)*

eign trade and investment as a form of economic warfare.

Many educated shapers of public opinion and ordinary people in Britain and Germany were increasingly locked in a fateful "love-hate" relationship between the two countries. Proud nationalists in both countries simultaneously admired and feared the power and accomplishments of their nearly equal rival. In 1909 the mass-circulation London *Daily Mail* hysterically informed its readers in a series of reports that "Germany is deliberately preparing to destroy the British Empire."[2] By then Britain was psychologically, if not officially, in the Franco-Russian camp. The leading nations of Europe were divided into two hostile blocs, both ill-prepared to deal with upheaval on Europe's southeastern frontier.

The Outbreak of War

In the early years of this century, war in the Balkans was as inevitable as anything can be in human history. The reason was simple: nationalism was destroying the Ottoman Empire and threatening to break up the Austro-Hungarian Empire. The only questions were what kinds of wars would occur and where they would lead.

Greece had long before led the struggle for national liberation, winning its independence in 1832. In 1875 widespread nationalist rebellion in the Ottoman Empire had resulted in Turkish repression, Russian intervention, and Great Power tensions. Bismarck had helped resolve this crisis at the 1878 Congress of Berlin, which worked out the partial division of Turkish possessions in Europe. Austria-Hungary obtained the right to "occupy and administer" Bosnia and Herzegovina. Serbia and Romania won independence, and a part of Bulgaria won local autonomy. The Ottoman Empire retained important Balkan holdings, for Austria-Hungary and Russia each feared the other's domination of totally independent states in the area (Map 27.1).

After 1878 the siren call of imperialism lured European energies, particularly Russian energies, away from the Balkans. This diversion helped preserve the fragile balance of interests in southeastern Europe. By 1903, however, Balkan nationalism was on the rise once again. Serbia led the way, becoming openly hostile toward both Austria-Hungary and the Ottoman Empire. The Serbs, a Slavic people, looked to Slavic Russia for support of their national aspirations. To block Serbian expansion and to take advantage of Russia's weakness after the revolution of 1905, Austria in 1908 formally annexed Bosnia and Herzegovina, with their large Serbian, Croatian, and Muslim populations. The kingdom of Serbia erupted in rage but could do nothing without Russian support.

Then in 1912, in the First Balkan War, Serbia turned southward. With Greece and Bulgaria, it took Macedonia from the Ottoman Empire and then quarreled with Bulgaria over the spoils of victory—a dispute that led in 1913 to the Second Balkan War. Austria intervened in 1913 and forced Serbia to give up Albania. After centuries, nationalism had finally destroyed the Ottoman Empire in Europe (Map 27.2). This sudden but long-awaited event elated the Balkan nationalists and dismayed the leaders of multinational Austria-Hungary. The former hoped and the latter feared that Austria might be next to be broken apart.

Within this tense context, Archduke Francis Ferdinand, heir to the Austrian and Hungarian thrones, and his wife, Sophie, were assassinated by Serbian revolutionaries living in Bosnia on June 28, 1914, during a state visit to the Bosnian capital of Sarajevo. The assassins were closely connected to the ultranationalist Serbian society the Black Hand. This revolutionary group was secretly supported by members of the Serbian government and was dedicated to uniting all Serbians in a single state. Although the leaders of Austria-Hungary did not and could not know all the details of Serbia's involvement in the assassination plot, they concluded after some hesitation that Serbia had to be severely punished once and for all. After nearly a month of maneuvering, on July 23 Austria-Hungary presented Serbia with an unconditional ultimatum.

The Serbian government had just forty-eight hours in which to agree to cease all subversion in Austria and all anti-Austrian propaganda in Serbia. Moreover, a thorough investigation of all aspects of the assassination at Sarajevo was to be undertaken in Serbia by a joint commission of Serbian and Austrian officials. These demands amounted to control of the Serbian state. When Serbia replied moderately but evasively, Austria began to mobilize and then declared war on Serbia on July 28. Thus a desperate multinational Austria-Hungary deliberately chose war in a last-ditch attempt to stem the rising tide of hostile nationalism within its borders and save the existing state. The "Third Balkan War" had begun.

Of prime importance in Austria-Hungary's fateful decision was Germany's unconditional support. Emperor William II and his chancellor, Theobald von

MAP 27.1 The Balkans After the Congress of Berlin, 1878 The Ottoman Empire suffered large territorial losses but remained a power in the Balkans.

MAP 27.2 The Balkans in 1914 Ethnic boundaries did not follow political boundaries, and Serbian national aspirations threatened Austria-Hungary.

Bethmann-Hollweg, gave Austria-Hungary a "blank check" and urged aggressive measures in early July, even though they realized that war between Austria and Russia was the most probable result. They knew Russian pan-Slavs saw Russia not only as the protector but also as the eventual liberator of southern Slavs. As one pan-Slav had said much earlier, "Austria can hold her part of the Slavonian mass as long as Turkey holds hers and vice versa."[3] At the very least, a resurgent Russia could not stand by, as in the Bosnian crisis, and simply watch the Serbs be crushed. Yet Bethmann-Hollweg apparently hoped that while Russia (and therefore France) would go to war, Great Britain would remain neutral, unwilling to fight for "Russian aggression" in the distant Balkans. After all, Britain had reached only "friendly understandings" with France and Russia on colonial questions and had no alliance with either power.

In fact, the diplomatic situation was already out of control. Military plans and timetables began to dictate policy. Russia, a vast country, would require much longer to mobilize its armies than Germany and Austria-Hungary. On July 28, as Austrian armies bombarded Belgrade, Tsar Nicholas II ordered a partial mobilization against Austria-Hungary. Almost immediately he found that this was impossible. All the complicated mobilization plans of the Russian general staff had assumed a war with both Austria and Germany: Russia could not mobilize against one without mobilizing against the other. Therefore, on July 29 Russia ordered full mobilization and in effect declared general war. For, as French general Boisdeffre had said to the agreeing

Russian tsar when the Franco-Russian military convention was being negotiated in 1892, "mobilization is a declaration of war."[4]

The same tragic subordination of political considerations to military strategy descended on Germany. The German general staff had also thought only in terms of a two-front war. The staff's plan for war—the Schlieffen plan, the work of Count Alfred von Schlieffen, chief of the German general staff from 1891 to 1906 and a professional military man—called for knocking out France first with a lightning attack through neutral Belgium before turning on Russia.

Thus on August 2, 1914, General Helmuth von Moltke, "acting under a dictate of self-preservation," demanded that Belgium permit German armies to pass through its territory. Belgium, whose neutrality had been solemnly guaranteed in 1839 by all the great states including Prussia, refused. Germany attacked. Thus Germany's terrible, politically disastrous response to a war in the Balkans was an all-out invasion of France by way of the plains of neutral Belgium on August 3. In the face of this act of aggression, Great Britain joined France and declared war on Germany the following day. The First World War had begun.

Nationalist Opposition in the Balkans This band of well-armed and determined guerrillas from northern Albania was typical of groups fighting against Ottoman rule in the Balkans. Balkan nationalists succeeded in driving the Ottoman Turks out of most of Europe, but their victory increased tensions with Austria-Hungary and among the Great Powers. *(Roger-Viollet)*

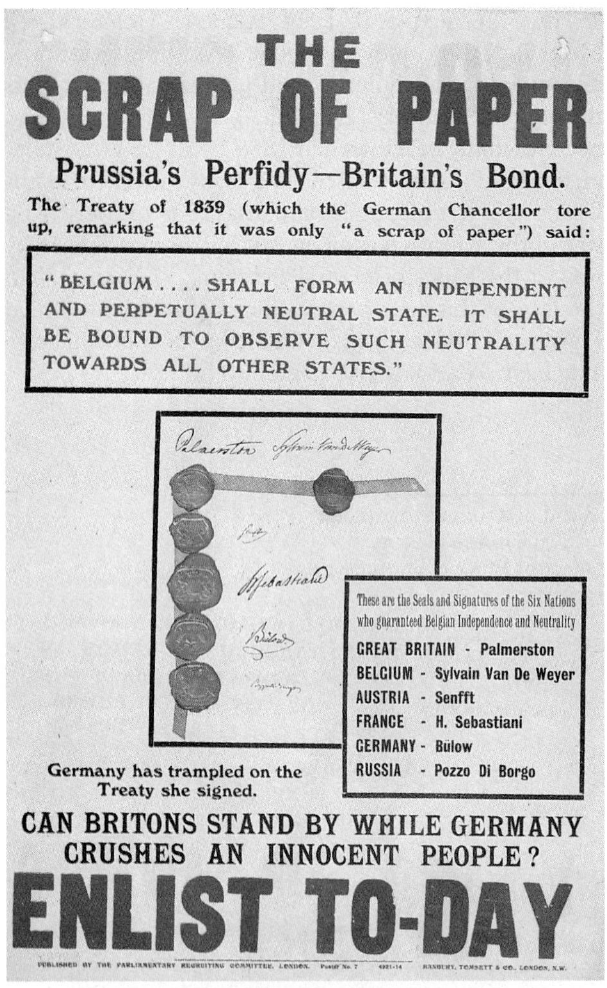

This British Poster shows the signature page of the 1839 treaty guaranteeing the neutrality of Belgium. When German armies invaded Belgium in 1914, Chancellor Bethmann-Hollweg cynically dismissed the treaty as a "scrap of paper"—a perfect line for anti-German propaganda. *(By courtesy of the Trustees of the Imperial War Museum)*

Reflections on the Origins of the War

Although few events in history have aroused such interest and controversy as the coming of the First World War, the question of immediate causes and responsibilities can be answered with considerable certainty. Austria-Hungary deliberately started the Third Balkan War. A war for the right to survive was Austria-Hungary's desperate, although understandable, response to the aggressive, yet understandable, revolutionary drive of Serbian nationalists to unify their people in a single state. Moreover, in spite of Russian intervention in the quarrel, it is clear that from the beginning of the crisis, Germany not only pushed and goaded Austria-Hungary but also was responsible for turning a little war into the Great War by means of a sledgehammer attack on Belgium and France. Why Germany was so aggressive in 1914 is less certain.

Diplomatic historians stress that German leaders lost control of the international system after Bismarck's resignation in 1890. They felt increasingly that Germany's status as a world power was declining, while that of Britain, France, Russia, and the United States was growing. Indeed, the powers of what officially became in August 1914 the Triple Entente—Great Britain, France, and Russia—were checking Germany's vague but real aspirations as well as working to strangle Austria-Hungary, Germany's only real ally. Germany's aggression in 1914 reflected the failure of all European leaders, not just those in Germany, to incorporate Bismarck's mighty empire permanently and peacefully into the international system.

Another more controversial interpretation, which has been developed by anticonservative German historians in recent years, argues that domestic conflicts and social tensions lay at the root of Germany's increasingly belligerent foreign policy from the late 1890s onward. Germany industrialized and urbanized rapidly after 1870 and established a popularly elected parliament. But German society was not democratized, and ultimate political power remained concentrated in the hands of the monarchy, the army, and the Prussian nobility. Determined to hold on to power and increasingly frightened by the rising socialist movement and in 1914 by a powerful new wave of strikes and grassroots working-class militancy, which was encouraged but never controlled by a few radical socialist intellectuals such as the fiery Rosa Luxemburg (see page 918), the German ruling class was willing to take chances. It was willing to gamble on diplomatic victory and even on war as the means of rallying the masses to its side and preserving its privileged position. Historians have also discerned similar, if less clear-cut, behavior in Great Britain, where leaders faced civil war in northern Ireland, and in Russia, where the revolution of 1905 had brought tsardom to its knees.

This stimulating debate over social tensions and domestic political factors correctly suggests that the triumph of nationalism was a crucial underlying precondition of the Great War. Nationalism was at the heart of the Balkan wars, in the form of Serbian aspirations and the grandiose pan-German versus pan-Slavic racism of some fanatics. Nationalism also drove the spiraling arms race. Broad popular commitment to "my country right or wrong" weakened groups that thought in terms of international communities and consequences. Thus the big international bankers, who were frightened by the prospect of war in July 1914, and the extreme-left socialists, who believed that the enemy was at home and not abroad, were equally out of step with national feeling. In each country, the great majority of the population enthusiastically embraced the outbreak of war in August 1914. In each country, people believed that their country had been wronged, and they rallied to defend it. Patriotic nationalism brought unity in the short run.

Nonetheless, the wealthy governing classes certainly underestimated the risk of war to themselves in 1914. They had forgotten that great wars and great social revolutions very often go hand in hand. Metternich's alliance of conservative forces in support of international peace and the social status quo had become only a distant memory.

The First Battle of the Marne

When the Germans invaded Belgium in August 1914, they and everyone else believed that the war would be short, for urban society rested on the food and raw materials of the world economy: "The boys will be home by Christmas." The Belgian army heroically defended its homeland, however, and fell back in good order to join a rapidly landed British army corps near the Franco-Belgian border. This action complicated the original Schlieffen plan of concentrating German armies on the right wing and boldly capturing Paris in a vast encircling movement. Moreover, the German left wing in Lorraine failed to retreat, thwarting the plan to suck French armies into Germany and then annihilate them. Instead, by the end of August, dead-tired German soldiers were advancing along an enormous front in the scorching summer heat. The neatly designed prewar plan to surround Paris from the north and west had been thrown into confusion.

French armies totaling 1 million, reinforced by more than 100,000 British troops, had retreated in orderly fashion before Germany's 1.5 million men in the field. Under the leadership of the steel-nerved General Joseph Joffre, the French attacked a gap in the German line at the Battle of the Marne on September 6. For three days, France threw everything into the attack. At one point, the French government desperately requisitioned all the taxis of Paris to rush reserves to the troops at the front. Finally, the Germans fell back. Paris and France had been miraculously saved.

Stalemate and Slaughter

The attempts of French and British armies to turn the German retreat into a rout were unsuccessful, however, and so were moves by both sides to outflank each other in northern France. As a result, both sides began to dig trenches to protect themselves from machine-gun fire. By November 1914, an unbroken line of trenches extended from the Belgian ports through northern France, past the fortress of Verdun, and on to the Swiss frontier.

In the face of this unexpected stalemate, slaughter on the western front began in earnest. The defenders on both sides dug in behind rows of trenches, mines, and barbed wire. For days and even weeks, ceaseless shelling by heavy artillery supposedly "softened up" the enemy in a given area (and also signaled the coming attack). Then young draftees and their junior officers went "over the top" of the trenches in frontal attacks on the enemy's line.

The cost in lives was staggering, the gains in territory minuscule. The massive French and British offensives during 1915 never gained more than 3 miles of blood-soaked earth from the enemy. In the Battle of the Somme in the summer of 1916, the British and French gained an insignificant 125 square miles at the cost of 600,000 dead or wounded, while the Germans lost 500,000 men. That same year, the unsuccessful German campaign against Verdun cost 700,000 lives on both sides. British poet Siegfried Sassoon (1886–1967) wrote of the Somme offensive, "I am staring at a sunlit picture of Hell."

Terrible 1917 saw General Robert Nivelle's French army almost destroyed in a grand spring attack at Champagne. At Passchendaele in the fall, the British traded 400,000 casualties for 50 square miles of Belgian Flanders. The hero of Erich Remarque's great novel *All Quiet on the Western Front* (1929) describes one attack:

> *We see men living with their skulls blown open; we see soldiers run with their two feet cut off. . . . Still the little piece of convulsed earth in which we lie is held. We have yielded no more than a few hundred yards of it as a prize to the enemy. But on every yard there lies a dead man.*

Such was war on the western front.

The Tragic Absurdity of Trench Warfare Soldiers charge across a scarred battlefield and overrun an enemy trench. The dead defender on the right will fire no more. But this is only another futile charge that will yield much blood and little land. A whole generation is being decimated by the slaughter. *(By courtesy of the Trustees of the Imperial War Museum)*

The war of the trenches shattered an entire generation of young men. Millions who could have provided political creativity and leadership after the war were forever missing. Moreover, those who lived through the slaughter were maimed, shell-shocked, embittered, and profoundly disillusioned. The young soldiers went to war believing in the world of their leaders and elders, the pre-1914 world of order, progress, and patriotism. Then, in Remarque's words, the "first bombardment showed us our mistake, and under it the world as they had taught it to us broke in pieces." For many, the sacrifice and comradeship of the battlefield became life's crucial experience, which "soft" civilians could never understand. A chasm opened up between veterans and civilians, making the hard postwar reconstruction all the more difficult.

Otto Dix: War Returning to Germany after the war, Dix was haunted by the horrors he had seen. This vivid expressionist masterpiece, part of a triptych painted in 1929–1932, probes the tormented memory of endless days in muddy trenches and dugouts, living with rats and lice and the constant danger of exploding shells, snipers, and all-out attack. Many who escaped death or dismemberment were mentally wounded forever by their experiences. *(Staatliche Kunstsammlungen Dresden)*

The Widening War

On the eastern front, slaughter did not degenerate into suicidal trench warfare. With the outbreak of the war, the "Russian steamroller" immediately moved into eastern Germany. Very badly damaged by the Germans under Generals Paul von Hindenburg and Erich Ludendorff at the Battles of Tannenberg and the Masurian Lakes in August and September 1914, Russia never threatened Germany again. On the Austrian front, enormous armies seesawed back and forth, suffering enormous losses. Austro-Hungarian armies were repulsed twice by Serbia in bitter fighting. But with the help of German forces, they reversed the Russian advances of 1914 and forced the Russians to retreat deep into their own territory in the eastern campaign of

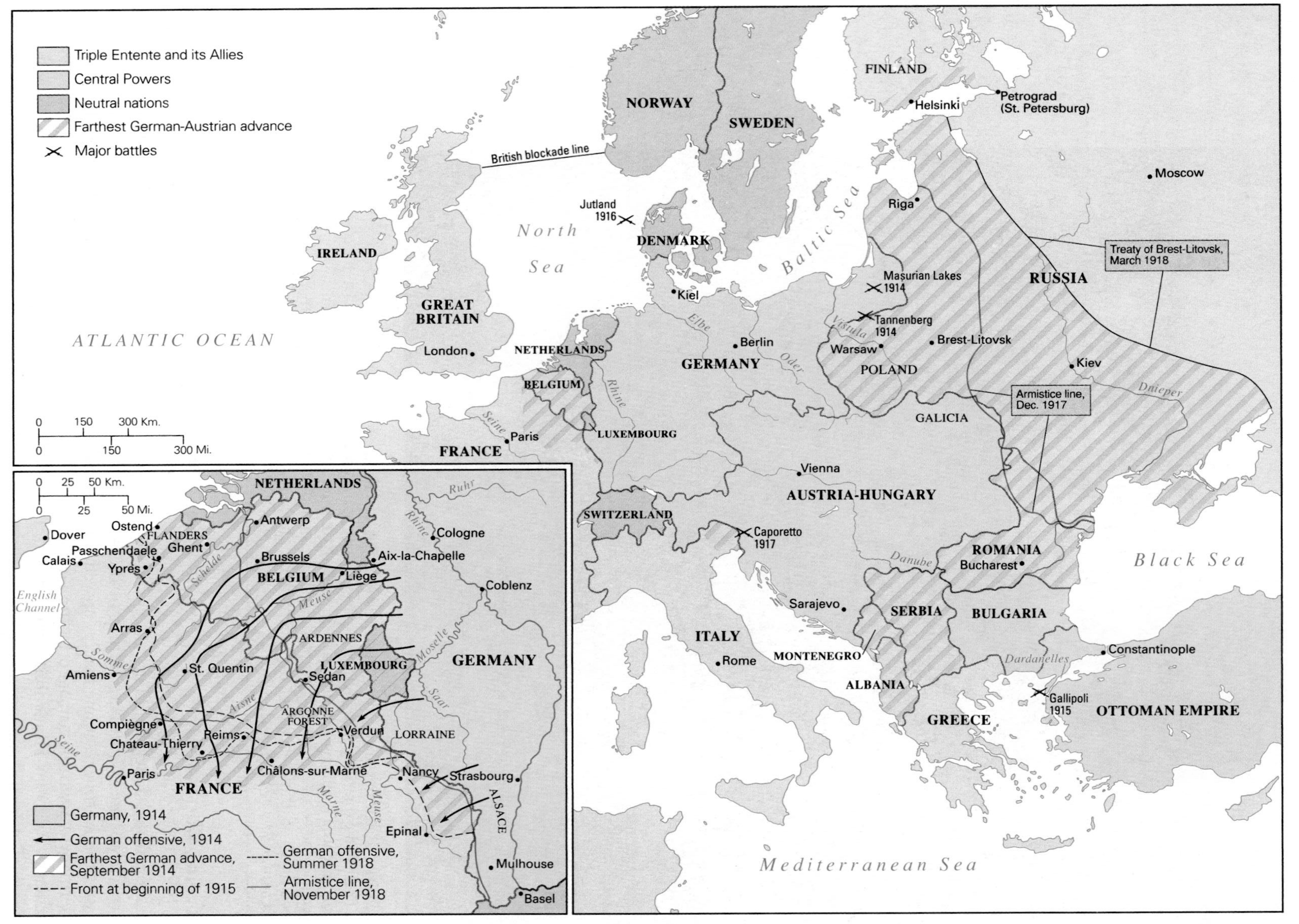
Triple Entente and its Allies
Central Powers
Neutral nations
Farthest German-Austrian advance
Major battles
0 150 300 Km.
0 150 300 Mi.
ATLANTIC OCEAN
IRELAND
GREAT BRITAIN
London
British blockade line
North Sea
Jutland 1916
NORWAY
SWEDEN
DENMARK
Kiel
FINLAND
Helsinki
Petrograd (St. Petersburg)
Moscow
Baltic Sea
Riga
Masurian Lakes 1914
Tannenberg 1914
Vistula
Warsaw
Brest-Litovsk
POLAND
RUSSIA
Treaty of Brest-Litovsk, March 1918
Kiev
Dnieper
Armistice line, Dec. 1917
GALICIA
Elbe
Oder
Berlin
GERMANY
NETHERLANDS
BELGIUM
Rhine
LUXEMBOURG
Seine
Paris
FRANCE
Vienna
AUSTRIA-HUNGARY
SWITZERLAND
Caporetto 1917
Danube
ROMANIA
Bucharest
Black Sea
Sarajevo
SERBIA
BULGARIA
ITALY
Rome
MONTENEGRO
ALBANIA
Dardanelles
Constantinople
Gallipoli 1915
GREECE
OTTOMAN EMPIRE
Mediterranean Sea
0 25 50 Km.
0 25 50 Mi.
NETHERLANDS
Ruhr
Dover
Ostend
FLANDERS
Antwerp
Rhine
Cologne
Passchendaele
Ghent
Calais
Brussels
Aix-la-Chapelle
Ypres
BELGIUM
Liège
Coblenz
English Channel
Scheldt
Meuse
Arras
ARDENNES
Moselle
Somme
LUXEMBOURG
GERMANY
Amiens
St. Quentin
Sedan
Aisne
Saar
ARGONNE FOREST
Compiègne
Reims
Verdun
LORRAINE
Chateau-Thierry
Seine
Paris
Châlons-sur-Marne
Nancy
Strasbourg
FRANCE
ALSACE
Marne
Meuse
Epinal
Mulhouse
Basel
Germany, 1914
German offensive, 1914
Farthest German advance, September 1914
Front at beginning of 1915
German offensive, Summer 1918
Armistice line, November 1918

Indian Soldiers from the so-called warrior castes had long been a critical factor in imperial Britain's global power. These Indian troops, preparing for the Battle of the Somme in 1916, ironically appear to be out for a pleasant bicycling excursion. Dispatched to France in October 1914, most Indian soldiers were moved to western Asia in 1915 to fight against the Ottoman Empire. *(By courtesy of the Trustees of the Imperial War Museum)*

1915. A staggering 2.5 million Russians were killed, wounded, or taken prisoner that year.

These changing tides of victory and defeat brought neutral countries into the war (Map 27.3). Italy, a member of the Triple Alliance since 1882, had declared its neutrality in 1914 on the grounds that Austria had launched a war of aggression. Then in May 1915, Italy joined the Triple Entente of Great Britain, France, and Russia in return for promises of Austrian territory. Bulgaria allied with Austria and Germany, now known as the Central Powers, in September 1915 in order to settle old scores with Serbia.

MAP 27.3 The First World War in Europe The trench war on the western front was concentrated in Belgium and northern France, while the war in the east encompassed an enormous territory.

The entry of Italy and Bulgaria in 1915 was part of a general widening of the war. The Balkans, with the exception of Greece, came to be occupied by the Central Powers, and British forces were badly defeated in 1915 trying to take the Dardanelles from Turkey, Germany's ally. More successful was the entente's attempt to incite Arab nationalists against their Turkish overlords. An enigmatic British colonel, soon known to millions as Lawrence of Arabia, aroused the Arab princes to revolt in early 1917. In 1918 British armies from Egypt smashed the Ottoman Empire once and for all. In the Middle East campaign, the British drew on forces from Australia, New Zealand, and India. Contrary to German hopes, the colonial subjects of the British (and French) did not revolt but loyally supported their foreign masters. The European war extended around the globe as Great Britain, France, and Japan seized Germany's colonies.

A crucial development in the expanding conflict came in April 1917, when the United States declared war on Germany. American intervention grew out of the war at sea, sympathy for the Triple Entente, and the increasing desperation of total war. At the beginning of the war, Britain and France had established a total naval blockade to strangle the Central Powers and prevent deliveries of food and raw materials from overseas. No neutral ship was permitted to sail to Germany with any cargo. The blockade annoyed Americans, but effective propaganda about German atrocities in occupied Belgium as well as lush profits from selling war supplies to Britain and France blunted American indignation.

Moreover, in early 1915 Germany launched a counter-blockade using the murderously effective submarine, a new weapon that violated traditional niceties of fair warning under international law. In May 1915, after sinking about ninety ships in the British war zone, a German submarine sank the British passenger liner *Lusitania,* which was also carrying arms and munitions. More than 1,000 lives, among them 139 Americans, were lost. President Woodrow Wilson protested vigorously. Germany was forced to relax its submarine warfare for almost two years; the alternative was almost certain war with the United States.

Early in 1917, the German military command—confident that improved submarines could starve Britain into submission before the United States could come to its rescue—resumed unrestricted submarine warfare. Like the invasion of Belgium, this was a reckless gamble. British shipping losses reached staggering proportions, though by late 1917 naval strategists had come up with an effective response: the convoy system for safe transatlantic shipping. In the meantime, an embattled President Wilson had told a sympathetic Congress and people that the "German submarine warfare against commerce is a warfare against mankind." Thus the last uncommitted great nation, as fresh and enthusiastic as Europe had been in 1914, entered the world war in April 1917, almost three years after it began. Eventually the United States was to tip the balance in favor of the Triple Entente and its allies.

 THE HOME FRONT

Before looking at the last year of the Great War, let us turn our attention to the people on the home front. They were tremendously involved in the titanic struggle. War's impact on them was no less massive than on the men crouched in the trenches. (See the feature "Listening to the Past: The Experience of War" on pages 924–925.)

Mobilizing for Total War

In August 1914, most people had greeted the outbreak of hostilities enthusiastically. In every country, the masses believed that their nation was in the right and defending itself from aggression. With the exception of a few extreme left-wingers, even socialists supported the war. Tough standby plans to imprison socialist leaders and break general strikes protesting the war proved quite unnecessary in 1914. In Germany, for example, the trade unions voted not to strike, and socialists in the Reichstag voted money for war credits in order to counter the threat of Russian despotism. A German socialist volunteered for the front, explaining to fellow members of the Reichstag that "to shed one's blood for the fatherland is not difficult: it is enveloped in romantic heroism."[5] Everywhere the support of the masses and working class contributed to national unity and an energetic war effort.

By mid-October generals and politicians had begun to realize that more than patriotism would be needed to win the war, whose end was not in sight. Each country experienced a relentless, desperate demand for men and weapons. In France, for example, the generals found themselves needing 100,000 heavy artillery shells a day, as opposed to the 12,000 they had anticipated using. This enormous quantity had to come from a French steel industry that had lost three-fourths of its iron resources in the first days of the war, when Germany seized the mines of French Lorraine. Each belligerent quickly faced countless shortages, for prewar Europe had depended on foreign trade and a great international division of labor. In each country, economic life and organization had to change and change fast to keep the war machine from sputtering to a stop. And change they did.

In each country, a government of national unity began to plan and control economic and social life in order to wage "total war." Free-market capitalism was abandoned, at least "for the duration." Instead, government planning boards established priorities and decided what was to be produced and consumed. Rationing, price and wage controls, and even restrictions on workers' freedom of movement were imposed by government. Only through such regimentation could a country make the greatest possible military effort.

Englishman George Orwell (1903–1950), however, had seen both that reality and its Stalinist counterpart by 1949, when he wrote perhaps the ultimate in anti-utopian literature: *1984.* Orwell set the action in the future, in 1984. Big Brother—the dictator—and his totalitarian state use a new kind of language, sophisticated technology, and psychological terror to strip a weak individual of his last shred of human dignity. The supremely self-confident chief of the Thought Police tells the tortured, broken, and framed Winston Smith, "If you want a picture of the future, imagine a boot stamping on a human face—forever."[4] A phenomenal bestseller, *1984* spoke to millions of people in the closing years of the age of anxiety.

Modern Art and Music

Throughout the twentieth century, there has been considerable unity in the arts. The "modernism" of the immediate prewar years and the 1920s is still strikingly modern. Like the scientists and creative artists who were partaking of the same culture, creative artists rejected old forms and old values. Modernism in art and music meant constant experimentation and a search for new kinds of expression. And though many people find the many and varied modern visions of the arts strange, disturbing, and even ugly, the twentieth century, so dismal in many respects, will probably stand as one of Western civilization's great artistic eras.

Architecture and Design

Modernism in the arts was loosely unified by a revolution in architecture. This revolution intended nothing less than a transformation of the physical framework of urban society according to a new principle: *functionalism.* Buildings, like industrial products, should be useful and "functional"—that is, they should serve, as well as possible, the purpose for which they were made. Thus architects and designers had to work with engineers, town planners, and even santitation experts. Moreover, they had to throw away useless ornamentation and find beauty and aesthetic pleasure in the clean lines of practical constructions and efficient machinery. Franco-Swiss genius Le Corbusier (1887–1965) insisted that "a house is a machine for living in."[5]

The United States, with its rapid urban growth and lack of rigid building traditions, pioneered in the new architecture. In the 1890s, the Chicago school of architects, led by Louis H. Sullivan (1856–1924), used cheap steel, reinforced concrete, and electric elevators to build skyscrapers and office buildings lacking almost any exterior ornamentation. In the first decade of the twentieth century, Sullivan's student Frank Lloyd Wright (1869–1959) built a series of radically new and truly modern houses featuring low lines, open interiors, and mass-produced building materials. Europeans were inspired by these and other American examples of functional construction, like the massive, unadorned grain elevators of the Midwest.

In Europe architectural leadership centered in German-speaking countries until Hitler took power in 1933. In 1911 twenty-eight-year-old Walter Gropius (1883–1969) broke sharply with the past in his design of the Fagus shoe factory at Alfeld, Germany—a clean, light, elegant building of glass and iron. After the First World War, Gropius merged the schools of fine and applied arts at Weimar into a single, interdisciplinary school, the Bauhaus. The Bauhaus brought together many leading modern architects, designers, and theatrical innovators. Working as an effective, inspired team, they combined the study of fine art, such as painting and sculpture, with the study of applied art in the crafts of printing, weaving, and furniture making. Throughout the 1920s, the Bauhaus, with its stress on functionalism and good design for everyday life, attracted enthusiastic students from all over the world. It had a great and continuing impact.

Another leader in the "international" style, Ludwig Mies van der Rohe (1886–1969), followed Gropius as director of the Bauhaus in 1930 and immigrated to the United States in 1937. His classic Lake Shore Apartments in Chicago, built between 1948 and 1951, symbolized the triumph of steel-frame and glass-wall modern architecture in the great building boom after the Second World War.

Modern Painting

Modern painting grew out of a revolt against French impressionism. The *impressionism* of such French painters as Claude Monet (1840–1926), Pierre Auguste Renoir (1841–1919), and Camille Pissarro (1830–1903) was, in part, a kind of "superrealism." Leaving exact copying of objects to photography, these artists sought to capture the momentary overall feeling, or impression, of light falling on a real-life scene before their eyes. By 1890, when impressionism was finally established, a few artists known as *postimpressionists,* or sometimes as *expressionists,* were already striking out in new directions. After 1905 art increasingly took on a

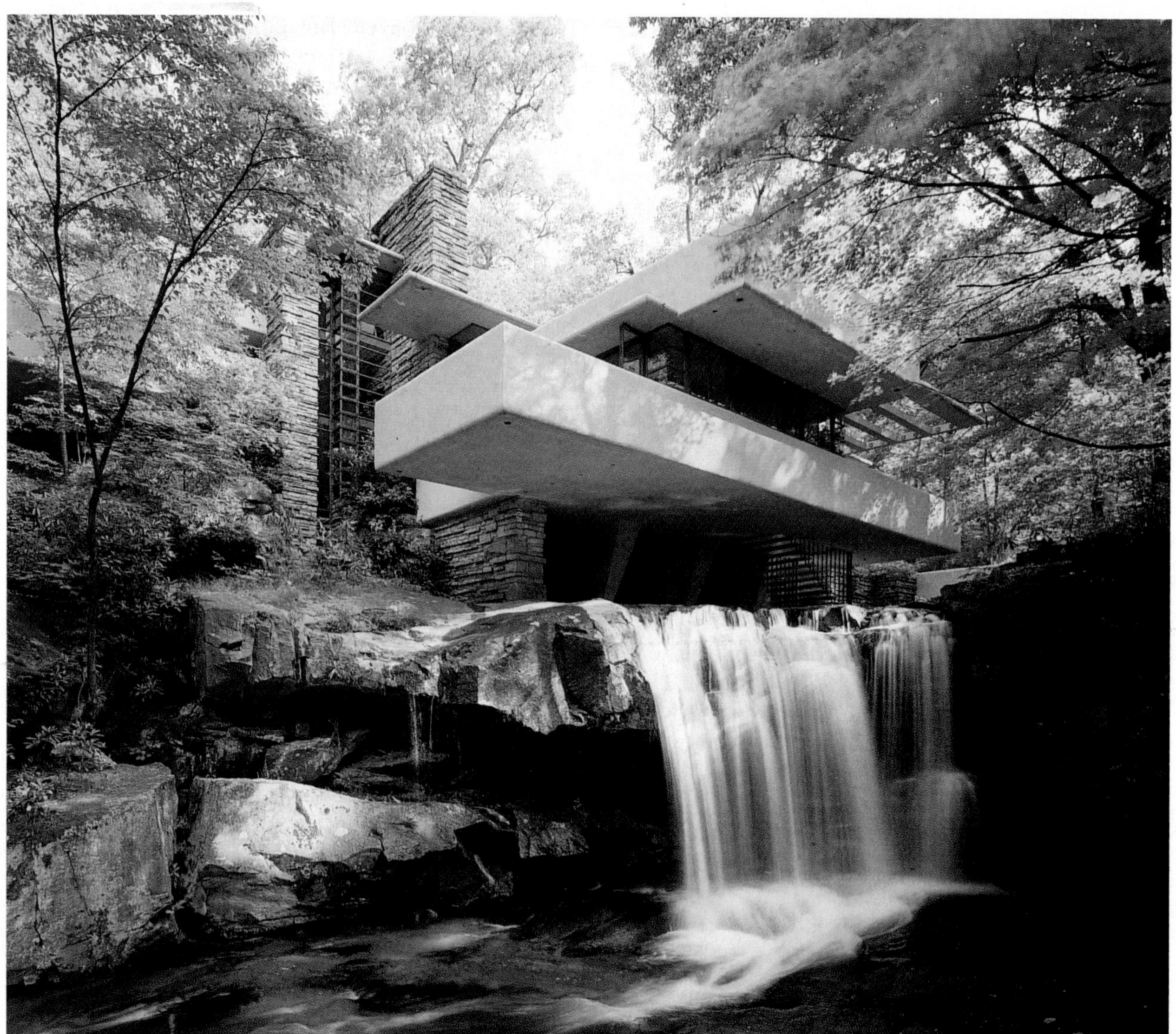

Frank Lloyd Wright: The "Falling Water" House Often considered Wright's masterpiece, Falling Water combines modern architectural concepts with close attention to a spectacular site. Anchored to a high rock ledge by means of reinforced concrete, the house soars out over a cascading waterfall at Bear Run in western Pennsylvania. Built in 1937 for a Pittsburgh businessman, Falling Water is now open to the public and attracts 70,000 visitors each year. *(Western Pennsylvania Conservancy/Art Resource, NY)*

nonrepresentational, abstract character, a development that reached its high point after World War II.

Though individualistic in their styles, postimpressionists were united in their desire to know and depict worlds other than the visible world of fact. Like the early-nineteenth-century romantics, they wanted to portray unseen, inner worlds of emotion and imagination. Like modern novelists, they wanted to express a complicated psychological view of reality as well as an overwhelming emotional intensity. In *The Starry Night* (1889), for example, the great Dutch expressionist Vincent van Gogh (1853–1890) painted the vision of his mind's eye. Flaming cypress trees, exploding stars, and a cometlike Milky Way swirl together in one great cosmic rhythm. Paul Gauguin (1848–1903), the French stockbroker-turned-painter, pioneered in expressionist techniques, though he used them to infuse his work with tranquillity and mysticism. In 1891 he fled to the

South Pacific in search of unspoiled beauty and a primitive way of life. Gauguin believed that the form and design of a picture were important in themselves and that the painter need not try to represent objects on canvas as the eye actually saw them.

Fascination with form, as opposed to light, was characteristic of postimpressionism and expressionism. Paul Cézanne (1839–1906), who had a profound influence on twentieth-century painting, was particularly committed to form and ordered design. He told a young painter, "You must see in nature the cylinder, the sphere, and the cone."[6] As Cézanne's later work became increasingly abstract and nonrepresentational, it also moved away from the traditional three-dimensional perspective toward the two-dimensional plane, which has characterized so much of modern art. The expressionism of a group of painters led by Henri Matisse (1869–1954) was so extreme that an exhibition of their work in Paris in 1905 prompted shocked critics to call them *les fauves*—"the wild beasts." Matisse and his followers still painted real objects, but their primary concern was the arrangement of color, line, and form as an end in itself.

In 1907 a young Spaniard in Paris, Pablo Picasso (1881–1973), founded another movement—*cubism.* Cubism concentrated on a complex geometry of zigzagging lines and sharply angled, overlapping planes. About three years later came the ultimate stage in the development of abstract, nonrepresentational art. Artists such as the Russian-born Wassily Kandinsky (1866–1944) turned away from nature completely. "The observer," said Kandinsky, "must learn to look at [my] pictures . . . as form and color combinations . . . as a representation of mood and not as a representation of *objects.*"[7] On the eve of the First World War, extreme expressionism and abstract painting were developing rapidly not only in Paris but also in Russia and Germany. Modern art had become international.

In the 1920s and 1930s, the artistic movements of the prewar years were extended and consolidated. The most notable new developments were *dadaism* and *surrealism.* Dadaism attacked all accepted standards of art and behavior, delighting in outrageous conduct. Its name, from the French word *dada,* meaning "hobbyhorse," is deliberately nonsensical. A famous example of dadaism is a reproduction of Leonardo da Vinci's *Mona Lisa* in which the famous woman with the mysterious smile sports a mustache and is ridiculed with an obscene inscription. After 1924 many dadaists were attracted to surrealism, which became very influential in art in the

Picasso: Guernica In this rich, complex work a shrieking woman falls from a burning house on the far right. On the left a woman holds a dead child, while toward the center are fragments of a warrior and a screaming horse pierced by a spear. Picasso has used only the mournful colors of black, white, and gray. *(© Copyright ARS, NY. Museo Nacional Centro de Arte Reina Sofia, Madrid, Spain)*

late 1920s and 1930s. Surrealists painted a fantastic world of wild dreams and complex symbols, where watches melted and giant metronomes beat time in precisely drawn but impossible alien landscapes.

Refusing to depict ordinary visual reality, surrealist painters made powerful statements about the age of anxiety. Picasso's twenty-six-foot-long mural *Guernica* (1937) masterfully unites several powerful strands in twentieth-century art. Inspired by the Spanish civil war, the painting commemorates the bombing of the ancient Spanish town of Guernica by fascist planes, an attack that took the lives of a thousand people—one out of every eight inhabitants—in a single night of terror. Combining the free distortion of expressionism, the overlapping planes of cubism, and the surrealist fascination with grotesque subject matter, *Guernica* is what Picasso meant it to be: an unforgettable attack on "brutality and darkness."

Modern Music

Developments in modern music were strikingly parallel to those in painting. Composers, too, were attracted by the emotional intensity of expressionism. The ballet *The Rite of Spring* by composer Igor Stravinsky (1882–1971) practically caused a riot when it was first performed in Paris in 1913 by Sergei Diaghilev's famous Russian dance company. The combination of pulsating, dissonant rhythms from the orchestra pit and an earthy representation of lovemaking by the dancers on the stage seemed a shocking, almost pornographic enactment of a primitive fertility rite.

After the experience of the First World War, when irrationality and violence seemed to pervade the human experience, expressionism in opera and ballet flourished. One of the most famous and powerful examples was the opera *Wozzeck,* by Alban Berg (1885–1935), first performed in Berlin in 1925. Blending a half-sung, half-spoken kind of dialogue with harsh, atonal music, *Wozzeck* is a gruesome tale of a soldier driven by Kafka-like inner terrors and vague suspicions of unfaithfulness to murder his mistress.

Some composers turned their backs on long-established musical conventions. As abstract painters arranged lines and color but did not draw identifiable objects, so modern composers arranged sounds without creating recognizable harmonies. Led by Viennese composer Arnold Schönberg (1874–1951), they abandoned traditional harmony and tonality. The musical notes in a given piece were no longer united and organized by a key; instead they were independent and unrelated. Schönberg's twelve-tone music of the 1920s arranged all twelve notes of the scale in an abstract, mathematical pattern, or "tone row." This pattern sounded like no pattern at all to the ordinary listener and could be detected only by a highly trained eye studying the musical score. Accustomed to the harmonies of classical and romantic music, audiences generally resisted modern atonal music. Only after the Second World War did it begin to win acceptance.

Movies and Radio

Until after World War II at the earliest, these revolutionary changes in art and music appealed mainly to a minority of "highbrows" and not to the general public. That public was primarily and enthusiastically wrapped up in movies and radio. The long-declining traditional arts and amusements of people in villages and small towns almost vanished, replaced by standardized, commercial entertainment.

Moving pictures were first shown as a popular novelty in naughty peepshows—"What the Butler Saw"—and penny arcades in the 1890s, especially in Paris. The first movie houses date from an experiment in Los Angeles in 1902. They quickly attracted large audiences and led to the production of short, silent action films such as the eight-minute *Great Train Robbery* of 1903. American directors and business people then set up "movie factories," at first in the New York area and then after 1910 in Los Angeles. These factories churned out two short films each week. On the eve of the First World War, full-length feature films such as the Italian *Quo Vadis* and the American *Birth of a Nation,* coupled with improvements in the quality of pictures, suggested the screen's vast possibilities.

During the First World War, the United States became the dominant force in the rapidly expanding silent-film industry. In the 1920s, Mack Sennett (1884–1960) and his zany Keystone Kops specialized in short, slapstick comedies noted for frantic automobile chases, custard-pie battles, and gorgeous bathing beauties. Screen stars such as Mary Pickford and Lillian Gish, Douglas Fairbanks and Rudolf Valentino, became household names, with their own "fan clubs." Yet Charlie Chaplin (1889–1978), a funny little Englishman working in Hollywood, was unquestionably the king of the "silver screen" in the 1920s. In his enormously popular role as a lonely tramp, complete with baggy trousers, battered derby, and an awkward, shuffling walk, Chaplin symbolized the "gay spirit of laughter in a cruel, crazy world."[8] Chaplin also demonstrated that in the hands of a genius, the new medium could combine mass entertainment and artistic accomplishment.

The early 1920s were also the great age of German films. Protected and developed during the war, the large German studios excelled in bizarre expressionist dramas, beginning with *The Cabinet of Dr. Caligari* in 1919. Unfortunately, their period of creativity was short-lived. By 1926 American money was drawing the leading German talents to Hollywood and consolidating America's international domination. Film making was big business, and European theater owners were forced to book whole blocks of American films to get the few pictures they really wanted. This system put European producers at a great disadvantage until "talkies" permitted a revival of national film industries in the 1930s, particularly in France.

Whether foreign or domestic, motion pictures became the main entertainment of the masses until after the Second World War. In Great Britain one in every four adults went to the movies twice a week in the late 1930s, and two in five went at least once a week. Continental countries had similar figures. The greatest appeal of motion pictures was that they offered ordinary people a temporary escape from the hard realities of everyday life. For an hour or two, the moviegoer could flee the world of international tensions, uncertainty, unemployment, and personal frustrations. The appeal of escapist entertainment was especially strong during the Great Depression. Millions flocked to musical comedies featuring glittering stars such as Ginger Rogers and Fred Astaire and to the fanciful cartoons of Mickey Mouse and his friends.

The Great Dictator In 1940 the renowned actor and director Charlie Chaplin abandoned the little tramp to satirize the "great dictator," Adolf Hitler. Chaplin had strong political views and made a number of films with political themes as the escapist fare of the Great Depression gave way to the reality of the Second World War. *(The Museum of Modern Art/Still Film Archives)*

Radio became possible with the transatlantic "wireless" communication of Guglielmo Marconi (1874–1937) in 1901 and the development of the vacuum tube in 1904, which permitted the transmission of speech and music. But only in 1920 were the first major public broadcasts of special events made in Great Britain and the United States. Lord Northcliffe, who had pioneered in journalism with the inexpensive, mass-circulation *Daily Mail,* sponsored a broadcast of "only one artist . . . the world's very best, the soprano Nellie Melba."[9] Singing from London in English, Italian, and French, Melba was heard simultaneously all over Europe on June 16, 1920. This historic event captured the public's imagination. The meteoric career of radio was launched.

Every major country quickly established national broadcasting networks. In the United States such networks were privately owned and financed by advertising. In Great Britain Parliament set up an independent, public corporation, the British Broadcasting Corporation (BBC), supported by licensing fees. Elsewhere in Europe the typical pattern was direct control by the government.

Whatever the institutional framework, radio became popular and influential. By the late 1930s, more than three out of every four households in both democratic Great Britain and dictatorial Germany had at least one cheap, mass-produced radio. In other European countries, radio ownership was not quite so widespread, but the new medium was no less important.

Radio in unscrupulous hands was particularly well suited for political propaganda. Dictators such as Mussolini and Hitler controlled the airwaves and could reach enormous national audiences with their frequent, dramatic speeches. In democratic countries, politicians such as President Franklin Roosevelt and Prime

Minister Stanley Baldwin effectively used informal "fireside chats" to bolster their support.

Motion pictures also became powerful tools of indoctrination, especially in countries with dictatorial regimes. Lenin himself encouraged the development of Soviet film making, believing that the new medium was essential to the social and ideological transformation of the country. Beginning in the mid-1920s, a series of epic films, the most famous of which were directed by Sergei Eisenstein (1898–1948), brilliantly dramatized the communist view of Russian history.

In Germany Hitler turned to a young and immensely talented woman film maker, Leni Riefenstahl (b. 1902), for a masterpiece of documentary propaganda, *The Triumph of the Will,* based on the Nazi party rally at Nuremberg in 1934. Riefenstahl combined stunning aerial photography, joyful crowds welcoming Hitler, and mass processions of young Nazi fanatics. Her film was a brilliant and all-too-powerful documentary of Germany's "Nazi rebirth." The new media of mass culture were potentially dangerous instruments of political manipulation.

The Search for Peace and Political Stability

As established patterns of thought and culture were challenged and mangled by the ferocious impact of World War I, so also was the political fabric stretched and torn by the consequences of the great conflict. The Versailles settlement had established a shaky truce, not a solid peace. Thus national leaders faced a gigantic task as they struggled with uncertainty and sought to create a stable international order within the general context of intellectual crisis and revolutionary artistic experimentation.

The pursuit of real and lasting peace proved difficult for many reasons. Germany hated the Treaty of Versailles. France was fearful and isolated. Britain was undependable, and the United States had turned its back on European problems. Eastern Europe was in ferment, and no one could predict the future of communist Russia. Moreover, the international economic situation was poor and greatly complicated by war debts and disrupted patterns of trade. Yet for a time, from 1925 to late 1929, it appeared that peace and stability were within reach. When the subsequent collapse of the 1930s mocked these hopes, the disillusionment of liberals in the democracies was intensified.

Germany and the Western Powers

Germany was the key to lasting peace. Yet to Germans of all political parties, the Treaty of Versailles represented a harsh, dictated peace, to be revised or repudiated as soon as possible. The treaty had neither broken nor reduced Germany, which was potentially still the strongest country in Europe. Thus the treaty had fallen between two stools: too harsh for a peace of reconciliation, too soft for a peace of conquest.

Moreover, with ominous implications for the future, France and Great Britain did not see eye to eye on Germany. By the end of 1919, France wanted to stress the harsh elements in the Treaty of Versailles. Most of the war in the west had been fought on French soil, and the expected costs of reconstruction, as well as repaying war debts to the United States, were staggering. Thus French politicians believed that massive reparations from Germany were a vital economic necessity. Also, having compromised with President Wilson only to be betrayed by America's failure to ratify the treaty, many French leaders saw strict implementation of all provisions of the Treaty of Versailles as France's last best hope. Large reparation payments could hold Germany down indefinitely, and France would realize its goal of security.

The British soon felt differently. Prewar Germany had been Great Britain's second-best market in the entire world, and after the war a healthy, prosperous Germany appeared to be essential to the British economy. Indeed, many English people agreed with the analysis of the young English economist John Maynard Keynes (1883–1946), who eloquently denounced the Treaty of Versailles in his famous *Economic Consequences of the Peace* (1919). According to Keynes's interpretation, astronomical reparations and harsh economic measures would indeed reduce Germany to the position of an impoverished second-rate power, but such impoverishment would increase economic hardship in all countries. Only a complete revision of the foolish treaty could save Germany—and Europe. Keynes's attack exploded like a bombshell and became very influential. It stirred deep guilt feelings about Germany in the English-speaking world, feelings that often paralyzed English and American leaders in their relations with Germany and its leaders between the First and the Second World Wars.

The British were also suspicious of France's army—momentarily the largest in Europe—and France's foreign policy. Ever since 1890, France had looked to Russia as a powerful ally against Germany. But with

Russia hostile and socialist, and with Britain and the United States unwilling to make any firm commitments, France turned to the newly formed states of eastern Europe for diplomatic support. In 1921 France signed a mutual defense pact with Poland and associated itself closely with the so-called Little Entente, an alliance that joined Czechoslovakia, Romania, and Yugoslavia against defeated and bitter Hungary. The British and the French were also on cool terms because of conflicts relating to their League of Nations mandates in the Middle East.

While French and British leaders drifted in different directions, the Allied reparations commission completed its work. In April 1921, it announced that Germany had to pay the enormous sum of 132 billion gold marks ($33 billion) in annual installments of 2.5 billion gold marks. Facing possible occupation of more of its territory, the young German republic, which had been founded in Weimar but moved back to Berlin, made its first payment in 1921. Then in 1922, wracked by rapid inflation and political assassinations and motivated by hostility and arrogance as well, the Weimar Republic announced its inability to pay more. It proposed a moratorium on reparations for three years, with the clear implication that thereafter reparations would be either drastically reduced or eliminated entirely.

The British were willing to accept a moratorium on reparations, but the French were not. Led by their tough-minded, legalistic prime minister, Raymond Poincaré (1860–1934), they decided they had to either call Germany's bluff or see the entire peace settlement dissolve to France's great disadvantage. So, despite strong British protests, in early January 1923, armies of France and its ally Belgium began to occupy the Ruhr district, the heartland of industrial Germany, creating the most serious international crisis of the 1920s. If forcible collection proved impossible, France would use occupation to paralyze Germany and force it to accept the Treaty of Versailles.

Strengthened by a wave of patriotism, the German government ordered the people of the Ruhr to stop working and start passively resisting the French occupation. The coal mines and steel mills of the Ruhr grew silent, leaving 10 percent of Germany's total population in need of relief. The French answer to passive resistance was to seal off not only the Ruhr but also the entire Rhineland from the rest of Germany, letting in only enough food to prevent starvation. The French also revived plans for a separate state in the Rhineland.

By the summer of 1923, France and Germany were engaged in a great test of wills. French armies could not collect reparations from striking workers at gunpoint. But French occupation was indeed paralyzing Germany and its economy and had turned rapid German inflation into runaway inflation. Faced with the need to support the striking Ruhr workers and their employers, the German government began to print money to pay its bills. Prices soared. People went to the store with a big bag of paper money; they returned home with a handful of groceries. German money rapidly lost all value, and so did anything else with a stated fixed value.

Runaway inflation brought about a social revolution. The accumulated savings of many retired and middle-

"Hands Off the Ruhr" The French occupation of the Ruhr to collect reparations payments raised a storm of patriotic protest in Germany. This anti-French poster of 1923 turns Marianne, the personification of French republican virtue, into a vicious harpy. *(International Instituut voor Sociale Geschiedenis)*

class people were wiped out. Catastrophic inflation cruelly mocked the old middle-class virtues of thrift, caution, and self-reliance. Many Germans felt betrayed. They hated and blamed the Western governments, their own government, big business, the Jews, the workers, and the communists for their misfortune. They were psychologically prepared to follow radical leaders in a crisis.

In August 1923, as the mark fell and political unrest grew throughout Germany, Gustav Stresemann (1878–1929) assumed leadership of the government. Stresemann adopted a compromising attitude. He called off passive resistance in the Ruhr and in October agreed in principle to pay reparations but asked for a re-examination of Germany's ability to pay. Poincaré accepted. His hard line was becoming increasingly unpopular with French citizens, and it was hated in Britain and the United States.

More generally, in both Germany and France, power was finally passing to the moderates, who realized that continued confrontation was a destructive, no-win situation. Thus after five long years of hostility and tension, culminating in a kind of undeclared war in the Ruhr in 1923, Germany and France decided to give compromise and cooperation a try. The British, and even the Americans, were willing to help. The first step was a reasonable compromise on the reparations question.

Hope in Foreign Affairs, 1924–1929

The reparations commission appointed an international committee of financial experts headed by American banker Charles G. Dawes to re-examine reparations from a broad perspective. The resulting Dawes Plan (1924) was accepted by France, Germany, and Britain. Germany's yearly reparations were reduced and depended on the level of German economic prosperity. Germany would also receive large loans from the United States to promote German recovery. In short, Germany would get private loans from the United States and pay reparations to France and Britain, thus enabling those countries to repay the large sums they owed the United States.

This circular flow of international payments was complicated and risky, but for a while it worked. The German republic experienced a spectacular economic recovery. By 1929 Germany's wealth and income were 50 percent greater than in 1913. With prosperity and large, continual inflows of American capital, Germany easily paid about $1.3 billion in reparations in 1927 and 1928, enabling France and Britain to pay the United States. In this way the Americans, who did not have armies but who did have money, belatedly played a part in the general economic settlement that, though far from ideal, facilitated the worldwide recovery of the late 1920s.

This economic settlement was matched by a political settlement. In 1925 the leaders of Europe signed a number of agreements at Locarno, Switzerland. Germany and France solemnly pledged to accept their common border, and both Britain and Italy agreed to fight either France or Germany if one invaded the other. Stresemann also agreed to settle boundary disputes with Poland and Czechoslovakia by peaceful means, and France promised those countries military aid if Germany attacked them. For years, a "spirit of Locarno" gave Europeans a sense of growing security and stability in international affairs.

Other developments also strengthened hopes. In 1926 Germany joined the League of Nations, where Stresemann continued his "peace offensive." In 1928 fifteen countries signed the Kellogg-Briand Pact, initiated by French prime minister Aristide Briand and U.S. secretary of state Frank B. Kellogg. This multinational pact "condemned and renounced war as an instrument of national policy." The signing states agreed to settle international disputes peacefully. Often seen as idealistic nonsense because it made no provisions for action in case war actually occurred, the pact was still a positive step. It fostered the cautious optimism of the late 1920s and also encouraged the hope that the United States would accept its responsibilities as a great world power and contribute to European stability.

Hope in Democratic Government

Domestic politics also offered reason to hope. During the occupation of the Ruhr and the great inflation, republican government in Germany had appeared on the verge of collapse. In 1923 communists momentarily entered provincial governments, and in November an obscure nobody named Adolf Hitler leaped onto a table in a beer hall in Munich and proclaimed a "national socialist revolution." But Hitler's plot to seize control of the government was poorly organized and easily crushed, and Hitler was sentenced to prison, where he outlined his theories and program in his book *Mein Kampf* (My Struggle). Throughout the 1920s, Hitler's National Socialist party attracted support only from a few fanatical anti-Semites, ultranationalists, and disgruntled ex-servicemen. In 1928 his party had an insignificant twelve seats in the Reichstag. Indeed, after

An American in Paris The young Josephine Baker suddenly became a star when she brought an exotic African eroticism to French music halls in 1925. American blacks and Africans had a powerful impact on entertainment in Europe in the 1920s and 1930s. *(Hulton-Getty/Tony Stone Images)*

1923 democracy seemed to take root in Weimar Germany. A new currency was established, and the economy boomed.

The moderate businessmen who tended to dominate the various German coalition governments were convinced that economic prosperity demanded good relations with the Western powers, and they supported parliamentary government at home. Stresemann himself was a man of this class, and he was the key figure in every government until his death in 1929. Elections were held regularly, and republican democracy appeared to have growing support among a majority of the Germans.

There were, however, sharp political divisions in the country. Many unrepentant nationalists and monarchists populated the right and the army. Members of Germany's recently formed Communist party were noisy and active on the left. The Communists, directed from Moscow, reserved their greatest hatred and sharpest barbs for their cousins the Social Democrats, whom they endlessly accused of betraying the revolution. The working classes were divided politically, but a majority supported the nonrevolutionary but socialist Social Democrats.

The situation in France had numerous similarities to that in Germany. Communists and Socialists battled for the support of the workers. After 1924 the democratically elected government rested mainly in the hands of coalitions of moderates, and business interests were well represented. France's great accomplishment was rapid rebuilding of its war-torn northern region. The expense of this undertaking led, however, to a large deficit and substantial inflation. By early 1926, the franc had fallen to 10 percent of its prewar value, causing a severe crisis. Poincaré was recalled to office, while Briand remained minister for foreign affairs. The Poincaré government proceeded to slash spending and raise taxes, restoring confidence in the economy. The franc was "saved," stabilized at about one-fifth of its prewar value. Good times prevailed until 1930.

Despite political shortcomings, France attracted artists and writers from all over the world in the 1920s. Much of the intellectual and artistic ferment of the times flourished in Paris. As writer Gertrude Stein (1874–1946), a leader of the large colony of American expatriates living in Paris, later recalled, "Paris was where the twentieth century was."[10] More generally, France appealed to foreigners and the French as a harmonious combination of small businesses and family farms, of bold innovation and solid traditions.

Britain, too, faced challenges after 1920. The wartime trend toward greater social equality continued, however, helping maintain social harmony. The great problem was unemployment. Many of Britain's best markets had been lost during the war. In June 1921, almost 2.2 million people—23 percent of the labor force—were out of work, and throughout the 1920s unemployment hovered around 12 percent. Yet the state provided unemployment benefits of equal size to all those without jobs and supplemented those payments with subsidized housing, medical aid, and increased old-age pensions. These and other measures kept living standards from seriously declining, defused class tensions, and pointed the way toward the welfare state Britain established after World War II.

Relative social harmony was accompanied by the rise of the Labour party as a determined champion of the working classes and of greater social equality. Committed to the kind of moderate, "revisionist" socialism that had emerged before World War I (see page 849), the Labour party replaced the Liberal party as the main opposition to the Conservatives. The new prominence of the Labour party reflected the decline of old liberal ideals of competitive capitalism, limited government control, and individual responsibility. In 1924 and 1929, the Labour party under Ramsay MacDonald (1866–1937) governed the country with the support of the smaller Liberal party. Yet Labour moved toward socialism gradually and democratically, so that the middle classes were not overly frightened as the working classes won new benefits.

The Conservatives under Stanley Baldwin (1867–1947) showed the same compromising spirit on social issues. The last line of Baldwin's greatest speech in March 1925 summarized his international and domestic programs: "Give us peace in our time, O Lord." In spite of such conflicts as the 1926 strike by hard-pressed coal miners, which ended in an unsuccessful general strike, social unrest in Britain was limited in the 1920s and in the 1930s as well. In 1922 Britain granted southern, Catholic Ireland full autonomy after a bitter guerrilla war, thereby removing another source of prewar friction. Thus developments in both international relations and the domestic politics of the leading democracies gave cause for optimism in the late 1920s.

The Great Depression, 1929–1939

Like the Great War, the Great Depression must be spelled with capital letters. Economic depression was nothing new. Depressions occurred throughout the nineteenth century with predictable regularity, as they recur in the form of recessions and slumps to this day. What was new about this depression was its severity and duration. It struck the entire world with ever-greater intensity from 1929 to 1933, and recovery was uneven and slow. Only with the Second World War did the depression disappear in much of the world.

The social and political consequences of prolonged economic collapse were enormous. The depression shattered the fragile optimism of political leaders in the late 1920s. Mass unemployment and failing farms made insecurity a reality for millions of ordinary people, who had paid little attention to the intellectual crisis or to new directions in art and ideas (Map 28.1). In desperation, people looked for leaders who would "do something." They were willing to support radical attempts to deal with the crisis by both democratic leaders and dictators.

The Economic Crisis

There is no agreement among historians and economists about why the Great Depression was so deep and lasted so long. Thus it is best to trace the course of the great collapse before trying to identify what caused it.

Though economic activity was already declining moderately in many countries by early 1929, the crash of the stock market in the United States in October of that year triggered the collapse into the Great Depression. The American economy had prospered in the late 1920s, but there were large inequalities in income and a serious imbalance between "real" investment and stock market speculation. Thus net investment—in factories, farms, equipment, and the like—actually fell from $3.5 billion in 1925 to $3.2 billion in 1929. In the same years, as money flooded into stocks, the value of shares traded on the exchanges soared from $27 billion to $87 billion. As a financial historian concludes in an important new study, "It should have been clear to everybody concerned that a crash was inevitable under such conditions."[11] Of course it was not. Irving Fisher,

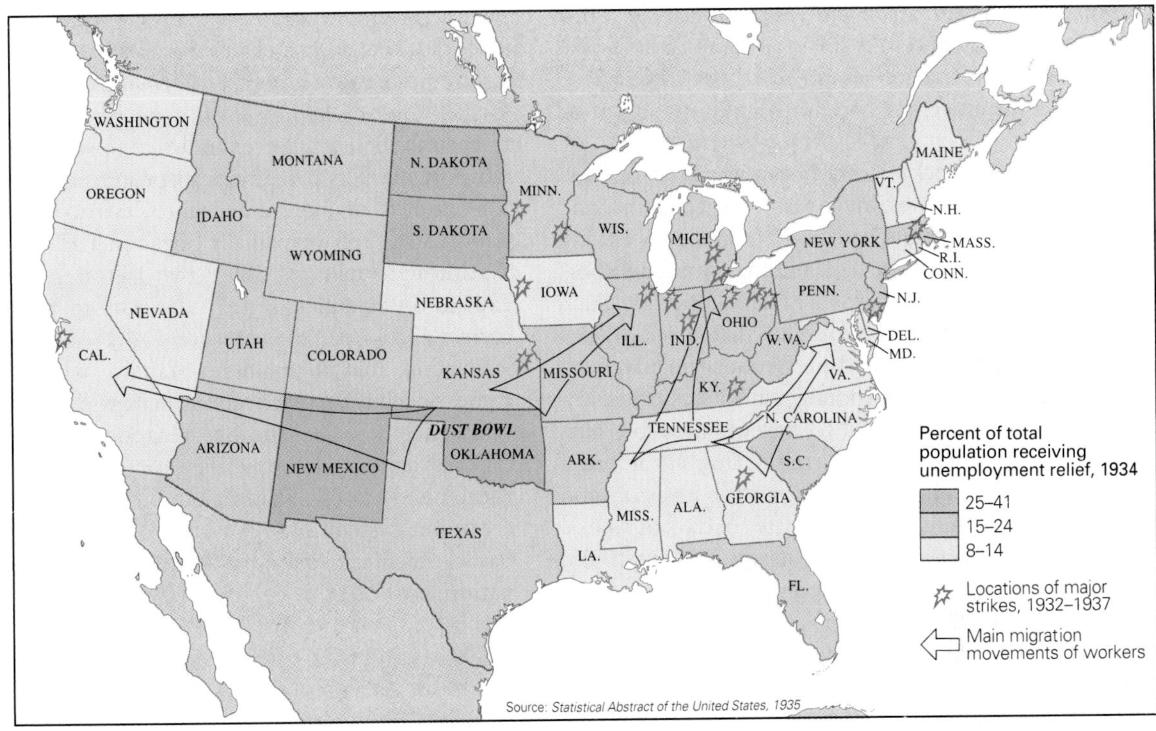

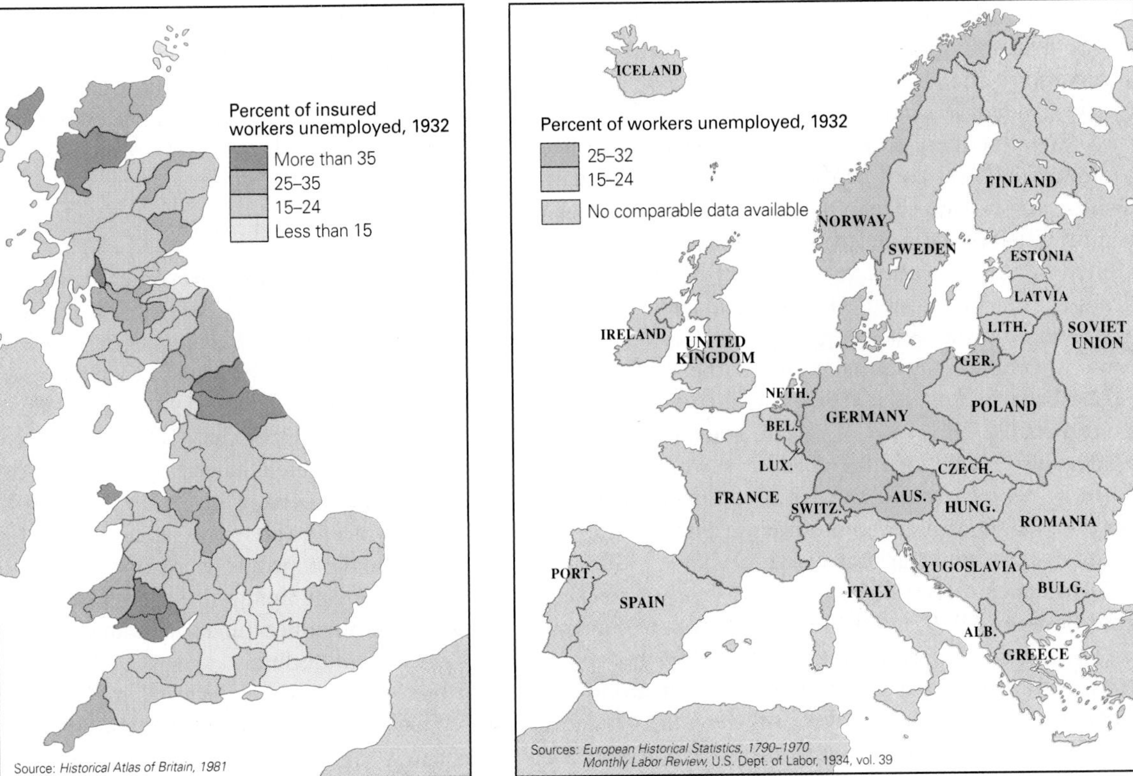

MAP 28.1 The Great Depression in the United States, Britain, and Europe National and regional differences were substantial. Germany, industrial northern Britain, and the American Midwest were particularly hard hit.

one of America's most brilliant economists, was highly optimistic in 1929 and fully invested in stocks. He then lost his entire fortune and would have been forced from his house if his university had not bought it and rented it to him.

The American stock market boom was built on borrowed money. Many wealthy investors, speculators, and people of modest means had bought stocks by paying only a small fraction of the total purchase price and borrowing the remainder from their stockbrokers. Such buying "on margin" was extremely dangerous. When prices started falling, the hard-pressed margin buyers either had to put up more money, which was often impossible, or sell their shares to pay off their brokers. Thus thousands of people started selling all at once. The result was a financial panic. Countless investors and speculators were wiped out in a matter of days or weeks.

The general economic consequences were swift and severe. Stripped of wealth and confidence, battered investors and their fellow citizens started buying fewer goods. Prices fell, production began to slow down, and unemployment began to rise. Soon the entire American economy was caught in a vicious, spiraling decline.

The financial panic in the United States triggered a worldwide financial crisis, and that crisis resulted in a drastic decline in production in country after country. Throughout the 1920s, American bankers and investors had lent large amounts of capital to many countries. Many of these loans were short-term, and once panic broke, New York bankers began recalling them. Gold reserves thus began to flow out of European countries, particularly Germany and Austria, toward the United States. It became very hard for European business people to borrow money, and the panicky public began to withdraw its savings from the banks. These banking problems eventually led to the crash of the largest bank in Austria in 1931 and then to general financial chaos. The recall of private loans by American bankers also accelerated the collapse in world prices, as business people around the world dumped industrial goods and agricultural commodities in a frantic attempt to get cash to pay what they owed.

The financial crisis led to a general crisis of production: between 1929 and 1933, world output of goods fell by an estimated 38 percent. As this happened, each country turned inward and tried to go it alone. In 1931, for example, Britain went off the gold standard, refusing to convert bank notes into gold, and reduced the value of its money. Britain's goal was to make its goods cheaper and therefore more salable in the world market. But because more than twenty nations, including the United States in 1934, also went off the gold standard, few countries gained a real advantage. Similarly, country after country followed the example of the United States when in 1930 it raised protective tariffs to their highest levels ever and tried to seal off shrinking national markets for American producers only. Within this context of fragmented and destructive economic nationalism, recovery finally began in 1933.

Although opinions differ, two factors probably best explain the relentless slide to the bottom from 1929 to early 1933. First, the international economy lacked a leadership able to maintain stability when the crisis came. Specifically, as a noted American economic historian concludes, the seriously weakened British, the traditional leaders of the world economy, "couldn't and the United States wouldn't" stabilize the international economic system in 1929.[12] The United States, which had momentarily played a positive role after the occupation of the Ruhr, cut back its international lending and erected high tariffs.

The second factor was poor national economic policy in almost every country. Governments generally cut their budgets and reduced spending when they should have run large deficits in an attempt to stimulate their economies. After World War II, such a "counter-cyclical policy," advocated by John Maynard Keynes, became a well-established weapon against downturn and depression. But in the 1930s, Keynes's prescription was generally regarded with horror by orthodox economists.

Mass Unemployment

The need for large-scale government spending was tied to mass unemployment. As the financial crisis led to cuts in production, workers lost their jobs and had little money to buy goods. In Britain unemployment had averaged 12 percent in the 1920s; between 1930 and 1935, it averaged more than 18 percent. Far worse was the case of the United States, where unemployment had averaged only 5 percent in the 1920s. In 1932 unemployment soared to about 33 percent of the entire labor force: 14 million people were out of work (see Map 28.1). Only by pumping new money into the economy could the government increase demand and break the vicious cycle of decline.

Along with economic effects, mass unemployment posed a great social problem that mere numbers cannot adequately express. Millions of people lost their spirit and dignity in an apparently hopeless search for work. Homes and ways of life were disrupted in millions of personal tragedies. Young people postponed marriages

between sick capitalism and cruel communism or fascism.

Recovery and Reform in Britain and France

In Britain MacDonald's Labour government and then, after 1931, the Conservative-dominated coalition government followed orthodox economic theory. The budget was balanced, but unemployed workers received barely enough welfare to live. Despite government lethargy, the economy recovered considerably after 1932. By 1937 total production was about 20 percent higher than in 1929. In fact, for Britain the years after 1932 were actually somewhat better than the 1920s had been, quite the opposite of the situation in the United States and France.

This good but by no means brilliant performance reflected the gradual reorientation of the British economy. After going off the gold standard in 1931 and establishing protective tariffs in 1932, Britain concentrated increasingly on the national, rather than the international, market. The old export industries of the Industrial Revolution, such as textiles and coal, continued to decline, but new industries, such as automobiles and electrical appliances, grew in response to British home demand. Moreover, low interest rates encouraged a housing boom. By the end of the decade, there were highly visible differences between the old, depressed industrial areas of the north and the new, growing areas of the south. These developments encouraged Britain to look inward and avoid unpleasant foreign questions.

Because France was relatively less industrialized and more isolated from the world economy, the Great Depression came late. But once the depression hit France, it stayed and stayed. Decline was steady until 1935, and a short-lived recovery never brought production or employment back up to predepression levels. Economic stagnation both reflected and heightened an ongoing political crisis. There was no stability in government. As before 1914, the French parliament was made up of many political parties, which could never cooperate for very long. In 1933, for example, five coalition cabinets formed and fell in rapid succession.

The French lost the underlying unity that had made government instability bearable before 1914. Fascist-type organizations agitated against parliamentary democracy and looked to Mussolini's Italy and Hitler's Germany for inspiration. In February 1934, French fascists and semifascists rioted and threatened to overturn the republic. At the same time, the Communist party and many workers opposed to the existing system were looking to Stalin's Russia for guidance. The vital center of moderate republicanism was sapped from both sides.

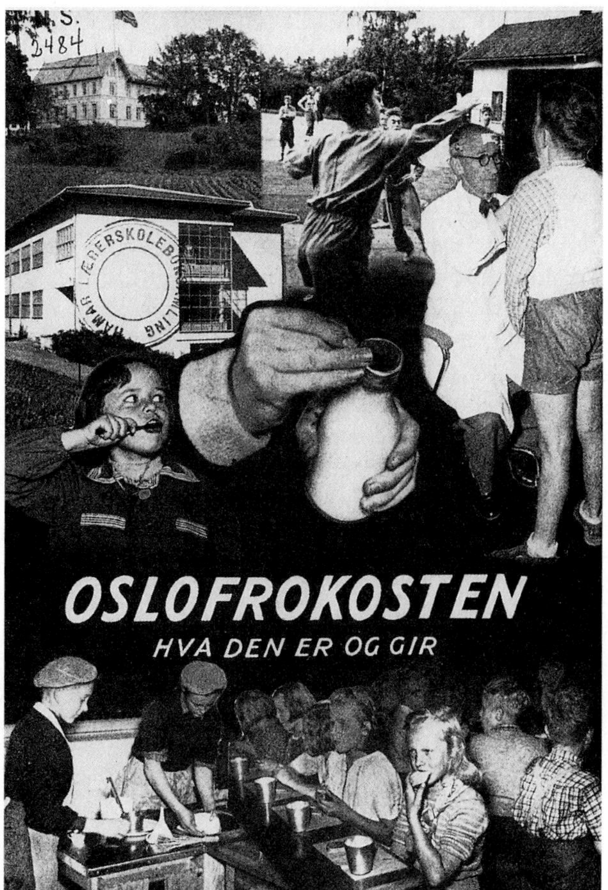

Scandinavian Socialism championed cooperation and practical welfare measures, playing down strident rhetoric and theories of class conflict. The Oslo Breakfast, depicted in the lower part of this poster, exemplified the Scandinavian approach. It provided every schoolchild in the Norwegian capital with a good breakfast free of charge. *(Universitets-biblioteket i Oslo)*

Frightened by the growing strength of the fascists at home and abroad, the Communists, the Socialists, and the Radicals formed an alliance—the Popular Front—for the national elections of May 1936. Their clear victory reflected the trend toward polarization. The number of Communists in the parliament jumped dramatically from 10 to 72, while the Socialists, led by Léon Blum, became the strongest party in France, with 146 seats. The really quite moderate Radicals slipped badly, and the conservatives lost ground to the semifascists.

In the next few months, Blum's Popular Front government made the first and only real attempt to deal with the social and economic problems of the 1930s in France. Inspired by Roosevelt's New Deal, the Popular Front encouraged the union movement and launched a far-reaching program of social reform, complete with paid vacations and a forty-hour workweek. Popular with workers and the lower middle class, these measures were quickly sabotaged by rapid inflation and cries of revolution from fascists and frightened conservatives. Wealthy people sneaked their money out of the country, labor unrest grew, and France entered a severe financial crisis. Blum was forced to announce a "breathing spell" in social reform.

The fires of political dissension were also fanned by civil war in Spain. Communists demanded that France support the Spanish republicans, while many French conservatives would gladly have joined Hitler and Mussolini in aiding the attack of Spanish fascists. Extremism grew, and France itself was within sight of civil war. Blum was forced to resign in June 1937, and the Popular Front quickly collapsed. An anxious and divided France drifted aimlessly once again, preoccupied by Hitler and German rearmament.

SUMMARY

After the First World War, Western society entered a complex and difficult era—truly an age of anxiety. Intellectual life underwent a crisis marked by pessimism, uncertainty, and fascination with irrational forces. Ceaseless experimentation and rejection of old forms characterized art and music, while motion pictures and radio provided a new, standardized entertainment for the masses. Intellectual and artistic developments that had been confined to small avant-garde groups before 1914, along with the insecure state of mind they expressed, gained wider currency.

Politics and economics were similarly disrupted. In the 1920s, political leaders groped to create an enduring peace and rebuild the prewar prosperity, and for a brief period late in the decade, they even seemed to have succeeded. Then the Great Depression shattered that fragile stability. Uncertainty returned with redoubled force in the 1930s. The international economy collapsed, and unemployment struck millions worldwide. The democracies turned inward as they sought to cope with massive domestic problems and widespread disillusionment. Generally speaking, they were not very successful, although relief measures and social concern eased distress and prevented revolutions in the leading Western nations. The old liberal ideals of individual rights and responsibilities, elected government, and economic freedom declined and seemed outmoded to many. And in many countries of central and eastern Europe, these ideas were abandoned completely, as we shall see in the next chapter.

NOTES

1. P. Valéry, *Variety,* trans. M. Cowley (New York: Harcourt Brace, 1927), pp. 27–28.
2. Quoted in S. Hughes, *The Obstructed Path: French Social Thought in the Years of Desperation, 1930–1960* (New York: Harper & Row, 1967), p. 82.
3. G. Greene, *Another Mexico* (New York: Viking Press, 1939), p. 3.
4. G. Orwell, *1984* (New York: New American Library, 1950), p. 220.
5. C. E. Jeanneret-Gris (Le Corbusier), *Towards a New Architecture* (London: J. Rodker, 1931), p. 15.
6. Quoted in A. H. Barr, Jr., *What Is Modern Painting?* 9th ed. (New York: Museum of Modern Art, 1966), p. 27.
7. Quoted ibid., p. 25.
8. R. Graves and A. Hodge, *The Long Week End: A Social History of Great Britain, 1918–1939* (New York: Macmillan, 1941), p. 131.
9. Quoted in A. Briggs, *The Birth of Broadcasting,* vol. 1 (London: Oxford University Press, 1961), p. 47.
10. Quoted in R. J. Sontag, *A Broken World, 1919–1939* (New York: Harper & Row, 1971), p. 129.
11. Dietmar Rothermund, *The Global Impact of the Great Depression, 1929–1939* (London and New York: Routledge, 1996), p. 50.
12. C. P. Kindleberger, *The World in Depression, 1929–1939* (Berkeley and Los Angeles: University of California Press, 1973), p. 292.
13. Quoted in S. B. Clough et al., eds., *Economic History of Europe: Twentieth Century* (New York: Harper & Row, 1968), pp. 243–245.
14. Quoted in D. Dillard, *Economic Development of the North Atlantic Community* (Englewood Cliffs, N.J.: Prentice-Hall, 1967), p. 591.
15. Quoted in Lois Scharf, *Eleanor Roosevelt: First Lady of American Liberalism* (Boston: Twayne, 1987), p. 110.

SUGGESTED READING

A. Bullock, ed., *The Twentieth Century* (1971), is particularly noteworthy because it is a lavish visual feast combined with penetrating essays on major developments. Two excellent accounts of contemporary history—one with a liberal and the other with a conservative point of view—are R. Paxton, *Europe in the Twentieth Century*, 3d ed. (1997), and P. Johnson, *Modern Times: The World from the Twenties to the Eighties* (1983). R. Clark, *Hope and Glory: Britain, 1900–1990* (1996), and J. McMillan, *Twentieth-Century France: Politics and Society, 1898–1991* (1992), are two recommended national surveys. Crucial changes in thought before and after World War I are discussed in three rewarding intellectual histories: S. Kern, *The Culture of Time and Space, 1880–1918* (1983); M. Berman, *All That Is Solid Melts into Air: The Experience of Modernity* (1982); and G. Masur, *Prophets of Yesterday* (1961). H. S. Hughes, *Consciousness and Society* (1956), and M. Biddiss, *Age of the Masses: Ideas and Society Since 1870* (1977), are stimulating and useful. R. Stromberg, *European Intellectual History Since 1789* (1986), is a clear general account. W. Kaufmann, *Nietzsche* (1974), is a sympathetic and justly famous older study, and S. Aschheim, *The Nietzsche Legacy in Germany, 1890–1990* (1992), considers the range of responses to the pioneering philosopher. W. Barrett, *Irrational Man: A Study in Existential Philosophy* (1958), is still useful.

N. Cantor, *The American Century: Varieties of Culture in Modern Times* (1997), is a pugnacious and stimulating survey. J. Rewald, *The History of Impressionism* (1961), and R. Golan, *Modernity and Nostalgia: Art and Politics in France Between the Wars* (1995), are excellent and also reflect changing tastes in art history. Barr, cited in the Notes, is helpful. P. Collaer, *A History of Modern Music* (1961), and H. R. Hitchcock, *Architecture: Nineteenth and Twentieth Centuries* (1958), are good introductions, whereas T. Wolfe, *From Bauhaus to My House* (1981), is a lively critique of modern architecture. L. Barnett, *The Universe and Dr. Einstein* (1952), is a fascinating study of the new physics. A. Storr, *Freud* (1989), and P. Rieff, *Freud* (1956), consider the man and how his theories have stood the test of time. S. Freud, *Civilization and Its Discontents* (1930), which is highly recommended, explores Freud's theory of instinct and repression, arguing that society's necessary repression of instinctual drives will always leave people unhappy. M. White, ed., *The Age of Analysis* (1955), opens up basic questions of twentieth-century psychology and philosophy. H. Liebersohn, *Fate and Utopia in German Sociology* (1988), analyzes developments in German social science. J. Willett, *The New Sobriety: Art and Politics in the Weimar Period, 1917–1933* (1978), considers the artistic renaissance and the political culture in Germany in the 1920s. M. Marrus, ed., *Emergence of Leisure* (1974), is a pioneering inquiry into an important aspect of mass culture. H. Daniels-Rops, *A Fight for God,* 2 vols. (1966), is a sympathetic history of the Catholic church between 1870 and 1939.

G. Ambrosius and W. Hibbard, *A Social and Economic History of Twentieth-Century Europe* (1989), and F. Tipton and R. Aldrich, *An Economic and Social History of Europe, 1890–1939* (1987), are recommended and interesting to compare. P. Fritzsche, *Rehearsals for Fascism: Populism and Political Mobilization in Weimar Germany* (1990), R. Wohl, *The Generation of 1914* (1979), and R. Kuisel, *Capital and State in Modern France: Renovation and Economic Management* (1982), are three important studies on aspects of the postwar challenge. S. Reynolds, *France Between the Wars: Gender and Politics* (1996), and J. Keiger, *Raymond Poincaré* (1996), are major reconsiderations of French politics from different perspectives. H. James, *The German Slump: Politics and Economics 1924–1936* (1986), is an excellent analysis of economic recovery and subsequent collapse. M. Childs, *Sweden: The Middle Way* (1961), applauds Sweden's efforts at social reform. L. Scharf, *Eleanor Roosevelt: First Lady of American Liberalism* (1987), is a pioneering interpretation, and J. Youngs, *Eleanor Roosevelt: A Personal and Public Life* (1985), is exceptionally well written. Both are highly recommended, as is Eleanor Roosevelt's own moving account, *This Is My Story* (1937). O. and L. Handlin, *Liberty in America Since 1600,* vol. 4 (1994), argues that the United States has erred in moving from equality of opportunity to equality of results since 1920. In addition to the contemporary works discussed in the text, the crisis of the interwar period comes alive in R. Crossman, ed., *The God That Failed* (1950), in which famous Western writers tell why they were attracted to and later repelled by communism; J. Ortega y Gasset's renowned *The Revolt of the Masses* (1932); and F. A. Hayek's *The Road to Serfdom* (1944), a famous warning of the dangers to democratic freedoms.

In addition to Rothermund's and Kindleberger's excellent studies of the Great Depression cited in the Notes, P. Temin, *Lessons from the Great Depression* (1987), is a judicious evaluation by an outstanding economic historian. J. Garraty, *Unemployment in History* (1978), is noteworthy, though novels best portray the human tragedy of economic decline. W. Holtby, *South Riding* (1936), and W. Greenwood, *Love on the Dole* (1933), are moving stories of the Great Depression in England. Hans Fallada, *Little Man, What Now?* (1932), is the classic counterpart for Germany. Also highly recommended as commentaries on English life between the wars are N. Gray, *The Worst of Times: An Oral History of the Great Depression in Britain* (1985); and George Orwell, *The Road to Wigan Pier* (1972). Among French novelists, André Gide painstakingly examines the French middle class and its values in *The Counterfeiters*; Albert Camus, the greatest of the existential novelists, is at his unforgettable best in *The Stranger* (1942) and *The Plague* (1947).

LISTENING TO THE PAST

A Christian View of Evil

The English philosopher C. E. M. Joad (1891–1953) stands out among intellectuals who turned toward religion in the age of anxiety. As a university student, he shed his faith and became a militant rationalist who was "frequently in demand for lectures and articles which adopted an attitude hostile to revealed religion in general, and to the Christian Church in particular." Only after intense reflection did Joad retrace his steps and come to reaccept Christianity. Ever the serious intellectual, he described and analyzed his "spiritual odyssey" in closely reasoned and influential writings.

The following selection is taken from God and Evil, *published in 1942 when Hitler's empire posed the problem of human depravity in the starkest terms. Reconsidering the modern secular faith in the primacy of environmental influences and in the perfectibility of humankind, Joad found these beliefs wanting. He reaffirmed the Christian focus on sin and the need for God's grace to escape from evil and find salvation.*

There is, we are told, a revival of interest in religious matters. . . . In this revival of interest I have shared. . . . As a young man at Oxford, I participated, as was natural to my age and generation, in prolonged and frequent discussions of religion which, finding me a Christian, left me as they did many of my generation, an agnostic, an agnostic who entertained a deep-seated suspicion of all dogmatic creeds. . . .

As an agnostic, I felt convinced of two things: first, . . . within the sphere of religion that we did not and probably could not know the truth; secondly, in regard to the so-called religious truths that I had been taught, as, for example, that God created the world as stated in Genesis [and] . . . sent His Son into it to redeem mankind, that it was improbable that they were true and certain that they could not be *known* to be true. In the confidence of this conviction I proceeded, to all intents and purposes, to turn my back upon the whole subject. . . .

It was only after the coming of the Nazis that my mind began again to turn in the direction of religion. . . . [With] the outbreak of [the Second World] war the subject leapt straight into the forefront of my consciousness where it has remained ever since. . . .

I take it [my spiritual odyssey] to be not untypical. From conversations and discussions, especially with students, I surmise that the revival of interest in religion is widespread. . . . This topical relevance of religion derives from two sources. [First, there is] the relation between religion and politics. This connection . . . subsists at all times, but in quiet times of peace it usually remains implicit. The peculiar circumstances of the last twenty-five years have, however, combined to thrust it into the foreground of men's consciousness. . . . Thus times of revolutionary political change are also times of religious questioning and discussion.

The other source of the specifically topical interest in religion is . . . the obtrusiveness of evil. [Perhaps] there is no more evil abroad in Western civilization than there was at the end of the last century, but it cannot be denied that what there is of it is more obtrusive. I am not referring to evils arising from the relation between the sexes upon which the Church has laid such exclusive stress. . . . I mean the evils of cruelty, savagery, oppression, violence, egotism, aggrandisement, and lust for power. So pervasive and insistent have these evils become that it is at times difficult to avoid concluding that the Devil has been given a longer rope than usual, . . . [and] it becomes correspondingly more difficult to explain it away by the various methods which have been fashionable during the last twenty years.

There was, for example, the explanation of evil in terms of economic inequality and injustice. So-

Nazi Mass Rally, 1936 This picture captures the essence of the totalitarian interpretation of dynamic modern dictatorship. The uniformed members of the Nazi party have willingly merged themselves into a single force and await the command of the godlike leader. *(Wide World Photos)*

the Bolsheviks during the Russian civil war. Lenin showed how a dedicated minority could make a total effort and achieve victory over a less-determined majority. Moreover, Lenin demonstrated how institutions and human rights might be subordinated to the needs of a single group—the Communist party—and its leader, Lenin. Lenin also provided a model for single-party dictatorship, and he inspired imitators, including Adolf Hitler. The modern totalitarian state then reached maturity in the 1930s in the Stalinist U.S.S.R. and Nazi Germany.

Embellishing on early insights, numerous Western political scientists and historians argued in the 1950s and the 1960s that the totalitarian state used modern technology and communications to exercise complete political power. But it did not stop there. Increasingly, the state took over and tried to control just as completely the economic, social, intellectual, and cultural aspects of people's lives. Deviation from the norm even in art or family behavior could become a crime. In theory, nothing was politically neutral; nothing was outside the scope of the state.

This grandiose vision of total state control broke decisively not only with conservative authoritarianism but also with nineteenth-century liberalism and democracy. Indeed, totalitarianism was a radical revolt against liberalism. Classical liberalism, which emerged decisively in the American and French Revolutions, sought to limit the power of the state and protect the rights of the individual. Moreover, liberals stood for rationality, peaceful progress, economic freedom, and a strong middle class. All of that disgusted totalitarians as sentimental slop. They believed in willpower, preached conflict, and worshiped violence. The individual was infinitely less valuable than the state, and there were no lasting rights, only temporary rewards for loyal and effective service.

Unlike old-fashioned authoritarianism, modern totalitarianism was based not on an elite but on people who had already become engaged in the political process, most notably through commitment to nationalism and socialism. Thus according to this interpretation, real totalitarian states built on mass movements and possessed boundless dynamism. Totalitarian societies were fully mobilized societies, moving toward some goal. And as soon as one goal was achieved at the cost of enormous sacrifice, another arose at the leader's command to take its place. Thus totalitarianism was in the end a *permanent* revolution, an *unfinished* revolution, in which rapid, profound change imposed from on high went on forever.

A second group of writers approached radical dictatorships outside the Soviet Union through the concept of *fascism.* A term of pride for Mussolini and Hitler, who used it to describe the supposedly "total" and revolutionary character of their movements, fascism was severely criticized by these writers and linked to reactionary forces, decaying capitalism, and domestic class conflict. Orthodox Marxists first argued that fascism was the way powerful capitalists sought to manipulate a mass movement capable of destroying the revolutionary working class and thus protect the enormous profits to be reaped through war and territorial expansion. Orthodox Marxists also rejected the totalitarian model, discerning at least some elements of the genuine socialism they desired in communist regimes such as that of Stalin.

Scholarly interest in fascism declined in the 1950s but revived thereafter. Comparative studies of fascist movements all across Europe showed that they shared many characteristics, including extreme, often expansionist nationalism; an antisocialism aimed at destroying working-class movements; alliances with powerful capitalists and landowners; mass parties, which appealed especially to the middle class and the peasantry; a dynamic and violent leader; and glorification of war and the military. European fascism remains a product of class conflict, capitalist crisis, and postwar upheaval in these more recent studies, but the basic interpretation has become less dogmatic and more subtle and convincing.

Historians today often adopt a third approach, which emphasizes the uniqueness of developments in each country. This approach has been both reflected and encouraged in recent years by an outpouring of specialized historical studies that stress change over time and challenge overarching interpretations like totalitarianism and fascism as too static and theoretical. This is especially true for Hitler's Germany, and a similar revaluation of Stalin's U.S.S.R. is in progress now that the fall of communism has opened the former Soviet Union's archives to new research. For this third school of historians, differences and changes in historical patterns are often more important than striking but frequently superficial similarities.

Four tentative judgments concerning these debates seem appropriate. First, as is often the case in history, leading schools of interpretation are rather closely linked to the political passions and the ideological commitments of the age. Thus modern Western "bourgeois-liberal" observers and moderate socialists, worried by the dual challenge of the Nazi and Soviet dictatorships, often found the totalitarian framework convincing in the 1930s and in the early cold war. At the same time, communists and orthodox Marxists saw profound structural differences between the continued capitalism in fascist countries and the socialism established in the Soviet Union, and starting in the 1960s New Left writers shared this view.

Second, as a noted scholar has recently concluded, the concept of totalitarianism retains real value for historical understanding. It correctly highlights that both Hitler's Germany and Stalin's Soviet Union made an unprecedented "total claim" on the belief and behavior of their respective citizens.[3] Third, antidemocratic, antisocialist movements sprang up all over Europe, but only in Italy and Germany (and some would say Spain) were they able to take power. Studies of fascist movements seeking power locate common elements, but they do not explain what fascist governments actually did. Fourth, the problem of Europe's radical dictatorships is complex, and there are few easy answers.

Stalin's Soviet Union

Many of Lenin's harshest critics claim that he established the basic outlines of a modern totalitarian dictatorship after the Bolshevik Revolution and during the Russian civil war. If this is so, then Joseph Stalin (1879–1953) certainly finished the job. A master of political infighting, Stalin cautiously consolidated his power and eliminated his enemies in the mid-1920s. Then in 1928, as undisputed leader of the ruling Communist party, he launched the first five-year plan—the "revolution from above," as he so aptly termed it.

The five-year plans were extremely ambitious. Often incorrectly considered a mere set of economic measures to speed up the Soviet Union's industrial development, the five-year plans actually marked the beginning of a renewed attempt to mobilize and transform Soviet society along socialist lines. The ultimate goal of the plans was to generate new attitudes, new loyalties, and a new socialist humanity. The means Stalin and the small Communist party elite chose in order to do so were constant propaganda, enormous sacrifice by the people, and the concentration of all power in party hands. Thus the Soviet Union in the 1930s became a dynamic, modern totalitarian state.

From Lenin to Stalin

By spring 1921, Lenin and the Bolsheviks had won the civil war, but they ruled a shattered and devastated land. Many farms were in ruins, and food supplies were exhausted. In southern Russia, drought combined with the ravages of war to produce the worst famine in generations. By 1920, according to the government, from 50 to 90 percent of the population in seventeen provinces was starving. Industrial production also broke down completely. In 1921, for example, output of steel and cotton textiles was only about 4 percent of what it had been in 1913. The Bolsheviks had destroyed the economy as well as their foes.

In the face of economic disintegration, riots by peasants and workers, and an open rebellion by previously pro-Bolshevik sailors at Kronstadt, the tough but ever-flexible Lenin changed course. In March 1921, he announced the New Economic Policy (NEP), which re-established limited economic freedom in an attempt to rebuild agriculture and industry. During the civil war, the Bolsheviks had simply seized grain without payment, in accordance with the extreme policies of "war communism." With the NEP, Lenin substituted a grain tax on the country's peasant producers, who were permitted to sell their surpluses in free markets. Peasants were also encouraged to buy as many goods as they could afford from private traders and small handicraft manufacturers, groups that were now allowed to reappear. Heavy industry, railroads, and banks, however, remained wholly nationalized.

The NEP was shrewd and successful both politically and economically. Politically, it was a necessary but temporary compromise with the Soviet Union's overwhelming peasant majority. Flushed with victory after the revolutionary gains of 1917, the peasants would have fought to hold on to their land. Realizing that his government was not strong enough to take land from the peasants and turn them into state workers, Lenin made a deal with the only force capable of overturning his government. Economically, the NEP brought rapid recovery. In 1926 industrial output surpassed the level of 1913, and Soviet peasants were producing almost as

Lenin and Stalin in 1922 Lenin re-established limited economic freedom throughout the Soviet Union in 1921, but he ran the country and the Communist party in an increasingly authoritarian way. Stalin carried the process much further and eventually built a regime based on harsh dictatorship. *(Sovfoto)*

much grain as before the war. Counting shorter hours and increased social benefits, urban workers as well as peasants were living somewhat better than they had in the past.

As the economy recovered and the government partially relaxed its censorship and repression, an intense struggle for power began in the inner circles of the Communist party, for Lenin had left no chosen successor when he died in 1924. The principal contenders were the stolid Stalin and the flamboyant Trotsky.

The son of a shoemaker, Joseph Dzhugashvili—later known as Stalin—studied for the priesthood but was expelled from his theological seminary, probably for rude rebelliousness. By 1903 he had joined the Bolsheviks. In the years before the First World War, he engaged in many revolutionary activities in the southern Transcaucasian area of the multinational Russian empire, including a daring bank robbery to get money for the Bolsheviks. This raid gained Lenin's attention and approval.

Stalin was a good organizer but a poor speaker and writer, with no experience outside of Russia. Trotsky, a great and inspiring leader who had planned the 1917 takeover (see page 913) and then created the victorious Red Army, appeared to have all the advantages. Yet it was Stalin who succeeded Lenin. Stalin won because he was more effective at gaining the all-important support of the party, the only genuine source of power in the one-party state. Rising to general secretary of the party's Central Committee just before Lenin's first stroke in 1922, Stalin used his office to win friends and allies with jobs and promises.

The practical Stalin also won because he appeared better able than the brilliant Trotsky to relate Marxian teaching to Soviet realities in the 1920s. Stalin developed a theory of "socialism in one country" that was more appealing to the majority of communists than Trotsky's doctrine of "permanent revolution." Stalin argued that the Russian-dominated Soviet Union had the ability to build socialism on its own. Trotsky maintained that socialism in the Soviet Union could succeed only if revolution occurred quickly throughout Europe. To many Russian communists, Trotsky's views seemed to sell their country short and to promise risky conflicts with capitalist countries by recklessly encouraging revolutionary movements around the world. Stalin's willingness to break with the NEP and "build socialism" at home appealed to young militants in the party, who detested the capitalist-appearing NEP.

With cunning skill, Stalin gradually achieved supreme power between 1922 and 1927. First, he allied with Trotsky's personal enemies to crush Trotsky, who was expelled from the Soviet Union in 1929 and eventually was murdered in Mexico in 1940, undoubtedly on Stalin's order. Second, Stalin aligned with the moderates, who wanted to go slow at home, to suppress Trotsky's radical followers. Third, having defeated all the radicals, he turned against his allies, the moderates, and destroyed them as well. Stalin's final triumph came at the party congress of December 1927, which condemned all "deviation from the general party line" formulated by Stalin. The dictator and his followers were then ready to launch the revolution from above—the real revolution for millions of ordinary citizens.

The Five-Year Plans

The party congress of 1927, which ratified Stalin's consolidation of power, marked the end of the NEP and the beginning of the era of socialist five-year plans. Building on planning models developed by Soviet economists in the 1920s, the first five-year plan had staggering economic objectives. In just five years, total industrial output was to increase by 250 percent. Heavy industry, the preferred sector, was to grow even faster. Agricultural production was slated to increase by 150 percent, and one-fifth of the peasants in the Soviet Union were scheduled to give up their private plots and join socialist collective farms. By 1930 economic and social change was sweeping the country.

Stalin unleashed his "second revolution" for a variety of interrelated reasons. There were, first of all, ideological considerations. Like Lenin, Stalin and his militant supporters were deeply committed to socialism as they understood it. They feared a gradual restoration of capitalism, and they burned to stamp out the NEP's private traders, independent artisans, and property-owning peasants. Purely economic motivations were also important. Although the economy had recovered, it seemed to have stalled in 1927 and 1928. A new socialist offensive seemed necessary if industry and agriculture were to grow rapidly.

Political considerations were most important. Internationally, there was the old problem, remaining from prerevolutionary times, of catching up with the advanced and presumably hostile capitalist nations of the West. Stalin said in 1931, when he pressed for ever-greater speed and sacrifice, "We are fifty or a hundred years behind the advanced countries. We must make good this distance in ten years. Either we do it, or we shall go under."[4]

Domestically, there was what communist writers of the 1920s called the "cursed problem"—the problem police arrested a mass of lesser party officials and newer members, also torturing them and extracting more confessions for more show trials. In addition to the party faithful, union officials, managers, intellectuals, army officers, and countless ordinary citizens were struck down. In all, at least 8 million people were probably arrested, and millions of these were executed or never returned from prisons and forced-labor camps.

Stalin and the remaining party leadership recruited 1.5 million new members to take the place of those purged. Thus more than half of all Communist party members in 1941 had joined since the purges. "These new men were 'thirty-something' products of the Second Revolution of the 1930s, Stalin's upwardly mobile yuppies, so to speak."[9] Often sons (and daughters) of workers, they had usually studied in the new technical schools, and they soon proved capable of managing the government and large-scale production. One of the most important products of the great purges, this new generation of Stalin-formed communists would serve the leader effectively until his death in 1953, and they would govern the Soviet Union until the early 1980s.

Stalin's mass purges remain baffling, for almost all historians believe that those purged posed no threat and confessed to crimes they had not committed. Possibly Stalin believed that the old communists, like the peasants under the NEP, were a potential threat to be wiped out in a preventive attack. Certainly the highly publicized purges sent a warning to the people: no one was secure; everyone had to serve the party and its leader with redoubled devotion. Some Western scholars have also argued that the terror reflected a fully developed totalitarian state, which must always be fighting real or imaginary enemies.

The long-standing Western interpretation that puts the blame for the great purges on Stalin, which became

Factory Workers Endorse the Moscow Trials Voicing opposition in public was a one-way ticket to a forced-labor camp. Yet revisionist historians also argue that genuine fears of foreign plots and widespread resentment of privileged elites created considerable popular support for the great purges among ordinary Soviet citizens. *(David King Collection)*

popular in Russia with both leading historians and the general public after the fall of communism, has nevertheless been challenged in recent years. Revisionist historians argue that Stalin's fears were exaggerated but real. Moreover, these fears and suspicions were shared by many in the party and in the general population. Bombarded with ideology and political slogans, the population responded energetically to Stalin's directives. Investigations and trials snowballed into a mass hysteria, a new witch-hunt that claimed millions of victims.[10] In short, in this view of the 1930s, a popular but deluded Stalin found large numbers of willing collaborators for crime as well as for achievement.

Mussolini and Fascism in Italy

Mussolini's movement and his seizure of power in 1922 were important steps in the rise of dictatorships in Europe between the two world wars. Like all the future dictators, the young Mussolini hated liberalism and wanted to destroy it in Italy. But although Mussolini began as a revolutionary socialist, like Stalin, he turned against the working class and successfully sought the support of conservatives. At the same time, Mussolini and his supporters were the first to call themselves "fascists"—revolutionaries determined to create a certain kind of totalitarian state. Yet few scholars today would argue that Mussolini succeeded. His dictatorship was brutal and theatrical, but it remained a halfway house between conservative authoritarianism and dynamic totalitarianism.

The Seizure of Power

In the early twentieth century, Italy was a liberal state with civil rights and a constitutional monarchy. On the eve of the First World War, the parliamentary regime finally granted universal male suffrage, and Italy appeared to be moving toward democracy. But there were serious problems. Much of the Italian population was still poor, and many peasants were more attached to their villages and local interests than to the national state. Moreover, the papacy, many devout Catholics, conservatives, and landowners remained strongly opposed to liberal institutions and to the heirs of Cavour and Garibaldi—the middle-class lawyers and politicians who ran the country largely for their own benefit. Relations between church and state were often tense. Class differences were also extreme, and a powerful revolutionary socialist movement had developed. Only in Italy among the main European countries did the radical left wing of the Socialist party gain the leadership as early as 1912, and only in Italy did the Socialist party unanimously oppose the war from the very beginning.[11]

The war worsened the political situation. Having fought on the side of the Allies almost exclusively for purposes of territorial expansion, the parliamentary government bitterly disappointed Italian nationalists with Italy's modest gains at Versailles. Workers and peasants also felt cheated: to win their support during the war, the government had promised social and land reform, which it did not deliver after the war.

The Russian Revolution inspired and energized Italy's revolutionary socialist movement. The Socialist party quickly lined up with the Bolsheviks, and radical workers and peasants began occupying factories and seizing land in 1920. These actions scared and mobilized the property-owning classes. Moreover, after the war the pope lifted his ban on participation by Catholics in Italian politics, and a strong Catholic party quickly emerged. Thus by 1921 revolutionary socialists, antiliberal conservatives, and frightened property owners were all opposed—though for different reasons—to the liberal parliamentary government.

Into these crosscurrents of unrest and fear stepped the blustering, bullying Benito Mussolini (1883–1945). Son of a village schoolteacher and a poor blacksmith, Mussolini began his political career as a Socialist party leader and radical newspaper editor before World War I. In 1914, powerfully influenced by antidemocratic cults of violent action, the young Mussolini urged that Italy join the Allies, a stand for which he was expelled from the Italian Socialist party. Later Mussolini fought at the front and was wounded in 1917. Returning home, he began organizing bitter war veterans like himself into a band of fascists—from the Italian word for "a union of forces."

At first Mussolini's program was a radical combination of nationalist and socialist demands, including territorial expansion, benefits for workers, and land reform for peasants. As such, it competed directly with the well-organized Socialist party and failed to get off the ground. When Mussolini saw that his violent verbal assaults on rival Socialists won him growing support from conservatives and the frightened middle classes, he shifted gears in 1920. In thought and action, Mussolini was a striking example of the turbulent uncertainty of the age of anxiety.

Mussolini and his growing private army of Black Shirts began to grow violent. Typically, a band of fascist toughs would roar off in trucks at night and swoop down on a few isolated Socialist organizers, beating them up and force-feeding them almost deadly doses of cleverly succeeded in gaining additional support from key people in the army and big business. These people thought they could use Hitler for their own advantage to get increased military spending, fat contracts, and tough measures against workers. Many conservative and nationalistic politicians thought similarly. They thus accepted Hitler's demand to join the government only if he became chancellor. There would be only two other National Socialists and nine solid conservatives as ministers, and in such a coalition government, they reasoned, Hitler could be used and controlled. On January 30, 1933, Adolf Hitler, leader of the largest party in Germany, was legally appointed chancellor by Hindenburg.

The Nazi State and Society

Hitler moved rapidly and skillfully to establish an unshakable dictatorship. Continuing to maintain legal appearances, he immediately called for new elections. In the midst of a violent electoral campaign, the Reichstag building was partly destroyed by fire. Although the Nazis themselves may have set the fire, Hitler screamed that the Communist party was responsible. On the strength of this accusation, he convinced President Hindenburg to sign dictatorial emergency acts that practically abolished freedom of speech and assembly as well as most personal liberties.

When the Nazis won only 44 percent of the vote in the elections, Hitler immediately outlawed the Communist party and arrested its parliamentary representatives. Then on March 23, 1933, the Nazis pushed through the Reichstag the so-called Enabling Act, which gave Hitler absolute dictatorial power for four years. Armed with the Enabling Act, Hitler and the Nazis moved to smash or control all independent organizations. Their deceitful stress on legality, coupled with divide-and-conquer techniques, disarmed the opposition until it was too late for effective resistance.

Germany soon became a one-party state. Only the Nazi party was legal. Elections were farces. The Reichstag was jokingly referred to as the most expensive glee club in the country, for its only function was to sing hymns of praise to the Führer. Hitler and the Nazis took over the government bureaucracy intact, installing many Nazis in top positions. At the same time, they created a series of overlapping Nazi party organizations responsible solely to Hitler.

As research in recent years shows, the resulting system of dual government was riddled with rivalries, contradictions, and inefficiencies. Thus the Nazi state lacked the all-compassing unity that its propagandists claimed and was sloppy and often disorganized. Yet this fractured system suited Hitler and his purposes. He could play the established bureaucracy against his private, personal "party government" and maintain his freedom of action. Hitler could concentrate on general principles and the big decisions, which he always made.

In the economic sphere, one big decision outlawed strikes and abolished independent labor unions, which were replaced by the Nazi Labor Front. Professional people—doctors and lawyers, teachers and engineers—also saw their previously independent organizations swallowed up by Nazi associations. Nor did the Nazis neglect cultural and intellectual life. Publishing houses were put under Nazi control, and universities and writers were quickly brought into line. Democratic, socialist, and Jewish literature was put on ever-growing blacklists. Passionate students and pitiful professors burned forbidden books in public squares. Modern art and architecture were ruthlessly prohibited. Life became violently anti-intellectual. As the cynical Joseph Goebbels put it, "When I hear the word 'culture' I reach for my gun."[14] By 1934 a brutal dictatorship characterized by frightening dynamism and obedience to Hitler was already largely in place.

Only the army retained independence, and Hitler moved brutally and skillfully to establish his control there, too. He realized that the army as well as big business was suspicious of the Nazi storm troopers (the SA), the quasi-military band of 3 million toughs in brown shirts who had fought communists and beaten up Jews before the Nazis took power. These unruly storm troopers expected top positions in the army and even talked of a "second revolution" against capitalism. Hitler decided that the SA leaders had to be eliminated. On the night of June 30, 1934, he struck.

Hitler's elite personal guard—the SS—arrested and shot without trial roughly a thousand SA leaders and assorted political enemies. His propagandists then spread lies about SA conspiracies. Shortly thereafter army leaders swore a binding oath of "unquestioning obedience . . . to the Leader of the German State and People, Adolf Hitler." The SS grew rapidly. Under its methodical, inhuman leader, Heinrich Himmler (1900–1945), the SS joined with the political police, the Gestapo, to expand its network of special courts and concentration camps. Nobody was safe.

From the beginning, Jews were a special object of Nazi persecution. By the end of 1934, most Jewish lawyers, doctors, professors, civil servants, and musicians had lost their jobs and the right to practice their professions. In 1935 the infamous Nuremberg Laws classified as Jewish anyone having one or more Jewish grandparents and deprived Jews of all rights of citizenship. By 1938 roughly 150,000 of Germany's half a million Jews had emigrated, sacrificing almost all their property in order to leave Germany.

Following the assassination of a German diplomat in Paris by a young Jewish boy trying desperately to strike out at persecution, the attack on the Jews accelerated. A well-organized wave of violence, known to history as "Kristallnacht," smashed windows, looted shops, and destroyed homes and synagogues. German Jews were then rounded up and made to pay for the damage. Another 150,000 Jews fled Germany. Some Germans privately opposed these outrages, but most went along or looked the other way. This lack of opposition reflected anti-Semitism to a degree still being debated by historians, but it certainly reflected the strong popular support Hitler's government enjoyed.

Hitler's Popularity

Hitler had promised the masses economic recovery—"work and bread"—and he delivered. Breaking with Brüning's do-nothing policies, Hitler launched a large public works program to help pull Germany out of the depression. Work began on superhighways, offices, gigantic sports stadiums, and public housing. Hitler also appointed as Germany's central banker a well-known conservative named Hjalmar Schacht, who skillfully restored credit and business. In 1936 an openly aggressive Hitler broke with Schacht, and Germany turned decisively toward rearmament and preparation for war. As a result of these policies (and plain good luck), unemployment dropped steadily, from 6 million in January 1933 to about 1 million in late 1936. By 1938 there was a shortage of workers, as unemployment fell to 2 percent, and women began to take jobs previously denied them by the antifeminist Nazis. Thus between 1932 and 1938, the standard of living for the average employed worker increased moderately. The profits of business rose sharply. For millions of people, economic recovery was tangible evidence that Nazi promises were more than show and propaganda.

For the masses of ordinary German citizens who were not Jews, Slavs, Gypsies, Jehovah's Witnesses, communists, or homosexuals, Hitler's government meant greater equality and more opportunities. In 1933 the position of the traditional German elites—the landed aristocracy, the wealthy capitalists, and the well-educated professional classes—was still very strong. Barriers between classes were generally high. Hitler's rule introduced changes that lowered these barriers. For example, stiff educational requirements, which favored the well-to-do, were relaxed. The new Nazi elite included many young and poorly educated dropouts, rootless lower-middle-class people like Hitler who rose to the top with breathtaking speed. More generally, the Nazis tolerated privilege and wealth only as long as they served the needs of the party. Even big business was constantly ordered around.

Yet few historians today believe that Hitler and the Nazis brought about a real social revolution, as an earlier generation of scholars often argued. Millions of modest middle-class and lower-middle-class people *felt* that Germany was becoming more open and equal, as Nazi propagandists constantly claimed. But quantitative studies show that the well-educated classes held on to most of their advantages and that only a modest social leveling occurred in the Nazi years. It is significant that the Nazis shared with the Italian fascists the stereotypic view of women as housewives and mothers. Only under the relentless pressure of war did they reluctantly mobilize large numbers of German women for work in offices and factories.

Hitler's rabid nationalism, which had helped him gain power, continued to appeal to Germans after 1933. Ever since the wars against Napoleon, many Germans had believed in a special mission for a superior German nation. The successes of Bismarck had furthered such feelings, and near-victory in World War I made nationalists eager for renewed expansion in the 1920s. Thus when Hitler went from one foreign triumph to another and a great German empire seemed within reach, the majority of the population was delighted and kept praising the Führer's actions well into the war.

Not all Germans supported Hitler, however, and a number of German groups actively resisted him after 1933. Tens of thousands of political enemies were imprisoned, and thousands were executed. But opponents of the Nazis pursued various goals, and they were never unified, a fact that helps account for their ultimate lack of success. In the first years of Hitler's rule, the principal resisters were the communists and the socialists in the trade unions. But the expansion of the SS system of terror after 1935 smashed most of these leftists. A second group of opponents arose in the Catholic and Protestant churches. However, their efforts were directed primarily at preserving genuine religious life, not at overthrowing Hitler. Finally in 1938 (and again in 1942 to 1944), some high-ranking army officers, who feared the consequences of Hitler's reckless aggression, plotted against him, unsuccessfully.

NAZI EXPANSION AND THE SECOND WORLD WAR

Although economic recovery and somewhat greater opportunity for social advancement won Hitler support, they were only byproducts of the Nazi regime. The guiding and unique concepts of Nazism remained space and race—the territorial expansion of the superior German race. As Germany regained its economic strength and as independent organizations were brought under control, Hitler formed alliances with other dictators and began expanding. German expansion was facilitated by the uncertain, divided, pacific Western democracies, which tried to buy off Hitler to avoid war.

Yet war inevitably broke out, in both the West and the East, for Hitler's ambitions were essentially unlimited. On both war fronts, Nazi soldiers scored enormous successes until late 1942, establishing a vast empire of death and destruction. Hitler's reckless aggression also raised a mighty coalition determined to smash the Nazi order. Led by Britain, the United States, and the Soviet Union, the Grand Alliance—to use Winston Churchill's favorite term—functioned quite effectively in military terms. By the summer of 1943, the tide of battle had turned. Two years later, Germany and its allies lay in ruins, utterly defeated. Thus the terrible Nazi empire proved short-lived.

The Glorification of Gender Difference The Nazi state favored traditional roles for women, believing that they should keep house and raise families, preferably large ones. Thus this propaganda poster starkly informs young women that their job is motherhood. Young men entering the State Labor Service are depicted as happy, self-confident "soldiers of work," bonding together and preparing for battle. *(AKG London)*

Aggression and Appeasement, 1933–1939

Hitler's tactics in international politics after 1933 strikingly resembled those he had used in domestic politics between 1924 and 1933. When Hitler was weak, he righteously proclaimed that he intended to overturn the "unjust system" established by the Treaties of Versailles and Locarno—but only by legal means. As he grew stronger, and as other leaders showed their willingness to compromise, he increased his demands and finally began attacking his independent neighbors (Map 29.1).

Hitler realized that his aggressive policies had to be carefully camouflaged at first, for Germany's army was limited by the Treaty of Versailles to only 100,000 men. As he told a group of army commanders in February 1933, the early stages of his policy of "conquest of new living space in the East and its ruthless Germanization" had serious dangers. If France had real leaders, Hitler said, it would "not give us time but attack us, presumably with its eastern satellites."[15] To avoid such threats to his plans, Hitler loudly proclaimed his peaceful intentions to all the world. Nevertheless, he felt strong enough to walk out of a sixty-nation disarmament conference and withdraw from the League of Nations in October 1933. Gustav Stresemann's policy of peaceful cooperation (see page 942) was dead; the Nazi determination to rearm was out in the open.

Following this action, which met with widespread approval at home, Hitler moved to incorporate independent Austria into a greater Germany. Austrian Nazis climaxed an attempted overthrow by murdering the Austrian chancellor in July 1934. They were unable to take power, however, because a worried Mussolini, who had initially greeted Hitler as a fascist little brother, massed his troops on Brenner Pass and threatened

EVENTS LEADING TO WORLD WAR II

1919	Treaty of Versailles is signed; J. M. Keynes publishes *Economic Consequences of the Peace*.
1919–1920	U.S. Senate rejects the Treaty of Versailles.
1921	Germany is billed $33 billion in reparations.
1922	Mussolini seizes power in Italy; Germany proposes a moratorium on reparations.
January 1923	France and Belgium occupy the Ruhr; Germany orders passive resistance to the occupation.
October 1923	Stresemann agrees to reparations based on Germany's ability to pay.
1924	Dawes Plan: German reparations are reduced and put on a sliding scale. Large U.S. loans to Germany are recommended to promote German recovery; occupation of the Ruhr ends; Adolf Hitler dictates *Mein Kampf*.
1924–1929	Spectacular German economic recovery occurs; circular flow of international funds enables sizable reparations payments.
1925	Treaties of Locarno promote European security and stability.
1926	Germany joins the League of Nations.
1928	Kellogg-Briand Pact renounces war as an instrument of international affairs.
1929	Young Plan further reduces German reparations; U.S. stock market crashes.
1929–1933	Great Depression rages.
1931	Japan invades Manchuria.
1932	Nazis become the largest party in the Reichstag.
January 1933	Hitler is appointed chancellor of Germany.
March 1933	Reichstag passes the Enabling Act, granting Hitler absolute dictatorial power.
October 1933	Germany withdraws from the League of Nations.
July 1934	Nazis murder the Austrian chancellor.
1935	Nuremberg Laws deprive Jews of all rights of citizenship.
March 1935	Hitler announces German rearmament.
June 1935	Anglo-German naval agreement is signed.
October 1935	Mussolini invades Ethiopia and receives Hitler's support.
March 1936	German armies move unopposed into the demilitarized Rhineland.
July 1936	Civil war breaks out in Spain.
1937	Japan invades China; Rome-Berlin Axis in effect.
March 1938	Germany annexes Austria.
September 1938	Munich Conference: Britain and France agree to German seizure of the Sudetenland from Czechoslovakia.
March 1939	Germany occupies the rest of Czechoslovakia; appeasement ends in Britain.
August 1939	Nazi-Soviet nonaggression pact is signed.
September 1, 1939	Germany invades Poland.
September 3, 1939	Britain and France declare war on Germany.

MAP 29.1 The Growth of Nazi Germany, 1933–1939 Until March 1939, Hitler brought ethnic Germans into the Nazi state; then he turned on the Slavic peoples he had always hated. He stripped Czechoslovakia of its independence and prepared for an attack on Poland in September 1939.

to fight. When in March 1935 Hitler established a general military draft and declared the "unequal" disarmament clauses of the Treaty of Versailles null and void, other countries appeared to understand the danger. With France taking the lead, Italy and Great Britain protested strongly and warned against future aggressive actions.

Yet the emerging united front against Hitler quickly collapsed. Of crucial importance, Britain adopted a policy of appeasement, granting Hitler everything he could reasonably want (and more) in order to avoid war. The first step was an Anglo-German naval agreement in June 1935 that broke Germany's isolation. The second step came in March 1936 when Hitler suddenly marched his armies into the demilitarized Rhineland, brazenly violating the Treaties of Versailles and Locarno. This was the last good chance to stop the Nazis, for Hitler had ordered his troops to retreat if France resisted militarily.

But an uncertain France would not move without British support, and the occupation of German soil by German armies seemed right and just to Britain. With a greatly improved strategic position, Germany handed France a tremendous psychological defeat.

British appeasement, which practically dictated French policy, lasted far into 1939. It was motivated by British feelings of guilt toward Germany and the pacifism of a population still horrified by the memory of the First World War. As in Germany, many powerful conservatives in Britain underestimated Hitler. They believed that Soviet communism was the real danger and that Hitler could be used to stop it. A leading member of Britain's government personally told Hitler in November 1937 that it was his conviction that Hitler "not only had accomplished great things in Germany itself, but that through the total destruction of Communism in his own country . . . Germany rightly had to be considered as a Western bulwark against Communism."[16] Such rigid anticommunist feelings made an alliance between the Western powers and Stalin unlikely.

As Britain and France opted for appeasement and the Soviet Union watched all developments suspiciously, Hitler found powerful allies. In 1935 the bombastic Mussolini decided that imperial expansion was needed to revitalize Italian fascism. From Italian colonies on the east coast of Africa, he attacked the independent African kingdom of Ethiopia. The Western powers and the League of Nations piously condemned Italian aggression without saving Ethiopia from defeat, while Hitler supported Italy energetically and overcame Mussolini's lingering doubts about the Nazis. The result in late 1936 was an agreement on close cooperation between Italy and Germany, the so-called Rome-Berlin Axis. Japan, which had been expanding into Manchuria since 1931, soon joined the Axis alliance.

At the same time, Germany and Italy intervened in the long, complicated Spanish civil war, where their support eventually helped General Francisco Franco's fascist movement defeat republican Spain. Only the Soviet Union gave aid to the leftist government that Franco fought, for public opinion in Britain and especially in France was hopelessly divided on the Spanish question.

In late 1937, while proclaiming peaceful intentions to the British and their gullible prime minister, Neville Chamberlain, Hitler told his generals his real plans. His "unshakable decision" was to crush Austria and Czechoslovakia at the earliest possible moment as the first step in his long-contemplated drive to the east for living space. By threatening Austria with invasion, Hitler forced the Austrian chancellor in March 1938 to put local Nazis in control of the government. The next day, German armies moved in unopposed, and Austria be-

Cartoonist David Low's biting criticism of appeasing leaders appeared shortly after Hitler remilitarized the Rhineland. Appeasement also appealed to millions of ordinary citizens in Britain and France, who wanted to avoid at any cost another great war. *(Reproduced by permission of London Evening/Solo Standard)*

came two more provinces of Greater Germany (see Map 29.1).

Simultaneously, Hitler began demanding that the pro-Nazi, German-speaking minority of western Czechoslovakia—the Sudetenland—be turned over to Germany. Yet democratic Czechoslovakia was prepared to defend itself. Moreover, France had been Czechoslovakia's ally since 1924; and if France fought, the Soviet Union was pledged to help. As war appeared inevitable—for Hitler had already told the leader of the Sudeten Germans that "we must always ask so much we cannot be satisfied"—appeasement triumphed again. In September 1938, Chamberlain flew to Germany three times in fourteen days. In these negotiations, to which the U.S.S.R. was deliberately not invited, Chamberlain and the French agreed with Hitler that the Sudetenland should be ceded to Germany immediately. Returning to London from the Munich Conference, Chamberlain told cheering crowds that he had secured "peace with honor . . . peace for our time." Sold out by the Western powers, Czechoslovakia gave in.

Confirmed once again in his opinion of the Western democracies as weak and racially degenerate, Hitler accelerated his aggression. In a shocking violation of his solemn assurances that the Sudetenland was his last territorial demand, Hitler's armies occupied the Czech lands in March 1939, while Slovakia became a puppet state. The effect on Western public opinion was electrifying. For the first time, there was no possible rationale of self-determination for Nazi aggression since Hitler was seizing Czechs and Slovaks as captive peoples. Thus when Hitler used the question of German minorities in Danzig as a pretext to confront Poland, a suddenly militant Chamberlain declared that Britain and France would fight if Hitler attacked his eastern neighbor. Hitler did not take these warnings seriously and decided to press on.

In an about-face that stunned the world, Hitler offered and Stalin signed a ten-year Nazi-Soviet nonaggression pact in August 1939. Each dictator promised to remain neutral if the other became involved in war. An attached secret protocol, which became known only after the war, ruthlessly divided eastern Europe into German and Soviet zones, "in the event of a political territorial reorganization." The nonaggression pact itself was enough to make Britain and France cry treachery, for they, too, had been negotiating with Stalin. But Stalin had remained distrustful of Western intentions, and Hitler had offered immediate territorial gain.

For Hitler, everything was set. He told his generals on the day of the nonaggression pact, "My only fear is that at the last moment some dirty dog will come up with a mediation plan." On September 1, 1939, German armies and warplanes smashed into Poland from three sides. Two days later, Britain and France, finally true to their word, declared war on Germany. The Second World War had begun.

Hitler's Empire, 1939–1942

Using planes, tanks, and trucks in the first example of a *blitzkrieg*, or "lightning war," Hitler's armies crushed Poland in four weeks. While the Soviet Union quickly took its part of the booty—the eastern half of Poland and the independent Baltic states of Lithuania, Estonia, and Latvia—French and British armies dug in in the west. They expected another war of attrition and economic blockade.

In spring 1940, the lightning war struck again. After occupying Denmark, Norway, and Holland, German motorized columns broke through southern Belgium, split the Franco-British forces, and trapped the entire British army on the beaches of Dunkirk. By heroic efforts, the British withdrew their troops but not their equipment.

France was taken by the Nazis. Aging marshal Henri-Philippe Pétain formed a new French government—the so-called Vichy government—to accept defeat, and German armies occupied most of France. By July 1940, Hitler ruled practically all of western continental Europe; Italy was an ally, and the Soviet Union and Spain were friendly neutrals. Only Britain, led by the uncompromising Winston Churchill (1874–1965), remained unconquered. Churchill proved to be one of history's greatest wartime leaders, rallying the British with stirring speeches, infectious confidence, and bulldog determination.

Germany sought to gain control of the air, the necessary first step toward an amphibious invasion of Britain. In the Battle of Britain, up to a thousand German planes attacked British airfields and key factories in a single day, dueling with British defenders high in the skies. Losses were heavy on both sides. Then in September Hitler angrily and foolishly changed his strategy, turning from military objectives to indiscriminate bombing of British cities in an attempt to break British morale. British aircraft factories increased production, anti-aircraft defense improved with the help of radar, and the heavily bombed people of London defiantly dug in. In September and October 1940, Britain was beating Germany three to one in the air war. There was no possibility of immediate German invasion of Britain.

In these circumstances, the most reasonable German strategy would have been to attack Britain through the

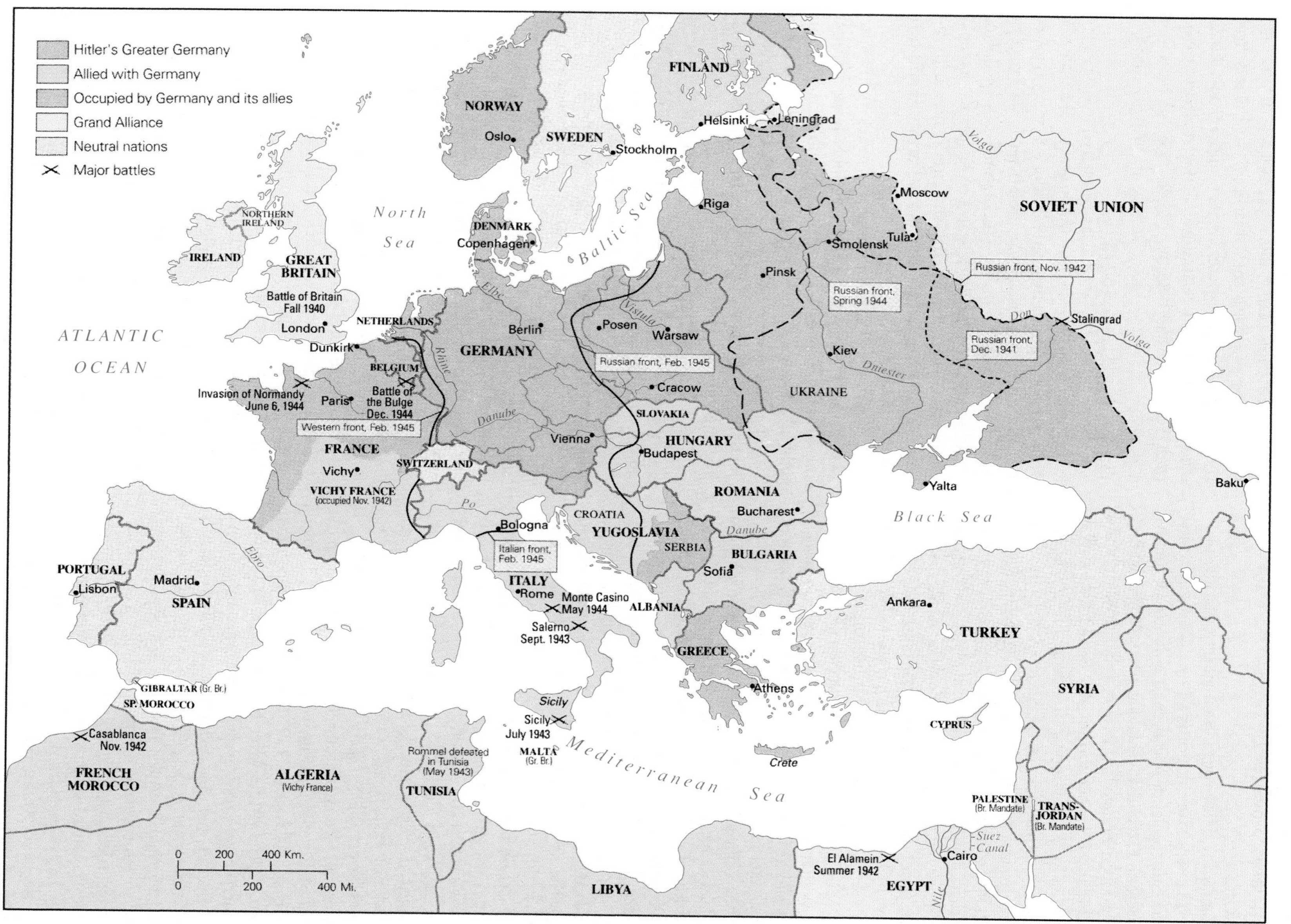

Hitler's Greater Germany
Allied with Germany
Occupied by Germany and its allies
Grand Alliance
Neutral nations
Major battles
NORWAY
Oslo
SWEDEN
Stockholm
FINLAND
Helsinki
Leningrad
Volga
Moscow
SOVIET UNION
Riga
NORTHERN IRELAND
North Sea
DENMARK
Copenhagen
Baltic Sea
Smolensk
Tula
IRELAND
GREAT BRITAIN
Pinsk
Russian front, Nov. 1942
Russian front, Spring 1944
Battle of Britain Fall 1940
Elbe
Vistula
Don
Stalingrad
ATLANTIC OCEAN
London
NETHERLANDS
Berlin
Posen
Warsaw
Volga
Dunkirk
GERMANY
Kiev
Russian front, Dec. 1941
Rhine
Russian front, Feb. 1945
Dniester
BELGIUM
Cracow
UKRAINE
Invasion of Normandy June 6, 1944
Paris
Battle of the Bulge Dec. 1944
Danube
SLOVAKIA
Western front, Feb. 1945
Vienna
HUNGARY
FRANCE
Budapest
Vichy
SWITZERLAND
Yalta
Baku
VICHY FRANCE (occupied Nov. 1942)
ROMANIA
Po
CROATIA
Bucharest
Black Sea
Bologna
YUGOSLAVIA
Danube
Ebro
SERBIA
Italian front, Feb. 1945
BULGARIA
PORTUGAL
Madrid
Sofia
Lisbon
ITALY
SPAIN
Rome
Monte Casino May 1944
ALBANIA
Ankara
TURKEY
Salerno Sept. 1943
GREECE
GIBRALTAR (Gr. Br.)
Athens
SYRIA
SP. MOROCCO
Sicily
Sicily July 1943
CYPRUS
Casablanca Nov. 1942
Rommel defeated in Tunisia (May 1943)
MALTA (Gr. Br.)
Crete
FRENCH MOROCCO
ALGERIA (Vichy France)
Mediterranean Sea
TUNISIA
PALESTINE (Br. Mandate)
TRANS-JORDAN (Br. Mandate)
Suez Canal
0 200 400 Km.
0 200 400 Mi.
El Alamein Summer 1942
Cairo
LIBYA
EGYPT
Nile

eastern Mediterranean, taking Egypt and the Suez Canal and pinching off Britain's supply of oil. By April 1941, Germany had already moved to the southeast, conquering Greece and Yugoslavia and forcing Hungary, Romania, and Bulgaria into alliances. But Hitler was not a reasonable person. His lifetime obsession with a vast eastern European empire for the "master race" dictated policy. So in June 1941, German armies suddenly attacked the Soviet Union along a vast front (Map 29.2). By October 1941, Leningrad was practically surrounded, Moscow was besieged, and most of Ukraine had been overrun. But with Britain still unconquered, Hitler's decision was a wild, irrational gamble epitomizing the violent, unlimited, and ultimately self-destructive ambitions of Nazism. The Soviets did not collapse, and when a severe winter struck German armies outfitted in summer uniforms, the invaders were stopped.

While Hitler's armies dramatically expanded the war in Europe, his Japanese allies did the same in Asia. Engaged in a general but undeclared war against China since 1937, Japan's rulers had increasingly come into diplomatic conflict with the Pacific basin's other great power, the United States. When the Japanese occupied French Indochina in July 1941, the United States retaliated by cutting off sales of vital rubber, scrap iron, oil, and aviation fuel. Tension mounted further, and on December 7, 1941, Japan attacked the U.S. naval base at Pearl Harbor in Hawaii. Hitler immediately declared war on the United States, and Japanese forces advanced swiftly into Southeast Asia (see Map 29.3 on page 986).

Meanwhile, though stalled in Russia, Hitler ruled over a vast European empire stretching from the outskirts of Moscow to the English Channel. Hitler, the Nazi leadership, and the loyal German army were positioned to greatly accelerate construction of their "New Order" in Europe, and they continued their efforts until their final collapse in 1945. In doing so, they showed what Nazi victory would have meant.

Hitler's New Order was based firmly on the guiding principle of Nazi totalitarianism: racial imperialism. Within this New Order, the Nordic peoples—the Dutch, Norwegians, and Danes—received preferential treatment, for they were racially related to the master race, the Germans. The French, an "inferior" Latin people, occupied a middle position. They were heavily taxed to support the Nazi war effort but were tolerated as a race. Once Nazi reverses began to mount in late 1942, however, all the occupied territories of western and northern Europe were exploited with increasing intensity. Material shortages and both mental and physical suffering afflicted millions of people.

Slavs in the conquered territories to the east were treated with harsh hatred as "subhumans." At the height of success in 1941 and 1942, Hitler set the tone. He painted for his intimate circle the fantastic vision of a vast eastern colonial empire where Poles, Ukrainians, and Russians would be enslaved and forced to die out, while Germanic peasants resettled the resulting abandoned lands. But he needed countless helpers and many ambitious initiators to turn his dreams into reality. These accomplices came forth.

Himmler and the elite corps of SS volunteers, supported (or condoned) by military commanders and German policemen in the occupied territories, pressed relentlessly to implement this program of destruction even before victory was secured. In western Poland, the SS arrested and evacuated Polish peasants to cleanse the region and create a "mass settlement space" for Germans. Polish workers and Soviet prisoners of war were transported to Germany, where conditions of slave labor were so harsh that four out of five Soviet prisoners did not survive the war.

Finally, the Nazi state condemned all European Jews to extermination, along with many Gypsies, Jehovah's Witnesses, and captured communists. After the fall of Warsaw, the Nazis stepped up their expulsion campaign and began deporting all German Jews to occupied Poland. There they and Jews from all over Europe were concentrated in ghettos, compelled to wear the Jewish star, and turned into slave laborers.

In 1941, as part of the "war of annihilation" in the Soviet Union, expulsion spiraled into extermination. On the Russian front, Himmler's special SS killing squads and also regular army units forced Soviet Jews to dig giant pits, which became mass graves as the victims were lined up on the edge and cut down by machine guns. Then in late 1941, Hitler and the Nazi leadership, in some still-debated combination, ordered the SS to stop all Jewish emigration from Europe and speeded up planning for mass murder. As one German diplomat put it, "The Jewish Question must be resolved in the course of the war, for only so can it be solved without a worldwide outcry."[17] The "final solution of the Jewish question"—the murder of every single Jew—had begun. All over the Nazi empire, Jews were systematically

MAP 29.2 World War II in Europe The map shows the extent of Hitler's empire at its height, before the Battle of Stalingrad in late 1942 and the subsequent advances of the Allies until Germany surrendered on May 7, 1945.

Prelude to Murder This photo captures the terrible inhumanity of Nazi racism. Frightened and bewildered families from the soon-to-be-destroyed Warsaw ghetto are being forced out of their homes by German soldiers for deportation to concentration camps. There they face murder in the gas chambers. *(Roger-Viollet)*

arrested, packed like cattle onto freight trains, and dispatched to extermination camps. Many Jews could hardly imagine the enormity of the crime that lay before them. (See the feature "Listening to the Past: Witness to the Holocaust" on pages 990–991.)

At the camps, the victims were taken by force or deception to "shower rooms," which were actually gas chambers. These gas chambers, first perfected in the quiet, efficient execution of seventy thousand mentally ill Germans between 1938 and 1941, permitted rapid, hideous, and thoroughly bureaucratized mass murder. For fifteen to twenty minutes came the terrible screams and gasping sobs of men, women, and children choking to death on poison gas. Then, only silence. Special camp workers quickly yanked the victims' gold teeth from their jaws, and the bodies were then cremated, or sometimes boiled for oil to make soap. At Auschwitz-Birkenau, the most infamous of the Nazi death factories, as many as twelve thousand human beings were slaughtered each day. The extermination of European Jews was the ultimate monstrosity of Nazi racism and racial imperialism. By 1945, 6 million Jews had been murdered.

Who was responsible for this terrible crime? An older generation of historians usually laid most of the guilt on Hitler and the Nazi leadership. Ordinary Germans had little knowledge of the extermination camps, it was argued, and those who cooperated had no alternative given the brutality of Nazi terror and totalitarian control. But in recent years, many studies have revealed a much broader participation of German people in the Holocaust and popular indifference (or worse) to the fate of the Jews. Yet exactly why so many perpetrated or condoned Nazi crimes has remained unclear.

In a controversial work, the American historian Daniel Goldhagen has reignited discussion of Nazi crimes by arguing that, above all, the extreme anti-Semitism of "ordinary Germans" led them to respond to Hitler and to become his "willing executioners" in World War II.[18] Yet in most occupied countries, local non-German officials also cooperated in the arrest and deportation of Jews to a large extent. As in Germany, only a few exceptional bystanders, like those in the French village of Le Chambon, did not turn a blind eye. (See the feature "Individuals in Society: Le Chambon, a Refuge for the Persecuted.") Thus some scholars have concluded that the key for most Germans (and most people in occupied countries) was that they felt no personal responsibility for Jews, and therefore they were not prepared to help them. This meant that many individuals, conditioned by Nazi racist propaganda but also influenced by peer pressure and brutalizing wartime violence, were psychologically prepared to perpetrate ever-greater crimes. They were ready to plumb the depths of evil and to spiral downward from mistreatment to arrest to mass murder.

The Grand Alliance

While the Nazis built their savage empire, the Allies faced the hard fact that chance, rather than choice, had brought them together. Stalin had been cooperating fully with Hitler between August 1939 and June 1941, and only the Japanese attack on Pearl Harbor in December 1941 and Hitler's immediate declaration of war had overwhelmed powerful isolationism in the United States. The Allies' first task was to overcome their mutual suspicions and build an unshakable alliance on the quicksand of accident. By means of three interrelated policies, they succeeded.

First, President Roosevelt accepted Churchill's contention that the United States should concentrate first on defeating Hitler. Only after victory in Europe was achieved would the United States turn toward the Pacific for an all-out attack on Japan, the lesser threat. The promise of huge military aid under America's policy of "Europe first" helped solidify the anti-Hitler coalition.

Second, within the European framework, the Americans and the British put immediate military needs first. They consistently postponed tough political questions relating to the eventual peace settlement and thereby avoided conflicts that might have split the alliance until after the war.

Third, to further encourage mutual trust, the Allies adopted the principle of the "unconditional surrender" of Germany and Japan. This policy cemented the Grand Alliance because it denied Hitler any hope of dividing his foes. It probably also discouraged Germans and Japanese who might have tried to overthrow their dictators in order to make a compromise peace. Of great importance for the postwar shape of Europe, it meant that Soviet and Anglo-American armies would almost certainly come together to divide all of Germany, and most of the continent, among the victorious allies.

The military resources of the Grand Alliance were awesome. The strengths of the United States were its mighty industry, its large population, and its national unity. Even before Pearl Harbor, President Roosevelt had called America the "arsenal of democracy" and given military aid to Britain and the Soviet Union. Now the United States geared up rapidly for all-out war production and drew heavily on a generally cooperative Latin America for resources. It not only equipped its own armies but also eventually gave its allies about $50 billion in arms and equipment. Britain received by far the most, but about one-fifth of the total went to the Soviet Union in the form of badly needed trucks, planes, and munitions.

Too strong to lose and too weak to win standing alone, Britain continued to make a great contribution as well. The British economy was totally and effectively mobilized, and the sharing of burdens through rationing and heavy taxes on war profits maintained social harmony. Moreover, by early 1943 the Americans and the British were combining small aircraft carriers with radar-guided bombers to rid the Atlantic of German submarines. Britain, the impregnable floating fortress, became a gigantic frontline staging area for the decisive blow to the heart of Germany.

As for the Soviet Union, so great was its strength that it might well have defeated Germany without Western help. In the face of the German advance, whole factories and populations were successfully evacuated to eastern Russia and Siberia. There war production was reorganized and expanded, and the Red Army was increasingly well supplied. The Red Army was also well led, for a new generation of talented military leaders quickly arose to replace those so recently purged. Most important of all, Stalin drew on the massive support and heroic determination of the Soviet people, especially those in the central Russian heartland. Broad-based Russian nationalism, as opposed to narrow communist ideology, became the powerful unifying force in what was appropriately called the "Great Patriotic War of the Fatherland."

Finally, the United States, Britain, and the Soviet Union were not alone. They had the resources of much of the world at their command. And, to a greater or lesser extent, they were aided by a growing resistance movement against the Nazis throughout Europe, even in Germany. Thus although Ukrainian peasants sometimes welcomed the Germans as liberators, the barbaric occupation policies of the Nazis quickly drove them to join and support behind-the-lines guerrilla forces. More generally, after the U.S.S.R. was invaded in June 1941, communists throughout Europe took the lead in the underground resistance, joined by a growing number of patriots and Christians. Anti-Nazi leaders from occu-

Individuals in Society

Le Chambon, a Refuge for the Persecuted

André and Magda Trocmé, resistance leaders at Le Chambon, in a family snapshot taken shortly before 1940. *(Papers of André and Magda Trocmé, Swarthmore College Peace Collection)*

On a cold night in February 1943, French officials arrived in Le Chambon-sur-Lignon in southern France. Known as a "nest of Jews in Protestant country," Le Chambon was a mountainous town of three thousand people that hid Jews and openly said so to the government.[1] Now the officials had finally come to arrest the Protestant minister André Trocmé, the assistant minister Edouard Theis, and the local school principal—the leaders of this defiant cell. Watching silently, the villagers demonstrated their unmistakable solidarity. They lined the streets, sang "A Mighty Fortress Is Our God," and then fell in behind their friends as they passed. As on other occasions, the people of Le Chambon showed the moral courage that would cause others in the region to search their hearts and examine their own conduct toward Jews.

Imprisoned in a camp with communists and resistance fighters, the three men led religious services, discussion groups, and classes that attracted prisoners and even guards. The camp administration, perhaps fearing that its authority was being subverted, offered the three men freedom in return for a signed oath of obedience to the Vichy government, which ruled southern France in collaboration with the Nazi occupiers in the north. Trocmé and his companions refused, but they were mysteriously released the next day. Returning home, Trocmé believed that the village had influential friends in the government.

The strength of the villagers and the quality of their leadership, so clearly evident in these confrontations with the state in early 1943, help explain how Le Chambon became one of the safest places for Jews in Europe in the first two years of the Nazi occupation and how it and the surrounding area successfully sheltered about thirty-five hundred Jewish refugees. Pastors Trocmé and Theis were inspired rebels who wanted to live an active, dangerous Christian love. They conceived of Le Chambon as a city of refuge for the innocent and as a means of overcoming evil with good through nonviolence. Magda Trocmé, André's spirited wife and the mother of four young children, was equally important. Warm and practical, she instinctively aided those in need. She welcomed Jews arriving at the parsonage, housed them, and helped find families to shelter them. She carried on after André himself fled in late 1943 to escape arrest by the Gestapo. Within the village, prayer meetings became conspiracies of goodness. A Jewish refugee printer forged papers and ration cards for the guests, and Theis and the local network helped them escape to Switzerland.

If the how is clear, the why is less so. Certainly a collective memory of persecution helped the Protestants of Le Chambon and nearby villages to identify with the Jews and feel a moral responsibility for their fate. They, too, were a tiny minority in France, the descendants of Protestant refugees who had fled to the mountains and been hounded and executed. But non-Protestants also joined the cause. Above all, the Trocmés, Theis, and the villagers responded because they had a strong moral philosophy rooted in their Christian belief. They believed that they should not obey evil laws but rather abide by God's commandments. They considered it evil to harm anyone, for God had instructed them to love and care for each other. Finally, Le Chambon was broadly representative of other exceptional groups and individuals who worked to help Jews in Nazi Europe. The common experience showed that a sense of moral responsibility was crucial, and that goodness, like evil, is contagious in life-and-death ethical situations.

Questions for Analysis

1. What did the people of Le Chambon-sur-Lignon do? Why did they do it?
2. What is the larger significance of the town's actions in terms of the Holocaust? Debate the idea that "goodness, like evil, is contagious."

1. Philip Hallie, *Lest Innocent Blood Be Shed: The Story of the Village of Le Chambon and How Goodness Happened There* (New York: Harper & Row, 1979), p. 18. In addition to this moving study, see *Weapons of Spirit* (1986), a documentary film by Pierre Sauvage.

cited in the Notes, is an important recent study. H. Arendt, *The Origins of Totalitarianism* (1951), is a classic interpretation. F. L. Carsten, *The Rise of Fascism* (1982), and W. Laqueur, ed., *Fascism* (1976), are also recommended. Z. Sternhell, *Neither Right nor Left: Fascist Ideology in France* (1986), is important and stimulating, stressing the antiliberal and antisocialist origins of fascist thinking in France.

Malia's work, cited in the Notes, is a provocative reassessment of Soviet history and an excellent introduction to scholarly debates. It may be compared with the fine synthesis M. Lewin, *The Making of the Soviet System* (1985). R. Stites, *The Women's Liberation Movement in Russia: Feminism, Nihilism, and Bolshevism, 1860–1930* (1978), and the works by Geiger and Deutscher, cited in the Notes, are highly recommended. R. McNeal, *Stalin: Man and Ruler* (1988), is useful. S. Cohen, *Bukharin and the Bolshevik Revolution* (1973), examines the leading spokesman of moderate communism, who was destroyed by Stalin. R. Conquest, *The Great Terror: A Reassessment* (1990), is an excellent account of Stalin's purges of the 1930s, and A. Solzhenitsyn, *The Gulag Archipelago* (1964), passionately condemns Soviet police terror. Three important reconsiderations of Soviet purges, peasants, and urban life are Thurston's revisionist work, cited in the Notes; S. Fitzpatrick, *Stalin's Peasants: Resistance and Survival in the Russian Village After Collectivization* (1994); and S. Kotkin, *Magnetic Mountain: Stalinism as Civilization* (1995). Arthur Koestler, *Darkness at Noon* (1956), is a famous fictional account of Stalin's trials of the Old Bolsheviks. Conquest's work, cited in the Notes, authoritatively recounts Soviet collectivization and the human-made famine. Two other remarkable books are J. Scott, *Behind the Urals* (1973), an eyewitness account of an American steelworker in the Soviet Union in the 1930s; and S. Alliluyeva, *Twenty Letters to a Friend* (1967), the amazing reflections of Stalin's daughter.

A. De Grand, *Italian Fascism: Its Origins and Development* (1989), and A. Lyttelton, *The Seizure of Power: Fascism in Italy, 1919–1929,* 2d ed. (1987), are excellent studies of Italy under Mussolini. D. Mack Smith, *Mussolini* (1982), is authoritative. Ignazio Silone, *Bread and Wine* (1937), is a moving novel by a famous opponent of dictatorship in Italy. E. Morante, *History* (1978), a fictional account of one family's divergent reactions to Mussolini's rule, is recommended. Two excellent books on Spain are H. Thomas, *The Spanish Civil War* (1977); and E. Malefakis, *Agrarian Reform and Peasant Revolution in Spain* (1970). In the area of foreign relations, G. Kennan, *Russia and the West Under Lenin and Stalin* (1961), is justly famous; A. L. Rowse, *Appeasement* (1961), powerfully denounces the policies of the appeasers. R. Paxton, *Vichy France* (1973), tells a controversial story extremely well.

On Germany, F. Stern, *The Politics of Cultural Despair* (1963), and W. Smith, *The Ideological Origins of Nazi Imperialism* (1986), are fine complementary studies on the origins of Nazism. Bracher's work, cited in the Notes, remains an outstanding account of Hitler's Germany. Two major studies by influential German historians are M. Brozat, *The Nazi State* (1981); and H. Mommsen, *From Weimar to Auschwitz* (1991). W. Shirer, *The Rise and Fall of the Third Reich* (1960), is a gripping popular account of an American journalist who experienced Nazi Germany firsthand. J. Fest, *Hitler* (1974), is engrossing, and A. Bullock, *Hitler and Stalin* (1993), is a fascinating comparison by a master biographer. I. Kershaw, *The "Hitler Myth": Image and Reality in the Third Reich* (1987), is a provocative reassessment of the limits of Hitler's power. M. Mayer, *They Thought They Were Free* (1955), probes the minds of ten ordinary Nazis and why they believed that Hitler was their liberator. A. Speer, *Inside the Third Reich* (1970), contains the fascinating recollections of Hitler's wizard of the armaments industry. C. Koonz, *Mothers in the Fatherland: Women, the Family, and Nazi Politics* (1987), and D. Peukert, *Inside Nazi Germany: Conformity, Opposition, and Racism in Everyday Life* (1987), are pioneering forays into the social history of the Nazi era. G. Mosse, *Toward the Final Solution* (1978), is a powerful history of European racism. Moving accounts of the Holocaust include Y. Bauer, *A History of the Holocaust* (1982); M. Gilbert, *The Holocaust: The History of the Jews During the Second World War* (1985); and R. Hilberg, *The Destruction of the European Jews, 1933–1945*, 3 vols., rev. ed. (1985), a monumental scholarly achievement. M. Marrus, *The Holocaust in History* (1987), is an excellent interpretive survey by a leading authority. Goldhagen's widely debated study, cited in the Notes, may be compared with C. Browning, *Ordinary Men: Reserve Police Battalion 101 and the Final Solution in Poland* (1992). E. Staub, *The Roots of Evil: The Origins of Genocide and Other Group Violence* (1989), is a profound study by a noted psychologist with a gift for history. Especially recommended are E. Weisel, *Night* (1961), a brief and compelling autobiographical account of a young Jew in a Nazi concentration camp; and A. Frank, *The Diary of Anne Frank*, is a remarkable personal account of a Jewish girl in hiding during the Nazi occupation of Holland. A. Fraser, *The Gypsies* (1992), considers a misunderstood people decimated by Nazi terror.

J. Campbell, *The Experience of World War II* (1989), is attractively illustrated and captures the drama of global conflict, as does G. Keegan, *The Second World War* (1990). G. Wright, *The Ordeal of Total War, 1939–1945* (1990), and C. Emsley, *World War II and Its Consequences* (1990), are also recommended. B. H. Liddell Hart, *The History of the Second World War* (1971), is an overview of military developments. G. Weinberg, *The Foreign Policy of Hitler,* 2 vols. (1970, 1980), is a thorough account of the diplomatic origins and course of World War II from the German perspective. Two dramatic studies of special aspects of the war are A. Dallin, *German Rule in Russia, 1941–1945* (1981), which analyzes the effects of Nazi occupation policies on the Soviet population; and L. Collins and D. La Pierre, *Is Paris Burning?* (1965), a best-selling account of the liberation of Paris and Hitler's plans to destroy the city.

LISTENING TO THE PAST

Witness to the Holocaust

The Second World War brought mass murder to the innocent. The Nazis and their allies slaughtered 6 million Jews in addition to about 5 million Slavs, Gypsies, Jehovah's Witnesses, homosexuals, and mentally ill persons. On the Russian front, some Jews were simply mowed down with machine guns, but most Jews were arrested in their homelands and taken in freight cars to unknown destinations, which were in fact extermination camps. The most infamous camp—really two camps on different sides of a railroad track—was Auschwitz-Birkenau in eastern Poland. There 2 million people were murdered in gas chambers.

The testimony of camp survivors helps us comprehend the unspeakable crime known to history as the Holocaust. One eyewitness was Marco Nahon, a Greek Jew and physician who escaped extermination at Auschwitz-Birkenau along with several thousand other slave laborers in the camp. The following passage is taken from Birkenau: The Camp of Death, *which Nahon wrote in 1945 after his liberation. Conquered by Germany in 1941, Greece was divided into German, Italian, and Bulgarian zones of occupation. The Nahon family lived in Dimotika in the Bulgarian zone.*

Early in March 1943, disturbing news arrives from Salonika [in the German occupation zone]: the Germans are deporting the Jews [of Salonika]. They lock them up in railway cattlecars . . . and send them to an unknown destination—to Poland, it is said. . . . Relatives and friends deliberate. What can be done in the face of this imminent threat? . . . My friend Vitalis Djivré speaks with conviction: "We must flee, cross over into Turkey at once, go to Palestine, Egypt—anywhere at all—but leave immediately.". . . A few friends and I held a completely different opinion. . . . [I say that] I am not going to emigrate. They are going to take us away to Germany or Poland [to work]? If so, I'll work. . . . It is certain that the Allies will be the victors, and once the war is over, we'll go back home. . . .

Until the end we were deaf to all the warnings. . . . [None of the warnings] would be regarded as indicating the seriousness of the drama in preparation. But does not the human mind find inconceivable the total extermination of an innocent population? In this tragic error lay the main cause, the sole cause, of our perdition. . . .

On Monday May 10, 1943, the bugles awaken us at a very early hour. We [have already been arrested and] today we are leaving for Poland. . . . As soon as a freight car has been packed to capacity with people, it is quickly locked up, and immediately the remaining passengers are pushed into the next one. . . .

Every two days the train stops in some meadow in open country. The car doors are flung open, and the whole transport spreads out in the fields. Men and women attend to their natural needs, side by side, without any embarrassment. Necessity and common misfortune have made them part of one and the same family. . . .

We are now in a small station in Austria. Our car door half opens; a Schupo [German police officer] is asking for the doctor. . . . He leads me to the rear of the convoy and shuts me inside the car where the woman is in labor. She is very young; this is her first child. The car, like all the others, is overcrowded. The delivery takes place in deplorable conditions, in front of everybody—men, women, and children. Fortunately, everything turns out well, and a few hours later a baby boy comes into the world. The new mother's family is very happy and passes candy around. Surely no one realizes that two days later the mother and her baby and more than half of the company will pass through the chimney of a crematorium at Birkenau.

It is May 16, 1943. We have reached the end of our journey [and arrived at Auschwitz-Birkenau]. The train stops along a wooden platform. Through the openings of the cars we can see people wearing strange costumes of blue and white stripes [the

Decolonization

In the postwar era, Europe's long-standing overseas expansion was dramatically reversed. Future generations will almost certainly see this rolling back of Western expansion as one of world history's great turning points (Map 30.3).

The most basic cause of imperial collapse—what Europeans called "decolonization"—was the rising demand of Asian and African peoples for national self-determination, racial equality, and personal dignity. This demand spread from intellectuals to the masses in virtually every colonial territory after the First World War. As a result, colonial empires had already been shaken by 1939, and the way was prepared for the eventual triumph of independence movements. Yet the new nations of Asia and Africa were deeply influenced by Western ideas and achievements, so that the "westernization" of the world rushed forward even as European empires passed into history.

European empires had been based on an enormous power differential between the rulers and the ruled, a difference that had declined almost to the vanishing point by 1945. Not only was western Europe poor and battered immediately after the war, but most Europeans regarded their empires very differently after 1945 than before 1914, or even before 1939. Empire had rested on self-confidence and self-righteousness; Europeans had believed their superiority to be not only technical and military but also spiritual and moral. The horrors of the Second World War destroyed such complacent arrogance and gave opponents of imperialism much greater influence in Europe. With its political power and moral authority in tatters, Europe could either submit to decolonization or enter into risky wars of reconquest. After 1945 many Europeans were willing to let go of their colonies more or less voluntarily and to concentrate on rebuilding at home.

Indian independence played a key role in decolonization. When the Labour party came to power in Great Britain in 1945, it was determined to leave India. British socialists had always opposed imperialism, and the heavy cost of governing India had become an intolerable burden. Empire in India ended in 1947, and most Asian colonies achieved independence shortly thereafter. Although the French obstinately tried to reestablish colonial rule in Indochina, they were defeated in 1954, and two independent Vietnamese states came into being. The French also fought a long, dirty war to keep Algeria, but Algeria won its independence in 1962 (see Map 30.3).

In much of Africa south of the Sahara, decolonization proceeded much more smoothly. Beginning in 1957, Britain's colonies achieved independence with little or no bloodshed and then entered a very loose association with Britain as members of the British Commonwealth of Nations. In 1958 the clever de Gaulle offered the leaders of French black Africa the choice of a total break with France or immediate independence within a kind of French commonwealth. All but one of

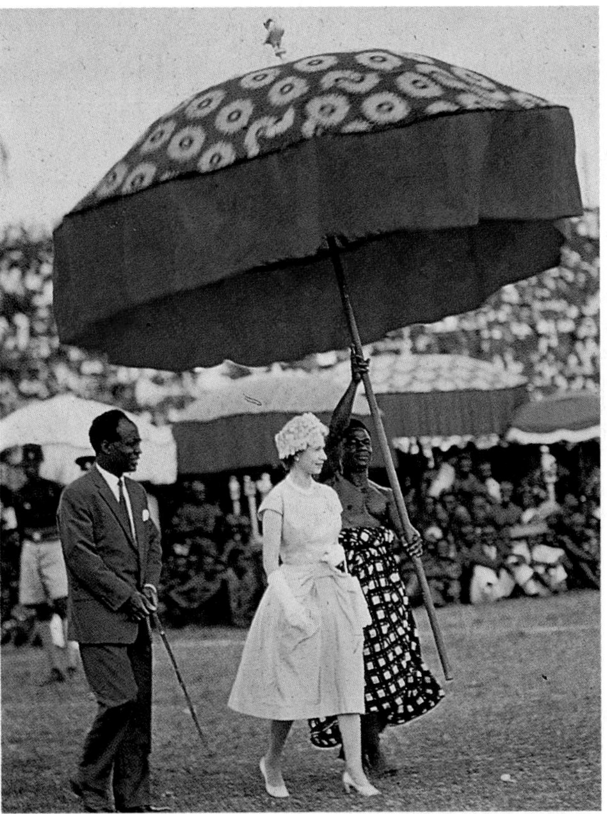

African Independence Britain's Queen Elizabeth II pays an official visit in 1961 to Ghana, the former Gold Coast colony. Accompanying the queen at the colorful welcoming ceremony is Ghana's popular Kwame Nkrumah, who was educated in black colleges in the United States and led Ghana's breakthrough to independence in 1957. *(UPI/Corbis-Bettmann)*

MAP 30.2 European Alliance Systems After the cold war divided Europe into two hostile military alliances, six western European countries formed the Common Market in 1957. The Common Market grew later to include most of western Europe. The communist states organized their own economic association—COMECON.

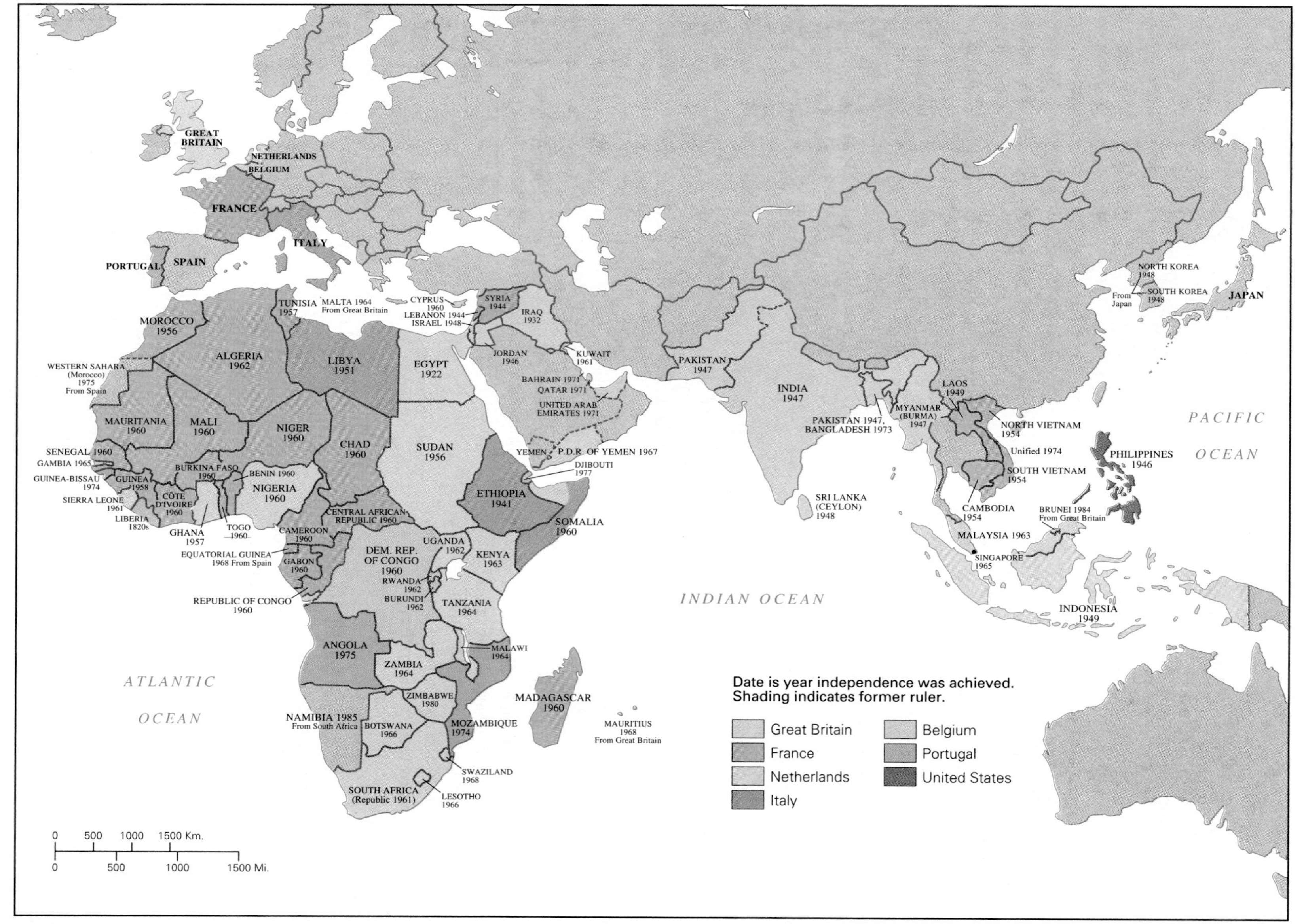
GREAT BRITAIN
NETHERLANDS
BELGIUM
FRANCE
ITALY
PORTUGAL
SPAIN
TUNISIA 1957
MALTA 1964 From Great Britain
CYPRUS 1960
LEBANON 1944
ISRAEL 1948
SYRIA 1944
IRAQ 1932
MOROCCO 1956
ALGERIA 1962
LIBYA 1951
EGYPT 1922
JORDAN 1946
KUWAIT 1961
BAHRAIN 1971
QATAR 1971
UNITED ARAB EMIRATES 1971
WESTERN SAHARA (Morocco) 1975 From Spain
MAURITANIA 1960
MALI 1960
NIGER 1960
CHAD 1960
SUDAN 1956
YEMEN
P.D.R. OF YEMEN 1967
DJIBOUTI 1977
SENEGAL 1960
GAMBIA 1965
GUINEA-BISSAU 1974
GUINEA 1958
BURKINA FASO 1960
BENIN 1960
NIGERIA 1960
SIERRA LEONE 1961
CÔTE D'IVOIRE 1960
LIBERIA 1820s
GHANA 1957
TOGO 1960
ETHIOPIA 1941
SOMALIA 1960
CENTRAL AFRICAN REPUBLIC 1960
CAMEROON 1960
EQUATORIAL GUINEA 1968 From Spain
GABON 1960
DEM. REP. OF CONGO 1960
UGANDA 1962
KENYA 1963
RWANDA 1962
BURUNDI 1962
TANZANIA 1964
REPUBLIC OF CONGO 1960
ANGOLA 1975
ZAMBIA 1964
MALAWI 1964
ZIMBABWE 1980
MADAGASCAR 1960
MAURITIUS 1968 From Great Britain
NAMIBIA 1985 From South Africa
BOTSWANA 1966
MOZAMBIQUE 1974
SWAZILAND 1968
SOUTH AFRICA (Republic 1961)
LESOTHO 1966
ATLANTIC OCEAN
PAKISTAN 1947
INDIA 1947
PAKISTAN 1947, BANGLADESH 1973
SRI LANKA (CEYLON) 1948
MYANMAR (BURMA) 1947
LAOS 1949
NORTH VIETNAM 1954
Unified 1974
SOUTH VIETNAM 1954
CAMBODIA 1954
MALAYSIA 1963
SINGAPORE 1965
BRUNEI 1984 From Great Britain
PHILIPPINES 1946
INDONESIA 1949
NORTH KOREA 1948
SOUTH KOREA 1948
From Japan
JAPAN
PACIFIC OCEAN
INDIAN OCEAN
Date is year independence was achieved.
Shading indicates former ruler.
Great Britain
France
Netherlands
Italy
Belgium
Portugal
United States
0 500 1000 1500 Km.
0 500 1000 1500 Mi.

the new states chose association with France. As in the past, the French and their Common Market partners, who helped foot the bill, saw themselves as continuing their civilizing mission in black Africa. More important, they saw in Africa untapped markets for their industrial goods, raw materials for their factories, outlets for profitable investment, and good temporary jobs for their engineers and teachers. The British acted somewhat similarly.

As a result, western European countries actually managed to increase their economic and cultural ties with their former African colonies in the 1960s and 1970s. Above all, they used the lure of special trading privileges and heavy investment in French- and English-language education to enhance a powerful Western presence in the new African states. This situation led a variety of leaders and scholars to charge that western Europe (and the United States) had imposed a system of neocolonialism on the former colonies. According to this view, *neocolonialism* was a system designed to perpetuate Western economic domination and undermine the promise of political independence, thereby extending to Africa (and much of Asia) the economic subordination that the United States had established in Latin America after the political revolutions of the early nineteenth century. At the very least, enduring influence in black Africa testified to western Europe's resurgent economic and political power in international relations.

America's Civil Rights Revolution

The Second World War cured the depression in the United States and brought about an economic boom. Unemployment practically vanished, and the well-being of Americans increased dramatically. Despite fears that peace would bring renewed depression, conversion to a peacetime economy went smoothly. As in western Europe, the U.S. economy proceeded to advance fairly steadily for a long generation.

Prosperity helps explain why postwar domestic politics consisted largely of modest adjustments to the status quo until the 1960s. Truman's upset victory in 1948 demonstrated that Americans had no interest in undoing Roosevelt's social and economic reforms. The Congress proceeded to increase Social Security benefits, subsidize middle- and lower-class housing, and raise the minimum wage. These and other liberal measures consolidated the New Deal. In 1952 the Republican party and the voters turned to General Dwight D. Eisenhower (1890–1969), a national hero and self-described moderate.

The federal government's only major new undertaking during the Eisenhower years (1953–1961) was the interstate highway system, a suitable symbol of the basic satisfaction of the vast majority. Some Americans feared that the United States was becoming a "blocked society," obsessed with stability and incapable of wholesome change. This feeling contributed in 1960 to the election of the young John F. Kennedy (1917–1963), who promised to "get the country moving again." President Kennedy captured the popular imagination, revitalized the old Roosevelt coalition, and modestly expanded existing liberal legislation before he was struck down by an assassin's bullet in 1963.

Belatedly and reluctantly, complacent postwar America did experience a genuine social revolution. After a long struggle, African Americans (and their white supporters) threw off a deeply entrenched system of segregation, discrimination, and repression. This civil rights movement advanced on several fronts. Eloquent lawyers from the National Association for the Advancement of Colored People (NAACP) challenged school segregation in the courts. In 1954 they won a landmark decision in the Supreme Court, which ruled in *Brown v. Board of Education* that "separate educational facilities are inherently unequal." Blacks effectively challenged institutionalized inequality with bus boycotts, sit-ins, and demonstrations. As civil rights leader Martin Luther King, Jr. (1929–1968), told the white power structure, "We will not hate you, but we will not obey your evil laws."[4]

In key northern states, African Americans used their growing political power to gain the support of the liberal wing of the Democratic party. A liberal landslide elected Lyndon Johnson (1908–1973) president in 1964. The Civil Rights Act of 1964 categorically prohibited discrimination in public services and on the job. In the follow-up Voting Rights Act of 1965, the federal government firmly guaranteed all blacks the right to vote. By the 1970s, substantial numbers of blacks had been elected to public and private office throughout the southern states, proof positive that dramatic changes had occurred in American race relations. The civil rights movement also provided an inspiring model for women and other groups seeking political and social change.

MAP 30.3 The New States in Africa and Asia Divided primarily along religious lines into two states, British India led the way to political independence in 1947. Most African territories achieved statehood by the mid-1960s, as European empires passed away, unlamented.

The March on Washington in August 1963 marked a dramatic climax in the civil rights struggle. More than 200,000 people gathered at the Lincoln Memorial to hear the young Martin Luther King, Jr., deliver his greatest address, his "I have a dream" speech. *(Francis Miller,* LIFE MAGAZINE © *Time Warner Inc.)*

African Americans enthusiastically supported new social legislation in the mid-1960s. President Johnson solemnly declared "unconditional war on poverty." Congress and the administration created a host of antipoverty projects, such as a domestic peace corps, free preschools for poor children, and community-action programs. Although these programs were directed to all poor Americans—the majority of whom were white—they were also intended to increase economic equality for blacks. Thus the United States promoted in the mid-1960s the kind of fundamental social reform that western Europe had embraced immediately after the Second World War. The United States became more of a welfare state, as government spending for social benefits rose dramatically and approached European levels.

Soviet Eastern Europe, 1945–1968

While western Europe surged ahead economically after the Second World War and increased its political power as American influence gradually waned, eastern Europe followed a different path. The Soviet Union first tightened its grip on the "liberated" nations of eastern Europe under Stalin and then refused to let go. Thus postwar economic recovery in eastern Europe proceeded along Soviet lines, and political and social developments were strongly influenced by changes in the Soviet Union. These changes went forward at a slow and uneven pace, and they appeared almost to halt after Leonid Brezhnev came to power.

Stalin's Last Years, 1945–1953

Americans were not the only ones who felt betrayed by Stalin's postwar actions. The "Great Patriotic War of the Fatherland" had fostered Russian nationalism and a relaxation of dictatorial terror. It also had produced a rare but real unity between Soviet rulers and most Russian people. Having made a heroic war effort, the vast majority of the Soviet people hoped in 1945 that a grateful party and government would grant greater freedom and democracy. Such hopes were soon crushed.

Even before the war ended, Stalin was moving his country back toward rigid dictatorship. As early as 1944, the leading members of the Communist party were being given a new motivating slogan: "The war on Fascism ends, the war on capitalism begins."[5] By early 1946, Stalin was publicly singing the old tune that war was inevitable as long as capitalism existed. Stalin's new foreign foe in the West provided an excuse for reestablishing a harsh dictatorship. Many returning soldiers and ordinary citizens were purged in 1945 and 1946, as Stalin revived the terrible forced-labor camps of the 1930s.

Culture and art were also purged in violent campaigns that reimposed rigid anti-Western ideological conformity. Many artists were denounced, including the composers Sergei Prokofiev and Dimitri Shostakovich and the outstanding film director Sergei Eisenstein. In 1949 Stalin launched a savage verbal attack on Soviet Jews, accusing them of being pro-Western and antisocialist.

In the political realm, Stalin reasserted the Communist party's complete control of the government and his absolute mastery of the party. Five-year plans were reintroduced to cope with the enormous task of economic reconstruction. Once again, heavy and military industry were given top priority, and consumer goods, housing, and collectivized agriculture were neglected. Everyday life was very hard. In short, it was the 1930s all over again in the Soviet Union, although police terror was less intense.

Stalin's prime postwar innovation was to export the Stalinist system to the countries of eastern Europe. The Communist parties of eastern Europe had established one-party states by 1948, thanks to the help of the Red Army and the Russian secret police. Rigid ideological indoctrination, attacks on religion, and a lack of civil liberties were soon facts of life. Industry was nationalized, and the middle class was stripped of its possessions. Economic life was then faithfully recast in the Stalinist mold. Forced industrialization, with five-year plans and a stress on heavy industry, lurched forward without regard for human costs. The collectivization of agriculture began.

Sergei Eisenstein: Ivan the Terrible Eisenstein's final masterpiece—one of the greatest films ever—was filmed during the Second World War and released in two parts in 1946. In this chilling scene, the crafty paranoid tyrant, who has saved Russia from foreign invaders, invites the unsuspecting Prince Vladimir to a midnight revel that will lead to his murder. The increasingly demonic Ivan seemed to resemble Stalin, and Eisenstein was censored and purged. *(David King Collection)*

Only Josip Broz Tito (1892–1980), the resistance leader and Communist chief of Yugoslavia, was able to resist Soviet domination successfully. Tito stood up to Stalin in 1948, and since there was no Russian army in Yugoslavia, he got away with it. Yugoslavia prospered as a multiethnic state until it began to break apart in the 1980s (see page 1054). Tito's successful proclamation of Communist independence led the infuriated and humiliated Stalin to re-enact the great show trials of the 1930s (see page 966). Popular Communist leaders who, like Tito, had led the resistance against Germany, were purged as Stalin sought to create absolutely obedient instruments of domination in eastern Europe. (See the feature "Individuals in Society: Tito and the Rise of Independent Communism.")

Reform and De-Stalinization, 1953–1964

In 1953 the aging Stalin finally died, and the dictatorship that he had built began to change. Even as Stalin's heirs struggled for power, they realized that reforms were necessary because of the widespread fear and hatred of Stalin's political terrorism. The power of the secret police was curbed, and many of the forced-labor camps were gradually closed. Change was also necessary for economic reasons. Agriculture was in bad shape, and shortages of consumer goods were discouraging hard work and initiative. Moreover, Stalin's belligerent foreign policy had led directly to a strong Western alliance, which isolated the Soviet Union.

On the question of just how much change should be permitted in order to preserve the system, the Communist leadership was badly split. Conservatives wanted to make as few changes as possible. Reformers, who were led by Nikita Khrushchev, argued for major innovations. Khrushchev (1894–1971), who had joined the party as an uneducated coal miner in 1918 at age twenty-four and had been one of the new people rising to a high-level position in the 1930s, emerged as the new ruler in 1955.

To strengthen his position and that of his fellow reformers within the party, Khrushchev launched an all-out attack on Stalin and his crimes at a closed session of the Twentieth Party Congress in 1956. In gory detail, he described to the startled Communist delegates how Stalin had tortured and murdered thousands of loyal Communists, how he had trusted Hitler completely and bungled the country's defense, and how he had "supported the glorification of his own person with all conceivable methods." Khrushchev's "secret speech" was read at Communist party meetings held throughout the country, and it strengthened the reform movement.

The liberalization—or "de-Stalinization," as it was called in the West—of the Soviet Union was genuine. The Communist party jealously maintained its monopoly on political power, but Khrushchev shook up the party and brought in new members. Some resources were shifted from heavy industry and the military toward consumer goods and agriculture, and Stalinist controls over workers were relaxed. The Soviet Union's very low standard of living finally began to improve and continued to rise substantially throughout the booming 1960s.

De-Stalinization created great ferment among writers and intellectuals who hungered for cultural freedom. The poet Boris Pasternak (1890–1960) finished his great novel *Doctor Zhivago* in 1956. Published in the West but not in Russia, *Doctor Zhivago* is both a literary masterpiece and a powerful challenge to communism. It tells the story of a prerevolutionary intellectual who rejects the violence and brutality of the revolution of 1917 and the Stalinist years. Even as he is destroyed, he triumphs because of his humanity and Christian spirit. Pasternak was denounced—but he was not shot. Other talented writers followed Pasternak's lead, and courageous editors let the sparks fly.

The writer Aleksandr Solzhenitsyn (b. 1918) created a sensation when his *One Day in the Life of Ivan Denisovich* was published in the Soviet Union in 1962. Solzhenitsyn's novel portrays in grim detail life in a Stalinist concentration camp—a life to which Solzhenitsyn himself had been unjustly condemned—and is a damning indictment of the Stalinist past.

Khrushchev also de-Stalinized Soviet foreign policy. "Peaceful coexistence" with capitalism was possible, he argued, and great wars were not inevitable. Khrushchev even made concessions, agreeing in 1955 to real independence for a neutral Austria after ten long years of Allied occupation. Thus there was considerable relaxation of cold war tensions between 1955 and 1957. At the same time, Khrushchev began wooing the new nations of Asia and Africa—even if they were not communist—with promises and aid.

De-Stalinization stimulated rebelliousness in the eastern European satellites. Having suffered in silence under Stalin, communist reformers and the masses were quickly emboldened to seek much greater liberty and national independence. Poland took the lead in 1956, when extensive rioting brought a new government that managed to win greater autonomy.

Hungary experienced a real and tragic revolution. Led by students and workers—the classic urban revolutionaries—the people of Budapest installed a liberal communist reformer as their new chief in October 1956. Soviet troops were forced to leave the country. But after the new government promised free elections and renounced Hungary's military alliance with Moscow, the Russian leaders ordered an invasion and crushed the national and democratic revolution. Fighting was bitter until the end, for the Hungarians hoped that the United States would come to their aid. When this did not occur, most people in eastern Europe concluded that their only hope was to strive for small domestic gains while following Russia obediently in foreign affairs.

The End of Reform

By late 1962, opposition in party circles to Khrushchev's policies was strong, and in 1964 Khrushchev fell in a bloodless palace revolution. Under Leonid Brezhnev (1906–1982), the Soviet Union began a period of stagnation and limited "re-Stalinization." The basic reason for this development was that Khrushchev's Communist colleagues saw de-Stalinization as a dangerous, two-sided threat. How could Khrushchev denounce the dead dictator without eventually denouncing and perhaps even arresting his still-powerful henchmen? Moreover, the widening campaign of de-Stalinization posed a clear threat to the dictatorial authority of the party. It was producing growing, perhaps uncontrollable, criticism of the whole communist system. The party had to tighten up considerably while there was still time. Khrushchev had to go.

Another reason for conservative opposition was that Khrushchev's policy toward the West was erratic and ultimately unsuccessful. In 1958 he ordered the Western allies to evacuate West Berlin within six months. In response, the allies reaffirmed their unity in West Berlin, and Khrushchev backed down. Then in 1961, as relations with communist China deteriorated dramatically, Khrushchev ordered the East Germans to build a wall between East and West Berlin, thereby sealing off West Berlin in clear violation of existing access agreements between the Great Powers. The recently elected U.S. president, John F. Kennedy, acquiesced to the construction of the Berlin Wall. Emboldened and seeing a chance to change the balance of military power decisively, Khrushchev ordered missiles with nuclear warheads installed in Fidel Castro's communist Cuba in 1962. President Kennedy countered with a naval blockade of Cuba. After a tense diplomatic crisis, Khrushchev agreed to remove the Soviet missiles in return for American pledges not to disturb Castro's regime. Khrushchev looked like a bumbling buffoon; his influence, already slipping, declined rapidly after the Cuban fiasco.

After Brezhnev and his supporters took over in 1964, they started talking quietly of Stalin's "good points" and ignoring his crimes. This change informed Soviet citizens that further liberalization could not be expected at home. Soviet leaders, determined never to suffer Khrushchev's humiliation in the face of American nuclear superiority, also launched a massive arms buildup. Yet Brezhnev and company proceeded cautiously in the mid-1960s and avoided direct confrontation with the United States.

In the wake of Khrushchev's reforms, the 1960s brought modest liberalization and more consumer goods to eastern Europe, as well as somewhat greater national autonomy, especially in Poland and Romania. In January 1968, the reform elements in the Czechoslovak Communist party gained a majority and voted out the long-time Stalinist leader in favor of Alexander Dubček (b. 1921), whose new government launched dramatic reforms.

Educated in Moscow, Dubček was a dedicated Communist. But he and his allies believed that they could reconcile genuine socialism with personal freedom and internal party democracy. Thus local decision making by trade unions, managers, and consumers replaced rigid bureaucratic planning, and censorship was relaxed. The reform program proved enormously popular.

Although Dubček remembered the lesson of the Hungarian revolution and constantly proclaimed his loyalty to the Warsaw Pact, the determination of the Czech reformers to build what they called "socialism with a human face" frightened hard-line Communists. These fears were particularly strong in Poland and East Germany, where leaders knew full well that they lacked popular support. Moreover, the Soviet Union feared that a liberalized Czechoslovakia would eventually be drawn to neutrality or even to the democratic West. Thus the Eastern bloc countries launched a concerted campaign of intimidation against the Czech leaders, and in August 1968, 500,000 Russian and allied eastern European troops suddenly occupied Czechoslovakia. The Czechs made no attempt to resist militarily, and the arrested Czech leaders surrendered to Soviet demands. The reform program was abandoned, and the Czechoslovak experiment in humanizing communism came to an end. Shortly after the invasion of Czechoslovakia,

Individuals in Society

Tito and the Rise of Independent Communism

Marshal Tito in 1940, planning operations for the liberation of Yugoslavia. *(Corbis-Bettmann)*

Josip Tito (1892–1980) was always a dedicated communist. But after fighting the Nazis and bringing revolution to Yugoslavia, he experienced Stalin's wrath. He then built an independent communist state and achieved remarkable influence as a world leader.

Tito was born into a peasant family of mixed ethnic background in northwest Croatia, in what was then Austria-Hungary. Leaving home as a teenager for work in towns, he became a communist labor organizer in the 1920s. Imprisoned for five years in the 1930s, Tito went to Moscow and in 1937 was charged by the Soviets to reorganize the Communist party of Yugoslavia and then to lead the resistance to Nazi and Italian occupation.

Communist revolution was always Tito's main goal. His guerrilla forces fought as much against the competing noncommunist resistance movement, centered in the Serbian region of Yugoslavia and loyal to the deposed monarchy, as against the Nazis and Italians and their collaborators in Croatia, Bosnia, and Serbia. Yet Tito played down his revolutionary objectives and appealed with some success to all ethnic groups in Yugoslavia. He promised "brotherhood and unity" when the carnage ended. Liberating Yugoslavia in 1945 in coordination with Stalin's Red Army, which moved on in pursuit of the retreating Germans, Tito and his followers quickly established the first Stalinist regime in eastern Europe. Yugoslavia's peasants were exploited to pay for heavy industry. Tito's picture was everywhere, and the Communists held all power.

Yet Stalin grew dissatisfied with his ally. Tito bubbled with revolutionary enthusiasm. He supported the Greek communists in their civil war, called for a communist federation in the Balkans, and enraged U.S. public opinion by shooting down an American "spy plane" over Yugoslavia. Stalin preferred cautious moderation in relations with the West, which would, he hoped, facilitate Soviet consolidation in eastern Europe and encourage a division of the world into spheres of influence. Above all, he demanded absolutely obedient Communist leaders. In 1948 he suddenly denounced Tito as a heretic and called on Yugoslavia's Communist party to oust him. Tito later described the rupture as his most traumatic experience, but he stayed calm, rallied party stalwarts, and survived.

At first, Tito's independent communism remained strictly Stalinist, imprisoning opponents and proclaiming its Marxist-Leninist orthodoxy. But Tito soon steered a middle course between East and West. He approved the introduction of "workers' self-management" in Yugoslavia, which loosened the state's hold on the economy and was trumpeted internationally as a radical step toward genuine communism. In the 1950s and 1960s, Tito's one-party dictatorship allowed greater personal freedom and presented would-be communist reformers in eastern Europe with an intriguing model.

Yugoslavia's independent, "nonaligned" communism became an influential model in world politics. Tito adroitly negotiated indispensable military commitments from the United States to keep Stalin's armies at bay, and he received massive U.S. aid. But he also re-established generally good relations with the Soviet Union after Stalin's death. Finally, Tito joined with India's Jawaharlal Nehru and Egypt's Gamal Abdel Nasser to lead and inspire the movement of nonaligned, newly independent countries. Pressing his case on many fronts, Tito strengthened the idea that Third World nations should avoid crippling cold war alliances and concentrate instead on building independent socialist states like his.

Questions for Analysis

1. Does the rupture between Tito and Stalin throw light on the origins of the cold war? In what ways?
2. What were the characteristics of Tito's independent communism? How did it enhance his status as a leader?

The End of Reform In August 1968 Soviet tanks rumbled into Prague to extinguish Czechoslovakian efforts to build a humane socialism. Here people watch the massive invasion from the sidewalks, knowing full well the suicidal danger of armed resistance. *(Joseph Koudelka PP/Magnum)*

Brezhnev declared the so-called Brezhnev Doctrine, according to which the Soviet Union and its allies had the right to intervene in any socialist country whenever they saw the need.

The 1968 invasion of Czechoslovakia was the crucial event of the Brezhnev era, which really lasted beyond the aging leader's death in 1982 until the emergence in 1985 of Mikhail Gorbachev. The invasion demonstrated the determination of the ruling elite to maintain the status quo in the Soviet bloc. In the U.S.S.R. that determination resulted in further repression, but the Soviet Union appeared quite stable in the 1970s and early 1980s.

Postwar Social Transformations, 1945–1968

While Europe staged its astonishing political and economic recovery from the Nazi nightmare, the patterns of everyday life and the structure of Western society were changing no less rapidly and remarkably. Epoch-making inventions and new technologies profoundly affected human existence. Important groups in society formulated new attitudes and demands, which were closely related to the changing class structure and social reforms. An international youth culture took shape and rose to challenge established lifestyles and even governments.

Science and Technology

Ever since the scientific revolution of the seventeenth century and the Industrial Revolution at the end of the eighteenth century, scientific and technical developments had powerfully influenced attitudes, society, and everyday life. Never was this influence stronger than after about 1940. Science and technology proved so productive and influential because, for the first time in history, "pure theoretical" science and "practical" technology (or "applied" science) were effectively joined together on a massive scale.

With the advent of the Second World War, pure science lost its impractical innocence. Most leading university scientists went to work on top-secret projects to help their governments fight the war. The development by British scientists of radar to detect enemy aircraft was a particularly important outcome of this new kind of sharply focused research. A radically improved radar system played a key role in Britain's victory in the battle for air supremacy in 1940. The air war also greatly stimulated the development of jet aircraft and spurred further research on electronic computers, which calculated the complex mathematical relationships between fast-moving planes and anti-aircraft shells to increase the likelihood of a hit.

The most spectacular result of directed scientific research during the war was the atomic bomb. In August 1939, physicist Albert Einstein wrote to President Franklin Roosevelt that recent work in physics suggested that "it may become possible to set up a nuclear chain reaction in a large mass of uranium" and to construct "extremely powerful bombs of a new type."[6] This letter and ongoing experiments by nuclear physicists led to the top-secret Manhattan Project, which ballooned into a mammoth crash. After three years of intensive effort, the first atomic bomb was successfully tested in July 1945. In August 1945, two bombs were dropped on Hiroshima and Nagasaki, thereby ending the war with Japan.

The atomic bomb showed the world both the awesome power and the heavy moral responsibilities of modern science and its high priests. As one Los Alamos scientist exclaimed as he watched the first mushroom cloud rise over the American desert, "We are all sons-of-bitches now!"[7]

The spectacular results of directed research during World War II inspired a new model for science—"Big Science." By combining theoretical work with sophisticated engineering in a large organization, Big Science could attack extremely difficult problems, from better products for consumers to new and improved weapons for the military. Big Science was extremely expensive, requiring large-scale financing from governments and large corporations.

Populous, victorious, and wealthy, the United States took the lead in Big Science after World War II. Between 1945 and 1965, spending on scientific research and development in the United States grew five times as fast as the national income, and by 1965 such spending took 3 percent of all U.S. income. It was generally accepted that government should finance science heavily in both the "capitalist" United States and the "socialist" Soviet Union.

One reason for the similarity was that science was not demobilized in either country after the war. Scientists remained a critical part of every major military establishment, and a large portion of all postwar scientific research went for "defense." New weapons such as rockets, nuclear submarines, and spy satellites demanded breakthroughs no less remarkable than those of radar and the first atomic bomb. After 1945 roughly one-quarter of all men and women trained in science and engineering in the West—and perhaps more in the Soviet Union—were employed full-time in the production of weapons to kill other humans.

Sophisticated science, lavish government spending, and military needs all came together in the space race of the 1960s. In 1957 the Soviets used long-range rockets developed in their nuclear weapons program to put a satellite in orbit. In 1961 they sent the world's first cosmonaut circling the globe. Embarrassed by Soviet triumphs and breaking with President Eisenhower's opposition to an expensive space program, President Kennedy made an all-out U.S. commitment to catch up with the Soviets and land a crewed spacecraft on the moon "before the decade was out." Harnessing pure science, applied technology, and up to $5 billion a year, the Apollo Program achieved its ambitious objective in 1969. Four more moon landings followed by 1972.

The rapid expansion of government-financed research in the United States attracted many of Europe's best scientists during the 1950s and 1960s. Thoughtful Europeans lamented this "brain drain" and feared that Europe was falling hopelessly behind the United States in science and technology. In fact, a revitalized Europe was already responding to the American challenge, pooling their efforts on such Big Science projects as the *Concorde* supersonic passenger airliner and the peaceful uses of atomic energy.

The rise of Big Science and of close ties between science and technology greatly altered the lives of scientists. The scientific community grew much larger than ever before. There were about four times as many scientists in Europe and North America in 1975 as in 1945. Scientists, technologists, engineers, and medical specialists counted after 1945, in part because there were so many of them.

One consequence of the growth of science was its high degree of specialization, for no one could possibly master a broad field such as physics or medicine. Intense specialization in new disciplines and subdisciplines increased the rates at which both basic knowledge was acquired and practical applications were made.

Highly specialized modern scientists and technologists normally had to work as members of a team, which completely changed the work and lifestyle of modern scientists. A great deal of work therefore went on in large bureaucratic organizations, where the individual was very often a small cog in a great machine. The growth of large scientific bureaucracies in government and private enterprise suggested how scientists and technologists permeated the entire society and many aspects of life.

Modern science became highly, even brutally, competitive. This competitiveness is well depicted in Nobel Prize winner James Watson's fascinating book *The Double Helix,* which tells how in 1953 Watson and an Englishman, Francis Crick, discovered the structure of DNA, the molecule of heredity. A brash young American Ph.D. in his twenties, Watson seemed almost obsessed by the idea that some other research team would find the solution first and thereby deprive him of the fame and fortune he desperately wanted. With so many thousands of like-minded researchers in the wealthy countries of the world, scientific and technical knowledge rushed forward in the postwar era.

The Changing Class Structure

Rapid economic growth went a long way toward creating a new society in Europe after the Second World War. European society became more mobile and more democratic. Old class barriers relaxed, and class distinctions became fuzzier.

Changes in the structure of the middle class were particularly influential in the general drift toward a less rigid class structure. In the nineteenth and early twentieth centuries, the model for the middle class had been the independent, self-employed individual who owned a business or practiced a liberal profession such as law or medicine. Ownership of property—usually inherited property—and strong family ties had often been the keys to wealth and standing within the middle class. After 1945 this pattern declined drastically in western Europe. A new breed of managers and experts replaced traditional property owners as the leaders of the middle class. Ability to serve the needs of a big organization largely replaced inherited property and family connections in determining an individual's social position in the middle and upper middle class. At the same time, the middle class grew massively and became harder to define.

There were several reasons for these developments. Rapid industrial and technological expansion created in large corporations and government agencies a powerful demand for technologists and managers. Moreover, the old propertied middle class lost control of many family-owned businesses, and many small businesses (including family farms) simply passed out of existence as their former owners joined the ranks of salaried employees.

Top managers and ranking civil servants therefore represented the model for a new middle class of salaried specialists. Well paid and highly trained, often with backgrounds in engineering or accounting, these experts increasingly came from all social classes, even the working class. Pragmatic and realistic, they were primarily concerned with efficiency and practical solutions to concrete problems. Everywhere successful managers and technocrats passed on the opportunity for all-important advanced education to their children, but only in rare instances could they pass on the positions

Claes Oldenburg: "Soft" Sculpture Emerging in the 1950s, pop (for *popular*) art recognized the presence and power of exploding technology. This was especially true in sculpture, where artists incorporated new materials and procedures and often offered a humorous view of mass culture. Oldenburg's influential one-man show in 1962 manipulated and confused perceptions of everyday facts, placing such things as this giant vinyl Floor Cake, among other whimsical objects, in a room of furniture. *(© Robert R. McElroy)*

they had attained. Thus the new middle class, which was based largely on specialized skills and high levels of education, was more open, democratic, and insecure than the old propertied middle class.

The structure of the lower classes also became more flexible and open. There was a mass exodus from farms and the countryside, as one of the most traditional and least mobile groups in European society drastically declined. Meanwhile, because of rapid technological change, the industrial working class ceased to expand, and job opportunities for white-collar and service employees grew rapidly. Such employees bore a greater resemblance to the new middle class of salaried specialists than to industrial workers, who were also better educated and more specialized.

European governments were reducing class tensions with a series of social security reforms. Many of these reforms—such as increased unemployment benefits and more extensive old-age pensions—simply strengthened social security measures first pioneered in Bismarck's Germany before the First World War (see pages 842–843). Other programs were new, like comprehensive national health systems directed by the state. Most countries also introduced family allowances—direct government grants to parents to help them raise their children. These allowances helped many poor families make ends meet. Most European governments also gave maternity grants and built inexpensive public housing for low-income families and individuals. These and other social reforms provided a humane floor of well-being. Reforms also promoted greater equality because they were expensive and were paid for in part by higher taxes on the rich.

The rising standard of living and the spread of standardized consumer goods also worked to level Western society, as the percentage of income spent on food and drink declined substantially. For example, the European automobile industry expanded phenomenally after lagging far behind the United States since the 1920s. In 1948 there were only 5 million cars in western Europe, but in 1965 there were 44 million. Car ownership was democratized and came within the range of better-paid workers.

Europeans took great pleasure in the products of the "gadget revolution" as well. Like Americans, Europeans filled their houses and apartments with washing machines, vacuum cleaners, refrigerators, dishwashers, radios, TVs, and stereos. The purchase of consumer goods was greatly facilitated by installment purchasing, which allowed people to buy on credit. Before the Second World War, Europeans had rarely bought "on time." But with the expansion of social security safeguards, reducing the need to accumulate savings for hard times, ordinary people were increasingly willing to take on debt. This change had far-reaching consequences.

Leisure and recreation occupied an important place in consumer societies. The most astonishing leisure-time development was the blossoming of mass travel and tourism. Before the Second World War, most people had neither the time nor the money for it. But with month-long paid vacations required by law in most European countries and widespread automobile ownership, beaches and ski resorts came within the reach of the middle class and many workers. By the late 1960s, packaged tours with cheap group flights and bargain hotel accommodations had made even distant lands easily accessible. A French company grew rich building imitation Tahitian paradises around the world. At Swedish nudist colonies on secluded West African beaches, officeworkers from Stockholm fleetingly worshiped the sun in the middle of the long northern winter. Truly, consumerism had come of age.

Youth and the Counterculture

Economic prosperity and a more democratic class structure had a powerful impact on youth throughout the Western world. The bulging cohort of youth born after World War II developed a distinctive and very international youth culture. Self-consciously different in the late 1950s, this youth culture became increasingly oppositional in the 1960s, interacting with a revival of leftist thought to create a "counterculture" that rebelled against parents, authority figures, and the status quo.

Young people in the United States took the lead. American college students in the 1950s were docile and often dismissed as the "Silent Generation," but some young people did revolt against the conformity and boredom of middle-class suburbs. These "young rebels" wore tightly pegged pants and idolized singer Elvis Presley and actor James Dean. The "beat" movement of the late 1950s expanded on the theme of revolt, and Jack Kerouac vividly captured the restless motion of the beatniks in his autobiographical novel *On the Road.* People like Kerouac clustered together in certain urban areas, such as the Haight Ashbury district of San Francisco or the Near North Side of Chicago. There the young (and the not-so-young) fashioned a highly publicized subculture that blended radical politics, unbridled personal experimentation (with drugs and communal living, for example), and new artistic styles. This subculture quickly spread to major American and western European cities.

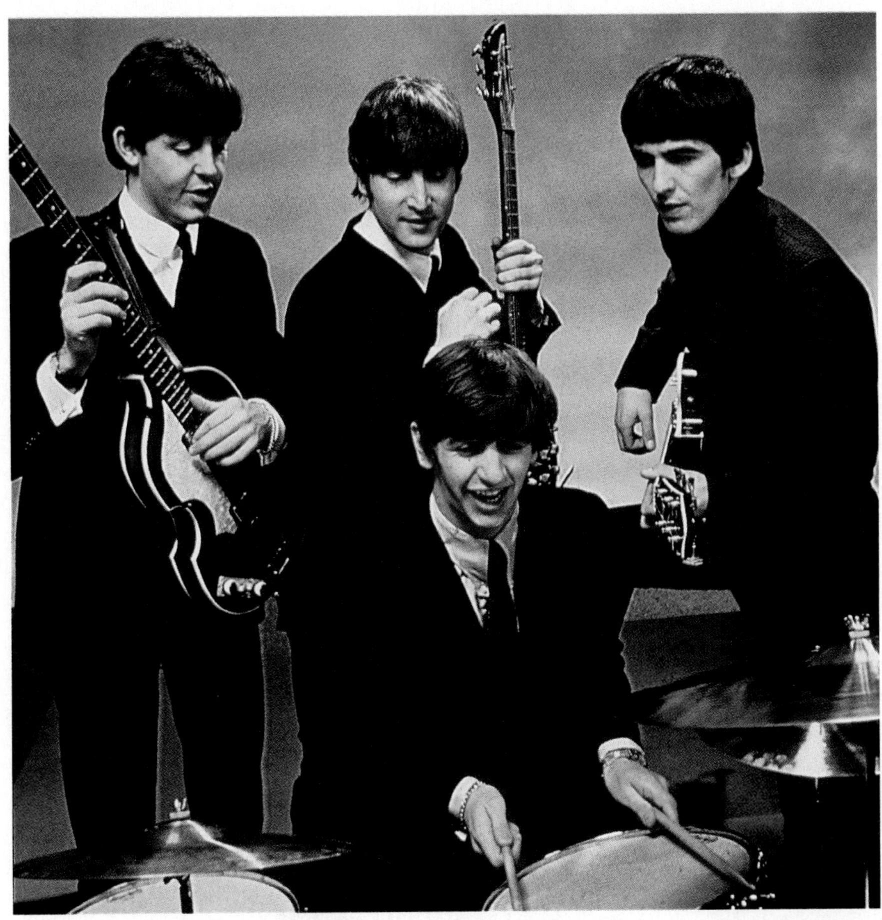

The Beatles The older generation often saw sexual license and immorality in the group's frank lyrics and suggestive style. But in comparison with all that came after them in the world of pop music, the Beatles were sentimental and wholesome. *(John Zimmerman/Camera Press/Retna Ltd.)*

Rock music helped tie this international subculture together. Rock grew out of the black music culture of rhythm and blues, which was flavored with country and western to make it more accessible to white teenagers. The mid-1950s signaled a breakthrough as Bill Hailey called on record buyers to "Rock Around the Clock" and Elvis Presley warned them to keep off of his "Blue Suede Shoes." In the 1960s, the Beatles thrilled millions of young people, often to their parents' dismay. Like Elvis, the Beatles suggested personal and sexual freedom that many older people found disturbing.

It was Bob Dylan, a young folksinger turned rock poet with an acoustic guitar, who best expressed the radical political as well as cultural aspirations of the "younger generation." In a song that became a rallying cry, Dylan sang that "the times they are a'changing."[8] The song captured the spirit of growing alienation between the generation whose defining experiences had been the Great Depression and World War II and the generation ready to reject the complacency of the 1950s. Increasing discontent with middle-class conformity and the injustices of racism and imperialism fueled the young leaders of social protest and reflected a growing spirit of rebellion.

Certainly the sexual behavior of young people, or at least some young people, appeared to change dramatically in the 1960s and into the 1970s. More young people engaged in sexual intercourse, and they did so at an earlier age. For example, a 1973 study reported that only 4.5 percent of West German youths born in 1945 and 1946 had experienced sexual relations before their seventeenth birthday but that 32 percent of those born in 1953 and 1954 had done so.[9] Perhaps even more significant was the growing tendency of young unmarried people to live together in a separate household on a semipermanent basis, with little thought of getting married or having children. Thus many youths, especially middle-class youths, defied social custom, claiming in effect that the long-standing monopoly of married couples on legitimate sexual unions was dead.

Several factors contributed to the emergence of the international youth culture in the 1960s. First, mass communications and youth travel linked countries and continents together. Second, the postwar baby boom meant that young people became an unusually large part of the population and could therefore exercise exceptional influence on society as a whole. Third, postwar prosperity and greater equality gave young people more purchasing power than ever before. This enabled them to set their own trends and mass fads in everything from music to chemical stimulants. Common patterns of consumption and behavior fostered generational loyalty. Finally, prosperity meant that good jobs were readily available. Students and young job seekers had little need to fear punishment from strait-laced employers for unconventional behavior.

The youth culture practically fused with the counterculture in opposition to the established order in the late 1960s. Student protesters embraced romanticism and revolutionary idealism, dreaming of complete freedom and simpler, purer societies. The materialistic West was hopelessly rotten, but better societies were being built in the newly independent countries of Asia and Africa, or so many young radicals believed. Thus the Vietnam War took on special significance. Many politically active students in the United States and Europe believed that the older generation in general and American leaders in particular were fighting an immoral and imperialistic war against a small and heroic people who wanted only national unity and human dignity. As the war in Vietnam intensified, so did worldwide student opposition to it.

Student protests in western Europe also highlighted more general problems of youth, education, and a society of specialists. In contrast to the United States, high school and university educations in Europe had been limited for centuries to a small elite. Whereas 22 percent of the American population was going on to some form of higher education in 1950, only 3 to 4 percent of western European youths were doing so. Then en-

Student Rebellion in Paris These rock-throwing students in the Latin Quarter of Paris are trying to force education reforms and even to topple de Gaulle's government. Throughout May 1968 students clashed repeatedly with France's tough riot police in bloody street fighting. De Gaulle remained in power, but a major reform of French education did follow. *(Bruno Barbey/Magnum)*

rollments skyrocketed. By 1960 at least three times as many students were going to some kind of university as had attended before the war, and the number continued to rise sharply until the 1970s. Reflecting the development of a more democratic class structure and a growing awareness that higher education was the key to success, European universities gave more scholarships and opened their doors to more students from the lower middle and lower classes.

The rapid expansion of higher education created problems as well as opportunities for students. Classes were overcrowded, and there was little contact with professors. Competition for grades became intense. Moreover, although more practical areas of study were gradually added, many students felt that they were not getting the kind of education they needed for jobs in the modern world and that basic university reforms were absolutely necessary. At the same time, some reflective students warned of the dangers of narrowly trained experts. They feared that universities would soon do nothing but turn out docile technocrats both to stock and to serve "the establishment."

The many tensions within the exploding university population came to a head in the late 1960s and early 1970s. Following the American example, European university students rose to challenge their university administrations and even their governments. The most far-reaching of these revolts occurred in France in 1968. Students occupied buildings and took over the University of Paris, which led to violent clashes with police. Most students demanded both changes in the curriculum and a real voice in running the university. Some student radicals went further, linking the attack on French universities to New Left critiques of capitalism and appealing to France's industrial workers for help. Rank-and-file workers ignored the advice of their cautious union officials, and a more or less spontaneous general strike spread across France in May 1968. It seemed certain that President de Gaulle's Fifth Republic would collapse.

In fact, de Gaulle stiffened, like an irate father. Declaring that he was in favor of university reforms and higher minimum wages but would oppose the "bed-wetting" of undisciplined students and workers, he moved troops toward Paris and called for new elections. Thoroughly frightened by the student-sparked upheaval and fearful that a successful revolution could lead to an eventual communist takeover, the masses of France voted overwhelmingly for de Gaulle's party and a return to law and order. Workers went back to work, and the mini-revolution collapsed. Yet the proud de Gaulle and the postwar European renaissance that he represented had been shaken, and within a year he resigned. Growing out of the counterculture and youthful idealism, the student rebellion of 1968 signaled the end of an era and the return of conflict and uncertainty in the 1970s and early 1980s.

Renewed Challenges in the Late Cold War, 1968–1985

Similar to but more important than the student upheaval in France and the crushing of socialist reform in Czechoslovakia, the Vietnam War marked the beginning of a new era of challenges and uncertainties in the late 1960s. The Vietnam War and its aftermath divided the people of the United States, shook the ideology of containment, and weakened the Western alliance. A second major challenge appeared when the great postwar economic boom came to a close in 1973 and opened up a long period of economic stagnation, widespread unemployment, and social dislocation.

The United States and Vietnam

President Johnson wanted to go down in history as a master reformer and a healer of old wounds. Instead, he opened new ones with the Vietnam War.

Although many student radicals believed that imperialism was the main cause, American involvement in Vietnam was more clearly a product of the cold war and the ideology of containment (see page 995). From the late 1940s on, most Americans and their leaders viewed the world in terms of a constant struggle to stop the spread of communism. As western Europe began to revive and China established a communist government in 1949, efforts to contain communism shifted to Asia. The bloody Korean War (1950–1953) ended in stalemate, but the United States did succeed in preventing a communist takeover in South Korea. After the defeat of the French in Vietnam in 1954, the Eisenhower administration refused to sign the Geneva Accords that temporarily divided the country into two zones pending national unification by means of free elections. President Eisenhower then acquiesced in the refusal of the anticommunist South Vietnamese government to accept the verdict of elections and provided it with military aid. President Kennedy greatly increased the number of American "military advisers" to sixteen thousand.

After successfully depicting his opponent, Barry Goldwater, as a trigger-happy extremist in a nuclear age and resoundingly winning the 1964 election on a peace platform, President Johnson greatly expanded the American role in the Vietnam conflict. As Johnson explained to his ambassador in Saigon, "I am not going to lose Vietnam. I am not going to be the President who saw Southeast Asia go the way China went."[10] American strategy was to "escalate" the war sufficiently to break the will of the North Vietnamese and their southern allies without resorting to "overkill," which might risk war with the entire Communist bloc. Thus South Vietnam received massive military aid, American forces in the South gradually grew to half a million men, and the United States bombed North Vietnam with ever-greater intensity. But there was no invasion of the North or naval blockade. In the end, the American strategy of limited warfare backfired. It was the Americans themselves who grew weary and the American leadership that cracked.

Divisions over the Vietnam War ran deep in the United States. Antiwar protesters captured the public's attention, but anti-Vietcong demonstrations like this one spoke for many Americans. Opinion polls showed that fewer than 20 percent of Americans supported withdrawal from Vietnam until after the November 1968 elections, by which time the decision to get out gradually had been made. *(Burt Glinn/Magnum)*

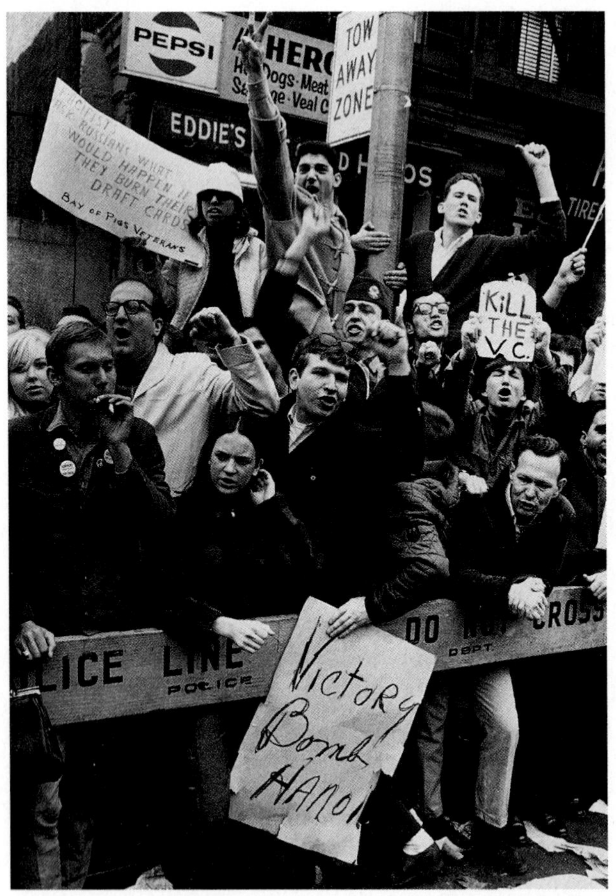

The undeclared war in Vietnam, fought nightly on American television, eventually divided the nation. Initial support was strong. The politicians, the media, and the population as a whole saw the war as part of a legitimate defense against communist totalitarianism in all poor countries. But an antiwar movement quickly emerged on college campuses, where the prospect of being drafted to fight savage battles in Asian jungles made male stomachs churn. In October 1965, student protesters joined forces with old-line socialists, New Left intellectuals, and pacifists in antiwar demonstrations in fifty American cities. By 1967 a growing number of critics denounced the war as a criminal intrusion into a complex and distant civil war.

Criticism reached a crescendo after the Vietcong Tet Offensive in January 1968. This, the communists' first comprehensive attack with conventional weapons on major cities in South Vietnam, failed militarily: the Vietcong suffered heavy losses, and the attack did not spark a mass uprising. But Washington had been claiming that victory in South Vietnam was in sight, and U.S. critics of the Vietnam War quickly interpreted the bloody combat as a decisive American defeat. America's leaders lost heart. In 1968, after a humiliatingly narrow victory in the New Hampshire primary, President Johnson called for negotiations with North Vietnam and announced that he would not stand for re-election.

Elected by a razor-slim margin in 1968, President Richard Nixon (1913–1994) sought to gradually disengage America from Vietnam and the accompanying national crisis. Intensifying the continuous bombardment of the enemy while simultaneously pursuing peace talks with the North Vietnamese, Nixon suspended the draft, so hated on college campuses, and cut American forces in Vietnam from 550,000 to 24,000 in four years. The cost of the war dropped dramatically. Moreover, President Nixon launched a flank attack in diplomacy. He journeyed to China in 1972 and reached a spectacular if limited reconciliation with the People's Republic of China. In doing so, Nixon took advantage of China's growing fears of the Soviet Union and undermined North Vietnam's position.

Fortified by the overwhelming endorsement of the voters in his 1972 electoral triumph, President Nixon and Secretary of State Henry Kissinger finally reached a peace agreement with North Vietnam. The agreement allowed remaining American forces to complete their withdrawal, and the United States reserved the right to resume bombing if the accords were broken. Fighting declined markedly in South Vietnam, where the South Vietnamese army appeared to hold its own against the Vietcong. The storm of crisis in the United States seemed to have passed.

On the contrary, the country reaped the Watergate whirlwind. Like some other recent American presidents, Nixon authorized spying activities that went beyond the law. Going further than his predecessors, he allowed special units to use various illegal means to stop the leaking of government documents to the press. One such group broke into the Democratic party headquarters in Washington's Watergate complex in June 1972 and was promptly arrested. Nixon and many of his assistants then tried to hush up the bungled job, but the media and the machinery of congressional investigation eventually exposed the administration's web of lies and lawbreaking. In 1974 a beleaguered Nixon was forced to resign in disgrace.

The consequences of renewed political crisis flowing from the Watergate affair were profound. First, Watergate resulted in a major shift of power away from the presidency and toward Congress, especially in foreign affairs. Therefore, as American aid to South Vietnam diminished in 1973 and as an emboldened North Vietnam launched a general invasion against South Vietnamese armies in early 1974, Congress refused to permit any American military response. A second consequence of the U.S. crisis was that after more than thirty-five years of battle, the Vietnamese communists unified their country in 1975 as a harsh dictatorial state. Third, the belated fall of South Vietnam in the wake of Watergate shook America's postwar confidence and left the country divided and uncertain about its proper role in world affairs.

Détente or Cold War?

One alternative to the badly damaged policy of containing communism was the policy of *détente,* or the progressive relaxation of cold war tensions. Thus while the cold war continued to rage outside Europe and generally defined superpower relations between the Soviet Union and the United States, West Germany took a major step toward genuine peace in Europe.

West German chancellor Willy Brandt (1913–1992) took the lead when in December 1970 he flew to Poland for the signing of a historic treaty of reconciliation. In a dramatic moment rich in symbolism, Brandt laid a wreath at the tomb of the Polish unknown soldier and another at the monument commemorating the armed uprising of Warsaw's Jewish ghetto against occupying Nazi armies. Standing before the ghetto memorial, a somber Brandt fell to his knees and knelt as if in prayer. "I wanted," Brandt said later, "to ask pardon in the name of our people for a million-fold crime which was committed in the misused name of the Germans."[11]

Brandt's gesture at the Warsaw ghetto memorial and the treaty with Poland were part of his policy of reconciliation with eastern Europe. Indeed, Brandt aimed at nothing less than a comprehensive peace settlement for central Europe and the two German states established after 1945. The Federal Republic of Germany (West Germany), formed out of the American, British, and French zones of occupation and based on freely expressed popular sovereignty, had long claimed that the communist German Democratic Republic (East Germany) lacked free elections and hence any legal or moral basis. West Germany also refused to accept the loss of German territory taken by Poland and the Soviet Union after 1945. However, Brandt, the popular socialist mayor of West Berlin when the Berlin Wall was built in 1961, believed that the wall showed the painful limitations of West Germany's official hard line toward communist eastern Europe and the need for a new foreign policy.

Winning the chancellorship in 1969, Brandt negotiated treaties with the Soviet Union, Poland, and Czechoslovakia that formally accepted existing state boundaries and the loss of German territory to Poland and the Soviet Union (see Map 30.1) in return for a mutual renunciation of force or the threat of force. Using the imaginative formula of "two German states within one German nation," Brandt's government also broke decisively with the past and entered into direct relations with East Germany, aiming for modest practical improvements rather than reunification, which at that point was completely impractical.

Brandt's bold initiatives encouraged President Nixon to sponsor a broader, American-led framework of reducing East-West tensions in the early 1970s. Thus Nixon's ambiguous policy of phased withdrawal from Vietnam was sold as part of détente, although it was designed mainly to end the conflict over the Vietnam War in the United States. After Nixon was forced to resign, détente reached its high point when all European nations (except isolationist Albania), the United States, and Canada signed the Final Act of the Helsinki Conference in 1975. Thirty-five nations agreed that Europe's existing political frontiers could not be changed by force, and they solemnly accepted numerous provisions guaranteeing the human rights and political freedoms of their citizens.

Optimistic hopes for détente in international relations gradually faded in the later 1970s. Brezhnev's So-

Willy Brandt in Poland, 1970 Chancellor Brandt's gesture at the Warsaw memorial to the Jewish victims of Nazi terrorism was criticized by some West Germans but praised by many more. This picture reached an enormous audience, appearing in hundreds of newspapers in both the East and the West. *(Bilderdienst Süddeutscher Verlag)*

viet Union ignored the human rights provisions of the Helsinki agreement, and East-West political competition remained very much alive outside Europe. Many Americans became convinced that the Soviet Union was taking advantage of détente, steadily building up its military might and pushing for political gains and revolutions in Africa, Asia, and Latin America. The Soviet invasion of Afghanistan in December 1979, which was designed to save an increasingly unpopular Marxist regime, was especially alarming. Many Americans feared that the oil-rich states of the Persian Gulf would be next, and once again they looked to the Atlantic alliance and military might to thwart communist expansion.

President Jimmy Carter (b. 1924), elected in 1976, tried to lead the Atlantic alliance beyond verbal condemnation and urged economic sanctions against the Soviet Union. Yet only Great Britain among the European allies supported the American initiative. The alliance showed the same lack of concerted action when the Solidarity movement rose in Poland. Some observers concluded that the alliance had lost the will to think and act decisively in dealing with the Soviet bloc.

The Atlantic alliance endured, however. The U.S. military buildup launched by Carter in his last years in office was greatly accelerated by President Ronald Reagan (b. 1911), who was swept into office in 1980 by a wave of patriotism and economic discontent. The new American leadership acted as if the military balance had tipped in favor of the Soviet Union, which Reagan anathematized as the "evil empire." Increasing defense spending enormously, the Reagan administration concentrated especially on nuclear arms and an expanded navy as keys to American power in the post-Vietnam age.

The broad swing in the historical pendulum toward greater conservatism in the 1980s gave Reagan invaluable allies in western Europe. In Great Britain a strong-willed Margaret Thatcher worked well with Reagan and was a forceful advocate for a revitalized Atlantic alliance. After a distinctly pro-American Helmut Kohl (b. 1930) came to power with the conservative Christian Democrats in 1982, West Germany and the United States once again effectively coordinated military and political policy toward the Soviet bloc.

Passing in the 1970s and early 1980s from détente to confusion to regeneration, the Atlantic alliance bent, but it did not break. In maintaining the alliance, the Western nations gave indirect support to ongoing efforts to liberalize authoritarian communist eastern Europe and probably helped convince the Soviet Union's Mikhail Gorbachev that endless cold war conflict was foolish and dangerous.

The Troubled Economy

For twenty years after 1945, most Europeans were preoccupied with the possibilities of economic progress and consumerism. The more democratic class structure also helped to reduce social tension, and ideological conflict went out of style. In the late 1960s, sharp criticism and social conflict re-emerged, however. As we have seen, the anti-Vietnam War movement and the international student rebellion of the late 1960s evidenced the passing of postwar social stability.

Yet it was the reappearance of economic crisis in the early 1970s that brought the most serious challenges for the average person. The postwar international monetary system was based on the American dollar, which foreign governments could exchange for gold at $35 an ounce and which was considered to be "as good as gold." Giving foreign aid and fighting foreign wars, the United States sent billions abroad. By early 1971, it had only $11 billion in gold left, and Europe had accumulated U.S. $50 billion. Foreigners then panicked and raced to exchange their dollars for gold. President Richard Nixon responded by stopping the sale of American gold, the value of the dollar fell sharply, and inflation accelerated worldwide. Fixed rates of exchange were abandoned, and great uncertainty replaced postwar predictability in international trade and finance.

Even more damaging was the dramatic reversal in the price and availability of energy. The great postwar boom was fueled by cheap oil, especially in western Europe. Cheap oil from the Middle East permitted energy-intensive industries—automobiles, chemicals, and electric power—to expand rapidly and lead other sectors of the economy forward. By 1971 the Arab-led Organization of Petroleum Exporting Countries (OPEC) had watched the price of crude oil decline consistently compared with the rising price of manufactured goods. OPEC decided to reverse that trend by presenting a united front against the oil companies. The stage was set for a revolution in energy prices during the fourth Arab-Israeli war in October 1973, when Egypt and Syria launched a surprise attack on Israel. OPEC then declared an embargo on oil shipments to the United States, which supported Israel with an emergency airlift of weapons, and in the course of a year crude oil prices quadrupled. It was widely realized that the rapid price rise was economically destructive, but the world's big powers did nothing. The Soviet Union was a great oil exporter and benefited directly; the United States was immobilized, its attention absorbed by the Watergate crisis in politics (see page 1017). Thus governments, industry, and individuals had no other choice than to deal piecemeal with the so-called oil shock—a "shock" that turned out to be an earthquake.

Coming on the heels of upheaval in the international monetary system, the revolution in energy prices plunged the world into its worst economic decline since the 1930s. The energy-intensive industries that had driven the economy up in the 1950s and 1960s now dragged it down. Unemployment rose; productivity and living standards declined. By 1976 a modest recovery was in progress. But when a fundamentalist Islamic revolution struck Iran and oil production collapsed in that country, the price of crude oil doubled in 1979, and the world economy succumbed to its second oil shock. Unemployment and inflation rose dramatically before another uneven recovery began in 1982. In the summer of 1985, however, the unemployment rate in western Europe rose to its highest level since the Great Depression. Nineteen million people were unemployed.

One telling measure of the troubled economy was the "misery index," first used with considerable effect by candidate Jimmy Carter in the 1976 U.S. presidential debates. The misery index combined rates of inflation and unemployment in a single, powerfully emotional number. Figure 30.1 shows a comparison of misery indexes for the United States, Japan, and the Common Market countries between 1970 and 1986. "Misery" increased on both sides of the Atlantic, but the increase was substantially greater in western Europe, where these hard times were often referred to simply as "the crisis." Japan did better than both Europe and the U.S. in this period.

Throughout the 1970s and 1980s, anxious observers, recalling the disastrous consequences of the Great Depression, worried that the Common Market would disintegrate in the face of severe economic dislocation and that economic nationalism would halt steps toward European unity. Yet the Common Market—now officially known as the European Economic Community—continued to exert a powerful attraction on nonmembers. In 1973 Denmark and Iceland, in addition to Britain, finally joined. Greece joined in 1981, and Portugal and Spain entered in 1986. The nations of the European

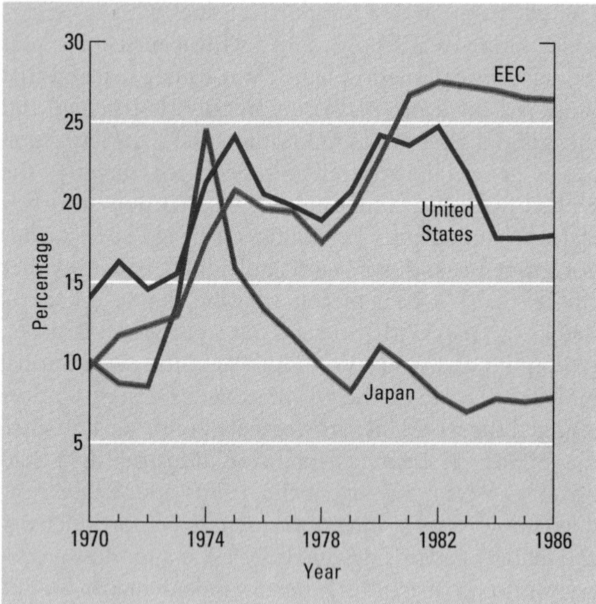

FIGURE 30.1 The Misery Index, 1970–1986 Combining rates of unemployment and inflation provided a simple but effective measure of economic hardship. This particular index represents the sum of two times the unemployment rate plus the inflation rate, reflecting the widespread belief that joblessness causes more suffering than higher prices. EEC = European Economic Community, or Common Market countries. *(Source: OECD data, as given in* The Economist, *June 15, 1985, p. 69.)*

Economic Community also cooperated more closely in international undertakings, and the movement toward unity for western Europe stayed alive.

Society in a Time of Economic Uncertainty

The most pervasive consequences of economic stagnation in the 1970s and early 1980s were probably psychological and attitudinal. Optimism gave way to pessimism; romantic utopianism yielded to sober realism. This drastic change in mood—a complete surprise only to those who had never studied history—affected states, institutions, and individuals in countless ways.

To be sure, there were heartbreaking human tragedies—lost jobs, bankruptcies, homelessness, and mental breakdowns. But on the whole, the welfare system fashioned in the postwar era prevented mass suffering and degradation through extended benefits for the unemployed, pensions for the aged, free medical care and special allowances for the needy, and a host of lesser supports. The responsive, socially concerned national state undoubtedly contributed to the preservation of political stability and democracy in the face of economic difficulties that might have brought revolution and dictatorship in earlier times.

The energetic response of governments to social needs helps explain the sharp increase in total government spending in most countries during the 1970s and early 1980s. In 1982 western European governments spent an average of more than 50 percent of gross national income, as compared to only 37 percent fifteen years earlier. In all countries, people were much more willing to see their governments increase spending than raise taxes. This imbalance contributed to the rapid growth of budget deficits, national debts, and inflation. By the late 1970s, a powerful reaction against government's ever-increasing role had set in, however, and Western governments were gradually forced to introduce austerity measures to slow the seemingly inexorable growth of public spending and the welfare state.

Part of a broad cultural shift toward greater conservatism, growing voter dissatisfaction with government and government spending helped bring Margaret Thatcher (b. 1925) to power in Britain in 1979. Thatcher had some success in slowing government spending and in "privatizing" industry—that is, in selling off state-owned companies to private investors. Of great social significance, Thatcher's Conservative government encouraged low- and moderate-income renters in state-owned housing projects to buy their apartments at rock-bottom prices. This privatization initiative created a whole new class of property owners, thereby eroding the electoral base of Britain's socialist Labour party.

President Ronald Reagan's success in the United States was more limited. With widespread popular support and the agreement of most congressional Democrats as well as Republicans, Reagan in 1981 pushed through major cuts in income taxes all across the board. But Reagan and Congress failed miserably at cutting government spending, which increased as a percentage of national income in the course of his presidency. Reagan's obsession with the Soviet threat and his massive military buildup were partly responsible, but spending on social programs also grew rapidly. First, the harsh recession of the early 1980s required that the government spend more on unemployment benefits, welfare benefits, and medical treatment for the poor. Second, Reagan's crude antiwelfare rhetoric mobilized the liberal opposition to defend the poor and eventually turned many moderates against him. Thus the budget deficit and the U.S. government debt soared, tripling in a decade.

The striking but temporary exception to the trend toward greater frugality was François Mitterrand (1916–

"The New Poor" Economic crisis and prolonged unemployment in the early 1980s reduced the status of many people from modest affluence to harsh poverty, creating a class of new poor. This photograph captures that human tragedy. After two years of unemployment, this homeless French officeworker (lower right) still dresses up and looks for work. But he must sleep each night in a makeshift shelter for the destitute. *(Dennis Stock/Magnum)*

1996) of France. After his election as president in 1981, Mitterrand led his Socialist party and Communist allies on a lurch to the left, launching a vast program of nationalization and public investment designed to spend France out of economic stagnation. By 1983 this attempt had clearly failed. Mitterrand's Socialist government was then compelled to impose a wide variety of austerity measures and to maintain those policies for the rest of the decade.

When governments were forced to restrain spending, large scientific projects were often singled out for cuts. These reductions reinforced the ongoing computer revolution. That revolution thrived on the diffusion of ever-cheaper computational and informational capacity to small research groups and private businesses, which were both cause and effect of the revolution itself. Big organizations lost some of their advantages as small firms and even individuals became able to link electronically with their region and most of the world.

Individuals felt the impact of austerity at an early date, for unlike governments, they could not pay their bills by printing money and going ever further into debt. The energy crisis of the 1970s forced them to reexamine not only their fuel bills but also the whole pattern of self-indulgent materialism in the postwar years. The result in both Europe and North America was a leaner, tougher lifestyle in the 1970s and early 1980s, featuring more attention to nutrition and a passion for exercise. Correspondingly, there was less blind reliance on medical science for good health and a growing awareness that individuals had to accept a large portion of the responsibility for illness and disease. More people began to realize that they could substantially increase their life spans simply by eating regular meals, sleeping seven or eight hours each night, exercising two or three times a week, maintaining moderate weight, forgoing smoking, and using alcohol only in moderation. For example, a forty-five-year-old American male who practiced three or fewer of these habits in the late 1970s could expect to live to be sixty-seven; one who adhered to five or six could expect to live eleven more years, to age seventy-eight.

Economic troubles also strengthened existing trends within the family. Men and women were encouraged to postpone marriage until they had put their careers on a firm foundation, so the age of marriage rose sharply for both sexes in many Western countries. Indeed, the very real threat of unemployment—or "underemployment" in a dead-end job—seemed to shape the outlook of a whole generation. The students of the 1980s were serious, practical, and often conservative. As one young woman at a French university told a reporter in 1985, "Jobs are the big worry now, so everyone wants to learn something practical."[12] In France as elsewhere, the shift away from the romantic visions and the political activism of the late 1960s was astonishing.

Harder times also meant that ever more women entered or remained in the workforce after they married. Although attitudes related to personal fulfillment were one reason for the continuing increase—especially for well-educated, upper-middle-class women (see the next section)—many wives in poor and middle-class families simply had to work outside the home because of economic necessity. As in preindustrial Europe, the wife's earnings provided the margin of survival for millions of hard-pressed families.

 THE CHANGING LIVES OF WOMEN

A growing emancipation of women in Europe and North America was unquestionably one of the most significant changes of the entire cold war era, and the 1970s and early 1980s were the period of breakthrough. The struggle for women's emancipation had distant roots, going back at least to the French Revolution, which stimulated pioneering feminists to formulate the first systematic demands for women's rights and gender equality. Yet a period of retrogression followed, and only in the later nineteenth century did the first wave of an organized women's movement win some modest rights, mainly for middle-class women (see pages 807–810). World War I also brought some gains for women, but many of those won in the workplace were then lost in the 1920s and 1930s. Nor did the economic expansion after World War II include many measures that were designed specifically to help women.

How then is one to explain the rise of a strong and remarkably effective women's movement in the 1970s and 1980s? Two sets of factors seem most important. First, as we shall see, long-term changes in the basic patterns of motherhood and work outside the home played a critical role because these changes had a major impact on women's life experiences and expectations. Second, a new wave of feminist thinkers and organizers convincingly interpreted these experiences, demanded gender equality, and mobilized a militant women's movement. This movement first assumed real significance in the late 1960s, gathered strength in the next decade, and won significant victories in the 1970s and 1980s.

Motherhood and Work Outside the Home

Before the Industrial Revolution, most men and women married late, and substantial numbers never married at all. Once a woman was married, however, she very often had children as long as she was fertile, and she bore several children, of whom a third to a half would not survive to adulthood. With the growth of industry and urban society, people began to marry earlier, and fewer remained unmarried. As industrial development led to higher incomes and better diets, more children survived to adulthood, and population grew rapidly in the nineteenth century. By the late nineteenth century, contraception within marriage was spreading.

In the twentieth century, and especially after World War II, these trends continued. In the 1950s and 1960s, the typical woman in the West continued to marry at an earlier age and have her children quickly. Indeed, women in Europe and North America were having about 80 percent of their children before age thirty. As for family size, the postwar baby boom made for larger families and a fairly rapid population growth of 1 to 1.5 percent per year in many European countries. In the 1960s, however, the long-term decline in birthrates resumed, and from the mid-1970s onward total population practically stopped growing or even declined in many European countries. The United States followed the same trend. The rate of population growth from natural increase (that is, excluding immigration) dropped by two-thirds, from 1.5 percent to 0.6 percent per year between the 1950s and the 1970s.

The culmination of the trends toward early marriage, early childbearing, and small family size in wealthy urban societies had revolutionary implications for women. Above all, pregnancy and child care occupied a much smaller portion of a woman's life than at the beginning of this century. By the early 1970s, about half of Western women were having their last baby by the age of twenty-six or twenty-seven. When the youngest child trooped off to kindergarten, the average mother still had more than forty years of life in front of her.

This was a momentous change. Throughout history male-dominated society insisted on defining most married women (and most young unmarried women) as mothers (and potential mothers). And motherhood was very demanding: pregnancy followed pregnancy, and there were many children to nurse, guide, and bury. In the postwar years, however, the period devoted to having babies and caring for young children became a relatively short phase in most women's total life span. Perhaps a good deal of the frustration that many women felt in the late 1960s and 1970s was due to the fact that their role as mothers no longer absorbed the energies of a lifetime, and that new roles in the male-dominated world of work outside the family were limited or simply unavailable.

For centuries before the Industrial Revolution, ordinary women worked hard and long on farms and in home industries while bearing and caring for their large families. With the growth of modern industry and large cities, young women continued to work as wage earners, but poor married women typically struggled instead to earn money at home by practicing some low-paid craft as they looked after their children. In the middle classes, it was a rare and tough-minded woman who worked outside the home for wages, although charity work was socially acceptable.

In the twentieth century and especially after World War II, the ever-greater complexity of the modern economy and its sophisticated technology meant that almost all would-be wage earners had to go outside the home to find cash income. Moreover, because child care took less of married women's lives, it often appeared that the full-time mother-housewife had less economic value for families. At the same time, young Western women shared fully in the postwar education revolution and could take advantage of the need for well-trained people in a more fluid society. The result was a sharp rise across Europe and North America in the number of married women who became full-time and part-time wage earners outside the home.

The trend went the furthest in eastern Europe before the collapse of communism. There women accounted for almost half of all employed persons in the postwar era. In noncommunist western Europe and North America, there was a good deal of variety, with the percentage of married women in the workforce rising from a range for different countries of roughly 20 to 25 percent in 1950 to a range of 40 to 70 percent in the early 1980s.

The rising employment of married women was undoubtedly a powerful force in the drive for women's equality and emancipation. Take the critical matter of the widespread differences between men and women in pay, occupation, and advancement. The young unmarried woman of sixty or a hundred years ago was more inclined to accept such injustices. She was conditioned to think of them as temporary nuisances and to look forward to marriage and motherhood for fulfillment. In the postwar era and recent past, a married wage earner in her thirties gradually developed a totally different perspective. She saw employment as a permanent condition within which she, like her male counterpart, sought not only income but also psychological satisfaction. Sexism and discrimination grew loathsome and evoked the sense of injustice that drives revolutions and reforms. When powerful voices arose to challenge the system, they found support among young working-women.

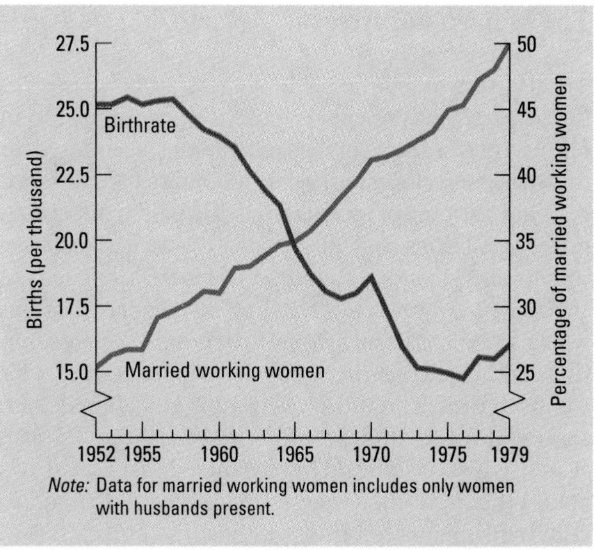

FIGURE 30.2 The Decline of the Birthrate and the Increase of Married Working Women in the United States, 1952–1979 The challenge of working away from home encouraged American wives to prefer fewer children and helped to lower the birthrate.

Rising employment for married women was a factor in the decline of the birthrate (Figure 30.2). Women who worked outside the home had significantly fewer children than women of the same age who did not. Moreover, survey research showed that young women who had held jobs and intended to do so again revised downward the number of children they expected to have after the first lovable but time-consuming baby was born. One reason was obvious: raising a family while holding down a full-time job was a tremendous challenge and often resulted in the woman's being grossly overworked. The fatiguing, often frustrating multiple demands of job, motherhood, and marriage simply became more manageable with fewer children.

The Women's Movement

The 1970s marked the birth of a revitalized grassroots, broad-based movement devoted to promoting the interests of women. Three basic reasons accounted for this major development. First, ongoing changes in underlying patterns of motherhood and paid work created novel conditions and new demands, as has just been suggested. Second, a vanguard of feminist intellectuals articulated a powerful critique of gender relations, which stimulated many women to rethink their assumptions and challenge the status quo. Third, taking a lesson from the civil rights movement in the United States and worldwide student protest against the Vietnam War, dissatisfied individuals recognized that they had to band together if they were to influence politics and secure fundamental reforms.

The first and one of the most influential major works produced by the second wave was *The Second Sex* (1949) by the French writer and philosopher Simone de Beauvoir (1908–1986). Characterizing herself as a "dutiful daughter" of the bourgeoisie in childhood, the adolescent Beauvoir came to see her pious and submissive mother as foolishly renouncing any self-expression outside of home and marriage and showing Beauvoir the dangers of a life she did not want. A brilliant university student, Beauvoir began at the Sorbonne a complex and generally fruitful relationship with an equally gifted classmate, future philosopher Jean-Paul Sartre, who became her lifelong intellectual companion and sometime lover.

Beauvoir analyzed the position of women within the framework of existential thought (see pages 928–930). She argued that women—like all human beings—were in essence free but that they had almost always been trapped by particularly inflexible and limiting conditions. (See the feature "Listening to the Past: A Feminist Critique of Marriage" on pages 1028–1029.) Only by means of courageous action and self-assertive creativity could a woman become a completely free person and escape the role of the inferior "other" that men had constructed for her gender. Drawing on history, philosophy, psychology, biology, and literature, Beauvoir's massive investigation inspired a generation of women intellectuals.

One such woman was Betty Friedan (b. 1924), who played a key role in reopening a serious discussion of women's issues in the United States. Unlike Beauvoir, who epitomized French individualism in believing that each woman had to chart her own course, Friedan reflected the American faith in group action and political solutions. As a working wife and the mother of three small children in the 1950s, Friedan became acutely aware of the conflicting pressures of career and family. Conducting an in-depth survey of her classmates at Smith College fifteen years after their graduation, she concluded that many well-educated women shared her growing dissatisfaction. In her pathbreaking study *The Feminine Mystique* (1963), Friedan identified this dissatisfaction as the "problem that has no name." According to Friedan, the cause of this nameless problem was a crisis of identity. Women were not permitted to become mature adults and genuine human beings. Instead, they were expected to conform to a false, infantile pattern of femininity and live (like Beauvoir's mother) for their husbands and children. In short, women faced what feminists would soon call *sexism,* a pervasive social problem that required drastic reforms.

When long-standing proposals to treat sex discrimination as seriously as race discrimination fell again on deaf ears, Friedan took the lead in 1966 in founding the National Organization for Women (NOW) to press for women's rights. NOW flourished, growing from seven hundred members in 1967 to forty thousand in 1974. Many other women's organizations of varying persuasions rose to follow NOW in Europe and the United States. Throughout the 1970s, a proliferation of publications, conferences, and institutions devoted to women's issues reinforced the emerging international movement.

Although national peculiarities abounded, this movement generally shared the common strategy of entering the political arena and changing laws regarding women. First, advocates of women's rights pushed for new statutes in the workplace: laws against discrimination, "equal pay for equal work," and measures such as maternal leave and affordable daycare designed to help women combine careers and family responsibilities. Second, the movement concentrated on gender and family questions, including the right to divorce (in some Catholic countries), legalized abortion, the needs of single parents (who were usually women), and protection from rape and physical violence. In almost every country, the effort to decriminalize abortion served as a catalyst in mobilizing an effective, self-conscious women's movement (and in creating an opposition to it, as in the United States).

In countries that had long placed women in a subordinate position, the legal changes were little less than revolutionary. In Italy, for example, new laws abolished restrictions on divorce and abortion, which had been strengthened by Mussolini and defended energetically by the Catholic church in the postwar era. By 1988 divorce and abortion were common in Italy, which had the lowest birthrate in Europe. More generally, the sharply focused women's movement of the 1970s won new rights for women. The movement became more diffuse in the 1980s and early 1990s, however, a victim of both its successes and the resurgence of an antifeminist opposition.

The accomplishments of the women's movement encouraged mobilization by many other groups. Homosexual men and lesbian women pressed their own demands, organizing politically and calling for an end to legal discrimination and social harassment. People with physical disabilities joined together to promote their interests. Thus many subordinate groups challenged the dominant majorities, and the expansion and redefinition of human liberty—one of the great themes of modern Western and world history—continued.

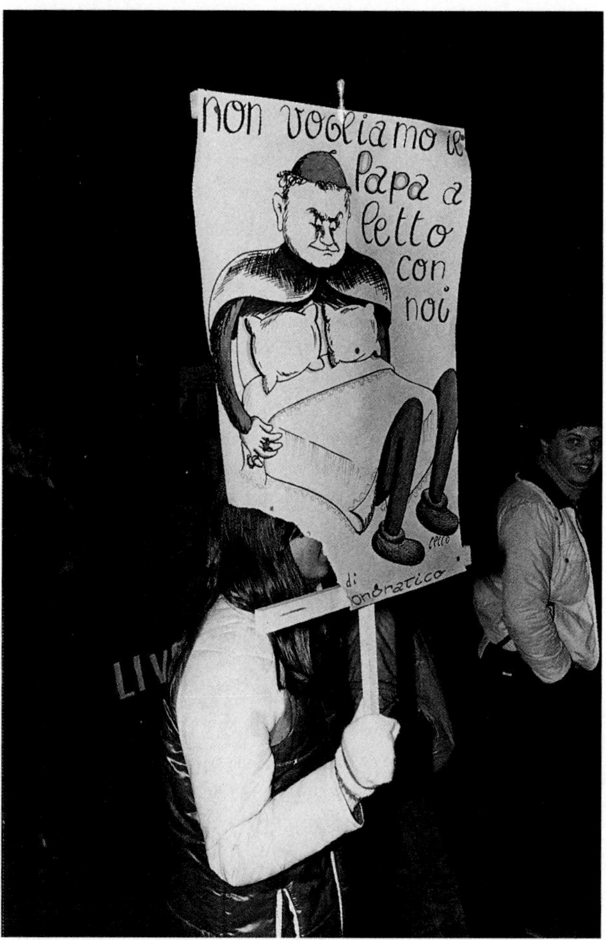

Italian Feminists demonstrate in Rome in 1981 for the passage of legislation legalizing abortion, which the pope and the Catholic church have steadfastly opposed. This woman's provocative sign says that she does not want the pope in her bed. *(Giansanti/Sygma)*

SUMMARY

The recovery of western Europe after World War II was one of the most striking chapters in the long, uneven course of Western civilization. Although the dangerous tensions of the cold war frustrated hopes for a truly peaceful international order, the transition from imperialism to decolonization proceeded rapidly, surprisingly smoothly, and without serious damage to western Europe. Genuine political democracy gained unprecedented strength in western Europe, and rapid economic progress marked a generation.

Fundamental social changes accompanied the political recovery and economic expansion after World War II. Pure science combined with applied technology to achieve remarkable success. The triumphs of applied science contributed not only to economic expansion but also to a more fluid, less antagonistic class structure, in which specialized education was the high road to advancement.

Postwar developments in eastern Europe displayed both similarities to and differences from developments in western Europe and North America. Perhaps the biggest difference was that Stalin imposed harsh one-party rule in the lands occupied by his armies, which led to the bitter cold war. Nevertheless, the Soviet Union became less dictatorial under Khrushchev, and the standard of living in the Soviet Union improved markedly in the 1950s and 1960s.

In the late 1960s and early 1970s, Europe and North America entered a time of crisis. Many nations, from France to Czechoslovakia to the United States, experienced major political difficulties, as cold war conflicts and ideological battles divided peoples and shook governments. Beginning with the oil shocks of the 1970s, severe economic problems added to the turmoil and brought real hardship to millions of people. Yet in western Europe and North America, the welfare system held firm, and both democracy and the movement toward European unity successfully passed through the storm. The women's movement also mobilized effectively and won expanded rights in the best tradition of Western civilization. Finally, efforts to achieve détente in central Europe while still maintaining a strong Atlantic alliance achieved some success. This modest progress helped lay the foundations for the sudden end of the cold war and the opening of a new era.

Notes

1. Quoted in N. Graebner, *Cold War Diplomacy, 1945–1960* (Princeton, N.J.: Van Nostrand, 1962), p. 17.
2. Quoted ibid.
3. Quoted in J. Hennessy, *Economic "Miracles"* (London: Andre Deutsch, 1964), p. 5.
4. Quoted in S. E. Morison et al., *A Concise History of the American Republic* (New York: Oxford University Press, 1977), p. 697.
5. Quoted in D. Treadgold, *Twentieth Century Russia,* 5th ed. (Boston: Houghton Mifflin, 1981), p. 442.
6. Quoted in J. Ziman, *The Force of Knowledge: The Scientific Dimension of Society* (Cambridge: Cambridge University Press, 1976), p. 128.
7. Quoted in S. Toulmin, *The Twentieth Century: A Promethean Age,* ed. A. Bullock (London: Thames & Hudson, 1971), p. 294.
8. Quoted in N. Cantor, *Twentieth-Century Culture: Modernism to Deconstruction* (New York: Peter Lang, 1988), p. 252.
9. M. Mitterauer, *The History of Youth* (Oxford: Basil Blackwell, 1992), p. 40.
10. Quoted in Morison et al., *A Concise History,* p. 735.
11. Quoted in Kessing's Research Report, *Germany and East Europe Since 1945: From the Potsdam Agreement to Chancellor Brandt's "Ostpolitik"* (New York: Charles Scribner's Sons, 1973), pp. 284–285.
12. *Wall Street Journal,* June 28, 1985, p. 1.

Suggested Reading

Three valuable general studies with extensive bibliographies are W. Laqueur, *Europe in Our Time: A History, 1945–1992* (1992); C. Black, *Rebirth: A History of Europe Since World War II* (1992); and P. Johnson, *Modern Times: The World from the Twenties to the Eighties* (1983). A good introduction to international politics is provided by W. Keylor, *The Twentieth Century: An International History* (1984). Winston Churchill and Charles de Gaulle both wrote histories of the war in the form of memoirs. Other interesting memoirs are those of Dwight Eisenhower, *Crusade in Europe* (1948); and Dean Acheson, *Present at the Creation* (1969), a defense of American foreign policy in the early cold war. K. Sainsbury, *Churchill and Roosevelt at War: The War They Fought and the Peace They Hoped to Make* (1994), is an excellent, very readable introduction. Valuable recent studies on the cold war include P. de Senarclens, *From Yalta to the Iron Curtain: The Great Powers and the Origins of the Cold War* (1995); and M. Walker, *The Cold War: A History* (1993).

D. Urwin, *The Community of Europe: A History of European Integration*, 2d ed. (1995), and R. Mayne, *The Recovery of Europe, 1945–1973* (1973), focus on steps toward western European unity. P. Lane, *Europe Since 1945: An Introduction* (1985), is an interesting combination of text and political documents. W. Leuchtenberg, *In the Shadow of FDR: From Harry Truman to Ronald Reagan* (1989), ably discusses developments in the United States. Postwar economic and social developments are analyzed in G. Ambrosius and W. Hibbard, *A Social and Economic History of Twentieth-Century Europe* (1989); and F. Tipton and R. Aldrich, *An Economic and Social History of Europe from 1939 to the Present* (1986).

Two outstanding works on France are J. Ardagh, *The New French Revolution* (1969), which puts the momentous social changes since 1945 in human terms; and S. Bernstein, *The Republic of de Gaulle, 1958–1969* (1993). On postwar West Germany, H. Turner, *The Two Germanies Since 1945: East and West* (1987), and W. Patterson and G. Smith, eds., *The West German Model: Perspectives on a Stable State* (1981), are good introductions. R. Dahrendorf, *Society and Democracy in Germany* (1971), is a classic interpretation. The spiritual dimension of West German recovery is probed by Günter Grass in his world-famous novel *The Tin Drum* (1963), as well as in the novels of Heinrich Böll. A. Marwick, *British Society Since 1945* (1982), and A. H. Halsey, *Change in British Society* (1981), are good on postwar developments. F. Zweig, *The Worker in an Affluent Society* (1961), probes family life and economic circumstances in the British working class on the basis of extensive interviews. R. von Albertini, *Decolonialization* (1971), is still a good history of the decline and fall of European empires, to be compared with T. von Laue, *The World Revolution of Westernization: The Twentieth Century in Global Perspective* (1987), a stimulating interpretation.

Z. Brzezinski, *The Grand Failure: The Birth and Death of Communism in the Twentieth Century* (1989), is a readable overview by a leading American scholar. L. Johnson, *Central Europe: Enemies, Neighbors, Friends* (1996), is an up-to-date synthesis discussing major developments, and H. Seton-Watson, *The East European Revolution* (1965), is a classic history of the communization of eastern Europe. J. Ridley, *Tito* (1994), is lively and learned. P. Zinner, *National Communism and Popular Revolt in Eastern Europe* (1956) and *Revolution in Hungary* (1962), are excellent on the tragic events of 1956. A. Amalrik, *Will the Soviet Union Survive Until 1984?* (1970), is a fascinating and prophetic interpretation of Soviet society and politics in the 1960s by a Russian who paid for his criticism with prison and exile. A. Lee, *Russian Journal* (1981), is a fine journalistic account by a perceptive American observer.

Ziman's volume, cited in the Notes, which has an excellent bibliography, is a penetrating look at science by a leading physicist. A. Bramwell, *Ecology in the Twentieth Century: A History* (1989), examines negative aspects of technical and industrial development. Two more stimulating works on postwar technology are J. J. Servan-Schreiber, *The World Challenge* (1981); and H. Jacoby, *The Bureaucratization of the World* (1973).

In addition to previously mentioned country studies, A. Simpson, *The New Europeans* (1968), provides a good guide to Western society in the 1960s. Mitterauer and Cantor, both cited in the Notes, are excellent on the youth culture and the trends that made it possible. W. Hampton, *Guerrilla Minstrels: John Lennon, Joe Hill, Woodie Guthrie, Bob Dylan* (1986), is highly recommended. L. Wylie, *Village in the Vaucluse* (1964), and P. J. Hélias, *The Horse of Pride* (1980), provide fascinating pictures of life in the French village before prosperity arrived. A. Kriegel, *The French Communists* (1972) and *Eurocommunism* (1978), are also recommended. D. Caute, *The Year of the Barricades: A Journey Through 1968* (1988), is a high-energy account that brings the upheavals of 1968 to life, while noted sociologist R. Aron's *The Elusive Revolution* (1969) is highly critical. Two outstanding works on the Vietnam War are N. Sheehan, *A Bright and Shining Lie: John Paul Vann and America in Vietnam* (1988); and A. Short, *The Origins of the Vietnam War* (1989). Among the many books to come out of the Czechoslovak experience in 1968, I. Svitak, *The Czechoslovak Experiment, 1968–1969* (1971), and Z. Zeman, *Prague Spring* (1969), are particularly recommended.

General studies on women include B. Smith, *Changing Lives: Women in European History Since 1700* (1989), which provides a good overview and a current bibliography. E. Sullerot, *Women, Society and Change* (1971), is an outstanding analysis of women's evolving roles after 1945. Two extremely influential books on women and their new awareness are S. de Beauvoir, *The Second Sex* (1962), and B. Friedan, *The Feminine Mystique* (1963). These may be compared with C. Lasch, *Haven in a Heartless World* (1977), and A. Cherlin, *Marriage, Divorce, Remarriage* (1981), which interpret changes in the American family.

On feminism and the women's movement, see N. Cott, *The Grounding of Modern Feminism* (1987). J. Lovenduski, *Women and European Politics: Contemporary Feminism and Public Policy* (1986), provides an extremely useful comparative study of similar developments in different countries. The women's movement in Italy is considered in L. Birnbaum, *Liberazione de la Donna* (1986), which is written in English despite the Italian title. C. Duchen, *Feminism in France: From May '68 to Mitterrand* (1986), is also recommended. L. Appignanesi, *Simone de Beauvoir* (1988), is a readable study of the life and thought of the famous thinker. Good studies on British women include E. Wilson, *Only Halfway to Paradise: Women in Postwar Britain, 1945–1968* (1980), and M. Barrett, *Women's Opposition Today* (1980). U. Frevert, *Women in German History: From Bourgeois Emancipation to Sexual Liberation* (1989), is both learned and engaging. Two good studies on Soviet women before the collapse of communism are F. DuPlessix Gray, *Soviet Women* (1989), and T. Mamonova, ed., *Women and Russia* (1986).

LISTENING TO THE PAST

A Feminist Critique of Marriage

Having grown up in Paris in a middle-class family and become a teacher, novelist, and intellectual, Simone de Beauvoir (1908–1986) turned increasingly to feminist concerns after World War II. Her most influential work was The Second Sex *(1949), a massive declaration of independence for contemporary women.*

As an existentialist, de Beauvoir believed that all individuals must accept responsibility for their lives and strive to overcome the tragic dilemmas they face. Studying the experience of woman since antiquity, de Beauvoir argued that man had generally used education and social conditioning to create a dependent "other," a negative nonman who was not permitted to grow and strive for freedom.

Marriage—on the man's terms—was part of this unjust and undesirable process. De Beauvoir's conclusion that some couples could establish free and equal unions was based in part on her experience with philosopher Jean-Paul Sartre, de Beauvoir's encouraging companion and sometime lover.

Every human existence involves transcendence and immanence at the same time; to go forward, each existence must be maintained, for it to expand toward the future it must integrate the past, and while intercommunicating with others it should find self-confirmation. These two elements—maintenance and progression—are implied in any living activity, and for *man* marriage permits precisely a happy synthesis of the two. In his occupation and his political life he encounters change and progress, he senses his extension through time and the universe; and when he is tired of such roaming, he gets himself a home, a fixed location, and an anchorage in the world. At evening he restores his soul in the home, where his wife takes care of his furnishings and children and guards the things of the past that she keeps in store. But she has no other job than to maintain and provide for life in pure and unvarying generality; she perpetuates the species without change, she ensures the even rhythm of the days and the continuity of the home, seeing to it that the doors are locked. But she is allowed no direct influence upon the future nor upon the world; she reaches out beyond herself toward the social group only through her husband as intermediary.

Marriage today still retains, for the most part, this traditional form. . . . The male is called upon for action, his vocation is to produce, fight, create, progress, to transcend himself toward the totality of the universe and the infinity of the future; but traditional marriage does not invite women to transcend herself with him; it confines her in immanence, shuts her up within the circle of herself. She can thus propose to do nothing more than construct a life of stable equilibrium in which the present as a continuance of the past avoids the menaces of tomorrow—that is, construct precisely a life of happiness. . . .

In domestic work, with or without the aid of servants, woman makes her home her own, finds social justification, and provides herself with an occupation, an activity, that deals usefully and satisfyingly with material objects—shining stoves, fresh, clean clothes, bright copper, polished furniture—but provides no escape from immanence and little affirmation of individuality. . . . Few tasks are more like the torture of Sisyphus than housework, with its endless repetition: the clean becomes soiled, the soiled is made clean, over and over, day after day. The housewife wears herself out marking time: she makes nothing, simply perpetuates the present. She never senses conquest of a positive Good, but rather indefinite struggle against negative Evil. . . . Washing, ironing, sweeping, ferreting out rolls of lint from under wardrobes—all this halting of decay is also the denial of life; for time simultaneously creates and destroys, and only its negative aspect concerns the housekeeper. . . .

Thus woman's work within the home gives her no autonomy; it is not directly useful to society, it does not open out on the future, it produces nothing. It takes on meaning and dignity only as it is linked with existent beings who reach out beyond themselves, transcend themselves, toward society in production and action. That is, far from freeing the matron, her occupation makes her dependent upon husband and children; she is justified through them; but in their lives she is only an inessential intermediary. . . .

The tragedy of marriage is not that it fails to assure woman the promised happiness—there is no such thing as assurance in regard to happiness—but that it mutilates her; it dooms her to repetition and routine. The first twenty years of woman's life are extraordinarily rich, as we have seen; she discovers the world and her destiny. At twenty or thereabouts mistress of a home, bound permanently to a man, a child in her arms, she stands with her life virtually finished forever. Real activities, real work, are the prerogative of her man: she has mere things to occupy her which are sometimes tiring but never fully satisfying. . . .

Marriage should be a combining of two whole, independent existences, not a retreat, an annexation, a flight, a remedy. . . . The couple should not be regarded as a unit, a close cell; rather each individual should be integrated as such in society at large, where each (whether male or female) could flourish without aid; then attachments could be formed in pure generosity with another individual equally adapted to the group, attachments that would be founded upon the acknowledgment that both are free.

This balanced couple is not a utopian fancy: such couples do exist, sometimes even within the frame of marriage, most often outside it. Some mates are united by a strong sexual love that leaves them free in their friendships and in their work; others are held together by a friendship that does not preclude sexual liberty; more rare are those who are at once lovers and friends but do not seek in each other their sole reasons for living. Many nuances are possible in the relations between a man and a woman: in comradeship, pleasure, trust, fondness, co-operation, and love, they can be for each other the most abundant source of joy, richness, and power available to human beings.

✣ Simone de Beauvoir at home in Paris, June 1985. *(Gerard Gastand/Sipa Press)*

Questions for Analysis

1. How did de Beauvoir analyze marriage and marriage partners in terms of existential philosophy?
2. To what extent does a married woman benefit from a "traditional" marriage, according to de Beauvoir? Why?
3. What was de Beauvoir's solution to the situation she described? Was her solution desirable? Realistic?
4. What have you learned about the history of women that supports or challenges de Beauvoir's analysis? Include developments since World War II and your own reflections.

CHAPTER

31 Revolution, Reunification, and Rebuilding: 1985 to the Present

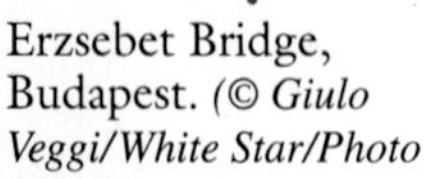

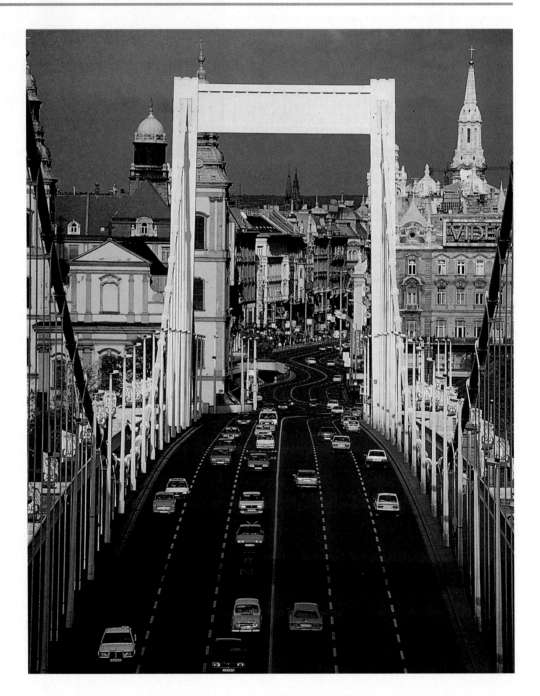

Erzsebet Bridge, Budapest. *(© Giulo Veggi/White Star/Photo Researchers)*

In the late twentieth century, massive changes swept through eastern Europe and opened a new era in human history. Efforts in the late 1980s to reform and revitalize the communist system in the Soviet Union snowballed out of control, and in 1989 revolutions swept away communist rule throughout the entire Soviet bloc. The cold war came to a spectacular end, West Germany absorbed East Germany, and the Soviet Union broke into fifteen independent countries. Thus after forty years of cold war division, Europe reestablished a basic underlying unity, as faith in democratic government and some kind of market economy became the common creed. Indeed, the peoples of Europe (and European settlement) were perhaps more united than at any time since the sixteenth-century Protestant and Catholic Reformations, which had split medieval civilization into opposing camps. In 1991 hopes for peaceful democratic progress were almost universal.

The 1990s saw the realization of some of these hopes, but the new era brought its own problems and even terrible tragedies. The cold war division of Europe had kept a lid on ethnic conflicts and nationalism, which suddenly burst into the open and led to a disastrous civil war in the former Yugoslavia and in parts of the old Soviet Union. Moreover, most western European economies were plagued by high unemployment and struggling to adapt to the extremely competitive global economy, which undermined cherished social benefits and also complicated the task of reconstruction in the former communist states. Thus in eastern Europe, the process of rebuilding shattered societies was much more difficult than optimists had envisioned in the post–cold war euphoria of 1991, and in western Europe, the road toward integration and monetary union proved bumpy.

- Why did efforts to reform the communist system fail and result in successful anticommunist revolutions throughout eastern Europe?
- What were the consequences of these revolutions and the end of the cold war?
- How, in the 1990s, did the different parts of a unifying Europe meet the challenges of postcommunist reconstruction, resurgent nationalism, and economic union?
- What are the prospects for Europe and Western civilization as they enter the third millennium?

These are the fundamental questions that this chapter will address.

The Decline of Communism in Eastern Europe

The Soviet bloc perplexed Western observers in the 1970s and early 1980s, and with good reason. On the one hand, attempts to liberalize the system continued, and the brutality of the Stalinist era was never reestablished after Nikita Khrushchev fell from power in 1964. These changes encouraged Western hopes of gradual liberalization and of a more democratic, less threatening Soviet eastern Europe.

On the other hand, hard facts frequently intervened to undermine these hopes. In addition to periodic threats and military action, the Soviet Union repeatedly demonstrated that it remained a harsh and aggressive dictatorship that paid only lip service to egalitarian ideology and was determined to uphold its rule throughout eastern Europe. Periodic efforts to achieve fundamental political change were doomed to failure sooner or later—or so it seemed to most Western experts into the mid-1980s.

And then Mikhail Gorbachev burst on the scene. The new Soviet leader opened an era of reform that was as sweeping as it was unexpected. Many believed that Gorbachev would soon fall from power and that his reforms would fail in the Soviet Union. As a matter of fact, Gorbachev's reforms rapidly transformed Soviet culture and politics, and they drastically reduced cold war tensions. But communism, which Gorbachev wanted so desperately to revitalize in order to save it, continued to decline as a functioning system throughout the Soviet bloc.

The Soviet Union to 1985

The 1968 invasion of Czechoslovakia (see page 1007) was the crucial event of the Brezhnev era, a period that actually lasted beyond the aging leader's death in 1982 until the emergence in 1985 of Gorbachev. The invasion demonstrated unmistakably the intense conservatism of the Soviet Union's ruling elite and its determination to maintain the status quo in the Soviet bloc.

"What's This? You Have Your Own Opinion?" This cartoon, published in the Soviet Union's enormously popular satirical magazine *The Crocodile,* shows a Soviet manager getting into trouble for drawing a nonstandard doodle at a meeting. Jokes poking fun at communist bosses and human foibles permeated Soviet culture, especially the oral culture, in the Brezhnev era. *(© Vneshtorgizdat, Moscow)*

Indeed, the aftermath of intervention in Czechoslovakia also brought a certain re-Stalinization of the U.S.S.R. But now dictatorship was collective rather than personal, and coercion replaced uncontrolled terror. This compromise seemed to suit the leaders and a majority of the people, and the Soviet Union appeared stable in the 1970s and early 1980s.

A slowly rising standard of living for ordinary people contributed to this stability, although the economic crisis of the 1970s greatly slowed the rate of improvement, and long lines and innumerable shortages persisted. The enduring differences between the life of the elite and the life of ordinary people also reinforced the system. Ambitious individuals had tremendous incentive to do as the state wished in order to gain access to special, well-stocked stores, to attend special schools, and to travel abroad.

Another source of stability was the enduring nationalism of ordinary Great Russians. Party leaders successfully identified themselves with Russian patriotism, stressing their role in saving the country during the Second World War and protecting it now from foreign foes, including eastern European "counterrevolutionaries." Moreover, the politically dominant Great Russians, who were concentrated in the central Russian heartland and in Siberia (which was formally designated as the Russian Federation) and who also held through the Communist party the commanding leadership positions in the non-Russian republics, constituted less than half of the total Soviet population. The Great Russians generally feared that greater freedom and open political competition might result in demands for autonomy and even independence not only by eastern European nationalities but also by the non-Russian nationalities of the smaller republics and the autonomous regions within the Soviet Union itself. Thus liberalism and democracy generally appeared to Great Russians as alien political philosophies designed to undermine the U.S.S.R.'s power and greatness.

The strength of the government was expressed in the re-Stalinization of culture and art. Free expression and open protest disappeared. In 1968, when a small group of dissenters appeared in Moscow's Red Square to protest the invasion of Czechoslovakia, they were arrested before they could unfurl their banners. This proved to be the high point of dissent, for in the 1970s Brezhnev and company made certain that Soviet intellectuals did not engage in public protest. Acts of open nonconformity and protest were severely punished, but with sophisticated, cunning methods.

Most frequently, dissidents were blacklisted and thus rendered unable to find decent jobs since the government was the only employer. This fate was enough to keep most in line. More determined but unrenowned protesters were quietly imprisoned in jails or mental institutions. Celebrated nonconformists such as Aleksandr Solzhenitsyn were permanently expelled from the country. Once again, Jews were persecuted as a "foreign" element, though some were eventually permitted to immigrate to Israel. As the distinguished Russian dissident historian Roy Medvedev explained in the mid-1970s,

The technology of repression has become more refined in recent years. Before, repression always went much further than necessary. Stalin killed millions of people when arresting 1,000 would have enabled him to control the people. Our leaders . . . found out eventually that you don't have to put people in prison or in a psychiatric hospital to silence them. There are other ways.[1]

Eliminating the worst aspects of Stalin's dictatorship strengthened the regime, and almost all Western experts concluded that rule by a self-perpetuating Communist party elite in the Soviet Union appeared to be quite solid in the 1970s and early 1980s.

Yet beneath the dreary immobility of political life in the Brezhnev era, the Soviet Union was actually experiencing profound changes. As a perceptive British journalist put it in 1986, "The country went through a social revolution while Brezhnev slept."[2] Three aspects of this revolution, which was seldom appreciated by Western observers at the time, were particularly significant.

First, the growth of the urban population, which had raced forward at breakneck speed in the Stalin years, continued rapidly in the 1960s and 1970s. In 1985 two-thirds of all Soviet citizens lived in cities, and one-quarter lived in big cities. Of great significance, this expanding urban population lost its old peasant ways, exchanging them for more education, better job skills, and greater sophistication.

Second, the number of highly trained scientists, managers, and specialists expanded prodigiously, increasing fourfold between 1960 and 1985. Thus the class of well-educated, pragmatic, and self-confident experts, which played such an important role in restructuring industrial societies after World War II (see pages 1011–1012), developed rapidly in the Soviet Union. Moreover, leading Soviet scientists and technologists, like their colleagues in the West, sought membership in the international "invisible college" of their disciplines. Correspondingly, they sought the intellectual freedom necessary to do significant work, and they often obtained it because their research had practical (and military) value.

Third, education and freedom for experts in their special areas helped foster the growth of Soviet public opinion, just as the reading revolution of the eighteenth century had encouraged the development of independent public opinion in France. Educated people read, discussed, and formed definite ideas about social questions. And if caution dictated conventional ideas (at least in public), many important issues could be approached and debated in "nonpolitical" terms. Developing definite ideas on such issues as environmental pollution or urban transportation, educated urban people increasingly saw themselves as worthy of having a voice in society's decisions, even its political decisions. This, too, was part of the quiet transformation that set the stage for the Gorbachev era.

Solidarity in Poland

Gorbachev's reforms interacted with a resurgence of popular protest in the Soviet Union's satellite empire. Developments in Poland were most striking and significant. There workers joined together en masse to fight peacefully for freedom and self-determination, while the world watched in amazement. Crushed in the short run but refusing to admit defeat, Polish workers waged a long campaign that inspired and reflected a powerful reform current in eastern Europe.

Poland had been an unruly satellite from the beginning. Stalin said that introducing communism to Poland was like putting a saddle on a cow. Efforts to saddle the cow—really a spirited stallion—led to widespread riots in 1956 (see page 1006). As a result, Polish Communists dropped their efforts to impose Soviet-style collectivization on the peasants and to break the Roman Catholic church. Most agricultural land remained in private hands, and the Catholic church thrived. With an independent peasant agriculture and a vigorous church, the Communists failed to monopolize society.

They also failed to manage the economy effectively. Even the booming 1960s saw little economic improvement. When the government suddenly announced large price increases right before Christmas in 1970, Poland's working class rose again in angry protest. Factories were occupied, and strikers were shot, but a new Communist leader came to power nevertheless. The government then wagered that massive inflows of Western capital and technology, especially from Willy Brandt's rich and now-friendly West Germany (see pages 1017–1019), could produce a Polish "economic miracle" that would win popular support for the regime. Instead, bureaucratic incompetence, coupled with worldwide recession after the first oil shock in 1973, put the economy into a nosedive in the mid-1970s. Workers, intellectuals, and the church became increasingly restive. Then the real Polish miracle occurred: Cardinal Karol Wojtyla, archbishop of Cracow, was elected pope in 1978. In June 1979, he returned from Rome for an astonishing pilgrimage across his native land. Preaching love of Christ and country and the "inalienable rights of man," Pope John Paul II drew enormous crowds and electrified the Polish nation. The economic crisis became a moral and spiritual crisis as well.

In August 1980, as scattered strikes to protest higher meat prices spread, the sixteen thousand workers at the gigantic Lenin Shipyards in Gdansk (formerly known as Danzig) laid down their tools and occupied the showpiece plant. As other workers along the Baltic coast joined "in solidarity," the strikers advanced truly revolutionary demands: the right to form free trade unions, the right to strike, freedom of speech, release of political prisoners, and economic reforms. After eighteen days of shipyard occupation, as families brought food to the gates and priests said Mass daily amid huge overhead cranes, the government gave in and accepted the workers' demands in the Gdansk Agreement. In a state where the Communist party claimed to rule on behalf of the proletariat, a working-class revolt had won an unprecedented victory.

Led by feisty Lenin Shipyards electrician and devout Catholic Lech Walesa (b. 1943), the workers proceeded to organize their free and democratic trade union. They called it "Solidarity." Joined by intellectuals and supported by the Catholic church, Solidarity became the union of a nation. By March 1981 it had a membership of 9.5 million, out of 12.5 million who were theoretically eligible. A full-time staff of 40,000 linked the union members together as Solidarity published its own newspapers and cultural and intellectual freedom blossomed in Poland. Solidarity's leaders had tremendous, well-organized support, and the ever-present threat of calling a nationwide strike gave them real power in ongoing negotiations with the Communist bosses.

But if Solidarity had power, it did not try to take the reins of government in 1981. History, the Brezhnev Doctrine, and virulent attacks from communist neighbors all seemed to guarantee the intervention of the Red Army and a terrible bloodbath if Polish Communists "lost control." Thus the Solidarity revolution remained a "self-limiting revolution" aimed at defending the cultural and trade-union freedoms won in the Gdansk Agreement, and it refused to use force to challenge directly the Communist monopoly of political power. (See the feature "Listening to the Past: A Solidarity Leader Speaks from Prison" on pages 1062–1063.)

Solidarity's combination of strength and moderation postponed a showdown. The Soviet Union, already facing sharp criticism for its European missile policy and condemned worldwide for its invasion of Afghanistan, played a waiting game of threats and pressure. After a crisis in March 1981 that followed police beatings of Solidarity activists, Walesa settled for minor government concessions, and Solidarity again dropped plans for a massive general strike. This marked a turning point. Criticism of Walesa's moderate leadership and calls for local self-government in unions and factories grew. Solidarity lost its cohesiveness. The worsening economic crisis also encouraged grassroots radicalism and frustration: a hunger-march banner proclaimed, "A hungry nation can eat its rulers."[3] With an eye on Western, and especially West German, opinion leaders, who generally preferred tyranny to instability in eastern Europe (although they seldom admitted this fact), the Polish Communist leadership shrewdly denounced Solidarity for promoting economic collapse and provoking Soviet invasion. In December 1981, Communist leader General Wojciech Jaruzelski suddenly struck in the dead of a subfreezing night, proclaiming martial law, cutting all communications, arresting Solidarity's leaders, and "saving" the nation.

Outlawed and driven underground, Solidarity fought successfully to maintain its organization and to voice the aspirations of the Polish masses after 1981. Part of the reason for the union's survival was the government's unwillingness (and probably its inability) to impose full-scale terror. Moreover, in schools and shops, in factories and offices, millions decided to continue acting as if they were free, even though they were not. Therefore, cultural and intellectual life remained extremely vigorous in spite of renewed repression. At the same time, the faltering Polish economy, battered by renewed global recession in the early 1980s and crippled by a disastrous brain drain after 1981, continued to deteriorate. Thus popular support for outlawed Solidarity

Lech Walesa and Solidarity An inspiration for fellow workers at the Lenin Shipyards in the dramatic and successful strike against the Communist bosses in August 1980, Walesa played a key role in Solidarity before and after it was outlawed. Speaking here to old comrades at the Lenin Shipyards after Solidarity was again legalized in 1988, Walesa personified an enduring opposition to Communist rule in eastern Europe. *(Merrillon/Liaison)*

remained strong and deep under martial law in the 1980s, preparing the way for the union's political rebirth toward the end of the decade.

The rise and survival of Solidarity showed again the fierce desire of millions of eastern Europeans for greater political liberty. The union's strength also demonstrated the enduring appeal of cultural freedom, trade-union rights, patriotic nationalism, and religious feeling. Not least, Solidarity's challenge encouraged fresh thinking in the Soviet Union, ever the key to lasting change in the Eastern bloc.

Gorbachev's Reforms in the Soviet Union

Fundamental change in Russian history has often come in short, intensive spurts, which contrast vividly with long periods of immobility. We have studied four of these spurts: the ambitious "westernization" of Peter the Great in the early eighteenth century (see pages 582–585), the great reforms connected with the freeing of the serfs in the mid-nineteenth century (see pages 837–838), the Russian Revolution of 1917 (see pages 908–916), and Stalin's wrenching "revolution from above" in the 1930s (see pages 961–965). To this select list of decisive transformations, we must now add the era of reform launched by Mikhail Gorbachev in 1985. Gorbachev's initiatives brought political and cultural liberalization to the Soviet Union, and they then permitted democracy and national self-determination to triumph spectacularly in the old satellite empire and eventually in the Soviet Union itself, although this was certainly not Gorbachev's original intention.

As we have seen, the Soviet Union's Communist party elite seemed secure in the early 1980s as far as any challenge from below was concerned. The long-established system of administrative controls continued to stretch downward from the central ministries and state committees to provincial cities, and from there to factories, neighborhoods, and villages. At each level of this massive state bureaucracy, the overlapping hierarchy of the Communist party, with its 17.5 million members, continued to watch over all decisions and manipulate every aspect of national life. Organized opposition was impossible, and average people simply left politics to the bosses.

Yet the massive state and party bureaucracy was a mixed blessing. It safeguarded the elite, but it also promoted apathy in the masses. Discouraging personal initiative and economic efficiency, it was ill suited to secure the effective cooperation of the rapidly growing class of well-educated urban experts. Therefore, when the ailing Brezhnev finally died in 1982, his successor, the long-time chief of the secret police, Yuri Andropov (1914–1984), tried to invigorate the system. Andropov introduced modest reforms to improve economic performance and campaigned against worker absenteeism and high-level corruption. Relatively little came of these efforts, but they combined with a sharply worsening economic situation to set the stage for the emergence in 1985 of Mikhail Gorbachev (b. 1931), the most vigorous Soviet leader in a generation.

Newly Elected President Mikhail Gorbachev vowed in his acceptance speech before the Supreme Soviet, the U.S.S.R.'s parliament, to assume "all responsibility" for the success or failure of *perestroika.* Previous parliaments were no more than tools of the Communist party, but this one actively debated and even opposed government programs. *(Vlastimir Shone/Liaison)*

Trained as a lawyer and working his way up as a Communist party official in the northern Caucasus, where he caught the attention of Andropov and other senior party members, Gorbachev was smart, charming, and tough. As long-time Soviet foreign minister Andrei Gromyko reportedly said, "This man has a nice smile, but he has got iron teeth."[4] Gorbachev believed in communism, but he realized it was failing to keep up with Western capitalism and technology. This was eroding the Soviet Union's status as a superpower. Thus Gorbachev (and his intelligent, influential wife, Raisa, a dedicated professor of Marxist-Leninist thought) wanted to save the Soviet system by revitalizing it with fundamental reforms. Gorbachev was also an idealist. He wanted to improve conditions for ordinary citizens. Understanding full well that the endless waste and expense of the cold war arms race had had a disastrous impact on living conditions in the Soviet Union, which remained much poorer than the United States and western Europe, he realized that improvement at home required better relations with the West.

In his first year in office, Gorbachev attacked corruption and incompetence in the bureaucracy, and he consolidated his power by packing the top level of the party with his supporters. He attacked alcoholism and drunkenness, which were deadly scourges of Soviet society. More basically, he elaborated his ambitious reform program.

The first set of reform policies was designed to transform and restructure the economy, which directed so much output to the military and failed to provide for the real needs of the Soviet population. To accomplish this economic "restructuring," this *perestroika,* Gorbachev and his supporters permitted an easing of government price controls on some goods, more independence for state enterprises, and the setting up of profit-seeking private cooperatives to provide personal services for consumers. These reforms initially produced a few improvements, but shortages then grew as the economy stalled at an intermediate point between central planning and free-market mechanisms. By late 1988, Gorbachev's timid economic initiatives had met with very little success, creating widespread consumer dissatisfaction and posing a serious threat to his leadership and the entire reform program.

Gorbachev's bold and far-reaching campaign "to tell it like it is" was much more successful. Very popular in a country where censorship, dull uniformity, and outright lies had long characterized public discourse, the newfound "openness," or *glasnost,* of the government and the media marked an astonishing break with the past. A disaster such as the Chernobyl nuclear accident in 1986, which devastated part of Ukraine and showered Europe with radioactive fallout, was investigated and reported with honesty and painstaking thoroughness. Long-banned and vilified émigré writers sold millions of copies of their works in new editions, while denunciations of Stalin and his terror became standard fare in plays and movies. Thus initial openness in government pronouncements quickly went much further than Gorbachev intended and led to something approaching free speech and free expression, a veritable cultural revolution.

Democratization was the third element of reform. Beginning as an attack on corruption in the Communist party and as an attempt to bring the class of educated experts into the decision-making process, it led to the first free elections in the Soviet Union since 1917. Gorbachev and the party remained in control, but a minority of critical independents were elected in April 1989 to a revitalized Congress of People's Deputies. Many top-ranking Communists who ran unopposed saw themselves defeated as a majority of angry voters struck their names from the ballot and prevented their election. Millions of Soviets then watched the new congress for hours on television as Gorbachev and his ministers saw their proposals debated and even rejected. Thus millions of Soviet citizens took practical lessons in open discussion, critical thinking, and representative government. The result was a new political culture at odds with the Communist party's monopoly of power and control.

Democratization ignited demands for greater autonomy and even for national independence by non-Russian minorities, especially in the Baltic region and in the Caucasus. These demands certainly went beyond anything that Gorbachev had envisaged. In April 1989, troops with sharpened shovels charged into a rally of Georgian separatists in Tbilisi and left twenty dead. But whereas China's Communist leaders brutally massacred similar prodemocracy demonstrators in Beijing in June 1989 and reimposed rigid authoritarian rule, Gorbachev drew back from repression. Thus nationalist demands continued to grow in the non-Russian Soviet republics.

Finally, the Soviet leader brought "new political thinking" to the field of foreign affairs and acted on it. He withdrew Soviet troops from Afghanistan and sought to reduce East-West tensions. Of enormous importance, he sought to halt the arms race with the United States and convinced President Ronald Reagan of his sincerity. In December 1987, the two leaders agreed in a Washington summit to eliminate all land-based intermediate-range missiles in Europe, setting the stage for more arms reductions. Gorbachev also encouraged reform movements in Poland and Hungary and pledged to respect the political choices of the peoples of eastern Europe. He thereby repudiated the Brezhnev Doctrine, which in 1968 had arrogantly proclaimed the right of the Soviet Union and its allies to intervene at will in eastern Europe. By early 1989, it seemed that if Gorbachev held to his word, the tragic Soviet occupation of eastern Europe might well wither away, taking the long cold war with it once and for all.

THE REVOLUTIONS OF 1989

Instead, history accelerated. In 1989 Gorbachev's plan to reform communism in order to save it snowballed out of control. A series of largely peaceful revolutions swept across eastern Europe (Map 31.1), overturning existing communist regimes and ending the communists' monopoly of power. Revolutionary mass demonstrations led to the formation of provisional governments dedicated to democratic elections, human rights, and national rejuvenation. Watched on television in the Soviet Union and around the world, these stirring events marked the triumph and the transformation of the long-standing opposition to communist rule and foreign domination in eastern Europe.

The revolutions of 1989 had momentous consequences, many of which are still unfolding. First, the peoples of eastern Europe joyfully re-entered the mainstream of contemporary European life and culture, after

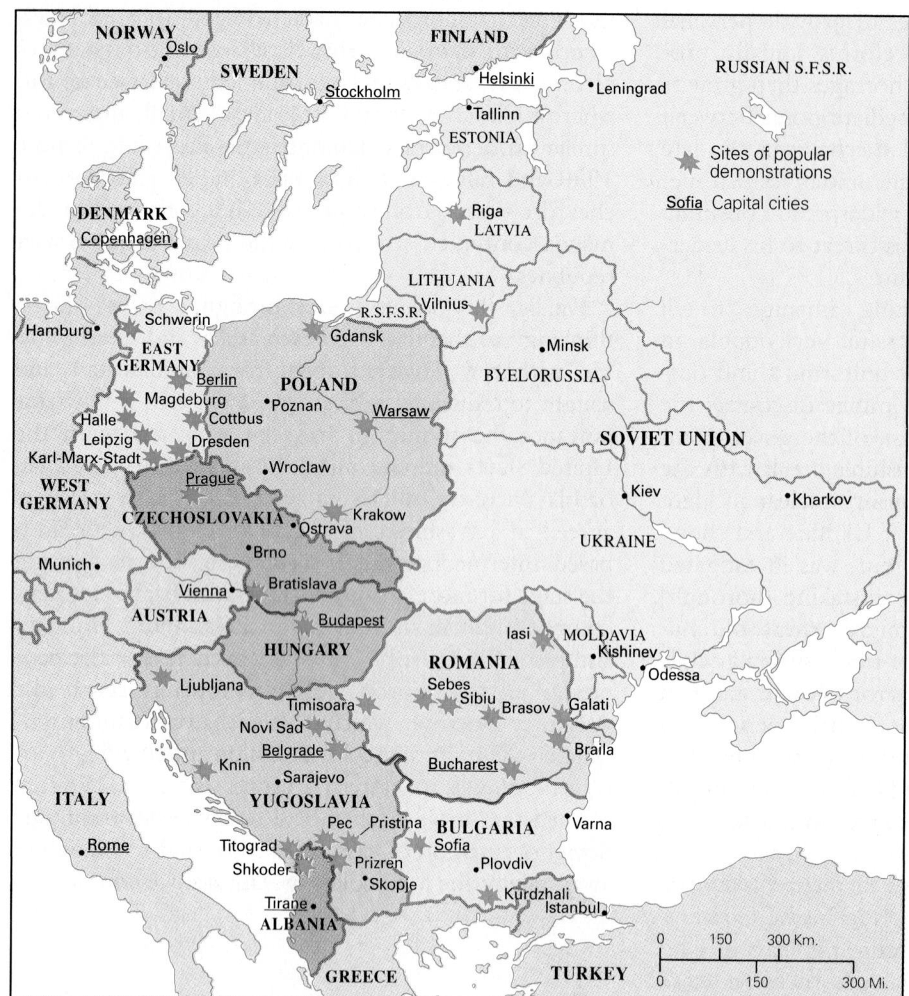

MAP 31.1 Democratic Movements in Eastern Europe, 1989 With Gorbachev's repudiation of the Brezhnev Doctrine, the revolutionary drive for freedom and democracy spread throughout eastern Europe. Countries that had been satellites in the orbit of the Soviet Union began to set themselves free to establish their own place in the universe of free nations.

having been been conquered and brutalized by Nazis and communists for almost sixty years. Second, Gorbachev's reforms now boomeranged, and a complicated anticommunist revolution swept through the Soviet Union, as the once mighty multinational empire committed suicide and broke into a large Russia and fourteen other independent states. Third, West Germany quickly absorbed its East German rival and emerged as the most influential country in Europe. Finally, the long cold war came to an abrupt end, and the United States suddenly stood as the world's only superpower.

The Collapse of Communism in Eastern Europe

Solidarity and the Polish people led the way to revolution in eastern Europe. In 1988 widespread labor unrest, raging inflation, and the outlawed Solidarity's refusal to cooperate with the military government had brought Poland to the brink of economic collapse. Profiting from Gorbachev's tolerant attitude and skillfully mobilizing forces, Solidarity pressured Poland's frustrated Communist leaders into another round of negotiations that might work out a sharing of power to resolve the political stalemate and the economic crisis. The subsequent agreement in early 1989 legalized Solidarity again after eight years. The agreement also declared that a large minority of representatives to the Polish parliament would be chosen by free elections in June 1989. The Communist party was still guaranteed a majority, and General Jaruzelski would be president for four years. Expecting to win many of the contested seats, the Communists believed that their rule was guaranteed for four years and that Solidarity would keep the workers in line.

Lacking access to the state-run media, Solidarity succeeded nonetheless in mobilizing the country and winning most of the contested seats in an overwhelming and largely unexpected victory. Moreover, many angry voters crossed off the names of unopposed party candidates, so that the Communist party failed to win the majority they had anticipated. Solidarity members jubilantly entered the Polish parliament as the first freely elected opposition in a communist country, and a dangerous stalemate quickly developed. But Solidarity leader Lech Walesa, a gifted politician who always repudiated violence, adroitly obtained a majority by securing the allegiance of two minor procommunist parties that had been part of the coalition government after World War II. Significantly, at a critical moment, Gorbachev told the Polish Communists again that Moscow would not intervene to save them. In August 1989, the editor of Solidarity's weekly newspaper was sworn in as the first noncommunist leader in eastern Europe since Stalin used Soviet armies to impose his system there after the Second World War.

In its first year and a half, the new Solidarity government cautiously introduced revolutionary political changes. It eliminated the hated secret police, the Communist ministers in the government, and finally Jaruzelski himself, but it did so step by step in order to avoid confrontation with the army or the Soviet Union. However, in economic affairs, the Solidarity-led government was radical from the beginning. Pointing to the disastrous economic condition of the country and its people, the new government applied "shock therapy" designed to make a clean break with state planning and ownership and to move quickly to market mechanisms and private property. Developed in the fall of 1989, the Solidarity government abolished controls on many prices on January 1, 1990, and reformed the monetary system with a "big bang." Showing for the first time how a communist economic system might be dismantled with breathtaking speed, the Polish program provided a model for similar radical action in other postcommunist countries.

Hungary followed Poland. Hungary's Communist party boss, János Kádár, had permitted liberalization of the rigid planned economy after the 1956 uprising in exchange for political obedience and continued Communist control. In May 1988, in an effort to retain power by granting modest political concessions, the party replaced Kádár with a reform communist. But opposition groups rejected piecemeal progress, and in the summer of 1989 the Hungarian Communist party agreed in a bold gamble to renounce one-party rule and to hold free elections in early 1990. Welcoming Western investment and moving rapidly toward multiparty democracy, Hungary's Communists now enjoyed considerable popular support and they believed, quite mistakenly it turned out, that they could defeat the opposition in the upcoming elections. In an effort to strengthen their support at home and also put pressure on East Germany's hard-line Communist regime, the Hungarians opened their border to East Germans and tore down the barbed-wire "iron curtain" with Austria. In doing so, Hungary repudiated its treaty commitment to prevent East Germans from escaping to the West, but Hungary's reform communists claimed that they were only following the United Nations convention on political refugees. Thus tens of thousands of dissatisfied East German "vacationers" began pouring into Hungary, crossed into Austria as refugees, and continued on to immediate resettlement in thriving West Germany.

The flight of East Germans led to the rapid growth of a homegrown protest movement in East Germany. Intellectuals, environmentalists, and Protestant ministers took the lead, organizing huge candlelight demonstrations and arguing that a truly democratic, independent, but still socialist East Germany was both possible and desirable. These "stayers" failed to convince the "leavers," however, who continued to flee the country en masse. In a desperate attempt to stabilize the situation, the East German government opened the Berlin Wall in November 1989, and people danced for joy atop that grim symbol of the prison state. East Germany's aging Communist leaders were swept aside, and a reform government took power, calling for a wide-ranging political dialogue and scheduling general elections for March 1990.

In Czechoslovakia, communism died in December 1989 in an almost good-humored ousting of Communist bosses in ten short days. This so-called Velvet Rev-

East Germans Escaping to the West After Hungary allowed more than 30,000 "vacationing" East Germans to pass into Austria and on to a tumultuous welcome in West Germany, Czechoslovakia followed suit. Hordes of East Germans, like those shown here, converged on the West German embassy in Prague. Then the East German government gave up, opening the Berlin wall and scheduling free elections. *(BUU/Saussier/Liaison)*

olution grew out of popular demonstrations led by students, intellectuals, and a dissident playwright turned moral revolutionary named Václav Havel. (See the feature "Individuals in Society: Václav Havel: Apostle of Regeneration.") The protesters practically took control of the streets and forced the Communists into a power-sharing arrangement, which quickly resulted in the resignation of the Communist government. As 1989 ended, the Czechoslovak assembly elected Havel president.

Only in Romania was revolution violent and bloody. There iron-fisted Communist dictator Nicolae Ceauşescu (1918–1989) had long combined Stalinist brutality with stubborn independence from Moscow. Faced with mass protests in December, Ceauşescu, alone among eastern European bosses, ordered his ruthless security forces to slaughter thousands, thereby sparking a classic armed uprising. After Ceauşescu's forces were defeated, the tyrant and his wife were captured and executed by a military court. A coalition government emerged from the fighting, although the legacy of Ceauseşcu's oppression left a very troubled country.

The Disintegration of the Soviet Union

As 1990 began, the revolutionary changes that Gorbachev had permitted, and even encouraged, had triumphed in all but two eastern European states—tiny Albania and the vast Soviet Union. The great question now became whether the Soviet Union would follow its former satellites and whether reform communism would give way to a popular anticommunist revolution. Near civil war between Armenians and Azerbaijanis in the Caucasus; assertions of independence in the Baltic States, including Lithuania's bold declaration of

Individuals in Society

Václav Havel, playwright, dissident leader, and the first postcommunist president of the Czech Republic. *(Chris Niedenthal/Black Star)*

Václav Havel: Apostle of Regeneration

On the night of November 24, 1989, the revolution in Czechoslovakia reached its climax. Three hundred thousand people had poured into Prague's historic Wenceslas Square to continue the massive protests that had erupted a week earlier after the police savagely beat student demonstrators. Now all eyes were focused on a high balcony. There an elderly man with a gentle smile and a middle-aged intellectual in jeans and sport jacket stood arm in arm and acknowledged the cheers of the crowd. "Dubček-Havel," the people roared. "Dubček-Havel!" Alexander Dubček, who represented the failed promise of reform communism in the 1960s (see page 1006), was symbolically passing the torch to Václav Havel, who embodied the uncompromising opposition to communism that was sweeping the country. That very evening, the hard-line Communist government resigned, and soon Havel was the unanimous choice to head a new democratic Czechoslovakia. Who was this man to whom the nation turned in 1989?

Born in 1936 into a prosperous, cultured, upper-middle-class family, the young Havel was denied admission to the university because of his class origins. Loving literature and philosophy, he gravitated to the theater, became a stagehand, and emerged in the 1960s as a leading playwright. His plays were set in vague settings, developed existential themes, and poked fun at the absurdities of life and the pretensions of communism. In his private life, Havel thrived on good talk, Prague's lively bar scene, and officially forbidden rock-and-roll.

In 1968 the Soviets rolled into Czechoslovakia, and Havel watched in horror as a tank commander opened fire on a crowd of peaceful protesters in a small town. "That week," he recorded, "was an experience I shall never forget."[1] The free-spirited artist threw himself into the intellectual opposition to communism and became its leading figure for the next twenty years. The costs of defiance were enormous. Purged and blacklisted, Havel lifted barrels in a brewery and wrote bitter satires that could not be staged. In 1977 he and a few other dissidents publicly protested Czechoslovak violations of the Helsinki Accord on human rights, and in 1989 this Charter '77 group became the inspiration for Civic Forum, the democratic coalition that toppled communism. Havel spent five years in prison and was constantly harassed by the police.

Havel's thoughts and actions focused on truth, decency, and moral regeneration. In 1975, in a famous open letter to Czechoslovakia's Communist boss, Havel wrote that the people were indeed quiet, but only because they were "driven by fear. . . . Everyone has something to lose and so everyone has reason to be afraid." Thus Havel saw lies, hypocrisy, and apathy undermining and poisoning all human relations in his country. "Order has been established—at the price of a paralysis of the spirit, a deadening of the heart, and a spiritual and moral crisis in society."[2]

Yet Havel saw a way out of the Communist quagmire. He argued that a profound but peaceful revolution in human values was possible. Such a revolution could lead to the moral reconstruction of Czech and Slovak society, where, in his words, "values like trust, openness, responsibility, solidarity and love" might again flourish and nurture the human spirit. Havel was a voice of hope and humanity, a voice who inspired his compatriots with a lofty vision of a moral postcommunist society. As president of his country, Havel continued to speak eloquently on the great questions of our time.

Questions for Analysis

1. Why did Havel oppose Communist rule? How did his goals differ from those of Dubček and other advocates of reform communism?
2. Havel has been called a "moralist in politics." Is this a good description of him? Why? Can you think of a better one?

1. Quoted in M. Simmons, *The Reluctant President: A Political Life of Václav Havel* (London: Methuen, 1991), p. 91.
2. Quoted ibid., p. 110.

national sovereignty; and growing dissatisfaction among the Great Russian masses were all parts of a fluid, unstable political situation. Increasingly, the reform-minded Gorbachev stood as a moderate besieged by both those who wanted revolutionary changes and hard-line Communists who longed to reverse course and clamp down.

In February 1990, as competing Russian politicians noisily presented their programs and nationalists in the non-Russian republics demanded autonomy or independence from the Soviet Union, the Communist party suffered a stunning defeat in local elections throughout the country. As in the eastern European satellites, democrats and anticommunists won clear majorities in the leading cities of the Russian Federation. Moreover, in Lithuania the people elected an uncompromising nationalist as president, and the newly chosen parliament declared Lithuania an independent state. Gorbachev responded by placing an economic embargo on Lithuania, but he refused to use the army to crush the separatist government. The result was a tense political stalemate, which undermined popular support for Gorbachev. Separating himself further from Communist hard-liners, a hard-pressed Gorbachev asked Soviet citizens to ratify a new constitution, which formally abolished the Communist party's monopoly of political

Celebrating Victory, August 1991 A Russian soldier flashes the victory sign in front of the Russian parliament, as the last-gasp coup attempt of Communist hard-liners is defeated by Boris Yeltsin and an enthusiastic public. The soldier has cut the hammer and sickle out of the Soviet flag, consigning those famous symbols of proletarian revolution to what Trotsky once called the "garbage can of history." *(Filip Horvat/Saba)*

power and expanded the power of the Congress of People's Deputies. Retaining his post as party secretary, Gorbachev convinced a majority of deputies to elect him president of the Soviet Union.

Gorbachev's eroding power and his unwillingness to risk a universal suffrage election for the presidency strengthened his great rival, Boris Yeltsin (b. 1931). A radical reform communist who had been purged by party conservatives in 1987 and had never forgiven Gorbachev's role in his fall, Yeltsin was a tough and crafty Siberian who had staged a remarkable comeback as the most prominent figure in the democratic movement in the Russian Federation. In May 1990, Yeltsin was elected leader of the Russian parliament. He boldly announced that Russia would declare its independence and put its laws and interests above those of the multinational Soviet Union. Yeltsin's declaration broadened the base of the anticommunist movement, skillfully joining the patriotism of ordinary Russians with the democratic aspirations of big-city intellectuals. Gorbachev countered by trying to save the Soviet Union with a new treaty that would link the member republics in a looser, freely accepted confederation. Nine republics agreed to join, but the three Baltic States (Lithuania, Latvia, and Estonia), as well as Armenia, Georgia, and Moldova, spurned Gorbachev's pleas. Thus the Soviet Union continued to unravel, and the country's economic decline accelerated.

Opposed by democrats and nationalists, Gorbachev was also challenged again by the Communist old guard. Defeated at the Communist party congress in July 1990, a gang of hard-liners kidnapped a vacationing Gorbachev and his family in the Caucasus and tried to seize the Soviet government in August 1991. But the attempted coup collapsed in the face of massive popular resistance, which rallied around Yeltsin, recently elected president of the Russian Federation by universal suffrage. As the world watched spellbound on television, Yeltsin defiantly denounced the rebels from atop a stalled tank in central Moscow and declared the "rebirth of Russia." The army supported Yeltsin, and Gorbachev was rescued and returned to power as head of the Soviet Union.

The leaders of the coup wanted to preserve Communist power, state ownership, and the multinational Soviet Union, but they succeeded only in destroying all three. An anticommunist revolution swept the Russian Federation as Yeltsin and his supporters outlawed the Communist party and confiscated its property. Locked in a personal and political duel with Gorbachev, Yeltsin and his democratic allies declared Russia independent and withdrew from the Soviet Union. All the other Soviet republics also left. The Soviet Union—and Gorbachev's job—ceased to exist on December 25, 1991 (Map 31.2).

To be sure, the independent republics of the old Soviet Union were bound together by innumerable ties. A loose but indispensable confederation, christened the Commonwealth of Independent States, was established as 1991 ended, but its prospects were anything but clear. Many foreign observers speculated that the new Russia, which was often harking back to nationalistic and prerevolutionary symbols, would eventually seek to reclaim the tsarist inheritance and bring the supposedly independent states of the commonwealth under Moscow's control. However, as 1992 opened, Russian dreams of empire seemed as dead as the Soviet Union. And throughout the rest of the 1990s, the enormous challenges inherent in building a market economy and a democratic society would fully absorb Russian energies.

German Unification and the End of the Cold War

The revolutions of 1989 and the collapse of communism transformed eastern Europe, as people tore down the walls and put in elected officials. The liberation of eastern Europe enhanced the prospect of ending the cold war, rooted above all in Stalin's brutal imposition of Soviet rule in eastern Europe after World War II (see pages 1004–1006). Yet the sudden death of communism in East Germany in 1989 also reopened the potentially dangerous "German question," for Gorbachev's rapidly changing but still powerful Soviet Union still had special rights in Germany, as did the Western allies. Renewed cold war conflict over Germany was still possible.

Taking power in October 1989, East German reform communists, enthusiastically supported by leading East German intellectuals and former dissidents, wanted to preserve socialism by making it genuinely democratic and responsive to the needs of the people. They argued for a "third way," which would go beyond the failed Stalinism they had experienced and the ruthless capitalism they saw in the West. These reformers supported closer ties with West Germany, but they feared unification and they wanted to preserve a distinct East German identity.

These efforts failed, and within a few months East Germany was absorbed into an enlarged West Germany,

MAP 31.2 Russia and the Successor States After the attempt in August 1991 to depose Gorbachev failed, an anticommunist revolution swept the Soviet Union. Led by Russia and Boris Yeltsin, the republics that formed the Soviet Union declared their sovereignty and independence. Eleven of the fifteen republics then formed a loose confederation called the Commonwealth of Independent States, but the integrated economy of the Soviet Union dissolved into separate national economies, each with its own goals and policies.

much like a faltering smaller company is merged into a larger rival and ceases to exist. Three factors were particularly important in this sudden absorption. First, in the first week after the Berlin Wall was opened, almost 9 million East Germans—roughly one-half of the total population—poured across the border into West Germany. Almost all returned to their homes in the East, but the joy of warm welcomes from long-lost friends and loved ones and the exhilarating experience of shopping in the well-stocked stores of the much wealthier West aroused long-dormant hopes of unity among ordinary citizens.

Second, West German chancellor Helmut Kohl and his closest advisers skillfully exploited the historic opportunity on their doorstep. Sure of support from the United States, whose leadership he had steadfastly followed, in November 1989 Kohl presented a ten-point plan for a step-by-step unification in cooperation with both East Germany and the international community. Building on his bold call for reunification without fanning fears of a dangerous greater Germany, Kohl then promised the ordinary citizens of a struggling, bankrupt East Germany an immediate economic bonanza—a one-for-one exchange of all East German marks in savings accounts and pensions into much more valuable West German marks. This generous offer helped a well-financed conservative-liberal "Alliance for Germany," which was set up in East Germany and was closely tied to Kohl's West German Christian Democrats, to overwhelm those who argued for the preservation of some kind of independent socialist society in East Germany. In March 1990, the Alliance outdistanced the Socialist party and won almost 50 percent of the votes in an East German parliamentary election. (The Communists ignominiously fell to fringe-party status.) The Alliance for Germany quickly negotiated an economic union on favorable terms with Chancellor Kohl, who wanted to complete the unification of the two Germanies as quickly as he could.

Finally, in the summer of 1990, the complicated international aspect of German unification was successfully resolved. This aspect was critical. Unification would once again make Germany the strongest state in central Europe and would directly affect the security of the Soviet Union and the general European balance of power. But Gorbachev swallowed hard—Western cartoonists delighted in showing Stalin turning over in his grave—and negotiated the best deal he could. In a historic agreement signed by Gorbachev and Kohl in July 1990, a uniting Germany solemnly affirmed its peaceful intentions and pledged never to develop nuclear, biological, or chemical weapons. In deference to Russian pride, Germany allowed the Soviet forces stationed in East Germany to withdraw gradually and with dignity. In side agreements, Germany sweetened the deal for Gorbachev by promising to make enormous loans to the hard-pressed Soviet Union. In doing so, Kohl continued Willy Brandt's strategy of buying favor in eastern Europe with aid and credit, a strategy that had proved highly effective. On October 3, 1990, East Germany merged into West Germany, forming henceforth a single nation under the West German laws and constitution.

The peaceful reunification of Germany accelerated the pace of agreements to reduce armaments and liquidate the cold war. With the Soviet Union's budget deficit rising rapidly in 1990, Gorbachev especially sought arrangements to justify massive cuts in military spending. Thus in November 1990, delegates from twenty-two European countries joined those from the United States and the Soviet Union in Paris and agreed to a scaling down of all their armed forces. The delegates also solemnly affirmed that all existing borders in Europe—from unified Germany to the newly independent Baltic republics—were legal and valid. The Paris Accord was for all practical purposes a general peace treaty, bringing an end to World War II and the cold war that followed.

The establishment of peace in Europe encouraged the United States and the Soviet Union to scrap a significant portion of their nuclear weapons. Having already agreed in 1987 to remove all land-based intermediate-range missiles from Europe, the two great nuclear superpowers pledged in July 1991 a major mutual reduction of intercontinental ballistic missiles with their multiple nuclear warheads in the START I agreement. In September 1991, a confident President George Bush unilaterally declared another major cut in American nuclear weapons. He also canceled the around-the-clock alert status for American bombers outfitted with atomic bombs. A floundering Gorbachev quickly followed suit. For the first time in four decades, Soviet and American nuclear weapons were no longer standing ready to destroy capitalism, communism, and life itself.

As anticommunist revolutions swept eastern Europe and East-West tensions rapidly disappeared, the Soviet Union lost both the will and the means to be a mighty superpower. Yet the United States retained the increased strength resulting from the Reagan arms buildup, as well as its desire to influence political and economic developments on a global scale. Thus the United States, still flanked by many allies, emerged rather suddenly as the world's only surviving superpower.

In 1991 the United States used its military superiority on a grand scale in a quick war with Iraq in western Asia. Emerging in 1988 from an eight-year war with neighboring Iran with a big, tough army equipped by the Soviet bloc, western Europe, and the United States, Iraq's strongman Saddam Hussein (b. 1937) set out to make himself the leader of the entire Arab world. Eyeing the great oil wealth of his tiny southern neighbor, Saddam Hussein suddenly sent his military forces into Kuwait in August 1990 and proclaimed Iraq's annexation of Kuwait.

Reacting vigorously, the United States called on the United Nations to turn back Iraqi aggression and free Kuwait. The five permanent members of the U.N. Security Council—the United States, the Soviet Union, China, the United Kingdom, and France—agreed in August 1990 to impose a strict naval blockade on Iraq. Naval forces, led by the United States but augmented by ships from several nations, then enforced the blockade and halted all trade between Iraq and the rest of the world. Receiving the support of ground units from some Arab states as well as from Great Britain and France, the United States also landed first 200,000, and then a total of 500,000, American soldiers in Saudi Arabia near the border of Kuwait. When a defiant Saddam Hussein refused to withdraw from Kuwait and pay reparations, the Security Council authorized the U.S.-led

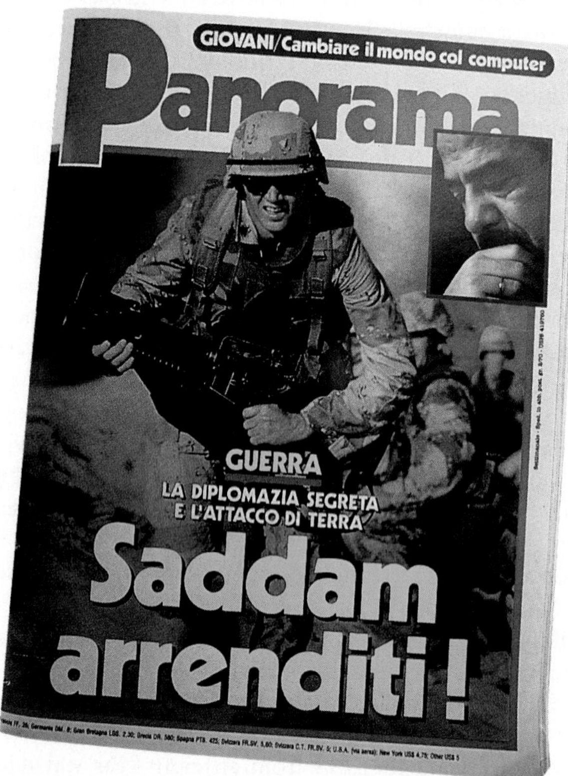

"Saddam, Surrender!" So reads the caption under the image of an advancing U.S. soldier on the cover of a leading Italian newsmagazine, which repeatedly featured the crisis over Kuwait and the war with Iraq. This heavy Italian coverage was symptomatic of enormous coverage worldwide. Although U.S. forces provided most of the muscle, twenty-eight countries, including Italy, participated in Operation Desert Storm. (U.S. News & World Report/ PANORAMA/*Mondadori. Courtesy, Madeline Grimoldi)*

military coalition to attack Iraq. The American army and air force then smashed Iraqi forces in a lightning-quick desert campaign, although the United States stopped short of toppling Saddam because it feared a sudden disintegration of Iraq more than Saddam's hanging on to power.

The defeat of Iraqi armies received saturation coverage by the world's media. The spectacularly efficient operation demonstrated the awesome power of the U.S. military, rebuilt and revitalized by the spending and patriotism of the 1980s. It showed with equal clarity the secondary status of a declining Soviet Union, which did not veto and even endorsed U.S. proposals in the U.N. Security Council. Little wonder that in the flush of yet another victory, President Bush spoke of a "new world order," an order that would apparently feature the United States and a cooperative United Nations working together to impose peace and security throughout the world.

Building a New Europe in the 1990s

The fall of communism, the end of the cold war, and the collapse of the Soviet Union opened a new era in European and world history. Few would disagree with this statement. Yet the dimensions and significance of this new era, opening suddenly and unexpectedly, are far from clear. A constant stream of information and events assails us, but what, we wonder, is truly significant and what is of only momentary importance? We are so close to what is going on that we lack vital perspective. Indeed, it is particularly difficult to interpret intelligently recent events. As the French philosopher Voltaire once said, "People who venture to write contemporary history must expect to be attacked for everything they have said and everything they have not said."[5]

Yet the historian must take a stand and find patterns of development and explanation. Thus we shall concentrate on two main themes of European development in the 1990s. First, considering that Europe has taken giant strides toward a loose unification of fundamental institutions and beliefs, we shall examine broad economic, social, and political trends that operated all across the continent in the 1990s. These trends include national economies increasingly caught up in global capitalism, the defense of social achievements under attack, and a powerful resurgence of nationalism and ethnic conflict. Second, with these common themes providing an organizational framework, we shall examine the course of development in the three overlapping but still distinct regions of contemporary Europe. These are Russia and the western states of the old Soviet Union; previously communist eastern Europe; and western Europe.

Common Patterns and Problems

The end of the cold war and the disintegration of the Soviet Union ended the division of Europe into two opposing camps with two different political and economic systems. Thus, although Europe in the 1990s was a collage of diverse peoples with their own politics, cultures, and histories, the entire continent shared an underlying network of common developments and challenges.

Of great importance, in economic affairs European leaders embraced, or at least accepted, a large part of the neoliberal, free-market vision of capitalist development. This was most strikingly the case in eastern Europe, where states such as Poland and Hungary implemented market reforms and sought to create vibrant capitalist economies. Thus postcommunist governments in eastern Europe freed prices, turned state enterprises over to private owners, and sought to move toward strong currencies and balanced budgets. Milder doses of this same free-market medicine were administered by politicians and big business to the lackluster economies of western Europe. These initiatives and proposals for further changes marked a considerable modification in western Europe's still-dominant welfare capitalism, which had been consolidated in the 1950s and 1960s and which featured a belief in government intervention, high taxes, and high levels of social benefits.

Two factors were particularly important in accounting for this ongoing shift from welfare state activism to tough-minded capitalism, which European socialists and leftist intellectuals regularly denounced as "savage capitalism," a dog-eat-dog throwback to the early industrial era. First, Europeans were only following practices and ideologies revived and enshrined in the 1980s in the United States and Great Britain (see page 1020). Western Europeans especially took American prescriptions more seriously in the 1990s. They did so because U.S. prestige and power were so high after the United States "won the cold war" (as American publicists liked to proclaim) and because the U.S. economy outperformed its western European counterparts in the Clinton years as it had in the Reagan era. Second, the deregulation of markets and the privatization of state-controlled enterprises in different European countries were an integral part of the powerful trend toward a wide-open, wheeler-dealer global economy. The rules of the global economy, which were laid down by powerful Western governments, multinational corporations, and big banks and international financial organizations such as the International Monetary Fund (IMF), called for the free movement of capital and goods and services, as well as low inflation and limited government deficits. Accepting these rules and attempting to follow them was the price of participating in the global economy.

In the 1990s, the ongoing computer and electronics revolution strengthened the move toward a global economy. That revolution thrived on the diffusion of ever-cheaper computational and informational capacity to small research groups and private businesses, which were both cause and effect of the revolution itself. Big organizations found it advantageous to farm out ever more work to small firms and home workers, who became able to link electronically with clients, regions, and most of the world. By the 1990s, an inexpensive personal computer had the power of a 1950s mainframe that filled a room and cost hundreds of thousands of dollars. The computer revolution reduced the costs of distance, speeding up communications and helping businesses tap cheaper labor overseas. Reducing the friction of distance made threats of moving factories abroad ring true and helped hold down wages at home.

The freer global economy, which probably did speed up world economic growth as enthusiasts invariably claimed, had powerful social consequences. Millions of ordinary citizens in western Europe saw global capitalism and freer markets as challenging hard-won social achievements. As in the United States and Great Britain in the 1980s, the public in other countries generally opposed the unemployment that accompanied corporate downsizing, the efforts to reduce the power of labor unions, and, above all, government plans to reduce social benefits. The difficulties with state-financed health care systems, with their costs rising as populations aged and more sophisticated treatments became available, provoked fierce debate and even upheaval. The reaction was particularly intense in France and Germany, where unions remained strong and socialists championed a minimum of change in social policies.

In the 1990s, political developments across the European continent were loosely unified by common patterns and problems. Most obviously, the demise of European communism brought the apparent triumph of liberal democracy everywhere. All countries embraced genuine electoral competition, with elected presidents and legislatures and the outward manifestations of representative liberal governments. With some notable exceptions, such as discrimination against Gypsies and illegal immigrants, countries also guaranteed basic civil liberties. Thus, for the first time since before the French Revolution, almost all of Europe followed the same general political model, although the variations were endless.

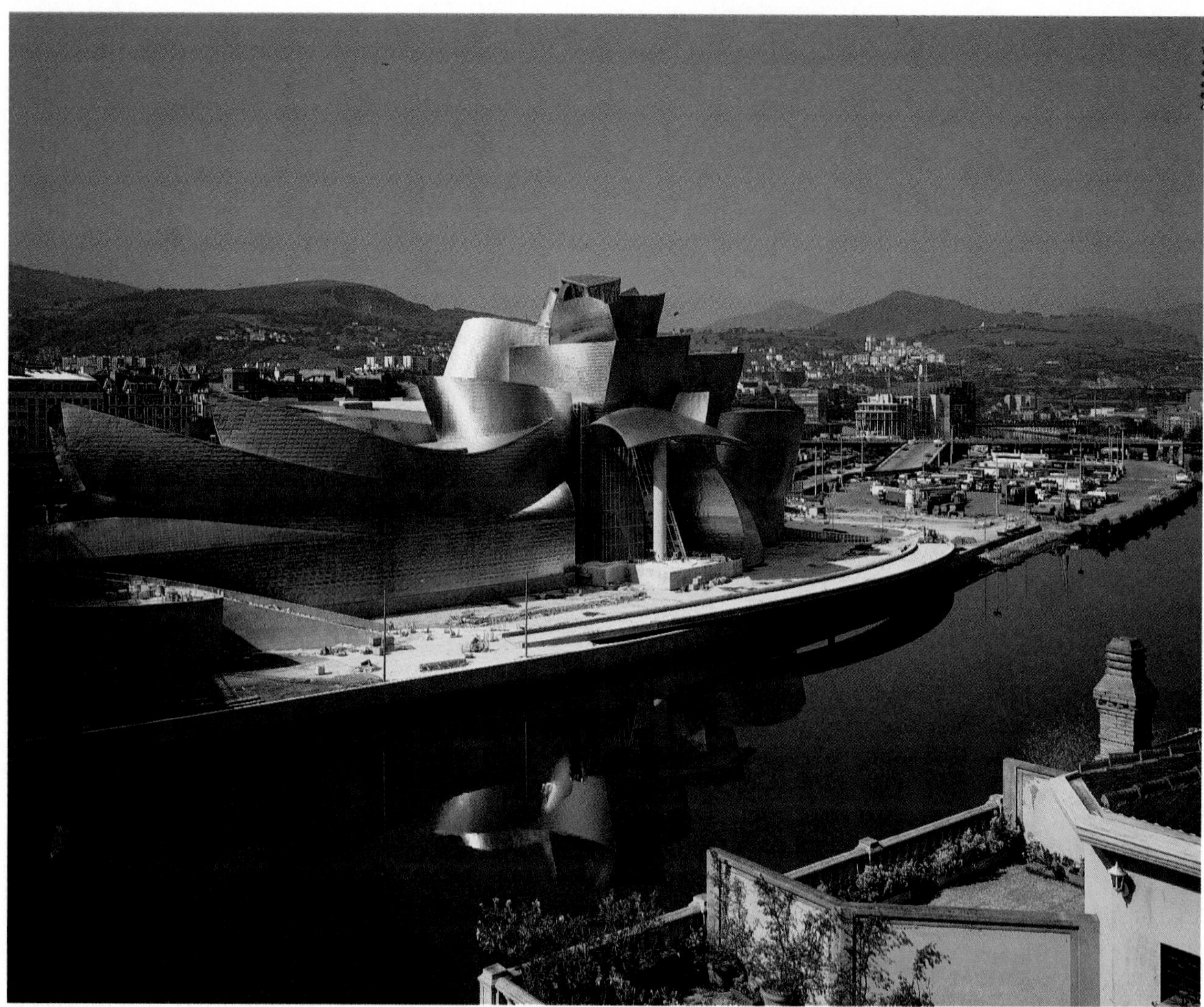

Guggenheim Museum, Bilbao, Spain Praised by admirers as the "first great building of the twenty-first century," Bilbao's exotic undulating museum of contemporary art is intended to revitalize the Basque region of northwestern Spain through international prestige, cultural renaissance, and tourism. Selected in a global competition, Frank Gehry's design relies heavily on three-dimensional computer modeling to hold dramatic opposites in delicate balance, as well as to translate complex forms into construction blueprints. *(Jeff Goldberg/Esto. All rights reserved)*

The triumph of the liberal-democratic program in Europe (and large parts of Latin America and Asia) led the American scholar Francis Fukuyama to discern the "end of history" in an influential book by that title. According to Fukuyama, first fascism and Nazism and then communism had been definitively bested by liberal-democratic politics and market economics. Conversely, as James Cronin perceptively noted, the fall of communism and the end of ideological competition also marked the return of nationalism and national history.[6] The cold war and the superpowers had generally kept their allies and clients in line, either by force or by granting them conditional aid. As soon as the cold war was over, nationalism and ethnic conflict re-emerged, and history, as the story of different peoples, began again.

The resurgence of nationalism in the 1990s led to terrible tragedy and bloodshed in parts of eastern Europe, as it did in several hot spots in Africa and Asia. During the civil war in Yugoslavia, many observers feared that national and ethnic hatreds would spread throughout eastern Europe and infect western Europe in the form of racial hostility toward minorities and immigrants. Yet if nationalist and racist incidents were a recurring European theme, they remained limited in the extent of their damage. Of critical importance in this regard was the fact that all states wished to become or remain full-fledged members of the European society of nations and to join eventually an ever-expanding European Community, renamed the European Union in 1993. States that embraced national hatred and ethnic warfare, most notably Serbia, were branded as outlaws and boycotted and isolated by the international community. The process of checking resurgent nationalism in Europe and generally keeping it from getting out of hand was almost as significant as the resurgence itself.

Recasting Russia

Politics and economics were closely intertwined in Russia after the attempted Communist coup in 1991 and the dissolution of the Soviet Union. President Boris Yeltsin, his democratic supporters, and his economic ministers wanted to create conditions that would prevent forever a return to communism and would also right the faltering economy. Following the example of some postcommunist governments in eastern Europe and agreeing with those Western advisers who argued that private economies were always best, the Russian reformers opted in January 1992 for breakneck liberalization. Their shock therapy freed prices on 90 percent of all Russian goods, with the exception of bread, vodka, oil, and public transportation. The government also launched a rapid privatization of industry and turned thousands of factories and mines over to new private companies. Within a year, 64 percent of the privatized firms were owned by their workers, and each citizen received a voucher worth 10,000 rubles (about $22) to buy stock in private companies. However, control of the privatized companies usually remained in the hands of the old bosses, the managers and government officials who had been running the factories and ministries in the communist era.

President Yeltsin and his economic reformers believed that shock therapy would revive production and bring prosperity after a brief period of hardship. As the president explained, "Everyone will find life harder for approximately six months, then prices will fall and goods will begin to fill the market. By the autumn of 1992 the economy will have stabilized."[7] The results of the reforms were in fact quite different. Prices increased 250 percent on the very first day, and they kept on soaring, increasing twenty-six times in the course of 1992. At the same time, Russian production fell a staggering 20 percent. Nor did the situation stabilize quickly. Throughout 1995 rapid but gradually slowing inflation raged, and output continued to fall. According to most estimates, in 1996 the Russian economy produced at least one-third and possibly as much as one-half less than in 1991. Only in 1997 did the economy stop declining. That year a respected expert concluded that "Russia has suffered a minimum of five years of economic travail. . . . It is necessary to acknowledge that the economic reforms in Russia have not been the success so many insisted they were for so long."[8]

Rapid economic liberalization worked poorly in Russia for several reasons. Perhaps most important, Soviet industry had been highly monopolized and strongly tilted toward military goods. Production of many items had been concentrated in one or two gigantic factories or interconnected combines that supplied the entire economy. With privatization these powerful state monopolies simply became powerful private monopolies. These private monopolies then cut production and raised prices in order to obtain large profits, as in the case of producers of raw materials, or to reduce losses in noncompetitive industries, such as steel and automobiles.

This was not what Yeltsin and the free-market ideologues around him had expected. According to standard economic theory, monopoly prices and profits should have encouraged new firms to enter production, thereby increasing Russian output and pushing down prices through competition. But this desirable process developed very slowly. Powerful managers and bureaucrats forced Yeltsin's government to hand out enormous subsidies and credits to reinforce the positions of big firms and to avoid bankruptcies and the discipline of a free market. The managerial elite also combined with criminal elements, which had already been strong in the late Soviet period, to intimidate would-be rivals and prevent the formation of new businesses. Not that most ordinary Soviet citizens were eager to start businesses.

For decades they had been told that all capitalists were "speculators" and "exploiters," and as Russian business became associated in popular culture with crime, corruption, and national decline, most people had little reason to change their minds. In short, enterprise directors and politicians combined to subvert Yeltsin's unrealistic "radical" liberalization. This group then succeeded in eliminating worker ownership and converted large portions of previously state-owned industry into their own private property.

Runaway inflation and poorly executed privatization brought a profound social revolution to Russia. A new capitalist elite acquired great wealth and power, while large numbers of people fell into abject poverty, and the majority struggled in the midst of decline to make ends meet.

Managers, former officials, and financiers who came out of the privatization process with large shares of the old state monopolies stood at the top of the reorganized elite. The richest plums were found in Russia's enormous oil and natural resources industries, headed in the Soviet era by Viktor Chernomyrdin, who later became Yeltsin's prime minister. In 1992 Chernomyrdin and his allies convinced Yeltsin to keep the price of oil sold in Russia frozen at only 1 percent of the world price. This enabled unscrupulous enterprise directors to divert oil abroad, selling it through Russian front men and dishonestly pocketing enormous gains. The president of one big Russian oil company, who was worth virtually nothing in 1991, was worth $2.4 billion in 1995. From all indications, crime and corruption permeated Russian business big and small. Russian (and foreign) business leaders always moved with their bodyguards, but murders of executives were nonetheless common. The new elite was more highly concentrated in Moscow than ever before, and westerners who visited only the capital had difficulty believing that there was a national economic decline. By 1996 Moscow, with 5 percent of the population, accounted for 35 percent of the country's national income and controlled 80 percent of its capital resources.

At the other extreme, the vast majority saw their savings become practically worthless. Pensions lost much of their value, and whole markets were devoted to people selling off their personal goods to survive. Unemployment rose, and in 1996 35 percent of the population was living in poverty. The quality of public services and health care declined precipitously. Perhaps the most telling statistic, summing up millions of hardships and tragedies, was the truly catastrophic decline in the life expectancy of the average Russian male from sixty-nine years in 1991 to only fifty-eight years in 1996. Only in 1997 did living conditions for ordinary people begin to improve a bit as the economy finally began to grow.

Yeltsin and his supporters proved more successful in politics. Rapid economic decline in 1992 and 1993 increased popular dissatisfaction. This encouraged the Russian parliament, dominated by former Communists elected in 1990, to oppose Yeltsin's plan for constitutional reform. Yeltsin and his coalition of democratic reformers and big business interests pressed for a strong presidential system, while an opposition of communists, nationalists, and populists defended the authority of the parliament. Winning in April 1993 the support of 58 percent of the population in a referendum on his proposed constitution, Yeltsin then brought in tanks to crush a parliamentary mutiny in October 1993 and literally blew away the last vestiges of Soviet power. Although Yeltsin's allies in the reform parties lost ground to the communists and the nationalists in two subsequent elections, in 1996 Yeltsin won re-election as president in an impressive come-from-behind victory.

Yeltsin's victory in 1996 suggested to some observers that free and open elections had become a regular and accepted core of Russian political life. To be sure, political problems remained. The constitution concentrated power in the hands of the president, and parliament was subordinate. Russian political parties were weak, and only Russia's superrich had organized effectively to pursue their interests. Russia still lacked a rule of law and a reorganized court system to deal with crime and corruption. Yet with all politicians looking to the ballot box for legitimacy, there was some reason to hope that a growing tradition of Russian democracy would eventually rise to meet these challenges.

Russia's moderation in relations with foreign countries also provided reasons for guarded optimism as the century came to a close. First, military spending continued to decline under Yeltsin. Second, Russia reluctantly accepted the enlargement of NATO in 1997 to include Poland, Hungary, and the Czech Republic and negotiated a treaty with NATO to provide a framework for cooperation in the future. Third, Russia generally respected the independence of the Soviet successor states, peacefully resolving disputes with Ukraine and the Baltic republics. Moreover, although bitter ethnic conflicts abounded in central Asia and the Caucasus and resulted in outbreaks of civil war in Georgia, Armenia, Azerbaijan, and central Asia, Russia generally played a

Battling to Survive These impoverished Russian women are selling their clothing and personal possessions in order to buy food for themselves and their families. Today's Russia is a relatively free society with a competitive electoral system, but begging, homelessness, and high crime rates have also taken root. *(Sovfoto)*

moderating role in these conflicts. Seldom did it use its position as dominant regional power to make matters worse.

The notable exception to this pattern was in Chechnya. In 1991 this tiny republic of 1 million Muslims on Russia's southern border with Georgia declared its independence from the Russian Federation (see Map 31.2). After a three-year stalemate, Yeltsin ordered the Russian army to crush the separatists. But Chechnya resisted with ferocious valor, and the unpopular war went poorly for Russia. In 1996 a wily Yeltsin accepted a face-saving truce and withdrew Russian soldiers, which helped him substantially in his close campaign for re-election. Thus the Russian people spurned military adventure and reinforced popular sovereignty as the ultimate authority in public life.

Progress and Tragedy in Eastern Europe

Developments in eastern Europe shared important similarities with those in Russia, as many of the problems were the same. First, the postcommunist states of the former satellite empire worked to replace state planning and socialism with market mechanisms and private property. Second, Western-style electoral politics took hold, and as in Russia these politics were marked by

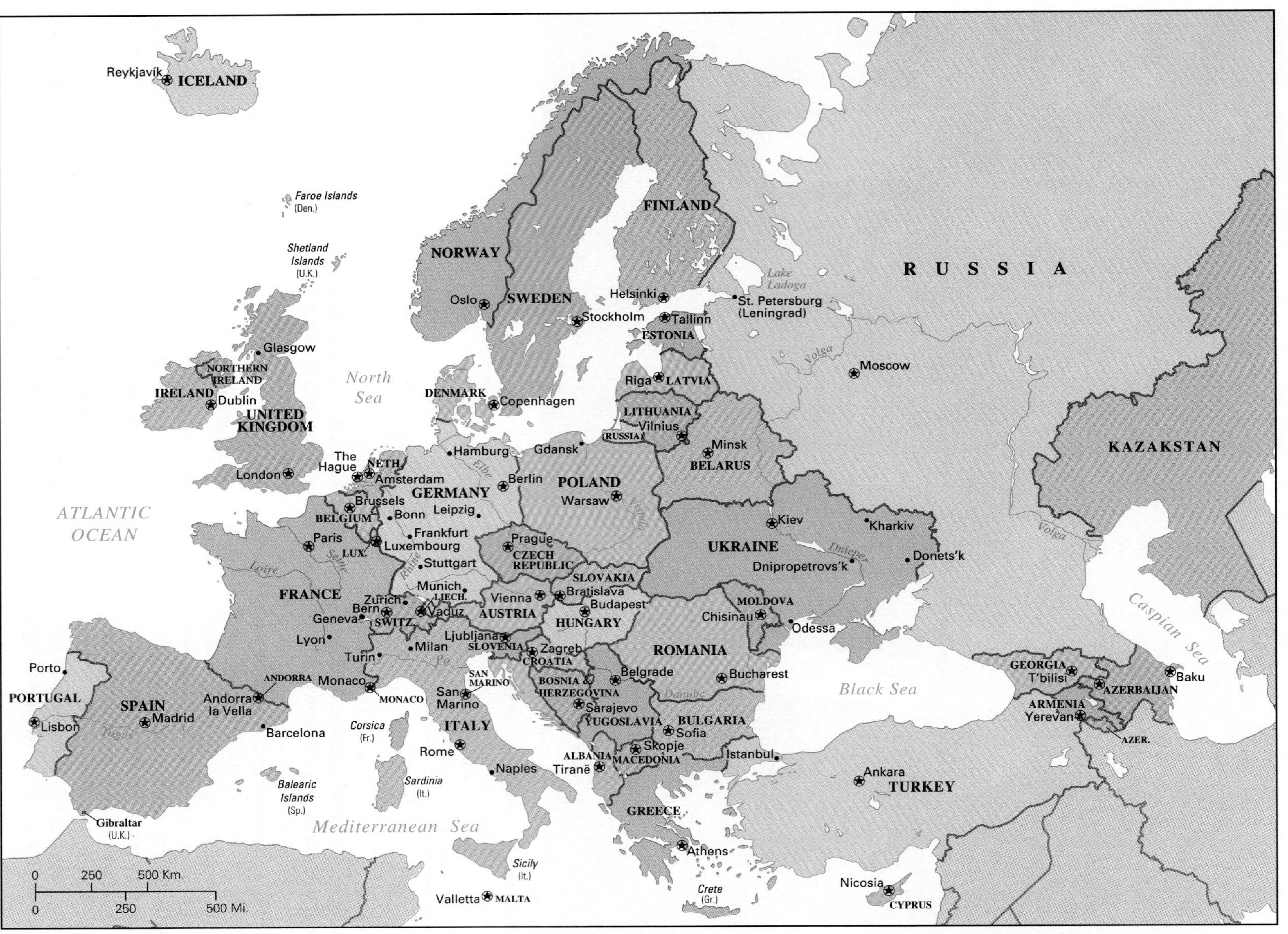

Reykjavík
ICELAND
Faroe Islands (Den.)
Shetland Islands (U.K.)
NORWAY
FINLAND
RUSSIA
Lake Ladoga
Oslo
SWEDEN
Helsinki
St. Petersburg (Leningrad)
Stockholm
Tallinn
ESTONIA
Glasgow
Volga
Moscow
NORTHERN IRELAND
North Sea
Riga
LATVIA
IRELAND
Dublin
DENMARK
Copenhagen
UNITED KINGDOM
LITHUANIA
Vilnius
(RUSSIA)
Minsk
BELARUS
KAZAKSTAN
Hamburg
Gdansk
The Hague
NETH.
Amsterdam
Elbe
London
Berlin
POLAND
GERMANY
Warsaw
ATLANTIC OCEAN
Brussels
Leipzig
Vistula
BELGIUM
Bonn
Kiev
Kharkiv
Paris
Frankfurt
Luxembourg
LUX.
Prague
UKRAINE
Volga
Rhine
Stuttgart
CZECH REPUBLIC
Dnieper
Donets'k
Loire
Seine
Dnipropetrovs'k
SLOVAKIA
Munich
Bratislava
FRANCE
Zurich
LIECH.
Vienna
Budapest
MOLDOVA
Caspian Sea
Bern
Vaduz
AUSTRIA
Chisinau
Geneva
SWITZ.
HUNGARY
Odessa
Ljubljana
Lyon
Milan
SLOVENIA
Zagreb
ROMANIA
Turin
Po
CROATIA
Porto
ANDORRA
SAN MARINO
Belgrade
Bucharest
GEORGIA
T'bilisi
Baku
Monaco
BOSNIA & HERZEGOVINA
Black Sea
PORTUGAL
SPAIN
Andorra la Vella
MONACO
San Marino
Danube
AZERBAIJAN
Madrid
Sarajevo
ARMENIA
Yerevan
Lisbon
Tagus
Barcelona
Corsica (Fr.)
ITALY
YUGOSLAVIA
BULGARIA
Sofia
AZER.
Rome
Skopje
ALBANIA
Istanbul
MACEDONIA
Naples
Tiranë
Ankara
TURKEY
Balearic Islands (Sp.)
Sardinia (It.)
GREECE
Gibraltar (U.K.)
Mediterranean Sea
Athens
Sicily (It.)
0 250 500 Km.
Nicosia
0 250 500 Mi.
Crete (Gr.)
Valletta
MALTA
CYPRUS

intense battles between presidents and parliaments and by weak political parties. Third, the social consequences of these revolutionary changes were similar to those in Russia. Inequality increased greatly. Ordinary citizens and the elderly were once again the big losers, while the young and the ex-Communists, whose privileges had included superior education and well-connected positions, were the big winners. Inequalities between richer and poorer regions also increased. Capital cities such as Warsaw, Prague, and Budapest concentrated wealth, power, and opportunity as never before, while provincial centers stagnated, and old industrial areas declined. Crime and gangsterism increased in the streets and in the executive suites, for it was frequently associated with big business and politicians.

Yet the 1990s saw more than a difficult transition, with high social costs, to market economies and freely elected governments in eastern Europe. As we have seen, the peoples of eastern Europe never fully accepted communism, which the opposition that triumphed in 1989 increasingly equated with Russian imperialism and the loss of national independence. The joyous crowds that toppled communist regimes in 1989 believed that they were liberating the nation as well as the individual. Thus communism died, and nationalism was reborn.

The surge of nationalism in eastern Europe recalled a similar surge of state creation after World War I. Then, too, authoritarian multinational empires had come crashing down in defeat and revolution, as the Austro-Hungarian Empire had broken apart and Russia's influence had receded. Then, too, peoples with long histories and rich cultures had drawn upon ideologies of popular sovereignty and national self-determination to throw off foreign rule and found new states, which contained ethnic minorities and conflicting nationalities to a greater or lesser extent. In the 1990s, the peoples of eastern Europe had a similar chance to create free, democratic, and peaceful national communities.

The response to this opportunity in the former communist countries was quite varied, but it was on a whole considerably better than the former Yugoslavia and the war in Bosnia (see page 1054) would suggest. Most observers agreed that Poland, the Czech Republic, and Hungary were the most successful in the 1990s (Map 31.3). Each of these three countries met the critical challenge of economic reconstruction more successfully than Russia. Each could claim to be the economic leader in eastern Europe, depending on the criteria selected. Poland had the fastest economic growth, the Czech Republic privatized the most completely and had the most foreign investment, and Hungary developed the most sophisticated market. The reasons for these successes included considerable experience with limited market reforms before 1989, flexibility and lack of dogmatism in government policy, and an enthusiastic embrace of capitalism by a rapidly rising entrepreneurial class. In the first five years of reform, Poland created twice as many new businesses as Russia, with a total population only one-fourth as large.

The three northern countries in the former Soviet bloc also did far better than Russia in creating new civic institutions, legal systems, and independent broadcasting networks that reinforced political freedom and national revival. Lech Walesa in Poland and Václav Havel in Czechoslovakia were elected presidents of their countries and proved as remarkable in power as in opposition. Continuing to call for ethical and spiritual regeneration after Czechoslovakia's "Velvet Revolution" in 1989, Havel and the Czech parliament accepted a "velvet divorce" in 1993 when Slovakian nationalists, dissatisfied with Czech majority rule and regional inequalities, wanted to break off and form their own state. In this instance, as in others in the 1990s, the three northern states managed to control national and ethnic tensions that might have destroyed their post-communist reconstruction. For all three countries, the horrors of war in the former Yugoslavia exemplified the dangers of playing with aggressive nationalism.

The popular goal of "rejoining the West" also was a powerful force toward moderation. Poles, Hungarians, and Czechs had been an integral part of medieval Christendom, and centuries later their opposition to communist rule was inspired in part by memories of liberal-democratic values in the 1920s. Now these nations wanted to complete the job, hoping to find security in NATO membership and prosperity in western Europe's ever-tighter economic union. Membership required many proofs of character and stability, however. Providing these proofs and endorsed by the Clinton administration, Poland, Hungary, and the Czech Republic were accepted into the NATO alliance in 1997.

MAP 31.3 Contemporary Europe No longer divided by ideological competition and the cold war, today's Europe features a large number of independent states. Several of these states were previously part of the Soviet Union and Yugoslavia, both of which broke into many different countries. Czechoslovakia also divided on ethnic lines, while a reunited Germany emerged, once again, as the dominant nation in central Europe.

Gaining admission to the European Union (EU) promised to be much more difficult. These three states (and others) could aspire to join the EU sometime in the future only if they continued to behave like "good Europeans."

Slovakia, Romania, and Bulgaria were the eastern European laggards in the postcommunist transition. Western traditions were much weaker there, and all three countries were much poorer than their neighbors to the north. In 1993 Bulgaria and Romania had per capita national incomes of $1,140, in contrast to Hungary ($3,830) and the Czech Republic ($2,710). But there was no going back, and progress was eventually made. After a slow start economically and politically, with grisly pictures of AIDS babies in grotesque orphanages and rampaging unpaid miners, the Romanian government claimed strenuously and with considerable justification that it was finally moving toward capitalism, democracy, and eventual integration with the West in NATO and the European Union. Slovakia and Bulgaria seemed to be following suit.

The great postcommunist tragedy was Yugoslavia. Under Josip Tito, Yugoslavia had been a federation of republics and regions under strict communist rule (see page 1008). But after Tito's death in 1980, power passed increasingly to the sister republics. This encouraged a revival of regional and ethnic conflicts, exacerbated by charges of ethnically inspired massacres during World War II and by a one-third decline in the Yugoslav standard of living between 1983 and 1988.

The revolutions of 1989 accelerated the breakup of Yugoslavia. The feuding Communist-turned-nationalist leaders of the different republics could not agree on a new constitution, and in January 1990 they abolished Yugoslavia's formerly all-powerful League of Communists. President Slobodan Milosevic of the Serbian republic speeded up preparations for a "greater Serbia," intending to grab territory from Yugoslavia's other republics and to combine all Serbs in a single state (Map 31.4). Milosevic's threats strengthened the cause of separatism, and in June 1991 Slovenia and Croatia declared their independence. Milosevic and Serbian separatists retaliated with a war of aggression, backed by the powerful Yugoslavian army and its largely Serbian officer corps. The Slovenes repulsed the invaders, but in Croatia the Serbian minority of about 12 percent and Milosevic's army seized about 30 percent of the territory, burning villages and pounding historic towns to pieces.

In 1992 the civil war spread to Bosnia-Herzegovina when it declared its independence. Serbs made up about 30 percent of Bosnia-Herzegovina's complex multiethnic society, and they adamantly refused to live under the Bosnian Muslims, who constituted 43 percent of the population (see Map 31.4). Local Serbian militias seized territory. Serbs, as well as Croats and Muslims to a far lesser extent, also ruthlessly drove "foreign" civilians from their homes with a combination of shelling, killing, raping, concentration camps, and torture. Cynically described as "ethnic cleansing," these atrocities were intended to send local minorities fleeing as traumatized refugees and to make each enclave ethnically homogeneous. The suffering was incalculable. Yugoslavia had been a tolerant and largely successful multiethnic state with groups living side by side and often intermarrying. The Bosnian war resulted in between 80,000 and 250,000 deaths and more than 3 million refugees.

Scenes of cruelty and slaughter on the nightly news shocked the world, but the Western nations had great difficulty formulating an effective response. By late 1994, a series of peace plans had failed and the Serbs controlled 70 percent of Bosnia-Herzegovina and 25 percent of Croatia. But the Muslims, strengthened by an alliance with the Croats and by American military aid, held on. Moreover, an isolated Milosevic wanted to ditch the Bosnian Serbs in order to hang on to power in his country, which had been isolated and impoverished by an effective international embargo.

The turning point came in July 1995, when Bosnian Serbs overran one of the United Nations' "safe areas," the predominately Muslim town of Srebrenica, and killed several thousand civilians. Western public opinion cried out for action, and a previously divided NATO bombed Bosnian Serb military targets as the Croatian army drove all the Serbs from Croatia. Reaffirming U.S. pre-eminence as the only superpower, President Bill Clinton brought the warring sides to Dayton, Ohio, where in November 1995 they reached a complicated accord. The Dayton Accord forced the Bosnian Serbs to remain in a loose federal state, where they administered only 49 percent of the country and the Muslim-Croatian alliance administered the rest. Troops from many NATO countries, including the United States, policed the agreement and maintained peace as 1998 opened. The civil war in Bosnia-Herzegovina was a monument to human cruelty and evil in the worst tradition of the twentieth century. But the belated fragile

MAP 31.4 The Ethnic Composition of Yugoslavia, 1991 Yugoslavia had the most ethnically diverse population in eastern Europe. The Republic of Croatia had substantial Serbian and Muslim minorities. Bosnia-Herzegovina had large Muslim, Serbian, and Croatian populations, none of which had a majority. In June 1991, Serbia's brutal effort to seize territory and unite all Serbs in a single state brought a tragic civil war.

peace and ongoing efforts to repatriate refugees and to try alleged war criminals before an international tribunal also testified to the regenerative power of liberal values and human rights as the century drew to a close.

Unity and Identity in Western Europe

The movement toward western European unity, which since the late 1940s had inspired practical politicians seeking economic recovery and idealistic visionaries wanting to construct a genuine European identity that transcends destructive national rivalries, received a powerful second wind in the mid-1980s. The Single European Act of 1986 laid down a detailed legal framework for establishing a single market, which would add the free movement of labor, capital, and services to the existing free trade in goods. With work proceeding vigorously toward the single market, which went into effect in 1993 as the European Community proudly rechristened itself the European Union (EU), French president François Mitterrand and German chancellor Helmut Kohl took the lead in pushing for a monetary union of EU members. After long negotiations and compromises, designed especially to overcome Britain's long-standing reluctance to cede aspects of sovereignty, in December 1991 the member states reached an agree-

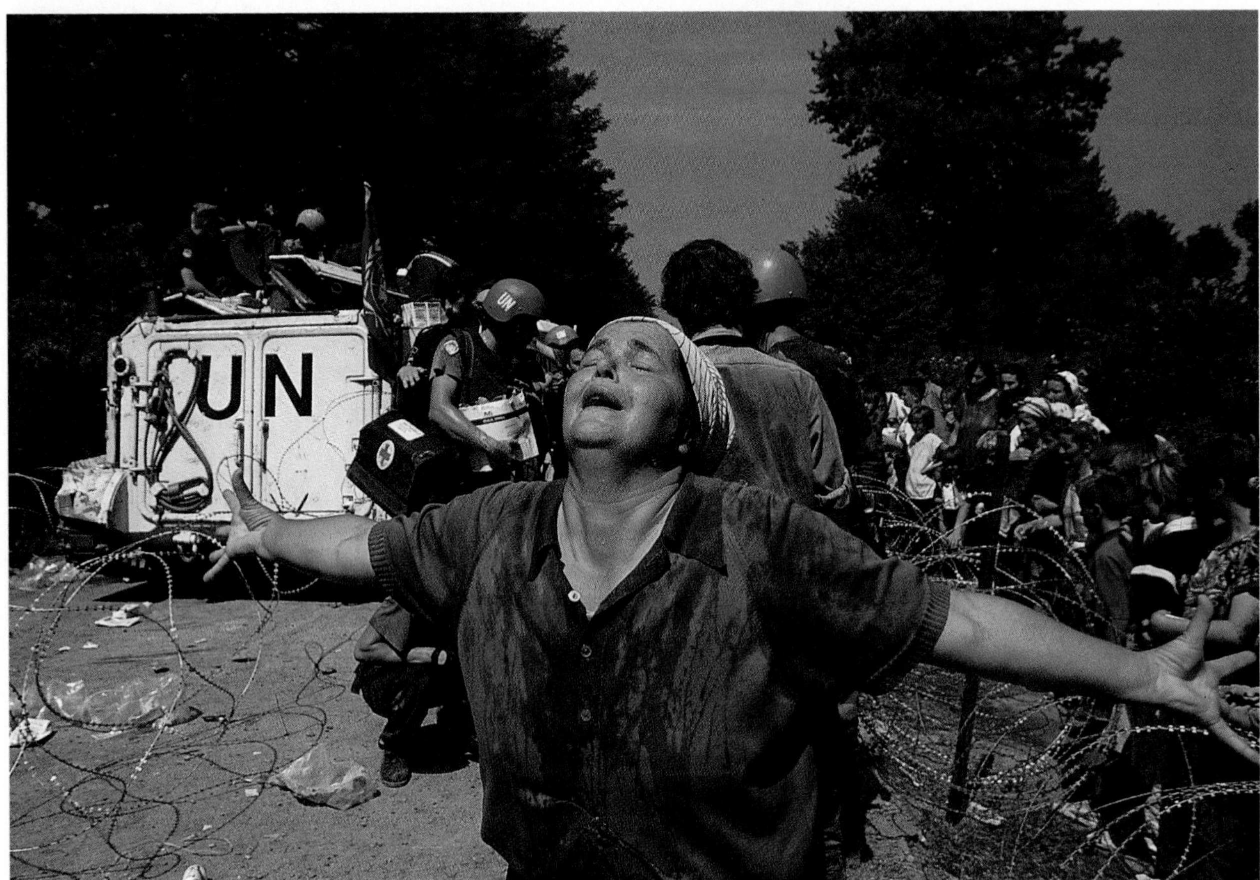

Escape from Srebrenica A Bosnian Muslim refugee arrives at the United Nations base in Tuzla and with her anguished screams tells the world of the Serbian atrocities. Several thousand civilians were murdered at Srebrenica, and Western public opinion finally demanded decisive action. Efforts continue to arrest those Serbs believed responsible and to try them for crimes against humanity. *(J. Jones/Sygma)*

ment in the Dutch town of Maastricht. The Maastricht treaty set strict financial criteria for joining the proposed monetary union, with its single currency, and set 1999 as the target date for its establishment. The treaty also anticipated the development of common policies on defense and foreign affairs after achieving monetary union.

Western European elites and opinion makers generally supported the decisive step toward economic integration embodied in the Maastricht treaty. They saw monetary union as a means of coping with Europe's ongoing economic problems, imposing financial discipline, cutting costs, and reducing high unemployment. And although European elites seldom stressed the point in public debates, they saw monetary union as an historic, irreversible step toward a basic political unity. This unity would allow western Europe as a whole to regain its rightful place in world politics and to deal with the United States as an equal. After campaigning effectively in their countries for ratification of the Maastricht treaty, Kohl and his new counterpart in France, President Jacques Chirac, continued to lead an all-European effort to reduce national budget deficits to 3 percent of gross national product (GNP), achieve low inflation, and curb the growth of national debt. Even Italy and Spain, long regarded by international financiers as profligate states, tightened their belts and met the tough Maastricht standards. In early 1998, it appeared very likely that all of the EU's large states, with the exception of still-reluctant Britain, would join the new monetary union on schedule in 1999.

The Maastricht plan for monetary union encountered widespread skepticism and considerable opposition from ordinary people, leftist political parties, and patriotic nationalists. Ratification votes were close, especially when the public rather than the politicians could vote yes or no on the question. French voters ratified the treaty with only 51 percent in favor, and Danish voters rejected it before narrowly approving it in a second referendum.

There were several interrelated reasons for this widespread popular opposition, which remained strong as 1998 opened. First, many people resented the unending flow of rules handed down by the EU's ever-growing bureaucracy in Brussels, which sought to impose common standards on everything from cheese to daycare and undermined national practices and local traditions. Second, the Maastricht treaty, the transnational "Euro" currency it promised, and vague plans for political unification gave still more power to distant bureaucrats and political insiders. Many people feared that these changes would undermine popular sovereignty and democratic control through national politics and electoral competition. Above all, many ordinary citizens feared that the new Europe was being made at their expense. Budget cuts and financial austerity meant reductions in health care and social benefits and apparently did nothing to reduce western Europe's high unemployment rate. Thus the road toward European monetary union was bumpy, as voters, protesters, and concerned citizens contested cuts in spending and defended the social achievements of the postwar welfare state.

Events in France dramatically illustrated these developments. Mitterrand's Socialist government had been forced to adopt conservative financial policies in the 1980s (see pages 1020–1022), and more cuts followed the Maastricht treaty. In early 1993, frustrated French voters elected Jacques Chirac president and gave a coalition of conservatives and moderates an overwhelming victory. The Socialist party suffered total defeat, and the once-powerful Communist party was reduced almost to fringe-party status. With unemployment climbing to a new high of 10.7 percent in the European Union by October 1993, and with industrial production and national income declining, the new French government faced a dilemma. Chirac had won by promising a vigorous attack on unemployment, but the Maastricht criteria demanded retrenchment. After some hesitation, Chirac's government chose deficit-reducing cuts in health benefits and transportation service. The Socialist opposition, the unions, and the railroad workers responded with massive protest marches and a crippling national strike, which closed down rail traffic throughout France for almost a month. Paris freeways became creeping parking lots as exhausted workers struggled with nightmare commutes. Yet the strike was widely supported by the public, despite the enormous inconvenience. Many ordinary people felt that the strikers were also fighting for them. The government had to back down, although it continued its austerity program with less provocative measures. In 1995 disgruntled French voters gave the Socialists control of the National Assembly. The Socialists quickly passed a controversial new law to reduce the legal workweek to 35 hours, in an attempt to reduce France's stubborn 12 percent unemployment rate without budget-busting spending. More generally, much of the western European public increasingly saw laws to cut the workweek and share the work as a way to reconcile desires for social welfare and a humane market economy with financial discipline and global competition.

Battles over budgets and high unemployment throughout the European Union raised profound questions about the meaning of European unity and identity. Would the European Union remain an exclusive Western club, or would it expand in the foreseeable future to include the postcommunist nations of eastern Europe, which aspired so ardently to EU membership? And if some eastern countries were admitted, how could Muslim Turkey's long-standing application be ignored? Conversely, how could a European Union of twenty-five to thirty countries have any real cohesion and common identity? These questions perplexed western Europeans throughout the 1990s.

The merging of East Germany into the German Federal Republic suggested the enormous difficulties of full East-West integration under the best conditions. After 1991 Helmut Kohl's Germany pumped massive investments into its new eastern provinces, but people in the east still saw factories closed, soaring unemployment, and social dislocation. Germany's generous social benefits cushioned the economic difficulties, but many ordinary citizens felt hurt and humiliated. West German practices weighed especially hard on eastern German women. Before unification, the overwhelming majority of these women had worked outside the home, effectively supported by cheap child care, flexible hours, and

French Commuters, 1995 Individuals and local governments improvised all manner of tactics to cope with the French transportation strike. Left without trains, city buses, and underground Metro service, these workers have been bused in from the suburbs on charter coaches. They are transferring to tourist boats being used to link temporarily a few points on the Seine. Many still face long walks to their jobs. *(Michel Verreault/Liaison)*

the prevailing socialist ideology. Now they faced expensive child care and a variety of pressures to stay at home and let men take the hard-to-find jobs. Many of these women, who had found autonomy and self-esteem in paid work, felt a keen sense of loss.

Instructed by the serious and largely unexpected difficulties of unification in Germany, where rising unemployment reached a postwar high of 12.8 percent in late 1997 and a catastrophic 20 percent in eastern Germany, western Europeans proceeded very cautiously in considering new requests for EU membership. Workers especially feared competition from low-paid but well-educated and hard-working eastern Europeans. Sweden, Finland, and Austria were admitted because they had strong capitalist economies and because they did not need to maintain the legal neutrality that the Soviet Union had required during the cold war. But of the former communist states, only Poland, the Czech Republic, and Hungary had any foreseeable chance of becoming EU members, and even they would need to wait until some unnamed time in the early twenty-first century. A former dissident in Hungary summed up the situation: the former Eastern bloc countries wanted to establish a road map leading toward integration and full membership, "but all they receive for their pains is mysterious *mañana* [tomorrow]. . . . 'Now! Now! Now!' says the East. 'No! No! No!' says the West."[9] Almost a decade after the revolutions of 1989 and the end of the cold war, a reunifying Europe was moving toward common institutions and groping for a common identity, but the process was far from complete.

 ENTERING THE NEW MILLENNIUM

What about the future? For centuries astrologers and scientists, experts and ordinary people, have sought to answer this question. Although it may seem that the study of the past has little to say about the future, the study of history over a long period is actually very useful in this regard. It helps put the future in perspective.

Certainly, history is full of erroneous predictions, a few of which we have mentioned in this book. Yet lack of success has not diminished the age-old desire to look into the future, and, as we enter not only a new century but a new millennium, that desire is stronger than ever. Self-proclaimed experts even pretend that they have created a new science of futurology. With great pomposity, they often act as if their hunches and guesses about future human developments are inescapable realities. Yet the study of history teaches healthy skepticism regarding such predictions, however scientific they may appear. Past results suggest that most such predictions will simply not come true or not in the anticipated way. Thus history provides some psychological protection from the visions of modern prognosticators.

This protection is particularly valuable when we realize that views of the future tend to swing between pessimistic and optimistic extremes from one generation, or even from one decade, to the next. These swings back and forth between optimism and pessimism, which one historian has aptly called "the great seesaw" in the development of the Western world, reflect above all the current situation of the observers.[10] Thus in the economic stagnation and revived cold war of the 1970s and 1980s, many projections into the future were quite pessimistic, just as they were very optimistic in the 1950s and 1960s. Many people in the Western world feared that conditions were going to get worse rather than better. For example, there were fears that trade wars would permanently cripple the world economy, that pollution would destroy the environment, and that the traditional family would disappear. Many experts and politicians predicted that the energy crisis—in the form of skyrocketing oil prices—meant disaster in the form of lower standards of living at best and the collapse of civilization at worst. In fact, oil prices collapsed in the early 1980s and they stayed low thereafter. It was heartening in that time of pessimism to know that most dire predictions do not prove true, just as the same knowledge of likely error is sobering in times of optimistic expectations.

Perhaps the most frightening source of pessimism and ominous predictions in recent times was the nuclear arms race. Not only did the United States and the Soviet Union accumulate unbelievably destructive nuclear arsenals, but Great Britain, France, China, India, and Israel also unlocked the secret of "the bomb." Other countries became equipped or desired to "go nuclear." Thus in the late 1970s and early 1980s, some gloomy experts predicted that twenty or thirty states might have nuclear weapons by the end of the century. In a world plagued by local wars and ferocious regional conflicts, these experts concluded that nuclear war was almost inevitable and speculated that the human race was an "endangered species."

Yet such predictions and the undeniable seriousness of the arms race jolted Western populations out of their customary fatalism regarding nuclear weapons. Efforts to reduce or even halt the nuclear buildup in the Soviet Union and the NATO alliance made some real progress. Above all, the Gorbachev era in the Soviet Union opened the way to new thinking and genuine superpower cooperation on nuclear arms questions. This cooperation accelerated after the fall of communism in Europe and the end of the cold war. Germany formally promised never to build nuclear arms as part of the price of German unification. Organized efforts to stop maverick states, such as Iraq and North Korea, from getting nuclear weapons made real progress. An optimistic projection from these developments could reasonably conclude that the global political will necessary to control nuclear proliferation will exist in the future.

Indeed, optimistic visions of the future were in the air after the end of the cold war. The pendulum definitely swung, most notably in the United States. Untroubled in the late 1990s by the high unemployment and early stages of corporate downsizing that soured the mood in western Europe, the United States celebrated its dynamic economy, its booming stock market, and the belated return in 1997 of rising real incomes for average workers. U.S. military power, leadership in world affairs, and excellence in advanced technologies also encouraged optimism and rosy projections. Little wonder that the large American contingent was riding high at the prestigious annual World Economic Forum of political leaders and top business executives at Davos, Switzerland, in February 1998. According to reports by journalists, the Americans explained in speeches and meetings that the world's future in the new millennium had already arrived in the United States, and they declared that future excellent. To repeat, just as it is heartening to know that most dire predictions do not prove true in pessimistic times, so is the same knowledge sobering in times of optimistic expectations.

Whatever does or does not happen, the study of history puts the future in perspective in other ways. We have seen that every age has its problems and challenges. Others before us have trod the paths of uncertainty and crisis. This knowledge helps save us from exaggerated self-pity in the face of our own predicaments.

Perhaps our Western heritage may rightly inspire us with pride and measured self-confidence. We stand, momentarily, at the head of the long procession of Western civilization. Sometimes the procession has wandered, or backtracked, or done terrible things. But it has also carried the efforts and sacrifices of generations of toiling, struggling ancestors. Through no effort of our own, we are the beneficiaries of those sacrifices and achievements. Now that it is our turn to carry the torch onward, we may remember these ties with our forebears.

To change the metaphor, we in the West are like a card player who has been dealt many good cards. Some of them are obvious, such as our technical and scientific heritage or our commitments to human rights and the individual. Others are not so obvious, sometimes half-forgotten or even hidden up the sleeve. Think, for example, of the Christian Democrats, the moderate Catholic party that emerged after World War II to play such an important role in the western European renaissance. And in the almost miraculous victory of peaceful revolution in eastern Europe in 1989—in what Czech playwright turned president Václav Havel called "the power of the powerless"—we see again the regenerative strength of the Western ideals of individual rights, representative government, and nationhood in the European homeland. We hold a good hand.

Our study of history, of mighty struggles and fearsome challenges, of shining achievements and tragic failures, gives a sense of what is the essence of life itself: the process of change over time. Again and again we have seen how peoples and societies evolve, influenced by ideas, human passions, and material conditions. As surely as anything is sure, this process of change over time will continue as the future becomes the present and then the past. And students of history are better prepared to make sense of this unfolding process because they have already observed it. They know how change is rooted in existing historical forces, and their projections will probably be better than many of the trendy speculations of futurologists. Students of history are also prepared for the new and unexpected in human development, for they have already seen great breakthroughs and revolutions. They have an understanding of how things really happen.

NOTES

1. Quoted in H. Smith, *The Russians* (New York: Quadrangle Books/New York Times, 1976), pp. 455–456.
2. M. Walker, *The Waking Giant: Gorbachev's Russia* (New York: Pantheon Books, 1987), p. 175.
3. T. G. Ash, *The Polish Revolution: Solidarity* (New York: Charles Scribner's Sons, 1983), p. 186.
4. Quoted in *Time,* January 6, 1986, p. 66.
5. Quoted in W. Laqueur, *Europe Since Hitler* (Baltimore: Penguin Books, 1972), p. 9. Rephrased slightly.
6. F. Fukuyama, *The End of History and the Last Man* (New York: Free Press, 1992); and J. Cronin, *The War the Cold War Made: Order, Chaos, and Return of History* (New York: Routledge, 1996), pp. 267–281.
7. Quoted in R. Suny, *The Soviet Experiment: Russia, the USSR, and the Successor States* (New York: Oxford University Press, 1998), p. 490.
8. M. Goldman, "Russia's Reform Effort: Is There Growth at the End of the Tunnel?" *Current History* 96 (October 1997): 313.
9. Quoted in L. Johnson, *Central Europe: Enemies, Neighbors, Friends* (New York: Oxford University Press, 1996), p. 286.
10. G. Blainey, *The Great Seesaw: A New View of the Western World* (London: Macmillan, 1988).

SUGGESTED READING

Many of the studies cited in the Suggested Reading for Chapters 29 and 30 are of value for the years since 1985 as well. Among other general works, F. Gilbert, *The End of the European Era: 1890 to the Present* (1991), is particularly helpful with its evenhanded account and extensive bibliography. Journalistic accounts in major newspapers and magazines are also invaluable tools for an understanding of recent developments. *Current History,* which devotes each monthly issue to either a geographical region or a contemporary issue, is especially recommended.

M. Dobbs, *Down with Big Brother: The Fall of the Soviet Empire* (1997), is a superb firsthand account by an inspired journalist who covered events in Russia and eastern Eu-

Britain's Millennium Dome will celebrate the arrival of the next thousand years in spectacular fashion. The lavish, 20-acre structure will offer visitors countless multimedia and interactive events, designed to entertain, thrill, and even stimulate thinking. This is an artist's rendering of "The Body Zone," one of the millennium exhibitions reveling in futuristic fantasies. *(NMEC/Hayes Division)*

rope between 1977 and 1993. On the Soviet Union, in addition to works cited in Chapter 30, the books by Smith and Walker cited in the Notes are fascinating eyewitness accounts of Soviet life in the 1970s and mid-1980s. The comprehensive history by Suny cited in the Notes is excellent on Russia in the 1990s and has up-to-date bibliographies. J. Hough and M. Fainsod, *How the Soviet Union Is Governed* (1979), is representative of Western scholarly thinking about the Soviet Union in the Brezhnev era. M. Lewin, *The Gorbachev Phenomenon: A Historical Interpretation* (1988), is excellent on the origins of the reforms. B. Eklof, *Soviet Briefing: Gorbachev and the Reform Period* (1989), focuses on 1987, a critical year. A. Shevchenko, *Breaking with Moscow* (1985), is the altogether fascinating autobiography of a top Soviet diplomat who defected to the United States. Two valuable studies by leading authorities on Russia today are M. Goldman, *Lost Opportunity: What Has Made Economic Reform in Russia So Difficult?* (1996); and M. McFaul, *Russia's 1996 Presidential Election: The End of Polarized Politics* (1996).

The recent work by Johnson cited in the Notes ably interprets developments in eastern Europe before and after the revolutions of 1989. For developments in Poland, M. Kaufman, *Mad Dreams, Saving Graces: Poland, a Nation in Conspiracy* (1989), carries developments through the summer of 1989; R. Leslie, *The History of Poland Since 1863* (1981), provides long-term perspective. T. Ash, *The Magic Lantern: The Revolution of '89 Witnessed in Warsaw, Budapest, Berlin, and Prague* (1990), is exciting instant history. Ash's book on Solidarity, cited in the Notes, is also recommended and may be compared with the less sympa-

(continued on page 1064)

LISTENING TO THE PAST

A Solidarity Leader Speaks from Prison

Solidarity built a broad-based alliance of intellectuals, workers, and the Catholic church, which was one reason it became such a powerful movement in Poland. Another reason was Solidarity's commitment to social and political change through nonviolent action. This enabled Solidarity to avoid a bloodbath in 1981 and thus maintain its structure after martial law was declared, although at the time foreign observers often criticized Lech Walesa's leadership for being too cautious and unrealistic.

One of Walesa's closest coworkers was Adam Michnik. Walesa was a skilled electrician and a devout Catholic, whereas Michnik was an intellectual and disillusioned Communist. But their faith in non-violence and gradual change bound them together. Trained as an historian but banned from teaching because of his leadership in student strikes in 1968, Michnik earned his living as a factory worker. In 1977 he joined with others to found the Committee for the Defense of Workers (KOR), which supported workers fired for striking. In December 1981, Michnik was arrested with the rest of Solidarity's leadership. While in prison until July 1994, he wrote his influential Letters from Prison, *from which the following is taken.*

Why did Solidarity renounce violence? This question returned time and again in my conversations with foreign observers. I would like to answer it now. People who claim that the use of force in the struggle for freedom is necessary must first prove that in a given situation it will be effective and that force, when it is used, will not transform the idea of liberty into its opposite.

No one in Poland is able to prove today that violence will help us to dislodge Soviet troops from Poland and to remove the communists from power. The U.S.S.R. has such enormous military power that confrontation is simply unthinkable. In other words, we have no guns. Napoleon, upon hearing a similar reply, gave up asking further questions. However, Napoleon was above all interested in military victories and not building democratic, pluralistic societies. We, by contrast, cannot leave it at that.

In our reasoning, pragmatism is inseparably intertwined with idealism. Taught by history, we suspect that by using force to storm the existing Bastilles we shall unwittingly build new ones. It is true that social change is almost always accompanied by force. But it is not true that social change is merely a result of the violent collision of various forces. Above all, social changes follow from a confrontation of different moralities and visions of social order. Before the violence of rulers clashes with the violence of their subjects, values and systems of ethics clash inside human minds. Only when the old ideas of the rulers lose this moral duel will the subjects reach for force—sometimes. This is what happened in the French Revolution and the Russian Revolution—two examples cited in every debate as proof that revolutionary violence is preceded by a moral breakdown of the old regime. But both examples lose their meaning when they are reduced to such compact notions, in which the Encyclopedists are paired with the destruction of the Bastille, and the success of radical ideologies in Russia is paired with the storming of the Winter Palace. An authentic event is reduced to a sterile scheme.

In order to understand the significance of these revolutions, one must remember Jacobin and Bolshevik terror, the guillotines of the sans-culottes, and the guns of the commissars. Without reflection on the mechanisms in victorious revolutions that gave birth to terror, it is impossible to even pose the fundamental dilemma facing contemporary freedom movements. Historical awareness of the possible consequences of revolutionary violence must be etched into any program of struggle for freedom. The experience of being corrupted by terror must be imprinted upon the consciousness of everyone who belongs to a freedom movement. [Or], as Simone Weil wrote, freedom will again become a refugee from the camp of the victors. . . .

Solidarity's program and ethos are inextricably tied to this strategy. Revolutionary terror has always been justified by a vision of an ideal society. In the name of this vision, Jacobin guillotines and

Bolshevik execution squads carried out their unceasing, gruesome work. The road to God's Kingdom on Earth led through rivers of blood.

Solidarity has never had a vision of an ideal society. It wants to live and let live. Its ideals are closer to the American Revolution than to the French. . . . The ethics of Solidarity, with its consistent rejection of the use of force, has a lot in common with the idea of nonviolence as espoused by Gandhi and Martin Luther King, Jr. But it is not an ethic representative of pacifist movements.

Pacifism as a mass movement aims to avoid suffering; pacifists often say that no cause is worth suffering or dying for. The ethics of Solidarity are based on an opposite premise: that there are causes worth suffering and dying for. Gandhi and King died for the same cause as the miners in Wujek who rejected the belief that it is better to remain a willing slave than to become a victim of murder [and who were shot down by police for striking against the imposition of martial law in 1981]. . . .

But ethics cannot substitute for a political program. We must therefore think about the future of Polish-Russian relations. Our thinking about this key question must be open; it should consider many different possibilities. . . .

The Soviet state has a new leader; he is a symbol of transition from one generation to the next within the Soviet elite. This change may offer an opportunity, since Mikhail Gorbachev has not yet become a prisoner of his own decisions. No one can rule out the possibility that an impulse for reform will spring from the top of the hierarchy of power. This is exactly what happened in the time of Alexander II and, a hundred years later, under Khrushchev. Reform is always possible, even in the face of resistance by the old apparatus. . . .

So what can now happen [in Poland]?

The "fundamentalists" say, no compromises. Talking about compromise, dialogue, or understanding demobilizes public opinion, pulls the wool over the eyes of the public, spreads illusions. Walesa's declarations about readiness for dialogue were often severely criticized from this point of view. I do not share the fundamentalist point of view. . . . The logic of fundamentalism precludes any attempt to find compromise, even in the future. It harbors not only the belief that communists are ineducable but also a certainty that they are unable to behave rationally, even in critical situations—that, in other words, they are condemned to suicidal obstinacy.

This is not so obvious to me. Historical experience shows that communists were sometimes forced by circumstances to behave rationally and to agree to compromises. Thus the strategy of understanding must not be cast aside. We should not assume that a bloody confrontation is inevitable and, consequently, rule out the possibility of evolutionary, bloodless change. This should be avoided all the more inasmuch as democracy is rarely born from bloody upheavals. We should be clear in our minds about this: The continuing conflict may transform itself into either a dialogue or an explosion. The TKK [the underground Temporary Coordinating Committee of outlawed Solidarity] and [Lech] Walesa are doing everything in their power to make dialogue possible. Their chances of success will be greater if the level of self-organization of independent Polish society increases. For street lynchings, angry crowds are enough; compromise demands an organized society.

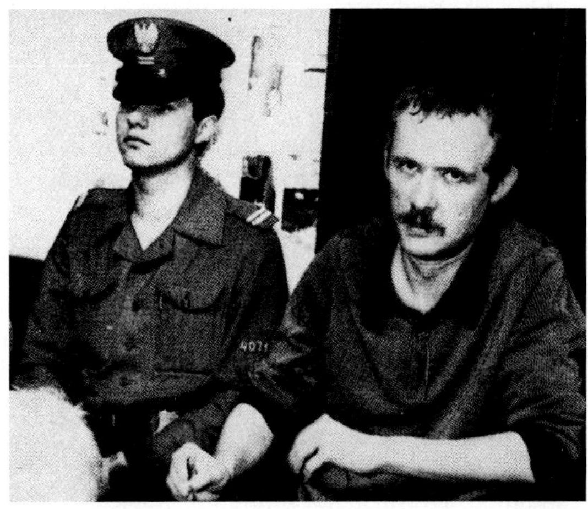

✣ Solidarity activist Adam Michnik in 1984, appearing under police guard in the military court that will sentence him to prison. *(Wide World Photos)*

Questions for Analysis

1. What arguments does Michnik present for opposing the government with nonviolent actions? Are his arguments convincing?
2. How did Michnik's study of history influence his thinking? What lessons did he learn?
3. Analyze Michnik's attitudes toward the Soviet Union and Poland's Communist leadership. What policies did he advocate? Why?

Source: Adam Michnik, *Letters from Prison and Other Essays,* trans. Maya Latynski (Berkeley and Los Angeles: University of California Press, 1985), pp. 86–89, 92, 95, by permission of the University of California Press.

thetic account by N. Ascherson, *The Polish August: The Self-Limiting Revolution* (1982). A. Bramberg, ed., *Poland: Genesis of a Revolution* (1983), is a valuable collection of documents with extensive commentary. G. Stokes, ed., *From Stalinism to Pluralism: A Documentary History of Eastern Europe Since 1945,* 2d ed. (1996), is another excellent collection. V. Havel, *The Art of the Impossible: Politics as Morality in Practice, Speeches and Writings, 1990–1996* (1997), reflects the hopes and worries of the Czech leader since 1989. Two excellent, judicious studies on the tragedy in Yugoslavia are J. Lampe, *Yugoslavia as History: Twice There Was a Country* (1996); and T. Judah, *The Serbs: History, Myth and the Destruction of Yugoslavia* (1997). M. Pinson, *The Muslims of Bosnia-Herzegovina,* 2d ed, is a useful brief history. T. Rosenberg, *The Haunted Land: Facing Europe's Ghosts After Communism* (1995), is a moving look at people's lives in postcommunist eastern Europe.

The work by Cronin cited in the Notes provides a stimulating view of the late cold war and the massive changes following it. K. Jarausch, *The Rush to Unity* (1994), considers German unification critically from the perspective of domestic politics. P. Zelikow and C. Rice, *Germany Unified and Europe Transformed: A Study in Statecraft* (1995), is an award-winning study of relations between the Great Powers and the peaceful resolution of the German question. P. Katzenstein, ed., *Tamed Power: Germany in Europe* (1997), examines united Germany's integration into the larger European Union. The culture and politics of protest are provocatively analyzed in H. Hughes, *Sophisticated Rebels: The Political Culture of European Dissent, 1968–1987* (1988). G. Rose, *Jacques Delors and European Integration* (1995), analyzes the controversies surrounding the European Union in the 1990s. L. Barzini, *The Europeans* (1983), draws engaging group portraits of the different European peoples, and W. Laqueur, *The Germans* (1985), is a contemporary report by a famous historian doubling as a journalist; both works are recommended. J. Ardagh, *Germany and the Germans: The United Germany in the Mid-1990s*, is another insightful study. P. Jenkins, *Mrs. Thatcher's Revolution: The End of the Socialist Era* (1988), and D. Singer, *Is Socialism Doomed? The Meaning of Mitterrand* (1988), are provocative studies on Great Britain and France in the 1980s.

The contemporary resurgence of nationalism is analyzed by R. Brubaker, *Nationalism Reframed: Nationhood and the National Question* (1996); and R. Caplan and John Feffer, *Europe's New Nationalism: States and Minorities in Conflict* (1996). D. Gompert and F. Larrabee, eds., *America and Europe: A Partnership in a New Era* (1997), features a number of European views of relations between the United States and Europe. N. Cantor, *The American Century: Varieties of Culture in Modern Times* (1997), is a lively consideration of many cultural developments that includes the 1990s. C. Goldin, *Understanding the Gender Gap: An Economic History of American Women* (1989), provides a provocative economic analysis of women's issues. Three important books on globalization are S. Strange, *The Retreat of the State: The Diffusion of Power in the World Economy* (1996); W. Greider, *One World, Ready or Not: The Manic Logic of Global Capitalism* (1997); and B. Eichengreen, *Globalizing Capital: A History of the International Monetary System* (1996). The November 1997 issue of *Current History,* "The Global Economy," provides an excellent introduction to this hotly debated issue. P. Kennedy, *Preparing for the Twenty-First Century* (1993), is a look into the future by a leading historian of international power politics. The work by Fukuyama cited in the Notes illustrates the widespread euphoria after the collapse of communism, arguing that democratic capitalism has defeated all its competitors. This optimistic projection may be compared with the somber future envisioned a generation ago in the influential and representative works by R. Heilbroner, *An Inquiry into the Human Prospect* (1974), and J. Revel, *The Totalitarian Temptation* (1977). The pathbreaking study of Blainey cited in the Notes examines the cycle of pessimism and optimism in Western history in fascinating detail.

Index

Religion and Philosophy	Science and Technology	Arts and Letters
Growth of anthropomorphic religion in Mesopotamia, ca 3000–2000 Emergence of Egyptian polytheism and belief in personal immortality, ca 2660 Spread of Mesopotamian and Egyptian religious ideas as far north as modern Anatolia and as far south as central Africa, ca 2600	Development of wheeled transport in Mesopotamia, by ca 3200 Use of widespread irrigation in Mesopotamia and Egypt, ca 3000 Construction of the first pyramid in Egypt, ca 2600	Sumerian cuneiform writing, ca 3200 Egyptian hieroglyphic writing, ca 3100
Emergence of Hebrew monotheism, ca 1700 Mixture of Hittite and Near Eastern religious beliefs, ca 1595	Construction of the first ziggurats in Mesopotamia, ca 2000 Widespread use of bronze in the ancient Near East, ca 1900 Babylonian mathematical advances, ca 1800	*Epic of Gilgamesh,* ca 1900 Code of Hammurabi, ca 1790
Exodus of the Hebrews from Egypt into Palestine, 13th c. Religious beliefs of Akhenaten, ca 1367	Hittites introduce iron technology, ca 1400	Phoenicians develop alphabet, ca 1400 Naturalistic art in Egypt under Akhenaten, ca 1367 Egyptian Book of the Dead, ca 1300
Era of the prophets in Israel, ca 1100–500 Intermixture of Etruscan and Roman religious cults, ca 753–509 Growing popularity of local Greek religious cults, ca 700 B.C.–A.D. 337 Babylonian Captivity of the Hebrews, 586–539	Babylonian astronomical advances, ca 750–400	Beginning of the Hebrew Bible, ca 9th c. Traditional beginning of the Olympic Games, 776 Babylonian astronomical advances, ca 750–400 Homer, traditional author of the *Iliad* and *Odyssey,* ca 700 Hesiod, author of the *Theogony* and *Works and Days,* ca 700 Archilochos, lyric poet, 648 Aeschylus, first significant Athenian tragedian, 525/4–456
Pre-Socratic philosophers, 5th c. Socrates, 469–399 Plato, 429–347 Diogenes, leading proponent of cynicism, ca 412–323 Aristotle, 384–322 Epicurus, 340–270 Zeno, founder of Stoic philosophy, 335–262 Emergence of Mithraism, ca 300 Spread of Hellenistic mystery religions, 2nd c. Greek cults brought to Rome, ca 200	Hippocrates, formal founder of medicine ca 430 Theophrastus, founder of botany, ca 372–288 Aristarchos of Samos, advances in astronomy, ca 310–230 Euclid codifies geometry, ca 300 Herophilus, discoveries in medicine, ca 300–250 Archimedes, works on physics and hydrologics, ca 287–212	Sophocles, tragedian who used his plays to explore moral and political problems, ca 496–406 Euripides, the most personal of the Athenian tragedians, ca 480–406 Thucydides, historian of the Peloponnesian War, ca 460–400 Aristophanes, the greatest writer of Old Comedy, ca 457–ca 385 Herodotus, the father of history, ca 450

	Government	Society and Economy
100 B.C.	Dictatorship of Sulla, 88–79 Civil war in Rome, 78–27 Dictatorship of Caesar, 45–44 Principate of Augustus, 31 B.C.–A.D. 14	Reform of the Roman calendar, 46
A.D. 300	Constantine removes capital of Roman Empire to Constantinople, ca 315 Visigoths defeat Roman army at Adrianople (378), signaling massive German invasions into the empire Bishop Ambrose asserts church's independence from the state, 380 Death of emperor Romulus Augustus marks end of Roman Empire in the West, 476 Clovis issues Salic law of the Franks, ca 490	Growth of serfdom in Roman Empire, ca 200–500 Economic contraction in Roman Empire, 3rd c.
500	Law Code of Justinian, 529 Dooms of Ethelbert, king of Kent, ca 604 Spread of Islam across Arabia, the Mediterranean region, Spain, North Africa, and Asia as far as India, ca 630–733	Gallo-Roman aristocracy intermarries with Germanic chieftains Decline of towns and trade, ca 500–700 Agrarian economy predominates in the West, ca 500–1500
700	Charles Martel defeats Muslims at Tours, 733 Pippin III anointed king of the Franks, 754 Charlemagne secures Frankish crown, r. 768–814	Height of Muslim commercial activity, ca 700–1300
800	Imperial coronation of Charlemagne, Christmas 800 Treaty of Verdun, 843 Viking, Magyar, and Muslim invasions, ca 845–900	Byzantine commerce and industry, ca 800–1000 Invasions and unstable conditions lead to increase of serfdom
1000	Seljuk Turks conquer Muslim Baghdad, 1055 Norman conquest of England, 1066 Penance of Henry IV at Canossa, 1077	Agrarian economy predominates in the West, 1000–1500 Decline of Byzantine free peasantry, ca 1025–1100 Growth of towns and trade in the West, ca 1050–1300 Domesday Book, 1086
1100	Henry I of England, r. 1100–1135 Louis VI of France, r. 1108–1137 Frederick I of Germany, r. 1152–1190 Henry II of England, r. 1154–1189 Thomas Becket murdered, 1170 Philip Augustus of France, r. 1180–1223	Henry I of England establishes the Exchequer, 1130 Beginnings of the Hanseatic League, 1159

Religion and Philosophy	Science and Technology	Arts and Letters
Mithraism spreads to Rome, 27 B.C.–A.D. 270 Dedication of the Ara Pacis Augustae, 9 Traditional birth of Jesus, ca 3	Pliny the Elder, student of natural history, 23 B.C.–A.D. 79 Frontinus, engineering advances in Rome, 30 B.C.–A.D. 104	Virgil, 70–19 B.C. Livy, ca 59 B.C.–A.D. 17 Ovid, 43 B.C.–A.D. 17
Constantine legalizes Christianity, 312 Theodosius declares Christianity the official state religion, 380 Donatist heretical movement at its height, ca 400 St. Augustine, *The City of God,* ca 425 Clovis adopts Roman Christianity, 496		St. Jerome publishes the Latin *Vulgate,* late 4th c. St. Augustine, *Confessions,* ca 390 Byzantines preserve Greco-Roman culture, ca 400–1000
Rule of St. Benedict, 529 Monasteries established in Anglo-Saxon England, 7th c. Muhammad preaches reform, ca 610 Publication of the Qu'ran, 651 Synod of Whitby, 664	Using watermills, Benedictine monks exploit energy of fast-flowing rivers and streams Heavy plow and improved harness facilitate use of multiple-ox teams; harrow widely used in northern Europe	Boethius, *The Consolation of Philosophy,* ca 520 Justinian constructs church of Santa Sophia, 532–537 Pope Gregory the Great publishes *Dialogues, Pastoral Care, Moralia,* 590–604
Missionary work of St. Boniface in Germany, ca 710–750 Iconoclastic controversy in Byzantine Empire, 726–843 Pippin III donates Papal States to the papacy, 756	Byzantines successfully use "Greek fire" in naval combat against Arab fleets attacking Constantinople, 673, 717	Lindisfarne Gospel Book, ca 700 Bede, *Ecclesiastical History of the English Nation,* ca 700 *Beowulf,* ca 700 Carolingian Renaissance, ca 780–850
Foundation of abbey of Cluny, 909 Byzantine conversion of Russia, late 10th c.	Stirrup and nailed horseshoes become widespread in shock combat Paper, invented in China ca 2nd c., enters Europe through Muslim Spain in 10th c.	Byzantines develop the Cyrillic script, late 10th c.
Beginning of reformed papacy, 1046 Schism between Roman and Greek Orthodox churches, 1054 Pope Gregory VII, 1073–1085 Peter Abelard, 1079–1142 St. Bernard of Clairvaux, 1090–1153 First Crusade, 1095–1099	Arab conquests bring new irrigation methods, cotton cultivation, and manufacture to Spain, Sicily, southern Italy Avicenna, Arab scientist, d. 1037	Romanesque style in architecture and art, ca 1000–1200 *Song of Roland,* ca 1095 Muslim musicians introduce lute, rebec—stringed instruments and ancestors of violin
Universities begin, ca 1100–1300 Concordat of Worms ends investiture controversy, 1122 Height of Cistercian monasticism, 1125–1175 Aristotle's works translated into Latin, ca 1140–1260 Third Crusade, 1189–1192 Pope Innocent III, 1198–1216	In castle construction Europeans, copying Muslim and Byzantine models, erect rounded towers and crenelated walls Windmill invented, ca 1180 Some monasteries, such as Clairvaux and Canterbury Cathedral Priory, supplied by underground pipes with running water and indoor latrines, elsewhere very rare until 19th c.	*Rubaiyat of Umar Khayyam,* ca 1120 Dedication of abbey church of Saint-Denis launches Gothic style, 1144 Hildegard of Bingen, 1098–1179 Court of troubador poetry, especially that of Chrétien de Troyes, circulates widely

	Government	Society and Economy
1200	Spanish victory over Muslims at Las Navas de Tolosa, 1212 Frederick II of Germany and Sicily, r. 1212–1250 Magna Carta, 1215 Louis IX of France, r. 1226–1270 Mongols end Abbasid caliphate, 1258 Edward I of England, r. 1272–1307 Philip IV (the Fair) of France, r. 1285–1314 England and France at war, 1296	Economic revival, growth of towns, clearing of wasteland contribute to great growth of personal freedom, 13th c. Agricultural expansion leads to population growth, ca 1225–1300
1300	Philip IV orders arrest of Pope Boniface at Anagni, 1303 Hundred Years' War, 1337–1450 Political chaos in Germany, ca 1350–1450 Merchant oligarchies or despots rule Italian city-states	European economic depression, ca 1300–1450 Black Death begins ca 1347; returns intermittently until 18th c. Height of the Hanseatic League, 1350–1450 Peasant and working-class revolts: France, 1358; Florence, 1378; England, 1381
1400	Appearance of Joan of Arc, 1429–1431 Medici domination of Florence begins, 1434 Princes in Germany consolidate power, ca 1450–1500 Ottoman Turks under Mahomet II capture Constantinople, May 1453 Wars of the Roses in England, 1453–1471 Ferdinand and Isabella complete reconquista in Spain, 1492 French invasion of Italy, 1494	Population decline, peasants' revolts, high labor costs contribute to decline of serfdom in western Europe Christopher Columbus reaches the Americas, October 1492 Portuguese gain control of East Indian spice trade, 1498–1511
1500	Charles V, Holy Roman emperor, 1519–1556 Imperial sack of Rome, 1527 Philip II of Spain, r. 1556–1598 Revolt of the Netherlands, 1566–1609 St. Bartholomew's Day massacre, August 24, 1572 Defeat of the Spanish Armada, 1588 Henry IV of France issues Edict of Nantes, 1598	Balboa discovers the Pacific, 1513 Magellan's crew circumnavigates the earth, 1519–1522 Spain gains control of Central and South America, ca 1520–1550 Peasants' Revolt in Germany, 1524–1525 "Times of Troubles" in Russia, 1598–1613
1600	Thirty Years' War, 1618–1648 Richelieu dominates French government, 1624–1643 Frederick William, Elector of Brandenburg, r. 1640–1688 English Civil War, 1642–1649	Chartering of British East India Company, 1600 Famine and taxation lead to widespread revolts, decline of serfdom in western Europe, ca 1600–1650 English Poor Law, 1601

Religion and Philosophy	Science and Technology	Arts and Letters
Crusaders capture Constantinople (Fourth Crusade), 1204 Maimonides, d. 1204 Founding of Franciscan order, 1210 Fourth Lateran Council, 1215 Founding of Dominican order, 1216 Thomas Aquinas (1225–1274) marks height of Scholasticism Pope Boniface VIII, 1294–1303	*Notebooks* of Villard de Honnecourt, a master mason (architect), a major source for Gothic engineering, ca 1250 Development of double-entry bookkeeping in Florence and Genoa, ca 1250–1340 Venetians purchase secrets of glass manufacture from Syria, 1277 Mechanical clock invented, ca 1290	*Parzifal, Roman de la Rose, King Arthur and the Round Table* celebrate virtues of knighthood Height of Gothic style, ca 1225–1300
Babylonian Captivity of the papacy, 1307–1377 John Wyclif, ca 1330–1384 Great Schism in the papacy, 1377–1418	Edward III of England uses cannon in siege of Calais, 1346	Petrarch, 1304–1374 Paintings of Giotto, ca 1305–1337 Dante, *Divine Comedy,* ca 1310 Boccaccio, *The Decameron,* ca 1350 Jan van Eyck, 1366–1441 Brunelleschi, 1377–1446 Chaucer, *Canterbury Tales,* ca 1385–1400
Council of Constance, 1414–1418 Pragmatic Sanction of Bourges, 1438 Expulsion of Jews from Spain, 1492	Water-powered blast furnaces operative in Sweden, Austria, the Rhine Valley, Liège, ca 1400 Leonardo Fibonacci's *Liber Abaci* (1202) popularizes use of Hindu-Arabic numerals, "a major factor in the rise of science in the Western world" Paris and largest Italian cities pave streets, making street cleaning possible Printing and movable type, ca 1450	Masaccio, 1401–1428 Botticelli, 1444–1510 Leonardo da Vinci, 1452–1519 Albrecht Dürer, 1471–1528 Michelangelo, 1475–1564 Raphael, 1483–1520 Rabelais, ca 1490–1553
Lateran Council attempts reforms of church abuses, 1512–1517 Machiavelli, *The Prince,* 1513 Concordat of Bologna, 1516 More, *Utopia,* 1516 Luther, *Ninety-five Theses,* 1517 Henry VIII of England breaks with Rome, 1532–1534 Loyola establishes Society of Jesus, 1540 Calvin establishes theocracy in Geneva, 1541 Merici establishes Ursuline order for education of women, 1544 Council of Trent, 1545–1563 Peace of Augsburg, 1555 Hobbes, 1588–1679 Descartes, 1596–1650	Copernicus, *On the Revolutions of the Heavenly Bodies,* 1543 Galileo, 1564–1642 Kepler, 1571–1630 Harvey, 1578–1657	Erasmus, *The Praise of Folly,* 1509 Castiglione, *The Courtier,* 1528 Cervantes, 1547–1616 Baroque movement in the arts, ca 1550–1725 Shakespeare, 1564–1616 Rubens, 1577–1640 Montaigne, *Essays,* 1598 Velazquez, 1599–1660
Huguenot revolt in France, 1625	Bacon, *The Advancement of Learning,* 1605 Boyle, 1627–1691 Leeuwenhoek, 1632–1723	Rembrandt van Rijn, 1606–1669 Golden Age of Dutch culture, 1625–1675 Vermeer, 1632–1675 Racine, 1639–1699

	Government	Society and Economy
1600 (cont.)	Louis XIV, r. 1643–1715 Peace of Westphalia, 1648 The Fronde in France, 1648–1660	Chartering of Dutch East India Company, 1602 Height of Dutch commercial activity, ca 1630–1665
1650	Protectorate in England, 1653–1658 Leopold I, Habsburg emperor, r. 1658–1705 Treaty of the Pyrenees, 1659 English monarchy restored, 1660 Siege of Vienna, 1683 Glorious Revolution in England, 1688–1689 Peter the Great of Russia, r. 1689–1725	Height of mercantilism in Europe, ca 1650–1750 Principle of peasants' "hereditary subjugation" to their lords affirmed in Prussia, 1653 Colbert's economic reforms in France, ca 1663–1683 Cossack revolt in Russia, 1670–1671
1700	War of the Spanish Succession, 1701–1713 Peace of Utrecht, 1713 Frederick William I of Prussia, r. 1713–1740 Louis XV of France, r. 1715–1774 Maria Theresa of Austria, r. 1740–1780 Frederick the Great of Prussia, r. 1740–1786	Foundation of St. Petersburg, 1701 Last appearance of bubonic plague in western Europe, ca 1720 Enclosure movement in England, ca 1730–1830 Jeremy Bentham, 1748–1823
1750	Seven Years' War, 1756–1763 Catherine the Great of Russia, r. 1762–1796 Partition of Poland, 1772–1795 Louis XVI of France, r. 1774–1792 American Revolution, 1776–1783 Beginning of the French Revolution, 1789	Start of general European population increase, ca 1750 Growth of illegitimate births, ca 1750–1850 Adam Smith, *The Wealth of Nations,* 1776 Thomas Malthus, *Essay of the Principle of Population,* 1798
1800	Napoleonic era, 1799–1815 Congress of Vienna, 1814–1815 "Battle of Peterloo," Great Britain, 1819	European economic imperialism, ca 1816–1880
1825	Greece wins independence, 1830 Revolution in France, 1830 Great Britain: Reform Bill of 1832; Poor Law reform, 1834; Chartists, repeal of Corn Laws, 1838–1848 British complete occupation of India, 1848 Revolutions in Europe, 1848	Height of French utopian socialism, 1830s–1840s German Zollverein founded, 1834 European capitalists begin large-scale foreign investment, 1840s Great Famine in Ireland, 1845–1851 Marx, *Communist Manifesto,* 1848
1850	Second Empire in France, 1852–1870 Crimean War, 1853–1856 Unification of Italy, 1859–1870 Civil War, United States, 1861–1865 Bismarck leads Germany, 1862–1890 Unification of Germany, 1864–1871 Britain's Second Reform Bill, 1867 Third Republic in France, 1870–1940	Crédit Mobilier founded in France, 1852 Japan opened to European influence, 1853 Mill, *On Liberty,* 1859 Russian serfs emancipated, 1861 First Socialist International, 1864–1871 Marx, *Das Capital,* 1867

Religion and Philosophy	Science and Technology	Arts and Letters
Patriarch Nikon's reforms split Russian Orthodox church, 1652 Test Act in England excludes Roman Catholics from public office, 1673 Revocation of Edict of Nantes, 1685 James II tries to restore Catholicism as state religion, 1685–1688 Montesquieu, 1689–1755 Locke, *Second Treatise on Civil Government,* 1690 Pierre Bayle, *Historical and Critical Dictionary,* 1697	Tull (1674–1741) encourages innovation in English agriculture Newton, *Principia Mathematica,* 1687 Newcomen develops steam engine, 1705	Construction of baroque palaces and remodeling of capital cities throughout central and eastern Europe, ca 1650–1725 J. S. Bach, 1685–1750 Fontenelle, *Conversations on the Plurality of Worlds,* 1686 The Enlightenment, ca 1690–1790 Voltaire, 1694–1778
Wesley, 1703–1791 Hume, 1711–1776 Diderot, 1713–1784 Condorcet, 1743–1794		
Ricardo, 1772–1823 Fourier, 1772–1837 Papacy dissolves the Jesuits, 1773 Church reforms of Joseph II in Austria, 1780s Reorganization of the church in France, 1790s	Hargreaves's spinning jenny, ca 1765 Arkwright's water frame, ca 1765 Watt's steam engine promotes industrial breakthroughs, 1780s War widens the gap in technology between Britain and the continent, 1792–1815 Jenner's smallpox vaccine, 1796	*Encyclopedia,* edited by Diderot and d'Alembert, published, 1751–1765 Mozart, 1756–1791 Rousseau, *The Social Contract,* 1762 Beethoven, 1170–1827 Wordsworth, 1770–1850 Romanticism, ca 1790–1850 Wollstonecraft, *A Vindication of the Rights of Women,* 1792
Napoleon signs Concordat with Pope Pius VII regulating Catholic church in France, 1801 Spencer, 1820–1903		
Comte, *System of Positive Philosophy,* 1830–1842 List, *National System of Political Economy,* 1841 Nietzsche, 1844–1900 Sorel, 1847–1922	First railroad, Great Britain, 1825 Faraday studies electromagnetism, 1830–1840s	Balzac, *The Human Comedy,* 1829–1841 Delacroix, *Liberty Leading the People,* 1830 Hugo, *Hunchback of Notre Dame,* 1831
Decline in church attendance among working classes, ca 1850–1914 Pope Pius IX, *Syllabus of Errors,* denounces modern thoughts, 1864 Doctrine of papal infallibility, 1870	Modernization of Paris, ca 1850–1870 Great Exhibition, London, 1851 Darwin, *Origin of Species,* 1859 Pasteur develops germ theory of disease, 1860s Suez Canal opened, 1869 Mendeleev develops the periodic table, 1869	Realism, ca 1850–1870 Freud, 1856–1939 Flaubert, *Madame Bovary,* 1857 Tolstoy, *War and Peace,* 1869 Impressionism in art, ca 1870–1900 Eliot (Mary Ann Evans), *Middlemarch,* 1872

	Government	Society and Economy
1875	Congress of Berlin, 1878 European "scramble for Africa," 1880–1900 Britain's Third Reform Bill, 1884 Berlin conference on Africa, 1884 Dreyfus affair in France, 1894–1899 Spanish-American War, 1898 Boer War, 1899–1902	Full property rights for women, Great Britain, 1882 Social welfare legislation, Germany, 1883–1889 Second Socialist International, 1889–1914 Witte directs modernization of Russian economy, 1892–1899
1900	Russo-Japanese War, 1904–1905 Revolution in Russia, 1905 Balkan wars, 1912–1913	Women's suffrage movement, England, ca 1900–1914 Social welfare legislation, France, 1904, 1910; England, 1906–1914 Agrarian reforms in Russia, 1907–1912
1914	World War I, 1914–1918 Easter Rebellion, 1916 U.S. declares war on Germany, 1917 Bolshevik Revolution, 1917–1918 Treaty of Versailles, 1919	Planned economics in Europe, 1914 Auxiliary Service Law in Germany, 1916 Bread riots in Russia, March 1917
1920	Mussolini seizes power, 1922 Stalin uses forced collectivization, police terror, ca 1929–1939 Hitler gains power, 1933 Rome-Berlin Axis, 1936 Nazi-Soviet Non-Aggression Pact, 1939 World War II, 1939–1945	New Economic Policy in the Soviet Union, 1921 Dawes Plan for reparations and recovery, 1924 The Great Depression, 1929–1939 Rapid industrialization in Soviet Union, 1930s Roosevelt's "New Deal," 1933
1940	United Nations, 1945 Cold war begins, 1947 Fall of colonial empires, 1947–1962 Communist government in China, 1949 Korean War, 1950–1953 "De-Stalinization" in Soviet Union, 1955–1962	The Holocaust, 1941–1945 Marshall Plan, 1947 European economic progress, ca 1950–1969 European Coal and Steel Community, 1952 European Economic Community, 1957
1960	The Berlin Wall goes up, 1961 United States in Vietnam, ca 1961–1973 Student rebellion in France, 1968 Soviet tanks end Prague Spring, 1968 Détente, 1970s Soviets in Afghanistan, 1979	Civil rights movement in United States, 1960s Collapse of postwar monetary system, 1971 OPEC oil price increases, 1973 and 1979 Stagflation, 1970s Women's movement, 1970s
1980	U.S. military buildup, 1980s Solidarity in Poland, 1980 Gorbachev takes power, 1985 Unification of Germany, 1989 Revolutions in eastern Europe, 1989–1990 End of Soviet Union, 1991 War in former Yugoslavia, 1991–1995	Growth of debt, 1980s Economic crisis in Poland, 1988 Maastricht Treaty proposes monetary union, 1990 Conservative economic policies in western Europe, 1990s

Religion and Philosophy	Science and Technology	Arts and Letters
Growth of public education in France, ca 1880–1900 Growth of mission schools in Africa, 1890–1914	Emergence of modern immunology, ca 1875–1900 Trans-Siberian Railroad, 1890s Marie Curie, discovery of radium, 1898 Electrical industry: lighting and streetcars, 1880–1900	Zola, *Germinal,* 1885 Kipling, "The White Man's Burden," 1899
Separation of church and state, France, 1901–1905 Jean-Paul Sartre, 1905–1980	Planck develops quantum theory, ca 1900 First airplane flight, 1903 Einstein develops relativity theory, 1905–1910	"Modernism," ca 1900–1929 Conrad, *Heart of Darkness,* 1902 Cubism in art, ca 1905–1930 Proust, *Remembrance of Things Past,* 1913–1927
Schweitzer, *Quest of the Historical Jesus,* 1906	Submarine warfare, 1915 Ernest Rutherford splits the atom, 1919	Spengler, *The Decline of the West,* 1918
Emergence of modern existentialism, 1920s Wittgenstein, *Essay on Logical Philosophy,* 1922 Revival of Christianity, 1920s and 1930s	"Heroic age of physics," 1920s First major public radio broadcasts in Great Britain and the United States, 1920 Heisenberg, "principle of uncertainty," 1927 Talking movies, 1930 Radar system in England, 1939	Gropius, the Bauhaus, 1920s Dadaism and surrealism, 1920s Woolf, *Jacob's Room,* 1922 Joyce, *Ulysses,* 1922 Eliot, *The Waste Land,* 1922 Remarque, *All Quiet on the Western Front,* 1929 Picasso, *Guernica,* 1937
De Beauvoir, *The Second Sex,* 1949 Communists fail to break Catholic church in Poland, 1950s	Oppenheimer, 1904–1967 "Big Science" in United States, ca 1940–1970 U.S. drops atomic bombs on Japan, 1945 Watson and Crick discover structure of DNA molecule, 1953 Russian satellite in orbit, 1957	Cultural purge in Soviet Union, 1946–1952 Van der Rohe, Lake Shore Apartments, 1948–1951 Orwell, *1984,* 1949 Pasternak, *Doctor Zhivago,* 1956 The "beat" movement in the United States, late 1950s
Catholic church opposes the legalization of divorce and abortion, 1970 to present Pope John Paul II electrifies Poland, 1979	European Council for Nuclear Research (CERN), 1960 Space race, 1960s Russian cosmonaut first to orbit globe, 1961 American astronaut first person on the moon, 1969	The Beatles, 1960s Solzhenitsyn, *One Day in the Life of Ivan Denisovitch,* 1962 Friedan, *The Feminine Mystique,* 1963 Servan-Schreiber, *The American Challenge,* 1967
Revival of religion in Soviet Union, 1985 to present Fukuyama proclaims "end of history," 1991	Reduced spending on Big Science, 1980s Computer revolution continues, 1980s and 1990s	Solzhenitsyn returns to Russia, 1994

GREENLAND
(DENMARK)
ICELAND
ALASKA
(U.S.)
CANADA
UNITED STATES
IRELA
PORTUGA
Azores
Bermuda
ATLANTIC OCEAN
Midway Is.
Hawaiian Is.
BAHAMAS
WESTERN
SAHARA
(MOROCCO)
MEXICO
CUBA
DOMINICAN REP.
Virgin Is.
JAMAICA
HAITI
ST. KITTS AND NEVIS
ANTIGUA AND BARBUDA
DOMINICA
BARBADOS
ST. LUCIA
GRENADA
ST. VINCENT AND
THE GRENADINES
BELIZE
HONDURAS
Puerto Rico
GUATEMALA
EL SALVADOR
NICARAGUA
COSTA RICA
PANAMA
PACIFIC OCEAN
VENEZUELA
TRINIDAD AND TOBAGO
GUYANA
FR. GUIANA
SURINAM
COLOMBIA
ECUADOR
Galapagos Is.
CAPE
VERDE
SENEGAL
GAMBIA
GUINEA-BISSAU
GUINEA
SIERRA
LEONE
LIBERIA
MAURIT
SAO TO
PERU
BRAZIL
BOLIVIA
PARAGUAY
CHILE
URUGUAY
ARGENTINA
WESTERN
SAMOA
TONGA
Easter Is.
Falkland Is.
Equator
80°N
60°N
40°N
20°N
0°
20°S
40°S
60°S
80°S
160°W
140°W
120°W
100°W
80°W
60°W
40°W
20°W